FOUNDATIONS OF LEGAL RESEARCH AND WRITING

Second Edition

The West Legal Studies Series

Your options keep growing with West Legal Studies

Each year our list continues to offer you more options for every area of the law to meet your course or on-the-job reference requirements. We now have over 140 titles from which to choose in the following areas:

- Administrative Law
- Alternative Dispute Resolution
- Bankruptcy
- Business Organizations/Corporations
- Civil Litigation and Procedure
- CLA Exam Preparation
- Client Accounting
- Computer in the Law Office
- Constitutional Law
- Contract Law
- Criminal Law and Procedure
- Document Preparation
- Environmental Law
- Ethics
- Family Law
- Federal Taxation
- Intellectual Property
- Introduction to Law
- Introduction to Paralegalism
- Law Office Management
- Law Office Procedures
- Legal Research, Writing, and Analysis
- Legal Terminology
- Paralegal Employment
- Real Estate Law
- Reference Materials
- Torts and Personal Injury Law
- Will, Trusts, and Estate Administration

You will find unparalleled, practical support

Each book is augmented by instructor and student supplements to ensure the best learning experience possible. We also offer custom publishing and other benefits such as West's Student Achievement Award. In addition, our sales representatives are ready to provide you with dependable service.

We want to hear from you

Our best contributions for improving the quality of our books and instructional materials is feedback from the people who use them. If you have a question, concern, or observation about any of our materials, or you have a product proposal or manuscript, we want to hear from you. Please contact your local representative or write us at the following address:

West Legal Studies, 3 Columbia Circle, P.O. Box 15015, Albany, NY 12212-5015

For additional information point your browser at

www.westlegalstudies.com

WEST

THOMSON LEARNING™

FOUNDATIONS OF LEGAL RESEARCH AND WRITING

Second Edition

CAROL BAST

MARGIE HAWKINS

WEST

THOMSON LEARNING

Australia Canada Mexico Singapore Spain United Kingdom United States

WEST LEGAL STUDIES

Foundations of Legal Research and Writing, 2E
by Carol Bast and Margie Hawkins

Business Unit Director:
Susan L. Simpfenderfer

Executive Editor:
Marlene McHugh Pratt

Senior Acquisitions Editor:
Joan M. Gill

Developmental Editor:
Andrea Edwards Myers

Editorial Assistant:
Lisa Flatley

Executive Production Manager:
Wendy A. Troeger

Production Manager:
Carolyn Miller

Production Coordinator:
Matthew J. Williams

Executive Marketing Manager:
Donna J. Lewis

Channel Manager:
Nigar Hale

Cover Image:
Comstock

Cover Design:
TDB Publishing Services

Printed in the United States
2 3 4 5 XXX 05 04 03 02

For more information contact Delmar,
3 Columbia Circle, PO Box 15015,
Albany, NY 12212-5015.

Or find us on the World Wide Web at
www.thomsonlearning.com or
www.westlegalstudies.com

Library of Congress Cataloging-in-Publication Data
Bast, Carol M.
Foundations of legal research and writing/Carol Bast, Margie Hawkins.—2nd ed.
p. cm.
Rev. ed. of: Legal research and writing. C1995.
Includes index.
ISBN 0-7668-3164-7
1. Legal research—United States. 2. Legal composition. I. Hawkins, Margie. II. Bast, Carol M. Legal research and writing. III. Title.

KF240 .B27 2001
340'.07'2073—dc21 2001026736

NOTICE TO THE READER

Publisher does not warrant or guarantee any of the products described herein or perform any independent analysis in connection with any of the product information contained herein. Publisher does not assume, and expressly disclaims, any obligation to obtain and include information other than that provided to it by the manufacturer.

The reader is notified that this text is an educational tool, not a practice book. Since the law is in constant change, no rule or statement of law in this book should be relied upon for any service to any client. The reader should always refer to standard legal sources for the current rule or law. If legal advice or other expert assistance is required, the services of the appropriate professional should be sought.

The Publisher makes no representation or warranties of any kind, including but not limited to, the warranties of fitness for particular purpose or merchantability, nor are any such representations implied with respect to the material set forth herein, and the publisher takes no responsibility with respect to such material. The publisher shall not be liable for any special, consequential, or exemplary damages resulting, in whole or part, from the readers' use of, or reliance upon, this material.

SUMMARY OF CONTENTS

TABLE OF CONTENTS

CHAPTER 10

Cyberlaw: Using the Internet as a Legal Research Tool 318

CHAPTER 11

Introduction to Legal Writing 331

CHAPTER 12

Fundamentals of Writing 347

Chapter 13

Transmittal Letter and Client Opinion Letter 365

CHAPTER 14

Writing Contracts 386

CHAPTER 15

Pleadings 419

CHAPTER 16

Law Office Memo 442

TABLE OF CASES

PREFACE

When I first started teaching legal research and legal writing, I found no single text in either legal research or legal writing that had what I needed. I was looking for a text that would contain:

(a) a clear explanation of basic information; and
(b) exercises to give the student the necessary practice in researching and writing.

The ideal text would also be "user-friendly" and readable while balancing the need for detail. Visual tools such as charts, tables, and flowcharts could be used for information that is hard to follow in narrative form. Sample pages from legal sources would be included so the students could see the format of the particular legal source and the professor would not have to supplement the text. Each chapter would cover only a manageable amount of material for someone who has not been previously exposed to the law.

This book attempts to fill that need for the paralegal and legal studies student and professor. The objectives of the legal research portion of the book are to teach the student how to:

1. competently perform legal research in the law library and on the computer;
2. use correct citation form; and
3. understand the fundamentals of legal research.

The objectives of the legal writing portion of the book are to:

1. explain the fundamentals of legal analysis and writing;
2. teach the student how to communicate clearly; and
3. explain how to eliminate mechanical errors.

ORGANIZATION OF THE TEXT

The legal research portion of the book includes sample pages of the legal sources discussed in the text and contains basic citation rules and research exercises. To facilitate the student's participation, this portion emphasizes the process of finding and using primary sources and gives the student "hands on" experience through completing legal research exercises. Chapters 1 and 2 give an important overview of the legal system and legal reasoning. Chapters 3 through 6 introduce legal encyclopedias, digests, American Law Reports, cases, constitutions, statutes, court rules, administrative law, and citators. The chapters also contain lengthy research assignments, allowing the professor to assign certain of the exercises one term and a different set of exercises another term. Chapter 7 gives an overview of the research process and explains how the various legal sources studied relate to each other. Chapter 8 introduces computer-assisted legal research, chapter 9 introduces legal research on the Internet, and chapter 10 explores the Internet as a legal research tool.

Primary and secondary sources are covered in separate chapters in the text. This organization allows the professor the freedom to choose which type of source to cover first. The chapters on secondary sources precede the chapters on primary sources because many legal research professors cover secondary sources before primary sources.

The sequence chosen for these chapters tracks the order in which a researcher who is unfamiliar with a particular area of the law commences a research assignment. Unless the legal researcher has somehow already found a primary source on point, the researcher will most likely begin research by referring to a secondary source first.

The legal writing portion of the book explains how to write legal documents and includes samples of various types of legal documents. Chapters 11 and 12 give an introduction to legal writing and legal writing fundamentals. Chapters 13 through 18 are each devoted to a different type of legal document, starting with the transmittal letter and the client opinion letter and continuing through the contract, pleadings and motions, the office memo, the memorandum of law, and the appellate brief. The chapter on contracts covers material rarely discussed in a legal writing class.

The various types of legal documents are explained in separate chapters, again to allow the professor to choose which chapters are to be covered, time permitting. A professor who does not usually cover a particular type of document may enjoy the challenge of teaching something a little different. In addition, the book is a good reference for the student who is asked later to write a type of legal document not studied in legal writing class.

The appendices contain additional material that could be profitably used in either legal research or legal writing. They provide the students with an explanation of and necessary practice in eliminating mechanical errors, quoting correctly, and writing short and long form citations correctly. The rules for quotations and short form citations are not covered in many other texts but are something the student should master. Appendix E contains four fact patterns. These fact patterns can serve as the subject of a legal research assignment, and then later, as the subject of a client opinion letter, office memo, memorandum of law, or appellate brief.

Making the book "user friendly" by including a search and seizure problem

A legal research and writing book could easily be the most boring textbook in the entire bookstore. My challenge was to write a book that would spark student interest and involve the student in the research and writing process. Students learn more if they are involved in the course materials. I found that students are keenly interested in "search and seizure" because the topic is easy to "picture" and understand. I decided to use the topic to make the book student friendly.

The text entices the student to participate in the learning process by including interesting and relevant examples of primary sources and documents relating to the search and seizure topic. Several of the newspaper articles concern racial profiling, an issue in the news at the time of the writing of this text. The search and seizure materials are fairly easy to understand, contain interesting and easy-to-grasp facts, and can be a basis for a number of class discussions. Students can be asked to determine whether their state has similar forfeiture statutes and to investigate whether racial profiling has been an issue in their state.

Appendix A introduces students to two brothers who have a legal problem. The Williams brothers were driving through Florida when law enforcement officers stopped the Williams' car and seized $35,000 in cash from the brothers. The brothers decided to consult an attorney to see if they could get their money back. References throughout the book to the search and seizure topic involve the students in the course materials and provide continuity. The topic also lends itself to some great class discussions. Where the search and seizure topic is not used, other topics appear several times in the text and in the exercises.

In addition to the search and seizure problem, appendix A contains examples of primary sources used in researching the issue. Moreover, the appendix includes an explanation of law on search and seizure, a flowchart on the issues involved in the search and seizure problem, and a suggested outline for a law office memo to be written after researching the search and seizure problem. By using this important topic, students will learn legal research and writing and some substantive law at the same time.

Appendix A is designed to be a vital part of the text, but the material was gathered together in a separate appendix rather than in a single chapter so the instructor could assign the entire appendix or portions of it at any time during the course. The whole appendix might be overwhelming to the novice researcher if it were assigned at the beginning of the course. The research problem and the newspaper articles could be assigned immediately, with the rest of the materials assigned as applicable legal research chapters are covered. An alternative is to assign appendix A after the student knows enough about legal research to pull the appendix A materials together. A third alternative is to assign the problem at the beginning of the course and ask students to glance over the rest of the material. After reading a particular chapter, students could be required to explain how appendix A illustrates the chapter material.

Decreasing professor preparation time

Legal research and legal writing are typically time-consuming courses in a paralegal/legal studies curriculum. Many professors shy away from teaching these courses because of the time commitment. Just keeping up with grading assignments leaves very little time for outside preparation of material.

The first few semesters I taught legal research and writing, I spent hours upon hours preparing additional student-friendly materials to supplement commercial texts. I also used several different texts and the *Bluebook* those first few semesters because I could not find one text that contained all the information I wanted my students to know. From this experience, I know that a "professor friendly" book would be self-contained and would eliminate the need for a great deal of professor-prepared materials.

This book is designed to be the only one the student and the professor need for legal research and legal writing. Basic citation rules are included, thus eliminating the need for the *Bluebook*. However, some professors may require students to purchase a *Bluebook* for reference. The citation rules are consistent with *Bluebook* form so that the advanced student can later refer to the *Bluebook* when necessary. As explained above, the legal research portion of the book contains sample pages from the various authorities and research exercises. The legal writing portion of the book contains sample documents, heavily footnoted to offer the student guidance on the writing process.

NEW TO THIS EDITION

This book's name, *Foundations of Legal Research and Writing*, indicates that substantial changes have been made from a prior version of the book, entitled *Legal Research and Writing*. Changes from the prior version include:

- Expanded discussion of the sources of law and law library resources in the first seven chapters
- New research exercises for legal encyclopedias, American Law Reports, digests, case law, statutes, and citators
- Legal analysis of statutes
- Legal analysis of constitutional law
- Discussion of KeyCite
- Three new chapters on computer-assisted legal research
- Discussion of changes in the legal publishing industry
- Discussion of universal citation form
- Cases illustrating the consequences of inadequate research and poor writing
- New sample documents
- More visual aids
- Cyberlaw exercises and references
- Discussion of ethics rules
- A second sample case in the case law chapter
- A second sample client opinion letter
- A second sample complaint and answer
- A second sample office memo
- A second sample memorandum of law
- A second sample appellate brief

SUPPLEMENTAL RESOURCES

- **Instructor's Manual with Test Bank** Written by the authors of the text, the Instructor's Manual contains a sample course syllabus, lecture outlines, teaching suggestions, answers to text exercises and questions, and test bank. The Instructor's Manual can also be found on-line at www.westlegalstudies.

com. Please click on Resources, then go into the Instructor's Lounge.

- **Computerized Test Bank** The Test Bank found in the Instructor's Manual is also available in a computerized format on CD-ROM. The platforms supported include Windows™ 3.1 and 95, Windows™ NT, and Macintosh. Features include:
  - Multiple methods of question selection
  - Multiple outputs—that is, print, ASCII, and RTF
  - Graphic support (black and white)
  - Random questioning output
  - Special character support
- **Online Resource** Come visit our Web site at www.westlegalstudies.com where you will find valuable information specific to this book such as hot links and sample materials to download, as well as other West Legal Studies products.
- **Survival Manual for Paralegal Students,** written by Bradene Moore and Kathleen Reed of the University of Toledo, covers practical and basic information to help students make the most of their paralegal courses. Topics covered include choosing courses of study and note-taking skills. ISBN 0-314-22111-5
- **Strategies and Tips for Paralegal Educators,** written by Anita Tebbe of Johnson County Community College, provides teaching strategies specifically designed for paralegal educators. A copy of this pamphlet is available to each adopter. Quantities for distribution to adjunct instructors are available for purchase at a minimal price. A coupon in the pamphlet provides ordering information. ISBN 0-314-04971-1
- **Citation-At-a-Glance** This handy reference card provides a quick, portable reference to the basic rules of citation for the most commonly cited legal sources, including judicial opinions, statutes, and secondary sources. *Citation-At-a-Glance* uses the rules set forth in *The Bluebook: A Uniform System of Citation.* A free copy of this valuable supplement is included with every student text.
- **Westlaw®** West's online computerized legal research system offers students "hands-on" experience with a system commonly used in law offices. Qualified adopters can receive ten free hours of Westlaw®. Westlaw® can be accessed with Macintosh and IBM PC and compatibles. A modem is required.
- **Court TV Videos** West Legal Studies is pleased to offer the following videos from Court TV. Available for a minimal fee:
  - New York v. Ferguson—Murder on the 5:33:The Trial of Colin Ferguson
    ISBN 0-7668-1098-4
  - Ohio v. Alfieri—Road Rage
    ISBN 0-7668-1099-2
  - Flynn v. Goldman Sachs—Fired on Wall Street: A Case of Sex Discrimination?
    ISBN 0-7668-1096-8
  - Dodd v. Dodd: Religion and Child Custody in Conflict
    ISBN 0-7668-1094-1
  - Fentress v. Eli Lilly & Co., et al—Prozac on Trial
    ISBN 0-7668-1095-X
  - In RE Custody of Baby Girl Clausen—Child of Mine: The Fight for Baby Jessica
    ISBN 0-7668-1097-6
- **West's Paralegal Video Library** includes:
  - *The Drama of the Law II: Paralegal Issues Video*
    ISBN 0-314-07088-5
  - *I Never Said I Was a Lawyer Paralegal Ethics Video*
    ISBN 0-314-08049-X

    These videos are available at no charge to qualified adopters.

> Please note the Internet resources are of a time sensitive nature and URL addresses may often change or be deleted.

Contact us at westlegalstudies@delmar.com

ACKNOWLEDGMENTS

I could not have written this book without the help of a number of people I would like to acknowledge here. Some of them provided me with valuable ideas along the way and others gave me the emotional support I needed.

I would first like to recognize those people whose contribution was both informational and inspirational: my colleagues at the University of Central Florida, Dr. Ransford Pyle and Dr. Daniel Hall. Dr.

Pyle wrote significant portions of chapters 1, 2, and 4. Dr. Hall wrote significant portions of chapters 1, 2, 4, 5, and appendix A.

Special thanks go to three important people in my life: my husband, Buddy, and my children, Christopher and Kathryn Elizabeth.

Early drafts and the final manuscript were read by the following reviewers:

Laura Barnard
Lakeland Community College

Mary Meinzinger Urisko
Madonna University

Eli Bortman
Suffolk University

Alex Yarborough
Virginia College at Birmingham

Sharon Lynch Norton
St. John's College of Professional Studies

Carole Olson
El Centro College

Barbara A. Ricker
Andover College

Paul Guymon
William Rainey Harper College

Richard T. Martin
Washburn University

Vickie Manton Brown
Carl Sandburg College

Joy Smucker
Highline Community College

Deborah Carr
University College

Lynne Dahlborg
Suffolk University

Janet Holt
Georgetown University

Carol M. Bast

First, I would like to thank my coauthor, Carol M. Bast, for giving me the opportunity to share my years of online legal research and Internet searching expertise. She has been a great collaborator and sounding board throughout this entire endeavor.

It is with fondness and gratitude that I thank my mentor, the late Orlando, Florida, attorney Lawrence G. Mathews, Jr., for his years of friendship, guidance, and support. Thanks, Larry, for teaching me the law and the power of the written word.

I would also like to extend special thanks to my family, friends, and colleagues, especially the staff and Board of Directors of the Central Florida Library Cooperative, Inc., and the law firm of Holland & Knight, LLP, for their support and encouragement.

Margie A. Hawkins

INTRODUCTION

If you are just starting your study of law you may be wondering what legal research and legal writing have to do with law. After all, you do not see television and movie lawyers performing legal research or writing legal documents. They are usually portrayed arguing eloquently to the judge and jury. What television and movies do not show is all the legal research and writing that took place before the lawyer entered the courtroom.

The job of the lawyer and those working with the lawyer is to competently deal with the client's problem. The client may need the lawyer to either help the client avoid a problem or help the client solve a problem. A client may ask the lawyer to write a will or contract or represent the client in a real estate closing. In these types of transactions, the lawyer helps the client avoid problems by advising the client of the client's rights and responsibilities, by helping the client plan the best course of action, and by drafting any necessary legal documents. Where a problem exists, the client may ask the lawyer to file a lawsuit on the client's behalf or defend the client in a lawsuit. In dealing with a litigation matter, the lawyer advises the client, drafts any necessary legal documents, and represents the client in court.

Legal research and writing are the basic skills necessary for avoiding and solving legal problems. To deal with a problem, the lawyer first has to know what the relevant law is. Discovering what the law is requires legal research. Inadequate knowledge of relevant law may cause the client to lose money or lose a lawsuit. Once the lawyer knows the relevant law, the lawyer avoids or solves problems by communicating—with the client, another lawyer, the court, the jury, and others. Many times the communication is oral, but the lawyer often must communicate using the lawyer's legal writing skills.

Besides causing the client problems, inadequate legal research or mistakes in written communication may cause the lawyer to be disciplined or disbarred because state lawyer ethics rules also govern lawyer legal research and communication. Each state has its own lawyer ethics rules required to be followed by lawyers admitted to practice law in the state. Many states, such as Florida, have lawyer ethics rules patterned on the American Bar Association's *Model Rules of Professional Conduct.* Rule 4-1.1 of the Rules Regulating the Florida Bar, similar to lawyer ethics rules of other states, generally describes the type of representation the lawyer must provide the client. It states:

Rule 4-1.1 Competence

> A lawyer shall provide competent representation to a client. Competent representation requires the legal knowledge, skill, thoroughness, and preparation reasonably necessary for the representation.

Incompetence may mean inadequate legal research or poor writing skills. A 1999 case from the federal Court of Appeals for the Second Circuit demonstrates both; the attorney failed to articulate a legal theory and failed to follow applicable court rules. The appellate court stated:

> The district court dismissed the complaint on the ground that ownership of a valid copyright had not been adequately alleged. Although the issues raised are complex, appellant's main Brief is only nine pages long and does not cite a single statute or court decision related to copyright. Nor does it present a coherent legal theory, even one unsupported by citation to authority, that would sustain the complaint. . . . Appellant's Brief is at best an invitation to the court to scour the record, research any legal theory that comes to mind, and serve generally as an advocate for appellant. We decline the invitation. . . . An attempt is made in the Reply Brief to supply what was conspicuously omitted in the main Brief. The Reply Brief is almost three times as long as the main Brief and contains some citations to pertinent legal authority. However, new arguments may not be made in a reply brief . . . and we decline to entertain the theories so proffered.

Erst Haas Studio, Inc. v. Palm Press, Inc., 164 F.3d 110, 111 (2d Cir. 1999).

The court held that the appellant's main brief was frivolous and sanctioned the attorney by requiring the attorney to pay opposing counsel's legal fees, estimated to be approximately $30,000. In addition, the court affirmed the dismissal of the complaint. Other cases and short passages illustrating incompetent legal representation caused by inadequate research and writing are included at various points in this book.

The provisions of a number of other lawyer ethics rules are summarized in this paragraph and the text of the relevant Florida ethics rules is printed in this introduction and in chapter 11. The lawyer generally may not reveal client confidential information. The lawyer has a duty to give the client honest advice. The lawyer may not represent the client if the claim or defense is frivolous. The lawyer must be truthful in dealing with the court and others and has a duty to explain the law to the court. The lawyer must respect the legal rights of others and not cause undue "embarrass[ment], delay or burden." The lawyer must supervise nonlawyer assistants and may be held responsible for the actions of the nonlawyer assistants. (See fig. I-1.) A lawyer may not falsely attack the reputation of a judge, a juror, or a legal official.

In today's competitive legal job market, you need to know how to competently research and write. Potential employers and colleagues are looking for someone who has these skills. Once on the job, those you come in contact with will assume that you know how to perform legal research and write legal documents. They may not have enough time to teach you those skills if you do not already have them. You will have to work hard to build credibility. You may easily lose this credibility if your colleagues sense you lack basic skills.

The legal researcher must find all law relevant to the legal question being researched, must apply the law to the legal question, and must reach an answer. An

Rule 4-5.3 Responsibilities Regarding Nonlawyer Assistants

With respect to a nonlawyer employed or retained by or associated with a lawyer:

(a) a partner in a law firm shall make reasonable efforts to ensure that the firm has in effect measures giving reasonable assurance that the person's conduct is compatible with the professional obligations of the lawyer;

(b) a lawyer having direct supervisory authority over the nonlawyer shall make reasonable efforts to ensure that the person's conduct is compatible with the professional obligations of the lawyer; and

(c) a lawyer shall be responsible for conduct of such a person that would be a violation of the Rules of Professional Conduct if engaged in by a lawyer if:

  (1) the lawyer orders or, with the knowledge of the specific conduct, ratifies the conduct involved; or

  (2) the lawyer is a partner in the law firm in which the person is employed, or has direct supervisory authority over the person, and knows of the conduct at a time when its consequences can be avoided or mitigated but fails to take reasonable remedial action.

FIGURE I-1 Rule 4-5.3 Responsibilities Regarding Nonlawyer Assistants.

answer to a legal question is inadequate if it is not supported by legal principles, if it is not based on current law, or if it is based on incomplete legal research. A lawyer's competency is immediately in question if the lawyer's argument does not take into account recent changes in the law or applicable legal principles.

The legal writer has the challenge of representing the best interests of the client while often facing a hostile audience. A court document will be closely scrutinized by the judge and opposing counsel. The details of a will will be studied when the decedent's estate is administered and may be challenged by relatives omitted from the will. The wording of a contract will be analyzed as the contract is performed, especially if a problem arises. Drafting legal documents is an important part of a lawyer's role; the reader judges the competency of the writer by the clarity and effectiveness of the legal document. Poor writing will deter and prejudice the reader and may cause problems if the writing is misunderstood; poor writing may cause litigation; unclear writing obscures the message the writer is attempting to communicate.

Legal research and legal writing are skills learned with practice. This book is written to give you basic information on legal research and legal writing; it contains research and writing exercises to help you learn how to perform legal research and write legal documents. The first half of the book describes basic legal research materials found in the law library and online. You will be searching these materials to find relevant legal principles. You will apply the legal principles you discover to answer legal research exercises. The second half of the book first helps you improve your basic writing skills by avoiding common errors, writing in plain English, and organizing. The book then introduces the traditional format of common legal documents—letters, contracts, office memos, pleadings, memoranda of law, and appellate briefs.

Now that you know why legal research and legal writing are important to someone dealing with the law, it is time for you to learn how to perform legal research and write legal documents. If you would like to get a taste of legal research by reviewing legal ethics rules, you may want to access http://www.legalethics.com.

CHAPTER 1*

LAW AND SOURCES OF LAW

INTRODUCTION

The information in this chapter provides a framework into which you can fit the pieces of the legal research puzzle. The chapter first explains how law relates to our tripartite system of government; the second part of the chapter discusses sources of law. You may find yourself referring to this chapter as you learn to perform legal research. You will be amazed how much better you understand it after you have covered a few more chapters.

THE AMERICAN SYSTEM OF LAW

Our common law heritage

"Common law" is the system of law developed in England and transferred to most of the English-speaking world. Many other countries are **civil law** jurisdictions. Louisiana is the only state in the United States that is a civil law jurisdiction. Because of the state's French and Spanish heritage, Louisiana's Civil Code is based on the French Code Napolean and the Spanish Fuero Real. Common law and civil law systems rely on different sources of law.

Common law is law developed case-by-case from court decisions. Legal principles are developed over time as cases are decided. Judges decide cases after examining what other courts have done in similar cases in the past. Judges may have to examine many cases before reaching a decision. Common law combines stability and flexibility. It is predictable, yet allows legal principles either to be expanded to fit new situations or to be replaced with a new legal principle that better accommodates new or changing social and economic conditions. The common law system considers prior case law to be a very high source of authority and follows the **doctrine of stare decisis.** Stare decisis means "let the decision stand." Under the doctrine of stare decisis, a court should follow the legal principle decided by that court or a higher court in a prior case where the facts of the prior case are substantially the same as the facts in the present case.

Civil law is based on a civil code, a systematic and comprehensive written set of rules of law. Judges look to the civil code to settle disputes, rather than rely on precedent. The civil law system considers the legislative code of laws to be a very high source of authority. The legislative code provides comprehensive coverage of all of the basic law of the country. In deciding a legal problem, the code must be reviewed to find the

*Grateful thanks to Ransford C. Pyle, Ph.D., J.D. and Daniel E. Hall Ed.D., J.D. who authored portions of this chapter. Reproduced by Permission. FOUNDATIONS OF LAW: CASES, COMMENTARY, AND ETHICS by Ransford C. Pyle. Delmar, Inc., Albany, New York. Second Edition, Copyright 1996. CONSTITUTIONAL LAW: CASES AND COMMENTARY by Daniel E. Hall. Delmar, Albany, New York. Copyright 1997.

appropriate code provision and the provision must be applied to solve the legal problem. In applying code provisions, judges rely primarily on scholarly articles and books written by professors rather than on prior case law. Cases may also be reviewed, but prior case law is not binding as it is in a common law system. Judges also consult the interpretive notes following court decisions. The professors writing the interpretive notes discuss the relationship of the court decision to applicable code provisions and legal principles.

For example, the Louisiana Civil Code is comprised of articles; the articles contain short, declarative sentences, without subparagraphs or internal definitions. Attorneys and judges faced with a legal problem consult the detailed rules of the Code; the Code contains a mixture of general legal principles and answers to specific legal problems. The Code governs wills, estates, succession law and marital property, sales, real property transactions, mortgages, conflicts of laws, statutes of limitation, co-ownership, contract formation and interpretation, tort liability, and allocation of loss. Louisiana follows the doctrine of **jurisprudence constante** rather than the doctrine of stare decisis. As explained earlier, courts following the doctrine of stare decisis are bound to follow a decision of the same court or a higher court where the facts in the prior decision are substantially the same as the facts in the present case. Under jurisprudence constante, a court respects a prior decision but is not bound to follow even the decision of a higher court where the higher court decision differs from the language of the Code. In applying a provision of the Louisiana Civil Code that is similar to a Code Napoleon provision, state courts might consult scholarly treatises interpreting the Code Napoleon.

At the founding of this country, common law was the primary source of law except in Louisiana. There was no important body of United States statutory law until the late nineteenth century. Until the turn of the century, the courts were more active than the legislatures in developing the law. Congress and the state legislatures played a subsidiary role to the courts until the late nineteenth and early twentieth centuries. Congress and the state legislatures began to be very active at the beginning of this century with the advent of the industrial revolution. Federal and state legislatures became more active with the increase in population, the change from a rural to an urban economy, and the increase in industrial accidents following the industrial revolution. The legislatures felt the need to provide broad and detailed solutions to problems of an increasingly industrialized society. Legislation could provide resolution of commonly-occurring disputes without waiting for the courts to decide disputes on a case-by-case basis. Statutory law changed many common law principles to reflect societal changes. The increasing legislative activity shifted the focus of lawmaking from the courts to federal and state legislatures. Legislatures were better able to deal with problems inherent in a rapidly-growing, increasingly- industrialized country. The federal and state legislatures began to pass statutes to safeguard the welfare of an increasingly industrialized workforce and to guarantee the safety of mass-produced products to the consumer. As federal and state legislatures became more active, statutory law increased in importance. Statutes have replaced the common law as the primary source of law.

Federalism

The United States **Constitution** contains the fundamental law for the country, establishes the framework of the government, and contains basic principles of law. Similarly, a state constitution contains the fundamental law for the state, establishes the state framework of government, and contains basic principles of law. The United States has a legal system for the federal government and a legal system for each state and the District of Columbia. In addition, local governments, such as counties, cities, and towns can enact local ordinances.

The United States Constitution divides power between the federal and state governments. This division is known as **federalism** (fig. 1-1). Federalism represents a vertical division of power between the federal government and the government of the states.

The Constitution specifically enumerates the powers of the federal government. Articles I, II, and III set forth the powers of Congress, the President, and the judiciary. The powers of the states are not specifically enumerated, for the most part. The absence of an enumeration of state powers concerned states rights advo-

		SEPARATION OF POWERS		
		Executive	*Legislative*	*Judicial*
FEDERALISM	United States	*President* ■ Second-level executive officials	*Congress* ■ Senate ■ House	*Federal courts* ■ Supreme Court ■ appeals court ■ trial courts ■ non-Article III courts
	States	*Governor* ■ Second-level officials	*State legislatures* ■ typically bicameral	*State courts* ■ highest court ■ intermediate appeal ■ trial

FIGURE 1-1 Dividing Governmental Power.

> The Tenth Amendment to the United States Constitution provides:
>
> The powers not delegated to the United States by the Constitution, nor prohibited by it to the States, are reserved to the States respectively, or to the people.

FIGURE 1-2 The Tenth Amendment to the United States Constitution.

cates at the time the Constitution was adopted. The Tenth Amendment (fig. 1-2) was included in the Bill of Rights to appease these concerns.

The Constitution gives the federal government certain powers. Figure 1-3 contains the text of Article I, sections 8 and 10, of the United States Constitution. Section 8 lists the powers explicitly granted to Congress. Section 10 prohibits the states from exercising certain powers granted to Congress. Powers exclusively granted to the federal government cannot be exercised by the states. Examples of exclusive national powers are coining money, declaring war, conducting foreign diplomacy, making treaties, regulating interstate and international commerce, establishing a post office, taxing imports and exports, regulating naturalization of citizenship, and establishing bankruptcy law (fig. 1-4).

In some circumstances, the federal government is deemed to have **pre-empted** state action. If it is determined that Congress has pre-empted a policy area, all state laws, even if consistent with federal law, are void. The **pre-emption doctrine** holds that in three instances state regulation is precluded or invalidated by federal regulation:

1. When Congress expressly states that it intends to pre-empt state regulation.
2. When a state law is inconsistent with federal law, even though no express pre-emption statement has been made by Congress.
3. When Congress has enacted a legislative scheme that comprehensively regulates a field.

The Constitution grants the federal government other powers on a non-exclusive basis. Granting a power on a non-exclusive basis means that the federal government can pass a statute and a state can pass a statute concerning similar activity within the state. These powers are held concurrently by the federal and state governments (fig. 1-4). The powers to tax citizens, charter banks and corporations, and build roads are examples.

If the power over a policy area has been delegated to the federal or state governments, the delegatee is generally permitted to engage in regulation of any type, civil, administrative, or criminal. Frequently, the result is an overlapping of administrative functions, as well as civil and criminal laws. For example, the United States Department of Transportation has overlapping jurisdiction with state agencies charged

FIGURE 1-3 Article I, Sections 8 and 10 of the United States Constitution.

Article I, section 8 of the United States Constitution provides:

(1) The Congress shall have Power To lay and collect Taxes, Duties, Imposts and Excises, to pay the Debts and provide for the common Defence and general Welfare of the United States; but all Duties, Imposts and Excises shall be uniform throughout the United States;

(2) To borrow Money on the credit of the United States;

(3) To regulate Commerce with foreign Nations, and among the several States, and with the Indian Tribes;

(4) To establish an uniform Rule of Naturalization, and uniform Laws on the subject of Bankruptcies throughout the United States;

(5) To coin Money, regulate the Value thereof, and of foreign Coin, and fix the Standard of Weights and Measures;

(6) To provide for the Punishment of counterfeiting the Securities and current Coin of the United States;

(7) To establish Post Offices and post Roads;

(8) To promote the Progress of Science and useful Arts, by securing for limited Times to Authors and Inventors the exclusive Right to their respective Writings and Discoveries;

(9) To constitute Tribunals inferior to the supreme Court;

(10) To define and punish Piracies and Felonies committed on the high Seas, and Offences against the Law of Nations;

(11) To declare War, grant Letters of Marque and Reprisal, and make Rules concerning Captures on Land and Water;

(12) To raise and support Armies, but no Appropriation of Money to that Use shall be for a longer Term than two Years;

(13) To provide and maintain a Navy;

(14) To make Rules for the Government and Regulation of the land and naval Forces;

(15) To provide for calling forth the Militia to execute the Laws of the Union, suppress Insurrections and repel Invasions;

(16) To provide for organizing, arming, and disciplining, the Militia, and for governing such Part of them as may be employed in the Service of the United States, reserving to the States respectively, the Appointment of the Officers, and the Authority of training the Militia according to the discipline prescribed by Congress;

(17) To exercise exclusive Legislation in all Cases whatsoever, over such District (not exceeding ten Miles square) as may, by Cession of particular States, and the Acceptance of Congress, become the Seat of the Government of the United States, and to exercise like Authority over all Places purchased by the Consent of the Legislature of the State in which the Same shall be, for the Erection of Forts, Magazines, Arsenals, dock-Yards, and other needful Buildings;—And

(18) To make all Laws which shall be necessary and proper for carrying into Execution the foregoing Powers, and all other Powers vested by this Constitution in the Government of the United States, or in any Department or Officer thereof.

Article I, section 10 of the United States Constitution provides:

(1) No state shall enter into any Treaty, Alliance, or Confederation; grant Letters of Marque and Reprisal; coin Money; emit Bills of Credit; make any Thing but gold and silver coin a Tender in Payment of Debts; pass any Bill of Attainder, ex post facto Law, or Law impairing the Obligation of contracts, or grant any Title of Nobility.

(2) No State shall, without the Consent of Congress, lay any Imposts or Duties on Imports or Exports, except what may be absolutely necessary for executing its inspection Laws; and the net Produce of all Duties and Imposts, laid by any State on Imports or Exports, shall be for the Use of the Treasury of the United States; and all such Laws shall be subject to the Revision and Controul of the Congress.

(3) No State shall, without the consent of Congress, lay any Duty of Tonnage, keep Troops, or Ships of War in time of Peace, enter into any Agreement or Compact with another State, or with a foreign Power, or engage in War, unless actually invaded, or in such imminent Danger as will not admit of Delay.

FIGURE 1-3 (continued)

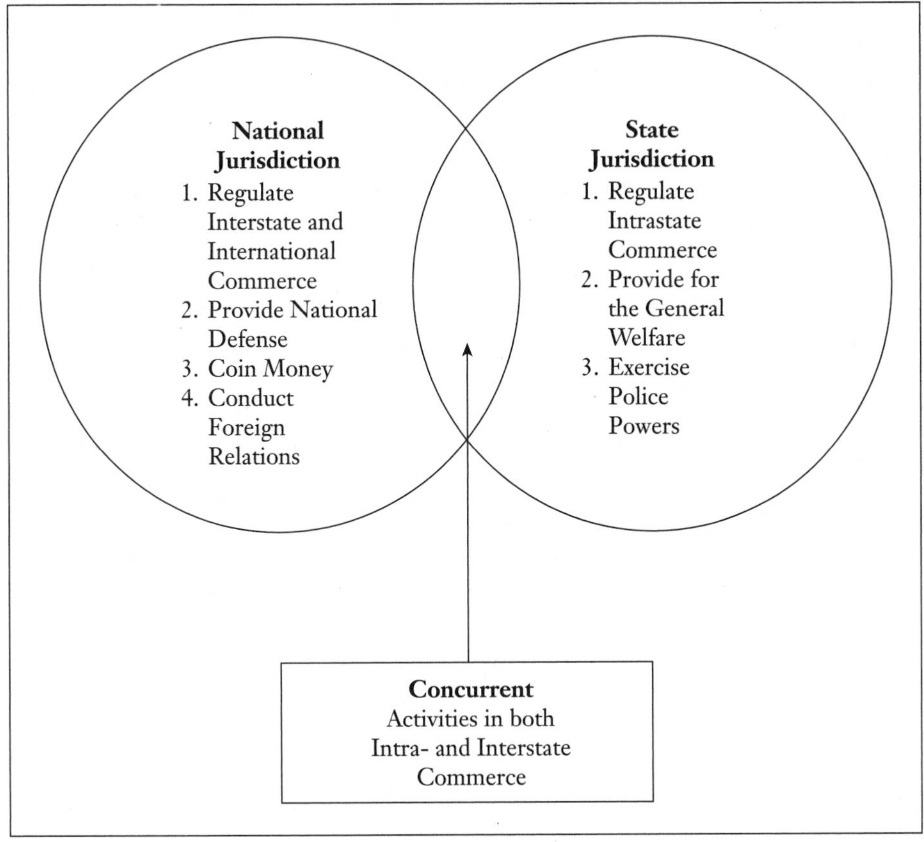

FIGURE 1-4 Federalism and Jurisdiction.

with highway administration. Also, robbery of a federally insured or chartered bank is a violation of both state and federal law. The state in which the robbery occurred has jurisdiction pursuant to its general police powers, and the federal government has jurisdiction by virtue of its charter or insurance coverage.

Article VI of the United States Constitution states in part:

> This Constitution, and the Laws of the United States which shall be made in Pursuance thereof . . . shall be the supreme Law of the Land; and the Judges in every State shall be bound thereby, any Thing in the Constitution or Laws of any State to the contrary notwithstanding.

Because of this provision, known as the **supremacy clause,** no federal statute, state constitution, or state statute may conflict with the United States Constitution. A constitutional or statutory provision found by a court to be in conflict would be held unconstitutional and thus ineffective.

When there is a conflict between a federal and a state statute in an area governed concurrently by both federal and state governments, the federal statute will control. For example, the Fair Labor Standards Act, a federal act, requires most employers to pay employees at least a specified minimum wage and prohibits employment of children under 14 years of age. A state statute that allows employers to pay less than the federal specified minimum wage or to employ 12- or 13-year olds would be in direct conflict with the federal act. A court would hold the state statute unconstitutional and unenforceable.

Powers not given to the federal government are reserved to the states under the Tenth Amendment to the United States Constitution (fig. 1-2). Although the sovereignty of the states has diminished since the Constitution was created, certain areas remain within the exclusive domain of the states (fig. 1-4). The areas of family law, real property law, and tort law are governed mainly by state statutes and case law. Regulating for the health and welfare of citizens is within the state sphere. Providing police and fire protection is another matter within a state's control. These functions make up what is generally referred to as the **police power.** The licensing of professions, such as physicians, plumbers, electricians, and attorneys, is regulated by the states. Education has also been a traditional state function. Just as the national government has the exclusive right to regulate interstate and foreign commerce, the states possess the exclusive right to regulate intrastate commerce.

The Constitution gives individuals rights that may not be taken away by federal or state government. These rights are often referred to as "civil rights." Figure 1-5 contains the text of the first nine amendments and section 1 of the Fourteenth Amendment to the United States Constitution. These provisions give individuals certain important rights.

The judiciary has dealt with federalism issues in three contexts, and through its decision in these contexts, it has advanced the supremacy of national power. First, under the pre-emption doctrine, state laws are invalidated if they interfere or conflict with national legislation. For example, the federal government has pre-empted state regulation of aviation. Thus, a state cannot enact airline safety regulations, because the federal government has completely regulated the area.

Second, state laws that interfere with interstate commerce, even if largely unregulated by the federal government, are invalidated. This is known as the dormant commerce clause doctrine. Pursuant to this doctrine, laws that discriminate against out-of-state market participants have been invalidated. Hence, a state law that prohibited the sale of milk produced outside New York at a lower price than milk produced within the state was held unconstitutional.

Third, through the intergovernmental immunity doctrine, the national government possesses greater immunity from state regulation than the states do from federal regulation. That is, the federal government has greater authority to impose obligations upon the states than vice versa. Accordingly, federal overtime and wage laws apply against the states, but similar state laws do not protect federal employees.

Another piece to fit into the research puzzle is local law. Counties, townships, municipalities, and other local governmental entities have laws governing matters such as zoning, occupational licenses, and construction permits, considered to be "local" in nature. Local laws include **charters** and **ordinances** (sometimes referred to as *resolutions*). A charter is similar to federal and state constitutions in that a charter is the fundamental document setting up the local government. Once formed, the local government passes ordinances to implement the power given it under its charter. Just as state statutes are grouped by subject matter into a state code, ordinances may be compiled into a code. If not available at the public library, a copy of the local government's charter and ordinances or code usually may be purchased from the local governmental entity or may be available without charge on the Internet.

OUR TRIPARTITE SYSTEM

The United States Constitution also allocates power horizontally among the three branches of government. State constitutions establish similar frameworks for the states. The federal and state governments are each divided into three branches: **legislative, judicial,** and **executive** (fig. 1-6). Each of the branches has a role in making law and there is an important interplay among the three branches. The chart in figure 1-7 shows these three branches

FIGURE 1-5 Amendments I through IX and XIV to the United States Constitution.

Amendment I.

Congress shall make no law respecting an establishment of religion, or prohibiting the free exercise thereof; or abridging the freedom of speech, or of the press; or the right of the people peaceably to assemble, and to petition the Government for a redress of grievances.

Amendment II.

A well regulated Militia, being necessary to the security of a free State, the right of the people to keep and bear Arms, shall not be infringed.

Amendment III.

No soldier shall, in time of peace be quartered in any house, without the consent of the Owner, nor in time of war, but in a manner to be prescribed by law.

Amendment IV.

The right of the people to be secure in their persons, houses, papers, and effects, against unreasonable searches and seizures, shall not be violated, and no Warrants shall issue, but upon probable cause, supported by Oath or affirmation, and particularly describing the place to be searched, and the persons or things to be seized.

Amendment V.

No person shall be held to answer for a capital, or otherwise infamous crime, unless on a presentment or indictment of a Grand Jury, except in cases arising in the land or naval forces, or in the militia, when in actual service in time of War or public danger; nor shall any person be subject for the same offence to be twice put in jeopardy of life or limb; nor shall be compelled in any criminal case to be a witness against himself, nor be deprived of life, liberty, or property, without due process of law; nor shall private property be taken for public use, without just compensation.

Amendment VI.

In all criminal prosecutions, the accused shall enjoy the right to a speedy and public trial, by an impartial jury of the State and district wherein the crime shall have been committed, which district shall have been previously ascertained by law, and to be informed of the nature and cause of the accusation; to be confronted with the witnesses against him; to have compulsory process for obtaining witnesses in his favor, and to have the Assistance of Counsel for his defence.

Amendment VII.

In Suits at common law, where the value in controversy shall exceed twenty dollars, the right of trial by jury shall be preserved, and no fact tried by a jury, shall be otherwise reexamined in any Court of the United States, than according to the rules of the common law.

Amendment VIII.

Excessive bail shall not be required, nor excessive fines imposed, nor cruel and unusual punishments inflicted.

Amendment IX.

The enumeration in the Constitution, of certain rights, shall not be construed to deny or disparage others retained by the people.

Amendment XIV.

Section 1. All persons born or naturalized in the United States, and subject to the jurisdiction thereof, are citizens of the United States and of the State wherein they reside. No State shall make or enforce any law which shall abridge the privileges or immunities of citizens of the United States; nor shall any State deprive any person of life, liberty, or property, without due process of law; nor deny to any person within its jurisdiction the equal protection of the laws.

	LEGISLATIVE BRANCH	EXECUTIVE BRANCH	JUDICIAL BRANCH
The Government of the United States (Federal Government)	United States Congress	President of the United States	Federal Courts
State Governments	State Legislatures	Governors	State Courts

FIGURE 1-6 Division of Governmental Power.

for the federal government. Legislatures pass statutes setting forth broad public policies. The legislative branch is discussed more fully below in this chapter and in chapter 5. The President is responsible for administering and enforcing the nation's laws, conducting foreign affairs, and negotiating treaties, and is the commander-in-chief of the military. **Administrative agencies,** often considered a part of the executive branch, promulgate detailed administrative rules and regulations that have the force of law. The executive branch is discussed more fully below and in chapter 5. The courts make law, interpret constitutions, statutes, and administrative regulations, and settle disputes based on the law. Federal courts can hold a statute that conflicts with the United States Constitution unconstitutional. Similarly, a state statute that conflicts with the United States Constitution or a state constitution can be held to be unconstitutional. The judicial branch is discussed more fully below and in chapter 4.

INTERPLAY AMONG THE THREE BRANCHES OF GOVERNMENT IN LAWMAKING

The three branches of government have different roles in the law-making process. These roles and the interplay among the three branches balance the law-making power, with each branch checking the law-making power of the other two (figs. 1-8 and 1-9).

Look first at the interplay between the legislative and judicial branches. Legislatures pass statutes to address a public problem. Where statutory language is very general, the courts have a lot of freedom to interpret statutes through cases in which the courts decide if and how a statute applies to a problem. Even where statutory language is much more specific, a court may be called upon to interpret particular statutory language or to decide if a statute applies to the problem before the court.

Legislatures enact statutes governing many different types of matters. However, statutes do not cover all legal problems that arise. Where a legal problem is not covered by a statute, attorneys and judges consult case law (common law). Judges make common law principles. Common law principles emerge as cases are decided.

The founders of the American legal system chose to adopt the common law system as the basis of our country's law. Common law is based on the doctrine of precedent. Precedent lends fairness, coherence, predictability, and reliability to the common law. The common law is stable, yet flexible, changing to meet the needs of a dynamic society. Historically, case law was emphasized over legislation, but this has changed with the rapid growth of and importance of legislation. Today, some areas of the law, such as torts, continue to be governed almost exclusively by case law; some areas are governed by statutes (as interpreted by the courts and administrative agencies); and other areas are governed partly by case law and partly by statutes.

In *Marbury v. Madison,* Chief Justice John Marshall wrote that federal courts could determine if a statute were invalid because it was in conflict with the United States Constitution. Judicial review of the constitutionality of a statute is grounded in the supremacy clause and the clause giving federal courts jurisdiction over cases "arising under this Constitution." Federal courts in the United States can declare a statute invalid if it conflicts with the United States

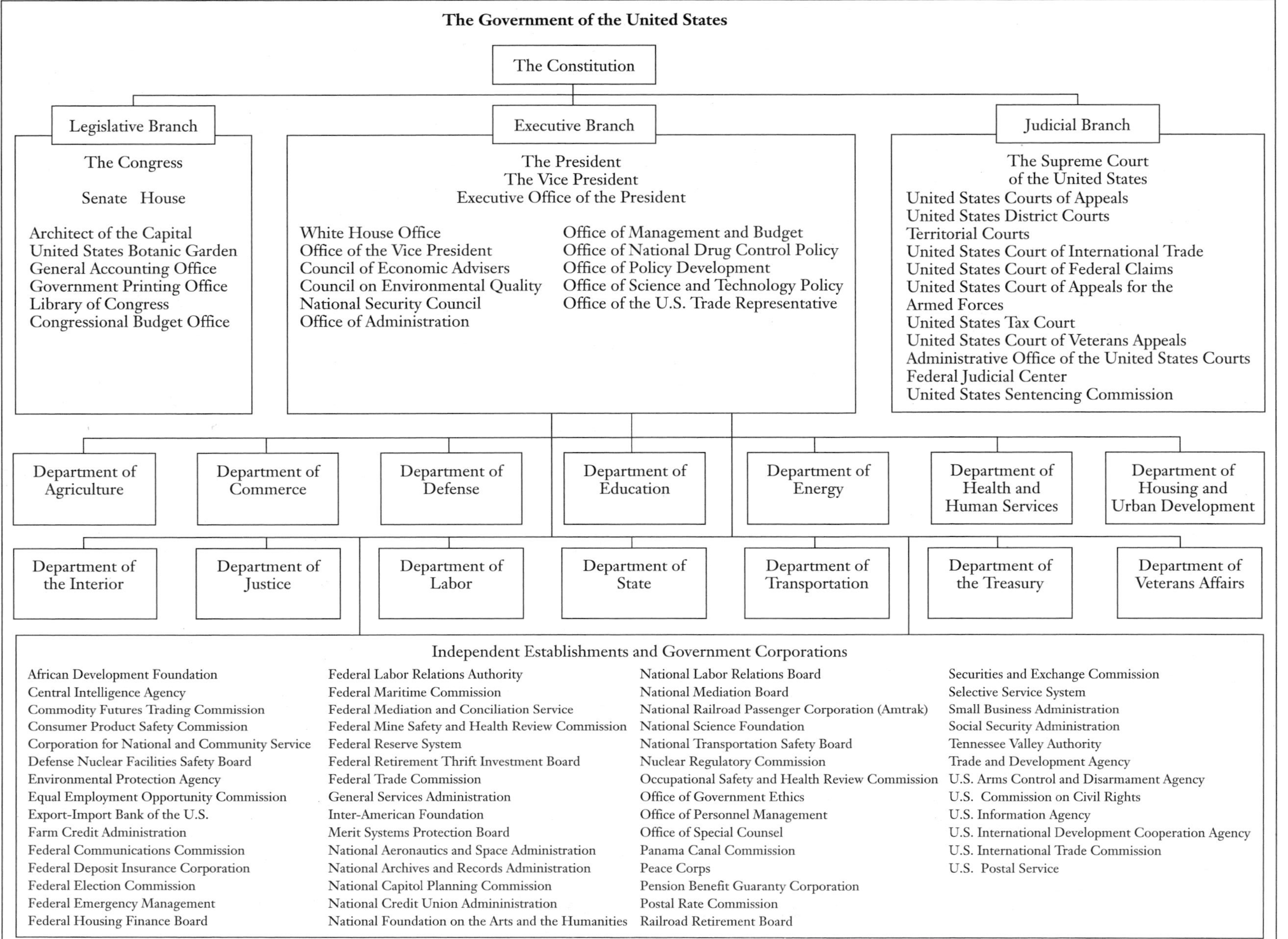

FIGURE 1-7 The Government of the United States.

FIGURE 1-8 Examples of Checks and Balances.

Power	Checked By
President negotiates treaties	Senate ratification
President nominates judges and officers	Senate confirmation
Congress enacts laws	Presidential approval and judicial review
Presidential veto	Congressional override
President is commander-in-chief of the military	Congress declares war and creates rules regulating the military
Courts exercise judicial review	Impeachment by Congress and constitutional amendment process
Courts decide cases	Congress enacts statutes changing the common law
Elected officials are not responsive to public	People, through the vote

FIGURE 1-9 Controls on Federal Judicial Power—Summary.

CONTROLS ON FEDERAL JUDICIAL POWER—SUMMARY

Formal

1. Presidential nomination and senate confirmation of Article III judges
2. Removal through impeachment
3. Congressional control of jurisdiction
4. Congressional control of number of justices and lower federal courts
5. Justiciability requirements
6. Constitution and statutory amendments intended to reverse judicial decisions
7. Congressional control of increases in salaries and provision of other resources

Informal

1. Judicial reliance on executive branch for the enforcement of orders
2. Public opinion
3. Interest in preserving the integrity of the judiciary

Constitution. State courts can declare a statute invalid if it conflicts with the United States Constitution or the state constitution. This is commonly known as the **doctrine of judicial review.**

The legislature can change the common law by passing statutes that supersede the common law. One reason to change the prior common law is because the legislature recognizes a need to systematically regulate an area of the law previously governed by case law. An example of this is the Uniform Commercial Code, at least a portion of which, in some form, has been adopted by all 50 states. Another reason to change the prior common law is to "overrule" unpopular court decisions. In 1989, the United States Supreme Court ruled that burning the United States flag was constitutionally protected as an expression of free speech. In response, several members of Congress proposed amending the United States Constitution to outlaw flag-burning. Because it generally takes such a long time to amend the Constitution, they suggested passing a federal statute prohibiting flag-burning in the meantime. Congress enacted a federal statute criminalizing the same conduct, in obvious contravention of the First Amendment. That statute might have been enforced until challenged in court. After the statute was challenged in court, the United States Supreme Court declared it unconstitutional in 1990.

Once enacted, constitutions, statutes, and regulations are then interpreted by the courts. In applying constitutions, statutes, and regulations to a particular case, a court in effect explains what a provision means. The court's interpretative role is such a significant one that constitutions, statutes, and regulations must be read in light of case law application of them. Sometimes a court is asked to determine the constitutionality of a statute or regulation. For example, in *Roe v. Wade*, 410 U.S. 113 (1973), the United States Supreme Court based its decision on an implied constitutional right to privacy. Although this right is not explicitly stated in the Constitution, the United States Supreme Court interpreted the Bill of Rights to require the existence of this unstated right under the theory that other important rights such as the right against unreasonable search and seizure would be meaningless without an implied right to privacy. The Court thus struck down Texas antiabortion statutes because they conflicted with the constitutional right to privacy.

Congress possesses considerable authority over the jurisdiction of the federal courts. Political concerns could, therefore, cause legislators to limit the jurisdiction of the judiciary over certain issues. Congress has the authority to remove cases from the appellate jurisdiction of the United States Supreme Court and, presumably, could limit the jurisdiction of lower courts. Also, because the courts inferior to the United States Supreme Court were created by Congress, they could be abolished by Congress.

The primary role of the *chief executive* is to enforce the law. Article II, section 1 of the United States Constitution provides:

> The executive Power shall be vested in a President of the United States of America.

Article II, section 2, clause 2 of the United States Constitution gives the President the following powers:

> He shall have Power, by and with the Advice and Consent of the Senate, to make Treaties, provided two thirds of the Senators present concur; and he shall nominate, and by and with the Advice and Consent of the Senate, shall appoint Ambassadors, other public Ministers and Consuls, Judges of the supreme Court, and all other Officers of the United States, whose Appointments are not herein otherwise provided for, and which shall be established by Law: but the Congress may by Law vest the Appointment of such inferior Officers, as they think proper, in the President alone, in the Courts of Law, or in the Heads of Departments.

In addition, the chief executive sets policy on enforcing the law. With limited resources, all laws cannot be enforced to the maximum. Policy set by the executive branch influences the extent to which different laws will be enforced. The chief executive can issue executive orders that direct the actions of agencies and officials. Several of the president's official roles, including United States military commander, give the President the power to issue proclamations and executive orders. These documents have the force of law, just like case law or statutory law.

No provision in the Constitution gives the President the power to directly make law. Regardless, all American presidents have made law through executive orders and presidential proclamations. Orders and proclamations are tools used by the President to perform executive functions. As such, they are not an independent source of presidential authority. A President only uses orders and proclamations to enforce otherwise lawful presidential power. If lawfully promulgated, orders and proclamations have the effect of statutes. Presidential proclamations and executive orders and administrative regulations are printed chronologically in the *Federal Register*. Later these documents are codified in the Code of Federal Regulations (C.F.R.).

The executive branch affects and is affected by the other two branches in a number of ways. The chief executive may veto legislation. Vetoed legislation can be enacted only if the legislature has sufficient votes to override the veto. The chief executive also greatly influences enforcement of legislation, in part through funding and publicity. Usually there is insufficient money and personnel to enforce all legislation, so the executive may direct that special attention be paid to certain laws. A priority in recent years has been the enforcement of criminal statutes prohibiting the illegal drug trade. The most lasting effect a President has may be from the constitutional mandate to nominate federal judges. Once confirmed by the Senate, such an appointment is for life, unless the judge resigns or is impeached.

The President conducts foreign affairs and negotiates treaties. Congress, the Senate in particular, must ratify treaties. The President is the commander-in-chief of the military, but Congress possesses significant authority over the military as well. It is charged with making rules regulating the military and is responsible for declaring war. The President has been delegated the authority to nominate federal judges and other governmental officers, but the appointments are final only after Senate confirmation. As a check on both the President and the judiciary, Congress holds the power of impeachment.

Many of the petitions filed with the Supreme Court are filed by the United States, by the Solicitor General of the United States. Such filings are examined with special care by the Court when it determines whether to hear the appeals. The executive branch therefore influences the Court by its partial control over the issues presented to the Court.

Although the United States Supreme Court is insulated from politics, it is generally believed that politics and public opinion play at least a minor role in influencing the Court's decision making. Because the Court has no method of enforcing its orders, it relies on the executive branch. This unenforceability, some contend, keeps the Court's decisions within the bounds of reason; that is, within a range the public will tolerate and the executive will enforce.

Politics also play a role in the selection of Article III judges. Supreme Court justices and judges of federal district and appellate courts are selected by the political branches of government; the President nominates and the Senate must confirm. In recent years, the process has been criticized as being too political, focusing on the political and ideological beliefs of nominees rather than on other qualifications, such as education, employment experience, prior judicial experience, intellectual ability, and the like. The confirmation hearings of Robert Bork (nominated by President Reagan and rejected by the Senate) and Clarence Thomas (nominated by President Bush and confirmed by the Senate) are used to illustrate this point.

Once appointed, an Article III judge maintains his or her position until one of three occurrences: retirement, death or **impeachment.** The power to impeach a judge rests with Congress. Congress may impeach for high crimes and misdemeanors. This is, therefore, another limitation upon the judiciary by an external force. Congress has been true to the purpose of impeachment and has not used the power to achieve political objectives.

By statute, federal and state legislatures can delegate some of their powers to administrative agencies. Statutes establish an administrative agency and allocate the administrative agency the power to promulgate **administrative regulations;** the agency is usually given the power to enforce the regulations and the quasi-judicial power for administrative law judges to decide disputes concerning the administrative regulations and impose sanctions.

Administrative agencies are an important source of law. Some consider these agencies a "fourth branch" of government; however, figures 1-10 and 1-11 place them under the executive branch because the heads of administrative agencies may be nominated by the chief executive (president or governor). Legislatures delegate rulemaking authority to administrative agencies. Administrative agencies have quasi-legislative, quasi-executive and quasi-judicial functions. They promulgate administrative rules and regulations, they enforce the rules and regulations, and they settle disputes concerning the rules and regulations. Administrative agencies are an important source of law—**administrative law.** Administrative rules and regulations have the force of law, just like case law or statutory law; however, administrative agencies can promulgate administrative rules and regulations only if a constitution or a statute gives them the power to do so.

Federal agencies include the Federal Trade Commission, the Environmental Protection Agency, the Internal Revenue Service, and the Food and Drug Administration. States have state administrative agencies. For example, Florida has the Department of Natural Resources, Department of Business and Professional Regulation, and the Department of Children and Families.

Administrative agencies promulgate administrative rules and regulations that have the force of law. These rules and regulations are in effect an interpretation of statutes passed by the legislature. To function, administrative agencies must interpret the law, often before any court has had an opportunity to address objections to that law. Further, the agencies' priorities in regulation and enforcement influence both the legislative and the judicial branches.

Now that you know something about the law produced by the three branches of our government, you need to know where to look to find it. The next section briefly introduces primary sources, secondary sources, and finding tools. Chapters 3 through 6 contain an in-depth discussion of primary sources, secondary sources, and finding tools.

FEDERAL GOVERNMENT		
Judicial Branch	**Legislative Branch**	**Executive Branch**
United States Supreme Court (9 Justices) *slip opinions* *looseleaf services* United States Law Week *reporters* United States Reports Supreme Court Reporter United States Supreme Court Reports, Lawyers' Edition	**Senate** **House of Representatives** *slip laws* *advance session law service* United States Code Congressional and Administrative News *session laws* United States Statutes at Large	**President** *Presidential Documents*
United States Courts of Appeals *reporter* Federal Reporter	*code* United States Code	**Administrataive Agencies** *daily publication* Federal Register *code* Code of Federal Regulations
United States District Courts *reporter* Federal Supplement	*annotated codes* United States Code Annotated United States Code Service	

FIGURE 1-10 The Three Branches of the Federal Government Are the Legislative, the Executive, and the Judicial.

STATE GOVERNMENT		
Judicial Branch	**Legislative Branch**	**Executive Branch**
court of last resort *slip opinion* *looseleaf service* *reporters* **intermediate appellate court** *looseleaf service* *reporter* **trial level courts** *reporters*	**state legislature** *slip laws* *advance session law service* *session laws* *code* *annotated codes*	**Governor** **Administrative Agencies** *daily or weekly publications* *code*

FIGURE 1-11 State Governments, Like the Federal Government, Have Three Co-equal Branches.

FIGURE 1-12 Legal Sources and Finding Tools.

Primary Sources	Secondary Sources	Finding Tools
constitutions†	treatises*	American Law Reports*
statutes†	law review articles*	legal encyclopedias*
court rulings†	legal periodicals*	digests*
administrataive regulations†	law dictionaries*	citators††
reporters**	legal thesaurus*	looseleaf services*
looseleaf services*	continuing legal education publications*	*Index to Legal Periodicals**
	Restatements*	
	hornbooks*	
	American Law Reports annotations*	
	legal encyclopedias*	
	looseleaf services*	

*See chapter 3
**See chapter 4
†See chapter 5
††See chapter 6

SOURCES OF LAW

Your first trip through the law library may seem overwhelming. The law library contains all kinds of sources you need to consult when researching a legal question. By the end of your legal research class, you will be familiar with many of these sources. Primary sources, secondary sources, and finding tools are all sources of law, but they are used in different ways. Their use depends on the information they contain and how authoritative they are. **Primary sources** contain the law itself, **secondary sources** contain commentary on the law, and **finding tools,** as the name implies, are used to find primary and secondary sources. Primary sources are given the most weight, but secondary sources may be used if no primary sources are available. Finding tools are not authoritative and may not be quoted or cited. Nevertheless, finding tools are an important part of legal research. You may be able to locate relevant primary and secondary sources only by using finding tools.

Figures 1-10 and 1-11 show the judicial, legislative, and executive branches for the federal and state governments. Figure 1-10 gives the names of the various entities within those branches and the reference materials containing the law made by each entity. You may want to add state-specific references to Figure 1-11 as a quick and handy guide for your state's law.

Primary sources and secondary sources.

The difference between primary sources and secondary sources is critical when working with the law. Figure 1-12 lists common and frequently used primary and secondary sources and finding tools. These sources are covered in greater depth in later chapters.

Primary sources contain the actual law. Figure 1-13 lists constitutions, cases (common law), statutes, administrative regulations, ordinances, and court rules as primary sources. Secondary sources, containing a commentary on the law, include treatises, legal periodicals, law review articles, legal encyclopedias, American Law Reports annotations, law dictionaries, legal thesauruses, continuing legal education publications, restatements, and hornbooks. Finding tools are reference publications used to find primary and secondary sources. They include American Law Reports

PRIMARY SOURCES OF LAW

SOURCE	COMMENT
Constitution	The United States and every state have a constitution. The United States Constitution is the supreme law of the land. Amendment of the federal constitution requires action by both the states and United States Congress.
Statutes	The written law created by legislatures, also known as codes. State statutes may not conflict with either their own constitution or the federal constitution. State statues are also invalid if they conflict with other federal law, and the federal government has concurrent jurisdiction with the states. Statutes of the United States are invalid if they conflict with the United States Constitution or if they attempt to regulate outside federal jurisdiction. Legislatures may change statutes at will.
Common Law	Law which evolved, as courts, through judicial opinions, recognized customs, and practices. Legislatures may alter, amend, or abolish the common law at will. In criminal law the common law is responsible for the creation of crimes and for establishing defenses to crimes.
Regulations	Created by administrative agencies under a grant of authority from a legislative body. Regulations must be consistent with statutes and constitutions and may not exceed the legislative grant of power. The power to make rules and regulations is granted to "fill in the gaps" left by legislatures when drafting statutes.
Ordinances	Written law of local bodies, such as city councils. Must be consistent with all higher forms of law.
Court Rules	Rules created by courts to manage their cases. Court rules are procedural and commonly establish deadlines, lengths of filings, etc. Court rules may not conflict with statutes or constitutions.

FIGURE 1-13 Primary Sources of Law.

annotations, legal encyclopedias, digests, citators, and the Index to Legal Periodicals. You may have noticed that American Law Reports annotations and legal encyclopedias are listed both as secondary sources and as finding tools in figure 1-12. American Law Reports annotations and legal encyclopedias are secondary sources, because of their commentary on the law, but they are also used to find primary and secondary authority. Looseleaf services are listed as a primary source, a secondary source, and a finding tool because they contain the text of primary sources and commentaries on the law, as well as features used to find primary sources.

A major goal in legal research is to locate the primary sources relevant to the problem you are researching. Secondary sources are often used to find primary sources. Another reason for consulting a secondary source is to gain a basic understanding of the subject matter being researched.

In legal writing always **cite** to the relevant primary source. Determining which primary sources are relevant and then deciding which of those sources to cite requires an understanding of legal reasoning and performance of legal analysis. (Legal reasoning and legal analysis are discussed in chapter 2). If you have found few or no relevant primary sources, you may cite certain types of secondary sources. The preferred secondary sources are treatises, legal periodicals, law review articles, law dictionaries, legal thesauruses, restatements, and continuing legal education publications. Digests should never be cited. Although you may cite legal encyclopedias and American Law Reports annotations, they are not a preferred citation source and you should do so with caution. It is always better to find ("pull") the primary authority referred to in the legal encyclopedia or annotation and cite that primary authority rather than the secondary authority.

Legal publishing

Legal publishing has been transformed during the 1990s in two different ways. First, the publishing vehicle has changed. Prior to the 1990s, print was the primary publication medium, although online legal research via Westlaw or Lexis was increasing in popularity. At the end of the century, legal materials were also available on CD-ROM and on the Internet. Chapters 8 through 10 discuss computer-assisted legal research in more detail.

Second, the legal publishers have changed. On one hand, a number of legal publishers were acquired by large corporations, resulting in two major legal publishing companies—Thomson Corp. and Reed Elsevier plc. On the other hand, recently-founded companies, such as Hyperlaw and Versuslaw, are marketing primary sources on CD-ROM and all levels of government are making primary sources available on the Internet.

In older legal research books you would find many references to Lawyers Cooperative Publishing Company and West Publishing Company. Lawyers Cooperative Publishing Company and West Publishing Company formerly were the two legal publishing giants. Both companies are now part of West Group. West Group is a division of Thomson Corp., an international information and publishing company.

West Group produces Corpus Juris Secundum, Supreme Court Reporter, Federal Supplement, Federal Reporter, United States Code Annotated, formerly published by West Publishing Company. In addition, West Group produces American Jurisprudence and American Law Reports, formerly published by Lawyers Cooperative Publishing Company.

The other giant in legal publishing is Reed Elsevier plc, an international publisher and information provider. Reed Elsevier, Inc. is the holding company for the majority of Reed Elsevier plc's United States business. LexisNexis, Matthew Bender, Martindale-Hubbell, Shepard's, and Lexis Law Publishing (formerly known as The Michie Company, LLP) are Reed Elsevier companies.

Lexis Law Publishing produces United States Code Service and United States Supreme Court Reports, Lawyers' Edition.

Print or electronic resources?

Many law firm libraries are shrinking in size because the firms are replacing some print sources with their electronic version. The smaller square footage of the library partly offsets rising real estate costs. Some law firms have reduced their library size by 30 to 40 per cent.

The move to electronic resources has some disadvantages. The fees for use of electronic resources can be equivalent to or more than the cost of print resources. While legal research classes taught the attorneys how to research in print sources, many attorneys may not be familiar with researching in the electronic sources. Efficient use of electronic sources requires adequate and updated hardware. Many sources, such as treatises, available in print are not yet available electronically.

CHAPTER 1 SUMMARY

- The federal and state governments are each made up of three branches: legislative, judicial, and executive.
- The judicial branch (the courts) produces what is called common law, case law, or judge-made law.
- Common law is law developed case-by-case from court decisions.
- The legislative branch (elected representatives) passes statutes.
- Administrative agencies (often considered part of the executive branch) promulgate administrative rules and regulations.
- The chief executive (the president or governor) issues proclamations and executive orders.

- Federal and state laws are a product of an important interplay among the three branches of government.
  - The legislature can pass statutes that supersede the common law.
  - The courts interpret and apply constitutions, statutes, and administrative regulations.
  - The chief executive may veto legislation, sets priorities in law enforcement, and appoints judges.
- The Supremacy Clause of the United States Constitution makes the United States Constitution the supreme law of the land. No federal or state statute or state constitution may conflict with it.
- In the law library primary sources contain the law itself while secondary sources and finding tools are used to locate relevant primary sources.
- In addition to books from the law library, many legal researchers use computers to assist them in legal research; computer-assisted legal research includes online services, services contained on CD-ROM, and the Internet.

EXERCISES FOR CHAPTER 1

1. Fill in the State Government chart on page 13 with the appropriate information from your state.
2. Visit the law library you will be using and identify the federal and state primary sources, secondary sources, and finding tools you will be using in your research. Compare the list on page 14 with the books available in your law library.
3. Find out what types of computer-assisted research are available to you.

CYBERLAW EXERCISES

1. Are you fairly new to the Internet? If so, you may like to use the tutorials offered at http://learnthenet.com.
2. The Federal Judiciary homepage is located at http://www.uscourts.gov/. Using the homepage, locate your federal district court and federal court of appeals through "links."
3. The United States Supreme Court's web page is located at http://www.supremecourtus.gov/. Using the homepage, read some of the information in its "Visitor's Guides," accessible from "Visiting the Court."
4. Thomas is the name of Congress' homepage, located at http://thomas.loc.gov/. Using Thomas, find the names of the senators and representatives from your state in the House and Senate directories.
5. The White House homepage is located at http://www.whitehouse.gov. Using the homepage, go into the news page and read several of today's releases.
6. The homepage of the National Center for State Courts links you to web sites for the courts of your state. The homepage is located at http://ncsc online.org. Use the page to locate information on the courts of your state. Try "Court Web Sites."
7. For more information on trial-level courts, try http://www.courts.net.

CHAPTER 2*

LEGAL REASONING AND ANALYSIS

When a legal distinction is determined, as no one doubts that it may be, between night and day, childhood and maturity, or any other extremes, a point has to be fixed or a line has to be drawn, or gradually picked out by successive decisions, to mark where the change takes place. Looked at by itself without regard to the necessity behind it the line or point seems arbitrary. It might as well or nearly as well be a little more to one side or the other. But when it is seen that a line or point there must be, and that there is no mathematical or logical way of fixing it precisely, the decision of the legislature must be accepted unless we can say that it is very wide of any reasonable mark.

***Louisville Gas. Co. v. Coleman*, 277 U.S. 32, 41 (1928)(Holmes, J., dissenting).**

INTRODUCTION

Attorneys and judges use the process of legal reasoning and analysis to plan transactions and to solve legal problems by applying cases and rules (constitutions, statutes, court rules, and administrative regulations). Legal reasoning and analysis involves **reasoning by analogy** and **deductive reasoning.**

When you research a legal problem you are looking for primary sources applicable to your problem. You must use legal reasoning and analysis to determine whether a source is in fact applicable and how it applies. Because we have a common law system, cases are central to legal reasoning and analysis. Although a case settles a particular dispute as to the parties to the case, the case may be applicable to future cases through the **doctrine of stare decisis.** Determining whether a past case should apply to a case presently before a court and what impact the earlier case has on the later cases involves reasoning by analogy. **Office practice attorneys** help clients plan transactions to make them as advantageous as possible to the client while avoiding potential legal problems. Office practice attorneys use reasoning by analogy to predict what a court would do, given a proposed fact pattern.

Legal rules (constitutions, statutes, court rules, and administrative regulations) are general statements of what the law permits, requires, and prohibits. Because the regulatory language is general, it may not

*Grateful thanks to Ransford C. Pyle, Ph.D., J.D. who authored the portion of this chapter entitled Legal Analysis of Statutory Law. Reproduced by Permsssion. FOUNDATIONS OF LAW: CASES, COMMENTARY, AND ETHICS by Ransford C. Pyle. Delmar, Inc., Albany, New York. Second Edition, Copyright 1996.

Grateful thanks to Daniel E. Hall Ed.D., J.D. who authored the portion of this chapter entitled Legal Analysis of Constitutional Law. Reproduced by Permission. CONSTITUTIONAL LAW: CASES AND COMMENTARY by Daniel E. Hall. Delmar, Inc., Albany, New York. Copyright 1997.

be clear whether a particular rule applies to a given factual situation. Deductive reasoning is used to determine if the rule applies. As more fully explained later in this chapter, deductive reasoning involves reasoning from the general (rule) to the specific (the impact of the rule on a particular fact pattern).

As explained in chapter 1, some areas of the law are governed solely by case law. Many areas are governed by a combination of rules and cases. Even if you find a constitutional or statutory provision that seems to apply, you must research the provision to see how it has been interpreted by the courts. Thus, the researcher will often be using a combination of reasoning by analogy and deductive reasoning to solve a legal problem.

The following section describes a hypothetical fact pattern. The fact pattern will be used at several points in this chapter to explain reasoning by analogy and deductive reasoning.

AN ILLUSTRATIVE FACT PATTERN

Imagine that you are a criminal defense attorney representing a woman arrested on federal criminal charges for drug possession. You will be researching several possible defenses for your client, Cruz Estrada.

Cruz was riding with her friend, Luis Briones, when Luis' car was pulled over. They were traveling south on I-95 toward Miami to visit friends. The officer said he had stopped the car because they were speeding.

The officer stood at the window on the driver's side and asked for Luis' license and car registration. While Luis searched his wallet for the documents, the officer noticed a glass vial containing small kernels of an off-white substance in Luis' lap. Believing the vial to contain crack cocaine, the officer announced that he was seizing it. He asked Luis and Cruz to exit the car and asked Luis for his wallet.

Cruz got out of the car with her purse strap slung over her shoulder. The officer approached her and said, "You don't mind if I search this, do you?" Without giving her time to respond, the officer grabbed her purse and began to search it. Inside her purse, he found a brown paper envelope. Cruz claimed that someone had given it to her to give to a friend in Miami.

Still holding Cruz' purse and Luis' wallet, the officer asked them to wait in the patrol car while he searched Luis' car. Cruz and Luis nervously waited in the back seat of the patrol car. Cruz admitted to Luis that the envelope was hers and that it contained illegal drugs.

After she and Luis were arrested, she discovered that the police officer had tape-recorded their conversation in the back of the patrol car. Luis told her that the reason the officer gave for stopping them must have been a pretext because, at the most, he was driving five miles over the speed limit. He said he suspected that he had been stopped for what is jokingly referred to as the offense of DWH or Driving While Hispanic.

The following section first discusses a number of terms central to understanding cases and then explains legal reasoning and analysis involving case law.

DOCTRINE OF STARE DECISIS

The doctrine of stare decisis states that when a court has set forth a legal principle, that court and all lower courts under it will apply that principle in future cases where the facts are substantially the same.

Reasoning by analogy first involves finding a past case with facts that appear to be similar to the case presently being decided. No two fact patterns are identical, even if they involve similarly situated parties or what appears to be the same issue. Therefore, there will always be similarities and differences between the two fact patterns. The second step is to compare the facts of the two cases to determine which facts are similar and which facts are different. The third step is to determine whether the facts of the two cases are so substantially similar that the past case should determine the result in the present case. If the facts in the two cases are substantially different, then the result in the present case might differ from the result in the past case. In examining factual differences and similarities, one must determine whether the similarities or differences are more significant. A few similarities between crucial facts in the two cases may outweigh numerous differences in unimportant facts.

The doctrine of stare decisis and reasoning by analogy can be illustrated with an example.

Griswold v. Connecticut, 381 U.S. 479 (1965) was a landmark case in which the United States Supreme Court first recognized an implied right to privacy under the United States Constitution. *Griswold* involved a Connecticut statute that banned the use of contraceptives, even between husband and wife. The constitutionality of the statute was first challenged in the Connecticut state courts. After the Supreme Court of Errors of Connecticut (the highest state court) affirmed the lower state court's enforcement of the state statute, the United States Supreme Court reviewed the case.

The Court found that "specific guarantees in the Bill of Rights have penumbras, formed by emanations from those guarantees that help give them life and substance . . . . Various guarantees create zones of privacy." The Court then determined that the Connecticut ban on the use of contraceptives "concerns a relationship lying within the zone of privacy created by several fundamental constitutional guarantees" and held the Connecticut statute unconstitutional.

Applying the above definition of the doctrine of stare decisis to *Griswold*, "that court" is the United States Supreme Court. The "legal principle" is that there is a constitutionally protected right to privacy. "Lower courts" to the United States Supreme Court are all federal courts and all levels of state courts in all fifty states. (See chapter 4 for a discussion of the hierarchical structure of the federal and state courts.) Because the Court has established this principle, it and all lower courts should reach the same decision in future cases but they only need to do so if "the facts are substantially the same."

Legal reasoning involves determining what the legal principle is and when the facts of the present case are "substantially the same" as the prior case so that the prior case would be used as precedent. This is sometimes called reasoning by analogy or *reasoning by example* because similar past cases are reviewed to determine the outcome of the present case. *Griswold* itself was binding only on the parties to the case. The doctrine of stare decisis makes the legal principle set forth in *Griswold* applicable to future cases. Although no two cases have material facts that are exactly the same, the facts of two cases may be similar.

Right to Privacy identified in *Griswold* applied to *Roe* to allow abortion

Roe v. Wade and the doctrine of stare decisis

The United States Supreme Court decided *Roe v. Wade* eight years after *Griswold*. *Roe v. Wade* was brought by a pregnant woman ("Jane Roe" was a pseudonym) challenging the constitutionality of Texas abortion laws. The laws made abortion a crime, except to save the mother's life. Before the case reached the United States Supreme Court, the federal district court had held the laws unconstitutional.

In *Roe*, the issue before the United States Supreme Court was whether the Texas laws were constitutional. Roe argued that a "woman's right [to an abortion] is absolute and that she is entitled to terminate her pregnancy at whatever time, in whatever way and for whatever reason she alone chooses." Texas argued that "life begins at conception and is present throughout pregnancy, and that therefore, the State has a compelling interest in protecting that life from and after conception."

In deciding *Roe* the United States Supreme Court was bound by the doctrine of stare decisis to use *Griswold* as precedent if the facts in *Griswold* were "substantially the same" as the facts in *Roe*. The Court apparently decided that the facts in *Griswold* and *Roe* were similar and found that the "right of privacy . . . is broad enough to encompass a woman's decision whether or not to terminate her pregnancy." The Court held that "the right of personal privacy includes the abortion decision, but that this right is not unqualified and must be considered against important state interests in regulation." The Court also held that the Texas statute was unconstitutional, but that the state could regulate the right to an abortion during the second trimester and prohibit it during the third trimester.

Application of *Roe v. Wade* to a later case

Would a state abortion statute requiring a twenty-four hour wait and spousal consent be constitutional? That was the issue in *Planned Parenthood of Southeastern Pennsylvania v. Casey*, 505 U.S. 833 (1992) after the Pennsylvania abortion statute containing these provisions was challenged in federal court.

The attorney for plaintiffs who challenged the statute might have characterized *Roe* by saying that it was "on point" with *Casey*. The plaintiffs' attorney probably urged the court to apply the doctrine of stare decisis and hold the Pennsylvania statute unconstitutional. The attorney would have argued that the facts in *Casey* were substantially the same as those in *Roe* because the waiting period and consent requirements effectively denied the right to an abortion to a woman who could not obtain her spouse's consent or who had to travel a great distance or could not afford to stay overnight.

"On all fours"—If a case is on all fours with a second case, facts and the applicable law in the two cases are very similar.

"On point"—If a case is on point with a second case, the facts and the applicable law are similar but not as similar as two cases on all fours.

In *Casey*, the attorney for the defendant—the state of Pennsylvania—might have argued that the facts in *Casey* were different from the facts in *Roe*. The state might have claimed the difference was that the Pennsylvania statute did not criminalize almost all abortions, as did the statute in *Roe*, and would have argued that the waiting period and consent requirements made sure the woman did not make hasty or ill-informed decisions. The state would thus be **distinguishing** *Casey* from *Roe* on the facts. The state might have then argued that because the two statutes were not substantially the same, holding the statute constitutional would not violate the doctrine of stare decisis.

In *Casey* the United States Supreme Court reaffirmed that *Roe* was still good law and applied the holding of *Roe* to *Casey*.

The United States Supreme Court ruled that the twenty-four hour wait was constitutional but that the spousal consent requirement was unconstitutional. The decision was a plurality opinion. Justices O'Connor, Kennedy, and Souter announced the judgment of the Court. Justices Stevens, Blackmun, and Scalia, and Chief Justice Rehnquist each wrote separate opinions concurring in part and dissenting in part. Justices White, Scalia, and Thomas joined in the separate opinion by Chief Justice Rehnquist, and Justices White and Thomas and Chief Justice Rehnquist joined in the separate opinion by Justice Scalia.

In deciding *Casey*, the Court explicitly reaffirmed *Roe* and restated *Roe*'s holding:

> It must be stated at the outset and with clarity that *Roe*'s essential holding, the holding we reaffirm, has three parts. First is the recognition of the right of the woman to choose to have an abortion before viability and to obtain it without undue interference from the State. Before viability, the State's interests are not strong enough to support a prohibition of abortion or the imposition of a substantial obstacle to the woman's effective right to elect the procedure. Second is a confirmation of the State's power to restrict abortion after fetal viability, if the law contains exceptions for pregnancies which endanger a woman's life or health. And third is the principle that the State has legitimate interests from the outset of the pregnancy in protecting the health of the woman and the life of the fetus that may become a child. These principles do not contradict one another; and we adhere to each.

At least two sides to every problem

In *Casey*, the state and the plaintiffs' attorneys reached opposite conclusions about the applicability of *Roe*. The state urged the court to hold the Pennsylvania statute constitutional, while the plaintiffs' attorney urged the court to hold the statute unconstitutional. They were pressing opposite decisions because their legal analysis of the effect of *Roe* on *Casey* was different. The state emphasized the differences between *Roe* and *Casey* while the plaintiffs' attorney emphasized the similarity between *Roe* and *Casey*.

Every legal problem has at least two sides. The job of each attorney is to represent the client's best interest. An attorney represents the client's best interest by explaining to the court which primary sources apply to the problem, why certain primary sources apply, and what decision the court should reach based on applicable primary sources. Assuming that both attorneys have competently performed their legal research of a problem, they both have the same primary sources on which to base their arguments. Although the attorneys are relying on the same primary sources, their answers will be much different because of the way they have applied the primary sources to the problem. Each attorney will argue that the primary authority favorable to the client's case is substantially similar to the problem and should control. In contrast, each attorney will argue that primary authority unfavorable to the client's case is readily distinguishable from the problem or that the court should change the law.

The doctrine of stare decisis has worked well over the centuries because it gives case law stability and predictability while at the same time allowing for gradual change. There is stability and predictability because courts are bound to look to prior cases in deciding present cases. Much of what an attorney does is to research the law to find cases on point and then predict how a court will decide—or try to convince the court to decide—based on those prior cases. Although the United States Supreme Court and the highest courts of the state have the power to **overrule** prior decisions, they hesitate to do so. A chronic practice of overruling prior decisions undermines the stability and predictability of the legal system.

Courts rarely state explicitly that they are overruling a prior case. Decades may pass between a precedent-setting case and a later case that overrules it. In *Plessy v. Ferguson*, 163 U.S. 537 (1896), the United States Supreme Court held that separate but equal accommodations for black and white railway passengers were constitutional. Over the years, *Plessy* was used to justify separate but equal public schools. It was not until over fifty years later that the Court overruled *Plessy*. In *Brown v. Board of Education of Topeka*, 347 U.S. 483 (1954), the Court held that separate but equal public school accommodations violated the Equal Protection Clause of the United States Constitution.

Instead of explicitly overruling a prior case, courts may limit its effect. The effect of a landmark case like *Roe* is unclear until the United States Supreme Court applies it in later cases. Many have argued that *Roe* was not the correct interpretation of the Constitution. In *Casey*, the Court was under great pressure to overrule *Roe*. The Court ruled only that the states may place certain limits, such as a twenty-four hour waiting period, on the abortion right.

The *Casey* plurality opinion contained some interesting comments on the Court's apparent struggle to decide whether *Roe* should be overturned and how it applied to *Casey:*

> [I]t is common wisdom that the rule of *stare decisis* is not an "inexorable command," . . . . Rather, when this Court reexamines a prior holding, its judgment is customarily informed by a series of prudential and pragmatic considerations designed to test the consistency of overruling a prior decision with the ideal of the rule of law, and to gauge the respective costs of reaffirming and overruling a prior case. Thus, for example, we may ask whether the rule has proved to be intolerable simply in defying practical workability . . . ; whether the rule is subject to a kind of reliance that would lend a special hardship to the consequences of overruling and add inequity to the cost of repudiation . . . ; whether related principles of law have so far developed as to have left the old rule no more than a remnant of abandoned doctrine . . . ; or whether facts have so changed or come to be seen so differently, as to have robbed the old rule of significant application or justification . . . .
>
> . . . .
>
> . . . Within the bounds of normal *stare decisis* analysis, . . . the stronger argument is for affirming *Roe*'s central holding, with whatever degree of personal reluctance any of us may have, not for overruling it.

Massey v. Prince George's County

The following case, *Massey v. Prince George's County*, presents another example of legal reasoning and analysis. In *Massey*, the judge chastises the county attorney's office for the failure of one of its attorneys to cite a "controlling case." In response to the judge's order to show cause why the case had not been cited, the defendants argued that the case was not controlling because facts were readily distinguishable from the facts in the case before the judge. The judge decided that the case should have been brought to the court's attention because the differences between the facts in the earlier case and the facts in the case before the judge were "immaterial."

Willie MASSEY, Plaintiff,

v.

PRINCE GEORGE'S COUNTY, et al., Defendants.

United States District Court,

D. Maryland.

March 4, 1996.

918 F.Supp. 905

MESSITTE, District Judge.

In this case alleging excessive use of force by police, the Court earlier granted Defendants' Motion for Summary Judgment. Subsequently a case from the United States Court of Appeals for the Fourth Circuit was brought to the Court's attention which the Court deemed controlling and directly adverse to Defendants' position. See *Kopf v. Wing*. Defendants had not cited *Kopf* in their motion nor had Plaintiff cited it in his opposition. Neither side raised the case at oral argument. Particularly troublesome to the Court was the fact that Prince George's County, Defendant here, had also been a defendant in *Kopf*. Sensing a possible violation of Rule of Professional Conduct 3.3(a)(3), which provides that "(a) lawyer shall not knowingly . . . fail to disclose to the tribunal legal authority in the controlling jurisdiction known to the lawyer to be directly adverse to the position of the client and not disclosed by opposing counsel," the Court ordered Defendants and defense counsel to show cause why the case had not been cited.

Respondents have now submitted their response to the Show Cause Order.

[Respondents'] response is that *Kopf* is not in fact "directly adverse" to their position; hence they had no obligation to disclose it in any event. As Respondents put it:

[a] close reading of *Kopf* reveals that it does not establish any new law; instead it applies the established law to a given set of facts. As such, *Kopf* is only "directly adverse" to the Defendants' position here if the cases are factually indistinguishable.

Respondents then proceed to cite a number of facts which they contend are readily distinguishable. The Court summarizes these purported distinctions in the following chart:

Kopf	Present Case
PA announcement made —Disputed	PA announcement made —Not disputed
Affidavits of experts on police dogs used	No such affidavits used
Suspect refused to surrender—Disputed	Suspect refused to surrender—Disputed
Head blows in addition to dog bites	No head blows—just single blow to back
Suspect had gun—Disputed	Suspect had no weapon—Not disputed
Where altercation occurred—Disputed	Where altercation occurred—Undisputed

The Court finds the response to be incorrect in at least two respects. *Kopf*, to some extent, did "make new law" at least as far as the Fourth Circuit is concerned. Moreover the factual distinctions Respondents make are either unconvincing or simply immaterial.

Whatever else *Kopf* says, it bluntly declares "that a jury could find it objectively unreasonable to require someone to put his hands up and calmly surrender while a police dog bites his scrotum." In other words,

Kopf goes on to say, "even if it found that force was necessary . . . a reasonable jury could nonetheless find the degree of force excessive," Indeed, if the law were otherwise, the fact that the slightest force might be justified would give the police license to have their dog chew a suspect to death. In the present case, Plaintiff maintains that he was not resisting arrest, merely defending himself, after the dog was set upon him. He contends that he received bites to his arms, legs, back, neck and other body parts, hardly a de minimis amount of force. Consistent with *Kopf*, these bites, together with Plaintiff's contention that he was only defending himself against the dog, suffice to raise a triable issue of excessive force.

Moreover, contrary to Respondents' position, in suggesting excessive force, certain facts of the present case not only match those of *Kopf*, they surpass them. For example, unlike *Kopf*, where the police had reason to believe the suspect was an armed robber, here, for all the police knew, the suspect could have been (indeed it turned out he was) merely a trespasser sleeping in a vacant building. Such a scenario would suggest the need for less rather than more force. Additionally, the fact that Plaintiff was asleep when the dog was set upon him tends to indicate that he may not have been actively resisting arrest. Finally, the undisputed absence of a weapon in this case also tends to suggest that the dog bites were less rather than more appropriate.

Other alleged factual distinctions between *Kopf* and the present case are simply immaterial. It can be assumed that any PA announcement made was not heard in the present case. That would still not license unlimited use of the police dog. Similarly, the presence or absence of expert testimony signifies nothing; no testimony is needed on the issue of whether the number of bites inflicted against a non-resistant subject is excessive. At the same time whether, in addition to the dog bites, the police struck one blow or several is of minimal import. The gist of the present claim of excessive force is dog bites. While in *Kopf* the excess was either dog bites or blows or both, clearly dog bites alone can be objectively unreasonable.

Thus, the Court remains firm in its view that, in key relevant respects, *Kopf* is very much on point, i.e. "directly adverse" to Respondents' position.

But Respondents' position is flawed in a more fundamental sense. Even if one assumes for the sake of argument that *Kopf* could be factually distinguished from the case at bar, there is always the possibility that a judge might disagree, that despite Respondents' view he might ultimately find the omitted case on point and directly adverse to their position. Respondents thus undertake a bold and risky gambit. They rely on their mere ipse dixit that the case is distinguishable and therefore unnecessary to call to the Court's attention. But careful lawyering demands greater sensitivity. In this district, whenever a case from the Fourth Circuit comes anywhere close to being relevant to a disputed issue, the better part of wisdom is to cite it and attempt to distinguish it. The matter will then be left for the judge to decide. While Respondents may still in time be judged unsuccessful in their attempt to distinguish the case, they will never be judged ethically omissive for failing to cite it.

The Court turns to Respondents' further answer to its Show Cause Order, namely that the Assistant County Attorney who filed the Motion for Summary Judgment in this case did not know about the *Kopf* case. That, of course, may well be true, but the question is, ought he to have known? As with Plaintiff's counsel in these proceedings, defense counsel had an obligation under Rule of Professional Conduct 1.1 to provide "competent representation," which includes an ability to research the law. Similarly, Rule 1.3 requires that "a lawyer shall act with reasonable diligence and promptness in representing a client," which includes pursuing applicable legal authority in timely fashion.

Thus, while it may be true that one Assistant County Attorney did not know about the *Kopf* case and others more senior did not know that attorney did not know, that is not the end of the matter. Individual attorneys may not merit sanctions, but it is clear that the Office of the Prince George's County Attorney overall needs to look to its internal organization. At a minimum, tighter oversight of each attorney's court filings is called for. The Office of the County Attorney would do well to see that the sort of omission that occurred here does not occur again.

JUDICIAL OPINIONS

The type of opinion (majority, plurality, concurring, dissenting, per curiam, or en banc opinion) in a case is important. A **majority** opinion is an opinion agreed upon by at least a majority of the judges deciding the case. Usually one judge writes the opinion and other judges who agree with the opinion join in it. A **plurality** opinion is an opinion agreed upon by more judges than any other opinion, although less than a majority. *Casey* is an example of a plurality opinion. In *Casey* only three Justices agreed upon the opinion. The only courts issuing plurality opinions are the United States Supreme Court, the highest court of the state, and intermediate appellate courts sitting *en banc*, because they are the only courts with enough members to have a plurality opinion. A **concurring** opinion is one agreeing with the result reached in the majority opinion but for different reasons. In *Casey* a number of Justices agreed with (concurred in) the result, but wrote separate concurring opinions to explain how their reasoning differed from the reasoning of the plurality opinion. A **dissenting** opinion is written by a judge who disagrees with the result reached by the majority opinion; it expresses the judge's reasons for the disagreement. One or more judges may join in a concurring or dissenting opinion. A judge may join in any part of any decision. For example, a judge may join in part in the majority opinion, write his or her own concurring opinion as to another part of the majority opinion, and join in part of another judge's dissenting opinion. A ***per curiam*** opinion is written by the whole court rather than by one particular judge. Usually you will see a per curiam opinion in a relatively unimportant case. In contrast, as discussed earlier, an ***en banc*** opinion is usually reserved for the most important or controversial cases, decided by the entire membership of the intermediate appellate court rather than by a three-judge panel.

Types of opinions:
majority
plurality
concurring
dissenting
per curiam
en banc

Except for *en banc* decisions, intermediate appellate courts sit in panels to decide cases. The panels are made up of three judges selected at random from the membership of the intermediate appellate court. Sometimes one of the judges on the panel may be a lower court judge specially designated to hear an intermediate appellate case. After the three judges review the appellate briefs and hear any oral argument, they meet to decide the case. One of the two or three judges agreeing on how the case should be decided is assigned to write the majority opinion. Any judge disagreeing may choose to write a concurring or dissenting opinion. Before the opinion is announced, it is circulated to the other judges. A judge disagreeing with the opinion may either negotiate with the judge who wrote the opinion, to attempt to change certain language, or may decide not to join in the opinion after all. A judge who originally intended to concur or dissent may decide to join in the majority opinion instead.

The entire membership of the United States Supreme Court and the highest state court in the state usually sit to decide a case. Each member of the United States Supreme Court is referred to as a "Justice" rather than a "judge," with the leader of the Court called the "Chief Justice." The members of the highest court in your state may also be referred to as "Justices." A Justice may be excused from hearing a case because of illness or because the Justice **recuses** himself or herself. The procedure for deciding a case in the United States Supreme Court or in the highest court of a state is similar to that described above for the intermediate appellate courts. Decisions of the United States Supreme Court and the highest state courts, sometimes referred to as **courts of last resort,** are not called *en banc* decisions, though, because the standard procedure is for the entire membership of the court to hear cases.

Most of the opinions you will use in research are published opinions of **appellate courts,** but not all opinions are published. If you learn of an unpublished opinion you would like to use as authority, you may obtain a copy of the opinion from the clerk of the court issuing the opinion, usually for a nominal fee. You very rarely see published opinions of trial courts in researching state case law of certain states. Perhaps this is because it is not customary to publish them since they are only persuasive authority for other courts. Published opinions of federal district courts are easily accessible in Federal Supplement.

Mandatory and persuasive authority

A **mandatory authority** is a case that must be followed under the doctrine of stare decisis. A **persuasive authority,** just as the term implies, is a case that is only persuasive and is not required to be followed. More precisely, the part of the case that is mandatory authority and therefore binding on other courts is the **holding** of the majority opinion.

Brown v. Board of Education is mandatory authority for the United States Supreme Court, unless the Court overrules it, and for all lower courts. (See chapter 4 for a discussion of the hierarchical structure of the federal and state courts.) This means that *Brown* must be followed; it is binding on all federal and all state courts because it is the most current interpretation of the United States Constitution.

A decision of a United States Court of Appeals is binding on that circuit and all federal district courts within that circuit. (See chapter 4 for a discussion of the hierarchical structure of the federal and state courts.) The decision of a United States Court of Appeals is not mandatory authority for another circuit because all circuits are on the same level. For example, the United States Court of Appeals for the Eleventh Circuit covers Alabama, Georgia, and Florida. The United States Court of Appeals for the Fifth Circuit covers Texas, Louisiana, and Mississippi. A decision of one three-judge panel of the Eleventh Circuit would be mandatory authority for any future Eleventh Circuit case and any federal district courts in Alabama, Georgia, and Florida. That decision would only be persuasive authority, however, for the Court of Appeals for the Fifth Circuit and federal district courts within Texas, Louisiana, and Mississippi. Interestingly enough, a decision of a United States district or circuit court is considered persuasive rather than mandatory authority for state courts, even state courts geographically located within the district or circuit. This is because a case that is appealed through the various state courts of a state to the highest court in the state would go up to the United States Supreme Court rather than to a United States circuit or district court. In practice, though, a state court may give great weight to decisions of United States district and circuit courts covering the same geographical area when the federal court decisions deal with constitutional issues.

Plurality, concurring, and dissenting opinions are considered persuasive authority as are all secondary sources. A decision of a court in one state is persuasive authority on the courts of another state. Although not binding, persuasive authority may be cited if there is no mandatory authority on point, or it may be cited to back up one's argument that the court should change the law by overruling a precedent.

Before becoming a United States Supreme Court Justice, Thurgood Marshall was one of the attorneys who argued *Brown* before the Court, claiming that *Plessy v. Ferguson* should be overruled. Marshall had only persuasive authority to rely on in his argument, because the only way the Court could rule in favor of his client was to overrule *Plessy v. Ferguson.* The Court accepted his argument that the law should be changed and did overrule *Plessy v. Ferguson.*

A decision of the highest court in the state is binding on all courts within the state. A decision of an intermediate appellate court is binding on the trial-level courts within the geographical area covered by the intermediate appellate court. If the intermediate appellate court in your state is divided into districts or circuits, it would be interesting for you to research whether the decision of one district or circuit is mandatory or persuasive authority for other districts or circuits. You will very likely find that the relationship between different intermediate appellate courts in your state is that of "sister courts," with the decision of one intermediate appellate court considered persuasive rather than mandatory. The United States Courts of Appeals have this same relationship.

Another question is what effect a decision of an intermediate appellate court has on the trial-level court geographically located outside the area covered by the intermediate appellate court. The decision of the intermediate appellate court could be considered either mandatory or persuasive authority.

Some examples will show the difference between mandatory and persuasive authority. In *Johnson v. Davis*, 480 So. 2d 625 (Fla. 1985), the Florida Supreme Court held that "where the seller of a home knows of facts materially affecting the value of the property which are not readily observable and are not known to the buyer, the seller is under a duty to disclose them to the buyer." In *Johnson* the homeowner knew that the roof leaked but failed to disclose this to the buyer. The court ruled that the seller's "fraudulent concealment" entitled the buyer to return of the buyer's deposit plus interest, costs, and attorneys' fees.

Johnson was a landmark case because the law in Florida had previously been that the **doctrine of caveat emptor** ("let the buyer beware") applied to home sales. The *Johnson* court cited decisions from California, Illinois, Nebraska, West Virginia, Louisiana, New Jersey, and Colorado in announcing its decision that the doctrine of caveat emptor would no longer apply to the sale of homes in Florida. These other state decisions constituted persuasive authority for the Florida court. After *Johnson*, a Florida trial court considering a similar case would have to follow *Johnson* and hold the home seller liable for fraud if the home seller knew the home had a leaky roof but failed to disclose it to the buyer. *Johnson* is mandatory authority in Florida for cases concerning material home defects undisclosed to the buyer.

DEDUCTIVE REASONING

Deductive reasoning involves reasoning from the general (rule) to the specific (the impact of the rule on a particular fact pattern). The principle of deductive reasoning will be illustrated by using the *Cruz* case described at the beginning of this chapter and the federal wiretapping and eavesdropping statutes.

The first step in deductive reasoning is identifying the rules that may apply to a particular fact pattern. A rule that may apply is referred to as the **major premise.** The second step is to state the facts in terms of the rule. This statement is called the **minor premise.** The facts must be weighed in light of the language of the rule to formulate the minor premise. In other words, should the language of the rule be interpreted to include the facts of the fact pattern? The last step is to reach a conclusion, after analyzing the relationship between the major premise and the minor premise.

The federal wiretapping and eavesdropping statutes may apply to *Cruz.* The federal statutes prohibit secretly tape-recording an "oral communication." An oral communication is defined as "any oral communication uttered by a person exhibiting an expectation that such communication is not subject to interception under circumstances justifying such expectation." A penalty for tape-recording an oral communication is that the tape-recording may not be used in court.

For *Cruz*, a major premise is:

> If an oral communication is secretly tape-recorded, the tape recording can be suppressed.

It might be helpful to state two alternative minor premises:

1. Cruz will be successful in having the tape-recording of her conversation with Luis suppressed because she had a reasonable expectation that the police officer would not tape-record their conversation while they sat in the back of the patrol car.
2. Cruz will not be successful in having the tape-recording of her conversation with Luis suppressed because it was not reasonable to expect that the police officer would not tape-record their conversation while they sat in the back of the patrol car.

The following are two alternative conclusions:

1. Because the conversation in the back seat of a patrol car was an oral communication, it should be suppressed.
2. Because the conversation in the back seat of a patrol car was not an oral communication, it should not be suppressed.

The researcher would have to determine which minor premise and which conclusion is the most likely to be employed by the court deciding *Cruz.* The determination hinges on the meaning of "reasonable" in "reasonable expectation of privacy." If Cruz and Luis' expectation of privacy in the rear seat of the patrol car was reasonable, then the tape should be suppressed; if not, then the tape would not be suppressed under the federal statute. If the facts were at one end or the other of the spectrum, formulation of the minor premise would be easy. An individual probably would have a reasonable expectation of privacy when conversing in the individual's home with the doors and windows closed; an individual probably would not have an expectation of privacy if conversing on a street corner in a loud voice. Were the facts toward the middle of the spectrum, it would be more difficult to determine whether an individual has a reasonable expectation of privacy. The word "reasonable" is vague when we attempt to determine whether Cruz and Luis have a reasonable expectation of privacy when conversing in the back of a patrol car.

The following section describes principles commonly used in statutory interpretation.

LEGAL ANALYSIS OF STATUTORY LAW

For the legal researcher, the most important problem with legislation is interpretation. Over the course of many years, a number of principles have been developed to guide the courts in resolving disputes over the meaning of statutes. The principles governing statutory interpretation are commonly called **rules of construction,** referring to the manner in which courts are to *construe* the meaning of the statutes. The overriding principle governing statutory interpretation is to determine the intent of the legislature and give force to that intent. This section discusses some of the rules and priorities employed to further this goal.

Legislative intent

The underlying purpose behind statutory construction is the search to determine **legislative intent.**

The plain meaning rule

This rule can actually be used to evade legislative intent. The **plain meaning rule** states simply that if the language of a statute is unambiguous and its meaning clear, the terms of the statute should be construed and applied according to their ordinary meaning. Behind this rule is the assumption that the legislature understood the meaning of the words it used and expressed its intent thereby. This rule operates to restrain the court from substituting its notion of what the legislature *really* meant if the meaning is already clear.

The application of the plain meaning rule may in fact undermine legislative intent. Although legislation is usually carefully drafted, language is by its nature susceptible to ambiguity, distortion, or simple lack of clarity. Because legislation is designed to control disputes that have not yet arisen, the "perfect" statute requires a degree of clairvoyance absent in the ordinary human being, including legislators, so that a statute may apply to a situation not foreseen by the legislators, who might have stated otherwise had they imagined such a situation.

The plain meaning rule obviates the need to pursue a lengthy inquiry into intent. Consider the nature of the legislative process. First, legislative intent is difficult to determine. The final product of the legislative process, the statute, would thus seem to be the best evidence of legislative intent. Legislatures are composed of numerous members who intend different things. In many instances, legislators do not even read the laws for which they vote. To believe there is a single legislative intent is to ignore reality. Many statutes are the result of compromise, the politics of which are not a matter of public record and cannot be accurately determined by a court. The precise language of the statute, then, is the best guide to intent. If, in the eyes of the legislature, the court errs in its application of the statute, the legislature may revise the statute for future application.

In the following case, the court interpreted an Augusta, Georgia, ordinance broadly enough to require Blackie the Talking Cat's owners to purchase a business license and dismissed their arguments that the ordinance was unconstitutional.

Carl M. MILES, et al., Plaintiffs-Appellants,

v.

CITY COUNCIL OF AUGUSTA, GEORGIA, et al., Defendants-Appellees.

United States Court of Appeals,

Eleventh Circuit.

Aug. 4, 1983.

710 F.2d 1542

PER CURIAM:

Plaintiffs Carl and Elaine Miles, owners and promoters of "Blackie the Talking Cat," brought this suit in the United States District Court for the Southern District of Georgia, challenging the constitutionality of the Augusta, Georgia, Business License Ordinance. Their complaint alleged that the ordinance is inapplicable in this case or is otherwise void for vagueness and overbroad, and that the ordinance violates rights of speech and association. The district court granted summary judgment in favor of the defendant City Council of Augusta. We affirm.

The partnership between Blackie and the Mileses began somewhat auspiciously in a South Carolina rooming house. According to the deposition of Carl Miles:

> Well, a girl come around with a box of kittens, and she asked us did we want one. I said no, that we did not want one. As I was walking away from the box of kittens, a voice spoke to me and said, "Take the black kitten." I took the black kitten, knowing nothing else unusual or nothing else strange about the black kitten. When Blackie was about five months old, I had him on my lap playing with him, talking to him, saying I love you. The voice spoke to me saying, "The cat is trying to talk to you." To me, the voice was the voice of God.

Mr. Miles set out to fulfill his divination by developing a rigorous course of speech therapy.

> I would tape the sounds the cat would make, the voice sounds he would make when he was trying to talk to me, and I would play those sounds back to him three and four hours a day, and I would let him watch my lips, and he just got to where he could do it.

Blackie's catechism soon began to pay off. According to Mr. Miles:

> He was talking when he was six months old, but I could not prove it then. It was where I could understand him, but you can't understand him. It took me altogether a year and a half before I had him talking real plain where you could understand him.

Ineluctably, Blackie's talents were taken to the marketplace, and the rest is history. Blackie catapulted into public prominence when he spoke, for a fee, on radio and on television shows such as "That's Incredible." Appellants capitalized on Blackie's linguistic skills through agreements with agents in South Carolina, North Carolina, and Georgia. The public's affection for Blackie was the catalyst for his success, and Blackie loved his fans. As the District Judge observed in his published opinion, Blackie even purred "I love you" to him when he encountered Blackie one day on the street.

Sadly, Blackie's cataclysmic rise to fame crested and began to subside. The Miles family moved temporarily to Augusta, Georgia, receiving "contributions" that Augusta passersby paid to hear Blackie talk. After receiving complaints from several of Augusta's ailurophobes, the Augusta police—obviously no ailurophiles themselves—doggedly insisted that appellants would have to purchase a business license. Eventually, on threat of incarceration, Mr. and Mrs. Miles acceded to the demands of the police and paid $50 for a business license.

The gist of appellant's argument is that the Augusta business ordinance contains no category for speaking animals. The ordinance exhaustively lists trades, businesses, and occupations subject to the tax and the amount of the tax to be paid, but it nowhere lists cats with forensic prowess. However, section 2 of Augusta's Business Ordinance No. 5006 specifies that a $50 license shall be paid by any "Agent or Agency not specifically mentioned." Appellants insist that the drafters of section 2 could not have meant to include Blackie the Talking Cat and, if they did, appellants assert that section 2, as drafted, is vague and overbroad and hence unconstitutional.

Upon review of appellants' claims, we agree with the district court's detailed analysis of the Augusta ordinance. The assertion that Blackie's speaking engagements do not constitute an "occupation" or "business" within the meaning of the catchall provision of the Augusta ordinance is wholly without merit. Although the Miles family called what they received for Blackie's performances "contributions," these elocutionary endeavors were entirely intended for pecuniary enrichment and were indubitably commercial. [FN3] Moreover, we refuse to require that Augusta define "business" in order to avoid problems of vagueness. The word has a common sense meaning that Mr. Miles undoubtedly understood.

FN3. This conclusion is supported by the undisputed evidence in the record that appellants solicited contributions. Blackie would become catatonic and refuse to speak whenever his audience neglected to make a contribution.

Appellants' attack on the vagueness of section 4 of the Augusta ordinance, which permits the mayor, in his discretion, to require a license, is not properly before this Court. As the district court indicated, defendants sought to enforce only section 2 of the ordinance in this case.

Finally, we agree with the district court that appellants have not made out a case of overbreadth with respect to section 2 of the ordinance. Appellants fail to show any illegal infringement of First Amendment rights of free speech [FN5] or assembly. The overbreadth of a statute must be "judged in relation to the statute's plainly legitimate sweep." *Broadrick v. Oklahoma.* Appellants' activities plainly come within the legitimate exercise of the city's taxing power.

FN5. This Court will not hear a claim that Blackie's right to free speech has been infringed. First, although Blackie arguably possesses a very unusual ability, he cannot be considered a "person" and is therefore not protected by the Bill of Rights. Second, even if Blackie had such a right, we see no need for appellants to assert his right *jus tertii.* Blackie can clearly speak for himself.

AFFIRMED.

Limitations on the plain meaning rule

Adherence to the plain meaning rule is neither blind nor simple-minded. A statute that is unambiguous in its language may be found to conflict with other statutes. Statutes are typically enacted in "packages," as part of a legislative effort to regulate a broad area of concern. Thus, alimony is ordinarily defined in several statutes embraced within a package of statutes covering divorce, which in turn may be part of a statutory chapter on domestic relations. The more comprehensive the package, the more likely some of its provisions may prove to be inconsistent. A sentence that seems unambiguous may be ambiguous in relation to a paragraph, a section, or a chapter.

Language must thus be interpreted in its *context.* In fact, this principle often operates to dispel ambiguity. Comprehensive statutes commonly begin with a **preamble** or introductory section stating the general purpose of the statutes collected under its heading. This statement of purpose is intended to avoid an overly technical interpretation of the statutes that could achieve results contrary to the general purpose.

The preamble is frequently followed by a section defining terms used in the statutes. This, too, limits the application of the plain meaning rules, but in a different way: the definitions pinpoint terms that have technical or legal significance to avoid what might otherwise be a non-technical, ordinary interpretation.

On occasion, a provision in a statute may turn out to defeat the purpose of the statute in a particular set of circumstances; the court is then faced with the problem of giving meaning to the purpose of the statute or the language of the clause within the statute. In *Texas & Pacific Railway v. Abilene Cotton Oil Co.*, 204 U.S. 426 (1907), the United States Supreme Court was called upon to interpret the Interstate Commerce Act, which set up the Interstate Commerce Commission (ICC) and made it responsible for setting rates and routes for the railroads. A disgruntled shipper sued the railroad under an old common law action for "unreasonable rates." The Act had a provision, commonly included in legislation, stating that the Act did not abolish other existing remedies. However, the court reasoned that if persons were able to bring such actions any time they were unhappy with the rates, the rate structures established by the ICC would have little meaning, depending instead upon what a particular jury or judge considered reasonable. The court limited the effect of the clause and argued that Congress could not have intended for the clause to be used to completely undermine the purpose of the Act: "in other words, the act cannot be held to destroy itself."

The court will not ordinarily disregard the plain meaning of a statute, especially in a criminal case.

Aids to statutory interpretation

Single statutes do not exist in a legal vacuum. They are part of a section, chapter, and the state or federal code as a whole. Historically, statutes developed as an adjunct to the traditional common law system that established law from custom.

Like case law, statutory construction relied heavily *on authority*. Interpretation is a formal reasoning process in the law, which in our legal tradition depends less on the creative imagination than on sources of the law. In the reasoning process, an overriding judicial policy insists that the body of laws be as consistent and harmonious as possible. It was for this reason that the court held in *Abilene Oil*, that the statute "cannot be held to destroy itself."

If a clause seems to conflict with its immediate statutory context, it will be interpreted so as to further the general legislative intent, if such can be ascertained. In a sense, this is simply intelligent reading; words and phrases take their meaning from their contexts. The principle can be extended further, however. Statutes taken from different parts of a state or federal code may be found to conflict. The court will interpret the language to harmonize the inconsistency whenever possible. Legislative intent may become quite obscure in such situations because the presumption that the legislature meant what it said is confronted by the problem that it said something different elsewhere. In reconciling the conflict, the court may use its sense of overall legislative policy and even the general history of the law, including the common law. The obvious solution to these conflicts is action by the legislature to rewrite the statutes to resolve the inconsistencies and provide future courts with a clear statement of intent.

Strict construction

Words by their nature have different meanings and nuances. Shades of meaning change in the context of other words and phrases. Tradition has determined that certain situations call for broad or liberal constructions, whereas others call for narrow or **strict construction,** meaning that the statute in question will not be expanded beyond a very literal reading of its meaning.

"Criminal statutes are strictly construed." This rule of construction has its source in the evolution of our criminal law, in particular, in the many rights we afford those accused of crime. Out of fear of abuse of the criminal justice system, we have provided protection for the accused against kangaroo courts, overzealous prosecutors, and corrupt police. It is an accepted value of our legal system that the innocent must be protected even if it means that the guilty will sometimes go free. For example in the following case, *McBoyle v. United States*, the United States Supreme

Court strictly construed a criminal statute to hold that "motor vehicle" did not include an airplane.

Although many basic crimes, such as murder, burglary, and assault, were formulated by the common law in the distant past, today most states do not recognize common law crimes but insist that crimes be specified by statute. Conversely, if a statute defines certain conduct as criminal, "ignorance of the law excuses no one" (***ignorantia legis neminem excusat***). If public notice of prohibited conduct is an essential ingredient of criminal law, strict construction is its logical conclusion. If conduct is not clearly within the prohibitions of a statute, the court will decline to expand its coverage.

A second category of statutes that are strictly construed is expressed by the principle that "statutes in derogation of the common law are strictly construed." State legislatures frequently pass laws that alter, modify, or abolish traditional common law rules. The principle that such changes are narrowly construed not only shows respect for the common law, but also reflects the difference between legislative and judicial decision making. Whereas judicial decisions explain the reasons for the application of a particular rule, allowing for later interpretations and modifications, statutes are presumed to mean what they say. The intent of the legislature is embodied in the language of the statute itself, which if well drafted can be seen to apply to the situations for which it was intended.

A statute should stand alone, its meaning clear. Unfortunately, this is not always possible. If there is some question of meaning, a statute that appears to conflict with prior principles of the common law can be measured against that body of law. In other words, the court has recourse to a wealth of time-tested principles and need not strain to guess legislative intent. This is particularly helpful when the statute neglects to cover a situation that was decided in the past. If the statute is incomplete or ambiguous, the Court will resolve the dispute by following the common law.

In the following case, Justice Holmes strictly construed a criminal statute to hold that "motor vehicle" did not include an airplane.

McBOYLE

v.

UNITED STATES.

Supreme Court of the United States

Decided March 9, 1931.

283 U.S. 25

Mr. Justice HOLMES delivered the opinion of the Court.

The petitioner was convicted of transporting from Ottawa, Illinois, to Guymon, Oklahoma, an airplane that he knew to have been stolen, and was sentenced to serve three years' imprisonment and to pay a fine of $2,000. The judgment was affirmed by the Circuit Court of Appeals for the Tenth Circuit. A writ of certiorari was granted by this Court on the question whether the National Motor Vehicle Theft Act applies to aircraft. That Act provides: 'Sec. 2. That when used in this Act: (a) The term 'motor vehicle' shall include an automobile, automobile truck, automobile wagon, motor cycle, or any other self-propelled vehicle not designed for running on rails. * * * Sec. 3. That whoever shall transport or cause to be transported in interstate or foreign commerce a motor vehicle, knowing the same to have been stolen, shall be punished by a fine of not more than $5,000, or by imprisonment of not more than five years, or both.'

Section 2 defines the motor vehicles of which the transportation in interstate commerce is punished in Section 3. The question is the meaning of the word 'vehicle' in the phrase 'any other self-propelled vehicle not designed for running on rails.' No doubt etymologically it is possible to use the word to signify a conveyance working on land, water or air, and sometimes legislation extends the use in that direction, e. g., land and air, water being separately provided for, in the Tariff Act. But in everyday speech 'vehicle' calls up the picture of a thing moving on land. Thus in Rev. St. s 4 (1 USCA s 4) intended, the Government suggests, rather to enlarge than to restrict the definition, vehicle includes every contrivance capable of being used 'as a means of transportation on land.' And this is repeated, expressly excluding aircraft, in the Tariff Act, June 17, 1930.

So here, the phrase under discussion calls up the popular picture. For after including automobile truck, automobile wagon and motor cycle, the words 'any other self-propelled vehicle not designed for running on rails' still indicate that a vehicle in the popular sense, that is a vehicle running on land is the theme. It is a vehicle that runs, not something, not commonly called a vehicle, that flies. Airplanes were well known in 1919 when this statute was passed, but it is admitted that they were not mentioned in the reports or in the debates in Congress. It is impossible to read words that so carefully enumerate the different forms of motor vehicles and have no reference of any kind to aircraft, as including airplanes under a term that usage more and more precisely confines to a different class. The counsel for the petitioner have shown that the phraseology of the statute as to motor vehicles follows that of earlier statutes of Connecticut, Delaware, Ohio, Michigan and Missouri, not to mention the late Regulations of Traffic for the District of Columbia, title 6, c. 9, s 242, none of which can be supposed to leave the earth.

Although it is not likely that a criminal will carefully consider the text of the law before he murders or steals, it is reasonable that a fair warning should be given to the world in language that the common world will understand, of what the law intends to do if a certain line is passed. To make the warning fair, so far as possible the line should be clear. When a rule of conduct is laid down in words that evoke in the common mind only the picture of vehicles moving on land, the statute should not be extended to aircraft simply because it may seem to us that a similar policy applies, or upon the speculation that if the legislature had thought of it, very likely broader words would have been used.

Judgment reversed.

Legislative history

If the application of a statute remains unclear in its language and in its written context, the intent of the legislature may be ascertained by researching the statute's **legislative history.** This includes the records and documents concerning the process whereby the statute became law. The purpose and application of the statute may sometimes become clear with these additional materials. Several committees may have held hearings or discussion on the law during its enactment that have become part of the public record and demonstrate the concerns of the legislators and the reasons for enactment. Inferences may be made based on different drafts of the statute and the reasons expressed for the changes. If two houses of the legislature began with different language, the final compromise language may also suggest conclusions. Legislative debates may similarly clarify legislative intent.

Research into legislative history can be a lengthy process involving extensive analytical skills; but an examination of the entire process for a particular enactment will tend to dispel plausible, but incorrect, interpretations of legislative intent. The informal politics of negotiation and compromise, however, are not always reflected in the record, so the reasons for the final decisions on the language of the statute may remain obscure.

A caveat on statutory interpretation

The preceding discussion touched on only a few of a multitude of rules of interpretation employed by the courts in resolving issues of statutory interpretation that a given court or judge favors. For example, any specific rule may be avoided by declaring that it conflicts with the primary intent of the legislature. There is a subjective element to this analysis that provides a court great discretion.

Courts ordinarily attempt to give force to legislative intent. They are assisted by a great variety of technical rules of construction that have been developed in the precedents of prior judges faced with the problem of statutory meaning. But judges differ in their thinking from legislators. They not only deal with abstract rules, but on a daily basis must also resolve difficult problems with justice and fairness. Very few judges will blindly follow a technical rule if the result would be manifestly unfair. They can justly reason that the legislature never intended an unjust result. When arguing the interpretation of a statute, a lawyer must keep in mind the importance of persuading the court that the proposed interpretation is not only correct but also fair and just.

LEGAL ANALYSIS OF CONSTITUTIONAL LAW

The Constitution does not state how it is to be interpreted. In many ways, the issue of what method of interpreting the Constitution should be used parallels the question of what is the role of the judiciary in the United States. The authority to make policy has been delegated to the legislative and, to a lesser degree, the executive branches, which are accountable to the people through the voting booth. However, federal judges are not elected, and once installed, they leave office only through death, retirement, or impeachment. Therefore, the issue is whether the Constitution should be interpreted in a manner that permits justices to consider policy matters. Should they be guided by their own ideologies or by the nation's? The following section describes methods of constitutional interpretation. (See fig. 2-1 for a summary of these methods.)

Originalism

Originalists follow the so-called doctrine of **original intent.** It is not truly a constitutional doctrine; rather it is an approach to interpreting the Constitution. Originalists hold that the Constitution should be interpreted to mean what the framers originally intended it to mean.

They contend that by examining the records from the Constitutional Convention, letters written by the framers, the *Federalist Papers* and related publications, the records from the state ratification debates, and other documents, it is possible to determine the framers' intent. Originalists assert that by using this approach, the Court's decision will be less normative. Said another way, decisions will not be the result of the personal opinions (beliefs, mores, biases, etc.) of Justices; they will be "objectively" arrived at. This being so, the Court's decisions will be more predictable and stable and will be perceived as objective, not as a product of the Court's ideological bent. Thereby, the institution itself will be more respected. Originalists argue that once the original intent has been declared, change can come only through the amendment process.

Opponents of the original intent approach argue that the very premise of originalism is unfounded. They ask how one intent can be attributed to the entire group of framers. Individual delegates may have had different reasons for supporting a particular provision of the Constitution.

Also, because the document was ratified by the states, should the intent of all the participants at the state conventions be considered? Maybe the intent of the framers is not even relevant—after all, the Constitution is a document of the people. Should an attempt to understand the people's general beliefs and attitudes be made? Furthermore, there is evidence that some provisions were intentionally drafted vaguely (such as the due process clause of the Fifth Amendment) so that the precise meaning could be developed at a later date. What of these provisions? There is also some evidence that the framers did not intend for their subjective intentions to live in perpetuity. For example, James Madison believed that a document must speak for itself and that any meaning derived from its reading should not be displaced by a contrary finding of original intent. He also stated, "[a]s a guide in expounding and applying the provisions of the Constitution, the debates and incidental decisions of the convention can have no authoritative character." He believed that the "public meaning" of the Constitution should prevail over the individual intentions of the framers. Public meaning

FIGURE 2-1 Methods of Interpreting the Constitution.

CONSTITUTION INTERPRETATION METHODS

Method	Description	Evidence
Originalism	Constitution is interpreted and applied in a manner consistent with the framers' intentions	■ Convention records ■ Writings of the framers and their contemporaries (e.g. *Federalist Papers*) ■ Ratification debate records ■ Laws of the era and preexisting constitution
Modernism/ Instrumentalism	Constitution is interpreted and applied in contemporary terms	■ Objective indicators of public values ■ Social scientific evidence
Literalism—historical	Constitution is interpreted and applied by focusing on its terms, syntax, and other linguistic features that were in use at the time of adoption/ ratification	■ Text of the Constitution ■ Evidence of language use at time of adoption/ratification
Literalism—contemporary	Constitution is interpreted and applied by focusing on its terms, syntax, and other linguistic features that are currently in use	■ Text of the Constitution ■ Evidence of contemporary language use
Democratic/normative reinforcement	Constitution is interpreted and applied in a manner that reinforces the document's underlying democratic themes	■ Evidence of framers' intentions ■ Structure/organization inherent in Constitution ■ Objective evidence of reinforcement of norms

could be shown, according to Madison, through precedent and consensus. That is, if there is consensus in the government and with the people as to what the Constitution means, and they have acted accordingly for some time, then the meaning is established, regardless of any original intent.

It is also argued that original intention cannot be discerned in most instances, because the framers did not consider every possibility. This is especially true when one considers the significant changes the nation has seen since the Constitution was ratified. The industrial revolution, technological revolution, rapid modernization, population explosion (there were fewer than four million people in the United States at the time the Constitution was ratified), and changes in social, political, and economic attitudes brought with them problems that could not have been foreseen by the framers.

Opponents also disagree with the conclusion that predictability and stability will be assured. Courts can differ in their interpretation of intent and even in the method of determining original intention; therefore, decisions could be changed because of differences in opinion concerning the framers' original intentions.

Modernism

Many of those who criticize originalism are **modernists,** also known as **instrumentalists.** Associate Justice William Brennan, Jr., was one of this ideological group. He contended that the Constitution should be interpreted as if it were to be ratified today—a "contemporary ratification" or "living constitution" approach. Originalists discover the meaning of the Constitution by examining the intent of the framers. Modernists find meaning by reading the language of the Constitution in light of contemporary life. Through this approach, the judiciary contributes to the social and moral evolution of the nation. Some oppose this method as countermajoritarian. That is, they contend that it is not the function of nine unelected individuals to make policy decisions for the nation. Proponents hold that, as an institution, the Court must engage in this form of decision making to perform its function of shielding the individual from governmental excesses and to assure that its decisions will be respected.

In addition to the philosophies previously mentioned, the adherents of this school oppose the doctrine of original intention because it causes the Constitution to become dated and out-of-touch with contemporary problems. They contend that the Constitution's strength comes from its dynamic, flexible nature. Although it affirmatively establishes certain principles, it does so in language that permits it to change as America changes—not drastic changes, but change within certain parameters. Change outside of the perimeters of reason must occur by amendment.

Modernists do not discard original intention or stare decisis; they recognize them as factors in judicial decision making. But the needs of society are also taken into account, as is the nature of the dispute that gave rise to the case before the Court. To the modernist, the framers could not anticipate every issue that would be presented to the Court, nor did they try. It is the duty of the Court to read the Constitution and apply its terms in a manner that gives due deference to the nation's history and customs, as well as contemporary conditions and public expectation.

The results of scientific research may also play a role in judicial decision making. Judges following the modernist tradition are more likely to be receptive to the use of scientific data than if they were following another method. For example, in *Brown v. Board of Education*, the evidence produced by social scientists indicating that segregation has detrimental effects on black people was relied upon in striking down the separate-but-equal doctrine. Critics charge that, by its nature, much scientific data, particularly the results of social science research, are unreliable and are used by the Court only to justify policy objectives (social engineering), a task better left to Congress and the states.

Reference to contemporary values may also be part of modern analysis. For example, the Eighth Amendment prohibits cruel and unusual punishments. The Court applies both original and modern approaches in Eighth Amendment cases. First, all punishments believed by the framers to be cruel and unusual are forever forbidden. Second, the Court has held that the Eighth Amendment is not "bound by the sparing humanitarian concessions of our forebears" and that punishments must be in accord with "evolving standards of decency that mark the progress of a maturing society." The Court has said that when necessary to determine contemporary values, it will look to "objective factors," such as how other states punish the crime in question, how the jurisdiction in question punishes other crimes, and (in death penalty cases) how often sentencing juries choose the punishment.

Historical and contemporary literalism

Another approach to interpreting the Constitution is **literalism,** also known as **textualism.** This method focuses on the actual text of the Constitution. Literalists believe that the words of the document must be examined first. Words have objective meaning that may differ from the drafters' intentions. Language is paramount, not the intentions of the framers. The framers were particular in their choice of language, and accordingly, those words should be respected. The first tenet of literalism is the plain meaning rule, which states that if the meaning of a word is immediately apparent, then that meaning must be accepted and applied, regardless of any other factors.

However, the meanings of words change. The phrase "modern means of production" is historically contextual. It has a different meaning today than it did in 1799. The same can be said of the language of the Constitution. Does the phrase "cruel and unusual punishment" mean the same today as it did in 1791?

Those in the historical literalism camp believe that the meaning of the words at the time the provision was ratified must be used. This approach is similar to originalism. However, do not confuse the two approaches. An originalist may transcend the language of the document in order to find the original intent; a literalist would not.

There is a second group of literalists that advocate contemporary literalism, that is, the view that contemporary definitions should be applied. They are similar to modernists, but focus on language more than a modernist does.

Historical literalists assert, as do originalists, that their method deemphasizes the effect the ideologies of judges have on decisions, and further, that it makes the law more predictable and stable. Contemporary literalists concede that because the meanings of terms evolve, this method may result in slightly less stability. Nevertheless, they believe that they strike the proper balance between keeping the Constitution current and preventing justices from engaging in policy making.

Democratic reinforcement

Another approach to interpreting the Constitution has been termed **democratic** or **representation reinforcement.** Proponents of this theory suggest that the framers did not intend to establish a set of specific substantive principles. Rather, they created a document that defines the processes, structures, and relationships that constitute the foundation of the American democracy. The first three articles of the Constitution, for example, establish the structure of the national government and its actors, and establish the procedures that must be followed in deciding who will occupy high government positions. Even rights usually thought of as purely substantive have procedural or structural aspects. For example, the First Amendment's religion clauses are recognized as protecting the individual's substantive right to choose and exercise religious beliefs, but it also establishes a structure separating governmental and religious institutions. Although structural components of the Constitution are generally easy to define, substantive portions are not. This is because the language of the Constitution is vague or broad when it comes to substance. "Due process," "equal protection," and "cruel and unusual punishments" are examples.

From these facts, some analysts glean that the framers did not intend to establish a precise set of substantive laws. Rather, they intended to define the who, what, where, and when of substantive rulemaking. Following this theory, judicial interpretation should be guided by the general republican principles underlying the Constitution. However, the analysis is contemporary. The basic republican themes established by the framers are used as a base, but those themes are interpreted within the context of contemporary society. By allowing change in this way, constitutional law actually reflects the will of people. Accordingly, the United States Supreme Court is not viewed as a countermajoritarian institution, but one that reinforces democracy and republicanism.

THE INTERPRETATION PROCESS

Few judges can be said to subscribe exclusively to any one approach. The same judge may favor originalism for one issue and modernism for another. This does not necessarily mean that the judge is inconsistent; rather, each judge develops his or her own approach to interpretation. For example, all judges must begin with the language of the Constitution. Nearly all judges believe they have an obligation to enforce language that is plain and clear on its face.

Although there are proponents and opponents of every approach discussed here, there is no one correct method. Justices differ in their approaches and legal scholars differ sharply on the subject as well. Be aware of the different methods; understanding them will increase your understanding of constitutional law and will also enhance your ability to predict the outcome of future cases.

Judicial restraint and judicial activism

In the American judiciary, a principle has evolved called **judicial restraint.** Because ultimate authority resides in the United States Supreme Court, which is made up of judges who are appointed for life subject only to removal by impeachment, it is necessary that judges restrain themselves from actively entering the political arena. This can be effectively accomplished by judges devoting themselves to deciding cases according to existing law. In simple terms, this means that judges interpret the law rather than make it, the latter function being reserved to the legislature. Ideally, judicial decisions are based on the authority of legal principles already in existence and not on the moral, political, or social preferences of the judges.

It is currently part of the American democratic folklore that judges merely interpret but do not "make" law. The fallacy of this notion lies in the fact that the power to interpret the law inevitably leads to making the law. Every time a judge is called upon to interpret the law, lawmaking occurs. Because judges ordinarily rely on the authority of existing law, judicial interpretation of the law invokes changes that are nearly imperceptible, but when faced with novel or difficult cases, judges formulate statements of the law that form important new principles.

Legal analysis

Legal analysis is a sequential process (see fig. 2-2). First, one must find all authority relevant to the problem. Some areas of the law are governed wholly by case law; other areas are governed by constitutions, statutes, court rules or administrative regulations, as applied and interpreted by the courts. When researching case law, one must search for a prior case decided by the highest possible court in the jurisdiction with the same issue as presented in the legal problem you are researching and with as similar as possible material facts. Any case found should be further researched to make sure it has not been later heard and decided by a higher court or overruled or that there is not a more recent case from the same or a higher court. When researching constitutions, statutes, court rules, and administrative regulations, one must search for an applicable primary source and any case law applying or interpreting the primary source. A statute should be further researched to make sure it has not been amended, repealed, or held unconstitutional. Constitutions, court rules, and administrative regulations should be further researched to make sure they have not been amended.

The *Cruz* problem found on page 19 in this chapter illustrates the process of legal analysis. Cruz Estrada and Luis Briones were tape recorded while seated in the back of the patrol car. Cruz was arrested on federal criminal charges for drug possession. Because Cruz' tape-recorded conversation contains incriminating statements, she would like to have the tape suppressed. The federal eavesdropping statutes may apply. These statutes were discussed in the section of this chapter entitled *deductive reasoning*.

The federal eavesdropping statutes prohibit secretly tape-recording an "oral communication." An oral communication is defined as "any oral communication uttered by a person exhibiting an expectation that such communication is not subject to interception under circumstances justifying such expectation."

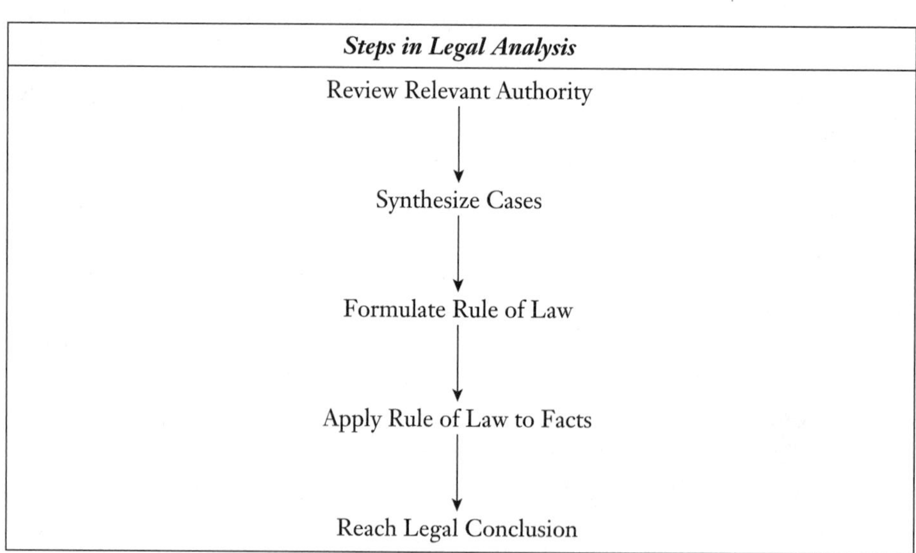

Steps in Legal Analysis
Review Relevant Authority
Synthesize Cases
Formulate Rule of Law
Apply Rule of Law to Facts
Reach Legal Conclusion

FIGURE 2-2 The Sequential Process of Legal Analysis Begins with Reviewing Relevant Legal Authority.

A penalty for tape-recording an oral communication is that the tape-recording may not be used in court.

Case law research has located a 1993 case from the Court of Appeals for the Eleventh Circuit, *United States v. McKinnon*, 985 F.2d 525 (11th Cir. 1993). *McKinnon* is reprinted and discussed in chapter 4. *McKinnon* may apply because it involved suspects tape recorded while conversing in the rear seat of a patrol car. It is the highest federal court that has discussed whether it is permissible for police officers to tape such conversations. *McKinnon* is binding on federal district courts within the eleventh circuit.

Relevant material, once found, must be read and synthesized. The facts in each case will be different from the facts in every other case, but from them you can formulate a rule of law. Synthesizing cases means extracting from the different fact patterns and holdings a rule of law. Once you know the rule of law, you can apply it to a present case to predict the outcome. If a constitution, statute, court rule, or administrative regulation controls, one must synthesize it with case law interpretations of it and extract the rule of law.

In the *deductive reasoning* section of this chapter, we determined that it was unclear whether the federal eavesdropping statutes would apply to *Cruz*. The determination hinged on the meaning of "reasonable" in "reasonable expectation of privacy" in the statutes. If Cruz and Luis' expectation of privacy in the rear seat of the patrol car was reasonable, then the tape should be suppressed; if not, then the tape would not be suppressed under the federal statute. In *McKinnon*, the eleventh circuit decided that the federal eavesdropping statutes did not apply to the tape-recorded conversation because the suspects had no reasonable expectation of privacy while seated in a patrol car. This is the rule of law.

The next step in legal analysis is to apply the rule of law to the facts of the problem. Application of law to facts requires one to determine how the rule of law and the authority backing it up is similar to or different from the facts in the problem. If the facts in prior cases are substantially the same, then the result in the problem should be the same as the result in the prior cases. *Massey v. Prince George's County* (pages 23–24 in this chapter) illustrates this process. In *Massey*, the judge compared the facts in the case to the facts of a case previously decided. Application of the law to the facts of the problem is the most important part of legal analysis. It is the step sometimes overlooked when students perform legal analysis. Students tend to carefully explain the rule of law and then skip directly from the rule of law to the conclusion. Instead, the reasoning followed must be explained. Written legal analysis should lead step by step from the rule of law through the application of the rule of law to the facts in the problem to the conclusion.

In comparing *McKinnon* and *Cruz*, there are many similarities. Both cars were stopped for alleged traffic violations. Both cars contained two occupants. In both cases, the occupants were asked to sit in the patrol car while their car was searched. In both cases, the officers recorded the suspects while seated in the rear seat of the patrol car. The tapes contained incriminating statements. The suspects were not under arrest at the time their conversations were recorded. There are also some differences. The alleged traffic violations were different. In *McKinnon*, the occupants of the car were males; in *Cruz*, one occupant was female and the other was male. In *McKinnon*, the driver consented to the search; in *Cruz*, the search was based on probable cause.

The last step is to reach a conclusion by tying the rule of law and the application of law to facts together. The conclusion is the solution to the problem and must be thoroughly supported by the rule of law and the application of the rule of law to the facts in the problem. The conclusion is also a prediction of what a court will do based on relevant authority.

The federal eavesdropping statutes could be used to suppress the tape-recorded conversation if there was a reasonable expectation of privacy. *McKinnon* can be used to determine if suspects have a reasonable expectation of privacy while seated in a patrol car. The *McKinnon* court held that there was no reasonable expectation of privacy under the facts presented in that case. *McKinnon* is mandatory authority for the eleventh circuit and for all federal district courts within the eleventh circuit.

Using the doctrine of stare decisis, the *Cruz* tape could not be suppressed under the federal eavesdropping statutes if the facts in *Cruz* are substantially similar to the facts in *McKinnon*. If the facts in the two cases are not substantially similar, then *McKinnon* would not be binding on *Cruz*. Although there are some factual differences between the two cases, the facts concerning the taping in the patrol car are virtually identical. While the police officers were conducting a car search, the car occupants were asked to sit in the patrol car. While in the patrol car, they made incriminating statements that were tape-recorded. Because the facts in the two cases were substantially similar, the court deciding *Cruz* should decide that the tape recording may not be suppressed under the federal eavesdropping statutes.

Although the tape may not be suppressed under the federal eavesdropping statutes, there may be another ground to suppress the tape. For a further discussion of *Cruz*, see chapters 13, 16, 17, and 18.

CHAPTER 2 SUMMARY

- The **doctrine of stare decisis** states that when a court has set forth a legal principle, that court and all lower courts under it will apply that principle in future cases where the facts are substantially the same.
- *Roe v. Wade* illustrates the doctrine of stare decisis:
  - In *Roe v. Wade* the United States Supreme Court held that a Texas statute making abortion a crime was unconstitutional but that the state could regulate the right to an abortion during the second trimester and prohibit it during the third trimester.
  - Applying the **doctrine of stare decisis,** *Roe v. Wade* is used as precedent in later cases where the facts are "substantially the same."
  - If the facts in a later abortion case in which a state abortion statute is challenged are substantially the same as the facts in *Roe v. Wade,* then the court in the later case should hold the challenged abortion statute unconstitutional.
  - However, if the challenged abortion statute in the later case is **distinguishable** from the *Roe* statute, a court may uphold the constitutionality of the challenged statute.
- The **doctrine of stare decisis** gives case law predictability while allowing gradual change.
- There are at least two sides to every problem and the attorney represents the client's best interest by arguing that authority favorable to the client's case should be applied and that unfavorable authority is distinguishable.
- When reading a court decision, note what type of opinion it is: majority, plurality, concurring, dissenting, per curiam, or en banc.
- A case may be mandatory authority, which must be followed under the doctrine of stare decisis, or a case may be persuasive authority, which may, but is not required, to be followed.
- In interpreting statutes, the legal researcher may consider legislative intent, the plain meaning of the statutory language, the immediate statutory context, strict construction of the statutory language, and legislative history.
- The methods of interpreting the United States Constitution include originalism, modernism, literalism, and democratic or representation reinforcement.
- Legal analysis involves three steps:
  - reading and synthesizing all relevant authority to extract a rule of law;
  - applying the rule of law to the facts of the problem; and
  - reaching a conclusion.

EXERCISES FOR CHAPTER 2

1. What was the holding (the central decision) of *Griswold v. Connecticut?*
2. What were the arguments of the two attorneys in *Roe v. Wade?*
3. Was *Griswold* used as precedent in *Roe?*
4. What was the issue (legal question before the court) in *Planned Parenthood of Southeastern Pennsylvania v. Casey?*
5. What were the arguments of the two attorneys in *Casey?*

6. Was *Roe* used as precedent in *Casey?*
7. What are the differences among majority, plurality, concurring, dissenting, per curiam and en banc court decisions?
8. What is a "court of last resort"?
9. Give an example of "mandatory authority" for federal courts and for the courts of your state.
10. Give an example of "persuasive authority" for federal courts and for the courts of your state.

CYBERLAW EXERCISES

1. Washburn University School of Law maintains Washlaw Web, a site with numerous links to other law-related web sites. Washlaw Web is accessible at http://www.washlaw.edu.
2. A well-known legal research site where you can start your legal research is http://ww.findlaw.com. Use this cite to find the full opinions of *Griswold v. Connecticut*, *Roe v. Wade*, and *Planned Parenthood of Southeastern Pennsylvania v. Casey* by using the volume and first page numbers of the cases. In a **case citation,** the first number is the volume number. The volume number is followed by an abbreviation of the set of books containing the opinion. The abbreviation is followed by the number of the first page of the case.
3. A comprehensive legal research site is American Law Sources Online, http://www.lawsource.com/also.
4. Another good starting point is Cornell Law School's Legal Information Institute, http://www.law.cornell.edu.
5. Try http://law.indiana.edu/law/v-lib for another site with links to other legal research sites.
6. Use the online legal dictionary linked to http://www.lawoffice.com to find definitions for key terms from this chapter. The online legal dictionary contains definitions for the terms in questions 7 through 10 above.

CHAPTER 3

SECONDARY SOURCES AND FINDING TOOLS

INTRODUCTION

This chapter introduces secondary sources and finding tools. It includes explanations of legal encyclopedias, American Law Reports, attorney general opinions, Restatements of the Law, treatises, legal dictionaries, legal directories, formbooks, looseleaf services, legal periodicals, and digests.

Secondary sources are designed to explain legal concepts. They can be used to understand basic legal terms and general concepts. They provide the researcher with background information and a framework of an area of the law, arranging legal principles in an orderly fashion. In contrast to primary authority (constitutions, cases, statutes, court rules, and administrative regulations), secondary sources do not have the force and effect of law. They function as citation finders, leading the researcher to relevant primary sources. It is preferable to cite to the primary authority found through secondary sources rather than citing to the secondary sources themselves.

Finding tools are used to find primary sources. Secondary sources can also be classified as finding tools because the legal researcher often uses citations found in secondary sources to find relevant primary sources. However, several legal publications function solely as finding tools; these include digests and citators. Citators are covered in chapter 6. Digests and citators are neither primary nor secondary authority and are never cited.

ENCYCLOPEDIAS

Legal encyclopedias offer a useful commentary on the law as it is and serve as a case finder to locate cases with which one can begin the research process. The legal encyclopedia is one of the many tools in the law library and should generally be used in combination with other legal research tools.

In organization, legal encyclopedias have much in common with general encyclopedias. Legal encyclopedias are organized like the multivolume encyclopedias found in schools and public libraries. They are multivolume sets covering broad topics arranged in alphabetical order, with the topics divided into sections. Index volumes are located at the end of the set. Each topic gives a textual explanation of the law relating to that topic. Topic coverage serves as a valuable frame of reference for more in-depth research in other sources.

The two widely-used national legal encyclopedias are ***Corpus Juris Secundum*** and ***American Jurisprudence 2d.*** They are designed to systematically explain the law as it exists in the United States; they may be consulted to gain an overview of the law from a national perspective. Each contains over 400 topics.

The researcher may begin to access the legal encyclopedia either in an index (the general index or the volume index) or in a topic table of contents.

Detailed subject index volumes are located at the end of the set, allowing the researcher to locate relevant material by looking up key terms. In addition, each volume is separately indexed and may contain more detailed information concerning the topics covered in that particular volume than the general index. Each legal encyclopedia topic is preceded by two tables of contents, the first listing major topic sections and the second listing topic sections and subsections in detail.

Legal encyclopedias can be used as a starting point for a researcher. They serve to educate the reader on the basic aspects of a topic with which the reader is unfamiliar; a more knowledgeable reader can refresh his or her understanding of the topic. The first sections of a topic in the legal encyclopedia give the reader a general basic statement of the law. Those sections are followed by a more detailed description of all aspects of the substantive law. The final sections generally describe available remedies.

In contrast to general encyclopedias, legal encyclopedias are heavily footnoted. The footnotes are a valuable feature of the legal encyclopedia, furnishing the legal researcher primary source citations useful in the research process. Legal encyclopedias were first published at a time when the emphasis of the law was on case law rather than statutes or regulations. Legal encyclopedias still tend to emphasize case law over statutes and regulations. A researcher should carefully search for relevant statutes and regulations; legal encyclopedias may not reference highly relevant statutes and regulations.

Each volume of the legal encyclopedia is annually updated with a cumulative pamphlet, generally referred to as a "pocket part." A **pocket part** is a paperbound "booklet" containing recent legal information. When researching, it is essential to check the pocket part for updated material. Pocket parts are usually reprinted annually and contain more recent information than the hardbound volume. The pocket part is inserted inside the back cover of the volume for easy reference and the pamphlet from the prior year is discarded; the pocket part contains textual material and citations, new since the copyright date of the hard bound volume. Over time, the information for the annual pocket part supplement becomes too voluminous to be easily stored inside the volume's back cover; when this happens, the information is printed either in a separate paperbound volume, shelved next to the hardbound volume or absorbed into the reprinted hardbound volume. The researcher should consult both the hardbound volume and the supplement.

When researching, note the copyright date of the hardbound volume and then the date on the front of the pocket part. Also note the date of coverage for the pocket part (this *currency date* tells the date on which research and update for that pocket part was cut off). This information is found in the first few pages of the pocket part. Because of its inherent datedness, a pocket part dated May of the current calendar year may only cover material through December of the preceding year.

The copyright date of the hardbound volumes varies greatly. As just stated, volumes are recompiled and reprinted from time to time when the supplementary material becomes unwieldy. A recompiled volume incorporates new material and eliminates out-of-date information; volumes relating to more rapidly changing areas of the law are reprinted more frequently than other volumes. There may be no pocket part published in the year in which the reprinted volume is published because the material in the hardbound volume would be current without reference to a pocket part.

Many states have state legal encyclopedias; they cover the law in a similar fashion, although from a state perspective, and are arranged similarly to the national legal encyclopedias. The state legal encyclopedia attempts to explain the law as it exists in that particular state. State legal encyclopedias generally provide more extensive treatment of state-specific topics, such as community property, homestead, and oil and gas law, and provide more state-specific citations. For example, Florida law is covered in Florida Jurisprudence 2d (Fla. Jur. 2d). If you were researching Florida law, Florida Jurisprudence would be your first choice. If your research did not locate any primary sources from Florida, you could consult the national encyclopedias to find authority from other states. You could use this authority as persuasive authority to answer your legal question.

FIGURE 3-1
Tips on Using Legal Encyclopedias.

Do—

1. use footnotes to locate relevant primary authority.
2. pull and read primary authority.
3. check pocket parts for recent information
4. update information found.

Do not—

1. rely on a legal encyclopedia alone as an accurate statement of the law.
2. generally cite to a legal encyclopedia.

Caveat on use of legal encyclopedias

Use legal encyclopedias while keeping in mind their limitations. The text provides a short summary of the law, without detail, which gives some background but is not usually specific enough to answer a legal question. You must look up a case cited in the legal encyclopedia. Do not rely on what the legal encyclopedia says about a case, because it may not be completely accurate. Researchers generally do not quote from legal encyclopedias. Because a legal encyclopedia only contains the publisher's interpretation of the law at the time it was written, it is preferable to use the primary source itself. Do not omit statutory research. Legal encyclopedias emphasize case law rather than statutory law and may not reference applicable statutes. See figure 3-1 for a summary of ways to use legal encyclopedias.

Once considered persuasive authority, legal encyclopedias are now considered a research tool, helpful in gaining a general understanding of a topic and locating case citations useful as a basis for further research. Because of the exponential growth of the law and the limits of the legal encyclopedia, topic coverage tends to be general, elemental, and oversimplified. Legal encyclopedias are not designed to put the law into a historical or sociological perspective. An exhaustive and complex treatment of the law would require a much larger set of books. Even with annual supplements, the information in the legal encyclopedia quickly becomes outdated and the cases cited may be a representative rather than exhaustive reference to all relevant cases.

No longer considered persuasive authority, legal encyclopedias are generally not cited as authority in legal documents. Information gleaned from the legal encyclopedia may be the starting point in the research of a legal problem, but certainly not the conclusion to the research process. A solution offered by the legal encyclopedia may be inapplicable because of the peculiar fact pattern, more recent case law, or applicable statutes or regulations not discussed in the legal encyclopedia.

Excerpts from a legal encyclopedia

The excerpted pages in figure 3-2 are from the "Searches and Seizures" topic of American Jurisprudence 2d. Figure 3-2 contains pages from the hardbound volume. Because the hardbound volume was published in 2000, the year in which this book was being written, there was no pocket part supplement to the volume. Ordinarily, you would check the pocket part supplement to determine if there was any relevant material added since the copyright date of the hardbound volume. The Searches and Seizures topic begins with the notes entitled, "Scope of Topic," "Federal Aspects," "Treated Elsewhere," and "Research References." As might be expected, the first three notes explain what is covered in the topic and give references to other topics in American Jurisprudence that contain related information. "Research references" lists citations to related material in primary and secondary sources.

Legal encyclopedias divide each topic into sections. An outline of section numbers and subjects appears at the beginning of the legal encyclopedia topic. Two outlines precede the topic text. The first is an abbreviated outline and the second is a detailed outline that functions as a table of contents.

Once you locate a relevant topic in the legal encyclopedia, it is a good idea to glance over the table of

FIGURE 3-2 Pages from the Searches and Seizures topic of American Jurisprudence 2d.

SEARCHES AND SEIZURES

by

John R. Kennel, J.D., and Jane E. Lehman, J.D., of the National Legal Research Group, Inc.

Beginning of topic

Scope of Topic: This article discusses the prohibitions against unreasonable searches and seizures found in the United States Constitution and in various state constitutions, and implemented in various federal and state statutes. In particular, the article will discuss questions regarding the scope or extent of such prohibitions, the requisites for compliance with the constitutional mandate of reasonableness, and the circumstances under which particular searches and seizures have been regarded as satisfying or failing to satisfy the constitutional requirements. The article also includes a discussion of the disposition of property seized and civil and criminal actions based on search and seizure. In addition to a treatment of searches and seizures of property or the person, the article also discusses electronic surveillance and wiretapping, including an examination of what constitutes an interception, the necessity of obtaining a warrant or order, the form and content of an application for an order and the order itself, execution of the order, post-execution procedures, and extensions of orders.

Explains topic coverage

Federal Aspects: The most commonly cited and applied statutory provision concerning searches and seizures is the prohibition of unreasonable searches and seizures contained in the Fourth Amendment to the United States Constitution. The issuance and execution of search warrants in federal criminal cases is governed by Rule 41 of the Federal Rules of Criminal Procedure and several federal statutes. Issues regarding electronic surveillance or wiretapping are in some instances governed by Title III of the Omnibus Crime Control and Safe Streets Act, and in certain other circumstances by the Foreign Intelligence Surveillance Act or the Communications Assistance for Law Enforcement Act. Federal statutes also provide for administrative inspections as a means of enforcing federal statutes regulating food, drugs, and cosmetics, and controlled substances. For USCA citations, see "Federal Legislation," below.

Treated Elsewhere:

Admissibility of evidence of property obtained through search and seizure, or communications intercepted through electronic surveillance, motions to suppress such evidence, and standing to raise such questions, see 29 Am Jur 2d, Evidence §§ 601–625

Aliens' rights respecting searches and seizures, see 3A Am Jur 2d, Aliens and Citizens §§ 98, 113, 114, 139–143; 3B Am Jur 2d, Aliens and Citizens §§ 1547, 1913, 2312–2320, 2384–2386; 3C Am Jur 2d, Aliens and Citizens §2614

Customs searches and seizures, generally, see 21A Am Jur 2d, Customs Duties and Import Regulations §§ 327–357

Debtor's property, seizure under warrant of attachment, see 6 Am Jur 2d, Attachment and Garnishment §§ 1 et seq.

Enemy-owned property, seizure and confiscation in time of war; seizure and capture in naval warfare, see 78 Am Jur 2d, War §§ 43–73, 95–113, 155–158

Forfeiture or destruction of property seized, generally, see 36 Am Jur 2d, Forfeitures and Penalties §§ 1 et seq.

Gambling devices, summary seizure and destruction of, see 38 Am Jur 2d, Gambling §§ 190–195

List of related topics

FIGURE 3-2 (continued)

SEARCHES AND SEIZURES 68 Am Jur 2D

Inmate or prisoner searches, generally, see 60 Am Jur 2d, Penal and Correctional Institutions §§ 98, 99

Intoxicating liquor and vehicles or other property used in connection therewith, search, seizure, and forfeiture rules applicable to, see 45 Am Jur 2d, Intoxicating Liquors §§ 431–486

Lewd, indecent, or obscene matter, search and seizure rules specifically applicable to, see 50 Am Jur 2d, Lewdness, Indecency, or Obscenity §14

Parolees' rights to be free from unreasonable searches, see 59 Am Jur 2d, Pardon and Parole §94

Shipping laws and regulations, particular rules pertaining to search and seizure of vessels in the enforcement of, see 70 Am Jur 2d, Shipping §§ 120–131

Tax enforcement, seizure or forfeiture of property as means of, see 35 Am Jur 2d, Federal Tax Enforcement §§ 25–37, 90–104

List of other resources a researcher could consult

Research References

Text References:

Burkoff, Search Warrant Law Deskbook
Cook, Constitutional Rights of the Accused (3d ed)
LaFave, Search and Seizure (3d ed)
Ringel, Searches and Seizures, Arrests and Confessions
Torcia, Wharton's Criminal Procedure (13th ed)
8 Federal Procedure, L Ed, Criminal Procedure

Annotation References:

ALR Digest: Search and Seizure

ALR Index: Abandonment of Property or Right; Administrative Law; Arrest; Automobiles and Highway Traffic; Eavesdropping and Wiretapping; Garbage and Refuse; Knock and Announce; Pen Registers; Physical and Mental Examinations; Privacy; Schools and Education; Search and Seizure

Practice References:

Hermann, Search and Seizure Checklists

7 Federal Procedural Forms, L Ed, Criminal Procedure

1A Am Jur Pl & Pr Forms (Rev), Administrative Law; 8 Am Jur Pl & Pr Forms (Rev), Criminal Procedure; 22 Am Jur Pl & Pr Forms (Rev), Searches and Seizures

29 Am Jur Proof of Facts 591, Wiretapping; 30 Am Jur Proof of Facts 113, Electronic Eavesdropping by Concealed Microphone or Microphone-Transmitter; 18 Am Jur POF2d 681, Third Party's Lack of Authority to Consent to Search of Premises or Effects; 26 Am Jur POF2d 465, Consent to Search Given Under Coercive Circumstances

59 Am Jur Trials 79, Driving Under the Influence: Tactical Considerations in Sobriety Checkpoint Cases

Federal Legislation:

U.S. Const. Amend. IV

Fed R Crim P 41 (authority to issue search warrants, property which may be seized thereunder, issuance and contents of warrant, execution and return with inventory, motion for return of property, etc.)

18 USCA §§ 913 (falsely representing oneself as an officer, agent, or employee of the United States and in such assumed character searching the person, buildings, or other property of any person); 2231 (resistance or interference with service or execution of search warrant); 2232 (destruction or removal of property to prevent seizure); 2233 (rescue of seized property); 2234 (exceeding authority in executing search warrant or exercising it with unnecessary severity); 2235 (procuring search

FIGURE 3-2 (continued)

68 Am Jur 2d SEARCHES AND SEIZURES

warrant maliciously and without probable cause); 2236 (searches without warrant); 2510–2521 (Title III of Omnibus Crime Control and Safe Streets Act, also known as the Electronic Communications Privacy Act or the Federal Wiretap Act); 3105 (persons authorized to serve search warrant); 3107 (seizures under warrant by Federal Bureau of Investigation) 3109 ("knock and announce" rule governing breaking of doors or windows of house by officer to execute search warrant or to liberate himself or another); 3121, 3112 (installation or use of pen registers or trap and trace device)

21 USCA §§ 374(a) (inspections, by persons designated by Secretary of Department of Health and Human Services, of places where food, drugs, devices, or cosmetics are processed, manufactured, packed, or held); 880(a), (b) (administrative inspections of records, documents, or reports required to be kept by facilities where controlled substances may be lawfully manufactured, distributed, dispensed, or administered)

42 USCA § 1988(b) (award of attorney's fees to prevailing party in civil rights action)

47 USCA §§ 1001 et seq. (Communications Assistance for Law Enforcement Act, governing duty of telecommunications carriers to cooperate in intercepting communications for law enforcement purposes)

50 USCA §§ 1802, 1805 (provisions of Foreign Intelligence Surveillance Act, governing electronic surveillance concerning activities of foreign governments or agents thereof)

KeyCite®: Cases and other legal materials listed in KeyCite Scope can be researched through West Group's KeyCite service on Westlaw®. Use KeyCite to check citations for form, parallel references, prior and later history, and comprehensive citator information, including citations to other decisions and secondary materials.

Some cases cited herein may be reported only on electronic media. The reader should consult local rules or statutes for any restrictions that may be imposed by a particular jurisdiction on the citation of such cases by parties to litigation.

Table of Parallel References

To convert General Index references to section references in this volume, or to ascertain the disposition (or current equivalent) of sections of articles in the prior edition of this publication, see the Table of Parallel References beginning at p ix.

Beginning of abbreviated topic outline

Outline

I. IN GENERAL; FOURTH AMENDMENT [§§ 1-15]
   A. GENERALLY [§§ 1-7]
   B. STANDING TO CHALLENGE [§§ 8, 9]
   C. UNREASONABLE SEARCHES AND SEIZURES PROHIBITED [§§ 10-12]
   D. APPLICATION OF FOURTH AMENDMENT TO STATES [§§ 13-15]

II. SEARCH AND SEIZURE OF PROPERTY OR PERSONS [§§ 16-326]
   A. WHAT CONSTITUTES SEARCH AND SEIZURE; SCOPE OF PROTECTION [§§ 16-108]
   B. THE WARRANT REQUIREMENT AND ITS EXCEPTIONS [§§ 109-165]
   C. VALIDITY OF WARRANT [§§ 166-228]

FIGURE 3-2 (continued)

Part of detailed topic outline

Beginning of material relevant to electronic surveillance and wiretapping

Sample pages provided for these sections

68 Am Jur 2d SEARCHES AND SEIZURES

b. AVAILABLE CAUSES OF ACTION

§ 308. Generally; federal civil rights action
§ 309. Replevin and trespass
§ 310. Mental and emotional distress
§ 311. Seizure of property as compensable taking
§ 312. Malicious prosecution

c. LIABILITY OF PARTICULAR PERSONS

§ 313. Generally; law enforcement officers and agents
§ 314. Private persons
§ 315. Private persons procuring warrants

d. DEFENSES

§ 316. Generally; consent to search
§ 317. —Consent from a third person
§ 318. Acting under authority of warrant
§ 319. —Property damage during search
§ 320. —Qualified immunity
§ 321. —Good faith

2. CRIMINAL ACTIONS

§ 322. Generally; resisting or impeding search
§ 323. Federal statutory offenses concerning resistance to the execution of warrants
§ 324. Contempt
§ 325. Wrongfully causing or conducting search
§ 326. Malicious procurement of warrant; related federal offenses

III. ELECTRONIC SURVEILLANCE; WIRETAPPING

A. IN GENERAL

§ 327. Generally
§ 328. Federal statutes; Federal Wiretap Act
§ 329. —Constitutional challenges
§ 330. —Communications Assistance for Law Enforcement Act
§ 331. State statutes

B. INTERCEPTION

1. COMMUNICATIONS SUBJECT TO INTERCEPTION

§ 332. Generally
§ 333. Under the Federal Wiretap Act
§ 334. Oral communications
§ 335. —Examples
§ 336. Wire communications
§ 337. Electronic communication

FIGURE 3-2 (continued)

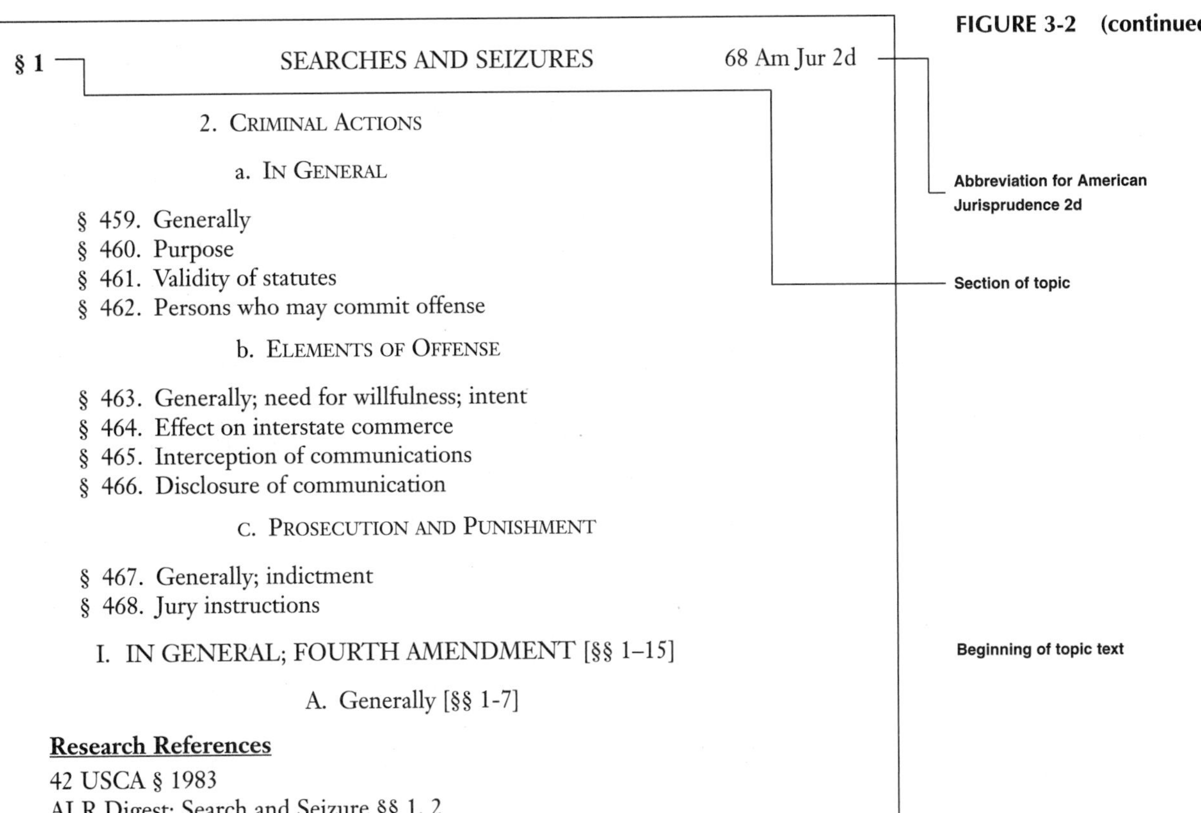

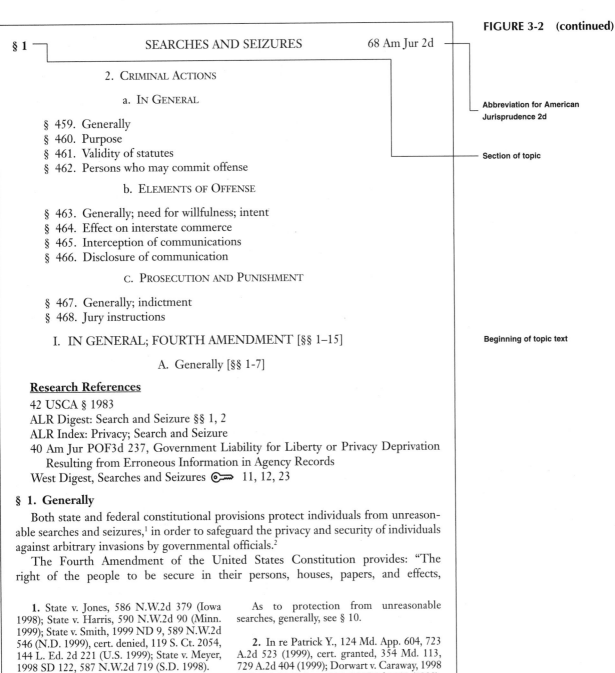

§ 1 SEARCHES AND SEIZURES 68 Am Jur 2d

2. Criminal Actions

a. In General

§ 459. Generally
§ 460. Purpose
§ 461. Validity of statutes
§ 462. Persons who may commit offense

b. Elements of Offense

§ 463. Generally; need for willfulness; intent
§ 464. Effect on interstate commerce
§ 465. Interception of communications
§ 466. Disclosure of communication

c. Prosecution and Punishment

§ 467. Generally; indictment
§ 468. Jury instructions

I. IN GENERAL; FOURTH AMENDMENT [§§ 1–15]

A. Generally [§§ 1-7]

Research References

42 USCA § 1983
ALR Digest: Search and Seizure §§ 1, 2
ALR Index: Privacy; Search and Seizure
40 Am Jur POF3d 237, Government Liability for Liberty or Privacy Deprivation Resulting from Erroneous Information in Agency Records
West Digest, Searches and Seizures 11, 12, 23

§ 1. Generally

Both state and federal constitutional provisions protect individuals from unreasonable searches and seizures,[1] in order to safeguard the privacy and security of individuals against arbitrary invasions by governmental officials.[2]

The Fourth Amendment of the United States Constitution provides: "The right of the people to be secure in their persons, houses, papers, and effects,

1. State v. Jones, 586 N.W.2d 379 (Iowa 1998); State v. Harris, 590 N.W.2d 90 (Minn. 1999); State v. Smith, 1999 ND 9, 589 N.W.2d 546 (N.D. 1999), cert. denied, 119 S. Ct. 2054, 144 L. Ed. 2d 221 (U.S. 1999); State v. Meyer, 1998 SD 122, 587 N.W.2d 719 (S.D. 1998).

Both the federal and state constitutions protect a person's right to be free from unreasonable searches and seizures by providing generally that a person may be searched only if the search is preceded by probable cause and the issuance of a warrant. State v. Martinson, 581 N.W.2d 846 (Minn. 1998).

As to protection from unreasonable searches, generally, see § 10.

2. In re Patrick Y., 124 Md. App. 604, 723 A.2d 523 (1999), cert. granted, 354 Md. 113, 729 A.2d 404 (1999); Dorwart v. Caraway, 1998 MT 191, 290 Mont. 196, 966 P.2d 1121 (1998), reh'g denied, (Nov. 12, 1998) and cert. denied, 119 S. Ct. 1358, 143 L. Ed. 2d 519 (U.S. 1909); State v. Bridges, 963 S.W.2d 487 (Tenn. 1997).

As to the protection of privacy interests, see § 5.

FIGURE 3-2 (continued)

§ 326 SEARCHES AND SEIZURES 68 Am Jur 2d

without reasonable cause, any other building or property without a search warrant, except when he or she is (a) serving a warrant of arrest; or (b) arresting or attempting to arrest a person committing or attempting to commit an offense in his presence, or who has committed or is suspected on reasonable grounds of having committed a felony; or (c) making a search at the request or invitation, or with the consent, of the occupant of the premises.[21]

In addition, it is a criminal offense to represent oneself falsely to be an officer, agent, or employee of the United States, and in such assumed character to search the person, buildings, or other property of any person.[22]

III. ELECTRONIC SURVEILLANCE; WIRETAPPING [§§ 327–468]

A. IN GENERAL [§§ 327–331]

Research References
18 USCA § 2511; 47 USCA §§ 1001 et seq.
28 CFR §§ 100.1 et seq.
ALR Digest: Telephones § 4
ALR Index: Eavesdropping and Wiretapping
29 Am Jur Proof of Facts 591, Wiretapping §§ 8–14
5 Am Jur Trials 331, Excluding Illegally Obtained Evidence § 2
West Digest, Telecommunications (key) 492

§ 327. Generally

With the possible exception of situations involving the national security,[23] electronic surveillance, such as attaching an electronic listening device to a telephone booth and recording the words of the occupant, constitutes a search and seizure within the meaning of the Fourth Amendment.[24] The Fourth Amendment protects an individual's reasonable expectation of privacy.[25] The test for determining whether a person has a reasonable or justifiable expectation of privacy has two prongs: first, whether the person's conduct exhibits a subjective expectation of privacy, and second, whether the person's subjective expectation of privacy is one that society is willing to recognize as reasonable.[26] Thus, whether warrantless eavesdropping by the police violates the Fourth

21. 18 USCA § 2236.

22. 18 USCA § 913.

23. § 347.

24. Katz v. U.S., 389 U.S. 347, 88 S. Ct. 507, 19 L. Ed. 2d 576 (1967); People v. Green, 63 Misc. 2d 435, 312 N.Y.S.2d 290 (City Crim. Ct. 1970) (abrogation recognized on other grounds by, People v. Rusciano, 171 Misc. 2d 908, 656 N.Y.S.2d 822 (J. Ct. 1997)).

As to particular methods of electronic surveillance, see §§ 338 et seq.

Law Reviews: Lennon, The Fourth Amendment's prohibitions on encryption limitation: Will 1995 be like "1984"? 58 Albany LR 2:467–508 (1995).

Dery, Remote frisking down to the skin: Government searching technology powerful enough to locate hole in Fourth Amendment fundamentals. 30 Creight LR 2:353 (1997).

Practice References: Search and seizure generally; searches without a warrant. 5 Am Jur Trials 331, Excluding Illegally Obtained Evidence § 2.

25. § 5.

26. U.S. v. McKinnon, 985 F.2d 525 (11th Cir. 1993).

Review footnotes for citations to relevant primary or secondary sources

Citation to case discussed in chapter 4

FIGURE 3-2 (continued)

68 Am Jur 2d SEARCHES AND SEIZURES § 329

Amendment depends on whether the defendant had a justified expectation of privacy at the place and time of the communication.[27]

- *Illustration:* Calling a beeper does not violate the Fourth Amendment under any circumstances because there simply is no reasonable expectation of privacy connected with a beeper.[28]
- *Observation:* The Fourth Amendment's protection of persons in their houses from unreasonable searches and seizures includes the right to be free from indiscriminate government video surveillance of the interior of an apartment.[29]

§ 328. Federal statutes; Federal Wiretap Act

The basic statute regulating wiretapping and electronic surveillance is Title III of the Omnibus Crime Control and Safe Streets Act, also known as the Electronic Communications Privacy Act or the Federal Wiretap Act.[30]

- *Observation:* Although the Wiretap Act does not specifically refer to covert entry, the language, structure, and history of the statute indicate that Congress has conferred upon the courts the power to authorize a law enforcement officer's covert entry into private premises to install "bugging" equipment.[31]

The Federal Wiretap Act regulates the interception of "electronic," as well as "wire" and "oral" communication.[32]

§ 329. —Constitutional challenges

Title III of the Omnibus Crime Control and Safe Streets Act is not unconstitutionally vague,[33] nor does it authorize such broad intrusions as to allow the obtaining of testimonial evidence in violation of the Fifth and Fourth Amendments.[34]

The failure of Title III to proscribe unconsented and unannounced entries does not render it unconstitutional,[35] nor does the provision permit an unconstitutional invasion of privacy,[36] or constitute a violation of equal protec-

27. People v. Palmer, 888 P.2d 348 (Colo. Ct. App. 1994), reh'g denied, (May 4, 1995).
As to the grounds for suppressing evidence involving illegal wiretapping and electronic surveillance, see 29 Am Jur 2d, Evidence §§ 609–625.

28. U.S. v. Diaz-Lizaraza, 981 F.2d 1216, 37 Fed. R. Evid. Serv. (LCP) 1095 (11th Cir. 1993).

29. U.S. v. Falls, 34 F.3d 674 (8th Cir. 1994).

30. 18 USCA §§ 2510–2520.
As to the necessity for an order or warrant, generally, see §§ 346 et seq.
As to the applicable rule where one party has consented to the interception, see § 356.

31. Dalia v. U. S., 441 U.S. 238, 99 S. Ct. 1682, 60 L. Ed. 2d 177 (1979).

Practice References: Wiretaps pursuant to statute. 29 Am Jur Proof of Facts 591, Wiretapping §§ 8–14.

32. 18 USCA § 2511.
As to what constitutes an electronic communication, see § 337.

33. U.S. v. Spy Factory, Inc., 951 F. Supp. 450 (S.D.N.Y. 1997), reconsideration denied, 960 F. Supp. 684 (S.D.N.Y. 1997).

34. U. S. v. Sklaroff, 506 F.2d 837 (5th Cir. 1975).

35. U. S. v. Giacalone, 455 F. Supp. 26 (E.D. Mich. 1977).

36. U. S. v. Sklaroff, 323 F. Supp. 296 (S.D. Fla. 1971).

Citation to statutes discussed in chapter 5

FIGURE 3-2 (continued)

tion.[37] The federal statute authorizing roving wiretap surveillance[38] is also constitutional.[39]

§ 330. —Communications Assistance for Law Enforcement Act

The Communications Assistance for Law Enforcement Act clarifies the duty of telecommunications carriers to cooperate in intercepting communications for law enforcement purposes.[40] The telecommunications carriers must provide equipment, facilities, or services that will allow the government to intercept the wire and electronic communications of a specific subscriber, without intercepting the communications of others.[41] The Attorney General has established regulations setting forth the procedures that telecommunications carriers must follow to receive reimbursement under the Act.[42]

The federal statute does not apply to a telephone system enclosed entirely within the walls of a jail which is operated by a local agency, when the system is not connected to any public utility system,[43] although monitoring of the system may be required under state law for institutional security purposes.[44]

§ 331. State statutes

Congress did not intend, by the enactment of federal laws, to pre-empt the field of wiretapping so as to supersede or exclude state legislation in the field.[45]

• *Observation:* If the state statutes aid in fulfilling the purposes of the federal law without impairing the federal objectives, the state statute is enforceable.[46]

In determining what construction to give to a state wiretap act, the court may weigh the fact that the state act is closely modeled after and is substantially parallel to the provisions of the Federal Wiretap Act.[47]

37. U. S. v. Horton, 601 F.2d 319 (7th Cir. 1979).

38. 18 USCA § 2518(11)(b).

39. U.S. v. Gaytan, 74 F.3d 545 (5th Cir. 1996).

40. 47 USCA §§ 1001 et seq.

41. 47 USCA § 1002(a).

42. 28 CFR §§ 100.10 et seq.

43. People v. Morgan, 197 Cal. App. 2d 90, 16 Cal. Rptr. 838 (4th Dist. 1961).

44. De Lancie v. Superior Court, 31 Cal. 3d 865, 183 Cal. Rptr. 866, 647 P.2d 149 (1982).

45. People v. Potter, 240 Cal. App. 2d 621, 49 Cal. Rptr. 892 (4th Dist. 1966); People v. Broady, 5 N.Y.2d 500, 186 N.Y.S.2d 230, 158 N.E.2d 817, 74 A.L.R.2d 841 (1959), remittitur amended, 6 N.Y.2d 814, 188 N.Y.S.2d 200, 159 N.E.2d 689 (1959).

As to the federal preemption of a legislative field generally, see 16A Am Jur 2d, Constitutional Law § 241.

Law Reviews: State statute applies to foreign wiretaps: Evidence governed by local use restrictions. 213 New York LJ 34:1 (1995).

46. State v. Verdugo, 180 Ariz. 180, 883 P.2d 417 (Ct. App. Div. 2 1993); Tavernetti v. Superior Court, 22 Cal. 3d 187, 148 Cal. Rptr. 883, 583 P.2d 737 (1978); Com. v. Birdseye, 543 Pa. 251, 670 A.2d 1124 (1996), related reference, 166 F.3d 1204 (3d Cir. 1998).

Law Reviews: Lansing & Bailey, Monitoring employee telephone conversations under the amended Illinois Eavesdropping Act. 47 Lab LJ 7:418 (1996).

47. PBA Local No. 38 v. Woodbridge Police Dept., 832 F. Supp. 808 (D.N.J, 1993).

As to the construction of statutes, see 73 Am Jur 2d, Statutes § 142.

As to the Federal Wiretap Act, see §§ 328–330.

FIGURE 3-2 (continued)

68 Am Jur 2d SEARCHES AND SEIZURES § 332

- *Practice Guide:* Wiretap statutes are exceptions to both federal and state constitutional rights to privacy and must therefore be strictly construed.[48]

Although a number of states have enacted wiretapping and eavesdropping statutes, by virtue of the Supremacy Clause of United States Constitution, the Federal Wiretap Act preempts the ability of states to adopt legislation that is less restrictive in allowing interceptions.[49] A state may, however, prohibit or more severely restrict electronic surveillance.[50]

B. INTERCEPTION [§§ 332-345]

Research References

18 USCA §§ 2510, 2518, 3121, 3122
ALR Digest, Telephones § 4
ALR Index: Eavesdropping and Wiretapping; Pen Registers
29 Am Jur Proof of Facts 591, Wiretapping §§ 22–26; 30 Am Jur Proof of Facts 113, Electronic Eavesdropping by Concealed Microphone or Microphone-Transmitter
West Digest, Telecommunications 🔑 493, 494, 540

1. COMMUNICATIONS SUBJECT TO INTERCEPTION [§§ 332-337]

§ 332. Generally

The term "intercept" is defined in federal law as the "aural or other acquisition of the contents of any wire, electronic, or oral communication through the use of any electronic, mechanical, or other device.[51] This definition of "intercept" equates "interception" with listening to, monitoring, or hearing described communications, either at the time such communications occur or at

48. Jackson v. State, 636 So. 2d 1372 (Fla. Dist. Ct. App. 2d Dist. 1994), review granted, 645 So. 2d 455 (Fla. 1994) and decision approved, 650 So. 2d 24 (Fla. 1995).

49. State v. Rivers, 660 So. 2d 1360 (Fla. 1995), reh'g denied, (Oct. 5, 1995); Com. v. Birdseye, 543 Pa. 251, 670 A.2d 1124 (1996), related reference, 166 F.3d 1204 (3d Cir. 1998) (applying Pennsylvania law).

50. U.S. v. Geller, 560 F. Supp. 1309 (E.D. Pa. 1983), judgment affd, 745 F.2d 49 (3d Cir. 1984), related reference, 1986 WL 9887 (E.D. Pa. 1986) (applying Pennsylvania law); Navarra v. Bache Halsey Stuart Shields Inc., 510 F. Supp. 831 (E.D. Mich. 1981) (applying Michigan law); People v. Stevens, 34 Cal. App. 4th 56, 40 Cal. Rptr. 2d 92 (6th Dist. 1995), reh'g denied, (May 19, 1995); State v. Thompson, 191 Conn. 360, 464 A.2d 799 (1983); State v. Rivers, 643 So. 2d 3 (Fla. Dist. Ct. App. 5th Dist. 1994), reh'g denied, (Sept. 29, 1994) and review granted, 651 So. 2d 1196 (Fla. 1995) and decision approved, 660 So. 2d 1360 (Fla. 1995), reh'g denied, (Oct. 5, 1995); Cox v. State, 152 Ga. App. 453, 263 S.E.2d 238 (1979); State v. Catania, 85 N.J. 418, 427 A.2d 537 (1981) (abrogation on other grounds recognized by, State v. Purnell, 161 N.J. 44, 735 A.2d 513 (1999)).

Annotations: Validity, construction, and effect of state legislation making wiretapping a criminal offense, 74 A.L.R.2d 855.

51. 18 USCA § 2510(4).

As to the general rule that law enforcement officials must obtain a warrant to intercept oral, wire, or electronic communications, see § 346.

contents for the topic to determine which sections might answer your question. If you had questions on electronic surveillance and wiretapping, you could start your research by reading §§ 327–468 in Searches and Seizures. (The symbol "§" stands for "section" and two section symbols (§§) stand for "sections." Double section symbols are used to reference two or more sections. Thus §§ 327–468 means sections 327 through 468.)

The footnotes are quite extensive compared to the text portion. For example, the footnotes on several sample pages cover at least a quarter of those pages.

The index volumes usually refer you to a topic and section number so that you can turn directly to that section. Using index volumes, you may encounter the terms "*infra*" and "*supra.*" *Infra* means "below" and is often used to reference information included on an index page located later in the index; *supra* means "above-mentioned" and is often used to reference information included on an index page located earlier in the index.

Use of legal encyclopedias

In summary, legal encyclopedias are best used:

1. To find primary authority; and
2. To give the researcher general background information.

For information on how to make legal encyclopedias a part of your research strategy, see chapter 7.

Citation to legal encyclopedias

Caveat: Do not assume that the legal citations found when researching are in correct citation form. Citations, even those included in cases may or may not comply with the citation rules your professor has asked you to use. Always check your citations against the appropriate citation rule for correct form.

Although legal encyclopedias are not usually cited in documents submitted to court or opposing counsel, you will need to cite legal encyclopedias for assignments and more informal documents such as office memos. (See chapter 16 for an explanation of the purpose and use of office memos.) Figure 3-3 is the citation for sections 327–468 of the American Jurisprudence Searches and Seizures topic. The number "68" is the volume in which sections 327 through 468 are located; "2000" is the copyright year of the volume. (Note: American Jurisprudence is now a West Group publication.)

Sections 327–468 of Searches and Seizures discuss electronic surveillance and wiretapping. An analogous discussion is found in sections 233–315 of the Telecommunications topic in Corpus Juris Secundum. Figure 3-4 contains the citation to those sections. The number "86" is the volume in which sections 233 through 315 are located; "1997" is the copyright year of the volume; "2000" is the year of the pocket part supplement. The ampersand ("&") indicates that the material you are referring to was found both in the hardbound volume and the pocket part supplement. The citation should be revised to show only "1997" in the parentheses if the material you are referring to was found only in the hardbound volume. Similarly, the parentheses should contain only "Supp. 2000" if the material you are referring to was found only in the pocket part supplement.

A citation to Corpus Juris Secundum or a state legal encyclopedia would be in similar form except for substituting the abbreviation for the legal encyclopedia used instead of "Am. Jur. 2d" as shown in figure 3-3.

AMERICAN LAW REPORTS

The first major attempt at case reporting as a commercial venture began in the late 1800s. The two major approaches to case reporting were the exhaus-

FIGURE 3-3 Citation to American Jurisprudence.

68 Am. Jur. 2d *Searches and Seizures* §§ 327-468 (2000).

FIGURE 3-4 Citation to Corpus Juris Secundum.

86 C.J.S. *Telecommunications* §§ 233–315 (1997 & Supp. 2000).

tive approach and the selective approach. As the names imply, the exhaustive approach undertook to publish all case opinions, from the most significant landmark decisions to the short, and often relatively unimportant decisions; the selective approach published a limited number of cases selected by the publisher as "leading cases," because of their landmark status or their treatment of a novel or interesting legal issue, and accompanied the selected cases with a commentary, called an "annotation." The annotation explored a particular legal issue in depth and referenced other cases concerning the same issue. The West Publishing Company followed the exhaustive approach. The American Law Reports Series ("ALR") typifies the selective approach.

The exhaustive approach to case reporting won out over the selective approach, but ALR survived as a valuable research tool. Each ALR volume contains approximately twenty cases, with accompanying annotations. Now the researcher consults ALR most frequently for the annotations and infrequently for the cases it reports. The ALR 5th reflects the diminishing importance of the cases reported and the increasing importance of the case annotations by printing the reported cases at the end of each volume, following the annotations.

American Law Reports, published by West Group (formerly published by Lawyers Cooperative Publishing), combines case reporter and legal encyclopedia features. This reference series is like reporters in that it contains cases, and the full text of selected cases is included. A case is selected for publication in American Law Reports because it contains an important, novel or interesting legal issue. American Law Reports are also similar to legal encyclopedias in that they contain textual explanations (called **annotations**) of the law with lengthy footnotes to relevant cases. A case selected for publication in American Law Reports illustrates a legal issue covered in the annotation.

While legal encyclopedias are designed to provide a comprehensive general treatment of the law, ALR provides a much more detailed and complex treatment of a particular legal issue. An ALR annotation provides a detailed discussion of cases concerning that legal issue from jurisdictions across the country. The cases are analyzed and the annotation is organized to provide a framework for further research of the issue. The researcher should consult the opening sections of the annotation to determine the often-narrow scope of the annotation. Those sections conveniently reference other annotations concerning related issues.

Because its coverage is not comprehensive, the researcher will not always be lucky enough to find an ALR annotation concerning the issue being researched. In those instances when a relevant ALR annotation exists, the annotation can significantly speed one's research by providing an extensive discussion of relevant legal principles, majority and minority rules, and a synthesis of relevant case law. Each annotation represents an extensive study of the development and treatment of a particular issue across the jurisdictions. Where there is no case law from the researcher's jurisdiction, case law from other jurisdictions furnishes persuasive authority.

In addition, the ALR annotation functions as a case-finder, giving citations to cases with which the researcher can start researching to find more cases from a particular jurisdiction.

Figure 3-5 shows that there are five series of ALR: ALR, ALR 2d, ALR 3d, ALR 4th, ALR 5th. There is another series, ALR Federal, which began in 1969 and which focuses on issues arising in federal courts. Prior to 1969, the first through third series of American Law Reports had covered both federal and state material. Since 1969, federal material has been covered in American Law Reports Federal. For state material since 1969, you would consult the third through the fifth series of American Law Reports.

Use the index and digest volumes of American Law Reports to find relevant annotations. Updates to the index and digest volumes are contained in pocket parts. The index also contains an "Annotation History Table," which reveals if an annotation has been supplemented or superceded. An annotation that supplements an earlier annotation should be read together with the earlier annotation. When an annotation supersedes an earlier annotation, only the later annotation should be read.

Figure 3-5 also shows how the various American Law Reports are updated. Update the third through the fifth series and ALR Federal annotations by consulting pocket parts. Update ALR 2d by consulting

FIGURE 3-5 Series of American Law Reports.

AMERICAN LAW REPORTS		
American Law Reports	(1919–1948)	supplemented by the ALR Bluebook of Supplemental Decisions
American Law Reports 2d	(1948–1965)	supplemented by the ALR Later Case Service volumes and pocket parts
American Law Reports 3d	(1965–1980)	pocket parts
American Law Reports 4th	(1980–1992)	pocket parts
American Law Reports 5th	(1992-present)	pocket parts
American Law Reports Federal	(1992–present)	pocket parts

the ALR Later Case Service volumes and the pocket parts to those volumes. Update the first series by consulting the ALR Bluebook of Supplemental Decisions.

ALR format has changed several times with the start of a new series, but the format in ALR 3d, ALR 4th, ALR 5th, and ALR Fed is relatively uniform. Hardbound volumes in ALR 3d, ALR 4th, ALR 5th, and ALR Fed are annually updated by pocket parts; the annotation in the hardbound volume should be reviewed in tandem with updated information from the pocket part. The researcher can find relevant annotations by searching key words in the ALR Index (covering ALR 2d, ALR 3d, ALR 4th, ALR 5th, and ALR Fed). From time to time, an annotation in an earlier ALR series is superceded in a later ALR series.

Unlike the topical arrangement of legal encyclopedias, annotations are published in the order they are written. The legal issues covered by annotations grow with developing case law. Extensive changes in case law may require a new "superceding" annotation. Annotations from one of the earlier series may be consulted for topics with little change.

Occasionally, the researcher may need to consult the first two series of ALR for issues not superceded in a later series. The researcher can find relevant annotations by searching key words in the ALR Index covering ALR and ALR 2d or searching under a relevant topic in the ALR Digest covering ALR and ALR 2d. ALR and ALR 2d are updated by separate volumes, called the "ALR Bluebook" for ALR and "ALR 2d Later Case Service," with accompanying pocket parts, for ALR 2d.

The structure of an ALR annotation

This section describes the structure of an ALR annotation using the annotation in figure 3-6 as an example. Figure 3-7 contains the case on which the annotation was based. The annotation is from ALR 5th. Although similar, the format for annotations from ALR 3d, ALR 4th, and ALR Fed varies slightly.

Each annotation is accompanied by a court opinion, with an issue from the court opinion the subject of the annotation. In ALR 5th, the accompanying court opinion is printed at the end of the volume rather than immediately preceding the annotation as it was in other series. In our example, the bottom of the first page of the annotation, *Propriety of Attorney's Surreptitious Sound Recording of Statements by Others Who Are or May Become Involved in Litigation*, indicates that the accompanying case, *Attorney M v. Mississippi Bar*, begins on page 891. The first page also contains an abstract of the annotation.

The following parts precede the body of the annotation text:

Table of Contents
Research References
Index
Jurisdictional Table of Cited Statutes and Cases

The Table of Contents, the Index, and the Jurisdictional Table of Cited Statutes and Cases help the researcher identify and locate relevant section of the annotation. These parts identify relevant sections by section and subsection number. The Research References aid the researcher in further research by cross-referencing

32 ALR5th 715

PROPRIETY OF ATTORNEY'S SURREPTITIOUS SOUND RECORDING OF STATEMENTS BY OTHERS WHO ARE OR MAY BECOME INVOLVED IN LITIGATION

by
Marjorie A. Caner, J.D.

An attorney may be disciplined for actions that contravene the ethics of the profession even though his conduct is neither criminal nor calculated to obstruct justice. However, it has been held that an attorney will not be disbarred soley because he fails to live up to the ideals of the canons of ethics of a bar association. Ethical problems are clearly presented by an attorney's tape recording of another party without his or her knowledge or consent. In Attorney M v Mississippi Bar (1992, Miss) 621 So 2d 220, 32 ALR5th 891, the court held that surreptitious tape recording by an attorney is not unethical when the information requested by the attorney is of such nature as reasonably to import to the person called the probability, if not certainty, that it will be taken down in some manner for future use, and the attorney's action, "considered within the context of the circumstances then existing, does not rise to the level of dishonesty, fraud, deceit or misrepresentation."

TABLE OF CONTENTS

ARTICLE OUTLINE

Research References

TOTAL CLIENT-SERVICE LIBRARY® REFERENCES

The following references may be of related or collateral interest to a user of this annotation.

Annotations

See the related annotations listed in the body of the annotation.

Encyclopedias and Texts

7 Am Jur 2d, Attorneys at Law § 60
7A Federal Procedure, L Ed §§ 20:222–20:224

FIGURE 3-6 Pages of 32 ALR 5th 715.

Volume 32 of American Law Reports 5th Series, page 715

Title of annotation

Author of annotation

Case summary

Citation to case annotated

Outline of annotation

Coverage of annotation

List of other annotations on related subjects

Summary of annotation

FIGURE 3-6 (continued)

ATTORNEYS—SOUND RECORDINGS 32 ALR5th

Practice Aids

2B Am Jur Pl & Pr Forms (Rev), Attorneys at Law Forms 11–22
31 Am Jur Trials 633, Defending Lawyers in Disciplinary Proceedings §§ 3, 5

Digests and Indexes

L Ed Digest, Attorneys §§ 5–8
ALR Digest, Attorneys §§ 9, 9.5, 10
ALR Index, Attorney-Client Privilege; Attorney or Assistance of Attorney; Disbarment of Attorney; Discipline and Disciplinary Actions; Eavesdropping and Wiretapping; Ethics and Ethical Matters; Malpractice by Attorney; Sound Recordings

Auto-Cite ®

Cases and annotations referred to herein can be further researched through the Auto-Cite® computer-assisted research service. Use AutoCite to check citations for form, parallel references, prior and later history, and annotation references.

RESEARCH SOURCES

The following are the research sources that were found to be helpful in compiling this annotation.

Texts

31 Am Jur Trials 633, Defending Lawyers in Disciplinary Proceedings §§ 3, 5

Citations to legal encyclopedia sections

Encyclopedias

7 Am Jur 2d, Attorneys at Law § 60
7 CJS, Attorney and Client § 44

Law Review Articles

Moliterna, Tape Recording Telephone Conversation—Is It Ethical For Attorneys?, 15 J Legal Prof 171, 1990

Suggested word search query for computer-assisted legal research

Electronic Search Query

counsel or attorney w/5 (sound or tape pre/1 record!) w/5 conversation or statement or telephon! w/5 client or party

Relevant digest topics and key numbers

West Digest Key Numbers

Attorney and Client 32(12), 38, 58
Criminal Law 639.1, 641.12(1)
Telecommunications 495

Index to this annotation

INDEX

FIGURE 3-6 (continued)

ATTORNEYS—SOUND RECORDINGS 32 ALR5th

Jurisdictional Table of Cited Statutes and Cases*

CALIFORNIA

Cal Code Penal Code § 632. See § 4
People v Wyrick (1978, 3rd Dist) 77 Cal App 3d 903, 144 Cal Rptr 38—§ 4

COLORADO

People v Selby (1979) 198 Colo 386, 606 P2d 45—§ 4
People v Smith (1989, Colo) 778 P2d 685—§ 4
People v Wallin (1981, Colo) 621 P2d 330—§ 4

IOWA

Committee on Professional Ethics & Conduct of Iowa State Bar Ass'n v Mollman (1992, Iowa) 488 NW2d 168—§ 4

MISSISSIPPI

Attorney M v Mississippi Bar (1992, Miss) 621 So 2d 220, 32 ALR5th 891—§ 3
Mississippi Bar v Attorney ST (1993, Miss) 621 So 2d 229—§ 3
National Life & Acci. Ins. Co. v Miller (1985, Miss) 484 So 2d 329—§ 3
Netterville v Mississippi State Bar (1981, Miss) 397 So 2d 878—§ 3
Shaw v Shaw (Miss) 603 So 2d 287, and J. C. Penney Co. v Blush (1978, Miss) 356 So 2d 590—§ 3

SOUTH CAROLINA

An Anonymous Member of the South Carolina Bar, In re (1984) 283 SC 369, 322 SE2d 667—§ 4
Anonymous Member of The South Carolina Bar, In re (1991) 304 SC 342, 404 SE2d 513—§ 4
Warner, In re (1985) 286 SC 459, 335 SE2d 90—§ 4

TENNESSEE

Cleckner v Dale (1986, Tenn App) 719 SW2d 535—§ 4

*Statutes, rules, regulations, and constitutional provisions bearing on the subject of the annotation are included in this table only to the extent, and in the form, that they are reflected in the court opinions discussed in this annotation. The reader should consult the appropriate statutory or regulatory compilations to ascertain the current status of relevant statutes, rules, regulations, and constitutional provisions.

For federal cases involving state law, see state headings.

Warning that statutes, administrative regulations and constitutional provisions used may not be only one's dealing with subject

FIGURE 3-6 (continued)

Explains what annotatiaon covers

Lists other American Law Reports annotations to consult

Summary of annotation

VIRGINIA

Gunter v Virginia State Bar (1989) 238 Va 617, 385 SE2d 597—§ 4

32 ALR5th ATTORNEYS—SOUND RECORDINGS § 1[b]

§ 1. Preliminary Matters

[a] Scope

This annotation collects and analyzes those state cases in which courts have decided the propriety of an attorney's[1] surreptitious sound recording of statements by others who are or may become involved in litigation.

A number of jurisdictions may have rules, regulations, constitutional provisions, or legislative enactments directly bearing upon this subject. These provisions are discussed herein only to the extent and in the form that they are reflected in the court opinions that fall within the scope of this annotation. The reader is consequently advised to consult the appropriate statutory or regulatory compilations to ascertain the current status of all statutes discussed herein, including those listed in the Jurisdictional Table of Cited Statutes and Cases.

[b] Related annotations

Appointment of counsel for attorney facing disciplinary charges. 86 ALR4th 1071.

Propriety of attorney's resignation from bar in light of pending or potential disciplinary action. 54 ALR4th 264.

Eavesdropping on extension telephone as invasion of privacy. 49 ALR4th 430.

Propriety of governmental eavesdropping on communications between accused and his attorney. 44 ALR4th 841.

Construction and application of state statutes authorizing civil cause of action by person whose wire or oral communication is intercepted, disclosed, or used in violation of statutes. 33 ALR4th 506.

Permissible warrantless surveillance, under state communications interception statute, by state or local law enforcement officer or one acting in concert with officer. 27 ALR4th 449.

Permissible surveillance, under state communications interception statute, by person other than state or local law enforcement officer or one acting in concert with officer. 24 ALR4th 1208.

Admissibility and necessity of expert evidence as to standards of practice and negligence in malpractice action against attorney. 14 ALR4th 170.

Admissibility, in criminal prosecution, of evidence obtained by electronic surveillance of prisoner. 57 ALR3d 172.

Investigations and surveillance, shadowing and trailing, as violation of right of privacy. 13 ALR3d 1025.

Eavesdropping as violating right of privacy. 11 ALR3d 1296.

What constitutes an "interception" of a telephone or similar communication forbidden by the Federal Communications Act (47 USCS § 605) or similar state statutes. 9 ALR3d 423.

§ 2. Summary and comment

An attorney may be disciplined for actions that contravene the ethics of the profession even though his conduct is neither criminal nor calculated to obstruct justice.[2] However, it has been held that an attorney will not be disbarred soley because he fails to live up to the ideals of the canons of ethics of a bar association.[3]

With regard to the propriety of an attorney's surreptitious sound recording of statements by others who are or may become involved in litigation, three Mississippi courts have held that an attorney did not act improperly in recording conversations with other

1. Excluded are cases involving district attorneys, federal agents, or state or local law enforcement officials acting as agents of prosecuting attorneys.

2. 7 Am Jur 2d, Attorneys at Law § 60.

3. 7 Am Jur 2d, Attorneys at Law § 60.

FIGURE 3-6 (continued)

individuals without their knowledge or consent (§ 3), although a number of other jurisdictions have held such conduct by an attorney to be improper (§ 4).

32 ALR5th ATTORNEYS—SOUND RECORDINGS § 3

§ 3. Surreptitious tape recording held proper

The courts in the following cases held, under the particular facts and circumstances presented, that it was not improper for an attorney to surreptitiously tape record a conversation with another individual.[4]

According to the court in Netterville v Mississippi State Bar (1981, Miss) 397 So 2d 878, an appeal of a private reprimand by the State Bar, where an attorney tape recorded a telephone conversation without informing the party being taped, his actions, when considered within the context of the circumstances, did not constitute dishonesty, fraud, deceit or misrepresentation, in violation of ABA Formal Op. 337, which proscribed the taping of conversations, since the information requested by the attorney, consisting of names and addresses, was of such a nature as reasonably to import to the party being called, the probability, if not certainty, that it would be taken down in some manner for future use.

In Attorney M v Mississippi Bar (1992, Miss) 621 So 2d 220, 32 ALR5th 891, an attorney disciplinary proceeding, the court held that, under certain circumstances, an attorney may tape a conversation with a potential party opponent without his knowledge or consent. An attorney taped two telephone conversations with a doctor who had treated a patient who later became a plaintiff in a malpractice action against another physician. Although the doctor testified that he assumed the conversations were taped, he did not know until he received a letter so indicating from the attorney. The court found that the attorney's conduct did not violate the ABA Code of Professional Responsibility, DR 1-102(A)(4), as interpreted by ABA Formal Op. 337, which proscribes the making of recordings without the prior knowledge or consent of all the parties. The court adopted a broader rule than that of the Bar, holding that surreptitious tape recording is not unethical when the information requested by the attorney is of such nature as reasonably to import to the person called the probability, if not certainty, that it would be taken down in some manner for future use, and the attorney's action, "considered within the context of the circumstances then existing, does not rise to the level of dishonesty, fraud, deceit or misrepresentation." The court concluded, in the case at bar, that, where the express purpose of each telephone call was to obtain a statement from the doctor concerning the physical condition of his client upon leaving the doctor's care; the information was of such a nature as reasonably to import to the doctor that it would be taken down for future use; the doctor admittedly assumed he was being taped; and, during one of the conversations, the attorney expressly stated that he wished to record the statement; and there was no indication that the attorney planned to use the recordings for any improper use, the attorney's actions were not violative of the rules of professional conduct.[5]

Also, according to the court in Mississippi Bar v Attorney ST (1993, Miss) 621 So 2d 229, an attorney disciplinary proceeding, an attorney who surreptitiously tape recorded telephone conversations with a city judge and the chief of police while representing a client whose civil rights he believed were being abused, did not act unethically, however, where the attorney untruthfully denied to one of the parties who was taped

4. Some bar associations have also issued formal opinions holding that, under certain circumstances, with various limitations, surreptitious sound recording by an attorney of a conversation is permissible, including: Arizona State Bar, Opinion No. 90-2; Idaho State Bar, Opinion No. 130 (1990); Kentucky Bar Association, Opinion No. E-279 (1984); New York City Bar Association, Opinion No. 80–95; Tennessee Board of Professional Responsibility, Opinion No. 81-F-14 (1986); Utah State Bar, Opinion No. 90.

5. For earlier cases, holding, in dicta, that surreptitious tape recording of telephone conversations by an attorney was improper, See: National Life & Acci. Ins. Co. v Miller (1985, Miss) 484 So 2d 329, app dismd 486 US 1027, 100 L Ed 2d 596, 108 S Ct 2007 and (criticized on other grounds by Shaw v Shaw (Miss) 603 So 2d 287), and J. C. Penney Co. v Blush (1978, Miss) 356 So 2d 590.

FIGURE 3-6 (continued)

that he was, in fact tape recording the conversation, the attorney was subject to private reprimand. The court stated that, under certain circumstances, an attorney may tape a

conversation with a potential party opponent without his knowledge or consent, and that surreptitiously tape recording a conversation is not unethical when the act, considered within the context of the circumstances then existing, does not rise to the level of dishonesty, fraud, deceit or misrepresentation. The court concluded that, looking at the context of the circumstances, the attorney was acting to protect his client's interests in surreptitiously tape recording his telephone conversations with the the judge and the police chief. However, where the attorney, when asked by the police chief if he was recording their conversation, denied so doing, the court held that the attorney violated the Mississippi Rules of Professional Conduct. Rule 4.1, which requires that a lawyer be truthful when dealing with others on a client's behalf, thereby warranting a private reprimand.

§ 4. Surreptitious tape recording held improper

According to the courts in the following cases, it was improper for an attorney to make a surreptitious tape recording of a conversation with another individual, under the particular facts and circumstances presented.[6]

An indictment charging an attorney with unlawfully recording a confidential communication without permission of both parties to the conversation, pursuant to Cal Code Penal Code § 632 was upheld by the court in People v Wyrick (1978, 3rd Dist) 77 Cal App 3d 903, 144 Cal Rptr 38. The attorney tape recorded an entire conversation with a physician who had refused to accept the attorney as a patient and who had refused to assist the attorney in settling a personal injury case. The court held that the attorney did not inform the physician that he was taping the conversation or obtain his permission to record the conversation, thus, the grand jury properly held that the attorney violated the statute prohibiting the recording by one party of a confidential telephone conversation without the other party's knowledge and consent. The court noted that the subjective expectation of the parties that the subject matter of the conversation was to be confidential was irrelevant to a determination of whether the evidence supported the indictment for the offense, since the statute proscribes taping of "any communication," without knowledge or consent of both parties, regardless of the content.

The court in People v Selby (1979) 198 Colo 386, 606 P2d 45, held that an attorney who surreptitiously tape recorded a conference between himself, the district attorney, and the judge in chambers was guilty of misconduct. The court stated, a lawyer may not secretly record any conversation he has with another lawyer or person, that candor is required between attorneys and judges, and that surreptitious recording suggests trickery and deceit. The court added, particularly reprehensible is the unauthorized recording of the private, informal discussions with a judge in chambers. The court concluded that the attorney's conduct, inter alia, violated the ABA Code of Professional Responsibility DR 1-102(A)(6), providing that an attorney shall not "engage in conduct involving dishonesty, fraud, deceit or misrepresentation."

Also, in People v Wallin (1981, Colo) 621 P2d 330, the court held that an attorney who surreptitiously tape recorded a telephone conversation with a witness to an offense with which his client was charged, was guilty of unethical conduct, in violation, inter alia, of the ABA Code of Professional Conduct, DR 1-102(A)(4) which proscribes conduct by an attorney "involving dishonesty, fraud, and deceit."

An attorney who surreptitiously tape recorded conversations with former clients in cooperation with a state drug investigation, soliciting a drug sale by one of the clients,

6. Several bar associations have also issued formal opinions which have taken the position that an attorney may not surreptitiously make a sound recording of a conversation, including: Alabama Bar Association, Opinion No. 84-22; Dallas Bar Association, Opinion No. 1981-5; Hawaii Disciplinary Board, Opinion No. 30 (1988); Idaho State Bar Opinion No. 130 (1990); Minnesota Professional Responsibility Board, Opinion No. 3 (1986).

FIGURE 3-6 (continued)

in exchange for leniency in the face of pending drug charges against himself, violated the ABA Code of Professional Responsibility, DR 1-102(A)(4), prohibiting conduct

involving dishonesty, fraud, deceit, or misrepresentation, according to the court in People v Smith (1989, Colo) 778 P2d 685. The court stated, while the attorney no longer represented the former clients, the conduct of the client probably would not have occurred had the attorney not relied upon the trust and confidence placed in him by the former client as a result of the recently completed attorney-client relationship between the two. The court added, the undisclosed use of a recording device necessarily involves elements of deception and trickery which do not comport with the high standards of candor and fairness to which all attorneys are bound. The court rejected the attorney's argument that his conduct should be deemed an exception to the ethical proscription against covert tape recordings, since he was acting under the direction of and pursuant to the advice of law enforcement officials in pursuit of their professional responsibilities, holding that the attorney was a private attorney, not a prosecutor, and that any policy considerations which may justify prosecutors' reliance on techniques such as tape recording of conversations did not apply to private counsel, so as to permit him to deal dishonestly and deceitfully with clients, former clients, and others.

Similarly, an attorney who wore a concealed microphone to record a conversation with a friend and former client, in order to obtain information for a government drug case in exchange for leniency in his own drug prosecution was misconduct warranting suspension, according to the court in Committee on Professional Ethics & Conduct of Iowa State Bar Ass'n v Mollman (1992, Iowa) 488 NW2d 168. The court held that, even absent an attorney-client relationship, the attorney violated, inter alia, the Iowa Code of Professional Responsibility, advisory opinion 83-16, which provides that "no lawyer should record any conversation whether by tapes or other electronic device, without the consent or prior knowledge of all parties to the conversation," modelled after the ABA Formal Opinion 337, which makes such recordings unethical even if legal under federal law. The court rejected the attorney's contention that an exception to the ABA opinion, permitting government prosecutors to make tape recordings of private conversations under "extraordinary circumstances," applied, since, in his case, the attorney was not a government agent or prosecutor, but a private citizen, when he made the recordings. The court likewise rejected the argument that the attorney cooperated with the government as a private citizen, not as an attorney, and thus, the code of professional responsibility should not apply to his conduct, since the attorney was able to draw incriminating statements out of his friend because their conversations centered on the legal implications of the way they had pooled their resources to purchase and share drugs in the past, and the friend looked to the attorney for guidance, if not legal advice.

According to the court in In re An Anonymous Member of the South Carolina Bar (1984) 283 SC 369, 322 SE2d 667, an attorney who, while representing a family member for the purpose of investigating an auto accident, telephoned the driver of the other vehicle, who was not represented by counsel, telling him that he was the injured driver's cousin, but not that he was an attorney, and secretly recorded the telephone conversation, was guilty of misconduct. The court stated that, pursuant to Formal Op. 337 of the ABA, a lawyer's secret recording of a conversation constitutes professional misconduct, warranting private reprimand.

An attorney who participated in a scheme with a client whom he represented in a divorce action to entrap and secretly record a family court judge by having an investigator place a tape recording device in a brief case, which the client carried to her conference with the judge, was guilty of misconduct, in violation of the ABA Code of Professional Responsibility DR 1-102, which provides that a lawyer shall not "engage in conduct involving dishonesty, fraud, deceit or misrepresentation," according to the court in In re Warner (1985) 286 SC 459, 335 SE2d 90. The court stated that attorneys may not participate in any manner in the furtive recording of judges in their chambers,

FIGURE 3-6 (continued)

and it is equally reprehensible and impermissible for an attorney to secretly record another attorney or, indeed, another person.

32 ALR5th ATTORNEYS—SOUND RECORDINGS § 4

The court in In re Anonymous Member of The South Carolina Bar (1991) 304 SC 342, 404 SE2d 513, later proceeding 308 SC 114, 417 SE2d 526, held that an attorney may not record a conversation of any person without the prior knowledge and consent of all the parties to the conversation. The court stated that this rule applied, irrespective of the purpose for which such recordings were made, the intent of the parties to the conversation, whether anything of a confidential nature was discussed, and whether any party gained an unfair advantage from the recordings.

In Cleckner v Dale (1986, Tenn App) 719 SW2d 535, a legal malpractice action against an attorney retained to represent the buyers in a real estate transaction, the court held that the attorney, who tape recorded a telephone conversation with his client, violated the ABA Code of Professional Responsibility, DR 1-102(A)(4), as interpreted by ABA Formal Op. 337, which proscribed tape recording any private conversation without the consent or prior knowledge of all parties to the conversation, and Tenn. Formal Op. 81-F-14, which prohibited an attorney's use against a client of a clandestine recording of a conversation with the client.

An attorney who authorized wiretapping of conversations of the wife of a client whom he was advising with respect to domestic difficulties engaged in "conduct involving dishonesty, fraud, or deceit" within the meaning of the ABA Code of Professional Responsibility, DR 1-102(A)(4), the court in Gunter v Virginia State Bar (1989) 238 Va 617, 385 SE2d 597, held. The court stated that the attorney's action was more than a departure from the standards of fairness and candor which characterize the traditions of professionalism, but was deceitful conduct, warranting suspension of the attorney's license.

Consult POCKET PART in the volume for later cases

Note reminds the researcher to consult the pocket part for supplementary information

parts of other sources in the law library that could be profitably consulted in further research.

The first two sections of the body of the annotation contain introductory material. Section 1[a] *Scope* identifies the issue covered in the annotation. Section 1[b] *Related annotations* lists other ALR annotations covering related issues. Section 2 *Summary and comment* briefly summarizes the information covered in the remainder of the annotation. The remainder of the annotation reviews cases concerning the issue that is the subject of the annotation, with the cases being organized around their facts and holdings. For example, for the annotation in figure 3-6, section 3 is entitled *Surreptitious tape recording held proper* and section 4 is entitled *Surreptitious tape recording held improper.* Thus, section 3 discusses cases allowing attorney tape recording and section 4 discusses cases not allowing attorney tape recording.

The annotation in figure 3-6 is supplemented by material in the pocket part and contains the following note at the end of the annotation: *Consult POCKET PART in the volume for later cases.* This annotation is one of the shorter ALR annotations, with most other annotations being longer.

Use of American Law Reports

The same cautions given about legal encyclopedias apply to American Law Reports. An annotation is a summary of the law and may not contain enough detail for your research. Be sure to review the cases cited in the annotation rather than relying on the annotation. The emphasis in the annotations is on case law, so do not omit statutory research. Never assume that the cases cited in the annotation—even in the pocket part to the annotation—are the most recent available. Use the cases cited in the annotation as starting points and use citators to locate more recent ones (see chapter 6).

Do not rely on the annotation as an accurate explanation of the law. The law may have changed since the annotation was written.

Generally, in legal writing, you would not quote from or refer to an ALR annotation because ALR annotations are not the law. They contain only the

SUBJECT OF ANNOTATION

Beginning on page 715

Propriety of attorney's surreptitious sound recording of statements by others who are or may become involved in litigation

ATTORNEY M

v

MISSISSIPPI BAR

Supreme Court of Mississippi

July 1, 1992

621 So 2d 220, 32 ALR5th 891

SUMMARY OF DECISION

An attorney representing a client with a potential malpractice claim against two physicians, who consecutively attempted to manipulate her dislocated shoulder back into its socket without realizing that she had sustained fractures therein, called the first physician, who did not have the benefit of X-rays clearly revealing the fractures, and in the course of conversations which were tape-recorded without the physician's knowledge or consent, informed the physician that he "didn't do anything wrong," but that the attorney might be forced to name him as a co-defendant in a malpractice action against the second physician unless he was willing to make a statement declaring that the client left his care in the same condition in which she arrived. Following a complaint filed by the recorded physician, and a hearing in which the physician admitted to assuming that his statements to the attorney were being recorded, an administrative tribunal found that by surreptitiously recording the physician, the attorney violated provisions of the Mississippi Code of Professional Conduct prohibiting a lawyer from engaging in conduct involving dishonesty, fraud, deceit, or

The annotation concerning this case begins on page 715 of this volume

Title of related annotation

FIGURE 3-7 First Page of Sample Case from American Law Reports.

publisher's interpretation of the law. It is preferable to refer to the primary source itself.

In summary, American Law Reports are best used:

1. To find primary authority; and
2. To give the researcher general background information.

Figure 3-8 provides useful tips on utilizing American Law Reports. For information on how to make American Law Reports a part of your research strategy, see chapter 7.

Citation to American Law Reports

Caveat: Do not assume that the legal citations found when researching are in correct citation form. Citations, even those included in cases may or may not comply with the citation rules your professor has asked you to use. Always check your citations against the appropriate citation rule for correct form.

FIGURE 3-8 Tips on Using American Law Reports.

Do—

1. use footnotes to locate relevant primary authority.
2. pull and read primary authority.
3. check pocket parts, Later Case Service, or ALR Bluebook for recent information.
4. update information found.

Do not—

1. rely on a American Law Reports alone as an accurate statement of the law.
2. generally cite to American Law Reports.

FIGURE 3-9 American Law Reports Citation.

Marjorie A. Caner, Annotation, *Propriety of Attorney's Surreptitious Sound Recording of Statements by Others Who Are or May Become Involved in Litigation,* 32 A.L.R. 5th 715 (1995).

Figure 3-9 is the proper citation for the annotation entitled *Propriety of Attorney's Surreptitious Sound Recording of Statements by Others Who Are or May Become Involved in Litigation* beginning on page 715 of volume 32 of American Law Reports Fifth Series, copyright 1995. The title of the annotation is fairly descriptive of the scope of the annotation. The case published in American Law Reports, which serves as a springboard for the annotation, is *Attorney M v. Mississippi Bar,* 621 So. 2d 220 (Miss. 1992).

The citation to an annotation from American Law Reports Federal would be similar in form except for substituting "A.L.R. Fed." for "A.L.R. 5th."

ATTORNEY GENERAL OPINIONS

The United States Attorney General is the chief law enforcement officer of the federal government and heads the United States Department of Justice. The Attorney General is the country's legal representative and gives opinions when requested by the President or heads of departments within the executive branch. Attorney General opinions are published in Official Opinions of the Attorneys General, containing opinions beginning with 1789. Few opinions of the Attorney General have been published in recent years. The following is an excerpt from an opinion of the Attorney General.

United States Attorney General

NATIONAL FLAG OF THE UNITED STATES.

May 15, 1925.

The placing of a fringe of the national flag, the dimensions of the flag and the arrangement of the stars in the union are matters of detail not controlled by statute, but are within the discretion of the President as Commander-in-Chief of the Army and Navy.

The desecration or improper use of the national flag outside the District of Columbia has not been made a Federal offense. This matter has been left to the States for action, but should Congress wish to assume such control it has the power under the Constitution to do so.

To the PRESIDENT.

SIR:

I am in receipt of a letter from the late President Harding, dated February 15, 1923, requesting from my predecessor then in office an opinion defining precisely what is the National Flag of the United States, and what official action is proper in order to preserve the flag from desecration. Accompanying this letter is a petition from officers of the Military Order of the Loyal Legion requesting the President to obtain such an opinion.

The only statute now in force which defines the flag or regulates its design is the Act of April 4, 1818, chapter 34 (3 Stat. 415), reenacted as sections 1791 and 1792 of the Revised Statutes of the United States. Section 1791 provides that 'the flag of the United States shall be thirteen horizontal stripes, alternate red and white; and the union of the flag shall be thirty-seven stars, white in a blue field.'

> Section 1792 provides that 'on the admission of a new State into the Union one star shall be added to the union of the flag; and such addition shall take effect on the fourth day of July then next succeeding such admission . . . . The effect of the two sections is that the number of stars now prescribed is forty-eight (48).
>
> . . .

The Office of Legal Counsel within the United States Department of Justice drafts Attorney General opinions requested by the President and heads of departments within the executive branch. In addition, the Office of Legal Counsel issues written opinions requested by the President's office and various governmental agencies. These opinions are published in the Opinions of the Office of Legal Counsel of the Department of Justice, containing opinions beginning with 1977. The following is an excerpt of an opinion from the Office of Legal Counsel.

> Office of Legal Counsel
>
> U.S. Department of Justice
>
> Constitutional Law—Fourth Amendment Interception of Oral Communications—Legality of Television Surveillance in Government Offices
>
> February 2, 1979
>
> MEMORANDUM OPINION FOR THE ATTORNEY GENERAL
>
> This responds to your request for our opinion concerning the legality of using concealed television cameras for surveillance in buildings owned by or leased to the Government, where the Government officer occupying the particular space has consented to the surveillance.
>
> While existing statutes govern certain aspects of television surveillance, no statute specifically regulates the surveillance for law enforcement purposes. The requirements of Title III of the Omnibus Crime Control and Safe Streets Act of 1968, 18 U.S.C. S 2510 et seq., would apply if a television device intercepts an oral communication 'uttered by a person exhibiting an expectation that such communication is not subject to interception under circumstances justifying such expectation.' 18 U.S.C. S 2510(2). In the area of foreign intelligence and foreign counterintelligence, the recently enacted Foreign Intelligence Surveillance Act of 1978 specifically encompasses television surveillance 'under circumstances in which a person has a reasonable expectation of privacy and a warrant would be required for law enforcement purposes.' 50 U.S.C. S 1801(b)(4). That Act generally requires that any such surveillance undertaken for foreign intelligence purposes be authorized by judicial order.
>
> . . .

Each state has an attorney general that performs a similar function as chief law enforcement officer for the state. The state attorneys general also issue written opinions. For example, in 1996 an Illinois state's attorney asked the Illinois Attorney General

> whether a person in police custody may be deemed to have consented to the recording of his or her conversation, for purposes of the Illinois eavesdropping statutes, when a law enforcement officer notifies the individual that his or her comments are being recorded and places the tape-recorder in full view, and, thereafter, the person continues to make unsolicited comments and statements.

The Illinois Attorney General opined that the person's consent might be inferred from the circumstances.

Citations to attorneys general opinions

Caveat: Do not assume that the legal citations found when researching are in correct citation form. Citations, even those included in cases may or may not comply with the citation rules your professor has asked you to use. Always check your citations against the appropriate citation rule for correct form.

Figure 3-10 contains sample citations to opinions of the United States Attorneys General and to the Office of Legal Counsel of the Department of Justice.

RESTATEMENTS OF THE LAW

The American Law Institute publishes ***Restatements of the Law***. The American Law Institute was founded in 1923 to "restate" or, in other words, to summarize major legal principles. Members of the American Law Institute are eminent legal scholars, judges, and attorneys. The American Law Institute aimed:

> To present an orderly restatement of the general common law of the United States, including in that term

FIGURE 3-10 Citations to Opinions of the United States Attorney General and to the Department of Justice's Office of Legal Counsel.

Official Opinions of the Attorneys General of the United States	34 Op.Atty. Gen. 483 (1925).
Opinions of the Office of Legal Counsel of the Department of Justice	3 Op. Off. Legal Counsel 64 (1979).

> not only the law developed solely by judicial decision, but also the law that has grown from the application by the courts of statutes that were generally enacted and were in force for many years.

The principles of law in the restatements often summarize the existing law; the principles of law are viewed by some as forward-thinking statements of what an enlightened court would do. Although a secondary source, the restatements have been highly persuasive in many of the cases citing to the restatements.

The following procedure was followed in preparing each restatement. The American Law Institute selected an accepted and well-known authority, called a "Reporter" to write a first draft of each restatement. The Reporter met with an advisory group of other recognized experts in the field (individually called "Advisors") who discussed and made recommendations concerning the draft. The draft was then submitted to the Council of the Institute and submitted for discussion and approval to the members of the Institute at a series of annual meetings.

Restatements have been published in the following specific areas of law:

Topic	Series
Agency	(First, Second)
Conflict of Laws	(First, Second)
Contracts	(First, Second)
Law of the Foreign Relations Law of the U.S.	(First, Second, Third)
Judgments	(First, Second)
Law Governing Lawyers	(First, Second, Third)
Property	(First, Second, Third)
Restitution	(First)
Security	(First)
Suretyship and Guaranty (superceding Security)	(First, Second, Third)
Torts	(First, Second, Third)
Trusts	(First, Second, Third)
Unfair Competition	(First, Second, Third)

Each restatement is divided into chapters, with the chapters divided into sections. The sections are numbered continuously throughout the restatement. Each section first contains a statement of a rule of law. The rule of law is followed by explanatory comments, with some comments followed by illustrations of the application of a comment. Reporter's Notes generally follow the comments or are included in an appendix. The Notes provide background information on the development of the section. An appendix contains summaries of and citations to cases citing the restatement. Cumulative annual pocket parts and supplements and semiannual interim citations pamphlets update the restatements.

Citations to Restatements

Caveat: Do not assume that the legal citations found when researching are in correct citation form. Citations, even those included in cases may or may not comply with the citation rules your professor has asked you to use. Always check your citations against the appropriate citation rule for correct form.

Figure 3-11 contains sample citations to section 1 of the Restatement (second) of contracts. The first citation is to section 1 and the second citation is to the illustration appearing in comment e of section 1.

TREATISES

Treatises are another legal resource. In the case excerpt on the following page, the court chastised the attorney for neglecting to consult available treatises.

Restatement (Second) of Contracts § 1 (1981).

Restatement (Second) of Contracts § 1 cmt. e, illus. 1 (1981).

FIGURE 3-11 Citations to the Restatements.

The Idaho Supreme Court suspended attorney Tway from the practice of law for five years based on various acts, including his failure to adequately research the statute of limitations on a section 1983 civil rights claim. The court stated:

Other than reviewing the annotations under section 5-218 of the Idaho Code, Tway had not consulted any of the Section 1983 treatises which he had in his office and had not Shepardized the cases he relied on regarding the statute of limitations before filing the claim. After learning from opposing counsel that the claim was governed by a two-year rather than a three-year statute of limitations, the record does not reveal whether Tway conducted any further research regarding the issue. The case was dismissed for inaction in January of 1993. . . . His reliance on a single case, without assuring the accuracy of the case, was not reasonable. *In re Tway*, 919 P.2d 323, 325, 327, 328 (Idaho 1996).

The treatise is a work, often multivolume, generally covering a single field of law and written by one or more legal scholars. The treatise contains text, explaining the field in detail, supported by citation to relevant authority. Like the legal encyclopedia, lengthy footnotes to the treatise text furnish the researcher citations to relevant cases. The treatise treatment of a topic is much more in depth than the treatment of the topic in a legal encyclopedia. Some treatises intended for the practitioner may contain relevant forms.

A treatise may be published in hardbound volumes, in loose-leaf binders or in paper bound pamphlets. The treatise usually has a table of contents, an index, and a table of cases. Hardbound treatises are usually updated with pocket parts; looseleaf publications are updated by newsletter-type supplements or by pages to be interfiled amongst the existing pages.

For example, the treatise *Wiretapping and Eavesdropping (Second Edition)*, written by Clifford S. Fishman and Anne T. McKenna, is published in two looseleaf binders. The treatise is updated annually with new pages and with cumulative paper pamphlet supplements. The new pages are filed among already-existing pages, often in the place of older pages, which are removed. The cumulative supplements are filed inside the back cover of the second ring binder. Figure 3-12 contains a page from the treatise concerning the statutory definition of "oral communication."

Citation to a treatise

Caveat: Do not assume that the legal citations found when researching are in correct citation form. Citations, even those included in cases may or may not comply with the citation rules your professor has asked you to use. Always check your citations against the appropriate citation rule for correct form.

Figure 3-13 contains a sample citation to section 2:15 of the treatise shown in figure 3-12.

LEGAL DICTIONARIES

The two major **legal dictionaries** used in the United States are Black's Law Dictionary and Ballentine's Law Dictionary. Each is a single volume and provides definitions to legal terms and their pronunciation (if necessary), with citations to relevant case law. Figure 3-14 contains the definition of "eavesdropping" from Black's Law Dictionary. Figure 3-15 contains a sample citation to figure 3-14.

FIGURE 3-12 A Page from a Treatise.

consents.[63] Where one or more participants to the conversation is clearly on notice that it is being monitored, however, that participant's use of the phone is often taken as implied consent to the monitoring.[64]

III. "ORAL COMMUNICATION"

§ 2:15 Statutory definition of oral communication

18 U.S.C.A. § 2510(2) provides:

> "oral communication" means any oral communication uttered by a person exhibiting an expectation that such communication is not subject to interception under circumstances justifying such expectation, but such term does not include any electronic communication, . . . [65]

The Electronic Communications Privacy Act of 1986 added the language following the comma to make it clear that "an oral communication is one carried by sound waves, not by an electronic medium."[66] Radio communications therefore are not to be analyzed in privacy terms to determine if they are oral communications.[67] Thus, an "oral communication" is a conversation unaided by any technology.

§ 2:16 Expectation of non-interception

18 U.S.C.A. § 2510(2) defines oral communications as being worthy of such protection only if "uttered by a person exhibiting an expectation that such communication is not subject to interception under circumstances justifying such expectation." If a person lacks such an

[63]See Anthony v. U.S., 667 F.2d 870, 876–877, (10th Cir. 1981); See also U.S. v. San Martin, 469 F.2d 5 (2d Cir. 1972); Sarno v. State, 424 So. 2d 829, 834 (Fla. Dist. Ct. App. 3d Dist. 1982).

[64]See § 6:42, subheading c. But see PBA Local No. 38 v. Woodbridge Police Dept., 832 F. Supp. 808, 818–819 (D.N.J. 1993), in which police officers sued their department for allegedly tapping and bugging their private conversations; the court held that, because plaintiffs did not evince a reasonable expectation of privacy as to wire communications, a cause of action existed as to conversations taped over telephone lines which emitted a beep audible to the users every five seconds. (The opinion does not discuss the issue of implied consent; perhaps defendants did not assert the defense.)

[65]"Electronic communication" is defined in 18 U.S.C.A. § 2510(12). See § 3:2.

[66]Senate Rpt. No. 99-541 at 13, reprinted in 1986 US Code, Cong & Admin News 3555, 3567.

[67]Id. Nevertheless, a few state courts, applying their own substantially identical statutes, have held that the radio transmissions from a cordless telephone are in fact "oral communications." State v. Mozo, 655 So. 2d 1115 (Fla. 1995); State v. Bidinost, 71 Ohio St. 3d 449, 644 N.E.2d 318 (1994).

FIGURE 3-13 Citation to a Treatise.

Clifford S. Fishman & Anne T. McKenna, Wiretapping and Eavesdropping § 2:15 (2d Ed. 1995).

Words and Phrases is a multivolume judicial legal dictionary. It is classified as a judicial legal dictionary because the definitions come from judicial opinions. The defined words and phrases are arranged in alphabetical order, with each word or phrase followed by paragraphs summarizing the way in which the word or phrase was defined in cases. Each summary paragraph ends with the corresponding case citation. *Words and Phrases* is updated by pocket parts. Figures 3-16 and 3-17 contain pages from the hardbound volume and pocket part of *Words and Phrases* defining "eavesdropping." The pocket part also defines "eavesdropping device."

Many digests include *Words and Phrases* volumes. Each word or phrase listed in those volumes is followed by citations to cases in which the word or phrase was defined.

529 **ecclessiastical authorities**

required to write a solar easement containing highly detailed, technical information often included in these easements." Sandy F. Kraemer, *Solar Law* 42 (1978).

timber easement. An easement that permits the holder to cut and remove timber from another's property.

easement appurtenant. See EASEMENT.

easement by estoppel. See EASEMENT.

easement by necessity. See EASEMENT.

easement in gross. See EASEMENT.

easement of convenience. See EASEMENT.

easement of natural support. See *lateral support* under SUPPORT.

Easter-offerings. *Eccles. law.* Small sums of money paid as personal tithes to the parochial clergy by the parishioners at Easter. • Under the Recovery of Small Tithes Act (1695), Easter-offerings were recoverable before justices of the peace. St. 7 & 8 Will. 3, ch. 6. — Also termed *Easter-dues.*

Easter sittings. *English law.* A term of court beginning on April 15 of each year and usu. ending on May 8, but sometimes extended to May 13. • This was known until 1875 as *Easter term.* Cf. HILARY SITTINGS; MICHAELMAS SITTING.

East Greenwich (eest **gren**-ich). *Hist.* The name of a royal manor in the county of Kent, England. • Historically, this manor was mentioned in royal grants or patents as descriptive of the tenure of free socage.

East India Company. *Hist.* The company that was originally established to pursue exclusive trade between England and India, and that later became more active in political affairs than in commerce. • In 1858, by the Government of India Act, the government of the company's territories was transferred to the Crown. The company was dissolved in 1874. St. 21 & 22 Vict., ch. 106.

EAT. *abbr.* Earnings after taxes.

eat inde sine die (**ee**-ət **in**-dee **sI**-nee **dI**-ee) [Latin] Let him go thence without day. • These words were used on a defendant's acquittal, or when a prisoner was to be discharged, to signify that the matter be dismissed without any further judicial proceedings. See GO HENCE WITHOUT DAY.

eaves-drip. 1. The dripping of water from the eaves of a house onto adjacent land. **2.** An easement permitting the holder to allow water to drip onto the servient estate. See DRIP RIGHTS; STILLICIDIUM.

eavesdropping. The act of secretly listening to the private conversation of others without their consent. Cf. BUGGING; WIRETAPPING.

ebba et fluctus (**eb**-ə et **flək**-təs), *n.* [Latin "ebb and flow"] *Hist.* The ebb and flow of tide; ebb and flood. • The time of one ebb and flood, plus an additional 40 days, was anciently granted to a person who was excused from court for being beyond seas. See EBB AND FLOW; ESSOIN; BEYOND SEAS.

ebb and flow. The coming in and going out of tide. • This expression was formerly used to denote the limits of admiralty jurisdiction.

ebdomadarius (eb-dom-ə-**dair**-ee-əs), *n.* [Latin "weekly"] *Eccles. law.* An officer in a cathedral church who supervises the regular performance of divine service and prescribes the duties of choir members.

EBIT. *abbr:* Earnings before interest and taxes.

EC. *abbr.* **1.** ETHICAL CONSIDERATION. **2.** European Community. See EUROPEAN UNION.

ecclesia (i-**klee**-z[h]ee-ə), *n.* [Latin "assembly"] **1.** A place of religious worship. **2.** A Christian assembly; a church.

ecclesiarch (i-**klee**-zee-ahrk), *n.* The ruler of a church.

ecclesiastic (i-klee-zee-**as**-tik), *n.* A clergyman; a priest; one consecrated to the service of the church.

ecclesiastical (i-klee-zee-*as*-ti-kəl), *adj.* Of or relating to the church, esp. as an institution. — Also termed *ecclesiastic.*

ecclesiastical authorities. The church's hierarchy, answerable to the Crown, but set apart from the rest of the citizens, responsible for superintending public worship and other religious ceremonies and for administering spiritual counsel and instruction. • In England, the several orders of the clergy are (1) archbishops

FIGURE 3-14 Page from a Treatise.

Black's Law Dictionary 529 (7th Ed. 1999).

FIGURE 3-15 Citation to Treatise.

FIGURE 3-16 Page from the Hardbound Volume of *Words and Phrases.*

EBONY

EAU DE VIE—Cont'd

"spiritus," meaning life. The discovery of the art of distillation belongs to the alchemists, who made it in the course of their investigations after what they called the "elixir vitae," a liquid the discovery of which was to render man immortal. When by distillation they had procured pure alcohol, judging from its effects, they for a time were deluded by the hope that the grand secret had been discovered, and called it "aqua vitae," water of life. Brandy is still so called by the French, "eau de vie." The English, in adopting the name, have taken the word "spiritus" as the root from which to form it, instead of the more common word "vitae." Caswell v. State, 21 Tenn. 402, 403, 2 Humph. 402, 403.

EAVES

Cross References

Building

The "eaves" of a building are the edges of the roof projecting beyond the face of the walls. Proprietors of Center St. Church v. Machias Hotel Co., 51 Me. 413, 414.

EAVESDROPPER

An "eavesdropper" is one who is secretly a listener to conversations between others, and would include a person who merely overheard communications or conversations between a husband and wife. Selden v. State, 42 N.W. 218, 219, 74 Wis. 271, 17 Am.St.Rep. 144.

" 'Eavesdroppers,' or such as listen under walls or windows or the eaves of a house to hearken after discourse and thereupon to frame slanderous mischievous tales," were a nuisance at common law and indictable, and were required, in the discretion of the court, to find sureties for their good behavior. Pavesich v. New England L. Ins. Co., 50 S. E. 68, 71, 122 Ga. 190, 69 L.R.A. 101, 106 Am.St.Rep. 1042, Ann.Cas. 561, quoting and adopting the definitions in 4 Blackstone, 168.

" 'Eavesdroppers' are such as listen under the walls or windows or eaves of houses to hearken to discourse and thereupon proclaim slanderous and mischievous tales." (4 Blk. 168.) Mr. Wharton, in his work on Criminal Law, says of the offense that: "In order to be indictable at common law, it should be habitual, and combine the lurking about dwelling houses and other places where persons meet for private discourse, secretly listening to what is said, and then tattling it abroad." State v. Davis, 51 S.E. 897, 139 N.C. 547, 111 Am.St.Rep. 816.

EAVESDROPPING

"Eavesdropping" consists in privately listening, but not looking or peeping, into the affairs of another. Eavesdropping is an indictable offense in Pennsylvania, but it seems that no prosecution would lie for such offense if it was proved to have been committed either by or under the authority of the husband of the prosecutrix, who was the subject of the offense, there being no law which can prevent a husband from setting a watch on his wife. Commonwealth v. Lovett, Pa., 4 Clark, 5.

Blackstone, defining the offense of "eavesdropping," says: "Eavesdroppers, or such as listen under walls or windows or the eaves of houses, and hearken for discourse, and thereupon frame slanderous and mischievous tales, are a common nuisance." 4 Bl.Comm. 168. Bishop says: "It consists in the nuisance of hanging about the dwelling house of another, hearing tattle, and repeating it, to the disturbance of the neighborhood." State v. Pennington, 40 Tenn. (3 Head) 299, 300, 75 Am.Dec. 771, citing 2 Bish.Cr.Law, 274.

EBB AND FLOW

Ebb and flow is an expression used formerly in this country to denote the limits of admiralty jurisdiction. See, 19 Corpus Juris.

EBONY

The terms "ebony" and "rosewood," as used in Tariff Act July 30, 1846, Schedule B, 9 Stat. 44, providing that manufacturers of ebony and rosewood, etc., should be subject to a duty of 40 per cent. ad valorem, did not mean articles manufactured from ebony and rosewood entirely, but included as well fancy boxes made of common wood, and veneered with rosewood or ebony, invoiced as rosewood and ebony boxes, and known to the trade by those names, and also as fancy boxes and furnishing boxes, it not appearing that there are any articles known as "ebony boxes" or "rosewood boxes" made wholly from those woods. Sill v. Lawrence, C.C.N.Y., Fed.Cas.No.12,850, 1 Blatchf. 605.

FIGURE 3-17 Pages from the Pocket Part Supplement to Volume 14 of *Words and Phrases.*

EAVESDROPPER **14 W&P—60**

privilege, in view of fact that the statement was made in presence of third party; husband, who had not made the statement in a low voice, could not have reasonably believed that the statement would not be overheard by such third party, who was seated next to wife in automobile, and the third party, who had not surreptitiously listened in on the conversation, was not an "eavesdropper." Rules of Evid., Rules 504, 504(a), 504 note.—State v. McMorrow, 314 N.W.2d 287.—Witn 193.

EAVESDROPPING

C.A.6 (Ohio) 1973. There is no "interception" or "eavesdropping" when party to conversation, or third person acting with consent of one of parties to conversation, records that conversation. 18 U.S.C.A. § 2520.—Smith v. Cincinnati Post and Times-Star, 475 F.2d 740, 25 A.L.R. Fed. 755.—Tel 495.

S.D.N.Y. 1966. There was no "eavesdropping" within meaning of section of New York Penal Law provision that person not present during conversation or discussion, who willfully and by means of instrument overhears or records such conversation or discussion without consent of party to such conversation or discussion, is guilty of felony, where federal officers, with consent of client, made recordings of conversations between client and defendant attorney in sheriff's office in jail. Penal Law N.Y. §§ 738 and subd. 2, 739.—U. S. v. Kahn, 251 F.Supp. 702.—Tel 495.

S.D.Ohio 1972. One who was party to telephone conversation was not "eavesdropping" or "wiretapping" when he recorded such conversation. 18 U.S.C.A. §§ 2510(5), (5)(a), 2511(2)(d), 2515.—Smith v. Wunker, 356 F.Supp. 44.—Tel 495.

Cal.App. 4 Dist. 1989. Although Penal Code sections which prohibit wiretapping and eavesdropping envision and describe the use of same or similar equipment to intercept communications, the manner in which such equipment is used is clearly distinguished and mutually exclusive; "wiretapping" is intercepting communications by an unauthorized connection to the transmission line whereas "eavesdropping" is interception of communications by the use of equipment which is not connected to any transmission line. West's Ann.Cal.Penal Code §§ 631(a), 632(a).—People v. Ratekin, 261 Cal. Rptr. 143, 212 C.A.3d 1165, review denied.—Tel 494.1.

Colo.App. 1980. Warrantless monitoring of defendant's conversations with her husband, which took place in jail visiting room while husband was confined in county jail, by jail officials did not violate statute requiring prior court authorization in order for a law enforcement officer to lawfully "engage in any wiretapping or eavesdropping," in that definitions of terms "wiretapping" and "eavesdropping" are synonymous with terms "wire communication" and "oral communication" as defined in statute concerning offenses involving communications, and defendant's conversations were not within statutory definition of a "wire communication" since they did not involve facilities of a common carrier, and they were not within statutory definition of an "oral communication" since there was no justifiable expectation of privacy. C.R.S. 1973, 16-15-101, 16-15-102(9, 10), 18-9-301, 18-9-301(8, 9), 18-9-303, 18-9-304, 18-9-304(1)(a), 18-9-305, 18-9-305(4).—People v. Blehm, 623 P.2d 411, 44 Colo.App. 472.—Tel 511.

Ga.App. 1972. Overhearing of defendant's telephone conversations with another named individual by police officers who were in motel room adjacent to defendant's room did not constitute "eavesdropping" and police officers were not required to seek prior judicial approval for surveillance. Code, §§ 26-3001, 26-3004, 26-3009; 18 U.S.C.A. §§ 2515–2519.—Satterfield v. State, 194 S.E.2d 295, 127 Ga.App. 528.—Tel 494.1.

Ill.App. 2 Dist. 1975. Statute proscribing offense of eavesdropping was enacted to protect individual from interception of communication intended to be private; term "eavesdropping" refers to listening to or recording of those oral statements intended by the declarant to be of private nature, and not merely listening to or recording of any oral communication. S.H.A. ch. 38, § 14-1 et seq.—People v. Klingenberg, 339 N.E.2d 456, 34 Ill.App.3d 705.—Tel 492.

Kan. 1972. Installation or use of an electronic device to record communications transmitted by telephone with consent of person in possession or control of the facilities for such communication does not constitute "eavesdropping" within purview of eavesdropping statute. K.S.A. 21-4001(1)(c).—State v. Wigley, 502 P.2d 819, 210 Kan. 472.—Tel 495.

N.Y.Sup. 1957. As respects the attorney-client privilege with respect to information obtained by "eavesdropping", such was offense of listening under walls or windows or the eaves of a house to harkening after discourse and thereupon frame slanderous and mischievous tales.—In re Lanza, 163 N.Y.S.2d 576, 6 Misc.2d 411, affirmed 164 N.Y.S.2d 534, 4 A.D.2d 252, appeal denied 166 N.Y.S.2d 302, 4 A.D.2d 831.—Witn 206.

FIGURE 3-17 (continued)

EAVESDROPPING

Utah 1978. Where undercover agent consented to procedure whereby the agent's conversation with defendant was transmitted to police officers via an electronic broadcasting unit attached to the agent's body, procedure did not constitute "eavesdropping" for purposes of the statute which defines "eavesdrop" to encompass overhearing, recording or transmitting any part of a communication of another "without the consent of at least one party thereto." (Per Ellett, C. J., with one Justice concurring and two Justices concurring in the result.) U.C.A. 1953, 76-9-401(2).—State v. Boone, 581 P.2d 571.—Tel 493.

EAVESDROPPING DEVICE

Ill.App. 1 Dist. 1990. Radio scanner used to overhear mobile telephone conversation was not "eavesdropping device" under Illinois statute making evidence obtained by means of eavesdropping inadmissible in any civil or criminal trial. S.H.A. ch. 38, ¶¶ 14-1(a), 14-2, 14-5.—People v. Wilson, 143 Ill.Dec. 610, 554 N.E.2d 545, 196 Ill.App.3d 997, appeal denied 149 Ill.Dec. 335, 561 N.E.2d 705, 133 Ill.2d 571, dismissal of post-conviction relief affirmed 240 Ill.Dec. 486, 717 N.E.2d 835.—Crim Law 394.3.

Ill.App. 1 Dist. 1987. In determining whether telephone is an "eavesdropping device" for purposes of applying eavesdropping statute, emphasis must be placed on whether telephone used to overhear conversation is capable, while being so used, of performing its ordinary functions of transmitting as well as receiving sound; when telephone cannot transmit sound while it is being used to receive, it is an illegal "eavesdropping device" regardless of method used to prevent such transmission. S.H.A. ch. 38, ¶¶ 14-1, 14-2, 108A-1, 108A-6; S.H.A. Const. Art. 1, § 6.—People v. Shinkle, 112 Ill.Dec. 463, 513 N.E.2d 1072, 160 Ill.App.3d 1043, appeal allowed 115 Ill.Dec. 407, 517 N.E.2d 1093, 117 Ill.2d 551, reversed 132 Ill.Dec. 432, 539 N.E.2d 1238, 128 Ill.2d 480.—Tel 494.1.

Ill.App. 1 Dist. 1984. A telephone extension is not an "eavesdropping device" as defined by Illinois law.—People v. Jenkins, 84 Ill.Dec. 118, 471 N.E.2d 647, 128 Ill.App.3d 853, appeal denied.—Tel 493.

Ill.App. 1 Dist. 1978. A camera is not an "eavesdropping device" within purview of eavesdropping statute because it is not capable of being used to hear or to record conversation. S.H.A. ch. 38, § 14-2.—Cassidy v. American Broadcasting Companies, Inc., 17 Ill.Dec. 936, 377 N.E.2d 126, 60 Ill.App.3d 831.—Tel 494.1.

Ill.App. 1 Dist. 1974. Unaided human ear listening to a telephone on which a conversation is being conducted does not constitute the use of an "eavesdropping device" within meaning of statute prohibiting the use of eavesdropping devices. S.H.A. ch. 38, §§ 14-1(a), 14-2(a).—People v. Giannopoulos, 314 N.E.2d 237, 20 Ill.App.3d 338.—Tel 494.1.

Ill.App. 1 Dist. 1970. Police officer, who obtained defendant's whereabouts by putting his ear to telephone while defendant's girl friend was talking with defendant, was not using an "eavesdropping device" within statute excluding evidence of oral conversation obtained by use of an eavesdropping device without consent of a party thereto. S.H.A. ch. 38, §§ 14-2, 14-5.—People v. Brown, 266 N.E.2d 131, 131 Ill.App.2d 244.—Crim Law 394.3.

Ill.App. 1 Dist. 1968. Apparatus which was placed on earphone of telephone and had extension permitting anyone other than telephone user to hear conversation was "eavesdropping device" within criminal code provision defining such a device as one capable of being used to hear telephone conversation. S.H.A. ch. 38, § 14-1.—People v. Perez, 235 N.E.2d 335, 92 Ill.App.2d 366.—Tel 493.

Ill.App. 2 Dist. 1997. Recording equipment installed on telephone line to police station which was used by officers for personal phone calls was used by police officers in ordinary course of their duties for proper purposes of recording any emergency calls made on line and, thus, was not "eavesdropping device" within meaning of statute defining eavesdropping offense, despite fact that it was unclear whether others officers were notified that line was being recorded, where there was no evidence. that line was taped for any illicit purpose and there was some evidence showing that officers knew that at least some of calls were being taped. S.H.A. 725 ILCS 5/108B-1(h)(1); Ill.Admin. Code title 83, § 725.503(e).—People v. Pitzman, 227 Ill. Dec. 653, 687 N.E.2d 1135, 293 Ill.App.3d 282, rehearing denied, appeal denied 232 Ill.Dec. 456, 698 N.E.2d 547, 177 Ill.2d 581.—Tel 494.1.

Ill.App. 5 Dist. 1983. Motel's switchboard operator did not violate the Illinois eavesdropping statute by overhearing drug-related conversation originating from defendant's room and reporting it to the police, since the switchboard was not an "eavesdropping device"; a prerequisite for criminal liability or exclusion of evidence under the eavesdropping statute is that a device which can hear or record conversations, but not transmit them, must have been used, but the switchboard did not fit this

FIGURE 3-17 (continued)

ECCLESIASTICAL

definition. S.H.A. ch. 38, ¶¶ 14-1 et seq., 14-1(a), 14-2, 14-5.—People v. Bennett, 75 Ill.Dec. 544, 457 N.E.2d 986, 120 Ill.App.3d 144.—Crim Law 394.3; Tel 494.1.

N.Y.Sup. 1996. Pen register with audio function, whether disabled or unused, is functional equivalent of "eavesdropping device," implicating probable cause strictures of statute. McKinney's CPL § 700.15.—People v. Salzarulo, 639 N.Y.S.2d 885, 168 Misc.2d 408.—Tel 521.

ECCLESIASTICAL ABSTENTION

C.A.9 (Wash.) 1987. "Ecclesiastical abstention" provides that civil courts may not redetermine correctness of interpretation of canonical text or some decision relating to government of religious polity; rather, civil courts must accept as given whatever entity decides.—Paul v. Watchtower Bible and Tract Soc. of New York, Inc., 819 F.2d 875, 93 A.L.R. Fed. 737, certiorari denied 108 S.Ct. 289, 484 U.S. 926, 98 L.E.2d 249.—Relig Soc 12(5), 14.

ECCLESIASTICAL ABSTENTION DOCTRINE

Hawai'i 1994. "Ecclesiastical abstention doctrine" embodied in both State and Federal Constitutions barred state court from considering Catholic newspaper publisher's claims against diocese and diocesan officials for defamation, unfair and deceptive acts and practices and monopoly, fraud, clergy malpractice, and negligence, all of which were based on diocese's alleged opposition to views expressed in publisher's newspaper, which opposition purportedly led to publisher's excommunication; each claim required resolution of controversies over church doctrine, law, or polity, which were matters beyond preview of state court. U.S.C.A. Const. Amends. 1, 14; Const. Art. 1, § 4.—O'Connor v. Diocese of Honolulu, 885 P.2d 361, 77 Hawai'i 383, reconsideration denied 889 P.2d 66, 77 Hawai'i 489.—Const Law 84.5(7.1).

LEGAL DIRECTORIES

The ***Martindale-Hubbell Law Directory*** has been published since 1868. It is an annual multivolume directory of attorneys and law firms, also available on CD-ROM and on the Internet. It provides extensive information on attorneys practicing in the United States and more selective coverage on attorneys and law firms in 160 other countries. Attorneys practicing in the United States are listed by city, with cities listed by state and the states arranged in alphabetical sequence. The directory contains biographical information on the attorneys and information on the law firms, such as representative clients and areas of practice. Another feature of the set is the "law digest." The law digest contains brief summaries of the law of all 50 states within the United States and of 75 other countries.

There are numerous other legal directories, including directories of attorneys practicing in a particular field of law or a particular state or region and judicial directories.

FORMBOOKS

Formbooks contain model forms that can be used as a basis in drafting documents. Commericially-prepared formbooks may be comprehensive, covering forms usable in a wide range of areas of practice; other commercially-prepared formbooks may be state-specific or topic-specific or both. A law office or individual attorney may have a file of frequently-used documents usable as forms.

Multivolume comprehensive **formbooks** include American Jurisprudence Legal Forms 2d, American Jurisprudence Pleading and Practice Forms Annotated, Fletcher Corporation Forms Annotated, and West's Legal Forms 2d. Figure 3-18 contains a form for an attorney's legal fee agreement from West's Legal Forms 2d. Formbooks are commonly indexed and checklists accompany many of the forms in formbooks. The careful drafter can use the checklist, modified to fit the particular transaction, to ensure that all relevant provisions are included in the document.

FIGURE 3-18 Pages from West's Legal Forms 2d.

WEST'S®
LEGAL FORMS

SECOND EDITION

VOLUME 24

EMPLOYMENT

AGENCY

SERVICE AGREEMENTS

By

JAMES H. WALZER
of the New Jersey Bar

Sections 1.1 to End
Tables and Index

ST. PAUL, MINN.
WEST PUBLISHING CO.
1986

FIGURE 3-18 (continued)

Ch. 4 ATTORNEY'S LEGAL FEE AGREEMENTS § 4.141

2. SPECIFIC FORMS

§ 4.141 General Format With Alternative Clauses

This agreement, dated ______ 19__, is made

BETWEEN
whose address is
referred to as the "Client",

AND
whose address is
referred to as the "Law Firm."

1. Subject Matter of Agreement.

a. (*First Alternative*) The law firm will represent the client in the following matter (here describe the matter and principal results to be achieved).

a. (*Second Alternative*) The law firm will represent the client in connection with the sale of the client's residence, located at ______.

a. (*Third Alternative*) The law firm will represent the client in the matrimonial dispute between the client and the client's spouse. Some of the issues which may be involved include grounds for divorce, custody of children, visitation of children, payments for alimony or child support, settlement of property rights between the parties, and the payment of counsel fees and costs.

a. (*Fourth Alternative*) The law firm will represent the client in the client's capacity as the executor or administrator of the estate of ______, who formerly resided at ______ and is referred to as the Deceased. The law firm will help the client to become appointed administrator or executor of the estate of the deceased and will guide the client with respect to carrying out the many functions of that office.

a. (*Fifth Alternative*) The law firm will represent the client with respect to the client's claim for injuries or damages suffered as a result of a certain automobile accident which took place on or about ______ 19__, in the town of ______ in the state of ______. The law firm will pursue the claim of the client with respect to those who may be responsible for the injuries or damages.

b. (*First Alternative*) Appeals. This agreement does not obligate the law firm to appeal on behalf of the client. If the client wishes to appeal and the law firm agrees to represent the client, an additional agreement will be entered into for that purpose.

b. (*Second Alternative*) Appeals. The rest of this agreement deals with the agreement between the law firm and the client with respect to the trial of the above matter. If an appeal is necessary, the law firm agrees to handle the appeal with the following financial arrangement: (See various alternatives under clause 4 below)

2. Legal Services to be Provided.

a. (*First Alternative*) The legal services to be provided include all necessary court appearances, legal research, investigation, correspondence, preparation of legal documents, trial preparation and all related work required to properly represent the client in this matter.

a. (*Second Alternative*) (*Real Estate*) The legal services to be provided include the preparation of a contract of sale or review of same if prepared by someone else. The law firm will also attempt to obtain reasonable amendments on your behalf and review any proposed amendments proposed by others. The law firm will prepare for the closing including obtaining necessary title work, review and prepare any closing documents, represent the clients at the closing itself and record all instruments after the closing. The law firm will also aid the client in obtaining a survey and the policy of title insurance.

a. (*Third Alternative*) (*Estates*) (See § 4.147, number 3 for a typical format in use in New Jersey. This should be tailored to the work your office customarily performs on behalf of such clients.)

FIGURE 3-18 (continued)

b. (*First Alternative*) The above legal services and others will be performed as needed by the law firm without need for consultation with or authorization from the client.

b. (*Second Alternative*) The law firm will not provide any additional legal services other than those specified above without first consulting with the client and obtaining authorization from the client.

3. Legal Services Not Covered by This Agreement.

(*First Alternative*) This agreement requires that the law firm represent the client with respect to the above subject matter only. Any other matters, except those incidental to and necessarily included with the above matter, must be the subject of a separate agreement between the law firm and the client.

(*Second Alternative*) If additional legal services are required by the client, which may or may not be related to the above matter, the client and the law firm may make an additional agreement with respect to those legal services.

(*Third Alternative*) The client and the law firm may make additional agreements to provide legal services not covered by this agreement. Unless such an agreement is made, the law firm will not be required to do any of the following:

a. Provide any services after the matter is disposed of at the trial level;
b. handle any appeal;
c. aid in the enforcement of any judgment or order of the trial;
d. represent the client with respect to the sale or transfer of any asset;
e. represent the client in any other court; or
f. prepare a will for the client.

4. Calculation of Legal Fees.

a. *Hourly Rate.*

The client agrees to pay the law firm for legal services at the following rates:

Rate per Hour *Services of*

These rates are subject to change from time to time, and the law firm agrees to notify the client of any such changes. The client will be billed at the hourly rates set forth above for all services rendered. This includes telephone calls, dictating and reviewing letters, travel time to and from meetings and the court, legal research, negotiations and all other legal services provided in this matter.

b. *Increased Fees in Exceptional Cases.*

(*First Alternative*) The rules of court allow attorneys to charge additional fees in certain cases. The client may be charged more where the urgency of the case, the amount involved, or the results obtained, reasonably justifies such an additional fee. For example, if emergency services are required by the client which require that the law firm work on a Sunday or a Holiday then an additional fee may be justified. If such an additional fee is charged, the client will be provided with a full list of all charges with a detailed explanation.

(*Second Alternative*) (*Real Estate*) The legal fees agreed upon may be increased to reflect extraordinary factors such as the necessity for scheduling a closing at a location distant from the law firm. Also if it is necessary to handle title problems on behalf of the client or if other matters require that the law firm devote unusual amounts of time and effort to properly represent the client, the client will be charged an additional fee for such extraordinary work.

(*Third Alternative*) The law firm may ask that the court require that the client pay an additional legal fee if the agreed upon fee is not adequate to fully compensate the law firm for the time and effort spent on behalf of the client. In this case, the court would decide whether or not such an increase is justified.

FIGURE 3-18 (continued)

Ch. 4 ATTORNEY'S LEGAL FEE AGREEMENTS § 4.141

c. *Fixed Fee Arrangement.*

(*First Alternative*) The estimated amount of legal fees for the services to be provided are $______. This fee will only be increased in exceptional circumstances as set forth above.

(*Second Alternative*) The total legal fee to be charged to the client for the legal services to be provided in accordance with this agreement is $______. If additional legal services are performed, they will be charged to the client. The charges will be agreed upon in advance, when possible, or otherwise the client will be charged a reasonable fee in light of the circumstances.

d. *Contingency Fee Arrangement.*

(*First Alternative*) If the law firm recovers money for the client which exceeds the client's costs and expenses of litigation, the client will pay the law firm a legal fee based on a percentage of the net recovery. The net recovery is the difference between the total amount received and the cost and expenses of litigation. The legal fee will be calculated as follows: ______% of the first $______ net recovery; ______% of the first $______ net recovery and _______% of the next $______ net recovery and ______% of the next $______ net recovery.

(*Second Alternative*) The client agrees to pay the law firm a fee contingent upon the outcome of the matter. If the law firm collects money on the client's behalf, the client will pay the law firm a fee for legal services as follows: ______% of all sums recovered by settlement prior to filing a law suit; ______% of any recovery if the law firm files a law suit on the client's behalf; or ______% of any amount recovered if there is an appeal either by the client or by the adverse party; or ______% of any recovery if a retrial is ordered by a trial or appellate court (regardless of whether or not the matter is settled prior to the completion of the retrial).

If there is no recovery, or if the recovery does not exceed the cost to the client, then the client would not be responsible for any legal fees.

e. *Fees in Estate Matters.* [See form § 4.147, for an example for fee arrangements to be used in relation to the handling of an estate].

5. Costs and Expenses Payable by the Client.

a. *Costs to Be Payable to the Law Firm.* The client agrees to compensate the law firm for the costs of photocopying, telephone toll charges, postage, messenger service or other out-of-pocket expenses required in the representation of the client.

b. *Other Charges Payable by the Client.*

(*First Alternative*) In addition to legal fees, the client is required to pay the following costs and expenses: charges for experts, court costs, fees for accountants or appraisers, fees for services of process, fees for investigators, costs of depositions, messenger service fees, and other necessary expenses in this matter.

(*Second Alternative*) (*Real Estate*).

The legal fees charged to the client are in addition to the client's obligation to pay for such items as homeowners insurance, charges to the title company or title searchers, charges to the client's lending institution, the cost of surveys, the cost of recording legal instruments, payments to real estate brokers and other charges to parties other than the law firm.

c. *Payment of Costs by Law Firm.* The law firm will pay all costs and expenses of litigation. The client will not be responsible for those costs except to the extent that the law firm recovers money on behalf of the client.

Comment: (Rules of Professional Conduct 1.8(e), if applicable in the jurisdiction—some jurisdictions refer to such an agreement as champerty and consider same to be illegal).

6. When Payments Are Due.

a. (*First Alternative*) All payments for costs and expenses including legal fees are due at or before the closing of title (insert other time or contingency as needed).

FIGURE 3-18 (continued)

Ch. 4 ATTORNEY'S LEGAL FEE AGREEMENTS § 4.141

a. (*Second Alternative*) The payment schedule is as follows:
Initial payment $______
Payment on filing of inheritance tax return on behalf of client $______.
Payment on service of final accounting of beneficiaries $______
Payment on making final distribution of estate $______
(Many other alternatives are possible depending upon the matter involved.)

a. (*Third Alternative*) Initial payment required. The law firm will begin work in representing the client upon the receipt of $______ This sum will be used to pay the client's fees and expenses according to this agreement. An additional sum of $______ will be due and payable on ______, 19.___ (Or within ______ days from the date of this agreement).

b. *Minimum Fee.* The client agrees to pay the law firm a minimum of $______ for legal services regardless of the actual amount of time spent by the law firm on this case. (Some limitations may be placed on the payment of the minimum fee to account for situations such as matrimonial litigation where the minimum fee world not apply if the client and the spouse reconcile before the law firm exerts much effort on behalf of the client.)

c. *Billing Practices.* The law firm will send the client itemized bills from time to time. The law firm may also require that costs and expenses of litigation be paid in advance. All such bills for costs and expenses are due upon receipt. The client will also be charged interest at a yearly rate of ______% on any balance due that is not paid within 30 days from the date of the bill.

7. Authorization and Decision Making.

(*First Alternative*) The law firm is authorized to take all actions which the law firm deems advisable on behalf of the client. However the following specific decisions must be made by the client: (Describe limitations in specific details). The law firm agrees to notify the client promptly of all significant developments in this matter and to consult with the client with respect to any significant decisions related to those developments.

(*Second Alternative*) The client shall have the right to settle this matter at any time the client considers to be in the client's best interest.

8. Client's Responsibility.

(*First Alternative*) a. The client must fully cooperate with the law firm in this matter. The client must provide all information relevant to the subject matter of this agreement. The client must also pay the bills as required by the agreement. If the client does not comply with these requirements, the law firm may withdraw from representing the client.

(*Second Alternative*) a. The client agrees to do the following:

1. To pay the law firm as agreed in this agreement.
2. To fully cooperate with the law firm and provide all information known to the client or available to the client which, in the opinion of the law firm, would aid the law firm in representing the client in this matter.

b. If the law firm is representing the clients jointly, then it is the client's individual responsibility to advise the law firm if any of the information provided to the law firm is to be kept confidential and to be withheld from the other clients. Otherwise the law firm will assume that all information is available to be disclosed to all clients.

9. No Guaranteed Result.

(*First Alternative*) The law firm shall act on behalf of the client in a courteous, conscientious and diligent manner at all times to achieve solutions which are reasonable and just for the client. However, the law firm does not guarantee or predict what the final outcome of this matter will be.

FIGURE 3-18 (continued)

Ch. 4 ATTORNEY'S LEGAL FEE AGREEMENTS § 4.141

(*Second Alternative*) The law firm agrees to use its best efforts in representing the client in this matter. However, the client recognizes that the firm cannot guarantee a particular outcome of this matter.

10. Termination of Services.

The law firm may terminate this agreement if the client is in breach of its obligations under this agreement or if the law firm is otherwise required to do so in accordance with the rules of professional conduct governing attorneys. The client is entitled to terminate this agreement, subject to its contractual liability to the law firm for services rendered.

11. Information to Be Made Available to the Client.

The law firm agrees to make every effort to inform the client at all times as to the status of the matter and as to the acts which are being taken on behalf of the client. The law firm will make the file available to the client and when possible will send copies of materials to the client at the client's expense.

12. Complete Agreement.

This writing includes the entire agreement between the client and the law firm regarding this matter. This agreement can only be modified with another written agreement signed by the client and the law firm. This agreement shall be binding upon both the client and the law firm and their respective heirs, legal representatives and successors in interest.

13. Signatures.

Both the client and the law firm have read and agreed to this agreement. The law firm has provided the client with answers to any questions and has further explained this agreement to the complete satisfaction of the client. The client has also been given a copy of this agreement.

Witnessed or Attested by:

____________________ ____________________

____________________ ____________________

The use of formbooks is explained in more detail in chapter 14.

LOOSELEAF SERVICES

Many sources in the law library are updated by pocket parts and pamphlet supplements. Looseleaf services present another format that is easily updated. The information in looseleaf services is stored in binders rather than formatted as hardbound volumes and paper pamphlet supplements. The binder format allows easy insertion of new material and removal of outdated material. With some looseleaf services, new material is received weekly.

Looseleaf services are generally of one of two types. One type is newsletter and the other type is interfiled. With the newsletter format, newsletter pamphlets contain new information. New pamphlets are filed at the end of a division within the binder to supplement pamphlets previously filed. With the interfiled format, new information is printed on individual pages. The individual pages are referenced by paragraph number or are numbered so they can be filed among already-existing pages, often in the place of older pages, which are removed.

The legal sources appearing in looseleaf format include state annotated codes, state administrative codes, formbooks, and services providing a collection of source material in a particular subject area. The looseleaf subject-specific services typically contain primary and secondary sources. The primary sources might include the text of relevant statutes and administrative regulations and summaries or the text of cases interpreting the statutes and regulations. The secondary sources might include a textual explanation and discussion of the area of law.

Bureau of National Affairs (BNA) and Commerce Clearing House (CCH) are well-known publishers of looseleaf services. BNA publishes United States Law Week. Federal Securities Law Reports is an example of a CCH publication.

United States Law Week is an example of a newsletter format looseleaf service. Current information is housed in two ring binders. One binder contains the General Law Section and the other binder contains the Supreme Court Section. The General Law Section contains a national survey of current developments in the law and summarizes and analyzes significant court opinions. The Supreme Court Section provides comprehensive coverage of the United States Supreme Court. It allows the researcher to monitor the status of cases, read the summaries of selected oral arguments before the Court, and read the full text of all United States Supreme Court opinions.

The Federal Securities Law Reports are comprised of eight looseleaf volumes. The material in the volumes includes the text of the Securities Act of 1933 and the Securities Exchange Act of 1934, relevant court decisions, Securities and Exchange Commission (SEC) rulemaking and interpretive releases, SEC administrative decisions, SEC no-action letters, annotations of securities law materials, and explanations of securities law topics.

LEGAL PERIODICALS

Legal periodicals can be a valuable source of information. They differ from other secondary sources in a number of ways. First, as the name implies, they are published periodically and contain articles, usually on a range of different issues and legal developments. The articles generally contain narrative text and citations to relevant primary sources.

There a number of different types of legal periodicals, ranging from law school **law reviews,** to bar association periodicals, to commercial **journals,** to **legal newspapers.**

Law school law reviews

Law reviews are considered by many to be the most prestigious legal periodical and are commonly cited in judicial opinions. Every accredited law school has at least one law review and many law schools have one or more specialized law reviews focusing on specific subject areas. An online *Directory of Law Reviews and Scholarly Legal Periodicals* is available at http://www.andersonpublishing.com/lawschool directory/.

Generally, there are three or four issues of a law review published annually. The majority of the issues contain articles on a wide range of topics; other issues may be devoted to a particular topic. Generally, legal scholars, judges, and practitioners author law review articles. The hallmarks of the typical law review article are a textual narrative of a particular issue or legal development and numerous footnotes containing citations to relevant primary and secondary authority. Law reviews also typically contain student notes and comments and book reviews. Student comments resemble law review articles in format, but may not be regarded as highly as law review articles because of the student authorship. Generally, student notes are shorter than articles and comments and each note usually focuses on a single case or statute.

Law reviews differ from scholarly journals in fields outside law in that they are edited and produced by law school students in their second and third years of study. Generally, student membership on the staff of the law school's primary law review is determined by high grade point average or writing ability demonstrated through a writing competition. Typically, students in their first year on law review perform tedious tasks, such as checking citations for accuracy. Students in their second year on law review often assume positions as editors.

Figure 3-19 contains selected pages from the Winter 1998 issue of The University of Chicago Law Review. The University of Chicago Law Review is one of the more prestigious law reviews. Figure 3-20 contains a sample citation to two pages of an article contained in that issue.

FIGURE 3-19 Pages from Chicago Law Review.

The University of Chicago Law Review

Volume 65 **Winter 1998** **Number 1**

ARTICLES

COMMENTS

REVIEWS

FIGURE 3-19 (continued)

Policing for Profit: The Drug War's Hidden Economic Agenda

Eric Blumenson†
Eva Nilsen††

TABLE OF CONTENTS

> Asset seizures play an important role in the operation of [multijurisdictional drug] task forces. One "big bust" can provide a task force with the resources to become financially independent. Once financially independent, a task force can choose to operate without Federal or state assistance.

Report commissioned by the Department of Justice (Oct 1993)[1]

> [W]hat reason can there be, that a *free people* should be expos'd to all the insult and abuse, . . . and even the *fatal consequences*, which may arise from the *execution* of a writ of assistance, only to put fortunes into private pockets . . . . [C]an a community be safe with an uncontroul'd power lodg'd in the hands of *such* officers . . .?

James Otis, Boston Gazette (Jan 4, 1762)[2]

†Professor, Suffolk University Law School; J.D. 1972, Harvard Law School.
††Associate Clinical Professor of Law, Boston University Law School; J.D. 1977, University of Virginia Law School; L.L.M. 1980, Georgetown University Law Center.
We presented an earlier version of this Article at the June 1997 meeting of the Law and Society Association and at faculty workshops at the Boston University School of Law and Suffolk University Law School. We are grateful to all participants and to the faculties at both institutions, who continued to provide thoughtful and valuable advice throughout the research and writing of the Article. We also thank Lawrence D. Weinberg for research assistance, and Dan Baum, Brenda Grantland, Eric Sterling, and Karen Tosh for leading us to much of the obscure but crucial data that appears herein. This research was supported by a grant from the Open Society Institute's Individual Project Fellowships Program.

[1]Justice Research and Statistics Association ("JRSA"), *Multijurisdictional Drug Control Task Forces: A Five-Year Review 1988–1992* 9 (Oct 1993).
[2]Attributed to James Otis, *Article*, Boston Gaz (Jan 4, 1762), reprinted in M.H. Smith, *The Writs of Assistance Case* 562, 565–66 (California 1978).

FIGURE 3-19 (continued

Introduction

The Nixon Administration officially declared the "War on Drugs" twenty-five years ago.[3] It has continued, at escalating levels, ever since.[4] Today we annually spend $15 billion in federal

[3]In 1973, the Administration created the Drug Enforcement Administration ("DEA") to prosecute its "declared[,] all-out, global war on the drug menace." *Message from the President of the United States Transmitting Reorganization Plan No. 2 of 1973, Establishing a Drug Enforcement Administration*, HR Doc No 69, 93d Cong, 1st Sess 3 (Mar 28, 1973).

[4]President Reagan affirmed his administration's "unshakable" commitment "to do what is necessary to end the drug menace" by, among other things, increasing the number of federal drug task forces. *Federal Initiatives Against Drug Trafficking and Organized Crime*, 18 Weekly Comp Pres Doc 1311, 1313–14 (Oct 14, 1982). Later, President Bush appointed a drug "czar," William Bennett, who, among other things, sought the death penalty for drug sellers. *Excerpts From News Session by Bush, Watkins and Bennett*, NY Times D16 (Jan 13, 1989); Philip Shenon, *Administration Offers a Tough New Drug Bill*, NY Times A21 (May 17, 1990). The Bush Administration also contributed ever more militant rhetoric and increased federal budgets to the war effort. Its 1991, $10.4 billion Drug War budget (of which 75 percent was earmarked for drug law enforcement) constituted a 62 percent increase over the 1989 budget, and a tenfold increase over the 1985 budget. John A. Powell and Eileen B. Hershenov, *Hostage to the Drug War: The National Purse, The Constitution, and the Black Community*, 24 UC Davis L Rev 557, 567 (1991). The Clinton Administration in turn has increased the antidrug budget by an additional 25 percent. Joshua Wolf Shenk, *The Phony Drug War*, The Nation 11, 12 (Sept 23, 1996). During Clinton's first term the number of marijuana-related arrests increased by 43 percent, and more Americans are in prison for such offenses than ever before. Eric Schlosser, *More Reefer Madness*, Atlantic Monthly 90 (Apr 1, 1997). The Clinton Administration also has proposed conditioning teenage drivers' licenses, parole, and welfare payments on manda

FIGURE 3-20 Citation to a Law Review.

Eric Blumenson & Eva Nilsen, *Policing for Profit: The Drug War's Hidden Economic Agenda*, 65 U. Chi. L. Rev. 35, 40–41 (1998).

Bar association periodicals

Most national and state bar associations publish bar journals. Many specialized and local bar associations publish bar journals or newsletters. The quality and prestige of the various bar journals varies widely; some are considered fairly scholarly, while others are more practitioner-oriented. The American Bar Association publishes a number of well-respected subject-specific journals. State bar association journals may be a good source of state-specific articles.

Non-student-edited journals

In addition to student-edited law reviews, some law schools produce peer-edited journals, each generally devoted to a specific topic. Commercial publishers produce a number of single-topic journals as well. These nonstudent-edited journals are listed in the online directory available at http://www.andersonpublishing.com/lawschool/directory/.

Legal newspapers and newsletters

Legal newspapers provide information on recent court decisions, changes in the law, legal publications, and other items of interest to the legal community. Some legal newspapers print recent court opinions. National legal newspapers include the *National Law Journal* and the *American Lawyer*. Local legal newspapers include the *Chicago Lawyer*, the *New Jersey Lawyer*, and the *New York Law Journal*.

Legal periodical indexes

The ***Index to Legal Periodicals*** and the ***Current Law Index*** are the most widely used print indexes used to locate legal periodicals. The researcher may locate relevant law journal articles online in Westlaw or LexisNexis using key word searches.

INTERNET MATERIAL

Many secondary sources are available on the Internet.

FIGURE 3-21 Citation to Article from the Internet.

David A. Harris, *Driving While Black: Racial Profiling on Our Nation's Highways* (visited Feb. 8, 2000) <http://www.aclu.org/profiling/report/index.html>.

Citation to Internet material

Figure 3-21 contains the citation to an article found on the Internet.

DIGESTS

The researcher is usually searching for cases containing facts and issues similar to those contained in the legal problem being researched. Finding similar cases would be almost impossible without **digests.** Digests have an essential role in the research process because of the manner in which cases are published. Cases are printed in rough chronological order in **reporters,** unorganized by subject matter, facts, or issues. A set of reporters contains no index volume. The case digest is a multivolume set of books that functions as an index, allowing the researcher to locate cases with similar subject matter, facts, and issues as that of the legal problem being researched. Digests contain summaries of cases and references to other research materials. The summaries are called "annotations." The case summaries are arranged by topic and subtopic to allow you to find cases related to a particular legal principle.

Your law library probably contains several sets of digests. Figure 3-22 contains a list of many of the most common digests. Usually, a digest set is shelved near the set of reporters with which it is used. As indicated in figure 3-22, West's *American Digest System* covers cases from all state and federal courts. There are two digests covering cases from the United States Supreme Court. The West federal digest series covers cases from various federal courts, including the district courts, courts of appeal, and the United States Supreme Court. Separate sets of digests accompany five of the seven regional reporters. State digests are published for most states. A state digest covers cases from the state courts of a particular state. In addition, there are subject-specific digests. For example, *Bankruptcy Law Digest, Second Edition* would allow the researcher to locate cases concerning issues in bankruptcy law.

Digests are organized by topics, with the topics arranged in alphabetical sequence. The West Key-Number System, the most commonly used arrangement of topics, contains over 400 topics. Other publishers use a similar alphabetical sequencing of topics in their digests. Each topic is further divided into subtopics, with some subtopics divided into sub-subtopics. Each subtopic and sub-subtopic represents a single point of law. Each subtopic and sub-subtopic receives a corresponding number, with a separate number sequence used for each topic. Thus, a topic and a number identify a single point of law. In a West publication, this is commonly referred to as the topic and "key number" because of the key outline preceding the number.

Digests have a number of advantageous as well as limiting characteristics. The extensive number of digest topics makes the digest comprehensive in scope; digests are an essential case-finding tool. The identical West key-number system is used throughout all West publications. The digest is devoid of the case commentary and analysis found in secondary sources; case law analysis and synthesis is left to the researcher. The digest summaries are not primary sources; the digest is a finding tool and digest material should never be cited to or quoted. The researcher relies on the summary alone at the researcher's peril. Instead, the researcher should read the case itself. The summary may be inaccurate, may take on a different meaning in the context of the entire case, or may have digested dictum rather than the holding of the case. Classification of a summary under a particular digest topic and number is an arbitrary decision made by the publisher; the text of the opinion supercedes any misleading digest classification. At the same time, an important point of law from a case may have been overlooked by the publisher and lack a corresponding headnote.

West key number system

The West key number system divides the law into over 400 topics and numerous subtopics within those

FIGURE 3-22 Digests.

Digests

West's American Digest System - state and federal courts
Century Digest
Decennial Digests (each covers a five to ten-year period)
General Digest (updates the latest Decennial Digest)
Digest for United States Supreme Court cases
United States Supreme Court Digest (West)
United States Supreme Court Digest, Lawyers' Edition (Lexis Law Publishing)
Federal Courts - (United States Supreme Court, courts of appeals, and district courts)(West)
Federal Digest (through 1939)
Modern Federal Practice Digest (1940–1960)
Federal Practice Digest 2d (1961–1975)
Federal Practice Digest 3d (1975–1983)
Federal Practice Digest 4th (1983–present)
Regional Digests—(West)
Atlantic Digest
North Western Digest
South Eastern Digest
Pacific Digest
State Digests
(West publishes digests for more states)

topics (see fig. 3-23 for topics). Each subtopic is assigned a key number. For example, if you were researching the hypothetical problem involving Cruz Estrada and wanted to find case law interpretation of the federal communications statutes that protect conversations against interception, you might look under key number 491 of "Telecommunications." Notice from the sample page in figure 3-24 that that key number is at the beginning of the key numbers grouped under "Interception or Disclosure of Communications; Electronic Surveillance" and is entitled "In general." To refer back to the same key number later, or to give an answer on a research assignment, you need to note both the topic and key number. There is a "key number 491" in hundreds of different topics. If you write down just "491" you may not remember that you looked at key number 491 of "Telecommunications" and if you write down just "Telecommunications" you may not remember you looked under key number 491. The topics comprising the West key number system are printed inside the cover of each West digest. A table of contents containing the key numbers and titles of subtopics appears at the beginning of each topic of the digest.

Lexis Law Publishing publishes digests to accompany reporters such as *United States Supreme Court Reports, Lawyers Edition*, published by Lexis Law Publishing. Lexis Law Publishing publications use similar topics and subtopics, even though they are not referred to as "key numbers."

The sample pages are from *Federal Practice Digest Fourth Series* (fig. 3-24), which contains summaries of federal cases. *Federal Practice Digest Fourth Series* uses the West Group key number system. This key number system is universal in West publications.

Relationship between digests and reporters

Digests are closely related to case headnotes. Before a case is published in a reporter, an attorney on the publisher's staff prepares a number of short paragraphs, each of which summarizes an important legal

FIGURE 3-23 Topics and Subtopics in the West Key Number System.

DIGEST TOPICS

See, also, Outline of the Law by Seven Main Divisions of Law, Page VII
The topic numbers shown below may be used in Westlaw searches for cases within the topic and within specified key numbers.

1 Abandoned and Lost Property
2 Abatement and Revival
3 Abduction
4 Abortion and Birth Control
5 Absentees
6 Abstracts of Title
7 Accession
8 Accord and Satisfaction
9 Account
10 Account, Action on
11 Account Stated
11A Accountants
12 Acknowledgment
13 Action
14 Action on the Case
15 Adjoining Landowners
15A Administrative Law and Procedure
16 Admiralty
17 Adoption
18 Adulteration
19 Adultery
20 Adverse Possession
21 Affidavits
22 Affray
23 Agriculture
24 Aliens
25 Alteration of Instruments
26 Ambassadors and Consuls
27 Amicus Curiae
28 Animals
29 Annuities
30 Appeal and Error
31 Appearance
33 Arbitration
34 Armed Services
35 Arrest
36 Arson
37 Assault and Battery
38 Assignments
40 Assistance, Writ of
41 Associations
42 Assumpsit, Action of
43 Asylums
44 Attachment
45 Attorney and Client
46 Attorney General
47 Auctions and Auctioneers
48 Audit a Querela
48A Automobiles
48B Aviation
49 Bail
50 Bailment
51 Bankruptcy
52 Banks and Banking
54 Beneficial Associations
55 Bigamy
56 Bills and Notes
57 Blasphemy
58 Bonds
59 Boundaries
60 Bounties
61 Breach of Marriage Promise
62 Breach of the Peace
63 Bribery
64 Bridges
65 Brokers
66 Building and Loan Associations
67 Burglary
68 Canals
69 Cancellation of Instruments
70 Carriers
71 Cemeteries
72 Census
73 Certiorari
74 Champerty and Maintenance
75 Charities
76 Chattel Mortgages
76A Chemical Dependents
76H Children Out-Of-Wedlock
77 Citizens
78 Civil Rights
79 Clerk of Courts
80 Clubs
81 Colleges and Universities
82 Collision
83 Commerce
83H Commodity Futures Trading Regulation
84 Common Lands
85 Common Law
86 Common Scold
88 Compounding Offenses
89 Compromise and Settlement
89A Condominium
90 Confusion of Goods
91 Conspiracy
92 Constitutional Law
92B Consumer Credit
92H Consumer Protection
93 Contempt
95 Contracts
96 Contribution
97 Conversion
98 Convicts
99 Copyrights and Intellectual Property
100 Coroners
101 Corporations
102 Costs
103 Counterfeiting
104 Counties
105 Court Commissioners
106 Courts
107 Covenant, Action of
108 Covenants
108A Credit Reporting Agencies
110 Criminal Law
111 Crops
113 Customs and Usages
114 Customs Duties
115 Damages
116 Dead Bodies
117 Death
117G Debt, Action of
117T Debtor and Creditor
118A Declatory Judgment
119 Dedication

FIGURE 3-23 (continued)

120 Deeds
122a Deposits and Escrows
123 Deposits in Court
124 Descent and Distribution
125 Detectives
126 Detinue
129 Disorderly Conduct
130 Disorderly House
131 District and Prosecuting Attorneys
132 District of Columbia
133 Disturbance of Public Assemblage
134 Divorce
135 Domicile
136 Dower and Curtesy
137 Drains
138 Drugs and Narcotics
140 Dueling
141 Easements
142 Ejectment
143 Election of Remedies
144 Elections
145 Electricity
146 Embezzlement
147 Embracery
148 Eminent Domain
148A Employers' Liability
149 Entry, Writ of
150 Equity
151 Escape
152 Escheat
154 Estates in Property
156 Estoppel
157 Evidence
158 Exceptions, Bill of
159 Exchange of Property
160 Exchanges
161 Execution
162 Executors and Administrators
163 Exemptions
164 Explosives
165 Extortion and Threats
166 Extradition and Detainers
167 Factors
168 False Imprisonment
169 False Personation
170 False Pretenses
170A Federal Civil Procedure
170B Federal Courts
171 Fences
172 Ferries
174 Fines
175 Fires
176 Fish
177 Fixtures
178 Food
179 Forcible Entry and Detainer
180 Forfeitures
181 Forgery
182 Fornication
183 Franchises
184 Fraud
185 Frauds, Statute of
186 Fraudulent Conveyances
187 Game
188 Gaming
189 Garnishment
190 Gas
191 Gifts
192 Good Will
193 Grand Jury
195 Guaranty
196 Guardian and Ward
197 Habeas Corpus
198 Hawkers and Peddlers
199 Health and Environment
200 Highways
201 Holidays
202 Homestead
203 Homicide
204 Hospitals
205 Husband and Wife
205H Implied and Constructive Contracts
206 Improvements
207 Incest
208 Indemnity
209 Indians
210 Indictments and Information
211 Infants
212 Injunction
213 Innkeepers
216 Inspection
217 Insurance
218 Insurrection and Sedition
219 Interest
220 Internal Revenue
221 International Law
222 Interpleader
223 Intoxicating Liquors
224 Joint Adventures
225 Joint-Stock Companies and Business Trusts
226 Joint Tenancy
227 Judges
228 Judgment
229 Judicial Sales
230 Jury
231 Justices of the Peace
232 Kidnapping
232A Labor Relations
233 Landlord and Tenant
234 Larceny
235 Levees and Flood Control
236 Lewdness
237 Libel and Slander
238 Licenses
239 Liens
240 Life Estates
241 Limitations of Actions
242 Lis Pendens
245 Logs and Logging
246 Lost Instruments
247 Lotteries
248 Malicious Mischief
249 Malicious Prosecution
250 Mandamus
251 Manufactures
252 Maritime Liens
253 Marriage
255 Master and Servant
256 Mayhem
257 Mechanics Liens
257A Mental Health
258A Military Justice
259 Militia
260 Mines and Minerals
261 Miscegenation
265 Monopolies
266 Mortgages
267 Motions
268 Municipal Corporations
269 Names
270 Navigable Waters
271 Ne Exeat
272 Negligence

FIGURE 3-23 (continued)

273 Neutrality Laws
274 Newspapers
275 New Trial
276 Notaries
277 Notice
278 Novation
279 Nuisance
280 Oath
281 Obscenity
282 Obstructing Justice
283 Officers and Public Employees
284 Pardon and Parole
285 Parent and Child
286 Parliamentary Law
287 Parties
288 Partition
289 Partnership
290 Party Walls
291 Patents
292 Paupers
294 Payment
295 Penalties
296 Pensions
297 Perjury
298 Perpetuities
299 Physicians and Surgeons
300 Pilots
301 Piracy
302 Pleading
303 Pledges
304 Poisons
305 Possessory Warrant
306 Post Office
307 Powers
307A Pretrial Procedure
308 Principal and Agent
309 Principal and Surety
310 Prisons
311 Private Roads
312 Prize Fighting
313 Process
313A Products Liability
314 Prohibition
315 Property
316 Prostitution
316A Public Contracts
317 Public Lands
317A Public Utilities
318 Quieting Title
319 Quo Warranto
320 Railroads
321 Rape
322 Real Actions
323 Receivers
324 Receiving Stolen Goods
325 Recognizances
326 Records
327 Reference
328 Reformation of Instruments
330 Registers of Deeds
331 Release
332 Religious Societies
333 Remainders
334 Removal of Cases
335 Replevin
336 Reports
337 Rescue
338 Reversions
339 Review
340 Rewards
341 Riot
342 Robbery
343 Sales
344 Salvage
345 Schools
346 Scire Facias
347 Seals
348 Seaman
349 Searches and Seizures
349A Secured Transactions
349B Securities Regulation
350 Seduction
351 Sequestration
352 Set-Off and Counterclaim
353 Sheriffs and Constables
354 Shipping
355 Signatures
356 Slaves
356A Social Security and Public Welfare
357 Sodomy
358 Specific Performance
359 Spendthrifts
360 States
361 Statutes
362 Steam
363 Stipulations
365 Submission of Controversy
366 Subrogation
367 Subscriptions
368 Suicide
369 Sunday
370 Supersedeas
371 Taxation
372 Telecommunications
373 Tenancy in Common
374 Tender
375 Territories
376 Theaters and Shows
378 Time
379 Torts
380 Towage
381 Towns
382 Trade Regulation
384 Treason
385 Treaties
386 Trespass
387 Trespass to Try Title
388 Trial
389 Trover and Conversion
390 Trusts
391 Turnpikes and Toll Roads
392 Undertakings
393 United States
394 United States Magistrates
395 United States Marshals
396 Unlawful Assembly
396A Urban Railroads
398 Usury
399 Vagrancy
400 Vendor and Purchaser
401 Venue
402 War and National Emergency
403 Warehousemen
401 Waste
405 Waters and Water Courses
406 Weapons
407 Weights and Measures
408 Wharves
409 Wills
410 Witnesses
411 Woods and Forests
413 Workers' Compensation
414 Zoning and Planning

FIGURE 3-24 Sample Pages from Federal Practice Digest 4th.

🔑 **476 TELECOMMUNICATIONS** 90B F P D 4th—468

For later cases see same Topic and Key Number in Pocket Part

tions Act. Communications Act of 1934, §§ 1 et seq., 201(b), 203(a), 414, 47 U.S.C.A. §§ 151 et seq., 201(b), 203(a), 414.

MCI Telecommunications Corp. v. Graphnet, Inc., 881 F.Supp. 126.

Filed rate doctrine did not preclude claim of telecommunications telex and facsimile transmission carrier against telecommunications company, alleging company breached agreement under which amounts owing to company for voice transmission services provided to carrier would be offset by amounts due to carrier from company's affiliate for services rendered, where neither carrier nor company had directly addressed issue of whether such practice was governed by provisions of tariff or was capable of existing as independent contract between the parties. Communications Act, §§ 1 et seq., 201(b), 203(a), 414, 47 U.S.C.A. §§ 151 et seq., 201(b), 203(a), 414.

MCI Telecommunications Corp. v. Graphnet, Inc., 881 F.Supp. 126.

Filed rate doctrine did not preclude breach of contract claim of telecommunications telex and facsimile transmission carrier against telecommunications company, alleging company deliberately and chronically withheld credits for traffic-minute and call-count discrepancies properly due to carrier under its agreement with company; claim did not directly implicate rates but, rather, claimed entitlement to credits for traffic-minute and call-count discrepancies due to service interruptions and disconnected calls, and neither party had directly addressed whether company's tariff controlled that matter. Communications Act of 1934, §§ 1 et seq., 201(b), 203(a), 414, 47 U.S.C.A. §§ 151 et seq., 201(b), 203(a), 414.

MCI Telecommunications Corp. v. Graphnet, Inc., 881 F.Supp. 126.

🔑 **477. Time and clock service.**

Library references

C.J.S. Telecommunications §217.

V. INTERCEPTION OR DISCLOSURE OF COMMUNICATIONS; ELECTRONIC SURVEILLANCE.

(A) IN GENERAL.

🔑 **491. In general.**

Library references

C.J.S. Telecommunications §§ 233, 234, 236–238, 240, 242, 244–246, 253, 258, 259, 261, 307.

C.A.D.C. 1975. Zweibon v. Mitchell, 516 F.2d 594, 170 U.S.App.D.C. 1, certiorari denied Barrett v. Zweibon, 96 S.Ct. 1684, 425 U.S. 944, 48 L.Ed.2d 187, certiorari denied 96 S.Ct. 1685, 425 U.S. 944, 48 L.Ed.2d 187, certiorari denied 96 S.Ct. 1685, 425 U.S. 944, 48 L.Ed.2d 187, on remand 444 F.Supp. 1296, affirmed in part, reversed in part 606 F.2d 1172, 196 U.S.App. D.C. 265, certiorari denied 101 S.Ct. 3147, 453 U.S. 912, 69 L.Ed.2d 997, rehearing denied 102 S.Ct. 892, 453 U.S. 928, 69 L.Ed.2d 1024, certiorari denied 101 S.Ct. 3147, 453 U.S. 912, 69 L.Ed.2d 997, rehearing denied 102 S.Ct. 892, 453 U.S. 928, 69 L.Ed.2d 1025, appeal after remand 720 F.2d 162, 231 U.S.App.D.C. 398, certiorari denied 105 S.Ct. 244, 469 U.S. 880, 83 L.Ed.2d 182, rehearing denied 105 S.Ct. 557, 469 U.S. 1068, 83 L.Ed.2d 442.

C.A.11 (Fla.) 1993. Test for determining whether person has reasonable or justifiable expectation of privacy, for purposes of Title III of the Omnibus Crime Control and Safe Streets Act and the Fourth Amendment, has two prongs: first, whether person's conduct exhibits subjective expectation of privacy, and second, whether person's subjective expectation of privacy is one that society is willing to recognize as reasonable. 18 U.S.C.A. §§ 2510(2), 2511; U.S.C.A. Const.Amend. 4.

U.S. v. McKinnon, 985 F.2d 525, certiorari denied 114 S.Ct. 130, 510 U.S. 843, 126 L.Ed.2d 94.

C.A.11 (Fla.) 1990. Statute prohibiting unauthorized receipt, assistance in receiving, or further transmission of radio communications for benefit by another applied to proscribe pirate chips and other unauthorized decoding devices which enable third parties to receive television satellite transmissions intended for paying subscribers. Communications Act of 1934, §§ 3(i), 705, 705(a), as amended, 47 U.S.C.A. §§ 153(i), 605, 605(a).

Cable/Home Communication Corp. v. Network Productions, Inc., 902 F.2d 829.

Sales of pirate chips and other unauthorized decoding devices which enabled third parties to receive television satellite transmissions intended for paying subscribers violated Federal Communications Act, though devices descrambled only video portion of satellite transmission and pirate chip overlaid portion of video picture with a black box; use of pirate chip permitted receipt of unauthorized programming. Communications Act of 1934, § 705, as amended, 47

For cited U.S.C.A. sections and legislative history, see United States Code Annotated

Same wording as headnote from McKinnon (*McKinnon* is included in chapter 4)

Citation to *McKinnon*

A 1990 case decided by the United States Court of Appeals for the Eleventh Circuit. The case originated in Florida.

Key number

FIGURE 3-24 (continued)

FEDERAL PRACTICE DIGEST

For references to other topics, see Descriptive-Word Index

U.S.C.A. § 605; § 705(c)(3), as amended, 47 U.S.C.(1982 Ed. Supp. V) § 605(c)(3).

Cable/Home Communication Corp. v. Network Productions, Inc., 902 F.2d 829.

Promotion of descrambling devices for subscription television programming, and creation, advertisement and sale of pirated chips to compromise copyrighted program within chip of descrambling program, which was in violation of both copyright and communications laws, was not protected by First Amendment; weak warnings by promoter of illegality were meaningless in overall sales pitch, particularly in light of fact that promoters were aware that pirate chips and decoding devices were unlawful and advised their audience of methods to evade American laws. U.S.C.A. Const.Amend. 1.

Cable/Home Communication Corp. v. Network Productions, Inc., 902 F.2d 829.

Commercial advantage or private financial gain is not pertinent to finding of violation of Communications Act section dealing with willful violation of statute, but is material in determining enhanced civil damages award. Communications Act of 1934, §§ 1 et seq., 705, 705(a), as amended, 47 U.S.C.A. §§ 151 et seq., 605, 605(a); § 705(d)(3)(C)(ii), as amended, 47 U.S.C.(1982 Ed. Supp. V) § 605(d)(3)(C)(ii).

Cable/Home Communication Corp. v. Network Productions, Inc., 902 F.2d 829.

Open promotion of purchase of pirate chips and other devices to compromise decoding program intended for pay television subscribers constituted willful violation of Communications Act, thus subjecting promoter to enhancement of civil damages award pursuant to statute; violations were willfully committed for direct and indirect financial gain given promoter's boastful statements to this effect as well as actual profits obtained from these violations. Communications Act of 1934, §§ 1 et seq., 705, 705(a), as amended, 47 U.S.C.A. §§ 151 et seq., 605, 605(a); § 705(d)(3)(C)(ii), as amended, 47 U.S.C.(1982Ed.Supp.V) § 605(d)(3)(C)(ii).

Cable/Home Communication Corp. v. Network Productions, Inc., 902 F.2d 829.

C.A.11 (Ga.) 1994. For offense of modifying device for assisting in unauthorized decryption of satellite cable programming, "satellite cable programming" and "private viewing" are not mutually exclusive, and defendant may be guilty of offense based upon modification of equipment permitting decryption of satellite signals intended for direct receipt by individuals with their own satellite dishes; although satellite cable programming may be primarily intended for direct receipt by cable operators, Congress plainly contemplated that such programming would also be received for private use by individuals with the necessary equipment. Communications Act of 1934, § 705(d)(1, 4), (e)(4), as amended, 47 U.S.C.A. § 605(d)(1, 4), (e)(4).

U.S. v. Howard, 13 F.3d 1500.

Affirmance of defendants' convictions on three grounds of assisting in unauthorized decryption of satellite cable programming would not cause manifest miscarriage of justice, even though evidence allegedly failed to show that they were each present and participating during all three of alleged violations and they were not charged with aiding and abetting; jury was properly instructed on aiding and abetting and evidence plainly established each defendant's active participation in and contribution to activity involving sale of illegal decryption devices. Communications Act of 1934, § 705(e)(4), as amended, 47 U.S.C.A. § 605(e)(4).

U.S. v. Howard, 13 F.3d 1500.

C.A.8 (Iowa) 1994. Fourth Amendment's protection of persons in their houses from unreasonable searches and seizures includes right to be free from indiscriminate government video surveillance of interior of apartment. U.S.C.A. Const.Amend. 4.

U.S. v. Falls, 34 F.3d 674. COURT OF APPEALS

C.A.7 (Wis.) 1988. Statute proscribing willfully and knowingly assisting in unauthorized interception and reception of cable service is not unconstitutionally vague or overbroad on ground that cable converter boxes have both legal and illegal applications and the statute accordingly provides inadequate notice that sales of such boxes are illegal; statute defines term "assist" to include manufacture or distribution of equipment intended by manufacturer or distributor for unlawful reception of cable service, and defendant could not be convicted if he sold boxes with intent that they would be used for lawful purposes. Communications Act of 1934, § 633, as amended, 47 U.S.C.A. § 553.

TO LOOK FURTHER

U.S. v. Gardner, 860 F.2d 1391, certiorari denied 109 S.Ct. 1751, 490 U.S. 1023, 104 L.Ed.2d 187.

Fact that cable converter boxes defendant sold allegedly had both legal and illegal uses did not preclude convicting seller of willfully and knowingly assisting in unauthorized interception and reception of cable service on theory

For cited U.S.C.A. sections and legislative history, see United States Code Annotated

A 1994 United States Court of Appeals for the Eighth Circuit case. The case originated in Iowa.

A 1994 case decided by the United States Court of Appeals for the Eleventh Circuit. The case originated in Georgia.

FIGURE 3-24 (continued)

491 TELECOMMUNICATIONS 90B F P D 4th—470

For later cases see same Topic and Key Number in Pocket Part

responsibility for illegal use of boxes should rest on buyer and user. Communications Act of 1934, § 633, as amended, 47 U.S.C.A. § 553.

U.S. v. Gardner, 860 F.2d 1391, certiorari denied 109 S.Ct. 1751, 490 U.S. 1023, 104 L.Ed.2d 187.

Defendant convicted of willfully and knowingly assisting in unauthorized interception and reception of cable service did not qualify as innocent and inadvertent facilitator of illegal transaction, for purposes of legislative intent that manufacturers and distributors who did not intend their equipment to be used illegally not be penalized, where jury found defendant did intend cable converter boxes he sold to be used illegally. Communications Act of 1934, § 633, as amended, 47 U.S.C.A. § 553.

U.S. v. Gardner, 860 F.2d 1391, certiorari denied 109 S.Ct. 1751, 490 U.S. 1023, 104 L.Ed.2d 187.

D.Conn. 1989. Eavesdropping invariably involves "broad" intrusion on privacy and must be carefully circumscribed.

U.S. v. D'Aquila, 719 F.Supp. 98.

D.D.C. 1989. Under California law, telephone company is generally required to obtain the consent of customer subscriber whose records are requested before they make that information available to the requester. West's Ann. Cal.Pub.Util.Code § 2891.

S.E.C. v. Pacific Bell, 704 F.Supp. 11.

N.D.Ill. 1983. U.S. v. Williams, 565 F.Supp. 353, affirmed 737 F.2d 594, certiorari denied 105 S.Ct. 1354, 470 U.S. 1003, 84 L.Ed.2d 377, certiorari denied O'Malley v. United States, 105 S.Ct. 1354, 470 U.S. 1003, 84 L.Ed.2d 377, certiorari denied Lombardo v. United States, 105 S.Ct. 1355, 470 U.S. 1003, 84 L.Ed.2d 377.

E.D.La. 1981. U.S. v. Marcello, 508 F.Supp. 586, affirmed U.S. v. Roemer, 703 F.2d 805, rehearing denied 707 F.2d 515, rehearing denied 708 F.2d 720, certiorari denied 104 S.Ct. 341, 464 U.S. 935, 78 L.Ed.2d 309, certiorari denied 104 S.Ct. 341, 464 U.S. 935, 78 L.Ed.2d 309, post-conviction relief granted 876 F.2d 1147.

D.Md. 1993. Federal Communications Act prohibits commercial establishments from intercepting and broadcasting to its patrons even unscrambled satellite cable programming. Communications Act of 1934, / 705(a), as amended, 47 U.S.C.A./605(a).

That's Entertainment, Inc. v. J.P.T., Inc., 843 F.Supp. 995.

W.D.N.Y. 1997. Cable television operator would be granted permanent injunctive relief against individual defendant, precluding future violations of federal statutory provisions governing unauthorized publication or use of communications and unauthorized reception of cable service, in operator's action against defendant, in which operator had shown that defendant had violated provisions through reception of operator's programming via unauthorized connection. Communications Act of 1934, // 633(a)(1), (c)(2)(A), 705(a), (e)(3)(B)(i), as amended, 47 U.S.C.A. // 553(a)(1), (c)(2)(A), 605(a), (e)(3)(B)(i).

International Cablevision, Inc. v. Cancari, 960 F.Supp. 28.

492. Constitutional and statutory provisions.

Library references

C.J.S. Telecommunications // 235–238, 240, 242–246, 253, 258, 259, 261, 262, 266, 270, 292, 307.

U.S.Cal. 1995. Government's interest in maintaining secrecy of wiretaps justified interpretation of wiretap disclosure statute to prohibit disclosure of expired wiretap applications without any artificial narrowing of statute's scope due to First Amendment concerns. U.S.C.A. Const.Amend. 1.

U.S. v. Aguilar, 115 S.Ct. 2357, 515 U.S. 593, 132 L.Ed.2d 520, on remand 80 F.3d 329.

C.A.D.C. 1975. Zweibon v. Mitchell, 516 F.2d 594, 170 U.S.App.D.C. 1, certiorari denied Barrett v. Zweibon, 96 S.Ct. 1684, 425 U.S. 944, 48 L.Ed.2d 187, certiorari denied 96 S.Ct. 1685, 425 U.S. 944, 48 L.Ed.2d 187, certiorari denied 96 S.Ct. 1685, 425 U.S. 944, 48 L.Ed.2d 187, on remand 444 F.Supp. 1296, affirmed in part, reversed in part 606 F.2d 1172, 196 U.S.App. D.C. 265, certiorari denied 101 S.Ct. 3147, 453 U.S. 912, 69 L.Ed.2d 997, rehearing denied 102 S.Ct. 892, 453 U.S. 928, 69 L.Ed.2d 1024, certiorari denied 101 S.Ct. 3147, 453 U.S. 912, 69 L.Ed.2d 997, rehearing denied 102 S.Ct. 892, 453 U.S. 928, 69 L.Ed.2d 1025, appeal after remand 720 F.2d 162, 231 U.S.App.D.C. 398, certiorari denied 105 S.Ct. 244, 469 U.S. 880, 83 L.Ed.2d 182, rehearing denied 105 S.Ct. 557, 469 U.S. 1068, 83 L.Ed.2d 442.

C.A.9 (Cal.) 1987. Probable cause showing required by Foreign Intelligence Surveillance Act is reasonable under Fourth Amendment as

For cited U.S.C.A. sections and legislative history, see United States Code Annotated

A 1997 United States district court case from the Western District of New York

Key number 492

A 1989 United States district court case from the District of Connecticut

A 1995 United States supreme court case originally from California

Western Dist. Louisiana

principle from the case. Each summary is assigned a corresponding topic and number from the publisher's topic classification scheme. Some summaries that correspond to more than one topic or number can be assigned multiple topics and numbers or multiple numbers within a single topic, or both. The summaries, with their corresponding topics and numbers are printed as "headnotes" at the beginning of the published opinion. The number of headnotes per case varies, based on the length and complexity of the case. Some cases have a single headnote, other cases may have as many as several dozen.

The headnote summaries are reprinted in the digests under the appropriate topic and number. Each summary is followed by its case citation. Thus, in the digest, the topic number is followed by a collection of paragraphs, each relating to the same point of law. The digest is comprised entirely of topic number headings and summary paragraphs reprinted from case headnotes.

Development of digest abstracts

To better understand the digests and their relationship to reporters, this section examines how the digest material is generated. Before a case such as *United States v. McKinnon* is published by West, an editor reads it and writes the syllabus (a summary) of the case. This syllabus may be in addition to the syllabus prepared by the official reporter. This is the reason some cases may be preceded by two syllabi. The editor also writes paragraphs, called **headnotes** summarizing the important principles contained in the case. Each headnote contains one legal principle. After completing the annotations, the editor assigns each one to one or more topics and key numbers. *McKinnon* has three headnotes (fig. 4-13). Headnote 1 was assigned the topic Criminal Law and key numbers 1139 and 1158(4). Headnote 2 was assigned the topic Searches and Seizures and key number 26 and the topic Telecommunications, key number 494.1. Headnote 3 was assigned the topic Telecommunications, key number 491. (See the sample digest page in fig. 3-24, which demonstrates how a case headnote is reproduced as a digest paragraph under the relevant topic.)

Each summary paragraph from a headnote of *McKinnon* is reprinted in a digest under the topic and key number to which it has been assigned. Because *McKinnon* was decided by a federal court, the headnotes from *McKinnon* are reprinted in Federal Practice Digest 4th (the latest series of the digest set covering federal courts). For example, the following summary paragraph from headnote 3 is reprinted under the topic Telecommunications, key number 491:

> Test for determining whether person has reasonable or justifiable expectation of privacy, for purposes of Title III of the Omnibus Crime Control and Safe Streets Act and the Fourth Amendment, has two prongs: first, whether person's conduct exhibits subjective expectation of privacy, and second, whether person's subjective expectation of privacy is one that society is willing to recognize as reasonable. 18 U.S.C.A. §§ 2510(2), 2511; U.S.C.A. Const. Amend. 4.

Digest page format

Examine the format for digest paragraphs using the sample page in figure 3-24. Under key number 491 you first see a library reference, which cites to Corpus Juris Secundum under various sections of the Telecommunications topic. Numerous case summary paragraphs follow the library reference. Case summaries from the highest court come first; then case summaries from other courts are arranged in descending order. If there was a paragraph summary from a United States Supreme Court case, that summary would come first, followed by paragraph summaries from the federal courts of appeals, followed by paragraph summaries from the federal district courts. Also notice that the summaries of cases of a particular court are arranged with the most current one first (reverse chronological order). The abbreviation in bold type at the beginning of the case summary identifies the court and the year of the decision. For example, "**C.A.D.C. 1975**" identifies a 1975 case decided by the United States Court of Appeals for the District of Columbia Circuit. "**C.A.11 (Fla.) 1993**" and "**C.A.11 (Fla.) 1990**" from the beginning of the next two paragraph summaries, identify case summaries from two cases decided by the United States Court of Appeals for the Eleventh Circuit. Both cases were originally from Florida. The material in bold is followed by the case summary, and the case summary is followed by the case citation.

The first case summary from the eleventh circuit is the reprint of the summary paragraph from headnote 3 of *McKinnon.* The wording contained in that paragraph is identical to the wording in headnote 3. The summary paragraph is followed by the citation to *McKinnon*.

Notice that the first and second sample pages contain a number of summary paragraphs from the 1990 eleventh circuit case, *Cable/Home Communication Corp. v. Network Productions, Inc.* The second sample page also contains summary paragraphs from cases from the United States Courts of Appeals for the Eleventh, Eighth, and Seventh Circuits. The 1994 eleventh circuit case originated in Georgia, the eighth circuit case originated in Iowa, and the seventh circuit case originated in Wisconsin. The third sample page contains summary paragraphs from the United States District Courts for the D.C. District, the Northern District of Illinois, the Eastern District of Louisiana, the District of Maryland, and the Western District of New York.

The third sample page continues with headnote 492, entitled "Constitutional and statutory provisions." The format for the information under headnote 492 is the same as that for the previous headnote, library references preceding paragraph summaries. **"U.S.Cal 1995,"** beginning the first summary paragraph identifies the paragraph as coming from a headnote of a case decided by the United States Supreme Court. The case was originally from California. That summary paragraph is followed by summary paragraphs from cases decided by the United States Court of Appeals for the District of Columbia Circuit and the Ninth Circuit.

Types of digests

The *Federal Practice Digest* sampled in figure 3-24 is just one of many digests published. A list of digests and their coverage appears in figure 3-22. When choosing which digest to use, pick the one that will give you results the quickest. The West *American Digest System* (comprised of the *Century Digest*, *Decennial Digests*, and the *General Digest*) is the most comprehensive digest, covering state and federal cases since 1658.

United States Supreme Court Digest, Lawyers' Edition covers United States Supreme Court cases. A note on *United States Supreme Court Digest, Lawyers' Edition* (L. Ed.): Because this digest is published by Lexis Law Publishing, it does not use the West key number system. It does use a similar classification system with topics and sub-topics.

The *Federal Practice Digest* (now in its fourth series) covers federal cases.

West's *Florida Digest* is an example of a state digest. It covers Florida cases.

Finding relevant material in digests

How would you choose which digest to consult? Look at a few examples. If you wanted to find a United States Supreme Court opinion you could consult the West *American Digest System*, West's *United States Supreme Court Digest*, *Federal Practice Digest*, or *United States Supreme Court Digest, Lawyers' Edition. United States Supreme Court Digest*, *Federal Practice Digest* or *United States Supreme Court Digest, Lawyers' Edition* would be your preferred choices because these digests are considerably less massive than the West *American Digest System.* If you wanted to find a United States circuit court opinion you could consult the West *American Digest System* or *Federal Practice Digest.* Your choice would be *Federal Practice Digest* rather than the West *American Digest System* because *Federal Practice Digest* contains only federal court case summaries. If you wanted to find a Florida Supreme Court opinion you could consult the *West American Digest System* or *Florida Digest.* Your choice would be *Florida Digest* rather than the West *American Digest System* because *Florida Digest* contains only Florida case summaries.

Currency is important in using digests. Digests are published in series. Each hard-bound volume in the series is updated by an annual pocket part. Paperbound supplementary pamphlets update the pocket parts. The pamphlets are updated by digest paragraphs found in any later hardbound volumes or advance sheets of the applicable reporter. Each hardbound volume of the digest is annually updated with a cumulative pamphlet, generally referred to as a "pocket part." The pocket part is inserted inside the back cover of the volume for easy reference and the pamphlet from the prior year is discarded; the pocket part contains headnote summaries from cases decided after the publication of the hardbound volume. Over time, the information for the annual pocket part supplement becomes too voluminous to be easily stored inside the volume's back cover; the information is printed in a separate paperbound volume, shelved next to the hard bound volume. The researcher should consult both the hardbound volume and the supplement.

The copyright date of the hardbound volumes varies greatly. Volumes are recompiled and reprinted from time to time to incorporate new material and eliminate out of date information; volumes containing topics frequently referenced in cases are reprinted more frequently than other volumes.

Start your digest research with the most recent series. If there are no case summaries printed for the digest subtopic you are researching, look in the prior series. For example, if you are looking for a search and seizure case from a United States circuit court, you would start with *Federal Practice Digest Fourth Series.* Review the "Searches and Seizures" topic in the hardbound volume, the pocket part to the volume, any available supplement pamphlet, and any later hardbound volumes or advance sheets of the applicable reporter. For summaries of earlier cases, consult a prior series of the digest.

Figure 3-25 contains some basic tips on digest use.

Using digests to find cases

There are three basic approaches to finding cases using a digest. They are:

1. Using a digest topic and number from a known case;
2. Using the digest subject indexes; and
3. Using a digest topic outline.

The first approach allows you to use a known case and its headnotes to find other cases with similar facts or issues. You might have a case that contains facts or issues similar to those contained in the legal problem you are researching. To find more cases with similar facts or issues, look for the corresponding headnote. Use the topic and number from that headnote and locate case summaries under the same topic and number in the digest. Once you find the case on point, determine the topic and key number from the case that are relevant to your search. Then look at the topic and key number in the digests. Cases concerning the same legal principle are grouped together under the same topic and key number.

The second approach requires you to use the digest's indexes, located at the end of the digest set. Identified as "Descriptive-Word Indexes" in West publications, these indexes are nothing more than subject indexes. The indexes supply a topic and key number when you look up key words in the indexes. Using key words from your legal problem, you can locate relevant digest topics and numbers. In brainstorming to find key words, you may consider the following case elements suggested by West:

1. the *parties* involved;
2. the *places* where the facts arose, and the *objects* or *things* involved;
3. the *acts* or *omissions* which form the *basis of action* or *issue;*
4. the *defense* to the action or issue; and
5. the *relief* sought.

A similar set of elements was suggested by Lawyers Cooperative Publishing Company (now part of West Group):

FIGURE 3-25 Tips on Using Digests.

Do—

1. use citations to locate relevant primary authority.
2. pull and read primary authority.
3. check pocket parts for recent information.
4. update information found.

Never—

1. rely on a digest entry as an accurate summary of a case.
2. cite to or quote from digests.

1. the *things* involved in the case;
2. the *acts* involved in the case;
3. the *persons* involved in the case; and
4. the *places* where the facts arose.

The third approach requires you to use digest topic outlines. If you know a topic relevant to your problem, look at the table of contents at the beginning of the topic. From the titles of the subtopics, identify relevant key numbers to research. Each digest topic in the hardbound volumes begins with two outlines. The first is an abbreviated topic outline and the second is a detailed topic outline. If you are fairly certain that a particular topic is relevant to the legal problem you are researching, you can review the topic outline for relevant topic numbers. Once you locate relevant topic numbers, review summaries following the relevant topic numbers.

Tables of Cases, Defendant-Plaintiff Tables, and Words and Phrases Index

You may have a case name and know that a particular court decided the case but have no other citation information. Each set of digests has volumes toward the end of the set marked "Table of Cases" and "Defendant-Plaintiff Table." A Table of Cases volume or volumes list cases alphabetically by the first-named party. Each case listing provides the corresponding case citation. The Defendant-Plaintiff Table volume lists cases alphabetically by the first-named opposing party (defendant, respondent, or appellee). Each case listing provides the corresponding citation.

If there is a particular term that is important to your research, you can look up the term in the Words and Phrases index located at the end of the digests. This index will give you citations to cases defining that term.

CHAPTER 3 SUMMARY

- Legal encyclopedias can be used as secondary authority and as finding tools.
- ***Corpus Juris Secundum*** and ***American Jurisprudence 2d*** are the two most widely used national encyclopedias. There may also be a legal encyclopedia for the law of your state.
- Legal encyclopedias contain a textual explanation of hundreds of legal topics, with the explanation heavily footnoted to give citations to relevant primary authority.
- Legal encyclopedias are best used to find primary authority and to give the researcher general background information.
- *American Law Reports* annotations contain selected cases, accompanied by a textual explanation (called an "annotation") of the law with lengthy footnotes to relevant cases.
- *American Law Reports* are best used to find primary authority and to give the researcher general background information.
- Restatements of the Law, another secondary source, summarize major common law legal principles.
- Other secondary sources include treatises, legal dictionaries, legal directories, formbooks, legal periodicals, law review articles, legal thesaurium, continuing education publications, and restatements.
- Digests are finding tools that contain case summaries and references to other research materials.
- Digests serve as indexes to cases and allow the researcher to locate relevant cases.
- When using digests, try to use the digest set that is most specific to the type of cases you are trying to find: a United States Supreme Court digest for cases from that court, a federal digest for cases from any of the federal courts, your state's digest for cases from your state, etc.
- Legal encyclopedias, digests, and other law books are updated by annual pocket parts and by paperbound supplementary pamphlets.
- Many secondary sources are also accessible using computer-assisted research.

CYBERLAW EXERCISES

1. The homepage for Martindale-Hubbell is located at http://www.martindale.com/. Use the homepage to learn more about the publication.
2. The National Law Journal is available on-line at http://www.nlj.com. Locate the National Law Journal and read a few of the current articles.
3. West Group (http://www.westgroup.com) and Lexis Law Publishing (http://www.michie.com) produce numerous series standard to the law library. Browse through their online bookstores to learn information on the two companies' publications. The online bookstores include pictures of many of the publications.
4. Many law journals are available online by accessing http://www.lawreview.org/ or http://usc.edu/dept/law-lib/legal/journals.html or http://findlaw.com.
5. Legal news is accessible at http://LegalNews.FindLaw.com.
6. Information concerning Bureau of National Affairs publications is available at http://www.bna.com.
7. The Practicing Law Institute homepage is located at http://PLI.EDU.
8. *Lawyers Weekly USA*, an online newsletter is located at http://www.lweekly.com.
9. Court TV is located at http://courttv.com.
10. *The Richmond Journal of Law & Technology* (http://www.richmond.edu/~jolt), published exclusively online, focuses on cyberlaw.
11. The *Internet Lawyer*, a newsletter concerning cyber law is available through The *Internet Lawyer* homepage (http://www.internetlawyer.com).
12. Nolo's legal encyclopedia is accessible from http://www.nolo.com.
13. A listing of law reviews and scholarly legal periodicals is available at http://www.andersonpublishing.com/lawschool/directory/.
14. Many law school librarians have written legal research guides and have posted them on the web. The guides attempt to introduce students to legal research and to answer commonly asked questions. Paul Richert, Law Librarian and Professor of Law at the University of Akron, School of Law Library, has compiled an "Internet Hotlist of Law Guides Organized by Subject" that links to many of the legal research guides. The Hotlist is accessible at http://www.uakron.edu/law/richert/index1.html.

LEGAL RESEARCH ASSIGNMENT—LEGAL ENCYCLOPEDIAS

1. Answer the following questions concerning legal encyclopedias:
   a. What are the names of the two most widely used national legal encyclopedias?
   b. What are the common abbreviations for those names?
   c. What is the legal encyclopedia for your state?
   d. What is the common abbreviation for the name of that encyclopedia?
   e. What type of authority is a legal encyclopedia?
   f. Is it proper to cite to a legal encyclopedia in legal writing? Why or why not?
2. Using *Corpus Juris Secundum* or *American Jurisprudence*,
   a. Who owns the land under navigable waters in the United States?
   b. What is the correct citation to your answer?
3. Using *Corpus Juris Secundum* or *American Jurisprudence*,
   a. What is the difference between a crime and a tort?
   b. What is the correct citation to your answer?
4. Using *Corpus Juris Secundum* or *American Jurisprudence*,
   a. What is an alibi as used in criminal law?
   b. What is the correct citation to your answer?
5. Using *Corpus Juris Secundum* or *American Jurisprudence*,
   a. How was arson defined at common law?
   b. What is the correct citation to your answer?
6. Using *Corpus Juris Secundum* or *American Jurisprudence*,
   a. What effect does disbarment or suspension have on an attorney?

b. What is the correct citation to your answer?

7. Using *Corpus Juris Secundum* or *American Jurisprudence*,
   a. What is the difference between "venue" and "jurisdiction"?
   b. What is the correct citation to your answer?
8. Using *Corpus Juris Secundum* or *American Jurisprudence*,
   a. What does Chapter 7 of the Bankruptcy Code deal with?
   b. What is the correct citation to your answer?
9. Using *Corpus Juris Secundum* or *American Jurisprudence*,
   a. What is the doctrine of stare decisis?
   b. What is the correct citation to your answer?
10. Using *Corpus Juris Secundum* or *American Jurisprudence*,
   a. What is an injunction?
   b. What is the correct citation to your answer?
11. Using *Corpus Juris Secundum* or *American Jurisprudence*,
   a. Are copyright matters governed exclusively by federal law, or by both federal and state law?
   b. What is the correct citation to your answer?
12. Using *Corpus Juris Secundum* or *American Jurisprudence*,
   a. What are defamation and libel?
   b. What is the correct citation to your answer?
13. Using *Corpus Juris Secundum* or *American Jurisprudence*,
   a. What is a quiet title action?
   b. What is the correct citation to your answer?
14. Using *Corpus Juris Secundum* or *American Jurisprudence*,
   a. Who owns wild animals?
   b. What is the correct citation to your answer?
15. Using *Corpus Juris Secundum* or *American Jurisprudence*,
   a. What is the judicial system in the District of Columbia?
   b. What is the correct citation to your answer?
16. Using *Corpus Juris Secundum* or *American Jurisprudence*,
   a. What is the difference between larceny and embezzlement?
   b. What is the correct citation to your answer?
17. Using *Corpus Juris Secundum* or *American Jurisprudence*,
   a. What is the general duty of a grand jury?
   b. What is the correct citation to your answer?
18. Using *Corpus Juris Secundum* or *American Jurisprudence*,
   a. What remedy does habeas corpus furnish?
   b. What is the correct citation to your answer?
19. Using *Corpus Juris Secundum* or *American Jurisprudence*,
   a. What are the reasons the inscription "In God We Trust" on United States currency does not violate the First Amendment?
   b. What is the correct citation to your answer?
20. Using *Corpus Juris Secundum* or *American Jurisprudence*,
   a. What is the difference between a unilateral and a bilateral contract?
   b. What is the correct citation to your answer?
21. Using *Corpus Juris Secundum* or *American Jurisprudence*,
   a. How long is a passport valid?
   b. What is the correct citation to your answer?
22. Using your state's legal encyclopedia,
   a. Name your state's trial and intermediate appellate courts and court of last resort.
   b. What is the correct citation to your answer?
23. Using your state's legal encyclopedia,
   a. How many years must a person have been a member of the state bar to be a justice on your state's highest court?
   b. What is the correct citation to your answer?
24. Using your state's legal encyclopedia,
   a. How many legislators comprise your state's legislature?
   b. What is the correct citation to your answer?
25. Using your state's legal encyclopedia,
   a. How long is the term for which someone can be elected as a legislator to your state's legislature?
   b. What is the correct citation to your answer?

LEGAL RESEARCH ASSIGNMENT—AMERICAN LAW REPORTS

1. a. What is the title of the annotation located at 62 A.L.R.5th 219?
   b. What is the citation to the case on which the annotation was based?
   c. In that case, what did the court hold?
2. a. What is the title of the annotation located at 62 A.L.R.5th 1?
   b. What is the scope of this annotation?
   c. What is the citation to a related annotation discussing surveillance of a fitting room as an invasion of privacy?
3. a. What is the title of the annotation located at 62 A.L.R.5th 475?
   b. What are four grounds on which the owner has been held liable?
   c. What are two affirmative defenses to the owner's liability?
4. a. What is the full citation of the annotation located at 20 A.L.R.5th 534?
   b. Using the annotation from *a*, when can the state remove the child from the parent's custody?
5. a. What is the citation to the annotation discussing the tort liability of public schools and institutions of higher learning for accidents occurring during school athletic events?
   b. What is the scope of the annotation?
   c. What are the citations to two related annotations discussing tort liability of schools for accidents occurring in physical education classes and during cheerleading activities?
6. a. What is the citation to the annotation discussing the defense of an inconsequential violation in criminal prosecution?
   b. What does "de minimus non curat lex" mean?
   c. What factors have courts looked to in applying the principle?
7. a. What is the citation to the annotation discussing the regulation of exposure of female, but not male breasts?
   b. What is the basis in the United States Constitution for challenging this type of regulation?
   c. What is the reasoning for concluding that this type of regulation does not violate the Constitution?
8. a. What is the citation to the annotation discussing a custodial parent's homosexual or lesbian relationship with a third person as justifying modification of a child custody order?
   b. What is the ground for modifying an original custody order?
   c. Who bears the burden of proof in a proceeding to modify custody?
9. a. What is the citation to the annotation discussing whether an individual has a reasonable expectation of privacy in a tent or campsite?
   b. What two factors have courts considered in determining whether a person has a reasonable expectation of privacy?
10. a. What is the citation to the annotation discussing the validity and construction of a statute or ordinance requiring installation of automatic sprinklers?
    b. Have the provisions generally been upheld?
    c. What did the court hold in *Third & Catalina Assocs. v. City of Phoenix?*
11. a. What is the citation to the annotation discussing homicide based on the killing of an unborn child?
    b. Is this the first annotation discussing this topic?
    c. What is the common law rule concerning this topic?
12. a. What is the citation to the annotation discussing the liability of a vendor for food or beverage spilled on the customer?
    b. What happened to the customer in the vast majority of lawsuits concerning this topic?
    c. In the McDonald's coffee case, how much did the jury award in compensatory and punitive damages?
13. a. What is the citation to the annotation discussing liability of the owner or operator of a self-service filling station for injury or death of patron?
    b. What is the key for imposing liability upon an owner or operator?
14. a. What is the citation to the annotation discussing conveyance of real property with

reference to a tree or similar monument as giving titles to the center thereof?
   b. Why is the issue a serious one?

15. a. What is the citation to the annotation discussing liability for an injury inflicted by a horse, dog, or other domestic animal exhibited at a show?
   b. What is the citation to the case on which the annotation was based?
   c. What were the facts in the case and what did the court decide?

16. a. What is the citation to the annotation discussing when the statute of limitations begins to run upon an action against an attorney for legal malpractice where there were deliberate wrongful acts or omissions?
   b. On what theories does a client's lawsuit against the attorney to turn over money sound either in contract or tort?
   c. Why is the distinction between a contract action and a tort action significant?

17. a. What is the citation to the annotation discussing the police surveillance privilege?
   b. What is the privilege and what are the reasons for the privilege?
   c. What are the interests in favor of nondisclosure and what are the interests in favor of disclosure?

18. a. What is the citation to the annotation discussing the propriety of a probation condition exposing the defendant to public shame or ridicule?
   b. What provisions of the United States Constitution have been used to challenge this type of probation condition?
   c. What are four particular probation conditions that have been the subject of examination?

19. a. What is the citation to the annotation discussing what constitutes obstructing or resisting an officer, in the absence of actual force?
   b. What is the citation of the case that is the basis for the annotation?
   c. What were the facts in the case and what did the court decide?

20. a. What is the citation to the annotation discussing excessiveness or adequacy of damages awarded for injuries to the trunk or torso, or internal injuries?
   b. In the case that is the basis for the annotation, was $245,000 considered excessive? Why or why not?
   c. What is the scope of the annotation?

21. a. What is the citation to the annotation discussing seizure or detention for purpose of committing rape, robbery, or other offense as constituting the separate crime of kidnapping?
   b. Is this the first annotation on this topic?
   c. What is the majority view as to whether there is a separate crime of kidnapping?

22. a. What is the citation of the annotation discussing insurance coverage for sexual contact with patients by physicians?
   b. Using the annotation from *a*, what is the scope of the annotation?

23. a. What is the citation of the annotation discussing whether a former employee is eligible for unemployment compensation where the former employee alleged that the work was illegal or immoral?
   b. Using the annotation from *a*, what is the citation to a related annotation discussing whether a former employee is eligible for unemployment compensation where the former employee refused to work at particular times or on particular shifts for domestic or family reasons?

24. a. What is the citation to the annotation discussing what constitutes a tenant holding over a leased premises?
   b. Using the annotation from *a*, what is the tenant's duty upon termination of the lease?

25. a. What is the citation to the annotation discussing whether a contractor who abandons a building project before completion can be liable for liquidated damages?
   b. Using the annotation from *a*, why are liquidated damages provisions included in construction contracts?

LEGAL RESEARCH ASSIGNMENT—DIGESTS

For questions 2–21, use West's *Federal Practice Digest 4th*.

Note: Because proper case citation form is not covered until the next chapter, where a question calls for a citation, write the citation as you find it in the digest.

1. Answer the following questions concerning digests:
   a. What is the name of the most current West Group digest you would use to research cases from federal courts?
   b. What is the name of the most current digest you would use to research cases from state courts of your state?
2. If you were looking for cases addressing the ownership by a state of the land under navigable waters, what topic and key number would you look under?
3. Give the *citation* to the 1998 United States Supreme Court case in which the Court found that New Jersey was sovereign over filled lands added to Ellis Island.
4. Give the *citation* to the 1997 United States Supreme Court case in which the Court found that the waters of Stefansson Sound, along Alaska's Arctic Coast, are not "inland waters" of which Alaska has ownership.
5. Give the *citation* to the 1992 United States Court of Appeals for the Eighth Circuit case in which the court found that under Missouri law, a radio broadcast tower constituted a fixture, where the tower was 2,000 feet tall, next to land subject to a renewable, 50-year lease, and taxed as leased real property.
6. Give the *citation* to 1992 United States Court of Appeals for the Eighth Circuit case in which the defendant alleged that he would have been labeled a prison "snitch" if he had reported to prison authorities that fellow inmate had threatened to kill him if he did not come up with the money to buy a gun to be used in the escape attempt.
7. Give the *citation* to the 1993 United States district court case from the Western District of Kentucky in which the court found that purchasers of horses were not bound by waiver of defenses clause appearing on the reverse side of one page purchase agreement; the front of the agreement above the signatures contained language incorporating only the terms on reverse side relating to express warranties.
8. Give the *citation* to 1998 United States Court of Appeals for the Tenth Circuit case in which the court found that the defendant's false statements that defendant had left Oklahoma before the alleged conspiracy was formed and had no contact with principal alleged conspirators was sufficiently material to venue decision to sustain perjury conviction.
9. Give the *citation* to 1997 United States Court of Appeals for the Third Circuit case in which the court found that acceptance of plaintiff's expert's survey in preference to that of defendant's expert was proper in Virgin Islands boundary dispute case; plaintiff's expert had greater familiarity with area and more extensive work on the survey.
10. Give the *citation* to the 1997 United States district court case from the Northern District of California in which the court found that a 48-hour search by hospital and coroner for next of kin of Danish tourist who had suffered fatal injuries, before harvesting organs of tourist was reasonable and did not give rise to negligent search claim on part of the tourist's parents.
11. Give the *citation* to the 1992 United States district court case from the District of South Carolina in which the court found that there was no violation of South Carolina blue law in service station leases requiring dealers to operate 24 hours a day, where dealers did not oppose working on Sunday but, rather, opposed being forced to operate during unprofitable hours.
12. Give the *citation* to 1998 United States Court of Appeals for the Seventh Circuit case in which the court found that the common law rule that Sunday is "dies non juridicus" means only that judicial acts performed on Sunday are void; the rule has nothing to do with the validity of contracts or the deadlines for performing them, unless the performance required by the contract

is the commencement of legal proceedings on a day on which the relevant court is not open.

13. Give the *citation* to 1992 United States district court case from the Southern District of New York in which the court found that the section of the New York Penal Law directed at vagrants providing that a person is guilty of loitering when he loiters, remains or wanders about in a public place with a purpose of begging violates the First Amendment.
14. Give the *citation* to 1994 United States district court case from the Northern District of Texas in which the court found that ordinances directed at vagrants that criminalized removal of waste from receptacles and coercive solicitation did not impermissibly punish homeless persons for mere status of homelessness, rather than conduct.
15. Give the *citation* to 1994 United States Court of Appeals for the Ninth Circuit case in which the court found that aircraft owners' refusal to hand over log books which had been removed from seized aircraft did not constitute offense of "forcible rescue" where log books were not in the government's possession during the refusal.
16. Give the *citation* to 1994 United States district court case from the Eastern District of California in which the court found that "Presidential Skill Contests" requiring listing of presidents in order of date of service, answering essay question and wordfind were contests, not illegal lotteries under California law.
17. Give the *citation* to 1992 United States district court case from the Southern District of New York in which the court found that a television sweepstakes was not an "unlawful gambling scheme" or "lottery" under New Jersey law; although the contest could be entered by calling "900" number, for which there was $2 charge, there were alternative cost-free methods of entering, and thus, the sweepstakes did not require that participants risk "something of value" necessary to gambling claim.
18. Give the *citation* to 1997 United States Court of Appeals for the First Circuit case in which the court found that the hotel did not "control" the rabid mongoose that emerged from the nearby swamp and bit the hotel guest in the hotel's pool area, thus precluding hotel's liability to the guest under the Puerto Rico statute that imposes strict liability on a possessor or user of the animal for any damages which the animal causes.
19. Give the *citation* to 1996 United States district court case from the Southern District of Indiana in which the court found that under Indiana law, the fact that the horse was blind in its left eye was not, in and of itself, a "dangerous propensity" or tendency of the horse which would potentially allow the owner of the horse or the premises at which horse was kept to be held liable for injuries suffered by an invitee who was thrown while attempting to mount the horse.
20. Give the *citation* to 1998 United States Court of Appeals for the Seventh Circuit case in which the court found that the landowner failed to prove a claim that adjoining landowner had contaminated landowner's property through spilled diesel fuel, given that the district court judge disbelieved the testimony that the landowner offered to show how fuel flowed on the surface onto the landowner's property.
21. Give the *citation* to 1990 United States Court of Appeals for the Seventh Circuit case in which the court found that an adjoining landowner has no duty to avoid building on property in such a way as to cut off a neighbor's natural light.
22. Using the Table of Cases volumes from the digest for United States Supreme Court cases, look up the following cases and give the citation to them:
    a. The 1998 United States Supreme Court case, *Minnesota v. Carter.*
    b. The 1998 United States Supreme Court case, *New Jersey v. New York.*
    c. The 1996 United States Supreme Court case, *Whren v. United States.*
    d. The 1999 United States Supreme Court case, *Florida v. White.*
23. Using the Table of Cases volumes from the appropriate series of the *Federal Practice Digest,* look up the following cases and give the citation to them:
    a. The 1998 Northern District of California case, *Apollomedia Corporation v. Reno.*

   b. The 1994 Court of Appeals for the Ninth Circuit case, *Kano v. National Consumer Cooperative Bank.*
   c. The 1997 Court of Appeals for the Ninth Circuit case, *N/S Corporation v. Liberty Insurance Company.*
   d. The 1996 Court of Appeals for the Ninth Circuit case, *Oregon Natural Desert Ass'n v. Bibles.*

24. Using the Table of Cases volumes from West's *Florida Digest 2d*, look up the following cases and give the citation to them:
   a. The 1997 Florida state court decision *State v. Conforti.*
   b. The 1995 Florida First District court of Appeals decision, *Department of Agriculture v. Edwards.*
   c. The 1994 Florida Fourth District Court of Appeals decision, *Cinci v. State.*

25. a. Using the Words and Phrases index in *Federal Practice Digest 4th*, give the *citation* to the case defining "insanity" and give the definition of insanity stated in the case.
   b. Using the Words and Phrases index in *Federal Practice Digest 4th*, give the *citation* to the case defining "vote denial" and give the definition of vote denial stated in the case.
   c. Using the Words and Phrases index in *Federal Practice Digest 4th*, give the *citation* to the case defining the "outpatient" and give the definition of outpatient stated in the case.
   d. Using the Words and Phrases index in *Federal Practice Digest 4th*, give the *citation* to the case defining the "doctrine of judicial immunity" and give the definition of doctrine of judicial immunity stated in the case.

CHAPTER 4

THE JUDICIAL BRANCH AND CASES

INTRODUCTION

In this chapter you will learn about the judicial branch and how to read a case, brief a case, locate cases in the law library, and cite to cases.

THE JUDICIAL BRANCH*

The judicial branch comprises the various levels of courts. The United States has a federal court system and a court system for each state and the District of Columbia. The courts in each system are arranged in a hierarchy. The federal courts are arranged in three tiers; many state court systems are arranged in three or four tiers. The lowest tier in a three-tier system is usually comprised of **trial courts.** In those systems with four tiers, the lower two tiers are usually trial courts. The next higher tier generally contains **intermediate appellate courts.** The highest tier usually contains one court, referred to as the **court of last resort.**

Jurisdiction

A court's **jurisdiction** is the power of the court to decide cases. To decide a case, a court must have geographical jurisdiction, subject matter jurisdiction, and hierarchical jurisdiction. **Geographical jurisdiction** refers to the geographical area within which cases arise. A court is restricted to deciding cases arising within a certain geographical area. For example, the United States District Court for the Middle District of Florida (a trial-level court) is restricted to hearing cases arising within the district covering the middle of the state (fig. 4-1). A party appealing a case from that court would appeal to the United States Court of Appeals for the Eleventh Circuit. The Eleventh Circuit is restricted to hearing cases arising in Florida, Georgia, or Alabama. Figure 4-2 shows the geographical arrangement of the federal circuits.

Subject matter jurisdiction refers to the type of case a court may hear. A court is a court of **general jurisdiction** or a court of **limited jurisdiction.** As the names imply, a court of limited jurisdiction is limited to hearing certain types of cases and a court of general jurisdiction may hear all other types of cases. For example, United States Bankruptcy Courts are restricted to hearing bankruptcy cases; therefore, they are courts of limited jurisdiction. United States district courts are considered courts of general jurisdiction, hearing civil and criminal cases not heard by specialized trial-level federal courts. Figure 4-3 shows an organizational chart of the federal courts.

*Grateful thanks to Daniel E. Hall, Ed. D., J.D. who authored portions of this section. Reproduced by Permission. CONSTITUTIONAL LAW: CASES AND COMMENTARY by Daniel E. Hall. Delmar, Albany, New York, Copyright 1997.

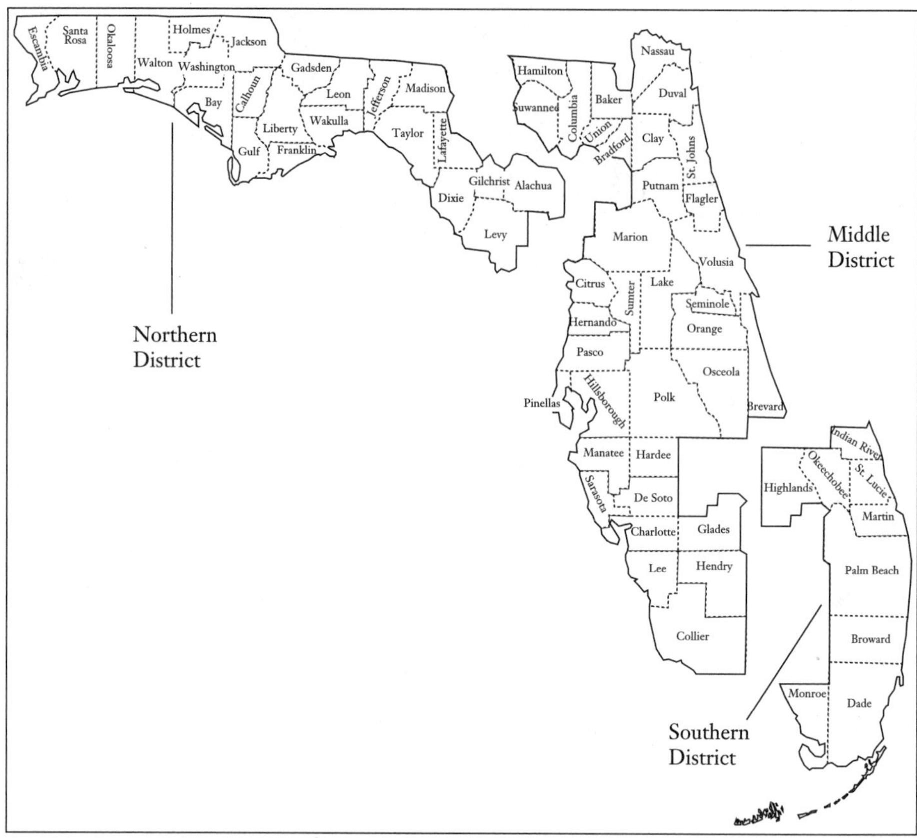

FIGURE 4-1 Federal Districts in Florida.

Hierarchical jurisdiction refers to the level of court deciding a case. A case begins in a court of **original jurisdiction.** The court of original jurisdiction initially hears and decides a case. When a court decision is appealed, the case is heard by a court with **appellate jurisdiction.** The court with appellate jurisdiction decides a case appealed from a lower court.

Trial courts usually are courts of original jurisdiction. However, in a state with a four-tier court system, the lower trial-level court may have original jurisdiction of a case and the upper-level trial court may have appellate jurisdiction of the case. Original jurisdiction is not restricted wholly to trial-level courts. For example, Article III, section 2 of the United States Constitution provides: "In all Cases affecting Ambassadors, other public Ministers and consuls, and those in which a State shall be a Party, the supreme Court shall have original jurisdiction."

The following sections consider the roles of a court of original jurisdiction (for simplicity referred to as a "trial court") and a court of appellate jurisdiction.

Trial court

In our adversary system, the two parties present their evidence at the trial level. The two parties may have different versions of the facts and the attorneys representing them may be relying on differing legal theories. An attorney tries to present the facts in the light most favorable to the client and the attorney will argue the law in the light most favorable to the client. The evidence may be **testimony,** documents, or tangible evidence. The role of a trial court is to determine the facts and to apply the applicable law to the facts. Usually, a single judge presides over the trial court. If there is a jury, the jury hears oral testimony and reviews documentary and tangible evidence. After considering the evidence, the jury determines the facts and applies the law to the facts, all in accordance with the judge's **charge** (instructions to the jury). The judge decides **questions of law,** such as the **admissibility** of evidence, the law to be applied, and whether a **motion,** such as a **motion for a directed verdict** or a **motion for summary judgment,** should

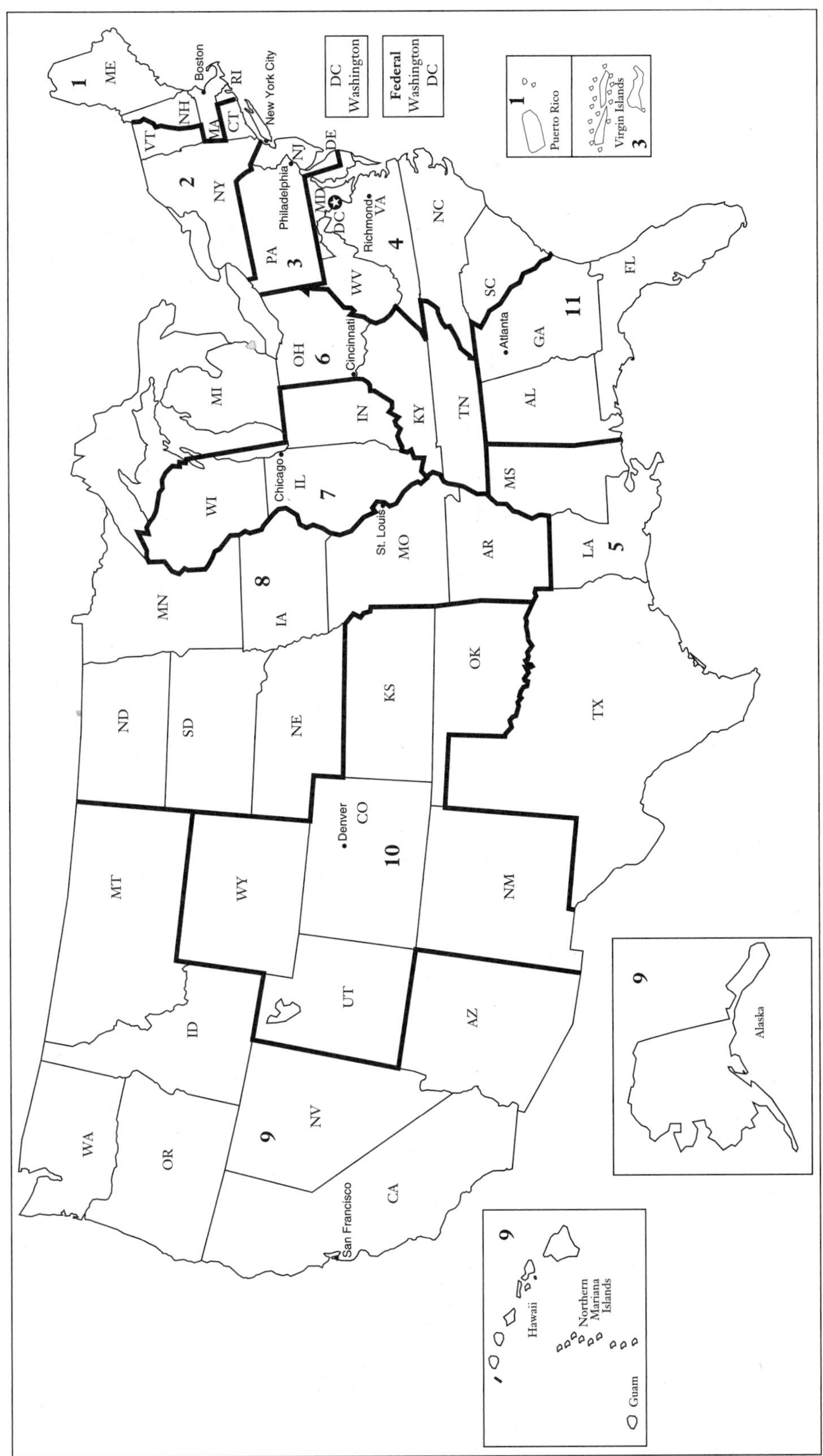

FIGURE 4-2 Map of Federal Courts of Appeals.
The Thirteen Federal Judicial Circuits.

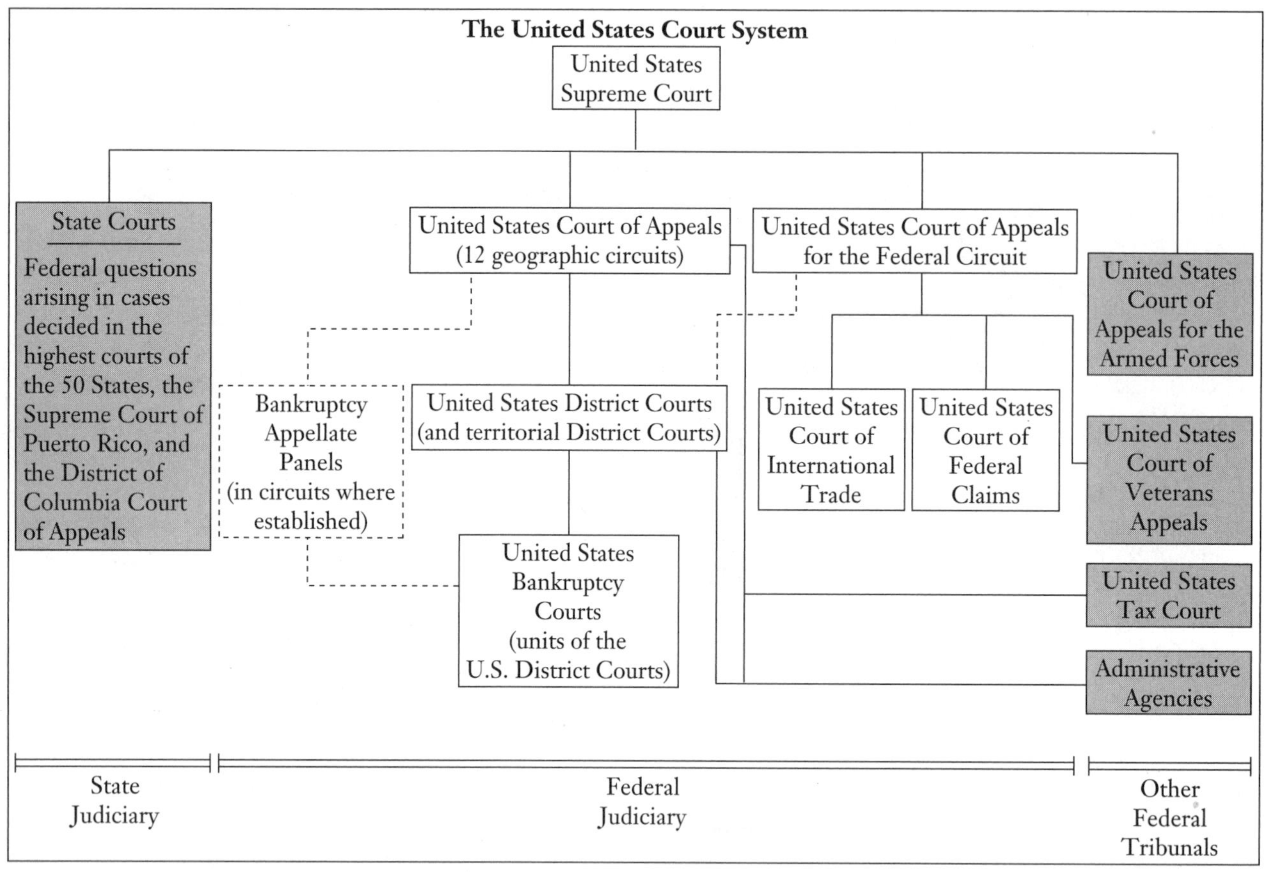

FIGURE 4-3 Structure of the Federal Courts.

be granted. The fact finder (the jury in a jury trial or the judge in a **bench trial**) determines the facts and the judge applies the law to the facts. If there is no jury (called a bench trial), the judge determines the facts and decides questions of law.

Appellate court

Generally, the losing party has the right to one appeal, from the trial court to an intermediate appellate court. Generally, review by the intermediate appellate court is mandatory, meaning that if a case is appealed to the intermediate appellate court, the court must hear the appeal.

The losing party in the intermediate appellate court may request that a higher court review the case. If in state court, the higher court may be the state court of last resort (referred to in many states as the state supreme court). If in federal court, the higher court may be the United States Supreme Court. Usually, jurisdiction of the state court and the United States Supreme Court is discretionary. **Discretionary jurisdiction** means that those courts can decide which cases they will review and typically review only a small percentage of the cases.

The role of the **appellate court** is to determine whether the lower court applied the law correctly. Appellate courts correct any errors made by lower courts. The appellate court defers to the trial court on **questions of fact** and may not substitute its judgment for that of the finder of fact unless the trial court's finding of fact was not supported by competent evidence. The appellate court may reverse a discretionary act of the trial court (for example admitting certain evidence) if the trial court abused its discretion. An appellate court will affirm a lower court ruling if the lower court ruling was correct or if any error was harmless. An appellate court will reverse the lower court if the lower court erred. Sometimes the appellate court reverses the lower court decision and **remands** the decision to the trial court for further proceedings. If several issues went up on appeal, the appellate court may affirm in part, as to those issues on which the court agrees with the lower court, and may reverse the lower court, as to those issues on which the appellate court disagrees with the lower court ruling.

At the intermediate appellate level, three judges are impaneled to decide an appeal. The three judges on the **panel** are randomly selected from the intermediate appellate court judges who are members of the court. The appellate court does not take testimony or consider evidence not introduced at trial. The appellate court may decide the appeal on the basis of the **appellate briefs** and the record alone. The record includes materials designated by the attorneys to be included, commonly including documents and exhibits from the trial and a transcript of a portion or all of the trial activities. Often, the court first hears **oral argument** from the attorneys representing the parties to the appeal. During the oral argument, each attorney has an allotted time period to present his or her case to the court and to answer questions from the judges.

The judges at the intermediate appellate level may decide to hear or rehear a case *en banc*. As explained in chapter 2, this means that all the members of the court sit to hear the case rather than the case being heard by a three-judge panel. For example, if the Eleventh Circuit Court of Appeals decides to hear a case *en banc* and there are twelve judges who are members of the Eleventh Circuit, all twelve judges would hear the case. Since very few cases are heard *en banc* and cases heard *en banc* deal with important legal issues, special attention should be paid to an *en banc* decision.

In a court of last resort, such as the United States Supreme Court or a state supreme court, all members of the court participate in deciding a case. The vast majority of opinions are written by appellate judges. Trial court judges, especially state trial court judges, write few opinions. In an intermediate appellate court, the three-judge panel assigns one judge in the **majority** to write the court opinion. A judge disagreeing with the majority may write a **dissenting opinion,** explicitly explaining the judge's reasons for disagreeing with the majority. In the United States Supreme Court the most senior justice in the majority assigns someone to write the opinion.

Federal courts

Article III, section 1 of the United States Constitution provides: "the judicial Power of the United States shall be vested in one supreme Court, and in such inferior Courts as the Congress may from time to time ordain and establish." The federal court system is hierarchical in structure (fig. 4-3). The Supreme Court of the United States is the highest court. The thirteen United States Courts of Appeals and the U.S. Court of Appeals for the Armed Forces are intermediate appellate courts. The United States District Courts are trial-level courts. The Tax Court, the Court of Federal Claims, the Court of Veterans Appeals, and the Court of International Trade are specialized federal courts at the same level as the United States District Courts.

Some federal courts are constitutional courts and some are legislative courts. Whether a court is legislative or constitutional largely depends on the status of the judges who sit on the court. If the judges are empowered under Article III of the Constitution—and therefore must undergo the nomination and confirmation process, are assured lifetime tenure, and cannot have their pay reduced—the court is constitutional. District, court of appeals, and United States Supreme Court judges are all constitutional judges.

In contrast, if the judges do not have these characteristics, they are empowered by Congress and not the Constitution. The Tax Court, the Court of Federal Claims, the Court of International Trade, and administrative law tribunals are examples of non-Article III courts. The judges of these courts are federal judicial officers, but they are not empowered by the Constitution; rather, their positions are created by Congress and are not formally part of the judicial branch. For this reason, they are commonly referred to as Article I judges.

Federal trial-level courts

Most federal cases are initially tried and decided in the **United States District Courts,** the federal courts of general trial jurisdiction. There are 94 district courts in the 50 states, the District of Columbia, the Commonwealth of Puerto Rico, and the territories of Guam, the United States Virgin Islands, and the Northern Mariana Islands. Each state has at least

FIGURE 4-4 Salary of the President, Federal Judges, and Members of Congress.

Position	Salary Rates Effective 1/1/2000
President of the U.S.	$200,000*
Chief Justice of the U.S.	$181,400
Associate Justices	$173,600
Judges, Courts of Appeals	$149,900
Members of Congress	$141,300
Judges, U.S. District Court	$141,300
Judges, Court of International Trade	$141,300
Judges, U.S. Court of Federal Claims	$141,300
Judges, U.S. Tax Court	$141,300
Bankruptcy Judges	$129,996
Magistrate Judges (full-time)	$129,996

*On January, 20, 2001, the President's salary changed to $400,000.

one district court. A district may itself be divided into divisions and may have several places where the court hears cases. Each district also has a bankruptcy unit. With the exception of the three territorial courts, all district court judges are appointed for life by the president with the advice and consent of the Senate. The 2000 salary rates for district court judges are shown in figure 4-4. In 1998, there were 57,691 criminal case filings and more than 250,000 civil case filings in the district courts. Figure 4-5 contains a directory of the United States District Courts.

The two bases of federal jurisdiction in United States district courts are **federal question jurisdiction** and **diversity jurisdiction** (fig. 4-6). Federal courts have federal question jurisdiction over cases concerning the United States Constitution, a federal law, or any treaty to which the United States is a party. Federal courts have diversity jurisdiction as long as the amount in controversy is more than $75,000 and the parties have the requisite diversity of citizenship. Diversity is met so long as the parties are citizens from different states or so long as one party is a citizen of a state and the other party is a citizen of a foreign country. Diversity must be complete. If there are multiple plaintiffs or multiple defendants, no plaintiff may be a citizen of the same state as any defendant.

District judges usually sit individually; however, Congress has provided for three-judge district courts in particular cases. Even when a three-judge court is statutorily mandated, one judge may be designated as the chief of the panel and be delegated the authority to make some decisions alone, such as whether preliminary injunctions or stays should be ordered. All three judges must sit, however, at trial. In most three-judge district court trials, appeal is taken directly to the United States Supreme Court.

Congress created the position of **United States Magistrate Judges,** which are Article I judgeships. The system of magistrates was created in an effort to reduce the burden on district judges without establishing new Article III judgeships. Under the Federal Magistrates Act, certain responsibilities are delegated to magistrates (although their actions are reviewable by district judges) and district judges are empowered to delegate further responsibilities. However, the United States Supreme Court has ruled that a magistrate may not preside over the critical stages of a criminal trial over the objection of one of the parties. Because Congress carefully drafted the Magistrates Act, however, magistrates may preside over nearly all other pretrial and trial proceedings, subject to review by a district judge.

Sometimes a plaintiff has a case that may be litigated in state or federal court. In that situation, the plaintiff would have to decide which is the more favorable forum. Certain types of cases, such as bankruptcy, copyright, and patent may only be litigated in federal court.

Federal Appellate Courts

The intermediate appellate courts in the federal judicial system are the courts of appeals (fig. 4-3). Twelve of these courts have jurisdiction over cases from

UNITED STATES DISTRICT COURTS

STATE	District	Number of Authorized Judgeships	Location
Alabama	Northern district	7	Birmingham, AL 35203
	Middle district	3	Montgomery, AL 36101
	Southern district	3	Mobile, AL 36602
Alaska		3	Anchorage, AK 99513
Arizona		8	Phoenix, AZ 85025
Arkansas	Eastern district	5	Little Rock, AR 72203
	Western district	3	Fort Smith, AR 72902
California	Northern district	14	San Francisco, CA 94102
	Eastern district	6	Sacramento, CA 95814
	Central district	27	Los Angeles, CA 90012
	Southern district	8	San Diego, CA 92189
Colorado		7	Denver, CO 80294
Connecticut		8	New Haven, CT 06510
Delaware		4	Wilmington, DE 19801
District of Columbia		15	Washington, DC 20001
Florida	Northern district	4	Tallahassee, FL 32301
	Middle district	11	Jacksonville, FL 32201
	Southern district	16	Miami, FL 33128
Georgia	Northern district	11	Atlanta, GA 30335
	Middle district	4	Macon, GA 31202
	Southern district	3	Savannah, GA 31412
Guam		1	Agana, GU 96910
Hawaii		3	Honolulu, HI 96850
Idaho		2	Boise, ID 83724
Illinois	Northern district	22	Chicago, IL 60604
	Southern district	3	East St. Louis, IL 62202
	Central district	3	Springfield, IL 62705
Indiana	Northern district	5	South Bend, IN 46601
	Southern district	5	Indianapolis, IN 46204
Iowa	Northern district	2	Cedar Rapids, IA 52401
	Southern district	3	Des Moines, IA 50309
Kansas		5	Wichita, KS 67202
Kentucky	Eastern district	4	Lexington, KY 40596
	Western district	4	Louisville, KY 40202
	Eastern and Western	1	
Louisiana	Eastern district	13	New Orleans, LA 70130
	Middle district	2	Baton Rouge, LA 70821
	Western district	7	Shreveport, LA 71101
Maine		3	Portland, ME 04101

FIGURE 4-5 Directory of the United States Courts—District Courts.

FIGURE 4-5 (continued)

STATE	District	Number of Authorized Judgeships	Location
Maryland		10	Baltimore, MD 21201
Massachusetts		13	Boston, MA 02109
Michigan	Eastern district	15	Detroit, MI 48226
	Western district	4	Grand Rapids, MI 49503
Minnesota		7	St. Paul, MN 55101
Mississippi	Northern district	3	Oxford, MS 38655
	Southern district	6	Jackson, MS 39201
Missouri	Eastern district	6	St. Louis, MO 63101
	Western district	5	Kansas City, MO 64106
	Eastern and Western	2	
Montana		3	Billings, MT 59101
Nebraska		3	Omaha, NE 68101
Nevada		4	Las Vegas, NV 89101
New Hampshire		3	Concord, NH 03301
New Jersey		17	Newark, NJ 07102
New Mexico		5	Albuquerque, NM 87103
New York	Northern district	4	Syracuse, NY 13261
	Eastern district	15	Brooklyn, NY 11201
	Southern district	28	New York, NY 10007
	Western district	4	Buffalo, NY 14202
North Carolina	Eastern district	4	Raleigh, NC 27611
	Middle district	4	Greensboro, NC 27402
	Western district	3	Asheville, NC 28801
North Dakota		2	Bismarck, ND 58502
N. Mariana Islands		1	Saipan, N. Mar. I. 96950
Ohio	Northern district	11	Cleveland, OH 44114
	Southern district	8	Columbus, OH 43215
Oklahoma	Northern district	3	Tulsa, OK 74103
	Eastern district	1	Muskogee, OK 74401
	Western district	6	Oklahoma City, OK 73102
	Northern, Eastern, and Western	1	
Oregon		6	Portland, OR 97205
Pennsylvania	Eastern district	22	Philadelphia, PA 19106
	Middle district	6	Scranton, PA 18501
	Western district	10	Pittsburgh, PA 15230
Puerto Rico		7	Hato Rey, PR 00918
Rhode Island		3	Providence, RI 02903
South Carolina		9	Columbia, SC 29201

FIGURE 4-5 (continued)

STATE	District	Number of Authorized Judgeships	Location
South Dakota		3	Sioux Falls, SD 57102
Tennessee	Eastern district	5	Knoxville, TN 37901
	Middle district	4	Nashville, TN 37203
	Western district	5	Memphis, TN 38103
Texas	Northern district	12	Dallas, TX 75242
	Southern district	18	Houston, TX 77208
	Eastern district	7	Tyler, TX 75702
	Western district	10	San Antonio, TX 78206
Utah		5	Salt Lake City, UT 84101
Vermont		2	Burlington, VT 05402
Virgin Islands		2	St. Thomas, V.I. 00801
Virginia	Eastern district	9	Alexandria, VA 22320
	Western district	4	Roanoke, VA 24006
Washington	Eastern district	4	Spokane, WA 99210
	Western district	7	Seattle, WA 98104
West Virginia	Northern district	3	Elkins, WV 26241
	Southern district	5	Charleston, WV 25329
Wisconsin	Eastern district	4	Milwaukee, WI 53202
	Western district	2	Madison, WI 53701
Wyoming		3	Cheyenne, WY 82001

FIGURE 4-6 Federal Judiciary—Jurisdiction.

FEDERAL JUDICIARY—JURISDICTION

Two forms of federal judicial jurisdiction are authorized by Article III of the Constitution. Both have been implemented by Congress via statute.

Federal Question

Law: 28 U.S.C. § 1331

Jurisdiction: Cases arising under the federal Constitution or other federal law

Diversity of Citizenship

Law: 28 U.S.C. § 1332

Jurisdiction: Cases in which all plaintiffs are from different states from all defendants (complete diversity) and there is a minimum amount in controversy ($75,000)

Removal: Cases originally filed in state court, but for which federal jurisdiction exists, may be removed to federal court by the defendant. 28 U.S.C. § 1441.

Remand: Improperly removed cases (no federal jurisdiction) may be returned to the state courts from which they were removed. 28 U.S.C. § 1447.

certain geographical areas. The First through the Eleventh Circuits each hear cases arising in the three or more states comprising the circuit. The United States Court of Appeals for the District of Columbia hears cases arising in the District of Columbia and has appellate jurisdiction assigned by Congress in legislation concerning many departments of the federal government. Figure 4-7 contains a directory of the United States Courts of Appeals for the twelve circuits. The Court of Appeals for the Federal Circuit has national jurisdiction over specific types of cases. Figure 4-3 shows the specialized federal courts for which the Court of Appeals for the Federal circuit has appellate jurisdiction.

The **United States Court of Appeals** for the Federal Circuit and the 12 regional courts of appeals are often referred to as circuit courts. That is because early in the nation's history, the judges of the first courts of appeals visited each of the courts in one region in a particular sequence, traveling by horseback and riding "circuit." These courts of appeals review matters from the district courts of their geographical regions, from the United States Tax Court, and from certain federal administrative agencies. A disappointed party in a district court case usually has the right to have the case reviewed in the court of appeals for the circuit. In 1998, there were 53,805 filings in the courts of appeals, a 3 percent increase over the prior year and the third consecutive year of increase.

The judges on the courts of appeals are appointed for life by the president with the advice and consent of the Senate. Figure 4-8 contains an article discussing the presidential appointment of federal district and circuit court judges. The 2000 salary for court of appeals judges is shown in figure 4-4.

United States Supreme Court

The **Supreme Court of the United States** consists of nine **justices** appointed for life by the president with the advice and consent of the Senate. One justice is appointed as the **Chief Justice** and has additional administrative duties related both to the Supreme Court and to the entire federal court system. Each justice is assigned on the courts of appeals for emergency responses. The 2000 salaries for the justices are shown in figure 4-4.

Review by the United States Supreme Court is discretionary for most cases. This means that it is within the discretion of the United States Supreme Court whether it will hear and decide a case. Only a very small percentage of the cases that are filed in the United States Supreme Court are heard. A case from the United States Court of Appeals would go to the United States Supreme Court by appeal or by **petition for writ of certiorari,** as set forth in federal statutes. Cases from the highest state courts and the United States Circuit Courts of Appeal reach the United States Supreme Court on petition for writ of certiorari (see fig. 4-9). The petition is granted if at least four justices vote to grant the writ. The article in figure 4-10 discusses the United States Supreme Court's case selection process.

FIGURE 4-7 Directory of the United States Courts—U.S. Courts of Appeals.

UNITED STATES COURTS OF APPEALS

Court of Appeals	Districts Included in Circuit	Number of Authorized Judgeships	Location/Postal Address
Federal Circuit	United States	12	Washington, DC 20439
District of Columbia Circuit	District of Columbia	12	Washington, DC 20001
First Circuit	Maine Massachusetts New Hampshire Rhode Island Puerto Rico	6	Boston, MA 02109

FIGURE 4-7 (continued)

Court of Appeals	Districts Included in Circuit	Number of Authorized Judgeships	Location/Postal Address
Second Circuit	Connecticut New York Vermont	13	New York, NY 10007
Third Circuit	Delaware New Jersey Pennsylvania Virgin Islands	14	Philadelphia, PA 19106
Fourth Circuit	Maryland North Carolina South Carolina Virginia West Virginia	15	Richmond, VA 23219
Fifth Circuit	Louisiana Mississippi Texas	17	New Orleans, LA 70130
Sixth Circuit	Kentucky Michigan Tennessee	16	Cincinnati, OH 45202
Seventh Circuit	Illinois Indiana Wisconsin	11	Chicago, IL 60604
Eighth Circuit	Arkansas Iowa Minnesota Missouri Nebraska North Dakota South Dakota	11	St. Louis, MO 63101
Ninth Circuit	Alaska Arizona California Hawaii Idaho Montana Nevada Oregon Washington Guam N. Mariana Islands	28	San Francisco, CA 94101
Tenth Circuit	Colorado Kansas New Mexico Oklahoma Utah Wyoming	12	Denver, CO 80294
Eleventh Circuit	Alabama Florida Georgia	12	Atlanta, GA 30303

FIGURE 4-8 Article—Also Up for Grabs: The Lower Courts.

THE WALL STREET JOURNAL MONDAY, JANUARY 31, 2000

ALSO UP FOR GRABS: THE LOWER COURTS

January ends with the emergence of judicial selection as an issue in the presidential campaign. To no one's surprise, Al Gore and Bill Bradley have indicated that they would pick judicial liberals while the Republican candidates have stressed their preference for judicial conservatives. There is a choice for voters here. And the contenders have been offering this choice by discussing the kind of Supreme Court justices they would select.

No one can blame them for that. The high court is our most important court, and the odds are strong that the next president will have at least a seat or two there to fill.

Rule of Law

By Terry Eastland

But the lower courts also deserve notice. And there can be no doubt that the next president will be able to influence their direction through repeated exercise of his appointment power.

There are 632 district judgeships and 179 seats on the 13 circuit courts of appeals. The judges who fill these positions don't serve as long as Supreme Court justices typically do, and district judges usually sit for fewer years than circuit judges. Vacancies quietly occur all the time in the lower courts and the next president will have even more seats to fill if Congress creates new judgeships, as it has several times since Jimmy Carter's presidency.

Ronald Reagan named 375 lower-court judges during his two terms, George Bush 187 during his single term, and Bill Clinton has appointed 331 federal judges to date. The math works out to a per-year average of 47 appointments; that's about one a week. Assuming no change in this rate, the next president will choose between 150 and 200 lower-court judges.

Most of these will be district judges. Presiding over federal trials, district judges make findings of fact that are rarely disturbed by reviewing courts. Sometimes they hand down rulings that attract national interest—recall the Clinton appointee in Ohio who recently declared unconstitutional that state's school-voucher program or the district judges in the '60s and '70s, who ruled on school-busing cases. It is fair to say that the justice most Americans experience in the federal courts is dispensed at the district court level.

Nonetheless, the decisions by district judges extend only to the parties before them, while the rulings by an appeals court bind the district courts—and thus the judges sitting on them—throughout the entire circuit. The circuits thus are the more important courts, and their significance has increased in recent years as the Supreme Court has reviewed fewer of their decisions. As a result, more of their decisions are final.

Many such "final" decisions are also extremely significant. In 1996, for example, the Fifth Circuit in the *Hopwood* case rejected the diversity rationale for preferences in admissions that many (wrongly) thought a Supreme Court majority had blessed in its landmark 1978 *Bakke* decision. Because the Supreme Court declined to review *Hopwood,* it became the law for the states in the Fifth Circuit—Texas, Louisiana and Mississippi.

Of the 153 judges now sitting on the appeals courts, 83 were named by Republican presidents and 70 by Democrats, including 54 by Mr. Clinton. There are 26 vacancies. Republican appointees have a numerical edge in nine circuits, Democratic appointees in three, and in the remaining circuit there is an equal number of both. Not all of the Republican appointees, however, merit description as judicial conservatives. And it is the rare Democratic appointee who routinely votes with his conservative colleagues. Conservatives have working majorities in five circuits—the Fourth, Fifth, Seventh, D.C., and Federal (which handles appeals from specialized courts, such as the one for international trade).

FIGURE 4-8 (continued)

Few if any of the 26 vacancies are likely to be filled this year, precisely because it is a presidential election year and the Republican-controlled Senate is loath to move Mr. Clinton's nominees. The next president will fill most of these vacancies as well as the bulk of those that occur this year and during his term. It is hardly rash to think that the next president will appoint 50 or more circuit judges. And it is possible to see what the ideological impact of these appointments could be.

The next president will choose between 150 and 200 lower court judges

A Democratic president could establish liberal majorities on the Fourth, Fifth and D.C. circuits, where currently there are a number of vacancies. That probably wouldn't happen on the Seventh and Federal circuits, unless there were an exceptional number of retirements. A Democratic president could also ensure liberal control of the Third, Sixth, Eighth, and 10th circuits—all of which have vacancies. Finally, assuming the necessary retirements, he could ensure clear liberal majorities on the First and the 11th circuits, and he could be expand the already considerable liberal majorities on the Second and Ninth circuits. In sum, a Democratic president could establish liberal dominance in all but two of the circuits.

A Republican president could not hope to do so well since he would be starting from further behind. Obviously, he could strengthen the conservative majorities on the Fourth, Fifth, and D.C. circuits, where there are vacancies. He might also do the same on the Seventh and the Federal circuits, where there are none. And he might have the chance to establish conservative majorities on the Third, Sixth, Eighth, 10th, and 11th circuits. But a GOP president would have little hope of shifting the balance of power in the First Circuit, and none at all in the Second and Ninth circuits.

Whether the next president successfully uses his appointment power to advance his judicial philosophy will be subject to many variables: the seriousness of his intention, the procedures he uses to vet prospects for the bench, and the extent to which he retains control of his nominating power (senators often try to share it). The most important variable will be the party that controls the Senate. A Senate of the same party as the president's will rarely vote to reject a nominee.

Sen. Orrin Hatch, who withdrew from the Republican race last week, has been the only candidate willing to discuss—in more than a sound bite or two—how he would go about appointing judges to the lower courts. Perhaps it is vain to hope that the remaining candidates, or even the eventual nominees, will take up this subject. Still, there is no question that the future of the lower courts will be riding on the outcome of this election.

Mr. Eastland is publisher and president of The American Spectator.

The Supreme Court meets on the first Monday of October each year and usually continues in session through June. The Supreme Court receives and disposes of approximately 5,000 cases each year, most by a brief decision that the subject matter is either not proper or not of sufficient importance to warrant review by the full court. Cases are heard en banc, that is by all of the justices sitting together in open court. Each year the court decides approximately 150 cases of great national importance and interest, with approximately two-thirds announced in full published opinions. The Court typically issues a number of opinions in June before it recesses for the summer. Figure 4-11 provides information on the caseload for the court for the October terms, 1994 through 1998.

State courts

The state court system varies from state to state. Some states have a simplified court structure (also called a **unified court structure**) with three or four tiers; the court structure of other states is more complex. A number of the four-tier state courts systems have two levels of trial courts; they are trial courts of limited jurisdiction, also called lower courts, and trial courts of general jurisdiction. The trial courts of limited jurisdiction typically are delegated certain

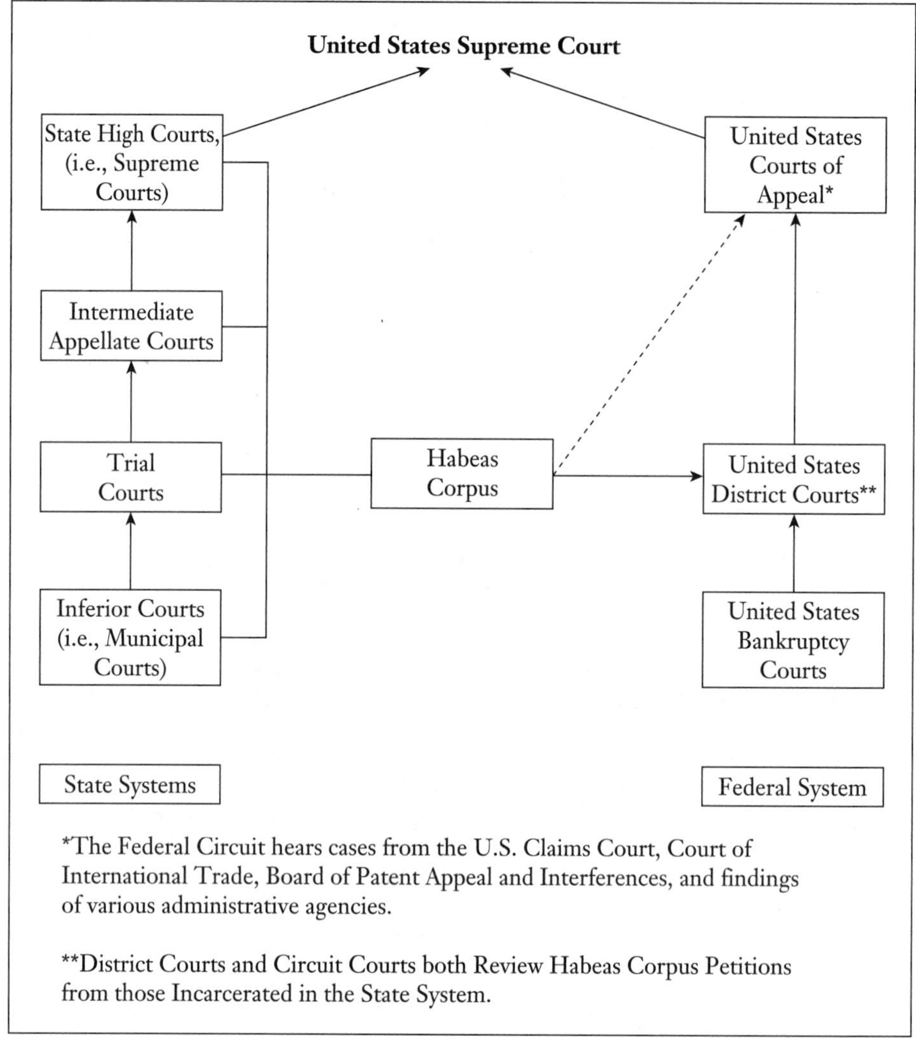

FIGURE 4-9 State and Federal Court Structures.

specific matters and the trial courts of general jurisdiction have jurisdiction over matters not delegated to the trial courts of limited jurisdiction. The state court structure in other states is more complex, with numerous courts, some with overlapping jurisdiction.

California and Illinois are examples of states with unified court structures. Illinois has a three-tier structure, with a single trial-level court, a single intermediate appellate court, and a single court of last resort. In the past, California had a four-tier structure, with two trial-level courts, a single intermediate appellate court, and a single court of last resort (fig. 4-12). Since 1998, judges in each county in California can vote to merge the two trial-level courts into a single trial court.

California's court of last resort is the Supreme Court of California. The court has one Chief Justice and six associate justices. California's intermediate appellate court, the Court of Appeal, has six appellate districts. Until 1998, California had two trial-level courts (the municipal court and the superior court), an intermediate appellate court (the Court of Appeal), and the court of last resort (the Supreme Court of California). California voters approved a constitutional amendment to the California Constitution that allows the superior courts and the municipal courts to be merged into a single "unified" superior court. Judges in a high percentage of the counties have voted for the unified superior court. In those counties with a unified superior court, all matters previously within

FIGURE 4-10 Article—Supreme Court Needs a Management Revolt.

WEDNESDAY, OCTOBER 13, 1993

SUPREME COURT NEEDS A MANAGEMENT REVOLT

Late last spring, the Supreme Court granted certiorari in a case involving 2 Live Crew's parody of Roy Orbison's 1960s hit, "Pretty Woman." 2 Live Crew's latter-day lyrics are Hobbesian—nasty, brutish and, mercifully, short. The serious legal issue now before the court in this case is whether 2 Live Crew's raunchy rendition of the song infringed Mr. Orbison's loftier lyrics.

At about the time it was sinking into 2 Live Crew's depths of vulgarity, the court was rebuffing the efforts of Quaker Oats Co. to bring order out of the chaos long characterizing trademark law. Turning a deaf ear to the company's importunings for review of the largest trademark judgment in history (the Gatorade litigation in Illinois), the court let stand a judgment tenuously supported by a confused set of lower court opinions. The Quaker Oats case is certainly less sexy than the 2 Live Crew case, but the subject matter—trademark law—is equally important.

Rule of Law

By Kenneth W. Starr

These are not isolated examples of the modern Supreme Court's peculiar system of selecting cases. All too often these days, the court is abdicating its responsibility to select complex cases with considerable practical importance; these are often cases of immense importance to business. Then there's the related mystery of the disappearing docket: The number of cases the court accepts each term is down a startling 30% over the past decade.

The explanation is not, as is commonly assumed, philosophy or ideology. The answer lies, rather, in two intertwined realities of modern court life: a lack of attention by the justices themselves to the review process and, relatedly, a ceding of power to clerks who typically have never practiced law or otherwise been involved in the world of free enterprise.

The court's system for selecting cases is simple. The justices themselves rarely read the certiorari documents that parties go to great trouble and expense to prepare; the law clerks do that for them. Like congressmen, justices have learned to rely on staff. And talented their staff is. Straight from leading law reviews and coveted federal appellate clerkships, these 36 or so bright, young lawyers wield enormous power.

They not only draft opinions in merits cases, but also inhabit the swamp internally dubbed the "cert pool." No matter how complex the case, a single law clerk writes a single memo on any given certiorari petition. A multibillion-dollar case is channeled into this bottleneck in exactly the same manner as child porno or 2 Live Crew cases. That memo is then consumed by eight of the nine justices (Justice Stevens is the lone holdout).

This judicial Bermuda Triangle has succeeded in choking off much of the important but unglamorous business-related issues from the contemporary court's docket. No matter how bright and promising the law clerks are, they are trapped in a system that is structurally impaired. The function of selecting 100 or so cases from the pool of 6,000 petitions is just too important to invest in very smart but brand-new lawyers.

My reinventing-government-style solution to this management problem is simple: Disband the cert pool. The bottleneck system was not agreed to at the Constitutional Convention in Philadelphia or included in the Judiciary Act of 1789. To the contrary, it is a newfangled contraption that began as a modest experiment but has grown into a Leviathan. It is at war with Justice Louis Brandeis's proud proclamation that the justices, unlike high government officials from the other branches, do their own work.

But how to do this without driving the justices blind, crazy, or both, from overwork? Perhaps the court should try the following formula: Circulate to the justices each week a number of cert petitions, enough to require a full day's (admittedly tedious) work by each justice. Then, on the heels of these individual reviews, the justices could assign a

FIGURE 4-10 (continued)

clerk to do follow-up work, including preparation of a full-length memo reflecting more detailed research and reflection. No pooling of information or sharing of work product would exist under this management system. The reason is fundamental: Judging should not be just another efficiency-driven joint venture.

This back-to-basics suggestion will doubtless be viewed within the court and perhaps elsewhere as unworkable or unnecessary. For skeptics, I offer a more modest suggestion: Keep the bottleneck, but break up the current monopoly into two or more equal-sized units competing with one another, accompanied by safety checks. The best check would be a quick initial look or screening of cert petitions by the individual justices themselves. This process could be completed in advance of the arrival of the pool memos in chambers, with the justice then determining, based on his or her own review and the pool memo, whether additional research or analysis should be done by an in-house "elbow" clerk.

Either of these options would create a process that is enriched and tempered by the wisdom, experience and maturity of the justices themselves. It is, after all, the justices, not their clerks, to whom the nation looks for careful, thoughtful and sober judgment.

Mr. Starr, a former federal judge, was President Bush's solicitor general.

the jurisdiction of the municipal and superior courts are within the jurisdiction of the unified superior court. An appellate division of the superior court hears cases that formerly would have been within the appellate jurisdiction of the superior court.

New York is an example of a state with a very complex court structure. New York has a single court of last resort, the Court of Appeals, and two intermediate appellate courts, the Appellate Division of Supreme Court and the Appellate Term of Supreme Court, generally divided along territorial lines. The trial-level courts include the Supreme Court, the County Court, the Court of Claims, the Family Court, the Surrogate's Court, the District Court, the City Court, the Civil Court of the City of New York, and the Town and Village Justice Court. Some trial courts have jurisdiction only in a certain geographical area, such as New York City or upstate New York; some are courts of special jurisdiction, having jurisdiction over specific types of cases; some have overlapping jurisdiction. Recent proposals for court simplification have suggested implementing a two-tier trial-court system, the higher tier with unlimited jurisdiction and the lower tier with limited jurisdiction.

The method for selecting state court judges varies from state to state and may differ for trial and appellate judges within a state. Three common methods for selecting judges are election, appointment (by the governor or the state legislature), and merit selection. Merit selection may involve the nomination of three candidates by an attorney and non-attorney judicial nominating committee, appointment of one of the three candidates by the governor, and a vote in the general election one to several years later whether the judge should be retained.

READING CASES*

Reported judicial decisions have a style and format all their own. The following discussion is designed to acquaint readers with the form and the nature of judicial decisions. While judges have considerable freedom in how they write opinions, some uniformity of pattern comes from the similarity of purpose for decisions, especially decisions of appellate courts, which frequently serve as authority for later cases. Similarity is also a product of custom. The influence of West Group, which publishes the regional **reporter** series as well as many of the federal reporters, has been great.

For whom are judicial opinions written?

In evaluating any written material, the reader should assess the audience the writer is addressing and the

*Grateful thanks to Ransford C. Pyle, Ph.D., J.D. who authored this portion of the chapter. Reproduced by Permission. FOUNDATIONS OF LAW: CASES, COMMENTARY, AND ETHICS by Ransford C. Pyle, Delmar Publishers Inc., Albany, New York, Second Edition, Copyright 1996.

SUPREME COURT OF THE UNITED STATES—CASES ON DOCKET, DISPOSED OF, AND REMAINING ON DOCKETS AT CONCLUSION OF OCTOBER TERMS, 1994 THROUGH 1998

Cases	Total	Original	Paid	In Forma Pauperis
1994				
Cases on docket	8,100	11	2,515	5,574
Disposed of	7,170	2	2,185	4,983
Remaining on dockets	930	9	330	591
1995				
Cases on docket	7,565	11	2,456	5,098
Disposed of	6,649	5	2,130	4,514
Remaining on dockets	916	6	326	584
1996				
Cases on docket	7,602	7	2,430	5,165
Disposed of	6,739	2	2,124	4,613
Remaining on dockets	863	5	306	552
1997				
Cases on docket	7,692	7	2,432	5,253
Disposed of	6,759	1	2,142	4,616
Remaining on dockets	933	6	290	637
1998				
Cases on docket	8,083	7	2,387	5,689
Disposed of	7,045	2	2,092	4,951
Remaining on dockets	1,038	5	295	738

	October Terms				
Cases	**1994**	**1995**	**1996**	**1997****	**1998**
Argued during term	94	90	90	96	90
Disposed of by full opinions	91	87	87	93	84
Disposed of by per curiam opinions	3	3	3	1	4
Set for re-argument	—	—	—	—	2
Granted review this term	93*	105*	87	90	81
Reviewed and decided without oral argument	69	120	82*	51	59
Total to be available for argument at outset of following term	39	52	48	41	30

*REVISED.
**TWO CASES DISMISSED UNDER RULE 46.1 ON 3/23/97 AND 5/15/97.

FIGURE 4-11 Caseload of the United States Supreme Court.

writer's goals. Judges write decisions for two reasons. The first is to inform the parties to the dispute who won and who lost, giving the rules and reasoning the judge applied to the facts. The second is to inform the legal profession, attorneys and judges, of the rules applied to a given set of facts and the reasons for the decision.

Attorneys and judges read judicial opinions

Very few laypersons ever enter a law library to find and read cases. The people found in the county law library are usually lawyers, paralegals, and judges. Cases are rarely intended to be entertaining, and judges are not motivated to make their cases

FIGURE 4-12 California State Courts.

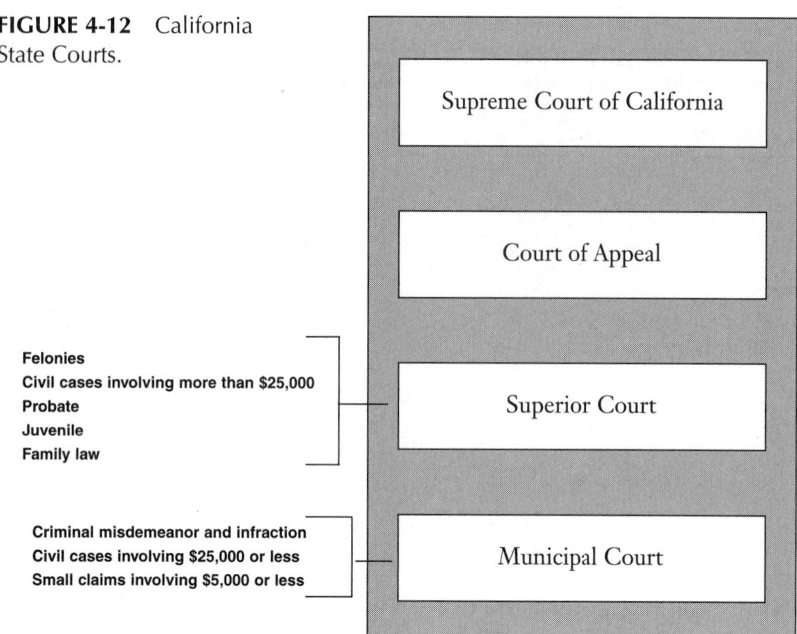

"reader-friendly." Their tasks are quite specific. Since any case may serve as precedent, or at least form a basis for subsequent legal arguments, judges are especially concerned with conveying a precise meaning by carefully framing the rules and providing the reasoning behind them. The higher the court, the greater this concern will be. Imagine writing an opinion for a highly skilled, highly intelligent readership that critically analyzes every word and phrase, an opinion that may very well affect important rights of citizens in the future.

Judicial writing is different from most other kinds of writing in that its goal is neither simply to pass on information nor persuade the reader of the author's point of view. Persuasion is past; the judge is stating the law, making a final judgment, but must do so with caution so that the statements are not misinterpreted or misused. An appreciation of the judge's dilemma is essential to critical evaluation of cases.

The effect of setting precedent

The cost of litigation is great, and appeal of a decision incurs significant additional cost. It makes sense to appeal if the losing party legitimately concludes that the lower court was incorrect in its application of the law. It would be quite foolish to spend large sums of money to go to the higher court if the chances of winning were slim and the stakes were small. This means that the cases we read from appellate courts, and especially from the highest courts, generally involve questions that have strong arguments on both sides. The judges of these cases are faced with difficult decisions and must respect the reasonable arguments of both sides in deciding which side prevails.

The format for a reported decision

The cases found in the reporters generally follow a uniform format with which researchers must become familiar. The first part of the case has no official authority. Authoritative statements begin with the actual text of the opinion.

Format preceding the opinion

West Group (formerly West Publishing Company), publisher of the regional reporters and many of the federal reporters, has established a quite uniform format. Lexis Law Publishing, publisher of *United States Supreme Court Reports, Lawyers' Edition* and other important law books, uses a similar format. To illustrate the West format, the pages of *United States v. McKinnon*, 985 F.2d 525 (11th Cir. 1993) and *Wyoming v. Houghton*, 526 U.S. 295 (1999) provide all the elements necessary. As you read the following explanation, it would be helpful for you to refer to figures 4-13 and 4-14 in this chapter. After you understand the West format, look up *Houghton*, starting on page 408

FIGURE 4-13 United States v. McKinnon.

U.S. V. MCKINNON

Cite as 985 F.2d 525 (11th Cir. 1993)

000 pound load of marijuana. De Los Santos inquired about the condition of the "equipment at the farm". The code terms referred to a radio and a radio base station. The corroborating evidence showed that on the day following the conversation, a search of Herrera's farm disclosed high frequency radios.

We have examined De Los Santos' other assignments of error which raise the issues of violation of the fair cross-section requirement of jury selection and the jury screening process. De Los Santos also assigns as error prejudicial prosecutorial comments which he asserts invited the jury to convict him for his failure to come forward with exculpatory evidence. We find these assignments of error to be without merit.

CONCLUSION

The convictions of all five coconspirators/defendants are AFFIRMED.

AFFIRMED.

UNITED STATES of America, Plaintiff-Appellee,
v.
Steve McKINNON, Defendant-Appellant.

No. 91-3944.

United States Court of Appeals, Eleventh Circuit.

March 9, 1993.

Defendant was convicted in the United States District Court for the Middle District of Florida, No. 91–7–Cr-Oc–16, John H. Moore, II, Chief Judge, pursuant to his guilty plea, of conspiracy to distribute cocaine and cocaine base, possession of cocaine and cocaine base, and aiding and abetting in possession of cocaine and cocaine base. Defendant appealed, challenging denial of motion to suppress prearrest portion of conversation recorded while defendant was in backseat of police car. The Court of Appeals, Hatchett, Circuit Judge, held that defendant did not have reasonable expectation of privacy for purposes of Title III of the Omnibus Crime Control and Safe Streets Act or the Fourth Amendment.

Affirmed.

1. Criminal Law 🔑 1139, 1158(4)

Whether district court erred in denying motion to suppress is mixed question of law and fact; district court's factual findings are reviewed under "clearly erroneous" standard, while its application of law to those facts is reviewed de novo.

2. Searches and Seizures 🔑 26
Telecommunications 🔑 494.1

Defendant did not have reasonable expectation of privacy while in backseat of police car and, therefore, tape recording of his prearrest conversations did not violate Title III of the Omnibus Crime Control and Safe Streets Act or his Fourth Amendment right to privacy. 18 U.S.C.A. §§ 2510(2), 2511; U.S.C.A. Const.Amend. 4.

3. Telecommunications 🔑 491

Test for determining whether person has reasonable or justifiable expectation of privacy, for purposes of Title III of the Omnibus Crime Control and Safe Streets Act and the Fourth Amendment, has two prongs: first, whether person's conduct exhibits subjective expectation of privacy, and second, whether person's subjective expectation of privacy is one that society is willing to recognize as reasonable. 18 U.S.C.A. §§ 2510(2), 2511; U.S.C.A. Const. Amend. 4.

H. Jay Stevens, Federal Public Defender and James H. Burke, Jr., Asst. Federal Public Defender, Jacksonville, FL, for defendant-appellant.

Robert W. Genzman, U.S. Atty. and Ernst D. Mueller, Asst. U.S. Atty., Jacksonville, FL, for plaintiff-appellee.

Appeal from the United States District Court for the Middle District of Florida.

Before HATCHETT, DUBINA and CARNES, Circuit Judges.

HATCHETT, Circuit Judge:

As a matter of first impression in this circuit, we hold that a person seated in a police car does not have a reasonable expectation of privacy under Title III of the Omnibus Crime Control and Safe Streets Act, 18 U.S.C. §§ 2510, *et seq.* nor the Fourth Amendment to the Constitution.

FACTS

On January 3, 1991, law enforcement officers stopped a pick-up truck in which Theodore Pressley was the driver, and the appellant, Steve McKinnon, was a passenger, for failure to drive in a single lane on the Florida Turnpike extension in Sumter County,

Page 525 of volume 985 of Federeal Reporter, Second Series

Headnote 2

Headnote 3

Caption

Attorneys representing Steve McKinnon

Docket Number

Attorneys for the United States

Court issuing the decision

Date of the decision

Judges deciding the case

Judge who authored the opinion

Opinion begins

Syllabus prepared by the publisher

Indexing topic

Key numbers

FIGURE 4-13 (continued)

985 FEDERAL REPORTER, 2d SERIES

Florida. After Pressley successfully performed sobriety tests, one of the officers asked Pressley if he could search the truck for narcotics. Pressley signed a form signifying his consent. After the officers began the search, they invited McKinnon and Pressley to sit in the back seat of the police car until completion of the search. Accepting the invitation, McKinnon and Pressley sat in the police car while the officers continued to search Pressley's truck.

Unbeknownst to McKinnon and Pressley, one of the law enforcement officers surreptitiously activated a tape recorder located in the police car which recorded McKinnon's and Pressley's incriminating conversations. Upon finding cocaine in the truck, the officers arrested McKinnon and Pressley. Following the arrest, the officers placed McKinnon and Pressley in the back seat of the police car, and again they engaged in incriminating conversations.

PROCEDURAL HISTORY

On February 6, 1991, a federal grand jury indicted McKinnon, charging in three counts that he: (1) knowingly, intentionally and willfully conspired with other persons to distribute cocaine and cocaine base pursuant to 21 U.S.C. § 846; (2) knowingly, intentionally and willfully possessed cocaine and cocaine base pursuant to 21 U.S.C. § 841(a)(1); and (3) aided and abetted in the possession of cocaine and cocaine base pursuant 18 U.S.C. § 2. McKinnon entered not guilty pleas.

On the morning of trial, McKinnon filed a motion to suppress the pre-arrest portion of the tape recorded conversation. After a hearing on the motion, the district court denied the motion to suppress. Later, McKinnon entered a plea of guilty to all three counts, but reserved the right to appeal the denial of the motion to suppress. The district court sentenced McKinnon to 150 months imprisonment on each count to run concurrently, plus five years of supervised release. McKinnon filed this appeal.

CONTENTIONS OF THE PARTIES

McKinnon contends that the admission of the tape recording of his pre-arrest conversation while he sat in the back seat area of a police car violates Title III of the Omnibus Crime Control and Safe Streets Act, 18 U.S.C. §§ 2510 *et seq.* ("Title III") and his right to privacy pursuant to the Fourth Amendment to the United States Constitution. The government contends that McKinnon could not have reasonably believed that he had a right to privacy in the back seat area of a police car; hence, neither Title III nor the Fourth Amendment apply.

ISSUE

The sole issue is whether the district court erred in denying the motion to suppress the tapes resulting from the secret recording of McKinnon's pre-arrest conversations while he sat in the back seat of the police car.

DISCUSSION

[1] Whether the district court erred in denying the motion to suppress is a mixed question of law and fact. *United States v. Wilson,* 894 F.2d 1245, 1254 (11th Cir.), *cert. denied sub nom. Levine v. United States,* 497 U.S. 1029, 110 S.Ct. 3284, 111 L.Ed.2d 792 (1990). We review the district court's factual findings under the clearly erroneous standard; we review *de novo* its application of the law to those facts. *Wilson,* 894 F.2d at 1254.

[2] McKinnon asserts that the tape recording of his pre-arrest conversations violates Title III and his Fourth Amendment right to privacy. Title III prohibits unauthorized interception and disclosure of oral communications. 18 U.S.C. § 2511. The government argues that the recording of McKinnon's conversation does not constitute the recording of an "oral communication" as defined in 18 U.S.C. § 2510(2). Title III defines "oral communication" as "any oral communication uttered by a person exhibiting an expectation that such communication is not subject to interception under circumstances justifying such exception, but such term does not include any electronic communication." 18 U.S.C. § 2510(2). Thus, we must decide the statutory question gleaned from Title III's language and the legislative history. That is, whether the person uttering the words has a reasonable or justifiable expectation of privacy. *See* 18 U.S.C. § 2510(2); S.Rep. No. 541, 99th Cong., 2d Sess. (1986), *reprinted in* 1986 U.S.C.C.A.N. 3555, 3567; *United States v. Harrelson,* 754 F.2d 1153, 1169 (5th Cir.), *cert. denied,* 474 U.S. 908, 106 S.Ct. 277, 88 L.Ed.2d 241 (1985) (framing the question as whether a reasonable expectation of privacy existed).

The legislative history of Title III directs that we consider "oral communication" in light of the constitutional standards expressed in *Katz v. United States,* 389 U.S. 347, 88 S.Ct. 507, 19 L.Ed.2d 576 (1967). S.Rep. No. 1097, 90th Cong., 2d Sess. (1968), *reprinted in* 1968 U.S.C.C.A.N. 2112, 2178. The constitutional question is "whether the person invoking its [Fourth Amendment] protection can claim a

FIGURE 4-13 (continued)

U.S. V. MCKINNON

Cite as 985 F.2d 525 (11th Cir. 1993)

'justifiable,' a 'reasonable,' or a 'legitimate expectation of privacy' that has been invaded by government action." *Smith v. Maryland*, 442 U.S. 735, 740, 99 S.Ct. 2577, 2580, 61 L.Ed.2d 220 (1979) (referring to *Katz*); *accord United States v. Shields*, 675 F.2d 1152, 1158 (11th Cir.), *cert. denied*, 459 U.S. 858, 103 S.Ct. 130, 74 L.Ed.2d 112 (1982) (citing *Katz*, 389 U.S. at 353, 88 S.Ct. at 512 and *United States v. White*, 401 U.S. 745, 752, 91 S.Ct. 1122, 1126, 28 L.Ed.2d 453 (1971)). Hence, the statutory and constitutional test is whether a reasonable or justifiable expectation of privacy exists.

[3] This test has two prongs. First, whether McKinnon's conduct exhibited a subjective expectation of privacy; second, whether McKinnon's subjective expectation of privacy is one that society is willing to recognize as reasonable. *Smith*, 442 U.S. at 740, 99 S.Ct. at 2580 (citing *Katz*, 389 U.S. at 361, 88 S.Ct. at 516).

McKinnon argues that he exhibited a subjective expectation of privacy because he could not exit the police car, did not consent to the surreptitious recording, was out of the officers' range for hearing his conversations, and was not under arrest. Furthermore, McKinnon argues that society is willing to recognize this subjective expectation of privacy because the government violated his rights because it did not have probable cause to conduct this secret search. Finally, McKinnon argues that the front seat of a police car is equivalent to the officer's office, but the back seat is the office of the arrestee.

The government counters that no expectation of privacy exists in a marked police car, which is tantamount to a police officer's office. Furthermore, the back seat of a police car is equivalent to a jail, and no reasonable expectation of privacy exists in a jail cell. Additionally, the government argues that McKinnon could hear police radio transmissions while in the back of the police car; hence, no reasonable or justifiable expectation of privacy existed.

Though we have no controlling authority in this circuit, one federal district court and several state courts have held that no reasonable expectation of privacy exists in the back seat area of a police care. *United States v. Sallee*, 1991 WL 352613, 1991 U.S.Dist. Lexis 20553 (N.D.Ill.1991); *State v. McAdams*, 559 So.2d 601, 602 (Fla. 5th D.C.A.1990); *State v. Hussey*, 469 So.2d 346, 351 (La.Ct.App.2d Cir.), *cert. denied*, 475 So.2d 777 (La.1985); *People v. Marland*, 135 Mich.App. 297, 355 N.W.2d 378, 384 (1984); *State v. Lucero*, 96 N.M. 126, 128, 628 P.2d 696, 698 (Ct.App.1981); *Brown v. State*, 349 So.2d 1196, 1197 (Fla. 4th D.C.A.1977), *cert. denied*, 434 U.S. 1078, 98 S.Ct. 1271, 55 L.Ed.2d 785 (1978). McKinnon fails to satisfy either prong of the test. Hence, we hold that McKinnon did not have a reasonable or justifiable expectation of privacy for conversations he held while seated in the back seat area of a police car.

Moreover, McKinnon concedes that his post-arrest conversations are not entitled to Title III or Fourth Amendment protection. He argues, however, that a person has broader rights pre-arrest than post-arrest. We find no persuasive distinction between pre-arrest and post-arrest situations in this case. *See Harrelson*, 754 F.2d at 1169–1170 (finding inmate and visiting wife had no reasonable expectation of privacy while conversing in a jail); *Marland*, 355 N.W.2d at 384 (holding detainees, not under formal arrest, had no reasonable expectation of privacy while conversing in a police car); *Hussey*, 469 So.2d at 351 (finding "guests" or "visitors" of arrestee had no reasonable and justifiable expectation of privacy while conversing in the back of a police car). Both situations require the same test.

We affirm the district court's denial of the motion to suppress.

AFFIRMED.

Lillie DAVIS, Plaintiff-Appellant
v.
Donna SHALALA, Secretary of Health and Human Services, Defendant-Appellee.
No. 91-7453.

United States Court of Appeals, Eleventh Circuit.

March 9, 1993.

Supplemental Security Income (SSI) claimant, who had IQ of 69, appealed denial of benefits. The United States District Court for the Southern District of Alabama, No. 87-00351-CB-M, Charles R. Butler, Jr., J., affirmed denial, and claimant appealed. The Court of Appeals, Hatchett, Circuit Judge, held that: (1) administrative law judge (ALJ) erred in failing to consider whether combined effect of claimant's allergies and mild carpal tunnel syndrome imposed significant limitations on her functional abilities as required under mental.

FIGURE 4-14 Wyoming v. Houghton.

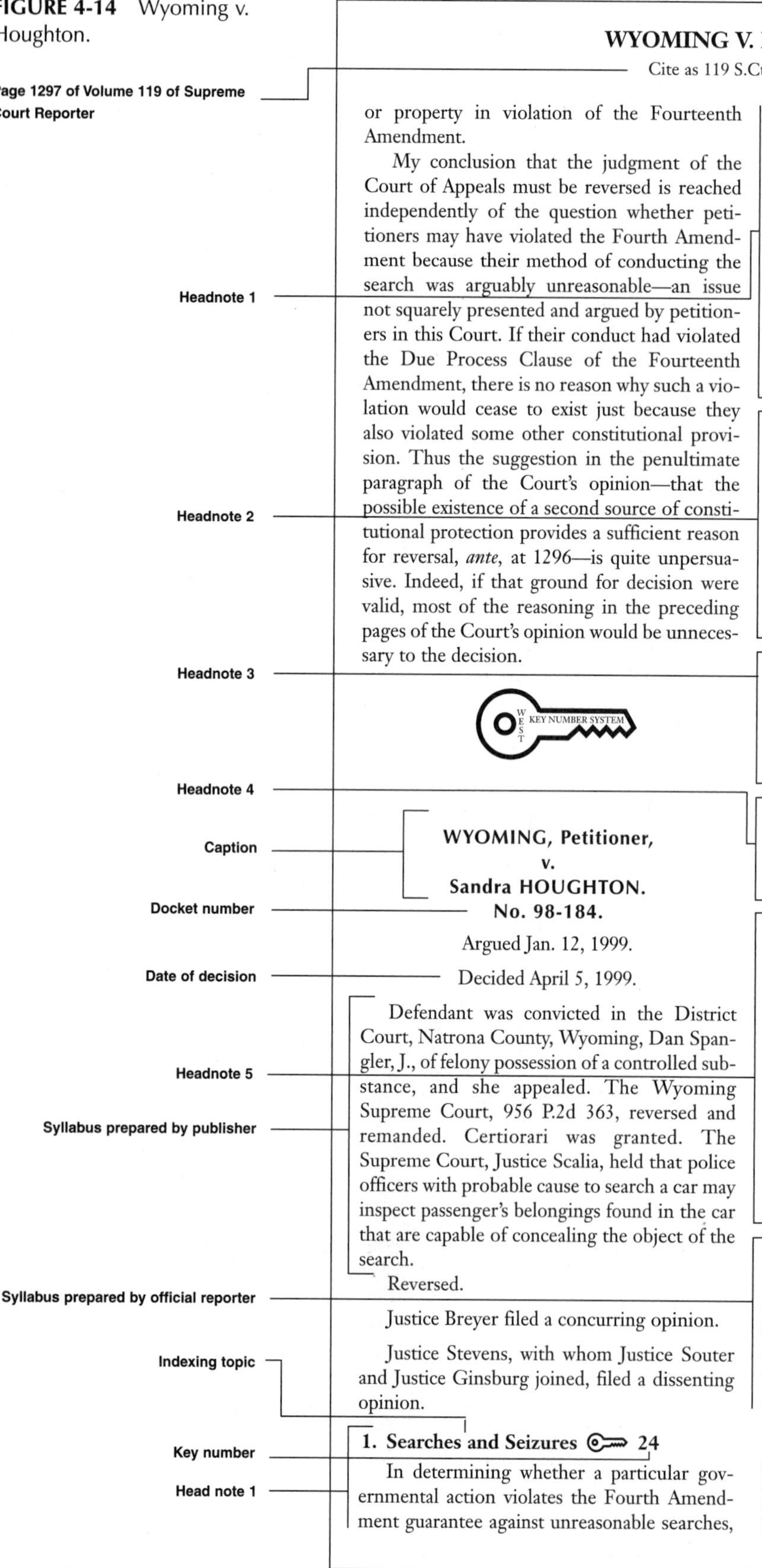

WYOMING V. HOUGHTON

Cite as 119 S.Ct. 1297 (1999)

or property in violation of the Fourteenth Amendment.

My conclusion that the judgment of the Court of Appeals must be reversed is reached independently of the question whether petitioners may have violated the Fourth Amendment because their method of conducting the search was arguably unreasonable—an issue not squarely presented and argued by petitioners in this Court. If their conduct had violated the Due Process Clause of the Fourteenth Amendment, there is no reason why such a violation would cease to exist just because they also violated some other constitutional provision. Thus the suggestion in the penultimate paragraph of the Court's opinion—that the possible existence of a second source of constitutional protection provides a sufficient reason for reversal, *ante*, at 1296—is quite unpersuasive. Indeed, if that ground for decision were valid, most of the reasoning in the preceding pages of the Court's opinion would be unnecessary to the decision.

WEST KEY NUMBER SYSTEM

WYOMING, Petitioner,
v.
Sandra HOUGHTON.
No. 98-184.

Argued Jan. 12, 1999.

Decided April 5, 1999.

Defendant was convicted in the District Court, Natrona County, Wyoming, Dan Spangler, J., of felony possession of a controlled substance, and she appealed. The Wyoming Supreme Court, 956 P.2d 363, reversed and remanded. Certiorari was granted. The Supreme Court, Justice Scalia, held that police officers with probable cause to search a car may inspect passenger's belongings found in the car that are capable of concealing the object of the search.

Reversed.

Justice Breyer filed a concurring opinion.

Justice Stevens, with whom Justice Souter and Justice Ginsburg joined, filed a dissenting opinion.

1. Searches and Seizures ⚿ 24

In determining whether a particular governmental action violates the Fourth Amendment guarantee against unreasonable searches, Supreme Court inquires, first, whether the action was regarded as an unlawful search or seizure under the common law when the Amendment was framed, and where that inquiry yields no answer, Court must evaluate the search or seizure under traditional standards of reasonableness by assessing, on the one hand, the degree to which it intrudes upon an individual's privacy and, on the other, the degree to which it is needed for the promotion of legitimate governmental interests. U.S.C.A. Const.Amend. 4.

2. Searches and Seizures ⚿ 65

If probable cause justifies the search of a lawfully stopped vehicle, it justifies the search of every part of the vehicle and its contents that may conceal the object of the search, and this rule applies to all containers within a car, without qualification as to ownership and without a showing of individualized probable cause for each container. U.S.C.A. Const.Amend. 4.

3. Searches and Seizures ⚿ 61

Passengers, no less than drivers, possess a reduced expectation of privacy with regard to the property that they transport in cars. U.S.C.A. Const.Amend. 4.

4. Searches and Seizures ⚿ 53.1

Unique, significantly heightened, protection is afforded against searches of one's person. U.S.C.A. Const.Amend. 4.

5. Searches and Seizures ⚿ 65

Police officers with probable cause to search a car may inspect passenger's belongings found in the car that are capable of concealing the object of the search, and the investigating officer need not have positive reason to believe that the passenger and driver were engaged in a common enterprise, or positive reason to believe that the driver had time and occasion to conceal the item in the passenger's belongings, surreptitiously or with friendly permission. U.S.C.A. Const. Amend. 4.

*Syllabus**

During a routine traffic stop, a Wyoming Highway Patrol officer noticed a hypodermic syringe in the driver's shirt pocket, which the driver admitted using to take drugs. The officer then searched the passenger compartment for contraband, removing and searching what

*The syllabus constitutes no part of the opinion of the Court but has been prepared by the Reporter of Decisions for the convenience of the reader. See *United States v. Detroit Timber & Lumber Co.*, 200 U.S. 321, 337, 26 S.Ct. 282, 50 L.Ed. 499.

FIGURE 4-14 (continued)

119 SUPREME COURT REPORTER

respondent, a passenger in the car, claimed was her purse. He found drug paraphernalia there and arrested respondent on drug charges. The trial court denied her motion to suppress all evidence from the purse as the fruit of an unlawful search, holding that the officer had probable cause to search the car for contraband, and, by extension, any containers therein that could hold such contraband. Respondent was convicted. In reversing, the Wyoming Supreme Court ruled that an officer with probable cause to search a vehicle may search all containers that might conceal the object of the search; but, if the officer knows or should know that a container belongs to a passenger who is not suspected of criminal activity, then the container is outside the scope of the search unless someone had the opportunity to conceal contraband within it to avoid detection. Applying that rule here, the court concluded that the search violated the Fourth and Fourteenth Amendments.

Held: Police officers with probable cause to search a car, as in this case, may inspect passengers' belongings found in the car that are capable of concealing the object of the search. In determining whether a particular governmental action violates the Fourth Amendment, this Court inquires first whether the action was regarded as an unlawful search or seizure under common law when the Amendment was framed, see, *e.g., Wilson v. Arkansas,* 514 U.S. 927, 931, 115 S.Ct. 1914, 131 L.Ed.2d 976. Where that inquiry yields no answer, the Court must evaluate the search or seizure under traditional reasonableness standards by balancing an individual's privacy interests against legitimate governmental interests, see, *e.g., Vernonia School Dist. 47J v. Acton,* 515 U.S. 646, 652–653, 115 S.Ct. 2386, 132 L.Ed.2d 564. This Court has concluded that the Framers would have regarded as reasonable the warrantless search of a car that police had probable cause to believe contained contraband, *Carroll v. United States,* 267 U.S. 132, 45 S.Ct. 280, 69 L.Ed. 543, as well as the warrantless search of containers *within* the automobile, *United States v. Ross,* 456 U.S. 798, 102 S.Ct. 2157, 72 L.Ed.2d 572. Neither *Ross* nor the historical evidence it relied upon admits of a distinction based on ownership. The analytical principle underlying *Ross*'s rule is also fully consistent with the balance of this Court's Fourth Amendment jurisprudence. Even if the historical evidence were equivocal, the balancing of the relative interests weighs decidedly in favor of searching a passenger's belongings. Passengers, no less than drivers, possess a reduced expectation of privacy with regard to the property they transport in cars. See, *e.g., Cardwell v. Lewis,* 417 U.S. 583, 590, 94 S.Ct. 2464, 41 L.Ed.2d 325. The degree of intrusiveness of a package search upon personal privacy and personal dignity is substantially less than the degree of intrusiveness of the body searches at issue in *United States v. Di Re,* 332 U.S. 581, 68 S.Ct. 222, 92 L.Ed. 210, and *Ybarra v. Illinois,* 444 U.S. 85, 100 S.Ct. 338, 62 L.Ed.2d 238. In contrast to the passenger's reduced privacy expectations, the governmental interest in effective law enforcement would be appreciably impaired without the ability to search the passenger's belongings, since an automobile's ready mobility creates the risk that evidence or contraband will be permanently lost while a warrant is obtained, *California v. Carney,* 471 U.S. 386, 105 S.Ct. 2066, 85 L.Ed.2d 406; since a passenger may have an interest in concealing evidence of wrongdoing in a common enterprise with the driver, cf. *Maryland v. Wilson,* 519 U.S. 408, 413–414, 117 S.Ct. 882, 137 L.Ed.2d 41; and since a criminal might be able to hide contraband in a passenger's belongings as readily as in other containers in the car, see, *e.g., Rawlings v. Kentucky,* 448 U.S. 98, 102, 100 S.Ct. 2556, 65 L.Ed.2d 633. The Wyoming Supreme Court's "passenger property" rule would be unworkable in practice. Finally, an exception from the historical practice described in *Ross* protecting only a passenger's property, rather than property belonging to *anyone* other than the driver, would be less sensible than the rule that a package may be searched, whether or not its owner is present as a passenger or otherwise, because it might contain the object of the search. Pp. 1300–1304.

Syllabus prepared by official reporter

956 P.2d 363, reversed.

SCALIA, J., delivered the opinion of the Court, in which REHNQUIST, C.J., and O'CONNOR, KENNEDY, THOMAS, and BREYER, JJ., joined. BREYER, J., filed a concurring opinion. STEVENS, J., filed a dissenting opinion, in which SOUTER and GINSBURG, JJ., joined.

Justice joining in majority opinion

Justice authoring concurring opinion

Justices joining in dissenting opinion

Paul S. Rehurek, Cheyenne, WY, for petitioner.

Attorney for State of Wyoming

Barbara B. McDowell, for United States as amicus curiae by leave of the Court.

Donna D. Domonkos, Cheyenne, WY, for respondent.

Attorney for Houghton

For U.S. Supreme Court briefs, see:
1998 WL 784283 (Pet.Brief)
1998 WL 876970 (Resp.Brief)
1998 WL 898902 (Reply.Brief)

WestLaw citations to the appellate briefs filed in the case

Justice SCALIA delivered the opinion of the Court.

Opinion begins

FIGURE 4-14 (continued)

WYOMING V. HOUGHTON

Cite as 119 S.Ct. 1297 (1999)

This case presents the question whether police officers violate the Fourth Amendment when they search a passenger's personal belongings inside an automobile that they have probable cause to believe contains contraband.

I

In the early morning hours of July 23, 1995, a Wyoming Highway Patrol officer stopped an automobile for speeding and driving with a faulty brake light. There were three passengers in the front seat of the car: David Young (the driver), his girlfriend, and respondent. While questioning Young, the officer noticed a hypodermic syringe in Young's shirt pocket. He left the occupants under the supervision of two backup officers as he went to get gloves from his patrol car. Upon his return, he instructed Young to step out of the car and place the syringe on the hood. The officer then asked Young why he had a syringe; with refreshing candor, Young replied that he used it to take drugs.

At this point, the backup officers ordered the two female passengers out of the car and asked them for identification. Respondent falsely identified herself as "Sandra James" and stated that she did not have any identification. Meanwhile, in light of Young's admission, the officer searched the passenger compartment of the car for contraband. On the back seat, he found a purse, which respondent claimed as hers. He removed from the purse a wallet containing respondent's driver's license, identifying her properly as Sandra K. Houghton. When the officer asked her why she had lied about her name, she replied: "In case things went bad."

Continuing his search of the purse, the officer found a brown pouch and a black wallet-type container. Respondent denied that the former was hers, and claimed ignorance of how it came to be there; it was found to contain drug paraphernalia and a syringe with 60 ccs of methamphetamine. Respondent admitted ownership of the black container, which was also found to contain drug paraphernalia, and a syringe (which respondent acknowledged was hers) with 10 ccs of methamphetamine—an amount insufficient to support the felony conviction at issue in this case. The officer also found fresh needle-track marks on respondent's arms. He placed her under arrest.

The State of Wyoming charged respondent with felony possession of methamphetamine in a liquid amount greater than three-tenths of a gram. See Wyo. Stat. Ann. § 35-7-1031(c)(iii) (Supp.1996). After a hearing, the trial court denied her motion to suppress all evidence obtained from the purse as the fruit of a violation of the Fourth and Fourteenth Amendments. The court held that the officer had probable cause to search the car for contraband, and, by extension, any containers therein that could hold such contraband. A jury convicted respondent as charged.

The Wyoming Supreme Court, by divided vote, reversed the conviction and announced the following rule:

> "Generally, once probable cause is established to search a vehicle, an officer is entitled to search all containers therein which may contain the object of the search. However, if the officer knows or should know that a container is the personal effect of a passenger who is not suspected of criminal activity, then the container is outside the scope of the search unless someone had the opportunity to conceal the contraband within the personal effect to avoid detection." 956 P.2d 363, 372 (1998).

The court held that the search of respondent's purse violated the Fourth and Fourteenth Amendments because the officer "knew or should have known that the purse did not belong to the driver, but to one of the passengers," and because "there was no probable cause to search the passengers' personal effects and no reason to believe that contraband had been placed within the purse." *Ibid.*

II

[1] The Fourth Amendment protects "[t]he right of the people to be secure in their persons, houses, papers, and effects, against unreasonable searches and seizures." In determining whether a particular governmental action violates this provision, we inquire first whether the action was regarded as an unlawful search or seizure under the common law when the Amendment was framed. See *Wilson v. Arkansas*, 514 U.S. 927, 931, 115 S.Ct. 1914, 131 L.Ed.2d 976 (1995); *California v. Hodari D.*, 499 U.S. 621, 624, 111 S.Ct. 1547, 113 L.Ed.2d 690 (1991). Where that inquiry yields no answer, we must evaluate the search or seizure under traditional standards of reasonableness by assessing, on the one hand, the degree to which it intrudes upon an individual's privacy and, on the other, the degree to which it is needed for the promotion of legitimate governmental interests. See, *e.g.*, *Vernonia School Dist. 47J v. Acton*, 515 U.S. 646, 652–653, 115 S.Ct. 2386, 132 L.Ed.2d 564 (1995).

[2] It is uncontested in the present case that the police officers had probable cause to believe there were illegal drugs in the car. *Carroll v. United States*, 267 U.S. 132, 45 S.Ct. 280, 69

FIGURE 4-14 (continued)

119 SUPREME COURT REPORTER

L.Ed. 543 (1925), similarly involved the warrantless search of a car that law enforcement officials had probable cause to believe contained contraband—in that case, bootleg liquor. The Court concluded that the Framers would have regarded such a search as reasonable in light of legislation enacted by Congress from 1789 through 1799—as well as subsequent legislation from the Founding era and beyond—that empowered customs officials to search any ship or vessel without a warrant if they had probable cause to believe that it contained goods subject to a duty. *Id.*, at 150–153, 45 S.Ct. 280. See also *United States v. Ross*, 456 U.S. 798, 806, 102 S.Ct. 2157, 72 L.Ed.2d 572 (1982); *Boyd v. United States*, 116 U.S. 616, 623–624, 6 S.Ct. 524, 29 L.Ed. 746 (1886). Thus, the Court held that "contraband goods concealed and illegally transported in an automobile or other vehicle may be searched for without a warrant" where probable cause exists. *Carroll, supra*, at 153, 45 S.Ct. 280.

We have furthermore read the historical evidence to show that the Framers would have regarded as reasonable (if there was probable cause) the warrantless search of containers *within* an automobile. In *Ross, supra*, we upheld as reasonable the warrantless search of a paper bag and leather pouch found in the trunk of the defendant's car by officers who had probable cause to believe that the trunk contained drugs. Justice STEVENS, writing for the Court, observed:

> "It is noteworthy that the early legislation on which the Court relied in *Carroll* concerned the enforcement of laws imposing duties on imported merchandise. . . . Presumably such merchandise was shipped then in containers of various kinds, just as it is today. Since Congress had authorized warrantless searches of vessels and beasts for imported merchandise, it is inconceivable that it intended a customs officer to obtain a warrant for every package discovered during the search; certainly Congress intended customs officers to open shipping containers when necessary and not merely to examine the exterior of cartons or boxes in which smuggled goods might be concealed. During virtually the entire history of our country—whether contraband was transported in a horse-drawn carriage, a 1921 roadster, or a modern automobile—it has been assumed that a lawful search of a vehicle would include a search of any container that might conceal the object of the search." *Id.*, at 820, n. 26, 45 S.Ct. 280.

Ross summarized its holding as follows: "If probable cause justifies the search of a lawfully stopped vehicle, it justifies the search of *every part of the vehicle and its contents* that may conceal the object of the search." *Id.*, at 825, 102 S.Ct. 2157 (emphasis added). And our later cases describing *Ross* have characterized it as applying broadly to *all* containers within a car, without qualification as to ownership. See, *e.g.*, *California v. Acevedo*, 500 U.S. 565, 572, 111 S.Ct. 1982, 114 L.Ed.2d 619 (1991) ("[T]his Court in *Ross* took the critical step of saying that closed containers in cars could be searched without a warrant because of their presence within the automobile"); *United States v. Johns*, 469 U.S. 478, 479–480, 105 S.Ct. 881, 83 L.Ed.2d 890 (1985) (*Ross* "held that if police officers have probable cause to search a lawfully stopped vehicle, they may conduct a warrantless search of any containers found inside that may conceal the object of the search").

To be sure, there was no passenger in *Ross*, and it was not claimed that the package in the trunk belonged to anyone other than the driver. Even so, if the rule of law that *Ross* announced were limited to contents belonging to the driver, or contents other than those belonging to passengers, one would have expected that substantial limitation to be expressed. And, more importantly, one would have expected that limitation to be apparent in the historical evidence that formed the basis for *Ross*'s holding. In fact, however, nothing in the statutes *Ross* relied upon, or in the practice under those statutes, would except from authorized warrantless search packages belonging to passengers on the suspect ship, horse-drawn carriage, or automobile.

Finally, we must observe that the analytical principle underlying the rule announced in *Ross* is fully consistent—as respondent's proposal is not—with the balance of our Fourth Amendment jurisprudence. *Ross* concluded from the historical evidence that the permissible scope of a warrantless car search "is defined by the object of the search and the places in which there is probable cause to believe that it may be found." 456 U.S., at 824, 102 S.Ct. 2157. The same principle is reflected in an earlier case involving the constitutionality of a search warrant directed at premises belonging to one who is not suspected of any crime: "The critical element in a reasonable search is not that the owner of the property is suspected of crime but that there is reasonable cause to believe that the specific `things' to be search for and seized are located on the property to which entry is sought." *Zurcher v. Stanford Daily*, 436 U.S. 547, 556, 98 S.Ct. 1970, 56 L.Ed.2d 525 (1978). This statement was illustrated by citation and

FIGURE 4-14 (continued)

WYOMING V. HOUGHTON

Cite as 119 S.Ct. 1297 (1999)

description of *Carroll, supra.* 436 U.S., at 556–557, 98 S.Ct. 1970.

In sum, neither *Ross* itself nor the historical evidence it relied upon admits of a distinction among packages or containers based on ownership. When there is probable cause to search for contraband in a car, it is reasonable for police officers—like customs officials in the Founding era—to examine packages and containers without a showing of individualized probable cause for each one. A passenger's personal belongings, just like the driver's belongings or containers attached to the car like a glove compartment, are "in" the car, and the officer has probable cause to search for contraband *in* the car.

[3] Even if the historical evidence, as described by *Ross*, were thought to be equivocal, we would find that the balancing of the relative interests weighs decidedly in favor of allowing searches of a passenger's belongings. Passengers, no less than drivers, possess a reduced expectation of privacy with regard to the property that they transport in cars, which "trave[l] public thoroughfares," *Cardwell v. Lewis*, 417 U.S. 583, 590, 94 S.Ct. 2464, 41 L.Ed.2d 325 (1974), "seldom serv[e] as . . . the repository of personal effects," *ibid.*, are subjected to police stop and examination to enforce "pervasive" governmental controls "[a]s an everyday occurrence," *South Dakota v. Opperman*, 428 U.S. 364, 368, 96 S.Ct. 3092, 49 L.Ed.2d 1000 (1976), and, finally, are exposed to traffic accidents that may render all their contents open to public scrutiny.

[4] In this regard—the degree of intrusiveness upon personal privacy and indeed even personal dignity—the two cases the Wyoming Supreme Court found dispositive differ substantially from the package search at issue here. *United States v. Di Re*, 332 U.S. 581, 68 S.Ct. 222, 92 L.Ed. 210 (1948), held that probable cause to search a car did not justify a body search of a passenger. And *Ybarra v. Illinois*, 444 U.S. 85, 100 S.Ct. 338, 62 L.Ed.2d 238 (1979), held that a search warrant for a tavern and its bartender did not permit body searches of all the bar's patrons. These cases turned on the unique, significantly heightened protection afforded against searches of one's person. "Even a limited search of the outer clothing . . . constitutes a severe, though brief, intrusion upon cherished personal security, and it must surely be an annoying, frightening, and perhaps humiliating experience." *Terry v. Ohio*, 392 U.S. 1, 24–25, 88 S.Ct. 1868, 20 L.Ed.2d 889 (1968). Such traumatic consequences are not to be expected when the police examine an item of personal property found in a car.[1]

Whereas the passenger's privacy expectations are, as we have described, considerably diminished, the governmental interests at stake are substantial. Effective law enforcement would be appreciably impaired without the ability to search a passenger's personal belongings when there is reason to believe contraband or evidence of criminal wrongdoing is hidden in the car. As in all car-search cases, the "ready mobility" of an automobile creates a risk that the evidence or contraband will be permanently lost while a warrant is obtained. *California v. Carney*, 471 U.S. 386, 390, 105 S.Ct. 2066, 85 L.Ed.2d 406 (1985). In addition, a car passenger—unlike the unwitting tavern patron in *Ybarra*—will often be engaged in a common

1. The dissent begins its analysis, *post*, at 1305, with an assertion that this case is governed by our decision in *United States v. Di Re*, 332 U.S. 581, 68 S.Ct. 222, 92 L.Ed. 210 (1948), which held, as the dissent describes it, that the automobile exception to the warrant requirement did not justify "searches of the passenger's pockets and the space between his shirt and underwear," *post*, at 1305. It attributes that holding to "the settled distinction between drivers and passengers," rather than to a distinction between search of the person and search of property, which the dissent claims is "newly minted" by today's opinion—a "new rule that is based on a distinction between property contained in clothing worn by a passenger and property contained in a passenger's briefcase or purse." *Ibid.*

In its peroration, however, the dissent quotes extensively from Justice Jackson's opinion in *Di Re*, which makes it very clear that it is *precisely* this distinction between search of the person and search of property that the case relied upon: "The Government says it would not contend that, armed with a search warrant for a residence only, it could search all persons found in it. But an occupant of a house could be used to conceal this contraband on his person quite as readily as can an occupant of a car." 332 U.S., at 587, 68 S.Ct. 222 (quoted *post*, at 1306).

Does the dissent really believe that Justice Jackson was saying that a house-search could not inspect *property* belonging to persons found in the house—say a large standing safe or violin case belonging to the owner's visiting godfather? Of course that is not what Justice Jackson meant at all. He was referring *precisely* to that distinction between property contained in clothing worn by a passenger and property contained in a passenger's briefcase or purse" that the dissent disparages, *post*, at 1305. This distinction between searches of the person and searches of property is assuredly *not* "newly minted," see *supra*, at 1302. And if the dissent thinks "pockets" and "clothing" do not count as part of the person, it must believe that the only searches of the person are strip searches.

FIGURE 4-14 (continued)

119 SUPREME COURT REPORTER

enterprise with the driver, and have the same interest in concealing the fruits or the evidence of their wrongdoing. Cf. *Maryland v. Wilson*, 519 U.S. 408, 413–414, 117 S.Ct. 882, 137 L.Ed.2d 41 (1997). A criminal might be able to hide contraband in a passenger's belongings as readily as in other containers in the car, see, *e.g., Rawlings v. Kentucky*, 448 U.S. 98, 102, 100 S.Ct. 2556, 65 L.Ed.2d 633 (1980)—perhaps even surreptitiously, without the passenger's knowledge or permission. (This last possibility provided the basis for respondent's defense at trial; she testified that most of the seized contraband must have been placed in her purse by her traveling companions at one or another of various times, including the time she was "half asleep" in the car.)

[5] To be sure, these factors favoring a search will not always be present, but the balancing of interests must be conducted with an eye to the generality of cases. To require that the investigating officer have positive reason to believe that the passenger and driver were engaged in a common enterprise, or positive reason to believe that the driver had time and occasion to conceal the item in the passenger's belongings, surreptitiously or with friendly permission, is to impose requirements so seldom met that a "passenger's property" rule would dramatically reduce the ability to find and seize contraband and evidence of crime. Of course these requirements would not attach (under the Wyoming Supreme Court's rule) until the police officer knows or has reason to know that the container belongs to a passenger. But once a "passenger's property" exception to car searches became widely known, one would expect passenger-confederates to claim everything as their own. And one would anticipate a bog of litigation—in the form of both civil lawsuits and motions to suppress in criminal trials—involving such questions as whether the officer should have believed a passenger's claim of ownership, whether he should have inferred ownership from various objective factors, whether he had probable cause to believe that the passenger was a confederate, or to believe that the driver might have introduced the contraband into the package with or without the passenger's knowledge.[2] When balancing the competing interests, our determinations of "reasonableness" under the Fourth Amendment must take account of these practical realities. We think they militate in favor of the needs of law enforcement, and against a personal-privacy interest that is ordinarily weak.

Finally, if we were to invent an exception from the historical practice that *Ross* accurately described and summarized, it is perplexing why that exception should protect only property belonging to a passenger, rather than (what seems much more logical) property belonging to *anyone* other than the driver. Surely Houghton's privacy would have been invaded to the same degree whether she was present or absent when her purse was searched. And surely her presence in the car with the driver provided more, rather than less, reason to believe that the two were in league. It may ordinarily be easier to identify the property as belonging to someone other than the driver when the purported owner is present to identify it—but in the many cases (like *Ross* itself) where the car is seized, that identification may occur later, at the station-house; and even at the site of the stop one can readily imagine a package clearly marked with the owner's name and phone number, by which the officer can confirm the driver's denial of ownership. The sensible rule (and the one supported by history and caselaw) is that such a package may be searched, whether or not its owner is present as a passenger or otherwise, because it may contain the contraband that the officer has reason to believe is in the car.

* * *

We hold that police officers with probable cause to search a car may inspect passengers' belongings found in the car that are capable of concealing the object of the search. The judgment of the Wyoming Supreme Court is reversed.

It is so ordered.

2. The dissent is "confident in a police officer's ability to apply a rule requiring a warrant or individualized probable cause to search belongings that are . . . obviously owned by and in the custody of a passenger," *post*, at 1306. If this is the dissent's strange criterion for warrant protection ("*obviously* owned by and in the custody of") its preceding paean to the importance of preserving passengers' privacy rings a little hollow on rehearing. Should it not be enough if the passenger *says* he owns the briefcase, and the officer has no concrete reason to believe otherwise? Or would the dissent consider *that* an example of "obvious" ownership? On reflection, it seems not at all obviously precisely what constitutes obviousness—and so even the dissent's on-the-cheap protection of passengers' privacy interest in their property turns out to be unclear, and hence unadministrable. But maybe the dissent does not mean to propose an obviously-owned-by-and-in-the-custody-of test after all, since a few sentences later it endorses, *simpliciter*, "a rule requiring a warrant or individualized probable cause to search passenger belongings," *ibid.* For the reasons described in text, that will not work.

FIGURE 4-14 (continued)

WYOMING V. HOUGHTON

Cite as 119 S.Ct. 1297 (1999)

Concurring opinion begins

Justice BREYER, concurring.

I join the Court's opinion with the understanding that history is meant to inform, but not automatically to determine, the answer to a Fourth Amendment question. *Ante*, at 1300. I also agree with the Court that when a police officer has probable cause to search a car, say, for drugs, it is reasonable for that officer also to search containers within the car. If the police must establish a container's ownership prior to the search of that container (whenever, for example, a passenger says "that's mine"), the resulting uncertainty will destroy the workability of the bright-line rule set forth in *United States v. Ross*, 456 U.S. 798, 102 S.Ct. 2157, 72 L.Ed.2d 572 (1982). At the same time, police officers with probable cause to search a car for drugs would often have probable cause to search containers regardless. Hence a bright-line rule will authorize only a limited number of searches that the law would not otherwise justify.

At the same time, I would point out certain limitations upon the scope of the bright-line rule that the Court describes. Obviously, the rule applies only to automobile searches. Equally obviously, the rule applies only to containers found within automobiles. And it does not extend to the search of a person found in that automobile. As the Court notes, and as *United States v. Di Re*, 332 U.S. 581, 586–587, 68 S.Ct. 222, 92 L.Ed. 210 (1948), relied on heavily by Justice STEVENS' dissent, makes clear, the search of a person, including even " 'a limited search of the outer clothing,' " *ante*, at 1302 (quoting *Terry v. Ohio*, 392 U.S. 1, 24–25, 88 S.Ct. 1868, 20 L.Ed.2d 889 (1968)), is a very different matter in respect to which the law provides "significantly heightened protection." *Ibid;* cf. *Ybarra v. Illinois*, 444 U.S. 85, 91, 100 S.Ct. 338, 62 L.Ed.2d 238 (1979); *Sibron v. New York*, 392 U.S. 40, 62–64, 88 S.Ct. 1889, 20 L.Ed.2d 917 (1968).

Less obviously, but in my view also important, is the fact that the container here at issue, a woman's purse, was found at a considerable distance from its owner, who did not claim ownership until the officer discovered her identification while looking through it. Purses are special containers. They are repositories of especially personal items that people generally like to keep with them at all times. So I am tempted to say that a search of a purse involves an intrusion so similar to a search of one's person that the same rule should govern both. However, given this Court's prior cases, I cannot argue that the fact that the container was a purse *automatically* makes a legal difference, for the Court has warned against trying to make that kind of distinction. *United States v. Ross*, *supra*, at 822, 102 S.Ct. 2157. But I can say that it would matter if a woman's purse, like a man's billfold, were attached to her person. It might then amount to a kind of "outer clothing." *Terry v. Ohio*, *supra*, at 24, 88 S.Ct. 1868, which under the Court's cases would properly receive increased protection. See *post*, at 1306 (STEVENS, J., dissenting) (quoting *United States v. Di Re*, *supra*, at 587, 68 S.Ct. 222). In this case, the purse was separate from the person, and no one has claimed that, under those circumstances, the type of container makes a difference. For that reason, I join the Court's opinion.

Dissenting opinion begins

Justice STEVENS, with whom Justice SOUTER and Justice GINSBURG join, dissenting.

After Wyoming's highest court decided that a state highway patrolman unlawfully searched Sandra Houghton's purse, the State of Wyoming petitioned for a writ of certiorari. The State asked that we consider the propriety of searching an automobile *passenger's* belongings when the government has developed probable cause to search the vehicle for contraband based on the *driver's* conduct. The State conceded that the trooper who searched Houghton's purse lacked a warrant, consent, or "probable cause specific to the purse or passenger." Pet. for Cert. i. In light of our established preference for warrants and individualized suspicion, I would respect the result reached by the Wyoming Supreme Court and affirm its judgment.

In all of our prior cases applying the automobile exception to the Fourth Amendment's warrant requirement, either the defendant was the operator of the vehicle and in custody of the object of the search, or no question was raised as to the defendant's ownership or custody.[1] In the only automobile case confronting the search of a passenger defendant—*United States v. Di Re*, 332 U.S. 581, 68 S.Ct. 222, 92 L.Ed. 210 (1948)—the Court held that the exception to the warrant requirement did not apply, *Id.*, at 583–587, 68 S.Ct. 222 (addressing searches of the passenger's pockets and the

1. See *e.g.*, *California v. Acevedo*, 500 U.S. 565, 111 S.Ct. 1982, 114 L.Ed.2d 619 (1991); *California v. Carney*, 471 U.S. 386, 105 S.Ct. 2066, 85 L.Ed.2d 406 (1985); *United States v. Johns*, 469 U.S. 478, 105 S.Ct. 881, 83 L.Ed.2d 890 (1985); *United States v. Ross*, 456 U.S. 798, 102 S.Ct. 2157, 72 L.Ed.2d 572 (1982); *Carroll v. United States*, 267 U.S. 132, 45 S.Ct. 280, 69 L.Ed. 543 (1925); 3 W. LaFave, Search and Seizure § 7.2(c), pp. 487–488, and n. 113 (3d ed.1996); *id.*, § 7.2(d), pp. 506 n. 167.

FIGURE 4-14 (continued)

119 SUPREME COURT REPORTER

space between his shirt and underwear, both of which uncovered counterfeit fuel rations). In *Di Re*, as here, the information prompting the search directly implicated the driver, not the passenger. Today, instead of adhering to the settled distinction between drivers and passengers, the Court fashions a new rule that is based on a distinction between property contained in clothing worn by a passenger and property contained in a passenger's briefcase or purse. In cases on both sides of the Court's newly minted test, the property is in a "container" (whether a pocket or a pouch) located in the vehicle. Moreover, unlike the Court, I think it quite plain that the search of a passenger's purse or briefcase involves an intrusion on privacy that may be just as serious as was the intrusion in *Di Re*. See, *e.g.*, *New Jersey v. T.L.O.*, 469 U.S. 325, 339, 105 S.Ct. 733, 83 L.Ed.2d 720 (1985); *Ex parte Jackson*, 96 U.S. 727, 733, 24 L.Ed. 877 (1878).

Even apart from *Di Re*, the Court's rights-restrictive approach is not dictated by precedent. For example, in *United States v. Ross*, 456 U.S. 798, 102 S.Ct. 2157, 72 L.Ed.2d 572 (1982), we were concerned with the interest of the driver in the integrity of "his automobile," *id.*, at 823, 102 S.Ct. 2157, and we categorically rejected the notion that the scope of a warrantless search of a vehicle might be "defined by the nature of the container in which the contraband is secreted," *id.*, at 824, 102 S.Ct. 2157. "Rather, it is defined by the object of the search and the places in which there is probable cause to believe that it may be found." *Ibid.* We thus disapproved of a possible container-based distinction between a man's pocket and a woman's pocketbook. Ironically, while we concluded in *Ross* that "[p]robable cause to believe that a container placed in the trunk of a taxi contains contraband or evidence does not justify a search of the entire cab," *ibid.*, the rule the Court fashions would apparently permit a warrantless search of a passenger's briefcase if there is probable cause to believe the taxidriver had a syringe somewhere in his vehicle.

Nor am I persuaded that the mere spatial association between a passenger and a driver provides an acceptable basis for presuming that they are partners in crime or for ignoring privacy interests in a purse.[2] Whether or not the Fourth Amendment required a warrant to search Houghton's purse, cf. *Carroll v. United States*, 267 U.S. 132, 153, 45 S.Ct. 280, 69 L.Ed. 543 (1925), at the very least the trooper in this case had to have probable cause to believe that her purse contained contraband. The Wyoming Supreme Court concluded that he did not. 956 P.2d 363, 372 (1998); see App. 20–21.

Finally, in my view, the State's legitimate interest in effective law enforcement does not outweigh the privacy concerns at issue.[3] I am as confident in a police Officer's ability to apply a rule requiring a warrant or individualized probable cause to search belongings that are—as in this case—obviously owned by and in the custody of a passenger as is the Court in a "passenger-confederate[']s," ability to circumvent the rule. *Ante*, at 1302. Certainly the ostensible clarity of the Court's rule is attractive. But that virtue is insufficient justification for its adoption. *Arizona v. Hicks*, 480 U.S. 321, 329, 107 S.Ct. 1149, 94 L.Ed.2d 347 (1987); *Mincey v. Arizona*, 437 U.S. 385, 393, 98 S.Ct. 2408, 57 L.Ed.2d 290 (1978). Moreover, a rule requiring a warrant or individualized probable cause to search passenger belongings is every bit as simple as the Court's rule; it simply protects more privacy.

I would decide this case in accord with what we *have* said about passengers and privacy, rather than what we *might have* said in cases where the issue was not squarely presented. See *ante*, at 1301. What Justice Jackson wrote for the Court fifty years ago is just as sound today:

2. See *United States v. Di Re*, 332 U.S. 581, 587, 68 S.Ct. 222, 92 L.Ed. 210 (1948) ("We are not convinced that a person, by mere presence in a suspected car, loses immunities from search of his person to which he would otherwise be entitled"): *Chandler v. Miller*, 520 U.S. 305, 308, 117 S.Ct. 1295, 137 L.Ed.2d 513 (1997) (emphasizing individualized suspicion); *Ybarra v. Illinois*, 444 U.S. 85, 91, 94–96, 100 S.Ct. 338, 62 L.Ed.2d 238 (1979) (explaining that "a person's mere propinquity to others independently suspected of criminal activity does not, without more, give rise to probable cause to search that person," and discussing *Di Re*); *Brown v. Texas*, 443 U.S. 47, 52, 99 S.Ct. 2637, 61 L.Ed.2d 357 (1979); *Sibron v. New York*, 392 U.S. 40, 62–63, 88 S.Ct. 1889, 20 L.Ed.2d 917 (1968); see also *United States v. Padilla*, 508 U.S. 77, 82, 113 S.Ct. 1936, 123 L.Ed.2d 635 (1993) *(per curiam)* ("Expectations of privacy and property interests govern the analysis of Fourth Amendment search and seizure claims. Participants in a criminal conspiracy may have such expectations or interests, but the conspiracy itself neither adds to nor detracts from them").

3. To my knowledge, we have never restricted ourselves to a two-step Fourth Amendment approach wherein the privacy and governmental interests at stake must be considered only if 18th-century common law "yields no answer." *Ante*, at 1300. Neither the precedent cited by the Court, nor the majority's opinion in this case, mandate that approach. In a later discussion, the Court does attempt to address the contemporary privacy and governmental interests at issue in cases of this nature. *Ante*, at 1302–1303. Either the majority is unconvinced by its own recitation of the historical materials, or it has determined that considering additional factors is appropriate in any event. The Court does not admit the former; and of course the latter, standing alone, would not establish uncertainty in the common law as the prerequisite to looking beyond history in Fourth Amendment cases.

FIGURE 4-14 (continued)

WYOMING V. HOUGHTON

Cite as 119 S.Ct. 1297 (1999)

"The Government says it would not contend that, armed with a search warrant for a residence only, it could search all persons found in it. But an occupant of a house could be used to conceal this contraband on his person quite as readily as can an occupant of a car. Necessity, an argument advanced in support of this search, would seem as strong a reason for searching guests of a house for which a search warrant had issued as for search of guests in a car for which none had been issued. By a parity of reasoning with that on which the Government disclaims the right to search occupants of a house, we suppose the Government would not contend that if it had a valid search warrant for the car only it could search the occupants as an incident to its execution. How then could we say that the right to search a car without a warrant confers greater latitude to search occupants than a search by warrant would permit?

"We see no ground for expanding the ruling in the *Carroll* case to justify this arrest and search as incident to the search of a car. We are not convinced that a person, by mere presence in a suspected car, loses immunities from search of his person to which he would otherwise be entitled." *Di Re*, 332 U.S., at 587, 68 S.Ct. 222; accord *Ross*, 456 U.S., at 823, 825, 102 S.Ct. 2157 (the proper scope of a warrantless automobile search based on probable cause is "no broader" than the proper scope of a search authorized by a warrant supposed by probable cause).[4]

Instead of applying ordinary Fourth Amendment principles to this case, the majority extends the automobile warrant exception to allow searches of passenger belongings based on the driver's misconduct. Thankfully, the Court's automobile-centered analysis limits the scope of its holding. But it does not justify the outcome in this case.

I respectfully dissent.

4. In response to this dissent the Court has crafted an imaginative footnote suggesting that the *Di Re* decision rested, not on Di Re's status as a mere occupant of the vehicle and the importance of individualized suspicion, but rather on the intrusive character of the search. See *ante*, at 1302, n. 1. That the search of a safe or violin case would be less intrusive than a strip search does not, however, persuade me that the *Di Re* case would have been decided differently if Di Re had been a woman and the gas coupons had been found in her purse. Significantly, in commenting on the *Carroll* case immediately preceding the paragraphs that I have quoted in the text, the *Di Re* Court stated: "But even the National Prohibition Act did not direct the arrest of all occupants but only of the person in charge of the offending vehicle, though there is better reason to assume that no passenger in a car loaded with liquor would remain innocent of knowledge of the car's cargo than to assume that a passenger must know what pieces of paper are carried in the pockets of the driver." *United States v. Di Re*, 332 U.S. 581, 586–587, 68 S.Ct. 222, 92 L.Ed. 210 (1948).

Amanda MITCHELL, petitioner,
v.
UNITED STATES.
No. 97-7541.

Argued Dec. 9, 1998.

Decided April 5, 1999.

Defendant was convicted in the United States District Court for the Eastern District of Pennsylvania, of conspiracy to distribute cocaine, and she appealed. The United States Court of Appeals for the Third Circuit, 122 F.3d 185, affirmed, and defendant petitioned for certiorari. The Supreme Court, Justice Kennedy, held that: (1) neither defendant's guilty plea nor her statements at plea colloquy functioned as a waiver of her right to remain silent at sentencing, and (2) sentencing court could not draw adverse inference from defendant's silence in determining facts relating to circumstances and details of the crime.

Reversed and remanded.

Justice Scalia filed dissenting opinion in which Chief Justice Rehnquist, Justice O'Connor, and Justice Thomas joined.

Justice Thomas filed dissenting opinion.

1. Witnesses ⊶ 305(1)

A witness, in a single proceeding, may not testify voluntarily about a subject and then invoke privilege against self-incrimination when questioned about the details; privilege is waived for the matters to which the witness testifies, and the scope of the waiver is determined by the scope of relevant cross-examination, U.S.C.A. Const.Amend. 5.

2. Criminal Law ⊶ 273.4(1), 393(1)

Neither defendant's guilty plea nor her statements at plea colloquy functioned as a waiver of her right to remain silent at sentencing. U.S.C.A. Const.Amend. 5; Fed. Rules Cr.Proc.Rule 11, 18 U.S.C.A.

3. Criminal Law ⊶ 393(1)

Where a sentence has yet to be imposed, entry of guilty plea does not complete the incrimination of defendant, so as to extinguish the privilege against self-incrimination. U.S.C.A. Const.Amend. 5.

of volume 143 of *United States Supreme Court Reports, Lawyers' Edition Second Series.* You will notice that the text of the opinion itself is exactly the same. However, the material prepared by the publisher and that precedes the opinion is different in format and longer than the West-prepared material preceding the same case in Supreme Court Reporter.

The citation

The heading (also called the running head) of the page for *McKinnon* indicates the citation "**U.S. v. McKINNON**" and "cite as 985 F.2d 525 (11th Cir. 1993)." This is the name of the case and where it can be found, namely on page 525 in volume 985 of the *Federal Reporter, Second Series.*

Similarly for *Houghton,* the heading of the page indicates the citation "**WYOMING v. HOUGHTON**" and "Cite as 119 S.Ct. 1297 (1999)." This is the name of the case and where it can be found, namely on page 1297 in Volume 119 of the Supreme Court Reporter. Cases from some courts are printed in more than one reporter with one of the reporters being designated as the "official reporter" because it is published by the government. Opinions of the United States Supreme Court are printed in *United States Reports* (abbreviated "U.S."), the official reporter, and in *Supreme Court Reporter* and *United States Supreme Court Reports, Lawyers' Edition,* two unofficial sources published by private publishers. The official citation is to volume 526, page 295 of *United States Reports* (526 U.S. 295).

The caption

The caption of *McKinnon* shows the parties as "UNITED STATES of America, Plaintiff-Appellee, v. Steve McKINNON, Defendant-Appellant." Note that the citation names only one party for each side and uses only the individual's surname, while the caption gives the Defendant-Appellant's first name "Steve." If there was more than one defendant-appellants, the other defendant-appellants might have been indicated by the use of "et al." meaning "and others." The caption also indicates the status of the United States as "Plaintiff-Appellee" and the status of Steve McKinnon as "Defendant-Appellant." We can surmise from this that the United States brought the case in federal district court and was successful at the trial level; Steve McKinnon defended the case in the trial level court and appealed the case to the United States Court of Appeals for the Eleventh Circuit. A common practice in the appellate court is to show the appellant as the first party and the appellee as the opposing party in the case name. This practice was not followed for this case.

The caption of *Houghton* shows the parties as "WYOMING, Petitioner, v. Sandra HOUGHTON." Note that the citation names only one party for each side and uses only the individual's surname, while the caption gives the respondent's first name "Sandra." The caption also indicates the status of Wyoming as "Petitioner." We can surmise from this that Wyoming lost in the lower court and filed a petition for certiorari for the case to be heard by the United States Supreme Court. Even though not stated, we know that Sandra Houghton is the "respondent" because that is the name given by the Court to the party who won below.

Because the caption for *Houghton* does not indicate, the reader must discover from the text who was the **plaintiff** and who was the **defendant** originally. It is important to note who is the respondent because the opinion refers to Houghton by that term.

Below the parties we find "No. 91-3944," as the docket number for *McKinnon;* "No. 98-184" is the docket number for *Houghton.* The docket number is a number assigned to the case upon initial filing with the clerk of the court and by which it is identified prior to assigning it a volume and page number in the reporter series. The docket number usually indicates the year in which the case was filed with the court and the sequence in which the case was filed. Thus, *McKinnon* was case number 3,944 filed with the court of appeals in 1991; *Houghton* was case number 184 filed with the United States Supreme Court in 1998. The docket number is important when attempting to research the case prior to its official publication. Below the docket number is the date of the decision for *McKinnon* and the date of oral argument and the date of the decision for *Houghton.*

The syllabus

Following the caption is a brief summary of the case called the *syllabus.* In *Houghton* there is another more detailed syllabus following the headnotes. In regional reporters, Federal Supplement, and Federal Reporter, cases usually include the first syllabus prepared by West but not the second. This is the format followed in *McKinnon;* the court opinion is preceded by a single syllabus. While the syllabi are sometimes written by the court or a reporter appointed by the Court, as indicated by the footnote to the second syllabus in *Houghton,* a syllabus is a narrow condensation of the court's ruling and cannot be relied upon as the precise holding of the court. The syllabus can be useful in obtaining a quick idea of what the case concerns—a summary of the issue and the holding of the court. Frequently legal researchers follow leads to cases, which upon reading prove to be unrelated to the issue of the research. Reading the syllabus may make reading the entire opinion unnecessary. On the other hand, if the syllabus suggests the case may be important, a careful reading of the entire text of the opinion is usually necessary.

Headnotes

There are three *headnotes* to *McKinnon* and five to *Houghton.* They are located on the first or first few pages of the case and are numbered consecutively, one through three in *McKinnon* and one through five in *Houghton.* The headnotes are statements of the major points of law discussed in the case. With limited editing, the headnotes tend to be nearly verbatim statements lifted from the opinion. The headnotes are listed in numerical order, starting at the beginning of the opinion, so that the reader may look quickly for the context of a point expressed by a headnote. For example, the part of the text that deals with a particular point made in the headnote will have the number of the headnote in brackets, e.g., [3], at the beginning of the paragraph or section in which it is discussed. This is very helpful when researching lengthy cases in which only one issue is of concern to the researcher.

To the right of the headnote number is a generic heading, such as "Searches and Seizures" and a *key* number. Since *Federal Reporter, Second Series* and *Supreme Court Reporter* are published by West Group, the two reporters use an indexing title and number that can be used throughout the many West indexes, reporters, and encyclopedias. Lexis Law Publishing uses a similar indexing title and number that can be used throughout the many Lexis Law publications.

Authorship of the opinion[s] and attorneys for the parties

In *McKinnon,* the second page of the opinion identifies the three judges who comprised the panel hearing the case and the judge who wrote the opinion. Circuit judges Hatchett, Dubina, and Carnes heard the case and Judge Hatchett wrote the opinion, which was joined in by the other two circuit judges. In *Houghton,* the roles of the justices are identified following both syllabi. This was a six to three decision, except that one justice joined in the majority opinion and wrote a separate concurring opinion. Justice Scalia wrote the majority opinion which was joined in by Chief Justice Rehnquist and Justices O'Connor, Kennedy, Thomas, and Breyer. Justice Breyer also wrote a separate concurring opinion. Justice Stevens wrote the dissenting opinion which was joined in by Justices Souter and Ginsburg. The attorneys of the parties are listed just above the beginning of the opinion. In *McKinnon,* the plaintiff-appellee had two attorneys as did the defendant-appellant. In *Houghton,* the petitioner had one attorney, the respondent had one attorney, and there was an attorney for the United States as ***amicus curiae.*** *Amicus curiae* means "friend of the court." This is a person, although not a party to the case, who is granted permission to file a brief in the case. Usually the person wants to present to the court a point of view which otherwise may not be represented in the case.

Format of the opinion

Following the names of the attorneys, the formal opinion (that is, the official discussion of the case) begins. In *McKinnon* as is common in cases other than United Supreme Court opinions, the opinion simply starts with the name of the judge writing the opinion rather than specifically explaining that that judge delivered the opinion. The beginning of *McKinnon* has a notation, "HATCHETT, Circuit Judge." In *Houghton,* the opinion states " Justice SCALIA delivered the opinion of the Court." The author of the opinion has considerable freedom in presentation. Some opinions are written mechanically, while a few are almost poetic. The peculiarities of any particular case may dictate a special logical order of its own. Nevertheless, the majority of opinions follow a standard format. When this format is followed, reading and understanding are simplified, but no judge is required to make an opinion easy reading (facts, procedure, issue, discussion, and holding).

As far as opinions of the United States Supreme Court are concerned, *Houghton* (fig. 4-14) is fairly brief, well organized, and easy to understand.

The facts

Most of the text of an opinion in appellate decisions is concerned with a discussion of the law, but because a case revolves around a dispute concerning events that occurred between the parties, no opinion is complete without some discussion of the events that led to the trial. Trials generally explore these events in great detail and judge or jury settle the facts; appellate opinions, however, usually narrow the fact statement to the most relevant facts. In an interesting case, the reader is often left wanting to know more about what happened; but the judge is not writing a story. The important element in the opinion concerns the application of law.

Procedure

Near or at the beginning of the opinion is a reference to the outcome of the trial in the lower court and the basis for appeal. For example in *McKinnon*, the history of the case is located in the left column on page 124 in a section entitled "PROCEDURAL HISTORY." That section states that McKinnon was charged in a three-count indictment with possessing and distributing cocaine. His motion to suppress the tape of his conversation recorded in the rear seat of a patrol car was denied and he entered a guilty plea, reserving his right to appeal the denial of the motion to suppress.

In *Houghton*, the opinion states that Houghton was charged with possession of methamphetamine. Her motion to suppress the evidence obtained from her purse was denied by the trial court and a jury convicted her. The Wyoming Supreme Court, by a divided vote, reversed.

Often the remarks about procedure are brief and confusing, especially if the reader is not familiar with the procedural rules. An understanding of the relevant state or federal court system and jurisdiction will help unravel procedural steps leading to the appellate decision. If the procedure is important to the opinion, a more elaborate discussion is usually found in the body of the opinion. Many things in the opinion become clear only upon further reading; and many opinions must be read at least twice for a full understanding. An opinion is like a jigsaw puzzle—the reader must put the parts together to see the full picture.

The issue

Many writers describe the questions of law that must be decided either at the beginning of the opinion or following the relevant facts.

In *McKinnon*, the issue is stated in a section on page 124 in the section entitled, "ISSUE." "The sole issue is whether the district erred in denying the motion to suppress the tapes resulting from the secret recording of McKinnon's pre-arrest conversations while he sat in the back seat of the police car."

In *Houghton*, Scalia states the issue very clearly in the first sentence. "This case presents the question whether police officers violate the Fourth Amendment when they search a passenger's personal belongings inside an automobile that they have probable cause to believe contains contraband."

Unfortunately, few writers pinpoint the issue in this fashion, so the reader must search the text for the issue. At this point it is appropriate to introduce a favorite term used by attorneys: *caveat.* This means "warning" or, literally, "Let him beware."

Caveat: The issue is the most important element in an opinion. If the issue is not understood, the significance of the rule laid down by the court can easily be misunderstood. This point cannot be emphasized too strongly. Law students study cases for three years with one primary goal: "Identify the issues." Anyone can fill out forms, but a competently trained person can go right to the heart of a case and recognize its strengths and weaknesses.

The discussion

The main body of the text of an opinion, often ninety percent of it, discusses the meaning of the issue(s) and offers a line of reasoning that leads to a disposition of the case and explains why a certain rule or rules must apply to the dispute. This part of the opinion is the most difficult to follow. The writer has a goal, but the goal is often not clear to the reader until the end. For this reason, it is usually helpful to look at the final paragraph in the case to see whether the appellate court affirmed (agreed with the lower court) or reversed (disagreed with the lower court).

The final paragraph of *McKinnon* states that the court "affirmed the district court's denial of the motion to suppress." The final paragraph of the *Houghton* majority opinion states that the Court reversed the Wyoming Supreme Court.

Many judges seem to like to hold the reader in suspense, but there is no reason the reader needs to play this game. By finding out the outcome of the decision, the reader can see how the writer of an opinion is building the conclusion. By recognizing the issue and knowing the rule applied, the reader can see the structure of the argument. The discussion section is the writer's justification of the holding.

The holding

The holding states the rule of the case, that is, the rule the court applies to conclude whether or not the lower court was correct. The rule is *the law*, meaning that it determines the rights of the parties until reversed by a higher court. It binds lower courts faced with a similar dispute in future cases. It is best to think of the holding as an answer to the issue.

The *McKinnon* holding is located at the end of the first paragraph in the second column of page 125. "Hence, we hold that McKinnon did not have a reasonable or justifiable expectation of privacy for conversations he held while seated in the back seat area of a police car."

The *Houghton* holding is located in the next to the last paragraph of the majority opinion on page 131. "We hold that police officers with probable cause to search a car may inspect passengers' belongings found in the car that are capable of concealing the object of the search."

Finding the Law

Research of cases is done for a number of reasons. The principles that apply to a dispute may be unknown, unfamiliar, or forgotten. With experience, legal professionals come to develop a knack for guessing how a dispute will be decided and can even predict what rules will be applied. Once the issues of a case are recognized, a reasonable prediction of a fair outcome can be made. This is, however, merely tentative; the researchers must check their knowledge and memory against definitive statements of the law. In some instances a statute will clearly define the rights and duties that pertain to the case at hand; in others the elaboration of the law in the cases will leave little room for doubt. Frequently, however, the issue in a client's case will be complex or unique, and no case can be found that is directly "on point." Ideally, research will result in finding a case that contains a fact situation so similar to that of the client that an assumption can be made that the same rule will apply.

Evaluating cases

Once the purpose, style, and structure of appellate decisions are grasped, mastering the content is a matter of concentration and experience. Researching cases generally has one or more of the following three goals:

1. Finding the statements of the law.
2. Assessing the law in relation to the client's case.
3. Building an argument.

These three goals can be illustrated using the Cruz search and seizure problem found in chapter 2. A researcher might look for cases stating what the law is concerning police officers opening a container belonging to a passenger. *Houghton* appears to be a good case to evaluate because it deals with this issue and is a very recent United States Supreme Court opinion.

Now the researcher would assess *Houghton* in relation to the Cruz situation. *Houghton* and *Cruz* contain similar facts and both consider the issue of whether the suspect's Fourth Amendment rights were violated when the officer opened a container belonging to the passenger. In both cases, the officer searched the female passenger's purse and found illegal drugs.

Although the issue and many of the facts in the two cases are similar, a number of crucial facts are different. In some instances the facts of a dispute are used to *distinguish* it from similar cases. For example, although *Houghton* and *Cruz* are on point on the issue of whether opening a container belonging to a passenger violated the passenger's rights, the facts concerning the location of the passenger's purse may be distinguished. In *Houghton*, the officer found the purse in the car after the passenger had exited the car;

the passenger initially disclaimed ownership of the purse. In *Cruz*, Cruz exited the car with her purse slung over her shoulder. The officer said, "you don't mind if I search this, do you?" Without giving Cruz a chance to answer, the officer grabbed the purse from her shoulder and began to search it. Cruz can argue that her case is different from *Houghton* because of the location of her purse. The purse more closely resembled an outer layer of clothing than a container abandoned in the car, as the purse was in *Houghton*. *Houghton* dealt with the search of a passenger's belonging rather than with a search of the passenger's person. The search therefore violated Cruz' Fourth Amendment right against unreasonable search and seizure.

Only experience and knowledge of the law will develop the keen sense it takes to separate cases that are on point from those that are distinguishable. It is often the advocate's job to persuade on the basis of threading a way through a host of seemingly conflicting cases.

BRIEFING A CASE

"Briefing a case" means taking notes of the most important parts of a case so that you can later refer to your "case brief" to quickly refresh your memory rather than have to read the case over again. When you write out a case brief, you have engaged in active learning as you write a summary in your own words. This leads to better understanding of the case than underlining or rereading. Professors may require you to brief cases, with class time spent discussing the cases and "synthesizing" them. Synthesizing involves analyzing how cases deal with a particular subject matter and extracting a "rule of law" from them.

> When attorneys refer to a "brief" they may be referring to a case brief, but more likely than not, they are referring to an "appellate brief." An appellate brief is the document containing the arguments of a party to a case which is usually prepared by the party's attorney and is submitted to the appellate court when a case is appealed.

A second reason to brief cases is as a research and writing tool. When researching a problem you should brief the cases found, synthesize them to determine the rule of law, and apply the rule of law to the problem.

Although some professors may require you to turn in your first few case briefs when you are learning how to brief a case, case briefs are generally read only by you. The format described below is a fairly standard one, but there is no one right way to brief a case. You may find yourself developing your own format for those case briefs you know you will not be required to turn in.

If a professor asks you to brief cases it may be a good idea to ask the professor if he or she prefers a particular format. The desired format may vary from professor to professor with some requiring a longer brief of three to four pages.

As the name suggests, a case brief should be fairly concise. If your case brief is as long as or longer than the case, you might just as well reread the entire case rather than refer to the case brief. For most cases, a good length is a page or less.

The parts of the case brief are depicted in figure 4-15 and the case brief format is explained in the following section.

Case brief format

A standard format for briefing a case is the following:

Correct case citation—Your professor will probably ask you to cite cases as in the examples provided below or by the citation rule for your state.

Facts—This section should only contain the significant facts in light of the legal question asked, but may state what facts are not known if the absence of facts is significant.

History—State briefly what happened at trial and at each level before the case reached the court whose opinion you are briefing.

Issue(s)—State the issue or issues considered by the court. Each issue should be one sentence in length and the issues should be numbered if there is more than one. An issue is easier to understand if it is stated in the form of a question, rather than beginning with the word "whether," and it should end with a question mark.

Holding(s)—Generally you will have the same number of holdings as you do issues, with each holding containing the answer to the corresponding issue. Sometimes you may have one issue and more than one holding if the issue is a broad one

FIGURE 4-15 Case Brief.

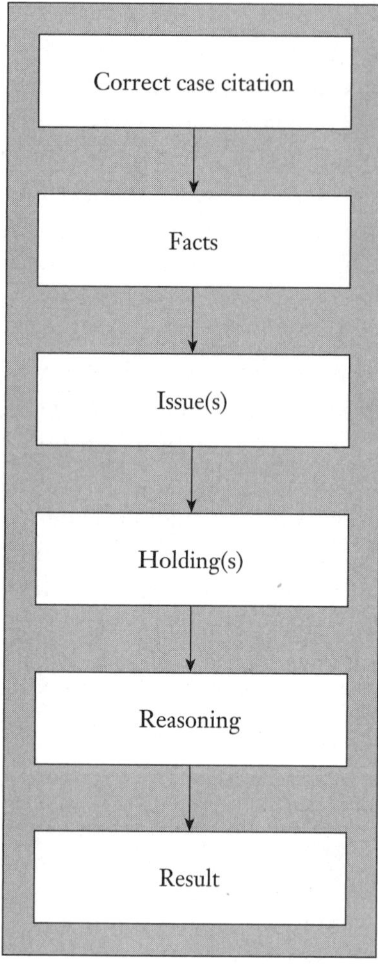

and there is more than one answer to it. Each holding should be one sentence. Even if the court does not explicitly state the holding or gives a simple "yes" or "no" answer to an issue, reread the case until you can write a one-sentence holding.

Reasoning—State the court's reasoning for reaching the holding from the issue considered. Your professor may require you to summarize the majority opinion.

Result—State what the court did with the lower court's decision: affirmed, reversed, vacated, etc.

Case briefs for McKinnon and Houghton

The following are suggested case briefs for *McKinnon* and *Houghton.* It would be good practice for you to try to brief *McKinnon* and *Houghton* yourself and compare your case briefs with the following case briefs.

United States v. McKinnon, *985 F.2d 525 (11th Cir. 1993).*

Facts—Police officers stopped a pick-up truck for failure to travel in a single lane on the Florida Turnpike. Theodore Pressley was driving and Steve McKinnon was the passenger. Pressley consented to the search of his vehicle. While the officers were searching, McKinnon and Pressley waited in the rear seat of the patrol car. There they made incriminating statements that were secretly recorded by the officers. The officers arrested McKinnon and Pressley after finding cocaine in the truck and they were placed in the rear seat of the patrol car. The officers again recorded McKinnon's and Pressley's incriminating statements.

History—McKinnon was charged in a three-count indictment with possessing and distributing cocaine. His motion to suppress the tape of his conversation recorded in the rear seat of a patrol car was denied and he entered a guilty plea, reserving his right to appeal the denial of the motion to suppress.

Issue—"The sole issue is whether the district erred in denying the motion to suppress the tapes resulting from the secret recording of McKinnon's pre-arrest conversations while he sat in the back seat of the police car."

Holding—"[W]e hold that McKinnon did not have a reasonable or justifiable expectation of privacy for conversations he held while seated in the back seat area of a police car."

Reasoning—The court considered the meaning of the term "oral communication" under the federal statutes. An oral communication is protected against taping. If a conversation is taped in violation of the statutes, the tape may be suppressed. A conversation is an oral communication only if the conversants exhibited a subjective expectation of privacy and the expectation of privacy was objectively reasonable. The court seemed to agree with the government's argument that a patrol car functions as the officer's office and the rear seat of the patrol car functions as a jail cell.

Results—The court "affirmed the district court's denial of the motion to suppress."

Wyoming v. Houghton, *526 U.S. 295 (1999).*

Facts—David Young was stopped for speeding and a faulty brake light. After the officer saw a hypodermic syringe in Young's pocket, Young admitted that he used it to take drugs. The officer asked the two female passengers seated in the front seat to exit the car and the officer searched the car. The officer found Houghton's purse on the back seat of the car. Searching the purse, the officer found a brown pouch that contained drug paraphernalia and a syringe containing methamphetamine in a large enough quantity for a felony conviction. Houghton claimed that the brown pouch was not hers. The officer also found a black container that contained drug paraphernalia and a syringe containing a smaller amount of methamphetamine, insufficient for a felony conviction. Houghton's arms showed fresh needle-marks. The officer arrested her.

History—Houghton was charged with possession of methamphetamine. Her motion to suppress the evidence obtained from her purse was denied by the trial court and a jury convicted her. The Wyoming Supreme Court, by a divided vote, reversed.

Issue—"This case presents the question whether police officers violate the Fourth Amendment when they search a passenger's personal belongings inside an automobile that they have probable cause to believe contains contraband."

Holding—"We hold that police officers with probable cause to search a car may inspect passengers' belongings found in the car that are capable of concealing the object of the search."

Reasoning—In an earlier case, the Court had found that, where there was probable cause to search a car, it was constitutionally permissible to search containers found in the car that might hold the object of the search. The Court noted that an individual carrying a package in a vehicle travelling on the public roads has a reduced expectation of privacy. Finally, the Court found no reason to afford more protection to a container owned by a passenger than a container owned by the driver.

Results—The Court reversed the Wyoming Supreme Court.

LOCATION OF CASES

Cases are generally found in the law library in **looseleaf publications, advance sheets,** or **reporters.** Libraries designated as government depositories may also have cases in slip opinion form. For the names of the looseleaf publications and reporters for federal court cases, refer to the chart in figure 4-16. You will need to obtain the names of the looseleaf publication (if any) and reporters for your state's cases from your professor or from your own research. You would use the looseleaf publication to read recently announced cases that are not yet contained in the advance sheets or reporters. Once a case is available in the advance sheets or the reporters, you would cite to the reporter

FIGURE 4-16 Publications and Reporters for Federal and State Court Cases.

Reporters and looseleaf services

FEDERAL

United States Supreme Court

United States Law Week (looseleaf)
United States Reports (official)
Supreme Court Reporter (unofficial—West)
United States Supreme Court Reports, Lawyers' Edition (unofficial—Lexis Law Publishing)

United States Circuit Courts of Appeal

Federal Reporter (unofficial—West)

United States District Courts

Federal Supplement (unofficial—West)

STATE

(fill in for your state)

Court of last resort

Intermediate appellate court

Trial court(s)

rather than to the looseleaf publication. Cases in looseleaf publications, advance sheets, and reporters are organized chronologically.

Cases from a particular court may be printed in more than one reporter. For example, United States Supreme Court opinions are printed in three different reporters: *United States Reports*, *Supreme Court Reporter*, and *United States Supreme Court Reports, Lawyers' Edition*. The text of the court opinion is identical in each of the three reporters but the material preceding the case, which is prepared by the publisher, is different. The reporter prepared by the government or under authority of the government is referred to as the "official reporter." The official reporter for United States Supreme Court opinions is *United States Reports*. Although *United States Reports* is considered the official reporter, many law libraries may only have one of the other two reporters. Because *United States Reports* is a government publication it lags considerably behind the other two reporters in publication date and does not contain the headnotes and other material prepared by the commercial publisher of the other two reporters.

West Group publishes seven different regional reporters (see figure 4-17). A particular regional reporter will contain state cases from courts in a particular region of the country. For example, Southern Reporter contains cases from Louisiana, Mississippi, Alabama, and Florida. With the wide availability of the regional reporters, many states that used to have official reporters as well as the regional reporters no longer publish official reporters.

There are three important pieces of information you need to find a case. First you need to know what series of what reporter it is in. You will find that many law books with multiple volumes are published in series. When the volume numbers of a reporter are so large that they become unmanageable, the publisher will start a new series of reporter beginning with volume 1. The series are designated by ordinal numbers with the highest series number containing the most recent information. For example, the most recent United States Supreme Court opinions are published in *United States Supreme Court Reports, Lawyers' Edition, Second Series*, abbreviated "L. Ed. 2d." Assume you wanted to find *Brown v. Board of Education* and you know the citation in Lawyers Edition is "98 L.Ed. 873." First of all, "L. Ed." tells you that you would need to look in the first series rather than the second series of the reporter. Each time you

The West regional reporters and the states covered are:

Pacific Reporter	Alaska, Hawaii, Washington, Oregon, Nevada, California, Montana, Idaho, Wyoming, Utah, Arizona, New Mexico, Colorado, Kansas, Oklahoma
North Western Reporter	North Dakota, South Dakota, Nebraska, Minnesota, Iowa, Wisconsin, Michigan
South Western Reporter	Texas, Arkansas, Missouri, Kentucky, Tennessee
North Eastern Reporter	Illinois, Indiana, Ohio, New York, Massachusetts
Atlantic Reporter	Maine, New Hampshire, Rhode Island, Connecticut, New Jersey, Delaware, District of Columbia, Vermont
South Eastern Reporter	Georgia, South Carolina, North Carolina, Virginia, West Virginia
Southern Reporter	Louisiana, Mississippi, Alabama, Florida

FIGURE 4-17 West Group's Regional Reporters and Their Coverage.

write a citation or pull a case, make sure you have the correct series.

The second and third things you need to know are the volume number and the page on which the case begins. In a citation, the volume number precedes the abbreviation for the reporter and the page number follows it. In the citation for *Brown*, "98" is the volume number and "873" is the first page of the case.

Citation tip: case names. In a reporter, a case begins with the full name of the case, a portion of the name appearing in all capital letters. Unless your reader requires Bluebook form for case names, use that portion of the case name that appears in all capitals, with the further modifications explained in this paragraph as the case name in your citation. You will have a very close approximation of Bluebook form without having to master a very complicated Bluebook rule. For case names, individuals are referred to only by their surnames. When the United States of America is a party to a case, the citation needs to show "United States" rather than "United States of America" or "U.S." If a state is a party to the case and the case is being decided by a court of the state, the citation should contain only "State," "Commonwealth," or "People." If a state is a party to the case but the case is being decided by a court other than a court of the state, then the citaion should contain only the name of the state, for example "Minnesota," not "State of Minnesota."

CASE CITATIONS

A citation is an abbreviation used to refer to a legal authority that allows the reader to find the legal authority in the law library. When you answer a research question or perform legal analysis, it is expected that your answer or analysis be backed up by a citation to your legal authority. It is important for you to learn correct citation form, because that form allows legal professionals to speak the same language. Correct usage is a sign of excellence.

Citations are integral to formal legal documents. Legal citations have several purposes. Legal writers use them to identify the source of a quotation or the authority for a statement. A legal researcher uses them to locate the cited source. The reader uses them to obtain information concerning the source. For example, case citations indicate the precedential authority by identifying the level of the deciding court and the year of the decision. A final purpose, perhaps more aspirational than realistic, is to allow the layperson access to the law.

Citation manuals

For years ***The Bluebook: A Uniform System of Citation*** published by several prominent law reviews has been the standard for citation. The seventeenth edition of *The Bluebook* was published in 2000. *The Bluebook* has been rightly criticized for being too detailed and hard to learn; *The Bluebook* is almost 400 pages long, with 7 practitioner's notes, 21 multipart citation rules, and 167 pages of tables and lists of abbreviations.

Many states have their own citation rules, which may be found in state statutes or court rules; law school students usually do not study the state-specific citation rules and must learn them on their own after law school. Even though use of these citation rules is mandatory in state courts, *The Bluebook* does not reference these rules.

The ***ALWD Citation Manual*** was published in 2000. Although slightly longer in page length than *The Bluebook*, the ALWD Citation Manual is considerably more reader-friendly and is more easily used in the classroom as a teaching tool. The Association of Legal Writing Directors hopes that the ALWD Citation Manual will be adopted by enough law schools and practicing attorneys that the ALWD Citation Manual will gradually supplant *The Bluebook*. Because the ALWD Citation Manual is so new, it is unclear what effect it will have on the legal community.

In this book, the abbreviation for Lexis Law Publishing, "Lexis L. Publg.," is used, where required in citations. This abbreviation comes from Rule 14.2(e) of the ALWD Citation Manual because *The Bluebook* does not contain an abbreviation for Lexis Law Publishing.

There is also a movement toward universal citation form. Traditional case citation form is tied to the print medium; it references a particular volume and page number. In addition, traditional citation form references the product of a particular publisher. Universal citation form is both medium and publisher neutral; it can be used with the CD-ROM, online, or print version of a case and does not reference any particular publisher's product.

The American Association of Law Libraries published its ***Universal Citation Guide*** in 1999. The *Universal Citation Guide* gives the recommended universal citation form for federal and state cases, constitutions, statutes, and administrative regulations. Because the ***Universal Citation Guide*** is so new, it is unclear what effect it will have on the legal community. Universal citation form had been adopted by a number of states prior to the publication of the *Universal Citation Guide*. If the trend continues, more states will adopt universal citation form.

Basic citation form

This section explains the basics of citation form for cases and then gives you sample citations for federal cases.

> **Caveat:** Do not assume that the legal citations found when researching are in correct citation form. Citations, even those included in cases may or may not comply with the citation rules your professor has asked you to use. Always check your citations against the appropriate citation rule for correct form.

Sample citation forms and an explanation of how to cite a particular type of legal authority are included in the chapter of this book in which each legal authority is introduced. For example, sample citations forms for secondary sources are included in chapter 3; sample citation forms for constitutions, students, court rules, and administrative regulations are included in chapter 5. The sample citation forms approximate Bluebook form. The suggestion is to either learn citation forms from this book or learn the citation forms contained in your state's citation rule. Your professor can tell you which he or she prefers. Those citation forms will be the only ones you will need much of the time. If the form for something you need to cite is not in this book or in your state's citation rule, you can refer to *The Bluebook*.

> **Citation tip: ordinal numbers.** In legal citations the ordinal number "second" and "third" are abbreviated to "2d" and "3d." For all other ordinal numbers use the standard abbreviations.

There is a certain framework for case citations that is fairly consistent for cases from all courts. Look at a typical citation in figure 4-18 and analyze its components:

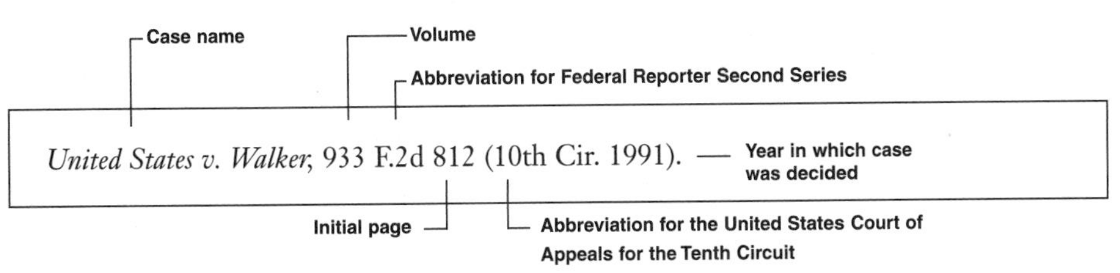

FIGURE 4-18 Citation for United States v. Walker.

The name of the case comes first, is italicized (or underlined), and is followed by a comma. Only the name of the first party on each side is given, with "v." (for versus) in between. The United States of America is the plaintiff-appellant. "Walker" is the last name of the defendant-appellee. The number "933" is the volume number, "F.2d" is the abbreviation for *Federal Reporter Second Series*, and "812" is the page on which the case begins. If needed, the first information within the parentheses identifies the court deciding the case. *Walker* was decided by the United States Court of Appeals for the Tenth Circuit, but only the number of the circuit is stated in the citation. You know it is a United States court of appeals case because the Federal Reporters contain only United States court of appeals cases. The year within the parentheses is the year in which the case was decided. Make sure you put the year of the decision in your citation rather than the year in which the case was argued.

Citation tip: subsequent history. Connect subsequent history to the end of the citation of the lower court decision by explaining what the higher court did, underlining the explanation, and setting it off by commas. "Certiorari denied" should be abbreviated to "*cert. denied*," "affrirmed" should be abbreviated to "*aff'd*," and "reversed" should be abbreviated to "*rev'd*." Otherwise the explanationshould be written out, for example, "*vacated*."

Subsequent history

After the United States Court of Appeals for the Tenth Circuit decided *Walker*, the United States petitioned for a rehearing. The petition was denied in a four-page order. *United States v. Walker*, 941 F.2d 1086 (10th Cir. 1991). The United States then petitioned for writ of certiorari to the United States Supreme Court. In *United States v. Walker*, 502 U.S. 1093 (1992), the petition was denied. The denial of the rehearing and the denial of the petition for writ of certiorari are called *subsequent history* because they happened subsequent to or after the Tenth Circuit's decision in *Walker*.

When citing to a case, you must give your reader all subsequent history *except for* denial of a rehearing, history on remand, and denial of certiorari or denial of review by a court with discretionary review if the case for which certiorari or review is sought is less than two years old. The reason you would not give the citation for the denial of a rehearing is that many parties routinely petition for a rehearing and the rehearing is routinely denied. A denial of a rehearing is different from a court denying review or the United States Supreme Court denying a petition for certiorari. A rehearing is denied by the same court that has already rendered a decision. In contrast, only a higher court can deny review or deny a petition for certiorari. Therefore, a denial of review or a denial of a petition for certiorari is important enough to be given as subsequent history for two years after the case has been decided, whereas denial of rehearing is not. The two year period was selected because the appeal of a case by a higher court is generally concluded within two years of the lower court decision. Subsequent history indicating denial of certiorari or denial of review within the two year period tells the reader the lower court decision is final. When an appellate court remands a case, it sends it back to the lower court to redo something the lower court did incorrectly before. The appellate decision in which the appellate court lays down the rule of law to be followed by the lower court on remand, and not the lower court decision in which the rule of law is carried out, is more important for its precedential value. For that reason history on remand is not usually cited in subsequent history.

The full citation of *Walker*, including subsequent history, is shown in Figure 4-19.

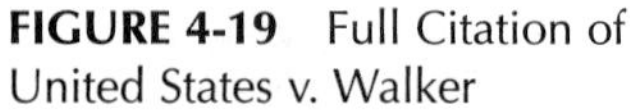

FIGURE 4-19 Full Citation of United States v. Walker

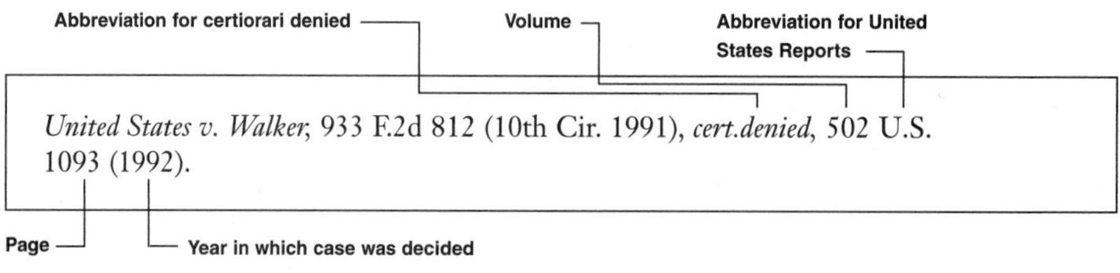

FIGURE 4-20 Page Reference within Walker.

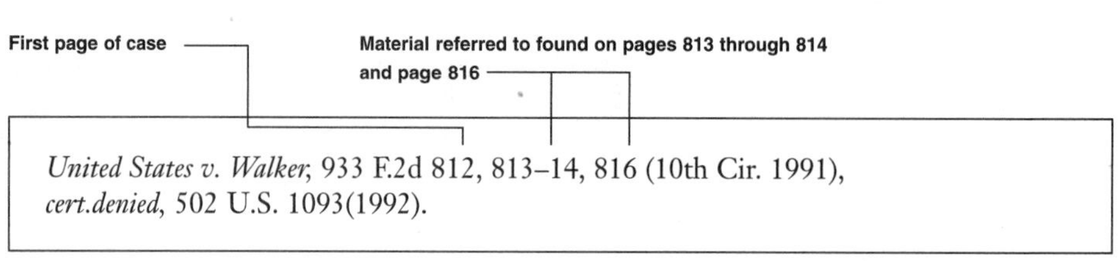

FIGURE 4-21 Citation to Wyoming v. Houghton in United States Law Week.

Wyoming v. Houghton, 67 U.S.L.W. 4225 (1999).

> **Caveat:** The subsequent history of certiorari being denied is included in figures 4-19, 4-20, 4-24, and 4-25 as an example of citation form only. According to the rule explained above, denial of certiorari would be included as subsequent history only for the two years after the 1991 decision by the Court of Appeals for the Tenth Circuit.

Notice that you place a comma after the first parentheses; italicize (or underline) the explanation of what happened in subsequent history ("*cert. denied*" explains that certiorari was denied); add a comma; identify the volume, reporter and page at which certiorari was denied; and give the year of the denial. As explained earlier, the citation to subsequent history includes the citation to where the United States Supreme Court denied the petition for certiorari, but not the citation to where the Court of Appeals for the Tenth Circuit denied the petition for rehearing.

Page numbers

When you are referring to specific information from a case or you are quoting from a case, you need to give a *pinpoint*, *locus*, or *jumpcite* page reference to the page or pages on which the material was found. Page references to material within a case can be made part of your full citation as shown in Figure 4-20.

The page numbers in this citation mean that 812 is the first page of the case and the material you are referring to is found on pages 813 through 814 and on page 816. If you wanted to refer to material on the first page of the opinion, you would repeat the number of the first page and separate the numbers by a comma. Notice that where you are referring to pages inclusive, such as pages 813 through 814, you join the page numbers by an en dash or a hyphen and retain only the last two digits of the second number.

United States Supreme Court cases

Cases appear in *United States Law Week* before they are printed in the reporters. Figure 4-21 contains the citation for *Wyoming v. Houghton* in *United States Law Week*. The citation to *United States Law Week* is used only until the case is published in one of the three reporters containing decisions of the United States Supreme Court.

If the case has been printed in a reporter you should give the citation to a reporter rather than to the looseleaf service. *The Bluebook* requires a citation to *United States Reports*, *Supreme Court Reporter*, or *United States Supreme Court Reports, Lawyers' Edition*, in that order of preference. At the time this book was being written, *Wyoming v. Houghton* was published in *United States Reports*, *Supreme Court Reporter*, and *United States Supreme Court Reports, Lawyers' Edition*. Because *The Bluebook* prefers *United States Reports* over *Supreme Court Reporter* and *United States Supreme Court Reports, Lawyers' Edition*, the citation would be to *United States Reports*. Figure 4-22 shows *The Bluebook*-required citation to *United States Reports*.

Wyoming v. Houghton, 526 U.S. 295 (1999).

FIGURE 4-22 Citation to Wyoming v. Houghton in Bluebook Form.

Wyoming v. Houghton, 526 U.S. 295, 119 S.Ct. 1297, 143 L. Ed. 2d 408 (1999).

FIGURE 4-23 Citation to Wyoming v. Houghton with Parallel Citations.

United States v. Walker, 933 F.2d 812 (10th Cir. 1991), *cert. denied*, 502 U.S. 1093 (1992).

FIGURE 4-24 Citation to United States v. Walker

Sexton v. Gibbs, 327 F. Supp. 134 (N.D. Tex. 1970), *aff'd*, 446 F.2d 904 (5th Cir. 1971), *cert. denied*, 404 U.S. 1062 (1972).

FIGURE 4-25 Citation to Sexton v. Gibbs

Although *The Bluebook* does not require you to give parallel citations to United States Supreme Court cases, you may give parallel citations to those cases, as shown in figure 4-23; they are often helpful to readers with more limited library resources.

If you are citing to only one reporter, cite to *United States Reports*, if the case is contained in it. If the case has not yet appeared in *United States Reports*, cite to *Supreme Court Reporter*. If the case has not yet appeared in *United States Reports* or *Supreme Court Reporter*, cite to *United States Supreme Court Reports, Lawyers' Edition*.

United States courts of appeals

Figure 4-24 shows a citation to a case reported in *Federal Reporter* from a United States court of appeals.

United States district courts

Figure 4-25 contains a citation to a case from the United States District Court for the Northern District of Texas.

Notice that "Northern District of Texas" has been abbreviated to "N.D. Tex." You know from this citation that Texas has more than one district. Some federal districts are divided into divisions. The parenthetical information should identify the district, but not the division within the district. Some of the less populous or smaller states, such as New Jersey, have only one United States district court to cover the whole state. The abbreviation for the United States District Court for the District of New Jersey would be "D. N.J." After the *Sexton* case was decided by the United States District Court for the Northern District of Texas in 1970, it was affirmed by the United States Court of Appeals for the Fifth Circuit in 1971 and certiorari was denied by the United States Supreme Court in 1972.

CHAPTER 4 SUMMARY

- A court's **jurisdiction** is the power of the court to decide cases. To decide a case, a court must have geographical jurisdiction, subject matter jurisdiction, and hierarchical jurisdiction.
- The **Supreme Court of the United States** is the highest federal court. The thirteen **United States Courts of Appeals** are federal intermediate appellate courts. The **United States District Courts** are federal trial-level courts.

- The state court system varies from state to state. Some states have a simplified court structure (also called a **unified court structure**) with three or four tiers; the court structure of other states is more complex.
- Cases are easier to read and understand once you are familiar with typical case style and format.
- The syllabus (case summary) and the headnotes (summaries of important legal principles contained in the case) that precede the opinion were prepared by the publisher and have no official authority.
- The main parts of a typical opinion are the facts, the procedural history of the case before it reached the court writing the opinion, the issue(s) (legal questions considered by the court), the holding(s) (the rules of the case), and the court's explanation of why it reached the particular holding (s).
- "Briefing a case" means taking notes of the most important parts of a case so that you can later refer to your "case brief" to quickly refresh your memory.
- A standard format for briefing a case contains:
  Correct case citation
  Facts
  History
  Issue(s)
  Holding(s)
  Reasoning
  Result
- Cases are organized chronologically in looseleaf publications, advance sheets, and reporters.
- A reporter contains cases from a particular court or courts; the reporters are published in "series" (1st, 2d, 3d, etc.).
- It is important to learn correct citation form to allow you to communicate with other legal professionals.
- Case citations contain the case name, the volume, first page of the case, and name and series of the reporter as well as information identifying the court writing the decision.
- A full case citation should contain the page number(s) on which the cited material is located and any subsequent history of the case.

CYBERLAW EXERCISES

1. From http://www.usscplus.com you can access current decisions of the United States Supreme Court. Use the page to locate the listing of United States Supreme Court decisions from the current term. Access one of the decisions and read it.
2. The Lexis law school site (http://lawschool.lexis.com) includes information on legal citation and researching cases.
3. The Law Library Resources Exchange (http://www.llrx.com) has become a well-known starting point for legal research.
4. The Center for Information Law and Policy was a joint initiative of Villanova University School of Law and the Illinois Institute of Technology's Chicago-Kent College of Law. A number of the "locators" formerly housed at the Center are now housed at Villanova or Chicago-Kent. For example, the Federal Courts Locator and the State Courts Locator are accessible through Villanova's The Internet Legal Research Compass (http://vls.law.vill.edu/compass/). The Federal Web Locator and State Web Locator are accessible through the Illinois Institute of Technology's Information Center (http://www.infoctr.edu/).
5. Northwestern University's The Oyez Project (http://oyez.nwu.edu) is a United States Supreme Court database. The site includes a virtual tour of the United States Supreme Court building and audiotapes of oral arguments before the United States Supreme Court.
10. The Emory University School of Law homepage (http://www.law.emory.edu) provides access to the Federal Courts Finder and the Electronic Reference Desk.
11. Many law school librarians have written legal research guides and have posted them on the

web. The guides attempt to introduce students to legal research and to answer commonly asked questions. Paul Richert, Law Librarian and Professor of Law at the University of Akron, School of Law Library, has compiled an "Internet Hotlist of Law Guides Organized by Subject" that links to many of the legal research guides. The Hotlist is accessible at http://www.uakron.edu/law/richert/index1.html.

LEGAL RESEARCH ASSIGNMENT—READING CASES

1. Please answer the following questions regarding *Florida v. Enio Jimeno* (case included in Appendix A, fig. A-6):
   a. What is the correct citation of the case?
   b. On what page does the court's decision begin?
   c. Is it proper to quote anything prior to this page?
   d. Which Justice wrote the opinion?
   e. Which Justice(s) joined in that opinion?
   f. Which Justice wrote the dissenting opinion?
   g. Which Justice(s) joined in the dissenting opinion?
   h. Is this a per curiam, majority, or plurality opinion?
   i. What are the important facts?
   j. Who won at the trial level?
   k. Where did the case go after it left the trial court and before it reached the United States Supreme Court?
   l. What was the issue before the United States Supreme Court?
   m. What did the Court hold?
   n. What was the Court's reasoning for reaching this holding?
   o. What was the result?
   p. Why did the dissent reason that the result should have been different?
   q. Using the answers to the above questions, write a case brief for *Jimeno*.
2. Answer the following questions regarding *Whren v. United States* (case included in Appendix A, fig. A-7):
   a. What is the correct citation of the case?
   b. What party brought the case in the trial level court?
   c. Who were the defendants in the trial level court?
   d. Who were the attorneys who represented the petitioners?
   e. Who were the attorneys who represented the respondent?
   f. Who wrote the opinion?
   g. How many justices joined in the opinion?
   h. What was the result at the trial level?
   i. What happened at the intermediate appellate level?
   j. What were the facts?
   k. According to the petitioners, what should the standard be for a stop for a traffic violation?
   l. What was the petitioners' reason for arguing for a higher standard?
   m. What was the issue before the United States Supreme Court?
   n. What was the holding of the United States Supreme Court?
   o. Why did the Court reject the petitioners' argument that a higher standard should apply to stops for traffic violations?
   p. What result did the United States Supreme Court reach?
   q. Using the answers to the above questions, write a case brief for *Whren*.

LEGAL RESEARCH ASSIGNMENT—CASE LAW

1. What are the names of the three reporters containing current decisions of the United States Supreme Court?
2. What is the name of the looseleaf publication containing current decisions of the United States Supreme Court?
3. What is the name of the reporter containing current decisions of the United States Courts of Appeals?
4. What is the name of the reporter containing current decisions of the United States District Courts?
5. What is the name of the highest court in your state and what is the name of the reporter containing current decisions of that court?
6. What is the name of your state's intermediate appellate court and what is the name of the reporter containing current decisions of that court?
7. What is the name of the looseleaf publication containing decisions of the state courts of your state?
8. What is the name of the trial-level court of your state? (If your state has more than one trial-level court, give the names of all trial-level courts.) What is the name of the reporter containing current decisions of that court/those courts?
9. Answer the following questions regarding the case found at 990 F. Supp. 657:
   a. What is the correct citation for this case?
   b. What does this decision deal with?
   c. Was the plaintiff successful on her claim? Explain.
10. Answer the following questions regarding the case found at 520 U.S. 681, 137 L. Ed. 2d 945, 117 S. Ct. 1636:
    a. What is the correct citation for this case?
    b. Can a president be subject to trial in a civil case while he is in office?
    c. Why or why not?
11. Answer the following questions regarding the case found at 164 F.3d 110:
    a. What is the correct citation for this case?
    b. What was the result in the trial court?
    c. What does Rule 28 require and why did the appellant's main brief fail to comply with the rule?
    d. Why didn't the court consider the appellant's reply brief?
    e. What did the appellee recover under Rule 38 and why?
12. Answer the following questions regarding the case found at 22 F.3d 899:
    a. What is the correct citation for this case?
    b. How did the appellant's opening brief exceed the page limit?
    c. What was the problem with the footnotes?
    d. How much did the attorney pay in sanctions?
13. Answer the following questions regarding the case found at 127 F.3d 1145:
    a. What is the correct citation for this case?
    b. What was wrong with N/S's brief?
    c. What was wrong with N/S's reply brief?
    d. What was the result?
    e. Why did the court feel that it had to enforce Rule 28?
14. Answer the following questions regarding the case found at 525 U.S. 83, 142 L. Ed. 2d 373, 119 S. Ct. 469:
    a. What is the correct citation for this case?
    b. What were the facts?
    c. What did the Court hold?
    d. How did the Court differentiate the respondents from overnight guests?
15. Answer the following questions regarding the case found at 19 F. Supp. 2d 1081:
    a. What is the correct citation for this case?
    b. What was the plaintiff seeking?
    c. Why was the case heard by a three-judge panel?
    d. What did the court hold?
    e. Look at 526 U.S. 1061, 143 L. Ed. 2d 538, 119 S. Ct. 1450 and explain what happened when the case went to the United States Supreme Court.
16. Answer the following questions regarding the case found at 526 U.S. 559, 119 S. Ct. 1555, 143 L. Ed. 2d 748:
    a. What is the correct citation for this case?

b. Why did the police believe that White's car was subject to forfeiture?
c. What did the officers do concerning White's car?
d. What did the Court hold?

17. Answer the following questions regarding the case found at 918 F. Supp. 905:
a. What is the correct citation for this case?
b. What was the matter before the court?
c. Why did the court rule that *Kopf* was controlling?

18. Answer the following questions regarding the case found at 710 F.2d 1542:
a. What is the correct citation for this case?
b. Why did the plaintiffs file this case?
c. Did the Augusta business ordinance apply to Blackie?

19. Answer the following questions regarding the case found at 283 U.S. 25:
a. What is the correct citation for this case?
b. What was the issue before the Court?
c. What did the Court hold?

20. Answer the following questions regarding the case found at 613 P.2d 398:
a. What was the issue in this case?
b. What were the facts?
c. According to the court, what did the term "traffic" include?

21. Answer the following questions regarding the case found at 247 N.W.2d 673:
a. How did the treatment of the inventory search of petitioner's vehicle differ under the United States Constitution and the state constitution?
b. What did the state constitution require concerning inventory searches?

22. Answer the following questions regarding the case found at 499 N.W.2d 512:
a. What was the issue?
b. What did Ms. Nelson argue?

23. Answer the following questions regarding the case found at 674 A.2d 1273:
a. Which court decided the case?
b. What was the issue?
c. What was the quality of attorney Shepperson's writing between 1985 and 1992?
d. How did the court punish Shepperson?

24. Answer the following questions regarding the case found at 445 So. 2d 1364:
a. What was the "primary issue" in this case?
b. What did the court hold?

25. Answer the following questions regarding the case found at 190 F. Supp. 116:
a. What is the correct citation to this case?
b. How do the plaintiff's and the defendant's definitions of "chicken" differ?
c. What did the court look to in determining the meaning of the word?
d. Did the court accept the defendant's or the plaintiff's definition of the word?

26. Answer the following questions regarding the case found at 602 F.2d 743:
a. What is the correct citation to the case?
b. What was the issue before the court?
c. What do subsections (a) and (e) of Rule 8 of the Federal Rules of Civil Procedure require?
d. What did the appellate court order the district court to do?

27. Answer the following questions regarding the case found at 463 F.2d 98:
a. What is the correct citation to the case?
b. Who are the plaintiffs seeking to represent?
c. What do the three counts of the complaint allege?
d. How much are the plaintiffs seeking in damages and attorneys fees?
e. What is wrong with count 1?

28. Answer the following questions regarding the case found at 377 N.Y.S.2d 448:
a. How long was attorney Slater's brief?
b. How long was the brief filed on behalf of the Tax Commission?
c. How did the court sanction Slater?

CHAPTER 5*

PRIMARY SOURCES: CONSTITUTIONS, STATUTES, COURT RULES, AND ADMINISTRATIVE LAW

INTRODUCTION

This chapter introduces constitutions, statutes, court rules, and administrative law and explains the correct citation form for those four primary sources.

CONSTITUTIONS

Because there is a United States Constitution and each state has its own **constitution,** constitutional law research may be done at the federal and the state level. As explained in chapter 1, Article VI of the United States Constitution contains the **supremacy clause.** The supremacy clause makes the Constitution prevail over any federal statute or state constitutional provision or statute in conflict with the Constitution. Congress is given certain **enumerated powers** in Article I, section 8 of the Constitution. Sections 9 and 10 of Article I prohibit the federal and state governments from taking certain actions (for example, passing any **ex post facto law**). The Tenth Amendment to the Constitution reserves all other powers to the states.

*Grateful thanks to Ransford C. Pyle, Ph.D., J.D. and Daniel E. Hall, Ed.D., J.D. who authored portions of this chapter. Reproduced by Permission. FOUNDATIONS OF LAW: CASES, COMMENTARY, AND ETHICS by Ransford C. Pyle. Delmar Publishers, Inc., Albany, New York. Second Edition, Copyright 1996. CONSTITUTIONAL LAW: CASES AND COMMENTARY by Daniel E. Hall. Delmar, Albany, New York. Copyright 1997.

A written constitution is the document setting forth the fundamental principles of governance. For example, Article I of the United States Constitution deals with the legislative branch, Article II deals with the executive branch, and Article III deals with the judicial branch of the federal government. A state constitution sets forth the basic framework of state government in a similar fashion.

Some people differentiate between the written and the **living** constitution. The written United States Constitution, including all amendments to it, is less than twenty pages in length. The living constitution would include those pages and all case law interpretations of the Constitution. If printed, the living constitution would require numerous volumes. Scholars and laypersons alike have hotly debated constitutional interpretation. Some believe that any interpretation should be based on the plain language of the Constitution and should not stray far from it. Others believe that the broad language of the Constitution should be interpreted as needed to deal with legal questions never dreamed of when the Constitution was first enacted.

The language of the United States Constitution is very broad, setting up a framework of government, often without much detail. For example, Article III of the Constitution establishes the United States Supreme Court with the establishment of other federal courts left to Congress. State constitutions may be much longer than the United States Constitution and may deal with many subjects that are dealt with on the federal level by statute. The only limit on state constitutions is that they may not conflict with the United States Constitution or any federal statute concerning a matter given exclusively to the federal government.

Constitutions generally have the same basic format. A constitution usually begins with a preamble. A preamble is a paragraph or clause explaining the reason for the enactment of the constitution and the object or objects it seeks to accomplish. The body of the document is divided into various parts (called "articles" in the United States Constitution and many state constitutions) corresponding to the various subjects dealt with in the constitution and the parts into subparts (called "sections" and "clauses" in the United States Constitution). Near the end of the constitution is a provision describing the procedure for amending it. Any amendments to a constitution are either printed at the end of the constitution (the procedure followed for the United States Constitution) or the new language is simply incorporated into the body of the document (the procedure followed for the Florida Constitution and the constitutions of many other states).

The United States Constitution is unique in that it was adopted in 1787 and has been the fundamental document of American government ever since. There are twenty-six amendments to it, with the first ten amendments known as the Bill of Rights. The Fourteenth Amendment, adopted in 1868, has been interpreted to make most of the provisions of the Bill of Rights applicable to the states. In contrast, many states have been governed under more than one constitution. For example, the present Constitution of the State of Florida is dated 1968 and is a revision of the constitution of 1885. The Florida Constitution has been amended a number of times since 1968.

Locating constitutions

The text of constitutions may be found in many reference books in the law library. If you just want to read the United States Constitution, you could read it from a constitutional law textbook or other source. (Even many dictionaries contain a copy of the United States Constitution). The text of your state's constitution may be printed in the set of books containing the official version of your state's statutory code.

An annotated version of the United States Constitution is found in the sets of books containing the annotated United States Code. If you want to know how the first amendment to the United States Constitution has been interpreted concerning restrictions on prayers in public schools, you would look at the case summaries of cases interpreting the first amendment. The case summaries are found in United States Code Service or United States Code Annotated following the text of the first amendment. You would follow a similar procedure to research your state's constitution. Often codes and annotated codes contain a separate index located at the end of a constitution. The index is designed to help you locate a particular provision within the constitution.

Don't forget to update your research. Hardbound volumes of the annotated codes are updated by pocket parts. The pocket parts are updated by quarterly supplements. Because of the lag time between the announcement of an important United States Supreme Court decision interpreting the Constitution and the printing of the annual pocket part to the annotated code, the annotated code may be as much as two years behind current case law. Update your research by using **citators** and **computer assisted legal research.**

When researching, you may find it helpful to consult one or more of the various treatises dealing with constitutional law in addition to reading the annotations in the annotated codes.

Citations for constitutions

Caveat: Do not assume that the legal citations found when researching are in correct citation form. Citations, even those included in cases, may or may not comply with the citation rules your professor has asked you to use. Always check your citations against the appropriate citation rule for correct form.

The clause prohibiting ex post facto laws and section 1 of the Fourteenth Amendment to the Constitution may be cited as follows:

U.S. Const. art. I, § 9, cl. 3.	(abbreviation for United States Constitution, Article I, section 9, clause 3)
U.S. Const. amend. XIV, § 1.	(abbreviation for United States Constitution, fourteenth amendment, section 1)

Give the section number when the Constitution specifically identifies a portion of an article as a section. When a section, such as section nine of article I, is long and contains a number of paragraphs, you can reference a particular paragraph as a "clause." Some copies of the United States Constitution identify the amendments as "articles" instead of "amendments." This is because the amendments are technically articles in amendment of the Constitution. To avoid confusion, cite the amendments to the Constitution as "amendments" rather than as "articles." State constitutions can be cited using the same citation form as above or using your state's citation rules.

Initiation of constitutional amendments

Article V of the Constitution states, in part:

> The Congress, whenever two thirds of both Houses shall deem it necessary, shall propose Amendments to this Constitution, or on the Application of the Legislatures of two thirds of the several States, shall call a Convention for proposing Amendments, which, in either Case, shall be valid to all Intents and Purposes, as Part of this Constitution, when ratified by the Legislatures of three fourths of the several States, or by Conventions in three fourths thereof, as the one or the other Mode of Ratification may be proposed by the Congress . . . .

Accordingly, there are two methods of initiating a constitutional amendment. Congressional resolution is the first. Two-thirds majorities in both houses of Congress are required. The President does not play a role in this process. Second, with two-thirds of the state legislatures or more, a convention can be convened to propose amendments. To date, initiation by Congress is the only method that has been successfully used to initiate amendments.

Regardless of which method of proposal is employed, Congress is empowered to decide the method of ratification. There are two methods: by concurrence of three-fourths of the state legislatures or by conventions in three-fourths of the states.

Congress holds considerable authority in the amendment process. It may establish a time limit for ratification of a proposal, regardless of the method of proposal, and it is empowered to decide whether an amendment has been ratified.

State constitutionalism and the new federalism

Every state has its own constitution. Like the federal Constitution, state constitutions contain declarations or bills of individual rights. In fact, many clauses in state bills of rights are worded identically or nearly so, to the federal Constitution.

State constitutional law may not decrease or limit federally secured rights, but a state may extend civil rights beyond what the federal Constitution secures. In some cases, this may occur expressly. For example, both the Florida and Alaska constitutions expressly protect privacy, whereas the federal constitution does not. Rather, a national right to privacy was only recently declared by the United States Supreme Court (as a penumbra or implied protection), and it is somewhat controversial because of the absence of express language in the Constitution establishing the right. The Washington state constitution protects "private affairs," which has been interpreted more broadly than privacy under the Fourth Amendment. Many states provide for a right to education through their constitutions, although the federal Constitution does not contain a right to education. In addition to protecting freedom of religion, as does the First Amendment of the federal Constitution, the Georgia Constitution protects freedom of "conscience."

In the following case, the South Dakota Supreme Court found that the search and seizure provision of the South Dakota Constitution provided more protection to its citizens than did the Fourth Amendment, even though the wording of the two provisions was identical.

STATE of South Dakota, Plaintiff and Respondent,

v.

Donald OPPERMAN, Defendant and Appellant.

Supreme Court of South Dakota.

Nov. 12, 1976.

247 N.W.2d 673.

WINANS, Justice.

On April 15, 1975, this court reversed a judgment against petitioner because we found that the contraband used to convict petitioner had been seized pursuant to an inventory search which was unreasonable under the Fourth Amendment to the United States Constitution. On November 3, 1975, the United States Supreme Court granted certiorari; in a 5–4 decision it reversed the judgment of this court and remanded for further proceedings not inconsistent with its opinion. On August 26, 1976, this court granted a rehearing to ascertain whether the inventory search of petitioner's automobile was in violation of his rights under Article VI, s 11 of the South Dakota Constitution. We find that the inventory procedure followed in this instance constitutes an unreasonable search under our state constitution; accordingly we reverse the decision of the trial court.

We are mindful that the United States Supreme Court found that the inventory procedure followed in this case did not amount to an 'unreasonable search' in violation of the Fourth Amendment. That decision is binding on this court as a matter of federal constitutional law. 'However, manifestly the question remains for us to decide whether it offends any of the provisions of our own constitution and we are under no compulsion to follow the United States Supreme Court in that regard.' House of Seagram v. Assam Drug Co.

There can be no doubt that this court has the power to provide an individual with greater protection under the state constitution than does the United States Supreme Court under the federal constitution. Oregon v. Hass, 1975, 420 U.S. 714, 95 S.Ct. 1215, 43 L.Ed.2d 570. This court is the final authority on interpretation and enforcement of the South Dakota Constitution. We have always assumed the independent nature of our state constitution regardless of any similarity between the language of that document and the federal constitution. Admittedly the language of Article VI, s 11 is almost identical to that found in the Fourth Amendment;[FN] however, we have the right to construe our state constitutional provision in accordance with what we conceive to be its plain meaning. We find that logic and a sound regard for the purposes of the protection afforded by S.D.Const., Art. VI, s 11 warrant a higher standard of protection for the individual in this instance than the United States Supreme Court found necessary under the Fourth Amendment.

FN. S.D.Const., Art. VI, s 11 provides:

'The right of the people to be secure in their persons, houses, papers and effects, against unreasonable searches and seizures shall not be violated, and no warrant shall issue but upon probable cause supported by affidavit, particularly describing the place to be searched and the person or thing to be seized.'

U.S. Const., Amend. 4 provides:

'The right of the people to be secure in their persons, houses, papers and effects, against unreasonable searches and seizures, shall not be violated, and no Warrants shall issue but upon probable cause, supported by Oath or affirmation, and particularly describing the place to be searched, and the persons of things to be seized.'

Article VI, s 11 of our state constitution guarantees our citizens the right to be free from 'unreasonable searches and seizures.' We have held that a determination of reasonableness requires a balancing of the need for a search in a particular case against the scope of the particular intrusion. State v. Catlette. In that opinion we relied on United States v. Lawson and held that an inventory was a search, but found that it was not an unreasonable search as long as it was conducted without investigative motive and its scope was limited to things within plain view.

We also find persuasive the reasoning in Lawson that for an inventory search to be reasonable, absent a warrant or circumstances constituting an exception to the warrant requirement, there must be a 'minimal interference' with an individual's protected rights. We now conclude that as a matter of protection under S.D.Const., Art. VI, s 11, 'minimal interference' with a citizen's constitutional rights means that noninvestigative police inventory searches of automobile without a warrant must be restricted to safeguarding those articles which are within plain view of the officer's vision. We therefore affirm the rationale of our original decision as a matter of state constitutional law.

Respondent argues that because petitioner failed to brief or argue the applicability of the state constitution before this court on the first appeal, this issue should be deemed abandoned. Admittedly petitioner did not contend that our state provision should be interpreted as giving greater individual protection than does the federal constitution; this court, however, granted a rehearing to consider that question and afforded both sides the opportunity to brief and argue that point. We find that this matter is properly before the court. Accordingly, we reverse the judgment of the trial court as a matter of state constitutional law.

STATUTES

The legislative branch

The United States Constitution gives Congress the power to pass legislation. Article I, section 1 of the United States Constitution provides:

> All legislative Powers herein granted shall be vested in a Congress of the United States, which shall consist of a Senate and House of Representatives.

Article I, section 7, clause 2 of the United States Constitution provides:

> Every Bill which shall have passed the House of Representatives and the Senate, shall, before it become a Law, be presented to the President of the United States; If he approve he shall sign it, but if not he shall return it, with his Objections to that House in which it shall have originated, who shall enter the Objections at large on their Journal, and proceed to reconsider it. If after such Reconsideration two thirds of that House shall agree to pass the Bill, it shall be sent, together with the Objections, to the other House, by which it shall likewise be reconsidered, and if approved by two thirds of that House, it shall become a Law. But in all such Cases the Votes of both Houses shall be determined by yeas and Nays, and the Names of the Persons voting for and against the Bill shall be entered on the Journal of each House respectively. If any Bill shall not be returned by the President within ten Days (Sundays excepted) after it shall have been presented to him, the Same shall be a Law, in like Manner as if he had signed it, unless the Congress by their Adjournment prevent its Return, in which Case it shall not be a Law.

Similarly, state constitutions give state legislatures power to pass legislation. Nebraska's legislature is unique among all state legislatures in the United States because it has a **unicameral** (single-house) system. All other states and the federal government have **bicameral** legislatures.

Today, the primary source of law-making is legislative bodies. Whereas courts are largely reactive (only become involved after a dispute has arisen), legislatures are largely proactive. When a court hears a case, it is concerned with individual facts; legislatures consider large systemic issues. Individual cases are used only as anecdotal evidence. Legislation is concerned with policy issues and large groups of people, whereas courts are usually concerned with dispensing justice among a small number of people. Courts look to the past in resolving disputes; legislatures are concerned with the future.

Often, legislation is proposed to address a perceived societal problem. The legislation is introduced and is assigned to a committee. The committee may investigate the need for the proposed legislation, gather information, and hold hearings. After the proposed legislation leaves the committee, it is subject to open debate and discussion in the legislature. During the discussion and debate, the legislature considers the need for the proposed legislation, the effect the legislation will have, and the appropriateness of the legislation's wording. After legislation is passed by both chambers of the legislature (or in Nebraska, if passed by the single legislative chamber), it is subject to being vetoed by the chief executive.

Legislatures are responsible for making law. In making law, legislators must consider competing policies and interests. Legislatures are free to enact any law, so long as that law is consonant with the United States Constitution. Legislatures are free to alter, amend, and abolish the common law of their jurisdictions if they wish, except for the common law that is now embodied in the United States Constitution.

The process of **legislation** and its effect differs significantly from **adjudication** (judges deciding cases). Adjudication resolves a dispute between particular parties based on the facts presented to the court and the law applied by the judge. The judge's opinion is directly binding only on the parties before the court. In the future, other courts may look to the judge's opinion as authority in deciding future cases.

In contrast, legislation is expected to have universal application. Universal application means that the legislation applies to all individuals subject to the legislation. The legislation applies as of its effective date and into the future unless amended, repealed, or held to be unconstitutional. Ex post facto laws are forbidden under the United States Constitution. (See fig. 1-3 for the wording of this provision.) Ex post facto laws are criminal statutes with retroactive effect. Civil statutes are usually interpreted to be **prospective** rather than **retrospective** in effect.

Congress

The Constitution creates the Senate and the House of Representatives as the two houses of Congress. The Senate comprises 100 senators, two from each state and the House of Representatives comprises 435 representatives, with at least one from each state and otherwise apportioned among the states according to population. Figures 5-1 and 5-2 depict the organization of the two houses of Congress. Effective January 1, 2000, the salary of senators and representatives was $141,300.

A Congress lasts for two years, beginning in January of the year following the biennial election of members. Each Congress is divided into two one-year sessions. For example, the first session of the 106th Congress began on January 1, 1999 and the second session of the 106th Congress began on January 1, 2000. The 107th Congress began on January 1, 2001 and lasts through calendar year 2002.

The Constitution provides that revenue bills must originate in the House of Representatives. By tradition, the House originates appropriation bills also.

The Constitution empowers each house to adopt procedural rules. The Senate considers itself a continuing body and operates under rules that are amended from time to time. The House adopts its procedural rules on the opening day of each Congress.

Most proposed legislation is introduced in the form of a bill. Congress also adopts resolutions, formal statements by Congress not intended to be statutes. For example, by resolution Congress may express its opinion to the President concerning a matter that is exclusively executive. Resolutions may be issued by a single house or both, in which case they are referred to as *concurrent.* A joint resolution is one passed by both houses and approved by the President. Such a resolution has the force of a statute.

During the 105th Congress (1997–1998), 4,874 bills and 140 joint resolutions were introduced in the House and 2,655 bills and 60 joint resolutions were introduced in the Senate. The concept for the proposed legislation originates from many sources,

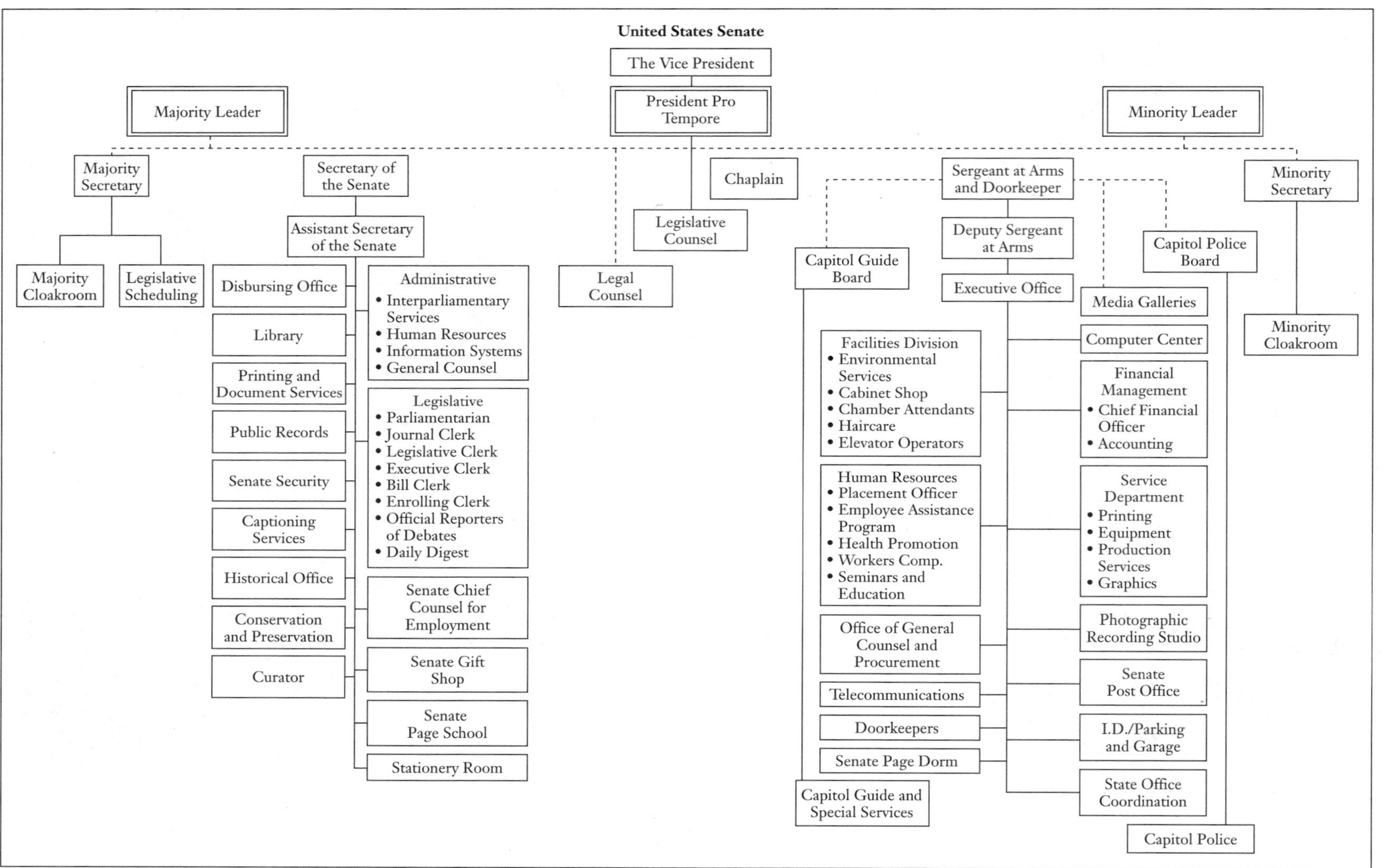

FIGURE 5-1 United States Senate.

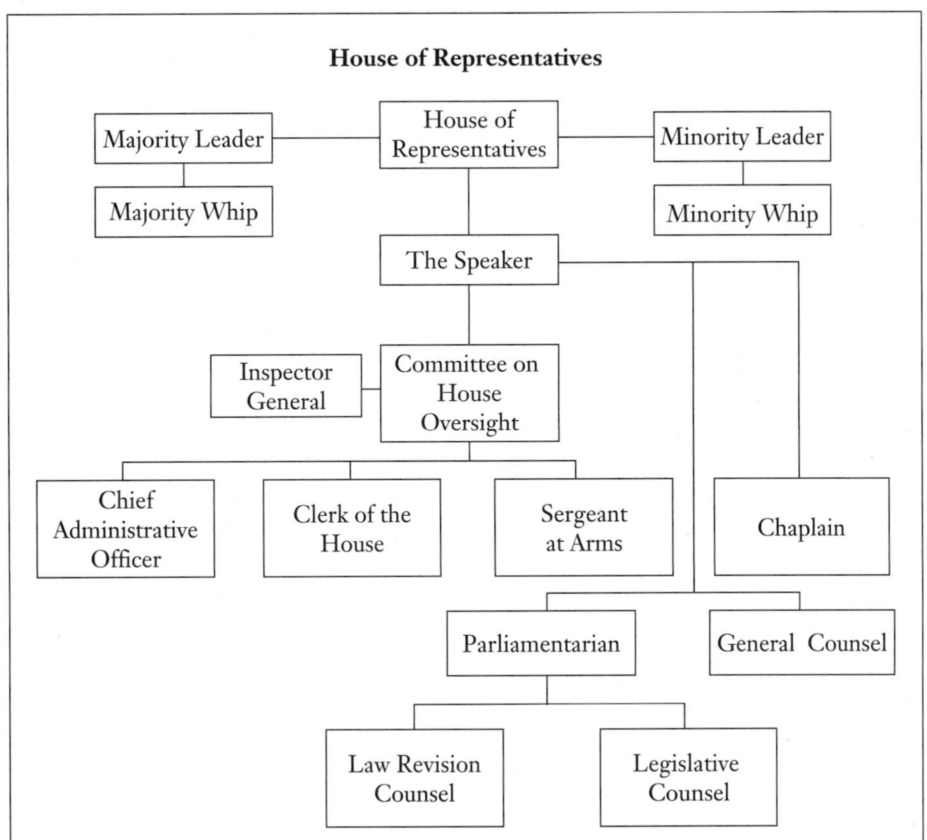

FIGURE 5-2 House of Representatives.

among which are members of Congress, congressional constituents, state legislatures, the president, executive departments, and administrative agencies.

Bills are public bills or private bills. A public bill applies to the general public. Sometimes, Congress authorizes relief to a named individual or an organization pursuant to a private bill. Common subjects of private bills are claims against the United States and immigration and naturalization matters. For example, a private bill may authorize the federal government to pay an individual's claim against the United States; a private bill is needed where the individual's claim would ordinarily be barred under sovereign immunity.

Bills in each house are identified by "H.R." (House of Representatives) or "S." (Senate), followed by sequential numbers identifying the order in which they are introduced in the house. Any member of either house may introduce a bill. The member introducing the bill is the "sponsor;" the bill may have an unlimited number of cosponsors. A member of the House of Representatives introduces a bill by signing and placing it in the "hopper," a wooden box located at the side of the House rostrum. A Senator introduces a bill by signing it and delivering it to one of the clerks at the Presiding Officer's desk; in the alternative, a Senator may orally introduce the bill from the Senate floor.

After being introduced, a bill is referred to the appropriate committee and copies of the bill are made available to the committee members and to the public. The House has 19 standing committees, the Senate has 16 standing committees, and four standing joint committees have oversight responsibilities. In addition, a house may form select committees and task forces as needed. Each committee has jurisdiction over certain matters; the committee may have a number of subcommittees to deal with particular issues within the jurisdiction of the committee. Committee members are assisted in their committee work by a professional staff.

A committee or a subcommittee may hold meetings or public hearings on a bill. After hearings have been held, a committee or subcommittee considers the bill in a "markup" session. A markup session is the committee or subcommittee members' opportunity to comment and then vote on a bill. A subcommittee may vote to report the bill favorably, with or without recommendation, unfavorably, or without recommendation to the committee. A bill would not leave the subcommittee if the vote were to table or postpone action on the bill. Similarly, a committee may vote to report a bill to the floor of the chamber, or may table or postpone action on the bill.

A committee staff member prepares the committee report once a committee has voted favorably to report the bill to the chamber floor. The committee report usually outlines the purpose and scope of the bill and provides a detailed explanation of each section of the bill.

After leaving a committee, a bill may be debated on the chamber floor; during the debate, the bill may be amended numerous times. Once a chamber passes a bill, the bill technically is transformed from a bill to an "act," signifying that it is the act of one chamber of Congress. Although it is technically an act, it is still commonly called a bill. The enrolling clerk prepares a copy of the bill, including all amendments adopted. The final copy of the bill is often referred to as the "**engrossed**" copy because it contains the definitive text approved by the chamber. If passed by the House of Representatives, the engrossed bill is printed on blue paper and the Clerk of the House signs it. If passed by the Senate, the engrossed bill is printed on white paper and is attested to by the Secretary of the Senate.

A bill approved by one chamber is delivered to the other chamber. There it is referred to the appropriate committee for study and public hearings. The second chamber may pass the bill, with or without amendments. If there were no amendments, the bill is enrolled for presentation to the president.

If the second chamber passes the bill with amendments, it is returned to the chamber in which it originated. The first chamber may approve the amendments. If the amendments are substantial, differing provisions may be resolved in a conference committee comprised of members from both chambers. The conference committee prepares a report containing the recommendations of the committee. A bill is considered approved by Congress if both chambers agree to the conference report.

An **enrolled** bill approved by both chambers in identical form is prepared for the president. The term "enroll" means to prepare the final perfect copy of the bill approved by both chambers in perfect final form. The enrolled bill is printed on parchment paper and is signed by the authorized member of each chamber.

The president may approve the bill by signing it, may veto the bill, or may take no action on the bill. If the president takes no action while Congress is in session, the bill becomes law ten days (Sundays excepted) after it was presented to him. If the president takes no action but Congress is not in session, the bill does not become law. This is commonly referred to as the "pocket veto." The president's veto can be overridden by the vote of two-thirds of each chamber.

State legislatures

Except for Nebraska, which has a unicameral legislature, all states have bicameral legislatures. The upper house in the state legislatures is called the Senate; the lower house is called the House of Representatives, General Assembly, or House of Delegates.

A primary role of state legislatures is enacting statutes. The legislative procedure followed to enact statutes differs from state to state but many states follow a procedure similar to that followed in Congress and described above. Figure 5-3 shows a flowchart tracing the route a bill takes through the Florida legislature.

As in Congress, the idea for a new statute may come from a variety of sources, including a constituent, a legislator, or an organization. A legislator introduces the bill and it is referred to a committee. After committee hearings and discussion, the bill is considered on the floor of the chamber. There it is debated and amended. If the bill passes in that chamber, it is transmitted to the other chamber for consideration. A similar procedure is followed in the second chamber. Once both chambers pass a bill, it may go to a conference committee to clear up any differences in wording. If both chambers passed the bill in identical form, it is transmitted to the governor. The governor may sign or veto the act. A veto may be overridden by the vote of two-thirds of each house.

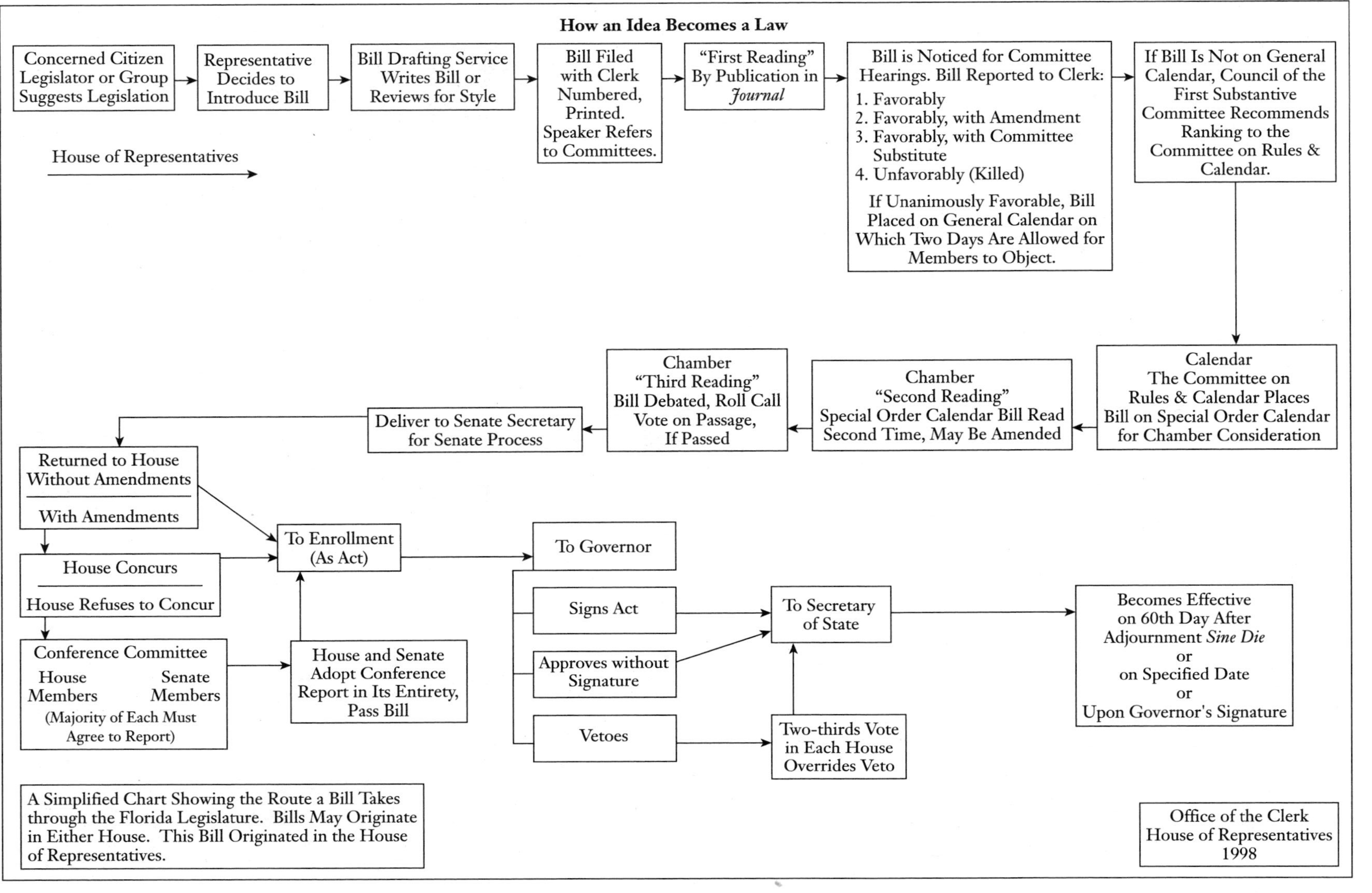

FIGURE 5-3 How an Idea Becomes a Law.

FIGURE 5-4 Federal Government Legislative Branch Reference Materials.

Senate
House of Representatives

slip laws

advance session law service

United States Code Congressional and Administrative News

session laws

United States Statutes at Large

code

United States Code

annotated codes

United States Code Annotated

United States Code Service

For example, the Florida Constitution provides for the governor's approval or veto:

> Every bill passed by the legislature shall be presented to the governor for approval and shall become a law if the governor approves and signs it, or fails to veto it within seven consecutive days after presentation. If during that period or on the seventh day the legislature adjourns sine die or takes a recess of more than thirty days, the governor shall have fifteen consecutive days from the date of presentation to act on the bill. In all cases except general appropriation bills, the veto shall extend to the entire bill. The governor may veto any specific appropriation in a general appropriation bill, but may not veto any qualification or restriction without also vetoing the appropriation to which it relates.

The Florida Constitution also specifies the effective date of a newly-passed statute:

> Each law shall take effect on the sixtieth day after **adjournment sine die** of the session of the legislature in which enacted or as otherwise provided therein. If the law is passed over the veto of the governor it shall take effect on the sixtieth day after adjournment sine die of the session in which the veto is overridden, on a later date fixed in the law, or on a date fixed by resolution passed by both houses of the legislature.

Publication of statutes

Although federal and state statutes are published in a number of different formats, there is a general pattern to the order in which the formats are used. The general names for the formats of statutory publication, in chronological order, are as follows:

slip law
advance session law service
session laws
code
annotated code

Figure 5-4 lists the types of reference materials and the names of the reference materials containing the law made by Congress. Figure 5-5 lists the types of reference materials produced by a state legislature, with room for you to add the names of the reference materials for your state. Once completed, use figure 5-5 as a quick and handy guide for the legislative reference materials for your state.

Slip law

A new statute is first published as a **slip law.** In this form, a single statute is printed in an unbound pamphlet, with each pamphlet individually paginated. Although the slip law is the first official form of publication, distribution of the slip law form of statutes is generally limited to law school libraries and libraries designated as official government depositories. A researcher would find researching slip laws cumbersome; they are unindexed and individual slip law pamphlets may easily be misshelved or misplaced.

slip laws

advance session law service

session laws

code

annotated code

FIGURE 5-5 State Government Legislative Branch Reference Materials.

Federal statutes are first published in slip law form. Each federal statute is numbered with a public law or a private law number, which contains the session number of Congress and is separated by a hyphen from the number corresponding to the statute's sequence. For example, the first public law in the 107th session of Congress would be "Public Law 107-1" and the first private law in that session would be "Private Law 107-1." Each slip law pamphlet is identified by a public or private law number, the approval date (or an explanatory notation if it became law without presidential approval), and the bill number.

Many states follow a similar procedure for state statutes. For example, the Florida legislature passes general laws (similar to public laws passed by Congress) and special laws (similar to private laws passed by Congress). These laws are first published in slip law form. Each statute is numbered with a general or special law number, which contains the year of passage and is separated by a hyphen from the number corresponding to the statute's sequence. For example, the first general law passed by the Florida legislature in 2001 was "Chapter 01-1."

Session laws

The next publishing format is called **session laws.** Session law format involves the publication of slip laws produced in a legislative session, with the laws published in chronological order. Each state and the federal government publish session laws, generally in hardbound volumes. As typical of a government publication, the session laws published by a state or the federal government appear some time after the end of the legislative session. In most states, commercial publishers produce **advance session law services** to fill the gap between the passage of the statutes and the appearance of the government-published session laws. The format for advance session law services for one legislative session may be a number of paperbound volumes, each volume with a numerical and subject index. The numerical index typically indexes the existing statute numbers, as codified, and indicates if the statutes have been amended or repealed.

The United States Code Congressional and Administrative News is an advance session law service for federal statutes. This publication contains the text of new statutes as well as selected legislative history information, such as House and Senate reports. Paperbound pamphlets (often referred to as advance pamphlets) produced to supplement United States Code Service and United States Code Annotated also contain the text of newly-passed federal legislation.

The United States Statutes at Large is the session law publication for federal statutes. The United States Statutes at Large contain the statutes, as enacted, arranged in chronological order. The United States Statutes at Large are the legal evidence of the laws contained in them; however, the legal researcher might find it difficult to determine the text of a statute currently in effect. The material in them is not arranged by subject matter and statutes are not consolidated with later amendments. Typically, publication lags two to three years behind passage of the statutes.

Florida is an example of a state with an advance session law service publication and a session law publication produced by the state. The advance session law service publication is West's *Florida Session Law Service* and the session law publication is *Laws of Florida*. West's *Florida Session Law Service* for a legislative session typically is comprised of eight to ten paperbound pamphlets, with the first several pamphlets published during or at the end of the legislative session. Each pamphlet contains a numerical and subject index at the end of the volume. The indexes are cumulative through the pamphlet in which the indexes appear, but do not index information contained in later pamphlets. Thus it is best to consult the indexes of the last pamphlet published.

Laws of Florida is a set of hardbound volumes that appear several months after the end of the legislative session. The set contains general laws and special laws in separate volumes. The set contains the text of the enacted statute. Where the legislature amended an existing statute, the language added is underscored and the language deleted is struck through. For each act, the set also contains the title of the act, the enactment clause, the effective date of the act, the date on which the governor acted, and the date on which the act was filed in the Secretary of State's office.

Statutory code

A **code** is the compilation of the existing statutes of a jurisdiction, with the statutes arranged by subject. The code is generally recompiled at regular intervals into a multivolume hardbound set; the recompilation incorporates statutes still in effect, statutory amendments, and newly passed statutes while omitting statutes that have been repealed and portions of statutes amended by deletion. Codes generally contain the text of the statutes, brief historical notes, and subject index volumes at the end of the set.

The official code containing federal statutes is the ***United States Code.*** The *United States Code* presents the laws in effect in a much more concise and usable form than the *United States Statutes at Large.* The *United States Code* presents the federal laws currently in effect organized according to subject matter under 50 "titles." The title headings are largely arranged in alphabetical order. Each title is divided into chapters and the chapters into sections. A new edition of the *United States Code* is published every six years. The edition contains the current text of the statutes, including all amendments and omitting all text previously amended. Cumulative supplements to the *United States Code* are published following each regular session of Congress. A cumulative supplement contains any statutory amendments and any new statutes passed since the last edition of the *United States Code.* As typical of a government publication, production of the volumes can lag eight months to two years behind the passage of legislation.

Look at your state's statutory code and determine the major subject groupings and what these groupings are called. For example, *Florida Statutes* are divided into over 900 "chapters," instead of into titles as is the *United States Code*, with the chapters further divided into sections. *Florida Statutes* are cited by decimal numbers with the numbers to the left of the decimal point identifying the chapter number and the numbers following the decimal point identifying the section number. For example the Florida Security of Communications statutes are located at §§ 934.01–934.10, Fla. Stat. (2000). (The preceding citation complies with the state citation rule.) If you had the citation to the statutes and wanted to read them you would look at sections 1 through 10 of chapter 934.

Florida recently made the decision to recodify *Florida Statutes* each year. Formerly, *Florida Statutes* were recodified every odd number year, with a supplement containing only the new statutory material passed during the even number years published at the end of those years. The material inside the parentheses at the end of the preceding citation tells the reader that the statutes are located in *Florida Statutes 2000.* To be current during 2001 you must consult *Florida Statutes 2000* and West's *Florida Session Law Service* for 2001. If you are doing your research in *Florida Statutes Annotated* instead of *Florida Statutes,* you need to check the hardbound volume and the pocket part. You may still have to check session laws if the pocket part does not contain statutes from the most current legislative session. The first few pages of the pocket part will tell the latest legislation covered in the pocket part. If the advanced session law service is more current, you will need to check session laws as well as *Florida Statutes Annotated.*

Statutes passed as an "act"

The legislature may either pass statutes singly or as part of an **act.** Single statutes are passed when the legislative provision is short. When the new statute is codified, it will be inserted into the statutory code with statutes concerning the same or related subject matter. Where the new statutory language is longer and, often, where it concerns matters not previously dealt with by statute, the legislature may pass an "act" comprised of a number of consecutively numbered statutes.

An act often is identified by a name given it by the legislature and for easy reference is often referred to by that name. This **short title** or **popular name** is usually found in one of the first sections of an act, at the beginning of a table of contents preceding the act, or, in annotated codes, in the historical references following each provision of the act. For example, 42 U.S.C. § 1983, which prohibits a state from depriving persons of their constitutional rights was passed as part of the Civil Rights Act of 1871. Other common provisions of an act are a **preamble,** which identifies the objective or the objectives of the act, and a **definitional section,** which defines terms used in the act.

Annotated code

The publication often used for statutory research is the **annotated code.** The annotated code is a commercial publication and often appears on a more timely basis than a code published by the federal or a state government; the annotated code is generally supplemented frequently by pocket parts and supplementary pamphlets. The annotated code contains the text of existing statutes, in language identical to that contained in the code for the jurisdiction. It is referred to as an annotated code because it contains annotated material after each statutory section. An **annotation** is a paragraph summary of a relevant court opinion, attorney general opinion, or administrative decision interpreting the preceding statutory section. The paragraph ends with a citation to the opinion or decision. A newly-passed statutory section may have no annotated material following it because the statute has not yet been interpreted in a published decision. Other research references following a statutory section may include citations to relevant administrative code sections, legal encyclopedia sections, law reviews, and treatises and references to digest sections and on-line services. There may be references to the legislative history of the statutory section and the text of the section prior to amendment or the text of amendments.

United States Code Annotated (*U.S.C.A.*)(published by West Group) and ***United States Code Service*** (*U.S.C.S.*) (published by Lexis Law Publishing and formerly published by Lawyers Cooperative Publishing) are the two annotated codes for federal statutes. Volumes of *U.S.C.A.* and *U.S.C.S.* contain the text of the United States Constitution, the Federal Rules of Civil, Criminal, Bankruptcy, and Appellate Procedure and the Federal Rules of Evidence. A volume in each set contains a popular name table, allowing the researcher to use the name under which a statute is popularly known to locate the statute's session law and code citations. The researcher may access the two sets by searching for key terms in the multivolume general index (located at the end of the set) or volume-specific indexes located at the end of the volumes.

Each volume of an annotated code is annually updated with a cumulative pamphlet, generally referred to as a "pocket part." The pocket part is inserted inside the back cover of the volume for easy reference and the pamphlet from the prior year is discarded; the pocket part contains textual material and citations, new since the copyright date of the hardbound volume. Over time, the information for the annual pocket part supplement becomes too voluminous to be easily stored inside the volume's back cover; the information is printed in a separate paperbound volume, shelved next to the hardbound volume. The researcher should consult both the hardbound volume and the supplement.

The copyright date of the hardbound volumes varies greatly. Volumes are recompiled and reprinted from time to time when the supplementary material becomes unwieldy. A recompiled volume incorporates new material and eliminates out-of-date information; volumes relating to more rapidly changing areas of the law are reprinted more frequently than other volumes.

Commercial publishers publish annotated versions of statutory codes. To research case law interpretations of the United States Code consult *United States Code Service* or *United States Code Annotated.* Look in your law library and identify the session law, codified and annotated code versions of your state's statutes. Then fill in that information on the chart in figure 5-5 so you have a record of it.

Statutory research

The first step in statutory research is to read the statute carefully and read any other statute or material cross-referenced in the first statute. Generally, statutes are drafted in broad language to set forth a legal principle rather than to deal with a specific problem. Great care must be taken in drafting statutory language so that the language is neither underinclusive nor overinclusive. A statute that is underinclusive may leave loopholes allowing practices that the statute was intended to preclude. A statute that sweeps too broadly may be held to be unconstitutionally vague.

As described more fully in chapter 2, a court faced with statutory interpretation will look first to the language of the statute itself and its context. A statute that is part of an act should be interpreted by the way it fits into the scheme of the act. Another tool for statutory interpretation is legislative history. Committee reports and other legislative documents may shed light on the meaning of a statute. A source of Congressional legislative history available in many law libraries is *United States Code Congressional and Administrative News*. This publication contains the text of federal acts and selected committee reports. *United States Code Congressional and Administrative News* was described more fully earlier in this chapter. A court will also look to prior case law interpretation of the statute. An interpretation by the same or a higher court would be mandatory authority while an interpretation by a lower court or the courts of another jurisdiction would be persuasive.

Remember to update your research. Once passed, a statute may be amended, repealed, or held to be unconstitutional. Pocket parts update hardbound volumes of the annotated codes. The pocket parts of *United States Code Service* and *United States Code Annotated* are updated by quarterly supplements. You can further update your research by Shepardizing or KeyCiting and using computer assisted legal research. (Shepardizing and KeyCiting are discussed in chapter 6.) If you are researching state statutes, update the annotated code by researching session laws.

In the following excerpt from *United States v. Vastola* the court considered whether Armenakis, an assistant United States attorney, had adequately researched the applicable statutes. Although the court found that her investigation did afford her the "minimum degree of certainty," the case illustrates how inadequate research can come back to haunt the attorney. The federal district court had found that Armenakis' research was not adequate.

The district court found that Armenakis herself had not adequately researched the law. The court reasoned as follows:

> Armenakis' research, which consisted of reading and outlining the statute and reviewing the relevant annotations, was enough to give an average attorney a basic understanding of the law. However, standing alone, this limited investigation cannot be considered a normally competent level of research that a reasonably prudent attorney would undertake.

We agree. Given the serious consequences which follow from the mistaken application of the Wiretap Act, i.e. suppression, a reasonable United States attorney should not be satisfied with a basic understanding of the Act and a summary review of applicable caselaw. In addition, as the district court reasoned, "the meaning of a complex statute, such as the Wiretap Act, is not always readily ascertainable from just the reading of the text; and the annotations often fail to fully reflect how caselaw has interpreted a statutory provision." Thus, Armenakis' research, standing alone, cannot be considered adequate. The inquiry, therefore, turns on whether Armenakis otherwise acted prudently.

The district court found that Armenakis acted as a reasonably prudent attorney, and based its conclusion on the "interaction between Armenakis' own research and the authoritative confirming advice she received from other, more experienced United States Attorneys." That is, Armenakis' research, standing alone was inadequate. This coupled with the confirmation of her initial understanding of the law by more experienced colleagues, however, convinced the district court that Armenakis acted reasonably under the circumstances.

We agree that when an attorney receives confirmation of legal theories from a number of proper sources, each consistent with the next, the attorney can act reasonably in relying on these theories in the course of legal research. The district court properly found that Armenakis' limited book research was inadequate. Moreover, her conversations with other attorneys, standing alone, were also insufficient. *Carson* (an attorney may not rely merely on conversations with peers or supervisors concerning developing area of law where incorrect answer could lead to suppression of important evidence). However, we believe that the combined impact of these concurring sources created a degree of certainty (albeit minimal) which a prudent attorney could have accepted in arriving at an appropriate procedure for sealing.

United States v. Vastola, 25 F.3d 164, 168–169 (3d Cir. 1994)(citations omitted).

Sample pages of wiretapping and eavesdropping statutes

As described above, the United States Code is divided into fifty broad subject categories called **titles.** For example, the federal wiretapping and eavesdropping statutes, 18 U.S.C. §§ 2510–2521, a portion of which are reprinted in this chapter, are part of title 18. Title 18 deals with crimes.

The federal wiretapping and eavesdropping statutes are in title 18 because the purposes of the statutes are to prohibit law enforcement officers and private individuals from intercepting certain types of conversations and to prohibit the use of devices capable of interception. The protected conversations include private face-to-face conversations and telephone conversations, whether made on landline, cellular, or cordless telephones. A law enforcement officer may intercept communications if the officer is a party to the conversation or obtains a **court order** authorizing the taping of a conversation of private individuals. Conversations intercepted in violation of the statutes may not be used as evidence in court. An individual who illegally intercepts a conversation may be subject to a fine and up to five years imprisonment. Someone whose conversation has been illegally intercepted may sue and collect **civil damages,** attorneys' fees, and costs.

Figure 5-6 contains a copy of the two-count indictment of Linda Tripp. The Maryland grand jury charged Tripp with violating Maryland statutes by recording telephone conversations with Monica Lewinsky and disclosing the tapes to *Newsweek* magazine. The Maryland statutes differ from the federal statutes by requiring consent of all parties to a private conversation. In contrast, the federal statutes allow a private individual to tape a conversation if the individual is a party to the conversation.

Federal statutes are further grouped by subject matter into chapters within a title of the *United States Code.* For example, the federal eavesdropping and wiretapping statutes are found in chapter 119 of title 18. Chapter 119 is entitled "Wire and Electronic Communications Interception and Interception of Oral Communications." Although the federal statutes are grouped into chapters within a title, the citation to the statutes references the title and section numbers; the citation does not reference the chapter. Notice in the *United States Code* that a number of statutes will appear numbered consecutively and then there may be a break in numbering before the next group of statutes; there is also a break in numbering between chapter numbers. The break in numbering allows new statutes to be inserted in the middle of a title without having to renumber existing statutes or chapters. For example, the federal wiretapping and eavesdropping statutes, comprising chapter 119, are numbered consecutively 2510 through 2521; they are preceded by chapter 117 "Transportation for Illegal Sexual Activity and Related Crimes," which contains sections 2421 through 2424, and are followed by chapter 121 "Stored Wire and Electronic Communications and Transactional Records Access," which contains sections 2701 through 2711. Often a table of contents precedes a group of consecutively numbered statutes. Figures 5-7 through 5-9 contain the table of contents for the federal wiretapping and eavesdropping statutes (Fig. 5-8), as well as the tables of contents for chapters 117 and 121. These tables of contents are helpful because they allow you to overview a series of statutes and to ascertain at a glance the general scope of those statutes. By examining figure 5-8, you see that section 2510 contains definitions, section 2511 prohibits the interception and disclosure of certain types of conversations,

FIGURE 5-6 Linda Tripp Indictment.

STATE OF MARYLAND,

HOWARD COUNTY, TO WIT:

The Grand Jurors of the State Of Maryland for the body of Howard County, do on their oath present that

LINDA R. TRIPP,

late of said Howard County, did, on or about 22nd day of December, 1997, at Howard County aforesaid, wilfully and unlawfully intercept a wire communication in violation of Section 10-402(a), *Courts and Judicial Proceedings Article, Annotated Code of Maryland,* to wit: did tape record a telephone conversation between the said LINDA R. TRIPP and Monica Lewinsky without the consent of the said Monica Lewinsky, a party to said conversation, contrary to the form of the Act of Assembly in such case made and provided and against the peace, government and dignity of the State.

(Illegal Interception, Section 10-402(a)(1), *Courts and Judicial Proceedings Article, Annotated Code of Maryland*)

SECOND COUNT

And the Jurors aforesaid, upon their oath aforesaid, do further present that the said

LINDA R. TRIPP,

did, between on or about 16th day of January, 1998 and on or about the 17th day of January, 1998, at Howard County aforesaid, through her agent, wilfully and unlawfully disclose the contents of the aforesaid wire communication to employees of *Newsweek* magazine and others, knowing and having reason to know that the information was obtained through the interception of a wire communication in violation of the Maryland Wiretapping and Electronic Surveillance Act, Sections 10-401, *et seq., Courts and Judicial Proceedings Article, Annotated Code of Maryland,* to wit: did authorize and instruct her agent and attorney, James Moody, Esquire, to play the contents of said unlawful tape recording for *Newsweek* magazine reporters and others, which was done by the said James Moody, Esquire at the offices of *Newsweek* magazine in Washington, District of Columbia, on or about the 17th day of January, 1998, contrary to the form of the Act of Assembly in such case made and provided and against the peace, government and dignity of the State.

(Illegal Disclosure of Intercepted Communication, Section 10-402(a)(2), *Courts & Judicial Proceedings Article, Annotated Code of Maryland*)

Stephen Montanarelli
State Prosecutor

section 2515 prohibits the use of intercepted conversations as evidence, and section 2520 authorizes civil damages.

Look at the sample pages of the federal wiretapping and eavesdropping statutes printed in figures 5-9 through 5-14. Figure 5-9 shows the table of contents for the federal wiretapping and eavesdropping statutes. Figure 5-10 contains the definitional section of the statutes. Figure 5-11 contains section 2511, which prohibits the interception and disclosure of conversations, provides exceptions, and provides a penalty for illegally intercepting conversations or disclosing illegally intercepted conversations. Figure 5-12 contains section 2515, which prohibits an illegally intercepted conversation from being used as evidence in court. Figure 5-13 contains section 2520, which authorizes civil damages. Figure 5-14 shows amendments to the federal wiretapping and

THE CODE OF THE LAWS

OF THE

UNITED STATES OF AMERICA

TITLE 18—CRIMES AND CRIMINAL PROCEDURE

CHAPTER 117. TRANSPORTATION FOR ILLEGAL SEXUAL ACTIVITY AND RELATED CRIMES

FIGURE 5-7 Page from United States Code Service Title 18, Chapter 117.

CHAPTER 121. STORED WIRE AND ELECTRONIC COMMUNICATIONS AND TRANSACTIONAL RECORDS ACCESS

FIGURE 5-8 Page from United States Code Service Title 18, Chapter 121.

eavesdropping statutes contained in the 2000 pocket part supplement to *United States Code Service*. The annotated materials for 18 U.S.C.S. § 2510 are included.

Section 2510 (1) contains the definition of a "wire communication." Although the definition is complex, a wire communication is a telephone conversation. A cordless telephone conversation did not used to be protected. The pocket part shows that section 2510 (1) was amended so that cordless telephone conversations are now protected against interception. Section 2510 (2) contains the definition of an "oral communication:"

> "oral communication" means any oral communication uttered by a person exhibiting an expectation that such communication is not subject to interception under circumstances justifying such expectation . . . .

This definition means that a face-to-face conversation is protected against someone recording it, so long as the conversants expect that the conversation is private and the expectation is reasonable.

Section 2511 (1), contained in figure 5-11, prohibits the intentional interception of telephone and face-to-face conversations:

> Except as otherwise specifically provided . . . any person who . . . intentionally intercepts . . . any

FIGURE 5-9 Page from United States Code Service Title 18, Chapter 119.

CHAPTER 119. WIRE AND ELECTRONIC COMMUNICATIONS INTERCEPTION AND INTERCEPTION OF ORAL COMMUNICATIONS

> wire [or] oral . . . communication . . . shall be punished as provided in subsection (4) . . . .

Section 2511 (4) provides that "whoever violates subsection (1) of this section shall be fined under this title or imprisoned not more than five years, or both."

There are certain exceptions to the prohibition against intercepting conversations. Those exceptions are found in section 2511 (2). Section 2511 (2)(c) allows a law enforcement officer ("a **person acting under color of law**") to intercept a conversation if the law enforcement officer is a party to the conversation. Section 2511 (2)(d) allows a private individual to intercept a conversation if the individual is a party to the conversation.

United States Code Service contains the text of the statutes and various research tools, including annotated material. Because of page constraints, you have only been given a portion of the research tools following 18 U.S.C.S. § 2515. Turn to the beginning of that statute to examine it and the research tools. The text of the statute is one paragraph:

> Whenever any wire or oral communication has been intercepted, no part of the contents of such communication and no evidence derived therefrom may be received in evidence in any trial . . . before any court . . . if the disclosure of that information would be in violation of this chapter [18 USCS §§ 2510 et seq.].

In legal documents, brackets ([ ]) generally enclose material not written by the original author, but added by an editor or publisher. Here, the publisher added the citation corresponding to "this chapter." The material on the next line is legislative history. The statute was first passed in 1968 as section 802 of title III of public law 90-351. If you wanted to look up the text of the statute as originally passed and the text of the amendments, you could use the information "82 Stat. 216" to look up the information in *United States Statutes at Large*. Apparently, this section has never been amended, which is unusual for a statute passed more than thirty years ago. If the statute had been amended, the statutory text would be followed by a section "HISTORY; ANCILLARY LAWS AND DIRECTIVES." This section would contain more references to legislative history.

Figure 5-14 shows a page of annotated material from section 2510. Look at the material following the text of the statute and "HISTORY; ANCILLARY LAWS AND DIRECTIVES." The following section, "RESEARCH GUIDE," cross-references you to related secondary sources, including an American Jurisprudence Federal annotation. For many statutes, this section cross-references you to primary sources, such as administrative law and other federal statutes.

§ 2510. Definitions

As used in this chapter [18 USCS §§ 2510 et seq.]—

(1) "wire communication" means any aural transfer made in whole or in part through the use of facilities for the transmission of communications by the aid of wire, cable, or other like connection between the point of origin and the point of reception (including the use of such connection in a switching station) furnished or operated by any person engaged in providing or operating such facilities for the transmission of interstate or foreign communications or communications affecting interstate or foreign commerce and such term includes any electronic storage of such communication, but such term does not include the radio portion of a cordless telephone communication that is transmitted between the cordless telephone handset and the base unit;

(2) "oral communication" means any oral communication uttered by a person exhibiting an expectation that such communication is not subject to interception under circumstances justifying such expectation, but such term does not include any electronic communication;

(3) "State" means any State of the United States, the District of Columbia, the Commonwealth of Puerto Rico, and any territory or possession of the United States;

(4) "intercept" means the aural or other acquisition of the contents of any wire, electronic, or oral communication through the use of any electronic, mechanical, or other device.

(5) "electronic, mechanical, or other device" means any device or apparatus which can be used to intercept a wire, oral, or electronic communication other than—

(a) any telephone or telegraph instrument, equipment or facility, or any component thereof, (i) furnished to the subscriber or user by a provider of wire or electronic communication service in the ordinary course of its business and being used by the subscriber or user in the ordinary course of its business or furnished by such subscriber or user for connection to the facilities of such service and used in the ordinary course of its business; or (ii) being used by a provider of wire or electronic communication service in the ordinary course of its business, or by an investigative or law enforcement officer in the ordinary course of his duties;

(b) a hearing aid or similar device being used to correct subnormal hearing to not better than normal;

(6) "person" means any employee, or agent of the United States or any State or political subdivision thereof, and any individual, partnership, association, joint stock company, trust, or corporation;

(7) "Investigative or law enforcement officer" means any officer of the United States or of a State or political subdivision thereof, who is empowered by law to conduct investigations of or to make arrests for offenses enumerated in this chapter [18 USCS §§ 2510 et seq.], and any attorney authorized by law to prosecute or participate in the prosecution of such offenses;

(8) "contents", when used with respect to any wire, oral, or electronic communication, includes any information concerning the substance, purport, or meaning of that communication;

(9) "Judge of competent jurisdiction" means—

(a) a judge of a United States district court or a United States court of appeals; and

(b) a judge of any court of general criminal jurisdiction of a State who is authorized by a statute of that State to enter orders authorizing interceptions of wire, oral, or electronic communications;

(10) "communication common carrier" shall have the same meaning which is given the term "common carrier" by section 153(h) of title 47 of the United States Code;

(11) "aggrieved person" means a person who was a party to any intercepted wire, oral, or electronic communication or a person against whom the interception was directed;

FIGURE 5-10 Pages from United States Code Service 18 U.S.C.S. 2510.

FIGURE 5-10 (continued)

18 USCS § 2510 **CRIMES & CRIMINAL PROCEDURE**

(12) "electronic communication" means any transfer of signs, signals, writing, images, sounds, data, or intelligence of any nature transmitted in whole or in part by a wire, radio, electromagnetic, photoelectronic or photooptical system that affects interstate or foreign commerce, but does not include—

(A) The radio portion of a cordless telephone communication that is transmitted between the cordless telephone handset and the base unit;

(B) any wire or oral communication;

(C) any communication made through a tone-only paging device; or

(D) any communication from a tracking device (as defined in section 3117 of this title);

(13) "user" means any person or entity who—

(A) uses an electronic communication service; and

(B) is duly authorized by the provider of such service to engage in such use;

(14) "electronic communications system" means any wire, radio, electromagnetic, photooptical or photoelectronic facilities for the transmission of electronic communications, and any computer facilities or related electronic equipment for the electronic storage of such communications;

(15) "electronic communication service" means any service which provides to users thereof the ability to send or receive wire or electronic communications;

(16) "readily accessible to the general public" means, with respect to a radio communication, that such communication is not—

(A) scrambled or encrypted;

(B) transmitted using modulation techniques whose essential parameters have been withheld from the public with the intention of preserving the privacy of such communication;

(C) carried on a subcarrier or other signal subsidiary to a radio transmission;

(D) transmitted over a communication system provided by a common carrier, unless the communication is a tone only paging system communication; or

(E) transmitted on frequencies allocated under part 25, subpart D, E, or F of part 74, or part 94 of the Rules of the Federal Communications Commission, unless, in the case of a communication transmitted on a frequency allocated under part 74 that is not exclusively allocated to broadcast auxiliary services, the communication is a two-way voice communication by radio;

(17) "electronic storage" means—

(A) any temporary, intermediate storage of a wire or electronic communication incidental to the electronic transmission thereof; and

(B) any storage of such communication by an electronic communication service for purposes of backup protection of such communication; and

(18) "aural transfer" means a transfer containing the human voice at any point between and including the point of origin and the point of reception.

The following section is entitled "INTERPRETIVE NOTES AND DECISIONS." Attorneys commonly refer to "INTERPRETIVE NOTES AND DECISIONS" as annotated material. Similar to digest annotated material, annotated material following a statute gives a summary of a legal principle contained in a case interpreting § 2510 and the citation to the case. If you would like to know how § 2510 has been interpreted, you can read through the annotations and use the citation to pull and read the case. Although the citations are usually to cases, sometimes they can be to other legal authority. When you are researching statutes, make sure to check the pocket part for later annotations. Also do not assume that an annotated code contains the most recent cases interpreting a statute. Use the cases you find from the annotated materials to find more recent cases through the digests or citators.

§ 2511. Interception and disclosure of wire, oral, or electronic communications prohibited

(1) Except as otherwise specifically provided in this chapter [18 USCS §§ 2510 et seq.] any person who—

(a) intentionally intercepts, endeavors to intercept, or procures any other person to intercept or endeavor to intercept, any wire, oral, or electronic communication;

(b) intentionally uses, endeavors to use, or procures any other person to use or endeavor to use any electronic, mechanical, or other device to intercept any oral communication when—

(i) such device is affixed to, or otherwise transmits a signal through, a wire, cable, or other like connection used in wire communication; or

(ii) such device transmits communications by radio, or interferes with the transmission of such communication; or

(iii) such person knows, or has reason to know, that such device or any component thereof has been sent through the mail or transported in interstate or foreign commerce; or

(iv) such use or endeavor to use (A) takes place on the premises of any business or other commercial establishment the operations of which affect interstate or foreign commerce; or (B) obtains or is for the purpose of obtaining information relating to the operations of any business or other commercial establishment the operations of which affect interstate or foreign commerce; or

(v) such person acts in the District of Columbia, the Commonwealth of Puerto Rico, or any territory or possession of the United States;

(c) intentionally discloses, or endeavors to disclose, to any other person the contents of any wire, oral, or electronic communication, knowing or having reason to know that the information was obtained through the interception of a wire, oral, or electronic communication in violation of this subsection; or

(d) intentionally uses, or endeavors to use, the contents of any wire, oral, or electronic communication, knowing or having reason to know that the information was obtained through the interception of a wire, oral, or electronic communication in violation of this subsection; shall be punished as provided in subsection (4) or shall be subject to suit as provided in subsection (5).

(2)(a)(i) It shall not be unlawful under this chapter [18 USCS §§ 2510 et seq.] for an operator of a switchboard, or an officer, employee, or agent of a provider of wire or electronic communication service, whose facilities are used in the transmission of a wire communication, to intercept, disclose, or use that communication in the normal course of his employment while engaged in any activity which is a necessary incident to the rendition of his service or to the protection of the rights or property of the provider of that service, except that a provider of wire communication service to the public shall not utilize service observing or random monitoring except for mechanical or service quality control checks.

(ii) Notwithstanding any other law, providers of wire or electronic communication service, their officers, employees, and agents, landlords, custodians, or other persons, are authorized to provide information, facilities, or technical assistance to persons authorized by law to intercept wire, oral, or electronic communications or to conduct electronic surveillance, as defined in section 101 of the Foreign Intelligence Surveillance Act of 1978 [50 USCS § 1801] if such provider, its officers, employees, or agents, landlord, custodian, or other specified person, has been provided with—

(A) a court order directing such assistance signed by the authorizing judge, or

(B) a certification in writing by a person specified in section 2518(7) of this title or the Attorney General of the United States that no warrant or court

FIGURE 5-11 Pages from United States Code Service 18 U.S.C.S. 2511.

FIGURE 5-11 (continued)

order is required by law, that all statutory requirements have been met, and that the specified assistance is required, setting forth the period of time during which the provision of the information, facilities, or technical assistance is authorized and specifying the information, facilities, or technical assistance required. No provider of wire or electronic communication service, officer, employee, or agent thereof, or landlord, custodian, or other specified person shall disclose the existence of any interception or surveillance or the device used to accomplish the interception or surveillance with respect to which the person has been furnished an order or certification under this subparagraph, except as may otherwise be required by legal process and then only after prior notification to the Attorney General or to the principal prosecuting attorney of a State or any political subdivision of a State, as may be appropriate. Any such disclosure, shall render such person liable for the civil damages provided for in section 2520. No cause of action shall lie in any court against any provider of wire or electronic communication service, its officers, employees, or agents, landlord, custodian, or other specified person for providing information, facilities, or assistance in accordance with the terms of a court order or certification under this chapter [18 USCS §§ 2510 et seq.].

(b) It shall not be unlawful under this chapter [18 USCS §§ 2510 et seq.] for an officer, employee, or agent of the Federal Communications Commission, in the normal course of his employment and in discharge of the monitoring responsibilities exercised by the Commission in the enforcement of chapter 5 of title 47 [47 USCS §§ 151 et seq.] of the United States Code, to intercept a wire or electronic communication, or oral communication transmitted by radio, or to disclose or use the information thereby obtained.

(c) It shall not be unlawful under this chapter [18 USCS §§ 2510 et seq.] for a person acting under color of law to intercept a wire, oral, or electronic communication, where such person is a party to the communication or one of the parties to the communication has given prior consent to such interception.

(d) It shall not be unlawful under this chapter [18 USCS §§ 2510 et seq.] for a person not acting under color of law to intercept a wire, oral, or electronic communication where such person is a party to the communication or where one of the parties to the communication has given prior consent to such interception unless such communication is intercepted for the purpose of committing any criminal or tortious act in violation of the Constitution or laws of the United States or of any State.

(e) Notwithstanding any other provision of this title or section 705 or 706 of the Communications Act of 1934 [47 USCS § 605 or 606], it shall not be unlawful for an officer, employee, or agent of the United States in the normal course of his official duty to conduct electronic surveillance, as defined in section 101 of the Foreign Intelligence Surveillance Act of 1978 [50 USCS § 1801], as authorized by that Act [50 USCS §§ 1801 et seq.].

(f) Nothing contained in this chapter [18 USCS §§ 2510 et seq.] or chapter 121 [18 USCS §§ 2701 et seq.], or section 705 of the Communications Act of 1934 [47 USCS § 605], shall be deemed to affect the acquisition by the United States Government of foreign intelligence information from international or foreign communications, or foreign intelligence activities conducted in accordance with otherwise applicable Federal law involving a foreign electronic communications system, utilizing a means other than electronic surveillance as defined in section 101 of the Foreign Intelligence Surveillance Act of 1978 [50 USCS § 1801], and procedures in this chapter [18 USCS §§ 2510 et seq.] and the Foreign Intelligence Surveillance Act of 1978 [50 USCS §§ 1801 et seq.] shall be the exclusive means by which electronic surveillance, as defined in section 101 of

FIGURE 5-11 (continued)

CRIMES **18 USCS § 2511**

such Act [50 USCS § 1801], and the interception of domestic wire, oral, or electronic communications may be conducted.

(g) It shall not be unlawful under this chapter [18 USCS §§ 2510 et seq.] or chapter 121 of this title [18 USCS §§ 2701 et seq.] for any person—

(i) to intercept or access an electronic communication made through an electronic communication system that is configured so that such electronic communication is readily accessible to the general public;

(ii) to intercept any radio communication which is transmitted—

(I) by any station for the use of the general public, or that relates to ships, aircraft, vehicles, or persons in distress;

(II) by any governmental, law enforcement, civil defense, private land mobile, or public safety communications system, including police and fire, readily accessible to the general public;

(III) by a station operating on an authorized frequency within the bands allocated to the amateur, citizens band, or general mobile radio services; or

(IV) by any marine or aeronautical communications system;

(iii) to engage in any conduct which—

(I) is prohibited by section 633 of the Communications Act of 1934 [47 USCS § 553]; or

(II) is excepted from the application of section 705(a) of the Communications Act of 1934 [47 USCS § 605(a)] by section 705(b) of that Act [47 USCS § 605(b)];

(iv) to intercept any wire or electronic communication the transmission of which is causing harmful interference to any lawfully operating station or consumer electronic equipment, to the extent necessary to identify the source of such interference; or

(v) for other users of the same frequency to intercept any radio communication made through a system that utilizes frequencies monitored by individuals engaged in the provision or the use of such system, if such communication is not scrambled or encrypted.

(h) It shall not be unlawful under this chapter [18 USCS §§ 2510 et seq.]—

(i) to use a pen register or a trap and trace device (as those terms are defined for the purposes of chapter 206 (relating to pen registers and trap and trace devices) of this title) [18 USCS §§ 3121 et seq.]; or

(ii) for a provider of electronic communication service to record the fact that a wire or electronic communication was initiated or completed in order to protect such provider, another provider furnishing service toward the completion of the wire or electronic communication, or a user of that service, from fraudulent, unlawful or abusive use of such service.

(3)(a) Except as provided in paragraph (b) of this subection, a person or entity providing an electronic communication service to the public shall not intentionally divulge the contents of any communication (other than one to such person or entity, or an agent thereof) while in transmission on that service to any person or entity other than an addressee or intended recipient of such communication or an agent of such addressee or intended recipient.

(b) A person or entity providing electronic communication service to the public may divulge the contents of any such communication—

(i) as otherwise authorized in section 2511(2)(a) or 2517 of this title;

(ii) with the lawful consent of the originator or any addressee or intended recipient of such communication;

(iii) to a person employed or authorized, or whose facilities are used, to forward such communication to its destination; or

FIGURE 5-11 (continued)

(iv) which were inadvertently obtained by the service provider and which appear to pertain to the commission of a crime, if such divulgence is made to a law enforcement agency.

(4)(a) Except as provided in paragraph (b) of this subsection or in subsection (5), whoever violates subsection (1) of this section shall be fined under this title or imprisoned not more than five years, or both.

(b) If the offense is a first offense under paragraph (a) of this subsection and is not for a tortious or illegal purpose or for purposes of direct or indirect commercial advantage or private commercial gain, and the wire or electronic communication with respect to which the offense under paragraph (a) is a radio communication that is not scrambled or encrypted, then—

(i) if the communication is not the radio portion of a cellular telephone communication, a public land mobile radio service communication or a paging service communication, and the conduct is not that described in subsection (5), the offender shall be fined under this title or imprisoned not more than one year, or both; and

(ii) if the communication is the radio portion of a cellular telephone communication, a public land mobile radio service communication or a paging service communication, the offender shall be fined not more than $500.

(c) Conduct otherwise an offense under this subsection that consists of or relates to the interception of a satellite transmission that is not encrypted or scrambled and that is transmitted—

(i) to a broadcasting station for purposes of retransmission to the general public; or

(ii) as an audio subcarrier intended for redistribution to facilities open to the public, but not including data transmissions or telephone calls, is not an offense under this subsection unless the conduct is for the purposes of direct or indirect commercial advantage or private financial gain.

(5)(a)(i) If the communication is—

(A) a private satellite video communication that is not scrambled or encrypted and the conduct in violation of this chapter [18 USCS §§ 2510 et seq.] is the private viewing of that communication and is not for a tortious or illegal purpose or for purposes of direct or indirect commercial advantage or private commercial gain; or

(B) a radio communication that is transmitted on frequencies allocated under subpart D of part 74 of the rules of the Federal Communications Commission that is not scrambled or encrypted and the conduct in violation of this chapter [18 USCS §§ 2510 et seq.] is not for a tortious or illegal purpose or for purposes of direct or indirect commercial advantage or private commercial gain, then the person who engages in such conduct shall be subject to suit by the Federal Government in a court of competent jurisdiction.

(ii) In an action under this subsection—

(A) if the violation of this chapter [18 USCS §§ 2510 et seq.] is a first offense for the person under paragraph (a) of subsection (4) and such person has not been found liable in a civil action under section 2520 of this title, the Federal Government shall be entitled to appropriate injunctive relief; and

(B) if the violation of this chapter [18 USCS §§ 2510 et seq.] is a second or subsequent offense under paragraph (a) of subsection (4) or such person has been found liable in any prior civil action under section 2520, the person shall be subject to a mandatory $500 civil fine.

(b) The court may use any means within its authority to enforce an injunction issued under paragraph (ii)(A), and shall impose a civil fine of not less than $500 for each violation of such an injunction.

§ 2515. Prohibition of use as evidence of intercepted wire or oral communications

Whenever any wire or oral communication has been intercepted, no part of the contents of such communication and no evidence derived therefrom may be received in evidence in any trial, hearing, or other proceeding in or before any court, grand jury, department, officer, agency, regulatory body, legislative committee, or other authority of the United States, a State, or a political subdivision thereof if the disclosure of that information would be in violation of this chapter [18 USCS §§ 2510 et seq.].
(Added June 19, 1968, P. L. 90–351, Title III, § 802, 82 Stat. 216.)

FIGURE 5-12 Pages from United States Code Service 18 U.S.C.S. 2515.

§ 2520. Recovery of civil damages authorized

(a) In general. Except as provided in section 2511 (2)(a)(ii), any person whose wire, oral, or electronic communication is intercepted, disclosed, or intentionally used in violation of this chapter [18 USCS §§ 2510 et seq.] may in a civil action recover from the person or entity which engaged in that violation such relief as may be appropriate.

(b) Relief. In an action under this section, appropriate relief includes—

(1) such preliminary and other equitable or declaratory relief as may be appropriate;
(2) damages under subsection (c) and punitive damages in appropriate cases; and
(3) a reasonable attorney's fee and other litigation costs reasonably incurred.

(c) Computation of damages. (1) In an action under this section, if the conduct in violation of this chapter [18 USCS §§ 2510 et seq.], is the private viewing of a private satellite video communication that is not scrambled or encrypted or if the communication is a radio communication that is transmitted on frequencies allocated under subpart D of part 74 of the rules of the Federal Communications Commission that is not scrambled or encrypted and the conduct is not for a tortious or illegal purpose or for purposes of direct or indirect commercial advantage or private commercial gain, then the court shall assess damages as follows:

(A) If the person who engaged in that conduct has not previously been enjoined under section 2511(5) and has not been found liable in a prior civil action under this section, the court shall assess the greater of the sum of actual damages suffered by the plaintiff, or statutory damages of not less than $50 and not more than $500.

(B) If, on one prior occasion, the person who engaged in that conduct has been enjoined under section 2511(5) or has been found liable in a civil action under this section, the court shall assess the greater of the sum of actual damages suffered by the plaintiff, or statutory damages of not less than $100 and not more than $1000.

(2) In any other action under this section, the court may assess as damages whichever is the greater of—

(A) the sum of the actual damages suffered by the plaintiff and any profits made by the violator as a result of the violation; or

(B) statutory damages of whichever is the greater of $100 a day for each day of violation or $10,000.

(d) Defense. A good faith reliance on—

(1) a court warrant or order, a grand jury subpoena, a legislative authorization, or a statutory authorization;

(2) a request of an investigative or law enforcement officer under section 2518(7) of this title; or

(3) a good faith determination that section 2511(3) of this title permitted the conduct complained of; is a complete defense against any civil or criminal action brought under this chapter [18 USCS §§ 2510 et seq.] or any other law.

(e) Limitation. A civil action under this section may not be commenced later than two years after the date upon which the claimant first has a reasonable opportunity to discover the violation.

FIGURE 5-13 Pages from United States Code Service 18 U.S.C.S. 2520.

FIGURE 5-14 Pages from United States Code Service Pocket Part.

18 USCS § 2441 **CRIMES & CRIMINAL PROCEDURE**

1949 or any protocol to any such convention, to which the United States is a party.". Although such Act purported to amend 18 USCS§2401, the amendments were executed to this section in order to effectuate the probable intent of Congress.

Short title:

Act Aug. 21, 1996, P. L. 104–192, § 1, 110 Stat. 2104, provides: "This Act [adding this chapter (18 USCS § 2441)] may be cited as the 'War Crimes Act of 1996'.".

CHAPTER 119. WIRE AND ELECTRONIC COMMUNICATIONS INTERCEPTION AND INTERCEPTION OF ORAL COMMUNICATIONS

Section
2522. Enforcement of the Communications Assistance for Law Enforcement Act [47 USCS §§ 1001 et seq.]

HISTORY; ANCILLARY LAWS AND DIRECTIVES

Amendments:

1994. Act Oct. 25, 1994, P. L. 103–414, Title II, § 201(b)(3), 108 Stat. 4290, amended the analysis of this chapter by adding item 2522.

§ 2510. Definitions

As used in this chapter [18 USCS §§ 2510 et seq.]—

(1) "wire communication" means any aural transfer made in whole or in part through the use of facilities for the transmission of communications by the aid of wire, cable, or other like connection between the point of origin and the point of reception (including the use of such connection in a switching station) furnished or operated by any person engaged in providing or operating such facilities for the transmission of interstate or foreign communications or communications affecting interstate or foreign commerce and such term includes any electronic storage of such communication;

(2)–(11) [Unchanged]

(12) "electronic communication" means any transfer of signs, signals, writing, images, sounds, data, or intelligence of any nature transmitted in whole or in part by a wire, radio, electromagnetic, photoelectronic or photooptical system that affects interstate or foreign commerce, but does not include—

(A) any wire or oral communication;

(B) any communication made through a tone-only paging device;

(C) any communication from a tracking device (as defined in section 3117 of this title); or

(D) electronic funds transfer information stored by a financial institution in a communications system used for the electronic storage and transfer of funds;

(13)–(15) [Unchanged]

(16) "readily accessible to the general public" means, with respect to a radio communication, that such communication is not—

(A)–(C) [Unchanged]

(D) transmitted over a communication system provided by a common carrier, unless the communication is a tone only paging system communication; or

(E) transmitted on frequencies allocated under part 25, subpart D, E, or F of part 74, or part 94 of the Rules of the Federal Communications Commission, unless, in the case of a communication transmitted on a frequency allocated under part 74 that is not exclusively allocated to broadcast auxiliary services, the communication is a two-way voice communication by radio;

(F) [Deleted]

(17), (18) [Unchanged] (As amended Oct. 25, 1994, P. L. 103–414, Title II, §§ 202(a), 203, 108 Stat. 4290, 4291; April 24, 1996, P. L. 104–132, Title VII, Subtitle B, § 731, 110 Stat. 1303.)

FIGURE 5-14 (continued)

CRIMES **18 USCS § 2510**

HISTORY; ANCILLARY LAWS AND DIRECTIVES

Amendments:

1994. Act Oct. 25, 1994, in para. (1), deleted ", but such term does not include the radio portion of a cordless telephone communication that is transmitted between the cordless telephone handset and the base unit" following "storage of such communication", in para. (12), deleted subpara. (A), which read: "the radio portion of a cordless telephone communication that is transmitted between the cordless telephone handset and the base unit;", and redesignated subparas. (B), (C), and (D), as subparas. (A), (B), and (C), respectively, and, in para. (16), in subpara. (D), deleted "or" after the concluding semicolon, in subpara. (E), inserted "or" after the concluding semicolon, and added subpara. (F).
1996. Act April 24, 1996, in para. (12), in subpara. (B), deleted "or" after the concluding semicolon, in subpara. (C), added "or" after the concluding semicolon, and added subpara. (D) and, in para. (16), in subpara. (D), added "or" after the concluding semicolon, in subpara. (E), deleted "or" after the concluding semicolon, and deleted subpara. (F), which read: "an electronic communication;".

Short title:

Act Nov. 21, 1997, P. L. 105–112, §1, 111 Stat. 2273, provides: "This Act [amending 18 USCS § 2512] may be cited as the 'Law Enforcement Technology Advertisement Clarification Act of 1997'.".

RESEARCH GUIDE

Federal Procedure:

19 Moore's Federal Practice (Matthew Bender 3d ed.), Appellate Jurisdiction in the Federal System § 201.52.
19 Moore's Federal Practice (Matthew Bender 3d ed.), Interlocutory Orders § 203.15.
24 Moore's Federal Practice (Matthew Bender 3d ed.), The Grand Jury § 606.04.
16 Fed Proc L Ed, Habeas Corpus §§ 41:155, 189.
31 Fed Proc L Ed, Telecommunications § 72:993.

Am Jur:

3 A Am Jur 2d. Freedom of Information Act (1994) §§ 123, 322.

Am Jur Trials:

70 Am Jur Trials, The Defense of a Computer Crime Case, p. 435.
4 Nimmer on Copyright, (Matthew Bender) Criminal Actions § 15.05.

INTERPRETIVE NOTES AND DECISIONS

26. Judge of competent jurisdiction

I. IN GENERAL

5. Construction, generally

Computer book/magazine/game publisher, is awarded judgment for more than $50,000 against U.S. Secret Service, where agents obtained warrant and seized computers, disks, and other materials of publisher under false notion that employee had sensitive, proprietary computer document that had been wrongfully made available to public via computer bulletin boards, because seizure of work product materials violated 42 USCS § 2000aa-6 and 18 USCS § 2703, even though seizure could not constitute interception of "electronic communication" so as to bring into play statutory scheme at 18 USCS §§ 2510 et seq. Steve Jackson Games, Inc. v United States Secret Serv. (1993, WD Tex) 816 F Supp 432.

6. —Definitions

No court order is required under 18 USCS § 3122 and 28 USCS § 1651 to use cellular telephone digital analyzer, where digital analyzer is to be used to detect electronic serial number, cellular telephone's own number, and numbers called by cellular telephone but not contents of any communication, because use of such device to detect these numbers does not violate proscriptions of 18 USCS §§ 2510 et seq., which define "contents" of communication as including any information covering substance, purport, or meaning of that communication. In re United States (1995, CD Cal) 885 F Supp 197.

FIGURE 5-14 (continued)

18 USCS § 2510 CRIMES & CRIMINAL PROCEDURE

II. CONSTRUCTION AND APPLICATION OF PARTICULAR DEFINITIONS

13. Oral communication

Section 1983 claim based on interception of neighbors' telephone calls via police scanner is partially dismissed, where cordless telephone conversations are not "oral communications" as defined by 18 USCS § 2510(2), because cordless telephone communication was also expressly excluded from definitions of wire and electronic communications prior to October 25, 1994. Quigley v Rosenthal (1999, DC Colo) 43 F Supp 2d 1163.

14. —Expectation of privacy, generally

Court did not commit plain error based on videotape surveillance of drug defendant which took place when number of persons were present and with consent of owner of premises. United States v Foster (1993, CA9 Cal) 985 F2d 466, 93 CDOS 820, 93 Daily Journal DAR 1586, remanded, on reh (CA9 Cal) 93 CDOS 4367.

Government did not show that complaint which was filed more than two years after conversations between plaintiff, a former Acting Assistant Secretary of State for Legislative Affairs, and former Assistant Secretary of State for Consular Affairs was time-barred under 18 USCS § 2520(e), where plaintiff submitted sworn affidavit that he discovered calls had been intercepted by officers at State Department communications center within limitations period, and government did not rebut affidavit but claimed that defendant must have realized that he had been monitored once one of his calls was broadcast throughout communications center. Berry v Funk (1998, App DC) 146 F3d 1003.

15. ——Miscellaneous

Police officers had no expectation that communications between police officers and prisoner in public jail would not be intercepted and thus communications were not "oral communications" within meaning of 18 USCS § 2510. Angel v Williams (1993, CA8 Mo) 12 F3d 786, 27 FR Serv 3d 1402.

Reference to *McKinnon*

Denial of motion to suppress tapes from secret recording of defendant's pre-arrest conversations while he sat in back seat of police car was proper since defendant did not have reasonable expectation of privacy. United States v McKinnon (1993, CA11 Fla) 985 F2d 525, 7 FLW Fed C 90, petition for certiorari filed (Jun 7, 1993).

Surreptitious tape recording of defendant's call from jail was not interception within meaning of 18 USCS § 2510 because police only recorded what defendant said in mouthpiece, not what was transmitted over wire, and admissibility of recording was not prohibited because defendant had no expectation of privacy, where defendant placed call while officer was standing three feet away and television camera was suspended eight feet from telephone and pointed toward phone, notwithstanding fact that defendant conducted conversation in Thai. Siripongs v Calderon (1994, CA9 Cal) 35 F3d 1308, 94 CDOS 5105, 94 Daily Journal DAR 9410, amd, reh, en banc, den (1994, CA9 Cal) 94 CDOS 7830, 94 Daily Journal DAR 14461.

Although drug defendant spoke in Spanish, he had no reasonable expectation that conversations between himself and his codefendants at tire shop, where they allegedly unloaded drug shipments, would not be subject to interception pursuant to 18 USCS § 2510, and thus court properly dismissed motion to suppress audio and video taped conversations surreptitiously recorded by informant under instructions from FBI. United States v Longoria (1999, CA10 Kan) 177 F3d 1179, 1999 Colo J C A R 2608, subsequent app (1999, CA10 Kan) 182 F3d 1156, 1999 Colo J C A R 4373 and cert den (1999, US) 1999 US Lexis 6101.

Employees at county rabies control center had reasonable expectation of privacy in their workplace under 18 USCS § 2510 and thus director who placed tape recorder in their common office violated statute, where entire office consisted of single room that could not be accessed without employees' knowledge, employees took great care to see that their conversations remained private, and frank nature of employees' conversations in which they criticized their boss makes it obvious that they had subjective expectation of privacy. Dorris v Absher (1999, CA6 Tenn) 179 F3d 420, 15 BNA IER Cas 193, 138 CCH LC § 58643, 1999 FED App 200P.

16. Intercept, generally

Interception includes both location of tapped telephone and of original listening post, and judges in either jurisdiction have authority under Title III to issue wiretap orders. United States v Denman (1996, CA5 Tex) 100 F3d 399.

17. —Telephone conversations

Surreptitious tape recording of defendant's call from jail was not interception within meaning of 18 USCS § 2510 because police only recorded what defendant said in mouthpiece,

FIGURE 5-14 (continued)

not what was transmitted over wire, and admissibility of recording was not prohibited because defendant had no expectation of privacy, where defendant placed call while officer was standing three feet away and television camera was suspended eight feet from telephone and pointed toward phone, notwithstanding fact that defendant conducted conversation in Thai. Siripongs v Calderon (1994, CA9 Cal) 35 F3d 1308, 94 CDOS 5105, 94 Daily Journal DAR 9410, amd, reh, en banc, den (1994, CA9 Cal) 94 CDOS 7830, 94 Daily Journal DAR 14461.

Recording of telephone conversation alone constitutes "aural acquisition" of that conversation within meaning of 18 USCS § 2510(4). Sanders v Robert Bosch Corp. (1994, CA4 SC) 38 F3d 736, 10 BNA IER Cas 1.

Interception of cordless telephone conversations was permissible at time plaintiffs' conversations took place, since cordless telephone transmissions were not wire, electronic or oral communications under 18 USCS § 2510, notwithstanding fact that one plaintiff used land-line telephone. McKamey v Roach (1995, CA6 Tenn) 55 F3d 1236.

Wife, who owned liquor store with husband, was properly held not liable for interceptions of telephone conversations at store, since defendant's listening to telephone conversations that her husband unlawfully recorded were not interceptions under 18 USCS § 2510(4), and defendant's acquiescence in husband's plans to tap his own telephone and her passive knowledge of interceptions were insufficient to impute liability to her for those interceptions in addition to husband's liability, and would result in potential double recovery for single interception. Reynolds v Spears (1996, CA8 Ark) 93 F3d 428.

Even assuming that newspaper and its editor knew that conversation had been illegally recorded by some unknown person, 18 USCS § 2510 could not be constitutionally applied to prohibit newspaper and its editor from publishing transcript of allegedly illegally wiretapped private conversation, where public school board trustee made numerous racial slurs and profane comments in conversation, written transcription of which was read into minutes of public school board meeting, and copy of minutes was obtained by newspaper through open records request. Peavy v New Times, Inc. (1997, ND Tex) 976 F Supp 532.

County employees' conversations were entitled to protection under 18 USCS § 2510(2), where office director placed tape recorder in office bathroom to tape employees' private and personal conversations, and although members of public visited office and used bathroom where tape recorder had been placed, recorded conversations took place only when no member of public had been present, and conversations had stopped when telephone was being used or when any car turned into road that was only entrance to office. Dorris v Absher (1997, MD Tenn) 959 F Supp 813.

19. —Miscellaneous

Security officer employed by company that provided corporate defendant with security services could not recover damages for period of time after defendant turned off voice logger, even though due to design defect device continued to transmit ambient noise from guard's office to defendant's security control room, since conversations in guard's office were not intercepted in violation of Federal Wiretapping Act under 18 USCS § 2511; corporation never acquired "contents" of any conversations taking place in guard's office under 18 USCS § 2510(4), and there was no "intentional interception" under 18 USCS § 2511. Sanders v Robert Bosch Corp. (1994, CA4 SC) 38 F3d 736, 10 BNA IER Cas 1, amd (1994, CA4) 10 BNA IER Cas 479 and reh, en banc, den (1995, CA4 SC) 10 BNA IER Cas 480.

Cordless telephone conversations between defendant and coconspirator were not protected from warrantless interception by Title III at time surveillance in case occurred, and thus defendant was properly held in contempt for not answering questions involving interception, even though defendant used either traditional wire based or cellular telephone and coconspirator used unprotected cordless phone; 18 USCS § 2510(1) and (12)(A) permitted interception of cordless radio waves and it was undisputed that case involved interception of radio component of cordless telephone transmissions by radio scanning device. United States v McNulty (In re Askin) (1995, CA4 W Va) 47 F3d 100.

Computer programmer could not be liable under Electronic Communications Privacy Act (18 USCS §§ 2510 et seq.), to extent he inadvertently glimpsed e-mail on computer screen while helping someone, because § 2510(4) defines "intercept" as "acquisition of contents of any wire, electronic, or oral communication through use of any electronic, mechanical, or other device." Wesley College v Pitts (1997, DC Del) 974 F Supp 375, 13 BNA IER Cas 355.

20. Electronic, mechanical, or other device, generally

Seizure of electronic transfer funds for forfeiture purposes was not prohibited intercep-

FIGURE 5-14 (continued)

tion under 18 USCS § 2511(1), since government did not use "device" within meaning of 18 USCS § 2510(4) to obtain electronic transfer funds or information. United Sates v Daccarett (1993, CA2 NY) 6 F3d 37, 72 AFTR 2d 93-6248, 93 TNT 212-11, petition for certiorari filed (Nov 15, 1993) and petition for certiorari filed (Dec 20, 1993) and petition for certiorari filed (Dec 22, 1993) and petition for certiorari filed (Dec 23, 1993) and petition for certiorari filed (Dec 27, 1993) and petition for certiorari filed (Dec 28, 1993) and petition for certiorari filed (Jan 3, 1994) and related proceeding (CA2) 1994 US App Lexis 3324.

Corporation's use of voice logger, which recorded all telephone conversations on some telephone lines with extensions in security office, did not fall within business-use exception of 18 USCS § 2510(5)(a)(i), since voice logger is not telegraph instrument, equipment or facility, or component thereof, and was not used in ordinary course of its business, even though corporation claimed that it feared bomb threats. Sanders v Robert Bosch Corp. (1994, CA4 SC) 38 F3d 736, 10 BNA IER Cas 1, amd (1994, CA4) 10 BNA IER Cas 479 and reh, en banc, den (1995, CA4 SC) 10 BNA IER Cas 480.

Covert monitoring of conversations between plaintiff, a former Acting Assistant Secretary of State for Legislative Affairs, and former Assistant Secretary of State for Consular Affairs concerning presidential candidate's passport by officers at State Department communications center was not shown to be within ordinary course of business under 18 USCS § 2510 so as to warrant dismissal of complaint; there was no reason presented as to need for secret monitoring nor was it shown to be routine and guidelines for center provided that calls should not be monitored unless parties so request. Berry v Funk (1998, App DC) 146 F3d 1003.

Prison intercepts of telephone conversations between inmate and his sister need not be suppressed, where interception and recording of calls occurred in conformity with pre-established institutional plan not specifically aimed at siblings, because prison officials are "investigative or law enforcement officers" and routine monitoring pursuant to established policy is "in ordinary course of their duties" within meaning of 18 USCS § 2510(5)(a)(ii) exemption from § 2511 blanket prohibition of interception of wire communications. United States v Cheely (1992, DC Alaska) 814 F Supp 1430, later proceeding (DC Alaska) 814 F Supp 1449, later proceeding (DC Alaska) 814 F Supp 1447, later proceeding (DC Alaska) 1992 US Dist Lexis 20607.

Employer is denied summary dismissal of employees' claims that it violated 18 USCS § 2511 by monitoring and recording their telephone calls at work, even though employer contends its monitoring was exempt under § 2510(4) and (5) or § 2511(2)(d), because (1) it is not at all clear that employees were aware of and consented to monitoring, and (2) employer does not offer legitimate business reason that, as matter of law, justifies indiscriminate recording of all business and personal telephone calls received or made during particular shift. Ali v Douglas Cable Communs. (1996, DC Kan) 929 F Supp 1362.

21. —Extension telephone exemption

Business extension exception did not apply to employer's interceptions of employees' phone calls because monitoring system used, which consisted of "alligator chips attached to a microphone cable" and "interface connecting microphone cable to a VCR and a video camera" was not "telephone or telegraph instrument, equipment or facility or component within meaning of 18 USCS § 2510(5). Williams v Poulos (1993, CA1 Me) 11 F3d 271, summary op at (CA1) 22 M.L.W. 729, 14 R.I.L.W. 682.

To meet business use exception of 18 USCS § 2510(5)(a)(i), both of that section's prongs must be met. Sanders v Robert Bosch Corp. (1994, CA4 SC) 38 F3d 736, 10 BNA IER Cas 1.

Tape recorder connected to extension phones in wife's home, which wife used to check on defendant husband's business dealings related to their funeral business and his possible marital infidelities, did not all fall within telephone or business extension exemption under 18 USCS § 2510(5), since recording mechanism does not qualify for exemption, and indiscriminate recording of both incoming and outgoing calls did not constitute conduct within ordinary course of funeral home business. United States v Murdock (1995, CA6 Mich) 63 F3d 1391, reh, en banc, den (1995, CA6) 1995 US App Lexis 28950.

Husband's attorneys and guardian ad litem are entitled to summary dismissal of ex-wife's civil action under federal and state eavesdropping statutes, where husband had recorded, by means of extension phone answering machine, and attorneys and guardian had disclosed, son's conversations with his mother, because, unlike typical circumstances of interspousal wiretapping, interception of minor child's telephone

FIGURE 5-14 (continued)

conversations by use of extension phone in family home is permitted by broad reading of exemption in 18 USCS § 2510(5)(a)(i). Scheib v Grant (1993, ND Ill) 814 F Supp 736, costs/fees proceeding (ND Ill) 1993 US Dist Lexis 10698.

Claim of former employees against former employer under 18 USCS §§ 2510–2521, arising out of employer's recording of employees' personal telephone conversations through voice-activated tape recorders attached to employer's telephones, is granted summarily, where recorders were attached to busboard installed by telephone company by means of wire installed by employer, because (1) wire, not busboard, was intercepting device so interception did not occur via instrument furnished by telephone company, and (2) recorders were not telephone instruments or equipment, so (3) business extension exception of 18 USCS § 2510(5) does not apply. Pascale v Carolina Freight Carriers Corp. (1995, DC NJ) 898 F Supp 276, 10 BNA IER Cas 1804.

22. Person

Dismissal of city as defendant was proper because Title III, 18 USCS § 2510(6), does not allow for suits against municipalities. Amati v City of Woodstock (1999, CA7 Ill) 176 F3d 952, 15 BNA IER Cas 1, 43 FR Serv 3d 351.

23. Investigative officers

Pursuant to 18 USCS § 2517, federal investigative officer may turn over wiretaps from federal investigation to state attorney grievance commission that is investigating potential misconduct by attorney, since commission was empowered to investigate attorney's commission of federal crimes, including, but not limited to, those listed in § 2516, and thus its personnel were "investigative officers" within meaning of 18 USCS § 2510(7) to whom disclosure could be made. Berg v Michigan Attorney Grievance Comm'n (In re Electronic Surveillance) (1995, CA6 Mich) 49 F3d 1188.

Prison intercepts of telephone conversations between inmate and his sister need not be suppressed, where interception and recording of calls occurred in conformity with pre-established institutional plan not specifically aimed at siblings, because prison officials are "investigative or law enforcement officers" and routine monitoring pursuant to established policy is "in ordinary course of their duties" within meaning of 18 USCS § 2510(5)(a)(ii) exemption from § 2511 blanket prohibition of interception of wire communications. United States v Cheely (1992, DC Alaska) 814 F Supp 1430, later proceeding (DC Alaska) 814 F Supp 1449, later proceeding (DC Alaska) 814 F Supp 1447, later proceeding (DC Alaska) 1992 US Dist Lexis 20607.

24. Law enforcement officers

Metropolitan Detention Center's routine taping of defendant's telephone conversations did not violate Title III, since center was law enforcement agency and interceptions were made in ordinary course of business and thus came within "law enforcement" exception, 18 USCS § 2510(5)(a). United States v Van Poyck (1996, CA9 Cal) 77 F3d 285, 96 CDOS 1091, 96 Daily Journal DAR 1850, subsequent app (1996, CA9 Cal) 1996 US App Lexis 4668.

Taping of confession to Catholic priest was in ordinary course of jailers' duties and did not violate Wiretap Act, since under 18 USCS § 2510(5)(a) statute does not apply to interceptions by law enforcement officers in ordinary course of his duties. Mockaitis v Harcleroad (1997, CA9 Or) 104 F3d 1522. 97 CDOS 602, 97 Daily Journal DAR 957.

Taping of police department's line, which had initially been left untapped to allow for person calls, came within statutory exclusion under 18 USCS § 2510(5)(a)(ii) for eavesdropping by investigative or law enforcement officer in ordinary course of his duties, notwithstanding claim by employees of police department that express notice was required; decision to tap was precipitated by an official use of the line which showed that it had been a mistake to leave it untapped. Amati v City of Woodstock (1999, CA7 Ill) 176 F3d 952, 15 BNA IER Cas 1, 43 FR Serv 3d 351.

Prison intercepts of telephone conversations between inmate and his sister need not be suppressed, where interception and recording of calls occurred in conformity with pre-established institutional plan not specifically aimed at siblings, because prison officials are "investigative or law enforcement officers" and routine monitoring pursuant to established policy is "in ordinary course of their duties" within meaning of 18 USCS § 2510(5)(a)(ii) exemption from § 2511 blanket prohibition of interception of wire communications. United States v Cheely (1992, DC Alaska) 814 F Supp 1430, later proceeding (DC Alaska) 814 F Supp 1449, later proceeding (DC Alaska) 814 F Supp 1447, later proceeding (DC Alaska) 1992 US Dist Lexis 20607.

Inmates' challenge to interception of calls originating from inmate telephone system at privately run detention facility will not be denied summarily, where nothing in state or federal law or contracts under which facility operates empowers private security guards to

FIGURE 5-14 (continued)

conduct investigations of or make arrests for offenses enumerated in 18 USCS § 2516, because employees intercepting inmate calls are not "investigative or law enforcement officers" for purposes of § 2510(5)(a)(ii). Huguenin v Ponte (1998, DC RI) 29 F Supp 2d 57.

26. Judge of competent jurisdiction

District court may not delegate review of Title III orders to magistrate judges; magistrate judge is not "judge of competent jurisdiction" under § 2510(9) authorized to issue wiretapping order. In re United States (1993, CA2 NY) 10 F3d 931.

§ 2511. Interception and disclosure of wire, oral, or electronic communications prohibited

(1) Except as otherwise specifically provided in this chapter [18 USCS §§ 2510 et seq.] any person who—

(a), (b) [Unchanged]

(c) intentionally discloses, or endeavors to disclose, to any other person the contents of any wire, oral, or electronic communication, knowing or having reason to know that the information was obtained through the interception of a wire, oral, or electronic communication in violation of this subsection:

(d) intentionally uses, or endeavors to use, the contents of any wire, oral, or electronic communication, knowing or having reason to know that the information was obtained through the interception of a wire, oral, or electronic communication in violation of this subsection; or

(e) (i) intentionally discloses, or endeavors to disclose, to any other person the contents of any wire, oral, or electronic communication, intercepted by means authorized by sections 2511(2)(a)(ii), 2511(2)(b)–(c), 2511(2)(e), 2516, and 2518 of this chapter, (ii) knowing or having reason to know that the information was obtained through the interception of such a communication in connection with a criminal investigation, (iii) having obtained or received the information in connection with a criminal investigation, and (iv) with intent to improperly obstruct, impede, or interfere with a duly authorized criminal investigation, shall be punished as provided in subsection (4) or shall be subject to suit as provided in subsection (5).

(2) (a) (i) It shall not be unlawful under this chapter [18 USCS §§ 2510 et seq.] for an operator of a switchboard, or an officer, employee, or agent of a provider of wire or electronic communication service, whose facilities are used in the transmission of a wire or electronic communication, to intercept, disclose, or use that communication in the normal course of his employment while engaged in any activity which is a necessary incident to the rendition of his service or to the protection of the rights or property of the provider of that service, except that a provider of wire communication service to the public shall not utilize service observing or random monitoring except for mechanical or service quality control checks.

(ii) [Unchanged]

setting forth the period of time during which the provision of the information, facilities, or technical assistance is authorized and specifying the information, facilities, or technical assistance required. No provider of wire or electronic communication service, officer, employee, or agent thereof, or landlord, custodian, or other specified person shall disclose the existence of any interception or surveillance or the device used to accomplish the interception or surveillance with respect to which the person has been furnished an order or certification under this subparagraph, except as may otherwise be required by legal process and then only after prior notification to the Attorney General or to the principal prosecuting attorney of a State or any political subdivision of a State, as may be appropriate. Any such disclosure, shall render such person liable for the civil damages provided for in section 2520. No cause of action shall lie in any court against any provider of wire or electronic communication service, its officers, employees, or agents, landlord, custodian, or other specified person for providing information, facilities, or assistance in accordance with the terms of a court order or certification under this chapter [18 USCS §§ 2510 et seq.].

(b)–(h) [Unchanged]

(3) [Unchanged]

(4) (a) [Unchanged]

(b) If the offense is a first offense under paragraph (a) of this subsection and is not for a tortious or illegal purpose or for purposes of direct or indirect commercial advantage or private commercial gain, and the wire or electronic communication with respect to which the offense under paragraph (a) is a radio communication that is not scrambled, encrypted, or transmitted

FIGURE 5-14 (continued)

CRIMES **18 USCS § 2511**

using modulation techniques the essential parameters of which have been withheld from the public with the intention of preserving the privacy of such communication, then—

(i) if the communication is not the radio portion of a cellular telephone communication, a cordless telephone communication that is transmitted between the cordless telephone handset and the base unit, a public land mobile radio service communication or a paging service communication, and the conduct is not that described in subsection (5), the offender shall be fined under this title or imprisoned not more than one year, or both; and

(ii) if the communication is the radio portion of a cellular telephone communication, a cordless telephone communication that is transmitted between the cordless telephone handset and the base unit, a public land mobile radio service communication or a paging service communication, the offender shall be fined under this title.

(c) [Unchanged]

(5) [Unchanged]

(As amended Sept. 13, 1994, P. L. 103-322, Title XXXII, Subtitle I, § 320901, Title XXXIII, § 330016(1)(G), 108 Stat. 2123, 2147; Oct. 25, 1994, P. L. 103-414, Title II, §§ 202(b), 204, 205, 108 Stat. 4290, 4291; Oct. 11, 1996, P. L. 104-294, Title VI, § 604(b)(42), 110 Stat. 3509.)

Notice under "**13. Oral Communications**" and "**15. -Miscellaneous**" there is a summary of facts from *United States v. McKinnon:* "Denial of motion to suppress tapes from secret recording of defendant's pre-arrest conversations while he sat in back seat of police car was proper since defendant did not have reasonable expectation of privacy." Those facts are similar to the facts in the hypothetical from chapter 2. This annotation seems to say that a conversation in the back seat of a patrol car is not protected as an oral communication because the conversants did not have a reasonable expectation of privacy. The researcher should read and update *McKinnon* through citators rather than rely on the annotated material; the one sentence summary of *McKinnon* may not do justice to the case, may be incorrect, or may have been taken out of context. The citation indicates that a petition for writ of certiorari was filed with the United States Supreme Court. A citator should be used to disclose whether the petition was granted and whether other cases cited to *McKinnon.* (Use of citators is explained in chapter 6.) A citator will show that the United States Supreme Court did not grant the petition. Other courts may or may not have followed *McKinnon. McKinnon* is binding authority only within the Eleventh Circuit and is not binding on the state courts. Thus, there could be a split in the federal circuits, with some circuits holding that there was a reasonable expectation of privacy. State courts could have held that there was a reasonable expectation of privacy in similar cases.

Citations for statutes

Citation tip: symbols for sections and paragraphs. The symbol § means "section." Use two section symbols (§§) when citing to two or more sections.

Caveat: Do not assume that the legal citations found when researching are in correct citation form. Citations, even those included in cases, may or may not comply with the citation rules your professor has asked you to use. Always check your citations against the appropriate citation rule for correct form.

Subsection (2)(c) of the federal eavesdropping and wiretapping statutes reprinted in this chapter may be cited as follows:

18 U.S.C. § 2511 (2)(c) (1994).	(abbreviation for volume 18 of *United States Code*, subsection (2)(c) of section 2511; 1994 is the date of the latest version of the Code containing the statute)

A citation to the *United States Code* is the preferred citation because the *United States Code* is the official code. If the statute had been amended since the latest version of the Code, the language of the amendment is included in a supplement to the Code. For example, section 2510 of title 18 is cited 18 U.S.C. § 2510 (1994 & Supp. III 1997). Because many law libraries do not have the *United States Code*, you may use the following citations to either *United States Code Service* or *United States Code Annotated:*

18 U.S.C.S. § 2511 (2)(c) (Lexis L. Publg. 1993 & Supp. 2000).	(*United States Code Service* is published by Lexis Law Publishing; part of the cited statute is in the 1993 hardbound volume and part is in the 2000 pocket part)
18 U.S.C.A. § 2511 (2)(c)(West 2000).	(West Group publishes *United States Code Annotated;* the cited statute is in the 2000 hardbound volume).

If you are referring to a portion of the statute rather than to the entire statute, pinpoint the portion by subsection. If you do give the subsection in your citation, be sure the subsection is designated just as it is in the statute, including whether letters are lower or upper case, whether numbers are Arabic or roman, and whether numbers and letters are enclosed in parentheses or not. For example, the above citation refers to sub-subsection (c) of subsection (2) of section 2511 of title 18 of the *United States Code.*

The parenthesis at the end of the citation gives an abbreviation of the commercial publisher's name and the location of the statute. In the two citations above, "Lexis L. Publg." is an abbreviation for "Lexis Law Publishing" and "West" is an abbreviation for "West Group." At the time this chapter was written, the hardbound volume of *United States Code Service* containing the statutes was copyrighted "1993" and the pocket part supplement was dated "2000." Similarly, the hardbound volume of *United States Code Annotated* was copyrighted "2000." Because this book was being written in 2000, there was no pocket part supplement. Include as much parenthetical information needed to locate the statutory language. In the first citation above, information was given for the hardbound volume and the pocket part supplement. The second citation above included information only for the hardbound volume. If the statutory language is found entirely in the hardbound volume (as was true for the second citation above), you need only include information on the hardbound volume in the parenthesis. Conversely, if the statutory language is found entirely in the pocket part supplement, you need only include information on the pocket part supplement in the parenthesis.

Local law

The many smaller units of government include counties, cities, and villages. Local laws passed by these units govern many areas of day-to-day concern. Matters regulated by local law include zoning, traffic, education, health, occupational licensing, and housing. Courts interpret these local laws, sometimes called **ordinances,** in a manner similar to statutes.

In chapter 2, the court deciding *Blackie the Talking Cat* determined whether the cat's owners were running a for-profit business. If so, the local ordinance required the owners to obtain an occupational license. In the following case, the court interpreted a local ordinance that prohibited livestock raising in the city to determine whether "livestock" included a woman's pet rooster.

STATE of Minnesota, Respondent,

v.

Tammie NELSON, Appellant.

Court of Appeals of Minnesota.

May 4, 1993.

499 N.W.2d 512

SCHUMACHER, Judge.

Tammie Nelson appeals her conviction under a Maplewood zoning ordinance, arguing that her pet rooster is not livestock prohibited by the ordinance. We reverse.

FACTS

Nelson keeps Jerry, an eight-year-old adult rooster, at her Maplewood residence as a pet. Jerry is housed in a cage in Nelson's yard and is prone to herald the breaking of dawn each day with a resounding cock-a-doodle-doo. The city alleges that neighbors have frequently complained about the rooster's crowing. In June of 1992, Nelson was cited by the city's environmental health officer for violation of Maplewood, Minn. Zoning Ordinance S 36- 66(c)(1) (1988), which prohibits the "raising or handling of livestock or animals causing a nuisance." The ordinance also provides that violations are misdemeanor offenses. Maplewood, Minn. Zoning Ordinance S 36-8 (1988).

The trial court found Nelson guilty of violating the ordinance and imposed a fine of $100, which was stayed provided Jerry was removed from the city within 10 days. Nelson admits that Jerry does, in fact, perform each morning in conformity with his nature but claims that the statute does not apply to her pet rooster because he is neither livestock nor an animal causing a nuisance under the ordinance.

ISSUE

Did the trial court correctly determine that Nelson's keeping a rooster as a pet violates Maplewood, Minn. Zoning Ordinance S 36–66(c)(1) (1988)?

ANALYSIS

The ordinance in dispute clearly prohibits (1) all livestock, and (2) any animal causing a nuisance. We acknowledge that a crowing rooster may well constitute a nuisance, but at trial the city expressly waived this issue and prosecuted its case solely on a theory that, under the ordinance, a rooster is livestock as a matter of law.

Since "livestock" is not defined in the ordinance, Maplewood relies on a dictionary definition of the term as "domestic animals kept for use on a farm or raised for sale and profit." Webster's *New Twentieth Century Dictionary* 1059 (2d ed. 1979). Other authorities have also defined livestock broadly enough to encompass roosters. At least as commonly, however, the term livestock is defined as separate from chickens. Minnesota's own statutes consistently define "livestock" as "cattle, sheep, swine, horses, mules and goats." See, e.g., Minn.Stat. S 17A.03, subd. 5 (1990). When the legislature intends to reach chickens, it uses the term poultry, often in conjunction with livestock. Clearly the lawmakers of this state understand livestock to be a category of animal distinct from poultry.

Other state statutes also define livestock to include four-legged animals, but not chickens or other poultry. Because the meaning of livestock is not entirely certain, we turn to rules of construction to resolve the ambiguity. Minnesota courts have often recognized that because zoning ordinances restrict common law rights, they should be strictly construed against the governmental unit and in favor of property owners. In light of this principle, we give "livestock" a less inclusive meaning than does the city and conclude that the term as used in the Maplewood Zoning Ordinance does not reach chickens or other poultry.

Our conclusion is further supported by the fact that the ordinance expressly establishes that violations will be misdemeanors and therefore punishable by up to $700 in fines and 90 days incarceration. The criminal consequences which attend violations of the ordinance also obligate us to construe its provisions strictly in favor of the accused.

Nelson should not bear the penal consequences of an ordinance the terms of which are reasonably capable of different meanings. Because a pet rooster does not plainly fall under the definition of livestock as used in the ordinance, we reverse Nelson's conviction.

DECISION

We reverse the trial court and hold that a pet rooster does not clearly constitute livestock for purposes of sustaining a conviction under the Maplewood Zoning Ordinance.

Reversed.

Court rules, discussed in the following section, govern the format of documents submitted to the court, among other matters. In the following case, the question was whether an attorney should be sanctioned for exceeding the specified word limit of a document.

PER CURIAM.

Our opinion in this case directed appellants' counsel to show cause why they should not be sanctioned for filing a brief that exceeded the type-volume limit. Counsel's attempt to incorporate some other document by reference led us to check whether this had been done in order to dodge the limit. Here's what we found: "The certificate under Fed. R.App. P. 32(a)(7)(C) represents that the brief contains 13,824 words, only 176 short of the maximum. Our check reveals that the certificate is false. The brief actually includes 15,056 words, substantially over the maximum. Appellants counted only the words in the text of the brief, although Rule 32 provides that '[h]eadings, footnotes, and quotations count toward the word and line limitations.' Fed. R.App. P. 32(a)(7)(B)(iii). Appellants' brief has 20 footnotes with a total of 1,232 words."

Appellants' brief was prepared with Microsoft Word 97, and an unfortunate interaction occurred between that software and the terms of Rule 32. All recent versions of Microsoft Word (Word 97 for Windows, Word 98 for Macintosh, and Word 2000 for Windows), and some older versions that we have tested, count words and characters in both text and footnotes when the cursor is placed anywhere in the document and no text is selected. In recent versions on both Windows and Macintosh platforms, choosing the Word Count function brings up a window listing the number of characters and words in the document. A checkbox at the bottom of the window reading "Include footnotes and endnotes," when selected, yields a word count for all text and notes. But if the user selects any text in the document this checkbox is dimmed, and the program counts only the characters and words in the selected text. Microsoft Word does not offer a way to count words in those footnotes attached to the selected text.

This complicates implementation of Fed. R.App. 32(a)(7), which limits the allowable length of a brief to 14,000 words, and of a reply brief to 7,000 words. Under Rule 32(a)(7)(B)(iii), footnotes count toward this limit, but the "corporate disclosure statement, table of contents, table of citations, statement with respect to oral argument, any addendum containing statutes, rules or regulations, and any certificates of counsel do not count toward the limitation." To determine the number of words that are included in the limit, counsel selects the "countable" body portions of the brief—which causes Microsoft Word to ignore countable footnotes. Counsel who do not notice that the count-footnotes box has been dimmed out may unintentionally file a false certificate and a brief that exceeds the word limits. That's what happened to appellants' lawyers. Older versions of Word have separate columns for text and footnote counts (plus a summation column), giving a visible cue that footnotes were not being counted when text had been selected, but current versions give only a consolidated count.

When the count-footnotes checkbox is dimmed, even counsel who are aware that the brief contains footnotes may suppose that the software included these automatically.

Current versions of Corel WordPerfect (for both Windows and Macintosh platforms) do not have this problem. WordPerfect does what lawyers may suppose that Word does (or should do): it automatically includes footnotes in its word and character counts. If no text is selected, the word count feature includes all words anywhere in the document; if text is selected, then WordPerfect includes words in footnotes that are attached to the selected text. We have not tested other programs, because the vast majority of briefs filed with the court are prepared using either Word or WordPerfect, but law firms that use other programs must find out how their software treats footnotes attached to selected text.

Lawyers who produce their documents with WordPerfect software have an easy job of things under Rule 32. They select the "countable" portions of the brief, and the program tells them how many words are in both text and footnotes. Lawyers who use Word, by contrast, must infer from the dimmed checkbox that footnotes have been omitted from the count. They must open a separate footnote window, select the footnotes attached to "countable" body text, and have the program count the words in these notes. Then they must add the text and footnote counts manually in order to determine compliance with Rule 32(a)(7).

Long-run solutions to this problem must come either from Microsoft Corporation—which ought to make it possible to obtain a count of words in footnotes attached to selected text—or from the national rulemaking process. We will send copies of this opinion to those responsible for such design decisions. In the meantime, we will flag this issue in the court's Practitioner's Guide and in materials distributed to counsel when an appeal is docketed. Law firms should alert their staffs to the issue pending a resolution at the software level. Our clerk's office will spot-check briefs that have been prepared on Microsoft Word, are close to the word limit, and contain footnotes. Noncomplying briefs will be returned, and if the problem persists after there has been ample time for news to reach the bar we will consider what else needs to be done. (Counsel who use Word are not entitled to a litigating advantage over those who use WordPerfect.) For now, however, sanctions are inappropriate, and the order to show cause is discharged.

DeSilva v. DiLeonardi, Nos. 99-1754, 99-1769, 1999 WL 517177 (7th Cir. July 21, 1999).

COURT RULES

Court rules govern the procedure of beginning a lawsuit and handling a case before a court. The rules cover such mundane matters as the size paper on which documents are to be submitted to the courts and the format for appellate briefs. They also set forth important time limitations such as the time period within which the defendant has to answer a complaint and the time period within which a party may appeal a decision.

Generally, each jurisdiction has a number of sets of court rules. **Rules of civil procedure** govern the conduct of civil cases at the trial level. **Rules of evidence** govern the gathering of information for use at trial and admission of information as evidence at trial. **Rules of criminal procedure** govern the conduct of criminal cases at the trial level. **Rules of appellate procedure** govern the conduct of cases before an appellate court. Courts of limited jurisdiction and specialized courts may have their own sets of court rules. In addition, a court may have promulgated **local court rules** that govern procedure in that court and supplement other court rules.

Each jurisdiction has its own procedures for promulgating court rules. In some jurisdictions, the legislature creates the court rules; in other jurisdictions, such as the federal courts, the highest court is responsible for creating court rules; and in other jurisdictions, the creation of court rules requires legislative and judicial action. In many jurisdictions, the judicial branch promulgates court rules under the statutory authority given to it by the legislative branch.

Congress has delegated the power to make court rules to the federal courts. The United States Supreme Court promulgates the rules for the Court and the rules for the lower federal courts. The United States Supreme Court is required to submit any proposed court rule to Congress by May 1 of the year in which the court rule is to take effect. Congress has until December 1 to review any proposed court rule. Congress must take action before a rule concerning an evidentiary privilege is effective. For any other proposed court rule, the proposed court rule becomes effective if Congress fails to act by December 1.

For federal courts, the basic court rules used at the trial level are the Federal Rules of Civil Procedure, the Federal Rules of Criminal Procedure, and the Federal Rules of Evidence. At the appellate level the Federal Rules of Appellate Procedure are used in the United States of Appeals Courts of Appeal and the Revised Rules of the Supreme Court of the United States are used in the United States Supreme Court. In addition, each federal court may promulgate its own supplementary local rules so long as the local rules do not conflict with the rules promulgated by the United States Supreme Court.

In the following case, which was dismissed on summary judgment, the court imposed sanctions on the plaintiff of $3,114.90 and on his attorney (Mr. Colvin) of $4,478.79 under rule 11 of the Federal Rules of Civil Procedure. Figure 5-15 contains the text of rule 11. The rule is discussed in the section of the text following this case.

Mr. Colvin actually attempts to place at least a portion of the blame for his ignorance of applicable law on defense counsel, complaining that "[n]ot once did defense counsel ever direct Plaintiff's attorney's attention to *Collings v. Longview Fibre Co.* . . or *Newland v. Dalton* . . . . If he had, due consideration would have been given to dismissing the case."

The responsibility for discovering relevant legal authority rested with Plaintiff's counsel himself. A lawyer admitted to practice before this court must apprise himself or herself of the relevant law. A lawyer may not diminish this responsibility by asserting his or her reliance on another lawyer.

Counsel insists that in September, 1995, when he researched Plaintiff's complaint, it was the law in this jurisdiction that an employer who discharges an employee for an act of misconduct related to a disability may be liable under the ADA. This statement is false. *Collings* was decided on August 14, 1995. In September 1995; therefore, *Collings* was the law.

Plaintiff's counsel failed to make the minimal pre-filing effort to ascertain the legal viability of Plaintiff's claim. None of counsel's arguments in his brief opposing Defendant's motion for sanctions is sufficient to shield him from sanctions under Section 12205, Section 1927, or Rule 11. In short, counsel's brief in opposition to the attorneys' fees motion offers no legitimate basis upon which to deny sanctions. He has had his chance to prepare a defense and to explain his questionable conduct. The court has considered the severity and propriety of the proposed sanctions in light of Mr. Colvin's explanation for his conduct.

It therefore appears to the court proper to apportion the blame, and hence the financial responsibility for the above-described abuses of this court's scant resources, between Plaintiff and his lawyer. The court does not expect the equivalent levels of legal knowledge from represented litigants and their attorneys. It is the lawyer's duty, both to the client and to the institutions of justice, to investigate the factual and legal bases for recovery on behalf of the client, to advise the client, and to act in accordance with the rules of substantive law and the rules of procedure. Plaintiff sued Defendant under the Americans with Disabilities Act for violation of his right not to be discriminated against solely by reason of a disability, seeking $50,000 in general damages, unspecified special damages, punitive damages and an award of attorney's fees. Given the ready availability of controlling judicial precedents authorizing employers to discharge even disabled employees who commit acts of misconduct, the legal and factual issues should have presented a competent attorney with no great challenge. Defendant won a motion for summary judgment.

But when lawyers shower the court with frivolous papers, everyone suffers. Defense counsel become cynical and hardened against all civil rights plaintiffs. The federal courts—which today face tremendous pressure from Washington and from the public to conserve costs and to deter unfounded litigation—must spend unnecessary time and effort disposing of baseless complaints. Legitimate civil rights plaintiffs pay part of the price for this intransigence, in the form of judges' and lawyers' decreasing patience with plaintiffs and their attorneys. As a result, the public itself understandably loses respect for our entire system of justice.

Conclusion

The court must devise a form of sanction sufficient to help defray Defendants' litigation expenses and also to deter future conduct similar to Mr. Colvin's and Mr. Schutts' in the course of this action, and thereby protect the public, the courts, the defense bar and the host of meritorious civil rights claimants whose causes languish beneath piles of pointless papers in the chambers of federal judges.

Schutts v. Bently Nevada Corporation, 966 F.Supp. 1549, 1563, 1564–1565, 1566 (D. Nev. 1997)(citations omitted).

Sample pages

Figure 5-15 shows the text of Rule 11 of the Federal Rules of Civil Procedure. Each federal court rule is followed by Advisory Committee notes from the committee that drafted the rules or an amendment to the rule. The notes may discuss the history and purpose of the rule.

Rule 11 of the Federal Rules of Civil Procedure does not directly reference inadequate research or poor writing skill as grounds for imposing sanctions under the rule. Nonetheless, inadequate research and poor writing are the basis of a number of Rule 11 cases; subsection (b)(2) requires that in documents filed with the court, "the claims, defenses, and other legal contentions therein are warranted by existing law or by a nonfrivolous argument for the extension, modification, or reversal of existing law or the establishment of new law." In *Wallace Computers Services, Inc. v. David Noyes & Company* the judge complained that the attorney had cited cases in a misleading manner and the attorney barely escaped monetary sanctions. In *Frederick v. Servicemaster, Limited Partnership*, the judge similarly complained that the attorney had misrepresented a case and threatened to impose Rule 11 sanctions, were the case misrepresentation repeated. In *Smith v. United Transportation Union Local No. 81* (which begins below on this pagae and continues on page 193), the court imposed monetary sanctions for violation of Rule 11.

Your state probably has similar sets of rules and may have sets of rules for courts of limited jurisdiction such as traffic court and small claims court. You will become familiar with some of your state's court rules by completing the legal research assignment on court rules.

Based on the following facts, the judge ordered counsel for the union to pay the plaintiff's attorney $1,500 as a sanction under Rule 11:

Defendants Transit District and Union cite only one case in their opposition papers in support of their laches defense. They rely upon *Nilsen v. City of Moss Point* for the proposition that the equitable portion of plaintiff's claim may be barred by laches even if the legal relief is timely. That case indeed endorses that proposition; however, it was vacated and reversed by the Fifth Circuit sitting en banc!

(Continued)

FIGURE 5-15 Rule 11 of the Federal Rules of Civil Procedure.

Rule 11. Signing of Pleadings, Motions, and Other Papers; Representations to Court; Sanctions

(a) **Signature.** Every pleading, written motion, and other paper shall be signed by at least one attorney of record in the attorney's individual name, or, if the party is not represented by an attorney, shall be signed by the party. Each paper shall state the signer's address and telephone number, if any. Except when otherwise specifically provided by rule or statute, pleadings need not be verified or accompanied by affidavit. An unsigned paper shall be stricken unless omission of the signature is corrected promptly after being called to the attention of attorney or party.

(b) **Representations to Court.** By presenting to the court (whether by signing, filing, submitting, or later advocating) a pleading, written motion, or other paper, an attorney or unrepresented party is certifying that to the best of the person's knowledge, information, and belief, formed after an inquiry reasonable under the circumstances,—

(1) it is not being presented for any improper purpose, such as to harass or to cause unnecessary delay or needless increase in the cost of litigation;

(2) the claims, defenses, and other legal contentions therein are warranted by existing law or by a nonfrivolous argument for the extension, modification, or reversal of existing law or the establishment of new law;

(3) the allegations and other factual contentions have evidentiary support or, if specifically so identified, are likely to have evidentiary support after a reasonable opportunity for further investigation or discovery; and

(4) the denials of factual contentions are warranted on the evidence or, if specifically so identified, are reasonably based on a lack of information or belief.

(c) **Sanctions.** If, after notice and a reasonable opportunity to respond, the court determines that subdivision (b) has been violated, the court may, subject to the conditions stated below, impose an appropriate sanction upon the attorneys, law firms, or parties that have violated subdivision (b) or are responsible for the violation.

(1) *How Initiated.* (A) By Motion. A motion for sanctions under this rule shall be made separately from other motions or requests and shall describe the specific conduct alleged to violate subdivision (b). It shall be served as provided in Rule 5, but shall not be filed with or presented to the court unless, within 21 days after service of the motion (or such other period as the court may prescribe), the challenged paper, claim, defense, contention, allegation, or denial is not withdrawn or appropriately corrected. If warranted, the court may award to the party prevailing on the motion the reasonable expenses and attorney's fees incurred in presenting or opposing the motion. Absent exceptional circumstances, a law firm shall he held jointly responsible for violations committed by its partners, associates, and employees. (B) On Court's Initiative. On its own initiative, the court may enter an order describing the specific conduct that appears to violate subdivision (b) and directing an attorney, law firm, or party to show cause why it has not violated subdivision (b) with respect thereto.

(2) *Nature of Sanction; Limitations.* A sanction imposed for violation of this rule shall be limited to what is sufficient to deter repetition of such conduct or comparable conduct by others similarly situated. Subject to the limitations in subparagraphs (A) and (B), the sanction may consist of, or include, directives of a nonmonetary nature, an order to pay a penalty into court, or, if imposed on motion and warranted for effective deterrence, an order directing payment to the movant of some or all of the reasonable attorneys' fees and other expenses incurred as a direct result of the violation.

(A) Monetary sanctions may not be awarded against a represented party for a violation of subdivision (b)(2).

(B) Monetary sanctions may not be awarded on the court's initiative unless the court issues its order to show cause before a voluntary dismissal or settlement of the claims made by or against the party which is, or whose attorneys are, to be sanctioned.

(3) *Order.* When imposing sanctions, the court shall describe the conduct determined to constitute a violation of this rule and explain the basis for the sanction imposed.

(d) **Inapplicability to Discovery.** Subdivisions (a) through (c) of this rule do not apply to disclosures and discovery requests, responses, objections, and motions that are subject to the provisions of Rules 26 through 37.

(Amended Aug. 1, 1983; Aug, 1, 1987; Dec. 1, 1993.)

(Continued)

Rule 11, as recently amended, requires a court to impose sanctions on attorneys who submit arguments which they know, or after "reasonable inquiry" should know, to be "[un]warranted by existing law or a good faith argument for the extension, modification, or reversal of existing law." The rule thus requires attorneys to inquire into the state of the law and the facts before making arguments to the court and to offer only those arguments which are supported by the law or a reasonable argument to change the law.

This minimal standard of practice has not been met by the attorneys representing the defendants in this case, value . . . . Transposing the numerals in a citation and even citing obiter dicta as actual holdings are common errors which the Court overlooks. But what we have here is misrepresentation of legal authority . . . . case. Counsel for the Union cited the original panel decision in *Nilsen* as an en banc opinion, which reveals that they knew that there had been an en banc decision in that case. Yet they did not favor the Court with a citation to the actual en banc opinion . . . which vacated the panel decision on which defendants relied. This is more than a merely sloppy failure to "Shepardize" a case.

Smith v. United Transportation Union Local No. 81, 594 F.Supp. 96 (S.D. Cal. 1984).

Sample pages of court rules

Court rules may be researched by using citators (see chapter 6) to determine how the court rules have been interpreted. *Federal Rules Decisions* is a reporter containing cases concerning the Federal Rules of Civil Procedure and the Federal Rules of Criminal Procedure. In the following passage, the court stated that the offending attorney failed to use Shepard's Citations, a well-known citator. The use of citators is covered in chapter 6.

Locating court rules

All the federal rules identified above, except for the local rules of the United States District Courts, may be found in *United States Code Service* or in *United States Code Annotated.* West also publishes paperbound volumes of certain of the federal court rules, including certain of the United States District Court local rules, and the court rules for certain states. The paperbound volumes have the virtue of being fairly inexpensive and easily transportable and contain an index following each set of rules. The paperbound volumes are not annotated, however. The paperbound volumes are printed annually. Be sure you are researching in the most current version available.

Besides being printed in a publication containing just court rules, you may find your state's court rules in volumes of the publication containing your state's annotated code. Court rules may be in separate volumes, or, if enacted by the legislature, they may be part of the statutory code. For example, the Florida Rules of Evidence comprise chapter 90 of the *Florida Statutes* while the balance of the state's court rules are printed in volumes at the end of *Florida Statutes Annotated.*

Local court rules

Most courts have local rules that must be followed, in addition to or in lieu of, federal or state rules. Some local court rules may be found in *United States Code Service* or in *United States Code Annotated.* Many are available on the Internet or for purchase from the clerk of the court. The attorney has a duty to research and be familiar with local rules. In the following three cases, the attorney's failure to follow the local rules had serious consequences.

On appeal of the following case, the court stated that the trial court did not err in refusing to consider the appellants' responses to appellees objections where the responses were not filed in accordance with local court rules:

In the instant case, Appellants' answers to both sets of preliminary objections were filed with the Prothonotary's office and appear on the docket as so filed. However, nothing on the docket or in the certified record indicates that Appellants ever followed the mandates of Rules 206.1 and 1028 by filing their response with Motions Court. Until Appellants filed their response to the preliminary objections with Motion Court, Motions Court personnel could not know that their response was available, and could not forward it to the appropriate judge for consideration. We note that the local rules, administrative regulations and filing requirements of the Philadelphia County Court System are widely publicized to the Bar through bound volumes, continuing education, court memoranda and lectures, and are available in the Motions Court filing office. Here, Appellants ignored critical filing procedures essential to proper motion court practice in Philadelphia County. Thus, Appellants did not ensure that their responses to Appellees' preliminary objections would be before the trial court for its consideration as Appellants simply did not follow the rules. Therefore, Appellants cannot now complain that the trial court erred when it failed to consider their responses to Appellees' preliminary objections. Accordingly, we agree with the trial court that Appellants' blunder is not excusable and does not constitute trial court error.

Schulykill Navy v. Langbord, 728 A.2d 964, 967–968 (Pa. Super. Ct. 1999).

Citations for court rules

Caveat: Do not assume that the legal citations found when researching are in correct citation form. Citations, even those included in cases may or may not comply with the citation rules your professor has asked you to use. Always check your citations against the appropriate citation rule for correct form.

The following are sample citations to the most important types of court rules identified above:

Fed. R. Civ. P. 23.	(Rule 23 of the Federal Rules of Civil Procedure)
Fed. R. Crim. P. 1.	(Rule 1 of the Federal Rules of Criminal Procedure)
Fed. R. App. P. 5.	(Rule 5 of the Federal Rules of Appellate Procedure)
Fed. R. Evid. 610.	(Rule 610 of the Federal Rules of Evidence)
Sup. Ct. R. 1.	(Rule 1 of the Rules of the United States Supreme Court)

WALLACE COMPUTERS SERVICES, INC., Plaintiff,

v.

DAVID NOYES & COMPANY, and Frank Colin, Defendants.

United States District Court, N.D. Illinois, Eastern Division.

March 9, 1994.

1994 WL 75201

PLUNKETT, District Judge.

Wallace filed the six-count complaint in the present case.

The Defendants moved to dismiss the Complaint. Upon review of the Defendants' motion, we granted it in part and denied it in part.

Unfortunately, the merits of the pleadings was not the only matter that required our attention. Upon our review of the Defendants' papers, we found what we considered to be a disturbing pattern: the repeated citation of authority in an inappropriate, out of context manner. Pursuant to the recently amended Rule 11, we issued a Rule to Show Cause why Defendants should not be sanctioned in the amount of $300.00 per occurrence for misrepresenting the following cases:

(1) *In re VMS Secur. Litig.;*

(2) *DeLeo v. Ernst & Young;*

(3) *Craig v. First American Cap. Resources.*

Defendants were ordered to respond to the Rule within thirty days, and they have done so with vigor. In fact, they spend fifteen pages explaining why their citation of these three cases was not improper. Indeed, the fact that it takes them so much text to explain how their use of three citations was not improper implies that the cases support them, if at all, in an indirect or convoluted manner.

There is a reason we are concerned with this type of conduct. The Northern District of Illinois is one of the most congested districts nationwide, and this court, with over 300 cases on its docket and dozens of motions pending at any given time, is sorely pressed for time and resources. Our job is only made all the more difficult when attorneys use authority out of context or in an otherwise questionable manner, a practice that not only slows down our efforts, but also serves to reduce our faith in the papers before us.

Upon expending even more of our time reviewing Defendants' lengthy Response to the Rule, we are unconvinced that they did not misrepresent the case law to us. Whether it was done deliberately or not, we cannot say and do not venture a guess. However, whether that conduct rises to a level of a Rule 11 violation is a close call. The Defendants' conduct is quite close to that gray area where good faith ends and either carelessness or deceit begins. Certainly, none of the Defendants' citations, standing alone, are sufficiently misleading to justify the imposition of sanctions. However, the pattern of conduct evidence by three such citations is another matter altogether.

The purpose of the Rule to Show Cause was not to punish the Defendants for misconduct, but rather to draw their attention to our requirement that authority not be cited for propositions that it does not support. It is clear that we have succeeded in that goal. Defendants undoubtedly are now aware of our expectations. With that mission accomplished, our zest to sanction them has faded, and we discharge the Rule to Show Cause. However, Defendants would be well advised to carefully scrutinize further submissions to this court. We trust that there will be no further such misunderstandings in the future.

ADMINISTRATIVE LAW

Since the beginning of this nation, administrative agencies have continuously increased in number, size and power. The daily lives of all citizens are affected by administrative agencies. Consider these examples: the processing, manufacturing, packing, labeling, advertising, and sale of nearly all products in the United States is regulated by agencies such as the Food and Drug Administration and the Department of Agriculture; the Internal Revenue Service oversees the collection of taxes from all citizens; the Federal Aviation Administration regulates commercial air transportation; the distribution of public welfare benefits (Aid to Dependent Children and food stamps) is regulated by the Department of Health and Human Services and the Department of Agriculture. These are only a few illustrations of the extent to which federal administrative agencies play a role in the daily lives of citizens. To get a complete picture, it is necessary to add state and local agencies. State departments of motor vehicles issue drivers' licenses, register cars, and issue automobile tags; doctors, lawyers, barbers, plumbers, and electricians are among the many whose professions and trades are regulated by state agencies; state departments of revenue collect taxes; state and local governments regulate building and construction; and federal, state, and local agencies regulate the environment.

Why do we need agencies at all? Why have they become so numerous and powerful? The answer to both questions is twofold. First, the job of governing has become too large for Congress, the courts, and the President to handle. There were four million citizens when the Constitution was adopted (1789). There are now over 260 million people in the United States. People are more mobile, technology is changing at unprecedented speed, and other social changes have increased the demands on government. Congress does not have the time to make all the laws, the President to enforce all the laws, or the courts to adjudicate all the cases.

Second, agencies possess expertise. Every year Congress must deal with a large and diverse number of issues. Discrimination, environmental concerns, military and national security matters, and funding for science and art are but a few examples. Congress is too small to be expert in every subject. Agencies, however, specialize and, as a result, they possess technical knowledge and experience in their subject areas. They can hire specialists and benefit from continuous contact with the same subjects.

There is no constitutional provision establishing administrative agencies, nor is the role of agencies in the United States governmental structure defined. Regardless, agencies have been part of the federal government since the beginning. Agencies have been analogized to a "fourth branch" of government. This is not accurate, as the Constitution establishes only three branches and does not permit the creation of a fourth. Even more, as you will learn, agencies are accountable to the three constitutional branches. Regardless, agencies are vital components of government. They are also unique. Though they are not a branch of government, they do perform the functions of all three branches of government, creating separation of powers problems.

Nearly every agency is created by Congress through its lawmaking power. Congress, the President, and constitutional courts are not "agencies." Legislation that created an agency and defines its powers is known as **enabling legislation.** Once created, agencies fall into the executive branch. An agency whose head cannot be terminated by the President without cause is known as an independent agency. The Interstate Commerce Commission, established in 1887, was the nation's first independent agency. An agency whose head serves at the pleasure of the President is known as an executive agency. There are many executive and independent agencies (see fig. 1-7).

As executive branch entities, administrative agencies perform executive functions. Also, agencies may perform quasilegislative and quasijudicial functions. For example, administrative agencies are empowered to create rules (a quasilegislative function) and to adjudicate cases (a quasijudicial function). The act of granting quasijudicial and quasilegislative authority to an agency is referred to as **delegation.**

To govern the procedures used by administrative agencies, Congress enacted the **Administrative Procedure Act** (APA) in 1946. The APA was intended to curb the growing power of agencies. Administrative regulations usually go through a **notice** and **hearing** procedure before being adopted. After they are adopted, administrative regulations have the force of law.

Publication of administrative regulations

Administrative regulations are published chronologically as they are adopted and they are later codified. Federal administrative regulations are published chronologically in the *Federal Register* and they are codified in the *Code of Federal Regulations.* The *Federal Register* is published each business day. The *Code of Federal Regulations* is divided into 50 titles, with the regulations contained within most of the titles roughly related to the same subject matter as contained in the same number title within the *United States Code.* For example, title 26 of both the *United States Code* and the *Code of Federal Regulations* concern the Internal Revenue Service. The regulations within a particular title are arranged by the agencies responsible for them rather than by subject matter. Regulations governing a particular topic are grouped in the same "part," with the parts divided into sections. As in the *United States Code,* where each section is considered a separate statute, one section of the *Code of Federal Regulations* contains one administrative regulation.

The *Code of Federal Regulations* is printed in hundreds of colorful paperbound volumes, with one fourth of the Code titles reissued quarterly and each year's reissue bound in a different color from that of the preceding year. The spine of each volume gives you the year of publication. Look at the front cover of the volume to determine the effective date within the year.

If you are looking for a regulation covering a particular subject matter, look in the index to the *Code.* Once you have located the regulation in the *Code,* note the effective date of the volume containing the regulation. The regulation must be updated with any amendments to the regulation contained in the *Federal Register.* The first step in updating is to check "LSA: List of CFR Section Affected," published monthly. Because the LSA is cumulative you need only check the latest LSA. When you check the LSA note the end of the period covered by the LSA. For the period between the latest date covered by the LSA and the latest Federal Register, check the last issue of the Federal Register for each month since the LSA. Each issue of the Federal Register contains a "List of CFR Parts Affected in [the name of the month of the particular Federal Register]." To find case law interpretations of administrative regulations, check "Shepard's Code of Federal Regulations Citations." See chapter 6 for an explanation of the use of citators.

Sample pages of administrative law

As explained earlier in this chapter, the federal wiretapping statutes prohibit interception of cellular telephone conversations. Figure 5-16 contains a portion of the table of contents for 47 C.F.R. part 15 (1999) and the text of 47 C.F.R. § 15.121 (1999). This regulation supplements the statutes by prohibiting the design or marketing of scanners capable of intercepting the radio frequencies allocated to cellular telephone signals.

Sample pages of LSA and Federal Register

The following figures show how you would update 47 C.F.R. § 15.121 (1999). You would first look at the latest LSA. The latest LSA available when this book was being written was July 2000 (fig. 5-17). The July 2000 issue of the LSA shows that 47 C.F.R. § 15.121 (1999) had not been revised since October 1, 1999. A notation at the end of 47 C.F.R. § 15.121 (1999) shows that the regulation was amended on April 27, 1999, and the effective date of the amendment was October 25, 1999. The notation "64 FR 22561" indicates the volume and page in the April 27, 1999 issue of the *Federal Register* on which the amended text of 47 C.F.R. § 15.121 begins.

Figure 5-18 shows the cover and pages 22559 through 22562 of the April 27, 1999 *Federal Register.* The introductory material on pages 22560 and 22561 summarizes the amendment to 47 C.F.R. § 15.121. The amended text of 47 C.F.R. § 15.121 appears on pages 22561 through 22562.

Because the coverage of the July 2000 ends with July 31, 2000, 47 C.F.R. § 15.121 must be researched to determine if there were any further revisions after July 31, 2000. The latest *Federal Register* available at the time this author was researching was September 21, 2000. Because the tables in the back of the *Federal Register* are cumulative for the month, you would only need to check the table in the August 31, 2000, issue and the September 21, 2000, issue of the *Federal Register.* The tables from those issues show that there were no amendments nor proposed amendments to 47 C.F.R. §§ 15.121 during that time period.

Citations for administrative law

Caveat: Do not assume that the legal citations found when researching are in correct citation form. Citations, even those included in cases may or may not comply with the citation rules your professor has asked you to use. Always check your citations against the appropriate citation rule for correct form.

The following are sample citations to the *Federal Register* and the *Code of Federal Regulations:*

64 Fed. Reg. 22561–62 (1999).	(pages 22561 through 22562 of volume 64 of the *Federal Register,* published in 1999)
47 C.F.R. § 15.121 (1999).	(section 121 of part 15 of volume 47 of the *Code of Federal Regulations,* 1999 version)

FIGURE 5-16 Pages from Code of Federal Regulations.

code of federal regulations

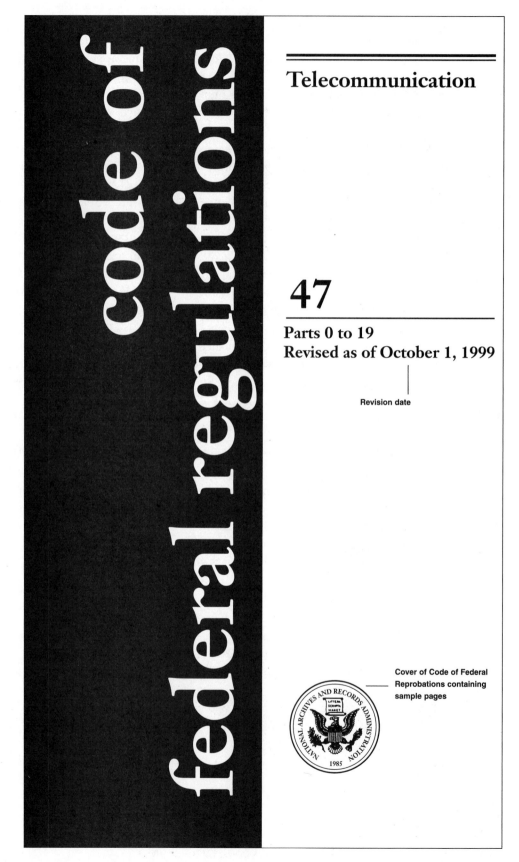

Telecommunication

47

Parts 0 to 19
Revised as of October 1, 1999

Revision date

Cover of Code of Federal Reprobations containing sample pages

FIGURE 5-16 (continued)

examination to the examinee and the COLEM must issue a PPC to an examinee who scores a passing grade on an examination element.

(f) A PPC is valid for 365 days from the date it is issued.

§ 13.213 COLEM qualifications.

No entity may serve as a COLEM unless it has entered into a written agreement with the FCC. In order to be eligible to be a COLEM, the entity must:

(a) Agree to abide by the terms of the agreement;

(b) Be capable of serving as a COLEM;

(c) Agree to coordinate examinations for one or more types of commercial radio operator licenses and/or endorsements;

(d) Agree to assure that, for any examination, every examinee eligible under these rules is registered without regard to race, sex, religion, national origin or membership (or lack thereof) in any organization;

(e) Agree to make any examination records available to the FCC, upon request.

(f) Agree not to administer an examination to an employee, relative, or relative of an employee.

§ 13.215 Question pools.

The question pool for each written examination element will be composed of questions acceptable to the FCC. Each question pool must contain at least 5 times the number of questions required for a single examination. The FCC will issue public announcements detailing the questions in the pool for each element. COLEMs must use only the most recent question pool made available to the public when preparing a question set for a written examination element.

§ 13.217 Records.

Each COLEM recovering fees from examinees must maintain records of expenses and revenues, frequency of examinations administered, and examination pass rates. Records must cover the period from January 1 to December 31 of the preceding year and must be submitted as directed by the Commission. Each COLEM must retain records for 1 year and the records must be made available to the FCC upon request.

PART 15—RADIO FREQUENCY DEVICES

Table of contents for part 15

Subpart A—General

Sec.

Subpart B—Unintentional Radiators

Relevant administrative regulation

FIGURE 5-16 (continued)

Federeal Communications Commission § 15.121

Prohibits designing or marketing scanning receivers capable of intercepting cellular telephone calls

Regulation was amended April 27, 1999

The amendment was effective October 25, 1999. The amended language was printed in volume 64 of the Federal Register page 22561.

Text of regulation prior to amendment

Subpart C—Intentional Radiators

(iii) The user should have the capability of overriding the automatic blocking described in paragraphs (e)(4)(i) and (4)(ii) of this section.

[63 FR 20133, Apr. 23, 1998]

§ 15.121 Scanning receivers and frequency converters used with scanning receivers.

(a) Except as provided in paragraph (c) of this section, scanning receivers and frequency converters designed or marketed for use with scanning receivers, shall:

(1) Be incapable of operating (tuning), or readily being altered by the user to operate, within the frequency bands allocated to the Cellular Radiotelephone Service in part 22 of this chapter (cellular telephone bands). Scanning receivers capable of "readily being altered by the user" include, but are not limited to, those for which the ability to receive transmissions in the cellular telephone bands can be added by clipping the leads of, or installing, a simple component such as a diode, resistor or jumper wire; replacing a plug-in semiconductor chip; or programming a semiconductor chip using special access codes or an external device, such as a personal computer. Scanning receivers, and frequency converters designed for use with scanning receivers, also shall be incapable of converting digital cellular communication transmissions to analog voice audio.

(2) Be designed so that the tuning, control and filtering circuitry is inaccessible. The design must be such that any attempts to modify the equipment to receive transmissions from the Cellular Radiotelephone Service likely will render the receiver inoperable.

(b) Except as provided in paragraph (c) of this section, scanning receivers shall reject any signals from the Cellular Radiotelephone Service frequency bands that are 38 dB or higher based upon a 12 dB SINAD measurement, which is considered the threshold where a signal can be clearly discerned from any interference that may be present.

(c) Scanning receivers and frequency converters designed or marketed for use with scanning receivers, are not subject to the requirements of paragraphs (a) and (b) of this section provided that they are manufactured exclusively for, and marketed exclusively to, entities described in 18 U.S.C. 2512(2), or are marketed exclusively as test equipment pursuant to §15.3(dd).

(d) Modification of a scanning receiver to receive transmissions from Cellular Radiotelephone Service frequency bands will be considered to constitute manufacture of such equipment. This includes any individual, individuals, entity or organization that modifies one or more scanners. Any modification to a scanning receiver to receive transmissions from the Cellular Radiotelephone Service frequency bands voids the certification of the scanning receiver, regardless of the date of manufacture of the original unit. In addition, the provisions of §15.23 shall not be interpreted as permitting modification of a scanning receiver to receiver Cellular Radiotelephone Service transmissions.

(e) Scanning receivers and frequency converters designed for use with scanning receivers shall not be assembled from kits or marketed in kit form unless they comply with the requirements in paragraph (a) through (c) of this section.

(f)(1) Scanning receivers shall have a label permanently affixed to the product, and this label shall be readily visible to the purchaser at the time of purchase. The label shall read as follows: WARNING: MODIFICATION OF THIS DEVICE TO RECEIVE CELLULAR RADIOTELEPHONE SERVICE SIGNALS IS PROHIBITED UNDER FCC RULES AND FEDERAL LAW.

(2) "Permanently affixed" means that the label is etched, engraved, stamped, silkscreened, indelibly printed or otherwise permanently marked on a permanently attached part of the equipment or on a nameplate of metal plastic or other material fastened to the equipment by welding, riveting, or permanent adhesive. The label shall be designed to last the expected lifetime of the equipment in the environment in which the equipment may be operated and must not be readily detachable. The label shall not be a stick-on, paper label.

[64 FR 22561, Apr. 27, 1999]

EFFECTIVE DATE NOTE: At 64 FR 22561, Apr. 27, 1999, §15.121 was revised, effective Oct. 25, 1999. For the convenience of the reader, the superseded text is set forth below.

§ 15.121 Scanning receivers and frequency converters designed or marketed for use with scanning receivers.

(a) Except as provided in paragraph (b) of this section, scanning receivers, and frequency converters designed or marketed for use with scanning receivers, must be incapable of operating (tuning), or readily being altered by the user to operate, within the frequency bands

FIGURE 5-16 (continued)

§ 15.201 **47 CFR Ch. 1 (10-1-99 Edition)**

allocated to the Domestic Public Cellular Radio Telecommunications Service in part 22 of this chapter (cellular telephone bands). Receivers capable of "readily being altered by the user" include but are not limited to, those for which the ability to receive transmissions in the cellular telephone bands can be added by clipping the leads of, or installing, a simple component such as a diode, resistor and/or jumper wire; replacing a plug-in semiconductor chip; or programming a semiconductor chip using special access codes or an external device, such as a personal computer. Scanning receivers, and frequency converters designed or marketed for use with scanning receivers, must also be incapable of converting digital cellular transmissions to analog voice audio.

(b) Scanning receivers, and frequency converters designed or marketed for use with scanning receivers, that are manufactured exclusively for, and marketed exclusively to, entities described in 18 U.S.C. 2512(2) are not subject to the requirements of paragraph (a) of this section.

[58 FR 25575, Apr. 27, 1993; 58 FR 29454, May 20, 1993]

Subpart C—Intentional Radiators

§ 15.201 Equipment authorization requirement.

(a) Intentional radiators operated as carrier current systems and devices operated under the provisions of §§15.211, 15.213 and 15.221 shall be verified pursuant to the procedures in subpart J of part 2 of this chapter prior to marketing.

(b) Except as otherwise exempted in paragraph (c) of this section and in §15.23 of this part, all intentional radiators operating under the provisions of this part shall be certificated by the Commission pursuant to the procedures in subpart J of part 2 of this chapter prior to marketing.

(c) For devices such as perimeter protection systems which, in accordance with §15.31(d), are required to be measured at the installation site, each application for certification must be accompanied by a statement indicating that the system has been tested at three installations and found to comply at each installation. Until such time as certification is granted, a given installation of a system that was measured for the submission for certification will be considered to be in compliance with the provisions of this chapter, including the marketing regulations in subpart I of part 2 of this chapter, if tests at that installation show the system to be in compliance with the relevant technical requirements. Similarly, where measurements must be performed on site for equipment subject to verification, a given installation that has been verified to demonstrate compliance with the applicable standards will be considered to be in compliance with the provisions of this chapter, including the marketing regulations in subpart I of part 2 of this chapter.

(d) For perimeter protection systems operating in the frequency bands allocated to television broadcast stations operating under part 73 of this chapter, the holder of the grant of certification must test each installation prior to initiation of normal operation to verify compliance with the technical standards and must maintain a list of all installations and records of measurements. For perimeter protection systems operating outside of the frequency bands allocated to television broadcast stations, upon receipt of a grant of certification, further testing of the same or similar type of system or installation is not required.

§ 15.203 Antenna requirement.

An intentional radiator shall be designed to ensure that no antenna other than that furnished by the responsible party shall be used with the device. The use of a permanently attached antenna or of an antenna that uses a unique coupling to the intentional radiator shall be considered sufficient to comply with the provisions of this section. The manufacturer may design the unit so that a broken antenna can be replaced by the user, but the use of a standard antenna jack or electrical connector is prohibited. This requirement does not apply to carrier current

In the above citation for the *Federal Register*, "64" is the volume, "22561–62" are the page numbers, and the year 1999 is the year of publication. In the above citation for the *Code of Federal Regulations*, "47" is the title, "15" is the part, "121" is the section, and the year 1999 is the year of publication.

FIGURE 5-17 Pages from LSA.

Cover of latest LSA available to author

Code of Federal Regulations

LSA

List of CFR Sections Affected

July 2000

United States
Government
Printing Office
SUPERINTENDENT
OF DOCUMENTS
Washington, DC 20402

OFFICIAL BUSINESS
Penalty for Private Use, $300

PERIODICALS
Postage and Fees Paid
U.S. Government Printing Office
(ISSN 0097-6326)

FIGURE 5-17 (continued)

78 **JULY 2000**

CHANGES OCTOBER 1, 1999 THROUGH JULY 31, 2000

Chapter IV—Federal Maritime Commission (Parts 500–599)

515 Authority citation amended 15253
515.2 (c) revised 15254
(m) revised 26512
515.11 (c) revised 15254
515.12 (a) revised 15254
515.23 (b)(2) revised 26512
Introductory text revised 33480
520.2 Amended 26513
530.3 (n) revised 26513
535 Authority citation amended 26513
535.101 Revised 26513
535.104 (u) revised 26513
545 Authority citation revised 33480
545.3 Added 33480

Proposed Rules:

2 . . . .**62018**
. 11410
5 . . . .**53970**
10 . . . . .11410, 37507
12 37507
15 . . . .**56720**
. . . . .6350, 11410, 37507, 45955
24 11410
25 11410
26 11410
28 11410
30 . . . .**62018**
. 11410
31 . . . .**62018**
52 . . . .**62018**
61 . . . .**62018**
67 46137
70 11410
71 . . . .**62018**
90 . . . .**62018**
. 11410
91 . . . .**62018**
98 . . . .**62018**
107 . . . .**62018**
110 . . . .**62018**
. . . . .6311, 35600, 39334, 46143
111 . . . . .6311, 35600, 39334, 46143
114 . . . .**62018**
. 11410
115 . . . .**62018**
125 . . . .**62018**
126 . . . .**62018**
132 . . . .**62018**
133 . . . .**62018**
134 . . . .**62018**
167 . . . .**62018**
169 . . . .**62018**
. 11410
175 . . . .**62018**
. 11410
176 . . . .**62018**
188 . . . .**62018**
. 11410
189 . . . .**62018**
195 . . . .**62018**
199 . . . .**62018**
. 11410
310 18957
356 646
401 20110
515 7335
520 31130

TITLE 47—TELECOMMUNICATION

Chapter I—Federal Communications Commission (Parts 0–199)

Chapter I Order **54561, 61527, 68053**
Petition reconsideration 5267
0.5 (a) revised **60716**
0.15 Undesignated center heading
and section revised **60716**
0.17 (g) added **60716**
0.31 (n) added **60716**
0.41 (k) revised **57585**
0.51 (s) added **60716**
0.61 (c) removed; (f) revised; (g)
added **60716**
0.91 (a), (c) and (h) revised **60716**
0.101 (d) revised **60716**
0.111 Undesignated center heading
and section revised **60716**
0.121 (a) revised **60718**
0.131 (a), (h) and (i) revised **60718**
(n) revised 375
0.141 Undesignated center heading
and section added **60718**
0.181 Introductory text, (c), (d)
and (h) revised **60720**
0.182 Revised **60720**
0.183 Removed **60721**
0.185 Introductory text, (a) and
(b) revised **60721**
0.251 (f) revised **57585**
0.261 (a)(15) revised **60721**
0.283 (b)(1)(iii) revised 7454
0.284 (a)(1) and (4) revised **60721**
0.285 Revised **60721**
0.302 Revised **60721**

NOTE: **Boldface page numbers indicate 1999 changes.**

FIGURE 5-17 (continued)

LSA—LIST OF CFR SECTIONS AFFECTED
CHANGES OCTOBER 1, 1999 THROUGH JULY 31, 2000

TITLE 47 Chapter 1—Con.

0.311 Undesignated center heading and section revised . . . . **.60721**
0.314 Revised . . . . **.60721**
0.317 Revised . . . . **.60722**
0.331 (d)(3) added 43715
0.332 (a) removed; (b) and (c) revised . . . . **.60722**
0.347 Revised . . . . **.60722**
0.357 Revised . . . . **.60722**
0.361 Undesignated center heading and section added . . . . **.60722**
0.387 (b) revised . . . . **.60722**
0.408 Revised (OMB numbers) . . . . **.55425**
0.413 Revised . . . . **.60722**
0.416 Revised . . . . **.60722**
0.422 Revised . . . . **.60722**
0.423 Revised . . . . **.60722**
0.431 Revised . . . . **.60722**
0.434 Revised . . . . **.60722**
0.441 Revised . . . . **.60722**
0.442 (a) and (b) amended; (d)(1), (3) and (e) revised . . . . **.55162**
0.443 Removed . . . . **.60723**
0.445 (b), (c) and (g) revised . . . . . . **.60723**
0.453 (a), (b), (d), (e) and (f) revised . . . . **.60723**
0.455 Revised . . . . **.60724**
0.459 (d)(1) and (g) amended; (i) added . . . . **.55163**
OMB number . . . . **.56269**
0.461 (i) revised . . . . **.55163**
0.465 (a) notes, (b) notes, (c)(1), (d)(1) and (3)revised; (d)(4) removed . . . . **.60725**
1 Authority citation revised . . . . . . **.63521**
Petition reconsideration . . . . **.69926**
Petition reconsideration 4891
Authority citation revised 10720, 19684, 31281
1.4 (b)(2) revised . . . . **.60725**
(b)(1) introductory text and (2) introductory text revised; (b)(1) note added 46108
1.13 (a)(1) amended 14476
1.47 (h) amended . . . . **.60725**
1.53 Added 7460
1.221 (b) and (c) revised . . . . **.60725**
1.720 Amended . . . . **.60725**
1.721 (b) amended . . . . **.60725**
1.722 (d)(1) amended . . . . **.60725**
1.730 Heading and (a) revised; (b), (c), (d) and (h) amended . . . . **.60725**
1.735 (b) revised . . . . **.60726**
1.774 Regulation at 64 FR 51264 eff. 11-4-99 . . . . **.60122**
1.923 (i) added; eff. 11-30-99 . . . . . . **.53238**
1.927 (a) revised; eff. 11-30-99 . . . . . **.53238**
1.928 Added; eff. 11-30-99 . . . . **.53238**
1.929 (b)(2), (c)(4)(i), (iii), (v) and (d) revised; eff. 11-30-99 . . . . **.53239**
1.939 (b) amended; eff. 11-30-99 . . . **.53240**
1.947 (b) revised; eff. 11-30-99 . . . . **.53240**
1.948 (d) revised . . . . **.62120**
1.955 (a)(1) and (b)(2) amended; eff. 11-30-99 . . . . **.53240**
1.1104 Table amended 30000
Regulation at 65 FR 30001 eff. date corrected to 6-9-00 34406
1.1152 Revised 44612
1.1153 Table amended 30001
Regulation at 65 FR 30001 eff. date corrected to 6-9-00 34406
Revised 44613
1.1154 Revised 44614
1.1155 Revised 44614
1.1156 Revised 44614
1.1202 (d)(2) revised . . . . **.63251**
(a) note, (d) introductory text and (1) through (5) revised; (d) note 5 added . . . . **.68947**
(d)(2) revised . . . . **.72571**
1.1203 (a) introductory text revised . . . . **.68947**
1.1204 (b)(5) revised . . . . **.63251**
(a) introductory text, (6), (9), (10)(iii) and (11) revised; (a)(12) and (b) note added . . . . . . **.68947**
1.1206 (a) note 1 and (a) note 2 redesignated as (a) note 2 and (a) note 3; new (a) note 1, (12), (13) and (14) added . . . . **.68948**
1.1208 Revised . . . . **.68948**
1.1210 Revised . . . . **.68949**
1.1307 (b)(2) revised . . . . **.69928**
(b)(2) revised; eff. 10-16-00 44001
1.1402 (c), (i), (j) and (1) revised; (n) added 31281
1.1404 (k) removed; (l), (m) and (n) redesignated as (k), (l), and (m); (g) and (h) revised; (j) amended (effective date pending) 31282
(g)(1)(vii) and (viii) corrected 34820
1.1409 (e)(3) redesignated as (e)(4); (e)(1) and (f) revised; new (e)(3) added (effective date pending) 31282
1.2105 (a)(2)(xi) revised . . . . **.59659**
1.4000 (g) revised . . . . **.60726**
1.6000-1.6012 (Subpart U) Added 10720

NOTE: **Boldface page numbers indicate 1999 changes.**

FIGURE 5-17 (continued)

No revision to 15.121

JULY 2000 79

CHANGES OCTOBER 1, 1999 THROUGH JULY 31, 2000

1.6010 Effective date pending 10721
1.7000–1.7002 (Subpart V)
Added 19684
Corrected 24654
1.7002 Corrected 24654
2 Petition reconsideration . . . . **.60123**
Authority citation amended . . . . . . **.72572**
Petition reconsideration 38431
2.100 Revised 4636
2.104 Revised 4636
2.105 Revised 4640
2.106 Table amended . . . . . . **.66409, 69928**
Table revised; footnotes amended 4640
2.106 Table amended; eff. 10-16-00 . . .44002
2.1093 (c) revised; eff. 10-16-00 44007
2.1204 (a)(9) added . . . . **.69929**
(a)(5) revised . . . . **.72572**
2.1205 (a) revised; note removed . . . **.72572**
6 Added . . . . **.63251**
6.18 Effective date pending . . . . . . **.63254**
7 Added . . . . **.63255**
7.18 Effective date pending . . . . . . **.63257**
11.11 (a), table and (b) amended 7639
Footnotes 4 and 5 removed 21657
(a) Amended; table revised 30001
Regulation at 65 FR 30001 eff.
date corrected to 6-9-00;
(a) table corrected 34406
11.17 Removed 21657
11.21 Introductory text revised 21657
11.41 (c) revised 21658
11.47 (b) revised 21658
11.51 (e) revised 7639
11.53 (a)(3) revised 7639
(a)(4) revised 30001
Regulation at 65 FR 30001 eff.
date corrected to 6-9-60 34406
11.54 (b)(2) removed; (b)(3)
through (15) redesignated as
(b)(2) through (14) 21658
11.55 (c)(4) revised 21658
11.61 (a)(1)(v) amended; (a)(2)(iii)
revised 7640
(a)(2)(i) removed; (a)(2)(ii)
through (v) redesignated as
(a)(2)(i) though (iv); (a)(6) revised 21658
11.62 (d) and (e)(2) revised 21658
13.8 Added; eff. 11-30-99 . . . . **.53240**
13.10 Added; eff. 11-30-99 . . . . **.53240**
15 Petition reconsideration 38431
15.37 (i) added; eff. 10-16-00 44008
20 Petition reconsideration 15559
Authority citation revised 19685
20.3 Amended . . . . **.60130**
20.6 Revised . . . . **.54574**
20.9 (a)(12) and (13) redesignated
as (a)(13) and (14); new (a)(12)
added . . . . **.59659**
20.12 Revised . . . . **.61027**
20.15 (b)(1) revised 19685
(b)(1) corrected 24654
20.18 (e) revised; (f) and (g)
redesignated as (j) and (k); (f)
through (i) added; eff. in
part 3-3-00 (OMB number
pending) . . . . **.60130**
(d)(1) and (j) revised . . . . **.72956**
21 Actions on petions 4136
21.2 Amended . . . . **.63730**
21.11 (d) and (e) amended . . . . **.63730**
21.23 (c)(1)(vi) revised; (c)(2) added . . **.63730**
(c)(2) revised 46617
21.31 (a) revised; (e)(6)(iv) removed . . **.63730**
(a) revised 46617
21.42 (c)(8) revised 46617
21.101 (a) footnote 2 revised . . . . . . **.63730**
21.106 (a)(2) revised 46617
21.201 Revised . . . . **.63731**
21.900 (a), (b) and (c) redesignated
as (a)(1), (2) and (3);
introductory text and
concluding text designated as
(a) introductory text and (b) . . . . . **.63731**
21.901 (d) revised . . . . **.63731**
21.902 (b)(3), (4), (7), (f)(1), (2)(i),
(ii), (i)(1), (2), (4) introductory text,
(iii), (iv), (v), (6)(i) introductory text,
(iii)(E), (F) and (iv) revised . . . . . . **.63731**
(c) introductory text and (i)(1)
revised; (m) added (effective date
pending in part) 46617
21.903 (d) revised . . . . **.63732**
21.904 Revised . . . . **.63732**
21.905 (b) and (d) introductory text
revised . . . . **.63732**
21.906 (a) revised; (d) amended . . . . **.63733**
(d) revised 46617
21.908 (d) revised 46617
21.909 (b), (c), (d), (g)(3), (6)(i), (ii),
(8), (h), (k), (m) and (n) revised;
(a) and (o) amended . . . . **.63733**

NOTE: **Boldface page numbers indicate 1999 changes.**

FIGURE 5-18 Pages from Federal Register.

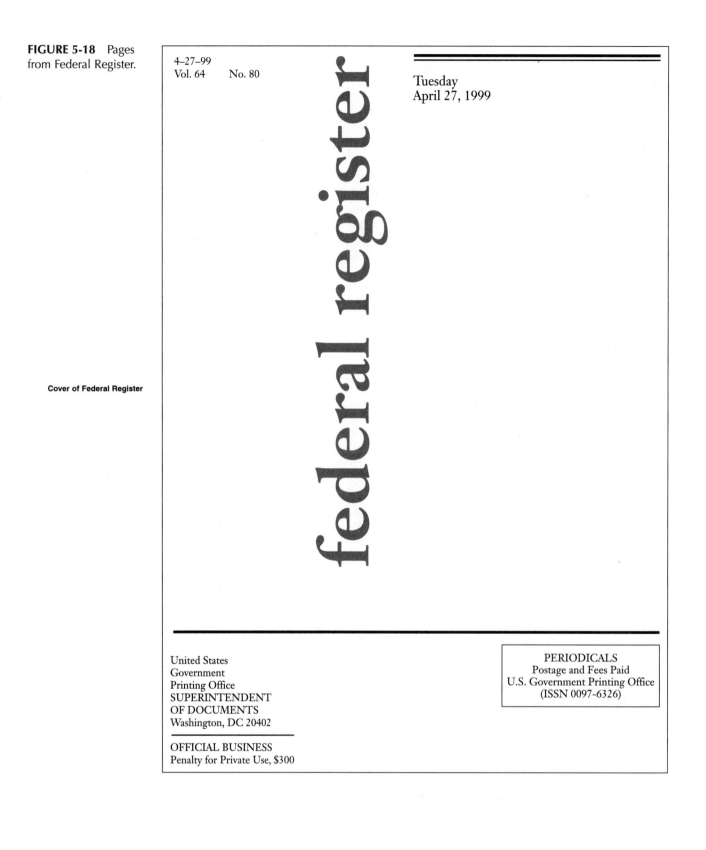

Cover of Federal Register

4-27-99
Vol. 64 No. 80

federal register

Tuesday
April 27, 1999

United States
Government
Printing Office
SUPERINTENDENT
OF DOCUMENTS
Washington, DC 20402

OFFICIAL BUSINESS
Penalty for Private Use, $300

PERIODICALS
Postage and Fees Paid
U.S. Government Printing Office
(ISSN 0097-6326)

FIGURE 5-18 (continued)

Federal Register/Vol. 64, No. 80/Tuesday, April 27, 1999/Rules and Regulations

For the reasons discussed in the preamble, the Coast Guard amends 46 CFR part 16 as follows:

PART 16—CHEMICAL TESTING

1. The authority citation for part 16 continues to read as follows:

Authority: 46 U.S.C. 2103, 3306, 7101, 7301, and 7701; 49 CFR 1.46.

2. Revise § 16.500 to read as follows:

§ 16.500 Management Information System requirements.

(a) *Data collection.* All marine employers must collect the following drug and alcohol testing program data for each calendar year:

(1) Total number of employees during the calendar year that were subject to the drug testing-rules in this part.

(2) Number of employees subject to testing under the anti-drug rules of both the Coast Guard and another DOT agency based on the nature of their assigned duties as identified by each agency.

(3) Number of drug and alcohol tests conducted identified by test type. Drug test types are pre-employment, periodic, random, post-accident, and reasonable cause. Alcohol test types are post-accident and reasonable cause.

(4) Number of positive drug test results verified by a Medical Review Officer (MRO) by test type and types of drug(s). Number of alcohol tests resulting in a blood alcohol concentration weight of .04 percent or more by test type.

(5) Number of negative drug and alcohol test results reported by MRO by test type.

(6) Number of applicants denied employment based on a positive drug test result verified by an MRO.

(7) Number of marine employees with a MRO-varified positive test result who returned to duty in a safety-sensitive position subject to required chemical testing, after meeting the requirements of § 16.370(d) and part 5 of this chapter.

(8) Number of marine employees with positive drug test results verified by a MRO as positive for one drug or a combination of drugs.

(9) Number of employees required under this part to be tested who refused to submit to a drug test.

(10) Number of covered employees and supervisory personnel who received the required initial training.

(b) *Data reporting.* (1) By March 15 of the year following the collection of the data in paragraph (a) of this section, marine employers must submit the data on Form CG-5573 to Commandant (G-MOA), 2100 Second Street, SW, Washington, DC, 20593-0001. Marine employers must complete all data fields on the form.

(2) Form CG-5573 is reproduced in Appendix B of this part and you may obtain the form from any Marine Inspection Office. You may also download a copy of Form CG-5573 from the U.S. Coast Guard Marine Safety and Environmental Protection web site at http://www.uscg.mil/hq/g-m.html.

(3) A consortium or other employer representative may submit data for a marine employer. Reports may contain data for more than one marine employer. Each report, however, must list the marine employers included in the report.

(4) Marine employers must ensure that data submitted by a consortium or other employer representative under paragraph(b)(3) of this section is correct.

(c) After filing 3 consecutive annual MIS reports since January 1, 1996, required by paragraph (b) of this section, marine employers with 10 or fewer covered employees may stop filing the annual report each succeeding year during which they have no more than 10 covered employees.

(d) Marine employers who conduct operations regulated by another Department of Transportation Operating Administration must submit appropriate data to that Operating Administration for employees subject to that Operating Administration's regulations.

Dated: April 18, 1999.

R.C. North,

Assistant Commandant for Marine Safety and Environmental Protection.

[FR Dec. 99-10553 Filed 4-26-99; 8:45 am]

BILLING CODE 4910-15-P

Beginning of introduction to revised regulation

FEDERAL COMMUNICATIONS COMMISSION

47 CFR Parts 0, 2 and 15

[ET Docket No. 98-76; FCC 99-58]

Rules To Further Ensure That Scanning Receivers Do Not Receive Cellular Radio Signals

AGENCY: Federal Communications Commission.

ACTION: Final rule.

SUMMARY: The *Report and Order* amends the Commission rules to further prevent scanning receivers from receiving cellular radio telephone

FIGURE 5-18 (continued)

This page and the following page explain the reasons for reviewing the rule

Federal Register/Vol. 64, No. 80/Tuesday, April 27, 1999/Rules and Regulations

signals. It also codifies the provisions of section 705(e)(4) of the Communications Act of 1934 into our rules and requires a label on scanning receivers to indicate that modification of the receiver to receive Cellular Service transmissions is a violation of FCC rules and Federal Law. These requirements will ensure the privacy of communications in the Cellular Service.

DATES: This final rule is effective October 25, 1999.

Compliance Dates: The manufacture or importation of scanning receivers, and frequency converters designed or marketed for use with scanning receivers, that do not comply with the provisions of § 15.121 shall cease on or before October 25, 1999. After July 26, 1999 the Commission will not grant equipment authorization for receivers that do not comply with the provisions of § 15.121. These rules do not prohibit the sale or use of authorized receivers manufactured in the United States, or imported into the United States, prior to October 25, 1999.

FOR FURTHER INFORMATION CONTACT: Rodney P. Conway (202) 418-2904 or via electronic mail: rconway@fcc.gov.

SUPPLEMENTARY INFORMATION: This is a summary of the Commission's *Report and Order*, ET Docket 98-76, FCC 99-58, adopted March 25, 1999 and released March 31, 1999. A full text of this Commission decision is available for inspection and copying during normal business hours in the FCC Reference Center (Room TW-A306), 445 12th Street, SW Washington, DC 20554, and also may be purchased from the Commission's duplication contractor, International Transcription Service, phone (202) 857-3800, facsimile (202) 857-3805, 1231 20th Street, NW Washington DC 20036.

Summary of the Report and Order

1. The *Report and Order* (R&O) amends the rules to modify the definition of a scanning receiver to include scanning receivers that switch among two or more frequencies to deter the manufacture of scanning receivers that automatically scan less than four frequencies to circumvent the Commission's rules.

2. The *R&O* also amends the rules to define test equipment as equipment that is intended primarily for purposes of performing measurements or scientific investigations: The definition is sufficiently clear to prevent individuals from marketing scanning receivers that receive Cellular Service transmissions as test equipment.

3. The *R&O* also amends the rules to require that scanning receivers provide at least 38 dB rejection of Cellular Service signals for any frequency to which the scanning receiver can be tuned. In addition, the *R&O* amends the rules to require that scanning receivers be designed so that tuning, control and filtering circuitry is inaccessible and the design must be such that any attempt to modify the scanning receivercircuitry to receive Cellular Service transmissions will likely render the scanning receiver inoperable.

4. The *R&O* also amends the rules to clearly prohibit the modification of scanning receivers to receive Cellular Service transmissions, regardless of the date of manufacture of number of units modified. The Commission finds that modifying scanning receivers to receive Cellular Service signals changes its operating characteristics, invalidates the equipment certification, and results in equipment that does not comply with Commission rules.

5. The *R&O* also amends the rules to require a labelling requirement for scanning receivers. The label will contain the following warning: Modification of this device to receive Cellular Service signals is prohibited under FCC Rules and Federal law. The Commission finds that the labelling requirement is an effective deterrent and is an expedient way to distribute information regarding Commission rules and Federal laws.

6. The *R&O* also amends the rules to require that information must be submitted with any application for certification of a scanning receiver to ensure that the proposed rule changes are satisfied. As a result, any application for certification of a scanning receiver must include a detailed showing which: describes the testing method used to determine compliance with the 38 dB rejection ration, contains a statement assessing the vulnerability of the scanning receiver to possible modification, describes the design features that prevent modification of the scanning receiver to receive Cellular Service transmissions, and describes the design steps taken to make tuning, control, and filtering circuitry inaccessible.

7. The *Report and Order* also amends the rules to keep certain portions of applications for equipment authorization for scanning receivers confidential. The Commission finds that any information that would be useful for modification of a scanning receiver to receive Cellular Service transmissions. This information includes schematic diagrams, technical narratives describing equipment operation, and design details taken to prevent modification of scanning receivers to receive Cellular Service frequencies. This will assist in preventing sensitive information regarding the design of scanning receivers from being distributed to the public via Commission filings.

FIGURE 5-18 (continued)

Federal Register/Vol. 64, No. 80/Tuesday, April 27, 1999/Rules and Regulations

Final Regulatory Flexibility Analysis

8. As required by Section 603 of the Regulatory Flexibility Act, 5 U.S.C. 603 ("RFA"), an Initial Regulatory Flexibility Analysis ("IRFA") was incorporated into the Notice of Proposed Rule Making (Notice), 63 FR 31684, June 10, 1998, in ET Docket No. 98-76. The Commission sought written public comments on the proposals in the *Notice* including the IRFA. The Commission's Final Regulatory Flexibility Analysis ("FRFA") in this Report and Order conforms to the RFA, as amended by the Contract with America Advancement Act of 1996 (CWAAA), Public Law 104-121, 110 Stat. 847 (1996). *See* Subtitle II of the CWAAA is "The Small Business Regulatory Enforcement Fairness Act of 1996" (SBREFA), codified at 5 U.S.C. 601 *et seq.*

9. Need for and Objective of the Rules. Our objectives are to adopt rules to ensure that scanning receivers do not receive signals from the cellular radiotelephone service frequency bands.

10. Summary of Significant Issues Raised by Public Comments in Response to the IRFAs. No comments were submitted in direct response to the IRFA.

11. Description and Estimates of the Number of Small Entities to Which the Rules Will Apply. For the purposes of this Report and Order, the RFA defines a "small business" to be the same as a "small business concern" under the Small Business Act, 15 U.S.C. 632, unless the Commission has developed one or more definitions that are appropriate to its activities. *See* 5 U.S.C. 601(3) (incorporating by reference the definition of "small business concern" in 5 U.S.C. 632). Under the Small Business Act, a "small business concern" is one that: 1) is independently owned and operated; 2) is not dominant in its field of operation; and 3) meets any additional criteria established by the Small Business Administration (SBA). *See* 15 U.S.C. 632.

12. The Commission has not developed a definition of small entities applicable to unlicensed communications devices. Therefore, we will utilize the SBA definition applicable to manufacturers of Radio and Television Broadcasting and Communications Equipment. According to the SBA regulations, unlicensed transmitter manufacturers must have 750 or fewer employees in order to qualify as a small business concern. *See* 13 CFR 121.201, (SIC) Code 3663. Census Bureau data indicates that there are 858 U.S. companies that manufacture radio and television broadcasting and communications equipment, and that 778 of these firms have fewer than 750 employees and would be classified as small entities. *See* U.S. Dept. of Commerce, *1992 Census of Transportation, Communications and Utilities* (issued May 1995), SIC category 3663. The Census Bureau category is very broad, and specific figures are not available as to how many of these firms will manufacture unlicensed communications devices. However, we believe that many of them may qualify as small entities.

13. Description of Projected Reporting, Recordkeeping and Other Compliance Requirements. The Commission has adopted rules that require scanning receivers to be manufactured to reduce the possibility of receiving signals from the cellular radiotelephone service frequency bands. The rules will require design details and test measurements to be reported to the Commission as part of the normal equipment authorization process under our certification procedure.

14. Significant Alternatives and Steps Taken to Minimize Significant Economic Impact on a Substantial Number of Small Entities Consistent with Stated Objectives. The Commission considered and rejected additional rules that would have significantly increased the costs of manufacturing scanning receivers. The rules adopted in the Report and Order represent the most efficient and least restrictive method to accomplish the Commission's policies and objectives.

15. Report to Congress. The Commission will send a copy of the Final Regulatory Flexibility Analysis, along with this Report and Order, in a report to Congress pursuant to the Small Business Regulatory Enforcement Fairness Act of 1996, 5 U.S.C. 801(a)(1)(A) and the Chief Counsel for Advocacy of the Small Business Administration.

List of Subjects

47 CFR Part 0

Freedom of information.

47 CFR Part 2

Communications equipment, Radio, Reporting and recordkeeping requirements.

47 CFR Part 15

Communications equipment, Labeling, Radio, Reporting and recordkeeping requirements.

Federal Communications Commission.

Magalie Roman Salas,

Secretary.

Rule Changes

For the reasons discussed in the preamble, the Federal Communications Commission amends 47 CFR parts 0, 2, and 15 as follows:

FIGURE 5-18 (continued)

Federal Register/Vol. 64, No. 80/Tuesday, April 27, 1999/Rules and Regulations

PART 0—COMMISSION ORGANIZATION

1. The authority citation for part 0 continues to read as follows:

Authority: Sec. 5, 48 Stat. 1068, as amended; 47 U.S.C. 155.

2. Section 0.457 is amended by revising paragraph (d)(1)(ii) to read as follows:

§ 0.457 Records not routinely available for public inspection.

(d) * * *

(1) * * *

(ii) Applications for equipment authorizations (type acceptance, type approval, certification, or advance approval of subscription television systems), and materials relating to such applications, are not routinely available for public inspection prior to the effective date of the authorization. The effective date of the authorization will, upon request, be deferred to a date no earlier than that specified by the applicant. Following the effective date of the authorization, the application and related materials (including technical specifications and test measurements) will be made available for inspection upon request (See § 0.460). Portions of applications for equipment certification of scanning receivers and related materials will not be made available for inspection. This information includes that necessary to prevent modification of scanning receivers to receive Cellular Service frequencies, such as schematic diagrams, technical narratives describing equipment operation, and relevant design details.

* * * * *

PART 2—FREQUENCY ALLOCATIONS AND RADIO TREATY MATTERS: GENERAL RULES AND REGULATIONS

3. The authority citation for part 2 continues to read as follows:

Authority: 47 U.S.C. 154, 302, 303, 307 and 336, unless otherwise noted.

4. Section 2.1033 is amended by revising paragraph (b)(11) to read as follows:

§ 2.1033 Application for certification.

(b) * * *

(11) Applications for the certification of scanning receivers shall include a statement describing the methods used to comply with the design requirements of all parts of § 15.121 of this chapter. The application must specifically include a statement assessing the vulnerability of the equipment to possible modification and describing the design features that prevent the modification of the equipment by the user to receive transmissions from the Cellular Radiotelephone Service. The application must also demonstrate compliance with the signal rejection requirement of § 15.121 of this chapter, including details on the measurement procedures used to demonstrate compliance.

* * * * *

PART 15—RADIO FREQUENCY DEVICES

5. The authority citation for part 15 continues to read as follows:

Authority: 47 U.S.C. 154, 302, 303, 304, 307 and 544A.

6. Section 15.3 is amended by revising paragraph (v) and adding paragraph (dd) to read as follows:

§ 15.3 Definitions

* * * * *

(v) *Scanning receiver.* For the purpose of this part, this is a receiver that automatically switches among two or more frequencies in the range of 30 to 960 MHz and that is capable of stopping at and receiving a radio signal detected on a frequency. Receivers designed solely for the reception of the broadcast signals under part 73 of this chapter or for operation as part of a licensed station are not included in this definition.

* * * * *

(dd) *Test equipment* is defined as equipment that is intended primarily for purposes of performing measurements or scientific investigations. Such equipment includes, but is not limited to, field strength meters, spectrum analyzers, and modulation monitors.

7. Section 15.37 is amended by revising paragraph (f) and adding a new paragraph (h) to read as follow:

§ 15.37 Transition provisions for compliance with the rules.

* * * * *

(f) The manufacture or importation of scanning receivers, and frequency converters designed or marketed for use with scanning receivers, that do not comply with the provisions of § 15.121(a)(1) shall cease on or before April 26, 1994. Effective April 26, 1993, the Commission will not grant equipment authorization for receivers that do not comply with the provisions of § 15.121(a)(1). These rules do not prohibit the sale or use of authorized receivers manufactured in the United States, or imported into the United States, prior to April 26, 1994.

* * * * *

FIGURE 5-18 (continued)

Federal Register/Vol. 64, No. 80/Tuesday, April 27, 1999/Rules and Regulations

(h) The manufacture or importation of scanning receivers, and frequency converters designed or marketed for use with scanning receivers, that do not comply with the provisions of §15.121 shall cease on or before October 25, 1999. Effective July 26, 1999 the Commission will not grant equipment authorization for receivers that do not comply with the provisions of § 15.121. This paragraph does not prohibit the sale or use of authorized receivers manufactured in the United States, or imported into the United States, prior to October 25, 1999.

8. Section 15.121 is revised to read as follows:

Revised regulation

§ 15.121 Scanning receivers and frequency converters used with scanning receivers.

(a) Except as provided in paragraph (c) of this section, scanning receivers and frequency converters designed or marketed for use with scanning receivers, shall:

(1) Be incapable of operating (tuning), or readily being altered by the user to operate, within the frequency bands allocated to the Cellular Radiotelephone Service in part 22 of this chapter (cellular telephone bands). Scanning receivers capable of "readily being altered by the user" include, but are not limited to, those for which the ability to receive transmissions in the cellular telephone bands can be added by clipping the leads of, or installing, a simple component such as a diode, resistor or jumper wire; replacing a plug-in semiconductor chip; or programming a semiconductor chip using special access codes or an external device, such as a personal computer. Scanning receivers, and frequency converters designed for use with scanning receivers, also shall be incapable of converting digital cellular communication transmissions to analog voice audio.

(2) Be designed so that the tuning, control and filtering circuitry is inaccessible. The design must be such that any attempts to modify the equipment to receive transmissions from the Cellular Radiotelephone Service likely will render the receiver inoperable.

(b) Except as provided in paragraph (c) of this section, scanning receivers shall reject any signals from the Cellular Radiotelephone Service frequency bands that are 38 dB or higher based upon a 12 dB SINAD measurement, which is considered the threshold where a signal can be clearly discerned from any interference that may be present.

(c) Scanning receivers and frequency converters designed or marketed for use with scanning receivers, are not subject to the requirements of paragraphs (a) and (b) of this section provided that they are manufactured exclusively for, and marketed exclusively to, entities described in 18 U.S.C. 2512(2), or are marketed exclusively as test equipment pursuant to § 15.3(dd).

(d) Modification of a scanning receiver to receive transmissions from Cellular Radiotelephone Service frequency bands will be considered to constitute manufacture of such equipment. This includes any individual, individuals, entity or organization that modifies one or more scanners. Any modification to a scanning receiver to receive transmissions from the Cellular Radiotelephone Service frequency bands voids the certification of the scanning receiver, regardless of the date of manufacture of the original unit. In addition, the provisions of § 15.23 shall not be interpreted as permitting modification of a scanning receiver to receiver Cellular Radiotelephone Service transmissions.

(e) Scanning receivers and frequency converters designed for use with scanning receivers shall not be assembled from kits or marketed in kit form unless they comply with the requirements in paragraph (a) through (c) of this section.

(f)(1) Scanning receivers shall have a label permanently affixed to the product, and this label shall be readily visible to the purchaser at the time of purchase. The label shall read as follows:

WARNING: MODIFICATION OF THIS DEVICE TO RECEIVE CELLULAR RADIOTELEPHONE SERVICE SIGNALS IS PROHIBITED UNDER FCC RULES AND FEDERAL LAW.

(2) "Permanently affixed" means that the label is etched, engraved, stamped, silkscreened, indelibly printed or otherwise permanently marked on a permanently attached part of the equipment or on a nameplate of metal plastic or other material fastened to the equipment by welding, riveting, or permanent adhesive. The label shall be designed to last the expected lifetime of the equipment in the environment in which the equipment may be operated and must not be readily detachable. The label shall not be a stick-on, paper label.

[FR Doc. 99-10118 Filed 4-26-99; 8:45 am]
BILLING CODE 6712-01-P

FEDERAL COMMUNICATIONS COMMISSION

47 CFR Part 52

[WT Docket No. 9??-229, CC Docket No. 95-116; FCC 99-19]

FIGURE 5-18 (continued)

Federal Register/Vol. 64, No. 80/Tuesday, April 27, 1999/Rules and Regulations

Cellular Telecommunications Industry Association's Petition for Forbearance From Commercial Mobile Radio Services Number Portability Obligations and Telephone Number Portability

AGENCY: Federal Communications Commission.

ACTION: Final rule.

SUMMARY: In this *Memorandum Opinion and Order*, the Commission grants a petition filed by the Cellular Telecommunications Industry Association (CTIA) requesting that the Commission forbear from imposing service provider local number portability (LNP) requirements on broadband commercial mobile radio service (CMRS) providers until the expiration of the five-year buildout period for broadband personal communications service (PCS) carriers. Accordingly, the *Memorandum Opinion and Order* extends the deadline for CMRS providers to support service provider LNP in the top 100 Metropolitan Statistical Areas (MSAs) until November 24, 2002. The *Memorandum Opinion and Order* finds that extension of the deadline will provide the industry with the flexibility to allocate its immediate resources toward network construction, a goal proven to promote a competitive marketplace.

DATES: Effective May 27, 1999.

FOR FURTHER INFORMATION CONTACT: David Furth at (202) 418-0632 or Joel Taubenblatt at (202) 418-1513 (Wireless Telecommunications Bureau).

SUPPLEMENTARY INFORMATION: This is a summary of the *Memorandum Opinion and Order*, FCC 99-19, adopted February 8, 1999 and released February 9, 1999. The complete text of the *Memorandum Opinion and Order* is available for inspection and copying during normal business hours in the FCC Reference Center, 445 12th Street, S.W., Washington, D.C. and also may be purchased from the Commission's copy contractor, International Transcription Services, (202) 857-3800, 1231 20th St., N.W., Washington, D.C. 20036. The document is also available via the Internet at http://www.fcc.gov/Bureaus/Wireless/ Orders/1999/index.html.

Introduction

1. In this *Memorandum Opinion and Order*, the Commission grants a petition filed by CTIA seeking forbearance from LNP requirements for CMRS carriers until the completion of the five-year buildout period for broadband PCS carriers. In granting the petition, the Commission extends the deadline for CMRS carriers to implement service provider LNP until November 24, 2002.

Background

2. Under the Commission's prior LNP decisions, broadband CMRS carriers (cellular, broadband PCS, and some specialized mobile radio (SMR) providers) were required to implement LNP in the top 100 MSAs, and to support nationwide roaming, by March 31, 2000. Implementation of LNP by CMRS providers would enable wireless customers to "port" their telephone numbers in the event that they switch from one wireless carrier to another, or from a wireless to a wireline carrier.

Findings

3. In this *Memorandum Opinion and Order*, the Commission finds that. extending the deadline is consistent with the statutory standard for granting forbearance under section 10 of the Communications Act of 1934, as amended, 47 U.S.C. 160. The Commission notes that the wireless industry requires additional time to implement LNP in part because, unlike wireline carriers (who are already required to provide LNP in the top 100 MSAs), wireless carriers face certain unique technical issues regarding implementation of LNP in their networks and in supporting roaming by customers with ported numbers. The Commission also states that extending the deadline until November 2002 is consistent with the public interest for competitive reasons because it will give CMRS carriers greater flexibility in that time-frame to complete network buildout, technical upgrades, and other improvements that are likely to have a more immediate impact on enhancing service to the public and promoting competition in the telecommunications marketplace.

4. The Commission emphasizes that its decision in the *Memorandum Opinion and Order* does not relieve CMRS carriers of their underlying obligation to implement LNP. As wireless service rates continue their downward trend and the use of wireless

CHAPTER 5 SUMMARY

- Constitutions, statutes, court rules, and administrative law, like cases, are primary authority.
- The United States Constitution sets forth the fundamental principles of governance for the country; State constitutions set forth the fundamental principles of governance for the states.
- To find how a provision of a constitution has been interpreted by the courts, you would consult an "annotated" version of the constitution.
- Federal and state statutes first appear as slip law, then as "session laws" (arranged chronologically), and later are "codified" (grouped by subject matter).
- To understand a statute you must read the text of the statute and any annotations summarizing how the statute has been interpreted by the courts.
- The Federal Rules of Civil Procedure, the Federal Rules of Criminal Procedure, and the Federal Rules of Evidence govern litigation procedure in federal trial courts.
- Similar sets of rules govern litigation procedure in state trial courts.
- Separate sets of courts rules govern litigation procedure in federal and state appellate courts.
- Administrative agencies promulgate administrative regulations that have the force of law.
- Federal administrative regulations are published chronologically in the *Federal Register* and are later codified in the *Code of Federal Regulations.*
- State administrative regulations are generally published in similar fashion.

CYBERLAW EXERCISES

1. From Washburn School of Law's homepage you can access state government and legislative information. The homepage is located at http://www.washlaw.edu. Using the homepage, locate information on your state's government and legislature.
2. The Louisiana State University libraries index (http://www.lib.lsu.edu/index.html) provides links to government information. Under "electronic resources" click on "government information."
3. The Law Guru (http://www.lawguru.com) is one of the hosts of the Internet Law Library and provides links to other legal research sites. Included are links to constitutions, codes, and statutes.
4. The Internet Legal Resource Guide (http://ilrg.com) is a comprehensive legal research site for accessing federal and state resources.
5. From Louisiana State University's homepage you can access The Constitution Page, maintained by the LSU political science department (College of Arts and Sciences). LSU's homepage is located at http://www.lsu.edu. The Constitution Page links you to the United States Constitution, the state constitutions and constitutions of the world. Locate the United States Constitution and your state's constitution.
6. The United State Code is accessible via the homepage of the United States House of Representatives. The homepage is located at http://www.house.gov/. Locate the page that allows you to search the United States Code and research one of the legal research questions at the end of this chapter using the page.
7. A number of municipal codes are accessible via the Municipal Code Corporation home page (http://www.municode.com/). Use this site to locate city codes for cities in your state.
8. Some old statutes, rarely enforced, remain a part of the state's body of statutes. A collection of these statutes may be accessed at http://www.dumblaws.com.
9. The Lexis law school site (http://lawschool.lexis.com) includes information on researching statutes (click on "My School," "Web Lectures," and "Legal Research 2 Writing").
10. The United States Code is also available through the Cornell Law School website. Go to

http://www.law.cornell.edu, point to "Constitutions & Codes" and click on "US Code (Acts of Congress)."

11. LLRX—ResearchWire:Litigator's Internet Resource Guide, located at <http://www.llrx.com>, offers access to federal and state court rules at http://www.llrx.com/courtrules/. See if you can access the various court rules for your state. Find local federal and state court rules that apply to the area in which you are located.
12. GPO Access homepage ("GPO" stands for government printing office) is located at http://www.access.gpo.gov. Using GPO, discover how you would access the *Code of Federal Regulations* and the *Federal Register.*
13. The *Code of Federal Regulations* is also available through the Cornell Law School website. Go to http://www.law.cornell.edu, point to "Constitutions & Codes" and click on "*Code of Federal Regulations.*"
14. Many law school librarians have written legal research guides and have posted them on the web. The guides attempt to introduce students to legal research and to answer commonly asked questions. Paul Richert, Law Librarian and Professor of Law at the University of Akron, School of Law Library, has compiled an "Internet Hotlist of Law Guides Organized by Subject" that links to many of the legal research guides. The Hotlist is accessible at http://www.uakron.edu/law/richert/index1.html.

LEGAL RESEARCH ASSIGNMENT—CONSTITUTIONS

1. What do the following articles of the United States Constitution deal with?
   a. Article I.
   b. Article II.
   c. Article III.
2. What is the citation to that portion of your state's constitution dealing with the following matters?
   a. The executive branch.
   b. The legislative branch.
   c. The judicial branch.
3. Which provision of the United States Constitution contains the "enumerated powers" of Congress?
4. Which provision of the United States Constitution is commonly known as the "supremacy clause"?
5. a. Which provision of the United States Constitution is frequently cited as giving people the right to own handguns?
   b. If your state constitution guarantees the same right, give the citation to that provision.
6. a. Which provision of the United States Constitution guarantees the right to a speedy and public trial?
   b. If your state constitution guarantees the same right, give the citation to that provision.
7. a. Which provision of the United States Constitution deals with freedom of the press?
   b. Which provision of your state constitution deals with freedom of the press?
8. What 1868 change to the United States Constitution made much of the Bill of Rights applicable to state governments as well as the federal government?
9. a. In what set of books would you be able to research how case law has interpreted the United States Constitution?
   b. In what set of books would you be able to research how case law has interpreted your state's constitution?
10. a. Which provision of the United States Constitution specifically guarantees a "right to privacy"?
    b. If your state constitution guarantees the right to privacy, give the citation to that provision.
11. a. Which provision of the United States Constitution guarantees "the right of the people to be secure in their persons, houses, papers and effects"?
    b. If your state constitution guarantees the same right, give the citation to that provision.
12. a. Which provision of the United States Constitution guarantees free speech?

b. If your state constitution guarantees the same right, give the citation to that provision.

13. a. Which provision of the United States Constitution prohibits laws "establishing" religion?
   b. If your state constitution guarantees the same right, give the citation to that provision?

14. a. Which provision of the United States Constitution prohibits cruel and unusual punishment?
   b. If your state constitution contains a similar prohibition, give the citation to that provision.

LEGAL RESEARCH ASSIGNMENT—STATUTES

Note: You may research questions 9 through 17 in *United States Code Service* or *United States Code Annotated* instead of *United States Code.*

1. Name the advance session law service containing federal statutes.
2. Name the set of books containing federal statutes arranged in chronological order.
3. Name the set of books containing the official codified version of federal statutes.
4. Name two sets of books containing the codified version of federal statutes and annotations to those statutes.
5. Name advance session law service for your state.
6. Name the set of books for your state containing state statutes arranged in chronological order.
7. Name the set of books for your state containing the official codified version of state statutes.
8. Name the set of books for your state containing the codified version of state statutes and annotations to those statutes.
9. a. What does Title 11 of the *United States Code* deal with?
   b. What does Title 28 of the *United States Code* deal with?
   c. What does Title 42 of the *United States Code* deal with?
10. a. What is the citation of the federal statute that designates the Federal Aviation Administration as an administration in the Department of Transportation?
   b. What is the citation of the federal statute that lists the purposes of the United States Olympic Committee?
   c. What is the citation of the federal statute that establishes the Food and Drug Administration as an administration in the Department of Health and Human Services?
11. a. What is the citation for the federal statute that designates the color and composition of the United States flag?
   b. What is the citation of the federal statute that allows final judgments of the highest court of a state to be reviewed by the United States Supreme Court on petition for writ of certiorari?
   c. What is the citation of the federal statute allowing final judgments of the courts of appeals to be reviewed by the United States Supreme Court on petition for writ of certiorari or on a certified question?
12. What penalty may Senators and members of the House of Representatives suffer if they are absent from Congress? State the authority for your answer.
13. What is the "universal" customary time for displaying the United States flag on buildings and on stationary flagstaffs in the open? State the authority for your answer.
14. What is the President's annual compensation and what is his expense allowance? State the authority for your answer.
15. What crime is it if one glues together parts of bills of different denominations? State the authority for your answer.
16. What may you do with merchandise you received without having ordered it? State the authority for your answer.
17. What is the Secretary of the Interior authorized to do with surplus elk, buffalo, bear, beaver, and predatory animals inhabiting Yellowstone National Park? State the authority for your answer.

LEGAL RESEARCH ASSIGNMENT—COURT RULES

1. Using the Federal Rules of Civil Procedure, answer questions *a* through *c:*
   a. Which courts are governed by the Federal Rules of Civil Procedure?
   b. What is the purpose of the rules?
   c. What is your authority? (Give the full citation to the rule.)
   d. Using your state's rules of civil procedure, what are the answers to *a* through *c?*
2. Using the Federal Rules of Civil Procedure, answer questions *a* and *b:*
   a. How does one begin a civil lawsuit?
   b. What is your authority?
   c. Using your state's rules of civil procedure, what are the answers to *a* and *b?*
3. Using the Federal Rules of Civil Procedure, answer questions *a* and *b:*
   a. Who may serve the summons?
   b. What is your authority?
   c. Using your state's rules of civil procedure, what are the answers to *a* and *b?*
4. Using the Federal Rules of Civil Procedure, answer questions *a* and *b:*
   a. What pleadings are allowed?
   b. What is your authority?
   c. Using your state's rules of civil procedure, what are the answers to *a* and *b?*
5. Using the Federal Rules of Civil Procedure, answer questions *a* and *b:*
   a. What are the prerequisites to a class action?
   b. What is your authority?
   c. Using your state's rules of civil procedure, what are the answers to *a* and *b?*
6. Using the Federal Rules of Civil Procedure, answer questions *a* and *b:*
   a. What is the number of jurors in a civil lawsuit?
   b. What is your authority?
   c. Using your state's rules of civil procedure, what are the answers to *a* and *b?*
7. Using the Federal Rules of Civil Procedure, answer questions *a* and *b:*
   a. What are the grounds for entering a default judgment?
   b. What is your authority?
   c. Using your state's rules of civil procedure, what are the answers to *a* and *b?*
8. Using the Federal Rules of Civil Procedure, answer questions *a* and *b:*
   a. What are the grounds for entering a temporary restraining order?
   b. What is your authority?
   c. Using your state's rules of civil procedure, what are the answers to *a* and *b?*
9. Using the Federal Rules of Evidence, answer questions *a* and *b:*
   a. What is the purpose of the rules?
   b. What is your authority?
   c. Using your state's rules of evidence, what are the answers to *a* and *b?*
10. Using the Federal Rules of Evidence, answer questions *a* and *b:*
    a. What type of fact may be judicially noticed?
    b. What is your authority?
    c. Using your state's rules of evidence, what are the answers to *a* and *b?*
11. Using the Federal Rules of Evidence, answer questions *a* and *b:*
    a. On what ground may relevant evidence be excluded?
    b. What is your authority?
    c. Using your state's rules of evidence, what are the answers to *a* and *b?*
12. Using the Federal Rules of Evidence, answer questions *a* and *b:*
    a. What is hearsay?
    b. What is your authority?
    c. Using your state's rules of evidence, what are the answers to *a* and *b?*
13. Using the Federal Rules of Criminal Procedure, answer questions *a* and *b:*
    a. What is the scope of the rules?
    b. What is your authority?
    c. Using your state's rules of criminal procedure, what are the answers to *a* and *b?*
14. Using the Federal Rules of Criminal Procedure, answer questions *a* and *b:*
    a. What is the purpose of the rules and how are they to be construed?
    b. What is your authority?
    c. Using your state's rules of criminal procedure, what are the answers to *a* and *b?*

15. Using the Federal Rules of Criminal Procedure, answer questions *a* through *c:*
a. How many members does a grand jury have?
b. Who may be present when the grand jury is in session?
c. What is your authority?
d. Using your state's rules of criminal procedure, what are the answers to *a* through *c?*

16. Using the Federal Rules of Criminal Procedure, answer questions *a* and *b:*
a. What happens during an arraignment?
b. What is your authority?
c. Using your state's rules of criminal procedure, what are the answers to *a* and *b?*

17. Using the Federal Rules of Criminal Procedure, answer questions *a* and *b:*
a. What are the reasons that allow trial in a district other than the one in which the offense was committed?
b. What is your authority?
c. Using your state's rules of criminal procedure, what are the answers to *a* and *b?*

18. Using the Federal Rules of Criminal Procedure, answer questions *a* and *b:*
a. How many members does a trial jury have?
b. What is the minimum number of jurors to return a valid verdict?
c. What is your authority?
d. Using your state's rules of criminal procedure, what are the answers to *a* through *c?*

19. Using the Federal Rules of Criminal Procedure, answer questions *a* and *b:*
a. What happens during closing argument?
b. What is your authority?
c. Using your state's rules of criminal procedure, what are the answers to *a* and *b?*

20. Using the Federal Rules of Appellate Procedure, answer questions *a* and *b:*
a. What courts are governed by these rules?
b. What is your authority?
c. Using your state's rules of appellate procedure, what are the answers to *a* and *b?*

21. Using the Federal Rules of Appellate Procedure, answer questions *a* and *b:*
a. What items constitute the record on appeal?
b. What is your authority?
c. Using your state's rules of appellate procedure, what are the answers to *a* and *b?*

22. Using the Federal Rules of Appellate Procedure, answer questions *a* and *b:*
a. How may service of papers be made?
b. What is your authority?
c. Using your state's rules of appellate procedure, what are the answers to *a* and *b?*

23. Using the Federal Rules of Appellate Procedure, answer questions *a* and *b:*
a. When must the appellant's brief be filed?
b. What is your authority?
c. Using your state's rules of appellate procedure, what are the answers to *a* and *b?*

24. Using the Federal Rules of Appellate Procedure, answer questions *a* and *b:*
a. When may an en banc hearing be ordered?
b. What is your authority?
c. Using your state's rules of appellate procedure, what are the answers to *a* and *b?*

25. Using the Rules of the Supreme Court of the United States, answer questions *a* and *b:*
a. When does the annual term of the Court begin and end?
b. What is your authority?

26. Using the Rules of the Supreme Court of the United States, answer questions *a* and *b:*
a. How many members of the Court constitute a quorum?
b. What is your authority?

27. Using the Rules of the Supreme Court of the United States, answer questions *a* and *b:*
a. Is review on writ of certiorari discretionary or mandatory?
b. What is your authority?

28. Using the Rules of the Supreme Court of the United States, answer questions *a* and *b:*
a. When must a petition for writ of certiorari be filed with the Court?
b. What is your authority?

29. Using the Rules of the Supreme Court of the United States, answer questions *a* and *b:*
a. How long does each side have for oral argument?
b. What is your authority?

30. Using the Rules of the Supreme Court of the United States, answer questions *a* and *b:*
a. What is the filing fee for a petition for writ of certiorari?
b. What is your authority?

LEGAL RESEARCH ASSIGNMENT—ADMINISTRATIVE LAW

1. a. What is the name of the set of books containing the codified version of federal administrative rules?
   b. What is the name of the publication containing new administrative rules not found in the code?
2. a. What is the name of the set of books containing the codified version of your state's administrative rules?
   b. What is the name of the publication containing new administrative rules not found in the code?
3. a. What federal government agency is the subject of Title 17 of the *Code of Federal Regulations?*
   b. What federal government agency is the subject of Title 26 of the *Code of Federal Regulations?*
   c. What federal government agency is the subject of Title 50 of the *Code of Federal Regulations?*
4. a. What is the purpose of the Note at 16 C.F.R. Part 17?
   b. What is the purpose of 16 C.F.R. §§1615.1–1616.65?
   c. What is the purpose of 16 C.F.R. §§1501.1–1501.5?
   d. What is the purpose of 16 C.F.R. §§238.0–238.4?
   e. What is the purpose of 16 C.F.R. §§233.1–233.5?
5. a. What is the citation to the rules promulgated under the Magnuson-Moss Warranty Act?
   b. What is the citation to the rules requiring care labels (stating whether the item is recommended to be machine washed or dry cleaned) in clothing?
   c. What is the citation to the rules requiring clothing labels to state the fabric content and the country of origin?
6. What is the definition in the *Code of Federal Regulations* for the following terms and what is the authority for your answer?
   a. "beer"
   b. "wine"
   c. "milk"
   d. "cream"
7. Locate the federal regulations concerning the *Code of Federal Regulations* and the *Federal Register* and answer the following questions:
   a. How often is each volume of the *Code of Federal Regulations* updated?
   b. What is the authority for *a?*
   c. What are the categories of documents published in the *Federal Register?*
   d. How often is the *Federal Register* published?
   e. What is the authority for *c* and *d?*
8. Locate the federal regulations in the *Code of Federal Regulations* concerning chewing tobacco and answer the following questions:
   a. What is the name of the federal act authorizing the enactment of the regulations?
   b. What is the wording for the three warnings, one of which is required to be placed on advertisements and packages of chewing tobacco?
   c. What is your authority for *a* and *b?*
9. Locate the federal regulations in the *Code of Federal Regulations* concerning labeling of alcoholic beverages and answer the following questions:
   a. What is the wording for the warning required to be placed on alcoholic beverages?
   b. What is the effective date of the labeling regulation?
   c. What is your authority for *a* and *b?*
10. Locate the federal regulations in the *Code of Federal Regulations* concerning inspection of meat and poultry and answer the following questions:
    a. What is the wording on the official inspection legend for beef carcasses?
    b. What is the wording on the official inspection legend for chicken?
    c. What is your authority for *a* and *b?*
11. Locate the federal regulations in the *Code of Federal Regulations* concerning grading of Florida oranges and answer the following questions:
    a. What types of fruit are covered by the regulations?

b. What are the names of the various grades of oranges?
c. What is the authority for *a* and *b?*

12. Answer the following questions and state the authority for your answers:
a. When may a petition for pardon be filed by someone seeking executive clemency?
b. Is a federal prisoner eligible for parole?
c. In whose name must a patent application be made?
d. May lawn darts be sold?

13. Answer the following questions and state the authority for your answer:
a. What is the maximum distance allowed between slats on full-size baby cribs?
b. What must a seller of mail order merchandise do when the seller is unable to ship merchandise within the applicable time period?
c. How long does a consumer who purchased a consumer item in "door-to-door" sale have to cancel the purchase and how long after receiving buyer's cancellation notice does the seller have to refund any money paid?
d. May someone operate a brewery in his or her home?

CHAPTER 6

CITATORS

INTRODUCTION

Although citators are one of the last sources to be studied in a legal research class, they are one of the most important tools in legal research. The attorney's failure to use citators will be quickly criticized by the court, as shown in the following judicial comments. The comments refer to the failure of the attorneys in the two cases to "Shepardize" or use Shepard's Citations. As explained in this chapter, the Shepard's Company produces sets of citators. (KeyCite, found on Westlaw, is another citator.) Thus, the court is saying that the attorney failed to use citators.

> As a peripheral matter, we address an issue that relates to appellate procedure before this court. In support of their argument that under the "universal rule," requests for attorney fees made for the first time by post-trial motions are timely, defendants' brief contains a series of citations to other jurisdictions. One of those cases upon which defendants rely, *Downs v. Stockman*, was quashed by *Stockman v. Downs.* The Utah Rules of Appellate Procedure require that "[a]ll briefs [under rule 24] be concise, presented with accuracy . . . and free from burdensome, irrelevant, immaterial or scandalous matters." Utah R.App. P. 24(j). The process of "Shepardizing" a case is fundamental to legal research and can be completed in a manner of minutes, especially when done with the aid of a computer. Though we do not consider counsel's actions to be egregious in this case, we admonish all attorneys to ensure the validity of all cases presented before this court.
>
> *Meadowbrook, LLC v. Flower*, 959 P.2d 115, 120 n.11 (Utah 1998)(citations omitted).
>
> Plaintiffs attest *Inryco* is no longer good law. The claim is disingenous. A glance at Shepard's Citations reveals *Inryco* has been both criticized and followed by other courts, including courts within the Seventh Circuit. Many courts continue to cite the case in a positive vein. This phenomenon reflects the schism RICO has engendered among the lower federal courts. Until the Tenth Circuit or the Supreme Court has spoken differently on this subject, I will continue to adopt the position taken by the other district courts of this circuit.
>
> *Behunin v. Dow Chemical Co.*, 650 F.Supp. 1387, 1390 n.3 (D. Colo. 1986)(citation omitted).

CITATORS

As explained in chapter 2, the doctrine of stare decisis requires judges to rely on past cases to decide controversies in front of them. Attorneys research case law to advise clients and to predict the outcome of a lawsuit. Judges and attorneys look for authoritative case law. Once the researcher locates a promising-looking case in a reporter, there is nothing to indicate the subsequent history of the case. Thus, the researcher cannot determine whether the case is still good law (is still authoritative) without consulting a citator.

A case, once authoritative, may no longer be good law for a number of reasons. It may have been reversed or overruled. A case may no longer be authoritative because subsequent decisions have created so many exceptions or so limited its effect, that the legal principle announced in the case is no longer viable. There is a difference between a court reversing a decision and a court overruling a decision. You might think of reversal as vertical in effect. A higher court reverses a case decided by a lower court; the result is that a higher court nullifies the decision of a lower court. Overruling a case is horizontal in effect. A case is overruled by the same court that originally decided the case. The result is that a court nullifies one of its past decisions. The court may decide, because of the passage of time or changes in society, that case law should be changed. The court accomplishes this by stating in a case presently before it, that it is overruling a prior case.

A case may have been appealed, with the case subsequently decided by a higher court. Even if the higher court affirmed the lower court, it is important to know that a higher court reached a decision in the case. If the lower court decided an issue and the higher court subsequently decided the same issue, the holding and reasoning of the higher court, rather than the lower court, is authoritative. One might want to cite to the lower court opinion for an issue not considered by the higher court or for facts or procedural history of the case not described in the higher court opinion. Even so, citation rules require the citation to the lower court opinion to include information informing the reader that the case was later decided by a higher court.

The consequences of not using citators can be quite serious. Without correctly using a citator, one may fail to ascertain that a case upon which he or she is relying has been reversed or overruled. This may result in an attorney giving a client incorrect legal advice, being admonished by a judge, or even losing a case. For a judge, it may mean being reversed on appeal and being chastised by the higher court. At the very worst, it may be the ground for a legal malpractice lawsuit against the attorney or disciplinary proceedings against the attorney or the judge. If this happened because the paralegal forgot to use the citator and the attorney relied on the paralegal's research, the paralegal can lose his or her job. In short, do not forget to use citators!

In a recent case, the court had been faced with an attorney who had failed to Shepardize. The court stated:

> It is really inexcusable for any lawyer to fail, as a matter of routine, to Shepardize all cited cases (a process that has been made much simpler today than it was in the past . . .). Shepardization would of course have revealed that the "precedent" no longer quailified as such.
>
> *Gosnell v. Rentokil, Inc.*, 175 F.R.D. 508, 510 n.1 (N.D. Ill. 1997).

The researcher uses the citator to verify the status of a case and update it. For many years citators have been published by Shepard's Company; Frank Shepard founded the company in 1873 in Illinois. The company publishes a separate set of citators for each jurisdiction. Shepard's citators are sets of indexes that enable you to look up cases, statutes, administrative regulations, and some secondary sources to discover if they have been cited. Thus the citator allows the researcher to verify the status of primary sources and ascertain whether and where sources were cited. A statute or administrative regulation may no longer be good law for a number of reasons; it may have been amended, repealed, or held to be unconstitutional.

Shepard's citators have been such an indispensable tool to the researcher for so long that the process of case verification and updating is commonly referred to as "Shepardizing." Recently, attorneys began to talk of "KeyCiting," to verify and update primary sources. KeyCite is the on-line citator introduced into Westlaw several years ago and became the exclusive citator on Westlaw in June 1999. The explanation of citators in this chapter will be limited to the procedure used for cases and statutes. Once you understand the procedure for those sources, the same procedure can be used for other materials. Shepard's is also available on-line on Lexis, as is KeyCite on Westlaw. KeyCite is discussed later in this chapter.

The scheme of the citator is quite simple. The citator lists each instance in which the case being Shepardized has been cited, with the information given as citations to the pages on which the case being Shepardized is cited. For example, imagine a case was later decided by a higher court in a published opinion and, in addition, the case was cited twice, once in another published opinion and once in a law review article. Shepardizing would yield three citations; one citation is to the higher court opinion, one is to the other case, and the third is to the law review article. The citations found by Shepardizing yield the page on which the Shepardized case was cited, which may not necessarily be the first page of the source.

The citator has two primary uses. It is used to determine the current status of a case, whether the case is still authoritative. The citator is also used as a case finding tool. You may have found an older case that is of interest because it contains facts and issues similar to those in the problem you are researching. If newer cases with similar facts and issues cited the case you are Shepardizing, Shepardizing will enable you to locate those cases.

The following are three important sets of Shepard's citators:

1. Shepard's United States Citations—used to Shepardize decisions of the United States Supreme Court in *United States Reports, Supreme Court Reporter*, and *United States Supreme Court Reports, Lawyers' Edition;*
2. Shepard's Federal Citations—used to Shepardize decisions of the United States district court and the United States courts of appeals; and
3. The appropriate state or regional Shepard's Citations—used to Shepardize decisions of the state courts in your state.

In the following case, the court expressed its irritation that neither counsel had Shepardized properly.

We believe a few more words are in order. We are distressed that neither appellant's counsel nor appellee's counsel favored us or the trial court with citation to any of the cases referred to in our opinion, which are completely dispositive of the issue presented. Worse, the appellee's counsel informs us in his brief that "[i]n a strikingly similar case, this court affirmed the trial court dismissal of a complaint where the Plaintiff, as in the case at bar, failed to deliver the process for service upon a defendant for 14 months after filing the Complaint."

By shepardizing the *Gonzalez* case, one would have been alerted that its soundness or reasoning had been questioned in a later case; and by reading that later case, *Rivera v. A.M.I.F., Inc.*, one would have discovered that *Gonzalez* is no longer the law.

If counsel did not observe Shepard's "questioned" signal (designated by a "q") and read *Rivera*, then they, at the least, performed inadequately: appellant's counsel (now the beneficiary of this court's own research) lost the opportunity to argue the controlling *Rivera* case; appellee's counsel, the opportunity to attempt to convince this court why we should not, as we do, find *Rivera* dispositive. [FN2] Without belaboring the point, we remind the bar that, as this case so dramatically shows, cases must be shepardized and that when shepardizing, counsel must mind the "p's" and "q's." [FN3]

FN2. If either counsel discovered but intentionally failed to disclose *Rivera*, the implications would be far more severe: appellant's counsel would be guilty of gross incompetence for failing to call our attention to an obviously controlling case; appellee's counsel would be in apparent violation of the Florida Bar Code of Professional Responsibility, D.R. 7-106(B)(1), which mandates that a lawyer disclose to a tribunal "[l]egal authority in the controlling jurisdiction known to him to be directly adverse to the position of his client and which is not disclosed by opposing counsel."

FN3. A "p" in Shepard's denotes "parallel" and refers to cases "substantially alike or on all fours with cited case in its law or facts." A "q" denotes "questioned" and refers to cases which question the "[s]oundness of decision or reasoning in cited cases . . . ."

Glassalum Engineering Corp. v. 392208 Ontario, Ltd., 487 So.2d 87, 88 (Fla. Dist. Ct. App. 1986).

The Shepard's sample pages contained in figures 6-1 through 6-12 are ones you would find if you were to Shepardize *United States v. McKinnon* and *Wyoming v. Houghton.* Shepardizing tells you the location of every subsequent citation to *United States v. McKinnon* and *Wyoming v. Houghton.* As explained below, Shepardizing even allows you to locate subsequent cases discussing the same legal principle contained in particular headnotes from *United States v. McKinnon* and *Wyoming v. Houghton.*

In the following cases, attorneys failed to discover relevant information through Shepardizing.

Defendant relies heavily upon *Matter of the Estate of Potts* (1925). Plaintiff's attorneys erroneously argue in their brief that Potts "has not been cited by any New York State court since 1940 (Search of Lexis and Shepards)." The Court must point to counsel's contention as a grievous error. *Potts* has been cited at least fifty times!

Mar Oil, S.A. v. Morrissey, 782 F.Supp. 899, 910 (S.D.N.Y. 1992)(citation omitted), *vacated on other grounds*, 982 F.2d 830 (2d Cir. 1993).

The record does not disclose that counsel for either party called *Wright*, *Evers*, and *Elliott* to the attention of the district court. These cases can be found quite readily by checking Shepard's citations starting with Parker, which Prudential claimed was the controlling case. Connelly's counsel, nevertheless, relied on the rationale of these cases.

Connelly v. Prudential Insurance Company, 610 F.2d 1215, 1220 n.3 (4th Cir. 1979).

FIGURE 6-1 Table of Abbreviations from a Shepard's volume.

ABBREVIATIONS

A2d—Atlantic Reporter, Second Series
ADC—Appeal Cases, District of Columbia Reports
AkA—Arkansas Appellate Reports
AL^{5}—American Law Reports, Fifth Series
ARF—American Law Reports, Federal
Ark—Arkansas Reports
Az—Arizona Reports
Bankr LX—United States Bankruptcy Court & United States District Court Bankruptcy Cases Lexis
BRW—Bankruptcy Reporter (West)
CAAF LX—U.S. Court of Appeals for the Armed Forces Lexis
C4th—California Supreme Court Reports, Fourth Series
CA4th—California Appellate Reports, Fourth Series
CA4S—California Appellate Reports, Fourth Series, Supplement
CaL—California Law Review
CaR2d—California Reporter, Second Series
CCA LX—U.S. Military Courts of Criminal Appeals Lexis
ChL—University of Chicago Law Review
CIT—United States Court of International Trade
CLA—University of California at Los Angeles Law Review
Cor—Cornell Law Review
CR—Columbia Law Review
CS—Connecticut Supplement
Ct—Connecticut Reports
CtA—Connecticut Appellate Reports
DC4d—Pennsylvania District and County Reports, Fourth Series
DPR—Decisiones de Puerto Rico
F2d—Federal Reporter, Second Series
F3d—Federal Reporter, Third Series
FCCR—Federal Communications Commission Record
FedCl—Federal Claims Reporter
FRD—Federal Rules Decisions
FS—Federal Supplement
FS2d—Federal Supplement, Second Series
Ga—Georgia Reports
GaA—Georgia Appeals Reports
Geo—Georgetown Law Journal
Haw—Hawaii Reports
HLR—Harvard Law Review
Ida—Idaho Reports
Il2d—Illinois Supreme Court Reports Second Series
IlA—Illinois Appellate Court Reports, Third Series
IlCCl—Illinois Court of Claims Reports
IlLR—University of Illinois Law Review
JTS—Jurisprudencia del Tribunal Supremo de Puerto Rico
KA2d—Kansas Court of Appeals Reports, Second Series
Kan—Kansas Reports
LCP—Law and Contemporary Problems
LE2—United States Supreme Court Reports, Lawyers' Edition, Second Series
MaA—Massachusetts Appeals Court Reports
MADR—Massachusetts Appellate Division Reports
Mas—Massachusetts Reports
MC—American Maritime Cases
McA—Michigan Court of Appeals Reports
Mch—Michigan Reports
McL—Michigan Law Review
Md—Maryland Reports
MdA—Maryland Appellate Reports
MJ—Military Justice Reporter
MnL—Minnesota Law Review
Mt—Montana Reports
NC—North Carolina Reports
NCA—North Carolina Court of Appeals Reports
NE2—Northeastern Reporter, Second Series
Neb—Nebraska Reports
Nev—Nevada Reports
NH—New Hampshire Reports
NJ—New Jersey Reports
NJS—New Jersey Superior Court Reports
NJT—New Jersey Tax Court Reports
NM—New Mexico Reports
NW2—Northwestern Reporter, Second Series
NwL—Northwestern University Law Review
NY2d—New York Court of Appeals Reports, Second
NYA2d—New York Appellate Division Reports, Second Series
NYL—New York University Law Review
NYM2d—New York Miscellaneous Reports, Second Series
NYS2d—New York Supplement, Second Series
OA3d—Ohio Appellate Reports, Third Series
OhM2d—Ohio Miscellaneous Reports, Second Series
OrA—Oregon Court of Appeals Reports
Ore—Oregon Reports
OS3d—Ohio State Reports, Third Series
P2d—Pacific Reporter, Second Series
Pa—Pennsylvania State Reports
PaC—Pennsylvania Commonwealth Court Reports
PaL—University of Pennsylvania Law Review
PaS—Pennsylvania Superior Court Reports
PQ2d—United States Patents Quarterly, Second Series
SC—Supreme Court Reporter
SE2—Southeastern Reporter, Second Series
So2d—Southern Reporter, Second Series
SoC—South Carolina Reports

StnL—Stanford Law Review	USDist LX—United States District Court Lexis
SW—Southwestern Reporter, Second Series	US LX—United States Supreme Court Lexis
TCM—Tax Court Memorandum Decisions	Va—Virginia Reports
TCt—Tax Court of the United States Reports; United States Tax Court Reports	VaA—Virginia Court of Appeals Reports
TPR—Official Translations of the Opinions of the Supreme Court of Puerto Rico	VaL—Virginia Law Review
TxL—Texas Law Review	VCO—Virginia Circuit Court Opinions
UCR2d—Uniform Commercial Code Reporting Service, Second Series	Vt—Vermont Reports
US—United States Reports	WAp—Washington Appellate Reports
USApp LX—United States Court of Appeals Lexis	Wis2d—Wisconsin Reports, Second Series
USClaims LX—United States Court of Federal Claims Lexis	WLR—Wisconsin Law Review
	Wsh2d—Washington Reports, Second Series
	WV—West Virginia Reports
	YLJ—Yale Law Journal

FIGURE 6-1 (continued)

SHEPARDIZING PROCEDURE

Although some students find the Shepardizing procedure difficult at first, you will gain confidence in your ability to Shepardize as you do it a few times. Sample pages from *Shepard's Federal Citations* have been reprinted for you in figures 6-1 through 6-9. These are the pages you would find if you were to Shepardize *United States v. McKinnon*, 985 F.2d 525 (11th Cir. 1993). In addition, sample pages from *Shepard's United States Citations* have been reprinted for you in figures 6-10 through 6-12. These are the pages you would find if you were to Shepardize *Wyoming v. Houghton*, 119 S. Ct. 1297 (1999).

The explanation of the Shepardizing procedure is designed to walk you through Shepardizing the two cases step by step. You will probably find yourself reading the procedure several times before you understand the concept. First, read the procedure step by step as you follow along, looking at the sample pages. Then read the procedure again by itself and test yourself by "Shepardizing" *McKinnon* and *Houghton* using the sample pages. After you have mastered the procedure, follow up by doing some of the Shepardizing exercises at the end of this chapter.

Getting organized

The first thing to do is get organized. If you do not Shepardize systematically, you may miss something. You must locate the correct set of Shepard's to use and be ready to record the results of your Shepardizing. The Shepard's set you will need is customarily located near the reporters containing cases Shepardized in that Shepard's set. The citators used to Shepardize United States Supreme Court decisions is called *Shepard's United States Citations. Shepard's United States Citations* is subdivided into *United States Citations: United States Reports, United States Citations: Supreme Court Reporter, United States Citations: United States Supreme Court Reports, Lawyers' Edition.* The Shepard's for *Federal Reporter* and *Federal Supplement* is called *Shepard's Federal Citations.* There are Shepard's for all the regional reporters as well. The Shepard's for *Southern Reporter* is *Shepard's Southern Citations.* Shepard's even publishes a Shepard's allowing you to Shepardize the cases from only one state, even though the state cases are printed in a regional reporter. For example, *Southern Reporter* contains cases from Louisiana, Mississippi, Alabama, and Florida. *Shepard's Southern Citations* allows you to Shepardize case from all four states, but *Shepard's Florida Citations* limits you to Shepardizing Florida cases. Some libraries carry the state-specific Shepard's rather than the Shepard's for the regional reporter because that is all that is usually needed for that state.

Once you find the correct Shepard's set, line up the volumes you will need to use. The set usually contains burgundy-colored hardbound volumes. It may also contain gold, red, and blue paperbound volumes. Take, for example, the front cover from the June 15, 1999, issue of *Shepard's Federal Citations* Part 1. Part 1 contains information on *Federal Reporter;* because Part 2

FIGURE 6-2 Table of Case Abbreviations from a Shepard's Volume.

HISTORY AND TREATMENT LETTERS

Abbreviations have been assigned, where applicable, to each citing case to indicate the effect the citing case had on the case you are Shepardizing. The resulting "history" (affirmed, reversed, modified, etc.) or "treatment" (followed, criticized, explained, etc.) of the case you are Shepardizing is indicated by abbreviations preceding the citing case reference. For example, the reference "f) 434F2d872" means that there is language on page 872 of volume 434 of the Federal Reporter, Second Series, that indicates the court is "following" the case you are Shepardizing. The abbreviations used to reflect both history and treatment are as follows.

History of Case

a (affirmed)	The decision in the case you are Shepardizing was affirmed or adhered to on appeal.
cc (connected case)	Identifies a different case from the case you are Shepardizing, but one arising out of the same subject matter or in some manner intimately connected therewith.
D (dismissed)	An appeal from the case you are Shepardizing was dismissed.
m (modified)	The decision in the case you are Shepardizing was changed in some way.
p (parallel)	The citing case is substantially alike or on all fours, either in law or facts, with the case you are Shepardizing.
r (reversed)	The decision in the case you are Shepardizing was reversed on appeal.
s (same case)	The case you are Shepardizing involves the same litigation as the citing case, although at a different stage in the proceedings.
S (superseded)	The citing case decision has been substituted for the decision in the case you are Shepardizing.
US cert den	Certiorari was denied by the U.S. Supreme Court
US cert dis	Certiorari was dismissed by the U.S. Supreme Court
US cert gran	Certiorari was granted by the U.S. Supreme Court
US reh den	Rehearing was denied by the U.S. Supreme Court.
US reh dis	Rehearing was dismissed by the U.S. Supreme Court.
v (vacated)	The decision in the case you are Shepardizing has been vacated.
W (withdrawn)	The decision in the case you are Shepardizing has been withdrawn.

Treatment of Case

c (criticized)	The citing case disagrees with the reasoning/decision of the case you are Shepardizing.
d (distinguished)	The citing case is different either in law or fact, for reasons given, from the case you are Shepardizing.
e (explained)	The case you are Shepardizing is interpreted in some significant way. Not merely a restatement of facts.
Ex (Examiner's decision)	The case you are Shepardizing was cited in an Administrative Agency Examiner's Decision.
f (followed)	The citing case refers to the case you are Shepardizing as controlling authority
h (harmonized)	An apparent inconsistency between the citing case and the case you are Shepardizing is explained and shown not to exist.
j (dissenting opinion)	The case you are Shepardizing is cited in a dissenting opinion.
L (limited)	The citing case refuses to extend the holding of the case you are Shepardizing beyond the precise issues involved.
o (overruled)	The ruling in the case you are Shepardizing is expressly overruled.
q (questioned)	The citing case questions the continuing validity or precedential value of the case you are Shepardizing.

Other

#	Citing references may be of questionable precedential value as review was granted by California Supreme Court or case was ordered not published.

FEDERAL REPORTER, 2d SERIES VOL. 985

Calif
22 CA4th1803
28 CA4th142
29 CA4th789
28 CaR2d805
34 CaR2d858
Fla
640 So2d88
Ga
211 GaA527
440 SE42
450 SE676
Kan
f 886 P2d876
f 886 P2d882
La
640 So2d367
Mich
201 McA235
505 NW902
NJ
267 NJS46
630 A2d811
NY
f 616 NYS2d540
Ohio
69 OS3d547
634 NE1003

—520—
United States v
Lopez
1993
Cir. 11
995 F2d 1025
17F3d 1385
W Va
190 WV325
438 SE505

—525—
United States v
McKinnon
1993
Cir. 4
22F3d559
Cir. 8
f 22F3d801
Cir. 11
34F3d[1]994
43F3d[2]1441
Fla
641 So2d852
Ore
129 OrA235
878 P2d1132

—528—
Davis v Shalala
1992

—535—
United States
v Kirkland
1993
Cir. 1
991F2d[3]912
Cir. 11
990F2d[2]1182
991F2d[1]732
991F2d[2]732
995 F2d[2]1025
2F3d[2]1110
2F3d[3]1110
30F3d[2]1458

—538—
Yeck v
Goodwin
1993
cc 174 GaA710
cc 331 SE76
Cir. 11
12F3d[2]1017
14F3d[2]561
24F3d[2]1304
24F3d[4]1306
36F3d1056
853FS[5]1523

—543—
Seaman v
Arvida
Realty Sales
1993
s 993F2d1556
Cir. 1
852FS[5]100
Cir. 7
869FS[2]1384
c 869FS1387
869FS[7]1390
Cir. 11
f 990F2d[6]1222
990F2d[5]1223
3F3d[5]1491

—547—
Barton v
Department
of Justice
1993

—549—
Harris v Office
of Personnel
Management
1993

—552—
Case 10
United States v
Nazzaro
1993
s 778FS1

—553—
Case 7
DeLong v
Thompson
1993
s 790FS594

—554—
Case 1
Cir. 4
845FS1129
845FS1132

—555—
Case 1
Hawkins
v Collins
1993
s 980F2d975

—555—
Case 2
McDermott
Inc. v
Clyde Iron
1993
s 979F2d1068
s 19UCR2d465
Cir. 11
172BRW412

—555—
Case 3
Parker &
Parsley
Petroleum
Co. v Dresser
Indus.
1993
s 972F2d580

—555—
Case 4
United States
v Crow
1993
s 981 F2d180

—555—
Case 5
Zapata Haynie
Corp. v Arthur
1993
s 980F2d287

—557—
Case 21
International
Bros. v
Quantum
Chem.
1993
s 806FS131

—559—
Case 15
Coleman
v Wirtz
1993
s 745FS434

—560—
Case 8
Hengesback v
Green River
Regional
Mental
Health/Mental
Retardation
Board Inc.
1993
s 753FS216

—563—
Case 20
United States
v LeBeau
1993
s 786FS761

—563—
Case 23
United States
v Watts
1993

—564—
Case 4
White v
Caterpillar Inc.
1991
s 765FS1418

—564—
Case 6
Gaines v
Nelson
1991
s 121BRW1015

—564—
Case 9
United States
v Lewis
1991
s 767FS1008

—564—
Case 12
Caleshu v
Merrill Lynch
Pierce Fenner
& Smith Inc.
1991
s 737FS1070
Cir. 8
835FS507

—565—
Case 9
Farmers &
Merchants v
Mid-Century
Insurance Co.
1991
s 752FS890

—565—
Case 20
Insurance Co.
of North
America v
Coast
Catamaran
Corp.
1991
s 753FS804

—565—
Case 30
Rally's v
International
Shortstop Inc.
1991
s 776FS451

—565—
Case 32
Kehr v
Aronowitz
1991
s 750FS400

—566—
Case 12
Sherpell v
Humnoke
1991
s 750FS971

—566—
Case 38
Roach v
Sullivan
1991
s 758FS1301

—567—
Case 11
Jaramillo v
Burkhart
1991
s 999F2d1241

—569—
Case 10
Henry v
Department
of Navy
1992
s 755FS1442

—569—
Case 38
Cheatham
v Indrie
1992
s 783FS1174

—574—
Case 12
Smith v Hurd
1993
s 699FS1433

—574—
Case 17
Tobkin v
Waltrip
1993
s 139BRW492

—575—
Case 5
United States
v Clark
1993
s 24F3d250

FIGURE 6-3 Page from a 1995 Bound Volume of *Shepard's Federal Citations.*

FIGURE 6-4 Page from a 1995–1996 Bound Volume of *Shepard's Federal Citations.*

FEDERAL REPORTER, 2d SERIES VOL. 985

—417—
Domino Group Inc. v Charlie Parker Memorial Foundation
1993
Cir. 7
56F3d[4]845
Cir. 8
881FS1419
881FS[4]1420
—421—
Woodyard v Hoover Group Inc.
1993
Cir. 8
62F3d[5]1114
—426—
Moutray v Butts
1993
US cert den
in 126LE38
in 114SC69
Cir. 8
50F3d534
—427—
United States v Cox
1993
Cir. 9
59F3d920
Cir. 10
Dk10 93-3372 [4
—434—
White v McDonnell Douglas Corp.
1993
Cir. 8
55F3d[6]1371
873FS[1]1333
873FS[2]1334
874FS[3]1580
875FS[1]573
875FS[2]573
875FS[3]573
875FS[4]574
877FS[1]1325
881FS[1]1336
881FS[2]1336
881FS[1]1362
881FS[2]1362
884FS[1]1300
884FS[2]1300
93McL2299
—437—
Wood v Omaha Sch. Dist.
1993
Cir. 1
882FS[4]1181
Cir. 8
47F3d[3]971
NY
84 NY706
646 NE442
622 NYS2d [221
—440—
Prior v United States Postal Service
1993
Tenn
891 SW591
—443—
United States v Sweet
1993
Cir. 8
56F3d[4]958
f 64F3d371
—446—
Standard Fire Insurance Co. v Peoples Church of Fresno
1993
Cir. 9
70F3d527
Calif
11 C4th26
34 CA4th [1188
f 34 CA4th [1192
40 CaR2d813
f 40 CaR2d815
44 CaR2d383
900 P2d632
—451—
Sayles Hydro Assoc. v Maughan
1993
j 128LE743
j 114SC1921
—456—
Palmer v Estelle
1993
US cert den
in 125LE735
in 113SC3051
Cir. 9
63F3d[3]814
881FS1426
f 881FS[3]1428
f 881FS[4]1428
88 1FS[5]1429
—459—
Empire Blue Cross and Blue Shield v Janet Greeson's A Place for Us Inc.
1993
NY
647 NE1315
—466—
United States v Foster
1993
Cir. 9
48F3d[5]1543
48F3d[6]1543
50F3d693
50F3d[1]694
62F3d[6]1194
62F3d[8]1194
884FS1448
83CaL494
—470—
Estate of Reynolds v Martin
1993
j 128LE290
j 114SC1520
Cir. 9
66F3d240
874FS1107
884FS1365
884FS[1]1366
887FS1314
—483—
United States v Canterbury
1993
Cir. 7
d 47F3d[4]907
Cir. 10
52F3d[2]889
52F3d[3]889
—487—
Exline v Gunter
1993
Cir. 4
57F3d1316
DC
651 A2d819
—491—
United States v Vasquez
1993
Cir. 5
63 F3d[1]1364
Cir. 10
Dk10 94-4227 [2
54F3d[9]1536
56F3d[10]1222
f 60F3d1481
60F3d[5]1481
60F3d[6]1481
60F3d[7]1481
69F3d[1]1066
69F3d[2]1066
69F3d[4]1066
69F3d[5]1066
—497—
United States v Evans
1993
US cert den
in 124LE690
in 113SC2942
Cir. 10
53F3d1143
—503—
Jones v New York Life & Annuity Corp.
1993
s 61F3d799
—510—
In re United States
1993
US cert den
in 126LE447
in 114SC545
Cir. 1
54F3d20
54F3d[1]21
Cir. 5
f 58F3d1060
—513—
Gulfside Distributors Inc. v Becco Ltd.
1993
Cir. 11
882FS[2]1032
—516—
Papas v Upjohn Co.
1993
US cert den
in 126LE248
in 114SC300
s 120LE892
s 112SC3020
Cir. 2
884FS[3]99
Cir. 4
47F3d[3]128
871FS[2]839
Cir. 5
880FS479
Cir. 7
887FS1106
Cir. 9
f 54F3d[2]560
f 54F3d[3]561
54F3d[5]563
Cir. 11
f 56F3d1343
Calif
32 CA4th606
33 CA4th823
38 CaR2d261
Ga
264 Ga738
Ill
f 271 IlA849
f 649 NE497
Iowa
f 534 NW387
Kan
f 256 Kan611
La
653 So2d199
Mass
f 421 Mas461
NY
f 204 NYAD11
f 205 NYAD [171
f 618 NYS2d [141
Tex
j 889 SW255
898 SW820
Wash
127 Wsh2d12
f 127 Wsh2d14
f 127 Wsh2d56
f 127 Wsh2d84
f 896 P2d677
f 896 P2d691
896 P2d702
f 896 P2d703
—525—
United States v McKinnon
1993
US cert den
in 126LE94
in 114SC130
Cir. 11
62F3d[1]1355
Colo
f 888 P2d351
SD
f 535 NW850
—538—
Yeck v Goodwin
1993
Cir. 11
52F3d926
—543—
Seaman v Arvida Realty Sales
1993
US cert den
in 126LE255
in 114SC308
Cir. 7
f Dk7 95-2159
Cir. 11
881FS[5]1575
—553—
Case 8
US cert den
in 126LE43
in 114SC74
—554—
Case 20
US cert den
in 126LE28
in 114SC59
—555—
Case 2
McDermott Inc. v Clyde Iron
1993
s 126LE246
s 114SC298
—556—
Case 3
US cert den
Continued

VOL. 985 FEDERAL REPORTER, 2d SERIES

—427—
United States v
Cox
1993
Cir. 10
72F3d[4]1478
—434—
White v
McDonnell
Douglas Corp.
1993
Cir. 8
97F3d[2]271
902FS[1]894
902FS[2]894
910FS[1]1419
910FS[2]1419
910FS[4]1421
—437—
Wood v
Omaha Sch.
Dist.
1993
Ohio
76OS3d176
666NE1385
—443—
United States v
Sweet
1993
Cir. 4
75F3d[3]947
Cir. 8
90F3d[4]300
96F3d334
—451—
Sayles Hydro
Assoc. v
Maughan
1993
Cir. 7
910FS[5]1381
f) 910FS[5]1382
Cir. 9
77F3d299
103F3d[1]746
f) 103F3d747
—456—
Palmer v
Estelle
1993
Cir. 9
932FS[2]1580

—459—
Empire Blue
Cross and Blue
Shield v Janet
Greeson's A
Place for Us
Inc.
1993
NY
85NY206
623NYS2d807
—463—
United States v
Donine
1993
Cir. 9
e) 80F3d401
—470—
Estate of
Reynolds v
Martin
1993
Cir. DC
78F3d653
D C
316ADC292
—478—
United States v
Brown
1993
Cir. 7
89F3d474
Cir. 9
103F3d70
106F3d1488
—483—
United States v
Canterbury
1993
Cir. 10
87F3d[2]1135
107F3d[2]826
107F3d[3]826
—491—
United States v
Vasquez
1993
Cir. 10
80F3d[1]1485
82F3d[1]976
82F3d[1]985
98F3d[7]530
948FS[10]1504
202BRW517

—497—
United States v
Evans
1993
Cir. 10
76F3d1153
100F3d[1]884
—500—
United States v
Ward
1993
Cir. 9
82F3d[1]893
Cir. 10
f) 81F3d[1]1007
f) 946FS[5]918
—510—
In re United
States
1993
Cir. DC
c) 100F3d1017
D C
c) 321ADC403
—513—
Gulfside
Distributors
Inc. v Becco
Ltd.
1993
Cir. 11
f) 917FS793
917FS[2]793
—516—
Papas v
Upjohn Co.
1993
Cir. 1
96F3d563
Cir. 5
909FS433
Cir. 6
926FS629
926FS[1]630
Cir. 7
f) 79F3d[2]628
f) 913FS[1]1240
f) 913FS[4]1241
913FS[5]1242
d) 927FS[4]295
Cir. 8
903FS[3]1283
f) 903FS1284
Cir. 11
922FS615
c) 26UCR2d92
f) 26UCR2d336
f) 26UCR2d740
f) 28UCR2d522
28UCR2d828
f) 28UCR2d
[1176

30UCR2d773
Calif
d) 53CA4th1389
d) 62CaR2d379
Ill
f) 169Il2d340
e) 278IlA780
f) 662NE405
662NE412
e) 663NE510
Ind
665NE598
La
666So2d620
Mass
f) 657NE1266
NJ
294NJS63
682A2d729
NY
e) 212NYAE
[136
e) 629NYS2d
[573
642NYS2d765
SD
542NW771
Tenn
922SW524
—525—
United States v
McKinnon
1993
Cir. 8
928FS[2]1483
Ga
475SE584
480SE589
Tenn
929SW383
—535—
United States v
Kirkland
1993
Cir. 7
77F3d 1549
—543—
Seaman v
Arvida Realty
Sales
1993
s) 910FS581
Cir. 5
934FS[5]232
Cir. 6
76F3d1412
Cir. 7
f) 71F3d257
940FS193
Cir. 8
936FS[5]1527
Cir. 9
80F3d[4]351

Cir. 11
932FS[2]1378
—561—
Case 3
Phillips v
United States
1993
US cert den
116SC135
s) 133LE507
s) 116SC585
—561—
Case 22
Stockenauer v
Deleeuw
1993
s) 133LE438
s) 116SC533
—562—
Case 20
United States v
Zack
1993
cc) 915FS913
—577—
Case 16
Washington
Public Power
Supply Sys. v
Pittsburgh-Des
Moines Corp.
1993
s) 72F3d136
—589—
Burlington
Northern
Railroad Co. v
Interstate
Commerce
Commission
1992
Cir. DC
89F3d882
91F3d[1]180
D C
319ADC241
319ADC[1]376
—604—
Forward v
Thorogood
1993
Cir. 1
943FS116
Cir. 2
940FS91

—612—
United States v
Savoie
1993
Cir. 1
70F3d[3]682
70F3d[4]683
70F3d[11]1411
75F3d20
75F3d[11]23
80F3d[15]22
80F3d[16]22
80F3d[12]28
f) 83F3d[19]16
87F3d[4]578
91F3d[8]277
96F3d532
99F3d[4]44
100F3d[11]1033
105F3d[4]777
901FS[11]31
Cir. 6
70F3d863
—621—
United States v
Portalla
1993
Cir. 1
82F3d532
906FS53
918FS41
—625—
Serrano-Perez
v FMC Corp.
1993
Cir. 1
95F3d[5]91
933FS128
—634—
United States v
Williams
1993
Vt
667A2d56
—640—
Newport Plaza
Associates L.P.
v Durfee
Attleboro Bank
1993
Cir. 1
915FS495
26UCR2d1213
—649—
PH Group Ltd
v Birch
1993
Cir. 1
82F3d[4]1189

FIGURE 6-5 Page from a 1996–1997 Bound Volume of *Shepard's Federal Citations.*

FIGURE 6-6 Page from a 1997–1998 Bound Volume of *Shepard's Federal Citations.*

VOL. 985 FEDERAL REPORTER, 2d SERIES

—323—
Brotherhood Shipping Company Ltd. v St. Paul Fire & Marine Insurance Co.
1993
Cir. 6
114F3d565

—330—
Tobey v Extel-JWP Inc.
1993
Cir. 6
212BRW[2]583
Cir. 7
137F3d952
977FS873
Colo
f) 956P2d554

—334—
Edwards v Sullivan
1993
Cir. 7
138F3d[1]1152
138F3d[4]1155
976FS756
977FS[3]871

—341—
United States v Campbell
1993
Cir. 7
127F3d[15]615
128F3d611
129F3d[14]913
129F3d[15]914

—348—
United States v Wilson
1993
Ohio
80OS3d606
687NE735

—354—
Lemons v Skidmore
1993
Cir. 2
118F3d[3]103
Cir. 7
125F3d[3]502
125F3d[5]502
125F3d[6]502
137F3d950
Colo
937P2d835

—360—
Kale v Obuchowski
1993
Cir. 2
128F3d[1]72
Cir. 7
138F3d[2]1225

—364—
Kristufek v Hussmann Foodservice Co.
1993
513US[3]356
Cir. 2
975FS465
Cir. 7
957FS1485
Cir. 8
980FS1310
Tex
949SW311

—379—
Frierdich v United States
1993
Cir. 7
976FS[1]783

—383—
Bowman v Western Auto Supply Co.
1993
Cir. 2
958FS[1]798
Cir. 5
130F3d152
Cir. 8
112F3d1354

—395—
United States v Womack
1993
US cert den
510US902

—401—
Pickner v Sullivan
1993
Cir. 8
970FS1455
976FS1246
978FS[4]1245
981FS1265
983FS[1]1267
985FS923

—406—
Boushel v Toro Co.
1993
Cir. 3
138F3d[4]515
Cir. 8
983FS824

—415—
IBEW Local 4 v KTVI-TV Inc.
1993
Cir. 8
133F3d668
Mo
962SW911

—417—
Domino Group Inc. v Charlie Parker Memorial Foundation
1993
Minn
f) 568NW869

—427—
United States v Cox
1993
Cir. 2
111F3d329

—443—
United States v Sweet
1993
81MnL340

—446—
Standard Fire Insurance Co. v Peoples Church of Fresno
1993
NC
c) 346NC746
c) 488SE238

—451—
Sayles Hydro Assoc. v Maughan
1993
j) 511US737
Cir. 9
125F3d1309

—456—
Palmer v Estelle
1993
Cir. 9
121F3d[3]1254

—459—
Empire Blue Cross and Blue Shield v Janet Greeson's A Place for Us Inc.
1993
Cir. 6
d) 119F3d398
119F3d[1]398
NY
238NYAD156
656NYS2d204

—466—
United States v Foster
1993
Cir. 9
136F3d652

—470—
Estate of Reynolds v Martin
1993
j) 511US315
Cir. 2
958FS917
Cir. 9
j) 114F3d1504
138ARF27n

—478—
United States v Brown
1993
Cir. 9
132F3d1315
Cir. 10
122F3d[5]1306

—483—
United States v Canterbury
1993
Calif
c) 62CA4th1093
c) 73CaR2d208

—491—
United States v Vasquez
1993
Cir. 8
120F3d[7]120

Cir. 10
137F3d[1]1187

—497—
United States v Evans
1993
Cir. 10
f) 115F3d781

—510—
In re United States
1993
Cir. 11
175FRD[4]348
Cir. DC
139F3d251
CIT
d) 958FS[4]634

—513—
Gulfside Distributors Inc. v Becco Ltd.
1993
Cir. 6
d) 964FS1163

—516—
Papas v Upjohn Co.
1993
US cert den
510US913
Cir. 3
965FS[1]570
Cir. 4
976FS397
Cir. 5
956FS31313
969FS403
Cir. 6
f) 984FS3592
Cir. 7
f) 131F3d[3]662
e) 131F3d663
Cir.11
956FS962
956FS[4]963
974FS[1]1470
974FS[3]1470
974FS[4]1470
32UCR2d109
34UCR2d326
Ariz
189Az48
938P2d97
Haw
f) 86Haw233
e) 86Haw237
f) 948P2d1074
e) 948P2d1078

Nebr
f) 252Neb279
f) 561NW577
NY
169NYM1452
Pa
705A2d850
d) 705A2d854
Wash
86WAp804
938P2d369

—520—
United States v Lopez
1993
Cir. 11
123F3d[3]1397

—525—
United States v McKinnon
1993
Fla
706So2d417
Ga
267Ga106
267Ga551
227GaA674
490SE204

—528—
Davis v Shalala
1992
Cir. 10
132F3d1353

—535—
United States v Kirkland
1993
Cir. 4
132F3d[3]1042
Cir. 11
123F3d[1]1403
123F3d[2]1403
129F3d[2]1438

—543—
Seaman v Arvida Realty Sales
1993
US cert den
510US916
137LE768
117SC1515
Cir. 5
f) 971FS1075
Cir. 10
121F3d570
Cir. 11
129F3d[1]559
961FS[3]264
961FS[5]265

FIGURE 6-7 Page from the February 1, 1999, Gold Cumulative Supplement to *Shepard's Federal Citations.*

VOL. 985 FEDERAL REPORTER, 2d SERIES

—261—
Cir. 6
146F3d[P]397
1998USDist
[LX19378
—271—
Cir. 6
f) 146F3d[10]326
—283—
Cir. 3
1998USDist
[LX17708
Cir. 4
1998USDist
[LX15491
—285—
Cir. 1
13FS2d[P]222
—305—
Cir. 7
1998USDist
[LX12923
997FS1183
—312—
Cir. 7
1998USDist
[LX14438
f) 1998USDist
[LX18728
6FS2d[P]925
21FS2d890
Cir. 11
5FS2d[P]1304
—318—
Cir. 4
220BRW[3]267
Cir. 7
180FRD352
223BRW[4]139
223BRW[4]157
—323—
Cir. 7
d) 144F3d468
—330—
Cir. 2
1998USDist
[LX14867
Cir. 7
1998USDist
[LX15814
1998USDist
[LX16839
1998USDist
[LX17820
1998USDist
[LX17856
1998USDist
[LX18161
990FS[2]1002

8FS2d[P]1079
16FS2d[P]938
—334—
Cir. 7
1998USDist
[LX15758
—341—
Cir.7
142F3d1019
—348—
d) 48MJ759
—354—
Cir. 10
2FS2d[P]1412
—360—
Cir. 7
221BRW[1]213
—364—
Cir. 7
1998USDist
[LX14937
f) 991FS[2]953
f) 991FS954
Cir. 10
152F3d1260
—371—
Cir. 3
2FS2d[P]625
—379—
Cir. 2
1998USDist
[LX18866
Cir. 4
7FS2d[P]763
Cir. 10
219BRW[2]613
—383—
Cir. 3
991FS712
Cir. 8
994FS1088
—395—
Cir. 8
141F3d873
—401—
Cir. 8
f) 1998USDist
[LX17191
991FS1103
f) 22FS2d1035
Cir. 9
16FS2d[P]1150
—406—
Cir. 8
988FS[5]1289

f) 988FS[4]1291
—417—
Cir. 7
c) 1998USApp
[LX27990
c) 161F3d427
Cir. 8
146F3d[1]579
—443—
Cir. 10
146F3d[3]818
81MnL340
—451—
Cir. 9
154F3d[3]1031
—470—
Cir. DC
1998USDist
[LX13847
45CLA1441
—478—
Cir. 9
1998USApp
[LX24702
152F3d[2]1095
Cir. 11
998FS1361
—491—
Cir. 10
1998USApp
[LX24848
1998USApp
[LX24849
1998USApp
[LX25780
148F3d[1]1192
149F3d[1]1105
153F3d[1]1126
154F3d[10]1239
1998Bankr LX
[1302
—503—
Cir. 10
12FS2d[P]1239
—510—
Cir. 11
1998USDist
[LX15370
179FRD[P]646
—516—
Calif
c) 65CA4th473
c) 76CaR2d469
Nebr
584NW[2]61
Tenn
970SW[2]474

—525—
Cir. 5
145F3d277
Minn
578NW[2]723
—528—
Cir. 11
14FS2d[P]1312
—535—
Cir. 11
d) 1998USDist
[LX19277
—543—
520US514
Cir. 7
141F3d[7]299
Cir. 10
1998USApp
[LX[P]30971
Cir. 11
998FS[5]1313
—547—
Cir. Fed.
1998USApp
[LX29641
—561—
Case 15
Mich
j) 458Mch133
j) 580NW[2]867
—562—
Case 14
s) 1998USApp
[LX20255
—569—
Case 16
cc) 1998USDist
[LX14946
cc) 20FS2d70
—589—
s) 1998USApp
[LX26584
s) 158F3d1294
Cir. DC
146F3d[3]943
f) 146F3d947
80MnL1423
—604—
Cir. 7
1998USDist
[LX14983
21FS2d896
—607—
Cir. 2
152F3d[1]126

—612—
Cir. 1
f) 141F3d[13]393
152F3d[15]7
152F3d[15]37
153F3d85
—634—
Cir. DC
e) 141F3d1211
—640—
Cir. 1
1998USApp
[LX24863
149F3d33
157F3d2
1998USDist
[LX17256
24FS2d218
—649—
Cir. 4
996FS[2]529
ClCt
41FedCl[P]365
—655—
Cir. 1
140F3d[3]315
1998USDist
[LX18934
Cir. 2
1998USDist
[LX15518
—662—
Cir. 2
13FS2d[P]537
—677—
Cir. 2
10FS2d[P]294
—680—
Cir. 2
995FS[5]320
d) 9FS2d[P]189
10FS2d[P]330
—685—
Cir. 1
1998USDist
[LX17576
Cir. 2
155F3d[3]139
155F3d[4]139
156F3d[11]145
156F3d[12]145
988FS[6]372
—707—
Cir. 3
988FS855
8FS2d[P]417
16FS2d[P]572
1997IILR154

—716—
Cir. 1
4FS2d[5]570
Cir. 7
156F3d[2]793
1997IIL 476
—729—
Cir. 3
1998USDist
[LX18799
—732—
c) 140F3d87
j) 140F3d89
2FS2d624
—736—
Cir. 1
152F3d[6]13
NY
676NYS2d178
676NYS2A620
676NYS2d635
—743—
Cir. 5
1998USApp
[LX272
141F3d139
158F3d[6]858
—749—
Cir. 5
141F3d140
145F3d276
151F3d[13]456
—758—
Cir. 5
1998USApp
[LX[2]30
141F3d[4]571
—770—
Cir. 3
148F3d281
Cir. 10
4FS2dP1327
Cir. DC
1998USApp
[LX299
160F3d[3]740
Iowa
f) 585NW[2]257
e) 585NW[2]258
—783—
Cir. 1
15FS2d153
Cir. 5
1998USDist
[LX1519
22FS2d558
f) 1998MC1806

FIGURE 6-8 Page from the June 1, 1999, Red Cumulative Supplement to *Shepard's Federal Citations.*

VOL. 985 FEDERAL REPORTER, 2d SERIES

—379—
Cir. 2
28FS2d[P]882
Cir. 3
1998USDist
[LX21118
Cir. 9
166F3d[2]1005
1999USDist
[LX4059
—383—
Cir. 4
1999USDist
[LX346
f) 1999USDist
[LX662
36FS2d267
f) 36FS2d279
Cir. 6
f) 1999USDist
[LX4619
Cir. 11
f) 162F3d1098
—391—
Cir. 8
1999USApp
[LX[1]5761
—401—
Cir. 8
1999USDist
[LX5598
1999USDist
[LX5606
f) 22FS2d[P]1053
—417—
Cir. 7
c) 161F3d430
—437—
Cir. 8
1999USApp
[LX[4]3041
j) 165F3d1219
169F3d[4]556
—446—
Cir. 9
1999USApp
[LX3101
—456—
Cir. 6
1999USDist
[LX3584
1999USDist
[LX5059
—478—
Cir. 9
1999USApp
[LX3343

—491—
35UCR2d642
—510—
Cir. Fed
165F3d1371
Cir. DC
329ADC214
—516—
Cir. 2
34FS2d193
Cir. 4
1999USApp
[LX475
Cir. 8
165F3d[5]608
35UCR2d1151
36UCR2d975
Iowa
f) 586NW212
Mo
f) 984SW180
—520—
Mich
232McA278
—535—
Cir. 11
d) 28FS2d[P]1369
—543—
Cir. 10
164F3d[9]1254
—554—
Case 16
cc) 1998USDist
[LX20863
—560—
Cir. 10
1999USDist
[LX4203
—562—
Case 14
s) 1998USApp
[LX36593
—566—
Case 33
US cert den
503US961
—567—
Case 22
US cert den
503US992
—567—
Case 28
US cert den
503US973

—569—
Case 16
cc) 20FS2d70
—589—
s) 158F3d1294
s) 332ADC388
Cir. DC
331ADC[3]2
f) 331ADC6
—604—
Cir. 7
21FS2d[P]903
—612—
Cir. 1
f) 164F3d[13]71
—634—
Cir. DC
e) 329ADC427
—640—
Cir. 1
157F3d5
24FS2d[P]221
36UCR2d856
—649—
Cir. 1
1999USApp
[LX7451
Cir. DC
162F3d1190
—655—
Cir. 1
1999USApp
[LX5219
1999USDist
[LX1657
183FRD338
—666—
j) 119SC1245
—677—
Cir. 2
1999USDist
[LX158
f) 1999USDist
[LX686
—685—
Cir. 1
26FS2d[P]278
Cir. 2
163F3d759
—707—
Cir. 3
f) 1999USDist
[LX5119
Mass
428Mas703
704NE1159

—716—
Cir. 3
163F3d773
—729—
Cir. 3
1999USDist
[LX1142
—732—
Cir. 3
161F3d[2]212
Tex
j) 979SW641
—743—
Cir. 5
1999USApp
[LX[4]5153
158F3d857
158F3d[6]858
—758—
Cir. 5
162F3d[2]836
—762—
Cir. 5
164F3d274
—763—
Cir. 5
f) 1999USApp
[LX7853
j) 1999USApp
[LX7853
—770—
s) 119SC1135
Cir. DC
160F3d[3]740
NM
c) 971P2d1280
—783—
Cir. 5
1999USDist
[LX210
22FS2d[P]563
—789—
Cir. 5
1999USDist
[LX2175
1999USDist
[LX2736
—840—
Cir. 6
29FS2d[P]767
Cir. 7
1999USDist
[LX1675

—844—
Cir. 6
1999USApp
[LX2874
—847—
Cir. 6
d) 1999USApp
[LX7219
1999USDist
[LX5184
—860—
Cir. 6
1999USApp
[LX2315
1999USApp
[LX5874
1999USApp
[LX5979
—869—
Cir. 7
1999USApp
[LX1613
—884—
Cir. 11
1999USApp
[LX[1]2595
168F3d[1]8
—908—
Cir. 7
1999USApp
[LX[8]1539
167F3d[8]381
1998USDist
[LX20242
1999USDist
[LX3495
32FS2d[P]1067
34FS2d736
226BRW[12]413
229BRW750
—916—
d) 36UCR2d202
—919—
Cir. 2
21FS2d[P]222
Cir. 3
27FS2d[P]559
Cir. DC
328ADC73
185ALRF149n
—946—
Cir. 8
1999USApp
[LX2550
Utah
f) 967P2d540

—951—
Cir. 8
162F3d980
—954—
Cir. 8
1999 Bankr LX
[182
1999 Bankr LX
[188
—962—
Cir. 8
157F3d1152
—970—
Cir. 8
1999USApp
[LX4570
—1001—
Cir. 10
f) 1999USApp
[LX5795
—1012—
Cir. 6
f) 165F3d[2]488
Cir. 7
f) 1999USApp
[LX 1665
f) 167F3d1142
22FS2d[P]866
22FS2d[P]870
—1021—
Cir. 3
1998Bankr LX
[1784
230BRW36
Cir. 6
1998Bankr LX
[1847
—1027—
Cir. 9
1999USApp
[LX144
1999USApp
[LX7878
—1031—
Cir. 3
24FS2d[P]359
—1036—
Cir. 5
1999USDist
[LX306
—1045—
Cir. 10
1998USApp
[LX32688
1999USApp
[LX2392

Continued

FIGURE 6-9 Page from the June 15, 1999, Blue Express Supplement to *Shepard's Federal Citations.*

VOL. 985 FEDERAL REPORTER, 2d SERIES

—1182—
Cir. Fed.
168F3d32
—1195—
ClCt
42FedCl 637
—1299—
Cir. 1
167F3d695
d) 167F3d696
—1359—
Cir. 3
36FS2d243
—1518—
Cir. 9
35FS2d764

Vol. 985

—94—
Cir. 1
1999USApp
[LX8368
Cir. 2
1999USApp
[LX8131
1999USApp
[LX8544
1999USDist
[LX5825
f) 1999USDist
[LX6252
1999USDist
[LX6532
35FS2d266
—102—
Cir. 4
36FS2d292
—151—
Cir. 4
d) 1998USDist
[LX21886
—175—
Cir. 4
1999USApp
[LX8345
—222—
Cir. 3
1998USDist
[LX21927
Cir. 5
168F3d866
—238—
Cir. 7
168F3d330

—241—
Cir. 6
f) 1999USApp
[LX8111
—312—
Cir. 6
1999USApp
[LX8801
—334—
Cir. 7
1999USDist
[LX6119
—383—
Cir. 4
36FS2d272
f) 36FS2d298
—401—
Cir. 8
f) 1999USDist
[LX5915
—406—
Cir. 2
1999USDist
[LX6031
—483—
Cir. 10
1999USApp
[LX8406
—583—
Case 22
ClCt
42FedCl 710
—655—
Cir. 1
1999USDist
[LX6231
184FRD230
—666—
j) 143LE388
j) 119SC1245
—880—
Cir. 7
1999USDist
[LX6207
—884—
Cir. 11
168F3d[1]18
—908—
Cir. 7
167F3d[8]383
1999USDist
[LX6195
f) 1999USDist
[LX6548
229BRW754

—930—
Cir. 4
f) 1999USApp
[LX8458
—1012—
Cir. 7
f) 167F3d1145
Cir. 9
35FS2d1210
—1067—
Cir. 11
1999USDist
[LX6093
—1113—
Cir. 1
1999USDist
[LX6345
—1148—
Cir. 2
1999USDist
[LX6382
Cir. 7
f) 35FS2d1081
—1175—
Cir. 3
f) 1999USDist
[LX5906
—1190—
Cir. 2
167F3d[4]131
167F3d[6]131
167F3d[9]132
—1275—
Cir. 6
1999USApp
[LX8463
—1320—
Cir. 6
1999USDist
[LX6181
—1362—
Cir. 7
1999USApp
[LX8578
35FS2d1061
35FS2d1093
—1471—
Cir. 11
168F3d[7]461
168F3d[8]461
168F3d[10]462
168F3d[11]462
—1565—
Cir. 11
d) 35FS2d1363

—1574—
ClCt
42FedCl 697
43FedCl 148

Vol. 986

—24—
Conn
d) 248Ct226
j) 248Ct278
—44—
Cir. 8
166F3d[4]1272
—86—
Cir. 4
1999USApp
[LX8602
—94—
Cir. 5
1999USDist
[LX5822
—115—
Cir. 5
167F3d[1]925
167F3d[6]925
—138—
Cir. 6
229BRW405
—154—
Cir. 4
c) 167F3d[4]859
—263—
Cir. 2
167F3d[6]780
—319—
Cir. 10
168F3d1178
—333—
Cir. 9
168F3d[2]391
—493—
Cir. 8
35FS2d725
—569—
Cir. 4
1999USDist
[LX5808
—580—
Cir. 1
167F3d711
167F3d[4]712
167F3d[11]712

1999USDist
[LX5882
35FS2d121
—607—
Cir. 1
1999USDist
[LX6345
—655—
Cir. 3
1999USDist
[LX5929
—700—
Cir. 4
36FS2d263
—725—
Cir. 10
1999USApp
[LX8362
—880—
Cir. 5
167F3d899
—940—
Cir. 4
f) 229BRW[1]668
—970—
Cir. 5
1999USApp
[LX8233
—990—
Mass
429Mas383
—1042—
Cir. 6
167F3d[1]1071
—1091—
Cir. 7
1999USApp
[LX8137
—1146—
Cir. 7
1999USApp
[LX8134
—1158—
Cir. 7
167F3d1127
—1197—
Cir. 8
q) 35FS2d724
—1208—
Cir. 8
167F3d[8]408

—1216—
ND
589NW[2]915
—1287—
s) 168F3d377
—1312—
Cir. 4
1999USDist
[LX6167
Cir. 10
1999USApp
[LX8282
1999USDist
[LX5798
1999USDist
[LX5817
—1416—
Case 10
cc) 1999USDist
[LX6065
—1446—
Cir. 6
1999USApp
[LX8592
—1459—
Md
352Md771
—1506—
Cir. 6
1999USDist
[LX5898
1999USDist
[LX5958
—1568—
Cir. 9
1999USApp
[LX8762

Vol. 987

—1—
Cir. 1
184FRD225
—129—
Cir. 2
1999USDist
[LX5784
—142—
Cir. 2
1999USDist
[LX6089
1999USDist
[LX6092
1999USDist
[LX6111

Continued

FIGURE 6-10 Page from the July 1, 1999, Red Cumulative Supplement to *Shepard's Federal Citations: Supreme Court Reporter.*

Vol. 119 SUPREME COURT REPORTER

—1187—
Minnesota v Mille Lacs Band of Chippewa Indians
1999
(143LE270)
s) 118SC2295
s) 119SC26
s) 119SC1333
s) 989F2d994
s) 48F3d373
s) 66F3d332
s) 68F3d253
s) 124F3d904
s) 853FS1118
s) 861FS784
s) 864FS102
s) 952FS1362
s) 140FRD390
s) 152FRD580
s) 152FRD583
s) 152FRD587
cc) 104SC53
cc) 700F2d341

—1215—
Jones v United States
1999
(143LE311)
s) 60F3d547
s) 116F3d1487

—1238—
Lowe v Pogue
1999
(143LE384)
cc) 119SC400
cc) 119SC401
cc) 119SC1111

—1239—
United States v Rodriguez-Moreno
1999
(143LE388)
s) 118SC725
s) 118SC894
s) 118SC1110
s) 118SC1327
s) 118SC2296
s) 119SC37
s) 121F3d841

—1292—
Conn v Gabbert
1999
(143LE399)
s) 119SC39
s) 131F3d793
1999US LX [3633
Cir. 2
1999USApp [LX9888
j) 1999USApp [LX9888
Cir. 6
1999USDist [LX6079
Cir. 8
1999USApp [LX7973

—1297—
Wyoming v Houghton
1999
(143LE408)
s) 119SC31
s) 119SC443
s) 119SC616
s) 956P2d363
1999US LX[1] [3172
j) 1999US LX [3172
Cir. 2
j) 1999USApp [LX9888

—1307—
Mitchell v United States
1999
(143LE424)
s) 118SC2318
s) 119SC38
s) 122F3d185

—1322—
Murphy Bros., Inc. v. Michetti Pipe Stringing, Inc.
1999
(143LE448)
s) 119SC401
s) 125F3d1396
s) 137F3d1357
Cir. 2
e) 1999USDist [LX5133

—1380—
UNUM Life Ins. Co. of Am. v Ward
1999
(143LE462)
s) 119SC334
s) 119SC900
s) 135F3d1276
Cir. 3
1999USDist [LX6335
Cir. 10
1999USApp [LX8231

—1392—
United States v Haggar Apparel Co.
1999
(143LE480)
s) 119SC30
s) 127F3d1460
s) 938FS868
Cir. Fed.
1999USApp [LX9710

—1402—
United States v Sun-Diamond Growers
1999
(143LE576)
s) 119SC402
s) 119SC409
s) 138F3d961
s) 329ADC149
s) 941FS1262
s) 941FS1277
s) 964FS486
cc) 23FS2d1
Cir. DC
1999USApp [LX10052

—1411—
Bank of Am. Nat'l Trust & Sav. Ass'n v 203 N. LaSalle St. Pshp.
1999
(143LE607)
s) 118SC1674
s) 118SC2314
s) 119SC24
s) 1997USApp [LX34046
s) 126F3d955
s) 190BRW567
s) 190BRW595
s) 195BRW692

—1430—
El Paso Natural Gas Co. v Neztsosie
1999
(143LE635)
s) 119SC334
s) 119SC900
s) 136F3d610

—1439—
INS v Aguirre-Aguirre
1999
(143LE590)
s) 119SC39
s) 121F3d521

FIGURE 6-10 (continued)

UNITED STATES SUPREME COURT Cross Reference Table by Lexis Citation	
1998	
LX8155	American Mfg. Mut. Ins. Co. v. Sullivan (No. 97-2000, 12/14/1998)
1999	
LX3170	Ruhrgas AG v. Marathon Oil Co. (No. 98-470, 05/17/1999)
LX3171	Hunt v. Cromartie (No. 98-85, 05/17/1999)
LX3172	Florida v. White (No. 98-223, 05/17/1999)
LX3173	Clinton v. Goldsmith (No. 98-347, 05/17/1999)
LX3174	Saenz v. Roe (No. 98-97, 05/17/1999)
LX3193	Rivera v. Florida Dep't of Corrections (No. 98-7450, 05/17/1999)
LX3450	New Jersey v. New York (No. 120, Orig., 05/17/1999)
LX3451	Cleveland v. Policy Mgmt. Sys. Corp. (No. 97-1008, 05/24/1999)
LX3452	Davis v. Monroe Bd. of Educ. (No. 97-834, 05/24/1999)
LX3606	California Dental Ass'n v. FTC (No. 97-1625, 05/24/1999)
LX3631	Monterey v. Del Monte Dunes, Ltd. (No. 97-1235, 05/24/1999)
LX3632	Cross v. Pelican Bay State Prison (No. 98-8486, 05/24/1999)
LX3633	Wilson v. Layne (No. 98-83, 05/24/1999)
LX3634	Hanlon v. Berger (No. 97-1927, 05/24/1999)

UNITED STATES COURTS OF APPEALS Cross Reference Table by Lexis Citation	
LX9859	Moore v. Molina (No. 98-1544, 7th Cir. 05/17/1999)
LX9860	Durham v. Roadway Packages Sys., Inc. (No. 98-5543, 6th Cir. 05/18/1999)
LX9861	Khalife v. United States (No. 98-1173, 6th Cir. 05/18/1999)
LX9862	Shaver v. Dixie Trucking Co. (No. 97-1954, 4th Cir. 05/21/1999)
LX9866	Salters v. Decipher, Inc. (No. 98-2717, 4th Cir. 05/21/1999)
LX9868	United States v. Cunningham (No. 98-4501, 4th Cir. 05/21/1999)
LX9869	United States v. Funchess (No. 98-4661, 4th Cir. 05/21/1999)
LX9885	L'anza Research Int'l, Inc. v. Quality King Distrib., Inc. (No. 98-56258, 9th Cir. 05/20/1999)
LX9886	Reynolds v. Williams (No. 98-2181, 10th Cir. 05/21/1999)
LX9887	Marathon Oil Co. v. United States (No. 97-5146, Fed. Cir. 05/13/1999)
LX9888	Horne v. Coughlin (No. 97-2047, 2nd Cir. 05/21/1999)
LX9889	Gray v. SLC Coal Co. (No. 97-4427, 6th Cir. 05/24/1999)
LX9890	Herman v. Collis Foods, Inc. (No. 97-646, 6th Cir. 05/24/1999)
LX9891	Jacklyn v. Schering-Plough Healthcare Prods. Sales Corp. (No. 98-1335, 6th Cir. 05/24/1999)
LX9892	Riggins v. Apfel (No. 98-2217, 8th Cir. 05/24/1999)
LX9976	United States v. Asher (No. 98-1700, 7th Cir. 05/21/1999)
LX9977	Ogden Martin Sys. v. Whiting Corp. (No. 98-2120, 7th Cir. 05/21/1999)
LX9978	Eaton v. United States (No. 98-3999, 7th Cir. 05/21/1999)
LX9979	Pischke v. Litscher (No. 98-4013, 7th Cir. 05/21/1999)
LX9980	FDIC v. Four Star Holding Co. (No. 98-6112, 2nd Cir. 05/21/1999)
LX9981	Miller v. Reed (No. 97-17006, 9th Cir. 05/24/1999)
LX9982	United States v. Deeb (No. 97-50157, 9th Cir. 05/24/1999)
LX9984	Harper v. Showers (No. 97-60822, 5th Cir. 05/24/1999)
LX9985	Fisher v. Johnson (No. 98-50566, 5th Cir. 05/24/1999)
LX9986	Electrosource, Inc. v. Horizon Battery Techs. (No. 97-50709, 5th Cir. 05/24/1999)
LX9995	Radecki v. Joura (No. 98-3606, 8th Cir. 05/24/1999)
LX9997	Roll v. Bowersox (No. 98-3465, 8th Cir. 05/24/1999)
LX9998	Ticor Title Ins. Co. v. Cohens (No. 98-7904, 2nd Cir. 03/31/1999)
LX10017	United States v. Johnson (No. 98-1455, 2nd Cir. 05/20/1999)
LX10021	Curro v. Kelly (No. 98-2483, 2nd Cir. 05/20/1999)
LX10024	Wilson v. Apfel (No. 98-6244, 2nd Cir. 05/20/1999)
LX10025	Johnson v. Delphi Energy & Engine Mgmt. Sys. (No. 98-7872, 2nd Cir. 05/20/1999)
LX10027	Moustakis v. New York City Police Dep't. (No. 98-7972, 2nd Cir. 05/20/1999)
LX10028	Sovak v. President & Members of the Bd. of Educ. (No. 98-9287, 2nd Cir. 05/20/1999)
LX10030	GMA Accessories v. Positive Impressions, Inc. (No. 98-9558, 2nd Cir. 05/18/1999)
LX10032	Sprint Spectrum, L.P. v. Willoth (No. 98-7442, 2nd Cir. 05/24/1999)
LX10033	Ostrzenski v. Seigel (No. 98-1717, 4th Cir. 05/24/1999)
LX10036	Quintero v. Encarnacion (No. 98-3129, 10th Cir. 05/24/1999)
LX10037	Christiansen v. APV Crepaco, Inc. (No. 98-1820, 7th Cir. 05/24/1999)

FIGURE 6-11 Cross Reference Table by Lexis Citation from *Shephard's United States Citations.*

FIGURE 6-12 Page from the July 1, 1999, Red Cumulative Supplement to *Shepard's United States Citations: United States Supreme Court Reports, Lawyers' Edition.*

UNITED STATES SUPREME COURT REPORTS, LAWYERS' EDITION, 2d SERIES — Vol. 143

1999USDist
[LX6236
f) 1999USDist
[LX6301
f) 1999USDist
[LX6574
Cir. 8
1999USApp
[LX6094
169F3d517
1999USDist
[LX4873
Cir. 9
1999USApp
[LX10366
Cir. 10
1999USApp
[LX[11]8711
f) 1999USApp
[LX8711
1999USApp
[LX[1]8711
1999USApp
[LX[5]8711
1999USApp
[LX[12]8711
j) 1999USApp
[LX8711
Cir. 11
f) 1999USApp
[LX9050
f) 1999USDist
[LX6421
f) 1999USDist
[LX6423
ClCt
1999USClaims
[LX91
1999USClaims
[LX96
1999CCA LX
[129

—258—
South Cent.
Bell Tel. Co. v
Alabama
1999
(119SC1180)
s) 141LE790
s) 711So2d1005
Cir. 2
1999USDist
[LX6915

—270—
Minnesota v
Mille Lacs
Band of
Chippewa
Indians
1999
(119SC1187)
s) 141LE156
s) 141LE786
s) 143LE497
s) 989F2d994
s) 48F3d373
s) 66F3d332
s) 68F3d253
s) 124F3d904
s) 853FS1118
s) 861FS784
s) 864FS102
s) 952FS1362
s) 140FRD390
s) 152FRD580
s) 152FRD583
s) 152FRD587
cc) 78LE72
cc) 700F2d341

—311—
Jones v United
States
1999
(119SC1215)
s) 60F3d547
s) 116F3d1487

—384—
Lowe v Pogue
1999
(119SC1238)
cc) 1999USLX
[1699
cc) 142LE325

—388—
United States
v Rodriguez-
Moreno
1999
(119SC1239)
s) 139LE664
s) 139LE880
s) 140LE162
s) 140LE489
s) 141LE156
s) 142LE29
s) 121F3d841

—399—
Conn v
Gabbert
1999
(119SC1292)
s) 142LE30
s) 131F3d793
1999US LX
[3633
Cir. 2
1999USApp
[LX9888
j) 1999USApp
[LX9888
Cir. 6
1999USDist
[LX6079
Cir. 8
1999USApp
[LX7973

—408—
Wyoming v
Houghton
1999
(119SC1297)
s) 141LE791
s) 142LE398
s) 142LE555
s) 956P2d363
1999US LX
[3172
j) 1999US LX
[3172
Cir. 2
j) 1999USApp
[LX9888

—424—
Mitchell v
United States
1999
(119SC1307)
s) 141LE693
s) 142LE29
s) 122F3d185

—448—
Murphy Bros.,
Inc. v Michetti
Pipe
Stringing, Inc.
1999
(119SC1322)
s) 142LE326
s) 125F3d1396
s) 137F3d1357
Cir. 2
e) 1999USDist
[LX5133

—462—
UNUM Life
Ins. Co. of
Am. v Ward
1999
(119SC1380)
s) 142LE275
s) 142LE900
s) 135F3d1276
Cir. 3
1999USDist
[LX6335
Cir. 10
1999USApp
[LX8231

—480—
United States
v Haggar
Apparel Co.
1999
(119SC1392)
s) 141LE790
s) 127F3d1460
s) 938FS868
Cir. Fed.
1999USApp
[LX9710

—576—
United States
v Sun-
Diamond
Growers
1999
(119SC1402)
s) 142LE326
s) 142LE332
s) 138F3d961
s) 329ADC149
s) 941FS1262
s) 941FS1277
s) 964FS486
cc) 23FS2d1
Cir. DC
1999USApp
[LX10052

—590—
INS v
Aguirre-
Aguirre
1999
(119SC1439)
s) 142LE30
s) 121F3d521

—607—
Bank of Am.
Nat'l Trust &
Sav. Ass'n v
203 N.
LaSalle St.
Pshp.
1999
(119SC1411)
s) 140LE812
s) 141LE156
s) 141LE785
s) 1997USApp
[LX34046
s) 126F3d955
s) 190BRW567
s) 190BRW595
s) 195BRW692

—635—
El Paso
Natural Gas
Co. v
Neztsosie
1999
(119SC1430)
s) 142LE275
s) 142LE900
s) 136F3d610

contains information on *Federal Supplement* and *McKinnon* is in *Federal Reporter*, you will not need to consult Part 2 to Shepardize *McKinnon*. The date is in the upper right-hand corner of the cover. Because Shepard's is fairly current, you should be looking for a month that is within three months of the month in which you are doing your research. Then look on the front cover for the legend "**WHAT YOUR LIBRARY SHOULD CONTAIN.**" Below that is the list of Shepard's volumes you need to Shepardize *McKinnon*. For example, the June 15, 1999, *Shepard's Federal Citations* Part 1 lists a number of hardbound volumes. Then it lists the February 1, 1999, gold cumulative supplement, the June 1, 1999, red cumulative supplement, and the June 15, 1999, blue express supplement.

The next step is to determine which volumes of the ones listed on the front cover of the June 1993 volume you will need to use. Because *McKinnon* is a 1993 case and there are no hardbound volumes earlier than 1995, you will have to consult all of the hardbound volumes. A more recent case, say a 1998 case, would not appear in any Shepard's prior to 1998. Look at the spines of the hardbound volumes. They will often give you the volume numbers of the reporters Shepardized in them. When you look at the spines of the hardbound volumes for volume 985 of F.2d, you find that volume 985 of F.2d is contained in one of the hardbound volumes for 1995, and the 1995–1996, 1996–1997, and 1997–1998 hardbound volumes.

It is important that you check each of the volumes (hardbound and paperbound) you have identified because they are *not* cumulative. This means that each of the Shepard's volumes listed on the front of the latest Shepard's issue contains different information from any other volumes. If you miss checking one of the Shepard's volumes, you may be missing information telling you that the case was reversed or affirmed on appeal. An easy way to make sure you do not miss checking any of the volumes is to make a chart like the one following. Along one edge of the chart, write the citation of the case you are Shepardizing and identify the Shepard's volumes to be checked along an adjoining side of the chart. As you check a particular issue, place a check mark next to it to show that you have checked that volume. A chart is especially helpful if you are Shepardizing a number of cases at the same time or you are not able to Shepardize the volumes in order because someone else is using the other volumes.

	1995	95–96	96–97	97–98
985 F.2d 525	X	X	X	X
	2/1/99	6/1/99	6/15/99	
	X	X	X	

Sometimes a Shepard's volume contains no references for the case you are Shepardizing. This simply means that no case or other authority cited to the case you are Shepardizing during the time period covered by the volume. As indicated in the following case excerpt, the lack of references may have some significance, in that the case being Shepardized may not be considered to carry great weight.

> This Court does not find the case to be persuasive as applied to the facts of this case. First, the case is a 1923 case that has not been cited by one other court. See Shepard's North Carolina Citations.
>
> *Medoil Corp. v. Clark*, 751 F.Supp. 88, 89 (W.D. N.C. 1990).

Abbreviations

The first few pages of each Shepard's volume contain useful information that you will be referring to often when you are learning how to Shepardize. There are several pages entitled "Abbreviations" (fig. 6-1). If you are not sure what an abbreviation used in Shepard's stands for, you should consult this table. For example, "A2d" is the abbreviation for "Atlantic Reporter, Second Series." Another page is entitled "History and Treatment Letters" (fig. 6-2). This page contains abbreviations dealing with the history of the case. For example, "a" stands for "affirmed," "r" stands for "reversed," "s" stands for "same case," and "v" stands for "vacated." Other abbreviations on this page deal with the treatment of the case. For example, "e" means that the case cited explained the case you are Shepardizing, "f" means that the case cited the case you are Shepardizing as controlling the later court's decision, "j" means that the case you are Shepardizing was cited in the dissenting opinion of the case cited, and "o" means that the cited case expressly overruled the case you are Shepardizing. If you are Shepardizing statutes, refer to the page that contains abbreviations for statutes.

In the following case excerpts, the attorneys were admonished for failing to Shepardize properly.

As a threshold matter, the Court admonishes Plaintiff's counsel for mischaracterizing the existing case law on this subject. Head counsel merely Shepardized the cases he cites in his Memorandum in Support of the Motion to Revise the Scheduling Order, he would have discovered that *In re Burg*, one of the cases upon which he relies for the proposition that requiring direct testimony by way of declaration or aworn affidavit is improper, was explicitly rejected by the United States Court of Appeals for the Ninth Circuit in *Adair v. Sunwest Bank*.

Saverson v. Levitt, 162 F.R.D. 407, 408 (D. D.C. 1995)(citations omitted).

In his brief on appeal, the plaintiff states that the court in *Kruzer* noted that expensive research failed to disclose any case directly on point. However, in Shepardizing the *Kruzer* case, we have been able to locate a very recent case taking the opposite view from *Kruzer*, and whose language, reasoning, and statements of law are persuasive.

Feola v. Valmont Industries, Inc., 304 N.W.2d 377, 382 (Neb. 1981).

Shepardizing

Look at a page from each of the 1995, 1995–1996, 1996–1997, 1997–1998, February 1, 1999, June 1, 1999, and June 15, 1999, Shepard's volumes that you would find if you were Shepardizing *United States v. McKinnon* and determine what the information on those pages means.

First look at the page from the 1995 volume (fig. 6-3). You know that you are looking at the right page because it says "Federal Reporter, 2d Series" and "Vol. 985" at the top. Be sure that you have the correct series and volume for the reporter. Then look down the columns until you see "**525**," the first page of the case, almost at the end of the last column. Everything after "**525**" and before the next number in bold, "**528**," has to do with *McKinnon*. It shows:

—525—
United States v
McKinnon
1993
Cir. 4
22 F3d559
Cir. 8
f22F3d801
Cir. 11
34F3d^{1}994
43F3d^{2}1441
Fla
641 So2d852
Ore
129 OrA235
878 P2d1132

Courts in the 4th, 8th, and 11th federal circuits and state courts in Florida and Oregon cited to *McKinnon* during the time period covered by the 1995 volume. The "f" in the left of the citation for the 8th circuit case indicates that that case followed the reasoning of *McKinnon*. The two citations from the 11th circuit contain superscript numbers between "F3d" and the page number. The superscript numbers refer to the headnote numbers of *McKinnon.* The superscript "1" in the first 11th circuit case citation indicates that that case discusses the same legal principle discussed in headnote 1 of *McKinnon.* Similarly, the superscript "2" in the second 11th circuit case citation indicates that that case discusses the same legal principle discussed in headnote 2 of *McKinnon.* There are two case citations from Oregon. Figure 6-1, which contains Shepard's pages of abbreviations, shows that "OrA" stands for Oregon Court of Appeals Reports and "P2d" stands for Pacific Reporter, Second Series. Oregon Court of Appeals Reports is the official reporter for Oregon state cases from the intermediate appellate court. Pacific Reporter, Second Series, a West regional reporter, is an unofficial reporter for Oregon state cases. It may be that the two citations listed under "Ore" are parallel citations to the same case. A researcher could determine if this is true from looking up the citations in the corresponding reporters.

Now, look at the page from the 1995–1996 volume (Figure 6-4). It shows:

—525—
United States
v McKinnon
1993
US cert den
In 126LE94
In 114SC130
Cir. 11
62f3d[1]1355
Colo
f888 P2d351
S D
f535 NW850

You know you are in the right place because the name of the case is given with the year of the decision. The abbreviation "US cert den" means that the United States Supreme Court denied the petition for writ of certiorari. Below that are the citations to the denial of certiorari at 126 L. Ed. 2d 94 and 114 S. Ct. 130. The case was cited by the federal Court of Appeals for the Eleventh Circuit and state courts in Colorado and South Dakota. As indicated in the preceding paragraph, the "f" means that the Colorado and South Dakota state courts followed the reasoning of *McKinnon.* The superscript 1 in "62F3d[1]1355" indicates that the 11th circuit discussed the same legal principle as that found in headnote 1 from *McKinnon.*

Now, look at the page from the 1996–1997 volume (fig. 6-5). It shows:

—525—
United States v
McKinnon
1993
Cir. 8
928FS[2]1483
Ga
475SE584
480SE589
Tenn
929SW383

The information shows that *McKinnon* was cited in a federal district court case at 928 F. Supp. 1483. The reference "Cir. 8" means that the federal district court was one within the geographical area of the Court of Appeals for the Eighth Circuit. That court discussed the same legal principle as that found in headnote 2 from *McKinnon. McKinnon* was also cited in state court cases, two from Georgia and one from Tennessee.

Now, look at the page from the 1997–1998 volume (fig. 6-6).

—525—
United States v
McKinnon
1993
Fla
706So2d417
Ga
267Ga106
267Ga551
227GaA674
490SE204

This information shows that *McKinnon* was cited by state courts in Florida and Georgia

Now, look at the page from the February 1, 1999 supplement (fig. 6-7).

—525—
Cir. 5
145F3d277
Minn
578NW723

This information shows that *McKinnon* was cited by the federal Court of Appeals for the Fifth Circuit and by a state court in Minnesota.

Now, look at the page from the June 1, 1999, and June 15, 1999, supplements (figs. 6-8 and 6-9). There is no reference on either of the pages to "**525.**" In the June 1 supplement the numbers skip from "**520**" to "**535**" and in the June 15 supplement, the pages skip from "**483**" to "**583.**" Lack of any reference to "**525**" means that no cases cited *McKinnon* during the time period covered by those supplements.

In summary, *McKinnon* is still good authority because the United States Supreme Court refused to hear the case and the case has not been reversed, overruled, superceded, modified, or limited. *McKinnon* was cited by a number of federal and state courts; several of those courts followed the reasoning of *McKinnon.*

Your next question may be how many cases do you have to read of the cases you found through Shepardizing. That depends on the reason you are Shepardizing. If your goal is to find if *McKinnon* is still good authority, you have already done that. If you had found a case marked with "m" for modified, "r" for reversed, "S" for superceded, "L" for limited, "o" for overruled, or "q" for questioned, you should read those cases. If you are using Shepard's as a case finder, to find similar cases, you might want to read as many of the cases as possible.

Now look at the Shepardizing information for *Wyoming v. Houghton. Houghton* was decided on April 5, 1999. The case is published in *United States Supreme Court Reports, Lawyers' Edition* and *Supreme Court Reporter* within a few weeks of the case being decided. Although *United States Reports* is the official reporter for decisions of the United States Supreme Court, publication of cases in *United States Reports* lags considerably behind publication in *United States Supreme Court Reports, Lawyers' Edition* and *Supreme Court Reporter.*

The July 1, 1999, supplement is the first issue of Shepard's to contain information on *Houghton.* A United States Supreme Court decision can be Shepardized using any of the three parallel citations. Thus *Houghton* could be Shepardized using the citation from *United States Reports, Supreme Court Reporter,* or *United States Supreme Court Reports, Lawyers' Edition.*

Use the citation for *Houghton* in *Supreme Court Reporter.* (The version of the case included in chapter 4 is from *Supreme Court Reporter.*) You would look at the cover of the paperbound July 1, 1999, *Shepard's United Stated Citations for Supreme Court Reporter* for the legend, "**WHAT YOUR LIBRARY SHOULD CONTAIN.**" Below that is the list of Shepard's you need to use to Shepardize. Beneath the legend, the cover lists a number of hardbound volumes. Then it lists the July 1, 1999, red cumulative supplement. The hardbound volumes need not be consulted because the hardbound volume with the most recent information for *Supreme Court Reporter* only gives information through volume 118 of *Supreme Court Reporter.*

Look at the page from the July 1, 1999, red cumulative supplement for *Supreme Court Reporter* (fig. 6-10). You know that you are looking at the right page because it says "Supreme Court Reporter" and "Vol. 119" at the top. Be sure that you have the correct volume for the reporter. Then look down the columns until you see "**1297,**" the first page of the case, in the second column. Everything after "**1297**" and before the next number in bold, "**1307,**" has to do with *Houghton.* It shows:

—1297—
Wyoming v
Houghton
1999
(143LE408)
s) 119SC31
s) 119SC443
s) 119SC616
s) 956P2d363
1999US LX[1]
[3172
j) 1999US LX
[3172
Cir. 2
j) 1999USApp
[LX9888

The parentheses around the first citation indicate that it is a parallel citation. Thus, the citation for *Houghton* in *United States Supreme Court Reports, Lawyers' Edition* is 143 L. Ed. 2d 408. The letter "s" to the left of the next four citations indicates that they are citations to the same case. The first three citations are to actions taken by the United States Supreme Court. They are likely short decisions, granting certiorari and taking other administrative actions concerning the case. The forth citation preceded by an "s" is the citation to the decision of the Wyoming Supreme Court before *Houghton* went up to the United States Supreme Court. The next two citations are to decisions of the United States Supreme Court reported in Lexis. Presumably, the citations are to Lexis because no citation is yet available to a print source. The same citation, "1999US LX3172," is given twice, the second time preceded by "j." The first citation means that the majority opinion of the case cited *Houghton* and the second means that *Houghton* was also cited in the dissenting opinion of the case. The superscript 1 in the first citation indicates that the United States Supreme Court discussed the same legal principle as that found in headnote 1 from *Houghton.* The last citation indicates that the Court of Appeals for the Second Circuit cited to *Houghton* in a dissenting opinion. The citation is to Lexis, again indicating that the citation information for the Court of Appeals for the Second Circuit case is not available for the print version.

Figures 6-10 and 6-11 contain pages from the July 1, 1999, red cumulative supplement for the *Supreme Court Reporter.* Figure 6-10 shows that 1999US LX 3172 is *Florida v. White*, a case decided by the United States Supreme Court on May 17, 1999. Figure 6-11 shows that 1999USAppLX 9888 is a United States Court of Appeals for the Second Circuit case, *Horne v. Coughlin*, decided on May 21, 1999.

Now look at the page from the July 1, 1999, red cumulative supplement for *United States Supreme Court Reports, Lawyers' Edition* and compare it with the information from the July 1, 1999, supplement for *Supreme Court Reporter* (fig. 6-12). You know that you are looking at the right page because it says "United States Supreme Court Reports, Lawyers' Edition, 2d Series" and "Vol. 143" at the top. Be sure that you have the correct series and volume for the reporter. Then look down the columns until you see **"408,"** the first page of the case, at the top of the next to the last column. Everything after **"408"** and before the next number in bold, **"424,"** has to do with *Houghton.* It shows:

—408—
Wyoming v
Houghton
1999
(119SC1297)
s) 141LE791
s) 141LE398
s) 142LE555
s) 956P2d363
1999US LX
[3172
j) 1999US LX
[3172
Cir. 2
j) 1999USApp
[LX9888

The first citation is the parallel citation for *Houghton* in *Supreme Court Reporter.* The next three citations are to *United States Supreme Court Reports, Lawyers' Edition,* 2d Series; they are parallel citations to the first three citations preceded by an "s" found through Shepardizing using the *Houghton* citation to *Supreme Court Reporter.* The balance of the citations are the same.

In the following case, the attorney would have found an "r," indicating that the case had been reversed, had the attorney Shepardized the case properly.

> In arguing that Jackson's conviction for fraudulent use of a credit card should be affirmed, the Commonwealth cited both *Gibson* . . . and *Gonsalves* . . . . While counsel for Jackson argued that *Gibson* had been modified by *Tarlton* . . . , upon Shepardizing *Gibson* the Court found that it was reversed by the Illinois Supreme Court in *People v. Gibson.*
>
> *Jackson v. Commonwealth*, 972 S.W.2d 286, 288 n.1 (Ky. Ct. App. 1997)(citations omitted).

Case Names Citator

What do you do if you have a case name, but not the corresponding citation? Chapter 3 explained that case names may be researched in the case names volumes of the applicable digest. Case names may also be researched in a Shepard's case names citator. Figure 6-13 shows the front cover of Shepard's Florida Case Names Citator.

Note on computer-assisted citators

Shepardizing may also be done on Lexis or a CD-ROM edition of Shepard's. As of July 1, 1999, Shepard's on Westlaw was replaced with KeyCite. KeyCite is discussed in the next section.

Using one of these computer-assisted legal research (CALR) services to cite check is much faster than manually checking all applicable issues of Shepard's and there is probably less chance of error. Cite checking using an on-line service will give more current information than Shepardizing using the print Shepard's. The Shepard's CD-ROMs may or may not give more current information than the hard copy Shepard's, depending on when the Shepard's CD-ROMs were last updated in comparison to the print version. Cite checking on-line using Shepard's or KeyCite will yield the most up-to-date information.

A comparison of the difference in cost to the client between Shepardizing using a CALR service and using the print Shepard's could be made by comparing the costs involved and the accuracy of the results obtained. The costs of the CALR service include the cost of the service and the amount of billable time expended. The costs of Shepardizing manually include the cost of the subscription and the amount of attorney time expended. The timeliness of Shepardizing using a CALR service may outweigh any additional cost over Shepardizing using the print version. In addition, the researcher Shepardizing using CALR can print out a copy of the Shepardizing request and the results. The printout could be kept in the appropriate file and referred to if there was a question later whether a particular authority had been Shepardized. Some attorneys now consider it legal malpractice to have missed a recent authority available on Westlaw or Lexis, but not yet available in the print Shepard's.

STATUTES

Once you know the Shepardizing procedure for cases, you can use the same procedure to Shepardize statutes, court rules, and administrative regulations. Figure 6-14 shows the cover for September 1999 issue of *Shepard's Federal Statute Citations*. There are Shepard's for numerous federal and statute primary sources as well. The next few sections will show you the procedure to shepardize primary sources other than cases, using a federal eavesdropping and wiretapping statute as an example.

Besides researching case law, attorneys research other primary sources, such as statutes, court rules, and administrative regulations, to advise clients and to predict the outcome of a lawsuit. Once the researcher locates an applicable statute, court rule, or administrative regulation, the researcher will perform further research to determine if the primary source is still good law (is still authoritative) and to determine how the primary source has been interpreted by the courts.

A primary source, once authoritative, may no longer be good law for a number of reasons. It may have been amended or held to be unconstitutional. A statute may have been repealed by the legislature. A primary source may have been interpreted in a unique way so as to make it inapplicable to the set of facts being researched.

The researcher can gather much information from consulting an annotated version of a statute or court rule. Often the research material and the annotations indicate whether the primary source is good law and give information on case law interpretation of the primary source. Although informative, the annotated version may not contain as current information as Shepard's on the primary source; the Code of Federal Regulations is not annotated.

The consequences of not using citators to determine the status of an applicable statute, court rule, or administrative regulation can be as serious as failing to use citators with applicable cases. In the following case, the court was careful to note that, although Shepardizing had indicated there were several cases interpreting a particular statute, none of the cases dealt with facts similar to the facts the court was reviewing (page 245):

VOL. 14 JUNE 1999 NO. 6

SHIP DATE
JUNE 17

Shepard's Florida Case Names Citator

ADVANCE SHEET

(USPS 767170)

WHAT YOUR LIBRARY SHOULD CONTAIN

1990 Bound Volumes, (Parts 1–3)*
Supplemented with:
—*May 1999 Cumulative Supplement Vol. 14 No.5*
—*June 1999 Advance Sheet Vol. 14 No. 6*

DESTROY ALL OTHER ISSUES

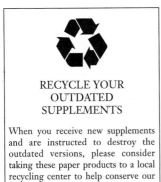

RECYCLE YOUR
OUTDATED
SUPPLEMENTS

When you receive new supplements and are instructed to destroy the outdated versions, please consider taking these paper products to a local recycling center to help conserve our nation's natural resources. Thank you.

Shepard's®

FIGURE 6-13 Cover of June 1999 *Shepard's Florida Case Names Citator.*

VOL. 98 SEPTEMBER 1, 1999 NO. 17

SHIP DATE
SEPTEMBER 1

Shepard's Federal Statute Citations

Cumulative Supplement

(USPS 605470)

IMPORTANT NOTICE:

The 1998–1999 three-volume Hardbound Supplement for *Shepard's Federal Statute Citations* was delivered in August.

IF YOU HAVE NOT RECEIVED THE 1998-1999 HARDBOUND SUPPLEMENT, RETAIN THE FOLLOWING:

1996 Bound Volumes 1–7*
1996–1997 Bound Supplement*

**Supplemented with:*
—September 1, 1998 Gold Cumulative Supplement (Vol. 97, No.17)
—July 1, 1999 Cumulative Supplement (Vol. 98, No. 13)
—July 15, 1999 Blue Express Supplement (Vol. 98, No.14)
—September 1, 1999 Red Cumulative Supplement (Vol. 98, No. 17)

IF YOU HAVE RECEIVED THE 1998-1999 HARDBOUND SUPPLEMENT, RETAIN THE FOLLOWING:

1996 Bound Volumes 1–7*
1996–1997 Bound Supplement*
1998–1999 Bound Supplement Volumes 1–3*

**Supplemented with:*
—September 1, 1999 Red Cumulative Supplement (Vol. 98, No.17)

DESTROY ALL OTHER ISSUES

NOTICE: If you do not have the 1996 revised edition, please see page vi of the preface.

RECYCLE YOUR
OUTDATED
SUPPLEMENTS

When you receive new supplements and are instructed to destroy the outdated versions, please consider taking these paper products to a local recycling center to help conserve our nation's natural resources. Thank you.

Shepard's®

FIGURE 6-14 Cover of September 1, 1999, Red Cumulative Supplement to Shepard's Federal Statute Citations.

> Congress enacted this provision in 1990, but counsel have pointed us to, and we have found, no opinions in this or any other Circuit interpreting its language. [FN4]
>
> FN4. Shepard's reveals seven citing cases in all, but they involve sentencing issues in cases where there is a much clearer violation of the law.
>
> *United States v. Seitz*, 952 F. Supp. 229, 233 (E.D. Pa. 1997).

Figure 6-15 contains an excerpt from a hearing in *State of California v. O.J. Simpson.* According to the judge's remarks, Ms. Clark may not have Shepardized an applicable court rule.

The scheme of the citator for primary sources other than statutes is similar to the case citator. The citator lists each instance in which the primary source being Shepardized has been cited, with the information given as citations to the pages on which the primary source being Shepardized is cited. For example, Shepardizing would yield one citation for each instance in which the primary source being Shepardized was cited by a court. The citations found by Shepardizing yield the page on which the Shepardized primary source was cited, which may not necessarily be the first page of the source.

Shepardizing statutes

This section discusses the process for Shepardizing statutes, which is similar to the process used to Shepardize cases. As with Shepardizing cases, the first step in Shepardizing statutes is to organize. Locate the correct set of Shepard's to use to Shepardize a federal eavesdropping and wiretapping statute and be ready to record the results of your Shepardizing. The Shepard's set you will need is customarily located near *United States Code*, *United States Code Annotated*, or *United States Code Service.* The Shepard's used to Shepardize federal statutes is called *Shepard's Federal Statutes Citations.*

Once you find the correct Shepard's set, line up the volumes you will need to use. Consult the front cover of the most recent Shepard's for the legend, **"WHAT YOUR LIBRARY SHOULD CONTAIN."** Below that is the list of Shepard's you need to use to Shepardize. For example, the September 1, 1999, *Shepard's Federal Statutes Citations* (fig. 6-14) lists hardbound volumes for 1996, 1996–1997, and 1998–1999. Then it lists the September 1, 1999, red cumulative supplement.

The next step is to determine which volumes you will need to use of the ones listed on the front cover of the September 1, 1999, Shepard's to Shepardize 18 U.S.C. § 2511 (2)(c). That statute allows a law enforcement officer to intercept a conversation if the law enforcement officer is a party to the conversation. Look at the spines of the hardbound volumes. They will often give you the citations of the federal statutes Shepardized in them. When you look at the spines of the hardbound volumes for 18 U.S.C. § 2511 (2)(c), you find that 18 U.S.C. § 2511 (2)(c) is contained in hardbound volume 3 for 1996, and is contained in the 1996–1997 and 1998–1999 hardbound supplements.

Check each of the Shepard's volumes (hardbound and paperbound) you have identified because they are not cumulative. A chart like the one below can be used to ensure that all of the volumes have been reviewed. After checking a particular volume, place a check mark next to it.

	1996	96–97	98–99	9/1/99
18 U.S.C. § 2511 (2)(c)	X	X	X	X

Sometimes a Shepard's volume contains no references for the statute you are Shepardizing. This simply means that no case or other authority cited to the statute you are Shepardizing during the time period covered by the volume.

Look at a page from each of the 1996, 1996–1997, 1998–1999, and September 1, 1999, Shepard's volumes that you would find if you were Shepardizing 18 U.S.C. § 2511 (2)(c) and determine what the information on those pages means.

First, look at the page from the 1996 volume (fig. 6-16). You know that you are looking at the right page because it says **"UNITED STATES CODE 1988 and 1994 Eds."** and **"TITLE 18 § 2511"** at

FIGURE 6-15 What Happens When You Don't Shepardize.

State of California vs. O.J. Simpson

Tuesday, September 5, 1995

Excerpt from a Hearing held at 1:03 p.m.

Ms. Clark:	There is no legal provision for motion to reconsideration in criminal law. That is only in civil law. It is recognized in Civil Code of Procedure Section 1008, and what they require in civil law is that the parties seeking reconsideration show newly discovered facts. In this case, we have no newly discovered facts with respect to the motion for reconsideration of Laura McKinney.
The Court:	But doesn't—don't the—doesn't the case law dealing with that particular code section include criminal cases; if you Shepardize that, you come up with some criminal cases?
Ms. Clark:	We did. I don't believe none were found, your honor. I didn't—we don't have any in our motion, which leads me to believe that no, there aren't any criminal cases under that section.
The Court:	All right.
Ms. Clark:	You asked me that question because you knew Miss Lewis wrote this motion, huh? But no, as far as I know, there are no criminal law cases that involve that section because it's not recognized in criminal law. So I mean, at least in theory, we didn't have to have all the argument.
The Court:	But my Pepperdine law clerks found some.
Ms. Clark:	Did they? Criminal cases? And what do they say?
The Court:	They say it's applicable in criminal law cases.
Ms. Clark:	Okay. Nevertheless—

the top. Then look down the columns until you see "**§ 2511 (2)(c)**" in the first column. Everything after "**§ 2511 (2)(c)**" and before the next statutory citation in bold, "**§ 2511 (2)(d),**" has to do with 18 U.S.C. § 2511 (2)(c).

Figure 6-16 shows that the United States Supreme Court and courts in the D.C., 1st, 2d, 3d, 4th, 5th, 6th, 7th, 8th, 9th, 10th, and 11th federal circuits cited to 18 U.S.C. § 2511 (2)(c) during the time period covered by the 1996 volume. The "C" to the left of three citations indicates that courts within the 7th and 9th circuits found the statute constitutional.

Figure 6-17 contains judicial and legislative treatment abbreviations as well as an explanation entitled "Illustrative Citations." These pages give you important information, such as "C" means Constitutional, "U" means Unconstitutional, and "R" means repealed. They also explain the use of a delta or an asterisk.

Now, look at the page from the 1996–1997 hardbound supplement (fig. 6-18). It shows that a federal district court within the second circuit cited to 18 U.S.C. § 2511 (2)(c) during the time period covered by the 1996–1997 hardbound supplement.

Now, look at the page from the 1998–1999 hardbound supplement (fig. 6-19). It shows that federal district courts and courts of appeals within the D.C., 1st, 2d, 3d, 5th, 6th, 7th, 9th, and 11th circuits cited to 18 U.S.C. § 2511 (2)(c) during the time period covered by the 1998–1999 hardbound supplement. The "i" to the left of one citation indicates that a federal district court within the 7th circuit interpreted the statute in some significant manner.

Now, look at the page from the September 1, 1999, supplement (fig. 6-20). It shows that federal district courts within the 2d and 11th circuits cited to 18 U.S.C. § 2511 (2)(c) during the time period

UNITED STATES CODE 1988 and 1994 Eds. TITLE 18 § 2511

814FS738
Cir. 8
546F2d247
951F2d944
Cir. 9
583F2d453
650F2d191
35F3d1320
343AR298n
§ 2511 (2) (a)(2)(A)
Cir. DC
718FS989
Cir. 2
792FS192
§ 2511(2)(b to e)
Cir. 6
981F2d1507
§ 2-511 (2) (b)
A 100St1851
Cir. DC
492FS701
Cir. 1
669F2d26
Cir. 3
573F2d855
Cir. 7
C 601F2d324
Cir. 9
488F2d194
448FS118
580FS1167
814FS1443
§ 2511(2)(c)
401US791
415US997
440US744
28LĒ481
39LĒ894
59LĒ738
91SC1145
94SC1600
99SC1467
67FRD345
Cir. DC
439F2d644
463F2d888
559F2d105
606F2d1203
337FS1263
366FS996
691FS1335
718FS989
774FS10
Cir.1
444F2d711
520F2d527
573F2d682
611F2d388
720F2d228
726F2d897
758F2d41
894F2d9
895F2d853
944F2d47
71F3d936
71F3d981
410FS1367
453FS819
502FS1195
538FS1047
592FS899
727FS684
848FS9
901FS490
Cir. 2
469F2d6
483F2d1202
487F2d654
558F2d677
692F2d859
705F2d620
706F2d376
831F2d378
860F2d19
913F2d49
80F3d693
466FS910
496FS367
497FS502
552FS483
565FS1437
609FS569
649FS990
660FS779
675FS167
755FS615
792FS192
842FS70
842FS1527
888FS1262
890FS202
Cir. 3
458F2d471
483F2d730
507F2d630
515F2d50
573F2d855
708F2d124
885F2d52
933F2d203
320FS198
327FS368
400FS286
405FS145
408FS196
448FS1103
456FS220
467FS284
553FS777
568FS116
574FS1042
651FS78
779FS369
Cir. 4
499F2d1377
589F2d158
594F2d12
594F2d984
717F2d1485
915F2d907
917F2d800
934F2d50
492FS585
502FS1162
554FS153
711FS280
836FS1196
Cir. 5
480F2d438
488F2d871
515F2d886
573F2d252
573F2d268
574F2d1373
592F2d854
603F2d507
610F2d299
651F2d337
656F2d976
693F2d347
706F2d592
835F2d94
839F2d1050
846F2d973
900F2d44
947F2d738
948F2d1426
19F3d1542
455FS181
508FS600
537FS1368
562FS465
787FS674
Cir. 6
511F2d31
788F2d379
800F2d88
813F2d110
859F2d1514
881F2d273
990F2d863
558FS999
737FS436
Cir. 7
506F2d1360
C 508F2d867
573F2d455
C 601F2d319
745F2d437
874F2d1218
875F2d1300
879F2d1565
891F2d1329
902F2d1245
958F2d1410
973F2d580
998F2d449
74F3d827
303FS644
350FS547
363FS1350
387FS807
397FS1087
520FS820
562FS648
610FS1475
722FS428
793FS840
Cir. 8
446F2d794
518F2d981
558F2d877
801F2d315
843F2d1115
963F2d1126
30F3d952
374FS327
374FS612
763FS1494
Cir. 9
470F2d1065
484F2d165
486F2d60
508F2d986
545F2d1183
548F2d792
548F2d847
582F2d1212
587F2d957
619F2d813
633F2d776
660F2d735
667F2d784
694F2d201
753F2d1435
77F3d292
526FS1200
C 531FS1121
536FS257
803FS362
814FS1441
883FS504
Cir. 10
493F2d347
536F2d315
604F2d1333
697F2d283
729F2d1260
730F2d1332
876F2d805
970F2d748
1F3d1016
69F3d1074
418FS819
424FS518
482FS826
529FS547
568FS1197
730FS1029
Cir. 11
662F2d739
664F2d104
675F2d1156
677F2d1380
693F2d1340
699F2d1100
725F2d1581
799F2d1492
939F2d1460
625FS659
764FS1491
791FS293
34MJ119
49A[4]35n
§ 2511(2)(d)
A 100St1850
Cir. DC
495F2d138
559F2d105
991F2d839
348FS1202
366FS996
537FS1173
555FS1182
691FS1335
Cir. 1
573F2d682
720F2d228
813F2d479
842F2d1323
904F2d115
918F2d1006
4F3d1021
11F3d281
465FS1284
639FS901
727FS686
796FS630
796FS633
801FS872
813FS116
848FS9
901FS490
Cir. 2
429F2d219
558F2d677
706F2d376
736F2d870
491FS36
496FS367
587FS1185
609FS570
837FS81
842FS1527
849FS164
890FS202
Cir. 3
448FS1118
568FS116
592FS193
698FS93
Cir. 4
589F2d158
704F2d1298
731F2d1131
502FS1162
554FS153
831FS1258
836FS1197
846FS453
Cir. 5
490F2d805
526F2d654
630F2d419
764F2d1066
8F3d1018
19F3d1542
455FS181
508FS600
537FS1368
562FS464
Cir. 6
475F2d741
542F2d662
731F2d337
813F2d108
U 881F2d268
884F2d266
893F2d858
937F2d1038
974F2d730
981F2d1503
981F2d1508
990F2d864
63F3d1400
356FS45
450FS250
510FS833
558FS999
694FS1305
732FS767
737FS436
71BRW1003
Cir. 7
581F2d1290
C 601F2d319
668F2d959
875F2d1300
33F3d1469
44F3d1353
74F3d827
400FS435
520FS821
731FS882
793FS842
851FS308
Cir. 8
446F2d794
540F2d320
564F2d33
801F2d315
841F2d1422
951F2d160
980F2d1156
685FS210
780FS621
51FRD5
Cir. 9
582F2d1212
589F2d960
968F2d910

Continued

FIGURE 6-16 Sample Page from a 1996 Bound Volume of *Shepard's Federal Statute Citations.*

FIGURE 6-17 Sample pages from *Shepard's Federal Statute Citations.*

Statute being Shepardized (Cited Reference)

Citing References

ILLUSTRATIVE CITATIONS

Various symbols and notations have been used to reflect Shepard's analysis of the cited authorities shown in *Shepard's Federal Statute Citations*. These symbols/notations are illustrated in the following diagram. The data contained in this diagram is provided solely for illustrative purposes, and should not be relied upon.

TITLE 18	— **Title Number.** The title of the statute to be Shepardized.
§2a	— **Section Number.** The section of the statute to be Shepardized.
Cir. 7	—**Circuit/State Designator.** Citations following are to cases
698F2d123*1996	of the circuit or state indicated.
724F2d457*1996	
f)878F2d599*1996	—**Judicial and Legislative Treatment Letters.** Citing
896F2d1290*1996	sources have been analyzed to determine what effect they
914F2d78*1996	have on the statute being Shepardized, or the use they made
i)930F2d786*1996	of the statute being Shepardized. The resulting legislative or
980F2d454Δ1988	judicial treatment is indicated by abbreviations preceding the
988F2d376*1996	citing case volume number. **A table of these abbreviations**
996F2d1267*1996	**appears on the inside cover.** Citations without legislative or
997F2d1268*1996	judicial treatment letters indicate that the statute being
13F3d1001*1996	Shepardized was referred to in a less significant manner.
15F3d528***1988**	—**Delta/Asterisk followed by a Year.** All citations to the
18F3d856Δ**1996**	United States Code will include either the year of the code
25F3d1002*1996	cited, or the year of the case in which the code was cited. An
26F3d98*1996	asterisk followed by a year indicates that the citing case
26F3d357*1996	referred to a specific edition of the United States Code. In
26 F3d 750*996	this example, the court in the decision reported at 15 F.3d
26F3d756*1996	528 specifically cited the 1988 edition of Title 18, Section 2a.
na)30F3d256*1996	If the court fails to clearly designate the edition of the code
30F3d968*1996	cited, Shepard's will report the year of the case, together with
31F3d741*1996	the delta symbol (Δ). In this example, the court in the
31F3d777*1996	decision reported at 18 F.3d 856 did not designate the
33F3d125*1996	edition of the code cited. Shepard's, therefore, will report
33F3d564*1996	"Δ1996" to indicate that the case was decided in 1996. You can use that reference to help determine which edition of the
Cir. 8	code was intended by the court.
1997USApp [LX28605	—**Lexis Numbers.** A Lexis number indicates that the citing case has not been published in a case reporter in time for
1998USApp [LX30195	publication of this issue. In this example, the statute being Shepardized was cited in an Eighth Circuit Court of Appeals
1997USDist [LX27848	opinion which is identified by its Lexis number, 1997USAppLX28605. For more information on Lexis numbers, please see page vi.
105ALRF13n	—**Annotation.** A small letter "n" to the right of the page
106ALRF35n	number indicates that the case being Shepardized has been
107ALRF76n	cited in an annotation. In this example, the case being
110ALRF102n	Shepardized was cited on page 13 of bound volume 105 of the *American Law Reports, Federal.*

FIGURE 6-17 (continued)

Arrangement of Citations

TITLE 21	The list of citations following each case being Shepardized has been ordered as follows:
§ 10(a)(3)	
Cir. 5	1. Federal cases, arranged by circuit;
f)J736F2d102*1995	
748f2d987*1996	
Cir. 9	
879F2d636*1996	
889FS335*1996	
Cl Ct	
16ClC480*1995	2. Federal administrative decisions; and
107TCt 9* 1998	
159ARF595n	3. Annotations.
162ARF125n	

JUDICIAL TREATMENT LETTERS

Each citing federal court case has been analyzed to determine whether the court passed upon the constitutionality or validity of any cited United States statute. The resulting judicial operation of the statute (constitutional, unconstitutional, valid, void, etc.) is indicated by a letter-form abbreviation preceding the citing reference. **A table of abbreviations used for that purpose appears on the inside *front* cover.**

LEGISLATIVE HISTORY LETTERS

With the publication of the 1998–1999 Hardbound Supplement (Volumes 1–3), *Shepard's* continues the usage of legislative treatment letters in its *Federal Statute* publications. Any analysis of the legislative history for statutes cited within this publication (added, amended, repealed, etc.) is indicated by a letter-form abbreviation preceding the citing reference. **A table of abbreviations used for that purpose appears on the inside *back* cover.**

ABBREVIATIONS—JUDICIAL

C	(Constitutional)	Statute upheld as constitutional by citing the citing case
DG	(Decision for Gov't)	Citing case holds for the Government in a dispute concerning the code section
DGp	(Decision for Gov't in part)	Citing case holds in part for the Government in a dispute concerning the code section
DT	(Decision for Taxpayer)	Citing case holds for the taxpayer in a dispute concerning the code section
DTp	(Decision for Taxpayer in part)	Citing case holds in part for the taxpayer in a dispute concerning the code section
f	(followed)	Statute was expressly relied upon as controlling authority
i	(interpreted)	Statute was interpreted in some significant manner (may include a discussion of the statute's legislative history)
j	(dissenting opinion)	Case or statute is cited in a dissenting opinion
na	(not applicable)	Statute has been found to be inapplicable to legal or factual circumstances of the citing case
rt	(retroactive/prospective)	Retroactive or prospective application of the statute has been discussed by the citing case

FIGURE 6-17 (continued)

U	(Unconstitutional)	Statute was declared to be unconstitutional by the citing case
Up	(Unconstitutional in part)	Part of the statute was declared to be unconstitutional by the citing case
V	(Void or invalide)	Citing case has concluded that the statute is not good law because it conflicts with a law that takes priority
Va	(Valid)	Citing case has concluded that the statute is good law and does not conflict with another statutory provision
Vp	(Void or invalid in part)	Citing case has concluded that part of the statute is not good law because it conflicts with a law that takes priority

ABBREVIATIONS—LEGISLATIVE

A	(amended)	Statute amended
Ad	(added)	New section added
E	(extended)	Provisions of an existing statute extended in their application to a later statute, or allowance of additional time for performance of duties required by a statute within a limited time
GP	(granted and citable)	Review granted and ordered published
L	(limited)	Provisions of an existing statute declared not to be extended in their application to a later statute
R	(repealed)	Abrogation of an existing statute
Re-en	(re-enacted)	Statute re-enacted
Rn	(renumbered)	Renumbering of existing sections
Rp	(repealed in part)	Abrogation of part of an existing statute
Rs	(repealed & superseded)	Abrogation of statute & substitution of new legislation
Rv	(revised)	Statute revised
S	(superseded)	Substitution of new legislation for an existing statute not expressly abrogated
Sd	(suspended)	Statute suspended
Sdp	(suspended in part)	Statute suspended in part
Sg	(supplementing)	New matter added to an existing statute

covered by the September 1, 1999, supplement. Now, look at the page from the September 15, 1999, supplement (fig. 6-21). It shows that federal district courts within the 2d and 7th circuits cited to 18 U.S.C. § 2511 (2)(c) during the time period covered by the September 15, 1999, supplement.

In summary, Shepardizing shows that § 2511 (2)(c) is still good authority because the statute has not been amended, repealed, or ruled unconstitutional. It also shows that the statute was cited by a number of federal courts.

Your next question may be how many cases do you have to read of the cases you found through Shepardizing. That depends on the reason you are Shepardizing. If your goal is to find if § 2511 (2)(c) is still good authority, you have not found anything to the contrary. If you had found a statute marked with "U" for "unconstitutional," "Up" for "unconstitutional in part," "V" for "void or invalid," "Vp" for "void or invalid in part," or "L" for "Limited," you should read those cases. If you are using Shepard's as a case finder, to find cases with facts similar to the facts you are researching, you might want to read as many of the cases as possible, especially those marked "C," "f," and "i." In addition, abbreviations indicating legislative action should be reviewed to determine if your research has located all legislative changes to the statute.

FIGURE 6-18 Sample Page from 1996–1997. Bound Supplement to *Sheperd's Federal Statute Citations.*

TITLE 18 § 2510 UNITED STATES CODE

§2510(5)(a)(1)
Cir. 10
f) 929FS1380Δ1996
§2510(5)(a)(2)
Cir. 2
88F3d120*1994
§2510(6)
Cir.4
83F3d690Δ1996
Cir. 6
959FS819Δ1997
Cir. 7
953FS937Δ1996
§2510(11)
Cir. 3
111F3d1069Δ1997
§2510(12)
Cir. 2
922FS836
Cir. 9
932FS1235Δ1996
Cir.10
936FS815Δ1996
§2510(16)
Cir. 10
936FS815Δ1996
§2510(17)
Cir. 2
922FS836
§2510(18)
Cir. 7
953FS940Δ1996
Cir. 9
932FS1235Δ1996
§2511 et seq.
Cir. 3
168FRD532Δ1996
§2511
Cir. 2
939FS145Δ1996
951FS454Δ1997
960FS687Δ1997
168FRD478*1988
Cir. 4
83F3d691Δ1996
Cir. 6
957FS1000Δ1997
959FS817Δ1997
Cir. 9
98F3d504Δ1996
104F3d1531Δ1997
Cir. 10
929FS1375Δ1996
936FS815Δ1996
§2511(1)
Cir. 6
957FS1000Δ1996
959FS819Δ1997

Cir. 10
936FS815Δ1996
139ARRF521nΔ1997
§2511(1)(a)
Cir. 2
922FS836
939FS145Δ1996
953FS86Δ1996
Cir. 3
111F3d1069Δ1997
Cir. 4
93F3d124Δ1996
Cir. 6
959FS817Δ1997
Cir. 7
953FS935Δ1996
Cir. 10
929FS1375Δ1996
na) 930FS505Δ1996
§2511(1)(b)
Cir. 2
953FS86Δ1996
§2511(1)(c)
Cir. 3
111F3d1069Δ1997
Cir. 4
93F3d124Δ1996
Cir. 6
959FS817Δ1997
Cir. 10.
na) 930FS506Δ1996
936F8S15Δ1996
§2511(1)(d)
Cir. 6
959FS817Δ1997
Cir. 10
na) 930FS506Δ1996
936F8S15Δ1996
§2511(1)(e)
Cir. 10
936FS816Δ1996
§2511(2)
Cir. 2
951FS475Δ1997
§2511(2)(a)(1)
Cir.11
i) 957FS216Δ1997
§2511(2)(c)
Cir. 2
923FS424Δ1996
§2511(2)(d)
Cir. 2
951FS473Δ1997
Cir. 10
f) 929FS1376Δ1996
§2511(2)(g)
Cir. 10
936FS811Δ1996

§2511(2)(g)(1)
Cir. 10
936FS815Δ1996
§2511(2)(g)(2)(2)
Cir. 10
i) 936FS811Δ1996
§2511(4)(a)
Cir. 2
953FS86Δ1996
§2512
Cir. 2
951FS453Δ1997
i) 951FS470Δ1997
C) 951FS471Δ1997
C) 960FS687Δ1997
Cir. 3
111F3d1069Δ1997
Cir. 10
936FS814Δ1996
§2512(1)(a)
Cir. 2
951FS453Δ1997
§2512(1)(b)
Cir. 2
951FS453Δ1997
960FS687Δ1997
§2512(2)
Cir. 2
951FS475Δ1997
§2513
Cir. 3
111F3d1069Δ1997
§2515
Cir. 1
113F3d291Δ1997
Cir. 2
103F3d236Δ1997
922FS837
Cir. 3
111F3d1069Δ1997
Cir. 9
938FS1521Δ1996
Cir. 11
957FS216Δ1997
§§ 2516 to 2519
Cir. 3
111F3d1069Δ1997
§§ 2516 to 2518
Cir. 1
113F3d291Δ1997
Cir. 7
88F3d465Δ1996
§2516
Cir. 2
924FS571*1982
Cir. 11
96F3d1584Δ1996

§2516(1)
Cir. 4
88F3d1357Δ1968
Cir. 9
88F3d703Δ1996
Cir. 10
920FS1543
§2517
Cir. 1
113F3d293Δ1997
§ 2517(4)
Cir. 9
938FS1547Δ1996
§2518
Cir. 2
924FS571*1982
Cir. 3
111F3d1070Δ1997
Cir. 7
953FS940Δ1996
Cir. 8
94F3d441Δ1996
Cir. 10
111F3d1484Δ1997
Cir. 11
96F3d1584Δ1996
§2518(1)
Cir. 10
920FS1543
§2518(1)(c)
Cir. 8
94F3d441Δ1996
Cir. 10
920FS1540
§2518(1)(d)
132LE533Δ1995
§2518(3)
Cir. 5
100F3d402Δ1996
Cir. 7
i) 112F3d852Δ1997
Cir. 10
920FS1543
§2518(3)(a to d)
Cir. 10
920FS1544
§2518(3)(a)
Cir. 2
954FS640Δ1997
§2518(3)(b)
Cir. 2
954FS640Δ1997
§2518(3)(c)
Cir. 2
954FS638Δ1997
Cir. 10
920FS1545

FIGURE 6-19 Sample Page from 1998–1999 Bound Supplement to *Shepard's Federal Statute Citations.*

TITLE 18 § 2511 UNITED STATES CODE

§2511(2)
Cir. 1
29FS2d61Δ1998
Cir. 6
1998USAppLX37797
[Δ 1999
160F3d348Δ1998
§2511(2)(a to f)
Cir. 5
1999USDist LX324
[Δ 1999
§ 2511(2)(a)
A) 108St4291
§ 2511(2)(a)(1)
Cir. DC
146F3d1010*1994
Cir. 1
118F3d5Δ1997
124F3d290Δ1997
Cir. 2
32FS2d639Δ1998
Cir. 7
991FS1042Δ1998
31FS2d618Δ1998
§2511(2)(a)(2)
Cir. 1
118F3d6Δ1997
Cir. 2
36FS2d112Δ1999
Cir. 3
124F3d427Δ1997
Cir. 7
1999USDist LX6177
[Δ1999
31FS2d618Δ1998
§ 2511(2)(c)
Cir. DC
146F3d1011*1994
31FS2d6Δ1998
Cir. 1
124F3d296Δ1997
1998USDist LX5846
[Δ1998
29FS2d66Δ1998
33FS2d63Δ1998
Cir. 2
124F3d360Δ1997
1999USDist LX3159
[Δ1999
1999USDist LX3713
[Δ1999
1999USDist LX7078
[Δ1999
994FS490Δ1998
182FRD416Δ1998
Cir. 3
968FS1051Δ1997
Cir. 5
1998USDist LX15088
[Δ1998
Cir. 6
1998USDist LX8635
[Δ1998
Cir. 7
1999USApp LX8448
[Δ1999
1999USDist LX6177
[Δ1999
i) 1999USDist LX6177
[Δ1999
Cir. 9
129F3d516Δ1997
Cir. 11
1999USDist LX3657
[Δ1999
968FS1541Δ1997
§ 2511(2)(d)
Cir. DC
146F3d1011*1994
1998USDist LX19497
[Δ1998
Cir. 1
1998USDist LX5846
[Δ1998
1998USDist LX12044
[Δ1998
29FS2d60Δ1998
Cir. 2
1998USApp LX22044
[*1998
153F3d57* 1994
182FRD416Δ1998
Cir. 4
1998USDist LX8106
[Δ1998
1998USDist LX21529
[*1998
Cir. 5
1998USDist LX15088
[Δ1998
1999USDist LX672
[Δ1999
Cir. 6
154F3d602Δ1998
1998USDist LX8635
[Δ1998
975FS977Δ1997
Cir. 7
1999USDist LX6177
[Δ1999
i) 1999USDist LX6177
[Δ 1999
Cir. 8
2FS2d1189Δ1998
Cir. 9
121F3d467Δ1997
971FS435Δ1997
30FS2d1205Δ1998
Cir. 10
1998USDist LX4716
[Δ1998
Cir. 11
1999USDist LX3657
[§ 1999
§ 2511(2)(e)
Cir. 7
1999USDist LX6177
[Δ1999
§ 2511(2)(g)
Cir. 7
991FS1042Δ1998
§ 2511(2)(g)(1)
Cir. 11
1999USDist LX3657
[Δ1999
§ 2511(2)(g)(2)
Cir. 11
1999USDist LX3657
[Δ1999
§ 2511(3)
Cir. DC
146F3d1014*1970
§ 2511(3)(a)
Cir. 2
124F3d360Δ1997
Cir. 11
129F3d1190Δ1997
§ 2511(3)(b)
Cir. 7
991FS1042Δ1998
§ 2511(4)
Cir. 7
31FS2d618Δ1998
§ 2511(4)(b)
A) 108S5t4290
A) 108St4291
Cir. 2
i) 36FS2d113Δ1998
Cir. 11
1999USDist LX3657
[Δ1999
§ 2511(4)(b)(2)
Cir. 2
36FS2d113Δ1998
Cir. 11
1999USDist LX3657
[Δ1999
§ 2511(4)(c)(2)
Cir. 7
991FS 1042Δ1998
§ 2512
A) 108St2147
Cir. 11
C) 143F3d1426Δ1998
22FS2d1315Δ1998
§ 2512(1)(a)
Cir. 11
C) 143F3d1422Δ1998
§ 2512(1)(b)
Cir. 11
C) 143F3d1422Δ1998
§ 2512(2)
A) 108St2150
A) 110St3509
§ 2512(2)(a)
Cir. 11
143F3d1425Δ1998
§ 2512(2)(b)
Cir. 11
143F3d1425Δ1998
§ 2512(3)
Ad) 111St2273
§ 2515
Cir. DC
136F3d829Δ1998
1998USDist LX19497
[Δ1998
Cir. 1
978FS366Δ1997
Cir. 2
991FS80Δ1998
Cir. 3
124F3d426Δ1997
Cir. 4
143F3d827Δ1998
29FS2d329Δ1998
37FS2d429Δ1998
f) 37FS2d431Δ1998
Cir. 5
1999USDist LX3090
[Δ1999
964FS1102Δ1997
37FS2d506Δ1998
Cir. 6
1998USDist LX8635
[Δ1998
989FS896Δ1997
Cir. 7
1999USDist LX6177
[Δ1999
Cir. 8
994FS1041Δ1998
Cir. 9
125F3d1298Δ1997
155F3d1054Δ1998
971FS433Δ1997
Cir. 10
1999USApp LX7969
[Δ 1999
117F3d1162Δ1997
117F3d1185*1994
1998USDist LX4716
[Δ1998
Cir. 11
1999USDist LX3657
[Δ1999
§§2516 to 2519
Cir. 5
37FS2d506Δ1998
§§2516 to 2518
Cir. 2
116F3d660Δ1997
Cir. 9
125F3d1299Δ1997
§ 2516
Cir. DC
11FS2d30Δ1998

UNITED STATES CODE TITLE 18 § 2511

§ 2262(b)
Cir. 6
1999USDist LX9109
[Δ1999
§ 2262(b)(2)
143LE321Δ1999
143LE311Δ1999
119SC1220Δ1999
§ 2262(b)(3)
j) 143LE336*1994
j) 143LE311*1994
j) 119SC1232*1994
§ 2311 et seq.
Cir. 2
1999USApp LX15679
§ 2314
Cir. 2
1999USDist LX9529
[Δ1999
Cir. 4
1999USApp LX12085
[*1998
Cir. 7
1999USApp LX14121
[Δ1999
Cir. 8
1999USApp LX13434
[Δ1999
Cir. 9
1999USApp LX11677
[*1998
Cir. 10
1999USApp LX 13230
[Δ1999
Cir. 11
1999USApp LX14884
[Δ1999
§ 2318
Cir. 3
1999USDist LX10017
[Δ1999
§ 2319
Cir. 3
1999USDist LX10017
[Δ1999
§ 2320(a)
523US236Δ1998
§ 2321(a)
Cir. 2
1999USApp LX11960
[Δ1999
§ 2322
143LE6Δ1999
143LE1Δ1999
119SC968Δ1999
§ 2326
Cir. 9
1999USApp LX11408
[Δ1999

§ 2331
et seq.
Cir. 2
172F3d178*1996
§ 2332b(b)(1)(A)
Cir. 2
1999 USApp LX15042
[Δ1999
§ 2339A
Cir. 11
42FS2d1321Δ1999
§ 2339B(a)(1)
Cir. DC
1999USApp LX14168
[Δ1999
§ 2340A
Cir. 7
39FS2d957Δ1998
§ 2390
j) 143LE13Δ1999
j) 143LE1Δ1999
j) 119SC974Δ1999
§ 2422
Cir. 10
171F3d1235Δ1999
§ 2422(a)
Cir. 10
C) 1999USApp LX14674
[Δ1999
1999USApp LX14674
[Δ1999
§ 2422(b)
Cir. 2
1999USDist LX8819
[Δ1999
Cir. 10
171F3d1233Δ1999
§ 2423
Cir. 1
1999US Dist LX9663
[Δ1999
§ 2423(a)
Cir. 6
1999USApp LX16967
[Δ1999
Cir. 10
1999USApp LX14902
[Δ1999
§ 2423(b)
Cir. 2
1999USDist LX8819
[Δ1999
Cir. 10
171F3d1233Δ1999
§ 2510
et seq.
Cir. 1
171F3d715Δ1999

Cir. 3
1999USDist LX7918
[Δ1999
Cir. 5
39FS2d789Δ1999
Cir. 7
1999USDist LX10626
[Δ1999
Cir. 11
41FS2d1368Δ1999
§§ 2510 to 2711
Cir. 4
1999USDist LX10384
[*1994
§§ 2510 to 2522
Cir. 6
1999USApp LX11164
[Δ1999
1999USApp LX13128
[Δ1999
Cir. 8
1999USDist LX7832
[Δ1999
Cir. 10
1999USDist LX9866
[*1998
Cir. 11
41FS2d1371*1998
§§ 2510 to 2521
Cir. 6
1999USApp LX13128
[Δ1999
§§ 2510 to 2520
Cir. 3
1999USApp LX16653
[Δ1999
§ 2510
Cir. 11
41FS2d1370Δ1999
§ 2510(2)
Cir. 6
1999USApp LX11164
[Δ1999
§ 2510(5)
Cir. 1
1999USApp LX16656
[Δ1999
§ 2510(5)(a)(2)
Cir. 6
1999USApp LX13128
[Δ1999
§ 2510(6)
Cir. DC
1999USApp LX11347
[Δ1999
§ 2510(8)
Cir. 5
39FS2d790Δ1999

§ 2510(16)
Cir. 11
41FS2d1373Δ1999
§ 2511 et seq.
Cir. 5
1999USDist LX7938
[Δ1999
§ 2511
Cir. 1
171F3d715Δ1999
Cir. 8
1999USDist LX7832
[Δ1999
Cir. 11
41FS2d1369Δ1999
§ 2511(1)(a to d)
Cir. 6
1999USApp LX13128
[Δ1999
§ 2511(1)(a)
Cir. 5
39FS2d789Δ1999
Cir. 8
1999USDist LX7832
[Δ1999
Cir. 11
41FS2d1372Δ1999
§ 2511(1)(b)
Cir. 1
1999USApp LX16656
[Δ1999
Cir. 11
41FS2d1372Δ1999
§ 2511(1)(c)
Cir. 5
39FS2d790Δ1999
§ 2511(1)(d)
Cir. 5
39FS2d794Δ1999
Cir. 8
1999US Dist LX7832
[Δ1999
§ 2511(2)(c)
Cir. 2
42FS2d283Δ1999
Cir. 11
41FS2d1369Δ1999
§ 2511(2)(d)
Cir. 11
41FS2d1369Δ1999
§ 2511(2)(g)(1)
Cir. 11
41FS2d1373Δ1999
§ 2511(2)(g)(2)
Cir. 11
41FS2d1373Δ1999

FIGURE 6-20 Sample page from September 1, 1999, Red Cumulative Supplement to *Shepard's Federal Statute Citations.*

FIGURE 6-21 Sample Page from September 15, 1999, Blue Express Supplement of *Shepard's Federal Statute Citations.*

UNITED STATES CODE TITLE 18 § 3500

§ 2510(12)(A)
Cir. 10
43FS2d1184Δ1999
§ 2511
Cir. 7
1999USDist LX11995 [Δ1999
§ 2511(1)
Cir. 7
1999USDist LX11995 [Δ1999
§ 2511(1)(a)
Cir. 10
43FS2d1183Δ1999
§ 2511(1)(c)
Cir. 10
43FSd1183Δ1999
§ 2511(1)(d)
Cir. 10
43FS2d1183Δ1999
§ 2511(2)(c)
Cir. 2
43FS2d373Δ1999
Cir. 7
1999USDist LX11995 [Δ1999
§ 2511(2)(d)
Cir. DC
1999USDist LX11409 [Δ1999
Cir. 7
1999USDist LX11995 [Δ 1999
§ 2511(5)
Cir. 7
1999USDist LX11995 [Δ1999
§ 2512(1)
Cir. 7
1999USDist LX11995 [Δ1999
§ 2515
Cir. 1
1999USApp LX18041 [Δ1999
§ 2518(4)
Cir. 1
1999USApp LX18041 [Δ1999
§ 2518(4)(a)
Cir. 1
1999USApp LX18041 [Δ1999
§ 2518(4)(b)
Cir. 1
1999USApp LX18041 [Δ1999

§ 2518(4)(c to e)
Cir. 1
1999USApp LX18041 [Δ1999
§ 2518(10)(a)
Cir. 1
1999USApp LX18041 [Δ1999
§ 3006A
Cir. 1
1999USDist LX11282 [Δ1999
§ 3006A(e)(1)
Cir. 8
1999USApp LX18206 [Δ1999
§ 3141 et seq.
Cir. 3
1999USDist LX11511 [1999
Cir. 9
43FS2d1119Δ1999
§ 3142
Cir. 3
1999USDist LX11511 [Δ1999
§ 3142(e)
Cir. 3
1999USDist LX11511 [Δ1999
§ 3142(f)
Cir. 3
1999USDist LX11511 [Δ1999
§ 3142(g)
Cir. 3
1999USDist LX11511 [Δ1999
§ 3145
Cir. 10
1999USDist LX12058 [Δ1999
§ 3145(b)
Cir. 3
1999USDist LX11511 [Δ1999
§ 3146
Cir. 2
1999USDist LX11232 [Δ1999
§§3161 to 3174
Cir. 11
1999USAppLX17875 [Δ1999
§ 3161
Cir. 6
173F3d984Δ1999

§ 3161(c)(1)
Cir. 10
1999USDist LX11951 [Δ1999
1999USDist LX12058 [Δ1999
Cir. 11
1999USApp LX17875 [Δ1999
§ 3161(h)(1 to 7)
Cir. 10
1999USDist LX12058 [Δ1999
§ 3161(h)(1)(D)
Cir. 10
1999USDist LX12058 [Δ1999
§ 3161(h)(1)(F)
Cir. 10
1999USDist LX12058 [Δ1999
Cir. 11
1999USApp LX17875 [Δ1999
§ 3161(h)(1)(J)
Cir. 5
1999USDist LX11496 [Δ1999
§ 3161(h)(7)
Cir. 11
1999USApp LX17875 [Δ1999
§ 3161(h)(8)
Cir. 10
1999USDist LX12058 [Δ1999
§ 3161(h)(8)(A)
Cir. 11
1999USApp LX17875 [Δ1999
§ 3162
Cir. 5
1999USDist LX11496 [Δ1999
§ 3162(a)(2)
Cir. 10
1999USDist LX11951 [Δ1999
1999USDist LX12058 [Δ1999
Cir. 11
1999USApp LX17875 [Δ1999
§ 3181
Cir. 5
1999USApp LX18253 [Δ1999

§ 3184
Cir. 5
1999USApp LX 18253 [Δ1999
§ 3186
Cir. 5
1999USApp LX18253 [Δ1999
§ 3190
Cir. 5
1999USApp LX18253 [Δ1999
§ 3231
Cir. 3
1999USApp LX17938 [Δ1999
Cir. 4
1999USApp LX17824 [Δ1999
§ 3237(a)
Cir. 2
1999USDist LX11430 [Δ1999
§ 3281
Cir. 8
1999USApp LX17921 [Δ1999
§ 3282
Cir. 8
1999USApp LX17921 [Δ1999
§ 3401(a)
Cir. 8
1999USDist LX11309 [Δ1999
§ 3401(b)
Cir. 8
1999USDist LX11309 [Δ1999
§ 3402
Cir. 2
1999USApp LX17878 [Δ1999
§ 3500
Cir. 2
1999USDistLX11232 [Δ1999
Cir. 3
1999USDist LX11425 [Δ 1999
Cir. 4
1999USApp LX17793 [*1994
Cir. 5
1999USDist LX11611 [Δ1999
1999USDist LX11612 [Δ1999

KEYCITE

Using KeyCite for cases

KeyCite serves the same function as Shepard's; it is used to determine if a case is still authoritative and it is used to find other cases that cited to the case you are cite checking. The information accessed through KeyCite is organized differently than the information in the print Shepard's. In the print Shepard's, citations concerning the history of the case are shown first and are followed by citations to cases that have cited the case being Shepardized, with those cases arranged by the court issuing the decision.

When viewing cases in Westlaw, it is good practice to check the upper left-hand corner of the screen for case **status flags,** a red triangular warning flag, a yellow triangular warning flag, a blue upper-case "H" symbol, and a green upper-case "C" symbol. The red flag indicates that the case is no longer good law in some respect; the yellow flag indicates there is some negative history concerning the case, but the case has not been reversed or overruled; the "H" indicates some history exists concerning the case, none of which is negative; the "C" identifies a case that has been cited but that has no direct or negative indirect history. Absence of status flags indicates that the case you are viewing has no direct or indirect history. Clicking the status flag accesses KeyCite and brings you to a screen containing the history of the case, both direct and negative indirect. The **direct history** of the case includes prior and subsequent history of that case. The **negative indirect history** includes cases outside the direct appellate line of the case being KeyCited that may have a negative impact on the precedential weight of the case. For example, cases listed under negative indirect history are later cases that may have questioned the reasoning of the earlier case or distinguished themselves on their facts.

Figure 6-22 shows the first screen of *United States v. McKinnon* on Westlaw. The case has a blue "H" in the upper left-hand corner. The status flag for the case was an "H" because the case has some history, but no negative history. Figure 6-23 shows the first screen of *Wyoming v. Houghton* on Westlaw. The case has a yellow flag in the upper left-hand corner. The status flag for the case was yellow because courts in later cases did not follow *Houghton.*

From figure 6-22, the first screen for *United States v. McKinnon,* the researcher can access KeyCite by clicking on the "H," by clicking on the "KC History" tab or the "KC Citations" tab to the left of the case. Clicking on the "H," or clicking on the "KC History" tab automatically brings the researcher to the full history of the case, shown in figure 6-24.

If one were to scroll down the lefthand screen in figure 6-24, it would show the citation to *McKinnon* in the Court of Appeals for the Eleventh Circuit and the United States Supreme Court. A review of the citations indicates that there was a reported decision by the Eleventh Circuit in *McKinnon* and the United States Supreme Court denied the petition for writ of certiorari. Apparently, the federal district court did not issue a reported decision because there is no citation to any district court opinion.

Clicking the "KC Citations" tab brings up the thirty-four documents that have cited to *McKinnon* (fig. 6-25). In contrast to the print Shepard's, KeyCite gives full citation information for all cases and secondary material. The citation information for cases that have cited the case being KeyCited includes the first page of the case and the page on which the KeyCited case is cited.

Thus, with KeyCite, citations concerning the history of the case are separated from citations to cases that have cited the case being KeyCited. Figure 6-24 shows cases concerning the case history of *McKinnon.* Figure 6-25 shows KeyCite screens containing cases and secondary sources citing to *McKinnon.*

"Citations to the Case" materials are separated into several sections. Typical sections are "Negative Cases," "Positive Cases," "Administrative Materials," and "Secondary Sources." As shown in figure 6-25, *McKinnon* has no section of "Negative Cases." *McKinnon* does have sections of "Positive Cases," "Administrative Materials," and "Secondary Sources." The "Positive Cases" section begins with the first screen of figure 6-25. The "Administrative Materials" and "Secondary Sources" sections follow.

The positive cases citing *McKinnon* are grouped by the depth of discussion of *McKinnon* they contain by **depth of treatment stars.** The cases containing the most in-depth discussion of the KeyCited case listed before cases containing a briefer discussion of the KeyCited case.

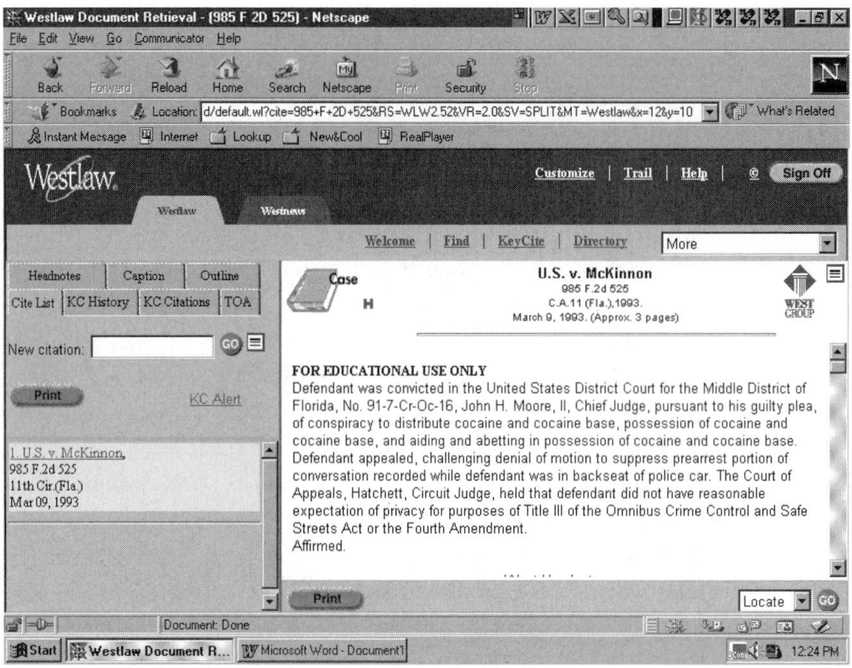

FIGURE 6-22 Westlaw Screen of *United States v. McKinnon.*

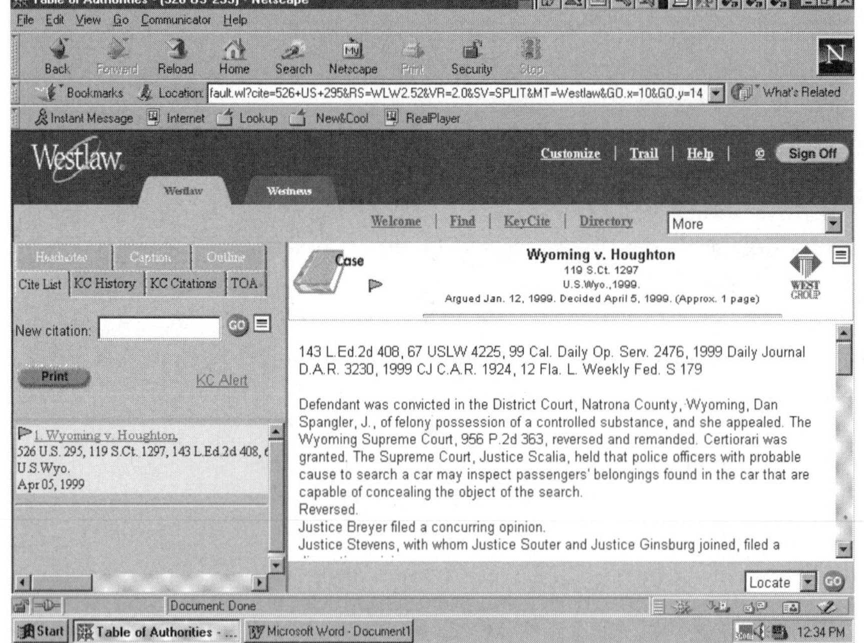

FIGURE 6-23 Westlaw Screen of *Wyoming v. Houghton.*

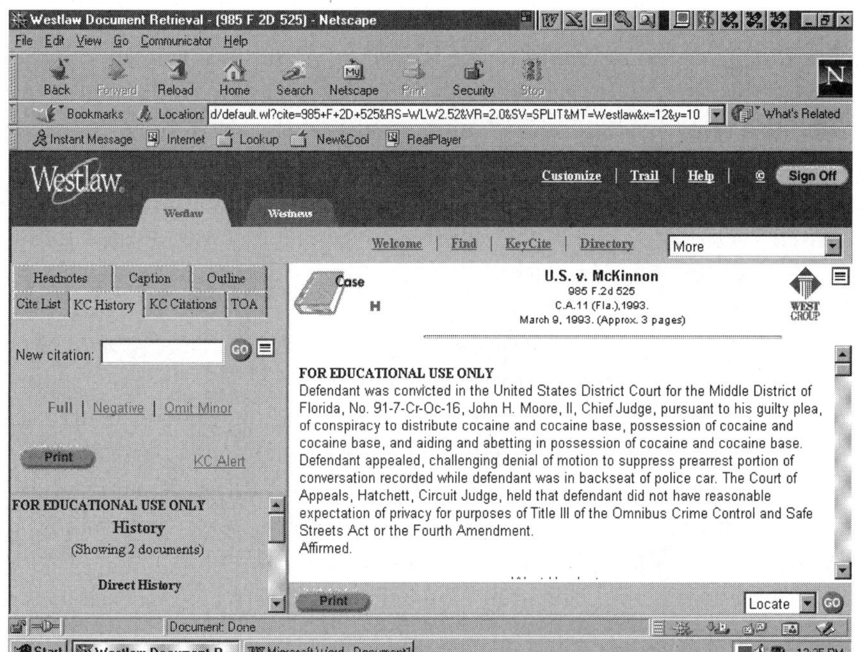

FIGURE 6-24 Full History Screen of *McKinnon.*

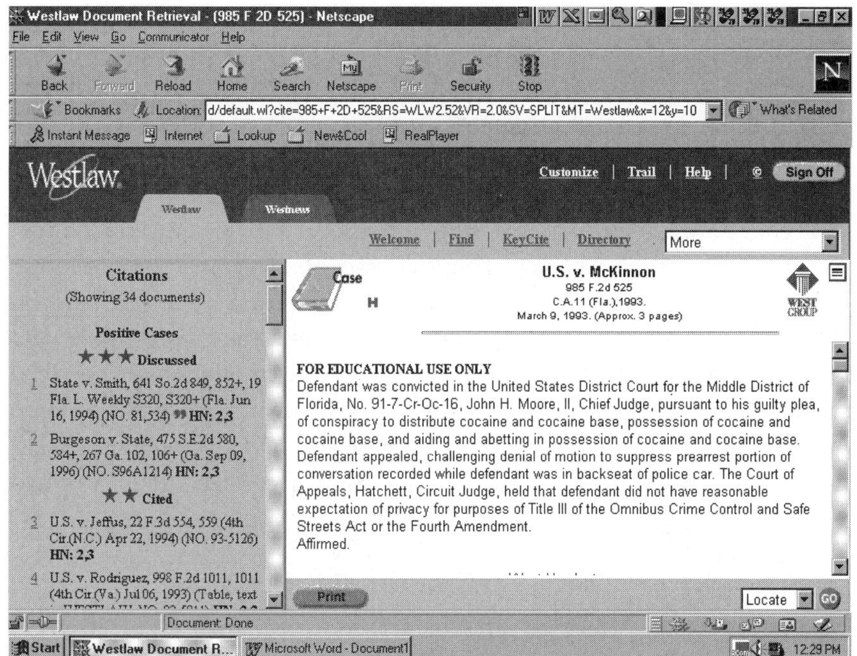

FIGURE 6-25 Documents That Have Cited to *McKinnon.*

Each case is identified with one to four depth of treatment stars. The cases with the fullest discussion of the case being KeyCited are marked "★★★★ Examined." A case in this category would include an in-depth discussion of the KeyCited case, usually more than a page. The cases in which the KeyCited case is discussed are marked "★★★ Discussed." A case in this category includes a substantial discussion of the KeyCited case, usually more than a paragraph but less than a page. The cases in which the KeyCited case is cited and discussed briefly are marked "★★ Cited." A case in this category includes a brief discussion of the KeyCited case, usually less than a paragraph. The cases that simply cite the KeyCited case are marked "★ Mentioned." A double quotation mark indicates that the KeyCited case is quoted in the listed case.

Figure 6-25 shows the information for *McKinnon* retrieved by clicking the "KC Citations" tab. Because the information begins "★★★ Discussed," there were no cases that examined *McKinnon.* The information following "★★★ Discussed" shows that two cases discussed *McKinnon.* The citation information for the two cases is followed by "**HN: 2,3.**" This means that the two cases discussed the legal principles covered in headnotes 2 and 3 of *McKinnon.* Cases 3 through 18 are grouped under "★★ Cited." Within that grouping, federal circuit case citations precede federal district court citations, which precede state court citations. Cases from the same level federal court are listed in reverse chronological order. State court cases are listed alphabetically by state, Delaware, Georgia, Kansas, Oregon, and Tennessee. Cases 19 through 24 are grouped under "★ Mentioned." There is one case from the District Court for the District of South Dakota and state court cases from Colorado, Florida, Georgia, Minnesota, and South Dakota. An opinion of the Texas Attorney General citing to *McKinnon* is listed under "Administrative Materials." A number of law review articles and other secondary sources citing *McKinnon* are listed under "Secondary Sources."

Now examine the KeyCite information for *Houghton.* Figure 6-26 shows the information retrieved by clicking the "KC History" tab or the yellow status flag for *Houghton.* The history of *Houghton* is divided into two sections, "Direct History" and "Negative Indirect History." "Direct History" gives the citation for the Wyoming Supreme Court decision, indicates that certiorari was granted ("Certiorari Granted by"), gives the citation information for the United States Supreme Court's grant of the petition for writ of certiorari, indicates that the United States Supreme Court reversed the Wyoming Supreme Court, and gives the citation to the United States Supreme Court opinion. "Negative Indirect History" shows that courts in several later cases did not follow *Houghton* and groups those cases to indicate why the courts did not follow *Houghton.* The categories are "*Not Followed on State Law Grounds,*" "*Declined to Extend By,*" and "*Distinguished by.*" In the "*Distinguished by*" category, there is one federal court case and the state cases are listed in alphabetical order, California and Illinois. Depth of treatment stars follow each "Negative Indirect History" case citation.

Figure 6-27 shows the information retrieved by clicking the "KC Citations" for *Houghton.* Figure 6-27 begins with a "Negative Cases" section. The cases in this section are the same cases that were found under "Negative Indirect History"; however, the cases in the "*Distinguished by*" category are listed in reverse chronological order. A "Positive Cases" section follows the "Negative Cases" section. The "Positive Cases" are grouped as "★★★★ Examined," "★★★ Discussed," "★★ Cited," and "★ Mentioned." Within each grouping, the cases are listed hierarchically, with United States Supreme Court cases preceding federal court of appeals cases, which precede federal district court cases, which precede state court cases. The federal court of appeals cases are listed in numerical order by circuit. The federal district court cases are listed in reverse chronological order. State court cases are listed alphabetically by state. An opinion of the Oklahoma Attorney General citing to *Houghton* is listed under "Administrative Materials." A number of law review articles and other secondary sources citing *Houghton* are listed under "Secondary Sources."

Using KeyCite for statutes

KeyCite can also be used with statutes. When viewing a statute on Westlaw, a red flag indicates that a section has been amended or repealed by a session law. A yellow flag indicates that pending legislation is available for a section. With KeyCite, citations concerning the history of the statute are separated from citations to cases and other materials that have cited the statute being KeyCited.

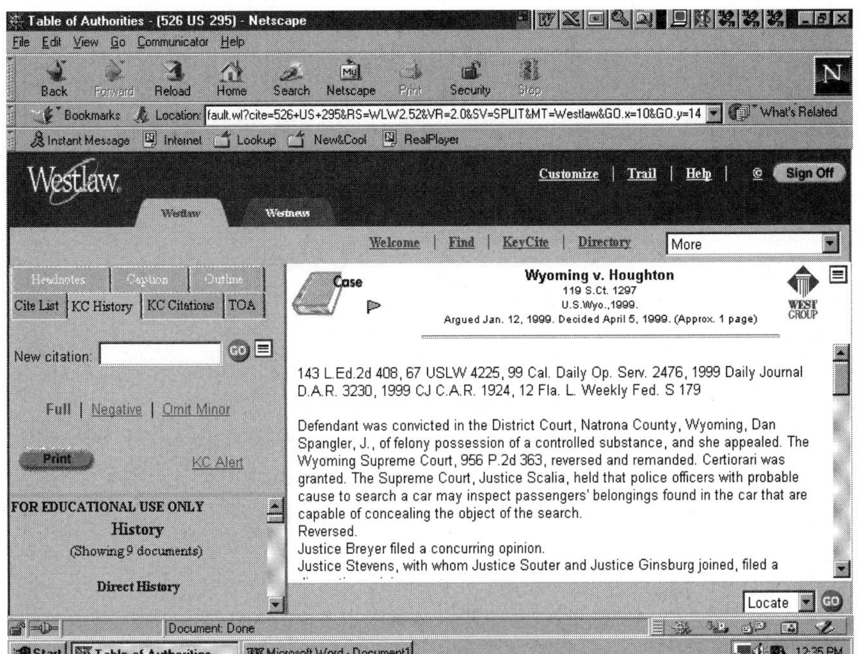

FIGURE 6-26 The History of *Houghton*.

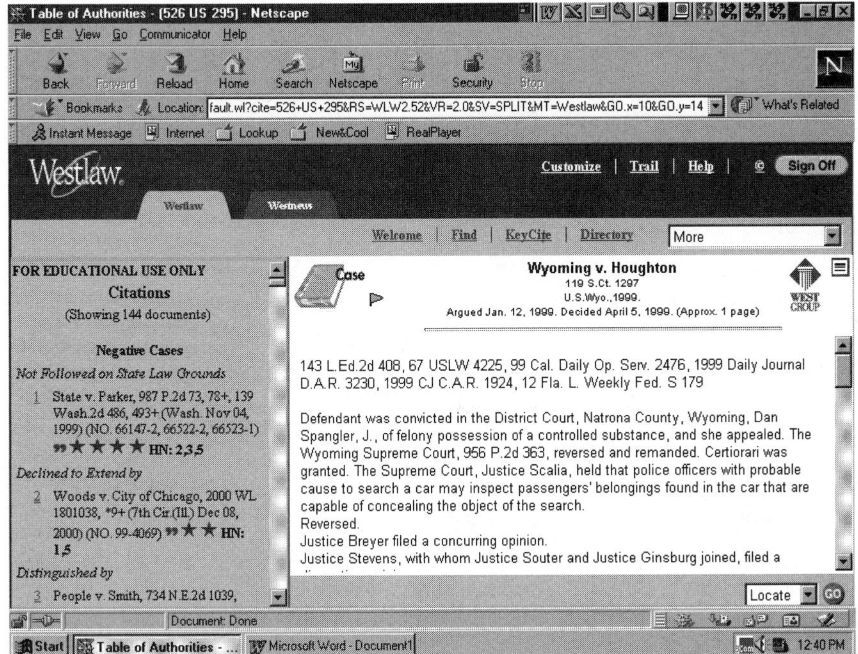

FIGURE 6-27 Negative Cases and Positive Cases Citing *Houghton*.

CHAPTER 6 SUMMARY

- Citators allow the legal researcher to determine whether and where the authority found has been cited in any source.
- The Shepard's company produces the best known set of citators; "Shepardizing" involves consulting Shepard's citators.
- The two reasons for consulting citators are to discover whether your authority is still good law and to locate more recent authority dealing with the same legal principle found in the found authority.
- To Shepardize an authority, consult each volume of the appropriate Shepard's set to see whether your authority has been cited in any other source.
- Shepardizing needs to be done systematically or you may miss something.
- Check to determine that you are Shepardizing under the correct volume and series of the correct reporter and that you have consulted every applicable Shepard's volume.
- Consult the abbreviation tables at the beginning of each Shepard's volume to determine what the abbreviation stands for.
- Single letter abbreviations in the left-hand margin of a column of Shepard's citations indicate whether an authority has been affirmed, reversed, or vacated.
- Other single letter abbreviations indicate the treatment of the authority you are Shepardizing in other sources.
- Shepard's case citations are grouped by court: federal courts in descending order and then state court decisions arranged alphabetically.
- Shepardizing may also be done on Lexis, or a CD-ROM edition of Shepard's.
- Westlaw uses KeyCite to perform the same function as performed by Shepard's on Lexis.

CYBERLAW EXERCISES

1. Shepard's homepage is located at http://www.shepards.com. Using the homepage, go to "helpcite" and take the on-line tutorial.
2. Westlaw's homepage is located at http://www.westlaw.com/. The homepage offers information on KeyCite. Take the product tour for KeyCite, exploring KeyCite for cases and KeyCite for statutes.

LEGAL RESEARCH ASSIGNMENT—CITATORS

1. What is the name of the Shepard's you would use to Shepardize decisions of the United States Supreme Court?
2. What is the name of the Shepard's you would use to Shepardize decisions of the United States District and Circuit Courts?
3. What is the name of the Shepard's you would use to Shepardize decisions of the state courts of your state?

To answer questions 4–12, consult your professor to determine whether you should use Shepard's or KeyCite.

4. The case found at 19 F. Supp. 2d 1081 later went to the United States Supreme Court.
   a. Give the proper citation to the case in the federal district court.
   b. Give the proper citation to the case in the United States Supreme Court. (Only use the citation to the amended decision.)

   c. Give the proper citation to the case in the federal district court, including subsequent history in the United States Supreme Court.
5. The case found at 53 F.3d 371 went to the United States Supreme Court.
   a. Give the proper citation to the case in the federal circuit court.
   b. Give the proper citation to the case in the United States Supreme Court.
   c. Give the proper citation to the case in the federal district court, including subsequent history in the United States Supreme Court.
6. The case found at 551 F.Supp. 349 went to the federal circuit court.
   a. Give the proper citation to the case in the federal district court.
   b. Give the proper citation to the case in the federal circuit court.
   c. Give the proper citation to the case in the federal district court, including subsequent history in the federal circuit court.
   d. Give the proper citation to the case that cited to the case found at 551 F.Supp. 349.
7. The case found at 830 F. Supp. 250 went to the federal circuit court.
   a. Give the proper citation to the case in the federal district court.
   b. Give the proper citation to the case in the federal circuit court.
   c. Give the proper citation to the case in the federal district court, including subsequent history in the federal circuit court.
8. Give the proper citation to the document that cited the case found at 562 F.Supp. 263.
9. Give the proper cittion to the case that cited to *Kano v. National Consumer Cooperative Bank*, 22 F.3d 899 (9th Cir. 1994) in a dissenting opinion.
10. Using Shepard's United States Case Names Citator or KeyCite, look up the 1998 United States Supreme Court case, *Minnesota v. Carter*, and give its proper citation.
11. Using Shepard's United States case Names Citator or KeyCite, look up the 1998 United States Supreme Court case, *New Jersey v. New York*, and give its proper citation.
12. Using Shepard's Federal Case Names Citator or KeyCite, look up the 1997 9th Circuit Court of Appeals case, *N/S Corporation v. Liberty Insurance Company*, and give its proper citation.

CHAPTER 7

OVERVIEW OF THE RESEARCH PROCESS

In the following case excerpts, the court chastises the attorney for failure to perform adequate research.

> On September 7, 1997, the Panel issued an Order in which we stated:
>
> It should also be noted that the Appellant failed to mention, let alone distinguish *Bonner Mall*, the Supreme Court's most recent pronouncement on the issue of vacatur. Had the case law been even perfunctorily researched and Shepardized, it would have been apparent that *Bonner Mall* limited the holding in *Munsingwear*, and precludes *Munsingwear*'s applicability to this case. Having filed the instant motion without a determination that it was warranted by existing law, the Fund and its counsel are subject to the imposition of sanctions for violation of Fed. Bankr.R. 9011. However, we will treat this infraction as a warning to the Fund that it has used its "one free bite."
>
> *In re Markarian*, 228 B.R. 34, 46 n.3 (B.A.P. 1st Cir. 1998).

> The City of New Haven omitted any reference to *Sestito* in its memorandum, despite the fact that *Sestito* is a leading Connecticut case on the issues raised by the motion and is discussed at some length in *Shore v. Stonington*, upon which the City heavily relies. Moreover, in another part of its memorandum the City represents to the court that the rule in *Massengill v. Yuma County* ought to be followed, yet failed to inform the court that that case was specifically overruled in *Ryan v. State*. The court is unable to discern whether sloppy research or warped advocacy tactics are responsible for these errors of omission, but the Corporation Counsel is admonished that diligent research, which includes Shepardizing cases, is a professional responsibility and that officers of the court are obliged to bring to its attention all important cases bearing on the matter at hand, including those which cut against their position. See Model Rules of Professional Conduct, Rule 3.3(a)(3).
>
> *Cimino v. Yale University*, 638 F.Supp. 952, 959 n.7 (D. Conn. 1986)(citations omitted).

INTRODUCTION

Now that you have learned about the basic types of law books a legal researcher would use it is time to discuss how to use them together. This chapter will also discuss basic research strategies. Throughout the chapter the Cruz search and seizure problem from chapter 2 will be used as an example.

Before you start researching you need to get organized. One way to organize your research is to keep a research journal in which you record any relevant information you have found. A research journal may seem time consuming at the beginning of your research. However, the time you spend writing in your research journal should help you focus your research. Refer to figure 7-1 for tips on keeping a research journal. Reviewing your research journal from time to time will remind you what avenues of research you have pursued. Keep thinking of other key words, topics, and sources you could use and remember to check each of the primary and secondary sources you have learned about in this book.

It might be useful to use the Research Checklist (fig. 7-2) as part of or in addition to your research journal to make sure that your research is as thorough as possible.

GATHERING INFORMATION

The length of time you spend researching in the law zlibrary will probably be shortened by the time you spend organizing and gathering information beforehand. If you start researching without gathering all relevant information, you may spend hours researching a question that could have been answered by reviewing pertinent documents or gathering more facts.

If you were given the assignment to research the Cruz search and seizure problem you would start by reviewing the information you have (fig. 7-3). This means that you would carefully read the fact pattern contained in chapter 2. Then you would gather all other relevant information. If possible, you would talk to Cruz, Luis, the officer, and anyone else who might have information. Gather any documents related to the incident. Any reports concerning the incident would be important. The incident may have been videotaped from the patrol car. If so, it would be extremely important to obtain a copy of the videotape.

Research Journal

Purposes:

1. To document your progress in researching a legal problem
2. To document the development of your factual and legal analysis of a legal problem

Procedure

1. Log in the date and time you spent on legal problem.
2. Note key terms, legal issues, citations, legal sources consulted, and other relevant information.
3. Describe how you spent your time (reading, researching, discussing, reflecting, writing) and how the understanding of the legal problem was affected.
4. Note any ideas you develop that may be useful in understanding the problem.
5. Pose questions frequently to keep your thinking focused.
6. Note what research avenues did and did not lead to answers.
7. Record the results of Shepardizing or KeyCiting.
8. Reread previous entries and comment on the facing page.

FIGURE 7-1 Research Journal.

FIGURE 7-2 Research Checklist.

Research Checklist

Name:

Re:

Research begun:

Research completed:

Key words:

Legal encyclopedia:

__ state

__ C.J.S.

__ Am. Jur. 2d

Topics checked:

________________________ __ pocket part checked

________________________ __ pocket part checked

________________________ __ pocket part checked

________________________ __ pocket part checked

American Law Reports:

Annotations checked:

________________________ __ pocket part checked

________________________ __ pocket part checked

________________________ __ pocket part checked

Digests:

Topic and key number checked:

____

____

____

____

FIGURE 7-2 (continued)

Statutes found:

______________________ __ pocket part checked __ citator used

______________________ __ pocket part checked __ citator used

______________________ __ pocket part checked __ citator used

Cases found:

______________________ __ citator used

______________________ __ citator used

______________________ __ citator used

______________________ __ citator used

______________________ __ citator used

Administrative regulations found:

______________________ __ updated

______________________ __ updated

______________________ __ updated

Constitutional provisions found:

______________________ __ updated

______________________ __ updated

______________________ __ updated

Court rules found:

______________________ __ citator used

______________________ __ citator used

______________________ __ citator used

Other sources checked:

__ Legal periodicals

__ Restatements

__ Treatises

__ Other

Notes on other sources:

____

____

____

____

____

____

____

FIGURE 7-3 Step 1 in Research Process.

Step 1—gather and study all relevant information for search and seizure problem:

statements of Cruz and Luis

statement of witnesses

police report

police videotape

FIGURE 7-4 Step 2 in Research Process.

Step 2—Identify key terms:

Fourth Amendment

search and seizure

car automobile

vehicle

container

purse

passenger

tape recording

patrol car

IDENTIFICATION OF KEY TERMS

The next step is to review all the information you have gathered and use it to identify key terms and issues (fig. 7-4). The key terms can be used to start your research in the indexes to secondary or primary sources. From the search and seizure problem you might make a list of the following terms: "search and seizure," "car," "drug courier profile," "Fourth Amendment," and "civil rights." Because the indexes you consult may use words other than the ones you have identified, brainstorm to identify other words with similar meanings or related words. A legal thesaurus might be helpful at this point. From brainstorming and consulting a legal thesaurus, you might think of "dispossession," "forfeit," "vehicle," "automobile," and "race discrimination." As you progress in your research, add any other key words you find to your list.

The explanation of digests in chapter 3 introduced two lists of elements that could profitably be used to generate key words; the key words could be used to access information in the descriptive word indexes of the digests. These lists can also be used at a preliminary stage in your research to generate key terms. West suggested the first list:

1. the *parties* involved;
2. the *places* where the facts arose, and the *objects* or *things* involved;
3. the *acts* or *omissions* that form the *basis of action* or *issue;*
4. the *defense* to the action or issue; and
5. the *relief* sought.

A similar set of elements was suggested by Lawyers Cooperative Publishing Company (now a part of West Group):

1. the *things* involved in the case;

2. the *acts* involved in the case;
3. the *persons* involved in the case; and
4. the *places* where the facts arose.

Examine the hypothetical problem from chapter 2 involving Cruz Estrada and Luis Briones in terms of generating key words.

Parties or persons

The persons involved are two private individuals, Cruz Estrada and Luis Briones, and the police officer. Cruz and Luis are Hispanic. Cruz is also the criminal defendant in the case prosecuted by the United States attorney's office.

Place

The case arose along the interstate highway. Cruz was first located in the car Luis was driving and then conversed with Luis in the rear seat of the patrol car.

Objects or things

The officer used a tape recorder to record Cruz and Luis' conversation in the rear seat of the patrol car. The officer searched Cruz' purse and found illegal drugs.

Acts or omissions forming the basis of the action or issue

The officer stopped Luis for driving a few miles over the speed limit and Luis suspects that they may have been pulled over because of their race. The officer searched Cruz' purse without her verbal consent. The officer secretly tape-recorded Cruz and Luis' conversation in the rear seat of the patrol car.

Defense

If the evidence against Cruz, the drugs and the tape-recorded conversation, were suppressed, the criminal charges would have to be dropped for lack of evidence.

Relief

Cruz would like the criminal charges against her dropped.

Key terms

Some key words relating to the stop and search might be: search and seizure, suppress, evidence, traffic violation, race, racial discrimination, car, highway, police officer, purse, drugs.

Also think of synonyms: speeding, automobile, vehicle, interstate, law enforcement officer, handbag.

Some key words relating to the tape-recording of the conversation might be: patrol car, privacy, conversation, tape-recorder, secret recording, evidence.

Also think of synonyms: police car, communication, surreptitious, tape.

BASIC APPROACHES TO LEGAL RESEARCH

As shown in Figure 7-5, most legal sources have an index. While reporters are not accompanied by indexes, digests function as indexes for reporters. Part of the research process involves researching the key terms you have developed through brainstorming in the appropriate index.

Often, the hardest part of the research process is locating the first piece of relevant information. Once you locate the first piece of relevant information, use some of the techniques discussed below to move from that information to more relevant information.

There are several approaches to the research process depending on the amount of knowledge you possess concerning the areas of law involved in your research problem and depending on whether you are starting with a known primary source. Whichever approach you use, a common method of accessing a research tool is to examine the index, using key terms you brainstormed at the beginning of your research.

Overview approach

If you have little or no knowledge about the areas of law you are researching, you may want to begin the research process in secondary sources to gain a basic understanding of the areas of law. The secondary sources should give you an overview of the areas of law related to your legal question. Your background reading may help you focus your later research and help you generate more key terms to use (fig. 7-6).

This overview may help you familiarize yourself with the key terms used in the areas of law you will be researching. Add these terms to the list of key terms you will use in further research. For example, the terms "interception" and "oral communication" are

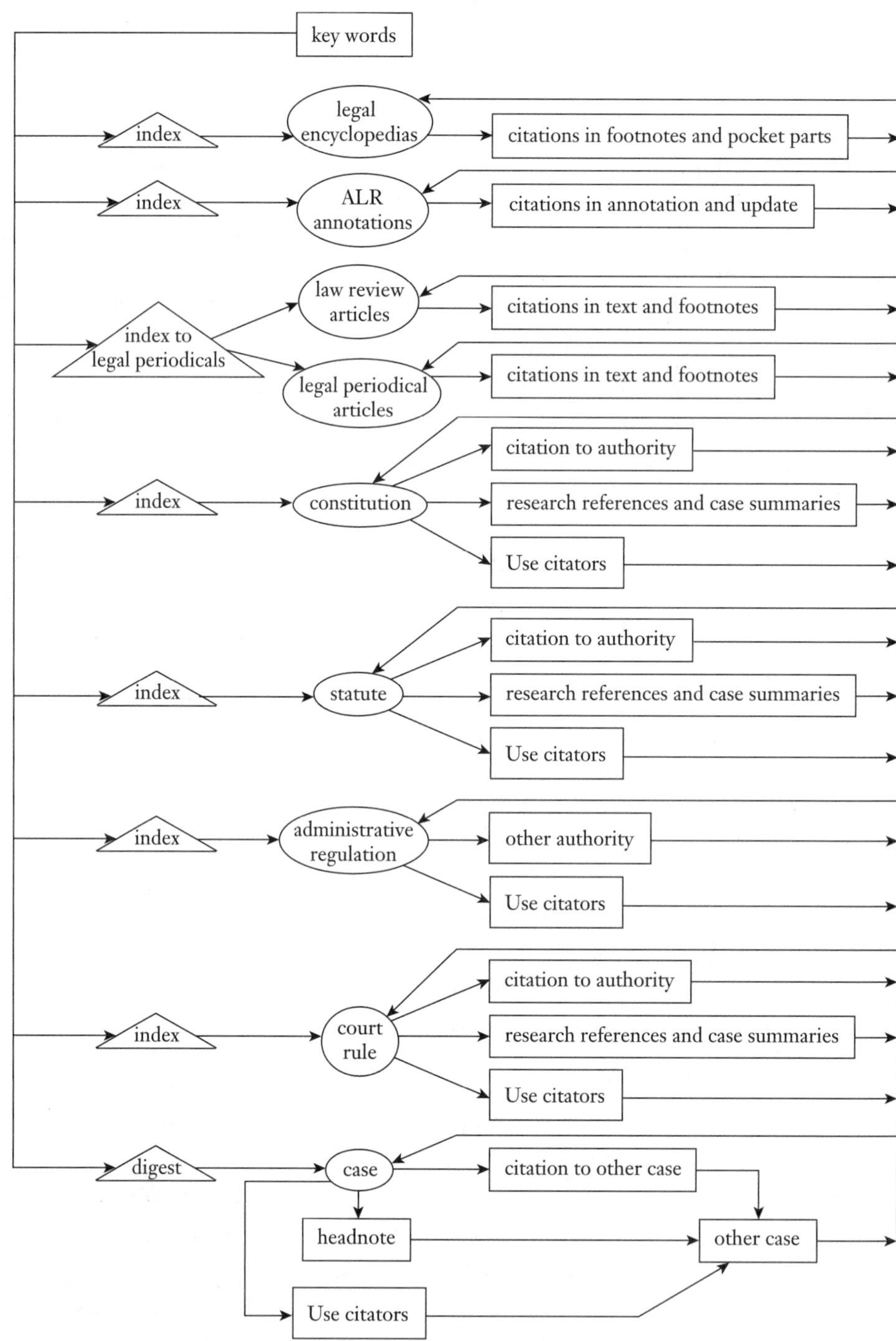

FIGURE 7-5 Research Flowchart.

key terms for the hypothetical problem involving Cruz and Luis. The overview may also give you a preliminary idea of the scope of your research. For the hypothetical problem, you might find that you will be researching federal rather than state law. The key to determining the legitimacy of the car stop and the search of Cruz' purse might be case law interpretations of the Fourth Amendment. The key to determining the legitimacy of the officer tape-recording Cruz and Luis' conversation might be the federal communications statutes and case law interpretations of those statutes. The hypothetical does not seem to raise issues governed by administrative regulations.

Step 3—learn more about the area of law you are researching through:

legal encyclopedias

ALR annotations

looseleaf services

treatises

hornbooks

textbooks

law review articles

articles in legal periodicals

Note the following in your learning journal:

citations to relevant authority

possible issues

applicable jurisdiction (federal, state, or local)

and make a checklist of publications to review

FIGURE 7-6 Step 3 in Research Process.

Topic approach

If you have knowledge about the areas of law you are researching, you may decide to begin the research process in primary sources to quickly locate relevant primary sources. If searching for case law, you might begin your research by examining the outline of a particular topic in a digest. If searching for statutes or administrative regulations, you might begin your research in the index to those statutes or regulations. The danger with focusing your research early on is that you may miss something in another area of law.

Known primary source

Sometimes you are starting with a known primary source. Read the primary source carefully and then explore links to other research tools. The relationship among research tools is described below.

CURRENCY

Currency is critical in legal research. Each source should be updated as you use it and any sources you intend to use as authority should be updated at the end of your research. Research should be updated again if there is a time lag between the completion of your research and the time you use the results of your research. If you have updated your sources as you have gone along, you only need update your authority from the date of your last update.

LEARNING ABOUT THE GENERAL TOPIC

If you know little or nothing about the area of law involved in the problem you are researching, a good beginning point in your research is to read a textual explanation of that area of the law. Legal encyclopedias and *American Law Reports* are the two most widely available sources giving you this type of information. Check to see whether your library has any looseleaf services that cover the area you are researching. Use the key words you have identified to locate relevant topics in the legal encyclopedias, relevant annotations in *American Law Reports*, and relevant materials in loose-leaf services.

By looking in the index to *American Jurisprudence* 2d and *American Law Reports* someone researching the search and seizure problem would locate the following materials:

> 68 Am. Jur. 2d Searches and Seizures §§ 327–468 (2000).
>
> Marjorie A. Caner, Annotation, *Propriety of Attorney's Surreptitious Sound Recording of Statements by Others Who Are or May Become Involved in Litigation*, 32 A.L.R. 5th 715 (1995).

FIGURE 7-7 Step 4 in Research Process.

Step 4—locate primary authority by:

1. using citations found in secondary authority;
2. using indexes to find relevant statutes, constitutional provisions, administrative regulations and court rules; and
3. using digests to find relevant cases.

Chapter 3 contains sample pages from the above *American Jurisprudence* topic and *American Jurisprudence* annotation.

Law review and legal periodical articles may give you even more specific information. ***Index to Legal Periodicals*** is a good source to use to locate these articles either by subject or by author. Familiarize yourself with other resources available in your library, including treatises and **hornbooks.** A legal textbook covering the area of law you are researching may be another good place to start. Appendix A contains a textual explanation of some aspects of search and seizure and the exclusionary rule, entitled "Search and Seizure and the Exclusionary Rule." This information was adapted from a criminal law textbook.

As you read about the topic you are researching, note in your research journal anything that may be helpful to you later (citations to relevant authority, possible issues, and applicable jurisdiction—federal, state or local). Also make a checklist of the publications to review. Make sure you list primary and secondary sources and finding tools for federal, state, and local jurisdictions.

If you are knowledgeable in the topic you are researching or have a primary source to work with, you may want to start researching in primary sources first. Even a knowledgeable researcher would be glad to quickly locate a law review or legal periodical article on point. The article usually saves the researcher time by summarizing the law in the area and citing relevant authority. The researcher can pull the cited authority, read it, update it, and pursue another avenue of research.

LOCATING PRIMARY SOURCES

By using secondary sources, indexes, and digests

Armed with general knowledge about search and seizure and civil forfeiture, you are ready to locate primary sources (fig. 7-7). There is no one right place to start to locate primary sources. You may first want to locate primary sources by using the citations noted in your research journal. If you think the problem involves a statute, constitution, administrative regulation or court rule, consult the appropriate index.

For example, you would find the text to the Fourth Amendment by looking in the index to the Constitution under "search and seizure." You would find the federal eavesdropping and wiretapping statutes (18 U.S.C. §§ 2510–2521) by looking in the index to the United States Code or an annotated code under "wiretapping"; you would find the federal court rule governing motions to suppress (Rule 12) by looking in the index to the Federal Rules of Criminal Procedure under "motion to suppress." Chapter 4 contains a copy of the federal wiretapping and eavesdropping statutes.

Consult a digest to find relevant cases. Locate cases in the digest either by consulting the Descriptive-Word Indexes (located at the end of the digest set) or reviewing a topic outline (printed at the beginning of each topic). When you locate a primary source, use the primary source to locate other primary sources. For example, you could look in the descriptive word index to *Federal Practice Digest* 4th under "search and seizure." The index would tell you that there is a digest topic "Searches and Seizures." You could look at the outline at the beginning of the topic to identify relevant key numbers. You would find *Wyoming v. Houghton* under various key numbers of the topic.

By using other primary authority

What do you do after you find a relevant statutory or constitutional provision? Once you find a relevant statutory or constitutional provision, there are three ways to use the provision to locate other primary authority (fig. 7-8). First, read the provision carefully and note any cross-references to other statu-

Step 5—once you have found primary authority, use the primary authority to locate other primary authority.

If you have a statute or constitutional provision:

1. Pull any primary authority referenced in the statute or constitutional provision.
2. Consult an annotated code or constitution.
3. Use a citator.

If you have a relevant case:

1. Pull any cases referenced in the known case.
2. Use the headnotes of the known case to locate other cases in the digest.
3. Use a citator.

FIGURE 7-8 Step 5 in Research Process.

Currency in research is crucial. Using a citator is a must to make sure primary sources are still good law. In the following passage, the court criticized the attorney for failing to Shepardize cases.

DeMyrick's motion is particularly distressing under the circumstances. It is not simply that DeMyrick's counsel are highly experienced in Illinois personal injury practice and might therefore be expected to keep themselves current on such issues that are of importance to the conduct of such practice and that arise with some frequency. Beyond that expectancy, no counsel ought to cite a case (such as *Comastro* in this instance) without Shepardizing that case (or without conducting the equivalent electronic search via Westlaw or Lexis). And any such search would immediately have revealed the decision in *Roth*, which expressly explains *Comastro* as holding that "defendants owed plaintiff ordinary, reasonable care to protect him from criminal attack" and as negating any notion of the "highest degree of care."

Demyrick v. Guest Quarters Suite Hotels, No. 93 C 1520, 1997 WL 177838, *1 (N.D.Ill. April 6,1997).

tory or constitutional authority. Then pull the authority referenced. Also examine how the provision fits with other statutory or constitutional provisions. You may find definitions of terms or related statutory provisions.

The second way is to consult an annotated code or constitution. Locate the applicable statute or constitutional provision and begin reading the references following the provision. The references may refer you to related constitutional provisions, statutes, and administrative regulations as well as digest topics, legal encyclopedia topics, and law review articles. Then read the case summaries. If a reference or case summary involves the same question you are researching, note the citation, pull the authority, and read it. A third way to locate other authority is to Shepardize or KeyCite your constitutional or statutory provision.

What do you do after you find a relevant case? Once you find a relevant case, there are three ways to use the case to locate other cases (fig. 7-8). The first way is to read the case and note the citations to earlier cases cited in it. Then pull and read any of those earlier cases that seem helpful. A second way is to make note of relevant headnotes from the case, locate the same digest topic in the digest, and read the digest abstracts to locate more cases. A third way of locating cases is to Shepardize or KeyCite the case. Using citators will give you citations to later cases citing the case. The case may also cite other primary sources such as statutes, constitutional provisions, court rules, or administrative regulations.

When are you finished with your research? You are probably finished when you have checked each of the main primary and secondary sources and you keep finding the same authorities. Before you stop, double-check to make sure you have updated any authorities you intend to use by using a citator and follow any other avenues of research suggested by the information you obtain from the citator.

In the preceding chapters, legal research tools (primary sources, secondary sources, and finding tools) have been discussed individually. When researching a legal problem, you must combine their use. This chapter discusses several research strategies as well as the relationship among the various research tools. Information in one research tool can lead to more information in the same or another research tool.

Legal research involves discovering what the law is and how it will affect the client's case. Your goal in legal research is to find all applicable constitutional provisions, statutes, court rules, and administrative regulations. As far as case law is concerned, your goal is to find cases that constitute mandatory authority; if there is no mandatory authority, you are searching for cases that constitute persuasive authority. Where primary authority is unavailable, you may look to secondary sources. Certain types of secondary sources, such as Restatements, law review articles, and well-respected treatises, generally carry more weight than other secondary sources and may be highly persuasive.

Your research process must be as efficient as possible to save you unnecessary wasted time and limit the client's fees; at the same time, the research must be as thorough as possible. You may have a limited amount of time to research a particular issue because you must meet a filing deadline. Your office may have quoted the client a certain amount in attorneys fees.

RELATIONSHIP AMONG RESEARCH TOOLS

Research tools are linked to each other in a variety of different ways. Note links to other research tools and follow up the links as you move through the research process. Look at some of the basic links among research tools. These links are illustrated in figure 7-5.

Use citations in the footnotes and pocket parts of legal encyclopedias, ALR annotations, and other secondary sources to lead you to relevant cases and statutes. Once you find a relevant case, read it, noting internal citations to other primary sources, including other cases, statutes, court rules, and administrative regulations. Note the digest topic and number from any relevant headnotes and use that information to locate summaries of relevant cases under the same topic and number of the appropriate digest. Use a citator to ascertain whether the case is still good authority and to find more recent relevant cases.

Once you find a relevant statute, read it, noting internal citations to other statutes. Carefully read the research references following the statute for citations to related constitutional provisions, statutes, administrative regulations, secondary sources, and digest topics. Read the case summaries to find relevant cases. Do not forget to check the pocket part to the volume and any interim pamphlets. Use a citator to double-check the status of the statute and to find relevant cases.

Once you find a relevant constitutional provision, locate it in an annotated code. Carefully read the research references following the provision for citations to related constitutional provisions, statutes, administrative regulations, secondary sources, and digest topics. Read the case summaries to find relevant cases. Do not forget to check the pocket part to the volume and any interim pamphlets. You probably do not need to use a citator to check the status of a provision from the United States Constitution, but do so for a state constitutional provision. Using a citator will allow you to find relevant cases.

In the following case, the attorney was found negligent in not having performed adequate research.

Charles E. BAIRD and Betty Baird, husband and wife, Third-Party

Plaintiffs/Appellees,

v.

Thomas M. PACE and Jane Doe Pace, husband and wife; Lawrence M. Hecker and Jane Doe Hecker, husband and wife; Steve W. Phillips and Jane Doe Phillips, husband and wife; dba Hecker & Phillips, a general partnership, Third-Party Defendants/Appellants.

Court of Appeals of Arizona,

Division 2, Department A.

Dec. 31, 1987.

Review Denied April 26, 1988.

752 P.2d 507

HATHAWAY, Judge.

Baird's third-party malpractice action against Pace was based on his alleged negligence in failing to adequately research how to perfect the security interest and where to file it. The case was tried to the court without a jury and the trial court entered judgment against Pace and his law firm, Hecker & Phillips, for the amount of the debt that remained unpaid and uncollectible because it was unsecured, together with attorney's fees incurred by Baird. We affirm.

Pace argues on appeal: (1) that the trial court's factual finding that he was negligent was not supported by the record, and (2) that his failure to properly file the financing statement was not the proximate cause of the harm Baird suffered.

Pace argues that the standard of negligence for legal malpractice was not met. We disagree. That standard requires an attorney to act for his client in a reasonably careful and skilled manner in view of his special professional knowledge. He must " . . . possess such a reasonable knowledge of the law as is ordinarily possessed by other attorneys, and to discover those additional rules of law which, although not commonly known, may be readily found by standard research techniques." 7A C.J.S. Attorney and Client, S 256 (1980) [footnotes omitted]. Whether that standard is met is a question of fact under the circumstances. At trial, both parties presented expert testimony from local attorneys regarding the "correct" procedure necessary to preserve a security interst in a liquor license. The experts expressed conflicing opinions as to the appropriate procedure.

Expert testimony is generally used to establish the standard of care by which the professional actions of an attorney are measured and to determine whether the attorney deviated from the proper standard. The testimony presented, subject to the factfinder's assessment, was a proper basis for the trial court's decision.

The trial court made the following pertinent findings:

> The court finds that Third-Party Defendant PACE neither undertook research nor made reasonable inquiry to determine the correct procedure for perfecting the security interest in the Liquor License.
>
> * * *
>
> The court further finds in the the [sic] present case, Mr. PACE failed to perform adequate research and thus was unable to exercise the informed judgment to which his client was entitled. He failed to meet the required standard of care, and the court finds that this was a proximate cause of the loss sustained by Mr. and Mrs. BAIRD. Supportive of those findings is Mr. Pace's testimony at trial in regard to his research in determining the proper place to record Baird's security interest.
>
> Q. And in determining how to perfect his security interest in the liquor license, did you undertake any research to determine how to do the perfection?
>
> A. Not at that time.
>
> Q. Had you previously undertaken any research in how to perfect a security interest in a liquor license?

A. I had reviewed the liquor regulations at some point in the past, and I'd also, I guess—although that's not research—seen how other people at Trew & Woodford had done it.

* * * * * *

Q. You didn't look at the statutes, in any event; you were relying on your practice at Trew & Woodford; is that right?

A. At Trew & Woodford and O'Connell, Hecker and Phillips, yes.Three of the lawyers testifying for Baird expressed their opinion that Pace fell below the appropriate standard of care when he failed to secure Mr. Baird's interest in the liquor license by filing a financing statement with the Secretary of State. Mr. Pace's own expert witness, an experienced attorney licensed in 1960 and frequently involved in liquor license transactions, testified that when he first began practicing law, he became involved in a liquor license transfer and set out to determine how it should be accomplished. He prepared by reading the law, checking with other attorneys and inquiring directly with the Director of the Department of Liquor Licenses to determine the appropriate way to secure an interest in a liquor license being transferred. He also spoke with the brother of the director, a Phoenix attorney, about transferring liquor licenses.

Pace cites Martin v. Burns, supra, as authority for the proposition that an attorney will not be held liable for a mistake of law or error in judgment regarding a point of law that has not been settled by the highest court of the jurisdiction and upon which reasonable lawyers may differ. He argues that the present case falls within the reasoning of Martin v. Burns, providing a basis for overruling the trial court. At first blush, this authority appears applicable; however, there is an important distinction. In Martin, there was no settled law upon which the attorney could have relied for guidance, whereas, in the instant case, a pertinent statutory provision exists. It is not important that there was no prior Arizona caselaw on point, because the statutory provision gives the necessary guidance. A.R.S. S 47-9401(A)(3) (formerly A.R.S. S 44-3140(A)(3)) provides that for collateral not falling within specific subsections, certain documents should be filed in the office of the Secretary of State. A reading of the statute clearly reveals that a liquor license is property falling within that category for filing with the Secretary of State.

Arizona caselaw available prior to 1980 provided that, as between a licensee and third parties, a liquor license is a property right with a "peculiar and special value." Hooper v. Duncan. It is reasonable to deduce that if a liquor license is a form of property, and if it does not fit within one of the specific categories provided in former A.R.S. S 44-3140(A), it must be perfected pursuant to the "catchall" provision and filed with the Secretary of State.

As we noted in Landon v. Stroud and Baird, supra, the statutory and regulatory provisions pertaining to the filing of statements of legal and equitable interests in liquor licenses did not address the creation or perfection of security interests. As noted above, former A.R.S. S 44-3140(A)(3) states that any collateral not provided for elsewhere in the Uniform Commercial Code should be filed pursuant to the "catchall" provision with the Secretary of State. A.R.S. S 4-112(B) pertains only to the duties of the board and superintendent of the liquor department, not to the procedure required for perfection of a security interest in a liquor license.

Further, Pace's action in filing only with the liquor department did not even constitute a good-faith filing in an improper place, see former A.R.S. S 44-3140(B), because as we pointed out in Landon:

The statement [of legal and equitable interest] merely identifies Baird's interest as arising under an agreement for sale and a promissory note. Nowhere is the term "security interest" or "security agreement" used, despite the directive in the form that the interest be so described and that the reasons for the granting of the interest be set forth.

As Baird argues, the safest method for perfecting a security interest, and that advocated by White and Summers, is that an attorney should " . . . file a financing statement in every conceivable place which could benefit him to do so; or he will buy insurance against the possibility that his client's interest will not be perfected." J. White and R. Summers, Uniform Commercial Code, S 23-12 at p. 943 (2d ed. 1980). Additionally, common precaution suggests the "cover all bases" approach. Pace's expert witness concurred in this theory. It is apparent that Pace's failure to file with the Secretary of State was not brought about by uncertainty as to where to file, but by a lack of research. We concur in the trial court's reliance on Smith v. Lewis, where the following reasoning was found persuasive:

> If the law on a particular subject is doubtful or debatable, an attorney will not be held responsible for failing to anticipate the manner in which the uncertainty will be resolved.
>
> [citation omitted] But even with respect to an unsettled area of the law, we believe an attorney assumes an obligation to his client to undertake reasonable research in an effort to ascertain relevant legal principles and to make an informed decision as to a course of conduct based upon an intelligent assessment of the problem.
>
> * * *
>
> Even as to doubtful matters, an attorney is expected to perform sufficient research to enable him to make an informed and intelligent judgment on behalf of his client.

Pace also contends that even if he was negligent in not properly filing a financing statement in 1980, his negligence was not the proximate cause of Baird's later injury because of Baird's "consent" to subsequent transfers of the liquor license.

We disagree. As a result of Pace's failure to perfect Baird's security interest in the license at the time of the original conveyance to Carrier and Maxwell, Baird was thereafter relegated to second position behind Landon. Neither the withholding of consent to subsequent transfers nor anything Baird's attorney, Chayet, could have done would have changed that. Pace suggests that there was a gap between the transfer from Lynch to Tull and Landon's filing of Tull's financing statement during which Baird would have obtained a security interest and filed ahead of Landon. First, although the Lynch-Tull agreement is dated two months before the date of filing, it is unclear exactly when the license was actually transferred, i.e., when the department approved the transfer. Second, Baird had no way to compel Tull to give him a security interest in the license. As for Pace's claim that Baird should have accelerated payment of the Carrier/Maxwell promissory note upon the sale to Lynch, such an action may or may not have been successful and, in any event, would have left him in second position behind Landon. The court was correct in finding that Pace's negligence was the proximate cause of Baird's damages.

CHAPTER 7 SUMMARY

- Before you start researching in the law library, gather and organize information and read all pertinent documents.
- Throughout the research process, take notes of what you have found, citations to relevant authority, and ideas for other avenues of research.
- Review all the information you have gathered and use it to identify key terms and issues.
- You may want to learn more about the area of law you are researching by consulting secondary sources such as legal encyclopedias, *American Law Reports* annotations, looseleaf services, and law review articles.
- Locate primary authority by using citations found in secondary authority, indexes, and digests.

- Use primary authority to locate other primary authority through reading cited primary authority, case summaries in annotated codes and constitutions, and Shepardizing or KeyCiting.
- You are probably finished with your research when you have checked each of the main primary and secondary sources and keep finding the same authorities.
- Consult the Research Flowchart printed in this chapter to develop a research strategy or explore other avenues of research.

CYBERLAW EXERCISES

1. Westlaw's homepage is located at http://www.westlaw.com/. The homepage offers information on those new to Westlaw. Take the product tour.
2. The Legal Information Institute at Cornell Law School maintains a homepage with a wealth of legal information. The home page is located at http://law.cornell.edu/. Explore some of the material accessible via this home page.
3. LexisNexis' homepage is located at http//www.lexis.com/. The homepage offers a tour of the site. Take the tour.
4. The Lexis law school site (http://lawschool.lexis.com) includes information on legal research strategies.
5. Two fee-based legal research sites offering alternatives to Westlaw and Lexis are VersusLaw (http://www.versuslaw.com) and Loislaw (http://www.loislaw.com/).
6. FindLaw (http://www.findlaw.com) is a well-known legal research starting point.
7. WashLaw Web (http://www.washlaw.edu) is another well-known legal research starting point.
8. For a different approach, try the "law" directory under government at http://yahoo.com.
9. The American Bar Association's homepage (http://www.abanet.org/lawlink/home.html) contains links to federal government sites, selected law libraries, and other on-line research sites.
10. Also try http://www.law.com. The site has current legal news plus links to multiple legal resources.
11. Many law school librarians have written legal research guides and have posted them on the web. The guides attempt to introduce students to legal research and to answer commonly asked questions. Paul Richert, Law Librarian and Professor of Law at the University of Akron, School of Law Library, has compiled an "Internet Hotlist of Law Guides Organized by Subject" that links to many of the legal research guides. The Hotlist is accessible at http://www.uakron.edu/law/richert/index1.html.

EXERCISES FOR CHAPTER 7

1. Pick one of the research problems from Appendix E.
2. Research the problem you have chosen.
3. List the citations to any relevant legal sources.
4. Using your research, write the answer(s) to the selected research problem.

In the following case, the federal district court awarded attorney fees totaling $14,736.95 against the union member's attorney, largely for the attorney's failure to perform adequate legal research:

After suit was filed, Taylor told his attorney that another union had voted on whether to make a job a house account. Plaintiff's attorney now argues that Local 41 was acting "ultra vires" when it agreed orally with Belger to treat Burlington Northern as a house account. Regardless of the merits of this position, counsel never explained how it had anything to do with the manner in which plaintiff's grievance was handled.

Furthermore, plaintiff's attorney never did any research to determine whether or not Local 41's business agent had authority to make such an oral agreement. He relied solely on his client's statement that another union had voted in a similar situation and on his client's conclusion that therefore it was unlawful not to vote.

Understandably, defendants filed motions for summary judgment based in large part on plaintiff's deposition testimony. Before opposing these motions plaintiff's attorney did not even read both defendants' suggestions in support of the motions for summary judgment. He conducted virtually no legal research in preparing his opposition to the motions. He never Shepardized his principle authority, *Baldini v. Local Union No. 1095*. Counsel explained that he felt there was no need to Shepardize *Baldini* because he was confident it was good law. Had he Shepardized *Baldini*, certainly he would have found that later decisions in the Seventh Circuit had restricted *Baldini* to its facts.

In summary, Taylor's counsel recommended filing a lawsuit against these defendants without determining the easily ascertainable standard for assessing whether Local 41 had fairly represented Taylor in processing his grievance. He recommended filing suit before the events had occurred that he had to assess to determine whether Taylor had a claim. After the arbitration procedure and before the suit was filed, plaintiff's counsel again failed to ascertain the proper legal standard and to analyze what had happened in light of this standard. Instead, he attempted to create, almost out of thin air, rationalizations for filing suit. After filing suit he did nothing to determine whether the facts really supported his view that Local 41 had breached its duty of fair representation. Even after Taylor's deposition confirmed what counsel had known for some time about the union's efforts on Taylor's behalf, he blindly and stubbornly opposed the motions for summary judgment. At no time did he counsel Taylor that he should get out of this case on the best terms possible; at no time did he seek to withdraw rather than pursue the claims against Local 41 and Belger, both of which were dependent on establishing that Local 41 failed to fairly represent Taylor. Rather than analyzing the facts available to him in light of the easily ascertainable and clear legal standard for determining whether plaintiff had been fairly represented, counsel relied primarily on his emotional belief that Taylor should have gotten the job because Taylor was a good union and family man.

Taylor v. Belger Cartage Service, Inc., 102 F.R.D. 172, 178 n.2, 180 (W.D. Mo. 1984)(citation omitted).

CHAPTER 8

CALR: COMPUTER-ASSISTED LEGAL RESEARCH

INTRODUCTION

Today, conducting legal research has become more and more computerized. While law schools and paralegal education programs continue to teach legal research "basics"—how to effectively use standard print tools to locate primary and secondary sources of the law—the use of computers has become an integral part of today's law practice.

The Internet and, in particular, its graphic component—the World Wide Web—offer enormous opportunities to improve the speed, currency, and cost-efficiency of both traditional legal research and factual research. Whether you prefer the software version—loaded on your computer's hard drive, a local area network (LAN), or a company intranet—or the convenience of logging on to an online vendor's web site from any computer with Internet access—conducting computer-assisted research has never been easier or more convenient.

In many cases, Internet resources are virtually free, although some sites are proprietary (requiring a user password) and may offer a combination of free and fee-based services. Often, web sites provide the most current information and may even offer resources that cannot be found in any other formats, such as print, CD-ROM, or commercial online databases. A good example is the trend toward "web-only" electronic publishing of many scholarly journals, newsletters, and law reviews.

HISTORY OF COMPUTER-ASSISTED LEGAL RESEARCH (CALR)

The first successful attempts at what we now call computer-assisted legal research (CALR) actually began in the late 1950s and early 1960s by John Horty, Director of the University of Pittsburgh Health Law Center and adjunct professor at the University of Pittsburgh School of Law. Horty had the texts of relevant statutes coded onto punch-cards and then put on computer tapes where they could be searched and retrieved by keyword—a electronic search technique that became known as "Key Words in Combination" or KWIC.

In 1967, in an effort to improve on Horty's system, the Ohio State Bar Association created a nonprofit corporation, the Ohio Bar Automated Research (OBAR). OBAR contracted with another Ohio company, Data Corporation, to develop the first commercially marketed legal research software.

In 1969, Data Corporation was acquired by Mead Corporation, a subsidiary of Mead Data Central. Mead Data Central continued the OBAR project and eventually acquired all rights to OBAR. By 1972, Mead Data Central had produced a second-generation version of the OBAR software, preserving many of the best features of Horty's original program. In April 1973, a modified version of this software (together with dedicated hardware) was introduced to the American legal community under the name Lexis. Lexis initially offered its subscribers a database of full-text federal statutes and case law, a federal tax library, and selected state databases. In 1980, it expanded to give its subscribers access to Nexis, a huge nonlegal database of news and business information. (Lexis™ and Nexis™ are registered trademarks of Reed Elsevier Properties, Inc.)

Lexis® went online nationally in 1973, and credits itself as the oldest full text CALR information service provider. That same year, West Publishing Company (now West Group) began work on its own computer-assisted legal database—Westlaw. Westlaw™ is a registered trademark of West Group, Inc. The earliest version of Westlaw, based on West's headnotes and key number system, was launched in the spring of 1975. But it was not until late the following year that Westlaw was positioned to compete with Lexis in the full text online service market. Over the years, both products have undergone major redesigns and enhancements in an effort to keep pace with technology, competitors and, most importantly, the demands of their users. In 1994, Mead Data sold the rights to LexisNexis to Reed Elsevier, Inc.

While initially the primary target market for both Lexis and Westlaw was lawyers, these vast online legal and factual databases are now widely used by business and industry. Both CALR products are an integral part of today's law school and paralegal education legal research training and are available to students and faculty at most colleges and universities, and many public libraries.

Together, Lexis and Westlaw have had a subtle yet profound impact on the way primary and secondary legal materials are distributed and accessed by millions of people worldwide. Today, these CALR "giants" offer timely, convenient access to the full text of federal and state court decisions, legislative information, law review articles, legal encyclopedias, and treatises. Their nonlegal databases now rival Dialog and other commercial online vendors for full text access to national and regional newspapers and scholarly journals, company and financial data, and public records.

ELECTRONIC INFORMATION FORMATS

Traditionally, when we refer to "computer-assisted" or "electronic" resources, we are actually referring to four distinctly different information formats: commercial online databases, CD-ROM products, computer disk programs, and the Internet and World Wide Web.

Commercial Online Databases

This category of resources includes proprietary databases accessible from software loaded on a single computer or network, or accessed from a vendor's Internet web site. These products generally require a user logon identification and/or password. Popular commercial online database providers include LexisNexis, Westlaw, VersusLaw, and Dialog.

Always check with your librarian, business manager, or other person responsible for negotiating database vendor licenses to determine what type of pricing arrangement applies to a particular product. Many vendors offer a number of pricing plans, including hourly, flat fee (a fixed price per month or annually based on use statistics), and transactional billing. In some cases, pricing may be different for the software and web versions of a vendor's product. For example, if your web access to a commercial product such as Westlaw or LexisNexis is based on transactional pricing, you will not be charged "by the minute" for reading retrieved data online—only for each new "transaction" (*i.e.*, executing a new search, editing a search query, changing databases or files, linking to a new document, or printing a document). Other products such as AutoTrack, CourtLink and CourtEXPRESS offer primarily transactional billing, often letting you know the cost of a particular search before incurring the charge.

CD-ROM Products

The vendor's databases are distributed to the customer on standard CD-ROM disks, which are loaded on a single stand-alone computer or network, depending on the "user access" provisions of your software license. CD-ROM products are generally updated with a new disk monthly, bimonthly, or quarterly, depending on the terms of your contract. No access fees are incurred when searching a CD-ROM database—your only costs are the initial price of the subscription and annual renewal fees. Today, most popular legal print titles can be purchased on CD-ROM. Many publishers such as Commerce Clearing House (CCH), Research Institute of America (RIA) and Matthew Bender (now part of Lexis Publishing) also market CD-ROM products that provide access to several related titles focusing on specific legal practice areas such as intellectual property, federal taxation, immigration, or commercial real estate transactions.

Computer disk programs

While CD-ROM technology—and now digital video disks (DVD)—have gained in popularity over the past few years, computer disks are still widely used. Originally marketed in large 5.25 inch "floppy" disks, the smaller 3.5 inch "hard" disk has become the most popular form of computer diskette. The term "floppy disk" is now used interchangeably regardless of size of diskette. Supplementary computer disks often accompany books and looseleaf sets and often provide access to forms referred to in the print text. Many publishers' print subscriptions to legal forms books, treatises, and texts on specific subject areas of the law (such as tax, products liability, domestic relations, and personal injury) frequently include a companion computer disk containing forms and, in some cases, a searchable, full text version of the print material.

Many state bar associations publish their practice forms and continuing education materials on computer disk, and various professional associations such as the American Institute of Architects (AIA) market law-related and industry specific forms on computer disk. Commercial CLE (continuing legal education) companies such as Professional Education System, Inc. (PESI, web site http://www.pesi.com/) and the Practising Law Institute (PLI, web site http://www.pli.edu/) also prefer to disseminate course materials on computer disk rather than using the more expensive CD-ROM format.

The Internet and the World Wide Web

A common misconception is that online databases and web-based resources are one and the same—they are not. This confusion is fostered by commercial online database providers like Westlaw, Lexis, Dialog, and Dun & Bradstreet who market their products in both proprietary software and web versions.

The term online typically refers to being connected to a remote service. For example, if you use the Internet, you are online when you have made the connection via a modem and logged on to your Internet provider with a username and password. When you log off the service, you are offline. This also applies when you access a commercial online vendor's remote computer database of information using the vendor's proprietary software installed on your computer. A common misconception is that software is data. It is not. Software tells the hardware how to process the data. Once a connection to the vendor's host computer system is made via a modem, you are prompted to enter a username and/or password. Once you exit the service, your modem connection disconnects and you are offline.

In some cases the two versions (web and proprietary software) of a vendor's product are identical in content, but not always. The look and feel of each version may also vary somewhat, depending on vendor and product. While some people favor using a web-based service, many still prefer the software version.

A major source for obtaining free primary and secondary legal information is law schools and, specifically, law libraries. Some premier law school web sites include the Cornell Law School Legal Information Institute (web site http://fatty.law.cornell.edu/), Washburn University School of Law's WashLaw WEB (web site http://www.washlaw.edu/) and the Center for Information Law and Policy (CILP, web site http://www.cilp.org/). While initially a joint initiative of the Villanova University School of Law and the Illinois Institute of Technology's Chicago-Kent College of Law, key portions of the CILP project are now being administered jointly by both law schools' libraries. These sites link to hundreds of original sources of primary and secondary legal materials, compiling them in a systematic and user-friendly web format.

Many federal government web sites such as FedWorld and GPO*Access*, and literally thousands of federal, state, and local governmental agencies, departments, and divisions also offer free access to legal and government information. In 1992, FedWorld was established by the National Technical Information Service (NTIS), an agency of the U.S. Department of

Commerce, to serve as the online locator service for a comprehensive inventory of information disseminated by the United States federal government. *See* Fed-World web site at http://www.fedworld.gov/. The United States Goverment Printing Office's GPO*Access* Internet site is located at http://www.access. gpo.gov/ and provides web access to hundreds of federal government publications. (*See* chapter 10 for a thorough discussion of legal and government Internet and web resources).

When purchasing electronic databases, regardless of the format, be sure to fully understand and comply with the terms of any applicable licensing agreements.

COMPUTER-ASSISTED LEGAL RESEARCH TOOLS

Today's law practice routinely incorporates both traditional legal and nonlegal computer-assisted research tools. While some vendors only provide access to a specific category of information (*i.e.*, legislative information, judicial opinions or public records), most large commercial information vendors offer a variety of legal and nonlegal databases as part of their online and web-based subscription services.

The following section highlights several popular electronic information providers for legal and nonlegal resources. It is not intended as an in-depth review of the many features of each product.

LexisNexis

In August 1999, LexisNexis Group announced the formation of Lexis Publishing, a division of Reed-Elsevier Inc. The combined LexisNexis database offers one of the world's largest full text collections for both legal and factual information.

The legal information products and services currently available through Lexis include:

- LexisNexis (computer-assisted legal research)
- *SHEPARD'S* (legal citators)
- Matthew Bender (secondary legal resources)
- Michie (annotated statutes)
- Martindale-Hubbell (directory of lawyers and law firms)

Lexis subscribers also have access to Nexis, a powerful news, public records, and reference database. Nexis offers current access to world, national, regional, and topical news covering a wide range of business and industry topics. Like Lexis, Nexis is full text and searchable. The LexisNexis database is arranged under various "libraries" of information, each with its own unique alpha-abbreviation (e.g. ALL-REC, COURTS, STATES, MARHUB). A library is a large collection of related materials for a given area of legal research or general topic. Libraries are comprised of files, individual or group. Examples of specific database files include: ASSETS (real estate assessment and deed transfer records, plus FAA [Federal Aviation Authority] aircraft and selected boat and motor vehicle registrations); FINDER (nationwide person and business locator files); LIENS (state UCC [Uniform Commercial Code] registrations, judgments and liens); VERDCT (state and national verdict and settlement reporters); and INCORP (state corporation and partnership filings).

Another popular feature on LexisNexis is ECLIPSE,™ an electronic clipping service that provides automatic updates to "saved" research sessions. This time-saving feature allows you to enter a search once and save it as an ECLIPSE search. You can then rerun the search at user-selected intervals (daily, weekly, monthly). Each ECLIPSE search is saved under the user's unique LexisNexis identification number and can be recalled from any computer with access to the Internet (or the LexisNexis software).

Shepard's Citations Service® is now available exclusively through LexisNexis. *Shepard's* offers comprehensive coverage of case law, federal and state statutes (all 50 states, the District of Columbia, and Puerto Rico), federal administrative regulations, court rules, law reviews, and even registered United States patents. The *Shepard's* database is updated daily to provide extremely current cite-validation information.

Some users of the traditional LexisNexis software may find the web version a bit intimidating at first, but people who are comfortable researching on the Internet will quickly adapt to the user-friendly web format. Regardless of which format you choose, the products are basically identical in scope and content. Use the web-based LexisNexis Source Locator, the directory of online resources, to locate the appropriate libraries and files for your specific research session at http://www. lexis-nexis.com;lncc/sources. There is no charge to search the Source Locator; online costs are incurred once you select a database to execute a search.

Westlaw

The other major electronic legal information database is Westlaw®, a registered trademark of West Group, Inc., a conglomerate of print and electronic legal resource tools, all integrated into a single research system. In addition to the Westlaw legal database, the West Group companies include Bancroft-Whitney (BW), Clark Boardman Callaghan (CBC), Lawyers Cooperative Publishing (LCP) and West Publishing. For purposes of this chapter, we will focus briefly on Westlaw, West Group's online resource of legal and business information (West Group Web site http://www.westgroup.com).

As with LexisNexis, Westlaw is available in a software (WestMate™) and web (westlaw.com™) product. Both versions offer similar content and open with the Westlaw Directory, an index of Westlaw databases and services and their alpha-identifiers, a series of letters used to identify the contents of the library or file. You can also search the Westlaw Directory free on the web at http://www.westlaw.com/DbOptions/directory. Once you select the appropriate databases for your search, you will be prompted to logon with a valid Westlaw password, and online charges will be incurred from that point forward in your research sessions. Westlaw contains over 10,000 individual databases covering every jurisdiction and practice area of law, including federal and state statutes and court decisions, law reviews, federal regulations, tax and securities law information, continuing legal education (CLE) materials from well-known national and state providers, news and business information, public records and court dockets. Court dockets are only available from selected jurisdictions whose courts provide this information. More and more federal and state courts are providing electronic access to their dockets and, in some cases, scanned images of actual court filings.

KeyCite® is a registered trademark of West Group and is West's counterpart for Lexis' *Shepard's.* While the term "shepardizing" has become synonymous with electronic legal citation research and cite-validation, it is a registered tradename of LexisNexis. Use KeyCite, a citator and case finder, to trace the history of a case and retrieve all citing references, including cases and secondary sources. KeyCite covers every case in West's National Reporter System® as well as more than one million unpublished cases. KeyCite also provides citing references from hundreds of law reviews, thousands of ALR annotations and Am Jur® 2d articles, *Couch on Insurance*, Merten's *Law of Federal Taxation*, Norton *Bankruptcy Law and Practice 2d*, publications of The Rutter Group, Witkin's California Treatises and Wright & Miller's *Federal Practice and Procedure.* KeyCite is convenient to use on the web version and through Westcheck®, an automated citation-checking software product that verifies citations in a legal document or in a manually-entered citations list. Westcheck can also verify citations directly from a Microsoft Word or Wordperfect document saved on your computer's hard drive or computer diskette.

Regardless of which Westlaw product you prefer or have access to—the software or web version—searching is easy with "Terms and Connectors" (Boolean) and "Natural Language" (plain English) search methods. *See* chapter 9 for a detailed discussion of Boolean search language.

Pricing depends on the type of contract negotiated with the vendor. Both Westlaw and Lexis offer transactional (flat fee charges based on each "transaction" as defined by the terms of the contract) and hourly (a flat rate per hour while logged on) pricing. It is important to know which type of billing arrangement your employer has subscribed to and whether it includes printing and downloading. In addition, make sure you know which databases (libraries, files, etc.) are included in your base plan. Many publishers, such as Commerce Clearing House (CCH), do not allow full access to all their products under standard, base pricing arrangements. Many public records databases, business and financial sources, and subject-specific legal resources are available only under "optional" pricing—over and above your base contract. Searching these sources can be very expensive, so know what is included in your contract before starting your research session.

In addition to the two industry giants, Westlaw and LexisNexis, there are several other computer-assisted legal information services that bear mentioning.

Law Office Information Systems (LOIS)

LOIS is a fee-based product, offering unlimited full text access to primary state and federal law, including United States Supreme Court opinions dating back to 1899. The law "libraries" accessible through the web version, Loislaw.com at http://www.loislaw.com/contain more than 8 million pages of state and federal primary law. The databases are duplications of the official law received from the state and federal courts, Congress and the state legislatures, administrative agencies, or other designated official government information sources.

Pricing is based on the specific databases you subscribe to (for example, all 50 states and all 18 federal libraries *or* the 18 federal libraries and your home state), and whether you opt for web or CD-ROM format.

VersusLaw

VersusLaw, Inc. was founded in 1985. Initially, the fledgling company's focus was to provide the legal community with accurate, current, and in-depth information exclusively on one topic—professional liability. In 1992, VersusLaw (at http://www.versuslaw.com/) began providing electronic access to federal and state appellate court decisions, with a goal of creating an online legal research service for small law firms. In the fall of 1995, VersusLaw was among the first web legal content provider, offering access to opinions from the U.S. Supreme Court, the federal circuit courts of appeals, and the various state appellate courts (including the District of Columbia).

VersusLaw currently provides access to the appellate decisions of all 50 states, all federal circuit courts of appeal, and the U.S. Supreme Court (opinions dating back to 1930). Archival coverage varies by jurisdiction. As with LOIS, there are no additional charges for online searching, downloading or printing. Both products offer a viable alternative for small law firms and sole practitioners to more expensive database products such as LexisNexis and Westlaw.

LEGISLATIVE DATABASES

While many online subscription services, including Lexis and Westlaw, cover legislative information, several other products focus exclusively on this type of information. Currency of the data supplied by reliable online information providers is a real plus over comparable print or even CD-ROM products, with most information updated within 24 hours of public availability—an important factor to consider when conducting legislative research.

Following are a few of the more popular online subscription and free web-based legislative information products.

CCH Access®

Commerce Clearing House (CCH), a major publisher of tax materials, produces ACCESS®, a electronic legal research and information retrieval system for conducting research in the areas of tax law and estate planning, with a focus on both federal and state laws. As with LexisNexis, the ACCESS database is organized by libraries. The CCH news library contains summaries of federal and state tax developments, plus electronic versions of popular print tax titles, including the *Standard Federal Tax Reporter, Federal Estate and Gift Tax*, and *Federal Excise Tax Reporter.* The news library also contains the full text of the current Internal Revenue Service Code, court decisions from 1913 to the present (tax-related), IRS rulings and *Cumulative Bulletin Documents.* There is also a state taxes library with coverage for all 50 states.

Electronic Legislative Search System (ELSS)

Another Commerce Clearing House (CCH) electronic database is ELSS, a legislative bill tracking system containing CCH summary notices of new bill introductions and their corresponding legislative histories for the current regular and special legislative sessions of the 50 states and the U.S. Congress. For more information about CCH and its electronic subscription and web-based products, consult the company's web site at http://www.cch.com.

Legi-Slate

Legi-Slate is a subscription database service used to conduct bill tracking and legislative histories. The federal legislative information segment of Legi-Slate was acquired by Congressional Quarterly, Inc., publishers of the *Congressional Quarterly*, and is marketed as "CQ.com OnCongress." The CQ web site is http:// www.oncongress.cq.com. This web-based product offers subscribers immediate access to the full text of government documents, legislative summaries, committee reports, vote analyses, plus congressional schedules and member profiles. CQ's news and analysis explains legislative developments as they occur. Customized e-mail updates continuously alert you to the latest legislative action on your areas of interest. (See chapter 9 for a discussion of e-mail "alerts").

The custom services end of Legi-Slate was acquired by State Net (at http://www.statenet.com), which delivers vital data, legislative intelligence, and in-depth reporting of all pending bills and regulations in the 50 states and Congress, including bill actions, full text of legislation, calendars, legislator biographies, and regulations.

THOMAS and GPO*Access*

Two of the most popular and reliable web resources offering free federal legislative information are THOMAS and GPO*Access*, both official government web sites. THOMAS web site is at http:// thomas.loc.gov and GPO*Access* web site is at http://www.access.gpo.gov.

THOMAS, a product of the U.S. Congress, is arranged under three major categories:

1. **Legislation** (bill summary and status, bill text, major legislation, public laws, and U.S. House and Senate roll call votes)
2. **Congressional Record** (full text, index, and session calendars)
3. **Committee Information** (committee reports, House and Senate hearing schedules, hearing transcripts, and related information)

THOMAS is also a good source of basic information on how the legislative process works, as well as the status of federal funding and appropriations bills. There are also links to key U.S. historical documents and the full text of congressional documents and debates from 1774–1873.

GPO*Access*, a service of the Government Printing Office (GPO) in Washington, DC, is another free web site providing the full text of selected information published by the federal government. Among the growing list of available publications are the *Federal Register*, the *Code of Federal Regulations (CFR)*, the *Congressional Record*, the *United States Code*, *congressional bills*, and *GAO Reports* published by the Government Accounting Organization, the federal watchdog agency. While searching the official GPO site has gotten easier, several GPO "gates" maintained by university and law school libraries tend to be more user friendly in their design and search capabilities. One example is the GPO Gate maintained by the Libraries of the University of California (http://www.gpo.ucop.edu/). See chapter 10 for a more detailed discussion of these and other legal web resources.

BUSINESS INFORMATION DATABASES

A wide range of business and industry-specific information is available from both subscription databases and free web sites. Of course, like any other information on the Internet, you should always verify the source and currency of the data before relying on it.

Business research many include:

- Locating corporate annual reports and other documents filed with the Securities and Exchange Commission (SEC)
- Compiling a corporate "family tree" showing the relationship between a parent company and its subsidiaries
- Obtaining background information on a company or corporate officer or director
- Accessing current company financial data
- Accessing statistical data such as the Consumer Price Index (CPI) for a specific industry on a given date
- Retrieving current or historical stock prices for a company
- Locating news articles about a specific company, product or individual associated with a U.S. or foreign business entity

You may also be asked to verify the registered agent for a company and the state of incorporation to effect valid service of process in a lawsuit. A prudent lawyer will have his/her paralegal confirm with the secretary of state's corporations division, in the state where the lawsuit will be filed, the legal name and status of a potential defendant. It is also a good idea to confirm the legal status of a corporate client before filing suit on its behalf. Many states have laws that bar a company from bringing or maintaining an action if it is not in "good standing" with the secretary of state's office in the jurisdiction where the suit will be filed (*i.e.*, has complied with all applicable corporate filing requirements).

Following are some popular online services offering business and financial information.

Datatimes

Datatimes (http://www.datatimes.com/) is a commercial subscription service providing access to a full text database of business and industry resources, international information, and major news sources, including newspapers, newswires, news magazines, company press releases, television and radio news transcripts, and U.S. regional news sources. Datatimes EyeQ™ is an electronic index to over 150 newspapers, including regional U.S. papers. It includes both general newspapers and financial news sources, plus many smaller local papers not found in other print or electronic newspaper databases (full text or abstracts).

Dialog and DataStar

Dialog™ and DataStar™ are registered trademarks of the Information Services division of The Dialog Corporation. One of the earliest multidiscipline information databases, Dialog remains one of the largest and most powerful online information storage and retrieval systems. It currently holds the distinction of being the world's largest commercial online collection of business, scientific, and technical information, available by subscription and "per-use" credit card access. Subscribers can access Dialog to locate information on almost any subject, using a computer, modem, and telecommunications software, or now on the web at http://www.dialogweb.com.

Dialog provides access to more than 1000 full text journals, magazines, newspapers, and newsletters, in addition to a wide range of company and financial data, trademarks and patents, and sources for scientific and technical research. Dialog contracts directly with hundreds of publishers and original information suppliers and then stores the data in hundreds of databases or files. While a very powerful research tool, searching the software version of Dialog requires a mastery of the unique commands and query formulation utilized by the system. However, this can generally be avoided by using the web version, which is considerably more user friendly than the software. Searching Dialog is expensive, with a combination of connect time charges, telecommunications charges, per-item viewing charges, and per-item print charges.

DataStar and its web inferface, DataStarWeb at www.datastarweb.com, are the European counterparts of Dialog. As Europe's leading online database service, DataStar provides access to over 350 databases with worldwide coverage.

One alternative to subscribing to Dialog is to access *select* Dialog databases (currently about 80 percent of the total offerings) through Westlaw. Consult a current Westlaw Database Directory for a list of available Dialog databases. This also allows you to search the Dialog information using standard Westlaw Boolean or free-style (natural language) searching. There is currently a nominal surcharge to access the Dialog databases through Westlaw, but this is usually offset by the time saved in searching.

Dow-Jones News/Retrieval

Dow-Jones.com, from the publishers of *The Wall Street Journal*, is a good example of a blend of free and fee-based information. From the DowJones.com web site (http://dowjones.wsj.com), you can access current financial data, and obtain stock quotes and selected industry-specific news reports and press releases. As with much of the free information available on the web, it is selective in its coverage and in no way comprehensive. Even with subscription services, not every news article from the print edition of a newspaper, magazine, or journal is available electronically. Often you will need to contact the original news source directly to see if they offer fee-based research services to obtain archived issues. Another option is to contact a public library or public university in a nearby major city to inquire whether they provide fee-based news and business research services.

Dun & Bradstreet

Dun & Bradstreet (D&B) is more than just stock ratings. D&B is the leading provider of business-to-business credit, marketing, purchasing, receivables management, and decision-support services worldwide. Access to the comprehensive D&B database, which now covers more than 57 million businesses in over 200 countries, is available through a software product or the popular web version http://www.dnb.com/. D&B claims to be the only worldwide information provider that collects financial statements on both publicly and privately held companies. D&B is an excellent source for researching complex corporate "family trees," containing eight levels of parents, subsidiaries, and branch locations.

The D&B D-U-N-S Number (**D**ata **U**niversal **N**umbering **S**ystem) is a 9-digit identification code, providing unique numerical identifiers of single business entities, while linking corporate family structures together. D&B uses the unique D-U-N-S Numbers to link parent companies, subsidiaries, headquarters and branches on more than 62 million corporate family members worldwide. Used by the world's most influential standards-setting organizations, it is recognized, recommended and/or required by more than 50 global, industry and trade associations, including the United Nations, the U.S. federal government, and the European Commission (EC).

As with other electronic information providers, D&B draws from a wide range of original sources for its data, including:

- All federal bankruptcy filing locations
- All U.S. secretaries of state
- Millions of trade and banking institutions
- Public utilities
- The U.S. Postal Service
- Over 2,500 state filing locations
- Daily newspapers, publications, and electronic news services

Reports generated using D&B will include up to 1,500 data elements on any given company, providing an thorough business and financial picture.

SEC's EDGAR Database

A free web-based product, the EDGAR (Electronic Data Gathering, Analysis, and Retrieval) system performs automated collection, validation, indexing, acceptance, and forwarding of submissions by companies and others who are required by law to file forms with the U.S. Securities and Exchange Commission (SEC). Its primary purpose is to increase the efficiency and fairness of the securities market for the benefit of investors, corporations, and the economy by accelerating the receipt, acceptance, dissemination, and analysis of time-sensitive corporate information filed with the agency. A short description of the most common corporate filings made with the SEC is available online from the Commission's web site at www.sec.gov/edaux/forms.htm. This *Guide to Corporate Filings* will help simplify your corporate research on EDGAR, by explaining the type of corporate and financial information reported in each form. The SEC also provides web access to the full text of its various rules and regulations, including proposed rules, at www.sec.gov/rulemake.htm.

However, when researching in the EDGAR database, it is important to remember that not all documents filed with the SEC by public companies are available on EDGAR, and that information on privately held companies is not included. Companies were phased in to the EDGAR system over a three-year period, ending May 6, 1996. As of that date, all public domestic companies were required to make their filings on EDGAR, except for filings made in paper because of a hardship exemption. A company is owned by its shareholders. A "public company" generally denotes companies whose securities (*i.e.* shares of stock) are publicly traded. A public company may (but is not required to) be listed on a stock exchange. Shares in public listed and unlisted companies are financial assets of the company. A "private company" is usually smaller [than a public company], often a family-owned business with between one and fifty shareholders, and a private company's securities cannot be offered to sale to the general public.

Foreign companies are not required to submit their filings on EDGAR, although some do so voluntarily. Therefore, you cannot rely exclusively on the EDGAR database when conducting this type of research. It is recommended that you run a broader search of the SEC filings databases available through both Lexis-Nexis and Westlaw.

Another source to access corporate and financial information is Disclosure,™ a product of Primark Corporation. Disclosure provides access to over one million documents covering thousands of publicly traded U.S. companies. Retrieve, view, and download company annual reports, SEC filings, stock price data, earnings estimates, and research reports. Another popular Primark product is EDGAR Direct,™ a real-time delivery service of all electronic SEC filings. For a complete list of electronic products and services offered by Primark, visit the company's web site at www.primark.com.

Other web sources

One of the most useful and reliable sites for locating company information on the Internet is *The Internet Lawyer* web site at www.internetlawyer.com. This web directory is efficiently arranged under major headings such as "starting points," "nonprofit organizations," "associations," and "annual reports" to name a few. Short abstracts are available for most of the links. Another helpful directory of corporate information resources on the web can be found at www.corporateinformation.com/ and includes information on thousands of U.S. and foreign companies. Hoover's Online at www.hoovers.com provides free and fee-based access to a wide range of business and financial information on both public and private U.S. corporations. See Appendix F for a list of additional web resources for obtaining company information.

INVESTIGATIVE AND PUBLIC RECORDS DATABASES

In addition to traditional legal research for case law, statutes, administrative rulings and regulations, attorney general opinions, and other primary and secondary legal resources, you may also need to locate various types of information in the public domain. Investigative research can be as simple as locating a current address for a potential witness or the registered agent for a corporation for service of process, to "locating everything you can find" on a person or company.

When conducting a thorough public records investigation on an individual, you will want to determine, among other things, current or last known addresses and telephone numbers, verify full name and any aliases, and whether other persons are reported to have used the subject's Social Security Number (SSN). If asked to conduct a thorough "assets search" on a person or business, you will need to ascertain all publicly recorded assets (*i.e.*, real property, tangible personal property, vehicles, boats, airplanes, trademarks, etc.). A search of "liabilities" (*i.e.*, liens, judgments, UCC filing statements) recorded nationwide or in a particular state under the subject's name is also recommended. It is also helpful to know whether the subject has any current or expired professional licenses, has filed for bankruptcy, or ever been a party to any pending or resolved litigation.

When researching a business, this would generally include a nationwide search of state corporation records, any Uniform Commercial Code (UCC) filings, and liens or judgments recorded against the corporation (and possibly any of its officers and directors). You will also want to locate all recorded real and personal property assets of the corporation. It may be helpful to compile a corporate family tree establishing the relationship between a parent corporation and any subsidiaries or divisions. Finally, you should include a current financial report of the company's holdings and economic viability. If the company is required by law to file with the SEC, copies of the company's recent annual reports (Form 10-K) and other key SEC filings are valuable sources of information (see previous section on the EDGAR database).

Searching national, regional, and local newspaper databases can often provide additional information and "leads" to other data sources. Locating a company's web site may also provide detailed information about the company, including recent press releases and financial reports.

While more and more public information is available free on the web, most legal professionals prefer the convenience, efficiency, and reliability of researching electronically available public data through a variety of subscription database products. You may wish to start your research with free web resources, and then use one or more subscription services to complete your investigation. Some of the more popular commercial electronic public records databases include the following.

AutoTrack

AutoTrack™ is available in both software (AutoTrack Plus) and web-based (AutoTrackXP™ at http://www.autotrackxp.com/) versions, although like many companies, the majority of research and development is focused on its web product. With AutoTrack, you can instantly access over 4 billion publicly available records nationwide. While initially marketed to law enforcement agencies, AutoTrack is currently used by private investigators, corporate legal departments and private law firms to search and cross-reference information from a variety of original sources. Always remember that, unless stated otherwise, all online information vendors merely obtain information directly from the *original* sources of the data and compile it in a user-friendly, searchable database. Disclaimers as to errors and omissions in content generally accompany the information provided to third parties such as lawyers.

AutoTrackXP also allows the researcher to conduct a variety of specialized searches for real property assets and court litigation, including bankruptcies, liens, and judgments (under "Popular Searches").

Additional offline searches are available, including:

- Criminal reports (supplied by state and federal law enforcement agencies)
- Moving Violations Records (MVRS)
- Detailed real property records
- State motor vehicle drivers license and vehicle registration records
- Professional licensing information recorded with state agencies that regulate professional licensure of physicians, real estate brokers, private investigators, lawyers, and hundreds of other occupations

This information is supplied to the commercial online vendor directly from the original reporting agencies. In most cases, the results of your offline searches are available at your computer for printing or downloading within a matter of hours. Most services offer a feature that notifies you by e-mail when your search results are available.

You can use many of these online databases to search for published telephone listings for individuals and businesses in the United States, Canada, and even worldwide, although this information is generally available from a variety of free web sites. Unlisted telephone numbers are generally not available from free web sites or most subscription services, since they are not part of the public domain. Some popular free web telephone directories include: Switchboard www.switchboard. com; InfoSpace www.infospace. com/; BigBook.com www.bigbook.com/ (businesses yellow pages); and AT&T Anywho.com www.anywho.com/ (white and yellow pages) and www.anywho.com/tf.html (toll free "800" numbers). It is also getting easier to locate international telephone numbers on the web using sites such as WorldPages, www.worldpages.com (U.S. and Canadian listings), and the global version, www.worldpages.com/global (international listings, arranged alphabetically).

There are also "reverse lookup" web directories that allow you to cross-reference residential and business telephone listings when all you have is a phone number and need to match it with a residential or business address. These include InfoSpace's Reverse Lookup at http://in-110.infospace.com/info/reverse.htm and the ReversePhoneDirectory www.reverse phonedirectory.com/.

Case*Stream*®

Case*Stream*, a registered trademark of MarketSpan, Inc. (http://www.marketspan.com), is a unique web-based information service that provides electronic litigation support to the legal, business, financial, and media communities. Case*Stream* is a subscription database containing civil and criminal case information. For example, use it to find out how a particular judge ruled in prior cases involving similar facts and legal issues, or what opposing counsel argued on similar matters—features not currently offered by other public records database services. You can also use Case*Stream* to request a court docket from a specific court, and be notified by e-mail when the docket is ready for you to retrieve electronically.

ChoicePoint

In the spring of 2000 DBT Online, Inc. (the "Auto-Track" company) merged with ChoicePoint, Inc. (http://www.choicepoint.net), another nationwide public records information provider. The combined companies form a major source of online and on-demand public records in the U.S.

ChoicePoint, originally used primarily by private investigators, government agencies, and law enforcement to obtain crucial background information on a person or company, now offers a wide range of legal, business, and financial information services, including online public records searches. The information contained in the ChoicePoint databases is accessible using MS-Windows® based software or the web-based Internet version.

CourtEXPRESS and CourtLink

CourtEXPRESS and CourtLink are two popular companies providing electronic access to federal, state, and local court records and, in some jurisdictions, scanned images of actual documents filed with the court. CourtLink at http:www.courtlink.com markets itself as "a research tool for professionals" with a primary focus on providing litigation history, discovery, case management and background checks. Similarily, CourtEXPRESS at http://www.court

express.com provides court litigation information from basically the same group of U.S. bankruptcy, appellate, and federal district courts as CourtLink. With these subscription services, you can locate litigation records, retrieve case dockets to track court filings, run criminal searches, and even order copies of court documents delivered to your desktop via e-mail, by fax, or express mail. Additional document delivery fees may apply. You can search both of databases from software that can be downloaded from their respective web sites, or simply log on and conduct your research using the subscription web-based products with your user identification and password.

PACER (Public Access to Court Electronic Records)

Both CourtLink and CourtEXPRESS often link directly to the PACER system to retrieve federal court filings. The most popular service provided by PACER is the U.S. Party Case Index, a national index for U.S. district, bankruptcy, and appellate courts, now available on the Internet at http://pacer.uspci.uscourts.gov. Use this system to conduct nationwide searches to determine whether a party (company or individual) is involved in any federal litigation. However, not every federal court participates in the Index, usually because they do not yet have their records available electronically for public access. Recently, a very small group of state courts made their records available on PACER, yet electronic access to state court dockets and party case information remains limited.

There is no fee to register for the Internet version of PACER, although a valid login and password are required. To register, contact the PACER Service Center at 1.800.676.6856. If you have an existing PACER account for the software version, you will still need to contact the PACER Service Center to activate that login and password on the U.S. Party Case Index web site. Once you logon to the web Index, you are billed a nominal per minute rate for dial-up access while online, and an additional per page charge for retrieved text.

The key benefit of using subscription services such as PACER, CourtLink, and CourtEXPRESS to search court records is the value-added features each vendor adds to its product. Of course, the major drawback is the cost—these services are not free. Most charge per transaction rather than on an hourly basis. Depending on how many individual searches you conduct, this can be costly. If you know that a particular court provides access to the same information from its web site, you should try and obtain the information from the court's free web site before turning to a fee-based service. However, many federal courts provide only limited access to a select group of "high profile" cases, and few offer access to court dockets, although this is continually improving. This same principal applies to state courts. As previously mentioned, access to state courts at the trial and even appellate levels is very limited at this time, although many jurisdictions are in the process of digitizing their records.

RACER (Remote Access to Electronic Court Records)

Taking electronic access of court records to the next level, some federal, district and backruptcy courts now offer remote access to actual full text scanned images of pleadings and papers filed in the official court file, excluding juvenile court records, and court files that have been "sealed" by court order and are therefore not public record. RACER, developed in cooperation with the U.S. Courts and Wade Systems, Inc. (http://www.wadesystems.com), is currently available in several federal district and bankruptcy courts and some state courts. The ability to access not only dockets and routine case information (*i.e.*, case number, parties, counsel for the parties, judge assigned to the case, nature of the suit, date filed, and current disposition), but also actual document images is the trend of the future in remote electronic access to court records. LLRX, the Law Library Resource Exchange, maintains a web site that has organized links to federal and state court dockets, court rules, and forms at www.llrx.com/courtrules.

A more in-depth discussion of these databases, including a comparison of PACER, CourtLink, CourtEXPRESS and Case*Stream*, was published in late 1999 by Julie Bozzell www.llrx.com/features/dockets3.htm.

Credit Reporting Laws

No discussion of electronic subscription database services would be complete without mentioning compliance with federal and state credit reporting laws. Access to the kind of information supplied to AutoTrack and other investigative information providers (generally by credit reporting companies and government agencies) is restricted pursuant to the Fair Credit Reporting Act (FCRA), 15 U.S.C. Sec. 1681 *et seq.*, Federal Trade Commission interpretations of the FCRA, and similar state statutes.

All consumer reporting agencies are required by law to adopt reasonable procedures to insure that information disseminated to the public is done in a manner which is "fair and equitable to the consumer, with regard to the confidentiality, accuracy, relevancy, and proper utilization of such information in accordance with the requirements of this subchapter," 15 U.S.C. 1681(b). The FCRA stipulates in section 1681(a)(4) that there is a "need to insure that consumer reporting agencies exercise their grave responsibilities with fairness, impartiality, and a respect for the consumer's right to privacy."

While not specifically mandated by law, most third-party information providers (*i.e.*, AutoTrack, Westlaw, LexisNexis, Case*Stream*) have voluntarily established policies and procedures to protect the privacy interests of individuals. The products and services (*i.e.*, information) provided by DBT (AutoTrack) Online and other information providers, are not "consumer reports," as such term is defined by the FCRA, and are not to be used for purposes specified under the Act. DBT Online is a founding member of the Individual Reference Services Group ("IRSG") http://www. irsg.org/, a group of information services companies with similar philosophies regarding the access and distribution or nonpublic information. Nonpublic information includes nonfinancial identifying information in a credit report (*i.e.*, social security number and date of birth). This information obtained from nonpublic sources may not be displayed to the general public (via free or fee-based subscriptions) on the Internet by IRSG companies. Since its formation in late 1997, IRSG members have worked closely with the Federal Trade Commission (FTC) to develop a comprehensive set of self-regulatory principles that govern dissemination of personally identifiable information. The IRSG principles, along with the December 1997 FTC Report to Congress on "Individual Reference Services," are available on the IRSG web site at http://www.irsg.org/ html/industry_principles_principles.htm.

For example, as a registered DBT Online subscriber, each time you log on to AutoTrackXP (web version), you are required to identify an appropriate use for your research session by selecting all possible choices from a list of permissible purposes. Agreement with the terms of this compliance statement is required to access the database and continue your research session. Individual privacy policies of IRSG members may differ slightly, but the goal of protecting consumers' privacy remains consistent. Individual privacy policies are available from the IRSG members page at http://www.irsg.org/. In an effort to protect the privacy of consumers, IRSG members provide only *truncated* personal data in their reports (*i.e.*, social security number, date of birth, drivers license number), when originally supplied by nonpublic information sources (*i.e.*, credit reporting agencies).

EXAMPLE: Social Security Number:
417-8275-XXXX

LEGAL CITATION: ELECTRONIC FORMATS

In recent years, online, CD-ROM, and web-based law collections have become major research tools for legal professionals. As a direct result of the emerging technologies and our increasing reliance on these nonprint formats, several jurisdictions have established new legal citation rules.

In 1996, the American Bar Association approved a resolution recommending that courts adopt a uniform public domain citation system equally effective for printed case reports and for case reports electronically published on computer disks or network services, and laying out several key elements of such a system. The American Association of Law Libraries had previously gone on record for "vendor and media neutral" citation. Several jurisdictions have, in fact, adopted citation schemes embodying the elements recommended by these national bodies.

Although no uniform citation standards for online resources currently exist, intense policy debates over citation norms continue in an effort to achieve some standardization to the rules governing electronic citation formats. In the interim, there are several good sources to guide you in citing to electronic resources in legal briefs and other writings.

One of the best is *The Columbia Guide to Online Style*, compiled by Janice Walker, a professor of English at the University of South Florida. Part 1 includes a guide to locating, translating, and using the elements of citation for electronically-accessed sources.

While this *Guide* offers several forms with examples, the basic component of reference citation style is:

- Author's Last Name, First Name.
- "Title of Document." (in quotation marks)
- *Title of Complete Work* (*if applicable*) (in italics)
- Document Date or Date of Last Revision. (*if different from access date*)
- Protocol and Address, Access Path or Directories,
- Date of Access.

Example: Walker, Janice R. and Taylor, Todd. *The Columbia Guide to Online Style.* 1998. http://www.columbia.edu/cu/cup/cgos/idx_basic.html, accessed 6-27-2001.

Another web resource guide for citing electronic resources is maintained by the cittions handbook published by the Writing Center at the University of Wisconsin–Madison at http://www.wisc.edu/writing/Handbook/ elecapa.html.

The seventeenth edition (2000) of *The Bluebook: A Uniform System of Citation*, compiled by the law review editors at Harvard, Yale, and the University of Pennsylvania law schools, includes a section on citation formats for electronic resources. The addition of this information was one of the major reasons for publishing a new edition.

The *ALWD Citation Manual: A Professional System of Citation*, published by the Association of Legal Writing Directors and Darby Dickerson, a law professor at Stetson University College of Law, includes an entire section (Part 4) on electronic and online citation formats.

CALR: PROS AND CONS

Today, technology and the Internet are an integral part of practicing law. The reality of a truly paperless "virtual" law library is not likely for many years, although a transition from paper, and even CD-ROMs and computer disk programs, to web-based databases is becoming a more attractive option. While web access to subscription databases may initially be more costly than other information formats, there is no physical deterioration or replacement costs, as with books and even computer disks and CD-ROMs. There are no costly routine updating expenses such as you have with books and looseleaf materials. All you need to do is periodically download or install upgraded versions of your web browser software.

Many factors need to be considered when deciding which format (*i.e.*, print, CD-ROM, computer diskette, or the Internet) will best meet your research needs. In large law firms and corporate legal departments, purchasing decisions for electronic resources are often made by the law librarian, with input from the lawyers and paralegals who use the products. However, small firms and sole practitioners often look to their paralegals and legal assistants to help make these decisions. Large law firms and corporate legal departments usually subscribe to both Westlaw and Lexis; smaller firms and sole practitioners will generally opt for one or the other, but may wish to consider other options such as LOIS or VersusLaw. However, most law firms will select a nice blend of print, CD-ROM, and web technology to best meet their specific needs and practice areas. Recognizing this, many legal publishers offer "dual-format" discounts of between 15 percent and 25 percent when purchasing the print and a companion electronic version of a particular title. Before making a purchasing decision, you should consult your law librarian or office manager, or contact the vendor directly to inquire about available discounts. Table 8-1 provides a summary of the advantages and disadvantages of electronic resources.

Online research is recommended when:

- Currency is very critical
- Comparable print source is unavailable
- Information is not published in paper or on CD-ROM
- Researching an emerging area of law or current event
- The online version is easier to use than its print counterpart
- You have a unique fact situation and search terms

- Cite checking (cite verification)

Manual research is recommended when:

- Researching older materials or historical data
- Print source is preferable to the online version
- Information is not available from a reliable online source
- You found too much (or irrelevant) information using online resources
- Establishing general knowledge of an area of law (more cost efficient)
- Exploring complex concepts and legal theories
- Search terms are too common, ambiguous, or have too many synonyms to effectively narrow your online search

CHAPTER 8 SUMMARY

- The first attempts at computer-assisted legal research (CALR) actually began in the late 1950s and early 1960s.
- LexisNexis and Westlaw remain the most popular online databases for accessing legal information. Their respective nonlegal databases are also increasing in popularity.
- CALR generally refers to four distinctly different formats: commercial online services; CD-ROM products; computer disks; and the Internet/ World Wide Web.
- Web sites often provide the most current information available.
- Today's law practice routinely incorporates both traditional legal and nonlegal computer-assisted research.
- Nexis is Lexis' news, public records and reference database. The combined LexisNexis database offers one of the world's largest full text collection of legal and factual information.
- *Shepard's Citations Service* is now available exclusively through LexisNexis. Westlaw's electronic cite-validation product is KeyCite.
- Another popular feature of LexisNexis is ECLIPSE, an electronic clipping service that provides automatic updates to "saved" research sessions.
- As with LexisNexis, Westlaw is available in a software (WestMate) and web-based (Westlaw.com) product. Both versions offer similar content. Which format you use often depends on cost, personal preference, convenience, and availability of Internet access.
- Other legal information database products include LOIS and VersusLaw, viable alternatives to Westlaw and LexisNexis for small law firms and sole practitioners.
- Some of the more popular online subscription and free web-based legislative information products include CCH Access, Legi-Slate, THOMAS and GPO*Access*.
- A wide range of business and industry-specific information is available from both subscription online database providers and free web sites. Some popular products include: Datatimes, Dialog, DataStar, Dow-Jones News/ Retrieval, Dun & Bradstreet, Hoover's Online and the SEC's EDGAR database.
- Business research may include locating company annual reports and SEC filings, obtaining background information on companies and individuals, locating financial and stock information (both current and historical), and retrieving news articles and statistical data about a company, product, or person associated with a U.S. or foreign business.
- Some of the more popular investigative and public records electronic databases include: AutoTrack, Case*Stream*, ChoicePoint, CourtEXPRESS, CourtLink, and PACER.
- Access to the types of public records information provided by these services is restricted by federal and state credit reporting laws. All states must comply with the Fair Credit Reporting Act, 15 U.S.C. Sec. 1681 *et. seq.*, and the Federal Trade Commission's interpretations of the FCRA. State statutes may also govern the availability of certain types of public records.
- Although no uniform citation standards for online resources currently exist, there are several

excellent sources to guide you in citing to electronic resources, including *The Columbia Guide to Online Style*, the seventeenth edition of *The Bluebook: A Uniform System of Citation*, and the *ALWD Citation Manual: A Professional System of Citation* include sections on electronic citations.

- As with any resource tool, print or electronic, you should be knowledgeable about the content and arrangement of the product. This is particularly important with sophisticated online databases, each with its own unique features and search capabilities.
- Take advantage of free training provided by most vendors and publishers, and keep current on new products and enhancements.
- Most electronic databases incorporate some variation of Boolean search logic, so being familiar with the basic concepts of grouping terms and connectors will make you a better online researcher.
- Well-organized, reliable sites will provide helpful hints on how to conduct a search and even include examples for framing a query. Always read the "Help" screen or "Search Tips" if you have not previously used the web site (or database), and are unfamiliar with its features and search capabilities.
- Online searching is a skill developed over time.
- A paralegal proficient in computer assisted research is a real asset to any employer.

EXERCISES FOR CHAPTER 8

INSTRUCTIONS: For all questions, use only Internet resources to obtain your answers. Note the source(s) for your answers, including Internet address/location.

1. Obtain a Quarterly Federal Excise Tax return form for the most recent federal tax filing year. HINT: When downloading tax forms, rely only on official government sites. You will also need to have the *Adobe Acrobat Reader* web browser plug-in loaded on your computer to print an official copy of the tax form.
2. What was the CPI (Consumer Price Index) figure for the most recent month for South Urban Consumers (all items) and cities with a population of more than 1.5 million. HINT: You are looking for CPI figures for a "selected area" of the country.
3. Retrieve a copy of the most recent SEC 10-K Annual Report for Compaq Computer Corp.
   a. What date was it filed with the Securities & Exchange Commission?
   b. When does the company's fiscal year end?
   c. Were there any significant mergers or acquisitions for the company during the reported fiscal year?
   d. What kinds of financial data are contained in a 10-K report?
4. Using only free web business information resources, locate the following for Compaq Computer Corp.:
   a. Corporate headquarters address;
   b. Internet address of the company's web site;
   c. Total annual sales (in millions) for the most recently reported year (include the year);
   d. Company's ranking in the most recent Fortune 500 list; and
   e. A list of the key officers and directors of the company.
5. Using the Municipal Code Corporation web site *www.municode.com*, locate the code or ordinances for the city or county where you live. If unavailable, select any nearby municipality.
   a. Does the code or local ordinance define what is meant by a "dangerous animal"?
   b. If so, what is the definition. Include the official citation to the specific code section that provides this information.
6. How would you respond to a supervising attorney's statement that the firm is thinking about canceling its subscriptions to Lexis and Westlaw now that "everything is free on the Internet?"
7. A client of the firm is traveling to Egypt soon on business. Are there any U.S. State Department warnings he should be aware of?

8. According to Section 3-304 of the Uniform Commercial Code:
   a. What is the definition of the term "instrument" as used therein?
   b. When does an instrument payable on demand become overdue?
9. Aside from qualifying under all applicable New York Stock Exchange (NYSE) standards, what must a foreign (non-U.S.) company do before it can be listed to trade securities on the Exchange?
10. What was the Consumer Price Index for all urban consumers (CPI-U) for October 1985?
    a. What year did the Bureau of Labor Statistics begin reporting semiannual CPI statistics?
11. What is the address and telephone number for Paradyne Corp.? All you know is the company is located somewhere in Florida.
12. What does Chapter 26, Section 20.2031-7 of the Code of Federal Regulations deal with?
    a. What subsection applies when determining valuations after 1975 but before 1980?
    b. How is Title 26 of the U.S. Code commonly referred (*i.e.*, the popular name)?
13. Using only free web resources, locate a copy of the *IBM v. U.S.* decision. All you know is the case was filed in the United States Court of Appeals for the Federal District, and was decided sometime in January 2000.
    a. What is the style of the case?
    b. What is the case number?
    c. When was the case decided (*i.e.*, what is the exact date the opinion was entered by the court)?
    d. What was the final ruling as to the judgment on appeal, rendered by the Court of International Trade?
14. In 1999, a major bill was introduced in the U.S. House of Representatives to amend the Internal Revenue Code of 1986.
    a. What is the number of this House bill?
    b. When was it introduced and which legislator sponsored the bill?
    c. Are there any related bills pending in the House or Senate? If so, what are their respective bill numbers?
    d. What is the current status of this legislation?
15. How many articles in the official Congressional Record for the 105th session of Congress focus specifically on legislation relating to children and the Internet?
    a. What are the three major child protection laws referred to in these Congressional Record articles?
    b. What is the current status of each of these three pieces of federal legislation?
16. Using the RACER public access for the Bankruptcy Court for the District of Idaho http://www.id.uscourts.gov/doc.htm, locate the following information for the case filed by debtor, Automated Structures, Inc.:
    a. Case number
    b. Type of case (*i.e.*, Chapter 7 or Chapter 11)
    c. Date the voluntary petition was filed with the court;
    d. Status of the case
    e. Number of creditors who filed claims in this case
    f. Were any other cases (adversary proceedings) associated with this action?
17. All you have is a public law number (104-260). The 104 indicates the session of Congress.
    a. What is the corresponding bill number?
    b. What was the subject matter of this legislation?
    c. Who was the sponsor of the bill?
    d. What was the effective date of the law (*i.e.*, the date it was signed by the President)?
    e. What is the *Statutes at Large* citation for this public law?
    f. What specific section of the U.S. Code was amended by this law?
18. Compaq Computer Corp. is an American manufacturer. Knowing this, use only one web site to answer the following:
    a. Year the company was established
    b. Wht types of goods does the company manufacture?

FORMAT	ADVANTAGES	DISADVANTAGES
PRINT	• Cost—inexpensive to buy and replace in comparison to electronic • Easily transportable • Comfort level—many attorneys are more comfortable using books • Reliability—easily identifiable author/publisher	• Space—many reporters, digests and legal encyclopedias take up costly library shelf space and continually expand • Single access—only one user at a time; staff time in locating missing volumes • Photocopying can be difficult from some volumes; handling older, fragile books can damage further; cost of copying • Updating—need to consider annual cost to update books and looseleaf sets
CD-ROM	• Take up little space and easily transportable • Depending on site license, can be loaded on more than one computer or on a network for multiple access points • Precise searching • Hyperlinks to related information, depending on product	• Currency of information—most CD-ROMs are only updated monthly or quarterly • Support hardware—newer versions of software require faster, more expensive computers • License agreements—always remember that a site license is a legal and binding contract; always abide by the terms that dictate the conditions for use • Display—both the product and the quality of your computer screen should be considered, especially when displaying and printing financial data, charts and graphs, maps, real estate plats, and oversized documents
ONLINE SERVICES	• Multiple access points—desktop access from multiple locations (depending on site license) • Currency—online is generally the most current source, often updated hourly or "real-time" • Takes up virtually no library shelf space • Very precise searching, often utilizing a combination of Boolean and natural search language • Hyperlinks—ability to link to related information with the click of a mouse	• Cost—usually high initial subscription fees and expensive updating costs • Accuracy—not a problem if a subscription service is through a reputable vendor, but a real concern with the Internet • Printing—is this included in base contract or an additional "per document" fee? • Speed—whenever you access remote data through a modem, telecommunications software, or an Internet service provider, you can expect connection problems to occasionally occur, without warning

TABLE 8-1 PROS and CONS of Electronic Resources.

CHAPTER 9

THE INTERNET IN A NUTSHELL

INTRODUCTION

The Internet was first conceived in the early 1960s. Under the leadership of the United States Department of Defense's Advanced Research Project Agency (ARPA), it grew into a small network (ARPANET) intended to promote the sharing of super-computers amongst researchers in the United States. Although originally designed to allow scientists to share data and access remote computers, e-mail quickly became the most popular application of the Internet, turning ARPANET into a "high-speed digital post office" as people began to use it to collaborate on research projects and discuss topics of various interests.

By 1971, ARPANET had grown to 23 host computers, computers directly connected to the network, linking together universities and government research centers around the country. A decade later, ARPANET had over 200 hosts, with a new host being added to the network approximately once every 20 days. Three short years later, the number of Internet host computers worldwide broke the 1,000 barrier, and by 1987 that number passed the 10,000 mark.

By 1988, the Internet had become an essential tool for personal and business communications, with the use of e-mail gaining popularity. It was also during the late 1980s that concern about privacy and security in the digital world began to surface.

A more responsible figure, which has been widely quoted, is the statement that the number of people using the Internet is doubling every year, with 13.5 million Internet users as of October 1994, a growth rate that has proven consistently accurate over the past decade. Growth statistics for Internet use continue to rise at an astronomical rate. In May 1998, an estimated 57 million people in the United States alone were using the World Wide Web, the Internet's popular graphic browsing tool, and the estimated number of web pages worldwide was 320 million.

The Internet has developed into the world's largest information network, penetrating into almost every corner of the globe and directly or indirectly impacting nearly every aspect of our daily lives. The number of commercial e-mail messages sent *each day* in the United States alone exceeds 10 billion. By the end of 1998, 52 percent of the over 147 million Internet users lived in the United States. Predictions for the number of people worldwide using the Internet by the year 2003 exceed 4 billion, or a staggering 71 percent of the world's population. While electronic commerce or "e-commerce"—purchasing goods and services via the World Wide Web—has become a buzzword for the late 1990s, using the Internet for business and research is equally important. The 1998 American Internet User Survey found that 77 percent of adults who use the Internet predominately for work agreed that online services made them more productive at their job.

Please refer to Appendix G at the end of this book, which includes brief definitions for many of the Internet-related terms in this textbook.

What is the Internet?

Today, the Internet exists as an intricate pattern of smaller networks linked together through servers. The servers transmit data through lines that, in most cases, are dedicated to Internet communications. Individual computers (clients) are connected to these servers either through direct lines or telephone lines and modems. Direct lines are generally high speed telecommunication lines that are dedicated to transferring data between the host server and remote sites. Standard telephone lines or, in increasing numbers, special digital lines called ISDN (Integrated Services Digital Network), an international telecommunications standard for transmitting voice, video, and data over digital lines. Today, existing underground cable lines are providing faster connections to the Internet for business and residential users.

One of the most common misconceptions is that the Internet and the World Wide Web are one and the same, a mistake that is fostered by the belief that these terms are interchangeable. In reality, the World Wide Web, commonly referred to as the "web" or simply by its acronym WWW, is the graphic component of the Internet. The web developed in the late 1980s as a computer program designed to link personal computers together using keywords. The technology quickly evolved to allow linking of documents stored in different computers, as long as they were connected to the Internet. The document formatting language used to link documents is called HTML (Hypertext Markup Language), a form of computer language used by programmers and web designers when creating web pages.

The web remained primarily text based until 1992, when two events occurred that would forever change the way the web looked. Marc Andreesen, while at the National Center for Supercomputing Applications at the University of Illinois, developed the first web browser. This new computer program, known as Mosaic, was a software application loaded directly on a computer's hard drive. Mosaic made it easier to view the growing number of Internet web sites. After enduring the early days of line-oriented "text only" browsers like Lynx, more sophisticated graphical browsers became the industry standard. Today, Netscape Navigator® and Netscape Communicator® (products of Netscape Communications, Inc.) and Internet Explorer® (Microsoft Corporation) allow us to view sites containing a combination of text, graphics, audio, and video.

Lack of Controls: The Information Frontier

But like all good things, there is always a downside. With the Internet, the current lack of standards or controls, combined with the vast available resources, have helped to create an "information frontier." While there is an underlying system of networks existing worldwide, each of these networks is responsible for the traffic that flows within it and can only route that traffic as necessary. Each network system is responsible for its own funding and must develop its own administrative procedures. Since there is no single Internet service provider, agencies fund their own networks, each becoming a singular part of the overall "network of networks"—the Internet. Add to this a series of private systems, and the result is a series of self-administering networks whose funding, management, and policies differ widely. It is important to understand that a lack of controls or standards should not be confused with an existing system of Internet protocols.

Loosely defined, a protocol is a system of rules or standards for communicating over a network, in this case the Internet. Computers and the Internet interact according to a system of protocols that determine the behavior each side expects from the other in the transfer of information. The protocol tells your web browser software which Internet tool to use to interpret the electronic information you are requesting. The protocol used for accessing hypertext web documents on current Internet web sites is http://. Web browsers no longer require *http://* when typing the web address. The browser "assumes" the web protocol when receiving a delivery address beginning with "www". Other examples of Internet protocols are telnet, gopher and ftp (file transfer protocol)—each followed by a colon and double forward slash (://) which comprises the protocol command.

Internet protocols govern *access* to the network—how we communicate—not the content of information posted on Internet web sites, chat rooms, message boards, or in electronic mail transmissions. There are presently no controls on how or what information can be posted on the web, and no private corporation or governmental agency currently charged with overseeing the content of information posted on Internet web pages.

The process of obtaining an Internet domain name (the Internet address of the host computer) is really quite simple. Contact InterNIC (the Internet Network Information Center, http://www. internic. net), the organization that handles Internet domain name registrations, complete an application for the name you wish to reserve (*e.g.* http://findlaw.com or http://www.findlaw.com—name has been registered both ways—with and without the "www"), and pay a nominal fee.

InterNIC was formed in 1993 by agreements between it, the National Science Foundation, General Atomics, and AT&T. Today, InterNIC is a cooperative venture between the U.S. Government and Network Solutions, Inc. (NSI), a private company located in Herndon, Virginia. NSI is responsible for managing InterNIC.

Since 1993, NSI has been the only provider of domain name registration services in the commercial (.com), network provider (.net), and nonprofit organization (.org) top-level domains, pursuant to a Cooperative Agreement with the United States Government. In October 1998, the Cooperative Agreement was amended to reflect NSI's commitment to develop a protocol and associated software supporting a system that permits multiple registrars to provide registration services within .com, .net and .org—known as the "Shared Registration System."

The registrar accreditation process is handled by the Internet Corporation for Assigned Names and Numbers (ICANN). ICANN is a not-for-profit corporation formed by the global Internet community to assume responsibility for certain Internet domain name system functions. In an effort to keep pace with the amazing popularity of the Internet and the increased demand for new web domain names, seven new top-lovel domains or TLDs were approved by ICANN in November 2000: .aero, .biz, .coop, .info, .museum, .name, and .pro. This marked the first new TLDs in nearly two decades, when a limited number of original domains were approved: .com, .mil, .int, .gov, .org, and .net (in addition to special two-letter codes assigned to countries, *i.e.*, .us for United States, .fr for France and .uk for the United Kingdom). ICANN began accepting registrations for the new .biz and .info TLDs in mid-2001. The U.S. Government expects that competition in domain name registration will provide the global Internet community with a number of benefits, including greater choice in services and prices.

Often in the course of litigation or representation of a client, it may be necessary to research the ownership of an Internet domain name. Basic information regarding a registered owner is public record, and can be obtained from searchable sites such as DomainSurfer www.domainsurfer.com and DomainWatch! www.domainwatch.com.

Additional information on the implementation of NSI's Shared Registration System is available at www.nsiregistry.com and information about ICANN and ICANN's registrar accreditation process is available at www.icann.org. Information regarding the United States Government's efforts to privatize the management of the domain name system and increase competition in domain name registration services is available at www.ntia.doc.gov. Whether these efforts will also yield some standards for control over the *content* of information posted on the Internet is a subject of heated, ongoing debate at all levels of the public and private sectors.

ACCESSING THE INFORMATION SUPERHIGHWAY

Accessing the wealth of information available on the Internet is quite simple, from a technical standpoint. At the "low end," all you need is a computer equipped with a modem and web browser software, a telephone connection, and an online service provider. Major commercial Internet providers include America Online, Prodigy, Compuserve, and the Microsoft Network (MSN)—proprietary online services that provide everything you need to access the Internet: software, services, and content. In addition, there are smaller, local and regional Internet access providers offering similar services at competitive prices. There are literally thousands of Internet service providers

(ISPs), offering a variety of services from basic e-mail to full, unlimited Internet access. Whether you work for a sole practitioner or small firm and access the Internet using a personal computer (PC) and a modem, or are employed by a large firm, government agency or multinational corporation using dedicated hosts and routers, the ISP is the vendor that supplies the needed connection point. Connectivity is generally through existing telephone lines via a local, toll-free phone number, although cable access is becoming a more affordable, commercially viable alternative to dial-up services for both residential and business use.

Commercial access to the Internet has dramatically improved in recent years. With over 9,700 service providers in mid-2001, this competition has helped reduce costs and improve quality. However, when choosing a commercial online vendor or ISP, always consider your overall needs: will you be accessing the Internet from a single, computer housed at one location, or frequently dialing up remotely from a laptop computer when travelling or working out of the office? If access from another city, state, or even outside the U.S. may be required, make sure to confirm your online vendor's service area and whether toll-free numbers are provided, to avoid incurring long distance telephone charges when dialing in from a remote location. Today, most reputable online vendors and ISPs charge a flat monthly fee for their services, which usually includes unlimited access. Remember, even if your employer is just starting to use the Internet as a resource, "per minute" charges can add up fast; 60 or even 120 "free" minutes per month can be used up in one research session. For this reason, it is best to go with an unlimited monthly access plan.

A good web source for locating ISPs in your area is The List at http://thelist.com, the self-proclaimed "buyer's guide to Internet Service". The List allows you to quickly search by provider's name, area code (U.S. and Canada), or international country code to find a provider that offers the access speed and computing services that satisfy your needs and budget. Another good source is the Internet Service Providers Meta-List at www.herbison.com/herbison/iap_meta_list.html, a web site providing links to ISPs in the U.S. and Canada (arranged by state/province) and worldwide (arranged by country).

NAVIGATING THE INTERNET

The Internet is comprised of several major components, each offering different access points to resources and information. Electronic mail, or e-mail, represents one of the most commonly used Internet tools. E-mail provides the ability to electronically communicate with colleagues, clients, court personnel, or literally anyone worldwide with an e-mail address (yourname@domain.com). Correspondence routed electronically has enormous advantages over conventional "snail" mail and even facsimile transmissions (faxes.) E-mail is received almost instantaneously after being transmitted from the sender's computer. You can program most Internet access software mail programs to automatically alert you when new mail is received. You can create a message, save it in your computer's hard drive (or to a disk), edit and send at your convenience. Messages can be copied and forwarded to others with ease. However, keep in mind that just as with other forms of correspondence (*i.e.*, letters, memoranda, faxes), e-mail messages are routinely subpoenaed in litigation and are considered discoverable material in most jurisdictions. Even after you delete a sent or received e-mail message, a copy may still remain on your computer's hard drive or on a network server. Therefore, it is a good idea to consult your systems administrator or a computer specialist to help your employer develop appropriate computer records retention policies. This is also an area where clients routinely consult attorneys for guidance.

Telnet [telnet://] and the World Wide Web [http://] are the two most common Internet protocols, in addition to electronic mail [mailto@]. Telnet provides a means to connect to, and interact with, other remote computers using standard Internet protocols. Generally, you will be asked to "logon" with a user identification and/or password to access the remote computer's database. Once you are logged on, your keyboard is connected directly to the remote computer.

The Internet address or Uniform Resource Locator (URL) for the remote site will begin with the protocol telnet:// rather than http:// or www used to access web sites. Today, most new computers come preloaded with the telnet executable file (telnet.exe) required to access remote computers using this protocol. To determine whether your computer has this software, simply click the START button (Windows 95/98 and NT), then use the FIND option to search the hard drive (usually the C:/ drive) for the telnet.exe applications file. By right-clicking with your mouse on the application file, you can easily create a telnet desktop shortcut.

Web Browsers

A web browser is a software program interface needed to access the web. In order to view a site, you simply type its web address or URL into the browser's location field (see fig. 9-1). For example, when you type in www.findlaw.com, the main or home page of FindLaw, the popular legal search directory, is retrieved and downloaded to your computer's hard drive for viewing. The home page is an index to other pages on that site that can be linked to by clicking your mouse pointer over the page's hyperlinks. Hyperlink is a connection that is found in web pages and other electronic documents that, when clicked with a mouse, automatically opens a file or web page in your web browser. A hyperlink may be a word, icon, or graphic. When a hyperlink is text, it typically displays in a different color and may also be underlined. A text hyperlink that has already been visited is usually displayed in a third color. Links may also take you directly to other related sites on remote servers around the world.

As previously mentioned, Lynx was the earliest form of line-based browser, followed by Mosaic, the first interface designed to browse web pages containing a combination of text and graphic data. Today, the two most popular commercial web browsers are

FIGURE 9-1 Web Browser.

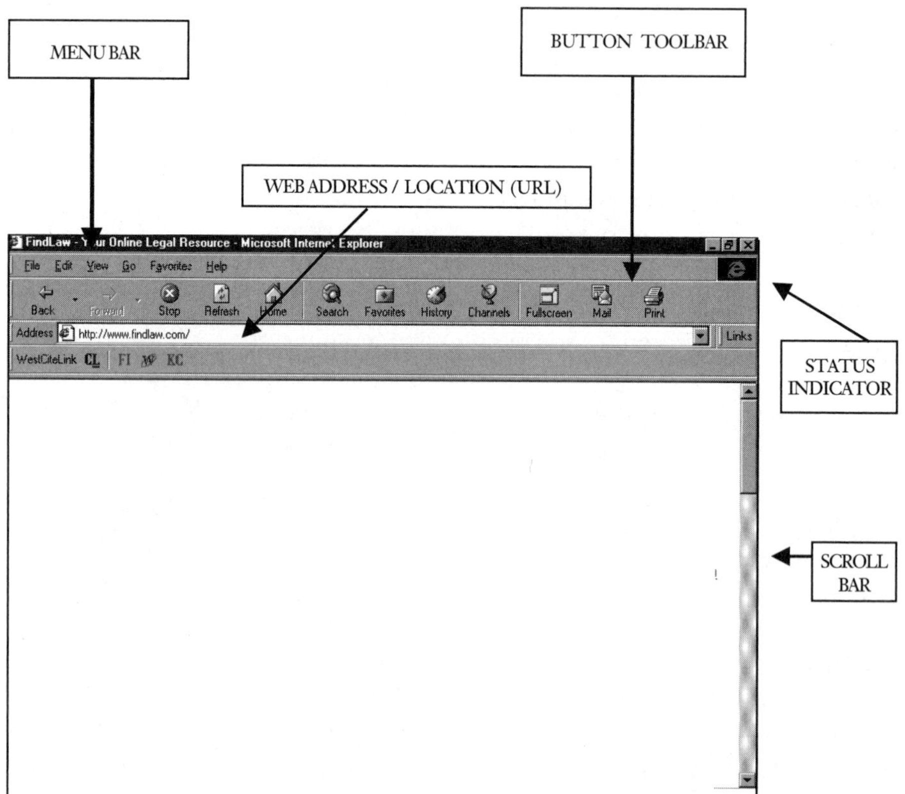

Source: Findlaw.com (http://www.findlaw.com)

Netscape Navigator and Netscape Communicator, products of Netscape Communications, Inc., and Microsoft Corporation's Internet Explorer. Netscape Navigator is a stand-alone browser that allows you to view web pages; it does not include e-mail or newsgroups. Netscape Communicator offers the complete set of Internet tools for browsing web content, plus e-mail, newsgroups and other Internet components. Each company vies for the biggest share of the market by regularly introducing new features and functions in the form of updated versions (*e.g.* Netscape Communicator 6.0, Internet Explorer 5.5). When a site indicates "best viewed by Netscape Navigator" or "best viewed by Internet Explorer", it means the pages were programmed for viewing using that particular browser. Using the other browser may ignore some of the page's special features until a subsequent release supports them. For more information on web browsers and easy download instructions for the most current versions, visit the Browser.com web site at http://www.browsers.com.

One very helpful feature of web browsers is the ability to "bookmark" web sites, allowing you to permanently store references to your favorite sites. Rather than typing in the URL each time to revisit a site, you simply select the link from your list of saved bookmarks, referred to as "bookmarks" in Netscape browsers and as "favorites" in Internet Explorer. Both features are accessed from the browser's menu bar (see fig. 9-1). This is a real timesaver for accessing frequently visited sites.

The major components of the two popular web browsers vary slightly, but generally consist of a menu bar and a button or toolbar situated horizontally across the top of the screen. Located on the far right margin of the toolbar, just above the scroll bar, is the status indicator. With some versions, when a page is in the process of being downloaded to your computer, "falling stars" appear in the Netscape "N" indicator and the "ring" around the Internet Explorer "E" spins. Once the page is successfully downloaded, the movement stops and it is safe to access hyperlinks on the page.

TIP: Wait until a page is completely downloaded before "bookmarking" it in your web browser for future reference.

The scroll bar runs vertically along the right margin of the entire web page and allows you to move up or down to view the entire contents of a page.

Directly below the toolbar is the location field where you type in the web address or URL. To access a home page of a web site, only the protocol and domain name is required. For example, http://www.whatis.com retrieves the home page for a popular dictionary of Internet and computer terminology. The http:// is the web protocol, and www.whatis.com is the domain name. (See fig. 9-2 for a graphic depiction of the components of a URL).

While the tendency to frequently change URLs has significantly diminished in recently years, especially with government (.gov) and educational (.edu) web sites, it can still present problems for the web researcher. Here are some tips for finding sites that have moved:

1. Use a web search engine (AltaVista, Google, InfoSeek, Lycos). Try phrase searching for the exact name of the old site or search keywords.
2. If the site includes several levels of directories and files (separated by a /), try typing just the root address (ending with .com/, .gov/, .edu/). The main page may not have changed; only the URL for the sub-directory or file.
3. Try the address again. The Internet may have "hiccuped" and missed some essential bit of information in the URL.
4. Check your spelling and punctuation. **Don't forget that URLs are case sensitive.** If you see something in capitals it must be typed in capitals. If you see something in lower case it must be in lower case.
5. Try adding or removing the "www." For example, if you typed in "abanet.org" or http://abanet.org and were unable to access the American Bar Association's web site, try using www.abanet.org. Alternatively, if the address you typed included "www" and was rejected, try it again without the "www." For the address to be interchangeable, both domain names would have to be registered with InterNIC [for the same site].

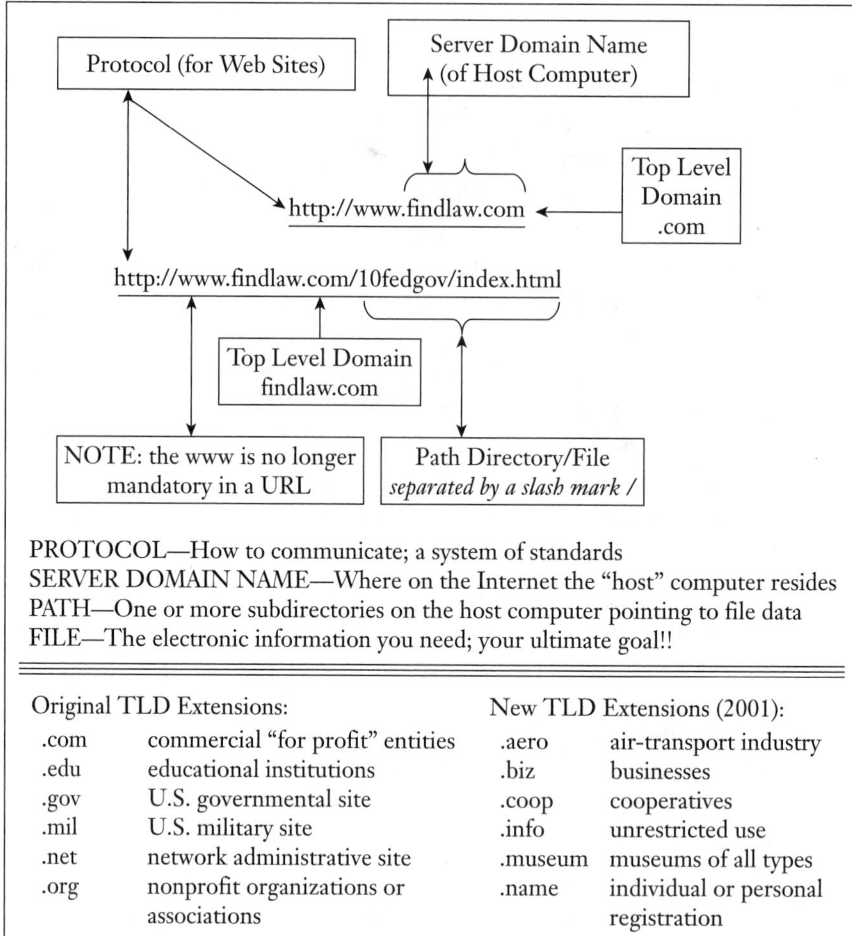

Protocol (for Web Sites)
Server Domain Name (of Host Computer)
Top Level Domain .com
http://www.findlaw.com
http://www.findlaw.com/10fedgov/index.html
Top Level Domain findlaw.com
NOTE: the www is no longer mandatory in a URL
Path Directory/File separated by a slash mark /
PROTOCOL—How to communicate; a system of standards
SERVER DOMAIN NAME—Where on the Internet the "host" computer resides
PATH—One or more subdirectories on the host computer pointing to file data
FILE—The electronic information you need; your ultimate goal!!
Original TLD Extensions:
.com commercial "for profit" entities
.edu educational institutions
.gov U.S. governmental site
.mil U.S. military site
.net network administrative site
.org nonprofit organizations or associations
New TLD Extensions (2001):
.aero air-transport industry
.biz businesses
.coop cooperatives
.info unrestricted use
.museum museums of all types
.name individual or personal registration

FIGURE 9-2
Dissecting a Web Address.

Browser Plug-ins

Plug-ins are software programs that extend the capabilities of a web browser in a specific way, such as giving you the ability to play audio samples or view video movies from within your browser. Popular plug-ins include:

- **Acrobat Reader by Adobe**—Adobe Acrobat Reader software allows you view and print Portable Document Format (PDF) files on all major computer platforms. Acrobat Reader also lets you fill in and submit PDF forms online.

  Download: http://www.adobe.com

- **Flash Player by Macromedia**—experience animation and entertainment on the web with Flash, the web standard for graphics and animation.

  Download: http://www.macromedia.com/

- **RealPlayer by RealNetworks**—with RealPlayer, you can play real-time audio, video, animations, and multimedia presentations on the web.

  Download: http://www.realplayer.com/

- **Shockwave by Macromedia**—Shockwave is the industry standard for delivering and experiencing quality interactive multimedia, graphics, and streaming audio on the web.

  Download: http://www.macromedia.com/

For more information about plug-ins and to download current versions of many plug-in products, visit the BrowserWatch Plug-in Plaza web site at http://browserwatch.internet.com/plug-in.html.

THE INTERNET AS A RESEARCH TOOL

We would all be lost in a vast sea of information if not for Internet search tools such as search engines, metasearch engines, web directories, and specialized or subject search engines. Yet even as these tools become more sophisticated in their search capabilities and more user friendly, we often feel as if we are wasting valuable time only to retrieve a list of useless sites. Search failures range from being swamped with literally hundreds of irrelevant and unusable "hits," to retrieving no results at all—the dreaded "404-Not Found" message—and everything in between.

This chapter provides a brief overview of several popular Internet search tools and takes a look at some future trends designed to make searching the Internet easier, faster, and more rewarding.

Search Engines

Search engines, not to be confused with web browsers which are computer software, are database programs designed to search the web for data based on some set of user-defined criteria. Web search engines constantly scour the Internet, visiting web sites and electronically creating catalogs of web pages. They are considered one of the primary ways to locate web resources. Popular examples include AltaVista (www.altavista.com), Excite (www.excite.com), Google (www.google.com), HotBot (www.hotbot.com), and Lycos (www.lycos.com).

The term "search engine" is often used synonymously with "spider" and "index," although these are separate components that work with the engine. The spider or robot component scans web documents and adds them to an index by following links. Simply stated, search engines are nothing more than full text indexes of web pages. When using a search engine, your goal is to retrieve a useful list of web sites (search "hits"), ultimately yielding files of pertinent data based on a simple search query. Of course, anyone who has ever used a web search engine knows this is often not the case. Trying to coax a search engine to find a good match from the keywords or phrases you type in and all of the words contained in the engine's index is often a monumental task. In essence, you are relying on a computer to do simple pattern-matching between your words and the words in the database index.

Web Directories

Similar to web search engines, web directories are collections of links to web sites compiled by people, not software robots. Sites must be submitted to the web directory site, reviewed, and approved for inclusion. Once a submission is approved, it is assigned [often by a subject expert] to an appropriate category or categories. Directories have the advantage over search engines in that they can be very precise in how they categorize web pages. Many directories annotate their links with brief descriptions or comments, so you get an idea of what a site is about before clicking through. While Yahoo! www.yahoo.com is probably the most popular web directory, others include Excite (www.excite.com/), NBC Interactive's Snap.com (http://home.nbci.com), Northern Light (www.northern light.com), Google (http://directory.google.com), and the Librarian's Index to the Internet (www.lii.org).

Many commercial search engines and web directories tend to focus on a particular collection of resources and often develop a unique focus or set of features. For example, Northern Light boasts a Special Collection™ of more than 7,000 full text web-based sources, and one-click access to a list of over thirty newswires with free real-time recent news articles. This directory is also a good source for locating legal and government resources, with a "Special Edition" offering in-depth coverage of major news stories and reports from Congress, when in session. From Northern Light's home page, you can link directly to Usgovsearch www.usgovsearch.com, a one-stop fee-based resource of government and military web sites that utilizes powerful searching, crawling, and classification technologies. Northern Light exemplifies a trend among search engines and directories to offer a combination of *free* and *fee-based* services. While most of its features are free, Northern Light does charge a nominal flat fee to download or print the full text of articles contained in its Special Collection (brief abstracts are provided free), and the cost of the article is clearly stated up front.

It is also common for the indexing and directory features to overlap—a search engine will include a small web directory, and many popular web directories include a search box that allows the researcher to search that particular site (or even the entire web). Google (www.google.com) is a good example.

While search engine indexes offer the advantage of size—indexes typically contain information on millions of web pages—the immense size of these indexes makes effective searching a real challenge, especially for the novice web searcher. The main advantage of a web directory is that, in most cases, the retrieved list of links will be of a much higher quality, although the universe from which links are pulled is much smaller than with search engines. Another key advantage of web directories is their hierarchical organizational format that lets the searcher move through a series of subject trees, browsing for categories and links in much the same way you browse the stacks of your library for a particular book. Often, the nature of your research project—what type of information you are looking for and in what degree of detail—will dictate whether you choose to use a search engine or a web directory.

Metasearch Engines

A metasearch is a "search of searches"—where a query is submitted to more than one search engine or directory, and results are reported from all the available engines, possibly after removal of duplicates and sorting. A metasearch engine is the server that passes these queries on to many search engines and/or directories and then summarizes all the results. Examples of popular metasearch engines are: Ask Jeeves® (www.askjeeves.com), c4.com (www.c4.com), Dogpile® (www.dogpile.com), Metacrawler (www.metacrawler.com), and Profusion® (www.profusion.com).

The major advantage to using a metasearch engine is the time you save by running your search once rather than several times using individual search engines. However, it is not uncommon to retrieve slightly different results from a particular search engine when running your query in a metasearch engine. This inconsistency is viewed by some as a disadvantage of metasearching; however, they continue to gain in popularity among web researchers. As with any search tool, always read the help screen or search "tips" before beginning to search in an unfamiliar search tool.

Subject or Specialized Engines

Another option for the web researcher is subject or specialized search engines that allow for more precise searching in collections of searchable resources dedicated to a particular subject or discipline. What we commonly refer to as "locators" or "finders"—those handy web directories that help us locate telephone numbers, street and postal addresses, e-mail and more on people and businesses—are examples of a specialized search engine. Specific examples of "locator" specialized search engines include: AnyWho Directories (www.anywho.com), Switchboard (www.switchboard.com), TelDir (www.teldir.com), WhoWhere? (www.whowhere.lycos.com), Yahoo! People Search (www.people.yahoo.com), and Yahoo! Yellow Pages (http://www.yp.yahoo.com).

There are even specialized "reverse" directories that let you to type in a telephone number (excluding unlisted telephone numbers) and cross-reference it to a person or business. For this service, try InfoSpace's Reverse Lookup www.infospace.com/info/ reverse.htm, or the Reverse Phone Directory at www.reversephonedirectory.com/.

Other types of specialized search engines are those dedicated to ferreting out Internet newsgroups, discussion and information lists (listservs), and even ftp (file transfer protocol) sites. Examples include CataList (www.lsoft.com/lists/listref.html), Liszt (www. liszt.com), and Tile.net (www.tile.net). For more about electronic discussion groups, listservs and bulletin boards, please refer to the section of this chapter discussing Internet e-mail discussion groups.

While many of the first specialized search engines were web versions of the white or yellow page directories, today there are many web search engines concentrating on a wide range of topics. These tools collect, and in some cases evaluate, hundreds of web resources covering subjects such as law and government, medicine and health, business and finance, news and current events, politics, real estate, and more. There is even a specialized search engine that searches for other specialized or subject search engines. SearchPower.com (www.searchpower.com) markets its site as "The World's Largest Search Engine Directory," a directory of thousands of links to subject search engines, organized under a wide range of categories and academic disciplines.

Law-Related Search Engines

For our purposes, we will focus briefly on three law-related subject search engines/directories: Findlaw's LawCrawler (http://lawcrawler.findlaw.com), the Meta-Index maintained by the Georgia State University College of Law (http://gsulaw.gsu.edu/metaindex), and FirstGov (http://www.firstgov.gov).

LawCrawler is a subject search engine powered by Google. Findlaw www.findlaw.com/, Lawcrawler's parent site, is a legal web directory, with thousands of links arranged under major and minor categories that actually make sense. By using simple Boolean operators or phrase searching, you can use LawCrawler to search the entire web for legal information sites matching your query. Limiting the searchable universe to only law-related sites greatly increases the accuracy and reliability of your search. Alternatively, you can choose to run your query by searching only federal government sites, the U.S. Code (1996–present), or in a database of U.S. Supreme Court decisions (1893–present). You can also limit your search to Findlaw's legal dictionary, legal news, or law reviews and journals. As part of the University Law Review Project, you type a query once and simultaneously search all web-based law reviews, electronic law journals, and legal periodicals published on the web. With more and more law-related publications available full text on the web, this is a real time-saver, and a very efficient, cost-effective research tool.

Another good metasearch engine for locating U.S. federal legal resources on the web is the Meta-Index maintained by the Georgia State University College of Law http://gsulaw.gsu.edu/metaindex. The index is arranged under major topics such as judicial opinions, legislation, federal regulation, people in the law and other legal sources, specific courts, and types of federal legislation (*i.e.*, House bills, Senate bills, and the Congressional Record). Each topic includes a separate search tool that includes a default entry as an example. If you want to see the kind of information returned by each tool, simply select the search button. If you have a specific search in mind, enter it in the space provided, and then select the search button.

FirstGov is a web portal designed to connect all of the federal government's online resources. Launced in September 2000, the site provides access to over 30 million government web pages. FirstGov allows users to browse a wealth of information, arranged in a directory format, or search the site using the search tool. The site will initially focus on providing information, but is expected to eventually enable web-based transactions between citizens and agency personnel, such as applying online for student loans, tracking Social Security benefits, comparing Medicare options, and even administering government grants and contracts. Developed by the nonprofit Federal Search Foundation, the Foundation will continue to manage FirstGov until approximately 2003, when responsibility for maintenance of the site will be turned over to the federal government, or outsourced to a private vendor.

If you are looking primarily for law review articles, the Tarlton Law Library at the University of Texas School of Law site (http://tarlton.law. utexas.edu/tallons/content_search.html) is a good place to start. This free web service includes an online version of the table of contents pages from hundreds of law reviews and other scholarly legal journals published in the U.S. and abroad. The files are updated daily and are very current. The downside is the site only contains contents pages from the most recent three months of a publication. Copies of actual full text articles are available through the Library's document delivery service for a nominal fee. You could also search the respective Westlaw or Lexis databases containing law reviews and legal journals to obtain the full text articles. Now that you have the citation information (*i.e.*, title, author, date, volume/ issue, and page numbers), you can quickly locate the article, saving time and money in expensive subscription database search charges.

Other Subject Areas

Just as with law and government information, other disciplines are well represented on the web. Refer to figure 9-3 for a list of several popular subject search engines. Obviously, the big advantage offered by all of these tools is the ability to narrow your web search to a smaller collection of sites—tools that offer a much better chance of yielding current, usable data.

As you can see, search engines and web directories offer a variety of ways for you to refine and control your searches. Some provide a menu system, while others require use of special commands as part of your query. Search Engine Watch, a web-based "watchdog" site, provides helpful information, including a handy glossary of search terminology (http://searchenginewatch.com/facts/glossary.html.) The Search Engine Watch web site also includes a user-friendly online tutorial (http://www.search enginewatch.com/facts/math.html). Taking a few minutes to review this tutorial will help improve your web search results, regardless of what search tool you use.

DISCIPLINE	SEARCH TOOL	WEB ADDRESS
Business and Finance	• FinancialWeb • Hoover's Online • MoneyCrawler • SmallBizSearch	• http://www.financialweb.com/rshIndex.asp • www.hoovers.com • www.moneycrawler.com • www.smallbizsearch.com
Clipart, Images & Photographs	• Barry's Clip Art Server • Clip Art Searcher • Photo/Images Finder	• www.barrysclipart.com/ • www.webplaces.com/search/ • www.altavista.com/cgi-bin/query?pg=q&stype=simage
Company Data	• Companies Online • Corporate Information • Hoover's Online • Internet Prospector • Kompass	• www.companiesonline.com/ • http://www.corporateinformation.com/ • www.hoovers.com • http://www.internet-prospector.org/company.html • www.kompass.com
Law and Government	• Findlaw • GSU MetaIndex	• www.findlaw.com • http://gsulaw.gsu.edu/metaindex/
Medical and Health	• Health A to Z • Medical World Search • Medscape • WebMD	• www.healthatoz.com • www.mwsearch.com • www.medscape.com • http://webmd.com
News and Current Events	• Newsbot • News Index • TotalNews	• www.newsbot.com • http://searchengines.net/newsindex_se.htm • www.totalnews.com

FIGURE 9-3 Specialized Search Engines.

Regardless of whether you are using a free web resource or a costly subscription database with transactional or per-hour pricing, it is a good idea to formulate a search strategy before beginning your online research. The query planner, Fig. 9-4, is designed to help plan your research question and improve the efficiency of your research session. Common Boolean "connectors" and "expanders" used in a variety of electronic databases are explained in detail on the second page of the query planner. Basic query tips and key definitions are also included.

Internet E-Mail Discussion Groups

The final component of the Internet discussed in this chapter is e-mail discussion groups. Electronic discussion groups simply take communicating with others via e-mail a step further by linking people with common interests and providing them with a format to discuss issues and share information related to a common topic, theme, or area of expertise. These groups are often referred to by other names, including discussion lists, interest groups, mailing lists, or listservs.

All communication in a discussion group is carried on by e-mail. A user "joins" or "subscribes" to a group. Once subscribed, you can send (post) and receive messages from other group members. It is important to remember that by posting a message to the group, it becomes a very public transmission—often being sent instantly to hundreds and even thousands of people. The exception is a moderated discussion group where a message sent to the group is first routed electronically to the person serving as moderator. The moderator either sends the message on to the group or takes other appropriate action (*i.e.*, returns message to the sender, edits message to comply with rules established by the moderator and/or group, etc.). Unsubscribing from a group is usually as simple as joining—send a message to the list proctor (listproc) at the host computer site asking to "unsubscribe [list name]." Simply follow the "unsubscribe" instructions provided [via e-mail] once you subscribe to a list.

QUERY? PLANNER

What is a QUERY? Just another name for a *Question!* When searching the World Wide Web (WWW) for quality sites, try using this handy Worksheet to plan your Query in advance.

Your Name____________________ Date__________ Time__________

Client Reference: ____________________ Client File Number__________

Question/Issue:______________________________

____

____

Restrict BY LANGUAGE *(Example: English ONLY sites)* YES____ NO____ Restrict BY DATE *(Example: 1997 or 1990-1997)*__________

Search Term/ Expander	Connector	Search Term/ Expander	Connector	Search Term/ Expander	Connector	Search Term/ Expander
Alternative(s)		Alternative(s)		Alternative(s)		Alternative(s)

Completed QUERY: ______________________________

____

____

FIGURE 9-4

Boolean CONNECTORS

Connector	Meaning
AND, &, +	Retrieves documents containing *both* terms. Use of AND *narrows* a search; a + sign before word makes it mandatory.
OR	Retrieves documents containing *at least one* of the search terms. Use of OR *broadens* a search; terms can be interchanged.
Space	A space between words (search terms) means the same as the word "OR."
NOT,—	The word NOT or a minus symbol *excludes (eliminates)* unwanted terms from your search results.
( ), " "	Parentheses or Quotation Marks retrieve documents containing search terms *in the same order* as they appear within these symbols.

Boolean EXPANDERS

*, +	Universal character or "wildcard" often used to replace letters at the end or within a word; also used to retrieve words with variations in spelling *(i.e. POTAT** retrieves POTATO and POTATOE; CENT** retrieves CENTER and CENTRE.)*
!, ?	Root Expansion symbols; also called truncation operators. Use these symbols at the end of a word to retrieve all forms of the term *(i.e. LIBRAR! retrieves LIBRARY, LIBRARIES, LIBRARIAN and LIBRARIANSHIP.)*

Copyright ©1998
Central Florida Library Cooperative

Basic QUERY Tips

1. A **Query** is simply a statement of the information you need to find.
2. **Relevancy** – use only words that are relevant to your query. All terms are equally weighted in a query.
3. **More is Usually Better** – don't worry about using too many words (terms) in your query.
4. **Specify Multiple Forms** of the same phrases (*i.e.*, CDROM, CD-ROM, CD).
5. **Common Words** are ignored so do not include in your query (a, and, the, at).
6. **Terms and Connectors** is a search method where you enter a query consisting of key *terms* from your issue; the *connectors* indicate the relationship between your terms.
7. **Know Your Sources** – always read the HELP or Query Formulation screens.
8. **Know Your Subject/Topic** – understand exactly what it is that you are looking for. A poor query will yield unwanted information. *Search only one (1) topic at a time!*
9. **Expect Limitations** – No web search tool is perfect in terms of accuracy or comprehensiveness. Search engines, directories and web databases vary greatly.
10. **Use Boolean Operators** *(and, or, not)* to fine-tune your search. But remember, not all sites and search engines support Boolean searching.
11. **Natural Language & Phrase Searching** – Use to refine your search, *if available.*
12. **Specialized Engines** – For more precise searching, use a "subject specific" site like FindLaw (legal resources) or Health AtoZ (medical and health information).

KEY DEFINITIONS

BOOLEAN SEARCH	A search based on combinations of keywords (terms) and connecting symbols or operators (AND, OR, NOT are the 3 basic).
KEYWORD SEARCH	A search for documents containing one or more words (terms) that are specified by a user.
PHRASE SEARCH	A search for documents containing words (terms) appearing in the *exact order* specified by the user. Most search engines and databases recognize parentheses ( ) or quotation marks " " to enclose a phrase.
PROXIMITY SEARCH	A search where users specify that documents should have search words (terms) NEAR each other or within a certain number of words ; not all search engines and databases allow proximity searching.
QUERY	Another name for a question; a simple statement of a user's question or the issue being researched; a completed query incorporates search words (terms), connectors and expanders.
RELEVANCY	How well a retrieved document provides the information a user is looking for; usually determined by the search engine or database.
SEARCH ENGINE	The software that searches an index and returns matches; often uses synonymously with "spider" and "index," although these are actually components of a search engine.
THESAURUS	A list of synonyms a search engine or database uses to find matches to particular words in documents.

FIGURE 9-4 (continued)

TIP: Be sure to retain a print or computer copy of instructions and other information received electronically from the listproc when you subscribe to a discussion group.

General rules of e-mail etiquette also apply to discussion groups. Discussions should always be conducted in a polite and civil manner. You should also avoid using the group as a format to air personal grievances or make lofty position statements, and never use profanity or take a hostile tone against others, e-mail conduct known as "flaming." Additionally, each group may disseminate additional rules of conduct for subscribers. These rules are generally sent to new subscribers via e-mail once you join the group.

While many busy professionals shun participation in electronic discussion groups to avoid receiving a proliferation of daily messages, the benefits often outweigh the drawbacks. Being a member of a discussion group allows you to communicate with colleagues worldwide. However, always remember that the attorney/client privilege extends to paralegals and other support staff and includes *all* forms of communication outside the office. When posting a question or comment to a listserv or discussion group, never refer to a client by name or make any statements that could in any way be construed as a breach of the privilege. Be very generic, such as requesting recommendations for print or online resources on a specific subject or posting questions or comments regarding continuing legal education programs in your region and practice area.

TIP: Always remember to post a "thank-you" to the group, thanking [by name/firm] those who came to your rescue.

There are literally hundreds of law-related discussion groups. Two very dependable web directories providing links to information on a variety of legal and government oriented lists are the Washburn University School of Law site at www.washlaw.edu/listserv.html, and from the D'Angelo Law Library at the University of Chicago Law School at www.lib.uchicago.edu/~llou/lawlists/info.html. The University of Chicago A–Z guide "is intended to facilitate person-to-person networking, legal research, and exchange and dissemination of legal information worldwide" and includes a handy introduction on how to use the guide and how to use electronic mailing lists generally for legal work.

Law-Lib is a very popular legal listserv. While geared toward law librarians, many lawyers, paralegals, and legal publishers subscribe to this list, sharing valuable information about publications, continuing education, recent court decisions, pending legislation, and issues of broad concern to the legal profession. Law-Lib is unmoderated. Topics of discussion vary, but include posting of difficult legal reference questions, interlibrary loan requests, announcements, information about legal vendors, and law office policy discussions. Occasionally, brief notices of new products or services from commercial vendors will be included.

How to Join a Listserv

In order to join a discussion group or listserv, you need to send a message to the administrative address (listproc) for the list you have selected. Following is an example of how to subscribe to Law-Lib:

List Name:	**Law-Lib**
Administrative Address:	*listproc@ucdavis.edu*
List Address:	*law-lib@ucdavis.edu*
To Subscribe:	Send e-mail to the administrative address:

subscribe LAW-LIB YourFullName

To unsubscribe:	Send e-mail to the administrative address. In the body of the message, type:

unsubscribe LAW-LIB *or* signoff LAW-LIB

To post messages:	Send e-mail message to the *List Address*

This format is generally utilized by most discussion groups. However, it is a good idea to review the specific instructions available from the Washburn or University of Chicago guides for the discussion group(s) you are interested in joining.

EVALUATIVE GUIDELINES FOR SELECTING INTERNET RESOURCES

One important goal when evaluating any information resource is to determine whether the information presented is accurate and timely. This is especially true with legal and government information, regardless of the format (*i.e.*, print, CD-ROM, Internet). Unlike most print and CD-ROM resources that go through a lengthy editorial or filtering process, information posted on the Internet and, specifically, the web, is mostly unfiltered. This places the burden of evaluating the authority of web-based resources squarely on the user.

Figure 9-5 summarizes the main criteria to consider when evaluating web resources, regardless of the type of information you are seeking. A bibliography of web sites designed as guides and checklists for evaluating Internet resources is also included in Appendix H.

The bottom line—when relying on Internet and web resources, be sure your site meets a majority of these criteria, especially the important "authority" and "currency" requirements.

FUTURE TRENDS

Now you know how the Internet and the World Wide Web began and evolved into an integral part of our daily personal and professional lives. What can we expect in the next decade? The possibilities are limitless. The way we practice law and do business in our global society is constantly changing. While the web continues to offer better content, the challenge becomes how to access and manage the wealth of information we now have at our fingertips.

E-commerce (electronic commerce) will impact the delivery of legal services, just as it has already had a tremendous effect on the way companies do business. Legal issues associated with web site development, including regulation, electronic fraud, copyright, and contractual and security issues will become very important, opening the way for a new area of practice for lawyers and legal assistants—computer and Internet law. Legal publishers have already recognized this trend, as evidenced by the prevalence of new publications geared toward the computer law practitioner. The *Computer Law Strategist*, a monthly newsletter published by Leader Publications, is a fine example, offering practical, informative articles on topics such as licensing software, negotiating antivirus warranties, trade secret protection, and dealing with high-tech clients.

It is already established procedure in all federal and most state jurisdictions that e-mail transmissions, computer files, even the contents of your computer's hard drive, are all discoverable in litigation proceedings. Therefore, appropriate language in the "definitions" section of any formal discovery (*i.e.*, interrogatories and requests to produce) should specifically include all possible electronic document sources.

Push Technology

As the role of the legal information professional expands to include knowledge management and global data integration, push technology will help make this possible. Push or webcasting technology as it is also known, automates the search and retrieval function. Based on user defined criteria, a push application will automatically search a database for specific information and deliver it when and where the user directs—usually straight to the desktop. Making use of push software is a convenient means of retrieving important information and a huge timesaver. Push technology keeps information on point and current, combining convenient delivery with intelligent filtering.

In keeping with our global society and the trend toward telecommuting and the remote office, push technology is a very portable form of information delivery, "pushing" data not only to your PC or laptop computer, but to users via voice and data pagers and cellular telephones. Today, all types of information are being pushed directly to users' desktops—corporate, financial, government and legal information, news and current events, and specialized industry data. In most cases, the software is a free download from the host site, and there is no change to receive information updates.

CRITERIA	KEY COMPONENTS
Authority of Source (Sponsorship)	• Who is the author? Is the author clearly identified? • What are the author's credentials? • Are the author and publisher the same entity? • Is there an organizational sponsor for the site? • Can you easily determine the author/publisher's reputation? • Can you easily contact the author with questions or comments? • Is the content author also the site webmaster? • Is the author and/or webmaster responsive to your questions?
Currency (Timeliness)	• Is the date of the last update or revision to the page content readily available? • Is the site current? • Is the information updated on a regular basis? • If the content is time sensitive, is it out of date? • Is the site archived?
Purpose and Usefulness	• Is the purpose (intent or focus) of the site clearly stated? • Is the intended audience easily determined from the main (home) page? • Does the site contain advertising (*i.e.*, a marketing focus)? If so, does it distract from the resource content? • Is the information too old [or too new] for your needs? • Is the information copyrighted?
Scope and Content	• Is the scope (time span, coverage) of the information easily determined? • Is the content easy to understand (*i.e.*, layman vs. expert level)? • Does the site include a variety of well organized links? • Does the site include advertisements or promotional material? Is it excessive? • If so, does it distract from the information content? • Is there a political, cultural or religious bias? • Are the sources for the content cited? • Does the author/sponsor's affiliation influence views presented on the site?
Objectivity and Balance	• Do you know the purpose of the site (news, personal, entertainment, informational, marketing, etc.)? • Is the author/publisher/sponsor's reason for publishing the information posted? • Is the information presented with a minimum of bias?
Accuracy and Reliability	• Is the information content accurate? [*How do you know?*] • Does the site contain technical errors (*spelling, grammar*)? • If the site contains links, are they reliable? • Does the site include any reviews or a rating system? • If so, are the reviewers' qualifications and/or rating criteria provided?
Technical Design	• Is the page well organized and easy to use? • Is the site design (*colors, background, fonts, layout*) appealing? • Does the page load reasonably fast? • If a highly graphic site, is there a "text only" option? • Is the site searchable? • Is there an index, table of contents and/or site map to help navigation? • How well does the page print out? • Are any required plug-ins or "helper" applications clearly identified [with links to any necessary software downloads]?
Uniqueness	• Is the information available elsewhere (*i.e.*, inprint, on CD-ROM or from another web site)? • If so, would using another resource be preferable?

FIGURE 9-5 Evaluative Criteria for Internet Resources.

Some popular push applications include:

- Infogate Entry Point News Ticker
  www.entrypoint.com
- TotalNEWS Feed Ticker
  www.totalnews.com/?_feed/install.html
- NewsPage
  www.individual.com/
- Web Ticker
  www.webticker.com
- WorldFlash News Ticker
  www.worldflash.com/

E-mail Alerts

Electronic mail (e-mail) is no longer limited to direct communications among individuals, select groups, or participants of a discussion group. You can also use your e-mail server to deliver news and up-to-the-minute information on a variety of topics, customized to *your* specific research needs. Many companies and online information providers such as newswires, research institutions and government agencies provide regular electronic information briefs covering subjects ranging from pending legislation, business news (in general or on a specific company), health and wellness issues, and breaking news stories. Anyone can take advantage of e-mail alerts, a popular research tool of professional journalists and research librarians, with a quick online registration. See figure 9-6 for examples of several e-mail alerts, a form of push technology.

Portable Document Format (PDF) Files

Adobe Portable Document Format (PDF) is the de facto standard for electronic document distribution worldwide and a universal file format that preserves all of the fonts, formatting, colors, and graphics of any original source document, regardless of the application and platform used to create it. PDF files are compact and can be shared, viewed, navigated, and printed exactly as intended by anyone with Adobe Acrobat Reader software loaded on their computer. Versions of Acrobat Reader run on most computer operating systems, including DOS, Windows, Macintosh, and UNIX.

FIGURE 9-6 Examples of Push Technology: E-mail Alerts.

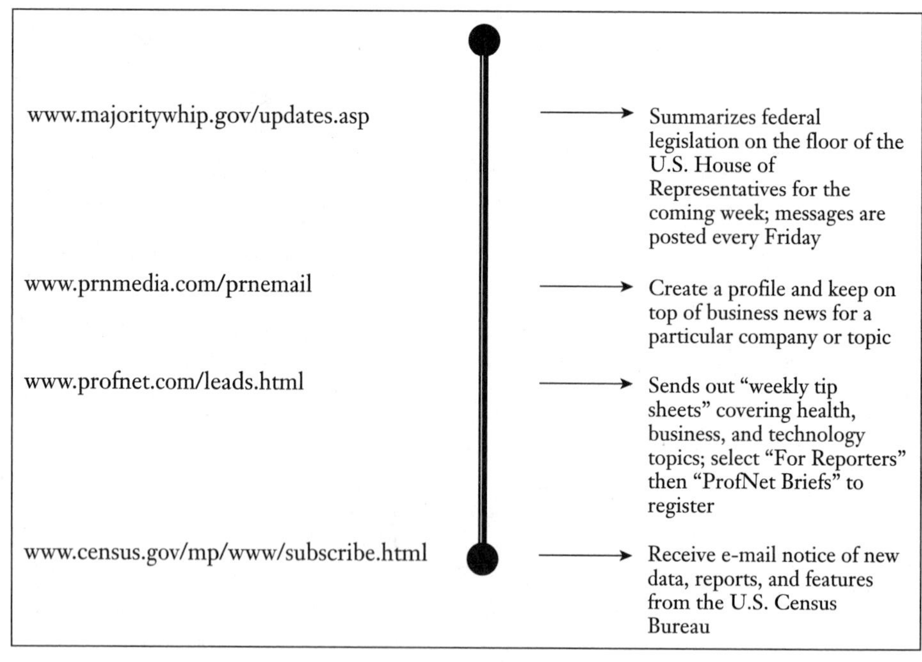

www.majoritywhip.gov/updates.asp
Summarizes federal legislation on the floor of the U.S. House of Representatives for the coming week; messages are posted every Friday
www.prnmedia.com/prnemail
Create a profile and keep on top of business news for a particular company or topic
www.profnet.com/leads.html
Sends out "weekly tip sheets" covering health, business, and technology topics; select "For Reporters" then "ProfNet Briefs" to register
www.census.gov/mp/www/subscribe.html
Receive e-mail notice of new data, reports, and features from the U.S. Census Bureau

Tax forms and tax publications, court forms, Federal Register Notices, and some court opinions available on the web, are all good examples of documents that must be viewed, navigated, and printed using the PDF format in order to preserve the original pagination and layout.

Adobe Acrobat Reader is a free download from the Adobe Systems web site at www.adobe.com/products/acrobat/readstep.html. Once you have downloaded and installed the software, you will be able to view and print documents created and saved as Portable Document Format files (.pdf extension). If you share documents electronically, you should be sending them in .pdf format.

Zipped Files—File Storage Compression

Have you ever tried to save a huge document or one with lots of graphics to a portable disk for storage or to send to a colleague or client, only to be unable to fit the entire contents on a single disk? You could invest in some expensive high-capacity storage disks, or simply save the document using a "zip" software program.

Zip is a compression and file packaging utility that works with all common computer operating software programs, UNIX, MSDOS, Microsoft Windows 95/98 and 2000, Windows NT, and Macintosh. The zip program puts one or more compressed files into a single zip archive, along with information about the files (*i.e.*, name, path, date, time of last modification). An entire directory can be packed into a zip archive with a single command. Compression ratios of 2:1 to 3:1 are common for text files. Zip has one compression method (deflation) and can also store files without compression. The software automatically chooses the better of the two for each file to be compressed. Both the person saving/ sending (zipping) and opening/retrieving (unzipping) a zipped document must have a [compatible] zip program loaded on their computer.

WinZIP®—the self-described "archive utility for Windows"—is one of the most popular zip software programs on the market today. From the company's web site at www.winzip.com, download a free shareware version. Shareware is software distributed on the basis of an honor system. Most shareware is delivered free of charge, but the author usually requests payment of a small fee if you like the program and use it regularly.

Intranets and Extranets

What.is (http://www.whatis.com/), an online techno-dictionary, defines intranet as "a private network that is contained within an enterprise". Typically, an intranet includes connections through one or more computers to the outside Internet. The main purpose of an intranet is to share company information and computing resources among employees. An intranet can also be used to facilitate working in groups and for teleconferences.

While similar to an intranet, an extranet is a private network that uses Internet protocols and a public telecommunication system to securely share part of a business's information or operations with suppliers, vendors, partners, customers, clients, or other businesses. An extranet can be viewed as part of a company's intranet that is extended to users outside the company. It has also been described as a state of mind in which the Internet is perceived as a way to do business with other companies as well as to sell products to customers.

The development of intranets is proliferating throughout corporate America, including law firms. An intranet, or internal networked corporate web site, is an application whose time has come. Today, most larger law firms either have intranets or are investigating the cost and mechanics of mounting one. The fact that clients increasingly expect their attorneys to be computer savvy and technologically advanced has clearly motivated many firms to develop intranets and extranets, mount web sites, and make e-mail the communications tool of choice. For law firms trying to keep up with the rush to embrace each new successive wave of technology, an intranet is a logical, positive step in the right direction.

The types of information available on company intranets is as varied as the organizations themselves. Examples include: policies and procedures manuals, company directories, office locations, maps and directions, news and press releases, library and research services, accounting forms, and, in law firms, online expert witness banks and forms files.

Intranets provide a timely, cost-efficient way for law firms and companies to disseminate information to employees. Intranet technology provides an excellent medium to significantly transform the way in which data is stored, published, and distributed within a company—whether to one office or multiple locations within a firm or organization. Efficient information knowledge management is the key to doing business in the future. Because of their training and organizational skills, legal assistants are routinely called upon to help develop and maintain law firm intranets.

Advanced "Smart" Search Engines

As previously stated, the key to using the Intranet and the web as a research tool is finding a way to efficiently locate, retrieve, organize, manage, and disseminate the wealth of available information. While this has often been a daunting task, considering the proliferation of resources, web searching is becoming easier and more exact as a result of new, more "intelligent" web search tools.

There are two fundamentally different types of search tools available for locating information on the web: search engines and web directories. However, developing technologies will allow you to interact with computers and search tools on a more personal level, making web searching easier and more responsive. The ultimate goal is to make ferreting out useful data easier and quicker by yielding better results, even if you are a novice web searcher. Ways to accomplish this include search tools that allow you to eliminate duplicate results, and limit your search to include only those sites that have been updated within a user-defined period of time.

Search Engine Watch at www.searchengine watch.com/ is a good source to learn more about the features and capabilities of new search tools. Greg Notess, a regular contributor to *Online* and *Database* magazines and author of *Government Information on the Internet, 2d Edition*, has developed a comprehensive web site with descriptions of the features of many of the major web engines and search tools. His site, www.notess.com, also includes news about many of the new "smart" engines and a handy bibliography of readings. For more information about this new breed of web search tools, please refer to figure 9-7.

CHAPTER 9 SUMMARY

- While in existence since the 1960s, the Internet has developed into the world's largest information network.
- Today, the Internet consists of a "network of networks" linked together by servers. Servers transmit data from host computers out to individual client computers.
- Data travels between the host and client computers via high-speed telecommunication lines, including standard telephone lines, special digital lines called ISDN, and underground cable lines.
- The Internet and the World Wide Web are not interchangeable terms. The web is the graphic component of the Internet.
- HTML (Hypertext Markup Language) is the document formatting language used by computer programers and web designers when creating web pages.
- A web browser is a software application loaded on your computer used to view web pages. Microsoft Internet Explorer and Netscape Communicator are the two most popular graphic web browsers.
- A protocol is a system of rules or standards for communicating over a network, such as the Internet. The protocol used for accessing hypertext web documents on the Internet is http://.
- Internet protocols govern access to the Internet, not the content.
- InterNIC, a cooperative venture between the U.S. Government and Network Solutions, Inc., is the organization that handles Internet domain name registrations.
- Basic information regarding a registered domain owner is public record and can be obtained from several searchable web sites.
- Plug-ins are software programs that extend the capabilities of a web browser such as adding the ability to play audio or video clips, or view and print a document in its original format.
- Search engines (not to be confused with browsers) are database programs designed to search the web for data based on some set of user-defined criteria.
- Web directories are collections of links to web sites compiled by people, not software robots.

SEARCH TOOL	DESCRIPTION	WEB ADDRESS
Alexa Internet	A web browser "add-on" that provides information about each site as you surf, plus recommendations about related sites you may want to visit; it learns and improves over time with the collective particiaption of its users.	http:/www.alexa.com/
Clever	The *CLEVER* search engine incorporates several algorithms that make use of hyperlink structure for discovering high-quality information on the web	http://www.almaden.ibm.com/cs/53/clever.html
Mirago	"Smart" web directory, providing access to the web with a 'United Kingdom' perspective.	http://www.mirago.co.uk/
NBCi New Zealand (formerly Global Brain)	Self-proclaimed "revolutionary new search technology" that captures the preferences of users to rank subsequent similar searches.	http://www.globalbrain.net/
Proteus	Proteus Internet search tools are designed to help you get the most out your Internet reseasrach through the interface you feel most comfortable with and your web browser can handle. with Proteus, you simply *Type Once, Search Everywhere.*	http://www.thrall.org/proteus.html
Searchapolis	Offers a filtered approach to searching, for both children and businesses.	http://www.searchopolis.com/

FIGURE 9-7 Advanced Search Engines Reference Guide.

Sites must be submitted to the web directory site, reviewed, and approved for inclusion.

- While search engine indexes offer the advantage of size, web directories generally retrieve lists of links of a much high quality. The organizational hierarchical format of web directories also benefits a novice searcher.
- Metasearch engines search multiple search engines and web directories simultaneously, with one simple query. Using a metasearch engine can save you time, but results may be inconsistent.
- Another option is subject or specialized search engines that allow for more precise searching in collections of searchable resources dedicated to a particular subject or discipline. People and business "locators" are examples of specialized search engines.
- Three popular law-related subject search engines are Findlaw's LawCrawler, the Meta-Index maintained by the Georgia State University College of Law, and FirstGov, the first government sponsored web site to provide the public with access to all online U.S. federal government resources. See figure 9-3 for a list of several popular subject search engines.
- Electronic discussion groups are often referred to as discussion lists, interest groups, mailing lists, or listservs. All communication in a discussion group is carried on by e-mail. Anyone with an e-mail address may join or "subscribe" to a group.
- Two reliable directories providing links to information on a variety of legal and government oriented lists are available from the Washburn University School of Law and the University of Chicago D'Angelo Law Library.
- There are several evaluative guidelines for selecting Internet and web resources. Of these, accuracy and timeliness are very important, especially with legal and government information. See figure 9-5 for a summary of the criteria to consider when evaluating web resources.
- Appendix H is a bibliography of web sites designed as guides and checklists for evaluating Internet resources.
- E-commerce—doing business via the Internet—will likely impact the delivery of legal services,

just as it has already had a tremendous effect on the way companies do business.

- It is already established procedure in all federal and most state jurisdictions that e-mail transmissions, computer files, and even the contents of your computer's hard drive, are all discoverable in litigation proceedings.
- A "push" application is software that automatically searches a web database for specific information, based on user defined criteria, and delivers the information when and where the user directs. Making use of push software is a convenient means of retrieving important information and a huge timesaver.
- E-mail alerts are electronic information "briefs" covering a wide range of topics, sent directly to you via e-mail. They are a form of push technology. See figure 9-6 for examples of some popular e-mail alerts.
- Adobe Portable Document Format (PDF) is the de facto standard for electronic document distribution and a universal file format that preserves all of the fonts, formatting, colors, and graphics of original source documents, regardless of the application used to create them. Adobe Acrobat Reader is a free download from the Adobe Systems web site.
- Zip is a compression and file packaging utility that works with all common computer operating software systems. The zip program puts one or more compressed files (text and graphics) into a single zip archive.
- WinZIP is one of the most popular zip software programs on the market, and is a free download from the company's web site.
- An intranet is a private network contained within a company, and typically includes connections through one or more computers to the outside Internet.
- The main purpose of an intranet is to share company information and computing resources among employees.
- An extranet is a private network that uses Internet protocols and a public telecommunications system to securely share part of a business's information or operations with suppliers, vendors, partners, customers, clients, or other businesses.
- Advanced "smart" search engines are the future of web research. New technologies will allow you to interact with computers and search tools on a more personal level, making web searching easier and more responsive.
- The Search Engine Watch web site is a good source to learn more about the features and capabilities of new search tools. See figure 9-7 for a guide to some of the new generation of web search tools.

LEGAL RESEARCH ASSIGNMENT—THE INTERNET

INSTRUCTIONS: For all questions, use only Internet resources to obtain your answers. Note the source(s) for your answers, including Internet address/location.

1. Explain what is meant by Internet protocol.
2. What is the major difference between the Internet and the World Wide Web?
3. Who owns the rights to the domain name: www.findlaw.com?
   a. Who is the administrative contact?
   b. How many host computers (domain servers) are associates with this web site?
   c. What free corporate information are you able to locate on the web relating to the owner of this domain name?
4. You are employed by a small law firm that is currently paying $25 per month for 5 accounts on America Online. All the firm really needs is dial-up access to the Internet for 5 computers, and occasional remote access from a laptop computer when someone is travelling out of the office. You have been asked to locate a less expensive Internet service provider for the firm and submit at least 3 possible alternatives to AOL.
5. How do a search engine and a web browser differ? Give two examples of each.
6. Adobe Acrobat Reader is an example of a browser plug-in. What does this mean, and why would you need it?

7. What are the major advantages and disadvantages of (1) a web search engine; (2) a metasearch engine; and (3) a web directory? Give two examples of each type of search tool.
8. What is a specialized or subject search engine? When might you use one?
9. Boolean searching, if done correctly, helps to focus your search, yielding more relevant results.
   a. Describe the difference between Boolean connectors and Boolean expanders. Give examples of each.
   b. What word and/or symbol would you use to *exclude* unwanted terms from your search results using Boolean searching?
   c. Which Boolean connector will *narrow* your search results, and which connector will broaden a search?
   d. What is meant by phrase searching?
   e. What is a proximity search?
10. Explain the key differences between electronic mail (e-mail) and e-mail discussion groups. Is a listserv the same as a discussion group?
11. Can you belong to more than one listserv at the same time? Explain your answer.
12. Locate a listserv that would benefit you in your work as a paralegal. Join the listserv, and describe the type of information posted on the list over the course of a few days. [*This exercise assumes you have an Internet e-mail account. If not, skip this exercise.*]
13. When choosing a web site as a source for primary federal or state legislative information, what three evaluative criteria would you consider most important? Explain your answer.
14. Describe the difference between a plug-in and push technology. Give examples of each.
15. Select one of the push applications discussed in chapter 9. How would this information benefit you as a paralegal?
16. What is an e-mail alert? Give an example of when this technology could be helpful in a law practice.
17. What is the difference between a PDF (.pdf) file and a zip (.zip) file?
18. Explain the key differences between "intranet," "internet," and "extranet." Give examples of how each type of technology might benefit a law practice.
19. Using the Query Planner in chapter 9 (Figure 9-4), develop a search strategy for each of the following research scenarios:
   a. Locate recent articles that discuss a possible connection between television violence and violent crimes committed by persons under the age of 21.
   b. Find any information you can that discusses a link between alcohol consumption and dementia.
20. Once you have formulated your search queries in Question 19 above, select *one* of these searches, run it using at least two different web search tools discussed in this chapter, and answer the following questions:
   a. Which search tools did you use, and why did you select them?
   b. What types of information did you locate?
   c. Did you get significantly different results from the two search tools, or were the results received from each basically consistent?
   d. Were the first 10–20 retrieved resources (hits) from each search mostly helpful or irrelevant?
   e. What might you do to make your search results more accurate?
   f. Which search tool did you like the best and why?

CHAPTER 10

CYBER-LAW: USING THE INTERNET AS A LEGAL RESEARCH TOOL

INTRODUCTION

Today, lawyers and paralegals must embrace technology to keep abreast of the ever-expanding amount of legal information being disseminated electronically worldwide. While computers made an impact in how we generate information, the Internet is perhaps the single most influential advancement in the delivery of information since the invention of movable type and the printing press. To ignore its value is to overlook a tremendous resource. Due to the need for up-to-the-minute information and data on a wide range of topics, the legal profession is well suited to benefit from reliance on electronic resources. Technology and the Internet offer lawyers and paralegals an opportunity to obtain the most current legal and factual information, communicate with clients and colleagues via e-mail, transfer documents and data files, and even improve their skills through web-based continuing education.

In her foreword to G. Burgess Allison's book, *The Lawyer's Guide to the Internet*, Roberta Cooper Ramo (president of the American Bar Association at the time of publication in 1995) stated that "today's lawyer requires an understanding of the fact that space on earth has been reduced to the distance between the computer on your desk or lap to the phone jack. . . . If you are computer-illiterate, you risk being unable to comprehend the world of your clients, many of whom are already sophisticated in the ways of the interactive world."

In this chapter we will focus on one particular format of electronic information—the Internet and, specifically, the World Wide Web. We will look at several primary and secondary legal resources currently available on the web and discuss the limitations of using the Internet as a legal research tool. A brief synopsis of some of the most popular and useful web sites for locating and accessing legal and government information is included, along with information on where to go to learn more about legal citation formats for electronic resources. Also included is a short overview of copyright concerns in a digital environment, and a discussion of some future trends that will impact the legal professional.

At the end of the book are several appendixes, all designed to facilitate efficient use of the Internet for legal research.

Appendix I is an annotated list of legal research "starting points"—sites that direct you to other sources of full text information on the web.

Appendix J highlights several important web resources providing access to primary legal and government information, including statutes, court opinions, administrative rulings, and municipal codes and ordinances.

Appendix K summarizes some of the best web sites for locating primary and secondary state and local (*i.e.* county and city) government resources.

Appendix L is a short annotated list of international law resources, sources for obtaining the full text of international treaties and foreign laws, as well as statistical data on foreign countries, and abstracts on various foreign legal topics such as taxation and commercial trade.

Appendix M is a list of links of popular commercial Internet sources for law-related information, including a law dictionary, interactive legal forms, directories, attorney "locators," and subject-specific web sites.

Appendix N incorporates many of the sites contained on the other lists and arranges them in a topical index. At least one recommended resource is listed under each major category.

AVAILABLE RESOURCES

When it comes to legal and government information, just about everything is available in some form on the Internet. You have probably heard or read commentaries about the value of web-based information, stating that the vast majority of web content is inaccurate, irrelevant, or basically useless data. Assuming this to be a fairly accurate assessment of the web, and working under the premise that only ten percent of the information posted on the Internet is of any real value, this leaves thousands of quality web resources at our disposal, much of it is free.

There are many excellent government and educational web sites providing current, full text, searchable access to most primary and many secondary federal law materials. While the availability of state and local government and law-related information is not as prevalent, this is improving every day. Soon, state-level web coverage of court decisions, court rules and forms, administrative rulings, and local codes and ordinances will be as comprehensive as federal materials are now.

Examples of federal government information currently accessible on the web include:

- All 50 Titles of the U.S. Code
- Code of Federal Regulations (CFR)
- Public Laws
- Federal Register
- Federal Acquisition Regulations (FARs)
- Congressional Record Transcripts
- Congressional Committee Reports and selected Hearing Transcripts
- Presidential Executive Orders

Intellectual Property Law

Researching intellectual property information on the web has become much easier in recent years. Although it is still recommended that you consult additional print and CD-ROM resources to insure a thorough copyright, patent, or trademark search, much of your initial research can now be done free from your desktop. The U.S. Patent & Trademark Office (USPTO) http://www.uspto.gov/ and the U.S. Copyright Office http://lcweb.loc.gov/copyright have greatly improved the scope and coverage of full text information available on their respective web sites. Selected pending and recorded U.S. trademark documents are searchable from the late 1980s to the present. The USPTO web site provides access to the trademark text data currently available on two of its Cassis CD-ROM products: *Trademarks Registered* and *Trademarks Pending*. Like the CD-ROM products, the web text is updated on a two-month cycle. The USPTO web site plans to add images as they become available. From the USPTO Web Patent Database http://www.uspto.gov/patft/ index.html you now have access to bibliographic information and searchable full text documents. The database covers the period from January 1, 1976 to the most recent weekly issue date (usually each Tuesday). A fairly new feature is the ability to search the actual patent images and link to an image directly from the full text document display.

The U.S. Copyright Office provides free web access to copyright forms, information circulars, *Federal Register* Notices relating to copyright issues, and other valuable information. In addition, Copyright Office records dating from 1978 to the present, including registration information and recorded documents, are available via a link to LOCIS (Library of Congress Information System). Electronic submission of applications and filings is also available from both the USPTO and U.S. Copyright Office web sites.

Administrative Law

Administrative codes and regulations, both federal and state, are very easy to access on the web. As previously mentioned, the *Code of Federal Regulations* and the *Federal Register* are both searchable online via the GPO*Access* site or any of several law school GPO "gateways" such as the University of California's GPO Gate http://www.gpo.ucop.edu, and DocLaw Web, a component of the WashlawWEB site hosted by Washburn University School of Law http://www.washlaw.edu/doclaw/doclawnew.html. DocLaw, a gateway to federal government Internet resources and other government related materials, has organized documents by subject and under a handy organizational chart. The site includes a search engine and a directory of federal agencies.

Another site with links to federal administrative decisions, federal agency administrative materials, and selected historic administrative law decisions of the U.S. Supreme Court is FindLaw's legal directory http://www.findlaw.com (select "Legal Subjects" and then "Administrative Law"). Two sources for locating state and local administrative law are the Municipal Code Corporation site http://www.municode.com and the Seattle Public Library http://www.spl.lib.wa.us/selectedsites/municode.html. The ABA Administrative Procedure Database http://www.law.fsu.edu/library/admin, developed and maintained as a cooperative effort of the American Bar Association's Section of Administrative Law and Regulatory Practice and the Florida State University College of Law, is another helpful web site for administrative law research. Another good resource is the Administrative Codes and Registers (ACR) Section of the National Association of Secretaries of State (NASS) page http://www.nass.org/acr/internet.htm. This site provides access to state administrative law materials, all arranged in an alphabetical state chart.

Law Reviews, Journals, and Legal Periodicals

Many legal periodicals—newsletters, magazines, journals, and law reviews—are now publishing electronic versions, full text and searchable. Most major law schools provide free web access to recent issues of their law reviews and journals. Prominent examples include the *Cornell Law Review* http://www.lawschool.cornell.edu/clr, the *Harvard Law Review* http://www.harvardlawreview.org, and the *Stanford Journal of International Law* http://www.stanford. edu/group/SJIL.

While most scholastic and scholarly materials published on the web are usually free, many commercial and private legal publishers only provide free access to the current edition, or selected articles or highlights. Archived (back) issues are often accessible only by paid subscribers. However, some publishers will include a "free" online password with each print subscription to a particular publication. This can be very helpful if a back issue is not readily accessible in print. Where free access is provided, it is often limited to the most recent 12–18 months. Two very good web directories for quickly locating and linking to law reviews and law-related e-journals are the law reviews page maintained by the D'Angelo Law Library at the University of Chicago http://www.lib.uchicago.edu/e/law/lawreviews.html, and Findlaw's law reviews page http://stu.findlaw.com/journals. Links to law reviews and legal journals are arranged by topic for easy reference. You may also sign up to receive free e-mail abstracts of new law review articles on a particular topic or subject. The Findlaw site also allows you to search the full text of *all* law journals published on the Internet with a single search query.

Case Law

The scope and coverage of federal court decisions still varies by jurisdiction. Initially, only selected U.S. Supreme Court and U.S. appellate court decisions were made available full text on the web. At the federal district court and federal bankruptcy court levels, access to actual cases was limited. Fortunately, this has improved. Today, court dockets, trial calendars, and the full text of nearly every U.S. Supreme Court decision from 1893 to the present and most U.S. appellate court opinions from the early 1990s are published on the web. Many federal trial and bankruptcy courts also offer full text access to their case opinions. The availability of court dockets at the trial court level is also improving, although access to this information is not always free. (See the *free vs. fee-based* discussion later in this chapter). Availability of case law at the state court level also varies greatly by state and local jurisdiction. Generally, you can expect to find the best coverage at the highest state court level, with scope and coverage decreasing as you move down the judicial court system.

THE BAD NEWS: WHAT IS [CURRENTLY] NOT AVAILABLE

Today, access to court decisions and dockets for most state trial courts is still not available on the web, or even through fee-based subscription services like PACER, CourtLink or CourtEXPRESS. Do not expect to find pre-1993 U.S. appellate court opinions on the web, although coverage varies by circuit. This also applies to pre-1994 federal legislative information, although it is getting easier to compile a thorough federal legislative history from the web. This is not the case with state legislative materials, which are still much less prevalent on the web than their federal counterparts. Most states do not have the funding to digitize older records. Therefore, bill text, bill history, staff analyses, and other legislative information are rarely available on the web prior to the mid-to-late 1990s for most states.

When conducting investigative research on a person, you will not find criminal histories, credit reports, tax records, driving records, or other similar information available free on the web. There are hundreds of private investigators and public records research companies advertising on the web who, for a fee, will obtain this information for you. You can also access much of this data from a variety of subscription databases, including LexisNexis, Westlaw and AutoTrack. (See chapter 8 for a discussion on these vendors and products).

Real property and tax records are available in many states, although access varies by county. However, few sites include maps or plats, and often the search options are limited, yielding inconsistent results. You will generally get more accurate information and wider coverage from a subscription database or CD-ROM product available from many title companies and vendors specializing in real property data. If your employer is currently purchasing property records, such as maps and plats in print, ask the vendor if an alternative online or CD-ROM product is available—but be sure to compare the cost of print vs. electronic, and verify the printer requirements needed to print oversized documents.

FREE VS. FEE-BASED

Not everything on the Internet is free, although this is a common misconception. Many commercial and private web pages (in contrast with educational and government web sites) attract you to their site with a sampling of free information and a selection of links to commonly used web resources. However, the primary purpose of their web site is to sell a product or services. For example, a site may offer free abstracts or summaries of recent court decisions or legislation, but to access the full text requires an existing account or payment in advance. As with any information provider, it is important to know how current the information is and who is the original source of the data. Always make sure the source of all information on the web page is clearly identified before relying on it. This is a good rule to follow, especially with commercial (.com) web sites.

As previously mentioned, if you subscribe to a print journal, newspaper, or magazine, you may be eligible for free access to the web edition, although there may be a charge to search back issues.

Even popular web search engines are getting into the "fee-based" business. A good example is Northern Light http://www.northernlight.com/, which combines a basic "search and retrieval" engine with a full text database. You can use the Northern Light search engine and other features at no cost, but to access the Special Collection™ of over 7,000 full text publications, you must have an existing account and a per-document fee is charged to view a document in this collection.

However, even if a particular web resource is not free, do not necessarily overlook it as a viable research tool. Often the fees charged to access full text information on the web (such as the Northern Light Special Collection) is less costly than obtaining the same information from other subscription databases, document delivery services, or directly from the original information provider. When time is a factor, using a fee-based web service may actually save time and money in the long run.

LEGAL RESOURCES ON THE INTERNET

No single vocation is better suited to using the Internet as a resource tool than the legal profession. After all, we are in the business of locating, retrieving, analyzing, organizing, and disseminating information, and the Internet is the single most comprehensive collection of data ever compiled. The Internet has created a real-time global database of information—text, graphics, financial and statistical data—delivered directly to your desktop from anywhere in the world. Information that once took hours, days, and even weeks to obtain, can now be viewed, downloaded and printed without ever leaving your office. The "virtual" aspect of the Internet provides access to a much broader collection of legal information than would be possible under normal circumstances. Even the largest law firm or corporate legal department must deal with rising costs and space constraints commonly associated with print materials.

Entire books have been written summarizing the wealth of law-related resources currently available on the Internet, although some still do not see the Internet as a serious legal research tool. This is a mistake that is quickly dispelled once you become familiar with the web resources presented in this book. The Internet is already delivering key information from original government sources. In fact, a significant number of information providers on the Internet are actually government agencies.

GOVERNMENT INFORMATION ON THE INTERNET

Information published and disseminated by government agencies has always been intended to be part of the public domain, easily accessible to all citizens. When available only in print, people had to either request the information directly from the publishing agency or the Government Printing Office (GPO), or visit the closest Government Depository Library. Today, with the advent of technology and the Internet, the vast majority of this information is just a mouse click away—from our homes, offices, classrooms, and local public library. While initially an experiment to try and reduce the bulk of print government publications and the expense of producing them, publishing on the Internet and the web has proven to be an effective means of sharing and disseminating a wide variety of information. In fact, discontinuing physical distribution of print products when reliable electronic alternatives are available was one of the key transition actions identified in a 1996 GPO study to help speed up the transition of federal government information into electronic formats. In the spring of 1999 at the annual Depository Library Council Meeting, a position statement was issued supporting the findings of this study and committing the resources of the Federal Depository Library Program toward a realization of the goals of the study.

For the most part, the U.S. Congress met its pledge to create and provide access to all of its documents electronically, including bills, resolutions, amendments, committee reports, and hearing transcripts, by the end of the twentieth century. This is also the case with the other branches of the federal government. Nearly every executive agency and many independent agencies and departments maintain a web site. While some provide nothing more than general contact information and possibly a brief synopsis of its functions, others are treasure troves of data, with links to hundreds of related Internet resources and full text documents. As previously discussed in this chapter, the judicial branch of the federal government is well-represented on the Internet. Federal court web sites offer full text coverage of legal opinions, court rules, administrative procedures, and other key primary law resources. Government information on the state level is not as comprehensive and varies greatly by jurisdiction, but the availability and content is continually improving.

While the scope of this chapter does not allow for a thorough discussion of international government information resources, there are many quality web of resources providing access to primary and secondary legal and government information for many foreign countries. Again, scope and coverage varies greatly by country. Although most foreign governmental web sites are in English, or with an "English language" option, it is not uncommon to find sites with information published only in the native language of the host country. For a list of international law web resources, please refer to Appendix L.

LITIGATION SUPPORT

The use of computers and technology for litigation support has become "standard operating procedure" in most law practices today. This includes everything from case management software programs to searchable real-time audio and video deposition transcripts available on diskette and CD-ROM. The high-tech "courtroom of tomorrow" is actually a reality in many jurisdictions throughout the country.

Using the Internet to find an expert witness or obtain information on the opposing side's experts is often an effective, cost-efficient alternative to Lexis, Westlaw, or referral services such as TASA (the Technical Advisory Service for Attorneys *http://www.tasanet.com/*. There are a growing number of web directories of expert witnesses. Some allow you to search their database at no cost. Three popular examples of free expert directories are Findlaw, Expert4Law, and the Hieros Gamos experts database.

From the Findlaw main page, select the "Consultants & Experts" option, then choose the "Expert Witnesses" link. This will take you to a directory of several dozen web resources. Each link includes a brief synopsis of the content of the linked page, and the directory is arranged alphabetically for easy searching. Another free web service is Expert4Law.com http://www. expert4law.org/. There are no fees for listing or searching, and attorneys contact experts and service providers directly. A link to litigation support services and ADR (alternative dispute resolution) arbitrators and mediators is also included.

The third example is the experts database maintained by the Hieros Gamos commercial web resource http://www.hg.org, one of the most comprehensive law and government web sites on the Internet. The HG expert database http://www.hg.org/ex_sel.html combines listings selected by the HG staff from advertisements in national and international publications, with a group of experts who have posted their own information in the free listings database. Categories include accident reconstruction to safety and security experts, and everything in between.

The Online Directory of Expert Witnesses http://www.claims.com/online.html is a continuously updated electronic version of the print edition of *The National Directory of Expert Witnesses*, and includes hundreds of experts and consultants from across the nation, organized in over 400 categories of technical, scientific, and medical expertise. Experts can be searched by keyword, browsed by detailed subject category, or by the expert's name or company name. Currently, there is no charge to access or search this web database, although online registration is required.

But "buyer beware"—as with most free web resources of this type, there is no prescreening of the content posted by any expert, professional consultant, or other service provider listed on these sites, and the "host" sites generally disclaim any responsibility for the content. An example is the disclaimer on the Hieros Gamos experts database web site that reads:

> **IMPORTANT:** *This information is provided as a public service. Before relying on the information contained in the Experts listings, you MUST perform due diligence by requesting references to assure appropriate credentials and expertise.*

The second category of expert databases available on the Internet is the fee-based directories. Similar to expert witness "files" available through Lexis or Westlaw, these web sites charge an expert witness a monthly or annual fee for inclusion in the directory. Usually, information can be searched free by attorneys. Examples of this type of resource include Law Info.com http://www.lawinfo.com, and ExpertPages.com http://www.expertpages.com. In addition to a searchable database of experts, LawInfo includes a directory of private investigators and links to court reporters, trial consultants, and process servers nationwide. ExpertPages offers one of the best selections of medical and industry-specific experts on the web.

Another way to locate experts on the Internet is from state and national bar associations' web pages, many of which include links to referral services and "expert banks." If you are looking for an expert in a particular region of the country, the web site for the state or local county bar association is a good place to begin your research. Expert referral services are also prominent on the Internet. Some provide access to their databases at no cost to attorneys, while others charge a nominal referral fee to put expert and attorney together. Two examples of this type of service are the TASA http://www.tasanet.com, and the American Medical Forensic Specialists (AMFS) http://www. amfs.com. For a fee or a percentage of their billings if retained, these services will provide a list of experts in a variety of specialty areas.

Another option for finding professionals who may be willing to serve as expert witnesses and consultants is to visit the home pages of professional associations and membership organizations. Examples include the American Medical Association (AMA) Doctor Finder http://www.ama-assn.org/aps/amahg. htm, and the American Institute of Architects (AIA) Architect Finder http://www. aiaaccess.com/. Nearly every major professional association has a web page; do not overlook these resources for locating experts and consultants, and as valuable tools for learning more about a particular industry or topic of interest. Many of these sites serve not only as "jump sites" with links to other related web pages, but as sources of reliable industry information and statistical data.

You can even download a shareware (also known as "freeware") version of a "Bates-type" sequential [label] numbering software program for use in organizing your documents for discovery and trial directly from the web at http://www.payneconsulting.com under ("Products" and "Freeware Utilities"). This is a good example of a commercial site whose primary purpose is to market fee-based products and services, but which also offers useful free product from its web site.

LIMITATIONS TO USING THE INTERNET AS A RESEARCH TOOL

As discussed in chapter 9, there are currently no controls on who can post information on the Internet and no laws or regulations governing web content. Therefore, the burden of evaluating the content of information retrieved on the Internet is solely the responsibility of the researcher. Always remember, there is no equivalent of a cyber-GAO (Government Accounting Office) monitoring the web for erroneous or outdated information.

When conducting Internet research, remember the evaluative guidelines discussed in detail in chapter 9, paying particular attention to author and/or publisher of the data, scope and content, and currency. You would not rely on a print or CD-ROM resource without a high level of confidence in the product and the vendor. The same is true with information published on the web. It is easy to loose track of the original source of data after hyper-linking your way through cyberspace. Always check your "final source" and make sure you are comfortable that it meets your criteria as a reliable resource. Simply proceed with caution, and only rely on quality, recommended sites, just as you would with other information resources.

TIP #1: The Internet is not always the best resource tool. If a current, reliable print or other resource is handy [and familiar to you]—use it. Unless you know exactly where to go, the Internet may not be the fastest way to find what you need.

TIP #2: Remember, like anything else, it takes time and practice to become a proficient Internet researcher.

CYBER-CITATION

In chapter 8, we discussed several traditional citation style guides that, in response to the proliferation of web and other electronic publishing, have incorporated guidelines for citing to electronically accessed sources, regardless of type. In this chapter, we will take a closer look at citing to electronic legal sources.

The Sixteenth Edition (1996) of *The Bluebook: A Uniform System of Citation*, the quintessential citations manual compiled by the editors of the *Columbia Law Review*, the *Harvard Law Review*, the *University of Pennsylvania Law Review*, and the *Yale Law Review*, did not adequately address "cyber citation" forms. However, the Seventeenth Edition, published in 2000, includes coverage of citation forms for electronic resources, and specifically the Internet. One of the main reasons for the revision was to expand the *Bluebook's* coverage of the Internet and electronic citations. Rule 10.3.3 has been added to provide a format for public domain citations, with a stipulation that if a state requires a format that differs from the *Bluebook's* suggested format, you should use that state's format. Rule 17 has been split into two rules creating a new Rule 18 for "Electronic Media and Other Sources." The Seventeenth Edition also includes several new tables with references to state web sites and information on state-specific public domain formats.

The *ALWD Citation Manual: A Professional System of Citation*, a new legal citations manual published in 2000 by the Association of Legal Writing Directors, includes an entire section (Part 4) on electronic and online citation formats. Sections 39 through 42 focus on electronic citation (including Lexis and Westlaw), web sites, electronic mail, and CD-ROM materials, respectively.

A good web-based legal citation resource is the University of Michigan's Documents Center http://www.lib.umich.edu/libhome/Documents.center/. This site provides links to several quality citation guides and manuals that specifically address how to correctly cite web and other electronic resources.

Web Citation Format:

- Author's Last Name, First Name.
- "Title of Document."
- *Title of Complete Work* [if applicable]
- Publisher [optional; if applicable]
- Version or File Number [*if applicable*]
- Document Date or Date or Last Revision [*if different from access date*]
- Protocol and Address, Access Path, or Directories
- Date of Access

Example of Web Citation Format (Government Agency as Author):

Author:	Administrative Office of the United States Courts.
Title:	"Electronic Cases Files in the Federal Courts Discussion Draft"
Document Date:	March 1997
Web Address:	http://www.uscourts.gov/casefiles/summ.htm
Date of Access:	November 1, 2000

Example of Web Citation Format (Individual Author):

Author:	Walker, Janice R. and Taylor, Todd
Title:	*The Columbia Guide to Online Style*
Publisher:	Columbia University Press
Document Date:	1998
Web Address:	http://www.columbia.edu/cu/cup/cgos/idx_basic.html
Date of Access:	November 2000

COPYRIGHT CONCERNS IN A DIGITAL ENVIRONMENT

The existing copyright law in the United States is governed by a nearly 30-year-old piece of legislation, the Copyright Law of the United States, contained in Title 17 of the U.S. Code. Since its enactment, there have been several key pieces of federal legislation passed by Congress in an attempt to address the omission of provisions covering copyright protection of electronic information. The most significant of these laws was passed in 1998.

On October 28, 1998, President Clinton signed into law the *Digital Millennium Copyright Act (DMCA)* Public Law 105-304 (1998). In addition to implementing existing international copyright law provisions, the DMCA created guidelines for online service providers, addressed certain computer maintenance issues, and facilitated Internet broadcasting. While the DMCA went a long way to help resolve copyright concerns brought on by the Internet and the advent of web publishing and e-journals, Congress continues to address this issue.

In a continuing effort to modify the existing U.S. Copyright Law to provide adequate protections for both publishers and consumers, several key bills were passed during the recent Sessions of the U.S. Congress.

The ultimate resolution to this matter will likely result in a completely overhauled federal copyright law—one that incorporates the DMCA and other subsequent federal copyright legislation, as well as implementing provisions of key international intellectual property treaties and laws. International copyright treaties are governed by the World Intellectual Property Organization (WIPO). To learn more about WIPO, visit http:/www.loc.gov/copyright/wipo/.

For now, with regard to the Internet, the rule to follow is simple—"when in doubt—DON'T." Publishers of original information on the Internet and the web are provided the same copyright protections as those who publish in other mediums, print and electronic. You should not reproduce or reprint in any manner the text or graphics from a web site, without permission of the author. This also applies to logos. Remember, unless it is a piece of public domain clip art, it is likely a registered trademark or service mark, so do not reproduce it (in print or on a web site) without express permission of the web author and/or owner of the mark. Many web sites will include copyright provisions on the main page, or links to additional information, including who to contact for reprint and copyright permission.

For more information about copyright protections, consult the Copyright Clearance Center http://www.copyright.com/Database/, the largest licenser of text reproduction rights in the world.

FUTURE TRENDS

Electronic Case Files Prototypes

One of the most exciting applications of the Internet for lawyers, particularly litigators, is the very real concept of the "paperless court." The prototype has already been in existence since the late 1990s. The Electronic Case Files (ECF) Project grew out of discussions at various regional and national meetings of federal judges and magistrates hoping to find a way to streamline the existing federal court filing system. At the March 1997 annual meeting of the Judicial Conference Committee on Automation and Technology, the Committee designated ECF as a top priority initiative, stating that the federal courts could reduce their reliance on paper records by using new technology to file, maintain, and retrieve case file information in "digitized" form. The transition towards electronic case files ("ECF") in the federal courts is well underway.

The major prototype goals of the ECF Project are:

- Paperless Courts
- Automated Dockets
- Electronic Access to Court Dockets
- Digital Document Images
- Electronic Filing of Court Papers

A number of federal and state courts are already operating prototype systems based on the ECF system developed by the Administrative Office of the United States Courts. For example, the Northern District of Ohio began receiving electronic filings in maritime asbestos cases via the Internet in January 1996. A similar Internet-based system began in the Bankruptcy Court for the Southern District of New York in November 1997. Many federal district and bankruptcy courts, including the Southern District of Texas, the Western District of Oklahoma, and the District of Kansas have been using electronic case files systems for several years.

In addition to prototypes developed in the judicial branch, commercial vendors like LexisNexis, West Group, CourtLink, CourtEXPRESS, and PACER are experimenting with products and offering services to courts and attorneys to provide their customers with Internet access to court dockets and court filings. These prototypes demonstrate not only that technology is available today, but also that many in the judiciary and the bar are ready to move forward and tackle the many cultural, legal, and policy issues that will likely result.

Internet access to courts allows lawyers, paralegals, and the general public to search and retrieve cases and court dockets directly from their computers. From the case docket, you can obtain basic information about the case such as the parties, case number, date the case was filed, type of action, the assigned judge, and the parties' attorneys. The ultimate goal of the ECF project is to allow public access not only to court dockets, but provide the ability to link from a docket entry to the digitized image of a document in the actual court case file. You could then read the document online, print it, save it to a disk, or download it to your computer's hard drive. The goal is to make access to this information free, although this may become a jurisdictional issue on both the federal and state levels as "electronic courts" become a reality. For an overview of the ECF initiative, visit the Administrative Office of the United States Courts' web site at http://www.uscourts.gov/casefiles/toc.htm.

The High-Tech Courtroom

Following closely behind the "electronic court" is the high-tech courtroom. The Roger A. Barker Courtroom located on the 23rd floor ("Courtroom 23") of the Orange County Courthouse in Orlando, Florida exemplifies the courtroom of the future that is already a reality in many jurisdictions across the country. Opened in March 1999, Courtroom 23 is an example of an integrated high-tech courtroom, a successful collaborative project involving government and private industry. The final plan for Courtroom 23 included these key technologies:

- Electronic evidence presentation system
- Internet and remote broadcast capabilities
- Real-time and digital court reporting
- Advanced audio system
- Plasma display monitors for the judge, jury, and counsel
- Videoconferencing that enables remote testimony
- Computerized legal research from counsel tables in the courtroom
- Touch screen computer integration

A virtual tour of Courtroom 23 is available from the Ninth Judicial Circuit Court's web site at http://www.ninja9.org/courtadmin/mis/courtroom_23.htm.

Videoconferencing

Videoconferencing is not just limited to the courtroom. The way lawyers conduct client conferences and confer with out-of-town opposing counsel, co-counsel, and colleagues, and even the manner in which depositions, witness interviews, mediations, and real estate closings are conducted is changing. Technology and state-of-the-art video communications hardware and software are already changing the way we practice law. Even though the initial cost of the equipment is an expensive investment, the savings in travel time and fees billed to clients are significant. Many technologically sophisticated clients, such as major corporations, are actually demanding these services from their outside legal counsel.

As paralegals, you will need to become familiar with and comfortable using technology and the Internet as more and more applications of new technology make their way into the practice of law. A good resource to keep abreast of current developments is *The Journal of Online Law* (JOL) at http://www.wm.edu/law/publications/ jol. Edited by Trotter Hardy, a professor at the William and Mary School of Law, the JOL is an electronic publication of scholarly essays about law and online communications and cyberspace. The focus is to explore key legal issues arising from networked communications, while speculating about future trends in cyber-law. Save time by having new issues of the JOL sent directly to your e-mail address.

CHAPTER 10 SUMMARY

- Technology and the Internet offer lawyers and paralegals an opportunity to obtain the most current legal and factual information, communicate with clients and colleagues via e-mail, transfer documents and data files, and even improve their skills through web-based continuing education.
- State and local law-related information is not as prevalent as its federal counterparts, but scope and coverage is improving.
- Examples of federal government information available full text on the Internet include all 50 Titles of the U.S. Code, the *Code of Federal Regulations*, Public Laws, the *Federal Register*, the *Congressional Record*, and Presidential Executive Orders.
- Both the U.S. Patent & Trademark Office and the U.S. Copyright Office provide searchable web access to the full text of recorded patents, trademarks, and copyrights.

- Administrative codes and regulations, both federal and state, are very easy to access on the web. The *Code of Federal Regulations* and the *Federal Register* are available online from the GPO*Access* web site, or several GPO gateways maintained by large academic institutions.
- The Municipal Code Corporation web site, the ABA's Administrative Procedure online database, and the National Association of Secretaries of State (NASS) site are good places to find state and local administrative law on the web.
- Law reviews, law journals, and legal periodicals can be searched full text on the web from a variety of sites, although generally only the most recent issues are available. For older articles, you may still need to use Lexis or Westlaw, or other subscription database service.
- Today, court dockets, trial calendars, and the full text of nearly every U.S. Supreme Court decision from the the late 1800s to the present, and most U.S. appellate court opinions from the mid-1990s, are available on the web.
- The availability of court dockets at the lower trial court level is improving, but are not as prevalent as comparable federal case information.
- Pre-1994 federal legislative information is generally not available on the Internet. Comparable state level information is even more difficult to find prior to the mid-late 1990s.
- Currently, criminal histories, credit reports, tax records, driving records, or other similar personal information is not available on the Internet, except through fee-based services, many of whom advertise on the web.
- Real property and tax records are available for most states, although access and coverage varies by state and county.
- Not all legal and government information posted on the Internet is free. Many sites include a combination of free information and fee-based services.
- Even if a particular web resource is not free, do not necessarily overlook it as a viable research tool. Often the fee charged to access full text information on the web is less costly than obtaining it from Lexis, Westlaw, or other subscription databases or expensive document delivery services.
- The "virtual" aspect of the Internet provides access to a much broader collection of legal information than would be possible otherwise.
- The Internet is already delivering free information from original government sources, with government agencies comprising a significant number of information providers on the web.
- The federal government continues to earmark funding to make even more documents available free on the web, with the ultimate goal to replace traditional print materials with web-based information.
- For the most part, the U.S. Congress met its pledge to create and provide electronic access to all bills, resolutions, amendments, committee reports, and hearing transcripts by the end of the twentieth century.
- The use of computers for litigation support has become "standard operating procedure" in most law practices. This includes using the web to locate experts and consultants, and downloading a free "Bates" sequential numbering software program for use in organizing documents for discovery and trial.
- There are currently no controls on who can post information on the Internet and no laws or regulations governing web content.
- When conducting Internet research, remember to use the evaluative guidelines discussed in chapter 9; always check your ultimate source and make sure you are comfortable that it meets the criteria for a reliable resource.
- Good sources for citation style guides for web and other electronic resources include: Rules 10.3.3, 17 and 18 of the Seventeenth Edition of *The Bluebook: A Uniform System of Citation;* Part 4 of the *ALDW Citation Manual: A Professional System of Citation;* and the web-based University of Michigan's Document Center.
- Always remember to include the "date of access" when citing to a web document. Since some web resources are not posted indefinitely, this provides validation of the date you last accessed the web site.
- Several pieces of federal legislation were passed during the recent sessions of Congress, all designed to address the omission of any provisions in the current U.S. Copyright Law covering

copyright protection of electronic information. The most significant of these laws is the *Digital Millennium Copyright Act of 1998*, Public Law 105–304.

- International copyright treaties are governed by the World Intellectual Property Organization (WIPO); these treaties influence but do not govern U.S. copyright laws.
- The Copyright Clearance Center is the largest licenser of text reproduction rights in the world.
- The prototype for the "paperless court" has existed since the late 1990s when the Electronic Case Files (ECF) Project was launched in several federal district and bankruptcy courts.
- In addition to prototypes developed in the federal and state courts, several commercial vendors, including LexisNexis, West Group (Westlaw), CourtLink, CourtEXPRESS, and PACER, are experimenting with products that will offer their customers Internet access to court dockets and actual court filings.
- From the court docket you can obtain basic information about the case such as the parties, the case number, the date the case was filed and the nature of the case, the judge the case is assigned to, and contact information for the parties' attorneys.
- Videoconferencing is becoming a popular way to conduct mediations, client and witness interviews, take depositions, confer with out-of-town counsel and colleagues, and even close real estate transactions.
- As paralegals, you need to become familiar with and comfortable using technology and the Internet as more applications of new technology make their way into the practice of law.

LEGAL RESEARCH ASSIGNMENT—THE INTERNET

INSTRUCTIONS: For all questions, use only Internet resources to obtain your answers. Note the source(s) for your answers, including Internet address/location.

1. What was the percentage increase/decrease in the national unemployment rate for December 1999 compared to December 1998?
2. When did the Administrative Dispute Resolution Act of 1996 become law, and what was the Public Law number for this federal legislation?
3. When was the current Japanese Constitution enacted?
4. What was the subject of H.R. 3494, who introduced in the bill in the U.S. House of Representatives during the 105th Congress, and when was this bill signed into law by the President?
5. With regard to the Public Law referred to in Question 4, what is the corresponding official U.S. Code cite (Title and Section)? What is the Statutes at Large cite?
6. Locate the full text of the *National Organ Transplant Act* and provide its official U.S. Code citation. HINT: You know the "popular name" of this federal law; locate using the fewest possible web resources.
7. Using the fewest possible sites, locate a copy of the FINAL DRAFT of the *Uniform Child Custody Jurisdiction and Enforcement Act* (approved at the 1997 Annual Meeting of the National Conference of Commissioners on Uniform State Laws).
8. Locate at least two recent law review articles, published on the web within the past 12–18 months, that discuss pornography and the Internet. Give the complete citation for each article.
9. Locate the landmark U.S. Supreme Court "Miranda decision" case, and give its official U.S. Code citation. HINT: You know the name of one of the parties to the litigation.
10. What is the subject matter of Chapter 50–27 of the Georgia Statutes? Try searching your state's statutes under the same topic. What did you find?
11. Search the 1999 *Federal Register* (Notices, Proposed Rules and Final Rules and Regulations) under the phrase "records retention." What kinds of information did you

retrieve, and what federal Act did most of the "hits" relate to?

12. Locate the following information on U.S. patents recorded during the years 1996–2000 for **self-cleaning litter** removal devices:
   a. How many patents were recorded during this 4-year period?
   b. Of these, only one is described as a "self-cleaning cat box." What is the number of this patent?
   c. When was the patent referred to in (b) above recorded and who is the inventor of record?
   d. When will this patent expire?

13. How many registered U.S. trademarks are associated with the name "Westlaw"?
   a. Of these, how many are currently active?
   b. What is the registration number for the "Westlaw.com" mark?
   c. What type of mark is "Westlaw.com" and when was it registered with the U.S. Patent & Trademark Office?
   d. When will this mark expire?

13. What is the European Commission's Directive on Data Privacy (a/k/a the European Data Directive)? HINT: It deals with international trade, and has been adopted by the United States Department of Commerce.
   a. When did the Directive take effect?
   b. What is meant by a "safe harbor," as referred to in the Directive?
   c. What country developed the "safe harbor" framework, and when did the European Union approve it?

14. Provide the complete electronic citation for the article published on the web at www.llrx.com/features/savvy.htm, discussing how to become a web-savvy researcher.

15. The U.S. Federal Trade Commission (FTC) is actively involved with public awareness of key online/Internet privacy initiatives. One of these initiatives concerns the *Children's Online Privacy Protection Act of 1998* and the FTC Rule that implements the Act. Knowing this, answer the following questions:
   a. On what date was the FTC's Children's Online Privacy Protection Final Rule published in the *Federal Register?*
   b. Give the complete *Federal Register* and *Code of Federal Regulations* citations for the publication of this Final Rule.
   c. According to the *Children's Online Privacy Protection Act of 1998*, the term "child" means an individual under what age?

16. Using only web resources, answer the following questions relating to the *Federal Rules of Civil Procedure:*
   a. What does Rule 11 cover?
   b. Which Rule (including subsection) sets out the prerequisites for filing a class action lawsuit?
   c. Chapter IX of the Rules deals with Special Proceedings. Which specific Rule discusses condemnation of property?

17. Are non-lawyers allowed to appear before the United States Tax Court? If so:
   a. What are the requirements for admission?
   b. Is the application form available on the web?

18. Using the web, locate at least two recent articles that discuss the prosecution of non-lawyers (including paralegals and legal assistants) for unauthorized practice of law (UPL). Provide a brief summary of each article and give the complete citation.

19. Locate a copy of the U.S. Ninth Circuit Court of Appeals *Apple Computer v. Microsoft* case.
   a. Give the complete *Federal Reporter* cite for this case.
   b. This case was taken on appeal from which lower United States district court?
   c. What date was oral argument heard, and when did the court render its decision?
   d. What United States Code provision is referred to in Footnote 11 of the court's opinion?
   e. Was this case appealed to the U.S. Supreme Court?

20. How many attorneys are listed as in-house general/corporate counsel for Microsoft Corporation, based in Redmond, Washington? Be sure to identify the web source used to locate this information, and the date the site was accessed.

CHAPTER 11

INTRODUCTION TO LEGAL WRITING

Supreme Court of Kentucky.

KENTUCKY BAR ASSOCIATION, Complainant,

v.

James Henry BROWN, Respondent.

No. 1999-SC-1043-KB.

April 20, 2000.

14 S.W.3d 916

OPINION AND ORDER

The respondent, Brown, represented a client in an appeal to the Kentucky Court of Appeals from a decision of the Jefferson Circuit Court. The Court of Appeals dismissed the appeal because of the substantial deficiencies contained in Brown's one and one-half page brief. While the style of the brief substantially conformed with the Kentucky Rules of Civil Procedure, the rest of the brief read:

INTRODUCTION

This is a second appeal in that the Appellee wasted the subject matter of the first appeal[handwritten line]prior to this Court's opinion.

FACTS

All references are to Video Tape Number 95-046. Appellee stated that the house had been torn down (1606). Appellant stated that the house was torn down on May 13, 1994, and that the Court of Appeals did not affirm the trial judgment until October 28, 1994. (1613) Appellant asked the trial court if an appeal stops everything. (1608) Trial judge stated that since the appeal went against the Appellant then no harm no foul. (1617) Appellant stated that a lien of $4800.00 has been placed against the property and this his redemption rights has been destroyed. (1610) The City of Louisville even stated by affidavit that a diligence search had been made for the owner of the property in question. (1611) Appellant stated that the real estate and improvements were taxed at $10,000. (1615)

Appellee stated that the City would put the property on the docket and let the City buy it. (Emphasis added) (1619)

The Court stated that it did not feel that the City acted maliciously or fraudulently (1621) and was not going to reopen the case. (1619) Trial Court stated that the Supreme Court deny revi [handwritten "e"]w April 13, 1994. (1619)

LAW

Section 13 of the Kentucky Constitution requires compensation for private property taken for public use. (1615) Furthermore Section two of the Kentucky Constitution prohibits injustices such as supra.

CONCLUSION

There is nothing in the record to show that the Appellant's property was destroyed because of emergency reasons and no order from the trial court permitting same, therefore Appellee has violated the laws of the land.

/s/James Henry Brown

In an order which described a portion of the brief as "virtually incomprehensible," the Court of Appeals dismissed the appeal and found that Brown's pleading failed to meet the basic requirements of CR 76.12(4)(c)(i), (iii), (iv) and (v) because it failed to contain a brief introduction, failed to include a statement of the case consisting of the chronological summary of facts and procedural events with ample reference to the record, failed to contain an argument with supporting references to the record and citations of authority and failed to contain a conclusion setting forth the specific relief sought from the court.

When Brown's brief was brought to the attention of the Inquiry Tribunal, it investigated the matter and issued a one-count Charge alleging that Brown violated SCR 3.130-1.1 when he filed the deficient brief:

COUNT I

1. Respondent represented [his client] in an appeal to the Court of Appeals of Kentucky from a decision of the Jefferson Circuit Court, the said appeal being identified as Court of Appeals Case No. 95-CA-001904-MR.

2. On or about December 6, 1996, the Court of Appeals entered an Opinion and Order dismissing the appeal because the brief submitted by the Respondent failed to comply with the basic requirements of CR 76.12.

3. SCR 3.130-1.1 states as follows:

A lawyer must provide competent representation to a client. Competent representation requires the legal knowledge, skill, thoroughness, and preparation reasonably necessary for the representation.

4. The Inquiry Tribunal charges that the Respondent violated SCR 3.130- 1.1 when the Respondent filed the aforesaid brief with the Court of Appeals of Kentucky, for all of the reasons set forth in [the Opinion and Order of the Court of Appeals which dismissed the action]

Brown responded to the Charge by asserting that his client had lost interest in the case before Brown filed the appeal and that, in any event, the client was satisfied with the representation he received. Brown also maintained that the Court of Appeals elevated "form over substance," alleged that the proper course of action might have been to seek "a mandamous [sic] from the Court of Appeals," and cited to authority interpreting RCr 11.42 to support his premise that "where the lawyer's client does not claim foul," disciplinary action is inappropriate.

At an evidentiary hearing on April 20, 1999, the Kentucky Bar Association introduced both a copy of Brown's pleading and Brown's testimony that he believed the claim involved in this appeal to be meritorious, that he believed his brief was adequate and substantially complied with the requirements of CR 76, and that the Court of Appeals adopted an overly technical view of pleadings which amounted to "We don't care if you've got the best case in the world, if you didn't dot all of your i's and cross all of your t's . . . ." Brown not only testified on his own behalf and introduced the testimony of his client regarding the client's opinion of Brown's efforts on his behalf, but also questioned three members of the Kentucky Judiciary whom he had subpoenaed before the Trial Commissioner. Brown focused much of his examination of these witnesses on the merits of actions which he had previously litigated before them, and the Trial Commissioner appropriately found that Brown's examination of the three judges "failed to produce any evidence that is relevant, material, and admissible in this proceeding." The Trial Commissioner found that "the Court's decision to strike the brief and dismiss the appeal was a foreseeable result of these serious deficiencies," and concluded that Brown had failed to provide competent representation to his client, and was therefore guilty as charged.

The Board of Governors agreed with the Trial Commissioner and recommended that Brown receive a suspension of sixty (60) days. Brown now petitions this Court to Review the KBA's recommendation and argues (1) that he provided competent representation to his client; and (2) that he has been found to be honest and trustworthy by his peers. Brown "does admit that the Court of Appeals would have been better served if he had styled his brief as a 'Writ of Mandamous [sic].'"

Brown cites his client's testimony from the evidentiary hearing before the Trial Commissioner to support his argument that he provided the client competent representation and specifically references the client's declaration that he would retain Brown in the future if he needed legal services performed on his behalf. In the face of such a grossly inadequate pleading, however, we find this testimony unpersuasive, and a close review of the record suggests to us that, after KBA counsel's cross-examination fully explained to the client why the Court of Appeals dismissed his case, this client would think twice before again seeking legal assistance from Brown. The fact remains that Brown filed a pleading in the Court of Appeals which the KBA correctly describes as "a little more than fifteen unclear and ungrammatical sentences, slapped together as two pages of unedited text with an unintelligible message." This "brief" would compare unfavorably with the majority of the handwritten pro se pleadings prepared by laypersons which this Court reviews on a daily basis. Despite the pleading's patent inadequacies, Brown continues to maintain that he prepared it in substantial compliance with the Civil Rules and in the course of competently representing his client.

We are mystified by Brown's conclusion that "the Court of Appeals would have been better served if he had styled his brief as a 'Writ of Mandamous [sic],'" and believe Brown's statement further demonstrates his unfamiliarity with the Rules of Civil Procedure.

Brown's contention that his peers consider him honest and trustworthy merely highlights his continued inability to grasp the concept of relevance which he demonstrated during the evidentiary hearing before the Trial Commissioner. As a preliminary matter, however, this Court must note that the equivocal testimony Brown cites to support his honesty comes from witnesses subpoenaed by Brown to testify in an unrelated evidentiary hearing before another Trial Commissioner in a disciplinary proceeding which is not a part of the record of this matter. Even if this testimony were properly before us, however, this Court believes it would be completely irrelevant. It appears that Brown may be trustworthy and honest, but we are convinced that he violated SCR 3.130- 1.1 by failing to provide competent representation to this client.

WHEREFORE, IT IS ORDERED that the respondent be, and he is, hereby suspended from the practice of law in the Commonwealth of Kentucky for a period of sixty (60) days.

We further order the respondent to pay the costs of this action in the amount of $1,090.95, for which execution may issue.

This order shall constitute a public record.

INTRODUCTION

Importance of good legal writing to the law

Good legal writing is vitally important to those professionally involved with the law. Attorneys, judges, and paralegals are in the business of communicating and their success depends in good measure on how well they write. As explained in this chapter, the goal of a legal document may be to inform, to persuade, or to record information, depending on the document. Serious problems with meeting any of these goals may have negative consequences. For the judge, a poorly written opinion or order may result in reversal on appeal. For the attorney, errors in legal writing may result in loss of a case, loss of a client, litigation of ambiguously written legal documents, legal malpractice lawsuits, or professional sanctions. A paralegal may lose a job over a poorly written document.

For example in *Kentucky Bar Association v. Brown*, the case that begins this chapter, attorney Brown filed a one and one half page appellate brief that was "virtually incomprehensible." The Kentucky Supreme Court declared that the brief "would compare unfavorably with the majority of the handwritten pro se pleadings prepared by laypersons which this Court reviews on a daily basis." Brown's brief was dismissed and the Kentucky Supreme Court suspended Brown from practicing law for sixty days for failing to provide competent representation to his client. In addition, the court ordered him to pay $1,090.95 in costs.

Chapter 12 discusses fundamentals of writing that apply to all types of legal documents. This chapter briefly discusses many different types of legal documents, and later chapters discuss some of the most important ones in detail—transmittal and client opinion letters (chapter 13), contracts (chapter 14), pleadings (chapter 15), law office memos (chapter 16), memoranda of law (chapter 17), and appellate briefs (chapter 18). Appendix B explains citation rules and appendix C explains rules for quotations and short form citations. Appendixes B and C also provide exercises for you to practice what you have learned. Appendix D explains how to avoid some of the most common mechanical errors in legal writing and provides exercises for you to practice what you have learned.

The article included at the end of this chapter highlights the type of problems faced by attorneys who fail to write clearly and follow applicable court rules. The article, by Wendy B. Davis, is entitled *An Attorney's Ethical Obligations Include Clear Writing*. In the cases referenced in the article, attorneys were fined and had their cases dismissed. Several ambiguously-worded contracts spawned lawsuits.

Do not be intimidated by legal writing. Although certain things, such as citation form and the format for some legal documents, are peculiar to legal writing, legal writing in many ways is not that different from writing you have done in the past. You can think of learning legal writing as fine tuning the writing skills you already have. In addition, just because you are doing legal writing does not mean that you leave your common sense behind. You will often have to pull on your own experiences in analyzing problems and in brainstorming to arrive at solutions.

Writing is not easy—not for good writers, nor even for professional writers. Your writing will improve with practice and a good grasp of the fundamentals. The following chapters are designed to give you practice in legal writing and to explain those fundamentals. In the following case, the attorney was suspended from practice for poor legal briefs and his failure to complete a legal writing tutorial.

In re Carlyle SHEPPERSON.

No. 95-133.

Supreme Court of Vermont.

Jan. 24, 1996.

674 A.2d 1273

ENTRY ORDER

Respondent Carlyle Shepperson appeals the Professional Conduct Board's recommendation that he be disbarred for violating DR 6-101(A)(1) (lawyer shall not handle legal matter that lawyer is incompetent to handle) and DR 6-101(A)(2) (lawyer shall not handle legal matter without adequate preparation). We suspend respondent indefinitely until he can demonstrate that he is fit to practice law.

In June 1991, a justice of this Court not taking part in this decision filed a complaint with the Board concerning the quality of respondent's legal submissions. In March 1993, the Board and respondent entered into a remedial stipulation in which respondent agreed not to engage in the practice of law while he completed a legal writing tutorial. The stipulation provided that respondent would participate in periodic tutoring sessions to develop skills in legal analysis, persuasive writing techniques, writing organization, and use of legal authority, proper citation form, and proper formatting for memoranda and briefs. At the end of the tutorial program, which was to last for a minimum of six months, respondent was to prepare a ten-page legal writing sample and a self-written evaluation of his progress. Respondent was given until September 1, 1993 to report on his progress with the tutor. On September 15, 1993, respondent wrote bar counsel that he would not be completing the tutorial, and that he had left the United States for an indefinite period of time. Bar counsel filed a petition of misconduct in June 1994, charging respondent with violating DR 6-101(A)(1) and (2). Respondent filed memoranda with the Board but did not appear for the disciplinary hearing held in December 1994. A majority of the Board adopted the hearing panel's recommendation that respondent be disbarred, with two dissenting members stating that they would suspend respondent indefinitely until he proved he was fit to practice law.

All members of the Board agreed with the hearing panel's findings that between 1985 and 1992 respondent repeatedly submitted legal briefs to this Court that were generally incomprehensible, made arguments without explaining the claimed legal errors, presented no substantiated legal structure to the arguments, and devoted large portions of the narrative to irrelevant philosophical rhetoric. The briefs contained numerous citation errors that made identification of the cases difficult, cited cases for irrelevant or incomprehensible reasons, made legal arguments without citation to authority, and inaccurately represented the law contained in the cited cases. All members of the Board also agreed with the hearing panel's conclusions that (1) respondent's briefs were not competently prepared and fell below the minimum standard for brief-writing expected of a practicing attorney in this state; (2) respondent failed to prepare adequately or give appropriate attention to his legal work; and (3) respondent did not use proper care to safeguard the interests of his clients.

A review of the exhibits in this case supports the Board's findings that respondent disserved his clients by preparing inadequate and incomprehensible legal briefs, in violation of DR 6-101(A)(1) and (2). Respondent's brief in this matter is a further example of the deficiencies noted by the Board. In over ninety pages, respondent fails to raise a legitimate legal issue or cite a single authority in support of his arguments. The gist of his harangue against the legal system is that the Board and this Court have violated his freedoms of speech and religion and limited his ability to think in diverse ways by dictating what is and what is not a proper legal argument. If we were to accept this argument, it would preclude any oversight of attorney competence in representing members of the public. Respondent may represent himself as he pleases, but he cannot be permitted to represent others in a manner that, under reasonable and accepted standards, fails to safeguard his clients' interests. Indeed, the primary purpose of the attorney disciplinary system is to protect the public.

The only real issue on appeal is whether respondent should be disbarred or suspended indefinitely. According to the American Bar Association Standards, which we have found helpful in determining appropriate sanctions, "Disbarment should be imposed on lawyers who are found to have engaged in multiple instances of incompetent behavior . . . [or] whose course of conduct demonstrates that they cannot or will not master the knowledge and skills necessary for minimally competent practice." Standard 4.51, Commentary. Here, respondent's course of conduct in filing several incomprehensible briefs over a period of seven years and his failure to follow through with the stipulated tutorial program designed to improve his skills demonstrate his inability or refusal to understand and apply fundamental legal doctrines and procedures. Nevertheless, because there is no indication that respondent's conduct was intentional or based on corrupt motives, we adopt the minority position of the Board and suspend respondent until he can prove that he is fit to practice law. In no event, however, shall respondent's suspension be less than six months.

Ethical obligations

The writer should be mindful of the attorney ethics rules; a number of them concern the contents of written documents. Boxes in this chapter contain the text of Florida's ethics rules that impact on the information included in written documents. For example, the attorney is prohibited from making false statements and must disclose certain information (fig. 11-1). The attorney ethics rules of your state may be similar in wording or intent.

A number of ethics rules, such as the rules in figures 11-4, 11-6, and 11-7 relate most directly to unethical litigation tactics. Others, such as the rules in figure 11-5 concern the attorney's relationship and dealings with the judge. Still others, such as the rule in figure 11-2 guide the attorney in determining the information the attorney is required to disclose, prohibited from disclosing, or permitted to disclose in written documents.

Writing as communication

The purpose of all writing, including legal writing, is to communicate. For centuries, legal writing has been criticized for being wordy and hard to understand because of the use of Latin phrases and legal terms. Although not universally accepted, the trend today is to write legal documents in plain English. (Statutes in some states require consumer contracts to be written

FIGURE 11-1 Rule 4-4.1 Truthfulness in Statements to Others.

Rule 4-4.1 of the Ruless Regulating the Florida Bar provides:

RULE 4-4.1 TRUTHFULNESS IN STATEMENTS TO OTHERS

In the course of representing a client a lawyer shall not knowingly:

(a) make a false statement of material fact or law to a third person; or

(b) fail to disclose a material fact to a third person when disclosure is necessary to avoid assisting a criminal or fraudulent act by a client, unless disclosure is prohibited by rule 4-1.6.

in plain English.) Writing in plain English means writing so the document can easily be understood. It requires good organization and format combined with elimination of excess words, Latin phrases, and unnecessary legal terms. Practice plain English whenever possible.

One common-sense thing you have probably done in your past writing is to think of your audience. You need to do the same in legal writing. Before you start writing, determine who your audience will be. For a client letter, it will be the client. For a memorandum of law, it will be the judge and opposing counsel. For a contract, it will be the parties to the contract. These are the obvious answers. Then think who else you need to make sure understands what you have written. For example, documents designed to record information, such as deeds, contracts and wills, may end up being litigated. A cautious writer of those types of documents will keep in mind the attorneys who might litigate and the judge who might interpret the meaning of those documents.

While writing ask yourself whether your intended (and perhaps your unintended) audience will understand what you have written. If you are writing to the client, will the client understand what you have written? If not, explain your message in simpler terms. Are the words you use too abstract or inexact? If so, use more specific words or explain yourself in more detail. Are any words too ambiguous? If so, try defining any ambiguous word.

Your ultimate goal is to have your reader understand what you have written. If you think your reader will have trouble understanding what you have written, revise your document. Even if your reader will understand what you have written, can you add more transitional language or signposts to make the document easier to understand? (The terms "transitional language" and "signposts" are explained in chapter 12.) One way to determine whether your writing is easy to understand is to read the document out loud. Revise the parts of the document that do not read well when being read out loud. Another way is to have someone else unfamiliar with the subject matter read your document. Ask that person which passages were hard to understand and revise them.

A warning against communicating too much

You must be careful not to communicate too much. If you were playing poker, you would not let the other

Rule 4-1.6 of the Rules Regulating the Florida Bar provides:

RULE 4-1.6 CONFIDENTIALITY OF INFORMATION

(a) Consent Required to Reveal Information. A lawyer shall not reveal information relating to representation of a client except as stated in subdivisions (b), (c), and (d), unless the client consents after disclosure to the client.

(b) When Lawyer Must Reveal Information. A lawyer shall reveal such information to the extent the lawyer reasonably believes necessary:

(1) to prevent a client from committing a crime; or
(2) to prevent a death or substantial bodily harm to another.

(c) When Lawyer may Reveal Information. A lawyer may reveal such information to the extent the lawyer reasonably believes necessary:

(1) to serve the client's interest unless it is information the client specifically requires not to be disclosed;
(2) to establish a claim or defense on behalf of the lawyer in a controversy between the lawyer and client;
(3) to establish a defense to a criminal charge or civil claim against the lawyer based upon conduct in which the lawyer was involved;
(4) to respond to allegations in any proceeding concerning the lawyer's representation of the client; or
(5) to comply with the Rules of Professional Conduct . . . .

FIGURE 11-2 Rule 4-1.6 Confidentiality of Information.

players see your hand. Just as you would guard your poker hand, an attorney representing the client's best interest will guard against certain information being disclosed and will be careful in the way information is presented. Care in word choice is extremely important because anything in writing may be used against the writer later. An attorney dealing with a confidential matter may refrain from putting the matter in writing for this reason. If the information is adverse to the client, it may be better to communicate the information orally rather than to put it in writing.

Another consideration is the attorney's duty of confidentiality to the client. Figure 11-2 contains Florida's ethics rule concerning confidentiality. Other states have similar ethics rules.

In contrast, a paper trail is often useful as proof of exactly what was communicated. Certain information needs to be written so it can have legal effect now and be referred to later (contracts, wills, deeds, court documents). An attorney may put advice or information in writing in case there is any question later as to what the attorney communicated. A client opinion is often put in writing so the client can study it in detail and refer to it later; putting the advice in writing protects the attorney if the client tries to apply the advice to some future situation beyond the scope of the opinion letter. Certain information may be given to the opposing attorney in writing to furnish proof that the opposing attorney was aware of the information.

Elimination of mechanical errors

Communicating is the fun part of legal writing. The other necessary, though tedious, part is eliminating mechanical errors. You need to do your best to eliminate mechanical errors for two reasons. First, you want your reader to concentrate on your message and not be distracted by mechanical errors. Second, a reader who spots a number of mechanical errors will begin to wonder if the writer was sloppy. If the writer did not take the time to proof for typographical and spelling errors, perhaps the writer's sloppiness extended to legal research, too. You do not want to lose your credibility over a few easily eliminated mechanical errors.

In this author's experience, students typically have trouble with three categories of mechanical errors. You are already familiar with the first category of mechanical errors from your previous writing experience. These errors, which include problems with apostrophes, antecedents, spelling, run-on sentences, sentence fragments, parallel construction, and sequence of tenses, are discussed in appendix D.

The second category of mechanical errors will be new to you if you have not had previous legal writing experience. This category includes problems with quotations and citations. The rules for quotations and citations are discussed in appendix C.

Third-category mechanical errors include errors other than second-category errors. This category includes errors such as quoting from a headnote or case syllabus, not using plain English, not giving a page reference to material from a primary or secondary source, not quoting exactly, plagiarizing, using contractions in more formal legal documents, using the word "I" in more formal legal documents, and elegant variation (using more than one word to refer to the same thing). These errors are discussed in chapter 12.

In the following case, the attorney was disciplined by being placed on inactive status because of his "incomprehensible" writing.

In re Dennis J. HOGAN, Respondent.

No. 62331.

Supreme Court of Illinois.

March 19, 1986.

490 N.E.2d 1280

Justice GOLDENHERSH delivered the opinion of the court:

On October 14, 1983, the Administrator of the Attorney Registration and Disciplinary Commission (Commission) filed a petition in this court seeking the interim suspension of respondent, Dennis John Hogan, who was licensed to practice law in Illinois on May 19, 1955.

On April 4, 1984, the Hearing Board filed its report in which it found that respondent lacked the fundamental skill of drafting pleadings and briefs, and although his deficiencies were remediable, respondent was incompetent to practice law and to properly represent clients. Although expressing doubt that disbarment was an appropriate remedy, the Hearing Board recommended that, for the protection of the public, respondent be disbarred, and upon being able to show further study and achievement of competence, apply for reinstatement pursuant to Rule 767.

The evidence presented by the Administrator consisted of 19 exhibits including pleadings filed in State and Federal trial courts, and briefs filed in reviewing courts. Respondent appeared pro se before the Hearing Board. The report of the Hearing Board states that respondent "did not testify but indulged in oral argument, much of which was incomprehensible."

The nature and cause of respondent's problem are somewhat difficult to ascertain. The reports of the physical and mental examinations ordered by the court indicate nothing of significance. He is a graduate of an accredited law school and has successfully completed a bar examination. Both of these accomplishments required that his writing be comprehensible. He appears to have practiced law for a number of years and presumably prepared pleadings and other documents before the problem developed. Nevertheless, the pleadings and briefs offered in evidence present the anomalous situation that portions are adequately clear, while others merit the description, by the courts with whom they were filed, of "incomprehensible."

In view of the finding that respondent's conduct did not involve a corrupt motive or moral turpitude and that his disability is remediable, we find it desirable that an effort be made to remedy the disability and, after a probationary period, restore respondent to the status of a licensed attorney.

The Administrator is directed to confer with respondent and his attorney and prepare a plan designed to remedy respondent's disability. In the preparation of the plan the parties may enlist the services of teachers or such other professions and disciplines as may be necessary. During the period of rehabilitation respondent will remain on inactive status. This court will retain jurisdiction, and when, in the opinion of the Administrator, respondent, or both, respondent has demonstrated competence sufficient to engage in the practice of law, either or both parties may petition for an order of probation pursuant to Rule 772.

The Administrator is further directed to report to the court within 90 days of the filing of this opinion the status of the plan and shall further report each six months thereafter the actions taken and the progress made.

Jurisdiction retained.

TYPES OF LEGAL WRITING

The purposes of legal documents are to inform, to persuade, to record information, and to set forth the law to be followed. The balance of this chapter will discuss the different types of legal documents falling within the first three categories—documents designed to inform, persuade, or record information. Cases, statutes, court rules, and administrative rules and regulations are specialized types of legal writing that set forth the law. You are already somewhat familiar with the substance and format of these documents from your legal research course, although further discussion of them is beyond the scope of this book.

FIGURE 11-3 Rule 4-2.1 Advisor.

> Rule 4-2.1 of the Rules Regulating the Florida Bar provides:
>
> **RULE 4-2.1 ADVISOR**
> In representing a client, a lawyer shall exercise independent professional judgment and render candid advice. In rendering advice, a lawyer may refer not only to law but to other considerations such as moral, economic, social, and political factors that may be relevant to the client's situation.

Legal writing designed to inform

The purpose of a transmittal letter, a client letter, a letter to a third party, an opinion letter, and an office memo is to inform. (The client letter and the letter to a third party are also dealt with in the following section because another purpose of those documents is to persuade.) As the name suggests, a client letter is written to the client. The subject matter of a client letter may be anything from a simple cover letter explaining a document attached to the letter, to a letter containing basic facts such as the time and date of a closing, to a letter answering a legal question the client has asked. The first two types of client letters are often referred to as *transmittal letters*. The purpose of a transmittal letter is to communicate basic information. The letter answering a legal question the client has asked is often referred to as a *client opinion letter*. It is the most complicated and takes care to write. The transmittal letter and the client opinion letter are the subject of chapter 13.

One of the roles of the attorney is that of advisor. Figure 11-3 contains Florida's ethics rule concerning the attorney's duty to advise the client. The advice can be oral; however, a transmittal letter may contain advice to the client and the client opinion letter may be used to render advice on a more complex matter.

A client letter and a letter to a third party may be similar in subject matter but usually differ in treatment of that subject matter. The two letters will likely differ in substance and wording because there are certain things which would be discussed in confidence with the client that would not be revealed to a third party. Care in word choice is essential, because anything contained in a letter may be later used against the writer should the matter be litigated.

Be careful not to confuse a client opinion letter with an opinion letter. When attorneys refer to an *opinion letter* they are usually referring to a formal letter written by an attorney in which the attorney gives the opinion that the transaction is legal. The attorney writing the opinion letter is the attorney for one of the parties to the transaction. For example, an opinion letter may be required in a loan closing, a securities offering, or a real estate closing. The opinion letter is usually addressed to one of the other parties to the transaction. Its status is that of a professional work product, and the party may sue the attorney who wrote the letter if the transaction does not result as the attorney has stated in the letter. This type of opinion letter is beyond the scope of this book, but the client opinion letter is discussed extensively in chapter 13.

The *law office memo* is used to inform the reader of the results of legal research. The information in the law office memo is used by the client or the attorney to solve the problem researched. The office memo is discussed extensively in chapter 16.

Legal documents designed to persuade

As previously discussed, a second purpose of the client letter and the letter to the third party is to persuade. This is also the purpose of a pleading, a memorandum of law, and an appellate brief. The job of the attorney is to represent the client's best interests by persuading others that the client's argument is the one that should be adopted.

Think for a moment how the client's argument is formulated. Imagine that two parties have a contract dispute. The attorneys have in front of them the same contract and, if they have competently performed their legal research, the same primary and secondary authority. Each attorney reviews the contract and any authority in the light most favorable to the client. Just as there are two sides to every story, there are at least two arguments that can be made on the same set of facts. Each attorney will argue that the contract interpretation

Rule 4-3.1 of the Rules Regulating the Florida Bar provides:

RULE 4-3.1 MERITORIOUS CLAIMS AND CONTENTIONS

A lawyer shall not bring or defend a proceeding, or assert or controvert an issue therein, unless there is a basis for doing so that is not frivolous, which includes a good faith marginal for an extension, modification, or reversal of existing law . . . .

FIGURE 11-4 Rule 4-3.1 Meritorious Claims and Contentions.

Rule 4-3.3 of the Rules Regulating the Florida Bar provides:

RULE 4-3.3 CANDOR TOWARD THE TRIBUNAL

(a) False Evidence Duty; to Disclose. A lawyer shall not knowingly:

(1) make a false statement of material fact or law to a tribunal;
(2) fail to disclose a material fact to a tribunal when disclosure is necessary to avoid assisting a criminal or fraudulent act by the client;
(3) fail to disclose to the tribunal legal authority in the controlling jurisdiction known to the lawyer to be directly adverse to the position of the client and not disclosed by opposing counsel; . . .

FIGURE 11-5 Rule 4-3.3 Candor Toward the Tribunal.

most favorable to the client applies and distinguish away any interpretation not supporting the client's position. If the law seems to be contrary to the client's position, the attorney can argue for a change in the law or can argue that the law should not be enforced because it is unconscionable or unconstitutional.

The client letter, the letter to the third party, a pleading, the memorandum of law, and the appellate brief may all contain the same legal argument. The differences among them is the time frame in which each is used and the format. Take a closer look at each of these documents.

Although the client letter and the letter to the third party may be used at any time, they are often used as persuasive documents prior to or in anticipation of litigation. Both types of letters analyze a problem and argue persuasively that the problem should be resolved in a certain way. The letter to the third party may conclude by saying that the client will be forced to file a lawsuit if the third party does not resolve the problem as suggested in the letter. After the lawsuit has been filed, the letter to a third party may also be used as a persuasive document in pre-trial settlement negotiations.

Pleadings are formal statements by the parties to a lawsuit setting forth their claims or defenses. Examples of pleadings include a complaint, an answer, and a counterclaim. The format and basic substance of civil law pleadings are governed by the Federal Rules of Civil Procedure for federal courts and are governed by the state rules of civil procedure for state courts.

A **memorandum of law** is a written document containing the attorney's argument substantiated by relevant authority. At the trial level, an attorney may prepare, or may be required to prepare a memorandum of law, the purpose of which is to persuade the judge to reach a particular decision. The format for the memorandum of law is discussed extensively in chapter 17.

An **appellate brief** is a formal statement by a party submitted to the appellate court. When a case is appealed, each attorney submits a written statement to the appellate court to persuade the court of the correctness of the client's position. An appellate brief argues the facts of the case and the applicable law, supported by citations to authority. The format for the appellate brief is discussed extensively in chapter 18.

Anyone writing persuasive documents must be mindful of ethics rules. Figures 11-4 through 11-7 contain the text of ethics rules especially relevant to litigation.

FIGURE 11-6 Rule 4-4.4 Respect for Rights of Third Persons.

Rule 4-4.4 of the Rules Regulating the Florida Bar provides:

RULE 4-4.4 RESPECT FOR RIGHTS OF THIRD PERSONS

In representing a client, a lawyer shall not use means that have no substantial purpose other than to embarrass, delay, or burden a third person or knowingly use methods of obtaining evidence that violate the legal rights of such a person.

FIGURE 11-7 Rule 4-8.2 Judicial and Legal Officials.

Rule 4-8.2 of the Rules Regulating the Florida Bar provides:

RULE 4-8.2 JUDICIAL AND LEGAL OFFICIALS

(a) Impugning Qualifications and Integrity of Judges or Other Officers. A lawyer shall not make a statement that the lawyer knows to be false or with reckless disregard as to its truth or falsity concerning the qualifications or integrity of a judge, mediator, arbitrator, adjudicatory officer, public legal officer, juror or member of the venire, or candidate for election or appointment to judicial or legal office . . . .

Legal documents designed to record information

The primary purpose of a deed, a contract, a will, a case brief, or a corporate document is to record information so the information can be reread later. These documents are sometimes referred to as planning documents because they set forth a plan of what will happen in the future so the parties can avoid litigation. Well-written planning documents should prevent rather than encourage litigation. Look at these planning documents.

A **deed** is a document by which real property or an interest in real property is transferred from one person to another. A deed contains the names of the parties, the date, the operative words transferring the property, and the property description. A warranty deed contains title covenants (promises made by the person transferring the property that certain things are true concerning title to the property) whereas the quitclaim deed does not. Although there are similarities in the format for deeds from state to state, real property transactions are largely creatures of state law, so the law of the state in which the property is located should be consulted as to any particular format required.

A **contract** is an agreement entered into to do or refrain from doing a particular thing. The contract must be supported by adequate consideration (that which is given in exchange for performance or the promise to perform), must involve an undertaking that is legal to perform, and must be based on mutuality of agreement and obligation between at least two competent parties. The format for the contract is extensively discussed in chapter 14.

A **will** is an instrument by which a person makes a disposition of his or her property, to take effect after death. A will contains the name of the person making the will, the date, the operative words willing that person's property, and the property description. In contrast to a deed, a will is revocable during a person's lifetime. While there are similarities in the format for wills from state to state, wills are also largely creatures of state laws, so the law of the state in which the property is located should be consulted as to any particular format required.

A **case brief** is an outline or summary of a published court opinion. One reason to brief a case is to understand the case better by identifying its important parts. The other reason to brief a case is to be able to refer to the case brief to refresh one's memory without having to read the whole case again. Although the format for a case brief varies from person to person, some standard parts of a case brief are the case citation, the facts, the history of the case, the issue(s), the holding(s), the reasoning, and the result.

FIGURE 11-8 An Attorney's Ethical Obligations Include Clear Writing.

Writing Clinic

An Attorney's Ethical Obligations Include Clear Writing

The power of a clear statement is the great power at the bar.—Daniel Webster[1]

By Wendy B. Davis

Writing clearly and concisely is not only good business practice, it should also be viewed as an ethical obligation of all attorneys.

Rule 1.1 of the ABA Model Rules of Professional Conduct requires an attorney to provide competent representation, and writing skills are one aspect of competence. Although no known case identifies an attorney who was disbarred for lack of writing skills, courts have reinforced the need for effective writing by imposing sanctions for verbosity, lack of organization, and errors in grammar and citations.[2]

Although it may once have been fashionable for legal writing to be filled with Latin and legalese in the belief that this would make all parties recognize the need for legal counsel, clients and courts now demand brevity and plain English.

Courts have commended parties for clear and concise writing.[3] A Massachusetts judge, quoting an appellate procedure textbook, stated that "[a]n attorney should not prejudice his case by being prolix . . . . Conciseness creates a favorable context and mood for the appellate judges."[4] Courts have indicated their displeasure with wordiness[5] and lack of clarity[6] in briefs and pleadings.

Poor writing by an attorney can result in court sanctions for the attorney, loss of the client's legal claim and unnecessary litigation.

Attorney Sanctions

Numerous regulations impose requirements on lawyers' writing. Federal Rule of Civil Procedure 8 requires a short and plain statement of the claim in a simple, concise and direct manner.[7] Under 28 USC § 1927, courts can impose costs and attorney's fees on lawyers who unreasonably multiply proceedings.[8] Many courts impose page limits on briefs.[9] Lawyers who exceeded the required page limits, or tried to come within the limits by using smaller margins or fonts, have been subject to sanction and fines that they were prohibited from passing on to their clients.[10]

In *Laitram Corp. v. Cambridge Wire Cloth Co.*,[11] the Court of Appeals for the Federal Circuit imposed a fine of $1,000 each on the lawyers who had signed briefs for both parties, directing that the fines be paid to the U.S. Treasury. The briefs lacked references to the record, relied on attorney argument as evidence, and cited inapplicable authority. The court said counsel had "wasted this court's resources by playing in the rarified atmosphere of a debating society."[12] It vacated and remanded the District Court's decision.

In *Julien v. Zeringue*,[13] the court imposed financial sanctions, equal to the defendant's attorney's fees, against the plaintiff's counsel. In addition to the numerous extensions and missed deadlines, the court noted that the attorney did not follow the court's rules of practice governing the preparation of a joint appendix.

Loss of Legal Claim

The inability of lawyers to write properly has a negative impact on clients. Courts have dismissed complaints with grammatical errors.[14] Courts have denied motions with misplaced punctuation marks.[15] These rejected claims have cost clients time and money, and could lead to loss of the client's legal rights.

In *Duncan v. AT&T Communications, Inc.*,[16] the court granted a motion to dismiss a complaint, stating that the plaintiff's complaint was so poorly drafted that it failed to state a claim on which relief could be granted. The court made no attempt to hide its displeasure with the plaintiff's pleadings, noting that "the court's responsibilities do not include cryptography, especially when the plaintiff is represented by counsel."[17] The

FIGURE 11-8 (continued)

court identified grammatical and stylistic shortcomings, adding that the allegations were written in a conclusory manner that failed to explain the facts to the court. Some of the allegations, the court said, might have been legally significant if they had been well-pleaded.

In *Feliciano v. Rhode Island*,[18] the plaintiff's claim under the Americans with Disabilities Act was dismissed because the complaint was too vague. The court found that the complaint did not describe the claim in sufficient detail, nor did it allege facts to support the claim of denial of constitutional rights. The complaint also alleged that there were differences in interpretation in the two applicable federal laws, but it did not articulate those differences. For that reason, the court did not consider this allegation.

In *Lennon v. Rubin*,[19] the court upheld a grant of summary judgment against the plaintiff. The court said that its review was made more difficult because the plaintiff's brief lacked analysis of the statute and identification of the lower court's reasoning. "[W]herever material uncertainties result from an incomplete or indecipherable record and impede or affect our decision, we resolve such uncertainties against appellants."[20] Finding the plaintiff's responses "weak" and his claims "cursory," the court affirmed the grant of summary judgment against the plaintiff.

Unnecessary Litigation

Lack of clarity in transactional documents can involve a client in a lawsuit that would not have been necessary if the drafting attorney had been more cautious or skilled in writing. Many lawsuits are caused by parties asking a court to determine the meaning of ambiguous terms.[21]

In both of the following cases, parties were involved in district court suits, which were appealed to a federal Circuit Court of Appeals. Neither case would have been necessary if the contracts had been drafted clearly and accurately.

Steps to Foster Clarity

Spell check programs have made it easier to detect common typographical errors, but they cannot be relied upon to catch certain peculiarities of the English language. The fact that a document passed a spell check is not a defense to an error that was missed. A checklist for items that deserve a close look after a spell check would include:

- Is a plural word something that should instead end with 's?
- Is *there* being used instead of *their?*
- Should *sea* instead read *see?*
- Has *an* crept in where *and* is meant?
- Has *he* been used when *the* or *her* is intended?
- Should *trail* instead be *trial?*
- Is *statue* used where *statute* is intended?
- Is each use of *its* correct? (Spell checkers will allow *its'* to pass as correct, and every use of *it's* should be the equivalent of saying *it is*.)

Headings and subheadings can give your reader a road map to approach the material with a better appreciation of how the argument is being constructed. Clear topic sentences at the start of each paragraph foster comprehension, particularly for speed readers and skimmers.

In *Bourke v. Dun & Bradstreet Corp.*,[22] employees sued their former employer for money due under a contractual incentive compensation plan. The contract provided for the employees to be paid if "targets" were achieved. Each employee had several targets and was entitled to increased compensation for each higher target. The employer interpreted the language to mean that the employee would be paid at the 100% level, and no higher. The employees contended that the phrase entitled them to payment at the

FIGURE 11-8 (continued)

200% and higher levels for higher targets. The two different interpretations resulted in a dispute worth nearly $2 million to the employees. The court found that, although the language was ambiguous, the employer's interpretation of the language was reasonable. The employees' complaint was dismissed, as it had been by the District Court.

In *Baybank v. Vermont National Bank*,[23] the loan participation contract at issue was inaccurate regarding the loan origination date, maturity date and loan amount. The plaintiff, a participant in the loan, refused to participate in the loan renewal, citing the inaccuracies as evidence that the contract was ambiguous. The court agreed that the inaccuracies made the contract ambiguous, but it found that the plaintiff's conduct indicated its consent to participate in the loan renewal.

1. Quote it! Memorable Legal Quotations 18 (Eugene C. Gerhart ed., 1987).
2. For an excellent discussion of this subject, see Judith D. Fischer, *Bareheaded and Barefaced Counsel: Courts React to Unprofessionalism in Lawyers' Papers*, 31 Suffolk U. L. Rev. 1 (1997).
3. *Commonwealth v. Angiulo*, 415 Mass. 502, 523 n.17, 615 N.E.2d 155, 169 n.17 (Mass. 1993).
4. *Id.* (quoting J.R. Nolan, Appellate Procedure § 24).
5. *See Gordon v. Green*, 602 F.2d 743, 744–45 (5th Cir. 1979).
6. *See Slater v. Gallman*, 38 N.Y.2d 1, 4, 377 N.Y.S.2d 448 (1975).
7. Fed. R. Civ. P. 8(a), (e)(1).
8. Section 1927 has been used by courts to impose fines on lawyers who violate page limits, thereby requiring the court and opposing counsel to read two sets of briefs. *Westinghouse Elec. Corp. v. NLRB*, 809 F.2d 419 (7th Cir. 1987).
9. *See, e.g.*, U.S. Sup. Ct. R. 33(1)(d), (g); Fed. Cir. R. 28(c).
10. *Westinghouse Elec. Corp.*, 809 F.2d 419.
11. 919 F.2d 1579 (Fed. Cir. 1990).
12. *Id.* at 1584.
13. 864 F.2d 1572 (Fed. Cir. 1989).
14. 668 F. Supp. 232, 237 (S.D.N.Y. 1987).
15. *People v. Vasquez*, 137 Misc. 2d 71, 76 n.2, 520 N.Y.S.2d 99, 103 n.2 (Crim. Ct., Bronx Co. 1987).
16. *Duncan*, 668 F. Supp. at 234.
17. *Id.*
18. 160 F.3d 780 (1st Cir. 1998).
19. 166 F.3d 6 (1st Cir. 1999).
20. *Id.* at 9 (quoting *Credit Francais International, S.A. v. Bio-Vita Ltd.*, 78 F.3d 698, 700–701 (1st Cir. 1996)).
21. *Bourke v. Dun & Bradstreet Corp.*, 159 F.3d 1032 (7th Cir. 1998); *Elkhart Lake's Rd. Am. v. Chicago Historic Races, Ltd.*, 158 F.3d 970 (7th Cir. 1998); *Baybank v. Vermont Nat'l Bank*, 118 F.3d 30 (1st Cir. 1997).
22. *Bourke*, 159 F.3d at 1037.
23. 118 F.3d 30 (1st Cir. 1997).

Corporate documents are those documents necessary, usual, or permitted for the establishment and operation of a corporation. Because the corporation is a creature of statute, it comes into existence only upon complying with requirements of state statute. Generally, state statutes require articles of incorporation or a corporate charter to be filed with the secretary of state and an incorporation fee be paid. Other corporate documents include bylaws, rules, and minutes. The format for corporate documents is beyond the scope of this book.

CHAPTER 11 SUMMARY

- Good legal writing is vitally important to attorneys, judges, and paralegals.
- The trend is to write legal documents in plain English (writing so the document can be easily understood).
- Your ultimate goal is to have your reader understand what you have written.
- Legal writing also involves eliminating mechanical errors; this book tells you how to eliminate mechanical errors common to writing in general and how to avoid errors with quotations and citations, as well as to avoid mechanical errors peculiar to legal writing.
- The purposes of legal documents are to inform, to persuade, to record information, and to set forth the law to be followed.
- This book devotes a chapter to the transmittal letter (designed to inform), and the client opinion letter (designed to inform and persuade), a chapter to the contract (designed to record information), a chapter to pleadings (designed to persuade), a chapter to the office memo (designed to inform), a chapter to the memorandum of law (designed to persuade), and a chapter to the appellate brief (designed to persuade).
- The purpose of a transmittal letter is to communicate information and the client opinion letter answers a client's legal question.
- A contract is an agreement between two or more parties entered into to do or refrain from doing a particular thing.
- Pleadings are formal statements by the parties to a lawsuit setting forth their claims or defenses.
- The office memo is used to inform the reader of the results of legal research.
- A memorandum of law is a written document usually filed with the court which contains the attorney's argument substantiated by relevant authority.
- An appellate brief is a formal statement by a party submitted to the appellate court.

CYBERLAW EXERCISES

1. The American Bar Association homepage allows you to access Internet sites for national, international, state, and local bar associations. The homepage is located at http://www.abanet.org/lawlink/. Use the page to locate information on your state and local bar.
2. The Lexis law school site (http://lawschool.lexis.com) includes information on developing effective writing skills.
3. The WashLaw Web site (http://www.washlaw.edu) allows you to access legal dictionaries. Go to the web site and click on "legal dictionaries."
4. If you are interested in researching legal ethics concerning the Internet, try http://www.legalethics.com. The site also contains links to other ethics sites.
5. For writing resources, including a legal dictionary and thesaurus, access http://www.legal.gsa.gov.

EXERCISES FOR CHAPTER 11

1. Why is good legal writing important to the legal profession?
2. How does legal writing resemble or differ from writing you have done in the past?
3. Who are the audiences for the different types of legal writing referred to in the chapter?
4. Is it always a good idea for legal writing to communicate as much as possible?
5. Where could you look in this book to find out how to eliminate mechanical errors from legal writing?
6. Name types of legal writing not covered in depth in this book.
7. What is the purpose of these types of legal writing?

CHAPTER 12

FUNDAMENTALS OF WRITING

INTRODUCTION

This chapter introduces you to certain writing fundamentals that apply to all types of legal writing. The first part of the chapter discusses the writing process, from the prewriting stage, to writing, to editing and proofing. The second part of the chapter discusses organization and then explains the use of topic sentences, transitional language and signposts, paragraphing, and format. The third part of the chapter discusses errors peculiar to legal writing other than errors in quotations and short form citations. These errors include quoting from a headnote or case syllabus, not using plain English, not giving a page reference to material from a primary or secondary source, not quoting exactly, plagiarizing, using contractions in more formal legal documents, using the word "I" in more formal legal documents, and elegant variation (using more than one word to refer to the same thing).

WRITING PROCESS

The writing process should have three steps:

1. prewriting
2. writing
3. editing and proofing

The novice writer plunges into writing without going through the prewriting step and may not spend enough time on the third step. Some of you will be slow to be convinced and some of you will never be convinced that all three steps are necessary. If your professor does not force you to proceed through all three steps by requiring you to turn in an outline, a written document, and a revision of the written document, try completing the three steps on your own. You will be pleased with the results.

Prewriting

Prewriting involves performing any necessary research, formulating a writing "plan," and outlining. Do not skimp on any of these activities. Your "research strategy" should include good notetaking and case briefing as you go along. You may spend a little more time doing research, but a little extra time on research should shorten the time you spend formulating your writing plan and outlining.

From time to time you may need to pause and collect your thoughts. Mentally review what you have accomplished and think about the direction you are heading. You need to pay attention to detail yet not lose sight of the big picture.

The research required to write letters, deeds, contracts, and wills may be limited to gathering facts and identifying the information to be included. In writing an office memo, a memorandum of law or an appellate brief, your research usually will be more extensive than for other types of documents. Performing research may mean various things, from gathering facts by reviewing documents and interviewing people to doing legal research in the law library. Research needs to have been completed as nearly as possible before you start writing or you may find yourself backtracking later.

As you do your research you should start to decide what your writing plan will be. In other words, how will you organize your facts and the results of your research to make sense to your reader? As you look at the information in front of you, you will probably identify a number of ideas you want to communicate to your reader. In formulating your plan you must decide on a scheme for arranging these ideas and developing them for the reader.

Your plan is somewhat dictated by the type of document you are writing. Research the standard format for the type of document you are writing. For certain documents, such as deeds and wills, you will probably want to follow the organizational format customarily used in your area but do not depend entirely on the recognized format. Make any organizational changes necessary to make sure your reader understands what you have written. The format for court documents may be dictated by court rule. Even though you must follow the overall organizational framework set out in the rule, make sure you have good internal organization.

If you are writing an office memo, a memorandum of law or an appellate brief, prewriting should involve developing a thesis. Think about your facts in relation to the results of your research. Then try to step back and look at the "whole picture." If you think about it long enough you will find a central idea that runs through your facts and research material. This is your thesis. Think of your thesis as the border to a puzzle. Once you have established your thesis, use it as a framework and fit your facts and research material within it.

Try to develop a "flow chart" or "road map" as part of your writing plan for your office memo, memorandum of law, or appellate brief. An example of a flow chart for a search and seizure problem is included in appendix A. A flow chart should help you to understand the legal analysis applicable to the legal problem you are researching. If you can complete a flow chart, you are probably on the right track with your legal analysis. Frequent reference to your flow chart will help you write your outline. If you cannot construct a flow chart because you cannot make sense of your research, you either need to spend more time to "fit the pieces" together or you need to do more research.

Once you have completed your flow chart, start writing an outline. The outline can be as brief or as detailed as you like. An outline that does not contain very much detail will not take as long to write but will be less helpful in the writing process. An outline that is too skeletal is not very useful. You need to include enough information in your outline to organize yourself before you start writing and determine whether your legal analysis flows. A more detailed outline will take more time to write but should speed up the writing process and cut down on revision time. An example of an outline for an office memo on the search and seizure problem is included in appendix A.

If your writing plan is not clear, your writing will be unclear. If your writing is unclear, your reader will end up doing the organization that should have been your job. A reader saddled with this task will not enjoy reading what you have written and may become very frustrated in the attempt.

STRUCTURE

Overall organization and organization within sections

Good organization is essential for readability. Depending on the complexity of your document, you may have various levels of organization. Your document must be well organized at each level. Section headings provide overall organization. Then you must organize your writing within each section and you must organize what you say within each paragraph and within each sentence.

A discussion or reasoning portion of a legal document should contain an introduction, explain the relevant law, and apply the law to the facts. The conclusion may be part of the body of the document or may be in a separate section. In explaining the relevant law and applying it to the facts, the body of the discussion should develop the idea introduced in the introduction and lead up to the conclusion. Develop the idea step by step so you do not lose your reader along the way, explaining even the most obvious steps. Just because you can see the connection between steps two and four does not necessarily mean that your reader will be able to unless the connection is spelled out. The development can be logical or chronological depending on the nature of the discussion.

Organization of an office memo

To understand what was explained in the preceding section, look at the various levels of organization of an office memo. The office memo is used to record the law found as a result of the research, to explain how the researcher analyzed the law and applied it to the facts, and to propose a solution to the problem. The overall organizational framework is set by the typical office memo format: facts, issue(s), answer(s), reasoning, and conclusion. This is the first level of organization. Figure 16-1 depicts this organization.

The key to the second level of organization is your formulation of the issue(s). An issue must be well organized to contain as much information as possible while still being readable. If you have more than one issue, you need to carefully consider the order in which you will present the issues. The way you formulate your issue(s) dictates everything else in the office memo. Look at your issue(s) and decide what facts are relevant or significant to the issue(s). These are the only ones that should be included in the facts section. Your answer(s), as the terms imply, are simply answer(s) to your issue(s) and should mirror your issues. The reasoning section flows from the issue(s) because it tells the reader how you got from your issue to your answer. The conclusion is a more detailed statement of your answer(s).

The reasoning section should contain a thesis paragraph, which serves as an introduction, an explanation of relevant law, and an application of the law to the facts. If you have more than one issue, you may want to follow the thesis paragraph with an explanation of the law that is applicable to all the issues first and then discuss each issue separately. For example, a section entitled "reasoning" may begin with a thesis paragraph that serves as an overall introduction and may continue with a statement of the law relevant to all issues. The balance of the reasoning portion of the office memo is broken up into the same number of sections as there are issues. You may visually break up the reasoning portion of the office memo for your reader by using headings for each issue such as "reasoning for issue one" and so on. Figures 16-4 and 16-5 depict ways in which you can organize the reasoning portion of an office memo. More levels of organization may be needed if you have sub-issues within issues.

Organization at the paragraph level

The final levels of organization are at the paragraph and sentence levels. You will lose your reader if your overall organization and the organization within the various sections is good but your paragraphs and sentences are not well organized. This section discusses organization at the paragraph level. The following section discusses organization at the sentence level.

Remember your English teacher talking to you about topic sentences? Most paragraphs need topic sentences. (A paragraph reciting a string of chronological events might get along without a topic sentence.) A topic sentence summarizes the topic being discussed in the paragraph. The rest of the paragraph should develop and expand on the idea introduced in the topic sentence. Because the reader will best remember the first and last sentences of the paragraph, the topic sentence is usually, but not always, in one of those two positions.

Look at the preceding paragraph. The first sentence in the paragraph caught the reader's attention. The second sentence is the "topic sentence" and contains the main idea of the paragraph: paragraphs usually need topic sentences. The rest of the paragraph expands on the idea contained in the topic sentence. The rest of the paragraph gives an exception to the use of topic sentences, explains what a topic sentence does, explains how the rest of the paragraph relates to the topic sentence, and gives the typical location of the topic sentence.

If your discussion sounds disjointed, check your paragraph structure. Do you deal with a single idea in each paragraph? If you have more than one idea in a paragraph, split up the paragraph so you give each idea its own paragraph. Do you have a topic sentence? If not, write a sentence that contains the essence of the rest of your paragraph. Did you develop the idea introduced in the topic sentence? If not, decide what else you can say about the idea and add it to the paragraph. If you cannot develop a topic sentence, perhaps the idea needs to be part of another paragraph or you need to eliminate it.

Word order within sentences

Although readers may enjoy a challenge, do not challenge your reader too often with unconventional word order. Most sentences should follow the conventional structure for English sentences: subject, verb, and object (if any). Your reader should easily understand your sentences without having to hunt for the subject and the verb. Help your reader by keeping the subject, verb, and object close together and near the beginning of the sentence. Every now and then you may want to vary the conventional subject/verb/object structure to emphasize certain words. Because your reader will remember the beginning and end of your sentence better than the middle of the sentence, put the information you want to emphasize either at the beginning or at the end of the sentence.

The following are "mixed-up" sentences from student writing. Read them, determine which word order rules have been broken, and decide how the sentences can be corrected.

1. The United States Supreme Court in two cases had to determine whether an investigatory stop was based on reasonable suspicion.
2. Trooper Vogel testified that the appellants, based on a reasonable suspicion created by a drug courier profile, were hauling drugs.
3. In *Smith*, relying on a drug courier profile Trooper Vogel stopped a car.

Here are suggested corrections to the above sentences. They are only suggestions. You may have come up with better answers.

1. In two cases the United States Supreme Court had to determine whether an investigatory stop was based on reasonable suspicion.
2. Trooper Vogel testified he had a reasonable suspicion that the appellants were hauling drugs and that his suspicion was based on the drug courier profile.
3. In *Smith* Trooper Vogel stopped the car in reliance on the drug courier profile.

Transitional language and signposts

Be kind to your reader by using transitional language and signposts as frequently as possible. Think of the textbooks you have been assigned to read this semester. You probably dread trying to read one or two of them and you may actually enjoy reading some of them. Even the most impenetrable subject matter can be made less so through use of transitional language and signposts. On the other hand, easier subject matter can seem just as impenetrable without transitional language and signposts. After reading this section, it would be interesting for you to take a look at your textbooks and analyze the author's writing style for use of transitional language and signposts.

Transitional language provides a "transition" or link between what you have just written and what you are going to write about. For example, the first sentence in this chapter provides a subject matter transition from chapter 11 to chapter 12 by explaining that chapter 12 introduces the reader to the fundamentals of legal writing. Although transitional language introducing a new topic can be used anyplace in the paragraph, it is usually used at the beginning of the paragraph (as it was in the example) or at the end of the paragraph. Use of transitional language at the end of a paragraph allows the writer to introduce the topic of the next paragraph. The writer can then emphasize the new topic by discussing it again immediately in the first sentence of the new paragraph. You can also use transitional words like "although," "even if," "after," "before," and "because" to show the reader the relationship between sentences in a paragraph.

Signposts are words or phrases that point the reader in the right direction and provide a framework for understanding the document. The signposts in the first paragraph of this chapter are the words "the first part of the chapter," "the second part of the chapter," and "the third part of the chapter." They make it easier for the reader to understand the chapter by preparing the reader to expect the chapter to discuss three main topics: the writing process, writing structure, and certain kinds of mechanical errors. Signposts can also highlight main points in a discussion. For example, the words "the main issue before the court . . ." tells the reader that that will be the central focus of the discussion and provides a context for the rest of the discussion.

Paragraphing and tabulation

To paragraph or not to paragraph: that is the question. There is no one right paragraph length. Some paragraphs may be one sentence long while other paragraphs may contain a number of sentences. One gauge of correct paragraph length is the subject matter of the paragraph. Each paragraph should discuss one main idea. If a paragraph is long and sounds disjointed, it may be because you are trying to discuss more than one idea in a single paragraph. Break up the paragraph into shorter paragraphs.

Another gauge of correct paragraph length is readability. Each page of print should contain a minimum of two or three paragraphs. A reader faced with a long, solid block of print will retain less of what you said than if the same material were broken up into a number of shorter paragraphs. A page containing a series of one- and two-sentence paragraphs is just as bad. If you find yourself with a series of one- and two-sentence paragraphs, see whether your text is easier to read if you combine several of the paragraphs.

Tabulation can be used very effectively in legal writing where you have a list of items or activities. When you tabulate, you place each item or activity on a separate line. Each line, except for the last and next to the last lines, ends with a semi-colon. The next to the last line ends with a semicolon and the word "and" or "or." The last line ends with a period.

The first page of this chapter contains the following example of tabulation:

The writing process should have three steps:

1. prewriting;
2. writing; and
3. editing and proofing.

Compare the tabulated material with the following:

> The writing process should have three steps: pre-writing, writing, and editing and proofing.

The only difference between the two sentences is tabulation. Tabulation makes the sentence much easier to read and understand.

In *In re Hawkins*, the Minnesota Supreme Court considered what type of disciplinary action was appropriate for the attorney's disregard of court rules and poor writing.

In re Petition for DISCIPLINARY ACTION AGAINST Patrick W. HAWKINS, an Attorney at Law of the State of Minnesota.

No. C1-92-1261.

Supreme Court of Minnesota.

July 9, 1993.

PER CURIAM.

On November 23 and 24, 1992 a hearing on the original petition and two supplementary petitions was held before our appointed referee, and on December 30, 1992 the referee issued his findings of fact, conclusions of law and a recommendation for suspension. Inasmuch as a transcript of the hearing has not been provided, the referee's findings are deemed conclusive.

The referee found that the Director had failed to prove the allegations of either the original or the first supplementary petition, although the written exhibits admitted in connection with those charges demonstrated respondent Hawkins' lack of skill as a communicator. With respect to the allegations of the second supplementary petition, however, the referee found that respondent's failure to comply with the Local Bankruptcy Rules of the United States Bankruptcy Court, District of Minnesota, and his repeated filing of documents rendered unintelligible by numerous spelling, grammatical, and typographical errors were sufficiently serious that they amounted to incompetent representation.

In short, the referee found that by regularly filing substandard bankruptcy documents containing numerous errors of various kinds, the respondent failed to represent his bankruptcy clients competently. The referee concluded, however, that respondent was well-versed in bankruptcy law and that his incompetence with respect to documentation had not harmed his clients. Nevertheless, the seriousness of respondent's noncompliance with the Local Bankruptcy Rules and respondent's attitude toward his shortcomings prompted the referee to recommend a three-month suspension followed by two years' supervised probation and completion of educational requirements.

It is apparent to us that Hawkins' repeated disregard of the Local Bankruptcy Rules, coupled with the incomprehensibility of his correspondence and documentation, constitutes a violation of Rule 1.1, Minnesota Rules of Professional Conduct. Although it is quite true that the deficiencies in the documents submitted to the bankruptcy court did not, as the referee concluded, cause harm to Hawkins' clients, the lack of harm is fortuitous. Compliance with the rules of the bankruptcy court ensures discharge of dischargeable debt. Even though Hawkins might be able to prove that a creditor who claims he did not receive notice of the bankruptcy proceedings was in fact notified, in the absence of appropriate documentation of service of proper notification, he might not. Therefore, Hawkins' contention that because there has been "no harm," there is "no foul" is unacceptable.

Moreover, harm has occurred: even though Hawkins' clients have not been harmed, administration of the law and the legal profession have been negatively affected by his conduct. Public confidence in the legal system is shaken when lawyers disregard the rules of court and when a lawyer's correspondence and legal documents are so filled with spelling, grammatical, and typographical errors that they are virtually incomprehensible.

We are of the opinion, however, that respondent's misconduct does not warrant suspension at this time. That is not to discount the seriousness of Hawkins' misconduct but only to recognize that suspension does not appear to be required for the protection of the public because, despite Hawkins' disregard of rules of court and lack of writing skill, he does—as the referee concluded—appear knowledgeable of the substantive law of bankruptcy. Hawkins' misconduct does, however, require the public reprimand we now issue, together with the admonition that there must be some changes in his attitude—blame for his misconduct cannot be laid at the feet of his clients. Neither can this disciplinary proceeding be characterized as persecution.

Respondent Patrick W. Hawkins is hereby publicly reprimanded for unprofessional conduct. He is ordered to pay costs and disbursements incurred in this proceeding in the amount of $250. Within two years after issuance of this opinion respondent shall successfully complete the following described CLE or other educational programs and shall report quarterly to the Director his progress in complying with these educational requirements:

(1) A program on bankruptcy rules, or if none is available, on the law of bankruptcy;

(2) A program of at least 10 hours in legal writing; and

(3) A program of at least 5 hours on law office management.

MECHANICAL ERRORS

Legal writing students typically have trouble with three categories of mechanical errors. The first and second categories of mechanical errors are discussed in the appendixes C and D. This section discusses a third category of mechanical errors—errors that are peculiar to legal writing other than errors in quotations and short form citations. This section will discuss the following errors:

1. quoting from a headnote or case syllabus;
2. not using plain English;
3. not giving a page reference to material from a primary or secondary source;
4. not quoting exactly;
5. plagiarizing;
6. using contractions in more formal legal documents;
7. using the word "I" in more formal legal documents; and
8. elegant variation.

Quoting from a headnote or case syllabus

The error that will most quickly identify you as a novice legal writer is quoting from a headnote or case syllabus. The reason that you should not use any material other than the opinion itself is that the material other than the opinion is not the law and may even be wrong because the publisher wrote it. It is appropriate to refer to or quote from the opinion because it is the law. The publisher or the official reporter for the court prepared the material in the reporter, other than the opinion itself. The non-opinion material is usually, but not always, accurate. It may on occasion contain outright errors. Because the non-opinion material is a summary of material from the case, you may have a different impression of what the law is from reading the non-opinion material than from reading the opinion itself. In addition, the summary may not refer to a part of the case important for your research. The only way to find that material is to read the whole case.

res ipsa loquitur—(Latin) "The thing speaks for itself." A rebuttal *presumption* (a conclusion that can be changed if contrary evidence is introduced) that a person is negligent if the thing causing an accident was in his or her control only, and if that type of accident does not "usually happen without negligence." It is often abbreviated "res ipsa" or "R.I.L." [pronounce: race ip-sal low-kwe-tur]

Not using plain English

Writing in plain English means writing so the document can easily be understood. It requires good organization and format combined with elimination of excess words, Latin phrases, and unnecessary legal terms and jargon. Organization and format were discussed in an earlier section of this chapter. The appendix entitled "Mechanical Errors" discusses elimination of excess words and contains exercises allowing you to practice what you learn.

Some attorneys seem to think that the more Latin phrases and legal terms they include, the better their writing will be. The contrary is usually true. Although there are some Latin terms (like "*res ipsa loquitur*") whose meanings are clear to attorneys but are hard to translate into English, use of most Latin terms is unnecessary and may alienate your reader. Eliminate all Latin terms if possible. Where you have to use a Latin term like *res ipsa loquitur*, do so with caution. If there is any question whether your reader will understand the term, define it. You can often slip in a definition in a parenthetical phrase within the sentence without insulting your reader's intelligence.

The same thing holds true with legal terms. Eliminate any legal terms or words you think your reader will have trouble understanding and replace them with words your reader will understand. For example, attorneys often speak of "drafting" a document and the client "executing" it. The client may be confused if the attorney's cover letter refers to the document the attorney has "drafted" and asks the client to "execute" the document. For the legally unsophisticated client, it would be preferable to refer to the document the attorney has "written" and ask the client to "sign" it.

Not giving a page reference to material from a primary or secondary source

Most students know they need to give a page reference when they quote from a case so the reader can quickly find and read the passage in the case. In legal writing, you must also give a page reference when you are referring to specific material from a case even if you are not quoting the material. For example, you may give the facts from the case in your own words. As a courtesy to your reader, you need to tell your reader the page or pages on which the facts are located so the reader can refer to that part of the case without reading the entire opinion. A reference to a specific page is sometimes referred to as a **pinpoint**

citation because the citation pinpoints or specifically locates the information for the reader. You do not have to give a page reference if you are referring to the case in general, rather than referring to specific material from the case, and you have previously given the full citation to the case.

A pinpoint citation may precede or follow the information to which it is referring. The location of the pinpoint citation (before or after the applicable information) is unimportant. You must provide the pinpoint citation and locate it so the reader is clear what information is being referenced. In the next paragraph the first pinpoint citation precedes the information being referenced and the second pinpoint citation follows the information being referenced. "*Terry*" appears by itself in the middle of the paragraph where the cases is being referred to in general terms.

> *Terry v. Ohio*, 392 U.S. 1, 27 (1968) was the landmark case which lowered the burden of proof necessary for a stop from probable cause to "reasonable suspicion." In *Terry* the United States Supreme Court held that police officers could stop someone on the street to investigate possible drug activity so long as the stop is based on something more than "inarticulate hunches." *Id.* at 22.

Not quoting exactly

A writer's stock in trade is his or her credibility. You will lose your credibility quickly if you do not quote accurately. It is important that anything you quote, but especially primary sources, be accurate. If your quotes are not accurate, your reader will think, at best, that you are sloppy and, at worst, that you are intentionally misleading the reader. You must disclose to your reader any intentional alteration of quoted material. Appendix C explains how to show alterations. If you quote a passage that was printed with a typographical error or other mistake, do not correct the passage. Instead, quote the passage as originally printed and insert "[sic]" after the mistake. "[Sic]" tells the reader that the mistake was that of the original author.

Plagiarizing

Plagiarism is adopting another writer's work as your own without giving proper credit to the other writer. Plagiarism exists when you quote from a primary or secondary source without putting the language in quotation marks. It also exists when you have generally followed another writer's style and word choice even though not every word is the other writer's. Instead of plagiarizing, you should either quote the other writer directly or put the material entirely in your own words. To put the material in your own words, you need to know the substance of it well enough that you can "retell" it without referring back to the text.

Using contractions in more formal legal documents

Most legal documents, except for letters and memos to business associates who are also friends, have at least a slightly formal tone of voice. Certain words, such as contractions, that are common in oral communication do not fit in formal legal documents because the tone of these words is too informal. When you are writing a legal document think twice before you use a contraction or informal word. Chances are it does not belong in your document.

Use of the word "I" in more formal legal documents

When giving an opinion in a document such as a client letter, an office memo, a memorandum of law, or an appellate brief, keep the word "I" out of your writing. Although you have a personal opinion and the legal opinion you give very likely coincides with your own opinion, your analysis must be backed up with the law rather than your personal opinion. Rephrase your sentences in third person (for example: "The virtual identity of the facts in the two cases means that . . .") instead of in first person singular (for example: "I think that . . ."). You can include your personal opinion in more formal legal documents so long as you state it in impersonal language.

Elegant variation

One English teacher or another in the past has probably suggested to you that you make your writing interesting by using as many different words as possible to refer to the same thing. This is called **elegant variation.** Elegant variation is terrific for most writing other than legal writing. In legal writing, pick a word to refer to something and use it whenever you refer to the same thing. For example, this book uses "attorney" to refer to a person licensed to practice law. It would be elegant variation to also refer to that person as a "lawyer," "counselor," and "practitioner." A legal thesaurus may profitably be used when you are trying to choose the right term. Once you chose your term, stick with it throughout your document.

Elegant variation is not appropriate in legal writing because attorneys focus so intently on word choice. If in writing a contract, you first referred to the document as a "contract," you have defined the document as a "contract." If you later referred to it as an "agreement," an attorney will wonder why you have changed the wording from "contract" to "agreement." The attorney will wonder whether the writer might have made a mistake or whether the writer was referring to two different documents, one of which was a "contract" and the other was an "agreement." Although it may seem uncomfortable at first to keep using the same word over and over again, you will soon get used to it.

MORE LEGAL WRITING ADVICE

The following article (in fig. 12-1), *Writing Clearly and Effectively: How to Keep the Reader's Attention*, was written for the practitioner (practicing attorney), but the advice is equally applicable to writing students. Much of the advice parallels information stated in this chapter.

FIGURE 12-1 Writing Clearly and Effectively.

New York State Bar Journal
July/August 1999
Vol. 71, No. 6

Writing Clinic

Writing Clearly and Effectively:
How to Keep the Reader's Attention

By Joshua Stein*

Lawyers write. They spend a good portion of their time communicating thoughts and ideas through documents, letters, memos or pleadings. Sometimes they make presentations or write articles and books that are not purely "legal."

Very often, however, lawyers write in a way that does not communicate effectively. As a small step toward changing that, this article summarizes some simple, classic principles that can help every lawyer turn weak, ineffective writing into strong, effective writing.

Most of these principles apply to all categories of written work. Others apply more selectively. But even the latter principles apply more generally than many lawyers think.

Few of these principles are new. Old or new, they are all worth remembering.

---

* **Joshua Stein,** a real estate and finance partner in the New York office of Latham & Watkins, serves on the Executive Committee of NYSBA's Real Property Law Section and is co-chair of its Commercial Leasing Committee. He was recently elected to the American College of Real Estate Lawyers and is national program chair of the Practising Law Institute annual seminar on commercial real estate finance. He is a graduate of the University of California at Berkeley and received his J.D. degree from Columbia University.

This article is an expanded and revised version of one previously published in The Practical Litigator. The author acknowledges with thanks the suggestions made by Mark T. Carroll, ALI-ABA, Philadelphia; Richard M. Frome, Jaffe, Segal & Ross; Andrew L. Herz, Richards & O'Neil, LLP; Richard A. Marks, Goulston & Storrs, Boston; Donald H. Oppenheim, West Coast director of Altman Weil, Inc.; and Sherman and Hannah Stein, Davis, California. The author's e-mail address is joshua.stein@lw.com.

FIGURE 12-1 (continued)

Catch the Reader's Attention

Begin with a short sentence that captures the reader's attention. Make the reader want to read what you're writing.

- *Identify the bigger picture.* Explain why your topic matters, and how it fits into the bigger picture of the reader's world.
- *Show why the reader should pay attention.* Readers care about themselves and their own lives. Tie your opening to your readers and their lives, or to the larger business context. After reading your first few paragraphs, a reader should know why they want or need to read whatever you're writing.
- *Be flexible about starting.* Don't feel you have to start writing at the beginning, however. You can start in the middle. Then figure out the beginning later. That way, you can prevent writer's block—the intimidating effect of a blank sheet of paper.
- *Know your audience.* Know your audience, what you want to tell them and why, before you put your first word on paper. Context dictates everything else. What does your audience already know? What does it want or need to read about?

Strong Verbs Strengthen Your Writing

Verbs mean action. When people do things, readers pay attention. When people sit around and have things done to them or when you talk about abstract or inanimate things, readers fall asleep. Keep your readers awake.

- *Seek active verbs.* Use active verbs. Don't use lame, static, sitting-around verbs such as "to have," "to be" or their variants. Instead of saying "there are available a significant range of meaningful options" (the reader envisions someone sitting and sleeping, and quickly falls asleep), say "a specific person can choose from four options" (the reader envisions someone doing something and stays awake).
- *Look for real events, real people.* Try to describe even the most abstract concepts in terms of real events happening to real people.
- *Don't turn verbs into nouns.* Say "she achieved" rather than "her achievements included." Don't add "ing" to the end of a verb to turn it into a semi-noun. A discussion of growing work force turnover (a thing) doesn't catch the reader's attention with the same force as a statement that turnover has exploded or that more employees than ever leave the company every year (actions). Rather than talk about "responses that some companies have experienced to be effective," discuss how "companies have responded." Someone is doing something. You're not just talking about static things and concepts.
- *Beware of technical terms.* Technical terms that mean something to you might not communicate as well to your audience. Many readers get snagged by words such as "mortgagee" and "mortgagor," which they have to translate in their minds to "bank" or "borrower," often incorrectly. Even though every reader should be able to understand words like these, in the real world they're an extra step. They get in the way. Make your reader's job as easy as you can.

Keep It Simple

Keep most of your sentences short. Break long sentences into shorter ones when you can. If you want to make two related points, write two sentences. Don't string them together into one sentence with the word "and."

- *Construct simple sentences.* Most sentences should contain no more than one idea. If you want to modify, clarify or qualify what you're saying, resist the temptation to do so in the middle of the discussion. It breaks the flow. Save it for somewhere else.
- *Avoid parentheses.* Anything you want to put in parentheses will create a legalistic complication and detour. If it's short, maybe use commas. If it's long, say it somewhere else.

FIGURE 12-1 (continued)

- *Strive for short paragraphs.* Keep most paragraphs short. Short paragraphs help readers digest ideas in bite-sized units.
- *Use a direct path.* Get to the point quickly and directly. Don't interrupt the logical flow while you talk about something else. Your readers don't want to hold their breath mentally. Rearrange your sentences as necessary. For example, if you are describing a general rule with some exceptions, explain the general rule first, then go talk about the exceptions. Don't strew the exceptions throughout your description of the general rule.
- *Conserve reader brainpower.* Don't make your reader spend too much brainpower deciphering your message. Readers need their brainpower to absorb your message once they have figured out what it is. Conserve that brainpower! Reading is hard work.
- *Be willing to start over.* If the presentation gets too complicated, maybe you should tear it up and start over again.
- *Provide options and alternative.* In a contract, you often need to set up multiple alternatives and allow someone to choose between them. To make things easier for yourself and your reader, try to address each alternative once, in a single, integrated discussion, rather than build the necessary flexibility (and complexity) into your discussion every place it might be relevant. For example, if a loan has two possible interest rates, you can refer to both of them every time the topic arises, which makes extra work for everyone, or you can set up a single definition of "interest rate" that describes the rate alternatives only once.
- *Provide graphic illustrations.* If you can use bullet points, charts and headings, do it.

Establish a Solid Structure

To build a house, you would dig the basement first, then pour the foundation, then frame the structure, install the systems to make it all livable and, finally, move toward your finishing touches. You should build most written work the same way.

- *Identify the overall purpose.* Start with a structure, an overall purpose for whatever you are doing. Make it clear in your first couple of paragraphs.
- *Remember your goal.* Don't lose sight of what you're trying to achieve, why and for whom.
- *Watch out for details.* Don't feel you have to go into every possible detail. Unnecessary little extras can confuse more than clarify. Properly used, however, details can help you turn abstractions into concrete examples and, hence, help you communicate better.
- *Provide a logical approach.* If you write about something complicated, introduce it in a logical order—usually the order in which your reader would encounter it in the real world.
- *Use an orderly scheme.* Use a logical and consistent system of headings and subheadings to impose order and help your readers understand that order. If your readers are lawyers, you may find that section numbers also help.
- *Seek consistency and coordination.* Present similar ideas in a similar way. If five conditions need to be satisfied before someone can do something, collect those five conditions in a single list. Don't randomly sprinkle them throughout the document like lost pieces of a jigsaw puzzle.
- *Say it once.* After the structure you have chosen identifies the points you wish to make, discuss each point once, all in one place. Don't force the reader to puzzle through and fit together several relevant provisions to understand what you are saying.

Use Powerful Words in a Powerful Way

Clear, straightforward words convey ideas more powerfully than stuffy, complicated phrases. See **Table 1** for some examples.

FIGURE 12-1 (continued)

Table 1	
Complicated	Powerful
Provide the requisite information	Tell
Suffer a numeric reduction in	Drop
Experience work force turnover	Lose people
Take the steps necessary to retain	Keep
Remain; continue in the status quo	Stay
Not found frequently to occur	Rare
Provide with	Give
Undesirable	Bad
With respect to; in connection with; applicable to	For

- **Accentuate the positive.** Write in the positive, not in the negative. A "negative" means not only the word "not" and its variations but also negative words such as "prohibit," "harm," "disapprove" and "undo." Any negative word will complicate your sentence and make your reader process one more concept, i.e., work harder. Positive words are easier to understand. An extreme example is set forth in **Table 2.**

Table 2	
Too Many Negatives (Plus Some Other Problems)	**Simpler Version**
Unless payment in currency other than United States dollars is the subject of any prohibition, limitation, or restriction imposed by a governmental authority, other than a governmental authority that is not a United States governmental authority, Borrower shall repay the obligations only in any form of currency other than United States dollars and shall be prohibited from repaying the obligations in United States dollars, provided however that notwithstanding the foregoing such requirement shall not be applicable and shall be of no force or effect if and only to the extent that such governmental authority, other than a governmental authority that is not a United States governmental authority, has not been duly authorized to enact such prohibition, limitation or restriction, or if such prohibition, limitation or restriction is not applicable or has been rescinded, canceled, terminated or waived, or has expired, or is otherwise not effective.	Subject to the terms of any valid United States law or regulation, Borrower shall repay the loan only in foreign currency.

- *Use active words.* Dramatic, active words get more attention than boring, sleepy words. See **Table 3** for some examples.

FIGURE 12-1 (continued)

Table 3	
Boring and Sleepy	**Dramatic and Active**
What can be done *in light* of some problem or *with reference* to the problem	How a specific person *has cut costs this quarter to save the company from the losses it suffered last quarter* because of some problem
Someone is *able to implement a program to mitigate the adverse impacts of* something	Someone can *solve the problem* by making specific changes and adopting a specific solution
Someone is *experiencing an adverse situation*	A specific business is *watching its profits evaporate* from some problem

- *Avoid word piles.* Don't build word piles, long strings of words piled together to express one concept. For example, instead of referring to alternative real estate business-based strategies, describe how the company manages its real estate.

Don't Take Yourself Too Seriously

Write the way you speak. Use simple language. Have a little fun, but not too much.

- *Avoid pomp.* Don't think your writing has to sound pompous, high-flown or archaic if you want to communicate important ideas effectively. Often, it's just the opposite.
- *Strive for normal language.* If appropriate, use the same informal phrases that your readers would use. This way, your readers won't need to translate from your language into theirs. If borrowers and lenders would talk about a "spread" in calculating an interest rate, do you really have to call it an "applicable adjustment factor"? Why can't you just call it a spread?
- *Have a little bit of fun.* Let your words sing a little sometimes. Play with alliteration, repetition, rhythm. Two examples—the last two sentences. Another example: The big companies not only pay more, they hire more.

Kill Unnecessary Words

Less is more. The fewer words you use, the more effectively you can communicate, if you choose the right words. You are probably clouding the picture when you use:

- *Glue.* Delete "glue" words such as "in sum," "clearly," "in order to," "however" and so on.
- *Intensifiers.* Avoid intensifiers such as "very," "really," much or the use of italics or boldface type to emphasize your point. They make you sound uncertain. Instead, use the rhythm of the sentence to accent what's important. The power positions in a sentence are at the beginning and end.
- *Throat clearing.* Watch out for "throat-clearing" phrases at the beginning of your work—extra phrases that add nothing but words. Although they can sometimes help you get started, they're easy to delete in your first round of editing.
- *Adjectives.* Adjectives weaken your words. Use them sparingly. Adverbs weaken them even more. Compare two sentences, one with, the other without, an adverb. The one without the intensifier is more intense. (Try it!)
- *Fad words.* Avoid fad words such as "arguably," which seems to have become a substitute for "perhaps" but isn't really.
- *Consultant-speak.* Don't use mushy and vague words such as "significant," "ongoing," "current," "arisen," "trend," "key," "actualization," "parameter," "activate," "situation," "in order to," "access" and similar consultant-speak. These words add little value.
- *Numbers:* To best communicate numbers 10 or higher, express them as numerals, not words.

FIGURE 12-1 (continued)

Keep Your Readers Involved

Readers love war stories, real-life examples and practical tips based on the experiences of specific people, including you.

- *Provide specific examples.* Give your readers ideas, suggestions and points to "take away" and use. Don't write in generalities relating to the world as a whole. Write in specifics that apply directly to your readers' own experiences.
- *Paint word pictures.* Use metaphors. They let your readers paint pictures in their heads and see connections and similarities.
- *Use effective quotations.* If you quote words spoken by a real person, your readers will appreciate it. But don't make your quotations too long.
- *Observe the "rule of three."* In any list of suggestions, examples, guidelines or points to remember, your readers want to see at least three items.

Tips for the Writing Process

First let your ideas flow freely onto paper, without being self-conscious about "writing well." Then edit and revise. That second process—making your writing simple and direct—is hard work, but you have the comfort of knowing that the raw material is there.

- *Find solid blocks of time.* For a substantial piece of work, try to prevent disruptions and reserve a solid block of time. If you can get away with it, close the door, hold your calls and reread the whole piece top to bottom (or bottom to top) one last time.
- *Be attuned to the sound of words.* Listen to your words. How do they sound in your head? How do they sound when you read them out loud? Make them sound better. Even if you accurately express your message, if your reader can't easily understand it or stumbles because your words don't sound right, then you've done only part of your job.
- *Weigh brevity vs. clarity.* Brevity is good. Clarity is better.
- *Let it sit.* After you've written your first draft, put it aside for a while. Look at it again as if you've never seen it before. Read it quickly for an overview, as a casual reader might. Does it work? Does it hang together? Does it flow? Then read it slowly, line-by-line and word-by-word. Have you made each point as effectively as you can? Did you leave out anything important? Do your words fit together?
- *Take the reader's perspective.* When you read through your work again, ask yourself whether you can easily grasp it. But don't assume you will. Assume the opposite. Approach your writing as a reader might—expecting to be confused, overwhelmed and lost. Look for opportunities to get confused, overwhelmed and lost. Fix them. Make your work clearer than it needs to be.
- *Cut, cut, cut.* Don't fall in love with a sentence, a paragraph, an idea. Do you need it? If not, dump it. Edit and edit again.
- *Bend the rules.* Ignore any of the suggestions in this article when it makes sense to do so. Every principle has its exceptions. Always use your judgment.

Your Conclusion

You don't have to end with a grand conclusion and a bow. If you can gracefully circle back to the point you made at the beginning, you'll give your readers a sense of closure.

- *Summarize.* Summarize your message briefly but without restating too much of what you've already said.
- *Avoid formulas.* Avoid trite or formulaic endings.
- *Stop.* Finish your job. Don't leave your reader hanging

CHAPTER 12 SUMMARY

- The three steps of the writing process are:
  prewriting;
  writing; and
  editing and proofing.
- Before you start writing you should perform any necessary research and formulate a writing plan.
- It is a good idea to develop a flow chart and/or outline before you start writing.
- Good organization is essential for readability.
- Carefully organize words within sentences, sentences into paragraphs, and paragraphs into an entire document.
- Overall organization may be dictated by the traditional format of the type of document you are writing.
- Most paragraphs need topic sentences.
- Do not challenge your reader too often with unconventional word order.
- Use transitional language to provide a link between what you have just written and what you are going to write about.
- Use signposts to point the reader in the right direction and provide a framework for understanding the document.
- Paragraph and tabulate to enhance readability.
- Make sure you know how to eliminate the eight mechanical errors discussed at the end of the chapter.

CYBERLAW EXERCISES

1. The Lexis law school site (http://lawschool.lexis.com) includes information on developing effective writing skills.
2. The WashLaw Web site (http://www.washlaw.edu) allows you to access legal dictionaries. Go to the web site and click on "legal dictionaries."
3. For writing resources, including a legal dictionary and thesaurus, access http://www.legal.gsa.gov.
4. The Michigan Bar has published numerous articles concerning writing in plain language. To access the article, go to http://www.michbar.org, click on "Member Resources," "Publications," and then access "Plain Language Articles."

EXERCISES FOR CHAPTER 12

1. What do you do before you write?
2. How can you improve your prewriting step?
3. Take a document you have written and analyze it:
   a. How is the overall organization?
   b. Do you use topic sentences?
   c. Is the word order within sentences logical?
   d. Can you use more transitional language and signposts?
   e. Do you paragraph about the right amount, too often, or too infrequently?
   f. Can you make more use of tabulation?
   g. Are you prone to any of the eight mechanical errors discussed in the chapter?

In the following case, mechanical errors almost resulted in a conviction being reversed.

Jacob HENDERSON

v.

STATE of Mississippi.

Supreme Court of Mississippi.

Feb. 8, 1984.

445 So.2d 1364

ROBERTSON, Justice, for the Court:

This case presents the question whether the rules of English grammar are a part of the positive law of this state. If they are, Jacob Henderson's burglary conviction must surely be reversed, for the indictment in which he has been charged would receive an "F" from every English teacher in the land.

Though grammatically unintelligible, we find that the indictment is legally sufficient and affirm, knowing full well that our decision will receive of literate persons everywhere opprobrium as intense and widespread as it will be deserved.

The primary issue presented on this appeal regards the legal adequacy of the indictment under which Henderson has been tried, convicted [of business burglary in violation of Miss.Code Ann. S 97-17-33 (1972)] and sentenced. That indictment, in pertinent part, reads as follows:

The Grand Jurors for the State of Mississippi, . . . upon their oaths present: That Jacob Henderson . . . on the 15th day of May, A.D., 1982.

The store building there situated, the property of Metro Auto Painting, Inc., . . . in which store building was kept for sale or use valuable things, to- wit: goods, ware and merchandise unlawfully, feloniously and burglariously did break and enter, with intent the goods, wares and merchandise of said Metro Auto Painting then and there being in said store building unlawfully, feloniously and then and there being in said store building burglariously to take, steal and carry away; And

One (1) Polaroid Land Camera,

One (1) Realistic AM/FM Stereo Tuner

One (1) Westminster AM/FM radio

One (1) Metal Box and contents thereof, . . .

the property of the said Metro Auto Painting then and there being in said store building did then and there unlawfully, feloniously and burglariously take, steal and carry away the aforesaid property, he, the said Jacob Henderson, having been twice previously convicted of felonies, to-wit: . . . .

The remainder of the indictment charges Henderson with being a recidivist.

Henderson, no doubt offended, demurred. In support, he presented an expert witness, Ann Dreher, who had been a teacher of English for nine years. Ms. Dreher testified that, when read consistent with accepted rules of English grammar, the indictment did not charge Jacob Henderson with doing anything; rather it charged that goods, ware and merchandise broke and entered the paint store. The trial judge overruled the objection and the motion, but not without reservation. He stated:

> [T]his same objection has been made numerous times. It is one of Mr. Hailey's pets. [B]ut as far as I know no one has elected to appeal and I'm going to follow the decision whether it is grammatically

correct or not. I have repeatedly begged for six years or five years for the district attorney not to use this form. It is very poor English. It is impossible English . . . . In addition to being very poor English, it also charges him with the crime of larceny, which is not necessary to include in an indictment for burglary. I never did understand the reason for that. I again ask the district attorney not to use this form. It's archaic. Even Shakespeare could not understand the grammatical construction of this indictment. But the objection will be overruled. Maybe it will take a reversal on a case of a similar nature where there is a serious offense as this one is by the fact that he is indicted as a habitual to get the district attorney's attention.

In the trial court and on this appeal, Henderson insists that the meaning of the indictment may be obtained only within the strait jacket of accepted rules of grammatical construction of the English language. From this point of view, we are asked to examine the indictment and concentrate on the words " . . . unlawfully, feloniously and burglariously did break and enter . . . . " Who, we are asked, when the rules of good grammar are employed, did this alleged breaking and entering?

There are two possible answers (again, looking at the indictment as would an English teacher). "Goods, ware and merchandise" are the most obvious choice. Those nouns proximately precede the verb(s) "did break and enter" (separated only by the familiar string of adverbs "unlawfully, feloniously and burglariously"—the district attorney, like other lawyers, never uses one word when two or three will do just as well). Thus read, the indictment charges that Goods, ware and merchandise, not Jacob Henderson, burglarized the Maaco Paint Shop on May 15, 1982.

More properly, however, the words "Goods, ware and merchandise" are seen as the tail end of a largely unintelligible effort to describe something else: the store building. A perceptive English grammarian would conclude that it is "the store building there situated . . . . " which is charged with the burglary, for those words seem to constitute the subject of the nonsensical non-sentence we are charged to construe.

Even so, whether the indictment charges that "Goods, ware and merchandise" or "The store building there situated" . . . "unlawfully, feloniously and burglariously did break and enter . . . . " matters not to Jacob Henderson. His point is merely that the indictment does not charge that he did the breaking and entering.

Were this a Court of nine English teachers, Henderson no doubt would prevail.

The indictment does contain at the outset the charge "That Jacob Henderson . . . on the 15th day of May, A.D., 1982." We have another non-sentence. The unmistakable period after 1982 is used by astute defense counsel to nail down the point—that the indictment fails to charge that Jacob Henderson did anything on May 15, 1982. Again, we must concede that grammatically speaking counsel is correct. The period after 1982 grammatically precludes the possibility that the indictment charges that Jacob Henderson did break and enter. Either the words "did break and enter" would have to precede the period, or the name Jacob Henderson would have to appear following it. Neither is the case.

Recognizing that the period is important, the State argues that in reality the indictment consists of one long sentence, written albeit in legalese instead of English. The State argues that "the period grammatically disjoined the first part of the sentence from the second", conceding that we are indeed confronted with "a patently inappropriate period". This, of course, prompts Henderson to analogize the state's argument to Lady Macbeth's famous "Out damned spot! Out, I say!" [FN1] W. Shakespeare, Macbeth, Act V, sc. 1, line 38. The retort would be telling in the classroom or in a court of the literati. Alas, it has meager force in a court of law.

FN1. It cannot be gainsaid that all the perfumes of Arabia would not eviscerate the grammatical stench emanating from this indictment. Cf. W. Shakespeare, Macbeth, Act V, sc. 1, lines 56–57.

With no little temerity, we insist that the correct statement of the question before this Court is: Does the indictment conform to the requirements of Rule 2.05, Uniform Criminal Rules of Circuit Court Practice. That rule provides:

> Rule 2.05
>
> FORM OF THE INDICTMENT
>
> The indictment upon which the defendant is to be tried shall be a plain, concise and definite written statement of the essential facts constituting the offense charged and shall fully notify the defendant of the nature and cause of the accusation against him. Formal or technical words are not necessary in an indictment, if the offense can be substantially described without them.

The instant indictment, however inartfully worded, clearly charges Jacob Henderson with the crime of business burglary. It informs Henderson that the burglary is alleged to have occurred on May 15, 1982. The indictment names the business burglarized as Maaco Paint Shop operated by Metro Auto Painting, Inc. It charges that the crime occurred within the First Judicial District of Hinds County. Further, the indictment identifies the items of property said to have been stolen in the course of the burglary.

Viewing the indictment under Rule 2.05, we find it legally adequate. It provides Henderson with a "written statement of the essential facts constituting the offense charged" in language which is "plain, concise and definite", albeit grammatically atrocious. Beyond that, the indictment notified Henderson of "the nature and cause of the accusation against him".

Establishment of a literate bar is a worthy aspiration. 'Tis without doubt a consummation devoutly to be wished. Its achievement, however, must be relegated to means other than reversal of criminal convictions justly and lawfully secured.

AFFIRMED.

CHAPTER 13

TRANSMITTAL LETTER AND CLIENT OPINION LETTER

INTRODUCTION

Two types of letters an attorney often writes to clients are the transmittal letter and the client opinion letter. This chapter explains the purpose and use of the letters and their proper format. It also includes a sample transmittal letter and two sample client opinion letters. The first sample client opinion letter has been footnoted to provide you with writing tips. It should be helpful to refer to the footnotes when writing client opinion letters.

PURPOSE OF THE TRANSMITTAL LETTER

One of the most common types of letters written in the law office is the transmittal letter, the cover letter used when forwarding a document or other information to the client or to a third party. The purposes of the transmittal letter are to explain the information being transmitted, to instruct the recipient in any further action to be taken, and to cover any related matters. For example, the sample transmittal letter in figure 13-1 is the cover letter for an attorney-client retainer agreement (the contract between the attorney and client memorializing the employment relationship between client and attorney). The transmittal letter explains to the client what the attached document is, asks the client to sign the two copies of the agreement and return one copy to the attorney, and suggests that the client schedule an appointment with the attorney.

Another purpose of the transmittal letter is to document that the information attached to the letter was sent to the client and to document the instructions given. Usually the attorney places a copy of the transmittal letter and attachment in the client file. Later, the attorney can refer to the file copy to learn what was sent to the client. If the client loses the transmittal letter or the attachment, the material can be resent.

STYLE OF LETTERS

Clients judge the competency of the attorney by the way the attorney presents himself or herself. Clients may lose confidence in the attorney if they spot errors in letters received from the attorney. In contrast, a clear but knowledgeable letter will strengthen the attorney-client relationship and may cause the client to recommend the attorney to others.

The ten style tips listed on the next page are applicable to the transmittal letter and the client opinion letter. The list probably contains nothing new. Most of the suggestions listed are a matter of common sense. They are things that you would wish someone writing a letter to you would do.

FIGURE 13-1 Sample Transmittal Letter.

Florida Attorney
101 Main Street
Anytown, Anystate
May 4, 2000

Via facsimile number: (000) 000-0000
Confirmation number: (000) 000-1000

Esteemed Client
201 Oak Street
Anytown, Anystate

Re: Attorney-Client Retainer Agreement

Dear Ms. Client:

It was a pleasure to meet with you in my office yesterday to discuss your potential lawsuit against Rack & Ruin, Inc. Enclosed are two copies of the Attorney-Client Retainer Agreement we had discussed. The Agreement states the terms of our attorney-client relationship.

Please sign both copies of the Agreement on page 2 in the space provided for your signature and keep one copy of the Agreement for your files. Please return the second signed copy to me in the enclosed stamped self-addressed envelope.

I would like to meet with you again to discuss any paperwork you are able to find on Rack & Ruin, Inc. Once you have gathered any applicable information, please call my office and schedule an appointment with me.

Very truly yours,

Florida Attorney

Glance over the style tips and try to keep them in mind as you write your transmittal or client opinion letter. As you revise the letter, use the list as a checklist and make sure you have complied with it.

Style

Do

1. Use plain English.
2. Be precise and specific.
3. Write at a level of formality appropriate for the recipient.
4. Be consistent in maintaining the same level of formality throughout the letter.
5. Keep your sentences fairly short.
6. Break up each page of the text with paragraphs.
7. State the purpose of the letter early in the letter (preferably in the "Re:" or in the opening line of the body of the letter).
8. Proofread the letter.
9. Double check that any enclosures are included.
10. Note any special transmittal method other than regular mail (facsimile, certified mail, etc.).

Practice tips for writing letters

The following article, *How to write letters nonlawyers will read* (fig. 13-2) was written to help practicing attorneys improve their letter writing skills. The practice tips are equally applicable to the student learning to write transmittal letters and client opinion letters.

FIGURE 13-2 How to Write Letters Nonlawyers Will Read.

22–The Florida Bar News/September 1, 1999

Practice Tips

HOW TO WRITE LETTERS NONLAWYERS WILL READ

By James W. Martin

Why do people hate to get letters from lawyers? They carry bad news. They mean serious business. They're hard to understand. They use strange words. They carry the inherent threat of suit.

Why do lawyers send such letters? They mean serious business, and they intend to sue.

But must they use those ancient, strange words and be so hard to understand, or can lawyers express serious business and imminent suit using words everyone knows?

Whether writing a demand letter to a contract breacher, an advice letter to a client, or a cover letter to a court clerk, the letter fails if the person receiving it cannot understand what it says.

All of these letters have one thing in common: They are not great literature. They will not be read in a hundred years and analyzed for their wit, charm or flowery words. With any luck they will be read just once by a few people, followed quickly by their intended result, whether that be compliance, understanding or agreement.

Lawyers Are Letter Factories

Lawyers write many, many letters. An average for me might be five letters a day. This includes advice letters, cover letters, demand letters, all sorts of letters. Some days have more, some have less, but five is a fairly conservative average, I would think. Five letters a day for five days a week for 50 weeks a year is 1,250 letters a year. This is my 25th year in practice, so it is quite conceivable that I have written 31,250 letters so far.

Why do lawyers write so many letters? A primary reason lies within the ethics of our profession. Florida Bar Rules of Professional Conduct Rule 4-1.4 says:

"A lawyer shall keep a client reasonably informed about the status of a matter and promptly comply with reasonable requests for information."

"A lawyer shall explain a matter to the extent reasonably necessary to permit the client to make informed decisions regarding the representation."

While clients can be kept informed and given explanations orally, lawyers certainly know the value of the printed word over the spoken word: It is not as easily forgotten or misunderstood. Letters also create a record of advice given, which is useful to both the lawyer and the client. That is why letters are the preferred method of keeping clients informed and giving clients explanations.

Some Things to Do before Writing

Before you start writing the letter it makes sense to do some preliminary background work.

- Find a letter form or find a similar letter you have sent in the past.
- Review prior letters to this recipient. In a busy world, it is easy to forget. Review prior letters to remind yourself where you are in the work process, what has already been said, and what remains to be said. This will give your letter direction and purpose.
- Do not send a letter to another lawyer's client without that lawyer's consent. Before sending the letter, find out if the nonlawyer is represented by someone else. Start by asking your client. Florida Bar Rules of Professional Conduct Rule 4-4.2 says:

"In representing a client, a lawyer shall not communicate about the subject of the representation with a person the lawyer knows to be represented by another lawyer in the matter, unless the lawyer has the consent of the other lawyer."

- Outline your thoughts in a checklist. Before turning on your computer or dictating machine, pull out a yellow pad and jot down the main points for your letter. List what you want the letter to say. Write the points in any order; write them as they

FIGURE 13-2 (continued)

come into your mind. You can rearrange them when you write the letter. Right now you're just making a checklist for writing the letter.

• Keep the legal pad close at hand. When you run out of ideas for the checklist, put the pad at the side of your desk. New ideas always spring forth when writing. Jot these down on the pad as you write the letter; they are easily forgotten.

Simple Stuff That Will Make You Look Dumb if It's Wrong

Letters begin with boring things like the date and recipient's name and address, but if any of these are missing or wrong the letter writer will look pretty careless, to say the least. So be careful when starting the letter, and you can even include some extra things that will make the letter even better than the regular letters the recipient receives.

• Date your letter. Date your letter the day you write it, and send it the same day. Undated letters are difficult to reply to. I usually reply to them by saying, "This is in reply to your undated letter that I received in the mail on 24 June 1999."

Consider using the international dating convention of day-month-year rather than the U.S. convention of month-day-year. As reported in the 1 June 1999 *Wall Street Journal:*

"The quirky U.S. style of date-writing is giving way to the day-first standard used by most of the world."

Both the MLA style guide and the Chicago Manual of Style support the day-first format. "You get rid of the comma that way," says Joseph Gibaldi, director of book acquisition for the MLA in New York.

If you are sending a fax or email, then type the time next to the date. While letters "cross in the mail" in days, faxes and emails "cross in the wires" in hours and minutes.

• Remind your client to preserve attorney-client confidentiality. Sometimes clients show your letters to others without realizing they can lose the attorney-client privilege of that communication. Add this phrase at the top of the letter to remind them not to do this:

CONFIDENTIAL ATTORNEY-CLIENT COMMUNICATION. DO NOT COPY OR DISCLOSE TO ANYONE ELSE.

If the letter is written during or in anticipation of litigation, the following phrase can be used:

CONFIDENTIAL ATTORNEY-CLIENT COMMUNICATION AND WORK PRODUCT. DO NOT COPY OR DISCLOSE TO ANYONE ELSE.

• Be sure to use the recipient's correct legal name and address. Your letter may be relied upon for its accuracy, so be accurate. Verification of names can be obtained from the public records, the phone book, or the Florida Division of Corporations website at http://ccfcorp.dos.state.fl.us/ index.html. And when it comes to middle initials, never rely on your memory or guess at it because most of the time you'll be wrong.

• Indicate the method of delivery if other than mail. If being faxed, include the fax number and telephone number. If being sent by FedEx, state whether it is by overnight or second day. If being sent by email, state the email address. This will make it easy for your staff person to send it to the correct place, and it will document for your file how it was sent.

• Include a fax notice. When sending by fax, include a notice in case it is sent to the wrong number. Here is the notice I use at the top of my letterhead when sending a fax:

NOTICE: This is privileged and confidential and intended only for the person named below. If you are not that person, then any use, dissemination, distribution or copying of this is strictly prohibited, and you are requested to notify us immediately by calling or faxing us collect at the numbers above.

Date Sent ______ Time Sent ______ Number of Pages ______ Person Who Conf'd Receipt ______

After sending a fax, call the recipient to confirm receipt and write that person's name in the space provided. Never rely on the fax machine itself to confirm a fax transmission; fax machines do not yet have the credibility of a human witness.

FIGURE 13-2 (continued)

The Corpus of the Litterae

The body of the letter is why you are writing it. You succeed by leaving the reader with full knowledge of why you wrote the letter and what it means. You fail by leaving the reader dumbfounded and clueless as to why you sent such a letter. While most letters fall somewhere in between these two extremes, following these suggestions will keep your letters on the successful end of the scale.

•Identify your client. It is important to let others know who is your client at the earliest opportunity. This accomplishes a great deal. First, it tells the reader that your client has a lawyer. This makes your client happy because most clients want the world to know they have a lawyer. Second, it tells the reader that you are not the reader's lawyer. This makes your malpractice carrier happy because it's one less person who's going to sue you claiming they thought you were representing them when, in fact, you were not.

Identifying your client is an ethical concern, as well. Florida Bar Rules of Professional Conduct Rule 4-4.3 says:

"In dealing on behalf of a client with a person who is not represented by counsel, a lawyer shall not state or imply that the lawyer is disinterested."

Therefore, the first time you write someone a letter, the letter should open with the following sentence: "I represent _____." After that, every time you write another letter reconfirm who you represent by referring to your client by name and as "my client."

• State the purpose of the letter. Why leave the reader guessing? Go ahead and say right up front why you are writing the letter. Here are some opening sentences:

"The purpose of this letter is to ______."

"This letter is to inform you that ______."

"My client has instructed me to ______."

"This is to confirm that ______."

"This confirms our phone conversation today in which ______."

• If there are any enclosures, list them first. Listing enclosures at the beginning of the letter will make it easier for your staff to assemble them and for the reader to check to be sure all was received. This is much easier than having to read an entire, perhaps lengthy, letter to ascertain what are the enclosures.

The enclosures should be described with specificity so that there is later no question as to what was enclosed. At a minimum, the title and date of each document should be listed. If the document was recorded, then the recording information should be included. Whether the document is an original or a copy should also be specified. The following is an example:

"Enclosed are the following documents from your closing held on __/__/1999 in which you purchased the home at ______, St. Petersburg, Florida, from ______:

1. Warranty Deed dated __/__/ 1999 and recorded on ___/___/1999 at O.R. Book ___, Page ___, ______, County, Florida (original)
2. Title Insurance Policy issued on ___/___/1999 by ______ on ______ as policy number ______ (original)
3. HUD-1 Settlement Statement dated ___/___/1999 (original)"

• Outline the letter as separately numbered paragraphs. Each paragraph of the letter should state a separate thought, comment, point or concept. No paragraph should be longer than four or five short sentences. If the paragraph is longer, then separate it into subparagraphs. The paragraphs should flow in logical, organized fashion. It is not necessary to write them all at once; you can write them as you think of them. Try to group related concepts in the same paragraphs or in adjacent paragraphs. See the Appendix for sample letters.

• Give each paragraph a title and underline that title. Think of this as the headline for a newspaper article. This makes it easy for the reader to scan the letter and choose how to more fully read and digest its contents. This also makes it easier for you later when you see the letter in your file and try to remember why you wrote it.

FIGURE 13-2 (continued)

• Complete each paragraph by writing what applies to that paragraph. This is simple. You learned this in elementary school. Just explain in words what you want to say about each concept or comment you placed in your outline.

• If this is a letter to your client, include ideas that occur to you as you write. Many ideas will occur to you as you write: things that could go wrong with a business deal, things that might happen in the future, things that happened in the past, ways to structure things better. Write these in your letter even if they are not strictly legal advice. Florida Bar Rules of Professional Conduct Rule 4-2.1 says:

"In rendering advice, a lawyer may refer not only to law but to other considerations such as moral, economic, social, and political factors that may be relevant to the client's situation."

• If this is a letter to a nonclient, do not offer any advice. The letter should accomplish its purpose of providing information, making a demand, etc., without giving legal advice to the recipient. The comment to Florida Bar Rules of Professional Conduct Rule 4-4.3 says:

"During the course of a lawyer's representation of a client, the lawyer should not give advice to an unrepresented person other than the advice to obtain counsel."

• State your assumptions. Whether or not this is an opinion letter, set forth the factual assumptions and statutes you rely upon in giving your opinion or advice. It is customary for opinion letters to recite the facts upon which the opinion is based and the statutes and case law, as well. This is something that every letter providing advice or opinion can include in order to avoid future misunderstanding. Every opinion and all advice is predicated upon facts and law. Stating the assumed facts and applicable law in the letter merely makes known to the reader what the writer understands to be true. This then places an obligation on the reader to inform the writer if any of the assumed facts is not accurate, which might change the opinion or advice.

• Place instructions to clients in bold type. This will make it easier for the client to follow up on your letter and do as advised.

• Close the letter with a final paragraph. The last paragraph will be one of the following:

A. Summary of advice: "To summarize, I advise that you . . ."

B. To do list: "Therefore, please do the following: . . ."

C. Demand: "Therefore, my client demands that you immediately cease and desist . . ."

D. Simple close: "If you have any questions, please call me."

Playing with the Words

Why does it take lawyers so long to write letters? Because we play with the words. We write, rewrite, move around, delete, cut and paste the words over and over and over again until we are happy with the way it sounds. That's the art of legal writing. It's like Picasso painting over the same canvas again and again, transforming it from one painting to another and then to another until finally he is satisfied with the result. Not always 100% satisfied, but good enough for it to go out the door and into the world. That's why writing is an art. And that's also why more copies of WordPerfect were sold to lawyers than any other industry. So here are some things to play with.

• Write in short sentences. Short sentences are easier to understand than long ones. "Short, crisp sentences in a language accessible to lay people." This is the Associated Press's description of the writing style of the late Lord Alfred Thompson Denning, who was one of Britain's longest-serving appeals judges when he died at the age of 100 in March 1999. The same style Lord Denning used in writing appellate opinions should be used in writing letters to nonlawyers.

• It's okay to use jargon; just explain it. We hear all the time that lawyers use too much jargon. But some concepts need the jargon. Like nunc pro tunc (which means now for then and is a wonderful concept that recognizes the inherent power of a court to correct its records by entering an order effective as of a prior date) and per stirpes (which means through representation and indicates a manner of taking title from a decedent).

FIGURE 13-2 (continued)

Every profession has its jargon. That's not bad. It's part of our identity. It's a form of shorthand. It's a form of common knowledge among professionals. If my physician failed to use jargon in describing a medical condition, I would probably wonder if I had the right expert. A good professional not only knows the jargon, but can also explain it to a layman. Therefore, show your expertise. Use the jargon when necessary, but explain it when you use it.

- Repeat yourself only when repetition is necessary to improve clarity or to emphasize a point. Ambiguity can be created by saying the same thing more than once; it is almost impossible to say it twice without creating ambiguity.
- When explaining a difficult concept, describe it from three directions. The only time repetition is helpful is when explaining a difficult concept. Each time you explain it you can make it a little more clear if you describe it from a different direction, perspective or point of view.
- Write in active tense, rather than passive. Active tense is interesting; passive is boring. Active tense sentences are shorter and use words more efficiently, and their meaning is more apparent.
- Watch where you place modifiers. When adding a modifier like "active" before a compound of nouns like "termites and organisms," be sure to clarify whether you intend the modifier to apply to both nouns or just the first one. If you intend it to apply to both, use parallel construction and write the modifier in front of each noun. If you intend it to apply to just one noun, place that one noun at the end of the list and the modifier directly in front of it.
- Write numbers as both words and numerals: ten (10). This will reduce the chance for errors. The Associated Press reported on 18 June 1999, that a comma in the wrong place of a sales contract cost Lockheed Martin Corp. $70 million: "An international contract for the U.S.-based aerospace group's C-130J Hercules had the comma misplaced by one decimal point in the equation that adjusted the sales price for changes to the inflation rate." Perhaps writing out the number would have saved the day.
- When you write "including" consider adding "but not limited to." Unless you intend the list to be all-inclusive, you had better clarify your intent that it is merely an example.
- Don't be creative with words. Legal letter writing is not creative writing and is not meant to provoke reflective thoughts or controversies about nuances of meaning. Legal writing is clear, direct and precise. Therefore, use common words and common meanings.
- Be consistent in using words. If you refer to the subject matter of a sales contract as "goods" use that term throughout the letter; do not alternately call them "goods" and "items." Maintaining consistency is more important than avoiding repetition.
- Be consistent in grammar and punctuation. Don't rely on the rules of grammar. The rules of grammar that you learned in school are not universal. The readers of your letter may have learned different rules. Write the letter so that no matter what rules they learned the letter is clear and unambiguous.

Be consistent in your use of grammar. Be aware of such things as where you put ending quote marks, whether you place commas after years and states, and similar variations in style. Many rules of grammar are a matter of choice, but your choice should be internally consistent within the letter.

- Define a word by capitalizing it and putting it in quotes. Capitalizing a word indicates that you intend it to have a special meaning. The following is a sample clause for defining a term:

"Wherever used in this letter, the word "Goods" shall mean the goods that _____ agreed to purchase from _____ under the Contract."

- Define words when first used. Instead of writing a section of definitions at the beginning or end of a long letter, consider defining terms and concepts as they appear in the letter. This will make it easier for the reader to follow.

FIGURE 13-2 (continued)

• Avoid needless and flowery words. Think of elementary school when you had to reduce fractions to the "lowest common denominator." That's what good writing is all about. A letter written for the lowest common denominator is understood by every reader. Eliminate needless words. Avoid flowery words.

• Be direct and frank. There is no sense beating around the bush in legal letter writing. Just say what you mean. If you leave the reader wondering what you mean, your letter will only stir the imagination instead of prompting some action.

• Study "The Elements of Style." The full text of the 1918 classic by William Strunk is now available on Columbia's Internet site at http://www.columbia.edu/acis/bartleby/strunk. This means that even if you left your copy on your bedstand at home, you can quickly go online and search the full text of "The Elements of Style," where you will find these simple rules among others (as you can see, I am a old student of this text):

"Make the paragraph the unit of composition: one paragraph to each topic.

"As a rule, begin each paragraph with a topic sentence; end it in conformity with the beginning.

"Use the active voice.

"Put statements in positive form.

"Omit needless words.

"Avoid a succession of loose sentences.

"Express coordinate ideas in similar form.

"Keep related words together.

"In summaries, keep to one tense.

"Place the emphatic words of a sentence at the end."

Cleaning Up

Now that you have the letter written, it's time to do some cleanup work before you hit the send button.

• Let your secretary or paralegal read it. Not only will your staff frequently find spelling and grammar errors missed by your word processor's spell checker, but they will find inconsistencies and confusing areas that you missed when drafting.

• Number every page of the letter, and staple the letter. If the letter is more than one page long, then it is important to number the pages because they will invariably get out of order. Place the following at the top left corner of each page after the first:

Recipient's name _____
Date _____
Page _____

• Sign the letter in blue ink, not black ink. This will make it easier to differentiate the signed original letter from photocopies, and it will make it more difficult for someone to change your letter after you send it.

Computerized Letter Writing Tips

My wife Cathy said I have to put this way at the end here because this article is about letter writing and not computers. She thinks I love wrestling with computers as much as I love playing with words. She's right. In my first three drafts this section was on page one.

But I think anyone who likes to play with words should play with them on a computer. That's where they really dance. And when you've written 31,250 letters, as my earlier calculations indicate I may have written in my practice so far, a fourth of them before I started writing letters on computer in 1980, you really begin to appreciate the ability to cut and paste text from prior letters. So here are my tips for anyone still around willing to listen:

• Write your own letters on a computer. If you have not yet joined the computer revolution, do it now. Get a computer for no other reason than writing letters. You will never again find yourself explaining to your client why the letter you dictated three days ago has not been mailed yet.

FIGURE 13-2 (continued)

• Get Microsoft Word or Corel WordPerfect. You will need good word processing software. The latest versions are Microsoft Word 2000 and Corel WordPerfect 2000. I have both, but I still use Wordperfect 5.1 for DOS for 99% of my work. My fingers know the special codes so well that it's faster for me to write in this older program. I can still convert the file format to any other one using one of the new 2000 programs which can read the old 5.1 files.

• Get voice recognition software if you cannot type. If you never learned to touch type, there is finally reliable software to do it for you. Voice recognition software allows you to dictate directly to your computer. The software is so good that WordPerfect 2000 is sold in a bundle with one brand. You can also purchase this software with an optional hand-held recorder so that you can dictate the old-fashioned way and then transfer it to your computer to transcribe. The two most-advertised brands of software are Dragon Naturally Speaking and L&H VoiceXpress.

• Set up a separate directory for each client. If you create a directory (folder) on your computer for every client, you can keep all letters, documents and work for that client in one easy-to-find place, just like your paper file folder. The client's last name can be used as the directory name. Thus, all letters, wills, contracts, spreadsheets, etc., for John Doe can be kept on your computer's directory named DOE.

• Keep all letters in one computer file. Just as you keep copies of all letters in a paper file folder, you should keep copies of all letters on your computer in the directory for that client. The easiest way to do this is not to start a separate computer file for each letter sent to someone. Instead you just add the new letter to the existing computer file containing other letters to that person. I find that it works best to add new letters at the top of old letters, rather than at the bottom. Then your computer file is like a paper folder since new letters are added at the top where you see them first. This is easy to do on your computer: You just start a new page at the top of the existing letter and write the new letter there.

• Name letters to clients LETTERCL and name letters to non-clients with the recipient's last name. If you name the file with the recipient's last name, you can easily find the letter later when you want to read it on your computer without having to pull the file. For example, a letter to non-client Mary Smith would be given the computer file name SMITH. The only exception is that I name all letters to my clients LETTERCL rather than the client's last name because their computer directory is already named their last name. I also do this because it saves me time finding the file if the client is a corporation or there are multiple clients.

• Copy text from prior letters. More than half the letters you write are not first letters to a recipient, but are follow-up letters that either remind the recipient of pending work to be done or continue discussion of a matter previously opened. The other half have at least one thing in common: the letter's opening with the recipient's name and address and the closing with your name. There is no need to retype all of this text in your new letter. Using block and copy (cut and paste) commands you can easily copy the recipient's name and address and usable text from a prior letter into your new letter. You can then modify that text to fit the current message. I even have macros that do the repetitive stuff for me.

• Print the envelope from the letter. Before we had a computer, we had a lot of errors in typing envelopes and mailing labels. Then when a client called to tell us the error, we would look at the letter and tell them we sent it to the correct address, only to be told that the envelope had a different address. This can easily be avoided by using the envelope printing features of word processing software, which takes the address right off the letter so that you know the letter and envelope will have the same address.

• Back up as you write. As wonderful as computers are, they are still powered by electricity, and when it goes off, the words disappear from the screen and if they have not been saved they disappear forever. The first time you lose an hour of work you get a backup device of some type. The second time you lose an hour of work you actually start to use the backup device. My recommendation for backing up is this:

FIGURE 13-2 (continued)

A. Hit the save button frequently while writing the letter.
B. If the letter is long, print hard copies of the letter frequently while writing it.
C. Copy all your work to a backup device at the end of every day.

Conclusion

Letters serve many purposes: advising clients, seeking compliance, sending documents, obtaining information. All letters benefit from clear writing and simple organization. Lawyers who write direct and concise letters to nonlawyers are more likely to achieve successful results.

Writing letters is no different from other lawyering skills. The demand letter that the recipient cannot understand is no more effective than a shouting match. If you want a shouting match, then by all means write long letters with big words that no one understands. But if compliance is what you really want, then writing a letter that the recipient understands is really the order of the day.

James W. Martin has practiced in St. Petersburg since graduating from Stetson University College of Law in 1974. Among his publications are West Publishing Company's *FLORIDA LEGAL FORMS* volumes on real estate, business organizations and specialized forms. This article was adapted from Mr. Martin's presentation to the 1999 Florida Bar Annual Meeting Seminar "Effective and Ethical: Keys to Better Writing" sponsored by The Florida Bar *Journal* and *News* Editorial Board.

PURPOSE OF THE CLIENT OPINION LETTER

From time to time, a client will ask an attorney a question that requires the attorney to do some research before giving the client the answer. After the attorney researches the question, the attorney may give the client the answer orally or in writing. The letter the attorney writes to the client explaining the answer is usually referred to as a client opinion letter because it gives the client the attorney's legal opinion. Another alternative is to tell the client the answer and follow up the conversation with a client opinion letter. The client opinion letter repeats what the client was told in the conversation and would add any additional information suggested by the conversation.

Generally, it is wise for the attorney to give the answer to the client's question in a client opinion letter. The client can reread the opinion letter as many times as necessary and refer to it later. Putting the opinion in writing means that the client will more likely understand the opinion as it was stated by the attorney. The client opinion letter usually states that the opinion it contains is limited by the facts stated in the letter and by the law as of the date of the letter. This language, and the fact that the opinion is in writing, protect the attorney to the extent possible from having the attorney's advice misconstrued or applied in the future to a different set of facts. An attorney might decide not to put the attorney's opinion in writing if the subject matter of the attorney's opinion is confidential. Another reason not to put the opinion in writing is that a written opinion may be discoverable in litigation.

The main purpose of the client opinion letter is to answer the client's question, but the opinion letter does not just contain the answer. A good client opinion letter also contains a statement of the facts on which the opinion was based, an explanation of applicable law, and an explanation of how the law applies to the facts. The tone of the client opinion letter is usually objective, rather than persuasive, because it explains the law, whether favorable or unfavorable to the client. There is no need to be persuasive and argue the client's position, because the letter is directed to the client.

Chapter 16, which discusses the law office memo, may sound very similar to what you read in this chapter. The reason is that both a client opinion letter and the office memo require the same type of research and analysis to answer a legal question or problem. The client opinion letter and the office memo differ in content because the audience is different. Unless the client is sophisticated, the client opinion letter should be stated in lay terms and include few quotations or citations. (If the client is sophisticated, he or she may be sent the office memo itself rather than a separate client opinion letter.) Another difference is format. A client opinion letter more closely resembles a business letter, although it may have internal headings similar to those of a law office memo.

FORMAT OF THE CLIENT OPINION LETTER

Although there is no one format for client opinion letters, the format given in this chapter is fairly standard. As you read the explanation in this chapter, compare it with the sample client opinion letters in figures 13-3 and 13-4.

Heading

The heading contains the name and address of the attorney, the date, the name and address of the client, and the subject matter (the "re"). The date is important because, unless otherwise stated in the letter, it is assumed that the opinion is based on the law current through the date of the letter. For ease of reading and reference, the "re" will identify the subject matter of the letter with a reasonable amount of detail.

Opening

The opening paragraph sets the stage. It typically reminds the client of the context of the client's question and reiterates the client's question. This is a good place to state any limitations on the opinion contained in the letter. The attorney typically states that the opinion is limited to the facts contained in the letter and the law of the state (or federal law, if federal law applies) as of the date of the letter. It is advisable to state that the opinion may be different given different facts or a different date.

Facts

The facts significant to the opinion are stated objectively in this section. If important facts are not known, this should be stated. It is wise to ask the client to review the facts and advise the attorney of any necessary additions or changes.

Answer

The answer section explains the answer to the client's question, with any necessary detail and clarification.

Explanation

In the explanation section, the attorney explains the law in lay terms and then explains how the law applies to the facts. The challenge is to support the answer with the law, yet explain it in a way the client can understand. Generally, the attorney would not use quotations or citations in this section, but they may be included if the client is sophisticated. Even if the client is not sophisticated, the opinion may quote the relevant portion of an important statute or case. If a source is quoted or a case is referred to specifically, the citation should be given. The subject matter content and the way it is presented must be geared to the particular client.

Closing

The closing is no different from the closing in any other business letter. The attorney may want to tell the client what action needs to be taken and may direct the client to contact the attorney with any further questions concerning the opinion.

SAMPLE CLIENT OPINION LETTERS

Introduction

This section contains two sample client opinion letters. The first sample letter has been footnoted to provide you with writing tips. Normally, the client opinion letter includes no footnotes; the footnotes in the first sample client opinion letter should not be considered part of the letter.

The sample client opinion letter in figure 13-3 was written to a mother whose son had been arrested for possession of cocaine. The cocaine was found in the car trunk when the son's car was stopped on Interstate 95 in Florida. The son is originally from Florida but had been attending an out-of-state university. Prior to the arrest, the son had returned to Florida with a friend to visit his mother and to enjoy spring break. The mother hired the attorney to represent the son and has asked the attorney whether the cocaine found can be suppressed.

The second sample client opinion letter in figure 13-4 was written to a client who had been arrested for possession of methamphetamines. The client was a passenger in a car stopped on the interstate. The

FIGURE 13-3 First Client Opinion Letter.

Florida Attorney
Main Street
Anytown, Florida
April 6, 2000

Ms. Mom Campbell
Oak Street
Anytown, Florida

Re: Whether cocaine found in the Campbell car when it was stopped on I-95 may be suppressed.

Dear Ms. Mom Campbell:

You hired me to represent your son who had been arrested for possession of cocaine on April 1, 2000. On April 3, 2000 I met with you and with your son and you asked me whether the cocaine could be suppressed. This opinion is limited to the facts contained in the facts section of this letter and to federal law as of the date of this letter and is solely for your benefit and for the benefit of your son.[1]

Facts

The following facts were gathered from the July 3, 2000 interview with you and Mike Campbell, your son, and a review of the police report. Please contact me or have your son contact me if there are any inaccuracies to be corrected or any additions to be made.[2]

Your son and his best friend, John Wright, were driving north on I-95 returning from spring break in Florida, when they were stopped by members of a drug task force made up of Volusia County Sheriff officers and federal drug enforcement agents. The agents requested permission to search the car. When your son refused consent, the agents brought in a drug dog that alerted to the trunk of the car. The agents then claimed that the dog's actions gave them probable cause to search the trunk and gave your son the choice of either opening the trunk or waiting until the agents obtained a search warrant. After your son opened the trunk, the agents found two kilograms of cocaine in a brown paper bag. Your son and Wright were arrested and charged with possession with intent to distribute cocaine.

The agents claimed they stopped your son's car because your son was following the car in front of him too closely and because the following facts fit a drug courier profile used by the Volusia County Sheriff officers:

1. The car was a large late model;
2. The car had out-of-state tags;
3. The car was being driven cautiously at the speed limit;
4. The car was being driven on a known drug corridor, I-95;
5. There were two passengers in the car;
6. The passengers were in their twenties;
7. The car was being driven in the early evening; and
8. The passengers were dressed casually.[3]

---

[1]This sentence protects the attorney by naming the persons who can rely on the opinion. Perhaps the attorney was trying to avoid having the other defendant (the son's best friend) rely on the letter, by stating that the letter's benefit is limited to the mother and son. This language is usually used when third parties not represented by the attorney may try to rely on the opinion.

[2]This language protects the attorney by requesting that both mother and son verify that the facts are accurate. The prior sentence identifies the source of the attorney's information.

[3]When you have a list of items, make it easier for your reader to skim down the list by tabulating. Number each item, follow each item except for the last one by a semi-colon, and place the word "and" after the semi-colon following the next-to-last item. Make sure that you follow parallel construction for all items. If you are unsure what *parallel construction* means, refer to Appendix D.

FIGURE 13-3 (continued)

Although not listed by the agents, your son and Wright believe the real reason they were stopped is because they are Afro-Americans.

Answer

The court should suppress the cocaine if it decides that your son did not commit a traffic violation. In opposition to the motion to suppress, the government will likely make two arguments.

One argument is that the agents had reasonable suspicion that your son's car contained illegal drugs. They may claim that their reasonable suspicion was based on a drug courier profile. The government should lose this argument because of the similarity between the facts in your son's case and another case. In the other case involving a car stop based on a drug courier profile, the court granted the defendant's motion to suppress the illegal drugs found because the stop violated the defendant's constitutional rights to be free from unreasonable search and seizure.

The second argument is that the agents had probable cause to stop your son's car for following too closely. In a 1996 case, the United States Supreme Court decided that a police officer may stop a car for any type of traffic violation, no matter how minor. This means that the traffic stop is valid so long as there is a technical violation; it does not matter if the reason the agents gave was a pretext for a stop based on race. The Court stated that a challenge to a stop allegedly based on race should be brought under the Equal Protection Clause and not under the Fourth Amendment. The Court did not explain that an Equal Protection Clause challenge is difficult to prove because it requires evidence of intentional discrimination.

The applicable Florida motor vehicle statute prohibits a vehicle from following another vehicle "more closely than is reasonable and prudent, having due regard for the speed of such vehicles and the traffic upon, and the condition of, the highway." Unfortunately, there is no simple test to determine if your son violated the statute. The court will have to determine from any evidence presented whether the distance at which your son was following the car in front of him was reasonable and prudent.

The court should grant the motion to suppress if we can convince the judge that your son was following the car at an appropriate distance; the cocaine would not have been found had the car not been stopped.

Explanation of the government's first argument

The Fourth Amendment to the United States Constitution protects your son "against unreasonable searches and seizures." The Fourth Amendment does not prohibit all searches and seizures—just *unreasonable* searches and seizures. The courts have allowed officers to stop cars on the highway to investigate a "reasonable suspicion" of illegal drug activity. In a case involving facts almost identical to those in your son's case, the court found that a highway stop was not reasonable under the Fourth Amendment even though the stop was made based on a drug courier profile. *United States v. Smith*, 799 F.2d 704, 712 (11th Cir. 1986).[4] (This was the drug courier profile case referred to in the answer section above.)

---

[4]"704" is the first page of *Smith* and "712" is the page on which the finding of the court referred to in the preceding sentence is located. As a courtesy to the reader, a page reference should be given when specific material from a case is referred to even if the material is not directly quoted.

The two types of sentences in legal writing are textual sentences and citation sentences. A **textual sentence** is the type of sentence you have been writing all your life. It is a complete grammatical sentence with a subject and a verb. A **citation sentence** contains only citations. A **string citation** is a citation sentence with more than one citation. In a string citation, the citations should be separated by semicolons.

A sentence is more difficult to read when it contains a full case citation, especially if the citation is long. To avoid including a full citation in a textual sentence, you can refer to a case in very general terms or refer to a legal principle from a case and give the full citation to the case in a citation sentence following the textual sentence.

FIGURE 13-3 (continued)

You will probably be interested to know more about *Smith* because the facts in that case are nearly identical to the facts in your son's case. This letter will first give you the facts from *Smith* and then compare them to the facts from your son's case.

Smith

One night in June of 1985, Trooper Robert Vogel, a Florida Highway Patrol trooper, and a DEA agent were observing cars traveling in the northbound lanes of I-95. They hoped to intercept drug couriers. When Smith's car passed through the arc of the patrol car headlights, Vogel noticed the following factors that matched his drug courier profile:

1. The car was traveling at 3:00 a.m.;
2. The car was a 1985 Mercury, a large late model car;
3. The car had out-of state tags;
4. There were two occupants of the car who were around 30; and
5. The driver was driving cautiously and did not look at the patrol car as the Mercury passed through the arc of the patrol car headlights.

Id. at 705–06.[5]

The above drug courier profile is almost identical to the profile used by the officers in your son's case.[6] In both *Smith* and your son's case the cars were traveling after dark, the cars were large late models with out-of-state tags, the cars were being driven "cautiously," and each car contained two passengers in their twenties or thirties. The differences between the two profiles are very minor. Your son and Wright were dressed casually while it is not known how Smith and Swindell were dressed. Smith and Swindell did not look at Vogel as they passed. It is not known whether your son and Wright looked in the agents' direction as your son drove past. Your son and Wright claim that race was a factor in their stop even though it was not listed as such by the agents. Smith and Swindell's race is unknown.[7]

In *Smith*, Vogel followed the Mercury for a mile and a half and noticed that the Mercury "wove" several times, once as much as six inches into the emergency lane. Vogel pulled Smith over. When a drug dog alerted on the car, a DEA agent searched the trunk and discovered one kilogram of cocaine. Smith and his passenger, Swindell, were arrested and were charged with conspiracy to possess cocaine with the intent to distribute it. *Id.* at 706. On appeal, the *Smith* court held that the stop of Smith's car vio-

---

[5]When you need to cite a block quote or other material set off from the rest of the text, as is the tabulation here, bring the citation back to the left margin. "*Id.*" is used here because "*id.*" refers back to the immediately preceding citation, *Smith*. When citing inclusive pages with three or more digits, drop all but the last two digits of the second number and place a hyphen between the numbers.

[6]This is an example of a topic sentence. A **topic sentence** contains one main idea summarizing the rest of the paragraph, with the rest of the paragraph developing the idea presented in the topic sentence. Most paragraphs should have topic sentences. The typical location of a topic sentence is the first sentence in the paragraph. Sometimes the topic sentence is the last sentence in the paragraph and pulls together the rest of the paragraph. Some paragraphs, typically narrative paragraphs, do not have a topic sentence.

If a paragraph sounds disjointed or unorganized, try it pulling together using a topic sentence. If a topic sentence does not help, think about breaking the paragraph up into more than one paragraph.

[7]This paragraph applies the facts in *Smith* to the facts in *Campbell*. Applying facts from one case to another case involves explaining the similarities and differences between the two sets of facts. Instead of simply stating that the facts from the two cases are very similar, the paragraph specifically states which facts are the same. Sometimes, in the application, you need to explain in what way the facts are similar if they are not identical.

You can either apply the *Smith* facts to *Campbell* as done here or you can wait until you have thoroughly discussed *Smith*. When you prepare your outline prior to starting to write the office memo, spend some time moving parts of your reasoning around to determine the best flow for your reasoning.

FIGURE 13-3 (continued)

lated Smith's constitutional rights and found that Smith's motion to suppress should have been granted. *Id.* at 712.

Just as there was nothing in your son's drug courier profile to differentiate your son and Wright from other innocent college students returning from spring break in Florida, there was nothing in Vogel's drug courier profile to differentiate Smith and Swindell from other law-abiding motorists on I-95. It is usual to drive after dark to avoid heavy traffic or to complete an interstate trip. Although many motorists speed on the highways, motorists driving "cautiously" at or near the speed limit are simply obeying traffic laws. Many people other than drug couriers drive large late model cars with out-of-state tags. A motorist between the ages of twenty and forty is not unusual.

Explanation for the government's second argument

In 1996, the United States Supreme Court decided that a stop for a traffic violation does not violate the driver's constitutional right against unreasonable search and seizure. *Whren v. United States*, 517 U.S. 806, 818 (1996). In *Whren*, Brown was driving a Pathfinder in which Whren was a passenger. Brown was stopped at a stop sign looking down into Whren's lap. Plain clothes police officers were patrolling this "high drug area" of the District of Columbia in an unmarked patrol car. The Pathfinder caught the attention of the officers because Brown remained stopped at the stop sign for approximately twenty seconds. When the patrol car made a U-turn to follow the Pathfinder, Brown turned right without signaling and started off at an "unreasonable speed." The patrol car stopped the Pathfinder. When one of the officers approached Brown's window and peered in, the officer saw that Whren had two plastic bags of crack cocaine on his lap. The officers arrested Whren and Brown. *Id.* at 808, 809.

Prior to *Whren*, some courts, including the court deciding *Smith*, had decided that a car stop for a traffic violation was unconstitutional unless a reasonable officer would have made the stop. The *Smith* court found that the cocaine should have been excluded from evidence because a reasonable officer would not have stopped Smith's car for the alleged traffic violation. 799 F. 2d at 711. However in *Whren*, the United States Supreme Court rejected the argument that the reasonable officer standard should apply. 517 U.S. at 813. The Court decided that the stop was constitutional because the officers observed Brown violate the traffic code. *Id.* at 819.

Whren and your son's case are very similar in that in both cases, the government claimed that the stop of a suspect's car did not violate the driver's right against unreasonable search and seizure because there was some irregularity in the way the car was being driven that gave the officer reason to stop the car. The driving "irregularities" are similar in that failure to use a turn signal in changing lanes, speeding, and following too closely are moving violations that can pose a severe safety hazard; under the circumstances, none appeared to adversely impact any other vehicle's safety.

After *Whren*, it would be very difficult to convince a court that a stop for an alleged traffic violation is unconstitutional. However, if the court finds that the driver did not violate any traffic regulation, then the stop would be unconstitutional.

The Florida motor vehicle statute identified by the officer in your son's case states: "The driver of a motor vehicle shall not follow another vehicle more closely than is reasonable and prudent, having due regard for the speed of such vehicles and the traffic upon, and the condition of, the highway." Fla. Stat. Ch. 316.0895 (1) (1999). No simple test determines if your son violated the statute. The court must determine from any evidence presented whether the distance at which your son was following the car in front of him was reasonable and prudent.

The alleged driving irregularities in *Whren* and your son's case are dissimilar in certain respects. While it was clear that Brown committed a traffic violation, the Florida statute cited in this case does not apply to your son if he was following at a safe distance. Determining whether one vehicle is following another vehicle too closely involved much more of a judgment call than determining whether the Pathfinder failed to signal when turning right and exceeded the speed limit. The position of the vehicles on the

FIGURE 13-3 (continued)

highway and the weather and road conditions must all be considered to determine if your son violated the statute.

I will be meeting with your son within the next few days to discuss the facts in more detail and I anticipate filing a motion to suppress after that meeting. Should you or your son have any questions concerning this matter do not hesitate to call me.

Very truly yours,

Florida Attorney

FIGURE 13-4 Second Client Opinion Letter.

Florida Attorney
Main Street
Anytown, Florida
March 23, 2000

Ms. Cruz Estrada
Main Street
Mytown, Florida

Re: whether drugs found in your purse may be suppressed

Dear Ms. Estrada:

You hired me to represent you after you were arrested for possession of methamphetamines on March 14, 2000. On March 17, 2000 I met with you and you asked me whether the drugs could be suppressed. This opinion is limited to the facts contained in the facts section of this letter and to federal law as of the date of this letter and is solely for your benefit.

Facts

The following facts were gathered from the March 17, 2000 interview with you and a review of the police report. Please contact me if there are any inaccuracies to be corrected or any additions to be made.

You were riding with your friend, Luis Briones, when Luis' car was pulled over. You and Luis were traveling south on I-95 toward Miami to visit friends. The officer said he had stopped the car because Luis was speeding.

After he stopped you, the officer stood at the window on the driver's side and asked for Luis' license and car registration. While Luis searched his wallet for the documents, the officer noticed a glass vial containing small kernels of an off-white substance in Luis' lap. Believing the vial to contain crack cocaine, the officer announced that he was seizing it. He asked you and Luis to exit the car and asked Luis for his wallet.

You got out of the car with your purse strap slung over your shoulder. The officer approached you and said, "You don't mind if I search this, do you?" Without giving you time to respond, the officer grabbed your purse and began to search it. Inside your purse, he found a brown paper envelope. You told the officer that someone had given it to you to give to a friend in Miami.

Still holding your purse, the officer asked you and Luis to wait in the patrol car while the officer searched Luis' car. You and Luis nervously waited in the back seat of the patrol car. You admitted to Luis that the envelope was yours and that it contained illegal drugs.

FIGURE 13-4 (continued)

After you were arrested, you discovered that the police officer had tape-recorded your conversation in the back of the patrol car. Luis believed that the reason the officer gave for stopping Luis' car must have been a pretext because, at the most, he was driving five miles over the speed limit. He said he suspected that he had been stopped for what is jokingly referred to as the offense of DWH or Driving While Hispanic.

You were charged under the federal drug statutes.

Answer concerning the motion to suppress the drugs found in your purse

The court should suppress the drugs if you file a motion to suppress. In opposition to the motion to suppress the drugs, the government will likely make two arguments.

One argument is that you consented to the search of your purse. If you had consented to the search, then the drugs would be admissible. Whether you consented is determined by what a reasonable person would believe. The government should lose this argument because a reasonable person would probably not believe that you had consented. The officer gave you no time to respond after he stated, "You don't mind if I search, do you?" You would not likely give the officer consent because your purse held personal items.

The second argument is that the officer had probable cause to search Luis' car after he discovered that Luis had drugs. Where an officer has probable cause to search the car, the officer can search containers found in the car that might hold the object of the search. Even though the officer can search containers found in the car, the officer would not be able to search your person, at least without more evidence than he had.

Once the court rules against the government on the government's two arguments, the court should grant the motion to suppress the drugs found in your purse.

Answer concerning the motion to suppress the tape recording

The court should deny the motion to suppress the tape recording if judged solely under the federal eavesdropping statutes; however, the court may suppress the tape of your conversation with Luis if the court finds that the tape was tainted by the unconstitutional search of your purse.

The federal eavesdropping statutes prohibit the taping of private conversations unless the officer was a party to the conversation and consented to the taping. The tape recording of a private conversation may not by used as evidence. To gauge whether a conversation is private, the federal statutes require the court to consider whether you expected the conversation to be private and whether society perceived the expectation to be reasonable.

In a case with similar facts, the court held that there is no reasonable expectation of privacy where the conversation took place in the rear seat of a patrol car. If a conversation in the rear seat of a patrol car is not considered private, then the tape may not be suppressed under the federal eavesdropping statutes.

Even though the tape of the conversation may not be suppressed under the federal eavesdropping statutes, we can use the argument that the unconstitutional search of your purse tainted the tape. The court might find that you would not have told Luis about the contents of your purse while you were in the patrol car, had your purse not been searched a few minutes earlier.

Explanation of the government's first argument

The Fourth Amendment to the United States Constitution protects you "against unreasonable searches and seizures." The Fourth Amendment does not prohibit all searches and seizures—just *unreasonable* searches and seizures. Although obtaining a search warrant before conducting a search is preferable, the courts have allowed a number of exceptions to the search warrant requirement over the years. The search of your purse is constitutional if you consented to the search.

FIGURE 13-4 (continued)

The United States Supreme Court has stated the standard for determining when an individual has consented to the search of a car. *United States v. Jimeno*, 500 U.S. 248, 251 (1991). "The standard for measuring the scope of a suspect's consent under the Fourth Amendment is that of 'objective reasonableness'—what would the typical person have understood by the exchange between the officer and the suspect?" *Id.* at 251.

Applying the objective reasonableness standard, it would not be objectively reasonable to believe that you consented to the search of her purse. You did not verbally consent nor did your actions demonstrate consent. A woman's purse often contains objects of a personal nature that the individual wants to guard from prying eyes. A purse is often considered an extension of the individual's outer clothing. Because of the private nature of your purse, it probably would take some overt action or response on your part before it would be reasonable to believe that you consented.

Explanation for the government's second argument

An exception to the search warrant requirement is stopping a vehicle to investigate a traffic violation. Once a vehicle is stopped, the officer can search the car if there is probable cause of criminal activity. Even without consent, the officer can search containers found in the car and suspected of holding the object of the officer's search, no matter who owns the container. An officer may not search someone's person without probable cause.

As far as the container exception is concerned, the United States Supreme Court recently held that "police officers with probable cause to search a car may inspect passengers' belongings found in the car that are capable of concealing the object of the search." *Wyoming v. Houghton*, 526 U.S. 295, 307 (1999). The facts of *Houghton* and your case will be compared to determine if the search of your purse was constitutional.

In *Houghton*, David Young was stopped for speeding and a faulty brake light. After the officer saw a hypodermic syringe in Young's pocket, Young admitted that he used it to take drugs. The officer asked the two female passengers seated in the front seat to exit the car and the officer searched the car. The officer found Sandra Houghton's purse on the back seat of the car. Searching the purse, the officer found a brown pouch that contained drug paraphernalia and a syringe containing methamphetamine in a large enough quantity for a felony conviction. Houghton claimed that the brown pouch was not hers. The officer also found a black container pouch that contained drug paraphernalia and a syringe containing a smaller amount of methamphetamine, insufficient for a felony conviction. Houghton's arms showed fresh needle-marks. The officer arrested her. 526 U.S. at 297–98.

In *Houghton* the Court held "that police officers with probable cause to search a car may inspect passengers' belongings found in the car that are capable of concealing the object of the search." *Id.* at 307. The Court noted that an individual carrying a package in a vehicle travelling on the public roads has a reduced expectation of privacy; however the Court did note the "unique, significantly heightened protection afforded against searches of one's person." *Id.* at 303. The Court found no reason to afford more protection to a container owned by a passenger than a container owned by the driver. *Id.* at 305.

The facts of *Houghton* and your case are similar in that the two cars were stopped for alleged traffic violations and the officers searched a passenger's purse. The facts of the two cases differ in that Houghton's purse was on the back seat of the car, Houghton had exited the car without taking the purse with her, and Houghton at first disclaimed ownership of the purse. In contrast, you took your purse with you when you exited the car and it was attached to you when the officer snatched it from your shoulder.

In *Houghton*, the Court drew a distinction between the permissible search of containers and the search of an individual. The officer would not have been permitted to search Houghton without probable cause that she was carrying drugs or weapon on her person.

FIGURE 13-4 (continued)

Explanation concerning the motion to suppress the tape recording

The federal eavesdropping statutes protect certain types of face-to-face conversations against interception. A conversation is not an oral communication unless the conversants expect that the conversation is private and an objective third party would consider that expectation reasonable. It is illegal to intercept an oral communication. If an oral communication is taped in violation of the eavesdropping statutes, the conversation cannot be used as evidence in court.

Thus, if your and Luis' conversation was an oral communication, it should be suppressed. Whether the conversation is an oral communication turns on whether you had a reasonable expectation of privacy while seated in the rear seat of the patrol car. One prong of the two-prong test is satisfied; you had an expectation of privacy or you would not have discussed the contents of your purse. The other prong of the test is whether your expectation was reasonable. On one hand, the conversation was not audible outside the patrol car. The only way the officer could have heard the conversation was by taping it. On the other hand, you were not sitting in Luis's car. You were sitting in the officer's car. While an expectation of privacy in Luis' car would have been reasonable, it is unclear from the statutes whether an expectation of privacy in the officer's car was reasonable. Some might equate the officer's car to the officer's office. If you were conversing in an office of a police station, it might not be reasonable to expect privacy.

In a case with similar facts, the issue before the United States Court of Appeals for the Eleventh Circuit was "whether the district erred in denying the motion to suppress the tapes resulting from the secret recording of McKinnon's pre-arrest conversations while he sat in the back seat of the police car." *United States v. McKinnon*, 985 F.2d 525, 526 (11th Cir. 1993).

In *McKinnon*, police officers stopped a pick-up truck for failure to travel in a single lane on the Florida Turnpike. Theodore Pressley was driving and Steve McKinnon was the passenger. Pressley consented to the search of his vehicle. While the officers were searching, McKinnon and Pressley waited in the rear seat of the patrol car. There they made incriminating statements that were secretly recorded by the officers. The officers arrested McKinnon and Pressley after finding cocaine in the truck and they were again placed in the rear seat of the patrol car. The officers again recorded McKinnon's and Pressley's incriminating statements. *Id.*

The *McKinnon* court considered the meaning of the term "oral communication" under the federal statutes. An oral communication is protected against taping. If a conversation is taped in violation of the statutes, the tape may be suppressed. A conversation is an oral communication only if the conversants exhibited a subjective expectation of privacy and the expectation of privacy was objectively reasonable. The court seemed to agree with the government's argument that a patrol car functions as the officer's office and the rear seat of the patrol car functions as a jail cell. *Id.* at 527. The court held "that McKinnon did not have a reasonable or justifiable expectation of privacy for conversations he held while seated in the back seat area of a police car." *Id.* at 528.

In examining the facts of *McKinnon* and your case, the facts concerning the taping seem virtually identical. In each case, an officer asked two individuals to wait in the patrol car prior to their arrest. The officer taped their conversation in the rear seat of the patrol car; the conversation contained incriminating statements. One difference between the two cases is that the officer in *McKinnon* also taped McKinnon's conversation following his arrest. This difference is not significant because an arrestee held in the back of a patrol car would have a lesser expectation of privacy than a person not under arrest.

Where a police officer obtained evidence in a unconstitutional manner, that evidence is excluded from use at trial. If that evidence leads the officer to other evidence, the other evidence is derivative of the first evidence. The derivative evidence is known as fruit of the poisonous tree and is also inadmissible. Generally, evidence that is tainted by the prior unconstitutional conduct is inadmissible; however, in some instances the

FIGURE 13-4 (continued)

second evidence is admissible because the connection between the unconstitutionally seized evidence and the subsequently obtained evidence is marginal.

We will argue that the tape is derivative of the evidence the officer discovered searching your purse. If the court finds that the tape is tainted from the unconstitutional search of your purse, the tape will also be inadmissible.

I will be meeting with you within the next few days and I anticipate filing a motion to suppress the drugs and the tape recording after that meeting. Should you have any questions concerning this matter do not hesitate to call me.

Very truly yours,

Florida Attorney

drugs were found in the client's purse. The client's conversation with the car's driver was tape-recorded while they sat in the patrol car as the officer searched their car. The passenger hired the attorney to represent her and has asked whether the methamphetamines and the tape recording can be suppressed.

CHAPTER 13 SUMMARY

- The transmittal letter is the cover letter used when forwarding a document or other information to the client or to a third party.
- The client judges the competency of the attorney by the way the attorney presents himself or herself. A client letter may either cause the client to lose confidence in the attorney or may strengthen the attorney-client relationship.
- The client opinion letter answers the client's question and contains a statement of the facts, an explanation of applicable law, and an explanation of how the law applies to the facts.
- The format of the client opinion letter generally contains a heading, an opening, the facts, an answer, an explanation, and a closing.
- The client opinion letter should state that it is limited to the facts in the letter, to federal and/or state law of a certain date and to the benefit of the client.
- Gear the language in the client opinion letter to the sophistication of the client.
- You may or may not want to include citations or quotations in the client opinion letter.

CYBER EXAMPLES

When writing legal documents for the first time, it may be helpful to look at examples. This chapter provides some examples. A number of law school professors have posted sample documents on the Internet. To find some of these documents you might access Jurist: The Law Professor Network (http://www.jurist.law.pitt.edu). (Under "Learning & Teaching Law", click on "Law School Courses" and then on "Legal Research & Writing.") At the time this book was being written, Professor Gregory Berry at Howard University School of Law had posted a number of student documents in his "Writing Hall of Fame" found under "Berry's Advice." Those documents included client letters, memoranda, motion reply briefs, a settlement agreement, and appellate briefs. Also, Professor Colleen Barger at the University of Arkansas at Little Rock School of Law had a web site that links to pages of other legal research and writing professors (http://www.ualr.edu/~cmbarger/).

EXERCISES FOR CHAPTER 13

1. What are important style tips to remember when writing a transmittal letter?
2. What does the heading of a client opinion letter contain?
3. What does the opening of a client opinion letter contain?
4. What facts should a client opinion letter contain?
5. What does the answer section of a client opinion letter contain?
6. What does the explanation section of a client opinion letter contain?
7. What does the closing of a client opinion letter contain?

WRITING CONTRACTS

CHAPTER 14

INTRODUCTION

On occasion you have probably been faced with a formidable-looking contract filled with legalese which someone expected you to sign. If you are like most people, you probably gave up reading after the first three "whereas" clauses, flipped to the signature line and signed, hoping that you had not signed your life or car away. Attorneys have rightly been criticized for adhering to their old forms and producing contracts that are almost unintelligible to the layperson and to many attorneys as well.

Contracts can be written in plain English so you can understand what you are signing without the help of an attorney. In fact, some states require consumer contracts to be written in plain English. Contracts need to be in plain English so the parties to the contract can read the contract and follow it in their performance.

WHAT IS COVERED IN THIS CHAPTER

This chapter is designed to give you:

1. basic information about writing contracts;
2. a few sample contract provisions; and
3. practice in writing a contract.

The focus is on two types of contracts: contracts for the sale of goods and employment contracts. These two types of contracts were selected because they are among the most common and because, from your own experience, you probably can think of terms that should be included in them.

A word of caution is advisable here. This chapter gives you some familiarity with writing contracts but does not license you to practice law. The sample contract provisions included in this chapter are very simple ones and may not be appropriate for certain situations. Statutory or case law may require inclusion of certain provisions not covered in this chapter. Only an attorney can advise someone how to adequately protect himself or herself under a contract.

Why be familiar with simple contracts?

This chapter gives you enough familiarity with simple contracts so that when you read a contract, you can start asking questions and identifying potential problems with the contract. Some problems may be created by the contract requiring too much or by the contract not addressing certain of your concerns. If there are problems with the contract, the time to solve them is before a party signs the contract. After signing, it is too late unless the other party is willing to amend the contract.

Read the contract carefully and decide whether a party can perform all that is expected of that party under the contract and whether the contract includes

COMPUTER CONTRACT

The parties to this Contract are Computer Sales, Inc., Anystreet USA, Anytown, Florida ("Seller") and J.A. Jones, Main Street, Anytown, Florida ("Buyer") and the date of this contract is July 3, 2000. Seller and Buyer agree as follows:

Seller will install the computer identified on Exhibit A to this contract (the "Computer") at the above address of the Buyer.

Buyer will pay Seller $2,000 for the Computer and the installation.

The Computer carries the manufacturer's warranty described in the Computer instruction manual.

Computer Sales, Inc.

By: ________________
Computer Whiz, President

____
J.A. Jones

FIGURE 14-1 Computer Contract.

everything the party expected. A contract term, though onerous, is enforceable unless it is so onerous that it is unconscionable. Absence of a particular contract term may create as big a problem. A party may not receive a benefit bargained for if it is not included in the contract. For example, if in an initial interview, the individual's prospective employer promised a bonus based on performance, make sure the written contract includes the terms of the bonus.

Why written contracts?

There are certain types of contracts that traditionally were required to be in writing to be enforceable. These included a contract for the sale of goods for $500 or more, an employment contract for the term of one year or more, and a contract for the sale of real property. A writing was required because these transactions were important enough that the temptation for fraud by an unscrupulous party was great. The contract was required to be in writing to furnish tangible proof of the parties' agreement in the event of a dispute. Contracts required to be in writing are generally referred to as falling within the **Statute of Frauds.** Your state has its own version of the Statute of Frauds. It might be interesting for you to research which types of contracts are required to be in writing in your state.

Even if a contract is not legally required to be in writing, it is advisable to put a contract of any importance in writing. The written contract furnishes tangible proof of the parties' agreement. A contract spells out the basic terms of a transaction, the respective rights and obligations of the parties, and the remedies in the event of a **breach.** A written contract also memorializes necessary information so that it is readily accessible later. Should a dispute arise later, it may be resolved simply by consulting the written contract. Should the contract go to litigation, a well-written contract will protect a party to the contract better than if the party had to rely on the party's recollection of the contract terms.

THE SUBSTANCE OF THE CONTRACT

A contract should include the material terms of the transaction. Think of the essential contract terms falling into three broad categories:

1. parties and subject matter;
2. operative provisions; and
3. contingencies.

For example, if J.A. Jones is purchasing a computer, the contract will contain his name and the name of the seller (**the parties**), the type of computer he is purchasing (the subject matter), the price and payment method (the **operative provisions**) and the warranty (**contingency provision**). Figure 14-1 is the bare bones contract containing these essential terms, written in plain English. The contract is fine if nothing goes wrong. After reading the contract, think what problems you might have purchasing the computer and what contract provisions could be added to deal with the problems. Potential problems with this contract will be discussed below.

Defined terms

The Computer Contract contains **defined terms,** Seller and Buyer. In the first sentence, "Seller" is defined as Computer Sales, Inc., Anystreet USA, Anytown, Florida and "Buyer" is defined as J.A. Jones, Main Street, Anytown, Florida. Throughout the contract (except for the signature lines), the defined terms are used instead of the full names of the Seller and Buyer. Defined terms are commonly used in contracts; use of defined terms shortens the length of the contract and makes it easier to read. In addition, if an attorney uses the Computer Contract as the basis for drafting a new contract with different parties, the names of the parties need only be changed in the first sentence and in the signature lines. In a long contract of 10 to 20 pages, use of defined terms shortens the contract considerably.

As explained later in this chapter, care must be taken that the same words are used as defined terms throughout the contract. For example, if the contract starts out referring to the buyer as "Buyer," the contract should always refer to that person as "Buyer." If a provision borrowed from another contract referred to the buyer as "Purchaser," the word "Purchaser" should be replaced by the word "Buyer" to be consistent.

Negotiated and unnegotiated terms

Negotiated terms, as the term implies, are the terms of the contract that the parties talked about and agreed to. For example, in the Contract above, Mr. Jones and the salesperson for Computer Sales, Inc. probably discussed which computer Mr. Jones should purchase and negotiated the price. These are the negotiated terms in this transaction.

In addition to including all material terms, a contract may contain terms the parties never formally negotiated, the unnegotiated terms. Certain contingencies happen often enough that the person writing the contract will provide for them. Whoever wrote the above Contract probably referred to the manufacturer's warranty because the Buyer would want to know the Computer is covered by the warranty if it malfunctions. Depending on the subject matter of the contract, state or federal law may mandate inclusion of certain terms or disclosure of certain information. For example, federal law requires certain consumer protection language to be inserted in the contract where the sale was solicited at the buyer's home or the purchase is made on credit. A contract also typically contains **boilerplate** provisions. Boilerplate provisions are provisions common to all legal documents of the same type. Typical contract boilerplate provisions include **notice, assignment, choice of law, attorneys' fees, saving clause,** and so on.

Notice—a notice provision contains the names and addresses of the persons to whom notice is to be sent. For example, a party terminating the contract may be required to give the other party notice of the termination. The notice should be sent as directed in the notice provision.

Assignment—an assignment is a party's transfer of that party's rights or duties (or both) under the contract. The original party to the contract is the assignor and the new party to the contract is the assignee. If an original party to a contract wants to deal only with the other party who originally signed the contract and not with an assignee, then the contract should prohibit assignment. If the contract contains no assignment provision, either party may assign the contract.

Choice of law—a choice of law clause sets forth which state's law will govern should a dispute arise.

Attorneys' fees—an attorneys' fee provision usually requires the losing party in a lawsuit to pay the prevailing party's attorneys' fees. In the absence of an attorneys' fee provision in a contract or statute, each party is responsible for that party's attorneys' fees.

Saving clause—a saving clause (also referred to as a **severability clause**) states that in the event part of the contract is held to be unenforceable, the valid portion of the contract will be enforced.

WRITING A CONTRACT

Where does one start in writing a contract?

Although a contract can be written entirely from scratch, a person writing a contract will usually try to find one or more contracts that are similar to the one the person is writing and use those contracts as a guide. An attorney may recall a similar matter the attorney has dealt with in the past and use the contract from that matter as a guide. In addition, attorneys typically maintain files of contracts that they use when appropriate.

Another option is to consult **forms** and **formbooks.** Attorneys may prepare their own forms or use commercially prepared forms. Some law firms develop their own formbooks for use by the attorneys in the firm. A law firm formbook may be a ring binder containing copies of documents contributed by various attorneys in the firm. If you are lucky, the forms may also be stored on the law firm central computer, accessible to everyone in the firm. You should check your law library to see whether it contains any commercially-prepared formbooks.

In addition, many forms are available online. Some are free and others may be purchased. The cyberlaw exercises at the end of this chapter may help you locate some of these online forms.

As the term implies, formbooks are volumes containing forms that may be referred to as guides. There is a wide variety of formbooks. The forms contained in a particular publication may be much simpler than those contained in another formbook. Some forms are written in plain English while others are not. Office supply stores sell forms, either singly or in packages. A law firm will stock certain of these forms for use in routine transactions. A number of formbooks are also available on computer disk.

Besides including forms, a formbook often contains **checklists** of typical provisions included in a particular type of contract. When writing a contract, it is helpful to glance down the checklist to make sure the writer has included all necessary provisions. Some writers actually use a checklist from a formbook and check off each item as either included in the contract or not needed. Later sections of this chapter contain a list of matters typically considered when writing a contract for the sale of goods and another list of matters typically considered when writing an employment agreement. You can use these lists as checklists in completing the exercises from this chapter.

In some states, the state bar association, or a bar-related not-for-profit corporation is active in preparing all sorts of helpful state-specific materials, including forms. It would be useful for you to determine what materials are prepared in your state and whether nonattorneys can purchase them.

In Florida, the Florida Bar has prepared and the Florida Supreme Court has approved forms for use by nonattorneys. The forms cover a number of matters commonly encountered by the average layperson. While the "Contract for Sale and Purchase" (designed to be used when someone is selling a home) was approved a number of years ago, the rest of the forms were approved much more recently. The forms were prepared in response to criticism that everyone needs legal assistance from time to time but few can afford to hire an attorney. Because the Florida Supreme Court approved these forms, a nonattorney using the forms cannot be prosecuted for unlicensed practice of law. The "Contract for Sale and Purchase" has been used so widely throughout Florida that it has become the standard form to use in the sale of residential property.

Use of contract forms

"Attorney-bashers" are fond of saying that all attorneys do is fill in forms and they do not even do that personally. They have their secretaries do it. Think about whether this criticism is valid.

The advantage in using forms is that they cut down on the time and expense of preparing a contract. For example, if an attorney represents a developer of a residential subdivision, the attorney will probably write a contract for the sale of lots in the subdivision and use it as a "form" when any lots in the subdivision are sold. This makes sense because there is very little that differs in the various sales, other than the buyer, the purchase price, and the lot number. These terms can be easily filled in to correspond to the particular transaction. Other changes to the form contract can be made either by writing in the change and having the parties initial it or attaching an **addendum** (an appendix or addition) to the contract.

The disadvantage in using forms is that they may not be tailored to a particular transaction. A form should be analyzed to determine whether there is a valid reason for including each provision and whether any other provisions are necessary for the particular transaction. Attorneys must stay current on the law or must do necessary legal research to make sure the contract reflects current law. A careless attorney who has a secretary or paralegal fill out a form without adequately supervising the work is looking for a legal malpractice lawsuit.

Ideally, an attorney will tailor the contract to the particular transaction by combining the best provisions from a number of "forms" with the negotiated terms and other information peculiar to the transaction. In doing this, the attorney must make sure the contract is consistent. Provisions taken from different forms should not contradict each other and the same "defined terms" should be used throughout the contract.

Research

Drafting documents must be accompanied by adequate research of the law. Inadequate research can easily be the basis for a legal malpractice action.

CHECKLIST OF MATTERS TO BE CONSIDERED WHEN WRITING A CONTRACT FOR THE SALE OF GOODS

Figure 14-2 is a list of matters to be considered when writing a contract for the sale of goods. As you read the list, keep in mind the above Computer Contract. In a later section of the chapter we will review the list and "brainstorm" to determine what provisions should be added to the Contract.

Test your "brainstorming" ability by making a list of provisions to add to the computer contract before you read the following sections.

FIGURE 14-2 Computer Contract Checklist.

Computer Contract Checklist

1. **Parties and subject matter.**
   a. Definitions.
   b. Parties.
   c. Date of the contract.
   d. Description of goods.
2. **Operative provisions.**
   a. Price.
   b. Obligations of seller.
   c. Obligations of buyer.
   d. Time for performance.
3. **Contingencies.**
   a. Warranties.
   b. Transfer of title to goods and risk of loss.
   c. Excuse of performance.
   d. Remedies of seller.
   e. Remedies of buyer.
4. **Provisions required by statute or case law.**
5. **Boilerplate.**
   a. Modification or amendment of contract.
   b. Assignment of contract.
   c. Notice provision.
   d. Choice of law provision.
   e. Attorneys fees.
   f. Saving clause.
6. **Signature lines**

THE PERFECT CONTRACT

If this were a perfect world, one would not need contracts because every transaction would be performed as planned. Because this is not a perfect world, there will be problems, hopefully very minor ones, with every contract. The challenge in writing a "perfect contract" is to accurately state the negotiated provisions, to include any provisions required by statute or case law, as well as to predict everything that will happen between the parties as the contract is performed.

In looking at a contract, you may have wondered why you recognize such a small portion of the provisions (the parties, subject matter, and operative provisions) and what the balance of the terms are doing in the contract. The provisions you were not familiar with are the ones included "just in case" something unanticipated happens. The "just in case" provisions are the ones categorized above as "contingencies," "provisions required by statute or case law," and "boilerplate."

If you were to compare a number of contracts for the sale of goods you would notice provisions, other than the negotiated ones, that are similar from contract to contract. Through the years certain problems in contract performance happened often enough that the "just in case" provisions began to be included in every contract. These provisions comprise a large portion of the contract because the potential problems are many and varied.

Although many of the "just in case" provisions are necessary, these provisions are probably the ones that make the contract hard to read. Someone attempting to write a plain English contract must analyze each provision of the traditional contract and determine whether there is a valid business reason for the provision. The choice should be made in light of the particular transaction covered by the contract. Certain detailed provisions may be necessary in a commercial transaction but may be overkill in a consumer transaction. The writer should not include provisions covering events that are extremely unlikely to occur so long as the risk of loss is minimal. Boilerplate provisions should be written to correspond to the specifics of the transaction, with any unnecessary provisions eliminated.

In addition to the standard "just in case" provisions, other "just in case" provisions peculiar to a particular transaction may be needed. The writer must study the transaction to determine whether other provisions are needed. Based on the course of dealings between the parties or a party's past experience or reputation, the writer may feel the need to avoid a potential problem peculiar to the parties or the subject matter of the contract.

Precise and imprecise language in the perfect contract

The language in a skillfully written contract precisely sets forth well-defined expectations and is purposefully imprecise when dealing with unknown future events. Usually, the material terms of a transaction are stated precisely to coincide with the parties' expectations. If a time period for performance is involved, it is wise to state it precisely. Otherwise performance within a "reasonable time" is sufficient and the transaction may never be completed. The language of "just in case" provisions is usually not precise because it is impossible to predict exactly what will happen.

The skill of an experienced attorney is knowing when to be precise and when to be imprecise. Although the material terms of the transaction are usually well-defined, sometimes even some of the material terms must be purposefully vague. For example, if the buyer wants to buy all that the seller can produce of a certain item, but it is not known how much the seller will produce, the contract can require the seller to sell and the buyer to buy all that the seller produces. On the other hand, a contingent provision may be written with a great deal of specificity if a particular contingency is fairly likely to occur. For example, if the seller has had great difficulty in the past obtaining an essential component of the item the seller is manufacturing, the contract may provide that the seller's performance is excused if the seller cannot obtain the essential component by a certain date.

An illustration of imprecise language

The following contract case illustrates the problems caused by not defining "chicken."

FRIGALIMENT IMPORTING CO., Ltd., Plaintiff,

v.

B.N.S. INTERNATIONAL SALES CORP., Defendant.

United States District Court S.D. New York.

Dec. 27, 1960.

190 F. Supp. 116

FRIENDLY, Circuit Judge.

The issue is, what is chicken? Plaintiff says 'chicken' means a young chicken, suitable for broiling and frying. Defendant says 'chicken' means any bird of that genus that meets contract specifications on weight and quality, including what it calls 'stewing chicken' and plaintiff pejoratively terms 'fowl'. Dictionaries give both meanings, as well as some others not relevant here. To support its [position], plaintiff sends a number of volleys over the net; defendant essays to return them and adds a few serves of its own. Assuming that both parties were acting in good faith, the case nicely illustrates Holmes' remark 'that the making of a contract depends not on the agreement of two minds in one intention, but on the agreement of two sets of external signs—not on the parties' having meant the same thing but on their having said the same thing.' The Path of the Law, in Collected Legal Papers, p. 178. I have concluded that plaintiff has not sustained its burden of persuasion that the contract used 'chicken' in the narrower sense.

The action is for breach of the warranty that goods sold shall correspond to the description, New York Personal Property Law, McKinney's Consol. Laws, c. 41, S 95. Two contracts are in suit. In the first, dated May 2, 1957, defendant, a New York sales corporation, confirmed the sale to plaintiff, a Swiss corporation, of 'US Fresh Frozen Chicken, Grade A, Government Inspected, Eviscerated 2 1/2–3 lbs. and 1 1/2–2 lbs. each all chicken individually wrapped in cryovac, packed in secured fiber cartons or wooden boxes, suitable for export

75,000 lbs. 2 1/2–3 lbs........ @$33.00

25,000 lbs. 1 1/2–2 lbs........ @$36.50

per 100 lbs. FAS New York

scheduled May 10, 1957 pursuant to instructions from Penson & Co., New York.'

The second contract, also dated May 2, 1957, was identical save that only 50,000 lbs. of the heavier 'chicken' were called for, the price of the smaller birds was $37 per 100 lbs., and shipment was scheduled for May 30. The initial shipment under the first contract was short but the balance was shipped on May 17. When the initial shipment arrived in Switzerland, plaintiff found, on May 28, that the 2 1/2–3 lbs. birds were not young chicken suitable for broiling and frying but stewing chicken or 'fowl'; indeed, many of the cartons and bags plainly so indicated.

Protests ensued. Nevertheless, shipment under the second contract was made on May 29, the 2 1/2–3 lbs. birds again being stewing chicken. Defendant stopped the transportation of these at Rotterdam.

This action followed. Plaintiff says that, notwithstanding that its acceptance was in Switzerland, New York law controls under the principle of Rubin v. irving Trust Co., 1953, 305 N.Y. 288, 305, 113 N.E.2d 424, 431; defendant does not dispute this, and relies on New York decisions. I shall follow the apparent agreement of the parties as to the applicable law.

Since the word 'chicken' standing alone is ambiguous, I turn first to see whether the contract itself offers any aid to its interpretation. Plaintiff says the 1 1/2–2 lbs. birds necessarily had to be young chicken since the older birds do not come in that size, hence the 2 1/2–3 lbs. birds must likewise be young. This is unpersuasive—a contract for 'apples' of two different sizes could be filled with different kinds of apples even though only one species came in both sizes. Defendant notes that the contract called not simply for chicken but for 'US Fresh Frozen Chicken, Grade A, Government Inspected.' It says the contract thereby incorporated by reference the Department of Agriculture's regulations, which favor its interpretation; I shall return to this after reviewing plaintiff's other contentions.

The first hinges on an exchange of cablegrams which preceded execution of the formal contracts. The negotiations leading up to the contracts were conducted in New York between defendant's secretary, Ernest R. Bauer, and a Mr. Stovicek, who was in New York for the Czechoslovak government at the World Trade Fair. A few days after meeting Bauer at the fair, Stovicek telephoned and inquired whether defendant would be interested in exporting poultry to Switzerland. Bauer then met with Stovicek, who showed him a cable from plaintiff dated April 26, 1957, announcing that they 'are buyer' of 25,000 lbs. of chicken 2 1/2–3 lbs. weight, Cryovac packed, grade A Government inspected, at a price up to 33 cents per pound, for shipment on May 10, to be confirmed by the following morning, and were interested in further offerings. After testing the market for price, Bauer accepted, and Stovicek sent a confirmation that evening. Plaintiff stresses that, although these and subsequent cables between plaintiff and defendant, which laid the basis for the additional quantities under the first and for all of the second contract, were predominantly in German, they used the English word 'chicken'; it claims this was done because it understood 'chicken' meant young chicken whereas the German word, 'Huhn,' included both 'Brathuhn' (broilers) and 'Suppenhuhn' (stewing chicken), and that defendant, whose officers were thoroughly conversant with German, should have realized this. Whatever force this argument might otherwise have is largely drained away by Bauer's testimony that he asked Stovicek what kind of chickens were wanted, received the answer 'any kind of chickens,' and then, in German, asked whether the cable meant 'Huhn' and received an affirmative response. Plaintiff attacks this as contrary to what Bauer testified on his deposition in March, 1959, and also on the ground that Stovicek had no authority to interpret the meaning of the cable. The first contention would be persuasive if sustained by the record, since Bauer was free at the trial from the threat of contradiction by Stovicek as he was not at the time of the deposition; however, review of the deposition does not convince me of the claimed inconsistency. As to the second contention, it may well be that Stovicek lacked authority to commit plaintiff for prices or delivery dates other than those specified in the cable; but plaintiff cannot at the same time rely on its cable to Stovicek as its dictionary to the meaning of the contract and repudiate the interpretation given the dictionary by the man in whose hands it was put. Plaintiff's reliance on the fact that the contract forms contain the words 'through the intermediary of,' with the blank not filled, as negating agency, is wholly unpersuasive; the purpose of this clause was to permit filling in the name of an intermediary to whom a commission would be payable, not to blot out what had been the fact.

Plaintiff's next contention is that there was a definite trade usage that 'chicken' meant 'young chicken.' Defendant showed that it was only beginning in the poultry trade in 1957, thereby bringing itself within the principle that 'when one of the parties is not a member of the trade or other circle, his acceptance of the standard must be made to appear' by proving either that he had actual knowledge of the usage or that the usage is 'so generally known in the community that his actual individual knowledge of it may be inferred.' 9 Wigmore, Evidence (3d ed. S 1940) 2464. Here there was no proof of actual knowledge of the alleged usage; indeed, it is quite plain that defendant's belief was to the contrary. In order to meet the alternative requirement, the law of New York demands a showing that 'the usage is of so long continuance, so well established, so notorious, so universal and so reasonable in itself, as that the presumption is violent that the parties contracted with reference to it, and made it a part of their agreement.' Walls v. Bailey.

Plaintiff endeavored to establish such a usage by the testimony of three witnesses and certain other evidence. Strasser, resident buyer in New York for a large chain of Swiss cooperatives, testified that 'on chicken

I would definitely understand a broiler.' However, the force of this testimony was considerably weakened by the fact that in his own transactions the witness, a careful businessman, protected himself by using 'broiler' when that was what he wanted and 'fowl' when he wished older birds. Indeed, there are some indications, dating back to a remark of Lord Mansfield, Edie v. East India Co., 2 Burr. 1216, 1222 (1761), that no credit should be given 'witnesses to usage, who could not adduce instances in verification.' 7 Wigmore, Evidence (3d ed. 1940). While Wigmore thinks this goes too far, a witness' consistent failure to rely on the alleged usage deprives his opinion testimony of much of its effect. Niesielowski, an officer of one of the companies that had furnished the stewing chicken to defendant, testified that 'chicken' meant 'the male species of the poultry industry. That could be a broiler, a fryer or a roaster,' but not a stewing chicken; however, he also testified that upon receiving defendant's inquiry for 'chickens,' he asked whether the desire was for 'fowl or frying chickens' and, in fact, supplied fowl, although taking the precaution of asking defendant, a day or two after plaintiff's acceptance of the contracts in suit, to change its confirmation of its order from 'chickens,' as defendant had originally prepared it, to 'stewing chickens.' Dates, an employee of Urner-Barry Company, which publishes a daily market report on the poultry trade, gave it as his view that the trade meaning of 'chicken' was 'broilers and fryers.' In addition to this opinion testimony, plaintiff relied on the fact that the Urner-Barry service, the Journal of Commerce, and Weinberg Bros. & Co. of Chicago, a large supplier of poultry, published quotations in a manner which, in one way or another, distinguish between 'chicken,' comprising broilers, fryers and certain other categories, and 'fowl,' which, Bauer acknowledged, included stewing chickens. This material would be impressive if there were nothing to the contrary. However, there was, as will now be seen.

Defendant's witness Weininger, who operates a chicken eviscerating plant in New Jersey, testified 'Chicken is everything except a goose, a duck, and a turkey. Everything is a chicken, but then you have to say, you have to specify which category you want or that you are talking about.' Its witness Fox said that in the trade 'chicken' would encompass all the various classifications. Sadina, who conducts a food inspection service, testified that he would consider any bird coming within the classes of 'chicken' in the Department of Agriculture's regulations to be a chicken. The specifications approved by the General Services Administration include fowl as well as broilers and fryers under the classification 'chickens.' Statistics of the Institute of American Poultry Industries use the phrases 'Young chickens' and 'Mature chickens,' under the general heading 'Total chickens' and the Department of Agriculture's daily and weekly price reports avoid use of the word 'chicken' without specification.

Defendant advances several other points which it claims affirmatively support its construction. Primary among these is the regulation of the Department of Agriculture, 7 C.F.R. S 70.300–70.370, entitled, 'Grading and Inspection of Poultry and Edible Products Thereof.' and in particular 70.301 which recited:

Chickens. The following are the various classes of chickens:

(a) Broiler or fryer . . .

(b) Roaster . . .

(c) Capon . . .

(d) Stag . . .

(e) Hen or stewing chicken or fowl . . .

(f) Cock or old rooster . . .

Defendant argues, as previously noted, that the contract incorporated these regulations by reference. Plaintiff answers that the contract provision related simply to grade and Government inspection and did not incorporate the Government definition of 'chicken,' and also that the definition in the Regulations is ignored in the trade. However, the latter contention was contradicted by Weininger and Sadina; and there is force in defendant's argument that the contract made the regulations a dictionary, particularly since the reference to Government grading was already in plaintiff's initial cable to Stovicek.

Defendant makes a further argument based on the impossibility of its obtaining broilers and fryers at the 33 cents price offered by plaintiff for the 2 1/2–3 lbs. birds. There is no substantial dispute that, in late April, 1957, the price for 2 1/2–3 lbs. broilers was between 35 and 37 cents per pound, and that when defendant entered into the contracts, it was well aware of this and intended to fill them by supplying fowl in these weights. It claims that plaintiff must likewise have known the market since plaintiff had reserved shipping space on April 23, three days before plaintiff's cable to Stovicek, or, at least, that Stovicek was chargeable with such knowledge. It is scarcely an answer to say, as plaintiff does in its brief, that the 33 cents price offered by the 2 1/2–3 lbs. 'chickens' was closer to the prevailing 35 cents price for broilers than to the 30 cents at which defendant procured fowl. Plaintiff must have expected defendant to make some profit—certainly it could not have expected defendant deliberately to incur a loss.

Finally, defendant relies on conduct by the plaintiff after the first shipment had been received. On May 28 plaintiff sent two cables complaining that the larger birds in the first shipment constituted 'fowl.' Defendant answered with a cable refusing to recognize plaintiff's objection and announcing 'We have today ready for shipment 50,000 lbs. chicken 2 1/2–3 lbs. 25,000 lbs. broilers 1 1/2–2 lbs.,' these being the goods procured for shipment under the second contract, and asked immediate answer 'whether we are to ship this merchandise to you and whether you will accept the merchandise.' After several other cable exchanges, plaintiff replied on May 29 'Confirm again that merchandise is to be shipped since resold by us if not enough pursuant to contract chickens are shipped the missing quantity is to be shipped within ten days stop we resold to our customers pursuant to your contract chickens grade A you have to deliver us said merchandise we again state that we shall make you fully responsible for all resulting costs.' [FN2] Defendant argues that if plaintiff was sincere in thinking it was entitled to young chickens, plaintiff would not have allowed the shipment under the second contract to go forward, since the distinction between broilers and chickens drawn in defendant's cablegram must have made it clear that the larger birds would not be broilers. However, plaintiff answers that the cables show plaintiff was insisting on delivery of young chickens and that defendant shipped old ones at its peril. Defendant's point would be highly relevant on another disputed issue—whether if liability were established, the measure of damages should be the difference in market value of broilers and stewing chicken in New York or the larger difference in Europe, but I cannot give it weight on the issue of interpretation. Defendant points out also that plaintiff proceeded to deliver some of the larger birds in Europe, describing them as 'poulets'; defendant argues that it was only when plaintiff's customers complained about this that plaintiff developed the idea that 'chicken' meant 'young chicken.' There is little force in this in view of plaintiff's immediate and consistent protests.

When all the evidence is reviewed, it is clear that defendant believed it could comply with the contracts by delivering stewing chicken in the 2 1/2–3 lbs. size. Defendant's subjective intent would not be significant if this did not coincide with an objective meaning of 'chicken.' Here it did coincide with one of the dictionary meanings, with the definition in the Department of Agriculture Regulations to which the contract made at least oblique reference, with at least some usage in the trade, with the realities of the market, and with what plaintiff's spokesman had said. Plaintiff asserts it to be equally plain that plaintiff's own subjective intent was to obtain broilers and fryers; the only evidence against this is the material as to market prices and this may not have been sufficiently brought home. In any event it is unnecessary to determine that issue. For plaintiff has the burden of showing that 'chicken' was used in the narrower rather than in the broader sense, and this it has not sustained.

What's wrong with the Computer Contract?

Review the checklist from figure 14-2 and brainstorm to determine what provisions should be added to the Computer Contract. In brainstorming, pull on your personal experience and your imagination of transactions that were not performed as planned. Think of the last time you purchased a large item. Did the item live up to the sales pitch? Was it delivered on time? Did the seller perform as expected? Were the payment terms satisfactory? And so on.

The following numbers correspond to the numbers in the checklist (fig. 14-2):

The title, "Computer Contract," tells what type of document it is and identifies the subject matter. You could add the names of the parties to the title also.

Parties and subject matter

1. a. The Computer Contract includes the "defined terms," "Seller," "Buyer," and "Computer." Once you have given the definition of a term, you need only capitalize the term later in the contract when you refer to it rather than give the whole definition each time. Be careful that you use the same defined term throughout the contract. If you start out using "Buyer," do not use "Purchaser" later to refer to the same person. If you have a number of defined terms, you may want to include a definition section near the beginning of the contract in which you give the definition of all the terms used in the contract. That way, the reader knows to refer back to the definition section when the reader sees a capitalized term. A definition section is probably not needed in the Computer Contract because there are not a great number of defined terms.

b. The parties are named. It is a good idea to also give their addresses and any other basic information in a contract. If you include the information in a contract, you can use the contract as a ready reference instead of having to consult a number of other sources.

c. The date of a contract is often the date when the later of the parties signs the contract or another date selected by the parties. The parties may have a reason for wanting the contract dated a certain date. The exact contract date would be important to know if time periods included in the contract start on the contract date.

d. In the Computer Contract it would be important for the Buyer to check Exhibit A and make sure that the Computer is the right one. If the Buyer was supposed to receive any other equipment, that equipment should also be listed on Exhibit A or Buyer may end up paying for it on top of the Contract price.

Operative provisions

2. a. The price is given, but the payment terms are not and should be. One payment option is having a portion of the purchase price due upon signing the Contract with the balance due upon installation of the Computer or the Buyer being billed for the balance. Another option is payment of the entire purchase price when the Contract is signed. This may be required when the goods are being designed and manufactured specially for Buyer. Another option is payment in full upon delivery.

b. From the Contract we know that Seller must supply and install the Computer. If the Seller has any other obligations they should be stated in the Contract. For example, the purchase price may include a certain number of hours of instruction and maintenance. It is to Buyer's benefit to have this clearly stated in the Contract.

c. The main obligation of the Buyer is to pay. As explained in 2.a. above, the payment terms should be included in the Contract. Any other obligation of the Buyer should be stated in the Contract.

d. The Contract does not state when the Computer is to be installed. If it is critical to the Buyer that the Computer be installed by a certain date, this should be stated in the Contract. Buyer may want to include a penalty that Seller would have to pay for each day Seller is late. Again, refer to 2.a. above for Buyer's payment terms.

Contingencies

3. a. The Contract does state that the Computer carries the manufacturer's warranties. If the Buyer expects any other warranties they should be stated in the Contract. If warranty service is vital to Buyer, Buyer may want to specify where the warranty service is to be done (does the service person come to Buyer or does Buyer have to take the computer in?) and how quickly any repairs will be made.

b. A transfer of title to goods and risk of loss provision most often is included where the goods are being manufactured specially for the Buyer. This provision would probably not be included in the Computer Contract unless the Seller was manufacturing the Computer for the Buyer. Should the specially manufactured goods be destroyed before they are delivered and paid for, two questions would be asked: "Who owned the goods when they were destroyed?" and "Who should bear the loss?" The parties can specify in a contract when ownership passes and who bears the risk of loss.

c. An excuse of performance provision is also often included where the goods are being manufactured specially for Buyer. An **act of God** may excuse the performance of the Seller. An act of God is an unusual, extraordinary, and unexpected act caused solely by the forces of nature or something outside the Seller's control. Examples would be a flood that destroys Seller's manufacturing facility or a war that makes it impossible for Seller to continue manufacturing. This provision would probably not be included in the Computer Contract unless the Seller was manufacturing the Computer for the Buyer.

d. In general, remedies for breach of a contract may include damages, consequential damages, liquidated damages, injunction, and specific performance.

Damages—Money that a court orders paid to a person who has suffered damage (a loss or harm) by the person who caused the injury (the violation of the person's rights).

Consequential damages—Indirect losses from a breach of contract. To recover, they usually have to be contemplated by the parties. It is wise for the person claiming them to have laid out this contemplation in the contract.

Liquidated damages—A sum agreed upon by the parties at the time of entering into the contract as being payable by way of compensation for loss suffered in the event of a breach of contract.

Injunction—A court order that commands or prohibits some act or course of conduct. It is preventative in nature and designed to protect a plaintiff from irreparable injury to the plaintiff's property or property rights by prohibiting or commending the doing of certain acts.

Specific performance—A court ordering performance of a contract. Specific performance may be ordered in circumstances where damages are an inadequate remedy because the goods are unique. Unless otherwise stated, it is assumed that a party may sue for damages. A party may also sue for specific performance if the goods are unique.

If there is a basis for a party demanding consequential or liquidated damages or an injunction, this information should be included in a contract. Because the only obligation of the Buyer under the Computer Contract is to pay the purchase price, the most likely remedy of the Seller is an action for damages to collect the balance of the purchase price. If the Seller would be satisfied with suing for damages, a remedy provision need not be included in the Contract. The Seller could also sue for specific performance to force the Buyer to purchase the computer if the computer is being specially manufactured for the Buyer. If Seller would like to sue for specific performance, it would be wise to specifically give Seller this remedy in the Contract.

e. If the Seller fails to deliver the Computer, the Buyer can sue for damages without having a damages provision included in the Contract. Following the explanation in 3.d. above, the basis for any other remedy should be stated in the Contract.

Provisions required by statute or case law

4. The Contract should be researched to determine what provisions, if any, are required by statute or case law.

Boilerplate

5. a. This provision typically states that it contains the parties' entire understanding regarding the subject matter of the contract and that any modification must be in writing.
   b. Assignment of a contract is usually prohibited where performance is of a personal nature or the seller relied on the creditworthiness of the person signing the contract as buyer.
   c. This provision contains the names and addresses of persons to whom notice is to be sent. This provision is probably not necessary in the Computer Contract because there is no requirement or mention of either party giving notice.
   d. Where the parties are from different states and the contract is to be performed in a third state, it may be helpful to specify which state's law is to govern. This provision is probably unnecessary in the Computer Contract because the parties are located in the same town where the Contract is to be performed.
   e. An attorneys' fee provision making the losing party responsible for the prevailing party's attorneys' fees is a very common provision. Otherwise each party pays that party's attorneys' fees absent a statute providing for attorneys' fees.
   f. This is a common provision stating that if one contract provision is ruled unenforceable, the rest of the contract should be enforced.

Signature lines

6. The Computer Contract contains the following signature lines:

Computer Sales, Inc.

By: ________________

Computer Whiz, President

____

J.A. Jones

The signature lines indicate that the parties to the contract are a corporation and an individual (Computer Sales, Inc. and J.A. Jones). Inclusion of "By:" preceding the first signature line and the title of the person signing on behalf of the corporation ("President") show that Computer Sales, Inc. is obligated. By signing, Computer Whiz has not personally obligated herself on the contract because she has not signed in her individual capacity; she has signed the contract only as a representative of the corporation. In contrast, J.A. Jones is personally obligated if he signs the contract.

CHECKLIST FOR AN EMPLOYMENT CONTRACT

Now that you have some familiarity with common provisions of a contract for the sale of goods, it would be interesting to see how those provisions differ from the common provisions of an employment contract. Figure 14-3 contains a checklist for a simple employment agreement.

Because an employment agreement governs an ongoing relationship between the employer and the employee, that relationship is much better defined than the relationship between the Seller and the Buyer in the Computer Contract. The employment agreement specifies the length of employment, the duties of the employee, the employee's compensation, and the reasons and procedure for terminating the agreement. The work product, non-disclosure, and non-competition provisions protect the employer against the employee taking advantage of what the employee has learned while on the job.

Think about a job you have held as you review the above checklist. What were the material terms of the employment agreement? Jot down notes of the material terms next to the sections of the checklist entitled

Employment Contract Checklist

1. **Parties and subject matter.**
   a. Definitions.
   b. Parties.
   c. Date of the contract.
   d. Statement establishing the employer / employee relationship.
2. **Operative provisions.**
   a. Duration of the employment.
      i. Employment term.
      ii. Renewal of term.
   b. Compensation.
      i. Wages.
      ii. Other benefits.
   c. When compensation payable.
   d. Reimbursement of business expenses paid by employee.
   e. Duties of employee.
   f. Time employee will devote to employer's business.
3. **Contingencies.**
   a. Termination of contract prior to end of contract term.
      i. Reasons.
      ii. Termination procedure.
   b. Work product provision (work produced by employee while employed is owned by employer).
   c. Employee's duty not to disclose trade secrets and other information important to the business.
   d. Non-competition provision (after leaving employer, employee may not compete with employer's business for a certain length of time and within a certain geographical area).
4. **Boilerplate.**
   a. Modification or renewal of contract.
   b. Notice provision.
   c. Choice of law provision.
   d. Saving clause.
5. **Signature lines.**

FIGURE 14-3 Employment Contract Checklist.

"Parties and subject matter" and "Operative provisions." Which of the "Contingencies" were spelled out in the employment agreement? If your employment agreement were written, which of the boilerplate provisions would be included? Now review the checklist again. Can you think of any terms that were omitted?

ORGANIZATION AND FORMAT

Deciding what provisions to include is only part of writing a contract. The reader will have an easier time understanding a contract that is well organized and has an inviting format. Organization and format go hand in hand. A well-organized contract may not be easy to understand if the format is poor. On the other hand, good format will not save poor organization.

Organization

The following are the traditional parts of a contract:

1. **Introduction** The introduction usually contains the names of the parties and the date. The contract must contain a statement that the parties agree to the remainder of the terms in the contract. This statement is typically contained either in the introduction or in the recitals.
2. **Recitals** This section of the contract states the basis for the contract and will state that the parties agree to the remainder of the terms in

the contract if this statement was not included in the introduction. In contracts not written in plain English, you can recognize this section because it is usually headed "WITNESSETH:," each paragraph of the section begins with "WHEREAS," and the section ends with some variation on the words: "Now therefore, in consideration of the mutual covenants herein contained, and other good and valuable consideration, the receipt of which is hereby acknowledged, the parties to this agreement hereby agree as follows."

Be kind to your reader by replacing the traditional "legalese" with plain English. Title this section, "Background of Contract" or simply "Background," instead of heading it "WITNESSETH:" and delete all use of "WHEREAS." If this is where you state the parties' agreement, state it simply: "The parties agree as follows." Unless you make this section part of the body of the contract, the section is not normally numbered or lettered.

Because the terms of the Computer Contract were so simple, the contract did not contain this section. If it had it might have looked something like this:

Background of Contract

Buyer desires to purchase a computer and Seller sells the type of computer Buyer desires.

3. **Body** The body of the contract contains the parts of the contract discussed earlier in the chapter: the subject matter, the definition section (if there is need for one), the operative provisions, the contingencies, and the boilerplate. For ease of reference the sections and divisions within sections are numbered or lettered as in an outline and the sections are introduced by a section heading.
4. **Signatures** The signature block contains signature lines for the parties signing and, if possible, should identify the persons signing. Preferably the identification can be typewritten, but may be handwritten legibly. Depending on the legal requirements of the contract, this section may contain lines for witnesses to sign and one or more notary blocks. State law typically requires each signature to be witnessed by two individuals and be notarized if the document is to be recorded in the public records. Other provisions of state or federal law contain requirements for certain types of contracts.

Good organization means that related terms are near each other and are placed in a logical order. Writing the contract using the four parts identified above provides a framework for the contract. Then the information within each of the four parts must be organized as well. The order may be chronological or functional or follow some other scheme suited to the subject matter and the intended audience.

Format

Select one of your textbooks whose pages look inviting to read and one whose pages look uninviting. Now compare the pages of the two texts. Chances are that the page that looks more inviting has wider margins, larger print, medium length lines and paragraphs, double spacing between sections, and underlined or boldfaced descriptive section headings. Reader-friendly format makes the page easier to read.

You can use that same reader-friendly format in writing contracts. Make your margins wide enough that they give the reader's eyes a place to rest. Line and paragraph length should be neither too long nor too short. The print should be no smaller than ten or twelve point. Give the contract a title that identifies the type of document it is. You may also want to include other information in the title such as the subject matter and the parties. Underlined or boldfaced descriptive section headings make it easy to find relevant terms. You may want to break up a longer section into a number of sections or tabulate to make the section easier to read.

When deciding on format, do not forget to check for any statutory requirements. The signatures on certain documents, typically those to be recorded in the public records, may require witnesses and may be required to be notarized.

The Cruise agreement of nondisclosure

Figure 14-4 contains a nondisclosure agreement signed by Tom Cruise and Nicole Kidman's former

FIGURE 14-4 Agreement of Nondisclosure.

AGREEMENT OF NONDISCLOSURE

By signing this Agreement of Nondisclosure, I, JUDITA T. GOMEZ, (Name of Employee) acknowledge and agree as follows:

1. I have been engaged by ODIN PRODUCTIONS, INC. to provide services for Tom Cruise and his wife, Nicole Kidman. I acknowledge that while performing such services, I may receive confidential information, whether oral or written, regarding the personal and/or business affairs of Tom Cruise and Nicole Kidman ("Confidential Information"). I further acknowledge that Mr. Cruise and Ms. Kidman (collectively "Cruise"), are prominent public persons whose reputations are of particular sensitivity due to their prominence as motion picture actors. I understand that disclosure of Confidential Information might embarrass or falsely injure the reputation of Cruise, which will cause irreparable harm. I also understand that disclosure will result in an invasion of the privacy of Cruise, which privacy I acknowledge they are entitled to maintain.

2. I agree to hold in strictest confidence and not to disclose, reveal or imply any Confidential Information which may be acquired by me, without the written consent of Cruise. My sole intention in signing this Agreement is to protect Cruise from the disclosure of information which may tend to harm, malign, damage, injure or otherwise adversely affect any of their respective activities.

3. I acknowledge and agree that any disclosure or misappropriation of any Confidential Information in violation of this Agreement will cause irreparable harm, the amount of which may be difficult to ascertain. I therefore agree that Cruise shall have the right to apply to a court of competent jurisdiction for an order restraining such disclosure, use or misappropriation and for such other relief as may be deemed appropriate, including, without limitation, damages, attorneys' fees and court costs.

I hereby acknowledge that I have read and understand the foregoing.

Dated ___July 26___ day of ________________, 1993.

____
(Signature of Employee)

Judita T. Gomez
(Print Name of Employee)

maid. The document is an exhibit in a lawsuit the maid filed, claiming that she was wrongfully terminated. A nondisclosure agreement is a type of contract. Read through the contract noting its organization and format. Note any potential problems or omissions.

Tips on writing contracts

The following article, *50 Tips for Writing the 21st Century Contract That Stays Out of Court*, provides a wealth of information on drafting contracts (fig. 14-5).

A TYPE OF EMPLOYMENT AGREEMENT—THE ATTORNEY-CLIENT RETAINER AGREEMENT

A common type of employment agreement an attorney drafts is the agreement between the attorney and the client. In this agreement the client retains the attorney to perform certain legal services and the attorney agrees to perform those services. The agreement is similar to other employment agreements in many respects. The attorney and the client mutually

FIGURE 14-5 50 Tips for Writing the 21st Century Contract That Stays Out of Court.

50 TIPS FOR WRITING THE 21ST CENTURY CONTRACT THAT STAYS OUT OF COURT

by James W. Martin

Welcome to the 21st Century, where practicing law requires us to don the garb of computers and the Internet. And where litigation is as costly as ever. Lawyer bills running $10,000 a month are not unusual in a hotly contested breach of contract lawsuit. With every word, phrase, and sentence carrying the potential for winning or losing, the stakes are high. Simple logic, therefore, directs us to cautious and thoughtful drafting.

Drafting contracts is actually one of the simple pleasures of practicing law. This article offers tips for drafting contracts in the context of our new tools and abilities. Following these suggestions could result in your writing a contract so clear no one will want to litigate it, saving your client from the trials and tribulations of litigation, truly a good reason to write the contract that stays out of court.

These tips apply to writing all kinds of agreements: office leases, real estate contracts, sales agreements, employment contracts, equipment leases, prenuptial agreements. They even apply to stipulations and settlements in litigation, where you want an agreement so clear that it avoids future litigation. Wherever clarity and simplicity are important, these tips will guide you there. The appendix provides a few sample forms to illustrate these tips.

Before You Write the First Word

1) Ask your client to list the deal points. This can be in the form of a list, outline, or narration. Doing this will help the client focus on the terms of the agreement.

2) Engage your client in "what if" scenarios. A good contract will anticipate many possible factual situations and express the parties understanding in case those facts arise. Talking to your client about this will generate many issues you may not otherwise consider.

3) Ask your client for a similar contract. Frequently, clients have had similar transactions in the past or they have access to contracts for similar transactions.

4) Search your office computer or the Internet for a similar form. Many times you can find a similar form on your computer. It may be one you prepared for another client or one you negotiated with another lawyer. Just remember to find and replace the old client's name. Starting with an existing form saves time and avoids the errors of typing. Here are some Web sites where you can find forms:

- The Florida Supreme Court links page, Self-Help Center: http://www.flcourts.org/
- The Florida Bar Real Property Probate and Trust Law Section links page: http://www.flabarrpptl.org/library.html
- Florida Law Online links page: http://www.gate.net/~wyman/flo.html
- West Publishing: http://www.westgroup.com
- Lexis: http://www.lexis.com/
- James W. Martin, P.A.: http://www.jamesmartinpa.com/pubs.htm
- Secretaries of State: http://www.jamesmartinpa.com/secst.htm
- Florida Clerks of Court: http://www.jamesmartinpa.com/clerks.htm

5) Typical forms of contracts can be found in form books, such as West's Legal Forms (a nationwide set) and Florida Jur Forms, as well as in treatises and Florida Bar CLE publications. These can be used as the starting point for drafting the contract or as checklists of typical provisions and wording to include in the contract. Many treatises and form books now come with forms on disk or CD-ROM.

James W. Martin practices in St. Petersburg. He received his B.S. from Stetson University (1971) and his J.D. from Stetson College of Law (1974). He has written numerous form books and articles and frequently participates in seminars.

FIGURE 14-5 (continued)

6) Don't let your client sign a letter of intent without this wording. Sometimes clients are anxious to sign something to show good faith before the contract is prepared. A properly worded letter of intent is useful at such times. Just be sure that the letter of intent clearly states that it is not a contract, but that it is merely an outline of possible terms for discussion purposes. See Appendix D.

Writing That First Word

7) Start with a simple, generic contract form. The form in Appendix A is such a form. It provides a solid starting point for the structure of the contract. Like a house, a contract must have a good, solid foundation.

8) State the correct legal names of the parties in the first paragraph. As obvious as this is, it is one of the most common problems in contracts. For individuals, include full first and last name, and middle initials, if available, and other identifying information, if appropriate, such as Jr. or M.D. For corporations, check with the Secretary of State where incorporated. (In Florida, call the Florida Division of Corporations at 850/488-9000 or search its database from its website at http://ccfcorp.dos.state.fl.us/index.html or for other states see the list of secretaries of state websites at http://www.jamesmartinpa.com/secst.htm).

9) Identify the parties by nicknames. Giving each party a nickname in the first paragraph will make the contract easier to read. For example, James W. Martin would be nicknamed "Martin."

10) Be careful when using legal terms for nicknames. Do not use "Contractor" as a nickname unless that party is legally a contractor. Do not use "Agent" unless you intend for that party to be an agent, and if you do, then you better specify the scope of authority and other agency issues to avoid future disagreements.

11) Include a blank for the date in the first paragraph. Putting the date in the first paragraph makes it easy to find after the contract is signed. It also makes it easy to describe the contract in other documents in a precise way, such as the "December 20, 2000, Contract for Sale of Real Estate."

12) Include recitals to provide background. Recitals are the "whereas" clauses that precede the body of a contract. They provide a simple way to bring the contract's reader (party, judge, or jury) up to speed on what the contract is about, who the parties are, and why they are signing a contract. The first paragraph in the body of the contract can incorporate the recitals by reference and state that they are true and correct. This will avoid a later argument as to whether the recitals are a legally binding part of the contract.

13) Outline the contract by writing out and underlining paragraph headings in their logical order. The paragraphs should flow in logical, organized fashion. It is not necessary to write them all at once; you can write them as you think of them. Try to group related concepts in the same paragraphs or in adjacent paragraphs. For example, write an employment contract's initial paragraph headings like this:

A. *Recitals.*
B. *Employment.*
C. *Duties.*
D. *Term.*
E. *Compensation.*

14) Complete each paragraph by writing the contract terms that apply to that paragraph. This is simple. You learned this in elementary school: Just explain in words what the parties agree to do or not do paragraph by paragraph.

15) Keep a pad at hand to remember clauses to add. It is normal to think of additional clauses, wording, and issues while writing a contract. Jot these down on a pad as you write; they are easily forgotten. Also keep your client's outline and other forms in front of you and check off items as you write them.

16) Repeat yourself only when repetition is necessary to improve clarity. Ambiguity is created by saying the same thing more than once; it is almost impossible to say it twice without creating ambiguity. Only if the concept is a difficult one should you write it in more than one way. In addition, if you use an example to clarify a

FIGURE 14-5 (continued)

difficult concept or formula, be sure that all possible meanings are considered and that the example is accurate and consistent with the concept as worded.

What to Watch for When Writing

17) Title it "Contract." Do not leave this one to chance. If your client wants a contract, call it a contract. A judge now sitting on the federal bench once ruled that a document entitled "Proposal" was not a contract even though signed by both parties. The lesson learned is, "Say what you mean." If you intend the document to be a legally binding contract, use the word "Contract" in the title.

If these 50 tips don't keep your contracts out of court, try mastering Strunk & White's *Elements of Style*, which is online at www.bartleby.com.

18) Write in short sentences. Short sentences are easier to understand than long ones.

19) Write in active tense, rather than passive. Active tense sentences are shorter and use words more efficiently, and their meaning is more apparent. Example of active: Sellers shall sell the Property to Buyer. Example of passive: The Property shall be sold to Buyer by Seller.

20) Don't use the word "biweekly." It has two meanings: twice a week and every other week. The same applies to "bimonthly." Instead, write "every other week" or "twice a week."

21) Don't say words like "active termites and organisms." Avoid ambiguity by writing either "active termites and active organisms" or "organisms and active termites." When adding a modifier like "active" before a compound of nouns like "termites and organisms," be sure to clarify whether you intend the modifier to apply to both nouns or just the first one. If you intend it to apply to both, use parallel construction and write the modifier in front of each noun. If you intend it to apply to just one noun, place that one noun at the end of the list and the modifier directly in front of it.

22) Don't say "Lessor" and "Lessee." These are bad nicknames for a lease because they are easily reversed or mistyped. Use "Landlord" and "Tenant" instead. The same applies to lienor and lienee, mortgagor and mortgagee, grantor and grantee, licensor and licensee, party *A* and party *B*. This is where you can use your creativity to come up with a different nickname for a party, as long as you use it consistently throughout the contract.

23) Watch out when using "herein." Does "wherever used herein" mean anywhere in the contract or anywhere in the paragraph? Clarify this ambiguity if it matters.

24) Write numbers as both words and numerals: ten (10). This will reduce the chance for errors.

25) When you write "including," consider adding "but not limited to." Unless you intend the list to be all-inclusive, you had better clarify your intent that it is merely an example.

26) Don't rely on the rules of grammar. The rules of grammar that you learned in school are not universal. The judge or jury interpreting the meaning of your contract may have learned different rules. Write the contract so that no matter what rules they learned, the contract is clear and unambiguous. Follow this test for clear writing: *Remove all periods and commas, then read it.* Choosing the right words and placing them in the right place makes the writing clear without punctuation.

27) Don't be creative with words. Contract writing is not creative writing and is not meant to provoke reflective thoughts or controversies about nuances of meaning. Contract writing is clear, direct, and precise. Therefore, use common words and common meanings. Write for the common man and the common woman.

28) Be consistent in using words. If you refer to the subject matter of a sales contract as "goods," use that term throughout the contract; do not alternately call them "goods" and "items." Maintaining consistency is more important than avoiding repetition. Don't worry about putting the reader to sleep; worry about the opposing lawyer a year from now hunting for ambiguities to get your contract into court.

FIGURE 14-5 (continued)

29) Be consistent in grammar and punctuation. The rules of grammar and punctuation you learned may differ from others, but you had better be consistent in your use of them. Be aware of such things as where you put ending quote marks, whether you place commas after years and states, and similar variations in style.

30) Consider including choice of law, venue selection, and attorneys' fee clauses. If your contract gets litigated, you might as well give your client some "ammunition" for the fight. Examples of these clauses appear in Appendices A and C.

Write for the Judge and Jury

31) Assume the reader is a knowledgeable layman. If your writing is so clear that a layman could understand it, then it is less likely it will end up in court.

32) Define a word by capitalizing it and putting it in quotes. Capitalizing a word indicates that you intend it to have a special meaning. The following are two sample clauses for defining terms:

> Wherever used in this contract, the word "Goods" shall mean the goods that Buyer has agreed to purchase from Seller under this contract.
>
> Buyer hereby agrees to purchase from Seller ten (10) frying pans, hereinafter called the "Goods."

33) Define words when first used. Instead of writing a section of definitions at the beginning or end of a contract, consider defining terms and concepts as they first appear in the contract. This will make it easier for the reader to follow.

34) Explain technical terms and concepts. Remember that the parties might understand technical jargon, but the judge and jury who interpret and apply the contract do not. Therefore, explain the contract's terms and concepts within the contract itself. Let the contract speak for itself from within its four corners.

Keep Your Client Informed While You Write

35) All contracts should come with a cover letter. This gives you a place to instruct your client on how to use and sign the contract.

36) Tell your client the ideas that come as you write. Many ideas will occur to you as you write: what could go wrong with the deal; what might happen in the future; what has happened in the past; what might structure things better. Write these in your letter to the client.

37) Inform your client of the risks. Writing a letter to the client as you write the contract is the perfect way to inform the client of the risks and rewards of entering into the contract. Frequently, problems do not become apparent until time is spent trying to word a contract.

After the First Draft Is Written

38) Check spelling, paragraph numbering, and cross references both manually and with your word processor's spelling and grammar checker. This almost goes without saying today, especially since Microsoft Word now checks your spelling and grammar as you type. (Unfortunately it also changes per stirpes to per stupid if you fail to watch it closely.) And now there are even computer programs that check contract documents for undefined terms. DealProof is packaged with Corel WordPerfect for law offices, and DocProofReader is available for download for MS Word 97 and 2000.

39) Let your secretary or paralegal read the contract. Not only will your staff frequently find spelling and grammar errors missed by your word processor's spell checker, but also they will find inconsistencies and confusing areas that you missed when drafting.

40) Stamp "Draft #1 6/22/2000" on it. This may be the first of many drafts, so avoid confusion early by numbering and dating all drafts at the top of the first page. A good idea is to write "DRAFT" across the face of each page to preclude the possibility of an impatient client signing a draft rather than waiting for the final version.

FIGURE 14-5 (continued)

41) Let your client read the contract. Letting the client in on reading the first draft assures that your drafting will stay in tune with the client's wishes.

42) Save the drafts as multiple files on your computer. If you save the first draft on your computer as two files, you will have one file identified as the first draft and the other identified as the current version. This can be done by naming the current version "contract" and the first draft as "contract.d1." Then, subsequent versions can be named "contract.d2," "contract.d3," etc., where the d in the extension indicates draft. (Of course, if you're not using WordPerfect 5.1 for DOS, as I do, you can use long file names to show the contract name, draft number and draft date, such as Contract Smith Jones draft 2 dtd 6 22 2000.

43) Compare the current version to prior versions. If you save draft versions, it is very easy to compare one version to another using the word processor's compare feature or using the CompareRite computer program. When you compare "contract.d1" to "contract.d2," save the comparison as "contract.c21" and print it to show the client what changes were made.

How to Print and Sign the Final Draft

44) Print the contract on 24 pound bond paper instead of 20 pound copier paper. Using a heavy bond paper will make it easy to tell the original contract from copies and the contract will also last longer.

45) Print on pages using the same paper, and if pages are changed, reprint the document using the same paper. This will avoid an argument that pages were substituted after the contract was signed.

46) Sign the contract in blue ink, not black ink. This, too, will make it easier to differentiate the signed original contract from photocopies.

47) Initial every page of the contract. Having each party initial each page of the contract will make it less likely that anyone could claim a page was changed after the contract was signed.

48) Identify the parties and witnesses who sign by providing blank lines below their signature lines for their printed names and addresses. This procedure will make it easier to find the witnesses if the contract is contested. And remember to include two witnesses for commercial leases.

49) Be sure that corporate officers include their titles, the corporation name, and the word "as." Failure to do this can result in personal liability of the officer. The proper way to sign in a representative capacity is as follows:

ABC Corporation, a Florida corporation
By: ________________________
John Jones, as its President

50) Add a notary clause that complies with the notary law. The notary acknowledgement in Appendix B is such a clause.

Appendix A (Basic Form of Contract)

CONTRACT

AGREEMENT made this __ day of _____ , 20 , between ___________ hereinafter called " ____________ ," and ____________ , hereinafter called "____________."

WHEREAS,____________ ;

WHEREAS, ____________ ; and

WHEREAS, ____________;

NOW THEREFORE, in consideration of their mutual promises made herein, and for other good and valuable consideration, receipt of which is hereby acknowledged by each party, the parties, intending to be legally bound, hereby agree as follows:

FIGURE 14-5 (continued)

1. *Recitals.* The parties agree that the foregoing recitals are true and correct and incorporated herein by this reference.

2. ________________________.

__. *Miscellaneous.* Time is of the essence of this agreement. This agreement is made in the State of Florida and shall be governed by Florida law. This is the entire agreement between the parties and may not be modified or amended except by a written document signed by the party against whom enforcement is sought. This agreement may be signed in more than one counterpart, in which case each counterpart shall constitute an original of this agreement. Paragraph headings are for convenience only and are not intended to expand or restrict the scope or substance of the provisions of this agreement. Wherever used herein, the singular shall include the plural, the plural shall include the singular, and pronouns shall be read as masculine, feminine or neuter as the context requires. The prevailing party in any litigation, arbitration or mediation relating to this agreement shall be entitled to recover its reasonable attorneys' fees from the other party for all matters, including but not limited to appeals. Pinellas County, Florida, shall be proper venue for any litigation involving this agreement. This agreement may not be assigned or delegated by either party without the prior written consent of the other party.

IN WITNESS WHEREOF, the parties have signed this agreement as of the day and year first above written.

______________________________ ______________________________ (Seal)

____

Witnesses

______________________________ ______________________________ (Seal)

____

Witnesses

Appendix B (Basic Form of Notary Acknowledgement)

STATE OF FLORIDA

COUNTY OF ____________

The foregoing instrument was acknowledged before me this __ day of _______ ,

20 __, by _____.

Notary Public-State of Florida:

sign ________________________

print ________________________

Personally Known __; OR Produced Identification ________________

Type of Identification Produced:

____

Affix Seal Below:

FIGURE 14-5 (continued)

Appendix C (Sample Hourly Attorneys' Fee Agreement for Probate)

IN THE CIRCUIT COURT FOR __________ COUNTY, FLORIDA

PROBATE DIVISION

FILE NUMBER _______________

IN RE: ESTATE OF

__________,

DECEASED.

_________________/

ATTORNEYS' HOURLY FEE AGREEMENT

AGREEMENT made between the following persons:

Personal Representative: ______________________________

Attorney: ______________________________

Residuary Beneficiaries: ______________________________

Whereas, Attorney is about to undertake the performance of substantial legal services on behalf of the Personal Representative, for which Attorney shall be paid fees and costs, and the Florida Bar's Rules of Professional Conduct encourage attorneys and clients to enter into fee agreements at the commencement of representation in order to avoid the possibility of misunderstandings, and the Florida Probate Code requires that attorney fee agreements be signed by the Personal Representative and by the persons bearing the impact of the fees;

Now therefore, in consideration of their mutual promises stated herein, the parties hereby agree that:

1. *Hourly Rates.* The Personal Representative has retained Attorney to provide legal services to the Personal Representative for administration of the above probate estate in Florida at hourly rates of $ ____ for attorney time and $ ____ for paralegal time for all matters handled, including but not limited to ordinary services and extraordinary services.
2. *Limitation on Fees.* Notwithstanding the foregoing, Attorney agrees not to bill fees for ordinary services of Attorney that would exceed the percentage fees provided for in Florida Statutes Section 733.6171.
3. *Monthly Bills.* Fees shall be billed by Attorney and paid by the Personal Representative out of the assets of the Estate on a monthly basis. Costs incurred for copies, postage, long distance, fax, FedEx, filing fees, and other items shall also be billed and paid at least monthly.
4. *No Statutory Percentage Fees.* The parties agree that the provisions of this Fee Agreement replace the provisions of the applicable statutes and case law and that Attorney will not charge fees based upon a percentage of ordinary services by the attorney for the Personal Representative: $1,500 for the first $40,000 plus $750 for the next $30,000 plus $750 for the next $30,000 plus 3% of the rest of the inventory value and income of the probate estate for ordinary services. The statute also provides that the attorney, personal representative and persons bearing the impact of the compensation may agree to compensation determined in a different manner. The statute also provides that attorneys are entitled to additional compensation for extraordinary services, such as real estate, adversary proceedings, homestead, tax matters, business, etc.)
5. *Fee Proceedings.* If the matter of fees and costs is submitted to the Court for review or determination at any time, fees and costs shall be billed by and paid to Attorney for such fee proceeding on the same basis as other fees under this Agreement; i.e., billed and paid at least monthly. In addition, attorneys testifying as expert witnesses on the

FIGURE 14-5 (continued)

matter of fees shall be entitled to fees at their usual hourly rates, which shall be paid out of the estate.

6. *Joint Representation.* The parties agree that Attorney represents __________ in his or her capacity as Personal Representative of the Estate and also in his or her capacity as Successor Trustee of THE _________ TRUST. The parties understand the potential conflict of interest arising from representation of multiple parties in multiple roles. They understand that if a conflict should ever develop between the multiple clients concerning the Estate or Trust, then Attorney would not be able to represent either of the clients in that conflict. The Personal Representative, Trustee and residuary beneficiaries are encouraged to engage his or her own separate lawyer before signing this agreement if they desire legal advice concerning this Fee Agreement or concerning any other aspect of the probate estate or Trust.

Under penalties of perjury, we declare that we have read the foregoing, and the facts alleged are true, to the best of our knowledge and belief.

Attorney:
___________________________ Date: ___ 20 ___
Personal Representative:
___________________________ Date: ___ 20 ___
Residuary Beneficiary:
___________________________ Date: ___ 20 ___

Appendix D (Sample Letter of Intent Form)

LETTER OF INTENT FOR POSSIBLE CONTRACT FOR SALE OF ASSETS

Possible Seller:

____

Possible Buyer:

____

Business:

____

Date:__________, 20 __

This is a nonbinding letter of intent that contains provisions that are being discussed for a possible sale of the Business named above from the possible Seller named above to the possible Buyer named above. This is not a contract. This is not a legally binding agreement. This is merely an outline of possible contract terms for discussion purposes only. This is being signed in order to enable the Possible Buyer to apply for financing of the purchase price. This letter of intent is confidential and shall not be disclosed to anyone other than the parties and their employees, attorneys and accountants and the possible lenders of the Possible Buyer. The terms of the transaction being discussed are attached hereto, but the terms (and the possible sale itself) are not binding unless and until they are set forth in a written contract signed by Possible Seller and Possible Buyer. The word "shall" is used in the attached terms only as an example of how a contract might read, and it does not mean that the attached terms are or ever will be legally binding.

____________________________ ____________________________

____

Witnesses

____________________________ ____________________________

____

Witnesses

agree to the employment relationship; the agreement sets forth the duties of the parties, the period of employment, and the attorney compensation.

Most attorney-client retainer agreements need not be in writing; however, it is advisable to reduce the agreement to writing to clarify the terms of the employment relationship, to avoid future disputes, and to handle any disputes that may arise. One law office management expert stated, "Over 50 percent of the complaints against lawyers arise from fee disputes, and about 90 percent of those would be alleviated with written fee agreements."

Florida Bar Rule 4-1.5 requires attorneys fees to be reasonable and sets certain limits on contingent fees. This rule is similar to the rule of many other state bar associations concerning attorneys fees. The rule requires contingent fee payment arrangements to be in writing and requires that the client sign and be given a copy of STATEMENT OF CLIENT'S RIGHTS FOR CONTINGENCY FEES. The rule prohibits the use of contingent fees in domestic relations and criminal defense matters. Florida Bar Rule 4-1.5 and the STATEMENT OF CLIENT'S RIGHTS FOR CONTINGENCY FEES are set forth in Figure 14-6.

Attorney employment agreement checklist

Figure 14-7 is a checklist of matters to be considered in drafting an employment agreement. The checklist was taken from American Jurisprudence Legal Forms 2d.

Many of the items in this checklist are similar to the items in the employment contract checklist from earlier in this chapter. The attorney employment checklist contains many more options as to the attorney compensation and addresses payment of costs and expenses and the attorney's lien; it does not contain the work product, non-disclosure, and non-competition provisions included in the employment contract checklist. Costs and expenses typically include items such as **filing fees,** long distance telephone charges, postage, copy charges, travel and meal expenses, **court reporter fees,** and **expert witness fees.**

Attorney compensation

Attorney compensation may be structured in a number of ways. Common types of attorney compensation include contingent fee, hourly fee, and flat fee. With a **contingent fee arrangement,** the attorney is paid a percentage of the amount the client recovers; thus with a contingent fee arrangement, the attorney will not collect attorney's fees if the client is not successful in being awarded damages. The contingent fee arrangement is prevalent in personal injury actions. In the typical personal injury action, the plaintiff has been injured and is seeking compensation for the injury. Ethics rules prohibit an attorney from using a contingent fee arrangement if the attorney is representing a party in a domestic relations case or a criminal defendant.

In an **hourly fee arrangement,** the attorneys (and often the paralegals in the firm) keep a detailed record of the amount of time the attorneys spend on the client's legal matters. The law firm bills the client on a monthly, or more frequent, basis for the time spent. Each attorney and paralegal has an hourly billing rate. The hourly rate is based on the experience of the attorney or paralegal, the type of legal matter, and the customary hourly rates in the area. The hourly attorney rates in a smaller legal community can range from $100 or $150 to $300 or $400 per hour. Hourly rates in a large city can be as much as $700 or more an hour. The client's bill is based on the amount of time an attorney or paralegal spent on the client's matter, multiplied by the attorney's or paralegal's hourly rate plus any costs and expenses. Many corporate clients pay for legal matters handled by an outside law firm (rather than by corporate staff attorneys) under an hourly fee arrangement.

In a **flat fee arrangement,** the attorney quotes the client one fee that will cover payment for a particular legal matter. The fee may or may not include costs and expenses. The flat fee arrangement is often used in criminal defense work. It may also be used if the attorney has been asked to draft a discrete legal document, such as a will, a trust, or a set of basic corporate documents.

To ensure payment, the attorney often requires the client to pay an amount of money prior to the attorney starting to work on the client matter. The money is generally referred to as a **retainer.** In criminal defense representation, the attorney may require the criminal defendant to pay the entire fee the attorney has quoted the prospective client before the attorney begins to work on the client's case. In other types

FIGURE 14-6 Florida Bar Rule 4-1.5 Fees for Legal Services.

Florida Bar Rule 4-1.5

FEES FOR LEGAL SERVICES

(a) Illegal, Prohibited, or Clearly Excessive Fees. An attorney shall not enter into an agreement for, charge, or collect an illegal, prohibited, or clearly excessive fee or a fee generated by employment that was obtained through advertising or solicitation not in compliance with the Rules Regulating The Florida Bar. A fee is clearly excessive when:

(1) after a review of the facts, a lawyer of ordinary prudence would be left with a definite and firm conviction that the fee exceeds a reasonable fee for the services provided to such a degree as to constitute clear overreaching or an unconscionable demand by the attorney; or

(2) the fee is sought or secured by the attorney by means of intentional misrepresentation or fraud upon the client, a nonclient party, or any court, as either entitlement to, or amount of, the fee.

(b) Factors to Be Considered in Determining Reasonable Fee. Factors to be considered as guides in determining a reasonable fee include:

(1) the time and labor required, the novelty, complexity, and difficulty of the questions involved, and the skill requisite to perform the legal service properly;

(2) the likelihood that the acceptance of the particular employment will preclude other employment by the lawyer;

(3) the fee, or rate of fee, customarily charged in the locality for legal services of a comparable or similar nature;

(4) the significance of, or amount involved in, the subject matter of the representation, the responsibility involved in the representation, and the results obtained;

(5) the time limitations imposed by the client or by the circumstances and, as between attorney and client, any additional or special time demands or requests of the attorney by the client;

(6) the nature and length of the professional relationship with the client;

(7) the experience, reputation, diligence, and ability of the lawyer or lawyers performing the service and the skill, expertise, or efficiency of effort reflected in the actual providing of such services; and

(8) whether the fee is fixed or contingent, and, if fixed as to amount or rate, then whether the client's ability to pay rested to any significant degree on the outcome of the representation.

(c) Consideration of All Factors. In determining a reasonable fee, the time devoted to the representation and customary rate of fee need not be the sole or controlling factors. All factors set forth in this rule should be considered, and may be applied, in justification of a fee higher or lower than that which would result from application of only the time and rate factors.

(d) Enforceability of Fee Contracts.

Contracts or agreements for attorney's fees between attorney and client will ordinarily be enforceable according to the terms of such contracts or agreements, unless found to be illegal, obtained through advertising or solicitation not in compliance with the Rules Regulating The Florida Bar, prohibited by this rule, or clearly excessive as defined by this rule.

(e) Duty to Communicate Basis or Rate of Fee to Client. When the lawyer has not regularly represented the client, the basis or rate of the fee shall be communicated to the client, preferably in writing, before or within a reasonable time after commencing the representation.

(f) Contingent Fees. As to contingent fees:

(1) A fee may be contingent on the outcome of the matter for which the service is rendered, except in a matter in which a contingent fee is prohibited by paragraph (f)(3) or by law. A contingent fee agreement shall be in writing and shall state the method by which the fee is to be determined, including the percentage or percentages that shall accrue to the lawyer in the event of settlement, trial, or appeal, litigation and other expenses to be deducted from the recovery, and whether such expenses are to be

FIGURE 14-6 (continued)

deducted before or after the contingent fee is calculated. Upon conclusion of a contingent fee matter, the lawyer shall provide the client with a written statement stating the outcome of the matter and, if there is a recovery, showing the remittance to the client and the method of its determination.

(2) Every lawyer who accepts a retainer or enters into an agreement, express or implied, for compensation for services rendered or to be rendered in any action, claim, or proceeding whereby the lawyer's compensation is to be dependent or contingent in whole or in part upon the successful prosecution or settlement thereof shall do so only where such fee arrangement is reduced to a written contract, signed by the client, and by a lawyer for the lawyer or for the law firm representing the client. No lawyer or firm may participate in the fee without the consent of the client, and by a lawyer for the lawyer or for the law firm representing the client. No lawyer or firm may participate in the fee without the consent of the client in writing. Each participating lawyer or law firm shall sign the contract with the client and shall agree to assume joint legal responsibility to the client for the performance of the services in question as if each were partners of the other lawyer or law firm involved. The client shall be furnished with a copy of the signed contract and any subsequent notices or consents. All provisions of this rule shall apply to such fee contracts.

(3) A lawyer shall not enter into an arrangement for, charge, or collect:

(A) any fee in a domestic relations matter, the payment or amount of which is contingent upon the securing of a divorce or upon the amount of alimony or support, or property settlement in lieu thereof; or

(B) a contingent fee for representing a defendant in a criminal case.

(4) A lawyer who enters into an arrangement for, charges, or collects any fee in an action or claim for personal injury or for property damages or for death or loss of services resulting from personal injuries based upon tortious conduct of another, including products liability claims, whereby the compensation is to be dependent or contingent in whole or in part upon the successful prosecution or settlement thereof shall do so only under the following requirements:

(A) The contract shall contain the following provisions:

(i) "The undersigned client has, before signing this contract, received and read the statement of client's rights and understands each of the rights set forth therein. The undersigned client has signed the statement and received a signed copy to refer to while being represented by the undersigned attorney(s)."

(ii) "This contract may be canceled by written notification to the attorney at any time within 3 business days of the date the contract was signed, as shown below, and if canceled the client shall not be obligated to pay any fees to the attorney for the work performed during that time. If the attorney has advanced funds to others in representation of the client, the attorney is entitled to be reimbursed for such amounts as the attorney has reasonably advanced on behalf of the client."

(B) The contract for representation of a client in a matter set forth in subdivision (f)(4) may provide for a contingent fee arrangement as agreed upon by the client and the lawyer, except as limited by the following provisions:

(i) Without prior court approval as specified below, any contingent fee that exceeds the following standards shall be presumed, unless rebutted, to be clearly excessive:

a. Before the filing of an answer or the demand for appointment of arbitrators or, if no answer is filed or no demand for appointment of arbitrators is made, the expiration of the time period provided for such action:

1. 331/3% of any recovery up to $1 million; plus
2. 30% of any portion of the recovery between $1 million and $2 million; plus
3. 20% of any portion of the recovery exceeding $2 million.

b. After the filing of an answer or the demand for appointment of arbitrators or, if no answer is filed or no demand for appointment of arbitrators is made, the expiration of the time period provided for such action, through the entry of judgment:

1. 40% of any recovery up to $1 million; plus
2. 30% of any portion of the recovery between $1 million and $2 million; plus

FIGURE 14-6 (continued)

3. 20% of any portion of the recovery exceeding $2 million.

c. If all defendants admit liability at the time of filing their answers and request a trial only on damages:

1. 331/3% of any recovery up to $1 million; plus
2. 20% of any portion of the recovery between $1 and $2 million; plus
3. 15% of any portion of the recovery exceeding $2 million.

d. An additional 5% of any recovery after notice of appeal is filed or postjudgment relief or action is required for recovery on the judgment relief or action is required for recovery on the judgment.

(ii) If any client is unable to obtain an attorney of the client's choice because of the limitations set forth in (f)(4)(B)(i), the client may petition the circuit court for approval of any fee contract between the client and an attorney of the client's choosing. Such authorization shall be given if the court determines the client has a complete understanding of the client's rights and the terms of the proposed contract. The application for authorization of such a contract can be filed as a separate proceeding before suit or simultaneously with the filing of a complaint. Proceedings thereon may occur before service on the defendant and this aspect of the file may be sealed. Authorization of such a contract shall not bar subsequent inquiry as to whether the fee actually claimed or charged is clearly excessive under subdivisions (a) and (b).

(iii) In cases where the client is to receive a recovery that will be paid to the client on a future structured or periodic basis, the contingent fee percentage shall only be calculated on the cost of the structured verdict or settlement or, if the cost is unknown, on the present money value of the structured verdict or settlement, whichever is less. If the damages and the fee are to be paid out over the long term future schedule, then this limitation does not apply. No attorney may separately negotiate with the defendant for that attorney's fee in a structured verdict or settlement where such separate negotiations would place the attorney in a position of conflict.

(C) Before a lawyer enters into a contingent fee contract for representation of a client in a matter set forth in this rule, the lawyer shall provide the client with a copy of the statement of client's rights and shall afford the client a full and complete opportunity to understand each of the rights as set forth therein. A copy of the statement, signed by both the client and the lawyer, shall be given to the client to retain and the lawyer shall keep a copy in the client's file. The statement shall be retained by the lawyer with the written fee contract and closing statement under the same conditions and requirements as subdivision (f)(5).

(D) As to lawyers not in the same firm, a division of any fee within subdivision (f)(4) shall be on the following basis:

(i) To the lawyer assuming primary responsibility for the legal services on behalf of the client, a minimum of 75% of the total fee.

(ii) To the lawyer assuming secondary responsibility for the legal services on behalf of the client, a maximum of 25% of the total fee. Any fee in excess of 25% shall be presumed to be clearly excessive.

(iii) The 25% limitation shall not apply to those cases in which 2 or more lawyers or firms accept substantially equal active participation in the providing of legal services. In such circumstances counsel shall apply for circuit court authorization of the fee division in excess of 25%, based upon a sworn petition signed by all counsel that shall disclose in detail those services to be performed. The application for authorization of such a contract may be filed as a separate proceeding before suit or simultaneously with the filing of a complaint. Proceedings thereon may occur before service of process on any party and this aspect of the file may be sealed. Authorization of such contract shall not bar subsequent inquiry as to whether the fee actually claimed or charged is clearly excessive. An application under this subdivision shall contain a certificate showing service on the client and The Florida Bar. Counsel may proceed with representation of the client pending court approval.

(iv) The percentages required by this subdivision shall be applicable after deduction of any fee payable to separate counsel retained especially for appellate purposes.

FIGURE 14-6 (continued)

(5) In the event there is a recovery, upon the conclusion of the representation, the lawyer shall prepare a closing statement reflecting an itemization of all costs and expenses, together with the amount of fee received by each participating lawyer or law firm. A copy of the closing statement shall be executed by all participating lawyers, as well as the client, and each shall receive a copy. Each participating lawyer shall retain a copy of the written fee contract and closing statement for 6 years after execution of the closing statement. Any contingent fee contract and closing statement shall be available for inspection at reasonable times by the client, by any other person upon judicial order, or by the appropriate disciplinary agency.

(g) Division of Fees Between Lawyers in Different Firms. Subject to the provisions of subdivision (f)(4)(D), a division of fee between lawyers who are not in the same firm may be made only if the total fee is reasonable and:

(1) the division is in proportion to the services performed by each lawyer; or

(2) by written agreement with the client:

(A) each lawyer assumes joint legal responsibility for the representation and agrees to be available for consultation with the client; and

(B) the agreement fully discloses that a division of fees will be made and the basis upon which the division of fees will be made.

(h) Credit Plans. Charges made by any lawyer or law firm under an approved credit plan shall be only for services actually rendered or cash actually paid on behalf of the client. No higher fee shall be charged and no additional charge shall be imposed by reason of a lawyer's or law firm's participation in an approved credit plan.

STATEMENT OF CLIENT'S RIGHTS FOR CONTINGENCY FEES

Before you, the prospective client, arrange a contingent fee agreement with a lawyer, you should understand this statement of your rights as a client. This statement is not a part of the actual contract between you and your lawyer, but, as a prospective client, you should be aware of these rights:

1. There is no legal requirement that a lawyer charge a client a set fee or a percentage of money recovered in a case. You, the client, have the right to talk with your lawyer about the proposed fee and to bargain about the rate or percentage as in any other contract. If you do not reach an agreement with one lawyer you may talk with other lawyers.

2. Any contingent fee contract must be in writing and you have 3 business days to reconsider the contract. You may cancel the contract without any reason if you notify your lawyer in writing within 3 business days of signing the contract. If you withdraw from the contract within the first 3 business days, you do not owe the lawyer a fee although you may be responsible for the lawyer's actual costs during that time. If your lawyer begins to represent you, your lawyer may not withdraw from the case without giving you notice, delivering necessary papers to you, and allowing you time to employ another lawyer. Often, your lawyer must obtain court approval before withdrawing from a case. If you discharge your lawyer without good cause after the 3-day period, you may have to pay a fee for work the lawyer has done.

3. Before hiring a lawyer, you, the client, have the right to know about the lawyer's education, training, and experience. If you ask, the lawyer should tell you specifically about the lawyer's actual experience dealing with cases similar to yours. If you ask, the lawyer should provide information about special training or knowledge and give you this information in writing if you request it.

4. Before signing a contingent fee contract with you, a lawyer must advise you whether the lawyer intends to handle your case alone or whether other lawyers will be helping with the case. If your lawyer intends to refer the case to other lawyers, the lawyer should tell you what kind of fee sharing arrangement will be made with the other lawyers. If lawyers from different law firms will represent you, at least 1 lawyer from each law firm must sign the contingent fee contract.

5. If your lawyer intends to refer your case to another lawyer or counsel with other lawyers, your lawyer should tell you about that at the beginning. If your lawyer takes

FIGURE 14-6 (continued)

the case and later decides to refer it to another lawyer or to associate with other lawyers, you should sign a new contract that includes the new lawyers. You, the client, also have the right to consult with each lawyer working on your case and each lawyer is legally responsible to represent your interests and is legally responsible for the acts of the other lawyers involved in the case.

6. You, the client, have the right to know in advance how you will need to pay the expenses and the legal fees at the end of the case. If you pay a deposit in advance for costs, you may ask reasonable questions about how the money will be or has been spent and how much of it remains unspent. Your lawyer should give a reasonable estimate about future necessary costs. If your lawyer agrees to lend or advance you money to prepare or research the case, you have the right to know periodically how much money your lawyer has spent on your behalf. You also have the right to decide, after consulting with your lawyer, how much money is to be spent to prepare a case. If you pay the expenses, you have the right to decide how much to spend. Your lawyer should also inform you whether the fee will be based on the gross amount recovered or on the amount recovered minus the costs.

7. You, the client, have the right to be told by your lawyer about possible adverse consequences if you lose the case. Those adverse consequences might include money that you might have to pay to your lawyer for costs and liability you might have for attorney's fees to the other side.

8. You, the client, have the right to receive and approve a closing statement at the end of the case before you pay any money. The statement must list all of the financial details of the entire case, including the amount recovered, all expenses, and a precise statement of your lawyer's fee. Until you approve the closing statement you need not pay any money to anyone, including your lawyer. You also have the right to have every lawyer or law firm working on your case sign this closing statement.

9. You, the client, have the right to ask your lawyer at reasonable intervals how the case is progressing and to have these questions answered to the best of your lawyer's ability.

10. You, the client, have the right to make the final decision regarding settlement of a case. Your lawyer must notify you of all offers of settlement before and after the trial. Offers during the trial must be immediately communicated and you should consult with your lawyer regarding whether to accept a settlement. However, you must make the final decision to accept or reject a settlement.

11. If at any time you, the client, believe that your lawyer has charged an excessive or illegal fee, you have the right to report the matter to The Florida Bar, the agency that oversees the practice and behavior of all lawyers in Florida. For information on how to reach The Florida Bar, call 904-561-5600, or contact the local bar association. Any disagreement between you and your lawyer about a fee can be taken to court and you may wish to hire another lawyer to help you resolve this disagreement. Usually fee disputes must be handled in a separate lawsuit, unless your fee contract provides for arbitration. You can request, but may not require, that a provision for arbitration (under Chapter 682, Florida Statutes, or under the fee arbitration rule of the Rules Regulating The Florida Bar) be included in your fee contract.

______________________	______________________
Client Signature	Atty. Signature
Date	Date

of matters, the attorney may require the client to pay a sizeable amount of money initially and pay the attorney more, smaller amounts as the first payment is expended. Often, upon receipt of the retainer, the money is deposited into a **client trust account.** The law firm holds the money in the client trust account in trust for the client until it is earned by the attorney. Money is withdrawn and transferred into the law firm account as needed to pay client costs and expenses and attorney fees as the client's legal work is performed.

FIGURE 14-7 Checklist of Matters to Be Considered in Drafting an Employment Agreement.

Attorney.
—Name.
—Address.
Client.
—Name.
—Address.
Effective date of agreement.
Statement of purposes for which attorney is employed.
Statement that attorney-client relationship is created for purposes stated in agreement.
Duration of employment [either by period of time or by extent to which services are to be provided].
Compensation of attorney.
—Amount.
—Manner of fixing and paying.
—Amount and payment of retainer, if any.
—Contingent fee arrangements, if any [including right of attorney to retain fee from proceeds of settlement or judgment].
—Fixed fee, if any.
—Compensation in event of dismissal of attorney by client.
Provision for lien in favor of attorney on any recovery made, or for a possessory lien on documents, and the like, to secure payment for general legal work.
Costs and expenses to be borne by client.
—Advances by attorney.
Authorization from client to employ associate or assistant counsel, investigators, and experts.
—Party responsible for fees.
Statement that favorable outcome is not warranted by attorney.
Termination of contract.
—Substitution or discharge of attorney.
—Withdrawal of attorney.
Grant by client of power of attorney to execute necessary documents.
Incorporation by reference of other documents into agreement.
Manner of giving notice.
Jurisdiction whose law is to govern agreement.
Disposition of disputes.
—Arbitration.
—Other method(s) of alternative dispute resolution.
Date of agreement.
Signatures.

Attorney employment agreement

Figure 3-18 in chapter 3 contains a form from West's Legal Forms 2d to be used when drafting an attorney employment agreement. The form is entitled "General Format With Alternative Clauses." The title indicates that someone using the form must choose one of the alternative clauses in writing the agreement. For example, section 4, entitled "Calculation of Legal Fees," allows the drafter to choose between an hourly, fixed fee, or contingency fee arrangement; there are also provisions for increased fees in certain circumstances and payment of fees in estate matters.

CHAPTER 14 SUMMARY

- You should be familiar with simple contracts so when you read a contract, you can start asking questions and identifying potential problems.
- Some contracts are required to be in writing. Even if not required, it is advisable to have a written contract.
- The three types of contract provisions are:
  parties and subject matter;
  operative provisions; and
  contingencies.
- Contract terms may be negotiated or unnegotiated.
- Often an attorney uses a contract form as a basis for writing the contract rather than writing the contract entirely from scratch.
- Contract forms may be helpful but should not be relied upon blindly.
- Besides the three types of contract provisions listed above, contracts often include provisions required by statute or case law and boilerplate provisions.
- The challenge in writing the "perfect contract" is to accurately state the negotiated provisions, to include any provisions required by statute or case law, and to predict everything that will happen between the parties as the contract is performed.
- The "perfect contract" also requires good organization and format.

CYBERLAW EXERCISES

1. The Lexis law school site (http://lawschool.lexis.com) includes information on developing effective writing skills.
2. The Lexis law school site (http://lawschool.lexis.com) also links you to search engines (click on "Legal Internet Guide" and then on "Internet Search Engines"). Try searching for "legal forms" using several of the search engines.
3. In addition, the Lexis law school site (http://lawschool.lexis.com) includes links to other sites useful in legal writing (click on "My School", "Web Lectures" and then on "legal research & writing").
4. The WashLaw Web site (http://www.washlaw.edu) allows you to access legal forms. Go to the web site and click on "legal forms."
5. LawCrawler (http://www.lawcrawler.com) is a highly-rated search engine that limits its searches to sites known to contain legal information. Try searching for "legal forms" using LawCrawler.

Contract exercises

Now use what you have learned in this chapter by completing the following exercises:

1. Rewrite the Computer Contract, supplying any missing terms. In rewriting, think about substance, organization, and format.
2. Find several form contracts for the sale of goods. Compare the terms in the forms to the checklist in figure 14-2.
3. Write a contract for the sale of goods using one of the forms you found. The terms can be taken

from a real-life transaction or an imaginary one. In writing, think about substance, organization, and format.

4. Find several form employment agreements. Compare the terms in the forms to the checklists in figures 14-3 and 14-7.
5. Write an employment agreement. The terms of the agreement can be based on real-life or can be imaginary. In writing, think about substance, organization, and format.
6. Write an attorney employment agreement. The terms should be tailored to the type of legal work the parties anticipate that the attorney will perform.

CHAPTER 15

PLEADINGS

INTRODUCTION

Pleadings are the formal statements by the parties to an action setting forth their claims or defenses. This chapter explains the purpose, use, and format of the "complaint" and the "answer" and includes two sample complaints and answers.

The sample pleadings have been extensively footnoted to provide you with writing tips. The footnotes in the sample pleadings are not part of the pleadings themselves. If the footnotes do not make sense to you right now, read them again when you are writing your own complaint and answer.

The chapter also includes a complaint Donald Trump filed against Marla Maples to have their prenuptial agreement enforced and a 1915 complaint claiming the value of 40 cases of Roquefort cheese lost on the Titanic (figs. 15-1 and 15-2).

PURPOSE AND USE

A civil lawsuit begins with the plaintiff filing the **complaint** with the court. The complaint is the initial **pleading** in a **civil action,** in which the plaintiff alleges a **cause of action** and asks the court to remedy the wrong done to the plaintiff. The purposes of the complaint are for the plaintiff to state what happened and to state the relief that the plaintiff is requesting from the court.

The **answer** is a pleading in response to the complaint. The answer may deny the allegations of the complaint, agree with them, state that the plaintiff is without knowledge of them, or introduce **affirmative defenses** intended to defeat plaintiff's lawsuit or delay it. The purposes of the answer are for the defendant to reply to the claims plaintiff raised in the complaint, to state defendant's affirmative defenses, and to state related claims (called **counterclaims**) that the defendant has against the plaintiff.

Look for a moment at the first sample complaint and answer included in this chapter. The plaintiff is Jake Carson and the defendant is Tom Harris. Jake and Tom ran against each other for the position of student body president at Collegiate University. The basis of Jake's suit was the statement Tom made about Jake in Tom's political skit, presented on the eve of the election. In the skit Tom stated to a student playing the part of Jake that "Jake" was HIV positive. Jake claims that the skit also depicted him as a homosexual. Jake was so outraged by the skit that he hired an attorney to sue Tom for slander and for depicting him in a "false light" as being a homosexual. The pleadings were filed in Florida state court.

A second sample complaint and answer follows the first set of pleadings. The second set of pleadings were filed in federal court because a federal statute

FIGURE 15-1 Complaint in *Trump v. Trump.*

SUPREME COURT OF THE STATE OF NEW YORK COUNTY OF NEW YORK

______________________________x

DONALD J. TRUMP,

Plaintiff, Index No. 311565/97

— against — VERIFIED COMPLAINT (Justice Lobie)

MARLA MAPLES TRUMP,

Defendant.

______________________________x

Plaintiff, Donald J. Trump, complaining of the defendant, as and for his Verified Complaint, alleges as follows:

ALLEGATION COMMON TO ALL CAUSE OF ACTION

1. Plaintiff and defendant are husband and wife, having been married in New York, New York on December 20, 1993.
2. Both plaintiff and defendant, are residents of New York State and City and have been so at all relevant times.
3. On December 15, 1993, plaintiff and defendant executed a prenuptial agreement (the "Agreement").

AS AND FOR A FIRST CAUSE OF ACTION

4. On August 1, 1997, plaintiff filed an action for divorce against the defendant. Service was effected upon defendant's then counsel pursuant to a stipulation and defendant has appeared in this action.
5. The commencement of said action for divorce by the service of a summons constitutes a "Permanent Separation" as defined in section 4.3 (b) of the Agreement.
6. The service of this Verified Complaint seeking a declaratory judgment also constitutes a "Permanent Separation" as defined in section 4.3 (b) of the Agreement.
7. The provisions of the Agreement with respect to defendant's property rights, maintenance and child support became operative upon the occurrence of the Permanent Separation.
8. On or about November, 5, 1997, plaintiff tendered $ 500,000 to defendant in accordance with the terms of Article 6 of the Agreement. Defendant refused to accept those funds and returned the check to plaintiff.
9. Defendant has accepted the monthly child support payments provided by plaintiff in accordance with the terms of section 5.1 (a) of the Agreement.
10. Defendant, both personally and through her attorneys, has advised plaintiff that she intends to assert that the Agreement is not valid, binding and enforceable.
11. By virtue of the foregoing, there is a real and justiciable controversy as to whether or not the Agreement is valid, binding and enforceable.
12. Plaintiff is entitled to a declaration that the Agreement is valid, binding and enforceable.
13. Plaintiff has no adequate remedy at law.

AS AND FOR A SECOND CAUSE OF ACTION

14. Plaintiff repeats and realleges the allegations contained in paragraphs 1 through 13 hereof as if fully set forth here.

FIGURE 15-1 (continued)

15. Section 9.1 (b) of the Agreement provides that

> If either party or the legal representatives of his or her estate (the "plaintiff") shall bring an action or proceeding to enforce the terms, conditions and covenants of this Agreement against the other party (the "defendant") or to declare the Agreement or any of its terms valid, binding and enforceable, and such action or proceeding is opposed or contested by the other party, if the action or proceeding results in a judgment, decree or order in favor of the plaintiff or a settlement substantially upon the terms, conditions and covenants of this Agreement, the defendant shall pay to the plaintiff the costs and expenses incurred by the plaintiff including actual attorneys' fees or shall permit such costs, expenses and fees to be completely offset against any obligation due from the plaintiff to the defendant hereunder or for my other reason whatsoever.

16. In the event that defendant in responding to this Verified Complaint, asserts that the Agreement is not enforceable, and the Court holds that it is enforceable, or this action is settled "substantially upon the terms, conditions and covenants" of the Agreement, defendant will be responsible to plaintiff for his costs and expenses incurred herein, including, without limitation, actual attorneys' fees.

WHEREFORE, plaintiff demands judgment;

(a) On the First Cause of Action, declaring that the Agreement is valid, binding and enforceable;

(b) On the Second Cause of Action, in the event that defendant asserts in this action that the Agreement is not valid, binding and enforceable, and the Court holds that it is enforceable, or this action is settled "substantially upon the terms, conditions and covenants" of the Agreement, awarding plaintiff the costs and expenses of this action together with his actual attorneys' fees in accordance with the terms of the Agreement;

(c) On both Causes of Action, awarding to plaintiff such other, further and different relief as to the Court may seem just and proper.

Yours etc.

Certified pursuant to 22 M.Y.C.R.R. § 130-1.1a

____

Jay Goldberg

JAY GOLDBERG, P.C.
250 Park Avenue
New York, New York 10177-0077
(212) 963-6000

and

____

Scanford G. Lotwin

TENZER GREENBLATT LLP
405 Lexington Avenue
New York, New York 10174
(212) 315-5000

Attorneys for Plaintiff

FIGURE 15-1 (continued)

STATE OF NEW YORK
COUNTY OF NEW YORK

DONALD J. TRUMP, being duly sworn, says:

I am the plaintiff in the action herein. I have read the foregoing Verified Complaint and know the contents thereof, and the same is true of my own knowledge, except as to the matters stated to be alleged upon information and belief, and as to those matters I believe them to be true.

____
DONALD J. TRUMP

Sworn to before me this
28th day of May 1998

____
Notary Public

gives the federal court jurisdiction over lawsuits alleging interception of telephone conversations. The plaintiff, Phone Addicted, alleges that the defendant, Nosy Neighbor, has used a scanner to listen to Phone Addicted's cordless telephone conversations.

> Trial judges are irritated by pleadings containing mechanical errors. On rare occasion, the errors are egregious enough to merit comment in a reported decision, as shown in the following passage:
>
> The amended complaint purports to allege violations of sections 5(a), 5(c), 12(1) and 12(2) of the Securities Act of 1933, together with violations of section 10(b) and rule 10b-5 of the 1934 Securities Exchange Act, and a multiplicity of state law violations. It is replete with misspellings, grammatical aberrations, non sequiturs and solecisms. [FN1]
>
> FN1. The most extreme example is found in plaintiff's response to the motions to dismiss: "Exercise of pendant jurisdiction is within trial courts [sic] desecration [sic]."
>
> *Gardner v. Investors Diversified Capital, Inc.*, 805 F.Supp. 874, 875 (D. Colo. 1992).

FORMAT

Court rules

Once you determine the court in which the complaint will be filed, you must carefully review any applicable court rules and statutes. The first sample set of pleadings should comply with the Florida Rules of Civil Procedure because they were filed in Florida state court; the second sample set of pleadings should comply with the Federal Rules of Civil Procedure. It

UNITED STATES DISTRICT COURT,
SOUTHERN DISTRICT OF NEW YORK.

IN THE MATTER
— of the —
Petition of the OCEANIC STEAM NAVIGATION COMPANY, LTD., for limitation of liability as owner of the Steamship "TITANIC".

Now appears VINCENZO VICARIO, of Providence, Rhode Island, and makes claim against the said Steamship "Titanic", as follows:

Claimant was the owner of the following property, of the kind and value hereinafter specified, which was aboard the Steamship "Titanic" when she was sunk as a result of a collision with an iceberg, in or about latitude 41.46 North, longitude 50.14 West, on or about the 14th day of April, 1912, while the said Steamship "Titanic" was proceeding towards the port of New York, United States of America, from Southampton, England. The character of the property and its value is set out in the following table:

Owner.	*Shipment.*	*Value.*
Vincenzo Vicario	40 cases Roquefort Cheese	$800.00

Claimant alleges that prior to April 14, 1912, the above-mentioned goods had been duly shipped aboard the Steamship "Titanic", for which bills of lading were duly issued and are now in the possession of claimant.

On April 14, 1912, said Steamship "Titanic", with all of the cargo hereinbefore specified on board, was sunk as the result of a collision with an iceberg at the place aforementioned, and as a result of the collision the said Steamship "Titanic", with all her cargo, including that hereinbefore specified, became a total loss. Said collision was caused and contributed to by the fault and negligence of the Steamship "Titanic", by reason of which your claimant as owner of the aforesaid cargo has sustained damage amounting to the sum of $800, for which he now makes claim against the Steamship "Titanic".

Dated, New York, July 7th, 1915.

VINCENZO VICARIO
By

As Attorney.

FIGURE 15-2 The Lost Roquefort Cheese.

might also be helpful to review court files to learn the format customarily used in the particular court.

Court rules may specify the contents of the complaint and the answer. For example, Rule 1.110 of the Florida Rules of Civil Procedure requires the complaint to "state a cause of action." The same rule requires the answer to "state in short and plain terms the pleader's defenses to each claim asserted and . . . [to] admit or deny the averments on which the adverse party relies." In *Kazmaier v. Central Intelligence Agency*, the plaintiff had requested that he be allowed to proceed in ***forma pauperis.*** This relief is requested when the plaintiff is unable to afford the fees to file the case. This case is reprinted in this chapter. The judge in *Kazmaier* found the lawsuit was frivolous and denied the plaintiff's request.

Commonly, the court rules and official forms accompanying the court rules specify the format of the caption (the heading of the court paper) and the body of the pleading. For example, Form 1.901 of the Florida "Forms for Use with the Rules of Civil Procedure" gives the general form of the caption. (See the caption of the sample pleadings contained in this chapter.)

Forms

Although pleadings can be written entirely from scratch, someone writing a pleading will usually try to find one or more pleadings that are similar to the one the person is writing and use those pleadings as a guide. An attorney may recall a similar lawsuit the attorney has dealt with in the past and use a pleading from that matter as a guide.

Another option is to consult "forms" and "formbooks." Court rules may have appended to them official forms. A number of commercial publishers publish formbooks. As the term implies, "formbooks" are volumes containing forms that may be referred to as a guide. There is a wide variety of formbooks. The forms contained in a particular publication may be much simpler than those contained in another formbook. Some formbooks are written in plain English while others contain a lot of "legalese." Many forms are now available on the Internet.

If you use a form you must tailor it to the particular situation you are dealing with. Just because material is contained in a form, it does not mean that the material is correct for your jurisdiction. Be sure to research the cause of action and defenses for your jurisdiction to ascertain you have all the elements of the cause of action, and have correctly stated the relief available and any affirmative defenses.

Besides including forms, a formbook often contains checklists of typical provisions included in a particular pleading. When writing a pleading, it is helpful to glance down the checklist to make sure you have included all necessary provisions.

John Wesley KAZMAIER, Plaintiff,

v.

CENTRAL INTELLIGENCE AGENCY and the United States Justice Dept. and the Federal Bureau of Investigation and the United States Government, Defendants.

United States District Court,

E.D. Wisconsin.

April 11, 1983.

562 F.Supp. 263

MYRON L. GORDON, Senior District Judge.

John Wesley Kazmaier, the plaintiff in this action, seeks leave of the court to proceed in forma pauperis. The complaint states that federal jurisdiction is based on 28 U.S.C. S 1983; because there is no such statute, it appears that Mr. Kazmaier may have intended to refer to 42 U.S.C. S 1983. Named as defendants are the Central Intelligence Agency (CIA), the Federal Bureau of Investigation (FBI), the United States Department of Justice, and the United States government.

The complaint sets forth in great detail the alleged wrongdoings of the defendants. Generally stated, Mr. Kazmaier claims that the CIA has subjected him to brainwashing and torture attacks since 1965 through the use of satellite beams, portable dental laser equipment, and other such means. The other defendants are alleged to have failed to investigate these incidents. As a result of these attacks, he contends that his high school career was ruined, he was prevented from receiving his college degree, his right ankle was broken, and he suffered tremendous agony. He seeks $7,308,089,250,000.00 in damages, employment as the director and assistant director of the FBI, protection from assassins, authorization to carry concealed weapons, and other forms of relief.

In several letters to the court, Mr. Kazmaier has "ordered" me to provide him with ridiculously large sums of money as loans or advances against his future court award. He has also "ordered" me to send him immediately a list of items, including:

"1. A 25 layer Kevlar bullet-proof vest with protection of both front and rear of body.

2. A 357 magnum caliber revolver in a right hand shoulder holster, preferably with a four inch barrel.

3. A selective-fire Beretta 9mm type 92 pistol in a left-hand shoulder holster.

4. An Uzi Submachine gun caliber 9mm with 5 large magazines, in a soft side case with a zipper top.

5. An M-16 rifle with 5 large magazines, caliber .223.

6. A .380 or .32 ACP caliber Gatling gun with one or more medium or large ammo-pak magazines. This gun is a multiple-barrel high speed gun capable of a high rate of fire, and it has an accurate range of 50 yards.

7. A United States Marshals Service Badge and I.D. set.

* * *

8. A bullet-proof car, such as a bullet-proof Lincoln Continental four door model from Ford Motor Company."

Based on the allegations of the complaint, the nature of the relief sought, and the contents of Mr. Kazmaier's letters, I find that this proposed lawsuit falls easily into the "frivolous" category. I will not grant the plaintiff permission to pursue this action without payment of fees, pursuant to 28 U.S.C. S 1915. Furthermore, the plaintiff has filed a nearly identical complaint in case no. 82-C-1384, now pending before Honorable John W. Reynolds, and he has paid the filing fee in that case. I see no reason to encourage duplication of judicial efforts, especially in a case as this one.

Therefore, IT IS ORDERED that the plaintiff's motion for leave to proceed in forma pauperis be and hereby is denied.

FORMAT OF THE COMPLAINT

This section gives a brief explanation of the various parts of the complaint and then the various parts of the answer. It might be helpful for you to read the rest of this section and the "format of the answer section" while comparing the explanation to the two sets of sample pleadings in this chapter.

Complaint—Caption, title, and introductory clause

This section (called the "caption") contains the name of the court, the names of the parties, and the case number. The title indicates the type of pleading. After the caption and title and before the first numbered paragraph an unnumbered sentence (called the "introductory clause" or "commencement") states who is filing the complaint and against whom it is being filed.

Complaint—Body

This section (called the "body" or "charging portion" of the complaint) contains a series of numbered paragraphs telling the court why it has jurisdiction of the case and what has happened. For example, Rule 1.110 of the Florida Rules of Civil Procedure requires the complaint to contain "(1) a short and plain statement of the grounds upon which the court's jurisdiction depends" and "(2) a short and plain statement of the ultimate facts showing that the pleader is entitled to relief." Rule 1.110 of the Florida Rules of Civil Procedure specifies the format for the body of the pleading:

> All averments of claim or defense shall be made in consecutively numbered paragraphs, the contents of each of which shall be limited as far as practicable to a statement of a single set of circumstances, and a paragraph may be referred to by number in all subsequent pleadings. Each claim founded upon a separate transaction or occurrence and each defense other than denials shall be stated in a separate count or defense when a separation facilitates the clear presentation of the matter set forth.

Complaint—Prayer for relief

This section of the complaint (called the "prayer for relief") states what the plaintiff wants the court to do. For example, Rule 1.110 of the Florida Rules of Civil Procedure requires the complaint to contain "demand for judgment for the relief to which the pleader deems himself or herself entitled." A plaintiff may ask the court for various types of damages, for an injunction, for specific performance, or for some other type of relief.

Complaint—Signature block

The signature block usually contains the name of the attorney, the name and designation of the person the attorney is representing, the attorney's address, and the attorney's telephone number. Many state courts require the attorney's bar membership number.

Complaint—Verification

The verification is a notarized statement of the party, rather than of the attorney, "verifying" the statements contained in the complaint. Some states dispense with verification of court documents unless specifically required by an applicable rule or statute. You should check to determine whether the court in which your complaint is being filed requires verification.

FORMAT OF THE ANSWER

Answer—Caption, title, and introductory clause

The caption is the same as the caption for the complaint. The title reflects that this is an answer. The introductory clause identifies the defendant and introduces the body of the answer.

Answer—Defenses

As stated above, the answer states the defendant's defense, admitting or denying plaintiff's claims. Rule 1.110 of the Florida Rules of Civil Procedure quite specifically states how any denial is to be made:

> If the defendant is without knowledge, the defendant shall so state and such statement shall operate as a denial. Denial shall fairly meet the substance of the averments denied. When the pleader intends in good faith to deny only a part of an averment the pleader shall specify so much of it as is true and shall deny the remainder. Unless the pleader intends in good faith to controvert all of the averments of the preceding pleading, the pleader may make denials as specific denials of the designated averments or may generally deny all of the averments except such designated averments as the pleader expressly admits, but when the pleader does so intend to controvert all of its averments, including averments of the grounds upon which the court's jurisdiction depends, the pleader may do so by general denial.
>
> . . .
>
> Averments in a pleading to which a responsive pleading is required, other than those as the amount of damages, are admitted when not denied in the responsive pleading. Averments in a pleading to which no responsive pleading is required or permitted shall be taken as denied or avoided.

Affirmative defenses and counterclaims

Again, Rule 1.110 of the Florida Rules of Civil Procedure specifies the format for any affirmative defenses or counterclaims:

All averments of claim of defense shall be made in consecutively numbered paragraphs, the contents of each of which shall be limited as far as practicable to a statement of a single set of circumstances, and a paragraph may be referred to by number in all subsequent pleadings. Each claim founded upon a separate transaction or occurrence and each defense other than denials shall be stated in a separate count or defense when a separation facilitates the clear presentation of the matter set forth.

A counterclaim, like the body of the complaint, would be followed by a prayer for relief.

Certificate of service

If the attorney for the defendant serves the answer on the plaintiff's attorney, a certificate of service must be included. There was no certificate of service included in the complaint because the complaint was served on the defendant by the court, not by the plaintiff's attorney.

The failure to follow format, as mandated by court rules, may have serious consequences, including dismissal of the complaint.

Edwin F. GORDON, Plaintiff-Appellant, Cross-Appellee,

v.

E. G. GREEN et al., Defendants-Appellees,

Gustave T. Broberg, Jr., Defendant-Appellee, Cross-Appellant.

United States Court of Appeals,

Fifth Circuit.

Sept. 18, 1979.

Rehearing Granted in Part and Denied in Part Nov. 19, 1979.

602 F.2d 743

JOHN R. BROWN, Chief Judge:

As we see it, the only issue currently before the Court in these five consolidated cases is whether verbose, confusing, scandalous, and repetitious pleadings totaling into the thousands of pages comply with the requirement of "a short and plain statement" set forth in F.R.Civ.P. 8. We think that the mere description of the issue provides the answer: we direct the District Court to dismiss the complaints with leave to amend because of appellant's failure to comply with F.R.Civ.P. 8(a) and (e).

The Pleadings: Gobbledygook

The appellant, Edwin F. Gordon, invested several million dollars in a series of Florida real estate syndications. When the promises of substantial profits failed to materialize, appellant filed suit against the sellers and promoters of the syndications, claiming various violations of the federal securities laws.

Under F.R.Civ.P. 8, a party seeking relief must submit a pleading containing "a short and plain statement of the grounds upon which the court's jurisdiction depends" and "a short and plain statement of the claim showing that the pleader is entitled to relief." In addition, F.R.Civ.P. 8(e)(1) states that "[e]ach averment of a pleading shall be simple, concise, and direct." As the following factual account demonstrates, nothing was further from the minds of appellant and his lawyer than the clear directions contained in F.R.Civ.P. 8(a) and (e).

These five consolidated cases were originally brought in the Southern District of New York in March and April of 1976. At this initial stage, appellant filed five separate long, verbose, and confusing verified complaints containing a total of 165 typewritten pages and an additional 413 pages of exhibits. In one of the five cases, appellant filed an amendment to the verified complaint (8 pages plus 39 pages of exhibits). By stipulation, the cases were transferred to the Southern District of Florida. The Florida Court proposed to dismiss appellant's complaints for violation of Rule 8, but did not actually do so when appellant introduced a single complaint and filed a motion to consolidate. The motion to consolidate was eventually denied.

In September 1976, the Trial Court ordered a hearing on various motions, primarily motions to dismiss under Rule 12(b). One week prior to the hearing and without seeking leave to amend appellant filed an "Amendment to Verified Complaint" for each of the actions. Each "Amendment to Verified Complaint" was 19 pages. On September 30, 1976, the Trial Court dismissed the action, but Not for failure to comply with Rule 8. Rather, after combing through the mountain of pages before him, the Trial Judge concluded that appellant failed to establish federal court jurisdiction. Subsequently, appellant topped his mountain of legal papers with a fourth set of complaints and a motion for leave to amend. The motion was summarily denied.

The various complaints, amendments, amended amendments, amendments to amended amendments, and other related papers are anything but short, totaling over 4,000 pages, occupying 18 volumes, and requiring a hand truck or cart to move. They are not plain, either. The Trial Court described the pleadings as being "extremely long and combin(ing) into single counts detailed recitation of evidence and legal arguments complete with extensive citations of authority." The Court also observed that a paragraph from one typical complaint was single spaced, "extend(ed) the full length of a legal page and constitute(d) a single sentence." Much of the pleadings are scandalous as well.

Moreover, we cannot tell whether complaints filed earlier in time are to be read in conjunction with those filed later or whether the amended versions supersede previous pleadings.

One option before us is to struggle through the thousands of pages of pleadings in an effort to determine (assuming we possibly could) whether the Trial Court correctly dismissed for lack of jurisdiction. However, such a course of action would be unwise from the standpoint of sound judicial administration. All would know that there is no longer any necessity for paying the least bit of heed to F.R.Civ.P. 8(a) in its demand for "a short and plain statement" reiterated by the 8(e) requirement that each averment "be simple, concise, and direct." Lawyers would see that in the face of even gross violations of Rule 8, we would undertake the burden of trying to parse out 18 volumes of words, disorganized and sometimes conflicting, with a mishmash of so-called evidentiary materials, citations of authority, and other things that a pleader, aware of and faithful to the command of the Federal Rules of Civil Procedure, knows to be completely extraneous. And the District Courts who come on the firing line are the first victims of this paper mill. We think that the Trial Court should have dismissed the complaints with leave to amend. While a Trial Court is and should be given great leeway in determining whether a party has complied with Rule 8, we think that as a matter of law, verbose and scandalous pleadings of over 4,000 pages violate Rule 8.

In finding a violation of Rule 8, we do not recede even one inch from the position expressed by this Court in Blue Cat, Plimsoll Club, and a host of other cases sounding an approach of liberality under F.R.Civ.P. 12 in reading a pleading as an adequate statement or claim. Appellant asks not that we adopt a liberal approach, but that we stand liberality on its head by accepting 4,000 pages of chaotic legal jargon in lieu of a short and plain statement. We would be hindering, not promoting, the underlying purpose of Rule 8, which is "to Eliminate prolixity in pleading and to achieve brevity, simplicity, and clarity." *Knox v. First Security Bank of Utah*, (emphasis added). We fully agree with the observation of the District Court for the Eastern District of Michigan that "the law does not require, nor does justice demand, that a judge must grope through (thousands of) pages of irrational, prolix and redundant pleadings." Passic v. State.

Our view that flagrant violations of Rule 8 should not be tolerated is shared by Courts throughout the country. There are numerous cases in which complaints have been dismissed as being contrary to the letter and spirit of the Rule. In *Carrigan v. California State Legislature*, the Ninth Circuit upheld the Trial Court's dismissal without prejudice of a complaint totaling 186 pages filled with hearsay statements, medical reports, and other extraneous material. In *Brown v. Knoxville News-Sentinel*, the District Court for the Eastern District of Tennessee dismissed without prejudice a complaint of 117 pages, indicating that "the Court is unable to separate the various charges."

As previously stated, in ordering the suits dismissed we do so with leave to amend. Appellant may file a Short and plain Statement in lieu of the 18 volumes of papers currently before us. We hold that under F.R.Civ.P. 15(c), the filing of a proper, decent, acceptable amendment will relate back to the original filing, thus eliminating any question concerning the statute of limitations. See, e. g., *Travelers Ins. Co. v. Brown*, (applying the "relation back" doctrine). We explicitly declare our "relation back" ruling to be the "law of the case," binding in all subsequent proceedings in both the district and appellate courts with respect to these consolidated cases.

If our holding results in more time and expense to the appellant, that would be fair recompense for these marked, unjustifiable violations of the letter and spirit of the Federal Rules of Civil Procedure and an indifference as though they had never been adopted 41 years ago.[FN13]

FN13. Counsel as scrivener would have been fair game for the discipline meted out by the Chancellor in 1596. As Professor Richard C. Wydick of Davis Law School reports: In 1596 an English chancellor decided to make an example of a particularly prolix document filed in his court. The chancellor first ordered a hole cut through the center of the document, all 120 pages of it. Then he ordered that the person who wrote it should have his head stuffed through the hole, and the unfortunate fellow was led around to be exhibited to all those attending court at West Minister Hall. Wydick, Plain English For Lawyers, 1978, 66 Calif.L.Rev. 727. Obviously this applies only to counsel who filed the papers, not to the appellate counsel who briefed and argued the case here.

We vacate the judgment of the District Court and remand for dismissal of the complaint without prejudice to the right promptly to file a complaint in compliance with Rule 8.

VACATED and REMANDED.

EVIDENTIARY FACTS, ULTIMATE FACTS, AND LEGAL CONCLUSIONS

An understanding of the terms **evidentiary facts, ultimate facts,** and **legal conclusion** is vital in drafting allegations of a complaint. This section will first explain what these terms mean. Then the section will explain the relationship among the terms and drafting allegations.

"Evidentiary facts" are facts admissible in evidence. "Ultimate facts" are the facts in a case upon which liability is determined or based. Ultimate facts establish the elements of the cause of action. A "legal conclusion" is a statement of the result in a situation that involves applying the law to a set of facts. A legal conclusion states an element of the cause of action. As shown in figure 15-3, there is an overlap between evidentiary facts and ultimate facts and there is an overlap between ultimate facts and conclusions of law. To understand these terms, examine how they relate to the first sample complaint.

FIGURE 15-3 The Relationship Among Facts and Conclusions.

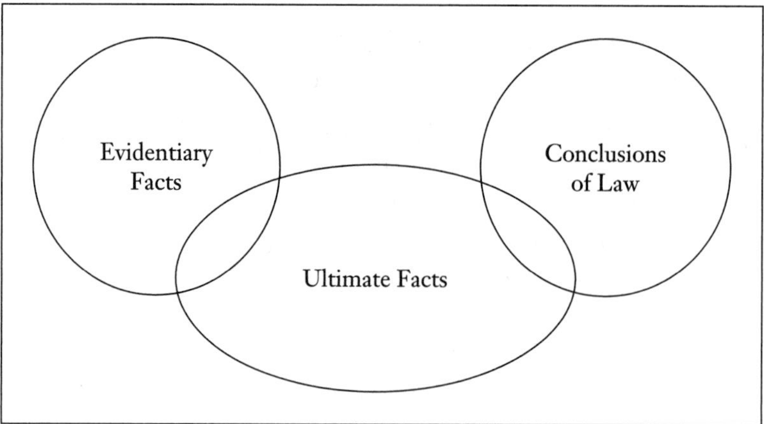

Evidentiary facts

Paragraphs 2 through 6 and 8 contain "evidentiary facts." For example:

> In October 1998 plaintiff was a student at Collegiate University, a member of the Collegiate Beta Fraternity, and a candidate for student body president of Collegiate University.
>
> In October 1998 defendant was a student at Collegiate University, a member of the Collegiate Alpha Fraternity, and a candidate for student body president of Collegiate University.
>
> In defendant's skit, defendant portrayed "plaintiff's doctor" and another student portrayed plaintiff.

Paragraph 7 contains a mixture of evidentiary and ultimate facts. The "kernel" of the ultimate facts has been bracketed:

> In defendant's skit, defendant, [in the presence and hearing of] plaintiff and the students and faculty watching the skit, [maliciously and falsely announced] that plaintiff had tested HIV positive, saying "you tested HIV positive."

Ultimate facts

Paragraphs 9 and 10 contain ultimate facts (establishing elements of defamation):

> Plaintiff at the time of defendant's statement was in good health and free from any disease, and the statements of defendant were wholly untrue.
>
> As a result of defendant's slanderous statement, plaintiff, suffered, and continues to suffer, great nervousness, and mental anguish.

Conclusions of law

Paragraph 11 contains conclusions of law:

> Plaintiff, as the direct result of defendant's statement, in addition to the nervousness and bodily injury, has been injured in plaintiff's good reputation in the Collegiate University community. Defendant published such false and slanderous statement about plaintiff to numerous students and faculty of Collegiate University, who have changed their attitude toward plaintiff, and who have begun to question plaintiff as to whether plaintiff has tested HIV positive, which the slanderous remark of defendant wrongly, maliciously, and untruthfully imputed to plaintiff.

The essence of paragraph 11 is that:

> Tom Harris made a defamatory statement about Jake Carson;
>
> Tom Harris published the statement to numerous students and faculty of Collegiate University; and
>
> The statement damaged Jake Carson's reputation.

Drafting allegations

Now that you have an idea of the difference among evidentiary facts, ultimate facts, and conclusions of law, notice how these terms relate to drafting allegations. The body of the complaint will contain evidentiary facts, ultimate facts, and conclusions of law. The complaint should be drafted so that defendant admits as much as possible and denies as little as possible. Defendant is more likely to admit evidentiary facts than to admit ultimate facts and will routinely deny conclusions of law. Therefore, the body of the complaint should as much as possible separate evidentiary facts from ultimate facts from conclusions of law. In the answer, defendant admitted paragraphs 2 through 6 and part of paragraph 7. The paragraphs defendant admitted contained evidentiary facts.

In the following case, one count of the complaint was dismissed because no facts were alleged supporting the legal claim and the attorney had already been permitted to amend the complaint.

HEART DISEASE RESEARCH FOUNDATION, a Charitable Trust of the State of New York, et al., Plaintiffs-Appellants,

v.

GENERAL MOTORS CORP. et al., Defendants-Appellees.

United States Court of Appeals,

Second Circuit.

Decided July 5, 1972.

463 F.2d 98

FEINBERG, Circuit Judge:

Plaintiffs Heart Disease Research Foundation, a charitable trust, and Robert R. Peters and Henry Sassone, two of the Foundation's trustees, appeal from an order of the United States District Court for the Southern District of New York, Harold R. Tyler, Jr., J., dismissing plaintiffs' amended complaint against General Motors Corp., Chrysler Corporation, Ford Motor Co. and American Motors Sales Corp. Plaintiffs seek to represent a class consisting of "the population of the United States residing in the metropolitan areas of the United States, amounting to approximately 125,000,000 persons." The amended complaint contains three counts: Count 1 alleges that defendants have committed antitrust violations by conspiring to suppress the development of motor vehicle pollution control devices; jurisdiction is grounded on the antitrust laws. Count 2 purports to add another cause of action "pursuant to common law principles of liability"; jurisdiction is based on "the 'general welfare' provisions of the Constitution of the United States . . . ." Count 3 asserts that the "United States Government is significantly involved in the production, manufacture and distribution of motor vehicles by reason of . . . [its] substantial purchases of motor vehicles . . ." and that such "continued purchase and operation of present motor vehicles . . . is adversely affecting the environment of the United States"; jurisdiction for this "claim" is premised on the "Environmental Quality Act," not otherwise identified. Plaintiffs seek injunctive relief and damages of "one hundred twenty five trillion dollars (trebled to three hundred and seventy five trillion dollars with respect to Count One)" and an attorney's fee of $3,000,000. Judge Tyler dismissed the complaint on the grounds that it failed to state any claims upon which relief could be granted and that plaintiffs' attorney failed to comply with Fed.R.Civ.P. 11. We affirm on the former ground.

Counts 2 and 3 of the complaint do not allege the essential elements of any cause of action. The purported jurisdictional basis for the former—the "general welfare" clause—is frivolous. As to count 3, plaintiffs now claim that "the sufficiency of this count need not be considered at this time" since count 2 "is also specifically bottomed on the 'Clean Air Act.'" This assertion is typical of the sloppy, scattershot manner in which this complaint was thrown together. Count 2 does not mention the "Clean Air Act." Neither does count 3 for that matter. The latter does refer to the "Environmental Quality Act," which Judge Tyler understandably took to mean the Environmental Quality Improvement Act of 1970, 42 U. S.C. S 4371 et seq. Plaintiffs now tell us they really were referring to 42 U.S. C. S. 1857, which the complaint nowhere mentions and which requires, in any event, allegations as yet unmade. Plaintiffs also now argue that count 2 is actually a nuisance or negligence action based upon diversity, allegations that they never bothered to make in the complaint. Even under the liberal Federal Rules of Civil Procedure, there is a limit to how much a court may be called upon to divine in assessing the sufficiency of the complaint before it, particularly when the plaintiff is represented by counsel.

As to count 1, it was well within the district court's discretion to dismiss the claim since no facts are alleged supporting an antitrust conspiracy. Although the Federal Rules permit statement of ultimate facts, a bare bones statement of conspiracy or of injury under the antitrust laws without any supporting facts permits dismissal. This is particularly true when, as here, the original plaintiff has already amended his complaint once with the approval of the court.

Judgment affirmed.

FIRST SAMPLE SET OF PLEADINGS

First sample complaint

IN THE CIRCUIT COURT
OF THE NINTH JUDICIAL CIRCUIT
IN AND FOR ORANGE COUNTY, FLORIDA

JAKE CARSON,	)	
Plaintiff,	)	
	)	CIVIL ACTION
- vs-	)	No. 99-000-00
	)	
TOM HARRIS,	)	
Defendant.	)[1]	

COMPLAINT[2]

Plaintiff, JAKE CARSON, sues defendant, TOM HARRIS, and alleges:[3]

[1]The caption contains the name of the court, the names of the parties, and the case number. There is one plaintiff and one defendant in this lawsuit. If there were more parties, all of them would be named in the caption of the initial complaint. In all other documents, only the first party on each side would be named, followed by "*et al.*" replacing all other parties. "*Et al*" is short for "*et alia*," meaning "and others." "JAKE CARSON, plaintiff vs. TOM HARRIS, Defendant" is often referred to as the **style** of the case. The case number is supplied by the court clerk. The number "99" indicates the year the case was filed. The next number indicates the order of filing. Cases are given consecutive numbers based on the order filed. For example, "100" would mean that the case was the one hundredth case filed in 1999. The sample complaint is unnumbered— "000"—to show that it is not an actual case.

[2]Rule 1.100 of the Florida Rules of Civil Procedure requires that court documents "indicate clearly the subject matter of the paper and the party requesting or obtaining relief." The form complaints at the end of the Florida Rules of Civil Procedure (see, for example Forms 1.936–1.942) are simply named "COMPLAINT." Some jurisdictions may require the pleading name to indicate the relief requested, for example, "COMPLAINT FOR DAMAGES."

[3]This introductory clause (also referred to as the "commencement") states who is suing whom. Notice that the introductory clause is not numbered.

COUNT I—DEFAMATION[4]

1. This is an action for damages that exceed $15,000.[5]

2. In October 1998 plaintiff was a student at Collegiate University, a member of the Collegiate Beta Fraternity, and a candidate for student body president of Collegiate[6] University.

3. In October 1998 defendant was a student at Collegiate University, a member of the Collegiate Alpha Fraternity and a candidate for student body president of Collegiate University.[7]

4. The October 20, 1998 issue of the Collegiate University student newspaper reported that plaintiff and defendant "were running neck and neck" in the student body president race.[8]

5. On October 20, 1998, the day before the student body president election, plaintiff and defendant presented skits to Collegiate University students and faculty at the Collegiate University football stadium.

6. In defendant's skit, defendant portrayed "plaintiff's doctor" and another student portrayed plaintiff.

This introductory clause is modeled on the one contained in the forms at the end of the Florida Rules of Civil Procedure: "Plaintiff, A.B., sues defendant, C.D., and alleges:" (see Forms 1.936–1.942). This plain English clause is much easier to read than the traditional introductory clause filled with legalese. For example, the introductory clause rewritten in legalese might look something like this:

> Now comes the above-named plaintiff, Jake Carson, by and through his attorney of record, Florida Attorney, and for cause of action and complaint against the defendant herein alleges unto this honorable court:Write your pleadings in plain English complying with the court rules of your jurisdiction. Plain English pleadings are easier for the client to understand and are less time consuming in the long run.

For simplicity sake, there is one plaintiff and one defendant in this sample complaint. For ease of reference they are referred to as "Plaintiff" and "Defendant" throughout the complaint. If this were a real complaint, Jake might have also named the Alpha Fraternity and Collegiate University as defendants. Multiple defendants could be referred to by short forms established in the introductory clause. For example:

> Plaintiff, JAKE CARSON, sues Defendants, TOM HARRIS ("Defendant Harris"), ALPHA FRATERNITY ("Defendant Fraternity"), and COLLEGIATE UNIVERSITY "Defendant University" and says:

or

> Plaintiff, JAKE CARSON, sues Defendants, TOM HARRIS ("Harris"), ALPHA FRATERNITY ("Fraternity"), and COLLEGIATE UNIVERSITY "University" and says:

Once you establish short forms, you should use them consistently throughout the rest of the complaint. For readability, you may want to put party names in all capital letters.

[4]In a complaint with more than one count, the counts are usually numbered for ease of reference. The count heading may also state the cause of action (here "COUNT I—DEFAMATION" and "COUNT II—FALSE LIGHT INVASION OF PRIVACY") or relief sought. The relief sought in another complaint, for example, may be "SPECIFIC PERFORMANCE" and "DAMAGES." If the complaint contains a single count, the count need not be headed.

In this complaint, the background for both counts is alleged in numbered paragraphs 1 through 8. Paragraph 12 of Count II realleges paragraphs 1 through 8. Another way to organize the complaint is to provide a heading "COMMON ALLEGATIONS" after the introductory paragraph. The "COMMON ALLEGATIONS" section of the complaint would contain numbered paragraphs 1 through 8. Then the complaint would state:

COUNT I—DEFAMATION

9. Plaintiff realleges and incorporates paragraphs 1–8 above.

[5]The paragraphs of the body of the complaint (sometimes referred to as the "charging portion" of the complaint) are numbered consecutively. In the body of the complaint the plaintiff alleges plaintiff's "ultimate facts." This paragraph establishes the court's jurisdiction. In Florida, the circuit court handles cases with more than $15,000 in controversy.

[6]Paragraphs 2 through 11 contain the ultimate facts on which plaintiff relies. The two purposes of the body of the complaint are to:

1. give the defendant notice of plaintiff's claims; and
2. include all the elements of the cause of action plaintiff alleges.

Before you write the body of the complaint, make a list of the elements of the cause of action. After you have completed the body of the complaint, double check to make sure you have included ultimate facts needed for all elements.

[7]Paragraphs 2 and 3 identify the parties. Usually the parties are identified early in the complaint.

[8]Plaintiff begins to narrate what happened. The narrative is written in past tense.

7. In defendant's skit, defendant, in the presence and hearing of plaintiff and the students and faculty watching the skit, maliciously and falsely announced that plaintiff had tested HIV positive, saying "you tested HIV positive."
8. In the student body president election on October 21, 1998, plaintiff received 10% of the vote and defendant received 90% of the vote.
9. Plaintiff at the time of defendant's statement was in good health and free from any disease, and the statements of defendant were wholly untrue.
10. As a result of defendant's slanderous statement, plaintiff suffered, and continues to suffer, great nervousness, and mental anguish.
11. Plaintiff, as the direct result of defendant's statement, in addition to the nervousness and bodily injury, has been injured in plaintiff's good reputation in the Collegiate University community. Defendant published such false and slanderous statement about plaintiff to numerous students and faculty of Collegiate University, who have changed their attitude toward plaintiff, and who have begun to question plaintiff as to whether plaintiff has tested HIV positive, which the slanderous remark of defendant wrongly, maliciously, and untruthfully imputed to plaintiff.

COUNT II—FALSE LIGHT INVASION OF PRIVACY

12. Plaintiff realleges and incorporates paragraphs 1–8 above.[9]
13. Prior to October 20, 1998, a rumor had circulated on the Collegiate University campus that plaintiff was a homosexual and the rumor was traced back to defendant's fraternity.
14. Defendant's statement during the skit and the manner of its presentation, in light of the rumor that plaintiff was a homosexual, falsely depicted plaintiff as a homosexual.
15. Plaintiff is not a homosexual and defendant's depiction of plaintiff as a homosexual was highly offensive to plaintiff.
16. Defendant's depiction of plaintiff as a homosexual was done with knowledge of its falsity or reckless disregard whether the depiction gave a false impression or not.
17. As a result of defendant's depiction of plaintiff as a homosexual, plaintiff suffered, and continues to suffer, great nervousness, and mental anguish.
18. Plaintiff, as the direct result of defendant's depiction of plaintiff as a homosexual, in addition to the nervousness and bodily injury, has been injured in plaintiff's good reputation in the Collegiate University community. Such false depiction has been circulated also among plaintiff's personal friends, who have changed their attitude toward plaintiff, and who have begun to question as to whether plaintiff is a homosexual, which depiction defendant wrongly, maliciously, and untruthfully imputed to plaintiff.

Plaintiff therefore requests judgment granting the following relief as to counts I and II:[10]

A. an award of compensatory damages in an amount to be set at trial;
B. an award of punitive damages in an amount to be set at trial;
C. an award of costs and attorney's fees; and
D. such other relief as the court deems appropriate.[11]

---

[9]Paragraph numbering is consecutive from one count to the next.

[10]This is the beginning line of plaintiff's prayer for relief. The line is not numbered but the various types of relief sought are lettered with capital letters. Traditionally, the first line of the prayer for relief would have read as follows:

WHEREFORE, Plaintiff, JAKE CARSON, demands that this honorable court grant judgment for the following relief:

This line has been rewritten in the sample complaint to eliminate legalese. Also the word "requests" (a word sounding less strident) has been substituted for "demands."

Another way to organize the complaint would be to have two prayer for relief sections—one following paragraph 11 and the other as it is in the sample complaint following paragraph 18.

[11]This "catchall phrase" typically is included in the player for relief. It allows the court to grant relief other than that specifically requested.

JURY DEMAND

Plaintiff demands trial by jury.[12]

____

Florida Attorney
101 Main Street
Anytown, Florida
Attorney for plaintiff
(407) 000-0000
Bar No. 0000000

First sample answer

IN THE CIRCUIT COURT
OF THE NINTH JUDICIAL CIRCUIT
IN AND FOR ORANGE COUNTY, FLORIDA

JAKE CARSON,	)	
Plaintiff,	)	
	)	CIVIL ACTION
- vs-	)	No. 99-000-00[13]
	)	
TOM HARRIS,	)	
Defendant.	)	

ANSWER[14]

Defendant TOM HARRIS answers Plaintiff's complaint and says:

1. He admits paragraph 1 for jurisdictional purposes only and otherwise denies it insofar as it is applied to him.
2. He admits paragraph 2.[15]
3. He admits paragraph 3.
4. He admits paragraph 4.
5. He admits paragraph 5.
6. With respect to paragraph 6, he denies making the quoted statement maliciously or falsely. Otherwise he admits paragraph 6.[16]

[12]Typically the plaintiff will request a jury trial. If plaintiff decides later against a jury trial, the right may be waived.

[13]The case number is copied from the complaint.

[14]Because there is a single defendant "ANSWER" is a sufficient title. If there were multiple defendants and the answer was that of all defendants, title the pleading "DEFENDANTS' ANSWER." If the answer was that of less than all the defendants, the title should indicate the party filing the answer. For example, "ANSWER OF DEFENDANT COLLEGIATE UNIVERSITY."

[15]Here the defendant's numbered paragraphs correspond to the numbering of the paragraphs in the complaint. Another way to organize the answer would be for the defendant to list in a single numbered paragraph the paragraphs of the complaint admitted, to list in a single numbered paragraph the paragraphs of the complaint denied, and to list in a single numbered paragraph the paragraphs of the complaint of which defendant has no knowledge. For example:

2. He admits paragraphs 2 through 6.
3. He is without knowledge of paragraphs 8 through 11, 13, 15, 17, and 18.
4. He denies paragraphs 14 and 16.

[16]Rule 1.110 of the Florida Rules of Civil Procedure requires the defendant to specify which part of the allegation is admitted and which part of the allegation is denied.

7. He is without knowledge of paragraph 7.
8. He is without knowledge of paragraph 8.
9. He is without knowledge of paragraph 9.
10. He is without knowledge of paragraph 10.
11. He is without knowledge of paragraph 11.
12. With respect to paragraph 12, he repeats his response to paragraphs 1 through 8.
13. He is without knowledge of paragraph 13.
14. He denies paragraph 14.
15. He is without knowledge of paragraph 15.
16. He denies paragraph 16.
17. He is without knowledge of paragraph 17.
18. He is without knowledge of paragraph 18.

FIRST AFFIRMATIVE DEFENSE

19. Defendant's skit was an obvious expression of humor and could not reasonably be understood as describing an actual fact about plaintiff or an actual event in which plaintiff participated.

SECOND AFFIRMATIVE DEFENSE

20. Plaintiff has failed to allege facts showing that defendant's skit was presented with falsity, negligence, actual malice, or reckless disregard for the truth.

CERTIFICATE OF SERVICE

I furnished a copy of this answer to Florida Attorney, attorney for plaintiff, 101 Main Street, Anytown, Florida, by U.S. mail on ________, 19__.

____
Unnamed Attorney
Attorney for defendant
TOM HARRIS
100 Court Street
Anytown, Florida
(407) 880-0000
Florida Bar No. 100000

SECOND SAMPLE SET OF PLEADINGS

Second sample complaint

UNITED STATES DISTRICT COURT
MIDDLE DISTRICT OF FLORIDA
ORLANDO DIVISION

PHONE ADDICTED,

Plaintiff,

v. Case No. 99-000-CIV-ORL-00

NOSY NEIGHBOR,

Defendants.

_____________________________________/

COMPLAINT

Plaintiff, PHONE ADDICTED, sues defendant, NOSY NEIGHBOR, and alleges:[17]

COUNT I—INTERCEPTION OF WIRE COMMUNICATION

1. This court has jurisdiction of this case pursuant to 28 U.S.C.S. § 1331 (Lexis L. Publg. 1986)[18] and 18 U.S.C.S. § 2520 (Lexis L. Publg. 1993).[19]

2. From 1982 to the present, plaintiff has resided at 200 Magnolia Street, Oviedo, Florida.[20]

3. From 1997 to the present, defendant has resided at 202 Magnolia Street, Oviedo, Florida.

4. Plaintiff regularly uses a cordless telephone to place and receive telephone calls at her residence.

5. Defendant owns a scanner capable of intercepting cordless telephone conversations.

6. In June and July of 1999, defendant intentionally intercepted and recorded a number of plaintiff's telephone calls.

7. Defendant's intentional interception of plaintiff's telephone calls violated 18 U.S.C.S. § 2511 (1) (Lexis L. Publg. 1993).

COUNT II—DISCLOSURE OF WIRE COMMUNICATION

8. Plaintiff realleges and incorporates paragraphs 1–6 above.

9. In June and July of 1999, defendant played tapes of several of plaintiff's conversations.

10. Defendant amplified the tapes so that plaintiff could hear them while she was on her property.

11. At least two other neighbors could hear the tapes from their properties.

12. In broadcasting the tapes, defendant intentionally disclosed to other persons the contents of plaintiff's conversations.

13. Defendant knew that he had obtained the tapes of plaintiff's conversations through the interception of plaintiff's cordless telephone calls.

14. Defendant's intentional disclosure of the tapes of plaintiff's cordless telephone conversations violated 18 U.S.C.S. § 2511 (1) (Lexis L. Publg. 1993).

---

[17]**Rule 8(a) of the Federal Rules of Civil Procedure provides:**

> (a) Claims for Relief. A pleading which sets forth a claim for relief, whether an original claim, counterclaim, cross-claim, or third-party claim, shall contain (1) a short and plain statement of the grounds upon which the court's jurisdiction depends, unless the court already has jurisdiction and the claim needs no new grounds of jurisdiction to support it, (2) a short and plain statement of the claim showing that the pleader is entitled to relief, and (3) a demand for judgment for the relief the pleader seeks. Relief in the alternative or of several different types may be demanded.

[18]Title 28 U.S.C.A. § 1331 (Lexis L. Publg. 1986) provides: "The district courts shall have original jurisdiction of all civil actions arising under the Constitution, laws, or treaties of the United States." This is commonly referred to as federal question jurisdiction.

[19]This statute authorizes a civil action by a person whose conversation has been wrongfully intercepted or disclosed.

[20]Rule 8(e)(1) of the Federal Rules of Civil Procedure provides: "(1) Each averment of a pleading shall be simple, concise, and direct. No technical forms of pleading or motions are required."

Plaintiff therefore requests judgment granting the following relief as to counts I and II:[21]

A. an award of compensatory damages in an amount to be set at trial;

B. an award of punitive damages in an amount to be set at trial;

C. an award of costs and attorney's fees;

D. an injunction prohibiting defendant from intercepting, tape-recording, and broadcasting plaintiff's telephone conversations; and

D. such other relief as the court deems appropriate.

JURY DEMAND

Plaintiff demands trial by jury.

____
Florida Attorney
101 Main Street
Anytown, Florida
Attorney for plaintiff
(407) 000-0000
Bar No. 0000000

Second sample answer

UNITED STATES DISTRICT COURT
MIDDLE DISTRICT OF FLORIDA
ORLANDO DIVISION

PHONE ADDICTED,

Plaintiff,

v. Case No. 99 - 000 - CIV - ORL - 00

NOSY NEIGHBOR,

Defendants.

__________________________________/

ANSWER

Defendant NOSY NEIGHBOR answers Plaintiff's complaint and says:[22]

---

[21]Title 18 U.S.C.S. § 2511 (1) (Lexis L. Publg. 1993) authorizes compensatory and punitive damages, reasonable attorney's fees and costs, and injunctive relief. The authorized compensatory damages are either actual damages or "statutory damages of the greater of $100 a day for each day of violation or $10,000."

[22]Rule 8 (b) of the Federal Rules of Civil Procedure provides:

> (b) Defenses; Form of Denials. A party shall state in short and plain terms the party's defenses to each claim asserted and shall admit or deny the averments upon which the adverse party relies. If a party is without knowledge or information sufficient to form a belief as to the truth of an averment, the party shall so state and this has the effect of a denial. Denials shall fairly meet the substance of the averments denied. When a pleader intends in good faith to deny only a part or a qualification of an averment, the pleader shall specify so much of it as is true and material and shall deny only the remainder. Unless the pleader intends in good faith to controvert all the averments of the preceding pleading, the pleader may make denials as specific denials of designated averments or paragraphs or may generally deny all the averments except such designated averments or paragraphs as the pleader expressly admits; but, when the pleader does so intend to controvert all its averments, including averments of the grounds upon which the court's jurisdiction depends, the pleader may do so by general denial subject to the obligations set forth in Rule 11.

1. He admits paragraph 1 for jurisdictional purposes only and otherwise denies it insofar as it is applied to him.
2. He admits paragraph 2.[23]
3. He admits paragraph 3.
4. He is without knowledge of paragraph 4.
5. He denies paragraph 5.
6. He denies paragraph 6.
7. He denies paragraph 7.
8. With respect to paragraph 8, he repeats his response to paragraphs 1 through 6.
9. He admits paragraph 9.
10. He admits paragraph 10.
11. He is without knowledge of paragraph 11.
12. He admits paragraph 12.
13. He denies paragraph 13.
14. He denies paragraph 14.

FIRST AFFIRMATIVE DEFENSE[24]

15. Defendant recorded only those portions of plaintiff's conversations audible from defendant's property

SECOND AFFIRMATIVE DEFENSE

16. Defendant broadcast only those portions of plaintiff's conversations recorded while defendant was on defendant's property.

CERTIFICATE OF SERVICE

I furnished a copy of this answer to Florida Attorney, attorney for plaintiff, 101 Main Street, Anytown, Florida, by U.S. mail on ________, 19__.

____

Unnamed Attorney
Attorney for defendant
100 Court Street
Anytown, Florida
(407) 880-0000
Florida Bar No. 100000

[23]Rule 8 (d) of the Federal Rules of Civil Procedure provides:

(d) Effect of Failure to Deny. Averments in a pleading to which a responsive pleading is required, other than those as to the amount of damage, are admitted when not denied in the responsive pleading. Averments in a pleading to which no responsive pleading is required or permitted shall be taken as denied or avoided.

[24]Rule 8 (c) of the Federal Rules of Civil Procedure provides:

(c) Affirmative Defenses. In pleading to a preceding pleading, a party shall set forth affirmatively accord and satisfaction, arbitration and award, assumption of risk, contributory negligence, discharge in bankruptcy, duress, estoppel, failure of consideration, fraud, illegality, injury by fellow servant, laches, license, payment, release, res judicata, statute of frauds, statute of limitations, waiver, and any other matter constituting an avoidance or affirmative defense. When a party has mistakenly designated a defense as a counterclaim or a counterclaim as a defense, the court on terms, if justice so requires, shall treat the pleading as if there had been a proper designation.

FIGURE 15-4 Tips for Drafting a Complaint.

In drafting the complaint, follow this list of things to do:

Do

1. Separate evidentiary facts, ultimate facts, and conclusions of law. (Defendant will be more likely to admit allegations if evidentiary facts are separated from ultimate facts).
2. Write in plain English. (Make your allegations clear to the judge).
3. Place only one or two sentences in each numbered paragraph. (If a number of facts are included in a paragraph and one of the facts is wrong, defendant may deny the whole paragraph).
4. Do not include more evidentiary facts than necessary. (Plaintiff will be faced with proving facts not admitted).
5. Use descriptive words for allegations favorable to plaintiff; use abstract words for allegations adverse to plaintiff. (The judge will more likely remember a description that brings a picture to mind than an abstract statement of adverse facts).
6. Use objective rather than subjective language. (It is harder for the defendant to deny objectively stated facts).
7. State facts precisely. (Defendant can easily deny inaccurate facts).

CHAPTER 15 SUMMARY

- The *complaint* is the initial pleading in a civil action, in which the plaintiff alleges a cause of action and asks that the court remedy the wrong done to the plaintiff.
- The *answer* is a pleading in response to the complaint.
- Pleadings must conform to applicable court rules and statutes.
- Pleading forms may be used to draft a pleading but must be tailored to the particular situation with which you are dealing.
- Generally the complaint contains a caption, claims, prayer for relief, and signature block.
- Generally the answer contains a caption, defenses, affirmative defenses and counterclaims, and a certificate of service.
- *Evidentiary facts* are facts admissible in evidence.
- *Ultimate facts* are the facts in a case upon which liability is determined or based.
- A *legal conclusion* is a statement of the result in a situation that involves applying the law to a set of facts.
- When drafting the complaint, follow these writing tips:
  1. Separate evidentiary facts, ultimate facts, and conclusions of law.
  2. Write in plain English.
  3. Place only one or two sentences in each numbered paragraph.
  4. Do not include more evidentiary facts than necessary
  5. Use descriptive words for allegations favorable to plaintiff; use abstract words for allegations adverse to plaintiff.
  6. Use objective rather than subjective language.
  7. State facts precisely.

CYBERLAW EXERCISES

1. The Smoking Gun (located at http://www.thesmokinggun.com) is a web site that posts documents "from government and law enforcement sources, via Freedom of Information requests, and from court files nationwide." A number of the documents are pleadings concerning famous individuals. View several of the documents posted at this web site.
2. The Lexis law school site (http://lawschool.lexis.com) includes information on developing effective writing skills (Click on "My School," "Web Lectures," and then on "Legal Research & Writing."
3. Before drafting a pleading, determine the format and content required by applicable court rules. The WashLaw Web site (http://www.washlaw.edu) allows you to access court rules. Go to the web site and click on "court rules."
4. The Lexis law school site (http://lawschool.lexis.com) also links you to search engines (Click on "Legal Internet Guide" and then on "Internet Search Engines.") Try searching for "pleadings" using several of the search engines.
5. The WashLaw Web site (http://www.washlaw.edu) allows you to access legal forms. Go to the web site and click on "Legal Forms."
6. LawCrawler (http://www.lawcrawler.com) is a highly-rated search engine that limits its searches to sites known to contain legal information. Try searching for "pleadings" using LawCrawler.

CYBER EXAMPLES

1. When writing legal documents for the first time, it may be helpful to look at examples in addition to those in this book. This chapter provides some examples. A number of law school professors have posted sample documents on the Internet. To find some of these documents you might access Jurist: The Law Professor Network (http://jurist.law.pitt.edu). (Click on "Law School," "Law School Courses," and then on "Legal Research and Writing.") Professor Gregory Berry at Howard University School of Law has posted a number of student documents in his "Writing Hall of Fame." Those documents include client letters, memoranda, motion reply briefs, a settlement agreement, and appellate briefs. Also, Professor Colleen Barger at the University of Arkansas at Little Rock School of Law had a web site that links to pages of other legal research and writing professors (<http://www.ualr.edu/~cmbarger/>).
2. Pleadings are increasingly available on the Internet. To find some pleadings, you might access http://www.llrx.com/extras/webpacers.htm. Some of the pleadings are available at no cost through this URL.
3. Numerous pleadings in *Anderson v. Beatrice Foods* are available through http://www.law.fsu.edu/library/faculty/gore/.

CHAPTER 16

LAW OFFICE MEMO

INTRODUCTION

One of the standard legal documents written by a paralegal or attorney is what will be referred to in this book as the "law office memo." (Sometimes it may be referred to as an "office memo" or "interoffice memorandum.") This chapter includes two sample office memos and explains the purpose and use of the office memo and its format. The first time you read this chapter, glance over the sample office memos, noting their format. Then refer back to the sample office memos as they are being analyzed in the balance of the chapter.

The first sample office memo has been extensively annotated to provide you with writing and citation tips. If the notes do not make much sense to you right now, read them again after you have reviewed the rules for citations and quotations contained in appendixes B and C. It might also be helpful to you to refer to the footnotes again when you are writing your own office memo.

PURPOSE AND USE

Legal research is required when the client or the attorney is confronted with a legal problem and the answer to the problem is unclear. A client who is planning a business deal may be wondering how the deal can be structured most advantageously to minimize taxes. Often a client is contemplating suing someone. It is important for both the client and the attorney to know what the chances are of the client obtaining a judgment and whether the client would be entitled to attorneys fees. After the lawsuit has been filed, there may be a procedural question that the attorney needs researched.

The main purposes of the office memo are to record the law found as a result of the research, to explain how the researcher analyzed the law and applied it to the facts, and to ultimately propose a solution to the problem. At the moment the research on the above problems has been completed, the researcher is the "expert" on the legal principles involved but the researcher will quickly forget many of the details of the research. Depending on the complexity of the above questions, one hour, several hours, or several weeks of research might have been required. For a client being billed at an hourly rate, research is expensive but necessary. Writing an office memo allows both the client and the attorney to benefit from the research. The office memo can be read several times and discussed before a decision is made. Although you will find that your first office memo seems to take days to write, edit, and rewrite, the time spent by an experienced writer on an office memo is fairly small in comparison to the time spent doing the research.

Usually, multiple copies of the office memo are made, with one copy being kept by the researcher, one copy going to the attorney in the office who had requested the research, one copy being placed in the client file, one copy going to the client (if the client is sophisticated enough to understand it), and one copy being placed in a research file in the office. The attorney and the client use their copies to decide how to resolve the problem discussed in the memo. The copy in the client file can be used later to quickly refer to the facts or to the analysis behind the decision made. Often the researcher has spent time pulling the facts together from various sources and organizing them. The memo may be referred to quickly to refresh one's memory on the facts without having to consult various sources or to understand later why the particular decision was made. The copy placed in the research file may be used to aid in later research; there may be further research to be done later on the same or a related problem. The researcher can quickly pull prior office memos and determine whether any of the research previously done can be used. If the researcher is lucky enough to find a prior office memo involving the same problem, all the researcher may have to do is to update the research from the date of the prior memo.

STYLE

A number of common style errors made in office memos can be easily avoided if you know what to do and what not to do. After you have written the first draft of your office memo, read this section again and make any necessary change to your memo.

First of all, the tone of the office memo should be objective rather than persuasive. Choose words that are fairly neutral. For example, referring to the illegal drug problem as a "serious menace" as the *Smith* court did in the last paragraph of the opinion is fine for an opinion, but that language sounds too persuasive for an office memo. Instead substitute "serious problem."

Secondly, keep yourself out of the memo. Even if the office memo contains your opinion, keep the tone of the office memo as impersonal as possible and do not use the word "I." Instead of saying: "I think that . . ." you might substitute: "Based on similar facts in *Smith* and *Campbell* it is obvious that . . . ."

A third style tip is to avoid using contractions, slang, or any other informal expressions that are normally used in spoken rather than in written communication. Although the tone of the office memo does not have to be so formal it is uninviting to read, it should be somewhat formal. Contractions and slang lend too informal a tone to your office memo.

A fourth error is use of elegant variation. Your English composition teacher probably told you not to use the same word twice and to use synonyms to make your writing more interesting. This is fine for English composition but not for legal writing. If you use two different words that mean the same thing, like "lawyer" and "attorney" or "purchaser" and "buyer," an attorney reading your writing will immediately want to know why you changed wording. The attorney will also assume there is some reason for the change. Perhaps you were referring to something different when you used a different word. If you are referring to the same thing a second time, use the same reference term.

The final style error is to use an abstract word when a more specific one is available. For example, in *Campbell* (the case on which the first sample office memo was based), the agents discovered cocaine in Campbell's car. Rather than talking about suppression of the "evidence" or the "drugs," tell your reader that Campbell filed a motion to suppress the "cocaine." It is just as easy to use the word "cocaine," it makes it easier for your reader to picture, and the word is more descriptive than "evidence" or "drugs."

FORMAT

Although there is no one correct format for office memos, the format given in this chapter is fairly standard. Figure 16-1 depicts this format. Another format frequently used has the same major sections but places the facts after the issues and answers. Ask your professor what format he or she prefers. You will need to do the same thing if you are asked to write an office

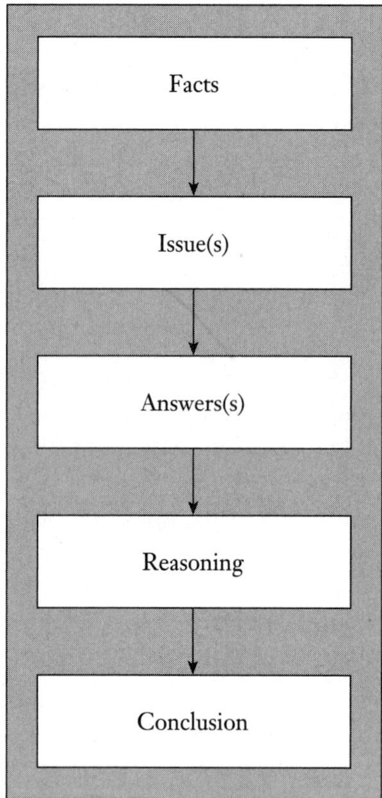

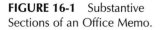

FIGURE 16-1 Substantive Sections of an Office Memo.

memo for your job. Many law offices have a format that the attorneys prefer.

The following portion of this chapter tells you in general terms what to put in each section of the office memo. You may want to read the following sections while comparing them to the sample office memos.

To and From

These two sections contain the name of the person who assigned you the office memo and your name. If the office memo will be read by persons other than the person who assigned you the memo, you may want to add their names as well.

Re

Identify the subject matter of the office memo in a phrase with sufficient detail so a reader will know whether to read further.

Date

The memo should be dated either the date you complete your research or the date you deliver it to your reader. The date is important for future reference because it is assumed that the research reflected in the memo is current with the date of the memo or shortly before.

Facts

Clearly state significant facts that the reader needs to know to understand the reasoning section of the memo and limit them to one or two paragraphs. The facts are the facts; do not invent facts. If you do not know important facts spend more time gathering them, or, if that is impossible, state what facts are not known. Where important facts are unknown, you may have to assume facts and then base your research and your office memo on the assumed facts. This is fine so

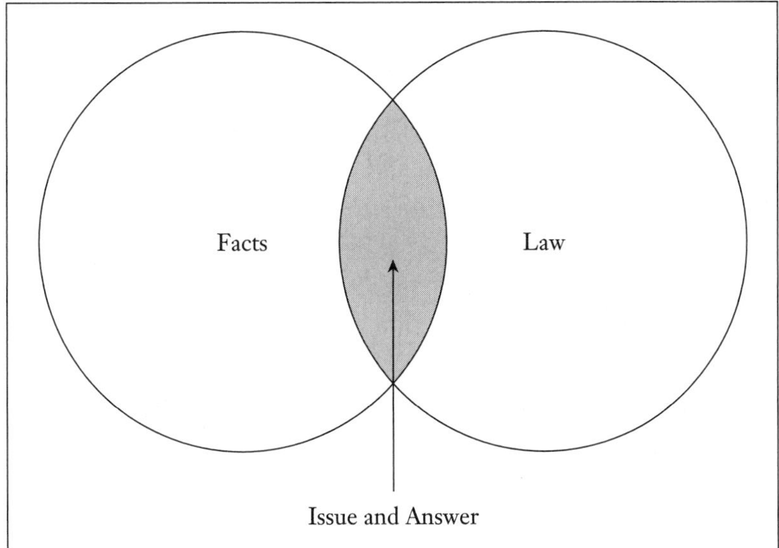

FIGURE 16-2 Issue and Answer.

long as you clearly state your assumption and explain that your discussion and conclusion are based on your assumption. You may even want to assume facts in the alternative and explain what conclusions you would reach based on the various assumptions.

Issue(s) and Answer(s)

You should spend considerable time writing your issues and answers because they are the heart of your memo. You may have an idea of what your issues will be before you begin your research, so write down your issues at this preliminary stage. As you perform your research and write your office memo, you will probably find yourself revising your issues and answers several times.

An issue and the corresponding answer should each be one sentence in length while giving the reader the most information possible. An issue is usually stated in the form of a question and the answer is a full sentence response to the issue. Usually there are the same number of issues as answers, with each issue being paired with an answer. Number your issues and answers to make it easier for your reader. If you find, in including as much information as possible in your issue and answer, that the issue and answer become unwieldy, experiment with splitting up an issue and answer into two issues and two answers.

An issue and answer contain a blend of fact and law, as depicted in figure 16-2. For example, the first issue and answer from the first sample office memo in this chapter are shown. The words relating to the facts are underlined and the words relating to the law are italicized. Some words are italicized and underlined because they relate both to law and to fact.

Issue:

1. Did the <u>agents</u> have *reasonable suspicion* to <u>stop</u> the <u>car</u> for an *illegal* <u>drug violation?</u>

Answer:

1. Because the *factors* in the *drug courier profile*, even if taken together, did not support *reasonable suspicion* of *illegal* <u>drug activity,</u> the <u>cocaine</u> should be *suppressed* unless the <u>agents</u> had *probable cause* to <u>stop</u> the <u>car</u> for a *traffic violation.*

Reasoning

The substance of the reasoning portion of the office memo usually is comprised of a thesis, a short

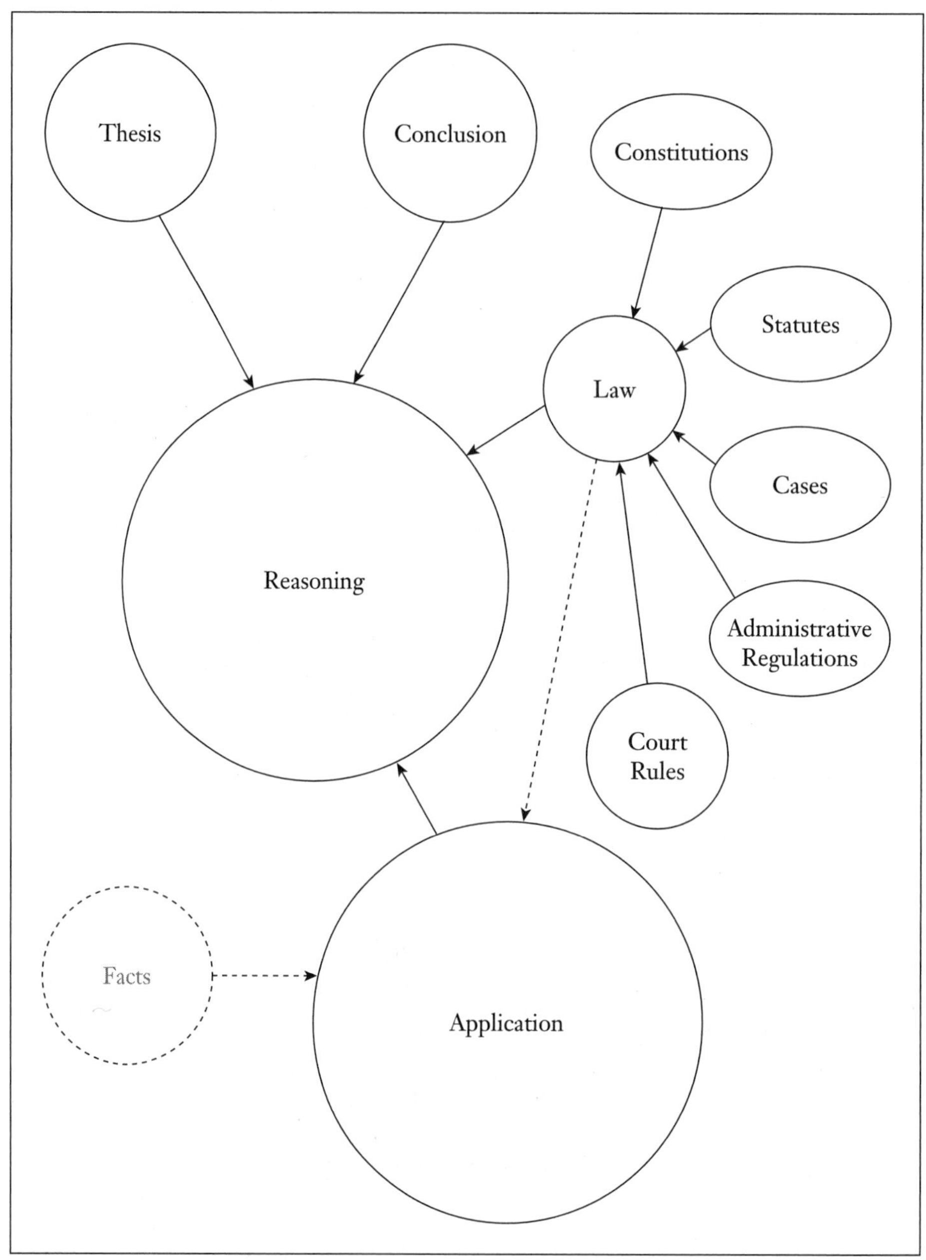

FIGURE 16-3 Reasoning Section of an Office Memo.

conclusion, the statement of the rule of law, and the application of the rule of law to the facts. Figure 16-3 depicts the substance of the reasoning portion of the office memo. This drawing shows the thesis, a short conclusion, the statement of the rule of law, and the application of the rule of law as belonging within the reasoning portion of the office memo. The drawing also shows the components of the statement of the rule of law and the application. Primary sources, such as constitutions, statutes, cases, court rules, and administrative regulations, are discussed in the statement of the rule of law; the law and the facts are analyzed extensively in the application.

Format for reasoning

Figure 16-4 depicts the parts of the reasoning portion of the office memo where the office memo contains one issue and one answer. Figure 16-5 depicts the parts of an office memo where the reasoning portion contains two issues and two answers. The reasoning portion of the first and second sample office memos in this chapter are examples of the way in which an

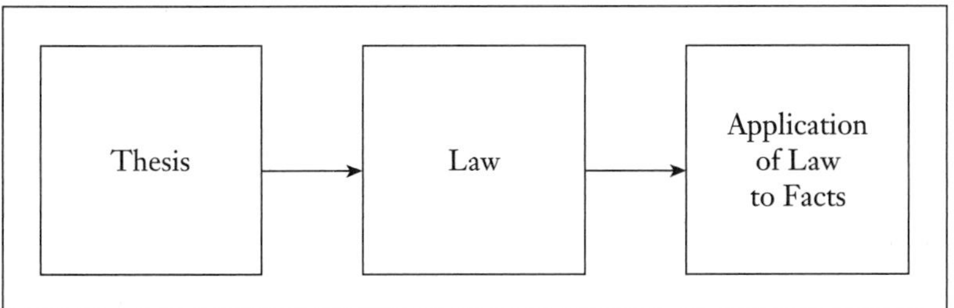

FIGURE 16-4 Reasoning Section of an Office Memo.

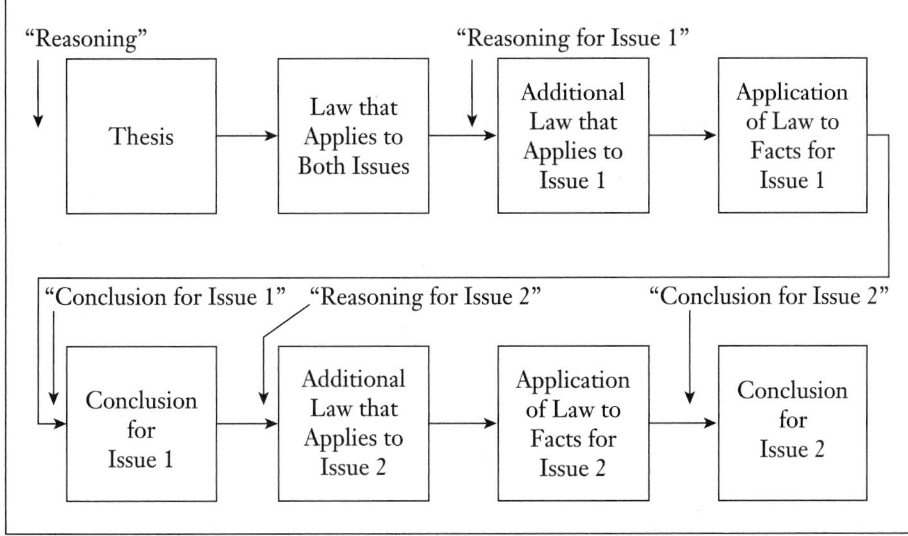

FIGURE 16-5 Reasoning Sections and Conclusion Sections of an Office Memo with Two Issues.

office memo with more than one issue and one answer can be organized. The first sample office memo contains two issues and two answers; the second sample office memo contains three issues and three answers.

Thesis paragraph

The reasoning portion of your office memo should begin with a **thesis paragraph.** This paragraph should contain your thesis—the central idea of your memo. It should serve as a road map, giving your reader the big picture of your memo. Besides stating your thesis in your thesis paragraph, you may want to state your final conclusion in simple terms.

Rule of law

The **statement of the rule of law** is the law contained in any legal sources and which will be applied to your facts later in your memo. Usually the law is contained in primary sources, but sometimes you may have to rely on secondary sources (such as law review articles or legal periodicals) if there are no primary sources on point.

You need to clearly explain the rule of law to the reader so the reader has a solid basis for understanding the rest of your reasoning. If your law is contained in constitutional or statutory provisions you may want to quote the relevant portions of those provisions. Leave out any portions of the provisions that are irrelevant and indicate any omission by the use of an ellipsis. If the provisions are very simple, you may want to explain them in your own words rather than quoting them. If your law is from case law, explain enough about the precedent case so the reader can understand what the case stands for and can better comprehend your application of the case to the facts of the current problem. You may need to devote one or more paragraphs to explaining the significant facts of an important case where you will later be comparing the facts of the case to the facts of the current problem. Your reader will be able to understand the rest of your reasoning better if you have first given the reader a good foundation in the rule of law.

Application of law to facts

Many students spend so much energy explaining the rule of law that they do not have energy for the application and may skip from the rule of law to the conclusion. This is a fatal error because the application is the most important part of the office memo. Omission of the application in the office memo results in a reduction of the student's grade, severely hampers the reader's understanding, and greatly lessens the memo's utility.

When applying the law to the facts, you must lead the reader step by step from the law to your conclusion. You must specifically explain why a constitutional or statutory provision applies or does not apply to the facts before explaining the consequences of the application. When applying case law, specifically tell your reader what facts from a case are similar to and what facts are different from the facts in the memo and *explain why*. It is not sufficient to simply state that facts are similar or different without telling your reader which facts you are referring to and why. You may not be conscious of some of the steps you used in concluding that a particular case is or is not controlling. Try to consciously think of the steps you went through in moving from the law to the conclusion and then write your steps down on paper so your reader can understand your analysis.

Figures 16-6 and 16-7 are charts you might use to help you brainstorm your application. Use figure 16-6 if you have a case you will be discussing in the application portion of your reasoning. Use a separate chart for each case discussed in your application. In the first column, list facts that are similar when comparing the facts of the problem you have researched. List facts that differ in the second column. In the last column, state the rule of law from the case and state a conclusion for your research problem. Remember the doctrine of stare decisis. If the case you are using is mandatory authority and the facts are substantially the same as the facts in your research problem, then the research problem should be decided the same way. If the facts are not substantially similar, then your research problem may be decided differently than the case.

Use figure 16-7 if you have one or more statutes you are applying to your research problem. In the first column, write the citations to your statutes. In the second column, list ways in which the statutory language applies or does not apply to your research problem. In the third column, write your conclusion as to the applicability of the statutes to your research problem.

Your writing of the statement of the rule of law and the application should be so clear that someone who has never read about the area of law before can understand your memo. You probably have a friend or relative who has a difficult time understanding a detailed explanation. Picture yourself with that person and imagine how you could explain your office memo to that person. Have someone else who has no knowledge of that area of the law read your memo and tell you if there are any passages he or she could not understand. Rewrite those passages so almost anyone can understand them. Try reading your office memo out loud either to yourself or to someone else. A passage that seems perfectly clear when you read it silently may not sound very clear when read out loud. Rewrite any passages that are unclear or awkward.

Conclusion

Your conclusion should be a final paragraph that ties everything together. Remember that in applying case law to your facts you are guided by the *doctrine of stare decisis*. If the facts in a prior case from the same or a higher court are substantially similar, then the answer to the problem should be the same as the result reached by the court in the prior case. Summarize the similarities and differences between the case law used as authority and the facts of the memo and explain what cases you are relying on to reach your conclusion.

NAME OF CASE		
Facts that Are Similar	Facts that Are Different	Rule of Law and Conclusion

FIGURE 16-6 Case Analysis Chart.

STATUTORY ANALYSIS		
Relevant Statutory Sections	Relevance	Conclusion

FIGURE 16-7 Statutory Analysis Chart.

FIRST SAMPLE OFFICE MEMO

To: legal research and writing classes

From: your author

Re: whether cocaine found in a car stopped on I-95 should be suppressed

Date: April 13, 2000

Facts:

Mike Campbell[1] and his best friend, John Wright, were driving north on I-95 returning from spring break in Florida, when they were stopped by members of a drug task force made up of Volusia County Sheriff officers and federal drug enforcement agents. The agents requested permission to search the car. When Campbell refused consent, the agents brought in a drug dog that alerted to the trunk of the car. The agents then claimed that the dog's actions gave them probable cause to search the trunk and gave Campbell the choice of either opening the trunk or waiting until the agents obtained a search warrant. After Campbell opened the trunk, the agents found two kilograms of cocaine in a brown paper bag. Campbell and Wright were arrested and charged with possession with intent to distribute cocaine. Prior to trial they filed a motion to suppress the cocaine claiming that it was the fruit of an unreasonable search and seizure.

The agents claimed they stopped the Campbell car because Campbell was following the car in front of him too closely and because the following facts fit a drug courier profile used by the Volusia County Sheriff officers:

1. The car was a large late model;
2. The car had out-of-state tags;
3. The car was being driven cautiously at the speed limit;
4. The car was being driven on a known drug corridor, I-95;
5. There were two passengers in the car;
6. The passengers were in their twenties;
7. The car was being driven in the early evening; and
8. The passengers were dressed casually.[2]

Although not listed by the agents, Campbell and Wright believe the real reason they were stopped is because they are Afro-Americans.

Issues[3]:

1. Did the agents have reasonable suspicion to stop the car for an illegal drug violation?
2. Did the agents have probable cause to stop the Campbell car for the driver's failure to follow at a safe distance?

Answers[4]:

1. Because the factors in the drug courier profile, even if taken together, did not support reasonable suspicion of illegal drug activity, the cocaine should be suppressed unless the agents had probable cause to stop the car for a traffic violation.
2. If Campbell failed to follow the vehicle in front of him at an appropriate distance, the stop did not violate the passengers' fourth amendment[5] right against unreasonable search and seizure and the cocaine cannot be suppressed on that ground.

---

[1]It is easier for your reader to understand if you refer to people by their names (a surname is sufficient) instead of as "plaintiff," "defendant," or similar terms. An alternative is to use terms such as "suspect" or "officer."

[2]When you have a list of items, make it easier for your reader to skim down the list by tabulating. Number each item, follow each item except for the last one by a semicolon, and place the word "and" after the semicolon following the next to last item. Make sure that you follow parallel construction for all items. (See appendix D for an explanation of parallel construction.)

[3]Each issue should be a single-sentence question. Between the issue and the answer you should give your reader the most information possible. Often a reader will read the issues and the answers first to determine if he or she should read the whole memo. It is very frustrating for the reader if the reader cannot make that determination without reading the rest of the memo.

[4]Each answer should be a complete, single-sentence answer responding to an issue. Usually there are the same number of answers as there are issues. An exception would be, for example, if the issue is so broad that there are two parts to the answer. As previously, between the issue and the corresponding answer, give your reader the most information possible. If you find an issue and answer getting so long as to be unwieldy, try splitting them up into two issues and answers.

[5]If you refer to a constitutional or statutory provision in an issue or answer by number, also give your reader a short explanation of the provision's subject matter. Otherwise your reader will be frustrated by not knowing why you cited a particular provision. It is usually better not to give case citations in issues or answers. Instead, state the rule of law from the case in your issue or answer and cite the case in the reasoning section of your memo.

Reasoning[6]:

Federal legislation makes possession of cocaine a crime and officers have the task of enforcing this legislation. One method used to check illegal drug activity is to cut down on the transportation of illegal drugs along the nation's highways.[7] Unfortunately, there is no accurate method to determine which cars on the highway are carrying drugs unless the cars are stopped and searched. The car driver and passengers expect that activities within the car will be private and not subject to the scrutiny of law enforcement officials. They may feel that their privacy is invaded if a law enforcement officer stops the car to investigate. A trained police officer may have a hunch that a car's occupants are engaged in illegal activity; however, a law enforcement officer may not constitutionally stop a car unless there is a reasonable suspicion of illegal activity or there is a traffic violation.[8]

The stop of Campbell's car to investigate for criminal activity was not permissible because the agents did not have reasonable suspicion of illegal drug activity. If Campbell violated a Florida statute by following too closely, the stop for a traffic violation was constitutionally justifiable.[9]

The Fourth Amendment[10] to the United States Constitution guarantees "[t]he[11] right of the people to be secure in their persons, houses, papers, and effects against unreasonable searches and seizures" and allows a search warrant to be issued only upon "probable cause."[12] The Fourth Amendment does not prohibit all searches and seizures—just *unreasonable* searches and seizures. Although obtaining a search warrant before conducting a search is preferable, the courts have allowed a number of exceptions to the search warrant requirement over the years. One exception[13] is for illegal drug activity and another exception is to investigate a traffic violation. These two exceptions are the ones involved in *Campbell* and are discussed in detail in this memo.

Terry v. Ohio, 392 U.S. 1 (1968)[14] was the landmark case that lowered the burden of proof necessary for a stop from probable cause to "reasonable suspicion." In *Terry*[15] the United States Supreme Court held that police officers could stop someone on the street to investigate possible drug activity so long as the stop was based on something more than an "unparticularized suspicion or 'hunch.'"[16] To reach the level of reasonable suspicion, the officer may rely on "reasonable inferences" from "unusual conduct." *Id.* at 27.[17] Such stops made on reasonable suspicion are often referred to as "Terry stops" after *Terry* and the definition of Terry stops has been broadened to

---

[6]You should begin the reasoning portion of your office memo with a thesis paragraph. A well-written thesis paragraph is a road map, providing the reader with a framework into which the balance of the memo can be placed. It also tells the reader your ultimate conclusion.

A *thesis* is the central idea running through the entire memo. The time you spend before you start writing in developing your thesis is well worth it. Once you find a central idea, it will be much easier to organize the writing of your memo. To find a thesis, think in broad terms of a problem or controversy which is the basis for your memo—the problem or controversy that caused you to do the research in the first place. This memo concerns the delicate balance between society's interest in enforcing criminal drug statutes against the individual's constitutional right against unreasonable search and seizure. The courts recognize society's interest by prosecuting those believed to have violated criminal drug statutes, but the courts also recognize the individual's constitutional right by excluding any evidence obtained in violation of the Fourth Amendment.

[7]Be sure to keep your tone objective rather than persuasive.

[8]This paragraph is the thesis paragraph.

[9]This paragraph contains a short conclusion.

[10]When quoting a constitutional or statutory provision, quote only the relevant portion. Set quotations of fifty words or more off from the rest of the text in a quotation block indented left and right but not enclosed in quotation marks. Other quotations should be run in as part of the paragraph, with the quoted language in quotation marks.

[11]The brackets indicate a change in the quotation from the original. Originally, the "t" was upper case.

[12]Periods and commas go inside quotation marks. Other punctuation is placed outside quotations marks unless it is part of the quotation.

[13]Signposts are words used to guide the reader in a particular direction. "One exception" and "another" are signposts clearly identifying the two exceptions that are discussed in much more detail later in the memo.

[14]The first time you are referring to a case by name you must give the full citation. After that you should use a short form citation.

Citations in the sample office memo are given in *Bluebook* form. Your professor may require you to cite according to some other citation rule (perhaps your state's citation rule). If so, always check the appropriate citation rule to make sure you are citing correctly.

[15]Once you have given the full citation for a case and are referring to the case in general terms, you can refer to it by using one or two of the words from the name of the case and underlining or italicizing it. Be sure the words you select are not so common as to cause confusion. Here, for example, use *Terry* rather than *Ohio*.

[16]To indicate quotes within quotes, alternate double and single quotation marks, with double quotations outermost.

[17]"*Id.*" means that you are referring to the immediately preceding authority cited and "27" tells you the page number on which your reader will find the material.

apply to car stops. Once a Terry stop is made, the officers would still need probable cause or consent to search a car.

In recent years, federal courts[18] have decided a number of cases in which the defendants filed motions to suppress claiming that the evidence seized from cars should be suppressed because of a violation of their right against unreasonable search and seizure. In a case involving almost identical facts to those in *Campbell*[19] above, the United States Court of Appeals for the Eleventh Circuit found that a highway stop was not reasonable under the Fourth Amendment even though the stop was made based on a drug courier profile and the driver had allegedly committed a traffic violation. *United States v. Smith*, 799 F.2d 704, 712 (11th Cir. 1986).[20] Although the *Smith* court found that the *Smith* drug courier profile did not support reasonable suspicion, the use of drug courier profiles is not *per se* unconstitutional. *Id.* at 708 n. 5.[21] The United States Supreme Court has allowed the use of drug courier profiles where all the factors of the drug courier profile taken together do support reasonable suspicion. *United States v. Sokolow*, 490 U.S. 1, 9 (1989).

In 1996, the United States Supreme Court decided that a stop for a traffic violation does not violate the driver's constitutional right against unreasonable search and seizure. *Whren v. United States*, 517 U.S. 806, 818 (1996). Under the Fourth Amendment, a police officer may stop a car for any type of traffic violation, no matter how minor. A traffic stop is constitutional so long as there is a technical violation of a traffic regulation; it does not matter if the reason the agents gave was a pretext for the stop based on race. If Campbell violated the Florida statute by following too closely, then the stop was constitutional. If Campbell did not violate the statute, then the stop was unconstitutional.

This memo will discuss *Smith*,[22] *Sokolow*, and *Whren* and apply them to the above facts to answer the two issues being considered.[23]

Reasoning for issue one:[24]
One night in June of 1985, Trooper Robert Vogel, a Florida Highway Patrol trooper, and a DEA agent were observing cars traveling in the northbound lanes of I-95, in hopes of intercepting drug couriers. When Smith's car passed through the arc of the patrol car headlights, Vogel noticed the following factors that matched his drug courier profile:

1. The car was traveling at 3:00 a.m.;
2. The car was a 1985 Mercury, a large late model car;
3. The car had out-of state tags;
4. There were two occupants of the car who were around 30; and
5. The driver was driving cautiously and did not look at the patrol car as the Mercury passed through the arc of the patrol car headlights.

---

[18]Capitalize the word "court" only when referring to the United States Supreme Court or to the full name of any other court.

[19]Refer to "*Campbell*" showing it is a case because Campbell and Wright have had charges filed against them.

[20]Page "704" is the first page of *Smith* and "712" is the page on which the finding of the court referred to in the preceding sentence is located. As a courtesy to the reader, a page reference should be given when specific material from a case is referred to even if the material is not quoted.

The two types of sentences in legal writing are textual sentences and citation sentences. A textual sentence is the type of sentence you have been writing all your life. It is a complete grammatical sentence with a subject and a verb. A citation sentence contains only citations. A "string citation" is a citation sentence with more than one citation. In a string citation, the citations should be separated by semicolons.

A sentence is more difficult to read when it contains a full case citation, especially if the citation is long. To avoid including a full citation in a textual sentence, refer to a case in very general terms or refer to a legal principle from a case and give the full citation to the case in a citation sentence following the textual sentence.

[21]This reference is to footnote 5 of *Smith* located on page 708.

[22]Delete excess words by writing "*Smith*" instead of "the *Smith* case" or "the case of *Smith*."

[23]This sentence contains transitional language helping the reader make the transition from the introductory material contained in the first part of the reasoning section to the reasoning for issue one. Your reader will understand your memo better if you make transitions from one paragraph to the next as smooth as possible by using transitional language.

[24]The material that applies to both issues was placed in the preceding section. The material in this section of the memo applies to issue one. Some of the material in this section, such as some of the facts from *Smith*, also apply to issue two. Rather than state the *Smith* facts all over again in the next section, you can refer the reader back to this section, if necessary.

799 F.2d at 705–06.[25]

The above drug courier profile is almost identical to the *Campbell* profile.[26] In both *Smith* and *Campbell* the cars were traveling after dark, the cars were large late models with out-of-state tags, the cars were being driven "cautiously," and each car contained two passengers in their twenties or thirties. The differences between the two profiles are very minor. Campbell and Wright were dressed casually while it is not known how Smith and Swindell were dressed. Smith and Swindell did not look at Vogel as they passed. It is not known whether Campbell and Wright looked in the agents' direction as Campbell drove past. Campbell and Wright claim that race was a factor in their stop even though it was not listed as such by the agents. Smith and Swindell's race is unknown.[27]

In *Smith*, Vogel followed the Mercury for a mile and a half and noticed that the Mercury "wove" several times, once as much as six inches in to the emergency lane. Vogel pulled Smith over. When a drug dog alerted on the car, a DEA agent searched the trunk and discovered one kilogram of cocaine. Smith and his passenger, Swindell, were arrested and were charged with conspiracy to possess cocaine with the intent to distribute it. Smith and Swindell's motions to suppress the cocaine were denied and they were tried and convicted. *Id.* at 706.

The issue before the appellate court was whether the stop of Smith's car was reasonable. *Id.*[28] This is the same basic issue that will be before the *Campbell* court when it considers Campbell and Wright's motion to suppress. The *Smith* court held that the stop of Smith's car could not be upheld as a valid Terry stop, *id.* at 708, finding that "Trooper Vogel stopped the car because [Smith and Swindell][29] . . . matched a few nondistinguishing characteristics contained on a drug courier profile and, additionally, because Vogel was bothered by the way the driver of the car chose not to look at him." *Id.* at 707.

Just as there was nothing in the *Campbell* drug courier profile to differentiate Campbell and Wright from other innocent college students returning from spring break in Florida, there was nothing in Vogel's drug courier profile to differentiate Smith and Swindell from other law-abiding motorists on I-95. It is usual to drive after dark to avoid heavy traffic and to complete an interstate trip.[30] Although many motorists speed on the highways, motorists driving "cautiously" at or near the speed limit are simply obeying traffic laws. Many people other than drug couriers drive large late model cars with out-of-state tags. A motorist between the ages of twenty and forty is not unusual.

---

[25]When providing a citation for a block quote or other material set off from the rest of the text, as is the tabulation here, bring the citation back to the left margin. "*Id.*" cannot be used here because "*id.*" would refer back to the immediately preceding citation, *Sokolow*, instead of to *Smith*. Where "*id.*" cannot be used, give the volume number of the reporter, the abbreviation for the reporter, "at," and the page number. You could precede this short form citation by "*Smith*," if *Smith* had not been cited for a page or more or the reader might confuse the citation with another case, especially one from the same volume of the same reporter. This is not necessary here because *Smith* has been cited fairly recently.

When citing inclusive pages with three or more digits, drop all but the last two digits of the second number and place a hyphen between the numbers.

[26]This is an example of a topic sentence. A topic sentence contains one main idea summarizing the rest of the paragraph, with the rest of the paragraph developing the idea presented in the topic sentence. Most paragraphs should have topic sentences. The typical location of a topic sentence is the first sentence in the paragraph. Sometimes the topic sentence is the last sentence in the paragraph and pulls together the rest of the paragraph. Some paragraphs, typically narrative paragraphs like the preceding paragraph, do not have a topic sentence.

If a paragraph sounds disjointed or unorganized, try pulling it together using a topic sentence. If a topic sentence does not help, think about breaking the paragraph up into more than one paragraph.

[27]This paragraph applies the facts in *Smith* to the facts in *Campbell.* Applying facts from one case to another case involves explaining the similarities and differences between the two sets of facts. Instead of simply stating that the facts from the two cases are very similar, the paragraph specifically states which facts are the same. Sometimes in the application you need to explain in what way the facts are similar if they are not identical.

You can either apply the *Smith* facts to *Campbell* as done here or you can wait until you have thoroughly discussed *Smith*. When you prepare your outline prior to starting to write the office memo, spend some time moving parts of your reasoning around to determine the best flow for your reasoning.

[28]When you are referring to material from the same page as the material you referred to in the last citation, use just "*id.*" Note that *id.* is capitalized only at the beginning of a sentence.

[29]"Smith and Swindell" are in brackets because this wording was inserted into the quotation by the person writing the memo. The ellipsis (. . .) shows that something was omitted from the original wording of the quotation. Your quotations must exactly match the wording and punctuation of the authority the quotation comes from. If you are sloppy in quoting and your reader discovers that you have taken "liberties" with the quotation, your reader may suspect that you are sloppy in other ways—perhaps even in your research. See appendix C for an explanation of quoting correctly.

[30]No page reference is needed where you have already given the facts in the cases you are using as authority and are referring to those cases in general.

The contrast between the *Campbell* and *Smith* drug courier profiles, which do not support reasonable suspicion, and the *Sokolow* drug courier profile, which was held to support reasonable suspicion, is instructive. *Sokolow*, 490 U.S. at 3. In *Sokolow*, DEA agents found 1,063 grams of cocaine inside Sokolow's carry-on luggage when he was stopped in Honolulu International Airport based on the following profile:

1. He had paid $2,100 in cash for two airplane tickets from a roll of $20 which appeared to contain $4,000;
2. He was ticketed under a name other than his own;
3. He traveled to Miami, a known drug source, and back;
4. Although his round trip flight lasted 20 hours, he stayed in Miami only 48 hours;
5. He appeared nervous;
6. He was about 25 years old;
7. He was dressed in a black jumpsuit and was wearing gold jewelry which he wore during both legs of the round trip flight; and
8. Neither he nor his companion checked any luggage.[31]

Id. at 3–5. The Court explained that the above drug courier profile must be evaluated in light of "the totality of the circumstances—the whole picture." *Id.* at 8 (quoting *United States v. Cortez*, 449 U.S. 411, 417 (1981)).[32] "Any one of these factors [in the drug courier profile] is not by itself proof of any illegal conduct and is quite consistent with innocent travel. But we think taken together they amount to reasonable suspicion." *Id.* at 9. The *Sokolow* dissent would have found that all of the factors even if "taken together" did not amount to reasonable suspicion. In criticizing the use of a drug courier profile to stop suspects, the dissent noted "the profile's 'chameleon-like way of adapting to any particular set of observations'" "subjecting innocent individuals to unwarranted police harassment and detention." *Id.* at 13 (Marshall, J., dissenting)[33] (quoting *Sokolow v. United States*, 831 F.2d 1413, 1418 (9th Cir. 1987), *rev'd*, 490 U.S. 1 (1989)[34]).

As predicted in the *Sokolow* dissent, Smith, Swindell, Campbell, and Wright were subjected to "unwarranted police harassment and detention" even though the factors in the respective drug courier profiles, even if "taken together," did not amount to reasonable suspicion. In contrast, several of the *Sokolow* factors, such as carrying such a large amount of cash and traveling a long distance to stay a relatively short period of time, are unusual or even suspicious in and of themselves. Each of the *Smith* and *Campbell* factors was not at all out of the ordinary alone and certainly taken together did not amount to reasonable suspicion.

Conclusion[35] for issue one:
Because the drug courier profiles in *Smith* and *Campbell* are virtually identical and are in sharp contrast to the *Sokolow* drug courier profile, the *Campbell* court should find that there was not reasonable suspicion to stop Campbell and the stop on that ground was an unconstitutional violation of Campbell and Wright's constitutional guarantee against unreasonable search and seizure. Unless the agents had probable cause to investigate the alleged traffic violation, the *Campbell* court should suppress the cocaine as the fruit of an unconstitutional search and seizure.

Reasoning for issue two:
An examination of *Whren v. United States* is necessary to answer the second issue. In *Whren*, Brown was driving a Pathfinder in which Whren was a passenger. Brown was stopped at a stop sign looking down into Whren's lap. Plain clothes police officers were patrolling this "high drug area" of the District of Columbia in an unmarked patrol car. The Pathfinder caught the attention of the officers because Brown remained stopped at the stop sign for approximately

[31]Only those facts from *Sokolow* that are relevant to the discussion of *Smith* are given.

[32]When you are quoting from a case that in turn quotes from another case, identify the second case by putting the citation to the second case in parentheses following the citation for the case you are quoting.

[33]You must identify the type of opinion you are quoting from if it is other than the majority opinion.

[34]Subsequent history must be given for the lower court decision in *Sokolow*.

[35]Your conclusion section at the end of a reasoning section ties together your previous discussion and reaches a conclusion. The difference between the conclusion section for issue one and answer one is that answer one is a more condensed one-sentence version of the conclusion section.

twenty seconds. When the patrol car made a U-turn to follow the Pathfinder, Brown turned right without signaling and started off at an "unreasonable speed." The patrol car stopped the Pathfinder. When one of the officers approached Brown's window and peered in, he saw that Whren had two plastic bags of crack cocaine on his lap. The officers arrested Whren and Brown. 517 U.S. at 808, 809.

Justice Scalia phrased the issue as "whether the temporary detention of a motorist who the police have probable cause to believe has committed a civil traffic violation is inconsistent with the Fourth Amendment's prohibition against unreasonable seizures unless a reasonable officer would have been motivated to stop the car by a desire to enforce the traffic laws." *Id.* at 808. The Court answered the question, "no." "[T]he district court found that the officers had probable cause to believe that petitioners had violated the traffic code. That rendered the stop reasonable under the Fourth Amendment, the evidence thereby discovered admissible, and the upholding of the convictions by the Court of Appeals for the District of Columbia Circuit correct." *Id.* at 819.

Whren and Brown, both black, had urged the Court to apply the reasonable officer standard. They argued that, because of the multitude of traffic ordinances, an officer could almost invariably find some reason to stop a particular vehicle for an alleged traffic violation. This might allow an officer to target a particular vehicle to be stopped on the pretext of a traffic violation, where the real reason for stopping the vehicle was an impermissible factor such as the race of the persons in the vehicle. *Id.* at 810. The Court dismissed this argument. "We of course agree with petitioners that the Constitution prohibits selective enforcement of the law based on considerations such as race. But the constitutional basis for objecting to intentionally discriminatory application of laws is the Equal Protection Clause, not the Fourth Amendment." *Id.* at 813. The Court did not explain that an Equal Protection Clause challenge is difficult to prove because it requires evidence of intentional discrimination.

Prior to *Whren*, some courts, including the court deciding *Smith*, had decided that a car stop for a traffic violation was unconstitutional unless a reasonable officer would have made the stop. The *Smith* court found that the cocaine should have been excluded from evidence because a reasonable officer would not have stopped Smith's car for the alleged traffic violation. 799 F. 2d at 711. However in *Whren*, the United States Supreme Court rejected the argument that the reasonable officer standard should apply. 517 U.S. at 813.

After *Whren*, it would be very difficult to convince a court that a stop for an alleged traffic violation is unconstitutional. However, if the court finds that the driver did not violate any traffic regulation, then the stop would be unconstitutional.

The applicable Florida motor vehicle statute states: "The driver of a motor vehicle shall not follow another vehicle more closely than is reasonable and prudent, having due regard for the speed of such vehicles and the traffic upon, and the condition of, the highway." Fla. Stat. Ch. 316.0895 (1) (2000). No simple test determines if Campbell violated the statute. The court must determine from any evidence presented whether the distance at which Campbell was following the car in front of him was reasonable and prudent.

Whren and *Campbell* are very similar in that in both cases, the government claimed that the stop of a suspect car did not violate the driver's right against unreasonable search and seizure because there was some irregularity in the way the car was being driven that gave the officer reason to stop the car. The driving "irregularities" are similar in the failure to use a turn signal in changing lanes and speeding in *Whren* and the following too closely in *Campbell* are moving violations that can pose a severe safety hazard; under the circumstances, neither appeared to adversely impact any other vehicle's safety.

The alleged driving irregularities in *Whren* and *Campbell* are dissimilar in several respects. While it was clear that Brown committed a traffic violation, the Florida statute that Campbell allegedly violated does not apply to Campbell if he was following at a safe distance. Determining whether one vehicle is following another vehicle too closely involved much more of a judgment call than determining whether the Pathfinder in *Whren* failed to signal when turning right and exceeded the speed limit. The position of the vehicles on the highway and the weather and road conditions must all be considered to determine if Campbell violated the statute by following the vehicle in front of him too closely.

Conclusion for issue two:
Whren rejected the argument that a pretextual traffic stop is unconstitutional. *Whren* is binding on the *Campbell* court. Following the mandatory authority of *Whren*, the *Campbell* court should hold that the stop was constitutional if the agents had probable cause of a traffic violation; the court should hold that the stop was unconstitutional if there was no traffic violation. If the *Campbell* stop violated the Fourth Amendment, Campbell and Wright's motion to suppress would be denied. If the stop were unconstitutional, the cocaine would be suppressed.

SECOND OFFICE MEMO

To: legal research and writing classes

From: your author

Re: whether drugs found in a car passenger's purse should be suppressed

Date: July 13, 2000

Facts:

Cruz Estrada was riding with her friend, Luis Briones, when Luis' car was pulled over. They were traveling south on I-95 toward Miami to visit friends. The officer said he had stopped the car because they were speeding.

The officer stood at the window on the driver's side and asked for Luis' license and car registration. While Luis searched his wallet for the documents, the officer noticed a glass vial containing small kernels of an off-white substance in Luis' lap. Believing the vial to contain crack cocaine, the officer announced that he was seizing it. He asked Luis and Cruz to exit the car and asked Luis for his wallet.

Cruz got out of the car with her purse strap slung over her shoulder. The officer approached her and said, "You don't mind if I search this, do you?" Without giving her time to respond, the officer grabbed her purse and began to search it. Inside her purse, he found a brown paper envelope. Cruz claimed that someone had given it to her to give to a friend in Miami.

Still holding Cruz' purse and Luis' wallet, the officer asked them to wait in the patrol car while he searched Luis' car. Cruz and Luis nervously waited in the back seat of the patrol car. Cruz admitted to Luis that the envelope was hers and that it contained illegal drugs.

After Cruz and Luis were arrested, she discovered that the police officer had tape-recorded their conversation in the back of the patrol car. Luis told her that the reason the officer gave for stopping them must have been a pretext because, at the most, he was driving five miles over the speed limit. He said he suspected that he had been stopped for what is jokingly referred to as the offense of DWH or Driving While Hispanic.

She has been charged under the federal drug statutes.

Issues:

1. Did the officer have probable cause to stop the Briones car for speeding where Luis was exceeding the speed limit by only a few miles and Luis suspects that his race (Hispanic) was the motivation for the stop?
2. Where the officer grabbed Cruz' purse from her shoulder, did the officer's search of Cruz' purse violate her Fourth Amendment right against unreasonable search and seizure and can the drugs found in her purse be suppressed?
3. Where the officer tape-recorded Cruz and Luis' conversation while they were seated in the back seat of the patrol car, is the tape admissible as evidence?

Answers:

1. Because an officer can stop the car for any traffic violation, no matter how minor, the stop did not violate Cruz' fourth amendment right against unreasonable search and seizure and the drugs cannot be suppressed on that ground.
2. Because Cruz did not consent to the search of her purse, she may be able to have the drugs suppressed if the court views her purse as an outer layer of clothing.
3. Because Cruz and Luis had no reasonable expectation of privacy in the back of the patrol car, their conversation was not an "oral communication," suppressible under the federal eavesdropping statutes; however, the tape may be suppressed if the court decides that the search of Cruz's purse was unconstitutional and the tape is derivative of the search.

Reasoning:

The *Estrada* facts illustrate the tension between an individual's expectation of privacy and a federal law enforcement officer's duty to enforce the federal drug statutes. Car occupants usually feel that items they transport in a car will remain private; however, the Fourth Amendment allows a police officer to stop a car for a traffic violation and question the occupants. The officer may search the car if the occupants consent or if the officer has probable cause that the car contains illegal drugs. During the search, the officer may ask the car occupants to wait in the patrol car for their safety or comfort. Suspects seated in the rear seat of a patrol car may expect the same amount of privacy they would have were they in a private car. With the patrol car doors and windows closed, the officer outside the patrol car cannot hear the suspects' conversation. However, the officer might tape the suspects' conversation in the belief that the patrol car is similar to the officer's office in a police station.

Cruz can allege that her Fourth Amendment rights were violated when the officer stopped the car in which she was riding and searched her purse. She can also claim that her conversation in the back seat of the patrol car should have been protected against being tape-recorded under the federal eavesdropping statutes. The stop of the car for a traffic violation was constitutionally justifiable. Because Cruz did not consent to the search of her purse, she may be able to have the drugs suppressed if the court views her purse as similar to an outer layer of clothing. The conversation in the back seat of the patrol car will not be suppressed under the federal eavesdropping statutes because Cruz and Luis had no reasonable expectation of privacy; however, if the search of Cruz's purse was unconstitutional and the incriminating statements on the tape were the fruit of the search, then the tape could be suppressed as well.

General reasoning for issues one and two:

The Fourth Amendment to the United States Constitution guarantees "[t]he right of the people to be secure in their persons, houses, papers, and effects against unreasonable searches and seizures" and allows a search warrant to be issued only upon "probable cause." The Fourth Amendment does not prohibit all searches and seizures—just *unreasonable* searches and seizures. Although obtaining a search warrant before conducting a search is preferable, the courts have allowed a number of exceptions to the search warrant requirement over the years. At least two exceptions apply to a vehicle search. One exception is for the occupants to consent to a search of the vehicle. *United States v. Jimeno*, 500 U.S. 248, 251 (1991). A second exception is that the officer can search the car if there is probable cause of criminal activity. Even without consent, the officer can search containers found in the car and suspected of holding the object of the officer's search, no matter who owns the container. *Wyoming v. Houghton*, 526 U.S. 295, 300–01 (1999). An officer may not search someone's person without probable cause. *Id.* at 303. These exceptions are the ones involved in *Estrada* and are discussed in detail in this memo.

Reasoning for issue one:

On June 10, 1996, the United States Supreme Court decided a landmark case in which the Court held that the Fourth Amendment allows a police officer to stop a vehicle for any type of traffic violation. *Whren v. United States*, 517 U.S. 806, 819 (1996). The facts of *Estrada* and *Whren* will be compared to determine if the *Estrada* vehicle stop was constitutional.

In *Whren*, plain clothes law enforcement officers were patrolling a high drug area of the District of Columbia when they passed a Pathfinder truck stopped at a stop sign. The driver was looking into the lap of the passenger and the truck paused an overly long period of time at the stop sign. As the patrol car made a U-turn to approach the truck, the truck turned right without signalling and started off at an "unreasonable" speed. The patrol car overtook the truck and stopped it. Whren was a passenger and Brown was the driver. When one officer looked through the driver's window, he saw plastic bags of something resembling crack cocaine in Whren's hands. *Id.* at 808.

In *Whren*, Justice Scalia phrased the issue as "whether the temporary detention of a motorist who the police have probable cause to believe has committed a civil traffic violation is inconsistent with the Fourth Amendment's prohibition against unreasonable seizures unless a reasonable officer would have been motivated to stop the car by a desire to enforce the traffic laws." *Id.* at 808. The Court answered the question, "no." "[T]he district court found that the officers had probable cause to believe that petitioners had violated the traffic code. That rendered the stop reasonable under the Fourth Amendment, the evidence thereby discovered admissible, and the upholding of the convictions by the Court of Appeals for the District of Columbia Circuit correct." *Id.* at 819.

Whren and Brown, both black, had urged the Court to apply the reasonable officer standard. They argued, that because of the multitude of traffic ordinances, an officer could almost invariably find some reason to stop a particular vehicle for an alleged traffic violation. This might allow an officer to target a particular vehicle to be stopped on the pretext of a traffic violation, where the real reason for stopping the vehicle was an impermissible factor such as the race of the persons in the vehicle. *Id.* at 810. The Court dismissed this argument. "We of course agree with petitioners that the Constitution prohibits selective enforcement of the law based on considerations such as race. But the constitutional basis for objecting to intentionally discriminatory application of laws is the Equal Protection Clause, not the Fourth Amendment." *Id.* at 813. The Court did not explain that an Equal Protection Clause challenge is difficult to prove because it requires evidence of intentional discrimination.

After *Whren*, it would be very difficult to convince a court that a stop for an alleged traffic violation is unconstitutional. One instance is if the facts, which the officer states violate a traffic ordinance, are found by a court not to violate the ordinance. For example, an officer could stop a car because the officer believes that the windows are too heavily tinted. A court could find the stop unconstitutional if the tinting, although dark, did comply with the applicable traffic ordinance. Another instance is if the court finds that the officer lied; no facts existed that could support the alleged violation.

Whren and *Estrada* are very similar in that in those cases, the government claimed that the stop of a suspect car did not violate the driver's right against unreasonable search and seizure because there was some irregularity in the way the car was being driven that gave the officer reason to stop the car. The driving "irregularities" are similar in that Brown's failure to signal a right turn and speeding off and Briones' speeding did not appear to cause any imminent safety hazard. From the facts of the two cases, it appears that Brown exceeded the speed limit for only a short distance and Luis may have been travelling only a few miles over the speed limit. In each case, the reason articulated for the stop may have been a pretext for stopping the vehicle on account of the occupants' race.

Conclusion for issue one:
Whren rejected the argument that a pretextual traffic stop is unconstitutional. *Whren* is binding on the *Estrada* court. Following the mandatory authority of *Whren*, the *Estrada* court should hold that the stop for speeding was constitutional because there was probable cause of a traffic violation. Because Cruz' fourth amendment right was not violated by the stop, the drugs would not be suppressed based on the Fourth Amendment.

Reasoning for issue two:
The search of Cruz' purse is constitutional if she consented to the search or the container exception to the search warrant requirement extends to her purse. The United States Supreme Court has stated the standard for determining when an individual has consented to the search of a car. *United States v. Jimeno*, 500 U.S. at 251. This portion of the office memo will examine whether the consent standard has been met. As far as the container exception is concerned, the United States Supreme Court recently held that "police officers with probable cause to search a car may inspect passengers' belongings found in the car that are capable of concealing the object of the search." *Wyoming v. Houghton*, 526 U.S. at 307. The facts of *Jimeno*, *Houghton*, and *Estrada* will be compared to determine if the search of Cruz' purse was constitutional.

In *Jimeno*, Officer Trujillo overheard a telephone call from a public telephone in which Jimeno was discussing a drug deal. Trujillo followed Jimeno's car and stopped Jimeno for failure to stop when turning right on red. After informing Jimeno about the traffic violation, Trujillo

> went on to say that he had reason to believe that respondent was carrying narcotics in his car, and asked permission to search the car. He explained that respondent did not have to consent to a search of the car.

> Respondent stated that he had nothing to hide, and gave Trujillo permission to search the automobile.

500 U.S. at 249–50. Trujillo found drugs in a brown paper bag on the car floorboard. *Id.* at 250.

The Court then set forth the test for determining whether consent was given. "The standard for measuring the scope of a suspect's consent under the Fourth Amendment is that of 'objective' reasonableness—what would the typical person have understood by the exchange between the officer and the suspect?" *Id.* at 251. Applying this standard, the Court found that Jimeno had consented to the search of the bag.

The facts of *Jimeno* and *Estrada* are similar in that the two cars were stopped for alleged traffic violations and the officers searched containers. The facts surrounding the consent issue differ greatly. Trujillo told Jimeno that the officer suspected that there were drugs in the car and explained that Jimeno did not have to consent to the search. When Trujillo asked Jimeno's permission, Jimeno claimed that he had nothing to hide and explicitly consented to the search. The officer in *Estrada* made a statement, "you don't mind if I search, do you?"; he did not ask Cruz for her consent. He gave Cruz no time to respond before snatching her purse. In *Jimeno* the container was a brown paper bag located on the floor of the car. In *Estrada*, the container was Cruz' purse, hanging from her shoulder.

Applying the objective reasonableness standard, it would not be objectively reasonable to believe that Cruz had consented to the search of her purse. She did not verbally consent and her actions did not imply consent. A woman's purse often contains objects of a personal nature that the individual wants to keep safe from prying eyes. A purse is often considered an extension of the individual's outer clothing. Because of the private nature of Cruz' purse, it presumably would take some overt action or response before it would be reasonable to believe that she had consented.

In *Houghton*, David Young was stopped for speeding and a faulty brake light. After the officer saw a hypodermic syringe in Young's pocket, Young admitted that he used it to take drugs. The officer asked the two female passengers seated in the front seat to exit the car and the officer searched the car. The officer found Houghton's purse on the back seat of the car. Searching the purse, the officer found a brown pouch that contained drug paraphernalia and a syringe containing methamphetamine in a large enough quantity for a felony conviction. Houghton claimed that the brown pouch was not hers. The officer also found a black container pouch that contained drug paraphernalia and a syringe containing a smaller amount of methamphetamine, insufficient for a felony conviction. Houghton's arms showed fresh needle-marks. The officer arrested her. 526 U.S. at 297–98.

The issue in *Houghton* was "whether police officers violate the Fourth Amendment when they search a passenger's personal belongings inside an automobile that they have probable cause to believe contains contraband." *Id.* at 297. The Court held "that police officers with probable cause to search a car may inspect passengers' belongings found in the car that are capable of concealing the object of the search." *Id.* at 307. The Court first relied on a 1982 case in which the Court had found that, where there was probable cause to search a car, it was constitutionally permissible to search containers found in the car that might hold the object of the search. *Id.* at 301–02. The Court noted that an individual carrying a package in a vehicle travelling on the public roads has a reduced expectation of privacy; however the Court did note the "unique, significantly heightened protection afforded against searches of one's person." *Id.* at 303. The Court found no reason to afford more protection to a container owned by a passenger than a container owned by the driver. *Id.* at 305.

In *Houghton*, Justice Breyer joined in the majority opinion and wrote a separate concurring opinion. In the concurring opinion, he stated that *Houghton* should be limited to vehicle searches and to containers found in a vehicle. He was troubled by the fact that it was Houghton's purse that was searched.

> [A]lso important is the fact that the container here at issue, a woman's purse, was found at a considerable distance from its owner, who did not claim ownership until the officer discovered her identification while looking through it. Purses are special containers. They are repositories of especially personal items that people generally like to keep with them at all times. So I am tempted to say that a search of a purse involves an intrusion so similar to a search of one's person that the same rule should govern both. However, given this Court's prior cases, I cannot argue that the fact that the container was a purse *automatically* makes a legal difference . . . . But I can say that it would matter if a

> woman's purse, like a man's billfold, were attached to her person. It might then amount to a kind of "outer clothing," which under the Court's cases would properly receive increased protection.

Id. at 308 (Breyer, J. concurring) (citations omitted).

The facts of *Houghton* and *Estrada* are similar in that the two cars were stopped for alleged traffic violations and the officers searched a passenger's purse. The facts of the two cases differ in that Houghton's purse was on the back seat of the car, Houghton had exited the car without taking the purse with her, and Houghton at first disclaimed ownership of the purse. In contrast, Cruz took her purse with her when she exited the car and it was attached to her when the officer snatched it from her shoulder.

In dicta in *Houghton*, the Court draws a distinction between the permissible search of containers and the search of an individual. The officer would not have been permitted to search Houghton without probable cause that she was carrying drugs or a weapon on her person. In the concurrence, Justice Breyer struggles with the fact that the container being searched is Houghton's purse. Were *Estrada* before him, he would likely find that the search of Cruz' purse was unconstitutional. As a concurrence, Justice Breyer's opinion is not mandatory authority. In addition, his opinion requiring the search of a purse attached to an individual to be treated similarly to the search of an individual's outer clothing is based on hypothetical facts.

Conclusion for issue two:
Applying the standard for consent enunciated in *Jimeno*, Cruz did not consent to the search of her purse. A reasonable person would not believe that Cruz' lack of response to the officer's statement, "you don't mind if I search, do you?," could be considered consent. Thus, the consent exception to the search warrant requirement does not exist in *Estrada*. Because Cruz did not consent to the search of her purse, the search on that ground was unconstitutional.

The comparison of *Houghton* and *Estrada* is more difficult. If the facts in the two cases are substantially similar, then the *Estrada* court should hold that the drugs found in Cruz' purse should not be suppressed. If the *Estrada* court finds that Cruz' purse can be likened to an item of clothing she was wearing, then the drugs found in her purse should be suppressed.

Although the facts in *Houghton* and *Estrada* are similar, they are different enough that a court could find that the drugs found in Cruz' purse should be suppressed. Because her purse was next to her body, Cruz had a heightened expectation of privacy in it. The officer could not have constitutionally searched Cruz without more evidence. Thus, the search of her purse should also be unconstitutional and the drugs found in the purse should be suppressed.

Reasoning for issue three:
To determine whether the audio recording of Cruz and Luis' conversation was permissible, the court must consider the federal eavesdropping statutes and their case law interpretation. The federal eavesdropping statutes protect certain types of face-to-face conversations against interception. To be protected, the conversation must qualify as an "oral communication." Under the statutes, an " 'oral communication' means any oral communications uttered by a person exhibiting an expectation that such communication is not subject to interception under circumstances justifying such expectation. . . ." 18 U.S.C.S. § 2510 (2) (Lexis L. Publg. 1993). Thus, a conversation is not an oral communication unless the conversants expect that the conversation is private and an objective third party would consider that expectation reasonable.

It is illegal to intercept an oral communication. "[A]ny person who . . . intentionally intercepts . . . any oral communication . . . shall be punished." 18 U.S.C.S. § 2511 (1) (Lexis L. Publg. 1993). One exception to this prohibition involves a police officer; however, the police officer must be party to the conversation or one conversant must have consented to the taping for the exception to apply. "It shall not be unlawful under this chapter for a person acting under color of law to intercept [an] . . . oral . . . communication where such person is a party to the communication or one of the parties has given prior consent to the interception." 18 U.S.C.S. § 2511 (2)(c) (Lexis L. Publg. 1993). If an oral communication is taped in violation of the eavesdropping statutes, the conversation cannot be used as evidence in court. "Whenever any . . . oral communication has been intercepted, no part of the contents of such communication and no evidence derived therefrom may be received in evidence in any trial, hearing, or other proceeding . . . before a court . . . if the disclosure of that information would be in violation of this chapter." 18 U.S.C.S. § 2515 (Lexis L. Publg. 1993).

Thus, if Cruz and Luis' conversation were an oral communication, it should be suppressed. Whether the conversation is an oral communication turns on whether Cruz and Luis had a reasonable expectation of privacy while seated in the rear seat of the patrol car. One prong of the two-prong test is satisfied; they appear to have had an expectation of privacy or they would not have made incriminating statements. The other prong of the test is whether their expectation was reasonable. On one hand, the conversation was not audible outside the patrol car. The only way the officer could have heard the conversation was by taping it. On the other hand, Cruz and Luis were not sitting in Luis's car. They were sitting in the officer's car. While an expectation of privacy in Luis' car would have been reasonable, it is unclear from the federal statutes whether an expectation of privacy in the officer's car was reasonable. Some might equate the officer's car to the officer's office. If Cruz and Luis were conversing in an office of a police station, it might not be reasonable to expect privacy.

In a case with similar facts, the issue before the United States Court of Appeals for the Eleventh Circuit was "whether the district court erred in denying the motion to suppress the tapes resulting from the secret recording of McKinnon's pre-arrest conversations while he sat in the back seat of the police car." *United States v. McKinnon*, 985 F.2d 525, 526 (11th Cir. 1993).

In *McKinnon*, police officers stopped a pick-up truck for failure to travel in a single lane on the Florida Turnpike. Theodore Pressley was driving and Steve McKinnon was the passenger. Pressley consented to the search of his vehicle. While the officers were searching, McKinnon and Pressley waited in the rear seat of the patrol car. There they made incriminating statements that were secretly recorded by the officers. The officers arrested them after finding cocaine in the truck and they were placed in the rear seat of the patrol car. The officers again recorded McKinnon's and Pressley's incriminating statements. *Id.*

The *McKinnon* court considered the meaning of the term "oral communication" under the federal statutes. An oral communication is protected against taping. If a conversation is taped in violation of the statutes, the tape may be suppressed. A conversation is an oral communication only if the conversants exhibited a subjective expectation of privacy and the expectation of privacy was objectively reasonable. The court seemed to agree with the government's argument that a patrol car functions as the officer's office and the rear seat of the patrol car functions as a jail cell. The court held "that McKinnon did not have a reasonable or justifiable expectation of privacy for conversations he held while seated in the back seat area of a police car." *Id.* at 527.

In examining the facts of *McKinnon* and *Estrada*, the facts concerning the taping seem virtually identical. In each case, an officer asked two individuals to wait in the patrol car prior to their arrest. The officer taped their conversation in the rear seat of the patrol car; the conversation contained incriminating statements. One difference between the two cases is that the officer in *McKinnon* also taped McKinnon's conversation following his arrest. This difference is not significant because an arrestee held in the back of a patrol car would have a lesser expectation of privacy than a person not under arrest.

A number of state and a number of federal courts, other than the *McKinnon* court, have faced the issue of whether an officer may secretly tape a conversation of individuals seated in the rear seat of a patrol car. In each case the court has said that taping is permissible. Carol M. Bast & Joseph B. Sanborn, Jr., *Not Just any Sightseeing Tour: Surreptitious Taping in a Patrol Car*, 32 Crim. L. Bull. 123, 130–31 (1996).

Cruz could make the argument that the search of her purse tainted the tape recording. Where a police officer obtains evidence in an unconstitutional manner, that evidence is excluded from use at trial. If that evidence leads the officer to other evidence, the other evidence is derivative of the first evidence. The derivative evidence is known as fruit of the poisonous tree and is also inadmissible. Generally, evidence that is tainted by the prior unconstitutional conduct is inadmissible; however, in some instances the second evidence is admissible because the connection between the unconstitutionally-seized evidence and the subsequently obtained evidence is marginal.

Conclusion for issue three:

Although persuasive authority in other circuits, *McKinnon* is mandatory authority in this circuit. The facts concerning the taping are virtually identical in

McKinnon and *Estrada*. A number of other state and federal courts have also held that there is no reasonable expectation of privacy for persons seated in the back of a patrol car. Therefore, a court should find that Cruz and Luis had no reasonable expectation of privacy while they were seated in the rear seat of the patrol car. Because they did not have a reasonable expectation of privacy, their conversation was not protected against taping as an oral communication.

If the court rules that the search of Cruz's purse was unconstitutional, then the tape may be suppressed if the search led Cruz to make the incriminating statements. Standard police procedure is to place a car's occupants in the rear seat of the police car while the officer is conducting a search and to tape their conversation. After the search of her purse, Cruz may have been more likely to discuss the drugs found in her purse. Cruz may have made reference to the drugs even if the officer had not found them in her purse. She might have commented that she was glad the officer did not search her purse.

The court will have to decide from the evidence the likelihood of Cruz making some type of incriminating statement without the officer having searched her purse. The court would not suppress the tape if the court decides that Cruz would have made the incriminating statements without the search of her purse.

COMMUNICATING CLEARLY WITH THE READER

The writer communicates with the reader through the written document. The communication must be clear to the reader because the reader does not have the opportunity to question the writer. A reader faced with unclear writing will have to spend additional time interpreting what the writer was trying to communicate. The following article (fig. 16-8) presents 10 tips for communicating clearly with your reader.

FIGURE 16-8 Article reprinted from March/April 2000 issue of the New York State Bar Journal.

Writing Clinic

ANALYZING THE WRITER'S ANALYSIS: WILL IT BE CLEAR TO THE READER?

*By Diana Roberto Donahoe**

Analysis is the cornerstone of lawyering. It is what we do every day. We are constantly asked to analyze a court decision, a legal issue, a client's problem. Yet, how often do we stop to analyze our own written analysis? Typically, we spend vast amounts of time analyzing an issue, but very little time thinking through the techniques we use to communicate that analysis to others.

All too often, we use certain methods merely because we have used them before—even though these comfortable techniques can be outdated, or worse, might never have been very effective. For some, it may be similar to continuing with the DOS system on a computer rather than changing to the Windows approach. To many Windows users, DOS appears to be Byzantine. Does your writing? Now may be the time to re-examine your analytical methods and try new techniques to present material clearly and logically.

Because it is difficult to change your personal approach to composition, the best method is to develop a critical editorial eye for rereading drafts. When reading the drafts, imagine you are the reader, not the writer. Step out of the worn-out "writer's" shoes and into the new shoes of the reader. This article provides 10 tips for creating a reader-based review of your documents.

***Diana Roberto Donahoe** is an associate professor of legal research and writing at Georgetown University Law Center. She also provides seminars and writing consulting services for law firms and in-house counsel. She is a graduate of Williams College and holds J.D. and L.L.M. degrees from Georgetown University Law Center.

FIGURE 16-8 (continued)

#1: Create a "Roadmap"

Create an effective large-scale organization. You have lived with the issues for weeks, months, even years, but readers are encountering this information for the first time. In addition, they are impatient, busy, and have short attention spans. They are not impressed by flowery writing and, for the most part, do not care what you think; instead, they want to be informed of the law as quickly and effectively as possible.

Present the rule of law in the beginning of your analysis. "Fronting" the law or creating a "roadmap" to your document allows the reader to understand the structure of the issue. Your "roadmap" should be a concise statement of the overarching rule of law you are analyzing. For example, in a document analyzing a particular statute, provide the reader with an immediate breakdown of the key elements of that statute. In a common law problem, state the rule from a synthesis of the cases.

An example of a "roadmap" from a document analyzing intentional infliction of emotional distress:

To prove intentional infliction of emotional distress, the plaintiff must prove the defendant's conduct is (1) extreme and outrageous, (2) intentional or reckless, and (3) the cause of emotional distress.

This "roadmap" provides a clear breakdown of the legal elements of intentional infliction and implicitly tells the reader that the document will be organized around each of the three elements.

#2: Follow Your "Roadmap"

In most situations, the discussion of the law should parallel your analysis in lock-step. If you follow your "roadmap" in the rest of the document, the reader will understand not only the breakdown of the law but also the layout of your document. If your roadmap is a three-part test, for example, analyze each part in the order in which you presented it. If it is a balancing test, address the first part of the balance immediately. The quickest way to confuse a reader is to set out the elements of the law and then fail to address each in turn.

#3: Use Topic Sentences to Follow Your "Roadmap"

Topic sentences notify the reader of the contents of the paragraph. Because the contents of the paragraph usually focus on a particular legal element, your topic sentence should refer to that element specifically. The language should parallel the language in your "roadmap" so that terms are consistent within the language of the law.

Topic sentences are also extremely useful in helping a reader focus quickly on a particular piece of the analysis. Think of the occasions when you have tried to develop just one facet of your argument and have searched for the analysis on that point in a case or legal article. It is very frustrating to spend unnecessary time searching for something you know is there but cannot find easily. Topic sentences can cure that problem. A clear topic sentence that identifies the argument being made in the paragraph helps readers focus on the parts of the document they find most relevant.

#4: Create a Reader-Based Outline

After you have finished your draft, create a reader-based outline developed from the topic sentences in the document. Then step into the shoes of a reader who knows nothing about this area of the law and read the result.

If you as the reader find that you have a coherent understanding of the law based on this outline, then you know that the large-scale organization of your document has presented the analysis clearly and efficiently. Better yet, if your reader-based outline matches your writer-based outline (assuming that you wrote one in advance), then

FIGURE 16-8 (continued)

your reader should understand your arguments simply by reading your topic sentences.

#5: Avoid a Simple Regurgitation of Cases

Too often, legal writers simply present a case-by-case method of analysis, methodically and thoroughly discussing applicable cases in sequence. Only then do they apply the law to the facts at hand. This technique is ineffective for at least three reasons.

First, it forces the reader to flip back and forth between the discussion of the cases and the later discussion of the facts. Second, it places the burden on the reader to perform the comparisons and to think through the analysis. Finally, it often results in unnecessary duplication as the writer is forced to discuss the case law twice—once in the case-by-case discussion and then again as the cases are applied to the facts at hand.

A more concise and effective technique involves applying the facts to each part of the law as it is presented. If a "roadmap" is provided up front, then the reader understands the structure of the law before the analysis begins and can appreciate the immediate comparison of prior holdings to present facts. If topic sentences effectively identify the legal proposition that will be discussed in the paragraph, the relevant facts of previous cases and their roles in your argument should fall into place within each paragraph. At times, the solution may be to begin with the anticipated bottom line of your analysis, followed by a presentation of cases that show how the facts and conclusions support the point you wish to make.

#6: Use Only Relevant Portions of the Law

When in doubt about how much of a prior case to discuss in a case comparison, lawyers often err on the side of using too much. This leaves the readers inundated with information that is not necessary to the analysis. Worse, the point the writer is trying to make is hidden in the interesting, but essentially irrelevant, facts of the other cases. Too many of these comparisons in a single document become a burden for readers as they struggle to discern the legal points being made.

Instead, the legal writer should strive for an approach to prior law that is well-balanced and effectively tied to the client's facts. The readers are not familiar with the relevant legal precedent, nor do they thoroughly understand the client's situation, even if presented earlier in a statement of the facts. Although readers might be exceptionally bright and well versed in the law, they cannot be expected to know all the intricacies of the issue. Therefore, the writer needs to distill the key elements from the previous cases and show how they serve as building blocks in the analysis for this case.

The following two-part analogy can illustrate how to balance the presentation of the law and the facts as you spell out your analysis. First, try to draw both sides of a penny from memory, and you will probably miss many intricacies of the coin that you thought you knew so well. Then look at a French two-franc piece and try to compare the franc to your drawing of the penny. The comparison is impossible; although you thought you knew the penny, you cannot compare an incomplete picture of a coin with a coin you have never seen (or saw years ago when visiting France).

In this analogy, the "penny" is the facts of your case. You think you know them just as you thought you knew the penny, but when you attempt to write about them, the picture is not clear to the readers, who cannot remember all the details from the statement of facts. Keep pulling the penny out of your pocket; be specific about each detail of your case. Do not let the statement of facts that appears earlier in your document substitute for a concise reminder of those facts during course of your analysis.

The "two-franc piece" is the prior case. Assume your reader has never been to France. Explain in detail the intricacies of the coin. As you are discussing the prior

FIGURE 16-8 (continued)

case, ask yourself if you have told the reader the facts, holding, and reasoning of the prior case (again, without inundating the reader with irrelevant information). Then compare those points specifically to your facts, tying the analysis together.

Instead of resorting to block quotes or case-by-case comparisons, ask whether the reader, who has not researched and lived with the issue, has enough information about the facts, the prior law, and how they fit together to understand the logic behind the analysis. Finally, ask yourself if everything you have mentioned is essential to your point. Do you, for example, really need the plaintiff's full name in your discussion of a prior case? If you critically read all your analysis with the "penny-franc" analogy in mind, you will ask the right questions—the questions a reader will ask when critically reading.

#7: Do Not Rely on Parentheticals for Comparisons

Although parentheticals after a citation can be useful tools in presenting a concise legal analysis, they are meant to contain secondary information. Because a reader's eyes instinctively skip over them, the writer's meaning may be lost if an important piece of analysis is presented in a parenthetical. For example:

Dr. Appleby's customer contacts at the clinic amount to the clinic's predictable interest making the covenant enforceable. If an employer invests a substantial amount of time, effort, and advertising to generate customers for its physician, the interest is predictable. See Pollack, 458 N.W.2d 591, 599 (1990); Wausau, 514 N.W.2d 34, 39 (1994) (four months not enough time to develop significant customer contacts). Dr. Appleby's seven years at the clinic where she associated the clinic with HMOs have given her substantial contacts with her patients.

The preceding paragraph uses a parenthetical where a full comparison in text would have been more appropriate. The writer is trying to compare four months to seven years as part of the analysis. Yet, because the "four months" portion is in parenthesis (and after a string quote to further hide its importance), the comparison is lost on the reader. Moving the comparison of four months vs. seven years into the text would make it easier for the reader to grasp the importance of the *Wausau* case.

In short, save the parentheticals for cases that are tangentially related, but not worthy of a full discussion or comparison.

#8: Avoid Block Quotes

Because there is a tendency to think that something is more persuasive if someone important said it, we frequently quote others. When we write, therefore, the temptation is to mistakenly assume that the way to be persuasive is to use block quotes. Readers, however, are busy, often impatient and prone to short attention spans. They do not have time to read words that are offset and single-spaced. Such masses of words are uninviting; they cause the eyes to avert and the attention to wander. Block quotes and footnotes are often the last things that will persuade a reader. Don't use either unless absolutely necessary.

To make matters worse, writers often instinctively underline parts of the quotation as if to say, "if your eyes do skip over this lengthy writing, at least read this part." For example:

Under the "customer contact theory," a threat is posed by the employee if she has enough control or influence over the customers that she would be able to take the customers away from the employer in a situation where the employee has worked for the employer for a number of years and gained particular customers who relate to her, not the company, due to her as an individual and not with the company as a unit.

First, the writer who inserted this block quote should have realized that the reader will not want to spend time digesting the message. That is the writer's job. Second, the underlining helps identify important terms, but it does not provide the important context. Instead, the writer should use those important terms in the text to explain their meaning and importance:

FIGURE 16-8 (continued)

Under the "customer contact theory" an employee is a threat if she has enough influence or control over customers to entice them from her employer.

The result is a concise statement of the law without the single-spaced distractions that can annoy and distract the reader.

#9: Take a Break From Your Document

Writing is personal; it becomes a part of you. You should take a step or two (in the form of days or weeks, if possible) away from your document to gain perspective and to depersonalize it. If you have not thought about your document for a while (the longer the better), upon your return, you will find the holes in your logic, the flaws in your reasoning, and the gaps in your large-scale organization that escaped your earlier review. In other words, by taking a step back from your document, you have, in a sense, become the reader who has not thought about these issues or the law at all. You will become an effective critical reader of your own writing.

#10: Read the Document Aloud

Another way to step into the reader's shoes is to read your document out loud. Better yet, have someone else read it to you. The goal here is to lose the writer's voice and hear the reader's voice. In doing so, you will gain a sense of the tone, purpose, and flow from the perspective of your audience as the reader, not the writer.

Although thinking like a lawyer is second nature for the experienced practitioner, problems arise when it is time to write these arguments down in a way that is logical, understandable and coherent. Too often the best arguments are lost in the transition from thoughts to words. Having someone else read your words out loud will help illuminate the communication gaps that inevitably develop when placing conceptual ideas on paper.

Conclusion

In sum, problems can be erased by taking the time to critically review your own writing. Step into the reader's shoes. Do not rely on old tricks and techniques that you understand; your reader might not. Weigh every word you write; your reader usually does. Question every legal proposition as if you were your opponent. You will then be ready to prove your points with an economical and precise analysis that no one will misunderstand or overlook.

The good news is that there is no need to change all your writing habits at once. Keep writing as you always have; if you try to write differently from the outset of a project, you can expect a case of writer's block and mounting frustration. The trick is to analyze your work after your first or second draft, during the rewrite stage. Use the techniques described here to ask yourself the right questions—the questions the reader asks. Analyze your own analysis just as you would analyze your opponent's arguments and supporting proof.

As you, the critical reader, begin to pinpoint problem areas, you, the writer, will be able to drop them from your repertoire and will eventually stop using ineffective techniques. As the new, effective ones you develop become second-nature, the methods you relied on for so long will appear to be as outdated as. . . DOS.

CHAPTER 16 SUMMARY

- The office memo records the results of legal research, explains how the researcher analyzed the law and applied it to the facts, and proposes a solution to the problem.
- The tone of the office memo is objective rather than persuasive.
- Generally the office memo contains a heading (to and from, re, and date), facts, issue(s) and answer(s), a thesis paragraph, the rule of law, the application of the law to the facts, and the conclusion.
- Refer to people by their names or terms such as "suspect" or "officer" instead of "appellant," "appellee," or similar terms.
- Each issue and each answer should be single sentences.
- Between the issue and the answer you should give your reader the most information possible.
- Usually there are the same number of answers as issues.
- If you refer to a constitutional or statutory provision in an issue or answer by number, also give your reader a short explanation of the provision's subject matter.
- A "thesis" is the central idea running through the entire memo.
- Quote only the relevant portion of constitutions or statutes.
- The first time you refer to a case by name, give the full citation; after that use a short form citation.

CYBER EXERCISES

1. When writing legal documents for the first time, it may be helpful to look at examples. This chapter provides some examples. A number of law school professors have posted sample documents on the Internet. To find some of these documents you might access Jurist: The Law Professor Network (http://jurist.law.pitt.edu). (Under "Learning & Teaching Law," click on "Courses" and then on "Legal Research & Writing.") At the time this book was being written, Professor Gregory Berry at Howard University School of Law had posted a number of student documents in his "Writing Hall of Fame" found under "Berry's Advice." Those documents included client letters, memoranda, motion reply briefs, a settlement agreement, and appellate briefs. Also, Professor Colleen Barger at the University of Arkansas at Little Rock School of Law had a web site that links to pages of other legal research and writing professors (http://www. ualr.edu/~cmbarger/).
2. The Lexis law school site (http://lawschool.lexis.com) includes legal writing information (click on "My School," "Web Lectures," and then on "Legal Research and Writing").

EXERCISES FOR CHAPTER 16

1. Pick one of the research problems from Appendix E.
2. Research the problem you have chosen.
3. Write an office memo summarizing and explaining your research.

CHAPTER 17

MEMORANDUM OF LAW

INTRODUCTION

One of the standard legal documents written by a litigation attorney for submission to court is what will be referred to in this book as the "memorandum of law." (Some attorneys refer to it as a "trial brief," a "trial level brief," or a "Memorandum of Points and Authorities.") This chapter explains the purpose, use, and format of the memorandum of law and includes two sample memorandums of law.

The first sample memorandum of law has been extensively annotated to provide you with writing and citation tips. If the notes do not make much sense to you right now, read them again after you have gone over the rules for citations and quotations contained in appendixes B and C. It might also be helpful to you to refer to the footnotes again when you are writing your own memorandum of law.

PURPOSE AND USE

In litigation an attorney may be required by court rule, may be asked by the judge, or may feel the need to submit a written document called a "memorandum of law." For example, some United States district courts require any party filing a motion to also file a legal memorandum with citation of authorities in support of the relief requested. Certain rules give the party opposing the motion a time period to file a legal memorandum in opposition. As a court document, the memorandum of law is a matter of public record and a copy of it is delivered to opposing counsel. The purposes of the memorandum of law are to explain the client's position in a lawsuit and to convince the judge to rule in the client's favor.

Look for a moment at the first sample memorandum of law in this chapter, written by Mike Campbell's attorney. You may recall from prior chapters that Mike had been arrested for possession of cocaine. The cocaine was found in Mike's car after he was stopped on the interstate by DEA agents. Mike's position is that, because the stop of his car was unconstitutional, the cocaine should be suppressed as the fruit of an unconstitutional search and seizure. If Mike's attorney can convince the judge that the cocaine should be suppressed, the charge against Mike will have to be dropped for lack of evidence. Mike's attorney would formally request the judge to suppress the cocaine by filing a "motion to suppress" and, as required by local rule, a memorandum of law supporting the motion. Once Mike's attorney has filed the motion to suppress the cocaine and the supporting memorandum of law, the government attorney will file a "motion in opposition to the motion to suppress" and a memorandum of law supporting the government's motion in opposition.

The circumstances surrounding Mike's arrest can be viewed from two perspectives: Mike's perspective and the perspective of the DEA agents. Mike would argue that the agents singled him out on the hunch that because he is Afro-American, he might be carrying illegal drugs. The agents then violated his constitutional right against unreasonable search and seizure by stopping and searching his car. The government would argue that the agents could have pulled Mike over either because of a traffic violation or because Mike fit a drug courier profile. In the agents' experience, persons who fit the drug courier profile often carry drugs. The drug courier profile, while not entirely accurate, has been one of the law enforcement officer's weapons in the war against the illegal drug trade.

The tone of the memorandum of law is persuasive. This in contrast to the office memo, which is objective in tone. In her memorandum of law, Mike's attorney will try to persuade the judge that Mike's view of the facts is more accurate and is supported by case law interpretation of the Fourth Amendment. In the government's memorandum of law in opposition to Mike's motion to suppress, the government attorney will try to persuade the judge that Mike's motion to suppress should not be granted because the government's view of the facts is more accurate and applicable case law supports denial of the motion to suppress.

Although Mike's attorney has to represent Mike's best interests, this duty is tempered by the attorney's ethical duty as an **officer of the court.** Rule 4-3.3 of the Rules Regulating the Florida Bar states: "A lawyer shall not knowingly . . . make a false statement of material fact or law to a tribunal . . . [or] fail to disclose to the tribunal legal authority in the controlling jurisdiction known to the lawyer to be directly adverse to the position of the client and not disclosed by opposing counsel. . . . " Attorney ethics rules in other states contain similar wording. Thus, Mike's attorney has a dual role. She is an advocate for Mike's best interests as well as an advisor to the court. Mike's attorney must present Mike's side of the story but may not invent or change facts. In presenting the law in support of Mike's position, the attorney may not intentionally mislead the court and must disclose law "directly adverse" to Mike's position that the government has failed to disclose.

In the following cases, an attorney failed to disclose adverse authority. In the first case, the court simply noted its displeasure. That, in itself, is rare in a published opinion. In the second case, the court ordered the offending attorney to pay the other side's reasonable attorney's fees and costs.

The government's brief is notable for its failure to cite or discuss the considerable authority that is adverse to its position, including *Broderson*, *Mullens*, and *Brunson*. Instead, it argues that Queen is "clearly applicable to the fraudulent scheme Jolly set up with regard to his investors." Gov't Br. at 12. Simply shepardizing the Tenth Circuit's decision in *Queen* would have disclosed the same circuit's decision in *Brunson*. Whether or not the defense cites or discusses applicable precedent, we expect the government to set out a fair and accurate description of relevant legal authority. That was not done in this case.

United States v. Jolly, 102 F.3d 46, 50 n.2 (2d Cir. 1996).

Our Supreme Court invalidated Section 21.701 of the Philadelphia's Code in City of Philadelphia, Police Department v. Gray and held that the waiver of governmental immunity in the Philadelphia's ordinance was invalid from the time of the enactment of the governmental immunity provisions of the Judicial Code on October 5, 1980. Subsequently, our Court in Davis v. City of Philadelphia, which was filed on November 10, 1994, before Robinson filed his brief with our Court, stated that decisions interpreting statutes apply retroactively to the date the particular statute became effective. Thus, Section 21.701 was invalidated as of the date Sections 8541 and 8542 of the Judicial Code were enacted. Accordingly, because Robinson's cause of action

> arose in 1989, a date well past the enactment date of the governmental immunity provisions in the Judicial Code, Section 21-701 is inapplicable and the City can assert the defense of governmental immunity.
>
> The City, in response to Robinson's argument based upon the applicability of Section 21-701, suggests that this Court impose sanctions against Robinson for failing to disclose legal authority that is controlling in the case . . . . In our view, Robinson's omission was not mere inadvertence. The City, in its motion for summary judgment, not only cited to *Gray*, but attached a copy of it to the motion. We must conclude that Robinson knowingly failed to disclose to this Court controlling legal authority in contravention of Rule 3.3 of the Rules of Professional Conduct. This Court finds that Robinson's conduct was irritating and frivolous. Robinson is hereby ordered to pay reasonable attorney fees and costs to the City, which will be determined by Judge Herron, the trial judge.
>
> *Robinson v. City of Phildelphia*, 666 A.2d 1141, 1142, 1143 (Pa. Commw. Ct. 1995)(citations omitted).

STYLE

An attorney must work very hard to build credibility with the judge and must work just as hard not to lose this credibility. The writer must build credibility by making absolutely sure that the facts and the law in the memorandum of law are stated accurately. Choose words that emphasize the client's position but are not obviously biased. The memorandum will be more credible if you include adverse facts and law as well as facts and law in the client's favor. The judge will be comparing your memorandum with that of opposing counsel's to see how you have dealt with adverse facts and law. Your failure to deal with adverse facts and law may make the judge think you are doing a sloppy job and you will quickly lose your credibility. Of course, adverse facts and law need only be mentioned and should not be dwelled upon. A well-organized memorandum will emphasize favorable facts and law and will downplay unfavorable ones. (See the next section of this chapter for tips on organization.)

The appearance of the memorandum should be inviting, with enough descriptive headings to allow the judge to glance through the memorandum and "see" the flow of your writing. When the first draft of the memorandum has been completed, review it critically. Does it appear reader-friendly? Are the pages broken up into a number of paragraphs? Is the print large enough to be easily read? Are the margins wide enough to give the reader's eyes a chance to rest? Can you make it easier to spot headings by putting them in bold type or underlining them? Make any necessary changes.

ORGANIZATION

When you are having trouble writing a memorandum of law, picture yourself as a busy judge with a heavy case load and ask yourself what you would find helpful in a memorandum of law. A busy judge does not have the luxury of time to pore over a lengthy, disorganized memorandum containing a convoluted legal argument. The judge will be more inclined to read a shorter memorandum that is straight-forward, well organized, and just long enough to get the point across. If you can squeeze the issues and short answers into the first two pages, you will have the judge's attention.

Remember that a reader will pay more attention to the beginning and the end than to the middle of sections within the memorandum. Put any information you want to emphasize either at the beginning or at the end of a section. For example, in the facts section focus the reader's attention on the client by referring to the client first and retelling the facts from the client's perspective. Diffuse the opposing party's thunder by including any significant adverse facts but downplay them by briefly mentioning them in the light most favorable to the client midway through the facts section.

Do something similar with the argument section. If there is an easy way for the judge to dispose of the case in the client's favor, put the argument supporting that easy ruling first. Otherwise, put the strongest argument first. "Bury" any adverse law that must be disclosed in the middle of the argument section. A duty to disclose adverse law does not mean that it has to be discussed in detail. Refer to it, distinguish it, and move on. Do the same with the opposing party's counterarguments. Refer to them briefly and then focus on the client's argument. The best defense is a good offense.

The organizational tip for sections of the memorandum applies for sentences and paragraphs. If you want your reader to focus on particular words in a sentence, rearrange your sentence to put the words first or last in the sentence. The focus will be even greater if rearranging the sentence changes the grammatical structure from the typical subject-verb-object structure of English sentences. Be careful that you do not change from the typical structure too often or the atypical structure will become routine and lose its impact. In addition, sentences are harder for the reader to understand if they differ from the typical subject, verb, and object order.

The reader will pay more attention to the first and last sentences in a paragraph than to the middle of the paragraph. For that reason, make your topic sentence either the first or last sentence in the paragraph. Put any information you want to make sure the reader does not miss in the first or last sentences. If the important information is more than can fit in the first and last sentences of the paragraph, consider splitting the paragraph into a number of paragraphs. Put adverse information three-quarters of the way through the paragraph to de-emphasize it.

FORMAT

Although there is no one right format for a memorandum of law, the format given in this chapter is fairly standard. The format should be modified to conform to any applicable court rules and to the format customarily used for a particular court. For example, applicable court rules may specify line spacing, paper size, margins, document length, and information concerning the attorney signing the document, including the attorney's name, bar identification number, firm name and address, and telephone number.

The balance of this section gives a brief explanation of the various parts of the memorandum of law. It might be helpful for you to read the rest of this section while comparing the explanation to the sample memorandums of law later in this chapter.

Caption

The caption contains the name of the court, the names of the parties, the case number and the title of the pleading. After the title of the pleading and before the questions presented section, it is customary to include a sentence stating who is submitting the memorandum and why it is being submitted.

Questions presented

The questions presented section contains several numbered questions for the judge to consider. The questions should be stated in the light most favorable to the client and should be worded so that the judge can easily reach an answer favorable to the client. Give as much information as possible in each question without sacrificing readability. There should be enough information so that the judge understands a question without having to refer to other sections of the memorandum.

Each question should contain a combination of law and facts, and should ask how the law applies to the facts. Because the facts section of the memorandum follows rather than precedes the questions presented section, the judge will not have read the facts before reading the questions. The judge will have an easier time understanding the facts if the law in each question precedes the facts. Using this order, the law will serve as a framework into which the judge can fit the facts.

Facts

The writer should create empathy for the client by painting a picture of the facts from the client's perspective. Choose descriptive words and incorporate a fair amount of detail when recounting facts favorable to the client. State the facts as specifically as possible to make them memorable. If the picture is created in sufficient detail, your picture will come to the judge's mind when considering the case. Relevant adverse facts which opposing counsel is likely to rely on can be mentioned briefly, in broad terms, and with little detail, using bland, uninteresting language.

Highlight your client's view of the facts. Focus the reader's attention on the client by referring to the client first and by calling the client by name. Try telling the facts in the order the client perceived them rather than in strict chronological order. This ordering of the facts will make it easier for the judge to understand the client's position.

Choose your words carefully. Words chosen should reflect favorably on the client without conveying an argumentative or adversarial tone. The writer's credibility may be lost if the language is too exaggerated or overly biased. Well-stated facts are so subtly persuasive that the judge can believe they are stated objectively.

Argument

The argument section is the longest and most complex portion of the memorandum of law. This section is divided into a number of subsections by headings called point headings. There may be an introductory portion of the argument section preceding the first main point heading. The introductory material contains a thesis paragraph and may explain law applicable to all the point headings in the memorandum. Each subsection following a point heading should explain the applicable rule of law and apply the rule of law to the facts.

Even though the tone of the memorandum of law is persuasive and the tone of the office memo is objective, the basic structure of the argument section of the memorandum of law should be similar to the structure of the reasoning section of an office memo. You should present one or more thesis paragraphs, you should set forth the rule of law, and you should apply the rule of law to the facts of the case. Refresh your memory of how to write the thesis paragraph(s), the rule of law, and the application of law to facts by rereading those portions of the "Format" section of chapter 16.

Although opposing counsel and others will read the memorandum of law, the intended and primary audience is the judge. The judge is not your adversary and may become your ally on the strength of the memorandum of law. Make the judge your ally by advising the judge as to why ruling in the client's favor is the correct solution to the problem. In most cases the judge has some discretion in making decisions. If you can convince the judge that he or she is your ally, the judge may use this discretion in your client's favor. Therefore, although the tone of the memorandum of law is persuasive, it should be subtly persuasive. Shy away from an argumentative or demanding tone of voice that may prejudice the judge against the client.

Thesis paragraph

If an introductory portion of the argument section precedes the first main point heading, it should begin with a thesis paragraph. Besides stating your thesis in your thesis paragraph, you may want to use this paragraph to state your final conclusion in simple terms. If your argument section begins with a point heading rather than with an introductory portion, you should either follow your first point heading with a thesis paragraph or include a short thesis paragraph after each of your point headings. For a more detailed explanation of how to write a thesis paragraph, reread the thesis paragraph portion of the "Format" section of chapter 16.

Rule of law

A busy judge does not have the time to do extensive independent research before ruling on a motion. A judge will appreciate a step by step explanation of the current status of applicable law—either to familiarize the judge with an unfamiliar area of the law or to update the judge's knowledge. Be careful to advise rather than to lecture the judge on the law. A judge will appreciate a clear explanation of the law, but a judge who is being "lectured" may take offense. For the judge's easy reference, you may want to provide copies of the cases you have cited in the memorandum. For a more detailed explanation of how to write the rule of law, reread the rule of law portion of the "Format" section of chapter 16.

Application of law to facts

After stating the rule of law, you must carefully lead the reader step by step from the law to your conclusion. For a detailed explanation of how to apply the rule of law to the facts, reread the application of law to facts portion of the "Format" section of chapter 16.

Either your argument section or the conclusion section should contain one or more paragraphs summarizing your argument. This summary serves the same purpose as the conclusion section of an office memo; it ties the facts to the rule of law and reaches a conclusion. Customarily, this summary is part of the argument rather than the conclusion section. Look through some recent memoranda of law filed with the court to determine what the custom is in your area. If the summary is part of the "argument" section, you can either put a summary of the answers to all of the question presented at the end of the argument section or have a summary paragraph at the end of each subsection within your argument.

Conclusion

The conclusion section of a memorandum of law specifically requests the judge to take a particular action or actions. The motion that accompanies Mike Campbell's memorandum of law is a motion to suppress the evidence found in Mike's car. If the evidence is suppressed, the government will be forced to drop the charge against Mike for lack of evidence. Therefore, the conclusion section of the memorandum of law should request the judge to suppress the evidence and to dismiss the charge against Mike.

As stated before, you should include a summary of your argument in the conclusion section if you have not included it in the argument section.

FIRST SAMPLE MEMORANDUM OF LAW

UNITED STATES DISTRICT COURT
MIDDLE DISTRICT OF FLORIDA
ORLANDO DIVISION

UNITED STATES OF AMERICA,

Plaintiff,

v. Case No. 00 - 000 - CR - ORL - 00[1]

MICHAEL CAMPBELL and JOHN WRIGHT,
Defendants.

______________________________/

MEMORANDUM IN SUPPORT OF DEFENDANT CAMPBELL'S MOTION TO SUPPRESS[2]

Defendant Michael Campbell submits this memorandum of law in support of defendant's motion to suppress the evidence seized from the defendant's car.[3]

Questions presented:[4]

1. Did the law enforcement officer violate Mike Campbell's constitutional right against unreasonable search and seizure when the law enforcement officer stopped Mike's out-of-state tagged Lincoln Continental that Mike was driving on I-95 in the early evening at the speed limit when the only other information the

---

[1]This is the docket number written as required by rule 1.03(a) of the Local Rules of the United States District Court for the Middle District of Florida. The first part of the docket number, "00," is an abbreviation for "2000" (the year in which the case was filed). Were this a real case, the number of the case would be substituted for "000," the second part of the docket number. Cases in the Orlando division of the district are consecutively numbered corresponding to the order in which they are filed. The third part of the docket number, "CR," indicates that this is a criminal rather than a civil case (abbreviated "CIV") and "ORL" indicates that this is an Orlando division case. The last two digits give the number of the judge to whom the case is assigned. As Middle District of Florida judges are appointed, they are numbered in sequence and the numbers are used to identify which judge is handling a particular case.

[2]Use a descriptive title to identify the type of document (a memorandum of law), why it is being filed (in support of a motion to suppress), and the party filing the document (defendant Campbell). From the title, the judge should learn at a glance important information about the document without having to read the text of the document.

[3]Use a short introductory sentence to explain to the judge why the document is being submitted. It does not hurt to lay out the explanation like this in a full sentence even though it repeats information from the title of the document.

[4]Each of these questions asks how the law applies to the facts. Notice the word choice. The questions are worded from Mike's perspective and Mike is referred to by name. Specific facts are included in the questions for a number of reasons. The judge's decision to grant or deny the motion to suppress turns on whether the facts were sufficient to justify the stop, making the facts extremely important. Because the factors in the drug courier profile and the nature of the alleged traffic violation are generally favorable to Mike, they are detailed so they are easy to remember. The way the questions are worded, they "paint" the judge a picture of the scene, which the judge can use as a framework when reading the rest of the memorandum. The most important facts need to be laid out in the questions, or the judge will not be familiar with them, because the facts section follows the questions presented section.

officer had was that Mike and his passenger were Afro-American, were in their twenties, and wore beach attire?

2. Did the officer violate Mike Campbell's constitutional right against unreasonable search and seizure when the officer followed the Campbell car for a distance and then pulled the car over, claiming that Mike was following the car in front of him too closely?

Facts:[5]
Mike Campbell and his best friend had decided, like thousands of other college students, to enjoy a Florida spring break. After Mike promised to drive carefully, Mike's father let Mike borrow his car, a brand new Lincoln Continental. After arriving in Florida, Mike and his friend spent every waking moment of their break on the beach. In the early evening on the last day of vacation they went straight from the beach to their car to begin the long trip back to school, calculating that they would have just enough driving time to make it back for their first class. Mike was driving north on I-95 thinking about the promise he had made to his father when he saw patrol cars parked in the median, one with its lights shining across the northbound lanes. Almost immediately after driving through the arc of the patrol car's headlights, Mike looked in the rear view mirror and saw the patrol car pull out behind him. The patrol car put on its flashing lights and pulled Mike over.

An officer got out of the patrol car, walked over to Mike's car, and asked for Mike's driver's license and car registration. As Mike handed over his license and the registration he noticed the officer eyeing Mike's beach attire suspiciously. When Mike told the officer they were heading back to school from spring break, the officer commented, "We don't see too many blacks down here over spring break." The officer added, "I stopped you for following the car in front of you too closely." Still holding the license and registration, the officer asked Mike whether the officer could search the car and said, "You don't have anything to hide, do you?" Hoping that if he answered "no" they could be on their way, Mike answered, "No." The officer said, "Wait here," turned around, walked back to the patrol car, and got in. Mike could not have left even if the officer had not told him to wait because the officer still had Mike's license and car registration.

Forty-five minutes later another patrol car pulled up and an officer got out with a dog. The officer led the dog around the car. The dog circled the car once and then stopped and pawed the car's trunk. The officer motioned Mike to roll down his window. The officer told him that the dog had detected drugs in the trunk of Mike's car. The officer told Mike that Mike could either open the car trunk or wait there whatever time was necessary for the officer to obtain a search warrant. Feeling that he had no choice, Mike opened the trunk. Both officers started pulling Mike's and his friend's belongings out of the trunk and tossing them on the ground. One of the officers found a brown paper bag containing cocaine wedged in a bottom corner of the trunk. Mike and his friend were arrested and were charged with possession with intent to distribute.

Argument[6]**:**
The car driver and passengers expect that activities within the car will be private and not subject to the scrutiny of law enforcement officials. They may feel that their privacy is invaded if a law enforcement officer stops the car to investigate. A trained police officer may have a hunch that a car's occupants are engaged in illegal activity; however, a law enforcement officer may not constitutionally stop a car unless there is either a reasonable suspicion of illegal activity or there is a traffic violation. The stop of Mike's car to investigate for criminal activity was not permissible because the agents did not have a reasonable suspicion of illegal drug activity.

[5]The facts are told from Mike's perspective and in the order he perceived them. Mike is referred to by name to create empathy, whereas the other persons are not. The wording was chosen to be subtly persuasive rather than obviously biased. Compare this statement of the facts with the facts contained in the office memo in chapter 16.

[6]You should begin the argument portion of your memorandum of law with a thesis paragraph. A well-written thesis paragraph is a road map, providing the reader with a framework into which the balance of the memo can be placed. It also tells the reader your ultimate conclusion.

The stop for a traffic violation was constitutionally justifiable only if Mike was following too closely.

The Fourth Amendment[7] to the United States Constitution guarantees "[t]he[8] right of the people to be secure in their persons, houses, papers, and effects against unreasonable searches and seizures" and allows a search warrant to be issued only upon "probable cause."[9] A search warrant requirement was spelled out in the amendment to safeguard this important right. Over the more than two hundred years since the amendment was adopted, the individual's right against unreasonable search and seizure has been jealously guarded.

Although the time and level of evidence needed to obtain a search warrant protects the individual's constitutional right, the courts have allowed two exceptions to the search warrant requirement, both of which the government argues are applicable here and allowed them to stop the Campbell car. The first exception[10] requires a minimum of "reasonable suspicion" of illegal activity to stop a car and question its occupants. *Terry v. Ohio*, 392 U.S. 1, 27 (1968).[11] The second exception allows an officer to stop a car to investigate a traffic violation. *Whren v. United States*, 517 U.S. 806, 818 (1996).

Defendant Campbell's motion to suppress should be granted because neither of the two exceptions to the search warrant requirement apply here. The officer stopped Campbell's car on a mere "hunch" and Campbell was following at a "reasonable and prudent" distance, as required by the Florida Statutes. Fla. Stat. Ch. 316.0895 (1) (2000). This memorandum will first explain why there was not enough evidence to justify an investigatory stop and then why there was no traffic violation.[12]

A. Because the information the officer relied on to stop the Campbell car was no more than a mere "hunch," the evidence should be suppressed unless the officer had probable cause to stop the car for a traffic violation.[13]

Terry[14] was the landmark case that lowered the burden of proof necessary for a stop from probable cause to "reasonable suspicion." Such stops made on reasonable suspicion are often referred to as "Terry stops," after *Terry*, and the definition of Terry stops has been broadened to apply to car stops. The new reasonable suspicion standard allows a police officer to stop and briefly question someone, but is still designed to protect the innocent traveler, singled out because of certain immutable personal characteristics such as race, sex, and age, from being subjected to "overbearing or harassing" law enforcement tactics. 392 U.S. at 14–15 n. 11. A stop made only on an "unparticularized suspicion or 'hunch'"[15] is unconstitutional. *Id.* at 27. Assuming the officer has the requisite reasonable suspicion for a Terry stop, the officer

[7]When quoting a constitutional or statutory provision quote only the relevant portion. Set quotations of fifty words or more off from the rest of the text in a quotation block indented left and right but not enclosed in quotation marks. Other quotations should be part of the paragraph with the quoted language in quotation marks.

[8]The brackets indicate a change in the quotation from the original. Here the "t" was upper case originally.

[9]Periods and commas go inside quotation marks; other punctuation is placed outside quotations marks unless it is part of the quotation.

[10]Signposts are words used to guide the reader in a particular direction. "The first exception" and "the second exception" are signposts clearly identifying the two exceptions, which are discussed in much more detail later in the memo.

[11]The first time you are referring to a case by name you must give the full citation. After that you should use a short form citation.

Citations in the sample office memo are given in *Bluebook* form. Your professor may require you to cite according to some other citation rule (perhaps your state's citation rule). If so, always check the appropriate citation rule to make sure you are citing correctly.

[12]This introductory portion of the argument section contains three paragraphs. The first paragraph is the thesis paragraph and quotes the relevant portion of the Fourth Amendment. The second paragraph lays out in general terms the law applicable to the rest of the memorandum. The third paragraph contains a statement of the conclusion. Do not leave the judge in suspense. Tell the judge your conclusion up front. The third paragraph also contains signposts. With these signposts, the reader will expect the portion of the memorandum following the first point heading to discuss the drug courier profile and the portion of the memorandum after the second point heading to discuss the alleged traffic violation.

[13]This point heading answers the first question presented.

[14]Once you have given the full citation for a case and are referring to the case in general terms, you can refer to it by using one or two of the words from the name of the case and underlining or italicizing them. Be sure the words you select are not so common as to cause confusion. Here, for example, use *Terry* rather than *Ohio*.

[15]To indicate quotes within quotes, alternate double and single quotation marks, with double quotations outermost.

would still need probable cause or consent to search a car.[16]

Smith involved almost identical facts to those being considered here. In *Smith* the government argued that a highway stop was constitutionally permitted based either on a drug courier profile or on Smith's alleged commission of a traffic violation. 799 F.2d at 705.[17] Smith filed a motion to suppress, claiming that the evidence seized from his car should be suppressed because of the violation of his right against unreasonable search and seizure. *Id.* at 706.[18] The United States Court of Appeals for the Eleventh Circuit found that the *Smith* drug courier profile did not support reasonable suspicion, reversed the lower court's denial of Smith's motion to suppress, and vacated Smith's conviction. *Id.* at 712.

One night in June of 1985, Trooper Robert Vogel, a Florida Highway Patrol trooper, and a DEA agent were observing cars traveling in the northbound lanes of I-95 in hopes of intercepting drug couriers. When Smith's car passed through the arc of the patrol car headlights, Vogel noticed the following factors that matched his drug courier profile:

1. The car was traveling at 3:00 a.m.;
2. The car was a 1985 Mercury, a large late model car;
3. The car had out-of state tags;
4. There were two occupants of the car who were around 30; and
5. The driver was driving cautiously and did not look at the patrol car as the Mercury passed through the arc of the patrol car headlights.

Id. at 705–06.[19]

The above drug courier profile is almost identical to the *Campbell* profile.[20] In both *Smith* and this case, the cars were traveling after dark, the cars were large late models with out-of-state tags, the cars were being driven "cautiously," and each car contained two passengers in their twenties or thirties. The differences between the two profiles are very minor. Campbell and his friend were dressed casually, while it is not known how Smith and Swindell were dressed. Smith and Swindell did not look at Vogel as they passed. It is not known whether Campbell looked in the agents' direction as Campbell drove past. Campbell claims that race was a factor in the stop even though it was not listed as such by the agents. Smith and Swindell's race is unknown.[21]

In *Smith*, Vogel followed the Mercury for a mile and a half and noticed that the Mercury "wove" several times, once as much as six inches into the emergency lane. Vogel pulled Smith over. When a drug dog alerted on the car, a DEA agent searched the trunk and discovered one kilogram of cocaine. Smith

[16]This discussion of *Terry* is written to support Mike's motion and to convince the judge to rule in Mike's favor. Compare it with the discussion of *Terry* contained in the office memo in the preceding chapter. There the *Terry* discussion was more balanced.

[17]Once you have cited a case in full, you should use a short form citation the next time you refer to material from the case. This short form citation contains the volume number and the abbreviation for the reporter in which *Smith* is printed, "at," and the page on which the "government's argument" is found in *Smith*. To learn more about short form citations, refer to appendix C, which explains short form citations.

[18]You should use "*id*" here instead of repeating "799 F.2d" because this citation is to the same volume of the same reporter cited in the immediately preceding citation. Retain "at 706" because the referenced material appears on page 706 instead of on page 705, the page of the previously-referenced material.

[19]When you need to give a citation for a block quote or other material set off from the rest of the text, as is the tabulation here, bring the citation back to the left margin. When citing inclusive pages with three or more digits, drop all but the last two digits of the second number and place a hyphen between the numbers.

[20]This is an example of a topic sentence. A topic sentence contains one main idea summarizing the rest of the paragraph, with the rest of the paragraph developing the idea presented in the topic sentence. Most paragraphs should have topic sentences. The typical location of a topic sentence is the first sentence in the paragraph. Sometimes the topic sentence is the last sentence in the paragraph and pulls together the rest of the paragraph. Some paragraphs, typically narrative paragraphs like the preceding paragraph, do not have topic sentences.

If a paragraph sounds disjointed or unorganized, try pulling it together using a topic sentence. If a topic sentence does not help, think about breaking the paragraph up into more than one paragraph.

[21]This paragraph applies the facts in *Smith* to the facts in *Campbell*. Applying facts from one case to another case involves explaining the similarities and differences between the two sets of facts. Instead of simply stating that the facts from the two cases are very similar, the paragraph specifically states which facts are the same. Sometimes in the application you need to explain in what way the facts are similar if they are not identical.

You can either apply the *Smith* facts to *Campbell* midway in discussing *Smith* as done here or you can wait until you have thoroughly discussed *Smith*. When you prepare your outline prior to starting to write the memorandum of law, spend some time moving parts of your "argument" section around to determine the best flow.

and his passenger, Swindell, were arrested and were charged with conspiracy to possess cocaine with the intent to distribute it. Smith and Swindell's motions to suppress the cocaine were denied and they were tried and convicted. *Id.* at 706.

The issue before the appellate court was whether the stop of Smith's car was reasonable. *Id.*[22] This is the same basic question to be answered by this court in determining whether Campbell's motion to suppress should be granted. The *Smith* court held that the stop of Smith's car could not be upheld as a valid Terry stop, *id.* at 708, finding that "Trooper Vogel stopped the car because [Smith and Swindell][23] . . . matched a few nondistinguishing characteristics contained on a drug courier profile and, additionally, because Vogel was bothered by the way the driver of the car chose not to look at him." *Id.* at 707.

Just as there was nothing in the *Campbell* drug courier profile to differentiate Campbell and his friend from other innocent college students returning from spring break in Florida, there was nothing in Vogel's drug courier profile to differentiate Smith and Swindell from other law-abiding motorists on I-95. It is usual to drive after dark to avoid heavy traffic or to complete an interstate trip.[24] Although many motorists speed on the highways, motorists driving "cautiously" at or near the speed limit are simply obeying traffic laws. Many people other than drug couriers drive large late model cars with out-of-state tags. A motorist between the ages of twenty and forty is not unusual.

The contrast between the *Campbell* and *Smith* drug courier profiles, which do not support reasonable suspicion, and another courier profile which was held to support reasonable suspicion is marked. *United States v. Sokolow*, 490 U.S. 1, 3 (1989).[25] In *Sokolow*, DEA agents found 1,063 grams of cocaine inside Sokolow's carry-on luggage when he was stopped in Honolulu International Airport based on the following profile:

1. He had paid $2,100 in cash for two airplane tickets from a roll of $20 which appeared to contain $4,000;
2. He was ticketed under a name other than his own;
3. He traveled to Miami, a known drug source, and back;
4. Although his round trip flight lasted 20 hours, he stayed in Miami only 48 hours;
5. He appeared nervous;
6. He was about 25 years old;
7. He was dressed in a black jumpsuit and was wearing gold jewelry which he wore during both legs of the round trip flight; and
8. Neither he nor his companion checked any luggage.[26]

Id. at 3–5. The Court held that the *Sokolow* drug courier profile did support reasonable suspicion. *Id.* at 11.

The *Sokolow* dissent would have found that all of the factors, even if "taken together," did not amount to reasonable suspicion. In criticizing the use of a drug courier profile to stop suspects, the dissent noted "the profile's 'chameleon-like way of adapting to any particular set of observations'" "subjecting innocent individuals to unwarranted police harassment and detention." *Id.* at 13 (Marshall, J., dissenting)[27] (quoting *Sokolow v. United States*, 831 F.2d 1413, 1418 (9th Cir. 1987), *rev'd*, 490 U.S. 1 (1989)[28]).

---

[22]When you are referring to material from the same page as the material you referred to in the last citation, use just "*id.*" *Id.* is capitalized only when it begins a sentence.

[23]"Smith and Swindell" are in brackets because this wording inserted into the quotation by the person writing the memo. The ellipsis (. . .) shows that something was omitted from the original wording of the quotation. Your quotations must exactly match the wording and punctuation of the authority the quotation comes from. If you are sloppy in quoting and your reader discovers that you have taken liberties with the quotation, your reader may suspect that you are sloppy in other ways—perhaps even in your research. See appendix C for an explanation of quoting correctly.

[24]No page reference is needed if you have already given the facts in the cases you are using as authority and are referring to those cases in general.

[25]To avoid including a full citation in a textual sentence, *Sokolow* is referred to in general terms and the citation to *Sokolow* is given in a separate citation sentence. Including the full citation in the sentence makes the sentence harder to read and understand.

[26]Only those facts from *Sokolow* that are relevant to the discussion of *Smith* are given.

[27]You must identify the type of opinion you are quoting from if it is other than the majority opinion.

[28]This explanatory parenthetical tells the reader that the material Marshall is quoting came from the lower court decision in *Sokolow*. If you are quoting something that in turn quotes another source, you should identify the original source as is done here. Subsequent history must be given for the lower court decision in *Sokolow*.

As predicted in the *Sokolow* dissent, Smith, Swindell, Campbell, and Campbell's friend were subjected to "unwarranted police harassment and detention" even though the factors in the respective drug courier profiles, even if "taken together," did not amount to reasonable suspicion. In contrast, several of the *Sokolow* factors, such as carrying such a large amount of cash and traveling a long distance to stay a relatively short period of time, are unusual or even suspicious in and of themselves. Each of the *Smith* and *Campbell* factors was not at all out of the ordinary alone and certainly taken together did not amount to reasonable suspicion.

B. Because Mike Campbell did not commit the traffic violation alleged by the officer, the evidence found in the trunk of Mike Campbell's car should be suppressed as the fruit of an unconstitutional search and seizure.

In *Whren*, Brown was driving a Pathfinder in which Whren was a passenger. Brown had stopped the vehicle at a stop sign and was looking down into Whren's lap. Plain clothes police officers were patrolling this "high drug area" of the District of Columbia in an unmarked patrol car. The Pathfinder caught the attention of the officers because Brown remained stopped at the stop sign for approximately twenty seconds. When the patrol car made a U-turn to follow the Pathfinder, Brown turned right without signaling and started off at an "unreasonable speed." The patrol car stopped the Pathfinder. When one of the officers approached Brown's window and peered in, he saw that Whren had two plastic bags of crack cocaine on his lap. The officers arrested Whren and Brown. 517 U.S. at 808, 809.

Justice Scalia phrased the issue as "whether the temporary detention of a motorist who the police have probable cause to believe has committed a civil traffic violation is inconsistent with the Fourth Amendment's prohibition against unreasonable seizures unless a reasonable officer would have been motivated to stop the car by a desire to enforce the traffic laws." *Id.* at 808. The Court answered the question, "no." "[T]he district court found that the officers had probable cause to believe that petitioners had violated the traffic code. That rendered the stop reasonable under the Fourth Amendment, the evidence thereby discovered admissible, and the upholding of the convictions by the Court of Appeals for the District of Columbia Circuit correct." *Id.* at 819.

Prior to *Whren*, some courts, including the court deciding *Smith*, had decided that a car stop for a traffic violation was unconstitutional unless a reasonable officer would have made the stop. The *Smith* court found that the cocaine should have been excluded from evidence because a reasonable officer would not have stopped Smith's car for the alleged traffic violation. 799 F.2d at 711. However in *Whren*, the United States Supreme Court rejected the argument that the reasonable officer standard should apply. 517 U.S. at 813.

After *Whren*, it would be very difficult to convince a court that a stop for an alleged traffic violation is unconstitutional. However, if the court finds that the driver did not violate any traffic regulation, then the stop would be unconstitutional.

The Florida motor vehicle statute identified by the *Campbell* officer states, "The driver of a motor vehicle shall not follow another vehicle more closely than is reasonable and prudent, having due regard for the speed of such vehicles and the traffic upon, and the condition of, the highway." Fla. Stat. Ch. 316.0895 (1) (2000). No simple test determines if Campbell violated the statute. The court must determine from any evidence presented whether the distance at which Campbell was following the car in front of him was reasonable and prudent.

The alleged driving irregularities in *Whren* and *Campbell* are dissimilar. While it was clear that Brown committed a traffic violation, the Florida statute cited in this case does not apply to Campbell. Determining whether one vehicle is following another vehicle too closely involved much more of a judgment call than determining whether the Pathfinder failed to signal when turning right and exceeded the speed limit. The position of the vehicles on the highway and the weather and road conditions must all be considered to determine if Campbell violated the statute.

The evidence that will be presented at the hearing on the motion to suppress will show that Fla. Stat. Ch. 316.0895 (1) does not apply to Campbell because Campbell was following the car in front of him at more than the appropriate distance given the vehicles' speed, the traffic, and the condition of the highway.

Following *Whren*, this court should find the stop of Campbell's car unconstitutional because there was no traffic violation. Because Campbell was following the car in front of him at a reasonable and prudent distance, the stop violated Campbell's right against unreasonable search and seizure. Because Campbell's fourth amendment right was violated by the stop and the agents would not have found the evidence if they had not first stopped the car on I-95, the evidence should be suppressed as the fruit of the poisonous tree.

Conclusion:
For the reasons set forth above, defendant Campbell requests this court to grant his motion to suppress and to dismiss the charge against him for lack of evidence.

Respectfully submitted,

____

Florida Attorney, Esq.
Florida Bar Number 000000
Law Firm
Main Street
Anytown, Fla.

SECOND SAMPLE MEMORANDUM OF LAW

UNITED STATES DISTRICT COURT
MIDDLE DISTRICT OF FLORIDA
ORLANDO DIVISION

UNITED STATES OF AMERICA,
Plaintiff,

v. Case No. 00 - 123 - CR - ORL - 00

LUIS BRIONES and CRUZ ESTRADA,
Defendants.

__________________________________/

MEMORANDUM IN OPPOSITION TO DEFENDANT'S MOTION TO SUPPRESS

Plaintiff the United States of America submits this memorandum of law in opposition to defendant's motion to suppress the methamphetamines seized from the defendant and the tape of her conversation.

Questions presented:

1. Was Officer Green's search of Defendant's purse permissible where the Defendant consented to the search?
2. Was Officer Green's search of Defendant's purse permissible where the officer had probable cause to search the car and the purse fell under the container exception to the search warrant requirement?
3. Where Officer Green had the defendant wait in his patrol car while he searched the car in which she had been riding, was it permissible for him to tape record any statements defendant made?

Facts:
Officer Green was patrolling the southbound lanes of I-95 when he observed a car travelling at an excessive rate of speed. The radar in the patrol car showed that the car was travelling 80 in a 65 mile per hour speed zone.

Officer Green approached the driver's side of the car and requested the driver's license and car registration. While the driver searched his wallet for the documents, Officer Green looked through the open window and noticed a glass vial containing small kernels of an off-white substance in the driver's lap. Believing the vial to contain crack cocaine, Officer Green announced that he was seizing it. He asked the driver and passenger to exit the car and asked the driver for his wallet. Officer Green identified the driver as Luis Briones from his driver's license.

As the passenger got out of the car, Officer Green struck up a conversation with her. She said that her name was Cruz Estrada. Officer Green explained that he would have to search their car but that they could wait in the patrol car for their comfort and safety. The defendant turned back to the car, explaining that she had to retrieve something. She reached into the car and pulled out her purse, which had fallen behind the front seat. As the defendant passed him on the way to the patrol car, Officer Green asked if he could search her purse. Without responding, the defendant held out her purse to him. Inside her purse, Officer Green found a brown paper envelope. When Officer Green asked her what was in the envelope, defendant claimed that she did not know, that someone had given it to her to give to a friend in Miami. When Officer Green opened the envelope, he found a quantity of white powder that he believed to be methamphetamines.

The two waited in the patrol car while Officer Green searched the car. The tape of their conversation contains several incriminating statements, including defendant's admission that the envelope was hers and that it contained illegal drugs.

Argument:

Over the years, courts have recognized a variety of exceptions to the search warrant requirement of the Fourth Amendment in recognition that exigent circumstances often do not allow an officer time to obtain a search warrant. This case illustrates the tension between the officer's duty to collect evidence of the illegal drug trade and the individual's privacy concerns. Consent had long enabled an officer to conduct a search, even without probable cause. Even without consent but upon probable cause, an officer may search a car and any containers within the car, without regard to their ownership. A standard law enforcement technique has been to ask suspects to wait in the officer's patrol car while the officer searches the suspects' car; to obtain evidence, the officer tape records any statements the suspects unwisely make while in the patrol car.

The government argues that two exceptions to the search warrant requirement allowed Officer Green to search the defendant's purse. Defendant's motion to suppress the contents of her purse should be denied either because defendant consented to the search or because probable cause to search the car allows Officer Green to search containers found in the car. Defendant has argued that the tape containing her incriminating statements should be suppressed because the tape was made in violation of the federal eavesdropping statutes. There is no ground to suppress the tape under the statutes; the statutes prohibit taping only if there is a reasonable expectation that the conversation is private. Society would not recognize any conversation of suspects in a patrol car to be private. This memorandum will first explain why the methamphetamines found in Defendant's purse should not be suppressed and then why the tape of defendant's incriminating statements should not be suppressed.

A. Because it was objectively reasonable for Officer Green to believe that Defendant had consented to the search when she held out her purse to him, the methamphetamines found should not be suppressed.

Once a vehicle is stopped, the officer can search the car if there is probable cause of criminal activity. An occupant can consent to the search of the occupant's belongings. *United States v. Jimeno*, 500 U.S. 248, 251 (1991). Even without consent, the officer can search containers found in the car and suspected of holding the object of the officer's search, no matter who owns the container. *Wyoming v. Houghton*, 526 U.S. 295, 300–01 (1999). An officer may not search someone's person without probable cause. *Id.* at 303.

The search of Cruz' purse is constitutional if she consented to the search or the container exception to the search warrant requirement extends to her purse. The United States Supreme Court has stated the standard for determining when an individual has consented to the search of a car. *Jimeno*, 500 U.S. at 251. This portion of the office memo will examine whether the consent standard has been met. As far as the container exception is concerned, the United States Supreme Court recently held that "police officers with probable cause to search a car may inspect passengers' belongings found in the car that are capable of concealing the object of the search." *Houghton*, 526 U.S. at 307. The facts of *Jimeno*, *Houghton*, and *Estrada* will be compared to determine if the search of Cruz' purse was constitutional.

In *Jimeno*, Officer Trujillo overheard a telephone call from a public telephone in which Jimeno was discussing a drug deal. Trujillo followed Jimeno's car and stopped Jimeno for failure to stop when turning right on red. After informing Jimeno about the traffic violation, Trujillo

> went on to say that he had reason to believe that respondent was carrying narcotics in his car, and asked permission to search the car. He explained that respondent did not have to consent to a search of the car. Respondent stated that he had nothing to hide, and gave Trujillo permission to search the automobile.

500 U.S. at 249–50. Trujillo found drugs in a brown paper bag on the car floorboard. *Id.* at 250.

The Court then set forth the test for determining whether consent was given. "The standard for measuring the scope of a suspect's consent under the Fourth Amendment is that of "objective" reasonableness—what would the typical person have understood by the exchange between the officer and the suspect?" *Id.* at 251. Applying this standard, the Court found that Jimeno had consented to the search of the bag. *Id.*

The facts of *Jimeno* and *Estrada* are similar in that the two cars were stopped for alleged traffic violations, the two defendants consented to searches, and the officers searched containers. The facts surrounding the consent issue are substantially similar. Trujillo told Jimeno that he suspected that there were drugs in the car and explained that Jimeno did not have to consent to the search. When Trujillo asked Jimeno's permission, Jimeno claimed that he had nothing to hide and explicitly consented to the search. Officer Green made a statement, "you don't mind if I search, do you?" Officer Green did not have time to explain that the defendant did not have to consent before she held out her purse to him.

In *Jimeno* the container was a brown paper bag located on the floor of the car. In *Estrada,* the container was defendant's purse, hanging from her shoulder. If anything, it was more objectively reasonable to believe that the defendant in this case had consented to the search of her purse than that Jimeno consented to the search of the brown paper bag. The defendant's implied consent of offering her purse to Officer Green made it clear that she was consenting to the search of that particular container. It was not as clear that Jimeno consented to the search of the brown paper bag when he consented to the search of the car. In *Jimeno,* the trial court had granted Jimeno's motion to suppress the contents of the brown paper bag. The Florida District Court of Appeal and the Florida Supreme Court affirmed. *Id.* at 250.

Applying the objective reasonableness standard, it is objectively reasonable to believe that the defendant in this case had consented to the search of her purse. Her overt action makes it objectively reasonable to believe that she consented.

B. Because the purse was found in a car that was searched upon probable cause that it contained illegal drugs, the container exception to the search warrant requirement applied and the methamphetamines should not be suppressed.

As far as the container exception is concerned, the United States Supreme Court in *Houghton* recently held that "police officers with probable cause to search a car may inspect passengers' belongings found in the car that are capable of concealing the object of the search." 526 U.S. at 307. The facts of *Houghton* and *Estrada* will be compared to determine that the search of Cruz' purse was constitutional.

In *Houghton,* David Young was stopped for speeding and a faulty brake light. After the officer saw a hypodermic syringe in Young's pocket, Young admitted that he used it to take drugs. The officer asked the two female passengers seated in the front seat to exit the car and the officer searched the car. The officer found Houghton's purse on the back seat of the car. Searching the purse, the officer found a brown pouch that contained drug paraphernalia and a syringe containing methamphetamine in a large enough quantity for a felony conviction. Houghton claimed that the brown pouch was not hers. The officer also found a black container pouch that contained drug paraphernalia and a syringe containing a smaller amount of methamphetamine, insufficient for a felony conviction. Houghton's arms showed fresh needle-marks. The officer arrested her. 526 U.S. at 297–98.

The issue in *Houghton* was "whether police officers violate the Fourth Amendment when they search a passenger's personal belongings inside an automobile that they have probable cause to believe contains contraband." *Id.* at 297. The Court held "that police officers with probable cause to search a car may inspect passengers' belongings found in the car that are capable of concealing the object of the search." *Id.* at 307. The Court first relied on a 1982 case in which the Court had found that, where there was probable cause to search a car, it was constitutionally permissible to search containers found in the car that might hold the object of the search. *Id.* at 301–02.

The Court noted that an individual carrying a package in a vehicle travelling on the public roads has a reduced expectation of privacy. *Id.* at 303. The Court found no reason to afford more protection to a container owned by a passenger than a container owned by the driver. *Id.* at 305. The *Houghton* Court foresaw the circumstance in which law enforcement efforts "would be appreciably impaired without the ability to search the passenger's belongings" because a passenger "will often be engaged in a common interprise with the driver, and have the same interest in concealing the fruits or evidence of their wrongdoing." *Id.* at 304–05. In addition, the driver "might be able to hide contraband in a passenger's belongings as readily as in other containers in the car." *Id.* at 305.

The facts of *Houghton* and this case are very similar in that the two cars were stopped for alleged traffic violations, the passengers exited the cars, leaving their purses in the back seat, and the officers searched a passenger's purse. The facts of the two cases differ slightly in that Houghton at first disclaimed ownership of the purse. In contrast, this defendant returned to the car to retrieve her purse and offered it to Officer Green.

Applying the holding in *Houghton* to *Estrada*, Officer Green's search of defendant's purse was constitutional. When Officer Green discovered the vial containing what he believed to be crack cocaine in the driver's possession, that gave Officer Green probable cause to search the car and all containers in the car that might contain illegal drugs. Defendant's purse was of the size that it might contain illegal drugs and it was initially found in the car. Either of the two occupants might have concealed illegal drugs in defendant's purse as Officer Green pulled them over. Because of the substantial similarities between *Houghton* and *Estrada*, this court should find that Officer Green's search was constitutional.

C. Because a patrol car is similar to an office in a police station, Defendant had no reasonable expectation of privacy while seated in the rear seat of a patrol car and the motion to suppress the tape containing Defendant's incriminating statements should be denied.

The federal eavesdropping statutes protect certain types of face-to-face conversations against interception; however, to be protected, the conversation must qualify as an "oral communication." Under the statutes, an " 'oral communication' means any oral communications uttered by a person exhibiting an expectation that such communication is not subject to interception under circumstances justifying such expectation. . . ." 18 U.S.C.S. § 2510 (2) (Lexis L. Publg. 1993). Thus, a conversation is not an oral communication unless the conversants expect that the conversation is private and an objective third party would consider that expectation reasonable.

It is illegal to intercept an oral communication. "[A]ny person who . . . intentionally intercepts . . . any oral communication . . . shall be punished." 18 U.S.C.S. § 2511 (1) (Lexis L. Publg. 1993). One exception to this prohibition involves a police officer; however, the police officer must be party to the conversation or one conversant must have consented to the taping for the exception to apply. "It shall not be unlawful under this chapter for a person acting under color of law to intercept [an] . . . oral . . . communication where such person is a party to the communication or one of the parties has given prior consent to the interception." 18 U.S.C.S. § 2511 (2)(c) (Lexis L. Publg. 1993). If an oral communication is taped in violation of the eavesdropping statutes, the conversation cannot be used as evidence in court. "Whenever any . . . oral communication has been intercepted, no part of the contents of such communication and no evidence derived therefrom may be received in evidence in any trial, hearing, or other proceeding . . . before an court . . . if the disclosure of that information would be in violation of this chapter." 18 U.S.C.S. § 2515 (Lexis L. Publg. 1993).

Thus, if defendant's conversation was an oral communication, it should be suppressed. Whether the conversation is an oral communication turns on whether the defendant had a reasonable expectation of privacy while seated in the rear seat of the patrol car. One prong of the two-prong test is satisfied; defendant and the driver appear to have had an expectation of privacy or they would not have made incriminating statements. The other prong of the test is whether their expectation was reasonable. On one hand, the conversation was not audible outside the patrol car. The only way the officer could have heard the conversation was by taping it. On the other hand, they were not sitting in a privately-owned car. They were sitting in the officer's car. While an expectation of privacy in a privately-owned car would have been reasonable, it is unclear whether an expectation of privacy in the officer's car was reasonable. Some might equate the officer's car to the officer's office. If defendant and the driver were conversing in an office of a police station, it might not be reasonable to expect privacy.

In a case with similar facts, the issue before the United States Court of Appeals for the Eleventh Circuit was "whether the district court erred in denying the motion to suppress the tapes resulting from the secret recording of McKinnon's pre-arrest conversations while he sat in the back seat of the police car." *United States v. McKinnon*, 985 F.2d 525, 526 (11th Cir. 1993).

In *McKinnon* police officers stopped a pick-up truck for failure to travel in a single lane on the Florida Turnpike. Theodore Pressley was driving and Steve McKinnon was the passenger. Pressley consented to the search of his vehicle. While the officers were searching, McKinnon and Pressley waited in the rear seat of the patrol car. There they made incriminating statements that were secretly recorded by the officers. The officers arrested them after finding cocaine in the truck and they were placed in the rear seat of the patrol car. The officers again recorded McKinnon's and Pressley's incriminating statements. *Id.*

The *McKinnon* court considered the meaning of the term "oral communication" under the federal statutes. An oral communication is protected against taping. If a conversation is taped in violation of the statutes, the tape may be suppressed. A conversation is an oral communication only if the conversants exhibited a subjective expectation of privacy and the expectation privacy was objectively reasonable. The court seemed to agree with the government's argument that a patrol car functions as the officer's office and the rear seat of the patrol car functions as a jail cell. *Id.* at 527. The court held "that McKinnon did not have a reasonable or justifiable expectation of privacy for conversations he held while seated in the back seat area of a police car." *Id.* at 528.

In examining the facts of *McKinnon* and *Estrada*, the facts concerning the taping seem virtually identical. In each case, an officer asked two individuals to wait in the patrol car prior to their arrest. The officer taped their conversation in the rear seat of the patrol car; the conversation contained incriminating statements. One difference between the two cases is that the officer in *McKinnon* also taped McKinnon's conversation following his arrest. This difference is not significant because an arrestee held in the back of a patrol car would have a lesser expectation of privacy than a person not under arrest.

A number of state and a number of federal courts, other than the *McKinnon* court, have faced the issue of whether an officer may secretly tape a conversation of individuals seated in the rear seat of a patrol car. In each case the court has said that taping is permissible. Carol M. Bast & Joseph B. Sanborn, Jr., *Not Just any Sightseeing Tour: Surreptitious Taping in a Patrol Car*, 32 Crim. L. Bull. 123, 130–31 (1996).

Although persuasive authority in other circuits, *McKinnon* is mandatory authority in this circuit. The facts concerning the taping are virtually identical in *McKinnon* and *Estrada*. A number of other state and federal courts have also held that there is no reasonable expectation of privacy for persons seated in the back of a patrol car. Therefore, a court should find that Cruz and Luis had no reasonable expectation of privacy while they were seated in the rear seat of the patrol car. Because they did not have a reasonable expectation of privacy, their conversation was not protected against taping as an oral communication. Therefore, a court would not suppress the tape under the federal eavesdropping statutes.

Defendant has also made the argument that the search of her purse tainted the tape recording. Obviously, were the court to deny the defendant's motion to suppress the illegal drugs, there would be no taint that could attach to the tape. Even were the court to grant the defendant's motion to suppress the methamphetamines, the court should not grant the motion to suppress the tape. In all probability, defendant would have made the incriminating statements even if Officer Green had not searched her purse.

Where a police officer obtains evidence in a unconstitutional manner, that evidence is excluded from use at trial. If that evidence leads the officer to other evidence, the other evidence is derivative of the first evidence. The derivative evidence is known as fruit of the poisonous tree and is also inadmissible. Generally, evidence that is tainted by the prior unconstitutional conduct is inadmissible; however, in some instances the second evidence is admissible because the connection between the unconstitutionally-seized evidence and the subsequently obtained evidence is marginal.

The tape is not derivative of the evidence the officer discovered searching Estrada's purse. The tape should not be suppressed.

Conclusion:
For the reasons set forth above, the United States requests this court to deny defendant's motion to suppress the methamphetamines and the tape of her incriminating statements.

Respectfully submitted,

____
Florida Attorney, Esq.
Florida Bar Number 000000
Law Firm
Main Street
Anytown, Fla.

CHAPTER 17 SUMMARY

- In litigation, an attorney may be required by court rule, may be asked by the judge, or may feel the need to submit a memorandum of law to court.
- The purposes of the memorandum of law are to explain the client's position in a lawsuit and to convince the judge to rule in the client's favor.
- The tone of the memorandum of law is persuasive.
- While the attorney has to represent the client's best interest, this duty is tempered by the attorney's ethical duty as "an officer of the court."
- Build your credibility by stating the facts and the law accurately.
- Use format that makes your memorandum of law reader-friendly.
- Organize the document to highlight important information and to obscure adverse information that you feel obligated to include.
- Comply with any court rules and format customarily used for the particular court.
- The parts of a standard memorandum of law are the caption, the question presented, the facts, the argument, the thesis paragraph, the rule of law, the application of law to the facts, and the conclusion.

CYBERLAW EXERCISES AND EXAMPLES

1. Materials concerning famous trials of the twentieth Century can be accessed at the University of Missouri–Kansas City School of Law homepage (http://www.law.umkc.edu). The web site was developed by Professor Douglas Linder and is accessible from the faculty directory under Professor Linder's name. The famous trials include the Leopold and Loeb trial, the Scopes "monkey" trial, and the Mississippi burning trial. View some of the materials collected at this web site.
2. When writing legal documents for the first time, it may be helpful to look at examples. This chapter provides some examples. A number of law school professors have posted sample documents on the Internet. To find some of these documents you might access Jurist: The Law Professor Network (http://jurist.law.pitt.edu). Click on "Law School," "Law School Courses," and "Courses on Legal Research and Writing." At the time this book was being written, Professor Gregory Berry at Howard University School of Law had posted a number

of student documents in his "Writing Hall of Fame" found under "Berry's Advice." Those documents included client letters, memoranda, motion reply briefs, a settlement agreement, and appellate briefs. Also, Professor Colleen Barger at the University of Arkansas at Little Rock School of Law had a web site that links to pages of other legal research and writing professors (http://www.ualr.edu/~cmbarger/).

3. The Lexis law school site (http://lawschool.lexis.com) includes legal writing information (click on "My School," "Web Lectures," and then on "Legal Research and Writing").

EXERCISES FOR CHAPTER 17

1. Pick one of the research problems from appendix E.
2. Research the problem you have chosen.
3. Write a memorandum of law using your research.

CHAPTER 18

APPELLATE BRIEF

"An ability to write clearly has become the most important prerequisite for an American appellate lawyer."

—William H. Rehnquist, Chief Justice of The United States Supreme Court, "From Webster to Word-Processing: The Ascendance of the Appellate Brief," 1 J. App. Prac. & Process 1, 3 (1999).

INTRODUCTION

When a case is appealed, the attorneys for the parties submit appellate briefs to the appellate court. This chapter explains the purpose, use, and format of the appellate brief and includes two sample appellate briefs.

Much of the substance of the sample appellate brief is similar to the sample memorandums of law from chapter 17. To save space, the footnotes from the first memorandum of law are not repeated in the first appellate brief. You may want to go back later and reread the footnotes to the first sample memorandum of law from chapter 17.

Because the appellate brief is so important in an appeals case, the substance of the appellate brief must be well researched. Sloppy research will cause the judge to lose faith in the argument presented, as indicated in the following passage.

The government's brief was most unsatisfactory, indeed misleading, in that it failed to cite the decision of the Sixth Circuit Court of Appeals in *United States v. Brown*, which is not so recent as to excuse the government's failure to find and discuss it. The *Brown* decision is critical to disposition of any motion for a preliminary injunction under 18 U.S.C. S 1345, because of its discussion of the appropriate standards and burdens of proof for issuance of such an injunction as well as such an injunction's proper scope. Thus, the government's brief is an example of the kind of gross oversight that can result from failure to update a "canned" brief, however repetitive a specialized practice may become. Merely "Shepardizing" the cases cited in the government's brief would have revealed the *Brown* decision. At worst, the government knew of the case, and intentionally failed to cite it; at best, the government was negligent in failing to find and discuss applicable case law. In either case, the court expects more from the government, particularly when the government attorneys involved are specialists.

United States v. Barnes, 912 F.Supp. 1187, 1189 n.1 (N.D. Iowa 1996)(citation omitted).

PURPOSE AND USE

When a party appeals a lower court ruling, the appellate court's job is to review what the lower court did to determine whether the lower court committed reversible error. In its review the appellate court examines the "record" of the lower court proceedings and reads the appellate briefs. Once the record on appeal is transmitted to the appellate court and appellate briefs are filed, the appellate court may rule on the appeal solely on the strength of the documents filed with the appellate court, or the court may hear oral argument. During oral argument, the attorney for each party has an allotted period of time to argue the client's position in the case and to respond to questions posed by the appellate judges.

In the following two passages, two courts criticize the attorneys for inaccurate citations. In the first case, the court ordered the offending attorney to pay the opposing counsel's reasonable costs and attorney fees.

This Court does not readily impose sanctions upon parties for filing frivolous appeals. However, given the inconsistent and conflicting positions John Deere has taken throughout this matter, its inaccurate citations to authority, and the lack of support for its claims on appeal, we conclude that sanctions are necessary and appropriate in this case.

Therefore, on the basis of the inconsistent and conflicting positions John Deere has taken throughout this matter, its baseless claims on appeal, and its inaccurate citations in its appellate brief, we assess sanctions against John Deere pursuant to Rule 32, M.R.App.P., and order it to pay Conifer's reasonable costs and attorney fees incurred in defending this appeal.

Federated Mutual Insurance Company v. Anderson, 920 P.2d 97, 102, 104 (Mont.1996).

FN6. We were not aided in our resolution of this appeal by the appellants' opening brief, which was riddled with inaccurate and incomplete case citations and which frequently referred to cases without reference to the pages on which the cited holdings appear. (See Cal. Style Manual (3d ed. 1986) S 99.)

Howard v. Oakland Tribune, 245 Cal.Rptr. 449, 451 (Cal. Ct. App. 1988).

The appellate briefs play a major role in the appeal. You might think of the appellate briefs as guidebooks to the case. They contain the arguments of the parties, they assist the appellate court in determining the issues to be decided on appeal, and they explain the applicable law and facts. Of course, because the appellate briefs are designed to persuade the appellate court of the correctness of the respective parties' positions, the **appellant's brief** is written from the appellant's perspective and the **appellee's brief** is written from the appellee's perspective.

The appellant's brief is filed first and gives the appellant's reasons the appellate court should reverse or otherwise modify the lower court decision. Court rules give the appellee a certain period of time after the appellant's brief is filed to file the appellee's brief. The appellee's brief gives the appellee's reasons why the lower court decision should be affirmed.

In reviewing a lower court decision, the appellate court must follow a standard of review. A standard of review is the nature and extent of the action the appellate court may take in reviewing the lower court decision. The standard is different depending on whether the appellate court is reviewing a **findings of fact,** a ruling of law, or a ruling on a question involving law and fact. Because the trial court was in the best position to judge the credibility of the witnesses, the trial court's findings of fact are given great deference. The appellate court is bound to follow the trial court's findings of fact unless a jury finding was unreasonable or a trial judge's finding was clearly erroneous. When deciding a question of law or a question involving law and fact, the appellate court is free to reach a ruling different from that of the trial court.

Keep in mind the standard of review when writing the appellate brief. If you represent the appellee and the question for review is one of fact, emphasize that the trial court's finding of fact must be deferred to unless unreasonable or clearly erroneous. Whether the issue is one purely of fact, purely of law, or of fact and law is rarely clear-cut. If you represent the appellant, try to characterize the issue as one of law or of fact and law so that the appellate court will not have to defer to the decision of the trial court.

If you represent the appellee, use the lower court decision in the appellee's favor to your advantage. Do not hesitate to rely on the reasoning of the lower court. You may even want to quote particularly well-worded passages of the lower court's opinion. Although an appellate court is not bound by the trial court's ruling on a question of law or a mixed question of fact and law, sometimes it helps to remind the appellate court that after studying the issue, the lower court ruled in the appellee's favor.

Compare the appellate brief with the memorandum of law. Of the legal documents covered in this book, the appellate brief is most similar to the memorandum of law. Because both the memorandum of law and the appellate brief are persuasive in tone and are designed to convince the reader of the correctness of the client's position, much of the substance of the two documents will be similar. Although similar in tone and purpose, the two documents differ in two respects. As explained above, the appellate brief differs from the memorandum of law in the standard of review by the appellate court. The different standard of review in the appellate court will probably dictate some change in the wording of the issues and argument of the appellate brief from the questions presented and argument of the memorandum of law. Another difference is format. Aside from complying with page size and other such mundane requirements, attorneys writing memoranda of law generally follow the format customary in their area rather than having to follow a certain detailed format specified by court rule. In contrast, the format for appellate briefs is usually specified in detail in the applicable court rules.

At this point it would be well for you to reread the preceding chapter on the memorandum of law (chapter 17). Except for differences in the standard of review and format, assume that the explanation of the memorandum of law from that chapter applies to the appellate brief.

The next section of this chapter discusses format for appellate briefs. In the following case excerpts, the judges criticized the attorneys for errors in format. A court may orally admonish an attorney for filing poorly-written briefs. However, such criticism in a published opinion is striking because its inclusion is so infrequent. Inclusion of the criticism in a published opinion is extremely embarassing to the attorney and is available for years to come in the law library.

> Finally, we note that plaintiffs-appellants have filed an overly long brief. Although the brief is less than the permissible fifty pages, it is not double spaced as required making the effective length of the brief considerably longer. Additionally, we are able to find no reason for the length of the brief. Despite the extra length, the brief failed to adequately present the claims of appellants or even to clearly identify the claims being appealed. "We believe it appropriate to discourage the filing of excessively long briefs in this court," and we believe it appropriate to discourage parties from attempting to flaunt the page limits by submitting briefs with improper line spacing. Accordingly, we assess double costs against appellants.
>
> *Doyle v. Hasbro, Inc*, 103 F.3d 186, 196 (1st Cir. 1996)(citations omitted).

FN2. Many of the cases upon which plaintiff relies most heavily contain citation errors. See cites to, *Gordon* and *Gens*, Brief in Support of Summary Judgment Motion p. 7, and *DeNiro* and *Estate of Fink*, Reply Brief at p. 9. Plaintiff's counsel is reminded that it is of paramount importance to cite cases accurately.

Hathaway v. United States, No. C92-628C, 1993 WL 207532, at *4 n.2 (W.D.Wash. Mar. 16, 1993).

After reviewing the briefs filed on Mathis' appeal, the Court finds the quality of Schofield's advocacy on Mathis' behalf to be disturbing. The brief is poorly organized and parts of it are inarticulate to the point of being incomprehensible.

Mathis v. Hood, No. 87 CIV. 6324 (RPP), 1990 WL 100869, at *7 n.14 (S.D.N.Y. July 11, 1990), *aff'd*, 937 F.2d 790 (2d Cir. 1991).

FORMAT

The first step in writing an appellate brief is to check applicable court rules to determine the format required by the court. For a case being appealed to a federal circuit court you would check the Federal Rules of Appellate Procedure. The United States Supreme Court has its own set of rules that must be consulted for documents submitted to it. For a case being appealed to the intermediate appellate court of your state, check the rules of appellate procedure for your state. The court of last resort of your state may have its own set of rules that must be consulted for documents submitted to it, or it may use the same rules as the state intermediate appellate courts. In addition to the rules referred to in this paragraph, many courts have local rules that must be complied with.

Failure to follow court rules for appellate briefs may have serious consequences. The least serious of the consequences is attorney embarrassment if the failure to comply is pointed out by the clerk of the court, by opposing counsel, or by a judge. A judge may impose monetary sanctions on an attorney who fails to comply with the rules. The most serious consequence is the clerk's office refusing to file an appellate brief that fails to comply with applicable appellate rules.

The following three cases concern sanctions for failure to follow the rules. In the first two cases, the judges imposed monetary sanctions. In the third case, the appeal was dismissed.

In re Ronald C. MacINTYRE; Mary M. Pikus, Debtors.

Philip A. DeMASSA, APC; Philip A. DeMassa, Appellants,

v.

Lyle BUTLER; Ronald MacIntyre; Mary Pikus; Prudential California Realty,

Appellees.

181 B.R. 420

United States Bankruptcy Appellate Panel

of the Ninth Circuit.

Decided Feb. 22, 1995.

RUSSELL, Bankruptcy Judge:

This appeal arises from a complaint seeking to have the debtors' discharge denied based on alleged fraudulent conduct by the debtors. The bankruptcy court ruled in favor of the debtors and granted the debtors a discharge. [FN1]

FN1. We affirmed the bankruptcy court on the merits of this case in an unpublished memorandum decision. In this opinion, we consider only one issue, whether appellants should be sanctioned for attempting to circumvent page limits by reducing the type size of footnotes in his brief in violation of BAP Rule 5 and Fed.R.App.P. 32(a).

The appellants, Philip A. DeMassa and his professional corporation ("DeMassa") moved to file an oversize brief exceeding the normal page limits set forth in BAP Rule 5(b). [FN2] Attached with that motion was a copy of DeMassa's oversized brief, which was sixty pages in length and contained twenty-eight footnotes. The motion was denied.

FN2. BAP Rule 5(b) provides that "[e]xcept with leave of a panel, the appellant's and the appellee's opening briefs shall not exceed thirty (30) pages, and reply briefs shall not exceed twenty (20) pages, exclusive of pages containing the table of contents, tables of citations and any addendum containing statutes, rules, regulations, or similar material."

The present opening brief filed by DeMassa is thirty-one pages in length and contains twenty-six footnotes. The present brief was printed in the same type size as the earlier brief, with the one exception that DeMassa changed the type size of his footnotes. In the first brief, the footnotes were printed in a type font similar to "courier 10," which contains ten characters per inch. In the present brief, DeMassa used a type font similar to "courier 12," which contains twelve characters per inch. This results in a minuscule type size which is much more difficult to read than the required type size. In addition, the reduced type size is in violation of our Rule 5(a) and Fed.R.App.P. 32(a). [FN3] Ironically, DeMassa's reply brief, which is twenty-one pages, contains the proper size footnotes.

FN3. BAP Rule 5(a) provides that "[b]riefs shall be submitted in general conformance with Bankruptcy Rule 8010 and Rule 32(a) of the Federal Rules of Appellate Procedure."

Fed.R.App.P. 32(a) in turn provides in relevant part, "(a) Form of Briefs and the Appendix . . . All printed matter must appear in at least 11 point type. . . ."

It is clear that DeMassa is utilizing the minuscule type size for the sole purpose of circumventing our page limits on opening briefs. Had DeMassa used the correct type size for the footnotes in his opening brief, he would have undoubtedly exceeded the thirty page limit by several pages.

It is also worth noting that DeMassa's use of footnotes is excessive and attempts to squeeze additional argument into his brief by utilizing the single spacing found in footnotes. The majority of his footnotes add additional argument which should have been included in the main text of DeMassa's brief.

Because page limits are important to maintain judicial efficiency and ensure fairness to opposing parties, we IMPOSE SANCTIONS in the amount of $250 upon DeMassa, which is payable to the United States Bankruptcy Appellate Panel of the Ninth Circuit.

In the following case, the court imposed $1,500 in sanctions against the appellant's attorney for failure to comply with the rule governing the form of the appellate brief.

Wayne H.T. KANO; Patricia Kano, Trustee and Phillip Kau, Trustee, Plaintiffs-

Appellants,

v.

NATIONAL CONSUMER COOPERATIVE BANK, et al.; Frank L. Torres, Defendants-

Appellees,

and

Jack L. Ayers, Jr. and Elsie M. Ayers, Third-party-plaintiffs-Appellees,

George R. Madden, Jr., Third-party-defendant-Appellee.

22 F.3d 899

United States Court of Appeals,

Ninth Circuit.

April 18, 1994.

The opening brief filed on behalf of appellant violated Fed.R.App.P. 32(a) in that the lines were not double-spaced, but were spaced only one-and- one half spaces apart. Furthermore, the footnotes were of a typeface much smaller than that permitted by the rule, and contained approximately eight lines per inch as opposed to six lines per inch in a normal single-spaced format. We estimate that the opening brief was the equivalent of at least sixty-five pages in length, far exceeding the fifty-page limit.

Counsel for appellant took full responsibility for the form of the brief. However, it is apparent from the reply brief filed by counsel that he knows what the spacing requirements are, even though the footnotes in the reply brief also do not comply with Rule 32. Consequently, we impose sanctions against counsel for the appellant in the amount of $1,500.

In the following case, the court held that N/S Corporation's briefs would be stricken and the appeal dismissed for failure to comply with the briefing rules.

N/S CORPORATION, a Pennsylvania corporation, Plaintiff-Appellant,

v.

LIBERTY MUTUAL INSURANCE COMPANY, Defendant-Appellee.

127 F.3d 1145

United States Court of Appeals,

Ninth Circuit.

Decided Oct. 23, 1997.

FERNANDEZ, Circuit Judge:

We will not spill ink detailing the substantive facts of this case because we need not discuss its merits. We are passing through a period in the history of this country when the pressures upon the courts are extremely high. They are so because of the volume of work as more and more people seek to have the courts resolve their disputes and vindicate their rights. But resources are limited. In order to give fair consideration to those who call upon us for justice, we must insist that parties not clog the system by presenting us with a slubby mass of words rather than a true brief. Hence we have briefing rules. By and large, we have been tolerant of minor breaches of one rule or another. Perhaps we are too tolerant sometimes. But there are times when our patience runs out. Then we strike an appellant's briefs and dismiss the appeal. This is one of those times. This is a time when an appellant has approached our rules with such insouciance that we cannot overlook its heedlessness.

The violations are legion. First, the standard of review section in the opening brief says nothing about the appellate standard of review and the omission is not corrected elsewhere in the brief. Second, while the opening brief is replete with assertions of fact and assertions about the record, it contains a mere handful of generalized record citations. The brief leaves it up to the court to attempt to find the asserted information; alas, much of it is not there at all. Third, the opening brief exceeds the word limits for proportionally spaced briefs. All of this is aside from lesser (?) matters like rather creative renditions of what actually occurred at the district court and the citation of California case authority which had been depublished many weeks before the brief was filed (and was without precedential value).

We might have been inclined to overlook all of that, but after Liberty Mutual pointed to these failures, and others, in a motion to dismiss, N/S did not even deign to respond. More than that, it filed a reply brief in which it entirely omitted the table of contents and the tables of authorities cited.

Enough is enough. We strike the N/S briefs and dismiss its appeal. Even so, we would feel most uneasy if this were an otherwise meritorious appeal, which cried out for reversal of the district court's decisions. "We acknowledge the apparent harshness . . . of our refusal to consider the merits of this appeal because . . . counsel failed to comply with the rules." Mitchel.

However, the appeal is not meritorious. We have carefully reviewed the district court's rulings, the facts, and the law, a process which N/S's failure to follow the rules made considerably more difficult than it ought to have been.

DISMISSED.

The rules for appellate briefs cover a number of matters. They usually specify the major sections required to be included in the appellate brief and may specify their content. The rules may also mandate certain more mundane matters such as paper size, type size, and maximum page length. For example, Rule 28 of the Federal Rules of Appellate Procedure states the sections required for the appellate brief, gives a brief explanation of the information to be included in each section, and limits appellate briefs to fifty pages. Rule 32 requires appellate briefs to be double-spaced in at least eleven point type on eight and one half by eleven inch paper with typed material not exceeding six and one half by nine and one half inches. (To save space, the sample appellate brief contained in this chapter was single rather than double-spaced.) Rule 32 also specifies the information required on the cover of the appellate brief and the color of the cover.

The format used in this chapter complies with Rule 28 of the Federal Rules of Appellate Procedure (except for being single-spaced rather than double-spaced). The following are the sections of an appellate brief required by Rule 28.

Table of contents

The table of contents includes the titles of the sections of the brief and the wording of the point headings as well as the page references.

Table of cases, statutes, and other authorities cited

This table (alphabetically arranged) contains references to the pages of the brief on which the listed authorities are cited.

Statement of subject matter jurisdiction

Rule 28 requires "a statement of the basis for subject matter jurisdiction in the district court or agency, with citation to applicable statutory provisions and with reference to the relevant facts to establish such jurisdiction."

Statement of appellate jurisdiction

Rule 28 requires:

> a statement of the basis for jurisdiction in the court of appeals, with citation to applicable statutory provisions and with reference to the relevant facts to establish such jurisdiction; the statement shall include relevant filing dates establishing the timeliness of the appeal or petition for review and
>
> (a) shall state that the appeal is from a final order or a final judgment that disposes of all claims with respect to all parties or, if not,
>
> (b) shall include information establishing that the court of appeals has jurisdiction on some other basis.

In the portion of the case reprinted below, the court expresses its disapproval of lengthy briefs in no uncertain terms.

Irwin SLATER, Appellant,

v.

Norman F. GALLMAN, Individually and as Acting Commissioner of the Department of Taxation and Finance of the State of New York, et al., Respondents.

Court of Appeals of New York.

Nov. 20, 1975.

377 N.Y.S.2d 448

JASEN, Judge.

In addition to considering the merits of this appeal, we feel that this case presents an appropriate opportunity to comment on a matter that concerns us greatly, namely, the quality, length and content of briefs presented to this court. Although this is an extreme example, unfortunately it is not always the rare case in which we receive poorly written and excessively long briefs, replete with burdensome, irrelevant, and immaterial matter. Although counsel candidly admits that his 284-page brief is 'unusually long', his claim that it is 'meticulously structured, thoroughly documented, exhaustively researched, carefully analyzed and comprehensively presented' seems too self-congratulatory. His argument wanders aimlessly through myriad irrelevant matters of administrative and constitutional law, pausing only briefly to discuss the issues raised by this appeal.* The brief pursues, in seemingly endless fashion, matters not properly before this court for the simple reason that they were not raised below. This is in contrast to the brief filed on behalf of the Tax Commission which, even though consisting of only 21 pages (including preliminary material in addition to a 14-page argument on the merits), cogently and concisely discusses all of the issues presented in this relatively uncomplicated appeal.

*[Footnote] The following breakdown of the contents of appellant's brief exemplifies the problem: statement of questions presented, 16 pages; statement of the nature of the case and facts, 50 pages; legal argument in support of contention that appellant has an appeal as of right, 23 pages (this despite the fact that he clearly has an appeal as of right pursuant to CPLR 5601 (subd. (a)), by virtue of the dissent below in his favor on a question of law); reproduction of statutes, 40 pages; table of contents, 14 pages; table of authorities, 11 pages; legal argument on the merits, 126 pages; and a purported explanation as to length of his brief, 4 pages. Concerned that his main brief may not have adequately ventilated the issues, the appellant also filed a 35-page reply brief. All of this, of course, in addition to a separate record on appeal which has been filed.

We are fully cognizant of the fact that the Federal appellate courts, faced with this same problem, have imposed a specific page limitation on briefs (Federal Rules of Appellate Procedure, rule 28, subd. (g)) and that the United States Supreme Court, by rule, requires that briefs be 'compact' and 'concise' and does, when appropriate, order that improper briefs be stricken. Nevertheless, we have avoided a specific rule in the belief that such a rule would be an insult to those appellate counsel who understand the functions of this court and their own role in pursuing appeals to this court, and whose briefs focus on the pertinent issues. Rather than now prescribe such a rule, we prefer to merely point out the problem, fully confident that counsel appearing before us will impose upon themselves a modicum of self-restraint.

We speak now on this matter only with some hesitancy lest counsel in the future be discouraged from vigorously and comprehensively urging their cases and, where appropriate, suggesting novel approaches to complex legal issues. However, in recent years we have witnessed great technological advances in the methods of reproduction of the written word. Too often this progress is merely viewed as a license to substitute volume for logic in an apparent attempt to overwhelm the courts, as though quantity, and not quality, was the virtue to be extolled. As we noted many years ago, for obvious reasons this problem never arose when 'every lawyer wrote his points with a pen'. Hopefully, the solution to this problem will not require that we return to that system, ignoring decades of technological advances.

The issues presented upon this appeal are neither novel nor complex; the brief and reply brief filed by counsel constitute an unwarranted burden upon this court. These briefs neither assist our deliberations nor serve the best interests of his client. Although recognizing this to be a wholly inadequate sanction, at a minimum, costs should be imposed against the appellant.

Statement of the issues presented for review

The issues are the questions you are suggesting the appellate court consider. Word the issues so the appellate court can easily reach the decision in your client's favor. Often the appellee will start an issue with the words, "Did the trial court properly find that" or "Did the trial court properly rule that." Such wording suggests that the trial court decision was correct. In contrast, the appellant would start the same issue with the words, "Did the trial court err in." That wording suggests that there was something wrong with the trial court's decision.

Statement of the case

Rule 28 requires that the statement "first indicate briefly the nature of the case, the course of proceedings, and its disposition in the court below."

Statement of the facts

Rule 28 requires that the statement contain "the facts relevant to the issues presented for review, with appropriate references to the record." For ease of reference, the appellant's brief usually has an appendix attached to it, containing copies of the parts of the record referenced in appellant's brief. The abbreviation "(A. 3)" would reference page three of the appendix.

Legal argument

Rule 28 states: "The argument may be preceded by a summary. The argument shall contain the contentions of the appellant with respect to the issues presented, and the reasons therefor, with citations to the authorities, statutes and parts of the record relied on." As in the memorandum of law, use point headings to make the brief reader-friendly. The brief should contain one or more major point headings for major sections and may contain subheadings within a major section to divide a major section into subsections. The major point headings should be equal in number to the issues presented, should answer the issues, and should appear in the same order as the issues presented.

Legal conclusion

Rule 28 requires "[a] short conclusion stating the precise relief sought."

FIRST SAMPLE APPELLATE BRIEF

IN THE
UNITED STATES COURT OF APPEALS
FOR THE ELEVENTH CIRCUIT

CASE NO. 00-0000

UNITED STATES OF AMERICA,

Appellee,

v.

MICHAEL CAMPBELL and JOHN WRIGHT,

Appellants.

APPEAL OF A CRIMINAL CONVICTION FROM THE

UNITED STATES DISTRICT COURT

ORLANDO DIVISION

BRIEF FOR APPELLANT CAMPBELL

Florida Attorney, Esq.

Florida Bar Number 000000

Law Firm

Main Street

Anytown, Fla.

TABLE OF CONTENTS

TABLE OF AUTHORITIES

CASES

FEDERAL RULES OF APPELLATE PROCEDURE

STATUTES

UNITED STATES CONSTITUTION

STATEMENT OF SUBJECT MATTER JURISDICTION
IN THE UNITED STATES DISTRICT COURT

The defendant, Michael Campbell, was indicted in the United States District Court for the Middle District of Florida on April 6, 2000. The indictment charged him with violating 21 U.S.C.S. § 841 (a)(1) (Lexis L. Publg. 1997 & Supp. 2000) for possession with intent to distribute a quantity of cocaine. (A. 21). Defendant received a jury verdict of guilty on June 7, 2000 and was sentenced on June 14, 2000 to a term of three years. (A. 25).

STATEMENT OF JURISDICTION

This is an appeal from the final judgment of the United States District Court for the Middle District of Florida in a criminal case pursuant to a Motion under Rule 4(b) of the Federal Rules of Appellate Procedure. Jurisdiction in the United States Court of Appeals for the Eleventh Circuit is invoked under 28 U.S.C.S. § 1291 (Lexis L. Publg. 1986), which provides that the Court of Appeals has jurisdiction from all final decisions of the United States District Court. Defendant was sentenced on June 14, 2000. On June 20, 2000, a timely Notice of Appeal was filed from which this appeal follows. (A. 25, 27).

STATEMENT OF THE ISSUE

Did the trial court err in admitting evidence seized from defendant Mike Campbell's car where a law enforcement officer pursued the Campbell car after he observed Mike and his friend, two Afro-American college students in their twenties in beach attire, traveling on I-95 in the early evening at the speed limit in an out-of-state tagged Lincoln Continental and where the law enforcement officer pulled the Campbell car over for following too closely? (A. 3–4).

STATEMENT OF THE CASE

On April 1, 2000, United States Drug Enforcement Agents stopped the defendant, Michael Campbell, on I-95 because he fit their drug courier profile and for following too closely. (A. 3–4). After the agents found cocaine in the trunk of Campbell's car, he was arrested and taken into custody. (A. 5). He was provided an initial detention hearing on April 2, 2000. (A. 20). On April 6, 2000, an indictment was filed charging him with a violation of 21 U.S.C.S § 841 (a)(1) for possession with intent to distribute a quantity of cocaine. He was arraigned the same day and he entered a plea of not guilty. (A. 21).

A trial date was set for June 7, 2000 for a jury trial. Prior to trial defendant filed a motion to suppress the cocaine found in the trunk of defendant's car. The district court denied the motion and the trial began on June 7, 2000. (A. 22). Defendant received a jury verdict of guilty on June 7, 2000. (A. 24). Defendant was sentenced on June 14, 2000 to a term of three years. (A. 25).

STATEMENT OF THE FACTS

Mike Campbell and his best friend had decided like thousands of other college students to enjoy a Florida spring break. After Mike promised to drive carefully, Mike's father let Mike borrow his car, a brand new Lincoln Continental. After arriving in Florida, they spent every waking moment of their break on the beach. In the early evening on the last day of vacation, they went straight from the beach to their car to begin the long trip back to school, calculating that they would have just enough driving time to make it back for their first class. (A. 1–2).

Mike was driving north on I-95, thinking about the promise he had made to his father, when he saw patrol cars parked in the median, one with its lights shining across the northbound lanes. Almost immediately after driving through the arc of the patrol car's headlights, Mike looked in the rear view mirror and saw the patrol car pull out behind him. The patrol car followed Mike for a distance before pulling Mike over. (A. 3–4).

An officer got out of the patrol car, walked over to Mike's car and asked for Mike's driver's license and car registration. As Mike handed over his license and the registration he noticed the officer eyeing Mike's beach attire suspiciously. When Mike told the officer they were heading back to school from spring break, the officer commented, "We don't see too many blacks down here over spring break." The officer added, "I stopped you for following the car in front of you too closely." Still holding the license and registration, the officer asked Mike whether the officer could search the car and said, "You don't have anything to hide, do you?" Hoping that if he refused they could be on their way, Mike answered, "No." The officer said, "Wait here," turned around, walked back to the patrol car, and got in. Mike could not have left even if the officer had not told him to "wait" because the officer still had Mike's license and car registration. (A. 3–4).

Forty-five minutes later another patrol car pulled up and an officer got out with a dog. The officer led the dog around the car. The dog circled the car once and then stopped and pawed the car's trunk. The officer motioned Mike to roll down his window. The officer told him that the dog had detected drugs in the trunk of Mike's car. The officer told Mike that Mike could either open the car trunk or wait there whatever time was necessary for the officer to obtain a search warrant. Feeling that he had no choice, Mike opened the trunk. Both officers started pulling Mike's and his friend's belongings out of the trunk and tossing them on the ground. Wedged in a bottom corner of the trunk one of the officers found a brown paper bag containing cocaine. Mike and his friend were arrested and were charged with possession with intent to distribute. (A. 4–5).

SUMMARY OF ARGUMENT

The car driver and passengers expect that activities within the car will be private and not subject to the scrutiny of law enforcement officials. They may feel that their privacy is invaded if a law enforcement officer stops the car to investigate. A trained police officer may have a hunch that a car's occupants are engaged in illegal activity; however, a law enforcement officer may not constitutionally stop a car unless there is a reasonable suspicion of illegal activity or there is a traffic violation. The stop of Mike's car to investigate for criminal activity was not permissible because the agents did not have reasonable suspicion of illegal drug activity. The stop for a traffic violation was constitutionally justifiable only if Mike was following too closely.

The Fourth Amendment to the United States Constitution guarantees "[t]he right of the people to be secure in their persons, houses, papers, and effects against unreasonable searches and seizures" and allows a search warrant to be issued only upon "probable cause." A search warrant requirement was spelled out in the amendment to safeguard this important right. Over the more than two hundred years since the amendment was adopted, the individual's right against unreasonable search and seizure has been jealously guarded.

Although the time and level of evidence needed to obtain a search warrant protects the individual's constitutional right, the courts have allowed two exceptions to the search warrant requirement, either of which the government argues is applicable here and allowed them to stop the Campbell car. The first exception requires a minimum of "reasonable suspicion" of illegal activity to stop a car and question its occupants. *Terry v. Ohio*, 392 U.S. 1, 27 (1968); *United States v. Smith*, 799 F.2d 704, 707 (11th Cir. 1986). The second exception allows an officer to stop a car to investigate a traffic violation. *Whren v. United States*, 517 U.S. 806, 818 (1996).

Defendant Campbell's motion to suppress should be granted because neither of the two exceptions to the search warrant requirement apply here. The officer stopped Campbell's car on a mere "hunch" and Campbell was following at a "reasonable and prudent" distance, as required by the Florida Statutes. Fla. Stat. Ch. 316.0895 (1)

(2000). The argument section of this brief will first explain why there was not enough evidence to justify an investigatory stop and then why the alleged traffic violation did not justify the stop.

ARGUMENT

THE EVIDENCE FOUND IN THE TRUNK OF DEFENDANT CAMPBELL'S CAR SHOULD HAVE BEEN SUPPRESSED AS THE FRUIT OF AN UNCONSTITUTIONAL SEARCH AND SEIZURE BECAUSE THE DRUG COURIER PROFILE DID NOT SUPPORT THE REASONABLE SUSPICION NECESSARY FOR AN INVESTIGATORY STOP AND CAMPBELL DID NOT COMMIT A TRAFFIC VIOLATION.

A. Because the information the officer relied on to stop the Campbell car was no more than a mere "hunch," the evidence should be suppressed unless the officer had probable cause to stop the car for a traffic violation.

Terry was the landmark case that lowered the burden of proof necessary for a stop from probable cause to "reasonable suspicion." Such stops made on reasonable suspicion are often referred to as "Terry stops," after *Terry*, and the definition of Terry stops has been broadened to apply to car stops. The new reasonable suspicion standard allows a police officer to stop and briefly question someone but is still designed to protect the innocent traveler, singled out because of certain immutable personal characteristics such as race, sex, and age, from being subjected to "overbearing or harassing" law enforcement tactics. 392 U.S. at 14–15 n. 11. A stop made only on an "unparticularized suspicion or 'hunch'" is unconstitutional. *Id.* at 27. Assuming the officer has the requisite reasonable suspicion for a Terry stop, the officer would still need probable cause or consent to search a car.

Smith involved almost identical facts to those being considered here. In *Smith*, the government argued that a highway stop was constitutionally permitted based either on a drug courier profile or on Smith's alleged commission of a traffic violation. 799 F.2d at 705. Smith filed a motion to suppress, claiming that the evidence seized from his car should be suppressed because of the violation of his right against unreasonable search and seizure. *Id.* at 706. The United States Court of Appeals for the Eleventh Circuit found that the *Smith* drug courier profile did not support reasonable suspicion, reversed the lower court's denial of Smith's motion to suppress, and vacated Smith's conviction. *Id.* at 712.

The *Smith* facts are very similar to the *Campbell* facts. In *Smith* one night in June of 1985, Trooper Robert Vogel, a Florida Highway Patrol trooper, and a DEA agent were observing cars traveling in the northbound lanes of I-95 with hopes of intercepting drug couriers. When Smith's car passed through the arc of the patrol car headlights, Vogel noticed the following factors that matched his drug courier profile:

1. The car was traveling at 3:00 a.m.;
2. The car was a 1985 Mercury, a large late model car;
3. The car had out-of-state tags;
4. There were two occupants of the car who were around 30; and
5. The driver was driving cautiously and did not look at the patrol car as the Mercury passed through the arc of the patrol car headlights.

Id. at 705–06.

The above drug courier profile is almost identical to the profile in this case. In both *Smith* and this case, the cars were traveling after dark; the cars were large late models with out-of-state tags; the cars were being driven "cautiously"; and each car contained two passengers in their twenties or thirties. The differences between the two profiles are very minor. Campbell and his friend were dressed casually while it is not known how Smith and

Swindell were dressed. Smith and Swindell did not look at Vogel as they passed. It is not known whether Campbell looked in the agents' direction as Campbell drove past. Campbell claims that race was a factor in the stop even though it was not listed as such by the agents. (A. 3–4). Smith and Swindell's race is unknown.

In *Smith*, Vogel followed the Mercury for a mile and a half and noticed that the Mercury "wove" several times, once as much as six inches into the emergency lane. Vogel pulled Smith over. When a drug dog alerted on the car, a DEA agent searched the trunk and discovered one kilogram of cocaine. Smith and his passenger, Swindell, were arrested and were charged with conspiracy to possess cocaine with the intent to distribute it. Smith and Swindell's motions to suppress the cocaine were denied and they were tried and convicted. *Id.* at 706.

The issue before the appellate court was whether the stop of Smith's car was reasonable. *Id.* This is the same basic question to be answered by this court in determining whether Campbell's motion to suppress should be granted. The *Smith* court held that the stop of Smith's car could not be upheld as a valid Terry stop, *id.* at 708, finding that "Trooper Vogel stopped the car because [Smith and Swindell] . . . matched a few nondistinguishing characteristics contained on a drug courier profile and, additionally, because Vogel was bothered by the way the driver of the car chose not to look at him." *Id.* at 707.

Just as there was nothing in the *Campbell* drug courier profile to differentiate Campbell and his friend from other innocent college students returning from spring break in Florida, there was nothing in Vogel's drug courier profile to differentiate Smith and Swindell from other law-abiding motorists on I-95. (A. 3–4). It is usual to drive after dark to avoid heavy traffic or to complete an interstate trip. Although many motorists speed on the highways, motorists driving "cautiously" at or near the speed limit are simply obeying traffic laws. Many people other than drug couriers drive large late model cars with out-of-state tags. A motorist between the ages of twenty and forty is not unusual.

The contrast between the *Campbell* and *Smith* drug courier profiles, which do not support reasonable suspicion, and another courier profile which was held to support reasonable suspicion is marked. *United States v. Sokolow*, 490 U.S. 1, 3 (1989). In *Sokolow*, DEA agents found 1,063 grams of cocaine inside Sokolow's carry-on luggage when he was stopped in Honolulu International Airport based on the following profile:

1. He had paid $2,100 in cash for two airplane tickets from a roll of $20 which appeared to contain $4,000;
2. He was ticketed under a name other than his own;
3. He traveled to Miami, a known drug source, and back;
4. Although his round trip flight lasted 20 hours, he stayed in Miami only 48 hours;
5. He appeared nervous;
6. He was about 25 years old;
7. He was dressed in a black jumpsuit and was wearing gold jewelry which he wore during both legs of the round trip flight; and
8. Neither he nor his companion checked any luggage.

Id. at 3–5. The Court held that the *Sokolow* drug courier profile did support reasonable suspicion. *Id.* at 11.

The *Sokolow* dissent would have found that all of the factors even if "taken together" did not amount to reasonable suspicion. In criticizing the use of a drug courier profile to stop suspects, the dissent noted "the profile's 'chameleon-like way of adapting to any particular set of observations'" "subjecting innocent individuals to unwarranted police harassment and detention." *Id.* at 13 (Marshall, J., dissenting)(quoting *Sokolow v. United States*, 831 F.2d 1413, 1418 (9th Cir. 1987), *rev'd*, 490 U.S. 1 (1989)).

As predicted in the *Sokolow* dissent, Smith, Swindell, Campbell, and Campbell's friend were subjected to "unwarranted police harassment and detention" even though the factors in the respective drug courier profiles, even if "taken together" did not amount to reasonable suspicion. In contrast, several of the *Sokolow* factors, such as carrying such a large amount of cash and traveling a long distance to stay a relatively short period of time, are unusual or even suspicious in and of themselves. Each of the *Smith* and *Campbell* factors was not at all out of the ordinary alone and certainly taken together did not amount to reasonable suspicion. (A. 3–4).

B. Because Mike Campbell did not commit the traffic violation alleged by the officer, the evidence found in the trunk of Mike Campbell's car should be suppressed as the fruit of an unconstitutional search and seizure.

An examination of *Whren v. United States* is necessary to answer the question whether the officer stopping Campbell on an alleged traffic violation was constitutional. In *Whren*, Brown was driving a Pathfinder in which Whren was a passenger. Brown was stopped at a stop sign looking down into Whren's lap. Plain clothes police officers were patrolling this "high drug area" of the District of Columbia in an unmarked patrol car. The Pathfinder caught the attention of the officers because Brown remained stopped at the stop sign for approximately twenty seconds. When the patrol car made a U-turn to follow the Pathfinder, Brown turned right without signaling and started off at an "unreasonable speed." The patrol car stopped the Pathfinder. When one of the officers approached Brown's window and peered in, he saw that Whren had two plastic bags of crack cocaine on his lap. The officers arrested Whren and Brown. 517 U.S. at 808, 809.

Justice Scalia phrased the issue as "whether the temporary detention of a motorist who the police have probable cause to believe has committed a civil traffic violation is inconsistent with the Fourth Amendment's prohibition against unreasonable seizures unless a reasonable officer would have been motivated to stop the car by a desire to enforce the traffic laws." *Id.* at 808. The Court answered the question, "no." "[T]he district court found that the officers had probable cause to believe that petitioners had violated the traffic code. That rendered the stop reasonable under the Fourth Amendment, the evidence thereby discovered admissible, and the upholding of the convictions by the Court of Appeals for the District of Columbia Circuit correct." *Id.* at 819.

Prior to *Whren*, some courts, including the court deciding *Smith*, had decided that a car stop for a traffic violation was unconstitutional unless a reasonable officer would have made the stop. The *Smith* court found that the cocaine should have been excluded from evidence because a reasonable officer would not have stopped Smith's car for the alleged traffic violation. 799 F.2d at 711. However in *Whren*, the United States Supreme Court rejected the argument that the reasonable officer standard should apply. 517 U.S. at 813.

After *Whren*, it would be very difficult to convince a court that a stop for an alleged traffic violation is unconstitutional. However, if the court finds that the driver did not violate any traffic regulation, then the stop would be unconstitutional.

The Florida motor vehicle statute identified by the *Campbell* officer states, "The driver of a motor vehicle shall not follow another vehicle more closely than is reasonable and prudent, having due regard for the speed of such vehicles and the traffic upon, and the condition of, the highway." Fla. Stat. Ch. 316.0895 (1) (2000). No simple test determines if Campbell violated the statute. The court must determine from any evidence presented whether the distance at which Campbell was following the car in front of him was reasonable and prudent.

The alleged driving irregularities in *Whren* and *Campbell* are dissimilar. While it was clear that Brown committed a traffic violation, the Florida statute cited in this case does not apply to Campbell. Determining whether one vehicle is following another vehicle too closely involved much more of a judgment call than determining whether the Pathfinder failed to signal when turning right and exceeded the speed limit. The position of the vehicles on the highway and the weather and road conditions must all be considered to determine if Campbell violated the statute.

The evidence presented at the hearing on the motion to suppress showed that Fla. Stat. Ch. 316.0895 (1) did not apply to Campbell because Campbell was following the car in front of him at more than the appropriate distance given the vehicles' speed, the traffic, and the condition of the highway.

Following *Whren,* this court should find the stop of Campbell's car unconstitutional because there was no traffic violation. Because Campbell was following the car in front of him at a reasonable and prudent distance, the stop violated Campbell's right against unreasonable search and seizure. Because Campbell's fourth amendment right was violated by the stop and the agents would not have found the evidence if they had not first stopped the car on I-95, the evidence should be suppressed as the fruit of the poisonous tree.

CONCLUSION

For the reasons set forth above, defendant Campbell requests this court to reverse the district court's denial of his motion to suppress, vacate his conviction and remand the case to the district court.

Respectfully submitted,

____

Florida Attorney, Esq.
Florida Bar Number 000000
Law Firm
Main Street
Anytown, Fla.

SECOND SAMPLE APPELLATE BRIEF

IN THE

UNITED STATES COURT OF APPEALS

FOR THE ELEVENTH CIRCUIT

CASE NO. 00-0000

UNITED STATES OF AMERICA,

Appellant,

v.

CRUZ ESTRADA,

Appellee.

APPEAL OF A SUPPRESSION ORDER FROM THE

UNITED STATES DISTRICT COURT

ORLANDO DIVISION

BRIEF FOR APPELLANT THE UNITED STATES OF AMERICA

Florida Attorney, Esq.
Florida Bar Number 000000
Law Firm
Main Street
Anytown, Fla.

TABLE OF CONTENTS

TABLE OF AUTHORITIES

CASES

FEDERAL RULES OF APPELLATE PROCEDURE

UNITED STATES CODE

UNITED STATES CONSTITUTION

MISCELLANEOUS

STATEMENT OF SUBJECT MATTER JURISDICTION IN THE UNITED STATES DISTRICT COURT

The defendant was indicted in the United States District Court for the Middle District of Florida on March 16, 2000. The indictment charged her with violating 21 U.S.C.S. § 841 (a)(1) (Lexis L. Publg. 1997) for possession with intent to distribute a quantity of methampetamines. (A. 21). On May 16, 2000, the trial court granted the defendant's motion to suppress the methamphetamines found in her possession and the tape recording of her incriminating statements. (A. 25).

STATEMENT OF JURISDICTION

This is an appeal from a suppression order of the United States District Court for the Middle District of Florida in a criminal case pursuant to a Motion under Rule 4(b) of the Federal Rules of Appellate Procedure. Jurisdiction in the United States Court of Appeals for the Eleventh Circuit is invoked under 28 U.S.C.S. § 1291 (Lexis L. Publg. 1986), which provides that the Court of Appeals has jurisdiction from all final decisions of the United States District Court. Defendant's motion to suppress was granted on July 12, 2000. On July 20, 2000, a timely Notice of Appeal was filed from which this appeal follows. (A. 25, 27).

STATEMENT OF THE ISSUES

1. Did the trial court err in granting the motion to suppress methamphetamines seized from defendant Estrada's purse after she gave the officer consent to search her purse? (A. 3–4).
2. Did the trial court err in granting the motion to suppress the tape recording of the defendants' conversation made while the defendants were seated in the rear seat of the patrol car? (A. 4).

STATEMENT OF THE CASE

On March 14, 2000 a highway patrol officer stopped the defendant and her driver on I-95 because the car was travelling 15 miles per hour over the speed limit. (A. 3–4). After the officer saw glass vials containing crack cocaine in the driver's lap, the officer asked them to wait in the patrol car while the officer searched the car. As she was walking towards the patrol car, defendant consented to a search of her purse. The officer found methamphetamine powder in a brown envelope in her purse. The officer recorded the defendant's statements while she was seated in the patrol car with the driver. The defendant was arrested and taken into custody. (A. 5). She was provided an initial detention hearing on March 15, 2000. (A. 20). On March 16, 2000 an indictment was filed charging her with a violation of 21 U.S.C.S. § 841 (a)(1) for possession with intent to distribute a quantity of methamphetamines. She was arraigned the same day and entered a not guilty plea. (A. 21).

A trial date was set for May 18, 2000 for a jury trial. Prior to trial defendant Estrada filed a motion to suppress the methamphetamines found in her purse and the defendants filed a motion to suppress the tape recording. The district court granted both motions at a suppression hearing on May 16, 2000. (A. 22).

STATEMENT OF THE FACTS

Officer Green was patrolling the southbound lanes of I-95 when he observed a car travelling at an excessive rate of speed. The radar in the patrol car showed that the car was travelling 80 in a 65 mile per hour speed zone. (A. 1–2).

After stopping the car, Officer Green approached the driver's side of the car and requested the driver's license and car registration. While the driver searched his wallet for the documents, Officer Green looked through the open window and noticed a glass vial containing small kernels of an off-white substance in the driver's lap. Believing the vial to contain crack cocaine, Officer Green announced that he was seizing it. He asked the driver and passenger to exit the car and asked the driver for his wallet. Officer Green identified the driver as Luis Briones from his driver's license. (A. 3–4).

As the passenger got out of the car, Officer Green struck up a conversation with her. She said that her name was Cruz Estrada. Officer Green explained that he would have to search their car but that they could wait in the patrol car for their comfort and safety. The defendant turned back to the car, explaining that she had to retrieve something. She reached into the car and pulled out her purse, which had fallen behind the front seat. As the defendant passed him on the way to the patrol car, Officer Green asked if he could search her purse. Without responding, the defendant held out her purse to him. Inside her purse, Officer Green found a brown paper envelope. When Officer Green asked her what was in the envelope, defendant claimed that she did not know, that someone had given it to her to give to a friend in Miami. When Officer Green opened the envelope, he found a quantity of white powder that he believed to be methamphetamines. (A. 4).

The two waited in the patrol car while Officer Green searched the car. The tape of their conversation contains several incriminating statements, including defendant's admission that the envelope was hers and that it contained illegal drugs. (A. 4–5).

SUMMARY OF ARGUMENT

Over the years, courts have recognized a variety of exceptions to the search warrant requirement of the Fourth Amendment in recognition that exigent circumstances often do not allow an officer time to obtain a search warrant. This case illustrates the tension between the officer's duty to collect evidence of the illegal drug trade and the individual's privacy concerns. Consent had long enabled an officer to conduct a search, even without probable cause. Even without consent but upon probable cause, an officer may search a car and any containers within the car, without regard to their ownership. A standard law enforcement technique has been to ask suspects to wait in the officer's patrol car while the officer searches the suspects' car; to obtain evidence, the officer tape records any statements the suspects unwisely make while in the patrol car.

The government argues that two exceptions to the search warrant requirement allowed Officer Green to search the defendant's purse. Defendant's motion to suppress the contents of her purse should be denied either because defendant consented to the search or because probable cause to search the car allows Officer Green to search containers found in the car. Defendant has argued that the tape containing her incriminating statements should be suppressed because the tape was made in violation of the federal eavesdropping statutes. There is no ground to suppress the tape under the statutes; the statutes prohibit taping only if there is a reasonable expectation that the conversation is private. Society would not recognize any conversation of suspects in a patrol car to be private.

ARGUMENT

I. THE MOTION TO SUPPRESS THE METHAMPHETAMINES FOUND IN DEFENDANT'S PURSE SHOULD HAVE BEEN DENIED EITHER BECAUSE DEFENDANT CONSENTED TO THE SEARCH OR THE PURSE FELL UNDER THE CONTAINER EXCEPTION TO THE SEARCH WARRANT REQUIREMENT.

A. Because it was objectively reasonable to believe that Defendant consented to the search of her purse, the motion to suppress the methamphetamines found in her purse should have been denied.

Once a vehicle is stopped, the officer can search the car with consent. An occupant can consent to the search of the occupant's belongings. *United States v. Jimeno*, 500 U.S. 248, 251 (1991). Even without consent, the officer can search the car if there is probable cause of criminal activity. The officer is entitled to search containers found in the car and suspected of holding the object of the officer's search, no matter who owns the container. *Wyoming v. Houghton*, 526 U.S. 295, 300–01 (1999). An officer may not search someone's person without probable cause. *Id.* at 303.

The search of defendant's purse is constitutional if she consented to the search or the container exception to the search warrant requirement extends to her purse. The United States Supreme Court has stated the standard for determining when an individual has consented to the search of a car. *Jimeno*, 500 U.S. at 251. This portion of this brief will explain why the consent standard has been met. As far as the container exception is concerned, the United States Supreme Court recently held that "police officers with probable cause to search a car may inspect passengers' belongings found in the car that are capable of concealing the object of the search.". *Houghton*, 526 U.S. at 307. The facts of *Jimeno*, *Houghton*, and *Estrada* will be compared to show that the search of the defendant's purse was constitutional.

In *Jimeno*, Officer Trujillo overheard a telephone call from a public telephone in which Jimeno was discussing a drug deal. Trujillo followed Jimeno's car and stopped Jimeno for failure to stop when turning right on red. After informing Jimeno about the traffic violation, Trujillo

> went on to say that he had reason to believe that respondent was carrying narcotics in his car, and asked permission to search the car. He explained that respondent did not have to consent to a search of the car. Respondent stated that he had nothing to hide, and gave Trujillo permission to search the automobile.

500 U.S. at 249–50. Trujillo found drugs in a brown paper bag on the car floorboard. *Id.* at 250.

The Court then set forth the test for determining whether consent was given. "The standard for measuring the scope of a suspect's consent under the Fourth Amendment is that of "objective reasonableness—what would the typical person have understood by the exchange between the officer and the suspect?" *Id.* at 251. Applying this standard, the Court found that Jimeno had consented to the search of the bag.

The facts of *Jimeno* and *Estrada* are similar in that the two cars were stopped for alleged traffic violations, the two defendants consented to searches, and the officers searched containers. The facts surrounding the consent issue are substantially similar. Trujillo told Jimeno that the officer suspected that there were drugs in the car and explained that Jimeno did not have to consent to the search. When Trujillo asked Jimeno's permission, Jimeno claimed that he had nothing to hide and explicitly consented to the search. Officer Green made a statement, "you don't mind if I search, do you?" Officer Green did not have time to explain that the defendant did not have to consent before she held out her purse to him.

In *Jimeno*, the container was a brown paper bag located on the floor of the car. In *Estrada*, the container was defendant's purse, hanging from her shoulder. If anything, it was more objectively reasonable to believe that the defendant in this case had consented to the search of her purse than that Jimeno consented to the search of the brown paper bag. The defendant's implied consent of offering her purse to Officer Green made it clear that she was consenting to the search of that particular container. It was not as clear that Jimeno consented to the search of the brown paper bag when he consented to the search of the car. In *Jimeno*, the trial court had granted Jimeno's motion to suppress the contents of the brown paper bag. The Florida District Court of Appeals and the Florida Supreme Court affirmed. *Id.* at 250.

Applying the objective reasonableness standard, it is objectively reasonable to believe that the defendant in this case had consented to the search of her purse. Her overt action makes it objectively reasonable to believe that she consented.

3

B. Because the purse was found in a car that was searched upon probable cause that it contained illegal drugs, the container exception to the search warrant requirement applied and the methamphetamines should not have been suppressed.

As far as the container exception is concerned, the United States Supreme Court recently held that "police officers with probable cause to search a car may inspect passengers' belongings found in the car that are capable of concealing the object of the search." *Houghton*, 526 U.S. at 307. The facts of *Houghton* and *Estrada* will be compared to determine that the search of Cruz' purse was constitutional.

In *Houghton*, David Young was stopped for speeding and a faulty brake light. After the officer saw a hypodermic syringe in Young's pocket, Young admitted that he used it to take drugs. The officer asked the two female passengers seated in the front seat to exit the car and the officer searched the car. The officer found Houghton's purse on the back seat of the car. Searching the purse, the officer found a brown pouch that contained drug paraphernalia and a syringe containing methamphetamine in a large enough quantity for a felony conviction. Houghton claimed that the brown pouch was not hers. The officer also found a black container pouch that contained drug paraphernalia and a syringe containing a smaller amount of methamphetamine, insufficient for a felony conviction. Houghton's arms showed fresh needle-marks. The officer arrested her. 526 U.S. at 297–98.

The issue in *Houghton* was "whether police officers violate the Fourth Amendment when they search a passenger's personal belongings inside an automobile that they have probable cause to believe contains contraband." *Id.* at 297. The Court held "that police officers with probable cause to search a car may inspect passengers' belongings found in the car that are capable of concealing the object of the search." *Id.* at 307. The Court first relied on a 1982 case in which the Court had found that, where there was probable cause to search a car, it was constitutionally permissible to search containers found in the car that might hold the object of the search. *Id.* at 301–02. The Court noted that an individual carrying a package in a vehicle travelling on the public roads has a reduced expectation of privacy. *Id.* at 303. The Court found no reason to afford more protection to a container owned by a passenger than a container owned by the driver. *Id.* at 305.

The facts of *Houghton* and this case are very similar in that the two cars were stopped for alleged traffic violations, the passengers exited the cars, leaving their purses in the back seat, and the officers searched a passenger's purse. The facts of the two cases differ slightly in that Houghton at first disclaimed ownership of the purse. In contrast, this defendant returned to the car to retrieve her purse and offered it to Officer Green.

Applying the holding in *Houghton* to *Estrada*, Officer Green's search of defendant's purse was constitutional. When Officer Green discovered the vial containing what he believed to be crack cocaine in the driver's possession, that gave Officer Green probable cause to search the car and all containers in the car that might contain illegal drugs. Defendant's purse was of the size that it might contain illegal drugs and it was initially found in the car. Either of the two occupants might have concealed illegal drugs in defendant's purse as Officer Green pulled them over. Because of the substantial similarities between *Houghton* and *Estrada*, this court should find that Officer Green's search was constitutional.

II. THE MOTION TO SUPPRESS THE TAPE OF THE DEFENDANT'S CONVERSATION IN THE REAR SEAT OF THE PATROL CAR SHOULD HAVE BEEN DENIED BECAUSE THE CONVERSATION WAS NOT PROTECTED AS AN ORAL COMMUNICATION UNDER 18 U.S.C.S §§ 2510–2515 (Lexis L. Publg. 1993 & Supp. 2000).

A. Because Defendant had no reasonable expectation of privacy while seated in the rear seat of a patrol car, the motion to suppress the tape containing Defendant's incriminating statements should have been denied.

The federal eavesdropping statutes protect certain types of face-to-face conversations against interception; however to be protected, the conversation must qualify as an "oral communication." Under the statutes, an " 'oral communication' means any oral communications uttered by a person exhibiting an expectation that such communication is not subject to interception under circumstances justifying such expectation. . . ." 18 U.S.C.S. § 2510 (2) (Lexis L. Publg. 2000). Thus, a conversation is not an oral communication unless the conversants expect that the conversation is private and an objective third party would consider that expectation reasonable.

It is illegal to intercept an oral communication. "[A]ny person who . . . intentionally intercepts . . . any oral communication . . . shall be punished." 18 U.S.C.S. § 2511 (1) (Lexis L. Publg. 1993). One exception to this prohibition involves a police officer; however, the police officer must be party to the conversation or one conversant must have consented to the taping for the exception to apply. "It shall not be unlawful under this chapter for a person acting under color of law to intercept [an] . . . oral . . . communication where such person is a party to the communication or one of the parties has given prior consent to the interception." 18 U.S.C.S. § 2511 (2)(c) (Lexis L. Publg. 1993). If an oral communication is taped in violation of the eavesdropping statutes, the conversation cannot be used as evidence in court. "Whenever any . . . oral communication has been intercepted, no part of the contents of such communication and no evidence derived therefrom may be received in evidence in any trial, hearing, or other proceeding . . . before an court . . . if the disclosure of that information would be in violation of this chapter." 18 U.S.C.S. § 2515 (Lexis L. Publg. 1993).

Thus, if defendant's conversation was an oral communication, it should be suppressed. Whether the conversation is an oral communication turns on whether the defendant had a reasonable expectation of privacy while seated in the rear seat of the patrol car. One prong of the two-prong test is satisfied; defendant and the driver appear to have had an expectation of privacy or they would not have made incriminating statements. The other prong of the test is whether their expectation was reasonable. They were not sitting in a privately-owned car. They were sitting in the officer's car. While an expectation of privacy in a privately-owned car would have been reasonable, an expectation of privacy in the officer's car was not reasonable. The officer's car is equivalent to the officer's office. If defendant and the driver were conversing in an office of a police station, it would not be reasonable to expect privacy.

In a case with similar facts, the issue before the United States Court of Appeals for the Eleventh Circuit was "whether the district court erred in denying the motion to suppress the tapes resulting from the secret recording of McKinnon's pre-arrest conversations while he sat in the back seat of the police car." *United States v. McKinnon*, 985 F.2d 525, 526 (11th Cir. 1993).

In *McKinnon*, police officers stopped a pick-up truck for failure to travel in a single lane on the Florida Turnpike. Theodore Pressley was driving and Steve McKinnon was the passenger. Pressley consented to the search of his vehicle. While the officers were searching, McKinnon and Pressley waited in the rear seat of the patrol car. There they made incriminating statements that were secretly recorded by the officers. The officers arrested them after finding cocaine in the truck and they were placed in the rear seat of the patrol car. The officers again recorded McKinnon's and Pressley's incriminating statements. *Id.*

The *McKinnon* court considered the meaning of the term "oral communication" under the federal statutes. An oral communication is protected against taping. If a conversation is taped in violation of the statutes, the tape may be suppressed. A conversation is an oral communication only if the conversants exhibited a subjective expectation of privacy and the expectation of privacy was objectively reasonable. The court seemed to agree with the government's argument that a patrol car functions as the officer's office and the rear seat of the patrol car functions as a jail cell. *Id.* at 527. The court held "that McKinnon did not have a reasonable or justifiable expectation of privacy for conversations he held while seated in the back seat area of a police car." *Id.* at 528.

In examining the facts of *McKinnon* and *Estrada*, the facts concerning the taping seem virtually identical. In each case, an officer asked two individuals to wait in the patrol car prior to their arrest. The officer taped their conversation in the rear seat of the patrol car; the conversation contained incriminating statements. One difference between the two cases is that the officer in *McKinnon* also taped McKinnon's conversation following his arrest. This difference is not significant because an arrestee held in the back of a patrol car would have a lesser expectation of privacy than a person not under arrest.

A number of state and a number of federal courts, other than the *McKinnon* court, have faced the issue of whether an officer may secretly tape a conversation of individuals seated in the rear seat of a patrol car. In each case the court has said that taping is permissible. Carol M. Bast & Joseph B. Sanborn, Jr., *Not Just any Sightseeing Tour: Surreptitious Taping in a Patrol Car*, 32 Crim. L. Bull. 123, 130–31 (1996).

Although persuasive authority in other circuits, *McKinnon* is mandatory authority in this circuit. The facts concerning the taping are virtually identical in *McKinnon* and *Estrada*. A number of other state and federal courts have also held that there is no reasonable expectation of privacy for persons seated in the back of a patrol car. Therefore, a court should find that Cruz and Luis had no reasonable expectation of privacy while they were seated in the rear seat of the patrol car. Because they did not have a reasonable expectation of privacy, their conversation was not protected against taping as an oral communication. Therefore, a court would not suppress the tape under the federal eavesdropping statutes.

Defendant has also made the argument that the search of her purse tainted the tape recording. Obviously, were the court to deny the defendant's motion to suppress the illegal drugs, there would be no taint that could attach to the tape. Even were the court to grant the defendant's motion to suppress the methamphetamines, the court should not grant the motion to suppress the tape. In all probability, defendant would have made the incriminating statements even if Officer Green had not searched her purse.

B. Because the officer followed standard procedure in requesting the defendants to wait in the patrol car, the defendants' incriminating statements were not related to the prior search of the car and the tape containing defendant's incriminating statements should not have been suppressed.

Where a police officer obtains evidence in a unconstitutional manner, that evidence is excluded from use at trial. If that evidence leads the officer to other evidence, the other evidence is derivative of the first evidence. The derivative evidence is known as fruit of the poisonous tree and is also inadmissible. Generally, evidence that is tainted by the prior unconstitutional conduct is inadmissible; however, in some instances the second evidence is admissible because the connection between the unconstitutionally-seized evidence and the subsequently obtained evidence is marginal.

The tape is not derivative of the evidence the officer discovered searching Estrada's purse. The tape should not have been suppressed.

CONCLUSION

For the reasons set forth above, the government requests this court to reverse the district court's order suppressing the methamphetamines and the tape recording and remand the case to the district court for trial.

Respectfully submitted,

____

Florida Attorney, Esq.
Florida Bar Number 000000
Law Firm
Main Street

CHAPTER 18 SUMMARY

- The appellate brief is a written statement submitted to an appellate court to persuade it of the correctness of one's position.
- When a party appeals, the appellate court's job is to review what the lower court did to determine whether the lower court committed reversible error.
- The standard of review is different depending on whether the appellate court is reviewing a finding of fact, a ruling of law, or a ruling on a question involving law and fact.
- The appellate court is bound to follow the trial court's finding of fact unless a jury finding was unreasonable or a trial judge's finding was clearly erroneous.
- When deciding a question of law or a question involving law and fact, the appellate court is free to reach a ruling different from that of the trial court.
- The appellate brief is persuasive in tone.
- Follow any applicable court rules (including local rules) governing the appellate brief.
- Rule 28 of the Federal Rules of Appellate Procedure requires:
  A table of contents;
  A table of authorities cited;
  A statement of subject matter jurisdiction;
  A statement of appellate jurisdiction;
  A statement of the issues;
  A statement of the case;
  A statement of the facts;
  An argument; and
  A conclusion.

CYBER EXAMPLES

1. When writing legal documents for the first time, it may be helpful to look at examples. This chapter provides some examples. A number of law school professors have posted sample documents on the Internet. To find some of these documents you might access Jurist: The Law Professor Network (http://jurist.law.pitt.edu). (Click on "Law School," "Law School Courses," and then on "Legal Research and Writing.") At the time this book was being written, Professor Gregory Berry at Howard University School of Law had posted a number of student documents in his "Writing Hall of Fame" found under "Berry's Advice." Those documents included client letters, memoranda, motion reply briefs, a settlement agreement, and appellate briefs. Also, Professor Colleen Barger at the University of Arkansas at Little Rock School of Law had a web site that links to pages of other legal research and writing professors (http://www.ualr.edu/~cmbarger/).
2. The Lexis law school site (http://lawschool.lexis.com) includes legal writing information. Click on "My School," "Web Lectures," and then on "Legal Research and Writing."
3. To take some tips on appellate writing from the North Dakota Supreme Court, access http://www.court.state.nd.us/Court/Filing/Tips.htm.
4. LLRX-ResearchWire:Litigator's Internet Resource Guide, located at <http://www.llrx.com>, offers access to federal and state court rules at http://www.llrx.com/courtrules/. See if you can access the various court rules for your state. Find local federal and state court rules that apply to the area in which you are located.

EXERCISES FOR CHAPTER 18

1. Pick one of the research problems from appendix E.
2. Research the problem you have chosen.
3. Write an appellate brief using your research.

APPENDIX A

SEARCH AND SEIZURE

INTRODUCTION

The search and seizure problem and the primary sources contained in this appendix can be used as the basis for research and writing exercises at the end of the appendix. The first time you read this appendix, read the problem carefully and skim the following section to gain some familiarity with the law you might find in the law library if you were researching the problem. The search and seizure topic was selected because it is fairly easy to understand and seems to be interesting to most students. In addition, you will be learning some substantive law as you read and work through the exercises.

THE WILLIAMS SEARCH AND SEIZURE PROBLEM

Ralph Williams is the owner of All-Right Paint Shop in a small town in Maine. The shop is in the business of repainting cars. Ralph had been operating the paint shop for 10 years when he decided that he would like to open a new business selling antique cars. (He had gotten the idea from advertisements for antique cars in car-trader magazines.) He thought that he would buy a few antique cars now and then would open the new business after he had a number of cars in stock. The money to buy the first cars would come from profits from the paint business and a home equity loan on his home. Ray Williams, Ralph's brother, offered to quit his job to manage the new business as soon as the brother had built up an inventory of a few cars.

After thoroughly reading the advertisements in the car-trader magazines, the brothers decided to head to Miami to look for antique cars. On a friend's advice, the brothers carried $35,000 in cash. The friend had told them that car dealers, especially in the Miami area, require cash. The friend also cautioned them that he had read articles about racial profiling, where law enforcement officers allegedly stop cars driven by blacks or hispanics. These stops occurred so often that many minorities joked that they had been stopped for the traffic offenses of DWB or DWH (driving while black or driving while hispanic).

In the early 1990s, a large number of cars were stopped by Volusia County sheriff officers on Interstate 95 in Florida. Cash was taken from a number of cars, although no arrests were made. The stops typically were made in the evening or early morning hours. Most of the cars stopped had rental or out-of-state tags. Almost three-quarters of the drivers were male, 85 percent were black, and just over half were between 18 and 29 years of age. Three-quarters of the cars stopped contained two or more occupants.

The trip was uneventful for a number of hours. The brothers stopped only for gasoline and food and took turns driving. As it grew dark, Ralph dozed off in the passenger seat, waking up off and on while Ray drove. Ralph noticed several times when he woke up that Ray seemed to be tired, too. He was driving below the 55-mph speed limit, and was letting the car weave ever so slightly within its lane. At one point Ralph grabbed the wheel and steered it back into the lane as the car's outside front tire crossed the center line. When Ralph asked Ray whether he was too tired to drive, Ray said that he was a little tired but would get some coffee at the next rest stop. Ray did not notice that, about the time his car was weaving, he had passed an unmarked police car parked on the shoulder of the road. The officer in the unmarked car had observed Ray weaving and the officer radioed ahead to other officers to be on the watch for Ray's car.

A few minutes later, Ray saw two marked patrol cars parked in the median, one with its lights shining across the southbound lanes of traffic and the other with its headlights shining across the northbound lanes of traffic. As Ray learned later, the patrol cars contained sheriff officers and DEA agents participating in a joint drug task force. Ray kept his eyes on the road while passing the patrol cars and then glanced in the rearview mirror. The patrol car pointing in his direction was pulling out onto the highway. As if in a bad dream, Ray watched as the patrol car came up behind him, put on its flashing lights, and pulled him over.

Ray was so nervous his hand was shaking as he handed over his driver's license and car registration. The officer examined Ray's driver's license and car registration and asked the brothers where they were going. They said they were going to Miami on business. The officer returned the license and registration and was turning back to the patrol car when he said,

> "You don't mind if I search your car, do you?"

The brothers were too surprised to say anything. Without giving them a chance to respond, the patrolman immediately opened the back door of the car and started examining the inside of the car with his flashlight. He picked up the cash box from the floorboard behind the front passenger seat, opened it, and found the $35,000 in cash.

When he saw the cash, the officer said, "This is an awful lot of cash to be carrying around. Where did you boys get this kind of money?" He looked at them in disbelief as they told him their story. Then he said, "I don't know whether I believe your story. I'll have to take this with me." When the brothers asked when they could get their money back, the patrolman suggested they contact the local Drug Enforcement Agency office in the morning and gave them the telephone number. The brother signed a receipt and the patrolman left.

The brothers decided to go to the nearest rest stop and wait until they could call the DEA office. When they called the office, they were told they would have to file suit to get the money back. They were understandably upset, believing that the patrolman chose not to believe their story because they are Afro-Americans. They decide to consult an attorney to determine what to do.

EXAMPLES OF PRIMARY AND SECONDARY SOURCES FOUND AFTER RESEARCHING SEARCH AND SEIZURE PROBLEM

As more fully explained in chapter 1, primary sources contain the law itself and secondary sources contain commentary on the law. Appendix A contains examples of primary and secondary sources you might find if you researched the search and seizure problem.

The text of the Fourth Amendment to the United States Constitution appears on the next page. Figures A-1 through A-5 contain newspaper articles concerning racial profiling and contraband forfeiture statutes. Figures A-6 and A-7 contain two United States Supreme Court cases. In the first case, *Florida v. Jimeno*, the Court determined whether the suspect had given a police officer consent to search a container found in a car. In the second case, *Whren v. United States*, the Court determined whether it is permissible for a police officer to stop a vehicle for a traffic violation; the vehicle's occupants claimed that the alleged reason for the stop was a pretext, allowing the police officer to stop the vehicle based on the occupants' race. Figures A-8, A-9, and A-10 contain the text of federal forfeiture statutes. Figure A-11 contains text excerpted from a criminal law and procedure textbook; the text gives background on search and seizure and the exclusionary rule. As you glance over these examples, try to understand the basic subject matter and notice the format of the various sources.

> The United States Constitution
> Amendment IV. Search and Seizure
>
> The right of the people to be secure in their persons, houses, papers, and effects, against unreasonable searches and seizures, shall not be violated, and no Warrants shall issue, but upon probable cause, supported by Oath or affirmation, and particularly describing the place to be searched, and the persons or things to be seized.

RESEARCH AND WRITING EXERCISES

1. The federal forfeiture statutes are included in this appendix. Many states also have forfeiture statutes. Research your state's statutes to determine if your state has forfeiture statutes. Compare your state's forfeiture statutes to the federal statutes in this appendix.
2. Over the years, the federal forfeiture statutes were amended a number of times, most recently in April 2000. Research whether the statutes were amended since this book was published.
3. Locate federal administrative regulations governing forfeiture procedure under 21 U.S.C. § 881.
4. To read more on racial profiling, go to the American Civil Liberties Union's web site (http://www.aclu.org) and search "racial profiling" and "driving while black."
5. To read more on forfeiture, go to Cornell Law School's web site (http://www.law.cornell.edu/background/forfeiture/) and access The LII backgrounder on forfeiture.
6. Write a law office memo concerning the Williams Brothers. You may want to use the outline at the end of this appendix as a guide.

FLOWCHART FOR OFFICE MEMO ON WILLIAMS BROTHERS

Background: to have a judge determine whether the money should be forfeited, the Williams brothers would first have to follow statutory requirements (file a claim). Once the judicial proceeding is filed, the brothers could file a motion to have the money excluded from evidence. They would allege that it should be excluded from evidence because the stop and seizure violated their right against unreasonable search and seizure. If the brothers did not file a claim, the government would declare their money forfeited in an administrative proceeding.

The following is a flowchart of the determinations the judge would have to make.

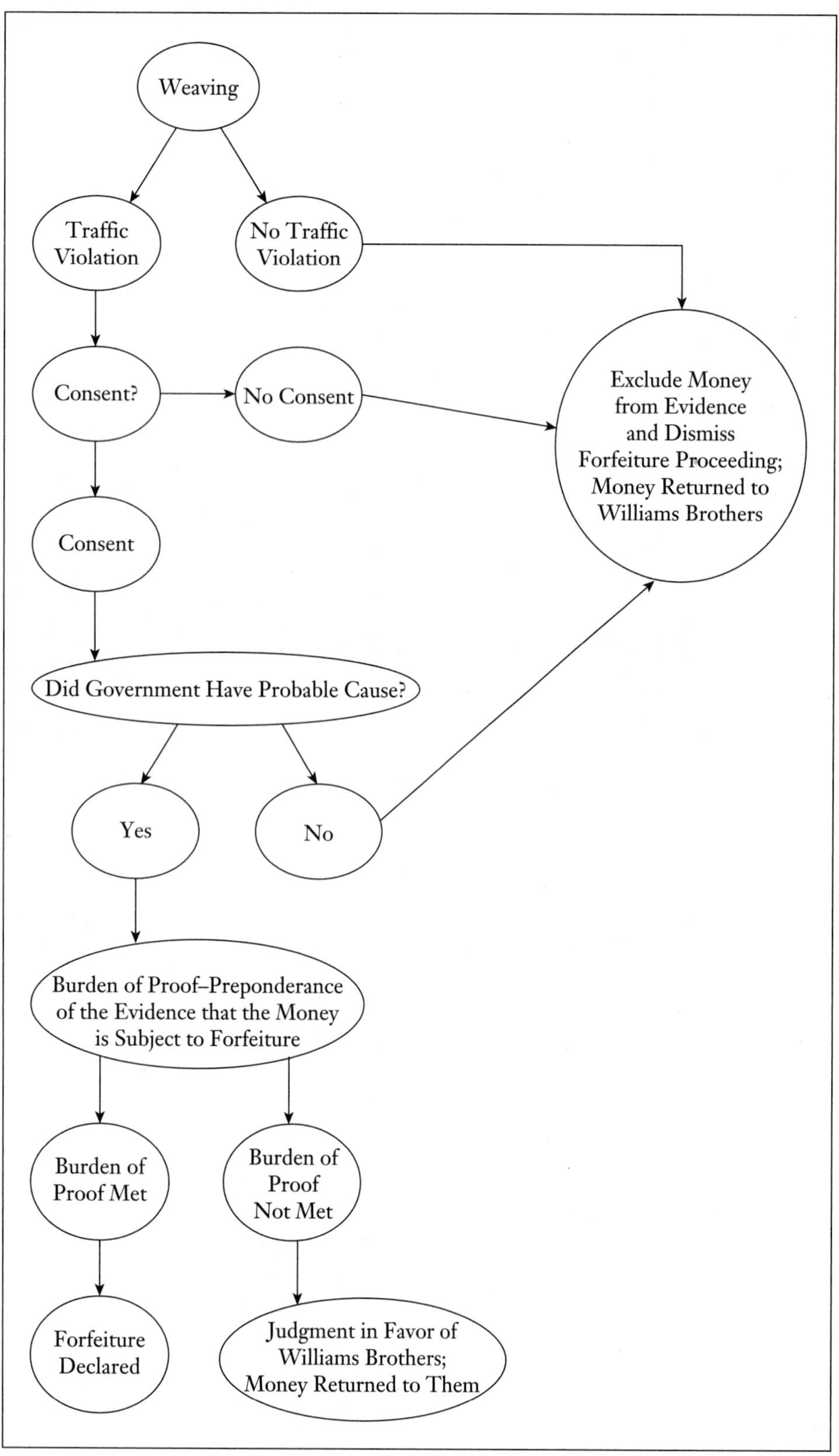
Weaving
Traffic Violation
No Traffic Violation
Consent?
No Consent
Exclude Money from Evidence and Dismiss Forfeiture Proceeding; Money Returned to Williams Brothers
Consent
Did Government Have Probable Cause?
Yes
No
Burden of Proof–Preponderance of the Evidence that the Money is Subject to Forfeiture
Burden of Proof Met
Burden of Proof Not Met
Forfeiture Declared
Judgment in Favor of Williams Brothers; Money Returned to Them

SAMPLE OUTLINE FOR OFFICE MEMO

The following is a sample outline for an office memo concerning the Williams brothers. Read through it and think how it could be expanded and what you would do differently.

To: [professor's name]
From: [writer's name]
Re: Whether the confiscated money will be returned to the Williams brothers.
Date: [date on which research completed or office memo written]

Facts: [state basic facts; be sure to describe in detail the interchange between the officer and the Williams brothers]

Issues:

1. Was the officer's stop of the Williams brothers car constitutional?
2. Did the officer have consent to search the Williams brothers car where the officer said, "You don't mind if I search do you ?" and proceeded with the search without giving the brothers a chance to respond?

Answers:

1. Because the officer observed the car weaving, the officer had probable cause to stop the car to investigate for possible careless driving, reckless driving, or driving under the influence.
2. Because the Williams brother did not consent to the search, the search was unconstitutional and the money should be returned to them.

Reasoning:

I. Thesis paragraph
   A. Drug courier or law-abiding citizen
   B. Racial profiling
   C. Violation of driver's right against search and seizure
II. Law common to issues 1 and 2—Fourth Amendment to the United States Constitution (quote)
III. Reasoning for issue 1
   A. Law—*Whren v. United States*
   B. Application of law to facts re alleged traffic violation
      1. similarities between *Whren* and *Williams*
         a. cars stopped for alleged traffic violation
         b. race claimed as a factor
         c. two occupants in each car
      2. differences between *Whren* and *Williams*
         a. Cocaine found in *Whren;* cash found in *Williams*
         b. *Whren*—turning without signaling and speeding; *Williams*—weaving
         c. *Whren*—D.C. area known for illegal drugs; *Willams*—highway
         d. *Whren*—unmarked patrol car; *Willams*—unmarked and marked patrol cars
   C. Conclusion for issue 1
      Checking for a sleepy or drunk driver is a legitimate reason for a traffic stop; because the Williams car swerved, the officer had probable cause of a traffic violation and the stop was constitutional.
IV. Reasoning for issue 2
   A. Law—*Jimeno*
   B. Application of law to facts
      1. Similarities between *Jimeno* and *Williams*
         a. cars stopped after alleged traffic violation
         b. officer asked to search car
         c. officer found something in car
         d. two passengers in car
      2. Differences between *Jimeno* and *Williams*
         a. officer explained to Jimeno that officer suspected drugs in car; officer did not explain to Williams brothers object of search
         b. Jimeno specifically gave consent to the search; Williams brothers remained silent
         c. officer waited until Jimeno consented to the search before beginning search; officer did not give the Williams brothers sufficient time to respond
         d. officer found cocaine in Jimeno's car; the officer found money in the Williams car
         e. Jimeno arrested; Williams brothers not arrested
   C. Conclusion for issue 2
      Differences between *Jimeno* and *Williams* show that Jimeno clearly consented to the search while the Williams brothers did not; therefore, because the Williams Brothers did not consent to the search, it was unconstitutional; the Williams brothers should be successful in having the money excluded from evidence, the case dismissed, and the money returned to them.

FIGURE A-1 " 'Racial Profiling' Is Bad Policing," article from *The Wall Street Journal,* June 2, 1999.

'Racial Profiling' Is Bad Policing

By Sophia A. Nelson And Brian W. Jones

Are America's cops on the verge of crisis? A cascade of revelations this year has further eroded many Americans' confidence that the nation's law-enforcement agencies function free of racial bias. But while police brutality makes most of the headlines, mainstream black Americans find themselves more intimately identifying with stories of a more common form of official bias: the use of race to "profile" suspects.

In April, New Jersey Attorney General Peter Verniero released a report finding that state troopers routinely used the race of drivers on the New Jersey Turnpike to decide whom to stop and search. Gov. Christine Todd Whitman declared that New Jersey had been "infected by [a] national problem." But rather than provoking surprise and outrage among blacks, the report elicited a familiar anger and frustration. Many black Americans have long swapped stories of confrontations with traffic-patrol officers, apparently precipitated by little more than a policeman's stereotypes about the types of cars and neighborhoods in which black citizens should be found. The phenomenon has a colloquial label—"DWB," or driving while black.

Given that black and Hispanic men commit a disproportionate share of violent and drug-related crimes in the U.S. today, reasonable people may ask why racial profiling should be so controversial. If black and Hispanic men are substantially more likely than others to commit serious crimes, is it not logical to include black or Hispanic ancestry in generalized criminal profiles? Perhaps. But a mere logical nexus between means and end is an insufficient governing principle for an institution—like law enforcement—that depends for its viability on the confidence of those that it serves.

Law-enforcement leaders and policy makers should be mindful of two significant social consequences of such official race-consciousness. First, allowing officers to use race as an element of probable cause places police departments on a slippery slope to civil-rights abuses. State-sanctioned race-consciousness—whether invidious or ostensibly benign—too frequently provides a pretext for officials to act on illegitimate biases. Accordingly, better to remove race from the tools of statecraft than risk sanctioning its impermissible official use.

Second and more important, permitting officers to use race as an element of probable cause encourages blacks and Hispanics to think that law-enforcement agencies cannot be trusted. These perceptions are often at odds with those held by most whites, which can create potentially volatile divisions within the community. Consider the racial perception gap laid bare in the wake of the trials of O.J. Simpson and the cops who beat Rodney King.

For a more recent example, look no further than the divergent attitudes of black and white New Jersey residents toward their state police. In a Star-Ledger/Eagleton Poll taken shortly after the release of the report on racial profiling, 84% of white New Jerseyites expressed confidence that state troopers were doing an excellent or good job patrolling the state's highways, a figure consistent with polls in prior years. By contrast, only 31% of black New Jerseyites surveyed expressed similar confidence in state troopers, down from 56% a year ago.

Black New Jerseyites' diminishing confidence in their law-enforcement officers should trouble anyone who believes that the authority of legitimate government derives from the consent of the governed. Clearly a substantial proportion of the governed in New Jersey and elsewhere lack confidence in the fundamental fairness of those purporting to protect them.

To make matters worse, the communities most in need of effective policing are those disproportionately populated by black and Hispanic citizens. Many of the nation's poorest urban communities are beset by crime and drugs. Honest, hardworking citizens in those cities are frequently the victims of crime. But those citizens frequently respond to the epidemic of crime not with crime-busting fervor, but with a pronounced ambivalence toward law-enforcement authorities, an ambivalence born of mistrust.

FIGURE A-1 (continued)

For honest cops seeking to make their urban beats safer, the ambivalence of law-abiding black and Hispanic citizens makes their jobs more difficult. Citizens who mistrust cops are less likely to provide tips and to cooperate with officers seeking information or assistance. Thus high-crime areas heavily populated by blacks and Hispanics are less safe than they would be if the police force enjoyed the support of law-abiding citizens.

How policy makers respond to the revelation that some police officers use race as a proxy for probable cause to stop and search certain citizens will tell us much about our civic commitment to effective crime fighting and about our commitment to genuinely representative government. So yes, America's cops *are* on the verge of a crisis. But sadly, as a result, so are those of us most in need of their protection.

Ms. Nelson, a senior fellow with the Center for New Black Leadership in Washington, served in the administration of Gov. Christine Todd Whitman. Mr. Jones, a San Francisco lawyer, is a director and former president of the Center for New Black Leadership.

FIGURE A-2 " 'Racial Profiling' Doesn't Prove Cops Are Racist," article from *The Wall Street Journal,* March 11, 1999.

'Racial Profiling' Doesn't Prove Cops Are Racist

By Jackson Toby

Late last month, New Jersey Gov. Christine Todd Whitman forced the resignation of Col. Carl A. Williams, superintendent of the New Jersey State Police, for "insensitivity" because of remarks he had made in a newspaper interview. In replying to accusations that the state police targeted black motorists for traffic stops on the New Jersey Turnpike, Col. Williams had insisted that there was no racial profiling and that stops were made only "on the basis of a traffic violation."

However, he also was quoted by the Newark Star-Ledger as saying that certain crimes were associated with certain ethnic groups and that it would be naive to think that race was not an issue in drug trafficking. "Two weeks ago," Mr. Williams reportedly said, "the president of the United States went to Mexico to talk . . . about drugs. He didn't go to Ireland. He didn't go to England."

Responding to that statement, a group of black state legislators, ministers and civil-rights advocates gathered to denounce Col. Williams as a racist. "His views are dastardly," said New Jersey Assemblyman Leroy J. Jones Jr. "He's unfit to hold such a critical, important office." Mr. Williams was dismissed hours later.

The Williams comments, along with the New York City police killing of Amadou Diallo, an unarmed black man, have contributed to the impression of widespread police racism. But neither Mr. Williams nor the officers involved in the Diallo shooting had to be racist to say or do what they did. A little perspective is in order here.

Begin with one of the most important ideas in modern criminology, and one that has revolutionized police practice—the belief that a good way to prevent robberies, murders and other serious felonies is to go after minor offenses. Thus, when William J. Bratton was chief of the Transit Police in New York City a decade ago, part of his strategy for controlling violence in the subway system was to order his officers to crack down on small infractions—fare beating, panhandling, graffiti, smoking, boisterous behavior.

Within two years of the policy's adoption, the number of felonies in the subway declined by more than 30%. Why? Well, one out of every six fare evaders stopped by the Transit Police in 1991 either was carrying a weapon or was wanted for another crime on an outstanding warrant. By paying attention to behavior that most people regard as not worth bothering about, the Transit Police prevented some violent crimes on the subways.

The same principle applies to drug traffickers on the highways: People who violate major laws are probably also inclined to violate minor ones, such as traffic regulations. Consequently, stopping motorists for traffic violations has led to the seizure of major

FIGURE A-2 (continued)

shipments of illegal drugs to Newark or New York—and even to the apprehension of a wanted murderer. The Oklahoma City bombing might have gone unpunished had the Perry, Okla., police not stopped Timothy McVeigh because he did not have a license plate on his pickup truck.

There is, of course, a civil-liberties cost to enlarging the police net. Cracking down on fare beaters on the New York subways snared (and embarrassed) passengers in a great hurry to get to appointments. Similarly, although the police have caught major drug traffickers by searching the vehicles of motorists stopped for traffic offenses on the New Jersey Turnpike, their success is counterbalanced by unsuccessful but intrusive vehicle searches of otherwise respectable citizens who made an illegal turn or drove faster than the speed limit. And a disproportionate number of those stopped were black or Hispanic. According to a survey sponsored by the New Jersey Office of the Public Defender, blacks accounted for 13% of drivers on the south end of the New Jersey Turnpike, 15% of speeders and 35% of those stopped by the state police.

Is this evidence of police racism? Not necessarily. True, most blacks and Hispanics are law-abiding. But if drug traffickers are disproportionately black or Hispanic, the police don't need to be racist to stop many minority motorists; they simply have to be efficient in targeting potential drug traffickers. It is an unfortunate fact that much higher proportions of black children than white grow up at a social disadvantage and are more tempted to break society's rules. Thus, although blacks are only 12% of the American population, in a recent year they comprised 56% of the arrests for murder, 42% of the arrests for rape, 61% of the arrests for robbery, 39% of the arrests for aggravated assault, 31% of the arrests for burglary, 33% of the arrests for larceny and 40% of the arrests for motor vehicle theft. Also 46% of state prison inmates—i.e., those actually convicted of crimes—were black (another 17% were Hispanic). Why should they not be equally overrepresented in drug trafficking, which is less easy to measure statistically?

Some police officers are no doubt racists and some are guilty of misconduct. But it is dangerous to make public policy on the basis of such horrible examples as the Amadou Diallo shooting. All professionals make mistakes: Surgeons operate on the wrong kidney; lawyers botch cross-examinations. Fairness requires that mistakes be looked at in the context of the more numerous examples of good judgment.

But the police deserve extra leeway for their mistakes because, unlike other professionals, they don't have the luxury of turning down unpleasant cases. They make house calls despite personal danger. They have to deal with not only criminals but also paranoid schizophrenics who have not taken their medication or suicidal people. The police come and do their best because the buck stops with them. Usually they succeed; occasionally, and sometimes tragically, they fail.

So should the New York City Police Department be convicted of racism? And should Mr. Williams have been fired as superintendent of the New Jersey State Police? Not in my opinion. True, the police in the Diallo case should have used better judgment, and Mr. Williams could have tiptoed more gently over the unpleasant reality that interdicting drug shipments on the New Jersey Turnpike requires stopping more black than white motorists. But he was defending his officers against what he considered a bum rap: that they were racists. By a wide margin, they are not.

Mr. Toby, a professor of sociology at Rutgers University, was director of the Institute for Criminological Research at Rutgers from 1919 to 1994.

FIGURE A-3 "Volusia to Pay Deputy $175,000 to End Suit," article from *The Orlando Sentinel,* September 11, 1999.

Volusia to pay deputy $175,000 to end suit

Frank Josenhans said his career had suffered since he helped a federal probe into Sheriff Bob Vogel's I-95 drug squad.

By Sandra Pedicini
OF THE SENTINEL STAFF

DELAND—A Volusia County deputy who said Sheriff Bob Vogel retaliated against him for assisting a federal investigation of the department will receive $175,000 in a settlement.

Frank Josenhans filed suit against the Volusia County Sheriff's Office last year, claiming his First Amendment rights had been violated. The 17-year veteran said he was unfairly disciplined and repeatedly transferred to undesirable jobs because he had angered Vogel years before, when he asked to be removed from the sheriff's controversial Interstate-95 drug squad.

The U.S. Justice Department eventually investigated charges that the squad had illegally targeted black and Hispanic drivers for traffic stops in order to search their cars. The team seized $8 million during a three-year period from motorists who were deemed suspicious.

A trial in Josenhans' case would likely have involved rehashing all the allegations of civil rights violations that had been made against the Sheriff's Office, County Attorney Dan Eckert said.

The settlement was the best option because the two trials—one in Circuit Court and another at the federal level—would have cost so much.

"The scope of the evidence on that would have caused a very lengthy trial, or trials," Eckert said. "So in the final analysis, we think this is a fair resolution of the thing."

As part of the settlement, Josenhans agreed to resign.

Sheriff's officials said they won't be sorry to see Josenhans depart. Josenhans, 46, has been working on a courthouse security detail.

"I'm sure Frank has made the decision he thinks is in the best interest of him and his family," Chief Deputy Leonard Davis said. "I certainly don't see that it's going to be detrimental to us at all."

During the federal investigation of the I-95 team, Josenhans had been portrayed by top sheriff's administrators as a disgruntled employee out to get his boss. The sheriff called Josenhans a liar after the deputy said Vogel specifically instructed the team to stop black and Hispanic drivers on a pretense, then search their cars.

Federal officials had begun reviewing Vogel's office in 1993 after an investigation by *The Orlando Sentinel.* In three of every four cases in which the drug squad took money from motorists, the newspaper reported, no charges were ever filed. And of that group, 90 percent were minorities.

Eighty percent of the cars searched were driven by minorities, although they represented a tiny fraction of all drivers on the interstate.

Under Florida's Contraband Forfeiture Act, officers can seize money and property, even if they merely suspect it has been—or may be—used for criminal purposes. Some of the Volusia seizures involved large amounts, along with hidden caches of drugs. The majority of the seizures, however, were relatively small amounts, with no drugs found. The squad was disbanded after the controversy.

The Justice Department ended its probe in 1997. It found direct evidence, as well as statistical and anecdotal evidence, that skin color was the primary reason drivers were stopped. But investigators decided there were gaps in the case and it could not be proved beyond a reasonable doubt.

Vogel said at the time that the probe was the work of unreliable witnesses and had never been objective.

The Volusia County Council will have to approve the settlement on Thursday. Council Chairwoman Pat Northey said she plans to vote in favor, but is not happy to pay so much.

"You could say I'm not happy about it, but it brings closure to it, and that's good for all of us," she said.

FIGURE A-3 (continued)

Josenhans said in his lawsuit that he was bounced around throughout the Sheriff's Office into jobs that paid less. Last year, he said he was making no more than he earned before Vogel's election in 1988.

Sheriff's officials said Josenhans' treatment wasn't unusual.

"I think, and I don't have the records here, I think some of the times Deputy Josenhans was moved were at his request," Davis said. "We have people that are moved frequently."

At one point, Josenhans said, he had to fingerprint inmates at the Volusia County Jail—a job usually done by jail personnel. He was not given a patrol car and was not given the electronic access code to enter the jail's operations center. In a strategy to cause him to lose his law enforcement certification, he said, the department denied him personal leave time to attend classes.

Josenhans also claimed he was the subject of internal affairs investigations.

Josenhans could not be reached for comment at his New Smyrna Beach home. His attorney, Frederick Morello, did not return phone calls.

FIGURE A-4 "Drug Evidence Can't Go to Court," article from *The Orlando Sentinel,* May 1, 1999.

Drug Evidence Can't Go to Court

A judge said the search was illegal. The case raised questions about racial profiling in traffic stops.

By Susan Jacobson

OF THE SENTINEL STAFF

KISSIMMEE—In a case that raises questions about the use of racial profiling in traffic stops, nearly 2 pounds of cocaine found during a stop on Florida's Turnpike can't be used in court, a judge has decided.

If the state does not appeal the ruling, Mac Dent, 22, likely will go free. He could have faced up to 15 years in prison.

Dent, a black construction worker from Tchula, Miss., was driving north on Florida's Turnpike Dec. 5 when Florida Highway Patrol Trooper Marlie Davis pulled him over, saying he was speeding at 85 mph.

Dent, who said his cruise control was set at 72 mph, was questioned and then given a traffic ticket after he was stopped south of St. Cloud.

Afterward, he was detained and queried further about matters including his level of education.

Trooper Dana Swatts of the drug interdiction squad patted Dent down and then walked his dog around the borrowed 1990 Oldsmobile Dent was driving.

The dog sniffed out 800 grams of cocaine in a plastic bag duct-taped under the hood and surrounded by coffee, an arrest report states. Drug agents estimated its street value at $40,000.

Troopers said Dent's behavior was suspicious because he acted nervous and was pacing and fidgeting. He also refused to allow his car to be searched, saying he was in a hurry to get home.

Circuit Judge Reginald K. Whitehead said that wasn't enough to constitute reasonable suspicion of illegal activity. He suppressed not only the drug, but statements Dent made.

The judge cited a 1997 case in which Florida's Fifth District Court of Appeal ruled a search is illegal if a traffic stop is unnecessarily prolonged so a dog can sniff a vehicle.

"They detained Mr. Dent after they were through with their legitimate reason to stop him," said his lawyer, Assistant Public Defender Marc Burnham.

Davis said she couldn't see into Dent's car and therefore didn't know his race when she pulled him over. However, Burnham said he suspected that race might have been an issue, as it has been in numerous cases in Florida and other states.

"If he was stopped because he was speeding, that's OK," Burnham said. "If she just stopped him because he was black and from Mississippi and driving north on the turnpike, that's wrong."

FIGURE A-5 "End Cash-Grab Abuse," article from *The Orlando Sentinel,* July 7, 1999.

End Cash-Grab Abuse

The U.S. House of Representatives' bold move would assure fair treatment of people whose cash police seize.

The U.S. House of Representatives has shown courage in voting overwhelmingly to tone down a law intended to allow law-enforcement authorities to seize assets, such as cash, from criminals.

Some lawmakers earlier had resisted challenging that law, out of fear that political opponents would brand them soft on crime.

But some law-enforcement authorities had twisted the law into a grab bag of abuse, making the House's recent action both necessary and long overdue.

The reforms would provide the badly needed assurance of fair treatment.

Under the existing law, officials have seized tens of millions of dollars in cash and property. In many cases, authorities never proved that the owners had taken part in a crime.

No one wins when the public views law enforcement as bullies who can take personal property on the basis of a flimsy suspicion.

That federal law has emboldened some local law-enforcement officials, such as Volusia County Sheriff Bob Vogel, to launch ruthless cash-seizure campaigns.

Volusia County deputies targeted minority motorists on Interstate 95, stopping drivers and searching their vehicles. In many cases, deputies seized any cash they found. Even when deputies couldn't tie the money to drugs, deputies pressured motorists to sign agreements that allowed the sheriff's office to keep some of the cash.

At hearings conducted during the past few years, House members heard a variety of complaints concerning the way federal agencies abused the law and victimized people whom they had not charged with a crime. Members also heard the process to challenge property seizures described as unfair, cumbersome and expensive.

Once House members understood the severity of the abuses, they responded impressively in approving a cash-seizure reform package 375 to 48, with strong bipartisan support. Many members who rarely agree with each other, such as U.S. Rep. Bill McCollum, R-Longwood, and Rep. Barney Frank, D-Massachusetts, voted in approval.

The reform package House members approved would not handcuff law-enforcement authorities. Police still can seize property if they find clear, convincing evidence that someone they stop has taken part in criminal activity, such as drug trafficking.

But under the reform package, owners of seized property would have more opportunity to challenge the police accusation.

Some key reform details include:

- Allowing judges to appoint legal counsel for poor people whose property is seized. Why should poor people not have the right to argue for the return of property?
- Dropping the requirement that, before challenging a seizure, a property owner must file a bond of 10 percent of the value of the item seized. That bond requirement would place an unfair burden on poor people.
- Allowing a property owner to sue the government if the seized property is destroyed while in government custody.
- Awarding interest to a property owner who wins the return of seized money.

If police use the asset-forfeiture law only on people actually involved in criminal activities, those changes should not hamper law enforcement. The changes are needed to protect those who are not criminals.

Now the U.S. Senate should join the reform movement.

FIGURE A-6 *Florida v. Jimeno*

FLORIDA v. JIMENO

Cite as 111 S.Ct. 1801 (1991)

500 U.S. 248, 114 L.Ed.2d 297
⊥248 FLORIDA, Petitioner
v.
Enio JIMENO et al.
No. 90-622.
Argued March 25, 1991.
Decided May 23, 1991.

State defendant's suppression motion for paper bag in defendant's automobile was granted by the Circuit Court, Dade County, Fredricka G. Smith, J., and State appealed. The Florida District Court of Appeal, 550 So.2d 1176, affirmed, and application for review was filed. The Florida Supreme Court, Grimes, J., 564 So.2d 1083, approved decision. Certiorari was granted. The Supreme Court, Chief Justice Rehnquist, held that criminal suspect's right to be free from unreasonable searches was not violated when, after he gave police officer permission to search his automobile, officer opened closed container found within car that might reasonably hold object of search.

Reversed and remanded.

Justice Marshall dissented and filed opinion in which Justice Stevens joined.

Opinion on remand, 588 So.2d 233.

1. Searches and Seizures ⚿ 23

Touchstone of Fourth Amendment is reasonableness. U.S.C.A. Const.Amend. 4.

2. Searches and Seizures ⚿ 23

Fourth Amendment does not proscribe all state-initiated searches and seizures; it merely proscribes those which are unreasonable. U.S.C.A. Const.Amend. 4.

3. Searches and Seizures ⚿ 186

Standard for measuring scope of suspect's consent to search under Fourth Amendment is that of "objective" reasonableness, i.e., what would typical reasonable person have understood by exchange between officer and suspect. U.S.C.A. Const.Amend. 4.

4. Searches and Seizures ⚿ 53.1, 147.1, 186

Scope of search is generally defined by its expressed object. U.S.C.A. Coast.Amend. 4.

5. Searches and Seizures ⚿ 186

Narcotics suspect's Fourth Amendment right to be free from unreasonable searches was not violated when, after he gave police officer permission to search his car, officer opened folded, brown paper bag on floorboard on passenger side and found kilogram of cocaine therein; suspect had not placed any explicit limitation on scope of search and it was objectively reasonable for officer to conclude that suspect's general consent included consent to search closed containers within car which might bear drugs. U.S.C.A. Coast.Amend. 4.

6. Searches and Seizures ⚿ 186

If police wish to search closed containers within car, they need not separately request permission to search each container, although suspect may delimit as he chooses the scope of a search to which he consents. U.S.C.A. Const.Amend. 4.

*Syllabus**

Having stopped respondent Jimeno's car for a traffic infraction, police officer Trujillo, who had been following the car after overhearing Jimeno arranging what appeared to be a drug transaction, declared that he had reason to believe that Jimeno was carrying narcotics in the car, and asked permission to search it. Jimeno consented, and Trujillo found cocaine inside a folded paper bag on the car's floorboard. Jimeno was charged with possession with intent to distribute cocaine in violation of Florida law, but the state trial court granted his motion to suppress the cocaine on the ground that his consent to search the car did not carry with it specific consent to open the bag and examine its contents. The Florida District Court of Appeal and Supreme Court affirmed.

Held: A criminal suspect's Fourth Amendment right to be free from unreasonable searches is not violated when, after he gives police permission to search his car, they open a closed container found within the car that might reasonably hold the object of the search. The Amendment is satisfied when, under the circumstances, it is objectively reasonable for the police to believe that the scope of the suspect's consent permitted them to open the particular container. Here, the authorization to search extended beyond the car's interior surfaces to the bag, since Jimeno did not place any explicit limitation on the scope of the search and was aware that Trujillo would be looking for narcotics in the car, and since a reasonable person may be expected to know that narcotics are generally carried in some form of container. There is no basis for adding to the Fourth Amendment's basic test of objective reasonableness a requirement that, if police wish to search closed containers within a car, they must separately request permission to search each container. Pp. 1803–1804.

564 So.2d 1083 (Fla. 1990), reversed and remanded.

*The syllabus constitutes no part of the opinion of the Court but has been prepared by the Reporter of Decisions for the convenience of the reader. See *United States v. Detroit Lumber Co.*, 200 U.S. 321, 337, 26 S.Ct. 282, 287, 50 L.Ed. 499.

FIGURE A-6 (continued)

111 SUPREME COURT REPORTER

REHNQUIST, C.J., delivered the opinion of the Court, in which WHITE, BLACKMUN, O'CONNOR, SCALIA, KENNEDY, and SOUTER, JJ., joined. MARSHALL, J., filed a dissenting opinion, in which STEVENS, J., joined, *post*, p. 1804.

⊥249 Michael J. Neimand, Miami, Fla., for petitioner.

John G. Roberts, Jr., Washington, D.C., for the U.S., as amicus curiae, supporting the petitioner, by special leave of Court.

Jeffrey S. Weiner, Miami, Fla., for respondent.

Chief Justice REHNQUIST delivered the opinion of the Court.

In this case we decide whether a criminal suspect's Fourth Amendment right to be free from unreasonable searches is violated when, after he gives a police officer permission to search his automobile, the officer opens a closed container found within the car that might reasonably hold the object of the search. We find that it is not. The Fourth Amendment is satisfied when, under the circumstances, it is objectively reasonable for the officer to believe that the scope of the suspect's consent permitted him to open a particular container within the automobile.

This case began when a Dade County police officer, Frank Trujillo, overheard respondent, Enio Jimeno, arranging what appeared to be a drug transaction over a public telephone. Believing that respondent might be involved in illegal drug trafficking, Officer Trujillo followed his car. The officer observed respondent make a right turn at a red light without stopping. He then pulled respondent over to the side of the road in order to issue him a traffic citation. Officer Trujillo told respondent that he had been stopped for committing a traffic infraction. The officer went on to say that he had reason to believe that respondent was carrying narcotics in his car, and asked permission to search the car. He explained that respondent did not have to consent to a search of the car. Respondent stated that he had nothing to hide and gave Trujillo ⊥250 permission to search the automobile. After two passengers stepped out of respondent's car, Officer Trujillo went to the passenger side, opened the door, and saw a folded, brown paper bag on the floorboard. The officer picked up the bag, opened it, and found a kilogram of cocaine inside.

Respondent was charged with possession with intent to distribute cocaine in violation of Florida law. Before trial, he moved to suppress the cocaine found in the bag on the ground that his consent to search the car did not extend to the closed paper bag inside of the car. The trial court granted the motion. It found that although respondent "could have assumed that the officer would have searched the bag" at the time he gave his consent, his mere consent to search the car did not carry with it specific consent to open the bag and examine its contents. No. 88-23967 (Cir. Ct. Dade Cty., Fla., Mar. 21, 1989); App. to Pet. for Cert. A–6.

The Florida District Court of Appeal affirmed the trial court's decision to suppress the evidence of the cocaine. 550 So.2d 1176 (Fla. 3d DCA 1989). In doing so, the court established a *per se* rule that "consent to a general search for narcotics does not extend to 'sealed containers within the general area agreed to by the defendant.'" *Ibid.* The Florida Supreme Court affirmed, relying upon its decision in *State v. Wells*, 539 So.2d 464 (1989), aff'd on other grounds, 495 U.S. 1, 110 S.Ct. 1632, 109 L.Ed.2d 1 (1990), 564 So.2d 1083 (1990). We granted certiorari to determine whether consent to search a vehicle may extend to closed containers found inside the vehicle, 498 U.S. 997, 111 S.Ct. 554, 112 L.Ed.2d 561 (1990), and we now reverse the judgment of the Supreme Court of Florida.

[1–3] The touchstone of the Fourth Amendment is reasonableness. *Katz v. United States*, 389 U.S. 347, 360, 88 S.Ct. 507, 516, 19 L.Ed.2d 576 (1967). The Fourth Amendment does not proscribe all state-initiated searches and seizures; it merely proscribes those which are unreasonable. *Illinois v. Rodriguez*, 497 U.S. 177, 110 S.Ct. 2793, 111 L.Ed.2d 148 (1990). Thus, we have long approved consensual searches because it ⊥251is no doubt reasonable for the police to conduct a search once they have been permitted to do so. *Schneckloth v. Bustamonte*, 412 U.S. 218, 219, 93 S.Ct. 2041, 2043, 36 L.Ed.2d 854 (1973). The standard for measuring the scope of a suspect's consent under the Fourth Amendment is that of "objective" reasonableness—what would the typical reasonable person have understood by the exchange between the officer and the suspect? *Illinois v. Rodriguez, supra*, at 183–189, 110 S.Ct., at 2798–2802; *Florida v. Royer*, 460 U.S. 491, 501–502, 103 S.Ct. 1319, 1326–1327, 75 L.Ed.2d 229 (1983) (opinion of WHITE, J.); *id.*, at 514, 103 S.Ct., at 1332 (BLACKMUN, J., dissenting). The question before us, then, is whether it is reasonable for an officer to consider a suspect's general consent to a search of his car to include consent to examine a paper bag lying on the floor of the car. We think that it is.

[4, 5] The scope of a search is generally defined by its expressed object. *United States v. Ross*, 456 U.S. 798, 102 S.Ct. 2157, 72 L.Ed.2d

FIGURE A-6 (continued)

FLORIDA v. JIMENO

572 (1982). In this case, the terms of the search's authorization were simple. Respondent granted Officer Trujillo permission to search his car, and did not place any explicit limitation on the scope of the search. Trujillo had informed respondent that he believed respondent was carrying narcotics, and that he would be looking for narcotics in the car. We think that it was objectively reasonable for the police to conclude that the general consent to search respondent's car included consent to search containers within that car which might bear drugs. A reasonable person may be expected to know that narcotics are generally carried in some form of a container. "Contraband goods rarely are strewn across the trunk or floor of a car." *Id.*, at 820, 102 S.Ct., at 2170. The authorization to search in this case, therefore, extended beyond the surfaces of the car's interior to the paper bag lying on the car's floor.

The facts of this case are therefore different from those in *State v. Wells, supra*, on which the Supreme Court of Florida relied in affirming the suppression order in this case. There the Supreme Court of Florida held that consent to search the trunk of a car did not include authorization to pry open a locked briefcase found inside the trunk. It is very likely ⊥252unreasonable to think that a suspect, by consenting to the search of his trunk, has agreed to the breaking open of a locked briefcase within the trunk, but it is otherwise with respect to a closed paper bag.

[6] Respondent argues, and the Florida trial court agreed with him, that if the police wish to search closed containers within a car they must separately request permission to search each container. But we see no basis for adding this sort of superstructure to the Fourth Amendment's basic test of objective reasonableness. Cf. *Illinois v. Gates*, 462 U.S. 213, 103 S.Ct. 2317, 76 L.Ed.2d 527 (1983). A suspect may of course delimit as he chooses the scope of the search to which he consents. But if his consent would reasonably be understood to extend to a particular container, the Fourth Amendment provides no grounds for requiting a more explicit authorization. "[T]he community has a real interest in encouraging consent, for the resulting search may yield necessary evidence for the solution and prosecution of crime, evidence that may insure that a wholly innocent person is not wrongly charged with a criminal offense." *Schneckloth v. Bustamonte, supra*, at 243, 93 S.Ct., at 2056.

The judgment of the Supreme Court of Florida is accordingly reversed, and the case is remanded for further proceedings not inconsistent with this opinion.

It is so ordered.

Justice MARSHALL, with whom Justice STEVENS joins, dissenting.

The question in this case is whether an individual's general consent to a search of the interior of his car for narcotics should reasonably be understood as consent to a search of closed containers inside the car. Nothing in today's opinion dispels my belief that the two are not one and the same from the consenting individual's standpoint. Consequently, an individual's consent to a search of the interior of his car should not be understood to authorize a search of closed containers inside the car. I dissent.

⊥253 In my view, analysis of this question must start by identifying the differing expectations of privacy that attach to cars and closed containers. It is well established that an individual has but a limited expectation of privacy in the interior of his car. A car ordinarily is not used as a residence or repository for one's personal effects, and its passengers and contents are generally exposed to public view. See *Cardwell v. Lewis*, 417 U.S. 583, 590, 94 S.Ct. 2464, 2469, 41 L.Ed.2d 325 (1974) (plurality opinion). Moreover, cars "are subjected to pervasive and continuing governmental regulation and controls," *South Dakota v. Opperman*, 428 U.S. 364, 368, 96 S.Ct. 3092, 3096, 49 L.Ed.2d 1000 (1976), and may be seized by the police when necessary to protect public safety or to facilitate the flow of traffic, see *id.*, at 368–369, 96 S.Ct., at 3096–3097.

In contrast, it is equally well established that an individual has a heightened expectation of privacy in the contents of a closed container. See, *e.g.*, *United States v. Chadwick*, 433 U.S. 1, 13, 97 S.Ct. 2476, 2484, 53 L.Ed.2d 538 (1977). Luggage, handbags, paper bags, and other containers are common repositories for one's papers and effects, and the protection of these items from state intrusion lies at the heals of the Fourth Amendment. U.S. Const., Amdt. 4 ("The right of the people to be secure in their . . . papers, and effects, against unreasonable searches and seizures, shall not be violated"). By placing his possessions inside a container, an individual manifests an intent that his possessions be "preserve[d] as private," *Katz v. United States*, 389 U.S. 347, 351, 88 S.Ct. 507, 511, 19 L.Ed.2d 576 (1967), and thus kept "free from public examination," *United States v. Chadwick, supra*, 433 U.S., at 11, 97 S.Ct., at 2483.

The distinct privacy expectations that a person has in a car as opposed to a closed container do not merge when the individual uses his car to transport the container. In this situation, the individual still retains a heightened expectation of privacy in the container. See *Robbins v. California* 453 U.S. 420, 425, 101 S.Ct. 2841, 2845, 69 L.Ed.2d 744 (1981) (plurality opinion);

FIGURE A-6 (continued)

111 SUPREME COURT REPORTER

Arkansas v. Sanders, 442 U.S. 753, 763–764, 99 S.Ct. 2586, 2592–2593, 61 L.Ed.2d 235 (1979). Nor does an individual's heightened expectation of privacy turn on the type of con⊥tainer$_{254}$ in which he stores his possessions. Notwithstanding the majority's suggestion to the contrary, see *ante;* at 1804, this Court has soundly rejected any distinction between "worthy" containers, like locked briefcases, and "unworthy" containers, like paper bags.

> "Even though such a distinction perhaps could evolve in a series of cases in which paper bags, locked trunks, lunch buckets, and orange crates were placed on one side of the line or the other, the central purpose of the Fourth Amendment forecloses such a distinction. For just as the most frail cottage in the kingdom is absolutely entitled to the same guarantees of privacy as the most majestic mansion, so also may a traveler who carries a toothbrush and a few articles of clothing in a paper bag or knotted scarf claim an equal right to conceal his possessions from official inspection as the sophisticated executive with the locked attaché case." *United States v. Ross,* 456 U.S. 798, 822, 102 S.Ct. 2157, 2171, 72 L.Ed.2d 572 (1982) (footnotes omitted).

Because an individual's expectation of privacy in a container is distinct from, and far greater than, his expectation of privacy in the interior of his car, it follows that an individual's consent to a search of the interior of his car cannot necessarily be understood as extending to containers in the car. At the very least, general consent to search the car is ambiguous with respect to containers found inside the car. In my view, the independent and divisible nature of the privacy interests in cars and containers mandates that a police officer who wishes to search a suspicious container found during a consensual automobile search obtain additional consent to search the container. If the driver intended to authorize search of the container, he will say so; if not, then he will say no.* The only objection that the police could have to such a ⊥$_{255}$rule is that it would prevent them from exploiting the ignorance of a citizen who simply did not anticipate that his consent to search the car would be understood to authorize the police to rummage through his packages.

According to the majority, it nonetheless is reasonable for a police officer to construe generalized consent to search an automobile for narcotics as extending to closed containers, because "[a] reasonable person may be expected to know that narcotics are generally carried in some form of a container." *Ante,* at 1804. This is an interesting contention. By the same logic a person who consents to a search of the car from the driver's seat could also be deemed to consent to a search of his person or indeed of his body cavities, since a reasonable person may be expected to know that drug couriers frequently store their contraband on their persons or in their body cavities. I suppose (and hope) that even the majority would reject this conclusion, for a person who consents to the search of his *car* for drugs certainly does not consent to a search of things *other than his car* for drugs. But this example illustrates that if there is a reason for not treating a closed container as something "other than" the car in which it sits, the reason cannot be based on intuitions about where people carry drugs. The majority, however, never identifies a reason for conflating the distinct privacy expectations that a person has in a car and in closed containers.

The majority also argues that the police should not be required to secure specific consent to search a closed container, because " '[t]he community has a real interest in encouraging consent.' " *Ante,* at 1804, quoting *Schneckloth v. Bustamonte,* 412 U.S. 218, 243, 93 S.Ct. 2041, 2056, 36 L.Ed.2d 854 (1973). I find this rationalization equally unsatisfactory. If anything, a rule that permits the police to construe a consent to search more broadly than it may have been intended would discourage individuals from consenting to searches of their cars. Apparently, the majority's real concern is that if the police were required to ask for additional consent to search a closed container found during the ⊥$_{256}$consensual search of an automobile, an individual who did not mean to authorize such additional searching would have an opportunity to say no. In essence, then, the majority is claiming that "the community has a real interest" not in encouraging citizens to *consent* to investigatory efforts of their law enforcement agents, but rather in encouraging individuals to be *duped* by them. This is not the community that the Fourth Amendment contemplates.

Almost 20 years ago, this Court held that an individual could validly "consent" to a search—or, in other words, waive his right to be free from an otherwise unlawful search—without being told that he had the right to withhold his consent. See *Schneckloth v. Bustamonte, supra.* In *Schneckloth,* as in this case, the Courts cited the practical interests in efficacious law enforcement as the basis for not requiring the police to take meaningful steps to establish the basis of an individual's consent. I dissented in *Schneck-*

*Alternatively, the police could obtain such consent in advance by asking the individual for permission to search both the car and any closed containers found inside.

FIGURE A-6 (continued)

500 U.S. 248 FLORIDA v. JIMENO 1805

loth, and what I wrote in that case applies with equal force here.

> "I must conclude, with some reluctance, that when the Court speaks of practicality, what it really is talking of is the continued ability of the police to capitalize on the ignorance of citizens so as to accomplish by subterfuge what they could not achieve by relying only on the knowing relinquishment of constitutional rights. Of course it would be "practical" for the police to ignore the commands of the Fourth Amendment, if by practicality we mean that more criminals will be apprehended, even though the constitutional rights of innocent people also go by the board. But such a practical advantage is achieved only at the cost of permitting the police to disregard the limitations that the Constitution places on their behavior, a cost that a constitutional democracy cannot long absorb." 412 U.S., at 288, 93 S.Ct., at 2079.

I dissent.

FIGURE A-7 *Whren v. United States.*

WHREN v. U.S.

Cite as 116 S.Ct. 1769 (1996)

517 U.S. 806, 135 L.Ed.2d 89

⊥806 Michael A. WHREN and James L. Brown, Petitioners,

v.

UNITED STATES.

No. 95-5841.

Argued April 17, 1996.

Decided June 10, 1996.

Defendants were convicted in the United States District Court for the District of Columbia, Norma Holloway Johnson, J., of drug offenses, and they appealed. The Court of Appeals affirmed, 53 F.3d 371, and certiorari was granted. The Supreme Court, Justice Scalia, held that: (1) constitutional reasonableness of traffic stops does not depend on the actual motivations of the individual officers involved; (2) temporary detention of motorist who the police have probable cause to believe has committed civil traffic violation is consistent with Fourth Amendment's prohibition against unreasonable seizures regardless of whether "reasonable officer" would have been motivated to stop the automobile by a desire to enforce the traffic laws; and (3) balancing inherent in Fourth Amendment inquiry does not require court to weigh governmental and individual interests implicated in a traffic stop.

Affirmed.

1. Arrest ⚷ 68(4)

Temporary detention of individuals during the stop of an automobile by the police, even if only for a brief period and for a limited purpose, constitutes "seizure" of persons within the meaning of Fourth Amendment. U.S.C.A. Const.Amend. 4.

See publication Words and Phrases for other judicial constructions and definitions.

2. Arrest ⚷ 63.5(6)

Automobiles ⚷ 349(2.1)

Automobile stop is subject to constitutional imperative that it not be unreasonable under the circumstances; as a general matter, decision to stop automobile is reasonable where police have probable cause to believe that traffic violation has occurred. U.S.C.A. Const.Amend. 4.

3. Searches and Seizures ⚷ 58

"Inventory search" is the search of property lawfully seized and detained, in order to ensure that it is harmless, to secure valuable items, and to protect against false claims of loss or damage. U.S.C.A. Const.Amend. 4.

See publication Words and Phrases for other judicial constructions and definitions.

4. Searches and Seizures ⚷ 79

"Administrative inspection" is the inspection of business premises conducted by authorities responsible for enforcing a pervasive regulatory scheme.

See publication Words and Phrases for other judicial constructions and definitions.

5. Searches and Seizures ⚷ 58, 79

Exemption from need for probable cause and warrant that is accorded to searches made for the purpose of inventory or administrative regulation is not accorded to searches that are not made for those purposes. U.S.C.A. Const.Amend. 4.

FIGURE A-7 (continued)

116 SUPREME COURT REPORTER

6. Automobiles ⊶ 349(2.1), 349.5(3)

Constitutional reasonableness of traffic stops does not depend on the actual motivations of the individual officers involved. U.S.C.A. Const.Amend. 4.

7. Constitutional Law ⊶ 211(3), 215

Constitution prohibits selective enforcement of the law based on considerations such as race.

8. Automobiles ⊶ 349(2.1, 17), 349.5(3)

Temporary detention of motorist who the police have probable cause to believe has committed civil traffic violation is consistent with Fourth Amendment's prohibition against unreasonable seizures regardless of whether "reasonable officer" would have been motivated to stop the automobile by a desire to enforce the traffic laws. U.S.C.A. Const.Amend. 4.

9. Automobiles ⊶ 349(2.1)

Balancing inherent in Fourth Amendment inquiry does not require court to weigh governmental and individual interests implicated in a traffic stop. U.S.C.A. Const. Amend. 4.

10. Searches and Seizures ⊶ 40.1

Probable cause justifies a search and seizure. U.S.C.A. Const. Amend. 4.

*Syllabus**

Plainclothes policemen patrolling a "high drug area" in an unmarked vehicle observed a truck driven by petitioner Brown waiting at a stop sign at an intersection for an unusually long time; the truck then turned suddenly, without signaling, and sped off at an "unreasonable" speed. The officers stopped the vehicle, assertedly to warn the driver about traffic violations, and upon approaching the truck observed plastic bags of crack cocaine in petitioner Whren's hands. Petitioners were arrested. Prior to trial on federal drug charges, they moved for suppression of the evidence, arguing that the stop had not been justified by either a reasonable suspicion or probable cause to believe petitioners were engaged in illegal drug-dealing activity, and that the officers' traffic-violation ground for approaching the truck was pretextual. The motion to suppress was denied, petitioners were convicted, and the Court of Appeals affirmed.

Held: The temporary detention of a motorist upon probable cause to believe that he has violated the traffic laws does not violate the Fourth Amendment's prohibition against unreasonable seizures, even if a reasonable officer would not have stopped the motorist absent some additional law enforcement objective. Pp. 1772–1777.

(a) Detention of a motorist is reasonable where probable cause exists to believe that a traffic violation has occurred. See, *e.g., Delaware v. Prouse,* 440 U.S. 648, 659, 99 S.Ct. 1391, 1399, 59 L.Ed.2d 660. Petitioners claim that, because the police may be tempted to use commonly occurring traffic violations as means of investigating violations of other laws, the Fourth Amendment test for traffic stops should be whether a reasonable officer would have stopped the car for the purpose of enforcing the traffic violation at issue. However, this Court's cases foreclose the argument that ulterior motives can invalidate police conduct justified on the basis of probable cause. See, *e.g., United States v. Robinson,* 414 U.S. 218, 221, n. 1, 236, 94 S.Ct. 467, 470, n. 1, 477, 38 L.Ed.2d.427. Subjective intentions play no role in ordinary, probable-cause Fourth Amendment analysis. Pp. 1772–1774.

(b) Although framed as an empirical question—whether the officer's conduct deviated materially from standard police practices—petitioners' proposed test is plainly designed to combat the perceived danger of pretextual stops. It is thus inconsistent with this Court's cases, which ⊥807 make clear that the Fourth Amendment's concern with "reasonableness" allows certain actions to be taken in certain circumstances, *whatever* the subjective intent. See, *e.g., Robinson, supra,* at 236, 94 S.Ct. at 477. Nor can the Fourth Amendment's protections be thought to vary from place to place and from time to time, which would be the consequence of assessing the reasonableness of police conduct in light of local law enforcement practices. Pp. 1774–1776.

(c) Also rejected is petitioners' argument that the balancing of interests inherent in Fourth Amendment inquiries does not support enforcement of minor traffic laws by plainclothes police in unmarked vehicles, since that practice only minimally advances the government's interest in traffic safety while subjecting motorists to inconvenience, confusion, and anxiety. Where probable cause exists, this Court has found it necessary to engage in balancing only in cases involving searches or seizures conducted in a manner unusually harmful to the individual. See, *e.g., Tennessee v. Garner,* 471 U.S. 1, 105 S.Ct. 1694, 85 L.Ed.2d

*The syllabus constitutes no part of the opinion of the Court but has been prepared by the Reporter of Decisions for the convenience of the reader. See *United States v. Detroit Lumber Co.,* 200 U.S. 321, 337 26 S.Ct. 282, 287,50 L.Ed. 499.

FIGURE A-7 (continued)

WHREN v. U.S.

1. The making of a traffic stop out of uniform does not remotely qualify as such an extreme practice. Pp. 1776–1777.

53 F.3d 371 (C.A.D.C.1995), affirmed.

SCALIA, J., delivered the opinion for a unanimous Court.

Lisa Burger Wright, Washington, DC, for Petitioners.

James A. Feldman, Washington, DC, for Respondent.

For U.S. Supreme Court briefs, see:

1996 WL 75758 (Pet.Brief)

1996 WL 115816 (Resp.Brief)

1996 WL 164375 (Reply Brief)

⊥808 Justice SCALIA delivered the opinion of the Court.

In this case we decide whether the temporary detention of a motorist who the police have probable cause to believe has committed a civil traffic violation is inconsistent with the Fourth Amendment's prohibition against unreasonable seizures unless a reasonable officer would have been motivated to stop the car by a desire to enforce the traffic laws.

I

On the evening of June 10, 1993, plainclothes vice-squad officers of the District of Columbia Metropolitan Police Department were patrolling a "high drug area" of the city in an unmarked car. Their suspicions were aroused when they passed a dark Pathfinder truck with temporary license plates and youthful occupants waiting at a stop sign, the driver looking down into the lap of the passenger at his right. The truck remained stopped at the intersection for what seemed an unusually long time—more than 20 seconds. When the police car executed a U-turn in order to head back toward the truck, the Pathfinder turned suddenly to its right, without signaling, and sped off at an "unreasonable" speed. The policemen followed, and in a short while overtook the Pathfinder when it stopped behind other traffic at a red light. They pulled up alongside, and Officer Ephraim Soto stepped out and approached the driver's door, identifying himself as a police officer and directing the driver, petitioner Brown, to put the vehicle in park. When Soto drew up to the driver's ⊥809 window, he immediately observed two large plastic bags of what appeared to be crack cocaine in petitioner Whren's hands. Petitioners were arrested, and quantities of several types of illegal drugs were retrieved from the vehicle.

Petitioners were charged in a four-count indictment with violating various federal drug laws, including 21 U.S.C. §§ 844(a) and 860(a). At a pretrial suppression hearing, they challenged the legality of the stop and the resulting seizure of the drugs. They argued that the stop had not been justified by probable cause to believe, or even reasonable suspicion, that petitioners were engaged in illegal drug-dealing activity; and that Officer Soto's asserted ground for approaching the vehicle—to give the driver a warning concerning traffic violations—was pretextual. The District Court denied the suppression motion, concluding that "the facts of the stop were not controverted," and "[t]here was nothing to really demonstrate that the actions of the officers were contrary to a normal traffic stop." App. 5.

Petitioners were convicted of the counts at issue here. The Court of Appeals affirmed the convictions, holding with respect to the suppression issue that, "regardless of whether a police officer subjectively believes that the occupants of an automobile may be engaging in some other illegal behavior, a traffic stop is permissible as long as a reasonable officer in the same circumstances *could have* stopped the car for the suspected traffic violation." 53 F.3d 371, 374–375 (C.A.D.C. 1995). We granted certiorari. 516 U.S. 1036, 116 S.Ct. 690, 133 L.Ed.2d 595 (1996).

II

[1,2] The Fourth Amendment guarantees "[t]he right of the people to be secure in their persons, houses, papers, and effects, against unreasonable searches and seizures." Temporary detention of individuals during the stop of an automobile by the police, even if only for a brief period and for a limited purpose, constitutes a "seizure" of "persons" within the ⊥810 meaning of this provision. See *Delaware v. Prouse*, 440 U.S. 648, 653, 99 S.Ct. 1391, 1395, 59 L.Ed.2d 660 (1979); *United States v. Martinez-Fuerte*, 428 U.S. 543, 556, 96 S.Ct. 3074, 3082, 49 L.Ed.2d 1116 (1976); *United States v. Brignoni-Ponce*, 422 U.S. 873, 878, 95 S.Ct. 2574, 2578, 45 L.Ed.2d 607 (1975). An automobile stop is thus subject to the constitutional imperative that it not be "unreasonable" under the circumstances. As a general matter, the decision to stop an automobile is reasonable where the police have probable cause to believe that a traffic violation has occurred. See *Prouse*, *supra*, at 659, 99 S.Ct., at 1399; *Pennsylvania v. Mimms*, 434 U.S. 106, 109, 98 S.Ct. 330, 332, 54 L.Ed.2d 331 (1977) *(per curiam)*.

Petitioners accept that Officer Soto had probable cause to believe that various provisions of the District of Columbia traffic code had been violated. See 18 D.C. Mun. Regs. §§ 2213.4 (1995) ("An operator shall . . . give full time and attention to the operation of the

FIGURE A-7 (continued)

116 SUPREME COURT REPORTER

vehicle"); 2204.3 ("No person shall turn any vehicle . . . without giving an appropriate signal"); 2200.3 ("No person shall drive a vehicle . . . at a speed greater than is reasonable and prudent under the conditions"). They argue, however, that "in the unique context of civil traffic regulations" probable cause is not enough. Since, they contend, the use of automobiles is so heavily and minutely regulated that total compliance with traffic and safety rules is nearly impossible, a police officer will almost invariably be able to catch any given motorist in a technical violation. This creates the temptation to use traffic stops as a means of investigating other law violations, as to which no probable cause or even articulable suspicion exists. Petitioners, who are both black, further contend that police officers might decide which motorists to stop based on decidedly impermissible factors, such as the race of the car's occupants. To avoid this danger, they say, the Fourth Amendment test for traffic stops should be, not the normal one (applied by the Court of Appeals) of whether probable cause existed to justify the stop; but rather, whether a police officer, acting reasonably, would have made the stop for the reason given.

⊥811A

[3–5] Petitioners contend that the standard they propose is consistent with our past cases' disapproval of police attempts to use valid bases of action against citizens as pretexts for pursuing other investigatory agendas. We are reminded that in *Florida v. Wells*, 495 U.S. 1, 4, 110 S.Ct. 1632, 1635, 109 L.Ed.2d 1 (1990), we stated that "an inventory search[1] must not be a ruse for a general rummaging in order to discover incriminating evidence"; that in *Colorado v. Bertine*, 479 U.S. 367, 372, 107 S.Ct. 738, 741, 93 L.Ed.2d 739 (1987), in approving an inventory search, we apparently thought it significant that there had been "no showing that the police, who were following standardized procedures, acted in bad faith or for the sole purpose of investigation"; and that in *New York v. Burger*, 482 U.S. 691, 716–717, n. 27, 107 S.Ct. 2636, 2651, n. 27, 96 L.Ed.2d 601 (1987), we observed, in upholding the constitutionality of a warrantless administrative inspection,[2] that the search did not appear to be "a 'pretext' for obtaining evidence of . . . violation of . . . penal laws." But only an undiscerning reader would regard these cases as endorsing the principle that ulterior motives can invalidate police conduct that is justifiable on the basis of probable cause to believe that a violation of law has occurred. In each case we were addressing the validity of a search conducted in the *absence* of probable cause. Our quoted statements simply explain that the exemption from the need for probable cause (and warrant), which is accorded to searches made for the purpose of inventory or administrative ⊥812regulation, is not accorded to searches that are *not* made for those purposes. See *Bertine, supra*, at 371–372, 107 S.Ct., at 740–741; *Burger, supra*, at 702–703, 107 S.Ct., at 2643–2644.

Petitioners also rely upon *Colorado v. Bannister*, 449 U.S. 1, 101 S.Ct. 42, 66 L.Ed.2d 1 (1980) (*per curiam*), a case which, like this one, involved a traffic stop as the prelude to a plain-view sighting and arrest on charges wholly unrelated to the basis for the stop. Petitioners point to our statement that "[t]here was no evidence whatsoever that the officer's presence to issue a traffic citation was a pretext to confirm any other previous suspicion about the occupants" of the car. *Id.*, at 4, n. 4, 101 S.Ct., at 44, n. 4. That dictum *at most* demonstrates that the Court in *Bannister* found no need to inquire into the question now under discussion; not that it was certain of the answer. And it may demonstrate even less than that: If by "pretext" the Court meant that the officer really had not seen the car speeding, the statement would mean only that there was no reason to doubt probable cause for the traffic stop.

It would, moreover, be anomalous, to say the least, to treat a statement in a footnote in the *per curiam Bannister* opinion as indicating a reversal of our prior law. Petitioners' difficulty is not simply a lack of affirmative support for their position. Not only have we never held, outside the context of inventory search or administrative inspection (discussed above), that an officer's motive invalidates objectively justifiable behavior under the Fourth Amendment; but we have repeatedly held and asserted the contrary. In *United States v. Villamonte-Marquez*, 462 U.S. 579, 584, n. 3, 103 S.Ct. 2573, 2577, n. 3, 77 L.Ed.2d 22 (1983), we held that an otherwise valid warrantless boarding of a vessel by customs officials was not rendered invalid "because the customs officers were

1. An inventory search is the search of property lawfully seized and detained, in order to ensure that it is harmless, to secure valuable items (such as might be kept in a towed car), and to protect against false claims of loss or damage. See *South Dakota v. Opperman*, 428 U.S. 364, 369, 96 S.Ct. 3092, 2097, 49 L.Ed.2d 1000 (1976).

2. Administrative inspection is the inspection of business premises conducted by authorities responsible for enforcing a pervasive regulatory scheme—for example, unannounced inspection of a mine for compliance with health and safelty standards. See *Donovan v. Dewey*, 452 U.S. 594, 599–605, 101 S.Ct. 2534, 2538–2542, 69 L.Ed.2d 262 (1981).

FIGURE A-7 (continued)

WHREN v. U.S.

accompanied by a Louisiana state policeman, and were following an informant's tip that a vessel in the ship channel was thought to be carrying marihuana." We flatly dismissed the idea that an ulterior motive might serve to strip the agents of their legal justification. In *United States v. Robinson*, 414 U.S. 218, 94 S.Ct. 467, 38 L.Ed.2d 427 (1973), we held that ⊥813a traffic-violation arrest (of the sort here) would not be rendered invalid by the fact that it was "a mere pretext for a narcotics search," *id.*, at 221, n. 1, 94 S.Ct., at 470, n. 1; and that a lawful postarrest search of the person would not be rendered invalid by the fact that it was not motivated by the officer-safety concern that justifies such searches, see *id.*, at 236, 94 S.Ct., at 477. See also *Gustafson v. Florida*, 414 U.S. 260, 266, 94 S.Ct. 488, 492, 38 L.Ed.2d 456 (1973). And in *Scott v. United States*, 436 U.S. 128, 138, 98 S.Ct. 1717, 1723, 56 L.Ed.2d 168 (1978), in rejecting the contention that wiretap evidence was subject to exclusion because the agents conducting the tap had failed to make any effort to comply with the statutory requirement that unauthorized acquisitions be minimized, we said that "[s]ubjective intent alone . . . does not make otherwise lawful conduct illegal or unconstitutional." We described *Robinson* as having established that "the fact that the officer does not have the state of mind which is hypothecated by the reasons which provide the legal justification for the officer's action does not invalidate the action taken as long as the circumstances, viewed objectively, justify that action." 436 U.S., at 136, 138, 98 S.Ct., at 1723.

[6, 7] We think these cases foreclose any argument that the constitutional reasonableness of traffic stops depends on the actual motivations of the individual officers involved. We of course agree with petitioners that the Constitution prohibits selective enforcement of the law based on considerations such as race. But the constitutional basis for objecting to intentionally discriminatory application of laws is the Equal Protection Clause, not the Fourth Amendment. Subjective intentions play no role in ordinary, probable-cause Fourth Amendment analysis.

B

[8] Recognizing that we have been unwilling to entertain Fourth Amendment challenges based on the actual motivations of individual officers, petitioners disavow any intention to make the individual officer's subjective good faith the touchstone of "reasonableness." They insist that the stand⊥814ard they have put forward—whether the officer's conduct deviated materially from usual police practices, so that a reasonable officer in the same circumstances would not have made the stop for the reasons given—is an "objective" one.

But although framed in empirical terms, this approach is plainly and indisputably driven by subjective considerations. Its whole purpose is to prevent the police from doing under the guise of enforcing the traffic code what they would like to do for different reasons. Petitioners' proposed standard may not use the word "pretext," but it is designed to combat nothing other than the perceived "danger" of the pretextual stop, albeit only indirectly and over the run of cases. Instead of asking whether the individual officer had the proper state of mind, the petitioners would have us ask, in effect, whether (based on general police practices) it is plausible to believe that the officer had the proper state of mind.

Why one would frame a test designed to combat pretext in such fashion that the court cannot take into account *actual and admitted pretext* is a curiosity that can only be explained by the fact that our cases have foreclosed the more sensible option. If those cases were based only upon the evidentiary difficulty of establishing subjective intent, petitioners' attempt to root out subjective vices through objective means might make sense. But they were not based only upon that, or indeed even principally upon that. Their principal basis—which applies equally to attempts to reach subjective intent through ostensibly objective means—is simply that the Fourth Amendment's concern with "reasonableness" allows certain actions to be taken in certain circumstances, *whatever* the subjective intent. See, *e.g.*, *Robinson*, *supra*, at 236, 94 S.Ct., at 477 ("Since it is the fact of custodial arrest which gives rise to the authority to search, it is of no moment that [the officer] did not indicate any subjective fear of the [arrestee] or that he did not himself suspect that [the arrestee] was armed") (footnotes omitted); *Gustafson*, *supra*, at 266, 94 S.Ct., at 492 (same). But even if our concern had been only an evidentiary one, ⊥815petitioners' proposal would by no means assuage it. Indeed, it seems to us somewhat easier to figure out the intent of an individual officer than to plumb the collective consciousness of law enforcement in order to determine whether a "reasonable officer" would have been moved to act upon the traffic violation. While police manuals and standard procedures may sometimes provide objective assistance, ordinarily one would be reduced to speculating about the hypothetical reaction of a hypothetical constable—an exercise that might be called virtual subjectivity.

FIGURE A-7 (continued)

Moreover, police enforcement practices, even if they could be practicably assessed by a judge, vary from place to place and from time to time. We cannot accept that the search and seizure protections of the Fourth Amendment are so variable, cf. *Gustafson, supra,* at 265, 94 S.Ct., at 491; *United States v. Caceres,* 440 U.S. 741, 755–756, 99 S.Ct. 1465, 1473–1474, 59 L.Ed.2d 733 (1979), and can be made to turn upon such trivialities. The difficulty is illustrated by petitioners' arguments in this case. Their claim that a reasonable officer would not have made this stop is based largely on District of Columbia police regulations which permit plainclothes officers in unmarked vehicles to enforce traffic laws "only in the case of a violation that is so grave as to pose an *immediate threat* to the safety of others." Metropolitan Police Department, Washington, D.C., General Order 303.1, pt. 1, Objectives and Policies (A)(2)(4) (Apr. 30, 1992), reprinted as Addendum to Brief for Petitioners. This basis of invalidation would not apply in jurisdictions that had a different practice. And it would not have applied even in the District of Columbia, if Officer Soto had been wearing a uniform or patrolling in a marked police cruiser.

Petitioners argue that our cases support insistence upon police adherence to standard practices as an objective means of rooting out pretext. They cite no holding to that effect, and dicta in only two cases. In *Abel v. United States,* 362 U.S. 217, 80 S.Ct. 683, 4 L.Ed.2d 668 (1960), the petitioner had been arrested by the Immigration and Naturalization Service (INS), on the basis of ⊥816an administrative warrant that, he claimed, had been issued on pretextual grounds in order to enable the Federal Bureau of Investigation (FBI) to search his room after his arrest. We regarded this as an allegation of "serious misconduct," but rejected Abel's claims on the ground that "[a] finding of bad faith is . . . not open to us on th[e] record" in light of the findings below, including the finding that " 'the proceedings taken by the [INS] differed in no respect from what would have been done in the case of an individual concerning whom [there was no pending FBI investigation],' " *id.,* at 226—227, 80 S.Ct., at 690–691. But it is a long leap from the proposition that following regular procedures is some evidence of lack of pretext to the proposition that failure to follow regular procedures *proves* (or is an operational substitute for) pretext. *Abel,* moreover, did not involve the assertion that pretext could invalidate a search or seizure for which there was probable cause—and even what it said about pretext in other contexts is plainly inconsistent with the views we later stated in *Robinson, Gustafson, Scott,* and *Villamonte-Marquez.* In the other case claimed to contain supportive dicta, *United States v. Robinson,* 414 U.S. 218, 94 S.Ct. 467, 38 L.Ed.2d 427 (1973), in approving a search incident to an arrest for driving without a license, we noted that the arrest was "not a departure from established police department practice." *Id.,* at 221, n. 1, 94 S.Ct., at 470, n. 1. That was followed, however, by the statement that "[w]e leave for another day questions which would arise on facts different from these." *Ibid.* This is not even a dictum that purports to provide an answer, but merely one that leaves the question open.

III

[9] In what would appear to be an elaboration on the "reasonable officer" test, petitioners argue that the balancing inherent in any Fourth Amendment inquiry requires us to weigh the governmental and individual interests implicated in a traffic stop such as we have here. That balancing, petitioners claim, does not support investigation of minor traffic in⊥fractions817 by plainclothes police in unmarked vehicles; such investigation only minimally advances the government's interest in traffic safety, and may indeed retard it by producing motorist confusion and alarm—a view said to be supported by the Metropolitan Police Department's own regulations generally prohibiting this practice. And as for the Fourth Amendment interests of the individuals concerned, petitioners point out that our cases acknowledge that even ordinary traffic stops entail "a possibly unsettling show of authority"; that they at best "interfere with freedom of movement, are inconvenient, and consume time" and at worst "may create substantial anxiety," *Prouse,* 440 U.S., at 657, 99 S.Ct., at 1398. That anxiety is likely to be even more pronounced when the stop is conducted by plainclothes officers in unmarked cars.

It is of course true that in principle every Fourth Amendment case, since it turns upon a "reasonableness" determination, involves a balancing of all relevant factors. With rare exceptions not applicable here, however, the result of that balancing is not in doubt where the search or seizure is based upon probable cause. That is why petitioners must rely upon cases like *Prouse* to provide examples of actual "balancing" analysis. There, the police action in question was a random traffic stop for the purpose of checking a motorist's license and vehicle registration, a practice that—like the practices at issue in the inventory search and administrative inspection cases upon which petitioners rely in making their "pretext" claim—involves police

FIGURE A-7 (continued)

WHREN v. U.S.

intrusion *without the probable cause that is its traditional justification.* Our opinion in *Prouse* expressly distinguished the case from a stop based on precisely what is at issue here: "probable cause to believe that a driver is violating any one of the multitude of applicable traffic and equipment regulations." *Id.*, at 661, 99 S.Ct., at 1400. It noted approvingly that "[t]he foremost method of enforcing traffic and vehicle safety regulations . . . is acting upon observed violations," *id.*, at 659, 99 S.Ct., at 1399, which afford the " 'quantum of individualized suspicion' " necessary to ensure that police $\perp_{818}$discretion is sufficiently constrained, *id*, at 654–655, 99 S.Ct., at 1396 (quoting *United States v. Martinez-Fuerte*, 428 U.S., at 560, 96 S.Ct., at 3084). What is true of *Prouse* is also true of other cases that engaged in detailed "balancing" to decide the constitutionality of automobile stops, such as *Martinez-Fuerte*, which upheld checkpoint stops, see 428 U.S., at 556–562, 96 S.Ct., at 3082–3085, and *Brignoni-Ponce*, which disallowed so-called "roving patrol" stops, see 422 U.S., at 882–884, 95 S.Ct., at 2580–2582: The detailed "balancing" analysis was necessary because they involved seizures without probable cause.

Where probable cause has existed, the only cases in which we have found it necessary actually to perform the "balancing" analysis involved searches or seizures conducted in an extraordinary manner, unusually harmful to an individual's privacy or even physical interests—such as, for example, seizure by means of deadly force, see *Tennessee v. Garner*, 471 U.S. 1, 105 S.Ct. 1694, 85 L.Ed.2d 1 (1985), unannounced entry into a home, see *Wilson v. Arkansas*, 514 U.S. 927, 115 S.Ct. 1914, 131 L.Ed.2d 976 (1995), entry into a home without a warrant, see *Welsh v. Wisconsin*, 466 U.S. 740, 104 S.Ct. 2091, 80 L.Ed.2d 732 (1984), or physical penetration of the body, see *Winston v. Lee*, 470 U.S. 753, 105 S.Ct. 1611, 84 L.Ed.2d 662 (1985). The making of a traffic stop out of uniform does not remotely qualify as such an extreme practice, and so is governed by the usual rule that probable cause to believe the law has been broken "outbalances" private interest in avoiding police contact.

Petitioners urge as an extraordinary factor in this case that the "multitude of applicable traffic and equipment regulations" is so large and so difficult to obey perfectly that virtually everyone is guilty of violation, permitting the police to single out almost whomever they wish for a stop. But we are aware of no principle that would allow us to decide at what point a code of law becomes so expansive and so commonly violated that infraction itself can no longer be the ordinary measure of the lawfulness of enforcement. And even if we could identify such exorbitant codes, we do not know by what standard (or what right) we would decide, as $\perp_{819}$ petitioners would have us do, which particular provisions are sufficiently important to merit enforcement.

[10] For the run-of-the-mine case, which this surely is, we think there is no realistic alternative to the traditional common-law rule that probable cause justifies a search and seizure.

* * *

Here the District Court found that the officers had probable cause to believe that petitioners had violated the traffic code. That rendered the stop reasonable under the Fourth Amendment, the evidence thereby discovered admissible, and the upholding of the convictions by the Court of Appeals for the District of Columbia Circuit correct. The judgment is

Affirmed.

DRUG ABUSE PREVENTION 21 USCS § 881

§ 881. Forfeitures

(a) Subject property. The following shall be subject to forfeiture to the United States and no property right shall exist in them:

(1) All controlled substances which have been manufactured, distributed, dispensed, or acquired in violation of this title.

(2) All raw materials, products, and equipment of any kind which are used, or intended for use, in manufacturing, compounding, processing, delivering, importing, or exporting any controlled substance or listed chemical in violation of this title.

(3) All property which is used, or intended for use, as a container for property described in paragraph (1), (2), or (9).

(4) All conveyances, including aircraft, vehicles, or vessels, which are used, or are intended for use, to transport, or in any manner to facilitate the transportation, sale, receipt, possession, or concealment of property described in paragraph (1), (2), or (9), except that—

(A) no conveyance used by any person as a common carrier in the transaction of business as a common carrier shall be forfeited under the provisions of this section unless it shall appear that the owner or other person in charge of such conveyance was a consenting party or privy to a violation of this title or title III;

(B) no conveyance shall be forfeited under the provisions of this section by reason of any act or omission established by the owner thereof to have been committed or omitted by any person other than such owner while such conveyance was unlawfully in the possession of a person other than the owner in violation of the criminal laws of the United States, or of any State; and

(C) no conveyance shall be forfeited under this paragraph to the extent of an interest of an owner, by reason of any act or omission established by that owner to have been committed or omitted without the knowledge, consent, or willful blindness of the owner.

(5) All books, records, and research, including formulas, microfilm, tapes, and data which are used, or intended for use, in violation of this title.

(6) All moneys, negotiable instruments, securities, or other things of value furnished or intended to be furnished by any person in exchange for a controlled substance or listed chemical in violation of this title, all proceeds traceable to such an exchange, and all moneys, negotiable instruments, and securities used or intended to be used to facilitate any violation of this title, except that no property shall be forfeited under this paragraph, to the extent of the interest of an owner, by reason of any act or omission established by that owner to have been committed or omitted without the knowledge or consent of that owner.

(7) All real property, including any right, title, and interest (including any leasehold interest) in the whole of any lot or tract of land and any appurtenances or improvements, which is used, or intended to be used, in any manner or part, to commit, or to facilitate the commission of, a violation of this title punishable by more than one year's imprisonment, except that no property shall be forfeited under this paragraph, to the extent of an interest of an owner, by reason of any act or omission established by that owner to have been committed or omitted without the knowledge or consent of that owner.

(8) All controlled substances which have been possessed in violation of this title.

(9) All listed chemicals, all drug manufacturing equipment, all tableting machines, all encapsulating machines, and all gelatin capsules, which have been imported, exported, manufactured, possessed, distributed, dispensed, acquired, or intended to be distributed, dispensed, acquired, imported, or exported, in violation of this title or title III.

(10) Any drug paraphernalia (as defined in section 1822 of the Mail Order Drug Paraphernalia Control Act [21 USCS § 857]).

FIGURE A-8 21 U.S.C.S. § 881 (Lexis Law Pub. 1997).

FIGURE A-8 (continued)

(11) Any firearm (as defined in section 921 of title 18, United States Code) used or intended to be used to facilitate the transportation, sale, receipt, possession, or concealment of property described in paragraph (1) or (2) and any proceeds traceable to such property.

(b) Seizure pursuant to Supplemental Rules for Certain Admiralty and Maritime Claims; issuance of warrant authorizing seizure. Any property subject to civil forfeiture to the United States under this title may be seized by the Attorney General upon process issued pursuant to the Supplemental Rules for Certain Admiralty and Maritime Claims by any district court of the United States having jurisdiction over the property, except that seizure without such process may be made when—

(1) the seizure is incident to an arrest or a search under a search warrant or an inspection under an administrative inspection warrant;

(2) the property subject to seizure has been the subject of a prior judgment in favor of the United States in a criminal injunction or forfeiture proceeding under this title;

(3) the Attorney General has probable cause to believe that the property is directly or indirectly dangerous to health or safety; or

(4) the Attorney General has probable cause to believe that the property is subject to civil forfeiture under this title.

In the event of seizure pursuant to paragraph (3) or (4) of this subsection, proceedings under subsection (d) of this section shall be instituted promptly. The Government may request the issuance of a warrant authorizing the seizure of property subject to forfeiture under this section in the same manner as provided for a search warrant under the Federal Rules of Criminal Procedure.

(c) Custody of Attorney General. Property taken or detained under this section shall not be repleviable, but shall be deemed to be in the custody of the Attorney General, subject only to the orders and decrees of the court or the official having jurisdiction thereof. Whenever property is seized under any of the provisions of this title, the Attorney General may—

(1) place the property under seal;

(2) remove the property to a place designated by him; or

(3) require that the General Services Administration take custody of the property and remove it, if practicable, to an appropriate location for disposition in accordance with law.

(d) Other laws and proceedings applicable. The provisions of law relating to the seizure, summary and judicial forfeiture, and condemnation of property for violation of the customs laws; the disposition of such property or the proceeds from the sale thereof; the remission or mitigation of such forfeitures; and the compromise of claims shall apply to seizures and forfeitures incurred, or alleged to have been incurred, under any of the provisions of this title, insofar as applicable and not inconsistent with the provisions hereof; except that such duties as are imposed upon the customs officer or any other person with respect to the seizure and forfeiture of property under the customs laws shall be performed with respect to seizures and forfeitures of property under this title by such officers, agents, or other persons as may be authorized or designated for that purpose by the Attorney General, except to the extent that such duties arise from seizures and forfeitures effected by any customs officer.

(e) Disposition of forfeited property. (1) Whenever property is civilly or criminally forfeited under this title the Attorney General may—

(A) retain the property for official use or, in the manner provided with respect to transfers under section 616 of the Tariff Act of 1930, transfer the property to any Federal agency or to any State or local law enforcement agency which participated directly in the seizure or forfeiture of the property;

(B) except as provided in paragraph (4), sell, by public sale or any other commercially feasible means, any forfeited property which is not required to be destroyed by law and which is not harmful to the public;

FIGURE A-8 (continued)

DRUG ABUSE PREVENTION **21 USCS § 881**

(C) require that the General Services Administration take custody of the property and dispose of it in accordance with law;

(D) forward it to the Bureau of Narcotics and Dangerous Drugs for disposition (including delivery for medical or scientific use to any Federal or State agency under regulations of the Attorney General); or

(E) transfer the forfeited personal property or the proceeds of the sale of any forfeited personal or real property to any foreign country which participated directly or indirectly in the seizure or forfeiture of the property, if such a transfer—

(i) has been agreed to by the Secretary of State;

(ii) is authorized in an international agreement between the United States and the foreign country; and

(iii) is made to a country which, if applicable, has been certified under section 490(b) of the Foreign Assistance Act of 1961 [22 USCS § 2291j(b)].

(2)(A) The proceeds from any sale under subparagraph (B) of paragraph (1) and any moneys forfeited under this title shall be used to pay—

(i) all property expenses of the proceedings for forfeiture and sale including expenses of seizure, maintenance of custody, advertising, and court costs; and

(ii) awards of up to $100,000 to any individual who provides original information which leads to the arrest and conviction of a person who kills or kidnaps a Federal drug law enforcement agent. Any award paid for information concerning the killing or kidnapping of a Federal drug law enforcement agent, as provided in clause (ii), shall be paid at the discretion of the Attorney General.

(B) The Attorney General shall forward to the Treasurer of the United States for deposit in accordance with section 524(c) of title 28, United States Code, any amounts of such moneys and proceeds remaining after payment of the expenses provided in subparagraph (A), except that, with respect to forfeitures conducted by the Postal Service, the Postal Service shall deposit in the Postal Service Fund, under section 2003(b)(7) of title 39, United States Code, such moneys and proceeds.

(3) The Attorney General shall assure that any property transferred to a State or local law enforcement agency under paragraph (1)(A)—

(A) has a value that bears a reasonable relationship to the degree of direct participation of the State or local agency in the law enforcement effort resulting in the forfeiture, taking into account the total value of all property forfeited and the total law enforcement effort with respect to the violation of law on which the forfeiture is based; and

(B) will serve to encourage further cooperation between the recipient State or local agency and Federal law enforcement agencies.

(4)(A) With respect to real property described in subparagraph (B), if the chief executive officer of the State involved submits to the Attorney General a request for purposes of such subparagraph, the authority established in such subparagraph is in lieu of the authority established in paragraph (1)(B).

(B)In the case of property described in paragraph (1)(B) that is civilly or criminally forfeited under this title, if the property is real property that is appropriate for use as a public area reserved for recreational or historic purposes or for the preservation of natural conditions, the Attorney General, upon the request of the chief executive officer of the State in which the property is located, may transfer title to the property to the State, either without charge or for a nominal charge, through a legal instrument providing that—

(i) such use will be the principal use of the property; and

(ii) title to the property reverts to the United States in the event that the property is used otherwise.

FIGURE A-8 (continued)

21 USCS § 883 FOOD AND DRUGS

(f) Forfeiture of schedule I or II substances. (1) All controlled substances in schedule I or II that are possessed, transferred, sold, or offered for sale in violation of the provisions of this title; all dangerous, toxic, or hazardous raw materials or products subject to forfeiture under subsection (a)(2) of this section; and any equipment or container subject to forfeiture under subsection (a)(2) or (3) which cannot be separated safely from such raw materials or products shall be deemed contraband and seized and summarily forfeited to the United States. Similarly, all substances in schedule I or II, which are seized or come into the possession of the United States, the owners of which are unknown, shall be deemed contraband and summarily forfeited to the United States.

(2) The Attorney General may direct the destruction of all controlled substances in schedule I or II seized for violation of this title; all dangerous, toxic, or hazardous raw materials or products subject to forfeiture under subsection (a)(2) of this section; and any equipment or container subject to forfeiture under subsection (a)(2) or (3) which cannot be separated safely from such raw materials or products under such circumstances as the Attorney General may deem necessary.

(g) Plants. (1) All species of plants from which controlled substances in schedules I and II may be derived which have been planted or cultivated in violation of this title, or of which the owners or cultivators are unknown, or which are wild growths, may be seized and summarily forfeited to the United States.

(2) The failure, upon demand by the Attorney General or his duly authorized agent, of the person in occupancy or in control of land or premises upon which such species of plants are growing or being stored, to produce an appropriate registration, or proof that he is the holder thereof, shall constitute authority for the seizure and forfeiture.

(3) The Attorney General, or his duly authorized agent, shall have authority to enter upon any lands, or into any dwelling pursuant to a search warrant, to cut, harvest, carry off, or destroy such plants.

(h) Vesting of title in United States. All right, title, and interest in property described in subsection (a) shall vest in the United States upon commission of the act giving rise to forfeiture under this section.

(i) Stay of civil forfeiture proceedings. The filing of an indictment or information alleging a violation of this title or title III, or a violation of State or local law that could have been charged under this title or title III, which is also related to a civil forfeiture proceeding under this section shall, upon motion of the United States and for good cause shown, stay the civil forfeiture proceeding.

(j) Venue. In addition to the venue provided for in section 1395 of title 28, United States Code, or any other provision of law, in the case of property of a defendant charged with a violation that is the basis for forfeiture of the property under this section, a proceeding for forfeiture under this section may be brought in the judicial district in which the defendant owning such property is found or in the judicial district in which the criminal prosecution is brought.

(k) [Omitted]

(l) Agreement between Attorney General and Postal Service for performance of functions. The functions of the Attorney General under this section shall be carried out by the Postal Service pursuant to such agreement as may be entered into between the Attorney General and the Postal Service.

§ 881. Forfeitures

(a) Subject property. The following shall be subject to forfeiture to the United States and no property right shall exist in them:

(1)–(3) [Unchanged]

(4) **[Caution: For provisions of this paragraph applicable to forfeiture proceedings commenced before the date that is 120 days after the date of the enactment of Act April 25, 2000, P. L. 106-185, see note below relating to April 25, 2000 amendments.]** All conveyances, including aircraft, vehicles, or vessels, which are used, or are intended for use, to transport, or in any manner to facilitate the transportation, sale, receipt, possession, or concealment of property described in paragraph (1), (2), or (9).

(5) [Unchanged]

(6) **[Caution: For provisions of this paragraph applicable to forfeiture proceedings commenced before the date that is 120 days after the date of the enactment of Act April 25, 2000, P. L. 106-185, see note below relating to April 25, 2000 amendments.]** All moneys, negotiable instruments, securities, or other things of value furnished or intended to be furnished by any person in exchange for a controlled substance or listed chemical in violation of this title, all proceeds traceable to such an exchange, and all moneys, negotiable instruments, and securities used or intended to be used to facilitate any violation of this title.

(7) **[Caution: For provisions of this paragraph applicable to forfeiture proceedings commenced before the date that is 120 days after the date of the enactment of Act April 25, 2000, P. L. 106-185, see note below relating to April 25, 2000 amendments.]** All real property, including any right, title, and interest (including any leasehold interest) in the whole of any lot or tract of land and any appurtenances or improvements, which is used, or intended to be used, in any manner or part, to commit, or to facilitate the commission of, a violation of this title punishable by more than one year's imprisonment.

(8)–(11) [Unchanged]

(b) Seizure procedures. [Caution: For provisions of this subsection applicable to forfeiture proceedings commenced before the date that is 120 days after the date of the enactment of Act April 25, 2000, P. L. 106-185, see note below relating to April 25, 2000 amendments.] Any property subject to forfeiture to the United States under this section may be seized by the Attorney General in the manner set forth in section 981(b) of title 18, United States Code.

(c)–(h) [Unchanged]

(i) [Caution: For provisions of this subsection applicable to forfeiture proceedings commenced before the date that is 120 days after the date of the enactment of Act April 25, 2000, P. L. 106-185, see note below relating to April 25, 2000 amendments.] The provisions of section 981(g) of title 18, United States Code, regarding the stay of a civil forfeiture proceeding shall apply to forfeitures under this section.

(j)–(l) [Unchanged]

(As amended April 25, 2000, P. L. 106–185, §§ 2(c)(2), 5(b), 8(b), 114 Stat. 210, 214, 216.)

FIGURE A-9 Amendments to Federal Forfeiture Statute. This Figure is from the July 2000 paperbound supplement to United States Code Service.

FIGURE A-10 New Federal Forfeiture Statute. From the July 2000 paperback supplement to United States Code Service.

18 USCS § 983 CRIMES & CRIMINAL PROCEDURE

§ 983. General rules for civil forfeiture proceedings [Caution: This section applies to any forfeiture proceeding commenced on or after the date that is 120 days after the date of enactment of Act April 25, 2000, P. L. 106-185, pursuant to § 21 of such Act, which appears as 8 USCS § 1324 note.]

(a) Notice; claim; complaint. (1)(A)(i)Except as provided in clauses (ii) through (v), in any nonjudicial civil forfeiture proceeding under a civil forfeiture statute, with respect to which the Government is required to send written notice to interested parties, such notice shall be sent in a manner to achieve proper notice as soon as practicable, and in no case more than 60 days after the date of the seizure.

(ii) No notice is required if, before the 60-day period expires, the Government files a civil judicial forfeiture action against the property and provides notice of that action as required by law.

(iii) If, before the 60-day period expires, the Government does not file a civil judicial forfeiture action, but does obtain a criminal indictment containing an allegation that the property is subject to forfeiture, the Government shall either—

(I) send notice within the 60 days and continue the nonjudicial civil forfeiture proceeding under this section; or

(II) terminate the nonjudicial civil forfeiture proceeding, and take the steps necessary to preserve its right to maintain custody of the property as provided in the applicable criminal forfeiture statute.

(iv) In a case in which the property is seized by a State or local law enforcement agency and turned over to a Federal law enforcement agency for the purpose of forfeiture under Federal law, notice shall be sent not more than 90 days after the date of seizure by the State or local law enforcement agency.

(v) If the identity or interest of a party is not determined until after the seizure or turnover but is determined before a declaration of forfeiture is entered, notice shall be sent to such interested party not later than 60 days after the determination by the Government of the identity of the party or the party's interest.

(B) A supervisory official in the headquarters office of the seizing agency may extend the period for sending notice under subparagraph (A) for a period not to exceed 30 days (which period may not be further extended except by a court), if the official determines that the conditions in subparagraph (D) are present.

(C) Upon motion by the Government, a court may extend the period for sending notice under subparagraph (A) for a period not to exceed 60 days, which period may be further extended by the court for 60-day periods, as necessary, if the court determines, based on a written certification of a supervisory official in the headquarters office of the seizing agency, that the conditions in subparagraph (D) are present.

(D) The period for sending notice under this paragraph may be extended only if there is reason to believe that notice may have an adverse result, including—

(i) endangering the life or physical safety of an individual;

(ii) flight from prosecution;

(iii) destruction of or tampering with evidence;

(iv) intimidation of potential witnesses; or

(v) otherwise seriously jeopardizing an investigation or unduly delaying a trial.

(E) Each of the Federal seizing agencies conducting nonjudicial forfeitures under this section shall report periodically to the Committees on the Judiciary of the House of Representatives and the Senate the number of occasions when an extension of time is granted under subparagraph (B).

(F) If the Government does not send notice of a seizure of property in accordance with subparagraph (A) to the person from whom the property was seized, and no

FIGURE A-10 (continued)

extension of time is granted, the Government shall return the property to that person without prejudice to the right of the Government to commence a forfeiture proceeding at a later time. The Government shall not be required to return contraband or other property that the person from whom the property was seized may not legally possess.

(2)(A) Any person claiming property seized in a nonjudicial civil forfeiture proceeding under a civil forfeiture statute may file a claim with the appropriate official after the seizure.

(B) A claim under subparagraph (A) may be filed not later than the deadline set forth in a personal notice letter (which deadline may be not earlier than 35 days after the date the letter is mailed), except that if that letter is not received, then a claim may be filed not later than 30 days after the date of final publication of notice of seizure.

(C) A claim shall—

(i) identify the specific property being claimed;

(ii) state the claimant's interest in such property (and provide customary documentary evidence of such interest if available) and state that the claim is not frivolous; and

(iii) be made under oath, subject to penalty of perjury.

(D) A claim need not be made in any particular form. Each Federal agency conducting nonjudicial forfeitures under this section shall make claim forms generally available on request, which forms shall be written in easily understandable language.

(E) Any person may make a claim under subparagraph (A) without posting bond with respect to the property which is the subject of the claim.

(3)(A) Not later than 90 days after a claim has been filed, the Government shall file a complaint for forfeiture in the manner set forth in the Supplemental Rules for Certain Admiralty and Maritime Claims or return the property pending the filing of a complaint, except that a court in the district in which the complaint will be filed may extend the period for filing a complaint for good cause shown or upon agreement of the parties.

(B) If the Government does not—

(i) file a complaint for forfeiture or return the property, in accordance with subparagraph (A); or

(ii) before the time for filing a complaint has expired—

(I) obtain a criminal indictment containing an allegation that the property is subject to forfeiture; and

(II) take the steps necessary to preserve its right to maintain custody of the property as provided in the applicable criminal forfeiture statute, the Government shall promptly release the property pursuant to regulations promulgated by the Attorney General, and may not take any further action to effect the civil forfeiture of such property in connection with the underlying offense.

(C) In lieu of, or in addition to, filing a civil forfeiture complaint, the Government may include a forfeiture allegation in a criminal indictment. If criminal forfeiture is the only forfeiture proceeding commenced by the Government, the Government's right to continued possession of the property shall be governed by the applicable criminal forfeiture statute.

(D) No complaint may be dismissed on the ground that the Government did not have adequate evidence at the time the complaint was filed to establish the forfeitability of the property.

(4)(A) In any case in which the Government files in the appropriate United States district court a complaint for forfeiture of property, any person claiming an interest in

FIGURE A-10 (continued)

the seized property may file a claim asserting such person's interest in the property in the manner set forth in the Supplemental Rules for Certain Admiralty and Maritime Claims, except that such claim may be filed not later than 30 days after the date of service of the Government's complaint or, as applicable, not later than 30 days after the date of final publication of notice of the filing of the complaint.

(B) A person asserting an interest in seized property, in accordance with subparagraph (A), shall file an answer to the Government's complaint for forfeiture not later than 20 days after the date of the filing of the claim.

(b) Representation. (1)(A) If a person with standing to contest the forfeiture of property in a judicial civil forfeiture proceeding under a civil forfeiture statute is financially unable to obtain representation by counsel, and the person is represented by counsel appointed under section 3006A of this title in connection with a related criminal case, the court may authorize counsel to represent that person with respect to the claim.

(B) In determining whether to authorize counsel to represent a person under subparagraph (A), the court shall take into account such factors as—

(i) the person's standing to contest the forfeiture; and

(ii) whether the claim appears to be made in good faith.

(2)(A) If a person with standing to contest the forfeiture of property in a judicial civil forfeiture proceeding under a civil forfeiture statute is financially unable to obtain representation by counsel, and the property subject to forfeiture is real property that is being used by the person as a primary residence, the court, at the request of the person, shall insure that the person is represented by an attorney for the Legal Services Corporation with respect to the claim.

(B)(i) At appropriate times during a representation under subparagraph (A), the Legal Services Corporation shall submit a statement of reasonable attorney fees and costs to the court.

(ii) The court shall enter a judgment in favor of the Legal Services Corporation for reasonable attorney fees and costs submitted pursuant to clause (i) and treat such judgment as payable under section 2465 of title 28, United States Code, regardless of the outcome of the case.

(3) The court shall set the compensation for representation under this subsection, which shall be equivalent to that provided for court-appointed representation under section 3006A of this title.

(c) Burden of proof. In a suit or action brought under any civil forfeiture statute for the civil forfeiture of any property—

(1) the burden of proof is on the Government to establish, by a preponderance of the evidence, that the property is subject to forfeiture;

(2) the Government may use evidence gathered after the filing of a complaint for forfeiture to establish, by a preponderance of the evidence, that property is subject to forfeiture; and

(3) if the Government's theory of forfeiture is that the property was used to commit or facilitate the commission of a criminal offense, or was involved in the commission of a criminal offense, the Government shall establish that there was a substantial connection between the property and the offense.

(d) Innocent owner defense. (1) An innocent owner's interest in property shall not be forfeited under any civil forfeiture statute. The claimant shall have the burden of proving that the claimant is an innocent owner by a preponderance of the evidence.

(2)(A) With respect to a property interest in existence at the time the illegal conduct giving rise to forfeiture took place, the term "innocent owner" means an owner who—

(i) did not know of the conduct giving rise to forfeiture; or

FIGURE A-10 (continued)

CRIMES **18 USCS § 983**

(ii) upon learning of the conduct giving rise to the forfeiture, did all that reasonably could be expected under the circumstances to terminate such use of the property.

(B)(i)For the purposes of this paragraph, ways in which a person may show that such person did all that reasonably could be expected may include demonstrating that such person, to the extent permitted by law—

(I) gave timely notice to an appropriate law enforcement agency of information that led the person to know the conduct giving rise to a forfeiture would occur or has occurred; and

(II) in a timely fashion revoked or made a good faith attempt to revoke permission for those engaging in such conduct to use the property or took reasonable actions in consultation with a law enforcement agency to discourage or prevent the illegal use of the property.

(ii) A person is not required by this subparagraph to take steps that the person reasonably believes would be likely to subject any person (other than the person whose conduct gave rise to the forfeiture) to physical danger.

(3)(A) With respect to a property interest acquired after the conduct giving rise to the forfeiture has taken place, the term "innocent owner" means a person who, at the time that person acquired the interest in the property—

(i) was a bona fide purchaser or seller for value (including a purchaser or seller of goods or services for value); and

(ii) did not know and was reasonably without cause to believe that the property was subject to forfeiture.

(B) An otherwise valid claim under subparagraph (A) shall not be denied on the ground that the claimant gave nothing of value in exchange for the property if—

(i) the property is the primary residence of the claimant;

(ii) depriving the claimant of the property would deprive the claimant of the means to maintain reasonable shelter in the community for the claimant and all dependents residing with the claimant;

(iii) the property is not, and is not traceable to, the proceeds of any criminal offense; and

(iv) the claimant acquired his or her interest in the property through marriage, divorce, or legal separation, or the claimant was the spouse or legal dependent of a person whose death resulted in the transfer of the property to the claimant through inheritance or probate,

except that the court shall limit the value of any real property interest for which innocent ownership is recognized under this subparagraph to the value necessary to maintain reasonable shelter in the community for such claimant and all dependents residing with the claimant.

(4) Notwithstanding any provision of this subsection, no person may assert an ownership interest under this subsection in contraband or other property that it is illegal to possess.

(5) If the court determines, in accordance with this section, that an innocent owner has a partial interest in property otherwise subject to forfeiture, or a joint tenancy or tenancy by the entirety in such property, the court may enter an appropriate order—

(A) severing the property;

(B) transferring the property to the Government with a provision that the Government compensate the innocent owner to the extent of his or her ownership interest once a final order of forfeiture has been entered and the property has been reduced to liquid assets; or

(C) permitting the innocent owner to retain the property subject to a lien in favor of the Government to the extent of the forfeitable interest in the property.

(6) In this subsection, the term "owner"—

FIGURE A-10 (continued)

(A) means a person with an ownership interest in the specific property sought to be forfeited, including a leasehold, lien, mortgage, recorded security interest, or valid assignment of an ownership interest; and

(B) does not include—

(i) a person with only a general unsecured interest in, or claim against, the property or estate of another;

(ii) a bailee unless the bailor is identified and the bailee shows a colorable legitimate interest in the property seized; or

(iii) a nominee who exercises no dominion or control over the property.

(e) Motion to set aside forfeiture. (1) Any person entitled to written notice in any nonjudicial civil forfeiture proceeding under a civil forfeiture statute who does not receive such notice may file a motion to set aside a declaration of forfeiture with respect to that person's interest in the property, which motion shall be granted if—

(A) the Government knew, or reasonably should have known, of the moving party's interest and failed to take reasonable steps to provide such party with notice; and

(B) the moving party did not know or have reason to know of the seizure within sufficient time to file a timely claim.

(2)(A) Notwithstanding the expiration of any applicable statute of limitations, if the court grants a motion under paragraph (1), the court shall set aside the declaration of forfeiture as to the interest of the moving party without prejudice to the right of the Government to commence a subsequent forfeiture proceeding as to the interest of the moving party.

(B) Any proceeding described in subparagraph (A) shall be commenced—

(i) if nonjudicial, within 60 days of the entry of the order granting the motion; or

(ii) if judicial, within 6 months of the entry of the order granting the motion.

(3) A motion under paragraph (1) may be filed not later than 5 years after the date of final publication of notice of seizure of the property.

(4) If, at the time a motion made under paragraph (1) is granted, the forfeited property has been disposed of by the Government in accordance with law, the Government may institute proceedings against a substitute sum of money equal to the value of the moving party's interest in the property at the time the property was disposed of.

(5) A motion filed under this subsection shall be the exclusive remedy for seeking to set aside a declaration of forfeiture under a civil forfeiture statute.

(f) Release of seized property. (1) A claimant under subsection (a) is entitled to immediate release of seized property if—

(A) the claimant has a possessory interest in the property;

(B) the claimant has sufficient ties to the community to provide assurance that the property will be available at the time of the trial;

(C) the continued possession by the Government pending the final disposition of forfeiture proceedings will cause substantial hardship to the claimant, such as preventing the functioning of a business, preventing an individual from working, or leaving an individual homeless;

(D) the claimant's likely hardship from the continued possession by the Government of the seized property outweighs the risk that the property will be destroyed, damaged, lost, concealed, or transferred if it is returned to the claimant during the pendency of the proceeding; and

(E) none of the conditions set forth in paragraph (8) applies.

(2) A claimant seeking release of property under this subsection must request possession of the property from the appropriate official, and the request must set forth the basis on which the requirements of paragraph (1) are met.

FIGURE A-10 (continued)

CRIMES **18 USCS § 983**

(3) (A)If not later than 15 days after the date of a request under paragraph (2) the property has not been released, the claimant may file a petition in the district court in which the complaint has been filed or, if no complaint has been filed, in the district court in which the seizure warrant was issued or in the district court for the district in which the property was seized.

(B) The petition described in subparagraph (A) shall set forth—

(i) the basis on which the requirements of paragraph (1) are met; and

(ii) the steps the claimant has taken to secure release of the property from the appropriate official.

(4) If the Government establishes that the claimant's claim is frivolous, the court shall deny the petition. In responding to a petition under this subsection on other grounds, the Government may in appropriate cases submit evidence ex parte in order to avoid disclosing any matter that may adversely affect an ongoing criminal investigation or pending criminal trial.

(5) The court shall render a decision on a petition filed under paragraph (3) not later than 30 days after the date of the filing, unless such 30-day limitation is extended by consent of the parties or by the court for good cause shown.

(6) If—

(A) a petition is filed under paragraph (3); and

(B) the claimant demonstrates that the requirements of paragraph (1) have been met,

the district court shall order that the property be returned to the claimant, pending completion of proceedings by the Government to obtain forfeiture of the property.

(7) If the court grants a petition under paragraph (3)—

(A) the court may enter any order necessary to ensure that the value of the property is maintained while the forfeiture action is pending, including—

(i) permitting the inspection, photographing, and inventory of the property;

(ii) fixing a bond in accordance with rule E(5) of the Supplemental Rules for Certain Admiralty and Maritime Claims; and

(iii) requiring the claimant to obtain or maintain insurance on the subject property; and

(B) the Government may place a lien against the property or file a lis pendens to ensure that the property is not transferred to another person.

(8) This subsection shall not apply if the seized property—

(A) is contraband, currency, or other monetary instrument, or electronic funds unless such currency or other monetary instrument or electronic funds constitutes the assets of a legitimate business which has been seized;

(B) is to be used as evidence of a violation of the law;

(C) by reason of design or other characteristic, is particularly suited for use in illegal activities; or

(D) is likely to be used to commit additional criminal acts if returned to the claimant.

(g) Proportionality. (1) The claimant under subsection (a)(4) may petition the court to determine whether the forfeiture was constitutionally excessive.

(2) In making this determination, the court shall compare the forfeiture to the gravity of the offense giving rise to the forfeiture.

(3) The claimant shall have the burden of establishing that the forfeiture is grossly disproportional by a preponderance of the evidence at a hearing conducted by the court without a jury.

(4) If the court finds that the forfeiture is grossly disproportional to the offense it shall reduce or eliminate the forfeiture as necessary to avoid a violation of the Excessive Fines Clause of the Eighth Amendment of the Constitution.

FIGURE A-10 (continued)

(h) Civil fine. (1) In any civil forfeiture proceeding under a civil forfeiture statute in which the Government prevails, if the court finds that the claimant's assertion of an interest in the property was frivolous, the court may impose a civil fine on the claimant of an amount equal to 10 percent of the value of the forfeited property, but in no event shall the fine be less than $250 or greater than $5,000.

(2) Any civil fine imposed under this subsection shall not preclude the court from imposing sanctions under rule 11 of the Federal Rules of Civil Procedure.

(3) In addition to the limitations of section 1915 of title 28, United States Code, in no event shall a prisoner file a claim under a civil forfeiture statute or appeal a judgment in a civil action or proceeding based on a civil forfeiture statute if the prisoner has, on three or more prior occasions, while incarcerated or detained in any facility, brought an action or appeal in a court of the United States that was dismissed on the grounds that it is frivolous or malicious, unless the prisoner shows extraordinary and exceptional circumstances.

(i) Civil forfeiture statute defined. In this section, the term "civil forfeiture statute"—

(1) means any provision of Federal law providing for the forfeiture of property other than as a sentence imposed upon conviction of a criminal offense; and

(2) does not include—

(A) the Tariff Act of 1930 or any other provision of law codified in title 19;

(B) the Internal Revenue Code of 1986 [26 USCS §§ 1 et seq.];

(C) the Federal Food, Drug, and Cosmetic Act (21 U.S.C. 301 et seq.);

(D) the Trading with the Enemy Act (50 U.S.C. App. 1 et seq.); or

(E) section 1 of title VI of the Act of June 15, 1917 (40 Stat. 233; 22 U.S.C. 401).

(j) Restraining orders; protective orders. (1) Upon application of the United States, the court may enter a restraining order or injunction, require the execution of satisfactory performance bonds, create receiverships, appoint conservators, custodians, appraisers, accountants, or trustees, or take any other action to seize, secure, maintain, or preserve the availability of property subject to civil forfeiture—

(A) upon the filing of a civil forfeiture complaint alleging that the property with respect to which the order is sought is subject to civil forfeiture; or

(B) prior to the filing of such a complaint, if, after notice to persons appearing to have an interest in the property and opportunity for a hearing, the court determines that—

(i) there is a substantial probability that the United States will prevail on the issue of forfeiture and that failure to enter the order will result in the property being destroyed, removed from the jurisdiction of the court, or otherwise made unavailable for forfeiture; and

(ii) the need to preserve the availability of the property through the entry of the requested order outweighs the hardship on any party against whom the order is to be entered.

(2) An order entered pursuant to paragraph (1)(B) shall be effective for not more than 90 days, unless extended by the court for good cause shown, or unless a complaint described in paragraph (1)(A) has been filed.

(3) A temporary restraining order under this subsection may be entered upon application of the United States without notice or opportunity for a hearing when a complaint has not yet been filed with respect to the property, if the United States demonstrates that there is probable cause to believe that the property with respect to which the order is sought is subject to civil forfeiture and that provision of notice will jeopardize the availability of the property for forfeiture. Such a temporary order shall expire not more than 10 days after the date on which it is entered, unless extended for good cause shown or unless the party against whom it

FIGURE A-10 (continued)

CRIMES 18 USCS § 983

is entered consents to an extension for a longer period. A hearing requested concerning an order entered under this paragraph shall be held at the earliest possible time and prior to the expiration of the temporary order.

(4) The court may receive and consider, at a hearing held pursuant to this subsection, evidence and information that would be inadmissible under the Federal Rules of Evidence.

(Added and amended April 25, 2000, P. L. 106–185, §§ 2(a), 9, 114 Stat. 202, 216.)

FIGURE A-11
Search and Seizure and the Exclusionary Rule.

Introduction

This section of the appendix gives you some background on search and seizure and the exclusionary rule. It should be of help in understanding the Williamses' problem and other search and seizure material in this book.

The Fourth Amendment[1]

Searches, seizures, and arrests are vital aspects of law enforcement. Because they involve significant invasions of individual liberties, limits on their use can be found in the constitutions, statutes, and other laws of the states and federal government.

The most important limitation is the fourth amendment to the United States Constitution, which reads:

> The right of the people to be secure in their persons, papers, and effects, against unreasonable searches and seizures, shall not be violated, and no warrants shall issue but upon probable cause, supported by oath or affirmation, and particularly describing the place to be searched and the persons or things to be seized.

Two remedies are available to the defendant whose fourth amendment rights have been violated by the government. First, in a criminal prosecution, the defendant may invoke the exclusionary rule. Second, he or she may have a civil cause of action against the offending officer under a rights statute or for a "constitutional tort."[2]

The concepts of reasonable expectation of privacy and probable cause are important throughout the law of searches, seizures, and arrests. Accordingly, they will be examined first. The Supreme Court has defined a *search* as occurring "when an expectation in privacy that society is prepared to consider reasonable is infringed" and a *seizure* as a "meaningful interference with an individual's possessory interest" in property.[3]

Probable Cause Defined

Probable cause is a phrase describing the minimum amount of evidence necessary before a search, seizure, or arrest is proper. Whether the issue concerns a search and seizure or an arrest, the same quantity of evidence is necessary to establish probable cause.

There is no one universal definition of probable cause. In fact, the definition of probable cause differs depending on the context. In all situations, it is more than mere suspicion and less than the standard required to prove a defendant guilty at trial (beyond a reasonable doubt). As the Supreme court has expressed, probable cause is present when the trustworthy facts within the law enforcement officer's knowledge are sufficient in themselves to justify a "person of reasonable caution" in the belief that seizable property would be found or that the person to be arrested committed the crime in question.[4]

FIGURE A-11 (continued)

Searches and Seizures

The Warrant Requirement

Depending upon the circumstances, a search may be conducted with or without a warrant. The Supreme Court has expressed a strong preference for the use of warrants, when possible, over warrantless actions.[5] The warrant preference serves an important purpose: it protects citizens from overzealous law enforcement practices.

Exceptions to the Search Warrant Requirement

Although the general rule is that a warrant must be obtained before a search may be undertaken, there are many exceptions. The exceptions to the warrant requirement are sometimes referred to as *exigent circumstances.*

Consent Searches

Voluntary consent to a search obviates the warrant requirement. A person may consent to a search of his or her person or property. The scope of the search is limited by the person consenting. Absent special circumstances, a consent to search may be terminated at any time by the person giving consent.

A person's consent must be voluntary. All of the circumstances surrounding the consent are examined to determine whether the consent was voluntary. There is no requirement that police officers inform a person that he or she may refuse to consent.[6]

Of course, a defendant who is threatened or coerced into consenting has not voluntarily consented. It is not coercion for a person to be told that, if he or she does not consent, a warrant will be obtained authorizing the desired search. It is coercion for officers to tell a person that, if he or she does not consent to a search, a warrant will be obtained and the officers will ransack the person's home.[7]

Motor Vehicles

Privacy in automobiles is protected by the Fourth Amendment. However, the Supreme Court has not extended full Fourth Amendment protection to the occupants of automobiles. The Court's rationale for decreased protection is twofold. First, because of the mobile nature of automobiles, evidence can disappear quickly. Second, automobiles are used on the public roads where they and their occupants are visible to the public; thus, an occupant of an automobile has a lesser expectation of privacy than does the occupant of a home.

Of course, a motorist may be stopped if an officer has probable cause. In addition, a *Terry* stop may be made if there is reasonable suspicion. As discussed earlier, *Terry* stops must be limited in duration and reasonable in method, and a frisk of the occupant is permissible only if the officer possesses a reasonable belief that the individual may have a weapon.

Where the Fourth Amendment's mandates have been reduced is in the context of the warrant requirement. In *Carroll v. United States,* 267 U.S. 132 (1925), it was announced that a warrantless search of a vehicle stopped on a public road is reasonable, provided the officer has probable cause to believe that an object subject to seizure will be found in the vehicle. The existence of probable cause is the key to the search. This authority has been extended to permit the search to continue after the vehicle is impounded.

The sticky question in this area is the scope of the search. Generally, an officer is given the scope that a magistrate would have if a warrant were sought. Thus, if an officer has probable cause to believe that a shotgun used in a crime will be found in a car, a search of the glove box is improper. The opposite would be true if the item sought was a piece of jewelry, such as a ring.

Officers may also search closed items found in the vehicle, provided probable cause exists to believe an item sought may be contained therein. The same rules apply as previously discussed. Rifling through a suitcase found in a car in search of a stolen painting that is larger than the suitcase is unreasonable and violative of the Fourth Amendment. Once the sought-after item is found, the search must cease.

FIGURE A-11 (continued)

An automobile may be searched incident to the arrest of its driver, but that search is also limited. If a motorist is arrested and removed from a vehicle, but there is no independent probable cause to search the vehicle, items contained therein may not be opened. This is true even if the vehicle is impounded and an inventory is performed. The inventory should note the luggage found, but no effort to discover its contents should be made.

May the occupants of a vehicle be searched incident to a proper search of the vehicle? The answer is no—but if an officer has probable cause to believe that one of the occupants has hidden the item sought on his or her person, a search of that occupant is permissible.

Fourth Amendment issues also arise in the context of roadblocks, which are used by law enforcement officers in two situations. First, they assist in the apprehension of a particular suspect. Second, serving the regulatory function of protecting the public from unsafe drivers, officers may stop vehicles to determine if the car satisfies the state's safety requirements, whether the driver is properly licensed, and whether the vehicle is properly registered. In regard to the former, reasonable suspicion is required before a stop can be made. As to the latter, temporary regulatory detentions are permitted so long as they are both objectively random and reasonable. That is, the police must use an objective system in deciding what automobiles will be stopped. Every car, or every tenth car, or some similar method is permissible.

Stop and Frisk

On October 31, 1963, in Cleveland, Ohio, a police detective observed three men standing on a street corner. Suspicious of the men, the detective positioned himself in order to watch their behavior. After some time, the officer concluded that the men were "casing a job, a stick-up."

The officer approached the men, identified himself, and asked them to identify themselves. After the men "mumbled something," the officer grabbed one of the men and conducted a *frisk*, or a pat-down, of the man's clothing. The officer felt a pistol in the man's coat pocket. He removed the gun from the coat and then patted down the other two men. Another gun was discovered during those frisks.

The officer testified that he conducted the frisks because he believed the men were carrying weapons. The first man frisked was defendant Terry. At trial, he was convicted of carrying a concealed weapon and was subsequently sentenced to one to three years in prison. His appeal made it to the United States Supreme Court.

In *Terry v. Ohio*, 392 U.S. 1 (1968), the Supreme Court was confronted with these issues: Did the officer's behavior amount to a search or seizure under the fourth amendment? If so, was the search and seizure by the officer reasonable?

The Court decided that defendant Terry had been seized under the fourth amendment. "It must be recognized that whenever a police officer accosts an individual and restrains his freedom to walk away, he has 'seized' that person." As to the frisk, the court stated that "it is nothing less than sheer torture of the English language to suggest that a careful exploration of the outer surfaces of a person's clothing all over his or her body in an attempt to find weapons is not a search."

With these statements, the Court made it clear that the police practice of stopping and frisking people is one governed by the fourth amendment. However, the Court then concluded that an exception to the probable cause requirement was justified because the intrusion upon a person's privacy is limited in a stop and frisk, as opposed to an arrest and full search.

Officers are not given carte blanche to stop and frisk. Although probable suspicion is not required, officers must have a "reasonable suspicion" that the person to be stopped has committed, is committing, or is about to commit a crime. The officer's suspicion must be supported by "specific and articulable facts which, taken together with rational inferences from those facts, reasonably warrant that intrusion." *Terry* 392 U.S. at 21. An officer's intuition alone is not enough suspicion to support a *Terry* seizure.

FIGURE A-11 (continued)

The stopping of a vehicle does fall within the reach of the fourth amendment. However, the Supreme Court has said that once a person is lawfully pulled over, he or she may be ordered out of the vehicle, even though there is no reason to believe that the driver is a threat.

In addition to requiring reasonable suspicion, the *Terry* court also stated that stops are to "last no longer than is necessary." and the investigative methods employed during the stop should be the "least intrusive means reasonably available to verify or dispel the officer's suspicion in a short period of time." If an officer detains a person longer than necessary, the investigatory detention turns into a full seizure (arrest), and the probable cause requirement of the Fourth Amendment is triggered.

Florida v. Royer, 460 U.S. 491 (1983), provides an example of the distinction between an investigatory detention and an arrest. The defendant, a suspected drug dealer, was questioned in a public area of an airport. After a few minutes, he was taken 40 feet away to a small police office, where he consented to a search of his luggage. The Court concluded that the search was the product of an illegal arrest, as less intrusive methods of investigation were available. As alternatives, the Court mentioned that the officers could have used narcotics dogs to inspect the luggage or could have immediately requested consent to search the defendant's luggage. The act of requiring the defendant to accompany the officers to a small room 40 feet away transformed the detention from a *Terry* stop to an arrest, which was violative of the fourth amendment because it was not supported by probable cause.

The Exclusionary Rule

An important constitutional development was the creation of the *exclusionary rule*. The rule is simple: Evidence that is obtained by an unconstitutional search or seizure is inadmissible at trial.

The rule was first announced by the Supreme Court in 1914.[8] However, at that time the rule had not been incorporated into the due process clause of the fourteenth amendment. As such, the exclusionary rule did not apply to state court proceedings. This was changed in 1961 when the Supreme Court declared that evidence obtained in violation of the Constitution could not be used in state or federal criminal proceedings. The case was *Mapp v. Ohio*, 367 U.S. 643 (1961).

The exclusionary rule has been the subject of intense debate. There is no explicit textual language in the Constitution establishing the rule. For that reason, many contend that the Supreme Court has exceeded its authority by creating it; that it is the responsibility of the legislative branch to make such laws.

On the other side is the argument that without the exclusionary rule the Bill of Rights is ineffective. Why have constitutional standards if there is no method to enforce them. For example, why require that the officers in the *Mapp* case have a search warrant, yet permit them to conduct a warrantless search and use the evidence obtained against the defendant? These questions go to the purpose of the exclusionary rule: it discourages law enforcement personnel from engaging in unconstitutional conduct. The exclusionary rule works to prevent the admission into evidence of any item, confession, or other thing that was obtained by law enforcement officers in an unconstitutional manner.

Most exclusionary rule issues are resolved prior to trial by way of a motion to suppress. In some instances the motion may be made at the moment the prosecutor attempts to introduce such evidence at trial. This is known as a *contemporaneous objection*.

Fruit of the Poisonous Tree

The exclusionary rule applies to *primary evidence*, evidence that is the direct result of an illegal search or seizure. It is possible that such primary evidence may lead the police to other evidence. Suppose that police officers beat a confession out of a bank robber. In that confession the defendant tells the police where he has hidden the stolen money. The confession is the primary evidence and is inadmissible under the exclusionary rule. The money (after it is retrieved by the police) is *secondary*, or *derivative, evidence*. Such evidence is known as *fruit of the poisonous tree* and is also inadmissible evidence. Gener-

FIGURE A-11 (continued)

ally, evidence that is tainted by the prior illegal conduct is inadmissible. The rule does not make all evidence later obtained by law enforcement inadmissible, though. In some instances, evidence may be admissible because the connection between the illegally seized evidence and the subsequently obtained evidence is marginal, or as the Supreme Court put it, "the causal connection . . . may have become so attenuated as to dissipate the taint."[9]

1. Grateful thanks is given to Dr. Daniel Hall who authored this portion of the appendix. Reproduced by permission. *Criminal Law and Procedure* by Daniel Hall, Delmar, Albany, New York, Coyright 1992.
2. *Biven v. Six Unknown Named Agents*, 403 U.S. 388 (1972).
3. *United States v. Jacobsen*, 466 U.S. 109, 113 (1984).
4. *Carroll v. United States*, 267 U.S. 132 (1934).
5. *Beck v. Ohio*, 379 U.S. 89 (1964).
6. *Schneckloth v. Bustamonte*, 412 U.S. 218 (1973).
7. *United States v. Kampbell*, 574 F.2d 962 (8th Cir. 1978).
8. The rule, as applied in federal courts, was announced in *Weeks v. United States*, 232 U.S. 383 (1914).
9. *Nardone v. United States*, 308 U.S. 338 (1939).

CITATION RULES

APPENDIX B

This appendix gives you a summary of basic citation rules. For a more detailed explanation of the citation rule for a particular authority, refer back to the chapter in which the authority was discussed.

Caveat: Do not assume that the legal citations found when researching are in correct citation form. Citations, even those included in cases, may or may not comply with the citation rules your professor has asked you to use. Always check your citations against the appropriate citation rule for correct form.

GENERAL CITATION TIPS

Citation tip: ordinal numbers. In legal citations the ordinal numbers "second" and "third" are abbreviated to "2d" and "3d." For all other ordinal numbers, use the standard abbreviations.

Citation tip: case names. In a reporter, a case begins with the full name of the case, a portion of the name appearing in all capital letters. Unless your reader requires *Bluebook* form for case names, use that portion of the case name that appears in all capitals, with the further modifications explained in this paragraph as the case name in your citation. You will have a very close approximation of *Bluebook* form without having to master a very complicated *Bluebook* rule. For case names, individuals are referred to only by their surnames. When the United States of America is a party to a case, the citation needs to show "United States" rather than "United States of America" or "U.S." If a state is a party to the case and the case is being decided by a court of the state, the citation should contain only "State," "Commonwealth," or "People." If a state is a party to the case but the case is being decided by a court other than a court of the state, then the citation should contain only the name of the state, for example "Minnesota," not "State of Minnesota."

Citation tip: subsequent history. Connect subsequent history to the end of the citation of the lower court decision by explaining what the higher court did, underlining the explanation, and setting it off by commas. "Certiorari denied" should be abbreviated to "*cert. denied,*" "affirmed" should be abbreviated to "*aff'd,*" and "reversed" should be abbreviated to "*rev'd.*" Otherwise the explanation should be written out, for example "*vacated.*" The *Bluebook* instructs you to omit information on denial of certiorari unless the case is less than two years old or there is a particular reason to include the information.

Citation tip: italics. Certain citations call for the use of italics. For example, in a case citation, the name of the case is in italics. You may substitute underlining for italics. Choose either italics or underlining; do not both underline and italicize.

Citation tip: pages and statutory sections. When citing to consecutive pages or statutory sections, give the first and the last page numbers or statutory numbers, joined by a hyphen. When citing to nonconsecutive pages or statutory sections, separate the pages and sections by commas. The first two examples illustrate the use of hyphens for consecutive pages (14 through 15) and statutory sections (2510 through 2515). The third and fourth examples illustrate the use of commas for nonconsecutive pages (249 and 251) and statutory sections (2515 and 2520).

Terry v. Ohio, 392 U.S. 1, 14-15 (1968).

18 U.S.C.S. §§ 2510-2515 (Lexis L. Publg. 1993 & Supp. 2000).

United States v. Jimeno, 500 U.S. 248, 249, 251 (1991).

18 U.S.C.S. §§ 2515, 2520 (Lexis L. Publg. 1993 & Supp. 1999).

Citation tip: symbols for sections and paragraphs. The symbol § means "section." Use two section symbols (§§) when citing to two or more sections.

UNITED STATES SUPREME COURT CASES

The following is an example of a citation for *Wyoming v. Houghton* as found in *United States Law Week*. The citation to *United States Law Week* would be used only until the case is published in *United States Reports*, *Supreme Court Reporter*, or *United States Supreme Court Reports, Lawyers' Edition:*

Wyoming v. Houghton, 67 U.S.L.W. 4225 (U.S. 1999).

If the case has been printed in a reporter you should give the citation to a reporter rather than to a looseleaf publication, such as *United States Law Week*. *The Bluebook* tells you to cite to *United States Reports* if the case has been published in *United States Reports*. If the case has not yet been published in *United States Reports*, you should cite to *Supreme Court Reporter*. If the case has not yet been published in *Supreme Court Reports*, you should cite to *United States Supreme Court Reports, Lawyers' Edition*. *Wyoming v. Houghton* has been published in *United States Reports*, *Supreme Court Reporter* and *United States Supreme Court Reports, Lawyers' Edition*. Therefore, the correct citation would be:

Wyoming v. Houghton, 526 U.S. 295 (1999).

Although *The Bluebook* does not require you to give **parallel citations** to United States Supreme Court cases, parallel citations to those cases are sometimes given, for example:

Wyoming v. Houghton, 526 U.S. 295, 119 S. Ct. 1297, 143 L. Ed. 2d 408 (1999).

Sometimes a parallel citation contains one or more blanks for information not yet known, such as the volume and page number of a case in a particular reporter.

UNITED STATES COURTS OF APPEALS

Whren v. United States, 53 F.3d 371 (D.C. Cir. 1995), *aff'd*, 517 U.S. 806 (1996).

United States v. McKinnon, 985 F.2d 525 (1993).

UNITED STATES DISTRICT COURTS

The following is an example of a citation to a case from the United States District Court for the Northern District of Texas:

Sexton v. Gibbs, 327 F.Supp. 134 (N.D. Tex. 1970), *aff'd*, 446 F.2d 904 (5th Cir. 1971).

Notice that "Northern District of Texas" has been abbreviated to "N.D. Tex." You know from this citation that Texas has more than one district. Some of the less populous or smaller states, such as New Jersey, have only one United States district court that covers the whole state. The abbreviation for the United States District Court for the District of New Jersey would be "D. N.J."

CITATIONS FOR CONSTITUTIONS

The clause prohibiting ex post facto laws and section 1 of the fourteenth amendment to the Constitution may be cited as follows:

U.S. Const. art. I, § 9, cl. 3.

U.S. Const. amend. XIV, § 1.

Give the section number when the Constitution specifically identifies a portion of an article as a section. When a section, such as section nine of article I, is long and contains a number of paragraphs, you can reference a particular paragraph as a "clause." Some copies of the United States Constitution identify the amendments as "articles" instead of "amendments." This is because the amendments are technically articles in amendment of the Constitution. To avoid confusion, cite the amendments to the Constitution as "amendments" rather than as "articles." State constitutions can be cited using the same citation form as above or using your state's citation rules.

Capitalize a state constitution only when naming it in full. Capitalize the United States Constitution or any reference to it. Do not capitalize the name of any portion of a constitution except for portions of the United States Constitution when referring to a portion of the United States Constitution in a textual sentence.

CITATIONS FOR STATUTES

Subsection (2)(c) of the federal eavesdropping and wiretapping statutes reprinted in chapter 5 of this book may be cited as follows:

18 U.S.C. § 2511 (2)(c) (1994).	(abbreviation for volume 18 of United States Code, subsection (2)(c) of section 2511, 1994 is the date of the latest version of the Code containing the statute)

A citation to the United States Code is the preferred citation since the United States Code is the official code. Because many law libraries do not have the United States Code, you may use the following citations to either *United States Code Service* or *United States Code Annotated:*

18 U.S.C.S. § 2511 (2)(c) (Lexis L Publg. 1993 & Supp. 2000.)	(*United States Code Service* is published by Lexis Law Publishing; part of the cite statute is in the 1993 hard bound volume and part is in the 2000 pocket part)
18 U.S.C.A. § 2511(2)(c) (West 2000).	(*United States Code Annotated* is published by West Group, the cited statute is in the 2000 hardbound volume)

If you are referring to a portion of the statute rather than to the entire statute, pinpoint the portion by subsection. If you do give the subsection in your citation, be sure the subsection is designated just as it is in the statute, including whether letters are lower or upper case, whether numbers are arabic or roman, and whether numbers and letters are enclosed in parentheses or not. For example, the above citation refers to subsubsection (c) of subsection (2) of section 2511 of title 18 of the United States Code.

The parenthesis at the end of the citation gives an abbreviation of the commercial publisher's name and the location of the statute. In the two citations above, "Lexis L. Publg." is an abbreviation for "Lexis Law Publishing" and "West" is an abbreviation for "West Group." At the time this chapter was written, the hardbound volume of *United States Code Service* containing the statutes was copyrighted "1993" and the pocket part supplement was dated "2000." Similarly, the hardbound volume of *United States Code Annotated* was copyrighted "2000." Include as much parenthetical information needed to locate the statutory language. In the citation to *United States Code Service,* information was given for the hardbound volume and the pocket part supplement. If the statutory language is found entirely in the hardbound volume, you need only include information on the hardbound volume in the parenthesis. Conversely, if the statutory language is found entirely in the pocket part supplement, you need only include information on the pocket part supplement in the parenthesis.

CITATIONS FOR COURT RULES

The following are sample citations to the most important types of court rules identified in chapter 5:

Fed. R. Civ. P. 23.	(Rule 23 of the Federal Rules of Civil Procedure)
Fed. R. Crim. P. 1.	(Rule 1 of the Federal Rules of Criminal Procedure)
Fed. R. App. P. 5.	(Rule 5 of the Federal Rules of Appellate Procedure)
Fed. R. Evid. 610.	(Rule 610 of the Federal Rules of Evidence)
Sup. Ct. R. 1.	(Rule 1 of the Rules of the United States Supreme Court)

CITATIONS FOR ADMINISTRATIVE LAW

64 Fed. Reg. 22561-62 (1999).	(pages 22561 through 22562 of volume 64 of the *Federal Register,* published in 1999)

47 C.F.R. § 15.121 (1999).	(section 121 of part 15 of volume 47 of the *Code of Federal Regulations*, 1999 version)

In the above citation for the *Federal Register*, "64" is the volume, "22561-62" are the page numbers, and the year 1999 is the year of publication. In the above citation for the *Code of Federal Regulations*, "47" is the title, "15" is the part, "121" is the section, and the year 1999 is the year of publication.

CITATIONS TO LEGAL ENCYCLOPEDIAS

Although legal encyclopedias are not usually cited in documents submitted to court or opposing counsel, you will need to cite legal encyclopedias for assignments and more informal documents such as office memos. See chapter 16 for an explanation of the purpose and use of office memos. The following is the citation for sections 327-468 of the *American Jurisprudence* Searches and Seizures topic. The number "68" is the volume in which sections 327 through 468 are located; "2000" is the copyright year of the volume. (Note: *American Jurisprudence* is now a West Group publication.)

68 Am. Jur. 2d *Searches and Seizures* §§ 327-468 (2000).

A citation to a state legal encyclopedia would be in similar form except for substituting the abbreviation for the legal encyclopedia used instead of "Am. Jur. 2d".

Sections 327-468 of Searches and Seizures discuss electronic surveillance and wiretapping. An analogous discussion is found in sections 233-315 of the Telecommunications topic in Corpus Juris Secundum. The following is the citation to those sections. The number "86" is the volume in which sections 233 through 315 are located; "1997" is the copyright year of the volume; "2000" is the year of the pocket part supplement. The ampersand ("&") indicates that the material you are referring to was found both in the hardbound volume and the pocket part supplement. The citation should be revised to show only "1997" in the parentheses if the material you are referring to was found only in the hardbound volume. Similarly, the parentheses should contain only "Supp. 2000" if the material you are referring to was found only in the pocket part supplement.

86 C.J.S. *Telecommunications* §§ 233-315 (1997 & Supp. 2000).

CITATIONS TO AMERICAN LAW REPORTS

The following is the citation to the annotation entitled "Effect of Forfeiture Proceedings under the Uniform Controlled Substances Act or Similar Statute on Lien against Property Subject to Forfeiture" beginning on page 317 of the first volume of *American Law Reports Fifth Series*, copyright 1995.

Marjorie A. Caner, Annotation, *Propriety of Attorney's Surreptitous Sound Recording of Statements by Others Who Are or May Become Involved in Litigation*, 32 A.L.R. 5th 715 (1995).

The citation to an annotation from *American Law Reports Federal* would be similar in form except for substituting "A.L.R. Fed." for "A.L.R. 5th."

CITATIONS TO ATTORNEYS GENERAL OPINIONS

The following are sample citations to opinions of the United States Attorneys General and to the Office of Legal Counsel of the Department of Justice.

Official Opinions of the Attorneys General of the United States	34 Op. Atty. Gen (1925).
Opinions of the Office of Legal Counsel of the Department of Justice	3 Op. Off. Legal Counsel 64 (1979).

CITATIONS TO RESTATEMENTS

The following are sample citations to section 1 of the Restatement of Contracts, Second Series. The first citation is to section 1 and the second citation is to the illustration appearing in comment e of section 1.

Restatement (Second) of Contracts § 1 (1981).

Restatement (Second) of Contracts § 1 cmt. e, illus. 1 (1981).

CITATION TO A TREATISE

The following is a sample citation to section 2:15 of the treatise *Wiretapping and Eavesdropping.*

Clifford S. Fishman & Anne T. McKenna, *Wiretapping and Eavesdropping* § 2:15 (2d Ed. 1995).

CITATION TO LEGAL DICTIONARY

The following sample citation is to the page containing the definition for "eavesdropping" in a legal dictionary.

Black's Law Dictionary 529 (7th Ed. 1999).

CITATION TO A LAW REVIEW ARTICLE

The following is the citation to a law review article.

Eric Blumenson & Eva Nilsen, *Policing for Profit: The Drug War's Hidden Economic Agenda*, 65 U. Chi. L. Rev. 35, 40-41 (1998).

CITATION TO INTERNET MATERIAL

The following is the citation to an article found on the Internet.

David A. Harris, *Driving While Black: Racial Profiling on Our Nation's Highways* (visited Feb. 8, 2000) <http://www.aclu.org/profiling/report/index.html>.

CYBER CITATIONS

For more information on legal citations, you may want to access http://www.law.cornell.edu and search for "basic legal citation."

APPENDIX C

RULES FOR QUOTATIONS AND SHORT FORM CITATIONS

INTRODUCTION

Many students have a mental block about using quotations and short form citations in their legal writing. They have so convinced themselves that they will never master the rules of quotations and short form citations that they structure their writing to avoid having to deal with quotations and short form citations at all. This appendix is designed to help you through this "writer's block." First, it gives you the most basic rules for quotations and short form citations and then it lets you practice applying the rules by working through some exercises. These basic rules should be sufficient for your writing assignments in a legal writing class. If you have questions not covered by the rules, refer the *Bluebook* or the *ALWD Citation Manual.*

The *Bluebook* rules for law review articles differ in many respects from rules used in the other types of legal writing you will be doing. The rules discussed in this appendix can be used for all types of legal writing other than law review articles. If you have the occasion to write a law review article, you will need to follow *Bluebook* form for law review articles.

QUOTATIONS

To quote or not to quote

When your authority is constitutional or statutory provisions, it is a good idea to quote the relevant portions of those provisions. The reason is that each word in those provisions has been carefully selected and a court interpreting those provisions will use the wording of those provisions as a starting point. Focus your reader's attention by quoting only those portions that are relevant. You may want to make sure your reader understands a complicated provision you have quoted by pairing the quotation with a summary of the provision in your own words. You do not need to quote constitutional or statutory provisions if they are simple and you can put them in your own words.

For example, if you are discussing several federal statutes, you would want to quote the relevant portion of the statutes. Because the statutory language would be difficult for your reader to understand, you might also summarize several of the quoted portions of the statutes in your own words. The following paragraph illustrates this use of quotations.

> It is illegal to intercept an oral communication. "[A]ny person who . . . intentionally intercepts . . . any oral communication . . . shall be punished." 18 U.S.C.S. § 2511 (1) (Lexis L. Publg. 1993). One exception to this prohibition involves a police officer; however, the police officer must be party to the conversation or one conversant must have consented to the taping for the exception to apply. "It shall not be unlawful under this chapter for a person acting under color of law to intercept [an] . . . oral . . . communication where such person is a party to the communication or one of the parties has given prior consent to the interception." 18 U.S.C.S. § 2511 (2)(c) (Lexis L. Publg. 1993). If an oral communication is taped in violation of the eavesdropping statutes, the conversation cannot be used as evidence in court. "Whenever any . . . oral communication has been intercepted, no part of the contents of such communication and no evidence derived therefrom may be received in evidence in any trial, hearing, or other proceeding . . . before an court . . . if the disclosure of that information would be in violation of this chapter." 18 U.S.C.S. § 2515 (Lexis L. Publg. 1993).

This paragraph uses ellipses (. . .) and brackets ([ ]). The use of ellipses and brackets is explained later in this appendix.

Quoting from cases is a little different from quoting from constitutions or statutes. Your own personal writing style determines to a great extent whether you use quotations in your legal writing and how many you use. You do not have to use any quotations at all if you can state everything in your own words. On the other hand, if you like to quote, do not use so many quotations that your writing is mostly quotations with very little in between. A reader who is faced with a number of long block quotes may be tempted to skip over the block quotes and read only what is between the quotes. Your goal is to keep your reader interested in what you have written. Quotations should be reserved for well-stated passages that you would have trouble stating in your own words. You may want to quote a portion of the issues, the holdings, and the reasoning. Usually you would not quote the facts, the case history, or the results because you can state those portions of the case better yourself.

Quote accurately

When you quote, your quote must be accurate down to punctuation and case of letters. (An "upper case" letter means a capital letter and a "lower case" letter means a small letter.) If your reader happens to check your quotation against the original source and finds differences, the reader will know you have been sloppy. Then the reader will wonder how far the sloppiness extended. If the writer did not take the time to quote accurately perhaps the writer did not take the time to research thoroughly. You will quickly lose your credibility and the reader's confidence by not quoting accurately.

Avoid plagiarism

Be wary of the possibility of plagiarism. Plagiarism occurs when you use portions of someone else's writing without indicating that you are quoting. It also occurs when your paraphrasing of portions of a case differs little from the wording of the case except for word order. One way to avoid this is to quote. A second way is to spend enough time with the case that you know it intimately ("internalize" it) and can write about it as if you were telling someone a story. Test yourself to see whether you understand a case by explaining it out loud to someone else. If you have trouble, go back and read the case again until you understand it.

Types of quotations

Quotations can appear:

1. as block quotations;
2. as complete sentences within your paragraph; or
3. as phrases within your sentence.

The following sections of this appendix will discuss the three types of quotations in that order.

Block quotations

A "block quotation" is a long quotation that looks like a "block" on the page. It is set off from the rest of your writing by double-spacing and is indented left and right. Do not use quotation marks around the outside of the block quote. You may use quotation marks inside the block quote if the passage you are quoting in turn quotes something else. If your citation follows the block quote, place your citation back at the left-hand margin. The *Bluebook* tells you to use a block quote if the quotation contains at least fifty words. This is a good rule of thumb that is frequently violated by block quoting shorter passages. Unless your professor wants you to adhere strictly to this rule, use a block quote when the block quote format makes the quotation easier to understand.

Rules for block quotations

1. Use if quotation is 50 words or more.
2. Indent left and right.
3. Do not enclose in quotation marks.
4. Place citation at lef-hand margin.

Sample block quotation

The following is a sample block quotation from *United States v. McKinnon*, 985 F.2d 525, 527 (11th Cir. 1993). The superscript numbers, which indicate editing changes, correspond to the numbered rules in figure C-1, and appear in the example to help you understand the changes from the original text.

> [9]McKinnon asserts that the tape recording of his prearrest conversations violates Title III and his Fourth Amendment right to privacy. . . . [1] The government

FIGURE C-1 Basic Quotation Rules.

Basic Quotation Rules Used for Block Quotes and for Quoting Sentences and Phrases

1. **Use of ellipses.** Delete any unnecessary wording. If the wording is in the **middle** of a quoted passage, indicate the deletion by using an ellipsis. Do not use an ellipsis when you are omitting something at the **beginning** of a quoted passage. Whether you use an ellipsis at the **end** of a quoted passage depends on whether you are quoting a complete sentence or a phrase used as part of your sentence. When quoting a complete sentence and omitting something at the end of the sentence, insert an ellipsis before the final punctuation of the sentence. When quoting a **phrase,** do not use an ellipsis at the end of the phrase.
2. **Use of brackets.** Add your own words to make the quotations easier to understand and place your words inside brackets. When you are changing a letter from upper to lower case or from lower to upper case, place the changed letter in brackets. You can replace a word in the quoted material with one of your own, so long as you bracket the word substituted for the original. Where a word is altered in this way, there is no need to include an ellipsis to indicate the omission.
3. **Omission of citations.** When you omit a citation, you do not need to replace it with an ellipsis if you use an explanatory parenthetical explaining this. (See 8 below.)
4. **Adding emphasis.** Add emphasis to quoted words by italicizing or underlining them and indicate this change in an explanatory parenthetical. (See 8 below.)
5. **Placement of punctuation and quotation marks.** Place periods and commas **inside** quotation marks and other punctuation **outside** the quotation marks unless the punctuation was part of the original quotation.
6. **Use of quotation marks.** Do not use quotation marks at the beginning and the end of a block quote; but do use quotation marks in block quotes when the passage you are quoting in turn quotes something else. For quotes other than block quotes, precede and follow the quoted language with quotation marks. Quotation marks for quotations within quotations alternate double and single quotation marks with the outermost quotation marks double.
7. **Placement of the citation to the quoted passage.** The citation to the quoted passage should be fairly close to the passage and may precede or follow it. The citation may appear in a textual sentence or in a citation sentence. A citation following a block quote should be placed back at the left-hand margin.
8. **Use of explanatory parentheticals.** When the case you are quoting in turn quotes a second case, identify the second case, including a page reference to the quoted material, by using an explanatory parenthetical. Explain you have underlined something or omitted citations by using an explanatory parenthetical.
9. **Paragraph structure.** In block quotes, indicate the paragraph structure by indenting the beginning of paragraphs; however, indent the beginning of the first paragraph, only if there were no words omitted from the beginning of the paragraph. Indicate the omission of language from the beginning of subsequent paragraphs by an indented ellipse (. . .). Within the block quote, indicate the omission of one or more entire paragraphs from the quoted language by indented four periods (. . . .).

> argues that the recording of McKinnon's conversation does not constitute the recording of an "oral communication" as defined in 18 U.S.C. § 2510(2). . . . [1]
>
> The legislative history of Title III directs that we consider "oral communication"[6] in light of . . . [1] constitutional standards . . . . [1] The constitutional question is "whether the person invoking its [Fourth Amendment][2] protection can claim a 'justifiable,' a 'reasonable,'[6] or a 'legitimate expectation of privacy' that has been invaded by government action."[6] Hence, the statutory and constitutional test is whether a *reasonable* or *justifiable*[4] expectation of privacy exists.
>
> This test has two prongs. First, whether McKinnon's conduct exhibited a subjective expectation of privacy; second, whether McKinnon's subjective expectation of privacy is one that society is willing to recognize as reasonable.

United States v. McKinnon, 985 F.2d 525, 527 (11th Cir. 1993)[2] (quoting *Smith v. Maryland*, 442 U.S. 735, 740 (1979)[8] (referring to *Katz*))(emphasis added)[4] (citations omitted)[3].

Now compare the block quote with the original case text:

> McKinnon asserts that the tape recording of his prearrest conversations violates Title III and his Fourth Amendment right to privacy. Title III prohibits unauthorized interception and disclosure of oral communications. 18 U.S.C. § 2511. The government argues that the recording of McKinnon's conversation does not constitute the recording of an "oral communication" as defined in 18 U.S.C. § 2510(2). Title III defines "oral communication" as "any oral communication uttered by a person exhibiting an expectation that such communication is not subject to interception under circumstances justifying such exception, but such term does not include any electronic communication." 18 U.S.C. S 2510(2). Thus, we must decide the statutory question gleaned from Title III's language and the legislative history. That is, whether the person uttering the words has a reasonable or justifiable expectation of privacy. *See* 18 U.S.C. § 2510(2); S.Rep. No. 541, 99th Cong., 2d Sess. (1986), reprinted in 1986 U.S.C.C.A.N. 3555, 3567; *United States v. Harrelson*, 754 F.2d 1153, 1169 (5th Cir.), *cert. denied*, 474 U.S. 908, 106 S.Ct. 277, 88 L.Ed.2d 241 (1985) (framing the question as whether a reasonable expectation of privacy existed).
>
> The legislative history of Title III directs that we consider "oral communication" in light of the constitutional standards expressed in *Katz v. United States*, 389 U.S. 347, 88 S.Ct. 507, 19 L.Ed.2d 576 (1967). S.Rep. No. 1097, 90th Cong., 2d Sess. (1968), reprinted in 1968 U.S.C.C.A.N. 2112, 2178. The constitutional question is "whether the person invoking its [Fourth Amendment] protection can claim a 'justifiable,' a 'reasonable,' or a 'legitimate expectation of privacy' that has been invaded by government action." *Smith v. Maryland*, 442 U.S. 735, 740, 99 S.Ct. 2577, 2580, 61 L.Ed.2d 220 (1979) (referring to *Katz*); *accord United States v. Shields*, 675 F.2d 1152, 1158 (11th Cir.), *cert. denied*, 459 U.S. 858, 103 S.Ct. 130, 74 L.Ed.2d 112 (1982) (citing *Katz*, 389 U.S. at 353, 88 S.Ct. at 512 and *United States v. White*, 401 U.S. 745, 752, 91 S.Ct. 1122, 1126, 28 L.Ed.2d 453 (1971)). Hence, the statutory and constitutional test is whether a reasonable or justifiable expectation of privacy exists.
>
> This test has two prongs. First, whether McKinnon's conduct exhibited a subjective expectation of privacy; second, whether McKinnon's subjective expectation of privacy is one that society is willing to recognize as reasonable. *Smith*, 442 U.S. at 740, 99 S.Ct. at 2580 (citing *Katz*, 389 U.S. at 361, 88 S.Ct. at 516).

Show your readers changes from the original text

The first block quote above is much more "reader friendly" because it is not clogged with citations and unnecessary words. Omitting citations and unnecessary words allows the reader to focus on what the court was trying to communicate. The rules on the preceding page explain how to indicate any editing of quotations by using ellipses (. . .), brackets ([ ]) and explanatory parentheticals (explanations within parentheses). The rules apply to all types of quotations, not just block quotations. The rule numbers coincide with the superscript numbers in the first sample block quotation.

Quoting complete sentences and quoting phrases

When the passage you are quoting contains less than fifty words and can stand alone as one or more complete sentences, the passage should be part of a paragraph rather than being set apart as a block quote. Capitalize the first letter of the quoted passage and bracket the capital letter if this is a change. When the passage you are quoting is not a complete sentence, use it as a phrase in your sentence without capitalizing the first letter of the quoted phrase unless it begins your sentence. Remember to use the eight quotation rules in figure C-1 when quoting complete sentences and phrases.

The following example contains both types of quotations—complete sentences and phrases. The superscript numbers appear in the example to help you understand the changes from the original text. The passage from which the quotations were taken follows the example. The explanation of the superscript numbers follows the original passage.

> In *Florida v. Jimeno,* 500 U.S. 248, 251 (1991)[1] the United States Supreme Court looked at the "expressed object"[2] of a search to determine "[t]he[3] scope of a search."[2] After the officer told the suspect that the officer suspected there were drugs in the suspect's car, the suspect consented to the search.[4] "[I]t[5] was objectively reasonable for the police to conclude that the general consent to search [the suspect's][6] car included consent to search containers within that car which might bear drugs . . . . [7] The authorization to search in this case therefore, extended beyond the surfaces of the car's interior to the paper bag . . . [8]." *Id.*[9]

Now compare the quotations contained in the preceding example with the text from which the quotations were taken:

> The scope of a search is generally defined by its expressed object. *United States v. Ross,* 456 U.S. 798, 102 S. Ct. 2157, 72 L. Ed. 2d 572 (1982). In this case, the terms of the search's authorization were simple. Respondent granted Officer Trujillo permission to search his car, and did not place any explicit limitation on the scope of the search. Trujillo had informed respondent that he believed respondent was carrying narcotics, and that he would be looking for narcotics in the car. We think it was objectively reasonable for the police to conclude that the general consent to search respondent's car included consent to search containers within that car which might bear drugs. A reasonable person may be expected to know that narcotics are generally carried in some form of a container. "Contraband goods rarely are strewn across the trunk or floor of a car." *Id.,* at 820, 102 S. Ct., at 2170. The authorization to search in this case therefore, extended beyond the surfaces of the car's interior to the paper bag lying on the car's floor.

This is an explanation of the superscript numbers included in the first block quote on the preceding page:

1. The citation to two quoted phrases precedes the phrases and gives the page reference to those phrases.
2. The quoted phrases are enclosed in quotation marks. Following basic quotation rule 1 of figure C-1, because these are phrases, no ellipsis is needed to indicate omission of words preceding or following the phrases.
3. The "t" is changed from upper to lower case because the phrase is in the middle of the author's sentence and the change is bracketed.
4. This sentence does not need quotation marks because it is stated in the author's own words. Even though the sentence is not a direct quote, it does need a page reference because the substance of the sentence is taken from the case. In this paragraph the two citations, one at the beginning and one at the end, give the page reference and are close enough to this sentence so that no additional citation is needed. If the sentence were not so near the two citations, a reference to page 251 should have been given.
5. Following basic quotation rule 1 of figure C-1, no ellipsis is needed to indicate omission of words at the beginning of the quoted complete sentence and the "i" is bracketed to indicate the letter was changed from lower to upper case.
6. The brackets indicate that the words "the suspect's" are added. "Suspect" is used instead of "respondent" because this reference makes it easier for the reader to understand who is being identified. There is no need to indicate the omission of "respondent" by inserting an ellipsis where the substituted wording is bracketed.
7. Following basic quotation rule 1 of figure C-1, the ellipsis indicates that wording has been omitted. Here a textual sentence and a citation sentence were omitted.
8. Following basic quotation rule 1 above, the ellipsis indicates that wording was omitted from the end of this quoted sentence and the ellipsis is followed by the final punctuation (a period).
9. Here the citation follows the quoted complete sentences and is placed in a citation sentence.

Exercises on quotations

A. Review a sample document from chapters 16, 17, or 18, noting the use of quotations.

B. Select a statute you might use in a legal document. Identify the relevant and irrelevant wording of the statute. Rewrite the statute to eliminate irrelevant wording, showing alterations from the original statutory wording. Write a paragraph containing the quoted statute.

C. Select a case you might use in a legal document. Identify significant wording, such as the issue, the holding, or a portion of the reasoning, that you might quote in your document. Imagine how you would show the alterations from the original passages. Write several paragraphs containing the quoted passages.

SHORT FORM CITATIONS

The first time you refer to a case, you must give its full citation. If you refer to the case again, you should use an abbreviation to the citation rather than give the full citation. This abbreviated citation is called a "short form citation." This section of the appendix uses the following citations in the examples and exercises:

Florida v. Jimeno, 500 U.S. 248 (1991).
Wyoming v. Houghton, 526 U.S. 295 (1999).
Whren v. United States, 517 U.S. 806 (1996).
United States v. McKinnon, 985 F.2d 525 (1993).

> The two types of sentences in legal writing are **textual sentences** and **citation sentences.** A textual sentence is the type of sentence you have been writing all your life. It is a complete grammatical sentence with a subject and a verb. A citation sentence contains only citations. The four citations above this box are written as citation sentences. Each is appropriately ended with a period.

This section of the appendix reviews examples of full and short form citations. In the examples, the citations are all followed by periods as they would be in citation sentences. If you are using the citations in textual sentences, you would not need a period at the end of a citation unless it is the end of the sentence.

Suppose in an office memo you first cite to the holding in *Whren* on page 819 of the case. You must give the full citation to *Whren* because you have not cited the case before. In the full citation, you can indicate the page of the case holding by adding a comma and the page of the holding after the first page of the case:

Whren v. United States, 517 U.S. 806, 819 (1996).

Suppose you now want to give another citation to *Whren*, this time to the facts on pages 808 and 809. Use "*id.*" to indicate that you are citing to the immediately preceding authority. "*Id.*" is always italicized or underlined. It is capitalized when it begins a sentence, but is not when it appears in the middle of a sentence. If you were referring to the same page again, page 819, the complete citation would be "*Id.*" Because you are referring to different pages, you must indicate the new page numbers by adding "at" and the new page numbers:

Id. at 808, 809.

Suppose now you give the following string cite to *Jimeno* and *Houghton* (a string cite is a citation to more than one case with the cases separated by a semicolon):

Florida v. Jimeno, 500 U.S. 248 (1991); *Wyoming v. Houghton*, 526 U.S. 295 (1999).

Then you want to cite to *Houghton* again, this time to page 1304. You might think that you could use *id.* as a short form citation for *Houghton* because you just cited it. However, if you used *id.*, you would be referring your reader back to the immediately preceding citation which is your string cite. Unless you want to refer to all the cases in the string cite, you must use another short citation form to cite to *Houghton.* Any one of the following short citation forms for *Houghton* is acceptable:

Wyoming v. Houghton, 526 U.S. at 307.
Houghton, 526 U.S. at 307.
526 U.S. at 307.

When using short form citations, try to use the shortest form possible so long as there is no confusion. If you had cited *Houghton* within the last few pages and there is no other United States Supreme Court case you had cited that is in volume 526 of United States Reports, use the third type of short citation form. If it had been several pages since you last cited *Houghton* or the reader might confuse *Houghton* with another case in the same volume of the reporter, use either the first or second versions of short form citations. When you are referring to a case by the name of only one of the parties, select a name that easily distinguishes the case from other cases. Because there are numerous case names that contain "Wyoming" but many fewer that contain "Houghton," you would use "Houghton" rather than "Wyoming."

If you wanted to refer to page 307 of *Houghton* again use:

Id.

If you want to refer to footnote 1 on page 303 of *Houghton*, use:

Id. at 303 n.1.

If you then wanted to refer to page 310 of *Houghton*, use:

Id. at 310 (Stevens, J., dissenting).

You must indicate the page number because it is not the same one referred to before. The explanatory parenthetical is needed because you are referring to something other than the majority opinion.

If you want to refer to pages 249 through 250 and 252 of *Jimeno*, you cannot use "*id.*" because *Jimeno* is not the immediately preceding citation. If you have recently cited *Jimeno*, use:

500 U.S. at 249–50, 252.

If you have not referred to *Jimeno* recently, precede the above short form citation by either "*Florida v. Jimeno*" or by "*Jimeno.*" Where material referred to spans more than one page, give the numbers of the first and last pages, joined by a hyphen. Retain only the last two digits of the second number. Where material appears on more than one page but does not span pages, separate the page numbers by a comma.

If you want to refer to *Jimeno* in general rather than to any specific material from *Jimeno*, use:

Jimeno.

When you are using *Jimeno* as an abbreviation to refer to the case, "Jimeno" is italicized or underlined. "Jimeno" would not be italicized or underlined if you are referring to the individual.

If you want to refer to pages 525 (the first page of the case), 526 and 528 of *McKinnon* and you had not given the full citation of *McKinnon* before, use:

United States v. McKinnon, 985 F.2d 525, 525, 526, 528 (1993).

Because you wanted to refer to the first page of the case in the full citation, the number "525" must be written twice, with the two numbers separated by a comma.

If you want to refer to pages 526 through 527 of *McKinnon*, use:

Id. at 526–27.

SHORT FORM CITATIONS FOR STATUTES

Just as for cases, you must use the complete citation the first time you cite to a statute. For example, you may cite to a federal wiretapping statute as follows:

18 U.S.C.S. § 2511 (Lexis L. Publg. 1993 & Supp. 2000).

Later, if you cite to the same statute you should use a short form citation. If you are citing to the immediately preceding statute, you use "*id.*" If you are citing to a statute you cited to previously, but it is not the immediately preceding statute, use a short citation that sufficiently identifies the statute for your reader. For a federal statute, you can either give the title and section number of the United States Code ("18 U.S.C.S. § 2511"), or just the section number ("§ 2511").

EXERCISES ON SHORT FORM CITATIONS

A. Review a sample document from chapters 16, 17, or 18, noting the use of short form citations.

B. Using the above citations to 18 U.S.C.S. § 2511, *Jimeno*, *Houghton*, *Whren*, and *McKinnon* give the correct citations called for by the following descriptions:

1. String cite to *Jimeno*, *Houghton*, and *Whren.*
2. Cite to pages 1302 and 1304 of *Houghton.*
3. Cite to pages 1299 through 1300 of *Houghton.*
4. Refer to *Jimeno* in general terms.
5. Cite to pages 1772 through 1773 of *Whren.*
6. Cite to page 251 of *Jimeno.*
7. Cite to page 252 of *Jimeno.*
8. Cite to note 1 on page 1302 of *Houghton.*
9. Cite to pages 526 and 528 of *McKinnon.*
10. Cite to 18 U.S.C.S. § 2511.
11. Cite to 18 U.S.C.S. § 2511.
12. Cite to pages 526 and 528 of *McKinnon.*
13. Cite to 18 U.S.C.S. § 2511.

C. If you have completed either of the exercises at the end of this chapter's section on quotations, insert citations as necessary.

APPENDIX D

MECHANICAL ERRORS

INTRODUCTION

Elimination of mechanical errors is the tedious, though necessary, part of writing. You need to do your best to eliminate mechanical errors for two reasons. The first reason is that you want your reader to concentrate on your message and not be distracted by mechanical errors. The second reason is that a reader who spots a number of mechanical errors will begin to wonder if the writer is sloppy. If the writer failed to proof for typographical and spelling errors, perhaps the writer's sloppiness extended to legal research too. Do not lose your credibility over a few easily eliminated mechanical errors.

You know your own writing and you probably know from past experience what types of mechanical errors give you problems. Keep in mind those types of mechanical errors that have given you problems in the past so you can eliminate them when editing and proofing your legal writing. If you have trouble spotting them yourself, ask a fellow student to help you proof your writing. Do the same for that student in return.

This appendix covers nine different mechanical errors. You have certainly been warned about a number of mechanical errors discussed in this appendix. They include incorrect use of apostrophes, sentence fragments, and run-on sentences. Problems with passive voice, parallel construction, and antecedents may be less familiar to you. Two other errors covered in this appendix are using excess words and changing tenses without reason.

Once you have mastered the material in this appendix and you are ready for a challenge, try completing the exercises in the last section of this appendix which involve a combination of mechanical errors.

EXCESS WORDS

Do not tire your reader by making the reader wade through excess words to understand your point. Your message will be easier to understand if you delete unnecessary wording. At the editing stage, look at each sentence again. Identify the meaning of the sentence and then attempt to eliminate any excess words.

The following sentences contain excess words. Review each sentence, identifying any excess words. Then compare your results with the suggested answers. The suggested answers are only suggested answers. Your results may be better.

1. The United States Constitution provides for protection against unreasonable search and seizure.
2. The similarities among *Smith*, *Forfeiture*, and *Nelson* are almost identical.
3. The Court found that the factors taken together as they were, amounted to reasonable suspicion.
4. In deciding the *Nelson* case, the court will have the difficult job of balancing Nelson's constitutional right against unreasonable search and seizure and society's interest in controlling drug trafficking on the nation's highways.
5. In regards to investigatory stops there must be a balance between an individual's right to privacy and society's interest in being safe.

Suggested answers:

1. The United States Constitution prohibits unreasonable search and seizure.
2. *Smith*, *Forfeiture*, and *Nelson* are almost identical.
3. The Court found that the factors taken together amounted to reasonable suspicion.

4. In deciding *Nelson*, the court will have the difficult job of balancing Nelson's constitutional right against unreasonable search and seizure and society's interest in controlling drug trafficking on the nation's highways.
5. Investigatory stops must balance an individual's right to privacy and society's interest in enforcing the law.

Now rewrite the following sentences to eliminate excess words:

1. They were having a private conversation of a business transaction involving drugs.
2. In this memo, the summarization of the facts under the particular circumstances shall begin with the parties.
3. Mario had a large order and he needed it for Bryce within three hours. Bryce needed two tons of marijuana and one hundred pounds of cocaine.
4. Did the detectives violate the Florida Security of Communications Act as well as the constitutional rights of privacy under sections 12 and 13 of the Florida Constitution when they intercepted phone calls of Bryce Canyon?
5. The phone call made by Mr. Canyon was to Mario Hernandez about a drug transaction that was to take place later on during the day.
6. The law enforcement officers were outside the building that Mario was in and were using a scanning device in an attempt to pick up any calls in the surrounding area.
7. The court granted a suppression of the evidence of the interception of the conversation on a cordless phone.
8. The case of *State v. Mozo* held that the cordless telephone conversation originating in the home was an oral communication protected by the Florida Statutes.
9. This concept does not apply to the *Canyon* case in that the *Mozo* case occurred before the federal statutes preempted the Florida Statutes.
10. Both telephone calls were each recorded by the answering machine by two distinct methods.
11. A common focus in these types of cases also looks to see whether or not the communicator who is seeking protection under the law has consented to the interception of his conversation.
12. This memorandum will first explain how James would meet the subjective and objective requirements of the statute and how the cases of *Stevenson* and *Brandin* do not apply to our case.
13. Therefore, under section 934.06 of the Florida Statutes, the evidence would be inadmissible as evidence in any trial and should be suppressed.
14. In order to do so, the state must produce evidence that has been acquired without violating the statutes.
15. In order for the tapes to be admissible into evidence against Mr. Johnson, there must have been an intentional interception coupled with Mr. Johnson's consent.
16. On appeal the issue was whether the profile used by Vogel provided reasonable suspicion to warrant a stop under the United States Supreme Court decision in *Terry*.
17. The *Smith* case is also based on the validity of a stop, and if the patrolman has reasonable suspicion to make such a stop.
18. Reasonable suspicion means that the officer must be able to articulate exactly what was suspicious to make him feel that illegal activity was taking place.
19. The stop was based on a personal drug courier profile Vogel had developed, with the following facts applying:
20. This particular stop was unconstitutional and any evidence seized as a product of this stop is deemed to be regarded as inadmissible in court.
21. When deciding this case the court will have to determine whether this particular stop made by Sheriff Vogel violates Nelson's right against an unreasonable search and seizure as provided under the United States Constitution and the Florida Constitution.
22. The court will apply the exclusionary rule which prohibits the court to use at trial any evidence

which was seized through an unconstitutional search and seizure to be used.

23. These three cases involve facts similar to the facts in this case, *Nelson.*

24. In deciding cases on the issue of search and seizure and the constitutionality of such, the courts will have to look to the Fourth Amendment.

25. According to the Fourth Amendment to the United States Constitution, individuals are guaranteed protection against unreasonable search and seizure.

26. Vogel proceeded to confiscate the amount of $6,003.00.

27. In the above facts in the *Sokolow* case, the suspect's behavior was consistent with the DEA's drug courier profile.

28. The stop cannot be upheld on the ground that Vogel did not have reasonable suspicion that the appellants were hauling drugs.

29. The use of a drug courier profile attempts to protect society from crime but the use of it may interfere with an individual's Federal and Florida Constitutional rights against unreasonable search and seizure.

30. The decision was based on facts that the traffic stop was rejected as pretextual and that the stop was not a valid drug investigation.

31. The Constitutions both have language stating that probable cause is needed to support a warrant.

32. In deciding this case, the court will have to consider and evaluate the essence of the drug courier profile used by police officers as a basis for reasonable suspicion.

33. Another case pertaining to the aspects of a drug courier profile is *United States v. Sokolow*, 490 U.S. 1 (1989).

USE OF APOSTROPHES

Apostrophes have two uses. They tell your reader that something belongs to someone (possessive use) and that letters have been omitted (use in contractions). This section will deal primarily with the use of apostrophes in possessives because contractions are generally too informal to be used in legal writing. The following contains rules for use of apostrophes.

Rule for use of apostrophes in possessives

1. To make a singular noun possessive, add an apostrophe and an "s." (If your noun already ends in an "s," refer to rule 2.)

   Example:

   the car of the officer = the **officer's** car

2. To make a plural noun (or a singular noun ending in "s") possessive, add an apostrophe.

   Example:

   the car of the officers = the **officers'** car

3. Do not, under pain of mortal embarassment, use an apostrophe with a pronoun like "its" to make it possessive. "It's" means "it is."

   Examples:

   the speed of it (when it refers to a car) = **its** speed

   it is a speedy car = **it's** a speedy car

Now rewrite the following sentences using the rules you have just read.

1. Should the police officers tape of Brice's cordless telephone conversation be suppressed? (Assume there are two officers.)

2. The police officers unlawfully intercepted the defendants cordless telephone conversation without their consent, which constitutes an unreasonable search and seizure.

3. He then refers to a "guy" who want's to make a large order and it must be received in three hours.

4. The officers interception and recording of a cordless telephone conversation without consent or a search warrant makes this recording illegal. (Assume there is one officer.)

5. The police should have had a search warrant when they scanned and recorded conversations in a lawyers office or the consent of the people in the office.

6. Defendant Bryce Dealer submits this memorandum of law in support of defendants' motion to suppress the evidence seized from the defendant's.

7. In *Stevenson*, surveillance equipment, a bionic ear, was used to record defendants conversation. (Assume there are two defendants.)

8. The officer's used the bionic ear lawfully to identify and deter drug activity. (Assume there are two officers.)
9. In *Stevenson*, the court affirms the lower courts decision to deny a motion to suppress evidence.
10. Should the second tape of my clients conversation with Bill Worth be suppressed for lack of consent to the interception? (Assume there is one client.)
11. Because Mr. Johnson did not give his prior consent to being recorded, Bill's recording of the conversation is illegal.
12. Defendant left a message on the victims answering machine of his own free will.
13. The mere fact that Johnson proceeded with his entire conversation does not mean that he consented to its' recording.
14. A few moments later the defendant appeared in front of the victim house to seek revenge.
15. This makes the interception of James communication by the police illegal.
16. *Stevenson* determined that the reasonableness of ones expectation of privacy in a conversation is based in part on the location of such conversation.
17. The police violated James expectation of privacy by recording his oral communication at a party on private property.
18. Privacy is an issue American's take to heart.
19. Bryce proceeded to use an office for privacy where he would not be disturbed with interference's.
20. The Mozo's were speaking on a cordless telephone in their home when the police intercepted the conversations.
21. For the reasons set forth above, the State requests this court to deny the defendants motion to suppress and allow the charge against him to stand.
22. He decided to make an investigatory stop since the driver matched the troopers drug courier profile.
23. The officers shone their lights on Smith's car but Smith did not look in the officers direction.
24. The judgments of conviction against the defendant's were vacated.
25. All the suspects were stopped because of Vogels' drug courier profile.
26. Trooper Vogels stop of the appellants vehicle was held not to be reasonable under the fourth amendment. (Assume there were three appellants.)
27. Although police officers have a duty to protect the community, sometimes the standards used violate citizens constitutional rights.
28. Public interest is at it's peak when contemplating the next step to combat the drug problem in this country.
29. The Eleventh Circuit reversed the district court's denial of appellants motion to suppress the evidence. (Assume there was one appellant.)
30. The court found Vogels courier profile to be too general and vague.
31. The dog sniffed defendants car and indicated the presence of drugs. (Assume there were two defendants.)
32. Although these stops may be warranted at times, the Court emphasized that the individuals constitutional right against unreasonable search and seizure must be safeguarded.

SENTENCE FRAGMENTS

A sentence fragment occurs when the writer attempts to write a sentence, but the thought is expressed incompletely. There are three common causes of sentence fragments. The first is omission of the verb; obviously, this can be easily corrected by supplying the verb. A second cause is beginning a sentence with a subordinating conjunction such as "while" or "although," and not following the dependent clause with an independent clause. "While" and "although" tell the reader: "I'm going to tell you something less important before I tell you the really important information." The reader reads what he or she was cued to think was the less important information and is left hanging when the sentence does not supply the "important information" promised. This error can be corrected either by deleting the subordinating conjunction or adding the "important information." The third cause of sentence fragments is incorrect punctuation. This happens when the writer puts a period where a comma should be and capitalizes the next word in the sentence. Correct this error by putting the comma back in and changing the capital to lower case. It can also happen when the writer puts a semicolon where a comma should be. A semicolon can be used to join two complete sentences that are related in subject matter. (Do not capitalize the word following the semicolon unless it is a proper noun or a word otherwise calling for capitalization.) A semicolon should not be used to join two phrases. Correct this error by changing the semicolon to a comma.

Rewrite the following sentences correcting any sentence fragments.

1. Regular price, plus $100,000, because he needs it so quickly.
2. They also discuss the price of the deal; the regular price plus $100,000, because it is such a large order.
3. Under the Florida Statutes, the interception of wire or oral communication when none of the parties to the communication has consented to the interception should not be allowed; unless it has been allowed by a court of competent jurisdiction.
4. Did the law enforcement officer violate chapter 934, Fla. Stat. (1997), in using a scanner to intercept the cordless telephone conversation between Bryce Smith and Mario Jones; when Bryce was alone in an office in a public building and when the officer had no court order?
5. Throughout this conversation, Mr. Johnson had some suspicion whether Bill was recording the conversation.
6. DeWayne and Bill had been friends for a long time, and for Bill's birthday some years ago; DeWayne had bought Bill an answering machine.
7. *State v. Sells*, 582 So. 2d 1244 (Fla. 4th DCA 1992), in which a similar set of circumstances applies.
8. Big Bill could have been aware of the message that Tiny had left on the first tape; maybe frightening Bill to the point where he had to take the necessary precautions to record Tiny's threats.
9. Under such situation, the State having the legal duty to seek justice and a responsibility to discover any admissible evidence against the defendant.
10. Section 934.02 (1), Fla. Stat. (1997). Does apply because the communication was transmitted by the aid of a wire.
11. Section 934.03 (2)(d), Fla. Stat. (1997). Does not apply because there was not an intentional interception of the conversation.
12. In *State v. Sells*, 582 So. 2d 1244 (Fla. 4th DCA 1991). In this case the facts are somewhat similar.
13. Was Defendant Johnson's first conversation intentionally intercepted without consent; therefore making the first tape recording inadmissible?
14. While, in *Johnson*, Mr. Dole intercepted their conversation through the use of his answering machine.
15. Because Bill had the answering machine set up for the purpose of recording phone calls, which is proof that Bill intentionally intercepted Tiny's first telephone conversation which is prohibited under this statute.
16. Still making the interception illegal.
17. Using the court's prior rules on a very similar case along with the Security of Communications Act.
18. Defendants charged with racketeering and prostitution.
19. Which would then mean that the interception is lawful.
20. The question is whether the evidence seized from the vehicle be suppressed.
21. The two main similarities between *Smith* and *Sokolow*.
22. While in *Sokolow* it was held that all the factors as a whole were enough for reasonable suspicion.
23. Looking at the two cases cited, it is apparent that the use of the drug courier profile has not been overwhelmingly embraced by the courts. Especially when it is the only reason given for the investigatory stop. As is *Nelson*, which factually is almost indistinguishable from the cases cited.
24. Whereas in *Smith* a traffic violation never occurred.

25. Order denying the motion to suppress reversed, judgments of conviction vacated, cases remanded to district court.
26. Because we are protected by the Fourth Amendment to the United States Constitution.
27. A Terry stop based on an Ohio case which eventually went to the United States Supreme Court.
28. The Court reasoned that the totality of the circumstances must be considered in evaluating the stop and that any one of the factors by itself was not proof of any illegal conduct. But when taken together they amount to a reasonable suspicion.
29. In *United States v. Sokolow*, 490 U.S. 1 (1989). Andrew Sokolow was stopped by DEA agents while trying to leave Honolulu International Airport.

RUN-ON SENTENCES

Run-on sentences are usually caused by trying to pack too much information into a sentence. The solution is to break up the run-on sentence into several sentences. Another cause of run-on sentences is wording. The wording of a sentence may make the reader think the reader is reading a run-on sentence. The solution is to reword and reorganize the sentence so the reader can handle the information as a single sentence.

Another solution might be to place a semicolon between two sentences closely related in subject matter. You would replace the period at the end of the first sentence with a semicolon. The initial word in the second sentence should not be capitalized unless it is a proper noun or a word otherwise requiring capitalization.

Analyze the following passages and rewrite them to eliminate run-on sentences.

1. Law enforcement officers were randomly scanning cordless telephone conversations in the area when they heard defendants talking on the telephone, the police officers recorded the conversation.
2. However, the Florida Supreme Court did not apply the "wire communication" definition of section 934.02(1) to the nonconsensual interception of conversations from the Mozos' home cordless telephone, instead the court set a precedent for application of the "oral communication" definition, section 934.01(2), Fla. Stat. (1991), to cordless telephone conversations.
3. The Florida Statutes exceptions are still there, it does not include cordless phones.
4. The police did not obtain consent or a search warrant, as a result the evidence should be deemed inadmissible in court.
5. Mr. Callahan did utter communication, however to determine if he did not intend for his communication to be intercepted, one must look to case law.
6. The first case is *Stevenson*, the court held that Stevenson had no reasonable expectation of privacy.
7. Furthermore, Hopper was impaired therefore he had no expectation of privacy and his actions prove that.
8. Pursuant to chapter 934, a cordless telephone conversation is a wire communication and the interception thereof is illegal therefore the conversation should be suppressed.
9. Bryce had no expectation of privacy therefore the officers did not intercept an oral communication.
10. Mr. Johnson denies knowing Bill was dead, to his best recollection Bill was still alive when he left.
11. There are state statutes that prevent citizens from recording conversation, there are also state statutes that protect citizens from having their conversations recorded.
12. Section 934.03 (2)(d), Fla. Stat. (1997), this statute states that it is lawful to record a conversation with the consent of all parties.
13. Based on this case, Johnson's conversation was obtained without his consent, the tape recording will be barred.
14. During this time Mr. Canyon received a page, he used the cordless telephone in the office to respond to the page.
15. When you read the above facts you might think this is a clear-cut case, that is not true.
16. Based solely upon these factors, no traffic violation was alleged, Vogel stopped and detained Nelson.

17. In *Forfeiture* Vogel observed Coleman driving on the interstate and because Coleman and Williams fit Vogel's drug courier profile he pulled them over even they had not broken any law.
18. The exclusionary rule prohibits the trial use of evidence secured through unreasonable search and seizure as applied to the federal courts in *Weeks v. United States*, 323 U.S. 383 (1914) and applied to the states, incorporated in the due process clause of the Fourteenth Amendment to the United States Constitution in *Mapp v. Ohio*, 367 U.S. 643 (1961).
19. Using a drug courier profile supported by only an "unparticularized suspicion or hunch" is prohibited by the United States Supreme Court in *Terry* which allows police stops when the officer has a reasonable suspicion.
20. The defendant filed a motion to suppress, motion denied, convicted, appealed. There was not reasonable suspicion therefore the stop is not lawful for reasons of carrying drugs or traffic violations.
21. Vogel did not have reasonable suspicion therefore the stop cannot be upheld on that ground.
22. The facts are too general to be of any value, they could be used for anyone driving on I-95, the same officer was Vogel in all three cases.
23. The motions to suppress were filed and denied, after jury trial both defendants were convicted.
24. Trooper Vogel had developed a reasonable suspicion of illegal activity based on the fact that the suspect, a thirty year old man, was driving at 3:00 a.m. on a known drug corridor highway and being very cautious by driving 50 miles per hour and did not look at the marked patrol car as the car went past.
25. In previous cases with similar facts court have found the drug courier profile to be too general to support reasonable suspicion therefore finding several searches and seizures unjustified and in violation of the individual's rights against unreasonable search and seizure.
26. Because the suspect produced an expired automobile rental contract Vogel called his dispatcher to verify the information given by the suspect, Vogel also requested that a drug dog be brought to the scene.
27. The federal appeals court held that the drug courier profile used in this case was too general and unparticularized to support a *Terry* stop, thus granted the return of the money to the suspects.
28. These are very general factors, there was no traffic ticket written, it was more of a hunch, combined with Vogel's experience that instigated the stop.

PARALLEL CONSTRUCTION

When you write about a series of items or activities, you must use parallel construction. This means that the wording of each item or activity must be similar in grammatical structure. For example, the following sentence discusses three different activities:

> The officers stopped the car, were questioning the occupants, and searched the car trunk.

The sentence is an example of poor parallel construction because the verb tense in the middle of the sentence does not match the verb tense at the beginning and at the end of the sentence. "Stopped" and "searched" are simple past tense while "were questioning" is past progressive tense. "Stopped" and "searched" describe two completed actions and "were questioning" describes an action in progress. The parallel construction problem can be corrected by changing the second verb to match the tense of the other two verbs in the sentence:

> The officers stopped the car, questioned the occupants, and searched the car trunk.

Now rewrite the following sentences, correcting any errors in parallel construction.

1. For the reasons stated above, Defendant Canyon requests that his motion to suppress be granted and to dismiss the charge against him for lack of evidence.
2. The use of the answering machine to record tape one and by Bill pushing the button of the recorder without Mr. Johnson's knowledge to record tape two, violates section 934.03 (1)(a).

3. After hearing the conversation, police were at the place of the transaction, arrested and brought charges against Bryce.
4. This memorandum will explain why the cordless telephone conversation is protected under Chapter 934 as a wire communication and therefore the interception was illegal and all evidence gained is inadmissible.
5. Furthermore, people in today's society use answering machines for intercepting calls when they are not home, too busy to answer the phone, just do not feel like answering the phone, or even to screen calls.
6. Under Florida statutes, the tapes must meet the following requirements to be suppressed:
   a. The conversation is an oral communication;
   b. Intentional interception occurred; and
   c. Consent did not exist.
7. The two conversations of Michael Johnson fall within the statutory definition of wire communication, and both are protected by statute from interception and inadmissible at trial.
8. After Tiny hung up the phone he had suspected that it could have been Bill's answering machine.
9. During the party, James was telling stories of killing people, how much money he made doing drug deals, and his next drop.
10. The court ruled that four grounds are actionable as slander per se:
    a. That a person has committed an infamous crime;
    b. Charges a person has an infectious disease;
    c. Tends to subject one to hatred, distrust, ridicule, contempt, or disgrace; and
    d. Tends to injure one in his trade or profession.
11. Margie Walker can hold the funeral homes liable for the tort of intentional infliction of emotional distress if she can prove that their actions of sending her dead husband's body parts in a plastic bag were:
    a. Outrageous and extreme in manner;
    b. With the intent to cause severe emotional distress to the victim or with reckless disregard for the victim; and
    c. Which results in the victim suffering severe emotional distress.
12. The employer had told its employees to attend the trade show because of the business benefits, paid for and deducted the employees' expenses, and reimbursed the employee for mileage.
13. Each party agrees that the confidential information is valuable, special and a unique asset of the party, has provided and will hereafter provide a substantial competitive advantage, and is a legitimate business interest of the party.
14. Such steps shall include: use of an alternative entrance for construction vehicles and equipment, requiring that all construction vehicles be cleaned of loose mud, gravel, dirt, and other debris prior to traversing the access road, and cleaning up any dirt gravel, construction materials and other debris deposited on the road.
15. This rule prescribes severe limitations on when a company can repurchase common stock, the maximum price the company can pay to repurchase common stock, and the amount of common stock the company can repurchase.
16. The differences consist of the time observed, the location, and the subject was investigated more thoroughly in *Sokolow*.
17. The motions to suppress was reversed, judgments of conviction was vacated, and the cases remanded.
18. The profile consists of a late model car, Florida rental tag, 2 persons about 35 years old, driver-male, car going Northbound on I-95, driving in a cautious manner, and not looking at the trooper while passing.
19. Did Vogel have reasonable suspicion that suspects were committing, has committed, or is about to commit a crime enough to make a valid stop?
20. The issue was whether Vogel had reasonable suspicion to believe that the defendants were committing, committed, or was about to commit a crime?
21. In this case the profile consisted of:
    a. traveling at 3:00 A.M.;
    b. traveling at 50 mph;
    c. car occupied by two individuals who were approximately 30 years of age;

   d. out of state tags;
   e. driving very cautiously;
   f. did not look in the trooper direction as he proceeded past them.

22. Both suspects were dressed casually and driving in the early morning.
23. It is not common to spend $2100 in cash for plane and making a long trip only to return forty-eight hours later.
24. Drug dogs alerted, search warrants obtained, and drugs were found in the luggage.

ANTECEDENTS

To understand the problem with antecedents, look at the following example:

> The DEA agents made an investigative stop of the suspect and his companion because they fit the drug courier profile as well as other information they had obtained.

There are three pronouns in the sentence: "his," "they," and "they." Out of context the reader would not know what these pronouns refer to. The reader will determine to whom the pronoun refers by assuming that it refers to the last person or persons identified (the antecedent). In the example above, "his" refers back to "suspect," "they" refers back to "the suspect and his companion," and "they" refers back to "the suspect and his companion." Do you see any problems? The problem is that the second "they" in the sentence should refer back to "the DEA agents" rather than to "the suspect and his companion." The way to correct this is to replace the second "they" with "the agents." Then the sentence would read:

> The DEA agents made an investigative stop of the suspect and his companion because they fit the drug courier profile as well as other information the agents had obtained.

The pronoun must agree in number with its antecedent. Many students have problems with antecedents and the word "court." Even though there are a number of judges making up the court, court is a singular noun. The proper pronoun to use with "court" would be "it" rather than "they."

Rewrite the following sentences correcting any antecedent problems.

1. Bryce Dealer had an appointment with Dr. Slaughter in his office. When he arrived at the officer his pager went off and he asked the secretary if he could use the office phone.
2. Mario tells Bryce he knows of someone who wants to make a large order, and he needs it in three hours.
3. Bryce asked the receptionist if he could use Dr. Slaughter's phone. She said, "Yes." Then he went into the office and closed the door.
4. Mario told Brice that he had a large order and he needed it for a friend within three hours.
5. The Florida Statutes explain that when one knowingly and illegally intercepts a conversation, they have committed a violation and can be punished according to the law in the state of Florida.
6. Because the conversation between Bryce and Mario was a wire communication, the information obtained from the officers illegally scanning their conversation cannot be used in court.
7. Next, the court illustrated the next factor in their determination of reasonableness.
8. The Florida statutes look to see what the person has done to show they expect privacy.
9. In the State of Florida, one has an expectation of privacy when conversing on the telephone. There is an expectation that what they say will not be recorded.
10. These laws protect wire communications from being intercepted without a prior court order. It also protects oral communications from interception without consent, if the person has a justifiable expectation of privacy.
11. It is reasonable to assume if a person has a mere suspicion that a conversation is going to be recorded and they do not want it to be recorded, then they should not engage in that conversation.
12. The State will argue that Johnson should have been aware of the fact that he was talking to an answering machine rather than to Dade himself. They will argue that Johnson should have been suspicious of the possible recording because of sounds made by the answering machine.

13. Because the sole purpose of an answering machine is to record messages, any reasonable person would conclude upon hearing the announcement that they have the choice to hang up and not be recorded.
14. When an individual endeavors to communicate with anyone they give implied consent to the recording of that communication when they are addressing an answering machine.
15. In *Sells*, the court reversed and held that there was a triable issue. They did not agree that mere suspicion or implied knowledge that a communication might be recorded makes unreasonable the expectation of privacy in that communication.
16. However, there are exceptions to these statutes when either party to the conversation gives either express or implied consent, or if the party being recorded has a reasonable suspicion that their conversation may be recorded.
17. Mr. Johnson admitted beating the decedent, but stated that he was alive when he left the house.
18. Though the caller has an expectation of privacy that their call is not being monitored or intercepted, their message has been legally intercepted through the answering machine of the person being called because the caller has consented.
19. In *Stevenson*, the court ruled that the intercepted conversation was not an oral communication. Their reasoning is that an oral communication requires a subjective and objective expectation of privacy.
20. The Florida Supreme Court cited to the district court for part of their reasoning.
21. In so holding, the Court relied heavily on their earlier decision in *Terry v. Ohio*, 392 U.S. 1 (1968).
22. The DEA agents escorted Sokolow and Norian to their office in the airport.
23. The appellants filed a motion to suppress the cocaine charge on the grounds that the stop of their car was unreasonable.
24. The patrolman stated that Coleman did not break any laws, but he was stopped because in his experience, people who fit the profile sometimes had drugs.
25. Smith and Swindell filed motions to suppress, but it was denied.
26. In their opinion, the court cited *Terry*.
27. Vogel stopped a driver and passenger because he thought he had reasonable suspicion that the driver fit a profile of a drug courier.
28. Vogel did not have enough facts to stop him.
29. The court stated that if they let officers stop vehicles based only on a hunch, there would be great potential for abuse.
30. The Court reasoned that they must consider all the factors, "the totality of the circumstances."

ACTIVE VERSUS PASSIVE VOICE

To understand active and passive voice look at the following sentences:

> The officer returned the money to the driver.
>
> The money was returned to the driver by the officer.

The first sentence is written in active voice. "Officer" is the subject, "returned" is the verb, "money" is the object, and "driver" is the indirect object. The "officer" is also the person taking the action of "returning"

> To find the direct object in a sentence, ask "what" or "who."
>
> To find the indirect object in a sentence, ask "to whom" or "for whom."
>
> So, to find the direct object in the first sentence above, "what" or "who" did the officer return? The officer returned the money; thus "money" is the direct object.
>
> To find the indirect object, "to whom" or "for whom" did the officer return the money? The officer returned the money to the driver; thus "driver" is the indirect object.

the money. Sentences written in active voice have the "performer" as the subject of the sentence, with the subject preceding the verb. The second sentence is written in passive voice. In passive voice sentences, the object of the action (the thing or person performed on) comes first, then the verb, and then the "performer."

Active voice is preferable in legal writing because it makes the sentence more powerful and easier to understand. See whether this it true by reading the two sentences above again. Which do you prefer? Passive voice is fine for those instances when you do not know or do not want to identify the performer. In the example above, if you did not know who returned the money you could write:

The money was returned to the driver.

When you edit your writing and you find a sentence in passive voice, rewrite it in active voice. Even if the "performer" is not specifically identified in the sentence, you may be able to identify the performer by the context of the sentence.

Now, rewrite the following sentences in active voice:

1. Also, it tells us that an intentional interception of the conversation by Bill occurred without prior consent from Mr. Johnson.
2. In both wire communications the interceptions of Bill were intentional.
3. Because of a button on Bill's answering machine which was used by Bill to intercept the conversation between Mr. Johnson and Bill, there was an intentional interception of the conversation.
4. The Longs were informed by the Browns that they wanted to build a small toy store on the commercial lot and live in the residence next door.
5. On April 1, 1997, a cordless telephone conversation was surreptitiously intercepted by police officers on the University of Central Florida campus with the use of a scanner.
6. Also stated by the Florida Supreme Court that federal pre-emption had the effect of amending state law to conform to the higher standard of protection under the federal statute.
7. In *Campbell v. Jacksonville Kennel Club*, 66 So. 2d 495 (Fla. 1953), the elements of slander were stated.
8. The joint venture will be owned equally by Arctic and Marine and governed by a five person board of directors, including two persons designated by Arctic, two persons designated by Marine, and one outside director agreed upon by both parties.
9. All profits of the joint venture will be split evenly between Arctic and Marine.
10. It is the intention of each party to protect its confidential and proprietary information.
11. The homeowners are hereby notified by the developer that the private roads constructed on the property must be maintained, resurfaced, and repaired by an association to be formed by the homeowners.
12. It is asserted that the ordinance is not applicable to the developer and the developer is exempt from concurrency based on its status as a Development of Regional Impact.
13. The fees charged by the doctors to the patients being seen at the office shall be consistent with the industry standard of the region.
14. The doctors shall reimburse the company for any claims made related to services provided by the doctors to company patients.
15. The applicable rule governing amendment of the agreement is found in section 10.
16. It has long been held that where writing expressly refers to and sufficiently describes another document, the other document is incorporated by reference.
17. Water management districts are enabled by part IV of the master agreement to issue permits for the construction and operation of surface water management systems.
18. All fees and costs associated with section 11, except for each party's attorneys' fees, shall be paid for by the corporation.
19. The regulations were issued and are administered by the Office of Foreign Affairs.
20. Unlike the other cases, it was held that the agents did have the needed suspicion to make a valid stop.

21. The application to the instant case detailing the similarities and differences will also be noted.
22. The money was ordered returned to the persons from whom it was taken.
23. Based entirely on these factors Nelson was detained by Vogel.
24. The cocaine seized was ordered by the court to be suppressed.
25. It was testified by Vogel that the appellees were stopped because they fit a drug courier profile.
26. Trooper Vogel testified that the vehicle was being driven by Mr. Johnson in an "overly cautious" manner.

CHANGE IN TENSES

Usually sentences and paragraphs are written in a single tense unless there is a reason for changing tenses. Your reader will be distracted from what you are trying to communicate if you change tenses in midstream without a reason. The following sentence contains a distracting change in tenses:

> DEA agents arrested Smith and Swindell and charged them with conspiracy to possess cocaine with intent to distribute. Defendants file motions to suppress. The motions were denied.

Why did the writer change from past tense ("arrested" and "charged"), to present tense ("file"), and back to past tense ("were denied")? Your reader may be wondering about that more than the writer's message. Keep your tenses consistent unless you have a reason for changing tenses.

Rewrite the following sentences keeping the verb tense consistent.

1. Bryce Canyon was waiting patiently for his appointment with Dr. Slaughter. While Bryce is waiting, his beeper goes off and he asked politely to use the telephone.
2. The receptionist lets him use a telephone in the office. Bryce closed the door so he could have some privacy while making his call.
3. Bryce called back his friend, Mario Hernandez. After minutes of small talk, Mario tells Bryce someone wants to make a large order.
4. The deal included the order from a customer who wanted two tons of marijuana and a hundred pounds of cocaine. They also discuss the price of the deal.
5. The law enforcement officers have violated Bryce's right of privacy when they did not get consent to intercept his wire communication.
6. Bryce and Mario agree to meet in two hours on Delaware Boulevard. The state police were outside the building during Bryce and Mario's conversation and intercepted and recorded their conversation.
7. Bryce Dealer had an appointment with Dr. Slaughter on the campus of UCF. Bryce receives a page on his beeper. Since Dr. Slaughter is not quite ready from Bryce, he asks if he could use a phone in one of the other offices. Bryce calls Mario. Mario needs a large order of drugs in about three hours. The order consisted of two tons of marijuana and one hundred pounds of cocaine.
8. Bryce and Mario were to meet in the office off of Delaware Boulevard. Bryce then hangs up the phone. What Bryce and Mario were not aware of was that a police officer had intercepted the cordless telephone conversation with a scanner.
9. After the conversation ended, Mr. Johnson went to Bill's house and brutally beats him.
10. At first it seemed he is trying to be calm, but immediately he burst out yelling.
11. Johnson did not fully know about the recording, but had more than a mere suspicion that it may be recorded.
12. Tiny told Bill Tiny wanted to beat him up. As soon as Tiny hears a voice he began yelling.
13. Bill had an answering machine for the sole purpose of recording telephone calls that may occur when he is not home.
14. James was in a screened porch attached to a house. James has an expectation of privacy that he will not be recorded.
15. Mario then asked Brice if he can supply the drugs in three hours.
16. Brice explained to Mario that he can get the order for the regular price.
17. The Orlando Police department's scanning is intentional when it continued to monitor the defendant's cordless telephone conversation.

18. The court looked at the totality of the circumstances in deciding this case and decided that any one of the reasons does not by itself support reasonable suspicion, but altogether they do amount to reasonable suspicion.
19. The suspect admitted that his real name is Sokolow.
20. The court held that the drug courier profile was too general and did not establish any more than a hunch which is condemned by the United States Supreme Court in *Terry*.
21. The issue in this case is whether the stop was a reasonable Terry stop. The court held that the stop was not supported by reasonable suspicion.
22. In *Smith*, the same officer is on a special operation to intercept drug couriers. He was parked in the median with his car's headlights shining into the northbound lanes.
23. The Court agreed that any one of these factors alone may not qualify as reasonable suspicion, but when combined they provide adequate proof for reasonable suspicion.
24. The Court of Appeals held that because Vogel did not have reasonable suspicion that the appellants were hauling drugs, the stop can not be upheld on that ground.
25. On appeal the stop was ruled unreasonable and any evidence obtained from the stop must be suppressed.
26. The court finds that there was no reasonable suspicion that the individual was committing, had committed, or was going to commit a crime. Therefore the evidence was suppressed.
27. The stop was not constitutionally permitted because the drug profile is too general and unparticularized to support a Terry stop.
28. The Fifth District Court of Appeal ruled the lack of reasonable suspicion and reliance upon a hunch, coupled with a drug courier profile too general to support a *Terry* stop, is inconsistent with the Florida Constitution.
29. The trial court denied a motion to suppress the evidence, and thus stipulating that the stop was a legal one.

COMBINATION OF ERRORS

Challenge yourself by rewriting the following sentences that contain a combination of errors:

1. Trooper stated that he initially stopped the car for a traffic violation, of weaving, to investigate for drunk driving, however, when the vehicle was stopped, no test for alcohol was conducted and a drug dog was called to the scene immediately, which leads to an obvious different scope for the reason of stopping the vehicle, upon which Vogel had no reasonable suspicion.
2. On June 5, 1985 at 3:00 AM, Trooper Robert Vogel and an unmarked DEA agent were stopped in the median of I-95 with the cars headlights shining into the northbound lane.
3. The Court reasoned that Vogel's profile could not reasonably infer that a vehicle meeting such criteria should be characterized as unusual.
4. Does the fact that driver fits a drug courier profile give the highway trooper reasonable suspicion that the driver was committing, committed or about to commit a crime and justify an investigatory Terry stop?

APPENDIX E

PROBLEMS

The following four problems were designed to give students practice in research and writing. Students can be assigned one or more of the problems to research. Writing assignments on the problems can include:

1. A client opinion letter (written to one of the persons named in a problem).
2. An attorney-client contract (the agreement one of the persons named in the problem signs to retain an attorney).
3. An office memo to a senior partner concerning one of the problems.
4. A memorandum of law in support of a motion for summary judgment or other litigation motion filed in a lawsuit concerning one of the problems.
5. An appellate brief filed after a judgment was reached in a lawsuit concerning one of the problems.

WAS SWIMMING POOL AN ATTRACTIVE NUISANCE?

John and Mary Cooke own a home in Anytown, Your State, with a private swimming pool in their back yard. Pursuant to local ordinances, their back yard is completely fenced by a five-foot wooden fence and the gate is kept closed with a latch at the top of the fence.

The Cookes live next door to the Andersons, a family with a two-year-old son Joseph. Joseph loved water and the Andersons had joined the Cookes swimming in the Cookes' pool on numerous occasions. Although not yet "swimming" on his own, Joseph greatly enjoyed splashing in the pool and looked forward to playing with the Cookes' dog Rover. From the moment Joseph woke up in the morning until he went to bed at night, his favorite topics were "pool" and "dog." Rover spent most of his days in the pool enclosure, relaxing on the pool deck or swimming. Joseph would become extremely excited anytime he heard Rover bark from next door.

One Saturday morning Joseph was playing on the screened-in porch of his home. He seemed quite content playing with his toys while his parents completed some odd jobs around the house. Once when his mother checked on him, he was gazing toward the Cookes' house and listening for Rover's bark. His mother told Joseph that they could go swimming and visit Rover later in the day.

The parents lost track of time, each assuming that the other had been checking on Joseph. All of a sudden the Andersons realized that neither one of them had checked on Joseph for a while. When they went to the screened-in porch Joseph was nowhere to be found and the outside screen door was sightly ajar. They called to Joseph but he didn't answer, even though he was usually very good about coming when called.

The Andersons immediately started looking outside for Joseph. He was not in the Anderson's yard. At that moment they noticed that the gate to the Cookes' pool fence was wide open. Fearing the worst, they rushed through the gate calling for Joseph. Initially nothing appeared out of the ordinary except that Rover was dashing around the outside of the pool and barking as if to attract someone's attention. Then they noticed the pool blanket was slightly pulled back from the side of the pool at the deep end.

The Cookes always kept the pool covered with a pool blanket when the pool was not in use. The blanket kept the water from losing heat during the night and kept debris from falling into the water. The pool blanket was constructed of two layers of blue plastic material with small air pockets between the layers. The blanket, floating on the surface of the water, covered the entire pool surface except for a small area left open so Rover could swim.

When the Cookes heard the Andersons yelling they rushed out to the pool to find out what was the matter. When they heard that Joseph was missing, the Cookes' first thought was that he might have fallen into the pool while following Rover. John Cooke called for Phil Smith so Phil could help remove the pool blanket. Phil was a fifteen-year-old neighbor who often came to play with Rover. Phil had been playing with Rover inside the pool fence that morning. Phil did not answer so the Cookes and the Andersons together started pulling back the pool blanket.

To their horror, they saw two bodies in the deep end of the pool. They all jumped into the pool and pulled out the bodies. The two women tried to revive Joseph and Phil while the two men called the police and fire departments. When they arrived, the police and fire fighters joined the Andersons and the Cookes in trying to revive the two boys. The two boys were rushed to the hospital but died a few hours later.

The police report of the incident showed that Mr. Cooke remembered opening the gate early in the morning while he was doing work around the pool. Joseph must have opened the outside screened door to his house and entered the pool enclosure looking for Rover. He may have fallen into the deep end of the pool while chasing Rover. The pool blanket would have parted enough from the side of the pool to allow Joseph to fall into the water. Although not a very good swimmer, Phil apparently jumped in to rescue Joseph at the same place Joseph had fallen in. The police theorized that Phil became disoriented while trying to rescue Joseph and couldn't get out from under the pool blanket.

The Cookes have just been told that their neighbors are planning to file suit against them, holding them responsible for Joseph and Phil's deaths. The Cookes hired your firm to represent them. The senior partner in your firm has asked you to research the law of your state and answer the following questions:

1. Does your state follow the attractive nuisance doctrine and, if so, how does it apply to private swimming pools?
2. Can the Andersons hold the Cookes responsible for Joseph's death?
3. What duty did the Cookes owe Phil and can the Smiths hold the Cookes liable for Phil's death?

DEFAMATION

Tom Harris and Jake Carson had been sports and political leaders and rivals ever since high school. They competed on the same sports teams and were of equal physical ability. In track and swimming races Tom would come in first in one race, Jake would come in first in the next race, and then they would tie each other for first in a third race. Either Tom or Jake had been class president each of four years in high school. Jake had been class president of his freshman and senior classes while Tom had been class president of his sophomore and junior classes.

Their friends speculated that the rivalry would continue in college. They both were to attend Collegiate University in nearby University Town. As freshmen they pledged two rival fraternities. Tom pledged Collegiate Alphas and Jake pledged Collegiate Betas. What had been friendly rivalry in high school gradually turned nasty during their years at the University. The Alphas pulled all sorts of pranks on the Betas and tried to discredit the Betas in the university community. The Betas did the same to the Alphas.

In the fall of their senior year at the University, Tom and Jake both decided to run for student body president. There was a lot of mudslinging during the campaign. At one point in the campaign, it was rumored that Jake was gay. The rumors were traced back to the Alphas. Although no one seemed to believe the rumor, Jake and his fraternity brothers were very upset about it.

The night before the election, the candidates participated in skits in the football stadium. Everyone eagerly looked forward to the skits each year, with most of the students and faculty of Collegiate University attending. The skits were usually half serious and half in jest. On skit night, the crowd in the stadium enjoyed the first skits while they speculated about Tom and Jake's skits. Jake's skit was the next-to-the-last and Tom's was the last of the evening. In Jake's skit, Jake neatly poked fun at Tom and emphasized how he, Jake, was the better candidate.

Then came time for Tom's skit. The scene was Jake's doctor's office. Tom played Jake's doctor and one of the Alphas played Jake. In the skit "Jake" walked into the doctor's office and said, "Well, doctor, now that I've completed my executive physical, I feel ready to complete my duties as Collegiate University student body president and lead the University to great achievements. How did my tests come out?" The "doctor" replied, "Well, Jake, you better sit down. I have good news and bad news for you. The good news is that most of your tests came back negative and you should make a fine student body president. The bad news is that you and Magic Johnson have something in common. Both of you tested HIV positive."

Those words were barely out of Tom's mouth when the stadium crowd gasped. A fight immediately broke out between the Alphas and Betas sitting near each other and the police were called in to clear the stands.

Although the student body president race had seemed almost even before the skits, Tom won with two-thirds of the vote. Jake was so outraged by Tom's skit that he hired your law firm to represent him. The senior partner in your firm has asked you to research the law of your state and answer the following questions:

1. Is it actionable per se as slander to announce that a person has tested HIV positive where the statement is not true?
2. Although Tom claims that his statement that Jake was HIV positive was made in jest, would the words give rise to an action for slander?
3. Could Jake be considered a public official or public figure in a slander action brought by him, and, if he is considered a public official or public figure, will it make any difference in the lawsuit?

THE NIGHTMARE PROPERTY

The Longs had purchased two adjoining lots on Nice Street in Anytown, Your State, as investment property. One of the lots was zoned residential and contained a three-bedroom, two-bathroom house which the Longs rented out. The other lot, zoned commercial, was vacant.

In September of 1988 the Longs rented the house to a 30-year-old business woman. Barely a month later the police called the Longs. A neighbor of the business woman had asked the police to investigate the Longs' Nice Street house. The neighbor reported he had heard a lot of yelling at the house and then a gun shot. The police found the front door open and the business woman dead, apparently shot by an intruder.

The Longs next rented the Nice Street house to a family. As soon as the family moved in, they reported that their television set repeatedly turned on and off, often in the middle of the night. The children claimed they had seen the ghost of the dead woman and were too terrified to sleep in their rooms. The neighborhood children started calling the Nice Street house the "haunted house" and refused to play with the children of the family renting the house. A few months later the family moved out complaining that they did not want to live with a ghost.

After that the Longs tried without success to rent the Nice Street house. At the same time the Longs posted a "For Sale" sign on the two lots. The Longs wanted to sell them for $250,000, the price at which the Longs had purchased them ten years earlier. The Longs received no offers until almost a year later. A retired couple, the Browns, called the Longs to ask the sale price on the two lots. The couple was looking to move to a warmer climate and open a small toy store. When the Browns heard the asking price of $250,000 they said they might be interested in purchasing the lots.

The Longs met the Browns at the lots and gave them a tour of the house. The Browns explained to the Longs that they wanted to build a small toy store on the vacant commercial property and live next door in the house. They said that they were attracted to the lots because of their location and because the asking price seemed reasonable. The Longs told the Browns that the only reason they had put such a low price on the property was because it had been on the market for a while. The Longs needed to sell the property quickly because they were in need of cash to pay for unexpected expenses.

The sale went through sixty days later and the Browns immediately started construction on the vacant lot. They hoped to have the construction finished by the time they moved to Anytown. Six months later the Browns moved into the Nice Street house and opened the then completed toy store. Business at the toy store seemed very slow. The Longs noticed that none of the children from the neighborhood came into the store. They did get some business from people vacationing in Anytown.

A week after the Browns moved into the house, their television turned on in the middle of the night.

They didn't think anything of it until it happened the next two nights in a row. When Mr. Brown got up to turn off the television, he thought he saw something white and filmy at the other end of the room. Then the same thing started happening to the small television in the toy store. The Browns made sure they had turned off the television before locking the store for the evening but they found the television turned on when they opened the store the next morning. Before they turned on the store lights in the morning, the Browns thought they glimpsed something white moving at the other end of the store. They didn't see anything out of the ordinary when they turned the lights on.

A few days later Mr. Brown struck up a conversation with the teenage clerk at the local grocery store. The clerk asked Mr. Brown whether he had just moved to town. When Mr. Brown told him he owned the new toy store and lived next door, the clerk said, "I didn't think the Longs would ever sell the haunted house." Mr. Brown said, "What do you mean?" The clerk said, "Everybody around here knows the house is haunted. Why do you think you paid such a low price for it?"

Understandably shaken, Mr. Brown went home and told his wife the news. They immediately called the Longs and accused them of tricking the retired couple. The Browns demanded their money back and demanded to be reimbursed for the cost of construction of the toy store. When the Longs refused, the Browns hired your law firm to represent them. The senior partner in your firm has asked you to research the law of your state and answer the following questions:

1. Did the Longs have a duty to disclose that the two lots were "haunted"?
2. What are the elements of fraud concerning the sale of real property?
3. Are there enough facts for the Browns to win if they sue the Longs for fraud?

I WONDER WHAT IS IN THE PACKAGE

Margie and Floyd Walker had been happily married for forty-five years. Even though past retirement age, Floyd continued to work for the railroad as a porter on its passenger trains. Margie was worried about Floyd's health and had been trying to get him to stop working for some time. She was concerned that the porter's job was too physically taxing for someone of Floyd's age.

One Monday morning as Floyd was getting ready for work, Margie had the uncomfortable feeling that something would happen to Floyd at work. Margie pleaded with Floyd to call in sick. Floyd said, "I feel fine. Why should I call in sick if I feel fine?" Floyd reported for work as usual. Margie tried to convince herself that she was worrying for nothing, but to no avail. She wandered through the house all day, not able to get anything done except worry.

At three o'clock in the afternoon the telephone rang. Margie was so frightened that her hand shook as she answered the telephone. Floyd's supervisor at the railroad said, "Margie, I think you better sit down. I have bad news for you. Floyd fell from the train as it was going full speed and was killed. It appears he became disoriented, opened the outside door of the train, and was pulled off the train step by a sudden gust of wind. Floyd's body is at the Near Town Funeral Home. I'll make arrangements if you like to have the body transferred to a funeral home in Any Town." Margie felt like she had been hit by a truck. She was glad that she was sitting down or she very likely would have fainted. She responded, "Please make the arrangements with Webury Funeral Home."

Margie's worst fear had come true. Somehow she made it through the funeral. She kept feeling that it must all be a bad dream. She kept imagining that she would wake up one morning with Floyd still alive. She did remember having to call the Near Town Funeral Home several times to have Floyd's personal effects forwarded to Webury. Webury delivered the personal effects to her the day after the funeral.

It was not until almost a week after Floyd's death when Margie went through Floyd's personal effects. To her horror, in a plastic bag labeled "personal effects" she found a kidney, teeth and fingers. At the sight of her dead husband's body parts she fainted. A neighbor lady friend found Margie an hour later collapsed on the floor. She was hospitalized for extreme exhaustion for two days and her doctor put her on antidepressant medication.

When she had recovered sufficiently, she called Webury to complain. Webury's owner disclaimed all responsibility. The owner said that Webury had simply forwarded the plastic bag, at Margie's insistence, from the Near Town Funeral Home. The owner added that the Webury employees had no reason to check what was in the bag.

Margie still suffers from depression and has not had a good night's sleep since she opened the plastic bag. She keeps having nightmares about the employees of Near Town Funeral Home placing Floyd's body parts in the plastic bag and imagines them laughing as they labeled the bag "personal effects." It also makes her angry that Webury seemed so unconcerned and did not even offer an apology. Margie has hired your law firm to represent her in a possible lawsuit against the funeral home. The senior partner in your firm has asked you to research the law of your state and answer the following questions:

1. What would Margie Walker have to prove to recover damages for the tort of interference with a dead body?
2. What are the elements of the tort of intentional infliction of emotional distress, sometimes called the "tort of outrage"?
3. Will Margie Walker be able to hold Near Town Funeral Home and Webury Funeral Home liable for the torts of interference with a dead body and intentional infliction of emotional distress?

APPENDIX F

WEB BIBLIOGRAPHY: COMPANY INFORMATION ON THE INTERNET

Associations on the Net
http://www.ipl.org/ref/AON/
A collection of over 2000 Internet sites providing information on a wide variety of professional and trade associations, cultural and art organizations, political parties and advocacy groups, labor unions, academic societies, and research institutions. Includes abstracts summarizing information about each site.

Companies Online
http://www.companiesonline.com/
Search information for over 100,000 public and private U.S. companies (by name or ticker symbol; narrow search by industry). *Requires free online registration.* Provides valuable information on annual sales, company size, ownership structure, web and e-mail addresses, and much more.

Company Sleuth
http://www.companysleuth.com/
This site offers a combination of free and subscription services. Obtain *free* real-time news and stock quotes and company briefs for publicly traded companies. Full reports include registered patents and trademarks, pending litigation, broker reports, insider trading; links to all SEC filings. Paid subscribers may also register for e-mail alerts for breaking news and information on companies you select to monitor.

Corporate Information (CI)
http://www.corporateinformation.com/
Research U.S. and foreign companies (search by name or stock ticker symbol), and obtain industry profiles. Other features include foreign currency exchange rates, and a list of the top 50 companies in the world, ranked by market capitalization. Highly recommended for conducting corporate research on foreign companies.

Corporation Records Online
http://www.internet-prospector.org/secstate3.html
Quickly locate official state corporation records online, or if not available electronically, contact information to obtain information by other means.

EDGAR Database of Corporate Information
http://www.sec.gov/edgar.shtml
EDGAR provides access to submissions by companies and others required by law to file forms with the U.S. Securities and Exchange Commission (SEC). Not all documents filed with the Commission by public companies will be available on EDGAR. Companies were phased in to EDGAR filing over a three-year period, ending May 6, 1996. As of that date, all public domestic companies were required to make their filings on EDGAR, except for filings made in paper because of a hardship exemption. Third-party filings with respect to these companies, such as tender offers and Schedules 13D, are also filed on EDGAR.

Fortune 500 List
http://www.fortune.com
Use the down arrow on drop menu box to browse the various Fortune Lists. Selct the "full list" button. Click on the company's name to get a snapshot of corporate and financial data.

Global 500 List
http://www.fortune.com
Use the down arrow on drop menu box to browse the various Fortune Lists. Select the "full list" button. The Global List includes the top 500 international companies, with same format as the Fortune 500 List.

Hoovers Online
http://www.hoovers.com/
While some resources are free, a fee-based membership allows full access to all that Hoover's Online has to offer, including the premium features such as in-depth company information on public and private companies (indicated throughout the site by the "key" icon). Reports include in-depth company information (public and private companies), including a list of officers, competitors, products/services, and current and historical financial data), plus real-time SEC documents through EDGAR Online *(see listing above).*

IPO Central
http://www.hoovers.com/ipo/0,1334,23,00.html
Latest filings, pricings and an IPO Scoreboard showing total number of IPO pricings and pricings by industry; includes a handy Beginners Guide. *Requires free online registration.* Register for free weekly e-mail updates of IPO filings, pricings, and scheduled offerings for the coming week.

Public Records Online
http://www.pac-info.com/
A web directory of thousands of free searchable public records databases, arranged by state.

The Public Registers Annual Report Service
http://www.prars.com/
Free annual reports for over thousands of public companies. PRARS is America's largest annual report service. Company financials, including annual reports, prospectuses, and 10-K's on public companies are available without charge to the public. Requests are generally processed within 24 hours and are shipped free of charge (U.S. mailing addresses only).

Thomas Register of American Manufacturers
http://www4.thomasregister.com/index.html
Search for information on American and Canadian manufacturers of industrial products and services. Requires *free* online registration.

Wall Street Research Network
http://www.wsrn.com/home/companyResearch.html
Search for links to web sites with data customized to the U.S. or Canadian company you have selected (*i.e*, SEC filings, business journal articles, stock quotes, stock price and volume history, earnings estimates, industry reports and financial data. The $ symbol next to link indicates a fee based service; otherwise free).

APPENDIX G

INTERNET TERMINOLOGY

Address The information used to identify a specific computer on the Internet (*see* URL).

ASCII Developed by the American National Standards Institute (ANSI), this is the most common format for text files in computers and on the Internet. In an ASCII file, each alpha, numeric, or special character is represented with a 7-digit binary number (a string of seven 0s or 1s). UNIX and DOS-based operating systems (except Windows NT) use ASCII for text files. Windows NT uses a newer code, Unicode.

BBS Short for "bulletin board service" where users dial in to access specialized information or services; semi-organized "chat" sessions on a common topic.

Baud The rate at which your modem transmits data. The higher the number, the faster the transmission.

Binary A numbering scheme in which there are only two possible values for each digit: 0 and 1.

Bookmarks Part of a web browser that allows you to store Internet addresses (URLs) for quick future recall; also known as Favorites (in Netscape browsers).

Boolean A system of logical, mathematical thought developed by the English mathematician and computer pioneer, George Boole (1815–1864). Its rules govern logical functions of word relationships; AND, OR and NOT are the primary operations of Boolean logic.

Browser Software used to browse hypertext documents on the web. Examples are Lynx (linear; line-based) and Netscape and Internet Explorer (graphical).

Cache *(pronounced CASH)* is a location on your computer's hard drive where data from web sites is temporarily stored. You can usually vary the size of your cache and the length of time information is stored, depending on your browser.

CGI (Common Gateway Interface) Programs or scripts executed on a web server that perform such tasks as manipulating databases.

Cookies Tiny messages sent out from some servers to get information from your machine. While not damaging like a virus, they do collect information about you and your browser. Users are advised *not* to accept "cookies" from unfamiliar servers.

Dedicated Server In web hosting, a dedicated server refers to the rental and exclusive use of a computer that includes a web server, related software, and connection to the Internet, housed in the web hosting company's premises (*see* Dedicated Host).

DHTML Dynamic HTML refers to web content that changes each time it is viewed. For example, the same URL could result in a different page depending on any number of parameters, such as geographic location of the reader, time of day, previous pages viewed by the reader, and profile of the reader.

DNS (Domain Name Server) A computer in a network or at an Internet Service Provider that contains an index of Internet addresses and domain names and converts these to Internet Protocol (IP) addresses to facilitate Internet connectivity.

DOS Disk Operating System was the first popular operating system for personal computers. A non-graphical line-oriented command or a menu-driven operating system. The prompt to enter a DOS command is C:>.

Download Downloading is the transmission of a file from one computer system to another, usually a smaller computer system. To download a file is to request it from another computer (or from a web page on another computer) and to receive it for storage on the requester's computer.

DVD (Digital Video Disk) High compression laser disc capable of storing complete programs on one side of a single disc; DVDs can hold up to four hours of video, plus soundtracks and more.

E-Mail Electronic mail sent via the Internet or another computer network; computer-to-computer exchange of electronic messages.

Firewalls A set of related computer programs located on a network server, designed to protect the private network from access by unauthorized users.

FTP (File Transfer Protocol) A standardized text-based method of transferring electronic files from one computer to another.

Hardware Like software, hardware is a collective term. Hardware includes not only the computer but also the cables, connectors, power supply units, and all peripheral devices such as the keyboard, mouse, audio speakers, scanners, and printers.

Home Page The gateway or "main menu" to a web site; usually the first screen you see when connecting to an Internet site; a starting point.

Host The term "host" has several related meanings. When referring to Internet protocol specifications, "host" means any computer that has full two-way access to other computers on the Internet. For companies or individuals with a web site, a host is a computer with a web server that serves the pages of one or more web sites (*see* Dedicated Server).

HTML (Hypertext Markup Language) The authoring language used to format and create documents on the World Wide Web. HTML formatting defines the structure and layout of a web document by using a variety of computer programming tags and attributes. The HTML code tells the web browser how to display a web page's words and images for the user.

HTTP (Hypertext Transfer Protocol) The set of rules (protocols) for exchanging files (text, graphics, images, sound, video, and other multimedia) on the web.

HTTPS (Secure Hypertext Transfer Protocol) The web protocol developed by Netscape and built into its browder software that encrypts and decrypts web page data. A means to provide secure transmission of personal or confidential data over the web.

Hypertext Highlighted text that, when selected, allows you to browse through related topics or Web sites.

IP Internet Protocol (see TCP/IP).

Internet An international "network of networks", interconnected to allow for sharing of information on a global scale.

ISDN Integrated Services Digital Network is an international telecommunications standard for transmitting voice, video, and data over digital lines.

ISP (Internet Service Provider) A telecommunications network provider (company) with which you contract for connectivity to the Internet.

JAVA A plug-in application that interfaces/interacts with web browsers such as Netscape Navigator and Microsoft Internet Explorer to execute simple programs known as applets.

Listserv Another name for mailing lists, they are organized around specific interest topics. While related to both electronic mail and bulletin boards, they are less interactive.

Lynx A line-based web browser that provides text-only display of data from the web.

Metasearch Engine A very powerful Internet tool that uses multiple search engines to locate resources on the web.

Modem A piece of computer equipment (hardware) that connects a computer to a data transmission line (typically a telephone or cable line).

Network Two or more computers connected to communicate with one another. The Internet is a "network of networks".

Newsgroup Any electronic discussion group that serves as a bulletin board for users to post universally accessible messages; allows you to read and reply to others' messages via the Internet.

PPP/SLIP (Point-to-Point Protocol/Serial Line Protocol) Special dial-up connection that allows computers to use TCP/IP (Internet) protocols via a standard telephone line and a high-speed modem.

PDF Portable Document Format is a computer file format that allows you to view and print a file exactly as the author designed it, without needing to have the same application or fonts used to create the file. The Internet standard for electronic distribution that preserves the look and feel of the original document, including fonts, colors, images and layout.

Packet The unit of data that is routed between an origin and a destination on the Internet (*see* Router).

Protocol A definition or standard for how computers will act when talking to each other.

Public Domain Material that is not copyrighted, and intended [by the author] for unlimited use by the general public.

Real Time A level of computer responsiveness that a user senses as sufficiently immediate or that enables the computer to keep up with some external process (for example, to present visualizations of the weather as it constantly changes). *Real-time* is an adjective pertaining to computers or processes that operate in real time. Real time describes a human rather than a machine sense of time.

Robots Web robots are computer software programs that traverse the web automatically, checking links and URLs; also called web wanderers, crawlers or spiders.

Router A device, or in some cases computer software, connecting two or more networks. The router determines which way to send each packet of information (data) being transmitted or routed via telephone or cable lines (*see* Packet).

Server The host computer that "serves" software or information to a user's (client) computer. A computer in a network shared by multiple users. The term may refer to both the hardware and software or just the software that performs the service (*see* Dedicated Server).

SGML Standard Generalized Markup Language is a system for organizing and tagging elements of a document. SGML was developed and standardized by the International Organization for Standards (ISO) in 1986. SGML itself does not specify any particular formatting; rather, it specifies the rules for tagging elements. These tags can then be interpreted to format elements in different ways.

Shell On a UNIX system, the software that accepts and processes command lines from your terminal or remote computer.

SHTML A web file with a suffix of .shtml (rather than .html or .htm) indicates the file includes some information that will be added "on the fly" by the server before it is sent to you. A typical example is a "Last modified" date at the bottom of a web page.

Software A general term for the various kinds of programs used to operate computers and related devices. Software is often packaged on CD-ROMs and computer diskettes, or downloaded over the Internet. Some software programs come preloaded when you purchase a computer.

Spiders *See* Robots.

TCP/IP (Transmission Control Protocol/Internet Protocol) The protocol (standard) on which all Internet communication is based.

Telecommunications Software Computer software that allows for all types of remote data transmissions, from voice to video.

Telnet A method of logging onto another computer remotely to access information (a password or user identification is usually required).

UNIX A popular operating system that is commonly used by Internet host computers.

URL (Uniform Resource Locator) An address to access web pages on the Internet, generally consisting of a protocol or program (*i.e.*, http, gopher, ftp, telnet) followed by the address one wishes to connect with (*Example:* http:www.findlaw.com is the home page for FindLaw, the legal web direcatory and search tool).

Usenet A conglomerate of bulletin boards, organized by subject; an avenue for discussion, announcements and questions/answers.

WWW (World Wide Web) A hypertext-based system for finding and accessing documents and resources on the Internet using a system of hypertext and hypermedia links.

APPENDIX H

BIBLIOGRAPHY OF EVALUATIVE CRITERIA WEB SITES

(all sites last accessed 10 June 2001)

Alexander, Janet E. and Marsha A. Tate. Evaluating Web Resources. http://www2.widener.edu/Wolfgram-Memorial-Library/webevaluation/webeval. htm (last revised: 21 July 2000).

Notess, Greg R. On the Net: Tips for Evaluating Web Databases. *Database*. http://www.onlineinc.com/database/DB1998/net4.html (Apr 1998).

Straiton, T. Harmon, Jr. The Auburn University Libraries. Evaluating Internet Resources: a Selected Bibliography. http://www.lib.auburn.edu/madd/docs/eir.html (6 Oct 1999).

Tillman, Hope. Evaluating Quality on the Net. Babson College. http://www. hopetillman.com/findqual.html (2 Jan 1999).

The Virginia Wing Library, The Winsor School. Evaluating Internet Resources; a Checklist for Students. http://www.winsor.edu/library/evalstud.htm (4 Apr 1999).

APPENDIX I

LEGAL RESEARCH "STARTING POINTS"

ABA LawLink
http://www.abanet.org/lawlink/
Maintained by the American Bar Association (ABA), this site provides links to a wide range of legal research and government information resources on the Internet. While not an exhaustive menu, the list is extensive and nicely organized under major categories.

Chicago Kent Law School Guide to Legal Resources on the Web
http://www.kentlaw.edu/clc/lrs/lawlinks/
This site provides links to a variety of legal resources available on the Internet, including specialized legal information relating to computer law, environmental law, intellectual property, litigation, alternative dispute resolution, and tax issues.

Cornell Law School Legal Information Institute
http://fatty.law.cornell.edu/
This site provides links to recent U.S. Supreme Court decisions and the full text of the U.S. Code, plus links to hundreds of excellent resources, arranged by legal topic.

Emory Law School Federal Courts Finder
http://www.law.emory.edu/FEDCTS/
This site contains links to full text decisions from the U.S. Supreme Court, and all 11 federal circuit courts of appeal, and the federal circuit for the District of Columbia. Opinions for most jurisdictions are generally available from November 1994 forward and are published in cooperation with the Federal Courts Publishing Project, which seeks to electronically publish federal court decisions and make them freely available to the public over the Internet.

Findlaw
http://www.findlaw.com/
A popular legal search engine and web directory. The site includes hundreds of links arranged under topics including legal resources, law schools, consultants and experts, state and federal law, legal news, and more.

Guide to Online Law
http://www.loc.gov/law.guide/index.html
Prepared by the U.S. Law Library of Congress for the Global Legal Information Network (GLIN), this is an annotated hypertext guide to full sources of government and legal information worldwide.

Hieros Gamos Comprehensive Legal Site
http://www.hg.org/usstates-govt.html
Provides easy access to government information for all 50 states, uniform laws, law-related organizations and associations, and online journals. Use the "Next State" button for easy movement from state to state in the database.

Internet Legal Resources Guide
http://www.ilrg.com/
A categorized index of more than 4,000 select web sites (domestic and international), representing a comprehensive directory of law-related information available on the Internet. This site is designed for lay persons and legal professionals. The index is annotated, providing handy summaries of linked web sites.

Villanova Center for Information Law and Policy
http://vls.law.villanova.edu/
This site offers a great graphical interface that allows you to link to a particular jurisdiction using a map of the United States. It also includes several "locators" to help direct you to the official web sites for federal and state courts and U.S. federal government information resources on the Internet.

Washburn University School of Law
http://www.washlaw.edu
WashLawWEB™ links to hundreds of law-related resources on the Internet. In addition to specialized subject areas, you can access information about law schools and law libraries, and search law library catalogs. The site includes a table of contents and a separate search option for locating pertinent full text materials.

FEDERAL LAW RESOURCES

APPENDIX J

Administrative Law
http://www.findlaw.com/01topics/00administrative/gov_laws.html
FindLaw has organized all major primary federal administrative legal resources (codes, regulations, orders, and agency rulings) into one easy-to-use site.

Bureau of Labor Statistics (BLS)
http://stats.bls.gov/
Keyword search the BLS web pages or link to information and resources organized under several major categories, including research papers, regional information, the economy, and BLS surveys and programs. The site provides detailed BLS data, information on BLS publications, and the most current Consumer Price Index.

Census Bureau
http://www.census.gov
The U.S. Census Bureau is the nation's chief statistical collection agency. The Census Bureau's home page contains social, demographic, and economic information. Thousands of reports and documents are instantly accessible from the Census Bureau's *CenStats* service located at http://tier2.census.gov/dbappweb.htm, including the *Annual Survey of Manufacturers*, building permits, county business patterns, a U.S. census tract street locator, and international trade data.

Documents Center—University of Michigan
http://www.lib.umich.edu/libhome/Documents.center/
Designed and maintained by the University of Michigan Libraries, the Documents Center is a central reference and referral point for federal, state, local, foreign, and international government information. The site combines keyword searching of the database with a typical directory hierarchical subject approach, and is a good starting point for locating government information on the Internet.

Federal Government Agencies
http://www.lib.lsu.edu/gov/fedgov.html
Maintained by the Louisiana State University (LSU) Libraries, this highly rated site offers an extensive list of federal agencies with web pages and information available on the Internet. A good place to locate information and resources related to, or issued by, federal agencies and their respective departments and divisions.

Federal Reference Desk
http://www.law.sc.edu/refdesk1.htm
Maintained as an information service of the Coleman Karesh Law Library at the University of South Carolina School of Law, this is one of the most comprehensive web directories for locating primary sources of law from all branches of the federal government.

Fedworld
http://www.fedworld.gov/
Established in 1992 by the National Technical Information Service (NTIS), an agency of the U.S. Department of Commerce, this popular site is a comprehensive central access point for locating and acquiring government information, offering access to over 130 government dial-up bulletin boards, and government agencies and services.

FirstGov
http://www.firstgov.gov
FirstGov is a web portal designed to connect all of the U.S. federal government's online resources. Launched in the fall of 2000, the site provides access to millions of government web pages. FirstGov allows users to browse information arranged in a directory format, or

search the site using the search tool. FirstGov will initially focus on providing information, but is expected to eventually enable web-based transactions between citizens and agency personnel, such as applying online for student loans, tracking Social Security benefits, comparing Medicare options and even administering government grants and contracts.

GODART—Government Documents Roundtable

http://www.library.vanderbilt.edu/central/staff/fdtf.html

This comprehensive site, a joint venture of the Federal Documents Task Force (FDTF), the Government Documents Round Table (GODART), and the American Library Association (ALA), is an index of frequently used sites containing U.S. federal government information. GODART includes annotated links to topics such as business and economics, the U.S. Congress, consumer information, education, foreign countries, health and welfare, federal laws and regulations, natural resources, the President and executive branch of the federal government, scientific and technical government reports, government statistics, and information relating to voting and elections.

GPO*Access*

http://www.access.gpo.gov/su_docs/index.html

The GPO*Access* web site is maintained as a service of the Superintendent of Documents of the United States Government Printing Office (GPO). There are quick links from the main page to the *Code of Federal Regulations*, *Federal Register*, *Congressional Record* and the *United States Code*. In addition, links to other official federal government documents are arranged under the three branches of the federal government (legislative, executive, and judicial), as well as federal regulatory agencies and administrative regulations. There is also a special group of important historical documents including the *Articles of Confederation*, *Bill of Rights*, and *The Federalist Papers*, plus executive orders and presidential proclamations.

GPO Gate—University of California

http://www.gpo.ucop.edu

Another way to access information published by the U.S. Government Printing Office (GPO) is through various GPO "gates"—web sites maintained by large academic institutions and law schools around the country. These sites are generally more user-friendly and easier to search. A good example is the gateway site hosted by the University of California. Use this site to access federal laws, regulations, reports, data, and other information provided through the official GPO system.

Government Documents and Information Center

http://www.library.yale.edu/govdocs/etitles.html

Hosted and maintained by the Social Science Libraries & Information Services at Yale University, this web directory is an alphabetical listing of electronic government documents on the web, arranged by topic or publication title. Although not as comprehensive as other resources, this site links to the electronic versions of many "core" traditional federal publications such as the *Budget of the United States*, *Catalog of Federal Domestic Assistance*, *CIA World Factbook*, *Uniform Crime Reports*, and the *Statistical Abstract of the United States*. Links do not include summaries or annotations of site content.

Securities and Exchange Commission (SEC)

http://www.sec.gov/

In addition to general information about the SEC, investor assistance and complaints, SEC digest statements, current rulemaking, and SEC enforcement actions, you can search and retrieve (most but not all) documents filed with the Commission by public companies since September 1995 via EDGAR, the Electronic Data Gathering, Analysis and Retrieval system database at http://www.sec.gov/edgarhp.htm. (See chapter 8 for discussion on EDGAR.)

Thomas Legislative Information

http://thomas.loc.gov/

A service of the U.S. Congress offered through the Library of Congress, this site contains the full text of pending and passed federal legislation, bill summaries and status, and summaries of major federal legislation and public laws (arranged by law number). In addition, you can access the full text of the Congressional Record, Senate and House committee reports, and congressional roll call votes on key legislation.

YAHOO! Government Information Locator
http://www.yahoo.com/Government/
This Yahoo! site links to accurate and current legal and government information on federal agencies, citizenship, U.S. foreign embassies and consulates, all branches of the federal government and the U.S. military, official government sites for all 50 states, and various international organizations.

APPENDIX K

STATE AND LOCAL RESOURCES

Administrative Codes and Registers
http://www.nass.org/acr/internet.html
Maintained as a service of the National Association of Secretaries of State (NASS), this site links directly to the official administrative codes and registers for all 50 states and the District of Columbia, plus various federal administrative law resources on the web.

Findlaw's State Resources Index
http://guide.lp.findlaw.com/11stategov
Choose a particular state from an alphabetical index to link directly to hundreds of sites. There are also direct links to state constitutions, state and local government information from the Library of Congress, the National Conference of Commissioners on Uniform State Laws web site (which includes drafts of uniform and model acts), and the official web sites of many state, county, and local governments around the country.

National Center for State Courts (NCSC)
http://www.ncsconline.org/
The National Center for State Courts (NCSC) is an independent, nonprofit organization founded in 1971 to provide assistance, information, and support to the state courts. The site includes information on court technology programs, and a comprehensive listing of state courts and law-related Internet sites.

State and Local Government Comprehensive Legal Site
http://www.hg.org/usstates-govt.html
Provides easy access to government information for all 50 states, uniform laws, law-related organizations and associations, and online journals. Use the "Next State" button to move easily from state to state in the database.

State and Local Governments Meta-Indexes
http://lcweb.loc.gov/global/state/stategov.html
Maintained by the Library of Congress, this meta-index is one of the most comprehensive resources of its kind on the web, with hundreds of links to state and local government resources.

APPENDIX L

INTERNATIONAL LAW RESOURCES

Embassy.org
http://embassy.org
Maintained as a resource for the Washington, DC foreign embassy community, this site includes links to information on foreign embassies in the United States, including country profiles and data. Detailed reports on over 190 countries can be ordered online for a nominal fee.

Global Legal Information Network (GLIN)
http://lcweb2.loc.gov/law/GLINv1/
GLIN maintains a database of laws, regulations, and other related legal sources, contributed by the governments of member nations from official texts deposited by the members in a server maintained at the Library of Congress. The full text of the documents is in the official language of the country of origin, with abstracts in English. The summaries or abstracts are linked directly to the corresponding text. Use the "Law-online" link to begin your research.

Multilaterals Project
http://fletcher.tufts.edu/multilaterals.html
Begun in 1992, the Multilaterals Project is an ongoing endeavor, of the Tufts University Fletcher School of Law and Diplomacy, to make available the texts of international multilateral conventions and other related instruments. Although the project was initiated to improve public access to environmental agreements, the current collection also includes treaties in the fields of human rights, commerce and trade, laws of war and arms control, and other areas. While the vast majority of treaties date from the second half of the twentieth century, the collection also includes historical texts, including the 1648 *Treaty of Westphalia*, and the *Covenant of the League of Nations.*

New York University School of Law
Guide to Foreign and International Legal Databases
http://www.law.nyu.edu/library/foreign_intl/
A simple yet comprehensive directory listing of links to foreign and international legal materials and law-related information. Links are arranged under major categories including constitutions, foreign databases arranged by jurisdiction, international trade, international treaties, and foreign tax laws.

United Nations Web Site
http://www.un.org/english/
A good place to start a search for foreign laws and treaties, or to obtain demographic or statistical data on a foreign country. Maintained by the United Nations Department of Public Information, this site provides original data as well as links to reliable web resources around the world. There is also a nice selection of official UN documents, maps, and geographic information.

Washburn University School of Law Guide to Foreign and International Legal Databases
http://www.washlaw.edu/forint/forintmain.html
A comprehensive collection of links to primary foreign and international legal materials and research aids to guide you in researching international law online, arranged alphabetically by country, author, subject, and document title.

APPENDIX M

COMMERCIAL LEGAL INFORMATION WEB SITES

American Association of Law Libraries (AALL)
http://www.aallnet.org/

American Bar Association (ABA) Home Page
http://www.abanet.org

Americans With Disabilities Act Document Center
http://janweb.icdi.wvu.edu/kinder/

Court TV Law Center
http://www.courttv.com/

Directory of Legal Academia (U.S. law schools, faculty & staff)
http://www.law.cornell.edu/dla

FOIA (Freedom of Information Act) Web Site
http://spj.org/foia/

Health Law Resource
http://www.netreach.net/~wmanning/index.html

Hieros Gamos Comprehensive Legal Site
http://www.hg.org/usstates-govt.html

The Internet Lawyer
http://www.internetlawyer.com/

Law Dictionaries
http://www.lectlaw.com/def.htm
http://www.duhaiame.org/diction.htm

LawOffice.com
http:www.lawoffice.com

Law World
http://www.lawworld.com/

Lectric Law Library
http://www.lectlaw.com

Legal Assistant Today Magazine
http://www.legalassistanttoday.com

Legaldocs®—Legal Documents Online ***(interactive forms)***
http://www.legaldocs.com/

Legal Dot Net
http://www.legal.net

Legal Forms
http://www.lectlaw.com/form.html

Martindale-Hubbell Law Directory Lawyer Locator
http://lawyers.martindale.com/marhub

National Association of Legal Assistants (NALA)
http://www.nala.org

National Federation of Paralegal Associations (NFPA)
http://www.paralegals.org

Virtual Medical Law Center
http://www-sci.lib.uci.edu/HSG/Legal.html

APPENDIX N

TOPICAL INDEX OF LEGAL AND GOVERNMENT WEB SITES

ADA (Americans with Disabilities Act)
ADA Document Center
http://janweb.icdi.wvu.edu/kinder/

Administrative Codes and Registers
National Association of Secretaries of State (NASS)
http://www.nass.org/acr/internet.html

Arbitration and Mediation
FedLaw
http://fedlaw.gsa.gov/legal89.htm

Attorney Locators
LawOffice.com (under "Consumer")
http://www.lawoffice.com/

Martindale-Hubbell Law Directory Lawyer Locator
http://lawyers.martindale.com/marhub

Basic Legal Citation
Cornell University Law School
http://www.law.cornell.edu:80/citation/citation.table.html

University of Michigan Documents Center Citation Guides
http://www.lib.umich.edu/libhome/Documents.center/cite.html

Budget of the U.S. Government
Washburn GPO Access Gateway
http://www.washlaw.edu/doclaw/gposearch.html

Bill of Rights (U.S. Constitution)
National Archives and Records Administration
http://www.nara.gov/exhall/charters/billrights/billmain.html

Bills and Bill History (U.S. Congress: 103rd Congress, 1993/94–current)
THOMAS
http://thomas.loc.gov/

Washburn GPO*Access* Gateway
http://www.washlaw.edu/doclaw/gposearch.html

Congressional Record (1994–current)
GPO*Access*
http://www.access.gpo.gov/su_docs/index.html

Washburn GPO*Access* Gateway
http://www.washlaw.edu/doclaw/gposearch.html

Constitution—United States of America
Washburn GPO*Access* Gateway
http://www.washlaw.edu/doclaw/gposearch.html

Constitutions—U.S. States and Foreign Countries
The Constitution Page
http://www.artsci.lsu.edu/poli/const.html

Cornell University Law School Legal Information Institute
http://fatty.law.cornell.edu/constitution/constitution.table.html

Copyrights (*see* Patents, Trademarks & Copyrights)

Core Documents of U.S. Democracy
GPO*Access*
http://www.access.gpo.gov/su_docs/locators/coredocs/index.html

Corporation Records (U.S.)
Internet Prospector
http://www.internet-prospector.org/secstate.html

Secretaries of State Links (NASS)
http://www.nass.org/sos/sos.html

Court Decisions and Opinions
Emory University Law School
http://www.law.emory.edu/FEDCTS/credit.html

National Law Library (federal and state court decisions)
http://www.itislaw.com/contlist.htm

State Court Locator
http://vls.law.vill.edu/Locator/statecourt/index.htm

United States Courts
http://www.wolfe.net/~dhillis/STATE3.HTM

United States Federal Courts
http://vls.law.vill.edu/Locator/fedcourt.html

Court Dockets (State & Federal)
LLRX Court Rules, Forms and Dockets
http://www.llrx.com/courtrules/

Court Rules and Court-Approved Forms
LLRX Rules, Forms and DOCKETS is name of the site.

Federal
Findlaw
http://www.findlaw.com/10fedgov/judicial/district_courts.html

Guide to Federal Local Rules
http://depo.com/uscourts.htm

Litigator's Internet Resource Guide *(includes Local Rules, where available)*
http://www.llrx.com/columns/litigat.htm

States
Court Web Sites
http://www.ncsonline.org/Information/info_court_web_sites.html

Litigator's Internet Resource Guide *(includes Local Rules, where available)*
http://www.llrx.com/columns/litigat.htm

Criminal Law/Criminology
Florida State University School of Criminology
http://www.criminology.fsu.edu/cjlinks/default.htm

Federal Acquisition Regulations
Federal Acquisition Regulations (FARs)
http://www.arnet.gov/far/

Defense Acquisition Deskbook
http://www.deskbook.osd.mil/

Department of Defense DFARS
http://farsite.hill.af.mil/vfdfara.htm

Federal Government Agencies
http://www.lib.lsu.edu/gov/fedgov.html

Federal Laws and Regulations
FedLaw
http://fedlaw.gsa.gov/intro2.htm

GPO*Access*
http://www.access.gpo.gov/su_docs/index.html

THOMAS
http://thomas.loc.gov

Federal Register (vol. 59 / 1994–current)
GPO*Access*
http://www.access.gpo.gov/su_docs/aces/aces140.html

Washburn GPO*Access* Gateway
http://www.washlaw.edu/doclaw/gposearch.html

Freedom of Information Act
Society of Professional Journalists
http://spj.org/foia/index.htm

Intellectual Property (*see* Patents, Trademark & Copyrights)

International Legal Resources
Cornell University Law School Legal Information Institute
http://www.law.cornell.edu/topics/international.html

University of Iowa Law Library
http://www.uiowa.edu/~lawlib/intlaw.html

Washburn University School of Law
http://www.washlaw.edu/forint/forintmain.html

United Nations System of Organizations
http://www.unsystem.org/

Law Dictionaries
Duhaime's Law Dictionary
http://duhaime.org/diction.htm

'Lectric Law Library
http://www.lectlaw.com/def.htm

Law Reviews and Law-Related Journals
Jurist—University of Pittsburgh School of Law
http://jurist.law.pitt.edu/lawrev.htm

Law Reviews Online
Law Library of Congress
http://www.loc.gov/low/guide/us-law-r.html

Search Engine
http://stu.findlaw.com/journals/

University Law Review Project
http://www.lawreview.org/

Legal Documents and Forms
'Lectric Law Library
http://www.lectlaw.com/form.html

Legaldocs®—Legal Documents Online
http://www.legaldocs.com/

Mediation and Arbitration
http://fedlaw.gsa.gov/legal89.htm

Member Directory: Legislature—U.S. Congress
House of Representatives (Members & Committees)
http://clerkweb.house.gov/mbrcmtee/mbrcmtee.html

Senate (Members & Committees)
http://www.senate.gov/senators/index.cfm

Municipal Codes and Ordinances
Municipal Code Corporation
http://www.municode.com/

Municipal Codes Online (Seattle Public Library)
http://www.spl.lib.wa.us/selectedsites/municode.html

Patents, Trademarks, and Copyright
U.S. Copyright Office
http://lcweb.loc.gov/copyright/

U.S. Patent and Trademark Office
http://www.uspto.gov/

Public Laws (P.L.)
GPO*Access*
http://www.access.gpo.gov/nara/nara005.html

THOMAS (arranged by Law Number, 1973–current)
http://thomas.loc.gov/

Search Engines (Law-Related Sites)
FindLaw
http://www.findlaw.com/

Internet Legal Resource Guide
http://www.ilrg.com/indices.html

LawCrawler
http://lawcrawler.findlaw.com/

LawGuru
http://www.lawguru.com/searchguru.html

State and Local Government Information
Secretaries of State Links (NASS)
http://www.nass.org/sos/sos.html

Secretaries of State (Incorporation Records)—Internet Prospector
http://www.internet-prospector.org/secstate.html

State Government and Legislative Information
http://www.washlaw.edu/uslaw/statelaw.html

State Government Web Servers
http://www.state.me.us/states.htm

State and Local Government Meta-Indexes
http://lcweb.loc.gov/global/state/stategov.html

Statutes and Codes—Federal
Code of Federal Regulations (CFR)
http://www.access.gpo.gov/nara/cfr/cfr-table-search.html

THOMAS Legislative Information
http://thomas.loc.gov/

U.S. Code Server (via House of Representatives)
http://uscode.house.gov/usc.htm

U.S. Code Table of Popular Names
http://www4.law.cornell.edu/uscode/topn/

Statutes—States
State Statutes and Legislation (Full Text)
http://www.prairienet.org/~scruffy/f.htm

State Statutes (Arranged by Topic)
http://www.law.cornell.edu/topics/state_statutes.html

Uniform Commercial Code Locator
Cornell University Law School Legal Information Institute
http://www.law.cornell.edu/uniform/ucc.html

Uniform State Laws and Model Acts
National Conference of Commissioners on Uniform State Laws (NCCUSL)
http://www.nccusl.org/

United Nations
United Nations Official Site
http://www.un.org/english/

United Nations System of Organizations
http://www.unsystem.org/

U.S. Supreme Court Decisions
Cornell University Legal Information Institute (1990–current)
http://supct.law.cornell.edu/supct/

Fedworld FLITE (1937–1975)
http://www.fedworld.gov/supcourt/index.htm

Findlaw U.S. Supreme Court Opinions (1893–current)
http:www.findlaw.com/casecode/supreme.html

Official U.S. Supreme Court Site (1999–current + slip opinions)
http://www.supremecourtus.gov/opinions/opinions.html

White House
http://www.whitehouse.gov

APPENDIX O

LAW-RELATED INTERNET DISCUSSION GROUPS (LISTS)

COMPLAW-L@complaw.com (computer law and related legal issues) Send the following message to: complaw-1-request@complaw.com
Subscribe http://www.complaw.com/

GDSIS@polecat.law.indiana.edu ***(Government Documents Special Interest Section of the American Association of Law Libraries)*** Send the following message to: listproc@polecat.law.indiana.edu
Subscribe gdsis Your Name
http://mason.gmu.edu/~ecarr/gdsis.html

GOVDOC-L@psuvm.psu.edu (Government Document Issues; U.S.-based) Send the following message to: listserv@psuvm.psu.edu
Subscribe govdoc-L Your Name

GOVPUB@listserv.nodak.edu (local and state government information, publications and documents on the Internet) Send the following message to: listserv@listserv.nodak.edu
Subscribe govpub Your Name

LAW-LIB@ucdavis.edu (U.S.-based law library list with discussion on issues related to law librarians and legal professionals, legal research, etc.) Send the following message to: listproc@ucdavis.edu
Subscribe law-lib yourfirstname yourlastname

LAWLIBREF-L@lawlib.wuacc.edu (list for legal reference librarians) Send the following message to: listserv@lawlib.wuacc.edu
Subscribe lawlibref-L yourfirstname yourlast-name

NET-LAWYERS@peach.ease.lsoft.com is a list for legal professionals who are interested in issues relating to the Internet. To subscribe send the following message to listserv@peach.ease.lsoft.com:
Subscribe net-lawyers Your Name
Related page at http://www.net-lawyers.org/
Archived at http://eva.dc.lsoft,com/Archives/net-lawyers.html

NEWLAWBOOKS-L@lawlib.wuacc.edu (includes publishers' notices) Send the following message to listserv@lawlib.wuacc.edu
Subscribe newlawbooks-L Your Name

NFPA Listservs, for members of the National Federation of Paralegal Associations. Join subject-specific lists on a variety of topics and areas of practice.
Subscribe at http://www.paralega.s.org/forum/listsubscribe.html

Paralegal-L@lawlib.wuacc.edu is a discussion list to duscuss topics related to paralegals and legal assistants. To subscribe send the following message to lisitserv@lawlib.wuacc.edu:
Subscribe PARALEGAL-L Your Name

TechnoLawyer Listserver is a discussion group that focuses on technology. To subscribe send the following message to commands@technolawyer.com:
Subscribe listserver
Information is also available at http://www.technolawyer.com/

GLOSSARY

Act A law passed by one or both houses of a legislature.

Act of God An event caused entirely by nature alone, especially a cataclysmic event. Also called force majeure. In contract law, however, *force majeure* is often defined as an unavoidable natural or *man-made event.*

Addendum An appendix or addition to a document.

Adjournment sine die An adjournment is the suspension of business and "sine die" means without day. Hence the term means ending a legislative or judicial session without setting a time for another session.

Adjudication The formal giving, pronouncing, or recording of a judgment for one side or another in a lawsuit.

Administrative agency A sub-branch of the government set up to carry out the laws. For example, the police department is a local *administrative agency* and the I.R.S. is a national one.

Administrative law (administrative regulations) 1. Laws about the duties and proper running of an administrative agency (see that word) that are imposed on agencies by legislatures and courts. 2. Rules and regulations written by administrative agencies.

Administrative Procedure Act (5 U.S.C. 500) A law that describes how U.S. agencies must do business (hearings, procedures, etc.) and how disputes go from these federal agencies into court. Some states also have administrative procedure acts.

Admissible Describes evidence that should be "let in" or introduced in court, or evidence that the jury may use.

Advance session law services Are publications that contain the text of recently-passed statutes and statutory amendments produced by commercial publishers to fill the gap between the passage of the statutes and the appearance of the government-published session laws.

Advance sheets "Hot off the press" unbound copies of case decisions that will later be printed with other cases in bound form.

Affirmative defense That part of a defendant's answer to a complaint that goes beyond denying the fact and arguments of the complaint. It sent out new facts and arguments that might win for the defendant even if everything in the complaint is true. The burden of proof for an *affirmative defense* is on the defendant. For example, an *affirmative defense* to a lawsuit for injuries caused by an auto accident might be the contributory negligence of the person who was hurt. Some other affirmative defenses in civil cases are *accord and satisfaction,* assumption of risk, and estoppel. Affirmative defenses in criminal cases include insanity and self-defense.

American Jurisprudence, 2d A multivolume legal encyclopedia. It is cross-referenced with American Law Reports.

Amicus curiae (Latin) "Friend of the court." A person allowed to give argument or appear in a lawsuit (usually to file a brief, but sometimes to take an active part) who is not a part to the lawsuit. [pronounce: a-me-kus cure-ee-I]

Annotated code The annotated code contains the text of existing statutes, in language identical to that contained in the code for the jurisdiction. It is referred to as an annotated code because it contains annotated material after each statutory section. An annotation is a paragraph summary of a relevant court opinion, attorney general opinion, or administrative decision interpreting the preceding statutory section. It is a commercial publication and often appears on a more timely basis than a code published by the federal or a state government; the annotated code is generally supplemented frequently by pocket parts and supplementary pamphlets.

Annotation 1. A note or commentary intended to explain the meaning of a passage in a book or document. 2. A legal *annotation* is usually an explanation of a case, including a comparison to other similar cases. It usually follows the text of the decision in a collection of cases.

Answer The first pleading by the defendant in a lawsuit. This pleading responds to the charges and demands of the plaintiff's complaint. The defendant may deny the plaintiff's charges, may present new facts to defeat them, or may show why the plaintiff's facts are legally invalid.

Appellate brief Written statement submitted to an appellate court to persuade the court of the correctness of one's position. An appellate brief argues the facts of the case, supported by specific page references to the record, and the applicable law, supported by citations of authority. (author supply definition)

Appellant The person who appeals a case to a higher court.

Appellant's brief Written from the appellant's perspective.

Appellate court Refers to a higher court that can hear appeals from a lower court.

Appellate jurisdiction The power and authority of a higher court to take up cases that have already been in a lower court and the power to make decisions about these cases. The process is called appellate review. Also, a trial court may have *appellate jurisdiction* over cases from an administrative agency.

Appellee The person against whom an appeal is taken (usually, but not always, the winner in the lower court). Compare with appellant.

Appellee's brief Written from the appellee's perspective.

Assignment The transfer of property, rights in property, or money to another person. For example, an *assignment of wages* involves an employer paying part of an employee's salary directly to someone whom the employee owes money.

Attorney fees The rule as followed in this country is that each party pays his or her own attorney's fees unless otherwise provided by contract or by statute. A typical contract provision is that the losing party would pay attorney's fees if the contract is litigated. Some statutes, especially consumer protection statutes, obligate the losing party to pay the winning party's attorney's fees. Attorney's fees are important because an attorney may decide not to take a case or the client may decide not to sue if the client has no chance of recovering attorney fees in the lawsuit.

Bench trial A case tried without a jury; in a bench trial, the judge determines the facts and decides questions of law.

Bicameral Having two chambers. A two-part legislature, such as the U.S. Congress is *bicameral:* composed of the Senate (the *"upper house"* or *"upper chamber"*) and the House of Representatives (the *"lower house"* or *"lower chamber"*).

Boilerplate Standardized, recurring language found in a document or a form for a document, such as those sold in formbooks. The word implies standardization or lack of tailoring to the individual legal problem.

Breach Breaking a law or failing to perform a duty. [pronounce: breech]

Case brief An outline or summary of a published court opinion.

Case names The full name of the case contains the names of the parties to the case. In a case citation, the case name is generally abbreviated.

Cause of action 1. Facts sufficient to support a valid lawsuit. For example, a *cause of action* for battery must include facts to prove an intentional, unconsented-to physical contract. 2. The legal theory upon which a lawsuit ("action") is based.

Charge The judge's final summary of a case and instructions to the jury.

Charters An organization's basic starting document (for example, a corporation's articles of incorporation).

Checklists A formbook contains checklists of typical provisions included in a particular type of contract.

Chief justice The presiding justice, usually of a court of last resort. The chief justice of the United States Supreme Court presides over the Court and has additional administrative duties related both to the Supreme Court and to the entire federal court system.

Choice of law Deciding which jurisdiction's laws apply to a lawsuit, to a document, etc.

Citation A reference to a legal authority and where it is found. For example, "17 U.DI.L.R. 247" is a *citation* to an article that begins on page 247 of volume 17 of the University of Dull Law Review. See also pinpoint citation.

Citation sentence A sentence that contains only one or more citations.

Citators A set of books or database that lists relevant legal events subsequent to a given case, statute, or other authority. It will tell, for example, if a case has been overruled, distinguished or followed. This is done by looking up the case by its citation (see that word) and checking whether there are citations to other cases listed under it. If there are, it means that the case was mentioned in these later cases. Two leading citators are *Shepherd's* and *KeyCite.*

Cite 1. Refer to specific legal references or authorities. 2. Short for "citation."

Civil action Every lawsuit other than a criminal proceeding. A lawsuit that is brought to enforce a right or to redress a wrong, rather than a court action involving the government trying to prosecute a criminal; in general, a lawsuit brought by one person against another.

Civil damages Money that a court orders paid to a person who has suffered damage (a loss or harm) by the person who caused the injury.

Civil law 1. Law handed down by the Romans. Law that is based on one elaborate document or "code," rather than a combination of many laws and judicial opinions. 2. "Noncriminal law."

Client trust account Upon the receipt of the retainers, the money is deposited into a client trust account.

Code 1. A collection of laws. 2. A complete, interrelated, and exclusive set of laws.

Common law 1. Either all caselaw or the caselaw that is made by judges in the absence of statutes. 2. The legal system that originated in England and is composed of caselaw and statutes that grow and change, influenced by ever-changing custom and tradition.

Complaint The first main paper filed in a civil lawsuit. It includes, among other things, a statement of the wrong or harm done to the plaintiff by the defendant, a request for specific help from the court, and an explanation why the court has the power to do what the plaintiff wants.

Computer assisted legal research Legal research performed on a computer.

Concurring Agree. A *"concurring opinion,"* or *"concurrence,"* is one on which a judge agrees with the result reached in an opinion by another judge in the same case but not necessarily with the reasoning that the other judge used to reach the conclusion.

Consequential damages Court-ordered compensation for *indirect* losses or other indirect harm. Also, in contract law, sometimes called *special damages.*

Constitution 1. A document that sets out the basic principles and most general laws of a country, states, or organization. 2. The U.S. Constitution is the basic law of the country on which most other laws are based, and to which all other laws must yield. Often abbreviated "Const." or "Con."

Contingency provision A contract term designed to deal with a potential problem.

Contingent fee arrangement Payment to a lawyer of a percentage of the "winnings," if any, from a lawsuit rather than payment of a flat amount of money or payment according to the number of hours worked. A *defense* (*or negative or reverse*) *contingent fee* is payment based on the money the lawyer saves a client compared to the potential losses the client thinks are likely.

Contract An agreement that affects or creates legal relationships between two or more persons. To be a *contract*, an agreement must involve: at least one promise, consideration (something of value promised or given) persons legally capable of making binding agreements, and a reasonable certainty about the meaning of the terms. A contract is called bilateral if both sides make promises (such as the promise to deliver a book on one side and a promise to pay for it on the other) or unilateral if the promises are on one side only. According to the Uniform Commercial Code, a contract is the "total legal obligation which results from the parties' agreement," and according to the Restatement of the Law of Contracts, it is "a promise or set of promises for the breach of which the law in some way recognizes a duty."

Corpus Juris Secundum A legal encyclopedia that is cross-referenced with the American Digest System. Corpus Juris Secundum is its most recent update.

Counter claim A claim made by a defendant in a civil lawsuit that, in effect, "sues" the plaintiff. It can be based on entirely different things from the plaintiff's complaint (a *permissive counterclaim*) and may even be for more money than the plaintiff is asking. A counterclaim often must be made if it is based on the same subject or transaction as the original claim (a *compulsory counterclaim*); otherwise, the person with the counterclaim may not be permitted to sue for it later.

Court of general jurisdiction Another term for trial court, that is, a court having jurisdiction to try all classes of civil and criminal cases excluding cases that can only be heard by a court.

Court of last resort The highest tier in the federal court system and the state court system, which usually contains one court, referred to as the court of last resort. The role of the appellate court is to determine whether the lower court applied the law correctly. In a court of last resort, such as the United States Supreme Court or a state supreme court, all members of the court participate in deciding a case.

Court of limited jurisdiction A court whose cases are limited to civil cases of certain types, or which involves a limited amount of money, or whose jurisdiction in criminal cases is confined to petty offenses.

Court order An order issued by the court requiring a party to do or not do a specific act.

Court report fees A fee charged by a court reporter to make a record of a legal proceeding. The fee can also include the fee charged by a court reporter to produce a transcript of the proceeding.

Court rules Govern the procedure of beginning a lawsuit and handling a case before a court. The rules cover such mundane matters as the size paper on which documents are to be submitted to the courts and the format for appellate briefs. They also set forth important time limitations such as the time period within which the defendant has to answer a complaint and the time period within which a party may appeal a decision.

Current Law Index A print index used to locate periodicals.

Damages 1. Money that a court orders paid to a person who has suffered damage (a loss or harm) by the person who caused the injury (the violation of the person's rights). See injury for more complete comparison of *damage*, *damages*, and *injury*. 2. A plaintiff's claim in a legal pleading for the money defined in definition no. 1. *Damages* may be actual and compensatory (directly related to the amount of the loss) or they may be, in addition, *exemplary* and punitive (extra money given to punish the defendant and to help keep a particularly bad act from happening again). Also, merely nominal *damages* may be given (a tiny sum when the loss suffered is either very small or of unproved amount).

Deductive reasoning Legal rules (constitutions, statutes, court rules, and administrative regulations) are general statements of what the law permits, requires, and prohibits. Because the regulatory language is general, it may not be clear whether a particular rule applies to a given factual situation. Deductive reasoning is used to determine if the rule applies; it involves reasoning from the general (rule) to the specific (the impact of the rule on a particular fact pattern).

Deed A document by which one person transfers the legal ownership of land to another person.

Defendant The person against whom a legal action is brought. This legal action may be civil or criminal.

Defined terms A shorthand way of referring to something, often to the parties, throughout a contract. For example, in a contract for sale and purchase, the initial paragraph may identify the seller as "Seller" and the Buyer as "Buyer." The balance of the contract will use "Seller" and "Buyer" to reference the parties to the contract.

Definitional section A common provision of a legislative act that defines terms used in the act.

Delegation The giving of authority by one person to another. *Delegation of powers* is the constitutional division of authority between branches of government and also the handing down of authority from the president to administrative agencies.

Democratic Government by the people, either directly or indirectly through representatives; ideally, as a basis for a system highly protective of individual liberties.

Depth of treatment stars In KeyCite, each case found as having cited the case being KeyCited is identified by one to four stars. These stars indicate how extensively the case being KeyCited is discussed by the cases that cite it.

Digests A collection of parts of many books, usually giving not only summaries, but also excerpts and condensations. For example, the American Digest System covers the decisions of the highest court of each state and of the Supreme Court. It is divided into volumes by time periods. It collects headnotes (summaries given at the top of each case) and is arranged by subject categories.

Direct history The direct history of the case includes prior and subsequent history of that case.

Discretionary jurisdiction A court with discretionary jurisdiction over a case can decide if the court should hear the case.

Dissenting opinion A judge's formal disagreement with the decision of the majority of the judges in a lawsuit. If the judge puts it in writing, it is called a dissenting opinion.

Distinguishing Point out basic differences. To *distinguish* a case is to show why it is irrelevant (or not very relevant) to the lawsuit being decided.

Diversity jurisdiction The two bases of federal jurisdiction in United States district courts are federal question jurisdiction and diversity jurisdiction. Federal courts have diversity jurisdiction as long as the amount in controversy is more than $75,000 and the parties have the requisite diversity of citizenship. Diversity is met so long as the parties are citizens from different states or so long as one party is a citizen of a state and the other party is a citizen of a foreign country. Diversity must be complete. If there are multiple plaintiffs or multiple defendants, no plaintiff may be a citizen of the same state as any defendant.

Doctrine of caveat emptor (Latin) "Beware"; warning. Caveat emptor means "let the buyer beware." While this is still an important warning, laws and court decisions provide many safeguards to the buyer. [pronounce: kav-ee-at]

Doctrine of stare decisis (Latin) "Let the decision stand." The rule that when a court has decided a case by applying a legal principle to a set of facts, the court should stick to the principle and apply it to all later cases with clearly similar facts unless there is a strong reason not to, and that courts below must apply the principle in similar cases. This rule helps promote fairness and reliability in judicial decision making.

Elegant variation Use of a number of different words to refer to the same thing.

En banc (French) All the judges of a court participating in a case all together, rather than individually or in panels of a few.

Enabling legislation Legislation that created an agency and defines its powers is known as enabling legislation.

Enroll Register or record a formal document in the proper office or file.

Enumerated powers The powers specifically granted to a branch of government in a constitution.

Evidentiary facts A fact that is learned directly from testimony or other evidence. Important factual conclusion inferred from *evidentiary facts* are called "*ultimate facts.*"

Ex post facto law (Latin) "After the fact." An *ex post facto law* is one that retroactively attempts to make an action a crime that was not a crime at the time it was done, or a law that attempts to reduce a person's rights based on a past act that was not subject to the law when it was done. *Ex post facto* laws are prohibited by the U.S. Constitution (Article 1, Section 9)

Executive The branch of government that carries out the laws (as opposed to the judicial and legislative branches). The administrative branch.

Expert witness fees A fee charged by a person possessing special knowledge or experience who is allowed to testify at a trial not only about the facts (like an ordinary witness) but also about the professional conclusions he or she draws from these facts.

Federal question jurisdiction A legal issue directly involving the U.S. Constitution, statutes, or treaties, Federal courts have jurisdiction in cases involving a *federal question.*

Federalism A system of political organization with several different levels of government (for example, city, state, and national) co-existing in the same area with the lower levels having some interdependent powers.

Filing fee A fee charged by the court for accepting a pleading or other legal document.

Findings of fact A ruling of law, or a ruling on a question involving law and fact.

Flat fee arrangement The attorney quotes the client one fee that will cover payment for a particular legal matter. The fee may or may not include costs and expenses. The flat fee arrangement is often used in criminal defense work. It may also be used if the attorney has been asked to draft a discrete legal document, such as a will, a trust, or a set of basic corporate documents.

Footnotes The footnotes in the sample office memo are not part of the office memo itself. Although an office memo may contain footnotes, there are not usually more than one or two.

Forma pauperis (Latin) "As a pauper". Describes a court filing that is permitted without payment of the customary fees or court costs, if the person filing proves he or she is too poor to pay.

Formbooks A collection of legal forms with summaries of relevant law and information on how to use the forms.

Forms A model to work from (or a paper with blanks to be filled in) of a legal document such as a contract or a pleading.

General jurisdiction The power of a court to hear and decide any of a wide range of cases that arise within its geographic area.

Geographical jurisdiction A court's jurisdiction is the power of the court to decide cases. To decide a case, a court must have geographical jurisdiction, subject matter jurisdiction, and hierarchical jurisdiction. Geographical jurisdiction refers to the geographical area within which cases arise. A court is restricted to deciding cases arising within a certain geographical area.

Headnotes A summary of a case, or of an important legal point made in the cases, placed at the beginning of the case when it is published. A case may have several headnotes.

Hearing A court proceeding.

Hierarchical jurisdiction Hierarchical jurisdiction refers to the level of court deciding a case. A case begins in a court of original jurisdiction. The court of original jurisdiction initially hears and decides a case. When a court decision is appealed, the case is heard by a court with appellate jurisdiction.

Holding The core of a judge's decision in a case. It is that part of the judge's written opinion that applies the law to the facts of the case and about which can be said "the case means no more and no less than this." When later cases rely on a case as precedent, it is only the *holding* that should be used to establish the precedent. A *holding* may be less than the judge said it was. If the judge made broad, general statements, the holding is limited to only that part of the generalizations that directly apply to the facts of that particular case.

Hourly fee arrangement The attorneys (and often the paralegals in the firm) keep a detailed record of the amount of time the attorneys spend on the client's legal matters. The client is billed for the time spent times the hourly billing rate of the persons who worked on the client matter.

Ignorantia legis neminem excusat (Latin) Ignorance of the law is no excuse.

Impeachment The first step in the removal from public office of a high public official such as a governor, judge, or president. In the case of the president of the United States, the House of Representatives makes an accusation by drawing up "*articles of impeachment*," voting on them, and presenting them to the Senate. This is *impeachment.* But *impeachment* is popularly thought to include the process that may take place after impeachment: the trial of the president in the Senate and conviction by two-thirds of the senators.

Index to Legal Periodicals A print index used to locate periodicals and law reviews by either subject or author.

Injunction A court order that commands or prohibits some act or course of conduct. It is preventative in nature and designed to protect a plaintiff from irreparable injury to the plaintiff's property or property rights by prohibiting or commending the doing of certain acts.

Instrumentalists See Modernists.

Intermediate appellate court An appellate court that is subject to judicial review by a higher appellate court.

Journals A periodical magazine such as a law journal.

Judicial 1. Having to do with a court. 2. Having to do with a judge. 3. Describes the branch of government that interprets the law and that resolves legal disputes.

Judicial restraint A judge's decision and decision-making that excludes the judge's personal views and relies strictly on precedent.

Jurisdiction 1. The geographical area within which a court (or a public official) has the right and power to operate. 2. The persons about whom and the subject matters about which a court has the right and power to make decisions that are legally binding.

Jurisprudence constante In deciding a legal problem, the code must be reviewed to find the appropriate code provision and the provision must be applied to solve the legal problem. In applying code provisions, judges rely primarily on scholarly articles and books written by professors rather than on prior case law. Cases may also be reviewed, but prior case law is not binding as it is in a common law system. A rule might be derived from a settled pattern of judicial decisions, but not from any single, individual case.

Justice A judge, especially an appellate judge such as a justice of the U.S. Supreme Court.

Landmark case A court case that makes major changes in the law, especially a U.S. Supreme Court case that resolves a major issue and has substantial practical impact.

Law office memo Is seen only by those in the law office and by the client and, therefore, can be objective.

Law reviews A publication put out by a law school (or bar association, etc.) with articles on legal subjects such as court decisions and legislation.

Legal conclusion 1. A statement about legal rights, duties, or results that is not based on specific facts. A conclusory statement. 2. A conclusion about legal rights, duties, or results that is drawn from specific facts, but those facts do not include the facts legally necessary to draw the conclusion. 3. Used loosely to mean a conclusion of law, the *opposite* of the meanings in no. 1 and no. 2.

Legal dictionaries Provide definitions of legal terms and their pronunciation, with citation to relevant case laws. The two major legal dictionaries used in the United States are the Blacks Law Dictionary and the Ballentine's Law Dictionary.

Legal encyclopedias Legal encyclopedias are a secondary source that offer a useful commentary on the law as it is and serve as a case finder to locate cases with which one can begin the research process. Legal encyclopedias are multivolume sets covering broad legal topics arranged in alphabetical order, with the topics divided into sections. Index volumes are located at the end of the set. Each topic gives a textual explanation of the law relating to that topic. Topic coverage serves as a valuable frame of reference for more in-depth research in other sources.

Legal newspapers Legal periodicals that provide information on recent court decisions, changes in the law, legal publications, and other items of interest to the legal community.

Legal periodicals Legal periodicals are a secondary source, published periodically, that contain articles, usually on a range of different issues and legal developments. The articles generally contain narrative text and citations to relevant primary sources.

Legislation 1. The process of thinking about and passing or refusing to pass bills into law (statutes, ordinances, etc.) 2. Statutes, ordinances, etc.

Legislative Lawmaking, as opposed to "executive" (carrying out or enforcing laws), or "judicial" (interpreting or applying laws). Concerning a legislature.

Legislative history The background documents and records of hearings related to the enactment of a bill. These documents may be used to decide the meaning of the law after it has been enacted.

Legislative intent The principle that when a statute is ambiguous, a court should interpret the statute by looking at its legislative history to see what the lawmakers meant or wanted when they passed the statute. This is one of several possible ways of interpreting statutes. Compare with legislative purpose rule.

Limited jurisdiction Subject matter jurisdiction refers to the type of case a court may hear. A court is a court of general jurisdiction or a court of limited jurisdiction. As the names imply, a court of limited jurisdiction is limited to hearing certain types of cases and a court of general jurisdiction may hear all other types of cases.

Liquidated damages A sum agreed upon by the parties at the time of entering into the contract as being payable by way of compensation for loss suffered in the event of a breach of contract.

Literalism 1. The process of discovering or deciding the meaning of a written document by studying only the document itself and not the circumstances surrounding it. 2. Studying the document and surrounding circumstances to decide the document's meaning.

Living (constitution) The written United States Constitution, including all amendments to it, is less than twenty pages in length. The living constitution would include those pages and all case law interpretations of the Constitution. If printed, the living constitution would require numerous volumes. Scholars and laypersons alike have hotly debated constitutional interpretation. Some believe that any interpretation should be based on the plain language of the Constitution and should not stray far from it. Others believe that the broad language of the Constitution should be interpreted as needed to deal with legal questions never dreamed of when the Constitution was first enacted.

Local court rules Court rules that govern procedure in a particular local court and supplement other court rules.

Looseleaf publications The legal sources appearing in looseleaf publication format include state annotated codes, state administrative codes, formbooks, and services providing a collection of source material in a particular subject area. The information in looseleaf services is stored in binders rather than formatted as hardbound volumes and paper pamphlet supplements. The binder format allows easy insertion of new material and removal of outdated material.

Looseleaf series for recent cases See looseleaf publications.

Major premise The basis for a logical deduction. The facts or arguments upon which a conclusion is based.

Majority More than half. Fifty-one is a *majority* vote when one hundred persons vote.

Mandatory authority Binding authority.

Martindale-Hubbell Law Dictionary A multivolume book that lists many lawyers by location and type of practice. Other volumes contain summaries of each major area of the law in each state and most foreign countries. A brief of law. It is often submitted to a judge in a case.

Memorandum of law A brief of law. It is often submitted to a judge in a case. The purpose of the memorandum of law is to support and argue the client's position in the lawsuit.

Minor premise The basis for a logical deduction. The facts or arguments upon which a conclusion is based.

Modernists Also known as Instrumentalists, they are those individuals who find meaning through reading the language of the constitution in light of contemporary life, and through this approach the judiciary contributes to judicial, social and moral evolution of the nation.

Motion A request that a judge make a ruling or take some other action. For example, a *motion to dismiss* is a request that the court throw the case out; a *motion for more definite statement* is a request that the judge require an opponent in a lawsuit to file a less vague or ambiguous pleading; a *motion to strike* is a request that immaterial statements or other things be removed from an opponent's pleading; and a *motion to suppress* is a request that illegally gathered evidence be prohibited. *Motions* are either *granted* or *denied* by the judge.

Motion for a directed verdict A verdict in which the judge takes the decision out of the jury's hands. The judge does this by telling them what the jury must decide or by actually making the decision. The judge might do this when the person suing has presented facts which, even if believed by a jury, cannot add up to a successful case.

Motion for a summary judgment A final judgment (victory) for one side in a lawsuit (or in one part of a lawsuit), without trial, when the judge finds, based on pleadings, deposition, affidavits, etc. that there is no genuine factual issue in the lawsuit (or in part of the lawsuit).

Negative indirect history The negative indirect history includes cases outside the direct appellate line of the case being KeyCited that may have a negative impact on the precedential weight of the case. For example, cases listed under negative indirect history are later cases that may have questioned the reasoning of the earlier case, distinguished themselves on their facts, or limited the effect of the earlier case.

Negotiated terms The terms of the contract that the parties talked about and agreed to.

Notice 1. Knowledge of certain facts. "*Constructive notice*" means a person is treated as if he or she knew certain facts. 2. Formal receipt of the knowledge of certain facts. For example, "*notice*" of a lawsuit usually means that formal papers have been delivered to a person (*personal notice*) or to the person's agent (*imputed notice*).

Obiter dictum (Latin) 1. Singular of dicta. 2. Short for "obiter dictum" (a remark by the way, as in "by the way, did I tell you . . ."); a digression; a discussion of side points or unrelated points.

Office practice attorneys Attorneys whose practice excludes litigation. Office practice attorneys help clients plan transactions to make them as advantageous as possible to the client while avoiding potential legal problems.

Officer of the court A court employee such as a judge, clerk, sheriff, marshal, bailiff, and constable. Lawyers are also *officers of the court* and must obey court rules, be truthful in court, and generally serve the needs of justice.

Operative provisions The essential terms of a contract including such things as parties to the contract, the subject matter of the contract, and payment terms.

Oral argument The presentation of each side of a case before an appeals court. The presentation typically involves oral statements by a lawyer, interrupted by questions from the judges.

Ordinal numbers A number describing the ranking of an item (i.e. first, second, third, etc.).

Ordinances A local or city law, rule, or regulation. (*Ordinance of 1787* providing for the government of the Northwest Territory).

Original jurisdiction The power of a court to take a case, try it, and decide it (as opposed to appellate jurisdiction, the power of a court to hear and decide an appeal).

Overrule To reject or supercede. For example, a case is *overruled* when the same court, or a higher court in the same system, rejects the legal principles on which the case was based. This ends the case's value as a precedent.

Panel A group of judges (smaller than the entire court) that decides a case.

Parallel citations An alternate reference to a case (or other legal document) that is published in more than one place. There is usually one official publication of a court case or a statute. If so, that is the *official or primary* citation, and all others are "parallel citations."

Parties 1. A person concerned with or taking part in any contract, matter, or affair, or proceeding. 2. A person who is either a plaintiff or a defendant in a lawsuit. A *real party* is a person who actually stands to gain or lose something from being a part of the case, while a *formal* or *nominal part* is one who has only a technical or "name only" interest.

Penumbra doctrine 1. The principle that the *"necessary and proper clause"* of the U.S. Constitution allows the federal government to take all actions to carry out legitimate government purposes, even if the powers needed to carry out these purposes are only implied from other powers (which themselves are not specifically mentioned in the Constitution, but only implied). 2. The principle that specific constitutional rights have less clear, but still real, implied rights, such as the right to privacy.

Per curiam (Latin) "By the court." Describes an opinion backed by all the judges in a particular court and usually with no one judge's name on it. [pronounce: per-cure-ee-am]

Person acting under color of law One taking an action that looks official or appears to be backed by law.

Persuasive authority All sources of law that a judge might use, but is not required to use, in making up his or her mind about a case; for example, legal encyclopedias or related cases from other states. A case may be strongly persuasive if it comes from a famous judge or a nearby, powerful court.

Petition for writ of certiorari (Latin) "To make sure." A request for *cretiorari* (or "cert." for short) is like an appeal, but one which the higher court is not required to take for decision. It is literally a writ from the higher court asking the lower court for the record of the case. [pronounce: sir-sho-rare-ee]

Pinpoint citation The page number of a specific quote, as opposed to the general citation (see that word). It follows the page number on which the quoted document begins. In the general citation 17 U.D.L.R. 247, 250 the **pinpoint citation** is page 250.

Plagiarism Taking all or part of the writing or idea of another person and passing it off as your own. [pronounce: play-jar-ism]

Plain meaning rule 1. The principle that if a law seems clear, you should take the simplest meaning of the words and not read anything into the law. This is one of several possible ways of interpreting statutes. 2. The principle that if a contract, statute, or other writing seems clear, the meaning of the writing should be determined from the writing itself, not from other evidence such as testimony.

Plaintiff A person who brings (starts) a lawsuit against another person.

Pleading 1. The process of making formal, written statements of each side of a civil case. First the plaintiff submits a paper with "facts" and claims; then the defendant submits a paper with "facts" (and sometimes counterclaims); then the plaintiff responds; etc., until all issues and questions are clearly posed for a trial. 2. *A pleading* is any one of the papers mentioned in no. 1. The first one is a complaint, the response is an answer, etc. *The pleadings* is the sum of all these papers. Sometimes, written motions and other court papers are called *pleadings*, but this is not strictly correct.

Plurality The greatest number. For example, if Jane gets ten votes and Don and Mary each get seven, Jane has a *plurality* (the most votes), but not a majority (more than half of the votes).

Pocket part An addition to a lawbook that updates it until a bound supplement or a new edition comes out. It is found inside the back (or occasionally, front) cover, secured in a "pocket," and should always be referred to when doing legal research.

Point heading A main point heading answers one of the questions in the questions present section of the memorandum, with the main point headings appearing in order corresponding to the order of the questions presented. The word "heading" is used because a point heading serves as a heading to one portion of the argument section. Main point headings are often written in all capitals or underlined to make them stand out from the rest of the memorandum. They may also be numbered with roman numerals or lettered with capital letters. A complex issue may call for several point headings for sub-issues under a main point heading.

Police power The government's right and power to set up and enforce laws to provide for the safety, health, and general welfare of the people; for example, *police power* includes the power to license occupations such as hair cutting.

Popular name An act often is identified by a name given it by the legislature and for easy reference is often referred to by that name. This is the "short title" or "popular name" of the act.

Preamble An introduction (usually saying why a document, such as a statute, was written).

Precedent A court decision on a *question of law* (how the law affects the case) that is binding authority on lower courts in the same court system for cases in which those courts must decide a similar question of law involving similar facts. (Some legal scholars include as *precedent* court decisions that are merely persuasive authority.) The U.S. court system is based on judges making decisions supported by past precedent, rather than by the logic of the judge alone. See stare decisis.

Pre-emption doctrine Describes the first right to do anything. For example, when the federal government pre-empts the field by passing laws in a subject area, the states may not pass conflicting laws and sometimes may not pass laws on the subject at all.

Privacy Describes the right to be left alone. The *right to privacy* is sometimes "balanced" against other rights, such as *freedom of the press.*

Prospective Looking forward; concerning the future; likely or possible. For example, a *prospective law* is one that applies to situations that arise after it is enacted. Most laws are *prospective* only.

Questions of fact A point in dispute in a lawsuit; an issue for decision by judge or jury.

Questions of the law A point in dispute in a lawsuit; an issue for decision by the judge.

Reasoning by analogy Is reasoning by applying the doctrine of stare decisis. First, the researcher must identify case law relevant to the legal problem being researched. Then the researcher compares the similarities and differences among the legal problem and relevant case law. Finally, the researcher reviews the significance of the various similarities and differences to determine if and how prior case law will control the answer to the legal problem being researched.

Reasoning by example See Reasoning by analogy.

Record 1. A formal written account of a case, containing the complete formal history of all actions taken, papers filed, rulings made, opinions written, etc. The *record* also can include all the actual evidence (testimony, physical objects, etc.) as well as the evidence that was *refused* admission by the judge. Courts of record include all courts for which permanent records of proceedings are kept. 2. A public record is a document filled with, or put out by, a government agency and open to the public for inspection. For example, a *title of record* to land is an ownership interest that has been properly filled in the public land records. The official who keeps these records is usually called the *recorder of deeds*, and the filing process is called *recordation*.

Recusal The process by which a judge is disqualified (or disqualifies himself or herself) from hearing a lawsuit because of prejudice or because the judge is interested.

Related annotations A section of an ALR annotation that identifies annotations covering related issues.

Remands Send back. For example, a higher court may *remand* (send back) a case to a lower court, directing the lower court to take some action. Also, a prisoner is *remanded to custody* when sent back to jail after failing to meet, or being denied release on, bail.

Reporters Sets of books containing published court decisions.

Representation reinforcement One approach to interpreting the United States Constitution. Some analysts glean that the framers did not intend to establish a precise set of substantive laws. Rather, they intended to define the who, what, where, and when of substantive rulemaking. Following this theory, judicial interpretation should be guided by the general republican principles underlying the Constitution. However, the analysis is contemporary. The basic republican themes established by the framers are used as a base, but those themes are interpreted within the context of contemporary society. By allowing change in this way, constitutional law actually reflects the will of people. Accordingly, the United States Supreme Court is not viewed as a countermajoritarian institution, but one that reinforces democracy and republicanism.

Res ipsa loquitur (Latin) "The thing speaks for itself." A rebuttable *presumption* (a conclusion that can be changed if contrary evidence is introduced) that a person is negligent if the thing causing an accident was in his or her control only, and if that type of accident does not usually happen without negligence. It is often abbreviated "res ipsa" or "R.I.L." [pronounce: race ip-sa low-kwe-tur]

Restatements of the Law Books put out by the American Law Institute that tell what the law in a general area is, how it is changing, and what direction the authors think this change should take; for example, the Restatement of the Law Contracts.

Retainer 1. Employment of a lawyer by a client. 2. The specific agreement in no. 1. 3. The first payment in no. 1 either for one specific case or to be available to unspecified future cases.

Retrospective A retrospective or retroactive law is one that changes the legal status of things already done or that applies to past actions.

Reverse Set aside. For example, when a higher court *reverses* a lower court on appeal, it sets aside the judgment of the lower court and either substitutes its own judgment for it or sends the case back to the lower court with instructions on what to do with it.

Rules of appellate procedure Court rules that govern the conduct of cases before an appellate court.

Rules of civil procedure Court rules that govern the conduct of civil cases at the trial level.

Rules of construction A decision (usually by a judge) about the meaning and legal effect of ambiguous or doubtful words that considers not only the words themselves but also surrounding circumstances, relevant laws and writings, etc. (Looking at just the words is called "interpretation," although interpretation is sometimes used to mean construction also.)

Rules of criminal procedure Court rules that govern the conduct of criminal cases at the trial level.

Rules of evidence Court rules that govern the gathering of information for use at trial and admission of information as evidence at trial.

Saving clause (separability or severability) A clause in a statute (or a contract) that states that if party of the statute (or contract) that states that if part of the statute (contract) is declared void, the remainder stays in effect.

Scope A section of an ALR annotation that identifies the issue covered in the annotation.

Secondary sources Secondary sources are designed to explain legal concepts and can be used to understand basic legal terms and general concepts. They provide the researcher with background information and a framework of an area of the law, arranging legal principles in an orderly fashion. In contrast to primary authority (constitutions, cases, statutes, court rules, and administrative regulations), secondary sources do not have the force and effect of law.

Session laws Statutes printed in the order that they were passed in each session of legislature. See also statutes at large.

Short title A legislative act often is identified by a name given it by the legislature and for easy reference is often referred to by that name. This is the "short title" or "popular name" of the act.

Signposts Words or phrases in a document that point the reader in the right direction and provide a framework for understanding the document.

Slip law A printed copy of a bill passed by Congress that is distributed immediately once signed by the president.

Slip opinions A court decision published singly shortly after the case has been decided.

Specific performance Being required to do exactly what was agreed to. A court may require specific performance of a contract if one person fails to perform and damages (money) will not properly compensate the other side for work done.

Statements of the rule of law The law contained in any legal sources.

Statutes at large—A collection of all statutes passed by a particular legislature (such as the U.S. Congress), printed in full and in the order of their passage. The U.S. *Statutes at Large* also contains *joint* resolutions, constitutional amendments, presidential proclamations, etc.

Status flags In KeyCite, a red or yellow triangular status flag located in the upper lefthand corner of a a primary source warns you of any negative history. A red flag appearing on a case means that the case is no longer good law for at least one of the points it contains. A yellow flag appearing on a case means that the case has some negative history, but has not been reversed or overruled.

Statute of frauds Any various state laws, modeled after an old English law, that requires many types of contracts (such as contract for the sale of real estate or of goods over a certain dollar amount, contracts to guarantee another's debt, and certain long-term contracts to be signed and in writing to be enforceable in court).

Strict construction Exact, precise; governed by exact rules. *Strict construction* of a law means taking it literally or "what it says, it means" so that the law should be applied to the narrowest possible set of situations. *Strict construction* of a contract means that any ambiguous words in the contract should be interpreted in the way least favorable to the side that wrote the words.

String citation A citation sentence with more than one citation.

Style Official name

Subject matter jurisdiction The person about whom and the subject matters about which a court has the right and power to make decisions that are legally binding.

Subsequent history The history of a case beginning after the decision cited.

Summary and comment A section of an ALR annotation that contains summary of information covered in the remainder of the annotation.

Supremacy clause The provision in *Article VI* of the U.S. Constitution that the U.S. Constitution, laws, and treaties take precedence over conflicting state constitutions or laws.

Supreme Court of the United States The highest of the United States courts.

Tabulation Can be used very effectively in legal writing where you have a list of items or activities. When you tabulate, you place each item or activity on a separate line. Each line, except for the last and next to the last lines, ends with a semi-colon. The next to the last line ends with a semi-colon and the word "and" or "or." The last line ends with a period.

Testimony Evidence given by a witness under oath. This evidence is *"testimonial"* and is different from demonstrative evidence.

Textual sentence A complete grammatical sentence with a subject and a verb.

Textualism 1. The process of discovering or deciding the meaning of a written document by studying only the document itself and not the circumstances surrounding it. But see no. 2. 2. Studying the document and surrounding circumstances to decide the document's meaning. See construction.

Thesis paragraph This paragraph should contain your thesis—the central idea of your memo.

Title The United States Code presents the federal laws currently in effect organized according to subject matter into 50 "titles." Thus a title is one of the major organizational divisions of the United States Code.

Topic sentence Contains one main idea summarizing the rest of the paragraph, with the rest of the paragraph developing the idea presented in the topic sentence.

Transitional language Provides a "transition" or link between what you have just written and what you are going to write about.

Treatises The treatise is a work, often multi-volume, generally covering a single field of law and written by one or more legal scholars. The treatise contains text, explaining the field in detail, supported by citation to relevant authority.

Trial courts The lowest tier in the federal court system and the state court system is usually comprised of trial courts. In our adversary system, the two parties present their evidence at the trial level. The two parties may have different versions of the facts and the attorneys representing them may be relying on differing legal theories. The evidence may be testimony, documents, or tangible evidence. The role of a trial court is to determine the facts and to apply the applicable law to the facts.

Ultimate facts Facts essential to a plaintiff's or a defendant's case. Often facts that must be inferred from other facts and evidence.

Unicameral A legislature with a single-house system.

Unified court structure A simplified state court structure with three or four tiers; the court structure of other states that do not have a unified court structure is more complex.

United States Code The official law books containing federal laws organized by subject. They are recompiled every six years, and supplements are published when needed.

United States Courts of Appeals Hear appeals from lower federal courts and administrative agencies; there is one court for each of twelve geographical *circuits* plus the *Federal Circuit*, which hears appeals nationwide from specialized federal courts and other appeals such as patent cases).

United States district courts The U.S. trial courts.

United States Magistrate Judges A judge, usually within limited functions and powers; for example, a police court judge. *U.S. magistrates* conduct pretrial prceedings, try minor criminal matters, etc. [pronounce: maj-eh-strate]

United States Supreme Court review of state court decisions The United States Supreme Court has jurisdiction to review final decisions of the highest state court rejecting claims based on federal constitutional law. Thus the United States Supreme Court makes the final interpretation of the meaning of the United States Constitution.

Will A document in which a person tells how his or her property is to be handed out after death. If all the necessary formalities have been taken care of, the law will help carry out the wishes of the person making the will.

Words and Phrases A multi-volume judicial legal dictionary in which defined words and phrases are arranged in alphabetical order, and each word or phrase is followed by a paragraph summary of the word or phrase as used in a case.

INDEX

Page numbers in italics indicate figures

T